Stepan Bandera

STEPAN BANDERA

The Life and Afterlife of a Ukrainian Nationalist

Fascism, Genocide, and Cult

Grzegorz Rossoliński-Liebe

ibidem-Verlag
Stuttgart

Bibliografische Information der Deutschen Nationalbibliothek
Die Deutsche Nationalbibliothek verzeichnet diese Publikation in der Deutschen Nationalbibliografie; detaillierte bibliografische Daten sind im Internet über http://dnb.d-nb.de abrufbar.

Bibliographic information published by the Deutsche Nationalbibliothek
Die Deutsche Nationalbibliothek lists this publication in the Deutsche Nationalbibliografie; detailed bibliographic data are available in the Internet at http://dnb.d-nb.de.

Cover photos: 1. Stepan Bandera, public domain. 2. SUM members in London in 1969, TShLA.

∞

Gedruckt auf alterungsbeständigem, säurefreien Papier
Printed on acid-free paper

ISBN-13 Paperbackausgabe / Paperback edition: 978-3-8382-0604-2

ISBN-13 Hardcoverausgabe / Hardback edition: 978-3-8382-0686-8

Printed in Germany

For Martina, Gustav, and Alma

and

in memory of civilians killed by the Ukrainian nationalists

CONTENTS

PREFACE AND ACKNOWLEDGMENTS

My interest in Stepan Bandera was awakened about a decade ago when I came across a picture of the Bandera monument in the eastern Galician town of Dubliany and read an article that described the unveiling ceremony. The solemn mood of the crowd in the picture and the highly respectful attitude of the article toward Bandera and his movement puzzled me. After this encounter I examined a number of academic and non-academic writings relating to Bandera, his role in Ukrainian and European history, and in the collective memory of Ukrainians, Jews, Poles, Russians, and other peoples. These publications, however, did not satisfy my curiosity. The characterizations of Bandera and his movement were intriguing but they lacked substance and many were superficial. Because of the lack of reliable information about the subject, it took me several years to define the bases and to comprehend its essentials. The more time I spent in the archives and libraries, the more I was astonished how mythical and escapist the Bandera images are. Interviewing various activists and investigating Bandera museums, I realized how much Bandera meant to people who had made him a part of their identity and how little they were interested in a more realistic understanding of the man and his movement. I also noticed a concealed hostility toward critical examination of the subject and deduced that the common representations of Bandera, whether apologetic or demonizing, were based on disavowal of certain aspects of his past and on collective misinformation, in particular in post-Soviet western Ukraine.

Investigating the early post-war period, I realized that our understanding of Bandera and his movement had been based to a substantial extent on that movement's propaganda, which had been modified after the Second World War and adjusted to the realities of the Cold War by the veterans of the movement and its sympathizers. Several thousand of these people had left western Ukraine together with the Germans during the last phase of the war and remained thereafter in various countries of the Western bloc. Their narrative of the events in western Ukraine during the Second World War was not challenged by professional historians until recently. On the contrary, some of the historians who studied Ukrainian nationalism during the Cold War adopted parts of this distorted and selective narrative in their own writings, taking the memories and self-representations of the veterans of the movement for granted. After the dissolution of the Soviet Union, a number of political activists and scholars based in western Ukraine presented explanations of the subject that were again very similar to those popularized previously by the movement's veterans and by some historians rooted in the Ukrainian diaspora. In other words the subject has remained unexplored for a long period of time, and its investigation has become difficult and even dangerous.

The theoretical part of my work, in particular the contextualization of Bandera and his movement among other East Central European fascist movements, evoked fierce reactions among far-right activists, and it irritated several historians and intellectuals, including experts in the fields of Polish, Soviet, and Ukrainian history. Equally intense emotions were aroused when I began to connect the apologetic commemorations and representations of Bandera and his followers with the involvement of Ukrainian nationalists and ordinary Ukrainians in the Holocaust and other forms of mass violence during and after the Second World War. To my surprise, some historians who had not worked in the field of Ukrainian history, but had specialized in subjects such as mass violence, fascism, nationalism, the Holocaust or its denial, had far fewer problems accepting the results of my research and following the narrative of this study.

When I was planning to investigate Bandera and his movement in depth and to write a comprehensive study about them, several scholars warned me that it would be better to choose a less contentious topic for a dissertation. As it turned out, the reactions to my research and to some of my findings exceeded their direst predictions. Especially in the last phase of writing this book, I was exposed to a number of unpleasant attacks on this study and sometimes also on my person. These attacks came both from the Ukrainian far right and from scholars who regarded Bandera as a national or local hero, and his followers as an anti-German and anti-Soviet resistance movement, or as the Ukrainian "liberation movement." Many people directly or indirectly expressed the opinion that the investigation of subjects such as the mass violence conducted by the Ukrainian nationalists, the Bandera cult, and the Holocaust denial among the Ukrainian diaspora and post-Soviet intellectuals constitutes an attack on Ukrainian identity, and they questioned the usefulness and integrity of such research.

When the Heinrich Böll Foundation, the German Academic Exchange Service, and the German embassy in Kiev invited me to deliver six lectures about Bandera in three Ukrainian cities in late February and early March 2012, organized hysteria was stirred up, not only among Ukrainian far-right activists and nationalist scholars but also among a number of "liberal" scholars in Ukraine and some scholars of East European history in other countries. The organizers of the lecture tour had great difficulty in finding universities or other institutions with sufficient courage to host my lectures. Venues were found in Kiev and Dnipropetrovs'k, but none in Lviv. In the event, even the four institutions (including the Tkuma Ukrainian Institute for Holocaust Studies) that had agreed to my appearance canceled the lectures a few hours prior to their planned start. As a result, only one lecture took place, in secure conditions in the premises of the German embassy in Kiev. In front of the building, about a hundred angry protesters tried to convince a few hundred interested students, scholars, and ordinary Ukrainians not to attend my lecture, claiming that I was "Joseph Goebbels' grandchild" and a "liberal fascist from Berlin," who did not understand anything about the subject he would talk about.

The lectures in Ukraine in early 2012 were prevented by two kinds of political and intellectual opponents. The first group consisted of far-right activists from the Svoboda Party who intimidated the universities and other institutions. The second group was composed of nationalist and "liberal" intellectuals and scholars, who contacted the institutions and also announced in public that it would be better not to allow me to speak on the subject of my research, because I was not a historian but a "propagandist" who would besmirch the country or attempt to spark a civil war and split Ukraine. During the wave of disturbing and hostile insults and protests, a number of people, including Antony Polonsky, Delphine Bechtel, Per Anders Rudling, Marco Carynnyk, Andreas Umland, Jared McBride, Mark von Hagen, Arnd Bauerkämper,

Christian Ganzer, Frank Golczewski, Anton Shekhovtsov, Gertrud Pickhan, Grzegorz Motyka, Omer Bartov, Simon Hadler, Susanne Heim, and especially my wife Martina, were very supportive. These people convinced me not to pay too much attention to the various kinds of nationalist and intellectual hysteria and to concentrate on finishing the study and publishing the book.

This study could not have been accomplished without the help and support of many people and institutions. At the very beginning of this undertaking, Philipp Ther convinced me to see it through. Heinz Dieter Kittsteiner († 2008), an inspiring theoretician and a remarkable critic of collective memories, did so too. During the entire project, my dissertation adviser Frank Golczewski supported me with advice on various academic matters and helped me to face sundry bureaucratic obstacles. In Ukraine, Leonid Zashkilniak, Iaroslav Hrytsak, Ostap Sereda, and a number of other colleagues helped me to locate and extract some essential documents and to overcome many kinds of administrative complications. Similarly, several archivists and librarians in Canada, Germany, Poland, Russia, Ukraine, the United Kingdom, and the United States were very helpful during my investigations. John-Paul Himka taught me a great deal about the Ukrainian diaspora and its nationalist misrepresentation of history. He and scholars such as Omer Bartov, Dieter Pohl, Grzegorz Motyka, and Per Anders Rudling drew my attention to the question of ethnic and political violence and its significance for this study. The writings on fascism by scholars such as Arnd Bauerkämper, Roger Eatwell, Roger Griffin, Constantin Iordachi, Michael Mann, Stanley G. Payne, Kevin Passmore, Robert Paxton, and Zeev Sternhell helped me to contextualize Bandera and his movement.

The book has profited from discussions and critical readings. I had the pleasure to present and discuss the project at academic seminars organized by Arnd Bauerkämper, Frank Golczewski, Heinz Dieter Kittsteiner, Gertrud Pickhan, Philip Ther, the German Historical Institute Warsaw, the working group "Holocaust and Memory Politics" at the University of Alberta, and the department of Eastern European History at the University of Giessen. Arnd Bauerkämper, Omer Bartov, Frank Golczewski, Mark von Hagen, John-Paul Himka, Iaroslav Hrytsak, Tanja Penter, Per Anders Rudling, Tomasz Stryjek, and Andrzej Zięba commented either on the whole manuscript or some of its parts. Ray Brandon, Franziska Bruder, Marco Carynnyk, John-Paul Himka, Jared McBride, Grzegorz Motyka, Dieter Pohl, and Per Anders Rudling assisted me with information and drew my attention to documents they had discovered during their own research on topics relating to this study. Marco Carynnyk and Michał Młynarz helped me by editing the manuscript. It would not have been possible to conduct the research for this study and to write this book, without the financial assistance of the Gerda Henkel Foundation, the University of Alberta, and the German Historical Institute Warsaw, or to have the manuscript edited without the assistance of the Gerda Henkel Foundation. I would therefore like to thank all the people who have helped me to publish this book. Given its subject and length it was a quite challenging task. Above all, I very sincerely thank my wife, who showed considerable patience and compassion during the extensive and exhaustive process of accomplishing this study. I devote this book to her and to my two children.

LIST OF ABBREVIATIONS

ASSS	Archives of the Shevchenko Scientific Society in New York
AAN	Archiwum Akt Nowych w Warszawie (Archives of Modern Records in Warsaw)
ABN	Anti-Bolshevik Bloc of Nations
AENM	Alliance of European National Movements
AK	Armia Krajowa (Polish Home Army)
ASBML	Archive of the Stepan Bandera Museum, London
ASSS	Archives of the Shevchenko Scientific Society, New York
ATsDVR	Arkhiv Tsentru doslidzhen' vyzvol'noho rukhu (Archives of the Institute for the Study of the Liberation Movement)
AUNR	Armia Ukraïns'koï Narodnoï Respubliky (Ukrainian People's Army)
AŻIH	Archiwum Żydowskiego Instytutu Historycznego (Archives of the Jewish Historical Museum, Warsaw)
BAB	Bundesarchiv Berlin (German Federal Archives, Berlin)
BAK	Bundesarchiv Koblenz (German Federal Archives, Koblenz)
BA-MA	Bundesarchiv—Militärarchiv (Military Archives in Freiburg)
BayHStA	Bayerisches Hauptstaatsarchiv (Bavarian Main State Archives)
BCh	Bataliony Chłopskie (Peasants' Battalions)
BMN	Blok Mniejszości Narodowych (Bloc of National Minorities, Blok fon Nashonal Minorities, Blok Natsional'nykh Menshyn, or Block der Nationalen Minderheiten)
BN	Biblioteka Narodowa w Warszawie (National Library, Warsaw)
BND	Bundesnachrichtendienst (Federal Intelligence Service)
BRD	Bundesrepublik Deutschland (Federal Republic of Germany)
BStU	Bundesbeauftragte für die Unterlagen des Staatssicherheits-dienstes (Federal Commissioner for the Stasi Archives)
CAW	Centralne Archiwum Wojskowe, Rembertów (Central Military Archives, Rembertów)
CIA	Central Intelligence Agency
CIUS	Canadian Institute of Ukrainian Studies
CŻKH	Centralna Żydowska Komisja Historyczna (Central Jewish Historical Commission)
DALO	Derzhavnyi Arkhiv L'vivskoï Oblasti (State Archives of Lviv Oblast)
DDR	Deutsche Demokratische Republik (German Democratic Republic)
DP	displaced person(s)
FNIe	Front natsional'noï iednosti (Front of National Unity)
FHO	Fremde Heere Ost (German Military Intelligence on the Eastern Front)
FSB	Federal'naia sluzhba bezopasnosti Rossiiskoi Federatsii (Federal Security Service of the Russian Federation
GARF	Gosudarstvennyi arkhiv Rossiiskoi Federatsii (State Archive of the Russian Federation)
Gestapo	Geheime Staatspolizei (Secret State Police)
HA	Hauptabteilung (Main Department—of the MfS)

HURI	Harvard Ukrainian Research Institute
HDA SBU	Haluzevyi Derzhavnyi arkhiv Sluzhby bezpeky Ukraïny (State Archives of the Security Service of Ukraine)
HJ	Hitlerjugend (Hitler Youth)
HRO	Hrvatska revolucionarna organizacija (Croatian Revolutionary Organization), or Ustaša
HSLS	Hlinkova slovenská ľudová strana (Hlinka's Slovak People's Party)
HUNM	Hrupa Ukraïns'koï Natsionalnoï Molodi (Group of the Ukrainian National Youth)
HURI	Harvard Ukrainian Research Institute
KAUM	Katolyts'ka aktsiia ukraïns'koï molodi (Catholic Action of Ukrainian Youth)
KAW	Karta, Archiwum Wschodnie in Warsaw (Karta Archives in Warsaw)
KGB	Komitet gosudarstvennoi bezopasnosti (Committee for State Security)
KiSPSB	Komitet iz sporudzhennia pam"iatnyka Stepanu Banderi (Society to Erect the Stepan Bandera Monument)
KONR	Komitet Osvobodzheniia Narodov Rossii (Committee for the Liberation of the Peoples of Russia)
KP(b)U	Komunistychna Partiia (bil'shovykiv) Ukraïny (Communist Party [Bolsheviks] of Ukraine)
KPSS	Kommunisticheskaia Partiia Sovetskogo Soiuza (Communist Party of the Soviet Union)
KPU	Komunistychna Partiia Ukrayïny (Communist Party of Ukraine)
KPZU	Komunistychna Partiia Zakhidnoï Ukraïny (Communist Party of West Ukraine)
KUK	Komitet Ukraïntsiv Kanady (Ukrainian Canadian Committee)
KUN	Kongres Ukraïns'kykh Natsionalistiv (Congress of Ukrainian Nationalists)
LAF	Lietuvos aktyvistų frontas (Lithuanian Activist Front)
LNAU	L'vivs'kyi Natsional'nyi Ahrarnyi Universytet (L'viv State Agrarian University)
LN-W	Landesarchiv Nordrhein-Westfalen (Provincial Archives, Nordrhein-Westfalen)
LUN	Lehiia Ukraïns'kykh Natsionalistiv (Legion of Ukrainian Nationalists)
MfS	Ministerium für Staatssicherheit, Stasi (Ministry for State Security)
MGB	Ministerstvo Gosudarstvennoi Bezopasnosti (Ministry of State Security)
MI6	Colloquial name for the Foreign Section of the (British) Secret Intelligence Service (SIS)
MSW	Ministerstwo Spraw Wewnętrznych (Ministry of Internal Affairs)
MSZ	Ministerstwo Spraw Zewnętrznych (Ministry of Foreign Affairs)
MVD	Ministerstvo Vnutrennikh Del (Ministry of Internal Affairs)
NARA	U.S. National Archives and Records Administration
NDH	Nezavisna Država Hrvatska (Independent State of Croatia)
NKGB	Narodnyi komissariat gosudarstvennoi bezopasnosti (People's Commissariat for State Security)

NKVD	Narodnyi komissariat vnutrennikh del (People's Commissariat for Internal Affairs)
NPD	Nationaldemokratische Partei Deutschlands (National Democratic Party of Germany)
NRU	Narodnyi Rukh Ukraïny (Popular Movement of Ukraine)
NSDAP	Nationalsozialistische Deutsche Arbeiterpartei (National Socialist German Workers' Party)
NSZ	Narodowe Siły Zbrojne (National Armed Forces)
NTS	Natsional'no Trudowoi Soiuz (National Alliance of Russian Solidarists)
OKW	Oberkommando der Wehrmacht (Supreme Command of the Armed Forces)
ONR	Obóz Narodowo-Radykalny (National Radical Camp)
OPC	Office of Policy Coordination
OSS	Office of Strategic Services
OUN-B	Orhanizatsia Ukraïns'kykh Natsionalistiv-Bandera (Organization of Ukrainian Nationalists-Bandera)
OUN-M	Orhanizatsia Ukraïns'kykh Natsionalistiv-Mel'nyk (Organization of Ukrainian Nationalists-Mel'nyk)
OUN-z	Orhanizatsia Ukraïns'kykh Natsionalistiv-za kordonom (Organization of Ukrainian Nationalists-abroad)
OVF	Orhanizatsiï Vyzvol'noho Frontu (Organizations of the Liberation Front)
ObVB	Ob"iednannia Ukraïntsiv u Velykii Brytaniï (Federation of Ukrainians in Great Britain)
OVKUH	Orhanizaciia Vyzhchykh Klias Ukraïns'kykh Himnazii (Organization of the Upper Grades of the Ukrainian High Schools)
PAA	Provincial Archives of Alberta
PAAA	Politisches Archiv des Auswärtigen Amtes in Berlin (Political Archives of the Foreign Office in Berlin)
PSPU	Prohresyvna sotsialistychna partiia Ukraïny (Progressive Socialist Party of Ukraine)
PUN	Provid Ukraïns'kykh Natsionalistiv (Leadership of the Ukrainian Nationalists)
PRL	Polska Rzeczpospolita Ludowa (People's Republic of Poland)
PZPR	Polska Zjednoczona Partia Robotnicza (Polish United Workers' Party)
RCMP	Royal Canadian Mounted Police
RFP	Rossiiskaia fashistskaia partiia (Russian Fascist Party)
RGASPI	Rossiiskii gosudarstvennyi arkhiv sotsial'no-politicheskoi istorii (Russian Soviet Federative Socialist Republic)
RGVA	Rossiiskii Gosudarstvennyi voennyi arkhiv (Russian State Military Archives)
ROA	Ruskaia Osvoboditelnaia Armia (Russian Liberation Army)
RGASOI	Rossiiskii gosudarstvennyi arkhiv sotsial'no-poiliticheskoi istorii (Russian State Archive of Socio-Political History)
RSHA	Reichssicherheitshauptamt (Reich Security Main Office)
SB	Sluzhba Bezpeky (Security Service)

SBU	Sluzhba Bezpeky Ukraïny (Security Service of Ukraine)
SD	Sicherheitsdienst (Security Service)
SED	Sozialistische Einheitspartei Deutschlands (Socialist Unity Party of Germany)
SIFAR	Servizio Informazioni Forze Armate (Italian Military Intelligence)
SIS	Secret Intelligence Service
SNPU	Sotsial-natsional'na partiia Ukraïny (Social-National Party of Ukraine)
SNUM	Spilka Nezalezhnoï Ukraïns'koï Molodi (Association of Independent Ukrainian Youth)
SS	Schutzstaffel (Protection Squadron)
StM	Staatsarchiv München (Munich State Archives)
SUB	Soiuz Ukraïntsiv u Velykii Brytaniï (Association of Ukrainians in Great Britain)
SUF	Soiuz Ukraïns'kykh Fashystiv (Union of Ukrainian Fascists)
SUM	Spilka Ukraïns'koï Molodi (Ukrainian Youth Organization)
SUN	Soiuz Ukraïns'kykh Natsionalistiv (Union of the Ukrainian Nationalists)
SUNM	Soiuz Ukraïns'koi Natsionalistychnoï Molodi (Union of the Ukrainian Nationalistic Youth)
SUOZUNzW	Stowarzyszenie Upamiętnienia Ofiar Zbrodni Ukraińskich Nacjonalistów z Wrocławia (Society to Commemorate the Victims of the Crimes of Ukrainian Nationalists in Wrocław)
TsDAHO	Tsentral'nyi derzhavnyi arkhiv hromads'kykh obiednan' Ukrainy (Central State Archives of Public Organizations of Ukraine)
TsDAVOV	Tsentral'nyi derzhavnyi arkhiv vyshchykh orhaniv vlady ta upravlinnia Ukrainy (Central State Archives of the Supreme Bodies of Power and Government of Ukraine)
TsDIAL	Tsentral'nyi derzhavnyi istorychnyi arkhiv u L'vovi (Central State Historical Archive of Ukraine in Lviv)
TsDVR	Tsentr doslidzhen' vyzvol'noho rukhu (Institute for the Study of the Liberation Movement)
TShLA	Taras Shevchenko Library and Archives (of the SUB in London)
TsNV	Tsentr Natsional'noho vidrodzhennia imeni Stepana Bandery (Stepan Bandera Centre of National Revival)
UNO	Ukraïns'ke Natsional'ne Obiednannia (Ukrainian National Association)
UNRRA	United Nations Relief and Rehabilitation Administration
UB	Urząd Bezpieczeństwa (Polish Department of Security)
UCC	Kongres Ukraïntsiv Kanady (Ukrainian Canadian Congress)
UHA	Ukraïns'ka Halyts'ka Armiia (Ukrainian Galician Army)
UHVR	Ukraïns'ka Holovna Vyzvol'na Rada (Ukrainian Supreme Liberation Council)
UINP	Ukraïns'kyi instytut natsional'noï pam"iati (Ukrainian Institute of National Memory)
UKKA	Ukraïns'kyi Kongresovyi Komitet Ameryky (Ukrainian Congress Committee of America)

Ukrainian SRR	Ukraïns'ka Radians'ka Sotsialistychna Respublika (Ukrainian Soviet Socialist Republic)
UKU	Ukraïns'kyi Katholyts'kyi Soiuz (Ukrainian Catholic Union)
UNA	Ukraïns'ka natsional'na asambleia (Ukrainian National Assembly)
UNA	Ukraïns'ka Natsional'na Armiia (Ukrainian National Army)
UNDO	Ukraïns'ke Natsional'no-Demokratychne Obiednannia (Ukrainian National Democratic Alliance)
UNDP	Ukraïns'ka Natsional'no-Demokratychna Partia (Ukrainian National-Democratic Party)
UNF	Ukrainian National Federation of Canada
UNK	Ukraïns'kyi Natsional'nyi Komitet (Ukrainian National Committee)
UNO	Ukraïns'ke Natsional'ne Obiednannia (Ukrainian National Association)
UNP	Ukraïns'ka Narodna Partia (Ukrainian National Party)
UNR	Ukrayins'ka Narodna Respublika (Ukrainian People's Republic)
UNR	Ukraïns'ka Natsionalna Rada (Ukrainian National Council)
UNRRA	United Nations Relief and Rehabilitation Administration
UNSO	Ukraïns'ka natsional'na samooborona (Ukrainian National Self-Defense)
UPA	Ukraïns'ka Povstans'ka Armiia (Ukrainian Insurgent Army)
USHMM	United States Holocaust Memorial Museum
USRP	Ukraïns'ka Sotsialistychno-Radykalna Partiia (Ukrainian Socialist Radical Party)
USSR	Soiuz Sovetskikh Sotsialisticheskikh Respublik (Union of Soviet Socialist Republics)
UTsK	Ukraïns'kyi Tsentral'nyi Komitet (Ukrainian Central Committee)
UVF	Ukraïns'kyi Vyzvol'nyi Front (Ukrainian Liberation Front)
UVO	Ukraïns'ka Viis'kova Orhanizatsiia (Ukrainian Military Organization)
UVU	Ukraïns'kyi Vil'nyi Universytet (Ukrainian Free University)
UWI	Ukrainisches Wissenschaftliches Institut (Ukrainian Scientific Institute)
UWVA	Ukrainian War Veteran's Association
VMRO	Vatreshna makedonska revoliutsionna organizatsia (Internal Macedonian Revolutionary Organisation)
VNN	Vereinigung der Verfolgten des Naziregimes (Society of People Persecuted by the Nazi Regime)
ZAIG	Zentrale Auswertungs- und Informationsgruppe des MfS (Central Evaluation and Information Group)
ZCh OUN	Zakordonni Chastyny OUN (Foreign Units of the OUN)
ZNiO	Zakład Narodowy im. Ossolińskich we Wrocławiu (National Ossoliński Institute in Wrocław)
ZP UHVR	Zakordonne Predstavnytsvo UHVR (Foreign Representation of the UHVR)
ZUNR	Zakhidno-Ukrayins'ka Narodna Respublika (West Ukrainian National Republic)

NOTE ON LANGUAGE, NAMES, AND TRANSLITERATIONS

The region in which Bandera lived for the first thirty years of his life was inhabited by peoples who spoke different languages and used various names for their cities, towns, and villages, and also for the regions in which they lived, such as Lemberg, Lwów, Lemberik, L'viv, L'vov for Lviv; or Kraków, Kroke, Krakau for Cracow; or Galizien, Halychyna, Galicja, Galitsye for Galicia. In this book I use well-established English names, such as Cracow, Galicia, Kiev, Lviv, Moscow, or Warsaw, if they exist. Otherwise I use the names in the language of the country in which they are currently located, such as Ivano-Frankivs'k, Ternopil' or Gdańsk. On first use, I also introduce the name used by the state administration at that time. The transliteration of Ukrainian and Russian words follows the standard of the Library of Congress (unless Latin characters were used in the original).

INTRODUCTION

This study investigates the life and the political cult of Stepan Bandera, a Ukrainian far-right leader who lived between 1909 and 1959. Bandera's cult emerged in the mid-1930s and has endured to the present. The person and the cult did not exist separately from each other but remained in a state of mutual dependency. They did not occur and function in a vacuum but in specific cultural, social, and political contexts. The investigation of these contexts is one of the crucial goals of this study. It will allow us to comprehend the interrelation between Bandera's life and the processes surrounding his mythologization. The book combines a political biography of the legendary Ukrainian leader, embedded in the history of his movement, with an analysis of the writers, historians, ideologists, film directors, politicians, and political activists who were involved in the process of creating the Bandera cult between the mid-1930s and the end of the first decade of this century.

The Person

Even without the cult that arose during his lifetime and flourished after his death, Stepan Bandera was an intriguing person. It was not purely by chance that he became one of the central symbols of Ukrainian nationalism, although the role of chance in history should not be underestimated. With his radical nature, doctrinaire determination, and strong faith in an ultranationalist Ukrainian revolution that was intended to bring about the "rebirth" of the Ukrainian nation, Bandera fulfilled the ideological expectations of his cohorts. By the time he was twenty-six, he was admired not only by other Ukrainian revolutionary ultranationalists but also by some other elements of Ukrainian society living in the Second Polish Republic. The same factors made him the leader (Ukr. *Providnyk* or *Vozhd'*), and symbol of the most violent, twentieth century, western Ukrainian political movement: the Organization of Ukrainian Nationalists (*Orhanizatsia Ukraïns'kykh Natsionalistiv*, OUN), which in late 1942 and early 1943 formed the Ukrainian Insurgent Army (*Ukraïns'ka Povstans'ka Armiia*, UPA). Despite, or perhaps because of the fact that Bandera spent a significant part of his life outside Ukraine, in prison or other confinement, he became a legendary personality after whom thousands of his followers, sympathizers and even ordinary western Ukrainians were called Banderites (Ukr. *banderivtsi*, Pol. *banderowcy*, Rus. *banderovtsi*). There are also those who think that his remarkable-sounding name, meaning "banner" in Polish and Spanish, contributed to his becoming the symbol of Ukrainian nationalism.

A biographical investigation of Bandera is challenging. His political myth is embedded in different ideologies, which have distorted the perception of the person. Not without reason do the Bandera biographies that have appeared in Poland, Russia and Ukraine since 1990 differ greatly from one another and inform us very little about the person and related history. Very few of them examine archival documents. Many are couched in various post-Soviet nationalist discourses. Their authors present Bandera as a national hero, sometimes even as a saint, and ignore or deny his radical worldview and his followers' contribution to ethnic and political violence. Others present Bandera as a biblical kind of evil and deny war crimes committed against Ukrainian civilians by the Poles, Germans, and Soviets. Earlier publications on Bandera written during the Cold War were either embedded in Soviet discourse or, more frequently, in the nationalist discourse of the Ukrainian diaspora.

The investigation of Bandera requires not only a comparison of his biographies and other publications relating to him, but, more important, the examination of numerous archival documents, memoirs written by persons who knew him, and documents and publications written by him personally. The study of these documents reveals how Bandera acted at particular stages of his life, and how he was perceived by his contemporaries. This enables us to understand Bandera's role in twentieth-century Ukrainian history and helps us look for answers to the most difficult questions related to his biography, such as if and to what extent he was responsible for OUN and UPA atrocities, in which he was personally not involved but which he approved of.

Cult, Myth, Charisma, and Rituals

The cult of the leader is a phenomenon created by and rooted within a particular society, group, or community that is prepared to accept the ideological dimensions of the cult. A leader often emerges in a time of crisis and his adherents believe that he will help the community weather it. The power and charisma of the leader derives usually only in part from him. In greater measure, it is a social product, a creation of social expectations vested in him.[1] The leaders around whom personality cults are established are therefore either charismatic or, more frequently, believed to be charismatic. Charisma might be a "personality gift, a situational coincidence, or a particular pact between leader and the followers."[2]

A charismatic leader cannot exist without a "charismatic community," which would accept, admire, celebrate, and believe in his "extraordinary" qualities. To achieve this state of mind and affairs, an emotional relationship between the leader and the community must be established. The community feels connected with its leader who, as his followers believe, takes care of them and leads them toward a better future.[3] One of the most effective ways to establish an emotional relationship between the leader and the community is through the performance of rituals. The practicing of political rituals is crucial for the formation of a collective identity that unites a group. Rituals influence the morality and values of the individuals practicing them, and transform the emotional state of the group.[4]

In practice, the process of creating charisma around the leader might proceed in different ways, depending on the nature of the movement. Small movements in

1 Ian Kershaw, *Hitler 1889–1936: Hubris* (New York: W. W. Norton & Company, 2000), xxvi.

2 Aristotle A. Kallis, "Fascism, 'Charisma' and 'Charismatisation': Weber's Model of 'Charismatic Domination' and Interwar European Fascism," Totalitarian Movements and Political Religions, Vol. 7, No. 1 (2006): 25.

3 Kallis, Fascism, 'Charisma' and 'Charismatisation', 25–26.

4 Albert Bergesen, "Die rituelle Ordnung," in *Ritualtheorien: Ein einführendes Handbuch*, eds. Andréa Belliger and David J. Krieger (Opladen: Westdeutscher Verlag, 1998), 50–51.

multiethnic states—such as the OUN or the Croatian Ustaša—would use methods different from those used by movements that took control of the state and established a regime, such as the Italian Fascists or the German National Socialists. Charisma may also be attributed to a leader after his death. A charismatic community might still be under the influence of its deceased leader and therefore continue to admire and commemorate him. Not only the body of the leader but also his personal objects, including his clothing, writing desk, or pen might become imbued with sacred meaning after his death. The members of the charismatic community might treat those objects as relics, the last remnants of their legendary leader and true hero.[5]

The cults of fascist and other totalitarian leaders emerged in Europe after the First World War. Their emergence was related to the disappearance of relevant monarchies and of the cults of emperors who had been regarded as the representatives of God on earth, and whose absence caused a void in the lives of many.[6] Several fascist movements regarded the Roman Catholic Church as an important institution to imitate because the head of the Church did not need his own charisma to appear charismatic.[7] Nazi Party Secretary Rudolf Hess wrote in a private letter in 1927: "The great popular leader is similar to the great founder of a religion: he must communicate to his listeners an apodictic faith. Only then can the mass of followers be led where they should be led. They will then also follow the leader if the setbacks are encountered; but only then, if they have communicated to them unconditional belief in the absolute rightness of their own people."[8] The legal philosopher Julius Binder argued in 1929: "The Leader cannot be made, can in this sense not be selected. The Leader makes himself in that he comprehends the history of his people."[9] The historian Emilio Gentile observed that the "charismatic leader is accepted as a guide by his followers, who obey him with veneration and devotion, because they consider that he has been invested with the task of realizing an idea of the *mission*; the leader is the living incarnation and mythical interpretation of his mission."[10] In this sense, the leader as an incarnation of a mission, or as a charismatic personality, might acquire the qualities of a saint or messiah that correspond to the community's needs.[11] Followers of a leader believe that he comes as "destiny from the inner essence of people,"[12] because he embodies the idea of the movement and personifies its politics. Roger Eatwell observed that the leader might help people

5 For worshiping a leader after his death, see Sergio Luzzatto, *The Body of Il Duce: Mussolini's Corpse and the Fortunes of Italy* (New York: Metropolitan Books, 2005).

6 Heidi Hein-Kircher, "Führerkult und Führermythos: Theoretische Reflexionen zur Einführung," in *Der Führer im Europa des 20. Jahrhunderts*, ed. Benno Ennker and Heidi Hein-Kircher (Marburg: Verlag Herder-Institut, 2010), 3.

7 Emilio Gentile, "Mussolini as the Prototypical Charismatic Dictator," *Charisma and Fascism in Interwar Europe*, ed. Roger Eatwell, Stein Ugevlik Larsen, and António Costa Pinto (London: Routledge 2007) 125.

8 Quoted in Ian Kershaw, *The 'Hitler Myth': Image and Reality in the Third Reich* (Oxford: Clarendon Press, 1987), 27.

9 Kurt Sontheimer, *Antidemokratisches Denken in der Weimarer Republik* (Munich: Nymphenburger Verlagshandlung, 1962), 273, quoted in Ian Kershaw, *The 'Hitler Myth'*, 19.

10 Gentile, Mussolini as the Prototypical Charismatic Dictator, 113.

11 Kallis, Fascism, 'Charisma' and 'Charismatisation', 29.

12 Kershaw, *The 'Hitler Myth'*, 19.

to "understand complex events" and "come to terms with complexity through the image of a single person who is held to be special, but in some way accountable."[13]

A fascist leader is expected to be an idealistic, dynamic, passionate, and revolutionary individual. He is the "bearer of a mission," who tries to overthrow the status quo and has a very clear idea of his foes. His mission is understood as a revolutionary intervention. He frequently presents himself as a person who is ready to sacrifice his life and the lives of his followers for the idea of the movement. His transformation into a myth is almost inevitable, and he may become the prisoner of his own myth.[14]

The interwar period witnessed the rise of a range of different charismatic leaders and personality cults. A few leaders, such as Tomáš Masaryk in Czechoslovakia, were neither fascist nor authoritarian.[15] Some of them, like Józef Piłsudski in Poland were authoritarian, but not fascist, and could best be described as military.[16] The cults sprang up in different political, cultural, and social circumstances. The most famous European personality cults were established around Adolf Hitler in Germany, Benito Mussolini in Italy, and Josef Stalin in the Soviet Union. Other cults surrounded Francisco Franco in Spain, Antonio de Oliveira Salazar in Portugal, Ante Pavelić in Croatia, Corneliu Zelea Codreanu and Ion Antonescu in Romania, Miklós Horthy in Hungary, Engelbert Dollfuss and Kurt Schuschnigg in Austria, Andrej Hlinka and Jozef Tiso in Slovakia.[17]

Unlike most of these personalities Bandera never ruled a state, nor was his cult institutionalized in a sovereign state during his lifetime. This changed, ironically enough, half a century after his death, when not only did his cult reappear in western Ukraine but the President, Iushchenko, designated him a Hero of Ukraine. Since the middle of the 1930s, Bandera has been worshiped by various groups, as *Providnyk*, as a national hero, and as a romantic revolutionary. The ideological nature of the Bandera cult did not differ substantially from that of other cults of nationalist, fascist, or other authoritarian leaders, but the circumstances in which the Bandera cult existed were specific. Moreover, the long period over which the Bandera cult has been cultivated is not typical of the majority of such European leader cults. Following his assassination, the Ukrainian diaspora commemorated Bandera, not only as the *Providnyk* but also as a martyr who died for Ukraine. After the dissolution of the Soviet Union, the cult re-emerged in Ukraine. One of the purposes of this study is to explain both the continuity of the Bandera cult, and its varieties.

The myth of a leader is related to the phenomenon of a leader cult but the two concepts are not synonymous. The leader myth is a story that reduces the personality

13 Roger Eatwell, "Concept and Theory of Charismatic Leadership," in *Charisma and Fascism*, ed. Eatwell, 13.

14 Gentile, Mussolini as the Prototypical Charismatic Dictator, 114, 117, 119, 127.

15 Masaryk was neither a fascist nor an authoritarian dictator, but his charisma was used to create a cult that helped to legitimize the existence of Czechoslovakia. Cf. Andrea Orzoff, "The Husbandman: Tomáš Masaryk's Leader Cult in Interwar Czechoslovakia," *Austrian History Yearbook* 39 (2008), 121–37.

16 For the Piłsudski cult, see Heidi Hein, *Der Piłsudski-Kult und seine Bedeutung für den polnischen Staat 1926–1939* (Marburg: Verlag Herder Institut, 2002).

17 For the cults of personality in Europe and the charismatic European leaders, see Roger Eatwell, Stein Ugevlik Larsen, and António Costa Pinto, ed., *Charisma and Fascism in Interwar Europe* (London: Routledge 2007); Benno Ennker and Heidi Hein-Kircher, *Der Führer im Europa des 20. Jahrhunderts* (Marburg: Verlag Herder-Institut, 2010); Bernd J. Fischer, ed., *Balkan Strongmen: Dictators and Authoritarian Rulers of South Eastern Europe* (West Lafayette: Purdue UP, 2007).

and history of the leader to a restricted number of idealized features. It may be expressed by means of a hagiographic article, book, image, film, song, or other form of media. The myth usually depicts the leader as a national hero, a brave revolutionary, the father of a nation, or a martyr. It describes the leader in a selective way, designed to meet and confirm the expectations of the "charismatic" or "enchanted" community. Like every myth, it mobilizes emotions and immobilizes minds.

The leader myth belongs to the more modern species of political myths, embedded in a particular ideology. Such myths emerged alongside modern politics, in the late eighteenth and early nineteenth century. According to Christopher Flood, there is a reciprocal relationship between political myths and ideologies. Ideology provides myths with a framework of meaning, and myths are a means of visualizing and manifesting ideology.[18]

For the purposes of this study, ideology is characterized as a set of ideas of authoritative principles, which provide political and cultural orientation for groups that suffer from temporary cultural, social or political disorientation.[19] Ideology oversimplifies the complexity of the world, in order to make it an understandable and acceptable "reality." It also deactivates critical and rational thought.[20] For Clifford Geertz, "it is a loss of orientation that most directly gives rise to ideological activity, an inability, for lack of usable models, to comprehend the universe of civic rights and responsibilities in which one finds oneself located."[21] Ideologies are more persistent in societies that have strong needs for mobilization and legitimization, such as totalitarian states and fascist movements, than in those without such needs. Owing to their unifying, legitimizing, and mobilizing attributes, ideologies can also be understood as belief-systems that unite societies or groups, provide them with values, and inspire them to realize their political goals.[22]

The political myth of Stepan Bandera was initially embodied in the ideology of Ukrainian nationalism, which, in the 1920s, 1930s, and early 1940s, underwent a process of fascistization. This ideology produced a whole mythology, consisting of a set of various political myths, of which the Bandera myth was perhaps the most significant. Examples of other important political myths embedded in far-right Ukrainian nationalist ideology are the myth of the proclamation of Ukrainian statehood on 30 June 1941 in Lviv; military myths, including the myth of the tragic but heroic UPA; and the myths of other OUN members and UPA insurgents such as Ievhen Konovalets', Roman Shukhevych, Vasyl' Bilas, and Dmytro Danylyshyn. Finally, it should be added that the Bandera myth was an important component of Soviet ideology and the ideology of Polish nationalism, each of which evaluated Bandera very differently from the way the Ukrainian nationalist ideology defined him.

18 Christopher Flood, *Political Myth: A Theoretical Introduction* (New York: Garland Publishing. Inc., 1996), 164; Yves Bizeul, "Theorien der politischen Mythen und Rituale," in *Politische Mythen und Rituale in Deutschland, Frankreich und Polen*, ed. Yves Bizeul (Berlin: Duncker & Humboldt, 2000), 18.

19 Clifford Geertz, *The Interpretation of Cultures* (New York: Basis Books, 1973), 218–20; Bizeul, Theorien der politischen Mythen, 16–17.

20 Anton Grabner-Haider, *Ideologie und Religion: Interaktion und Sinnsysteme in der modernen Gesellschaft* (Vienna: Herder, 1981), 23–31; Flood, *Political Myth*, 26. On this question, see also Hubert Schleichert, *Wie man mit Fundamentalisten diskutiert, ohne den Verstand zu verlieren: Anleitung zum subversiven Denken* (Munich: C.H. Beck, 1997).

21 Geertz, *Interpretation of Cultures*, 219.

22 Terry Eagleton, *Ideology: An Introduction* (New York: Verso, 1991), 43–44.

Ukrainian Nationalism and Integral Nationalism

The concept of integral nationalism has been attractive to many scholars who have investigated the OUN. The notion of integral nationalism was shaped around 1900 by Charles Maurras, a leader and ideologist of Action Française, a French royalist, conservative, and antidemocratic movement. Fifty years later, John Armstrong published *Ukrainian Nationalism*, the first comprehensive and authoritative study of the OUN and the Second World War. The American historian classified the extremist form of Ukrainian nationalism as "integral nationalism," and specified that "the theory and teaching of the Nationalists were very close to Fascism, and in some respects, such as the insistence on 'racial purity,' even went beyond the original Fascist doctrines."[23] According to him, integral nationalism "never had much appeal in France or other Western European countries, but, in modified forms, it became a dominant force in the 'dissatisfied' countries of Central and Southern Europe in the twenties."[24] Before Armstrong, historians such as Carlton Joseph Huntley Hayes applied the concept of integral nationalism to far-right movements and authoritarian regimes in Hungary and Poland, as well as to Fascist Italy and Nazi Germany. This method allowed Hayes and Armstrong to avoid using the contested term "fascism" but it did not contribute to the analytical and comparative understanding of the analyzed movements and regimes. As Armstrong explained, integral nationalism was "by definition a movement of individual nations rather than a universal ideology."[25]

In his early years as a scholar, Armstrong elaborated a number of important characteristics of the ideology of the Ukrainian nationalists and also a few significant differences and similarities between the OUN and other East Central European far-right movements. He defined "integral nationalism" in terms of five characteristics: "(1) a belief in the nation as the supreme value to which all others must be subordinated, essentially a totalitarian concept; (2) an appeal to mystically conceived ideas of the solidarity of all individuals making up the nation, usually on the assumption that biological characteristics or the irreversible effects of common historical development had welded them into one organic whole; (3) a subordination of rational, analytic thought to the 'intuitively correct' emotions; (4) expression of the 'national will' through a charismatic leader and an elite nationalist enthusiasts organized in a single party; (5) glorification of action, war, and violence as an expression of the superior biological vitality of the nation."[26]

Analyzing the ideology of Ukrainian nationalism, Armstrong argued that "the essential irrationalism of the ideology was expressed by fanatical romanticism, which was, however, among the comparatively unsophisticated Ukrainians more spontaneous and genuine than the cynical rejection of reason by the Germans and Italians."[27] In an article published in 1968 he broadened the scope of his analysis to include other East Central European movements, such as the Hlinka Party and the Croatian Ustaša. He admitted that all of them were influenced by Italian Fascism but empha-

[23] John A. Armstrong, *Ukrainian Nationalism* (New York: Columbia University Press, 1963), 280.
[24] Armstrong, *Ukrainian Nationalism*, 20.
[25] Armstrong, *Ukrainian Nationalism*, 20; Carlton Joseph Huntley Hayes, *The Historical Evolution of Modern Nationalism* (New York: The Macmillan Company, 1950), 167.
[26] Armstrong, *Ukrainian Nationalism*, 20.
[27] Ibid., 22.

sized that "at least as a start, it seems preferable to not call OUN's ideology 'fascism' but to designate it 'integral nationalism.'"[28]

Armstrong rightly analyzed the OUN in the context of the Ustaša, but the classification of the ideologies of the OUN, the Ustaša, and the Hlinka Party as "integral nationalism" is, at least from the contemporary point of view, problematic and not entirely convincing. First, neither did the OUN use the term "integral nationalism," nor did it identify itself with the ideology of "integral nationalism." Second, the OUN and its leaders did not claim the "traditional hereditary monarchy" and a number of other features typical of integral nationalism, as did Maurras, the father of this ideology. The OUN was integral in the sense of being exclusive: it anticipated the establishment of an ethnic Ukrainian state without Jews, Poles, Russians, and other minorities. Ukrainian extreme nationalism featured some of the elements of integral nationalism, such as placing the country above all. Similarly, Horthy's regime in Hungary, Piłsudski's in Poland, Mussolini's in Italy, or Hitler's in Germany were to some extent influenced by Action Française and Maurras' writings, but they were neither united by, nor were they a form of integral nationalism, as Armstrong and Hayes argued.[29]

If Armstrong's theoretical approach to the subject was not entirely useful for the contextualization of the OUN, the empirical part of his study—which has significantly influenced later studies of the OUN and UPA—appears today to be truly problematic. Limited access to sources concerning the OUN and UPA, and some of his methods of studying and selecting documents led Armstrong to depict only a part of the history of the movement, while purporting to present the whole. Like many historians at that time, Armstrong had no access to Soviet archives and did not use testimonies and memoirs left by survivors of the OUN and UPA terror. Armstrong based his study mainly on German documents, and on interviews with Ukrainian émigrés who had served in the OUN and UPA. In so doing, he was not able to detect, investigate, and understand many of the atrocities committed by the OUN and UPA during the Second World War. This prevented him from providing an appropriate evaluation of extremist Ukrainian nationalism, affected his understanding of the movement as a whole, and channeled the subsequent study of Ukrainian nationalism into a particular direction.

28 John Armstrong, "Collaborationism in World War II: The Integral Nationalist Variant in Eastern Europe," *The Journal of Modern History*, Vol. 40, No. 3 (1968): 400.

29 Armstrong, *Ukrainian Nationalism*, 20. On Charles Maurras and integral nationalism, see Steve Bastow, "Integral Nationalism," in *World Fascism: A Historical Encyclopedia*, ed. Cyprian P. Blamires (Santa Barbara, CA: ABC-CLIO, 2006), 1:338.

The OUN and Fascism

Of all of the ideologies investigated in this study, the most controversial, especially when related to Bandera and the OUN, is fascism. Constantin Iordachi correctly remarked that "fascism continues to be one of the most intriguing and most debated radical political phenomena of the twentieth century."[30] To use the term appropriately and to avoid misunderstandings, it is necessary to elucidate its meaning and to explain how it will be applied in this study. This will allow us to determine in which sense the OUN was a fascist phenomenon and Bandera a leader of a fascist movement. It will also enable us to place the OUN on the map of interwar European far-right, fascist, and other authoritarian movements and regimes. This approach should not narrow our analysis of Bandera and the OUN but should provide an appropriate theoretical context.

The term "fascism" is derived from the Latin word "fasces," meaning a bundle of rods tied around an axe. The fasces were carried by the Roman lictors, symbolized the juridical authority of the magistrate, and represented the unity and strength of the community. In the late eighteenth century, the Italian Jacobins used the word "fascism" as an expression of political freedom and national unity. In the nineteenth century, the term "fascism" was used by various socialist and nationalist political groups. In March 1919 in Milan, Mussolini used the term "fascism" when he founded the *Fascio di Combattimento*, to the ranks of which he recruited a number of ex-soldiers, syndicalists and futurists. At the end of October 1922, the National Fascist Party (*Partito Nazionale Fascista*, PNF) conducted the March on Rome, as a result of which Mussolini became prime minister of Italy. In this position, he began to seize power and to create the first fascist regime. Although the establishment of a full-scale dictatorship in Italy was accomplished only in 1926, fascism had been admired by a plethora of European politicians, writers and intellectuals, at least since Mussolini's 1922 coup d'état.[31]

During the interwar period the term "fascism" was used in at least three ways. First, it described the political regime in Italy. Second, it was extended to other far-right movements and regimes that held values and ideas similar to those of the Italian Fascists. By the end of the 1920s, Mussolini had declared fascism an "export product" and undertaken its popularization and attempted globalization. He argued that fascism is "Italian in its particular form—universalist in spirit."[32] The seizure of power by the National Socialists in Germany in 1933 significantly reinforced the expansion and popularization of fascism in Europe and on other continents. Third,

30 Constantin Iordachi, "Comparative Fascist Studies: An Introduction," in *Comparative Fascist Studies: New Perspectives*, ed. Constantin Iordachi (London: Routledge 2009), 1.

31 Iordachi, *Comparative Fascist Studies*, 16; Kevin Passmore, *Fascism. A Very Short Introduction* (Oxford: Oxford University Press, 2002), 10; Arnd Bauerkämper, *Die "radikale Rechte" in Großbritanien* (Göttingen: Vandenhoeck & Ruprecht, 1991), 13–15, 143; Roger Eatwell, "Introduction: New Styles of Dictatorship and Leadership in Interwar Europe," in *Charisma and Fascism*, ed. Eatwell, xxi.

32 Samuel Huston Goodfellow, "Fascism as a Transnational Movement: The Case of Inter-War Alsace," *Contemporary European History* Vol. 22, No. 1 (2013): 93; Philip Morgan, *Fascism in Europe, 1919–1945* (London: Routledge, 2003), 168.

the term "fascist" was used in particular by communists and socialists to discredit political opponents of various orientations.[33]

The earliest interpretations and condemnations of fascism came from Marxist intellectuals, communists, and liberals. In the early 1920s, the Communist International (Comintern) used the term "fascism" in connection with the fascists in Italy and the Nazis in Germany. It soon, however, began to apply it to various conservative, authoritarian, or military regimes, such as those of Józef Piłsudski in Poland, the Antanas Smetona regime in Lithuania, the Miklós Horthy authoritarian government in Hungary, and the Ion Antonescu regime in Romania. Although these regimes borrowed some trappings from fascism, they were at odds—or even in open combat—with fascist movements in their respective states. By labeling Piłsudski's authoritarian regime as "fascist," the Comintern sought to emphasize how disappointed it was with the Polish leader. Piłsudski in his earlier life had been a socialist, but after his seizure of power in 1926, he showed no interest in collaboration with communists.[34] Similarly, even socialists were sometimes labeled as "fascists." In 1924, Stalin announced that "Social Democracy is objectively the moderate wing of fascism." Because the Social-Democrat government in Germany took action against the May Day march in 1929, during which several communists were killed, the Comintern argued that "Social Democracy is preparing ... the establishment of a fascist dictatorship."[35]

Equally important for orthodox Marxists was the identification of capitalism with fascism. In the Comintern report of 1935, Georgi Dimitroff claimed that fascist regimes were "the open terrorist dictatorship of the most reactionary, most chauvinistic and most imperialist elements of finance capital."[36] Only a few Marxist thinkers, such as Antonio Gramsci and Palmiro Togliatti, interpreted fascism in a more nuanced and non-dogmatic manner. On the other hand, some liberal commentators perceived fascism as "a sort of illness of national culture."[37]

In Soviet discourse during the Cold War, democratic countries of the Western bloc were frequently portrayed as fascist. Outside the Soviet Union, leftist groups used "fascist" as a derogatory term to discredit their enemies.[38] In the 1950s, the theory of totalitarianism, which compared and sometimes even equated communism with fascism, concentrating on the Soviet Union and Nazi Germany, became very popular. This approach explained the origins and features of totalitarian regimes but neglected the political, social, and cultural differences between fascism and communism.[39]

33 Stanley G. Payne, "Fascism and Communism," *Totalitarian Movements and Political Religions* Vol. 1, No. 3 (2000): 1–15; Stanley G. Payne, "Soviet anti-fascism: Theory and practice, 1921–45," *Totalitarian Movements and Political Religions* Vol. 4, No. 2 (2003): 1–62; Leonid Fuks, *Entstehung der kommunistischen Faschismustheorie: Die Auseinandersetzung der Komintern mit Faschismus und Nationalsozialismus 1921–1935* (Stuttgart: Deutsche Verlags-Anstalt, 1984).

34 Fuks, *Entstehung der kommunistischen Faschismustheorie*, 109–11.

35 Fuks, *Entstehung der kommunistischen Faschismustheorie*, 137; Payne, Soviet anti-fascism, 10, 15.

36 Georgi Dimitroff, *The United Front Against War and Fascism: Report to the Seventh World Congress of the Communist International 1935* (New York: Gama, 1974), 7.

37 Stanley G. Payne, *A History of Fascism 1914–1915* (London: University College London, 1995), 123–25.

38 Iordachi, *Comparative Fascist Studies*, 7–8; Daniel Ursprung, "Faschismus in Ostmittel- und Südosteuropa: Theorien, Ansätze, Fragestellungen," in *Der Einfluss von Faschismus und Nationalsozialismus auf Minderheiten in Ostmittel- und Südosteuropa*, ed. Mariana Hausleitner and Harald Roth (Munich: IKGS-Verlag, 2006), 12–13; Payne, *A History of Fascism*, 128.

39 Hannah Arendt, *The Origins of Totalitarianism* (New York: Harcourt Brace Jovanovich, 1951); Zbigniew Brzezinski and Carl Joachim Friedrich, *Totalitarian Dictatorship and Autocracy* (Cambridge,

The first non-Marxist studies on the subject of European fascist movements and regimes appeared in the 1960s. Authors such as Ernst Nolte, Eugen Weber, and George L. Mosse dealt with countries including Austria, Britain, France, Germany, Italy, Romania, Spain, as well as movements such as the Russian Fascist Party (*Rossiiskaia fashistskaia partia*, RFP) and the Croatian Ustaša.[40] From the outset, the extreme and genocidal form of Ukrainian nationalism was not classified and investigated as a fascist movement, although the OUN, especially in the 1930s and early 1940s, had felt an ideological affinity with Italian Fascism, National Socialism, the Ustaša, the British Union of Fascists, the Romanian Iron Guard, and a number of related movements. Scholars such as Armstrong, who began investigating the OUN in the 1950s, were frequently misled by the fact that the OUN emphasized its own national uniqueness and indigenous roots. This feature, however, was typical of all fascist movements. In particular, small and weak movements tended to stress the uniqueness of national traditions, because their leaders and ideologists were concerned about the independence of their countries and wished to avoid being labeled as national "traitors" or agents of international movements.[41]

Like the National Socialists and Ustaša, but unlike the British Union of Fascists and the Russian Fascist Party, the OUN did not use the term "fascist" as part of the name of the organization. OUN members and ideologists referred to themselves as nationalists but felt, especially in the late 1930s and early 1940s, that Ukrainian nationalism was the same type of movement as National Socialism or Italian Fascism. They also perceived themselves as a "liberation movement." Its aims were to combat and remove the "occupiers" of Ukrainian territories and to establish an independent Ukrainian state. With this in mind, the OUN was closely related to "liberation movements" such as the Ustaša and the Hlinka Party, which were also rooted in societies without nation states.

The way of interpreting and understanding fascism was altered in the 1990s by scholars such as Robert Paxton, Roger Griffin, Roger Eatwell, and Stanley G. Payne, who tried to elaborate a concept of generic fascism. A huge difficulty, when developing such a concept, was the heterogeneity of interwar far-right, authoritarian, and fascist movements, the uneven empirical research of the particular movements and regimes, and the inconsistent nature of fascism. The concept of generic fascism was derived from early studies by Nolte, Mosse, and Weber. It provided a basic theoretical framework for comparative fascist studies but it did not finish the debates on fascism and its diverse aspects, including for example the questions as to whether fascism appeared only in Europe and only in the interwar period or whether it was a

Mass.: Harvard University Press, 1956). See also Fuks, *Entstehung der kommunistischen Faschismustheorie*, 12; Iordachi, *Comparative Fascist Studies*, 29–32.

40 Ernst Nolte, *Der Faschismus in seiner Epoche* (Munich: Piper, 1963); Eugen Weber, *Action Française: Royalism and Reaction in Twentieth Century France* (Stanford, Calif.: Stanford University Press, 1962); *Varieties of Fascism. Doctrines of Revolution in the Twentieth Century* (Princeton, NJ: Van Nostrand, 1964). The first issue of *Journal of Comparative History* was devoted to fascism. Cf. *Journal of Comparative History* Vol. 1, No. 1 (1966).

41 On the transnationalism of fascist movements and regimes, see Arnd Bauerkämper, "Transnational Fascism: Cross-Border Relations between Regimes and Movements in Europe, 1922–1939," *East Central Europe* 37 (2010): 215–16, 236.

global phenomenon not limited in time, or if there was a clear difference between fascist movements and revolutionary ultranationalist non-fascist movements.[42]

First of all, it is important to point out the differences between a fascist movement and a fascist regime. Only a few movements became regimes in the sense that the Italian Fascists and the National Socialists did. Others, such as the Ustaša and the Hlinka Party, formed a regime only with the help of Nazi Germany and were dependent upon it. There were also long-lasting regimes like Franco's in Spain, and Salazar's in Portugal, which at times adopted many fascist features, but in the long term were a combination of national-conservative and fascist regimes. Robert Paxton proposed five stages of fascism: "(1) the initial creation of fascist movements; (2) their rooting as parties in a political system; (3) the acquisition of power; (4) the exercise of power, and finally in the longer term, (5) radicalization or entropy." Although logical and instructive, Paxton's concept was not entirely relevant to the study of some East Central European movements, such as the Ustaša or the OUN, which first needed to establish a state in order to establish a regime. His concept was deduced from fascist movements in democratic states. Paxton suggested that "fascism can appear wherever democracy is sufficiently implemented to have aroused disillusion" and argued that the Ku Klux Klan was the "earliest phenomenon that seems functionally related to fascism."[43]

Griffin, who adopted a Weberian ideal-type methodology, emphasized the myth, its mobilizing force, and its revolutionary, populist, and ultranationalist framework: "Fascism is a genus of political ideology whose mythic core in its various permutations is a palingenetic form of populist ultranationalism."[44] Crucial to Griffin's conception of fascism is the notion of palingenesis, meaning the rebirth or redemption of a nation by means of new populist ultranationalist policies after a period of supposed decline. Simultaneously, Griffin also pointed out the limits of an ideal-type definition and suggested that "such a model is essentially a utopia, since it cannot correspond exactly to anything in empirical reality, which is always irreducibly complex, 'messy', and unique. Definitions of generic terms can thus never be 'true' to reality, but they can be more or less useful in investigating it ('heuristically useful') when applied as conceptual tools of analysis."[45]

42 For debate on and criticism of the new consensus and Griffin's theory of fascism, see Roger Griffin, Werner Loh, and Andreas Umland, ed., *Fascism Past and Present, West and East. An International Debate on Concepts and Cases in the Comparative Study of the Extreme Right* (ibidem-Verlag: Stuttgart, 2006).

43 Robert Paxton, "The Five Stages of Fascism," *The Journal of Modern History* Vol. 70, No. 1. (1998): 11–12. On the difference between a fascist regime and a fascist movement, see Aristotle A. Kallis, "The 'Regime-Model' of Fascism," in *Comparative Fascist Studies*, ed. Iordachi, 217. Some other scholars of fascism like Wolfgang Wippermann held the view that the earliest fascist regime appeared in the Second Empire of Louis Napoleon between 1849 and 1852. This interpretation was invented by August Thalheimer and Otto Bauer. Cf. Payne, *A History of Fascism*, 125–26. For Wolfgang Wippermann, see Wolfgang Wippermann, *Faschismus: Eine Weltgeschichte vom 19. Jahrhundert bis heute* (Darmstadt: Primus, 2009), 16–21.

44 Roger Griffin, *The Nature of Fascism* (London: Printer, 1991), 26. Later Griffin extended his definition to a "revolutionary form of nationalism bent on mobilizing all 'healthy' social and political energies to resist the onslaught of 'decadence' so as to achieve the goal of national rebirth, a project that involves the regeneration (palingenesis) of both the political culture and the social and ethical culture underpinning it." See Roger Griffin, "General Introduction," in *Fascism: Critical Concept in Political Science*, ed. Roger Griffin and Matthew Feldman (London: Routledge, 2004), 1:6.

45 Roger Griffin, "General Introduction," in *International Fascism: Theories, Cases, and the New Consensus*, ed. Roger Griffin (Oxford: Oxford University Press, 1998), 2.

Roger Eatwell observed that Griffin's early definition of fascism omitted "fascism's 'negation,'" the six points of "fascist minimum" first formulated by Nolte. These points were: anti-Marxism, antiliberalism, anticonservatism, *Führerprinzip*, a party army, and the aim of totalitarianism.[46] Griffin seems to have omitted these points because he had developed an "empathetic approach" inspired by the writings of George Mosse and Emilio Gentile.[47] This was one of the weaknesses of Griffin's concept of fascism because it detached fascism from its violent and disastrous nature, while emphasizing fascism's creative strengths related to palingenesis.[48] Seeking an appropriate definition of fascism, we should not only complement Griffin's definition with Nolte's "fascist minimum" but also point out further negative features typical of fascism, such as anti-democracy, ultranationalism, populism, racism, antisemitism, militarism, and the cult of ethnic and political violence.

In his definition of fascism, similarly to Griffin, another leading scholar, Stanley G. Payne, emphasized the revolutionary and ultranationalist core: "Fascism may be defined as a form of revolutionary ultranationalism for national rebirth that is based on a primarily vitalist philosophy, is structured on extreme elitism, mass mobilization, and the Führerprinzip, positively values violence as end as well as means and tends to normalize war and/or the military virtues."[49] Also like Griffin, Payne advised that such definitions of common characteristics should be used with great care. Discussing palingenesis, he pointed out another weak point of Griffin's theory. Payne indicated that palingenesis is typical not only for fascist but also for leftist, moderate, conservative, and extreme right-wing nationalisms, and that there were also "non-fascist populist revolutionary forms of nationalism," such as the Revolutionary Nationalist Movement (*Movimiento Nacionalista Revolucionario*, MNR) in Bolivia. According to Payne, it is necessary to "clearly distinguish between fascist movements per se, and the non-fascist (or sometimes protofascist) authoritarian right." Such a distinction is, however, difficult to make because "the heyday of fascism coincided with a general era of political authoritarianism" and because "it would be grossly inaccurate to argue that this process proceeded independent of fascism, but neither was it merely synonymous with fascism." In a table including fascists, radical right, and conservative right movements, he did not consider the OUN and Ukraine, but classified similar and better-known movements, such as the Ustaša, the Iron Guard, and the Polish National Camp Falanga, as fascist.[50]

Ian Kershaw, the author of several excellent studies on the Third Reich, including a superb biography of Hitler, pointed out the limits of the concept of generic fascism. He argued that he has "no difficulty in describing German National Socialism both as a specific form of fascism and as a particular expression of totalitarianism" but remarked that "when it comes to explaining the essence of the Nazi phenomenon, it is less than satisfying." This observation is very important because all fascist move-

46 Ernst Nolte, *Die Krise des liberalen Systems und die faschistischen Bewegungen* (Munich: Piper, 1968), 385.

47 Roger Eatwell, "The Nature of 'Generic Fascism'. The 'Fascist Minimum' and the 'Fascist Matrix,'" in *Comparative Fascist Studies*, ed. Iordachi, 137.

48 Griffin later complemented his concept of fascism with negations and negative values. Cf. Iordachi, *Comparative Fascist Studies*, 118–24.

49 Payne, *A History of Fascism*, 14.

50 Ibid., 5, 14–15.

ments and regimes had their own unique features, sight of which should not be lost while analyzing them in the framework of fascist studies.[51]

Somewhat similarly to Kershaw, Georg Mosse argued in favor of studying fascism "from the inside out," or trying to reconstruct how its followers perceived it. He defined fascism as a complex phenomenon, which cannot be reduced only to politics and can be comprehended through empathy: "Fascism considered as a cultural movement means seeing fascism as it saw itself and as its followers saw it, to attempt to understand the movement in its own terms. Only then, when we have grasped fascism from the inside out, can we truly judge its appeal and its power. ... The cultural interpretation of fascism opens up a means to penetrate fascist self-understanding, and such empathy is crucial in order to grasp how people saw the movement, something which cannot be ignored or evaluated merely in retrospect."[52]

Michael Mann reminded us of a very simple but extremely important aspect of fascism. He wrote that "fascist ideology must be taken seriously, in its own terms. It must be not dismissed as crazy, contradictory, or vague." He also argued that historians of fascism need to take the values of fascists seriously; they should not excuse or relativize them but seek to understand fascists' worldviews and deeds. Furthermore, he remarked that "fascism was a movement of high ideals, able to persuade a substantial part of two generations of young people (especially the highly educated) that it could bring about a more harmonious social order," and that the fascist movements were "hierarchical yet comradely."[53]

A very significant element of fascism was revolution. Movements such as the German National Socialists took over power and established a regime by cooperating with conservative politicians. Hitler perceived this process as a "national revolution."[54] Other movements took power by a coup d'état, such as the March on Rome by the Italian Fascists, which was staged to frighten liberal and conservative politicians and brought Mussolini to power. Fascist movements and regimes viewed revolution as a means not only of taking over power but also of altering society, changing its values and mindsets, and destroying opponents. Griffin called this process the "permanent revolution."[55] As this study will show, the OUN's leaders, including Bandera, used both concepts—"national revolution" and "permanent revolution"—to prepare a revolutionary act, take over power, and establish a fascist dictatorship.

Although fascist movements and regimes shared similar values and felt that they belonged to the same family of political movements, we certainly should not look at them as equal or identical. Kevin Passmore pointed out the inconsistent and contradictory nature of fascism. He reminded us that fascist ideology combined various elements, including contradictory ones, such as modernism and fascination with

51 Ian Kershaw, "Hitler and the Uniqueness of Nazism," in *Comparative Fascist Studies*, ed. Iordachi, 241.

52 George L. Mosse, *The Fascist Revolution: Toward a General Theory of Fascism* (New York: H. Fertig, 1999), x-xi.

53 Michael Mann, *Fascists* (Cambridge: Cambridge University Press, 2004), 2–4.

54 Kershaw, *Hitler 1889-1936: Hubris*, 466.

55 Roger Griffin, "Revolution from the Right: Fascism" in *Revolutions and the Revolutionary Tradition in the West 1560–1991*, ed. David Parker (Routledge, London, 2000), 196.

traditions, or secularism and obsession with religion. It also united very different types of people such as street fighters, intellectuals, and terrorists.[56]

Zeev Sternhell observed that fascism was a "pan-European phenomenon," which "existed at three levels—as an ideology, as a political movement, and as a form of government."[57] Given that fascism appeared in various countries and in different societies, it must have varied on all three levels in terms of culture, national tradition, economy, social structure, and political culture. Fascist movements appeared in industrialized countries, such as Britain and Germany, and also in rural and economically less developed countries, such as Romania, Croatia, or Slovakia. It also appeared in nation states, such as Italy, France, and Germany, and in societies without states, such as Croatia and Slovakia. Antisemitism and other forms of racism were central to National Socialism and several East Central European fascist movements, but not to the Italian Fascists. Romanticism, mysticism, and irrationality were more typical of the OUN and the Iron Guard than they were of Italian Fascism.

It is very important to emphasize that fascist movements and regimes—despite their cultural and ideological similarities—did not always collaborate with each other and were not always sympathetic to each other. Major and minor conflicts between fascist, far-right, and authoritarian leaders, movements, and regimes were not uncommon, because practical matters, such as the control of a particular territory, were seen as more important than ideological connections. The clash between the Austrian National Socialists on the one side, and the Fatherland Front (*Vaterländische Front*) and its Home Guard (*Heimwehr*), collectively known after the Second World War as "Austrofascists," on the other, is just one example of this. In July 1934 during the failed putsch against his Austrofascist regime, Chancellor Engelbert Dollfuss was assassinated by Austrian Nazis. Almost four years later, in March 1938, Nazi Germany invaded Austria. After the Anschluss, the absorption of Austria into Nazi Germany, the Germans arrested Dollfuss's successor, Kurt Schuschnigg, and kept him as a special political prisoner (*Ehrenhäftling* or *Sonderhäftling*). Together with his family, Schuschnigg was held from 1941 in a house in a special area of the Sachsenhausen concentration camp. Bandera was subsequently detained as a special political prisoner in another section of the same camp,[58] as was Horia Sima—the leader of the Romanian fascist Iron Guard, founded in 1927 by Corneliu Zelea Codreanu as the Legion of the Archangel Michael.[59]

On the one hand, the new consensus on fascism—and in particular Griffin's concept of the theory of generic fascism—stimulated new interest in fascism, inspired new studies of the uninvestigated, neglected, or heavily mythologized fascist movements, and other features of European and global fascism, and brought forward comparative and transnational fascist studies. On the other hand, the new consensus

56 Passmore, *Fascism. A Very Short Introduction*, 11–12, 25, 30–31.

57 Zeev Sternhell, "fascism," in *Comparative Fascist Studies*, ed. Iordachi, 57.

58 Ian Kershaw, *Hitler 1936–45: Nemesis* (London: The Penguin Press, 200), 69–72, 75–77; Payne, *A History*, 245–52; Volker Koop, *In Hitlers Hand: Sonder- und Ehrenhäftlinge der SS* (Köln: Böhlau, 2010), 95–109.

59 Armin Heinen, *Die Legion "Erzengel Michael" in Rumänien Soziale Bewegung und politische Organisation: Ein Beitrag zum Problem des internationalen Faschismus* (Munich: Oldenbourg, 1986), 461, 522; Koop, *In Hitlers Hand*, 190–96.

was met with criticism. One important argument of its critics was that palingenesis or national rebirth is typical not only for fascist movements but also for almost all forms of nationalism. Another criticism was that scholars of fascism tend to level the differences between various fascist movements and regimes. In particular, German and East European historians questioned the relevance of fascist studies to the investigation of their own national history.[60]

This study will refer to a movement, regime, or ideology as fascist if it meets the main criteria enclosed in the above-explained concepts of fascism. First, we will regard movements as fascist, only if they adopted the Führerprinzip, practiced the cult of ethnic and political violence, regarded mass violence as an extension of politics, and were entirely or in great part antidemocratic, anti-Marxist, antiliberal, anticonservative, totalitarian, ultranationalist, populist, racist, antisemitic, and militarist. Second, we will regard movements as fascist, only if they tried to take over power and intended to introduce a fascist dictatorship, and if they planned the palingenesis, or a radical political and cultural regeneration of a nation in order to prevent its "degeneration." Third, we should bear in mind the difference between conservative or military regimes like Antonescu's, Horthy's or Piłsudski's, and fascist regimes like Mussolini's Italy and Hitler's Germany, and also regimes, which at times were fascist but in the long term combined national-conservatism with fascism, like Franco's and Salazar's. Similarly, we should also be aware that far-right nationalist movements, which tried to take over power and establish a dictatorship, might in the course of the years have changed their ideologies and their attitude toward fascism. When it was convenient for them, they might have fascistized themselves and have represented themselves as fascist. Later they might have claimed that they have never been fascist. Similarly, they might have combined nationalism with fascism and other far-right ideologies, such as racism or antisemitism in different proportions and thus be neither typically fascist nor typically nationalist or racist.

Fascism, Nationalism, and the Radical Right

Having explained fascism, it is necessary to briefly explain the difference between fascism and nationalism, two quite closely related phenomena. The modern form of nationalism, defined as a political program that instrumentalizes and mystifies the past to form a national community and establish a nation state, has its origins in the late eighteenth and early nineteenth centuries.[61] Nationalism was a byproduct of the French Revolution and the modern politics generated by it. In addition, it was also

60 In German academia, fascism and fascist studies had been marginalized because many scholars of contemporary history were preoccupied with National Socialism and the singularity of the National Socialist regime. This preoccupation also led to the marginalization of Holocaust studies in post-war Germany. For a discussion between Roger Griffin and a number of scholars critical of his concept of fascism, see Griffin, et al., *Fascism Past and Present,* and especially Klaus Holz, and Jan Weyand, "'Wiedergeburt' – ein nationalistisches Geschichtsbild"; Bärbel Meurer, "Ernst Nolte oder May Weber: Braucht die Wissenschaft einen (Gott-)Vater?", Stanley G. Payne, "Commentary of Roger Griffin's 'Fascism's new faces," Griffin, *Fascism Past and Present,* 125, 151, 177. For Ukrainian historians and fascism, see chapter 9 and 10.

61 In general on nationalism, see Benedickt Anderson, *Imagined Communities: Reflections on the Origin and Spread of Nationalism* (London: Verso, 1983); Eric J. Hobsbawm, *Nations and Nationalism since 1780: Programme, Myth, Reality* (Cambridge: Cambridge University Press, 1992); Ernest Gellner, *Nations and Nationalism* (Oxford: Blackwell, 1983).

influenced by Romanticism. Nationalist movements took very different forms, depending on the social and political circumstances of the groups that invented or adopted this ideology. Nationalism became radicalized, especially during the late nineteenth and early twentieth centuries. According to George Mosse nationalism became the "life-system which provided the foundation for all fascist movements." The mass violence caused by and experienced during the First World War contributed to the development of fascism, which was in its first stage, according to Sternhell, a "synthesis of organic nationalism and anti-Marxist socialism." Fascism became the most radical form of nationalism, but its own ideology and goals differed from those of nationalism. Although nationalism and fascism were influenced by racism and antisemitism, they were not racist or antisemitic to the same extent. Finally, we should keep in mind that, although nationalism and fascism are distinct in nature, the boundaries between them became blurred, especially in the case of such movements as the OUN and Ustaša, which both understood themselves as nationalist "liberation movements" related to other fascist movements.[62]

During the interwar period, Bandera and the OUN called themselves "nationalists," but regarded the OUN as a movement related to the Italian Fascists, the National Socialists, the Iron Guard, and similar movements. In this study, therefore, they will be called either nationalist or fascist, depending on the context. Individuals or groups during the Cold War or after the dissolution of the Soviet Union, who established a cultural, spiritual, or emotional continuity between themselves and the interwar OUN, its leaders and members, or its politics, will be referred to as "nationalist," "neo-fascist," "radical right," or "far right," depending on the context. "Neo-fascism" in this study means the rebirth of fascist ideas and aesthetics after the end of the Second World War, when the main fascist states had disappeared, and fascism as an ideology was completely discredited on account of the atrocities committed by Nazi Germany and other similar movements and regimes.

The terms "fascism" and "radical right" or "far right" do not mean the same thing. The term "radical right" is also an ambiguous one. On the one hand, it has been used since the 1950s, especially by political scientists, to describe ultranationalist, anticommunist, fundamentalist, or populist parties. On the other hand, scholars use it in a more general context to refer to modern radical nationalist movements, which have been emerging in Europe since the late nineteenth century. In general, the term "radical right" is a broader one than "fascism." "Fascism" bears a more specific meaning than "radical right." It refers to a specific kind of "radical right" movement that emerged after the First World War, such as the Italian Fascists, the National Socialists, and a number of other smaller parties or organizations that sought to take power and introduce fascist dictatorships.[63]

62 Mosse, *Fascist Revolution*, xi–xii; Sternhell, "fascism," 575.

63 For the use of the terms "radical right," "extreme right," and "far right," see Uwe Backes, "'Rechtsextremismus'—Konzeption und Kontroversen," in *Rechtsextreme Ideologien in Geschichte und Gegenwart*, ed. Uwe Backes (Köln: Böhlau, 2003), 23–25, 30.

Sacralization of Politics and the Heroization-Demonization Dichotomy

The sacralization of politics is a theoretical concept related to the previously discussed notions of cult, myth, charisma, and fascism. Emilio Gentile, one of the leading theorists of this concept, argued that totalitarian movements and regimes have the tendency to sacralize politics and to create political religions. According to Gentile, the "sacralisation of politics takes place when politics is conceived, lived and represented through myths, rituals, and symbols that demand faith in the sacralised secular entity, dedication among the community of believers, enthusiasm for action, and a warlike spirit and sacrifice in order to secure its defense and its triumph."[64]

When analyzing the radical and revolutionary form of Ukrainian nationalism, which was deeply influenced by religion, it is important to keep in mind that the "sacralization of politics does not necessarily lead to conflict with traditional religions, and neither does it lead to a denial of the existence of any supernatural supreme being."[65] On the contrary, the relationship between political and traditional religion is very complex. Political religions take over religious elements and "transform them into a system of beliefs, myths and rituals," in consequence of which, the boundaries between them frequently blur: ordinary individuals are transformed into worshipers, political symbols became sacralized, and national heroes are perceived as secular saints.[66]

Gentile correctly observed that the sacralization of politics in the twentieth century was catalyzed by the First World War, during which several countries used God and religion to legitimize violence. After the war, even movements that had been declared to be atheist or anti-religious used religious symbols to legitimize their ideologies and to attract the masses. The cult of the fallen, heroes and martyrs, the symbolism of death and resurrection, dedication to and exaltation of the nation, and the mystic qualities of blood and sacrifice were very common elements of militarist and totalitarian movements.[67] The sacralization of the state was another significant variety of political religion, which became especially important in the Ukrainian context. When Ukrainians did not succeed in establishing a state, the attempt to do so became, for the Ukrainian revolutionary nationalists, a matter of life and death.[68]

After the Second World War, because of specific political circumstances, elements of the Ukrainian revolutionary nationalists continued to sacralize politics, especially in the diaspora. Both before and after Bandera's assassination, his cult was composed of various religious elements. After his death, the transformation of Bandera into a martyr was one of them. In order to explore this matter, Gentile's approach will be combined with Clifford Geertz's concept of "thick description." Using descriptive analyses of its rituals and its creation of various hagiographic items, we will try to

64 Emilio Gentile, "The Sacralisation of Politics: Definitions, Interpretations and Reflections on the Question of Secular Religion and Totalitarianism," *Totalitarian Movements and Political Religions* Vol.1, No.1 (2000), 21–22.

65 Gentile, The Sacralisation of Politics, 23.

66 Ibid., 23, 36–37.

67 Ibid., 38.

68 For the sacralization of the state, see Emilio Gentile, "Fascism as Political Religion," *Journal of Contemporary History* Vol. 25, No. 2–3 (1990): 248.

understand the meaning of the Bandera cult, and the role it has played in the invention of Ukrainian tradition.[69]

Related to the question of sacralization is the heroization-demonization dichotomy. This notion will be explored in this study, but it should not prevent us from uncovering Bandera's life and the history of his movement. The depiction of individuals as heroes and villains, or friends and enemies, is an intrinsic element of totalitarian ideologies. The main question to be investigated in this context is: Which ideology met what kind of needs, while depicting Bandera as a hero, or as a villain, and what kind of hero or villain did Bandera become?[70]

The investigation of Bandera, the OUN, and Ukrainian nationalism must also relate to the Soviet Union and Soviet ideology. The OUN perceived the Soviet Union as its most important enemy, before—and especially after—Jews and Poles had largely disappeared from Ukraine. Bandera's ultranationalist revolution after the Second World War was intended to take place in Soviet Ukraine and was directed against Soviet power. What is more, Soviet propaganda created its own Bandera image, which, during the Cold War, affected the perception of Bandera in the Western bloc and, after the dissolution of the Soviet Union, in post-Soviet Ukraine. Therefore, the investigation of Soviet questions concerning Bandera and Ukrainian revolutionary nationalism is an important aspect of this study.[71]

Memory, Identity, Symbol, and Denial

The last theoretical notion that needs to be shortly introduced—before we move to the empirical part of this book—is memory. Bandera's image in the collective memories of different communities has varied from the very beginning. Bandera was remembered in an idealized and heroic way by people who participated in his cult and who believed in his myth. The way that Polish, Jewish, and other survivors of the OUN and UPA terror remembered Bandera was very different from the way his worshipers among the Ukrainian diaspora did. Soviet propaganda shaped a very negative and offensive way of remembering and presenting Bandera and the OUN-UPA. After

69 Geertz, *Interpretation of Cultures*, 3–30. For invention of tradition, see Eric Hobsbawm and Terence Ranger, *The Inventing of Tradition* (Cambridge: Cambridge University Press, 1992).

70 For the heroization-demonization dichotomy in totalitarian movements and regimes, see Peter Lambert and Robert Mallett, "Introduction: The Heroisation-Demonisation Phenomenon in Mass Dictatorships," *Totalitarian Movements and Political Religions* Vol. 8, No. 3–4, (2007), 453–63. In the Ukrainian context, see David Marples, *Heroes and Villains: Creating National History in Contemporary Ukraine* (Budapest: Central European University Press, 2007).

71 On Soviet Ukraine and the ideology and propaganda in the Soviet Union, see Katrin Boeckh, *Stalinismus in der Ukraine: Die Rekonstruktion des sowjetischen Systems nach dem Zweiten Weltkrieg* (Wiesbaden: Harrassowitz, 2007); Terry Martin, *The Affirmative Action Empire: Nations and Nationalism in the Soviet Union, 1923–1939* (London: Cornell University Press, 2001); William Jay Rish, *The Ukrainian West: Culture and the Fate of Empire in Soviet Lviv* (Cambridge, Mass.: Harvard University Press, 2011); Alexander Statiev, *The Soviet Counterinsurgency in Western Borderlands* (Cambridge: Cambridge University Press, 2010); Amir Weiner, *Making Sense of War: The Second World War and the Fate of the Bolshevik Revolution* (New Jersey: Princeton University Press, 2001); Serhy Yekelchyk, *Stalin's Empire of Memory: Russian–Ukrainian Relations in the Soviet Historical Imagination* (Toronto: University of Toronto Press, 2004). On Soviet partisans in Ukraine, see Aleksandr Gogun, *Partyzanci Stalina na Ukrainie: Nieznane działania 1941–1944* (Warsaw: Bellona, 2010).

the dissolution of the Soviet Union, the memory of Bandera has divided post-Soviet Ukraine.

In order to analyze the different memories of Bandera, we must differentiate between at least three concepts: individual memory, collective memory, and the politics of memory. A number of people knew Bandera and thus possessed some kind of personal memory of him. The publication and dissemination of their memories allowed other individuals, who did not know Bandera in person, to familiarize themselves with his life and to develop some emotional bond with him, if they had not already done so through the cult and myth. This obviously influenced the collective memory of a community who shared a similar identity and a similar realm of experience. Both kinds of memories were influenced by the politics of memory, which defined how to conduct official commemorations, or how a biography, film, or exhibition should present the *Providnyk*, in order to meet the political expectations of a community, a society, or a state.[72]

The investigation of memory—like the investigation of the cult and myth—should not, however, obstruct the investigation of the "real" history of Ukrainian nationalism and the "real" personality of Bandera. Neglecting actual history or trying to understand history through the framework of memory is a dangerous tendency in contemporary historiography which, especially in fields like the Second World War or the Holocaust, opens doors to various radical right activists and other abusers of history. To avoid such problems, we should examine a memory also in the light of Holocaust denial and Holocaust obfuscation and pay particular attention to the question whether those far-right groups and nationalist communities that commemorated Bandera, the OUN, and the UPA recalled, ignored, or deliberately denied the Ukrainian contribution to the Holocaust, and other atrocities committed by the Ukrainian nationalists.[73] With this in mind, we should examine the "archives of silence," which are the result of collective ignorance of history. These archives are full of suppressed and forgotten—but very important—elements of national history, particularly history related to ethnic and political violence, and other elements that do not correspond with a patriotic interpretation of history.[74] "'I did that,' says my memory. I couldn't have done that—says my pride, and stands its ground. Finally, memory gives in," remarked Friedrich Nietzsche in 1886.[75]

72 On the concepts of memory, see Jeffrey K. Olick, *The Politics of Regret: On Collective Memory and Historical Responsibility* (New York: Routledge, 2007), 17–35; Aleida Assmann, *Der lange Schatten der Vergangenheit: Erinnerungskultur und Geschichtspolitik* (Bonn: C.H.Beck, 2007), 21–37.

73 On Holocaust denial, see Deborah Lipstadt, *Denying the Holocaust: The Growing Assault on Truth and Memory* (New York: Free Press, 1993); Michael Shermer and Alex Grobman, *Denying History: Who Says the Holocaust Never Happened and Why Do They Say It?* (Berkeley: University of California Press, 2000); Michael Shafir, "Between Denial and 'Comparative Trivialization.' Holocaust Negationism in Post-Communist East Central Europe," *Analysis of Current Trends in Antisemitism* 19 (2002): 1–83.

74 For the archives of silence, see Moritz Csáky, *Ideologie der Operette und Wiener Moderne: Ein kulturhistorischer Essay* (Vienna: Böhlau, 1998), 228; Jacques Le Goff, *Geschichte und Gedächtnis* (Frankfurt: Campus Verlag, 1992), 228. For the ethnization of history and memory, see Gerlach, *Extremely Violent Societies*, 255–65; Jeffrey Burds, "Ethnicity, Memory and Violence: Reflections on Special Problems in Soviet & East European Archives," *Comma. International Journal of Archives* No. 3–4 (2002): 69.

75 Friedrich Nietzsche, "Beyond Good and Evil. Prelude to a Philosophy of Future," in *Cambridge Texts in the History of Philosophy*, ed. Rolf-Peter Horstmann and Judith Norman (Cambridge: University Press, 2002), 59. In the German original: "'Das hab ich getan', sagt mein Gedächtnis. Das kann ich nicht getan haben—sagt mein Stolz und bleibt unerbittlich. Endlich gibt das Gedächtnis nach."

Genocide, Mass Violence, and the Complexity of the Holocaust

"Genocide" is a contested term and a concept that makes more sense in legal and political discourse than in historical studies. The use of the term may interfere with academic analysis, by obscuring links between different forms of mass violence conducted by the same group of perpetrators against various ethnic and political enemies.[76] It is not the purpose of this book to argue that some atrocities committed by the OUN, the Nazis, or the Ustaša were genocidal and that others were not, or to equate the Holocaust with other mass crimes in order to elevate the status of suffering of a particular group. My use of the term "genocide" assumes the intention of the perpetrators to annihilate a group or a community because of its national or ethnic identity. By the same token it is important to emphasize the multifarious nature of OUN violence, which was directed against all kinds of ethnic enemies and political opponents, but not against each of them to the same extent. Depending on the context, I frequently prefer terms such as "mass violence," "ethnic cleansing," or "crimes against humanity." In the last two chapters I explain how various groups of political activists and even scholars have abused the term "genocide" by promoting the narrative of victimization.

For a long time, historians who studied the Holocaust, or movements such as the OUN, concentrated on perpetrator documents and overlooked the testimonies, memoirs, reports, and other accounts left by survivors. Those historians believed that the perpetrator documents hold much more reliable data than the documents left by survivors, victims, and bystanders. In the view of such historians, perpetrators were objective, exact and emotionally detached. Survivors, on the other hand, were considered to be emotional, traumatized, and not able to produce any reliable account of the events. This approach was typical of historians such as the OUN specialist John Armstrong, and some German historians such as Martin Broszat, Thilo Vogelsang, and Andreas Hillgruber, who had grown up in Nazi Germany and served in the German army. Similarly, some leading Holocaust historians such as Raul Hilberg and the first director of Yad Vashem, Ben-Zion Dinur, also applied this approach. Historians such as Joseph Wulf or Léon Poliakov, who objected to the perpetrator-oriented approach, were mainly Holocaust survivors themselves. They were discredited especially by the German historians as "unscholarly."[77]

The first public discussion of this methodological problem took place in 1987–1988 between the director of the Institute for Contemporary History (*Institut für Zeitgeschichte*) in Munich, Martin Broszat, who had joined the NSDAP on 4 April 1944, and the Holocaust survivor and leading Holocaust historian Saul Friedländer. One of the main issues in this debate was "rational" German scholarship versus the "mythical memory" of the victims.[78] The discussion, did not undo the distrust of survi-

76 Christian Gerlach, *Extremely Violent Societies: Mass Violence in the Twentieth-Century World* (Cambridge: Cambridge University Press, 2010), 2–3, 5–6; Alexander Korb, "Understanding Ustaša violence," *Journal of Genocide Research* Vol. 12, No. 1–2 (2010): 1–14.

77 Laura Jockusch, *Collect and Record! Jewish Holocaust Documentation in Early Postwar Europe* (Oxford: Oxford University Press, 2012), 196–201. On Wulf, see also Nicolaus Berg, *Der Holocaust und die westdeutschen Historiker: Erforschung und Erinnerung* (Göttingen: Wallstein, 2003), 337–63.

78 Jockusch, *Collect and Record!*, 196–201. On the debate between Freidländer and Broschat, see also Saul Friedländer, *Nachdenken über den Holocaust* (Munich C. H. Beck, 2007), 78–124.

vor accounts but the situation began to change a decade later. In 1997 Friedländer returned to the debate in his study *Nazi Germany and the Jews*. He pointed out the methodological problems that were the result of neglecting survivor perspectives, and pleaded for the use of documents of both perpetrators and survivors, in order to achieve an integrated and comprehensive history.[79] Four years later, Jan Tomasz Gross published a study about the Polish town of Jedwabne. Relying on survivor testimonies Gross proved that the local Polish population killed the Jews of this locality on their own initiative and without any significant help from the Germans.[80] In the following years, historians such as Christopher Browning and Omer Bartov, who had previously concentrated on perpetrators, questioned the alleged uselessness of accounts left by victims and survivors, and provided a methodological foundation for the study of the neglected issues with the help of these documents.[81]

In this study we will follow Freidländer's plea for an integrated history, and will use two kinds of documents: those left by perpetrators and those left by victims and survivors. This approach will enable us to obtain a full picture of the events. We will obviously deal with both kinds of documents critically. With regard to perpetrator documents, it is necessary to distinguish between propaganda documents, internal documents relating to practical matters, and apologetic postwar memoirs. We must examine the intentions of their authors and consider the circumstances under which they were written. The survivor testimonies and memoirs, on the other hand, should be read against each other and placed in context with perpetrator and bystander documents. Similarly, when analyzing records of NKVD interrogations, we should be aware that such investigations were sometimes conducted under coercive circumstances that affected the content of the records.[82]

79 Saul Friedländer, *The Years of Extermination: Nazi Germany and the Jews 1933–1939* (New York: Harper Collins, 1997), 2.

80 Jan Tomasz Gross, *Neighbors: The Destruction of the Jewish Community in Jedwabne, Poland* (Princeton: Princeton University Press, 2001).

81 Christopher Browning, *Remembering Survival: Inside a Nazi Labor Camp* (New York: Norton, 2010), 1–12; Omer Bartov, "Eastern Europe as the Site of Genocide," *The Journal of Modern History* Vol. 80, No. 3 (2008): 562, 572.

82 On the methodology of using survivor testimonies and the records of Soviet interrogations, see Vladimir Solonari, "Patterns of Violence. The Local Population and the Mass Murder of Jews in Bessarabia and Northern Bukovina, July-August 1941," *Kritika: Explorations in Russian and Eurasian History* Vol. 8, No. 4 (2007): 753–55; Jan Grabowski, *Hunt for the Jews: Betrayal and Murder in German-Occupied* (Bloomington: Indiana University Press, 2013), 11–15; Grzegorz Rossoliński-Liebe, "Der Verlauf und die Täter des Lemberger Pogroms vom Sommer 1941. Zum aktuellen Stand der Forschung," *Jahrbuch für Antisemitismusforschung* 22 (2013): 210–11; Alexander Prusin, "'Fascist Criminals to the Gallows!': The Holocaust and Soviet War Crimes Trials, December 1945–February 1946," *Holocaust and Genocide Studies* Vol. 17, No. 1 (2003): 1–30; Tanja Penter, "Collaboration on Trial: New Source Material on Soviet Postwar Trials against Collaborators," *Slavic Review* Vol. 64, No. 4 (2005): 782–90. The first monograph about the Second World War in Ukraine which used survivor testimonies was written by Franziska Bruder. See Franziska Bruder, *"Den ukrainischen Staat erkämpfen oder sterben!" Die Organisation Ukrainischer Nationalisten (OUN) 1929–1948* (Berlin: Metropol Verlag, 2007). Earlier publications did not use survivor testimonies but mainly German and Soviet documents. See for example Armstrong, *Ukrainian Nationalism*; Dieter Pohl, *Nationalsozialistische Judenverfolgung in Ostgalizien 1941–1944: Organisation und Durchführung eines staatlichen Massenverbrechens* (Munich: Oldenbourg, 1997); Frank Grelka, *Die ukrainische Nationalbewegung unter deutscher Besatzungsherrschaft 1918 und 1941/42* (Wiesbaden: Harrassowitz, 2005).

Documents, Interpretations, and Manipulations

The investigation of Bandera's life, his cult, and the history of the OUN and UPA are highly contingent upon the study of archival documents and original publications. Because of the extremist nature of the OUN and its involvement in the Holocaust and other kinds of ethnic and political mass violence during and after the Second World War, OUN émigrés and UPA veterans began producing forged or manipulated documents during the Cold War, by means of which they whitewashed their own history. They removed undesirable and inconvenient phrases from republished documents, especially those relating to fascism, the Holocaust, and other atrocities. In 1955, for example, in a new edition of documents entitled *The OUN in the Light of the Resolutions of Great Congresses*, the OUN reprinted the resolutions of the Second Great Congress of the OUN in Cracow in April 1941. According to the original resolutions, the OUN adopted a fascist salute, consisting of raising the right arm "slightly to the right, slightly above the peak of the head," while saying "Glory to Ukraine!" (*Slava Ukraïni!*), and answering "Glory to the Heroes!"(*Heroiam Slava!*). The 1955 edition left out this particular part of the text.[83]

Such an approach to history resembles the Soviet approach, and to the question of how to represent Bandera and the OUN. For example, the Cultural Department of the Central Committee of the Communist Party of Ukraine (*Komunistychna Partiia Ukraïny*, or KPU) advised the producers of the film *The Killer Is Known* to show Bandera only at the moment when he metamorphoses into a swastika.[84] But not only OUN or Soviet publications related to the Bandera discourse contain striking misrepresentations. The book *Alliance for Murder: The Nazi-Ukrainian Nationalist Partnership in Genocide* contains a picture of Archbishop Andrei Sheptyts'kyi with a swastika and suggests that the head of the Greek Catholic Church carried it during the Second World War because he sympathized with Nazi Germany. The picture, however, must have been taken in the 1920s. It shows Sheptyts'kyi with two men in the uniforms of Plast, the Ukrainian scouting organization. Plast used the swastika as a symbol in the 1920s but the organization was outlawed in 1930. Moreover, Sheptyts'kyi is shown standing on his own two feet, whereas he was already confined to a wheelchair before the Second World War.[85]

Other indications of this process can be found in post-war memoirs. Mykola Klymyshyn, a close companion of Stepan Bandera, was the author of several important historical and autobiographical publications related to the *Providnyk*, and an im-

83 Compare *OUN v svitli postanov Velykykh Zboriv* (n.p.: Zakordonni Chastyny Orhanizatsiï Ukraïns'kykh Natsionalistiv, 1955), 44–45 with the original publication of 1941 "Postanovy II. Velykoho Zboru Orhanizatsiï Ukraïns'kykh Natsionalistiv," TsDAHO f. 1, op. 23, spr. 926, 199.

84 "Pro vnesennia vypravlen' do fil'mu 'Vbyvca vidomii,'" TsDAHO f. 1, op. 25, spr. 869, 32, reprinted in Liubov Krypnyk, "Formovannia svitohliadnykh ustanovok pro Druhu svitovu viinu zasobamy radians'koho kino (materialy TsDAHO Ukraïny, 1973 r.)," *Moloda Natsia. Almanakh* Vo. 41, No. 4 (2006): 116–17.

85 Cf. B. F. Sabrin, *Alliance for Murder: The Nazi-Ukrainian Nationalist Partnership in Genocide* (New York: Sarpedon, 1991), 172. On Sheptyts'kyi, see Julian J. Bussgang, "Metropolitan Sheptytsky: A Reassessment," *Polin. Studies in Polish Jewry* 21 (2009): 401, 404; Iuliian Busgang, *Mytropolyt Sheptyts'kyi: Shche odyn pohliad na zhyttia i diial'nist'* (L'viv: Drukars'ki kunshty, 2009), 18, 19. I am grateful to Marco Carynnyk for this observation. I was also misled by the picture in *Alliance for Murder*. See Grzegorz Rossoliński-Liebe, "The 'Ukrainian National Revolution' of Summer 1941," *Kritika: Explorations in Russian and Eurasian History* Vol. 12, No.1 (2011): 98.

portant progenitor of his cult. Klymyshyn was honest enough to admit that dark spots in his publications had been whitewashed at the personal request of Stepan Bandera. He admitted this with the object of warning future generations, who would question the omission of certain aspects in his descriptions.[86] Ievhen Stakhiv, another OUN member and the author of important autobiographical publications, admits that Mykola Lebed', another important OUN leader, asked him to forget and not to mention uncomfortable elements of the past, such as Bandera's direction to the movement in late 1941 to repair relations with Nazi Germany and to attempt further collaboration with the Nazis.[87] To review the different kinds of "forgotten" or instrumentalized history, it is necessary to study the original documents. Some of them, and their locations, are briefly introduced here.

The Central Archives of Modern Records in Warsaw (*Archiwum Akt Nowych*, AAN) holds collections of documents concerning the history of the UVO and OUN in the inter-war period. Documents relating to the investigation of OUN members involved in Bronisław Pieracki's assassination, and to the Warsaw and Lviv trials, can be found in the Central State Historical Archive of Ukraine in Lviv (*Tsentral'nyi derzhavnyi istorychnyi arkhiv*, TDIA) and in the State Archives of Lviv Oblast (*Derzhavnyi arkhiv L'vivs'koï oblasti*, DALO). A number of documents—including the twenty-four volumes of the investigation records prepared for the Warsaw trial—could not be found. In all probability, they were lost during the Second World War.

Many important documents relating to Bandera and the OUN-UPA during the Second World War are located in two Kiev archives: the Central State Archives of the Supreme Bodies of Power and Government of Ukraine (*Tsentral'nyi derzhavnyi arkhiv vyshchykh orhaniv vlady ta upravlinnia Ukrainy*, TsDAVOV) and the Central State Archives of Public Organizations of Ukraine (*Tsentral'nyi derzhavnyi arkhiv hromads'kykh obiednan' Ukrainy*, TsDAHO). The State Archives of the Security Service of Ukraine in Kiev (*Haluzevyi Derzhavnyi arkhiv Sluzhby bezpeky Ukraïny*, HDA SBU) holds collections of NKVD interrogation files, which also contain some information on the Ukrainian nationalists. Because NKVD interrogations were coercive, and in some cases torture was applied, such documents should be used carefully and checked against other sources. The Provincial Archives of Alberta, in Edmonton, also hold essential documents on the "Ukrainian National Revolution" and the conduct of the OUN and UPA during the Second World War.[88]

Other crucial documents relating to Bandera, the OUN-UPA, and the German occupation of Ukraine are located in the German Federal Archives (*Bundesarchiv*, BA) in Berlin and Koblenz, in the Military Archives (*Militärarchiv*, MA) in Freiburg, and in the Political Archives of the Foreign Office in Berlin (*Politisches Archiv des Auswärtigen Amtes*, PAAA). In the Provincial Archives of Nordrhein-Westfalen (*Landesarchiv Nordrhein-Westfalen*, LN-W), one can study documents from the preliminary proceedings against Theodor Oberländer. The Oberländer records are important for the study of the Lviv pogrom in 1941 and of the campaign against the Adenauer government's Federal Minister for Displaced Persons, Refugees, and War Victims.

86 Mykola Klymyshyn, *V pokhodi do voli* (Detroit: Ukrainska Knyharnia, 1987), 1:333.
87 Ievhen Stakhiv, *Kriz' tiurmy, pidpillia i kordony* (Kiev: Rada, 1995), 100.
88 For the "Ukrainian National Revolution," see chapter 4, and Rossoliński-Liebe, "'Ukrainian National Revolution,'" 83–114.

In Moscow, the State Archive of the Russian Federation (*Gosudarstvennyi arkhiv Rossiiskoi Federatsii*, GARF) and the Russian State Archive of Socio-Political History (*Rossiiskii gosudarstvennyi arkhiv sotsial'no-poiliticheskoi istorii*, RGASOI) are two further important sources of document collections relating to Ukraine during the Second World War. The Archives of the Jewish Historical Museum in Warsaw (*Archiwum Żydowskiego Instytutu Historycznego*, AŻIH) hold a huge collection of Jewish survivor testimonies, mainly collected between 1944 and 1947 in Poland by the Central Jewish Historical Commission (*Centralna Żydowska Komisja Historyczna*, CŻKH).[89] Two other important collections of survivor testimonies are located in the archives of the Holocaust Memorial Museum in Washington and in the archives of Yad Vashem. The Shoah Foundation Institute Visual History Archive, which was founded in 1994, also collected a huge number of survivor testimonies. The early documents collected by the AŻIH are especially important for this study.[90]

The Bavarian Main State Archives (*Bayerisches Hauptstaatsarchiv*, BayHStA) and the Munich State Archives (*Staatsarchiv München*, StM) mainly hold police documents relating to Bandera and the OUN after the Second World War. Documents in the possession of the intelligence services are another important source for the study of Bandera and the OUN during the Cold War, but not all intelligence services have made them accessible. Some documents on Bandera during the Cold War may be found in the National Archives and Records Administration in Washington. A number of important interrogation records of OUN members and UPA partisans, and other documents relating to the Cold War are located in the HAD SBU. The Federal Security Service of the Russian Federation (*Federal'naia sluzhba bezopasnosti Rossiiskoi Federatsii*, FSB) has informed me that its archives do not contain any documents concerning Bandera's assassination. The Federal Intelligence Service of Germany (*Bundesnachrichtendienst*, BND) has not made most of the relevant documents available to researchers who are interested in its collaboration with the OUN.

The archives of the Stepan Bandera Museum in London hold some documents relating to Bandera's assassination and about OUN émigrés in the Cold War period. During the last two decades, several important editions of documents relating to Stepan Bandera and the OUN-UPA have appeared in Ukraine. Some of these, such as the three volumes of *Stepan Bandera in the Documents of the Soviet Organs of the State Security*, together with documents from the State Archives of the Security Service of Ukraine, were an important source of information for this study.[91]

89 For the history of the CŻKH and other institutions that collected survivor testimonies in the early postwar period, see Jockusch, *Collect and Record!*, 5–7, 36–37, 89–98.

90 See the subsection "Genocide, Mass Violence, and the Complexity of the Holocaust" in this Introduction.

91 Volodymyr Serhiichuk, ed., *Stepan Bandera u dokumentakh radians'kykh orhaniv derzhavnoï bezpeky (1939–1959)*, Vol. 1–3 (Kiev: Vipol 2009). It is difficult to estimate how selective, if at all, were the edition of Serhiichuk's volumes or those edited by the Academy of Science in Kiev.

Literature

Until the current study, no academic biography and no study of the Bandera cult had been written, but in the last two decades a number of important studies on related subjects have appeared in German, English, Polish, Russian, Ukrainian, and other languages. These studies include subjects such as the OUN, the UPA, the Second World War in Ukraine, the Holocaust in Ukraine, the Soviet occupation of Ukraine, and the Polish-Ukrainian conflict during the interwar period. Because of their huge volume, only the most relevant for the purposes of this study will be briefly introduced at this point.

The complications of the interwar period and of relations between the Jews, Poles, and Ukrainians in the Second Polish Republic, and the political situation of the Ukrainians in particular were investigated by historians such as Christoph Mick, Maksym Hon, Timothy Snyder, Jerzy Tomaszewski, and Robert Potocki.[92] Frank Golczewski published a monumental and very informative monograph on German-Ukrainian relations between 1914 and 1939.[93] The fate of Ukrainians in the Habsburg and Russian Empires, and the subject of Ukrainian nationalism in the nineteenth century were explored in the 1980s, among others by John-Paul Himka, and later by historians such as Iaroslav Hrytsak.[94] The multiethnic character of the Ukrainian territories was portrayed by scholars such as Andreas Kappeler, Natalia Yakovenko, Mark von Hagen, and a number of other scholars.[95] Bohdan Bociurkiw published an important monograph on the Greek-Catholic Church.[96] Antony Polonsky wrote a three-volume study about the Jews in Poland, Ukraine, and Russia.[97]

Until now, three scholars have published monographs on the OUN. In 1955 John Armstrong published his classic and meanwhile problematic study. Roman Wysocki's and Franziska Bruder's monographs appeared after the dissolution of the Soviet Union, when it became possible to investigate Soviet archives. Wysocki concentrated

92 Christoph Mick, *Kriegserfahrungen in einer multiethnischen Stadt: Lemberg 1914–1947* (Wiesbaden: Harrassowitz, 2010); Maksym Hon, *Iz kryvdoiu na samoti: Ukraïns'ko-ievreis'ki vzaiemyny na zakhidnoukraïns'kykh zemiakh u skladi Pol'shchi (1935–1939)* (Rivne: Volyns'ki oberehy, 2005); Timothy Snyder, *The Reconstruction of Nations: Poland, Ukraine, Lithuania, Belarus, 1569–1999* (New Haven: Yale University Press, 2003), *Sketches from a Secret War: A Polish Artist's Mission to Liberate Soviet Ukraine* (New Haven: Yale University Press, 2005); Potocki Robert, *Polityka państwa wobec zagadnienia ukraińskiego w latach 1930–1939* (Lublin: Instytut Europy Środkowo Wschodniej, 2003); Jerzy Tomaszewski, *Ojczyzna nie tylko Polaków: Mniejszości narodowe w Polsce w latach 1918–1939* (Warsaw: Młodzieżowa Agencja Wydawnicza, 1985).

93 Frank Golczewski, *Deutsche und Ukrainer 1914–1939* (Paderborn: Ferdinand Schöningh, 2010).

94 John-Paul Himka, *Socialism in Galicia: The Emergence of Polish Social Democracy and Ukrainian Radicalism (1860–1890)* (Cambridge: HURI, 1983), "Serfdom in Galicia," *Journal of Ukrainian Studies* Vol. 9, No. 2 (1984): 3–28, *Galician Villagers and the Ukrainian National Movement in the Nineteenth Century* (Basingstoke: Macmillan, 1998); Iaroslav Hrytsak, *Narys istorii Ukraïny: Formuvannia modernoï ukraïns'koï natsiï XIX–XX stolittia* (Kiev: Heneza, 2000).

95 Natalia Yakovenko, "Choice of Name versus Choice of Path: The Names of Ukrainian Territories from the Late Sixteenth to the Late Seventeenth Century," in *A Laboratory of Transnational History: Ukraine and Recent Ukrainian Historiography*, ed. Georgiy Kasianov and Philipp Ther (Budapest: Central European University Press, 2009), 117–48; Andreas Kappeler, "From an Ethnonational to a Multiethnic to a Transnational Ukrainian History," in *A Laboratory of Transnational History*, ed. Kasianov, 51–80; Mark von Hagen, "Revisiting the Histories of Ukraine," in *A Laboratory of Transnational History*, ed. Kasianov, 25–50.

96 Bohdan Bociurkiw, *Ukraïns'ka Hreko-Katolyts'ka Tserkva i Radians'kak derzhava (1939–1950)* (Lviv: Vydavnytsvo Ukraïns'koho Katolyts'koho Universytetu, 2005).

97 Antony Polonsky, *The Jews in Poland and Russia, 1350–2008*, Vol. 1–3 (Oxford: The Littman Library of Jewish Civilization, 2010–12).

on the OUN in Poland between 1929 and 1939. Bruder wrote a critical and thoroughly researched study of OUN ideology, paying particular attention to antisemitism and political and ethnic violence.[98] Another scholar who investigated the antisemitism of the OUN is Marco Carynnyk.[99] Alexander Motyl in 1980 and Tomasz Stryjek in 2000 presented studies on Ukrainian political thinkers, including Dmytro Dontsov, the main ideologist of the Bandera generation.[100] Grzegorz Motyka published the most comprehensive monographs on the UPA, in which he also investigated the Polish-Ukrainian conflict during the Second World War, the anti-Polish atrocities in eastern Galicia and Volhynia, and the conflict between the UPA and the Soviet authorities. Motyka's study, however, analyzes the anti-Jewish violence only marginally.[101] Important articles on the Ukrainian police, OUN, UPA, and ethnic violence were published by Alexander Prusin.[102] Jeffrey Burds published articles on the conflict between the Ukrainian nationalists and the UPA, and on the early Cold War in Ukraine.[103] Alexander Statiev published a very well researched monograph on the conflict between the Ukrainian nationalists and the Soviet authorities, as did Katrin Boeckh on Stalinism in Ukraine.[104]

An important monograph on the German occupation of eastern Ukraine (Reichskommissariat Ukraine) during the Second World War, which also pays attention to the ethnic violence of the OUN and UPA in Volhynia, was written by Karel Berkhoff.[105] Dieter Pohl published a significant and authoritative monograph on the German occupation of eastern Galicia in which he investigated in depth how the Germans, with the help of the local Ukrainian police persecuted and exterminated the Jews. The roles of the OUN, the UPA, and the local population in the Holocaust, however, are analyzed only as a sideline in this book.[106] Thomas Sandkühler, who also published a monograph on the German occupation of western Galicia, took the

98 Armstrong, *Ukrainian Nationalism*; Roman Wysocki, *Organizacja Ukraińskich Nacjonalistów: Geneza, struktura, program, ideologia* (Lublin: Wydawnictwo uniwersytetu Marie Curie-Skłodowskiej, 2003); Bruder, *"Den ukrainischen Staat.*

99 Marco Carynnyk, "Foes of Our Rebirth: Ukrainian Nationalist Discussions about Jews, 1929–1947," *Nationalities Papers* Vol. 39, No. 3 (2011): 315–52.

100 Alexander Motyl, *The Turn to the Right: The Ideological Origins and Development of Ukrainian Nationalism, 1919–1929* (Boulder: East European Monographs, 1980); Tomasz Stryjek, *Ukraińska idea narodowa okresu międzywojennego: Analizy wybranych koncepcji* (Wrocław: FUNNA, 2000).

101 Grzegorz Motyka, *Tak było w Bieszczadach: Walki polsko-ukraińskie 1943–1948* (Warsaw: Oficyna Wydawnicza Volumen, 1999), *Ukraińska partyzantka 1942–1960: Działalność Organizacji Ukraińskich Nacjonalistów i Ukraińskiej Powstańczej Armii* (Warsaw: Rytm, 2006).

102 Alexander V. Prusin, "Revolution and Ethnic Cleansing in Western Ukraine: The OUN-UPA Assault against Polish Settlements in Volhynia and Eastern Galicia, 1943–1944," in *Ethnic Cleansing in Twentieth-Century Europe*, ed. Steven Béla Várdy, T. Hunt Tooley (New York: Boulder: Social Science Monographs, 2003), 517–35; Gabriel N. Finder and Alexander V. Prusin, "Collaboration in Eastern Galicia: The Ukrainian Police and the Holocaust," *East European Jewish Affairs* Vol. 34, No. 2 (2004): 95–118.

103 Jeffrey Burds, "AGENTURA: Soviet Informants' Networks and the Ukrainian Underground in Galicia, 1944–1948," *East European Politics and Societies* Vol. 11, No. 1 (1996): 89–130; "The Early Cold War in Soviet West Ukraine, 1944–1948," *The Carl Beck Papers in Russian & East European Studies*, Number 1505. Pittsburgh: The Center for Russian and East European Studies, 2001; "Gender and Policing in Soviet West Ukraine, 1944–1948," *Cahiers du Monde russe* Vol. 42, No. 2–4 (2001), 279–320.

104 Statiev, *Soviet Counterinsurgency*; Boeckh, *Stalinismus in der Ukraine.*

105 Karel Berkhoff, *Harvest of Despair: Life and Death in Ukraine under Nazi Rule* (Cambridge: Belknap Press of Harvard University, 2004).

106 Dieter Pohl, *Nationalsozialistische Judenverfolgung in Ostgalizien 1941–1944: Organisation und Durchführung eines staatlichen Massenverbrechens* (Munich: Oldenbourg, 1997). For a similar perspective, see also Grelka, *Die ukrainische Nationalbewegung.*

role of the OUN more seriously to some extent, but also concentrated on the German perpetrators.[107] Both Dieter Pohl and Frank Golczewski published several important articles on the Ukrainian police and on Ukrainian collaboration with the Germans.[108] Shmuel Spector investigated the Holocaust in Volhynia, paying special attention to survivor accounts, on the basis of which he published an important study that does not marginalize the non-German perpetrators.[109] A decade ago, Hans Heer published an article about the Lviv pogrom of 1941, and John-Paul Himka, Christoph Mick, and I did so more recently.[110] The Holocaust survivors and historians Philip Friedman and Eliyahu Yones also conducted significant studies of various aspects of the extermination of the Jews in western Ukraine, including the Lviv pogrom, and the attitude of the UPA toward the Jews.[111] The Holocaust survivor and historian Aharon Weiss published an important analytical article about Ukrainian perpetrators and rescuers.[112] In 2012 Witold Mędykowski published a transnational study of pogroms in the summer of 1941 in Belarus, the Baltic states, Poland, Romania and Ukraine.[113] Omer Bartov, Wendy Lower, Kai Struve, and Timothy Snyder have published on various issues relating to the Holocaust in western Ukraine.[114]

Several scholars published material on the subject of the Ukrainian diaspora, but with the exception of articles written by John-Paul Himka, Per Anders Rudling, and myself, the history of the OUN and Ukrainian nationalism in the Ukrainian diaspora has remained untouched.[115] Diana Dumitru, Tanja Penter, Alexander Prusin, and

107 Thomas Sandkühler, *"Endlösung" in Galizien: Der Judenmord in Ostpolen und die Rettungsinitiativen von Berthold Beitz 1941–1944* (Bonn: Diert, 1996).

108 Dieter Pohl, "Ukrainische Hilfskräfte beim Mord an den Juden," in *Die Täter der Shoah: Fanatische Nationalisten oder normale Deutsche?* ed. Gerhard Paul (Göttingen: Wallstein-Verlag, 2002), 205–34; Frank Golczewski, "Shades of Grey: Reflections on Jewish-Ukrainian and German-Ukrainian Relations in Galicia," in *The Shoah in Ukraine: History, Testimony, Memorialization*, ed. Ray Brandon and Wendy Lower (Bloomington: Indiana University Press, 2008), 114–55; Frank Golczewski, "Die Ukraine im Zweiten Weltkrieg," in *Geschichte der Ukraine*, ed. Frank Golczewski (Vandenhoeck & Ruprecht: Göttingen, 1993), 241–60; Frank Golczewski, "Die Kollaboration in der Ukraine," in *Kooperation und Verbrechen: Formen der "Kollaboration" im östlichen Europa 1939–1945*, ed Christoph Dieckmann, Babette Quinkert, and Tatjana Tönsmeyer (Göttingen: Wallstein, 2003), 151–82.

109 Shmuel Spector, *The Holocaust of Volhynian Jews 1941–1944* (Jerusalem: Achva Press, 1990).

110 John-Paul Himka, "The Lviv Pogrom of 1941: The Germans, Ukrainian Nationalists, and the Carnival Crowd," *Canadian Slavonic Papers* Vol. LIII, No. 2–4 (2011): 209–43; Christoph Mick, "Incompatible Experiences: Poles, Ukrainians and Jews in Lviv under Soviet and German Occupation, 1939–44," *Journal of Contemporary History* Vol. 46, No. 2 (2011): 336–63; Hans Heer, "Einübung in den Holocaust: Lemberg Juni/Juli 1941," *Zeitschrift für Geschichtswissenschaft* Vol. 49, No. 5 (2001): 409–27; Rossoliński-Liebe, Der Verlauf und die Täter, 207–43.

111 Philip Friedman, "Ukrainian-Jewish Relations during the Nazi Occupation," in *Roads to Extinction* (New York: Jewish Publication Society, 1980). This article was first published in YIVO Annual of Jewish Social Science Vol. 12 (1958–1959), 259–63; Eliyahu Yones, *Smoke in the Sand: The Jews of Lvov in the War Years 1939–1944* (Jerusalem: Gefen Publishing House, 2004).

112 Aharon Weiss, "Jewish-Ukrainian Relations in Western Ukraine During the Holocaust," in *Ukrainian-Jewish Relations in Historical Perspective*, ed. Peter J. Potichnyj and Howard Aster (Edmonton: CIUS, 2010), 409–20.

113 Witold Mędykowski, *W cieniu gigantów: Pogromy 1941 r. w byłej sowieckiej strefie okupacyjnej* (Warsaw: Instytut Studiów Politycznych Polskiej Akademi Nauk, 2012).

114 Omer Bartov, "Wartime Lies and Other Testimonies: Jewish-Christian Relations in Buczacz, 1939–1944," *East European Politics and Societies* Vol. 26, No. 3 (2011): 486–511; Wendy Lower, "Pogroms, Mob Violence and Genocide in Western Ukraine, Summer 1941: Varied Histories, Explanations and Comparisons," *Journal of Genocide Research* Vol. 13, No. 3 (2011): 114–55; Timothy Snyder, "The Life and Death of Western Volhynian Jewry, 1921–1945," in *Shoah in Ukraine*, ed. Brandon, 77–113; Kai Struve, "Rites of Violence? The Pogroms of Summer 1941," *Polin. Studies in Polish Jewry* 24 (2012): 257–74.

115 John-Paul Himka, "A Central European Diaspora under the Shadow of World War II: The Galician Ukrainians in North America," *Austrian History Yearbook* 37 (2006): 17–31; Grzegorz Rossoliński-

Vladimir Solonari published articles about the Soviet postwar investigation and trial records, and about the methodological problems related to their analysis.[116] Tarik Cyril Amar published an article about the Holocaust in Soviet discourse in western Ukraine.[117] Scholars such as Per Anders Rudling, Anton Shekhostov, and Andreas Umland published several articles about radical right groups and parties after 1990 in Ukraine.[118] Whether Ukrainian nationalism is a form of fascism has been discussed in publications by Frank Golczewski, Anton Shekhovtsov, Oleksandr Zaitsev, and myself.[119]

As already mentioned, a number of volumes of reprinted archival documents appeared in Ukraine during the last two decades.[120] They included much significant material, and should not be excluded solely because their authors, such as Volodymyr Serhiichuk, deny the ethnic and political violence of the OUN and UPA, or, like Ivan Patryliak, quote the former Ku Klux Klan Grand Wizard David Duke as an "expert" on the "Jewish Question" in the Soviet Union.[121] In addition to the above-mentioned academic studies, many books have been written by veterans of the OUN, UPA, and Waffen-SS Galizien, some of whom became professors at Western universities. After the dissolution of the Soviet Union, the apologetic and selective narrative

Liebe, "Celebrating Fascism and War Criminality in Edmonton: The Political Myth and Cult of Stepan Bandera in Multicultural Canada," *Kakanien Revisited*, 12 (2010): 1–16; Grzegorz Rossoliński-Liebe, "Erinnerungslücke Holocaust. Die ukrainische Diaspora und der Genozid an den Juden," *Vierteljahrshefte für Zeitgeschichte* Vol. 62, No. 3 (2014): 397–430; Per Anders Rudling, "Multiculturalism, Memory, and Ritualization: Ukrainian Nationalist Monuments in Edmonton, Alberta," *Nationalities Papers* 39, 5 (2011): 733–68; Per Anders Rudling, "The OUN, the UPA and the Holocaust: A Study in the Manufacturing of Historical Myths," *The Carl Beck Papers in Russian & East European Studies*, Number 2107 (Pittsburgh: The Center for Russian and East European Studies, 2011).

116 Diana Dumitru, "An Analysis of Soviet Postwar Investigation and Trial Documents and Their Relevance for Holocaust Studies," in *The Holocaust in the East: Local Perpetrators and Soviet Responses*, ed. Michael David-Fox, Peter Holquist, and Alexander M. Martin (Pittsburgh: University of Pittsburgh Press, 2014), 142–57; Penter, Collaboration on Trial, 782–90; Prusin, 'Fascist criminals to the gallows!', 1–30; Solonari, Patterns of Violence, 749–87.

117 Tarik Cyril Amar, "A Disturbed Silence: Discourse on the Holocaust in the Soviet West as an Anti-Site of Memory," in *The Holocaust in the East*, ed. David-Fox, 158–84.

118 Per Anders Rudling, "The Return of the Ukrainian Far Right. The Case of VO Svoboda," in Analysing Fascist Discourse. European Fascism in Talk and Text, ed. Ruth Wodak and John E. Richardson (New York: Routledge, 2013), 228–55; Per Anders Rudling, "Anti-Semitism and the Extreme Right in Contemporary Ukraine," in *Mapping the Extreme Right in Contemporary Europe: From Local to Transnational*, ed. Andrea Mammone, Emmanuel Godin, and Brian Jenkins (London: Routledge, 2012), 189–205; Anton Shekhovtsov and Andreas Umland, "Pravoradikal'naia partiinaia politika v postsovetskoi Ukraine i zagadka elektoral'noi marginal'nosti ukraïns'kikh ul'tranatsionalistov v 1994–2009 gg.," *Ab Imperio* 2 (2010): 1–29; Anton Shekhovtsov, "The Creeping Resurgence of the Ukrainian Radical Right? The Case of the Freedom Party," *Europe-Asia Studies* Vol. 63, No. 2 (2011): 203–208.

119 Golczewski, *Deutsche und Ukrainer*, 571–92; Rossoliński-Liebe, "'Ukrainian National Revolution,'" 83–114; Anton Shekhovtsov, "By Cross and Sword: 'Clerical Fascism' in Interwar Western Ukraine," *Totalitarian Movements and Political Religions* Vol. 8, No. 2 (2007): 271–85; Alexander Zaitsev, ed., *Natsionalizm i relihiia: Hreko-katolyts'ka tserkva ta ukraïns'kyi natsionalistychnyi rukh v Halychyni (1920–1930-ti roky)* (L'viv: Vydavnytstvo Ukraïns'koho Katolyts'koho Universytetu, 2011); Alexander Zaitsev, *Ukraïns'kyi integral'nyi natsionalizm (1920–1930-ti) roky: Narysy intelektual'noï istoriï* (Kiev: Krytyka, 2013).

120 Two very important document collections for this study are: I. K. Patryliak, *Viis'kova diial'nist' OUN (B) u 1940–1942 rokakh* (Kiev: Instytut Istoriï Ukraïny, 2004); and Volodymyr Serhiichuk, ed., *Stepan Bandera u dokumentakh radians'kykh orhaniv derzhavnoï bezpeky (1939–1959)*, Vol. 1–3 (Kiev: Vipol 2009).

121 Patryliak, *Viis'kova diial'nist' OUN (B)*, 326. For Serhiichuk, see Grzegorz Rossoliński-Liebe, "Der polnisch–ukrainische Historikerdiskurs über den polnisch-ukrainischen Konflikt 1943–1947," *Jahrbücher für Geschichte Osteuropas* 57 (2009): 65–66. See also Grzegorz Rossoliński-Liebe, "Debating, Obfuscating and Disciplining the Holocaust: Post-Soviet Historical Discourses on the OUN-UPA and other Nationalist Movements," *East European Jewish Affairs* Vol. 42, No. 3 (2012): 218.

initiated by these historians and other writers was taken over mostly by young Ukrainian patriotic historians and activists based in western Ukraine. On the one hand, works by Ukrainian patriotic historians such as Mykola Posivnych, and OUN veterans such as Petro Mirchuk, contain important material for a Bandera biography. On the other hand, they propagate the Bandera cult and are therefore analyzed in chapters 9 and 10, in which the Bandera cult is examined.[122]

Objectives and Limitations

This book investigates Bandera's life and cult. It concentrates on Bandera's political, and not his private life. It pays attention to Bandera's thoughts and his worldview, which can be reconstructed from books and newspapers that he read, published, or edited, opinions that he held and that he expressed in public, as well as the combat and propagandist activities that he organized or participated in. The history of the OUN and UPA takes up a substantial part of the study, in order to provide important background knowledge. The form of this book is determined by the major questions, the long period covered by the narrative, and the methods applied. It thereby differs from studies that ponder the advantages and disadvantages of nationalism or socialism for the life of a nation, or that explore short-term processes such as collaboration in a particular region or country during the Second World War.

The book is written "against the grain" in order to uncover several covered-up, forgotten, ignored, or obfuscated aspects of Ukrainian and other national histories. Obviously, the study does not seek to exonerate the Germans, Soviets, Poles, or any other nation or group for the atrocities committed by them during or after the Second World War but it cannot present and does not pretend to present all relevant aspects in an entirely comprehensive way. It pays more attention to subjects such as the ethnic and political violence of the OUN and UPA than it does to German or Soviet occupation policies in Ukraine. This method of presenting history is determined by the main subject of this study, which is Bandera and his role in the Ukrainian ultranationalist movement. Parts of the book may therefore evoke the impression that the major Holocaust perpetrators in western Ukraine were the Ukrainian nationalists and not the occupying Germans and the Ukrainian police. It is not the aim of this study to argue this. This study makes clear estimates of the percentages of people who were killed by the Germans and the Ukrainian police on the one hand, and by the OUN and UPA and other Ukrainian perpetrators on the other.

It is not the aim of this book to argue that all eastern Galician and Volhynian Ukrainians (and logically not all Ukrainians) supported the politics of the OUN,

122 Petro Mirchuk's most important publications about or relating to Bandera are: *Stepan Bandera: Symvol revoliutsiinoï bezkompromisovosty* (New York: Orhanizatsiia oborony chotyr'okh svobid Ukraïny, 1961); *Narys istoriï OUN: 1920–1939* (Kiev: Ukraïns'ka Vydavnycha Spilka, 2007). For Posivnych publications about Bandera, see Mykola Posivnych, ed., *Stepan Bandera: Dokumenty i materialy (1920–1930 rr.)* (Lviv: Afisha, 2006); Mykola Posivnych, *Stepan Bandera—zhyttia, prysviachene svobodi* (Toronto: Litopys UPA, 2008); Mykola Posivnych, ed., *Zhyttia i diial'nist' Stepana Bandery: Dokumenty i materialy* (Ternopil': Aston, 2008); Mykola Posivnych ed., *Zhyttia i diial'nist' Stepana Bandery: Dokumenty i materialy* (Ternopil: Aston, 2011); Mykola Posivnych, *Varshavs'kyi akt obvynuvachennia Stepana Bandery ta tovaryshiv* (Lviv: Tsentr doslidzhen' vyzvol'noho rukhu, 2005); Mykola Posivnych and Bohdan Hordasevych, eds., *Stepan Bandera: 1909–1959–2009: Zbirnyk statei* (Lviv: Triada Plius, 2010).

fought in the UPA, were involved in the Holocaust, the ethnic cleansing against Polish population, and other forms of ethnic and political violence conducted by the OUN and UPA, or that they agreed with such actions. The study explores the interrelation between nationalism and the violence committed in its name, but it does not ignore the economic, social, and political factors that contributed to ethnic conflicts or to the formation of fascist movements.

This monograph does not negate the fact that, during the Second World War, Ukrainians were both victims and perpetrators, and that the same persons who were involved in ethnic and political violence became the victims of the Soviet regime. Moreover, the study does not suggest that all Ukrainians who were in the OUN or UPA were fascists or radical nationalists. There were different reasons for joining the OUN and UPA, and various kinds of people joined these organizations, some of them under coercion. Logically, the study does not imply that all Ukrainians who joined the OUN or UPA committed atrocities, or that among Ukrainians, only OUN and UPA members were involved in the Holocaust or other atrocities. Such an assumption would distort reality, and exonerate groups such as non-nationalist Ukrainians, the Ukrainian police, and Ukrainians who participated primarily for economic and other non-political reasons. Finally, Ukrainian political parties and organizations other than the OUN appear only marginally in this study, because the monograph concentrates on Bandera and the OUN. As a result, readers might receive the impression that the OUN was the organization that dominated the entire political life of Ukraine. This, of course, is not true. Many other nationalist, democratic, conservative, and communist organizations and parties existed in Ukraine before the Second World War, and also impacted political life there, but they are not the subject of this book.

Chapter 1

HETEROGENEITY, MODERNITY, AND THE TURN TO THE RIGHT

"Longue Durée" Perspective and the Heterogeneity of Ukrainian History

Stepan Bandera was born on 1 January 1909 in the village of Staryi Uhryniv, located in the eastern part of Galicia, the easternmost province of the Habsburg Empire. Galicia, officially known as the Kingdom of Galicia and Lodomeria (*Regnum Galiciae et Lodomeriae*), was created in 1772 by the bureaucrats of the House of Habsburg at the first partition of the Polish-Lithuanian Commonwealth (*Res Publica Utriusque Nationis*). The province was an economically backward region with a heterogeneous population: according to statistics from 1910, 47 percent of the population were Polish, 42 percent Ukrainian, and 11 percent Jewish. The eastern part of Galicia, which the Ukrainian national movement claimed as a part of the Ukrainian nation state, and where the political cult of Stepan Bandera was born, was no less heterogeneous: 62 percent of the population were Ukrainian, 25 percent Polish, and 12 percent Jewish (Maps 1 and 2).[1]

At the time of Bandera's birth, close to 20 percent of "Ukrainians," or people who began to perceive themselves as Ukrainians as a result of the invention of Ukrainian national identity, lived in the Habsburg Empire (in Galicia, Bukovina and Transcarpathia). At the same time, 80 percent of Ukrainians lived in the Russian Empire (in eastern Ukraine, also known as "Russian Ukraine").[2] This division and other political, religious, and cultural differences caused Galician Ukrainians to become a quite different people from the Ukrainians in Russian Ukraine. The division posed a difficult challenge, both for activists of the moderate, socialist-influenced, nineteenth-century national movement, such as Mykhailo Drahomanov (1841–1895), Mykhailo Hrushevs'kyi (1866–1934), and Ivan Franko (1856–1916), and later for the extreme, violent, and revolutionary twentieth-century nationalists such as Dmytro Dontsov (1883–1973), Ievhen Konovalets' (1891–1938), and Stepan Bandera (1909–1959). These political figures tried to establish a single Ukrainian nation that would live in one Ukrainian state.[3]

1 Rudolf A. Mark, *Galizien unter österreichischer Herrschaft: Verwaltung-Kirche-Bevölkerung* (Marburg: Herder Institut, 1994), 70, 80. The Habsburg statistics were based on religion. In Galicia, Poles generally identified themselves as Roman Catholics, and Ukrainians as Greek Catholics.

2 The Habsburg Empire was, from 1867 until its demise in 1918, an Austro-Hungarian monarchy, and was divided into two parts: Cisleithania (capital Vienna), and Transleithania (capital Budapest). Galicia and Bukovina belonged to Cisleithania, and Transcarpathia to Transleithania. Ukrainians constituted about 40 percent of Bukovina's population. Other ethnic groups in Bukovina were Romanians (34 percent), Jews (13 percent), and Germans (8 percent). Cf. Kerstin Jobst, "Die ukrainische Nationalbewegung bis 1917," in *Geschichte der Ukraine*, ed. Frank Golczewski (Göttingen: Vandenhoeck & Ruprecht, 1993), 171.

3 For the political and cultural division of Ukraine in the nineteenth century, see Wolfdieter Bihl, "Aufgegangen in Großreichen: Die Ukraine als österreichische und russische Provinz," in *Geschichte*

To some extent, the dual and heterogeneous state of affairs was a continuation of earlier pre-modern political and cultural divisions of the territories that the Ukrainian national movement claimed as its own. In the twentieth century, the East-West division and the separate development of the two Ukrainian identities did not narrow and, due to new geopolitical circumstances, even widened. One of the most important factors that contributed to the increase of cultural and religious differences between western and eastern Ukrainians was the military conflict between the OUN-UPA and the Soviet regime during the 1940s and early 1950s. This conflict was followed by a powerful propaganda battle between nationalist factions of the Ukrainian diaspora and the Soviet Union; as a consequence, each side demonized and hated the other. In Soviet and Soviet Ukrainian discourse, the personality of Stepan Bandera acquired a significance completely different from that perceived by Galician Ukrainians. As a result, two contradictory myths relating to Stepan Bandera marked the cultural and political division of Ukraine.[4]

In nineteenth- and early twentieth-century Habsburg Galicia, the local Ukrainians identified themselves—and were identified by others—as "Ruthenians" (Ger. *Ruthenen*, Pol. *Rusini*, Ukr. *Rusyny*). In the Russian Empire, Ukrainians were called "Little Russians" (Rus. *malorossy*, Ukr. *malorosy*). "Ukraine" as the term for a nation only came into use in Galicia in about 1900. Although the word obviously existed long before this time, it was not the term for a nation, despite the fact that the Ukrainian national movement purported retroactively to impose such an identity on the medieval or even ancient inhabitants of "Ukrainian territories." In the pre-modern era the term "Ukraine" referred to the "border territories" of the Polish-Lithuanian Commonwealth and Kievan Rus'. Such terms as Rosia, Russia, Rus', Ruthenia, and Roxolonia were also used for the Ukrainian territories.[5]

In 1916 the historian Stanisław Smołka, son of the Austrian conservative and Polish nationalist politician Franciszek Smołka, to whom he dedicated his book *Die Reussische Welt*, argued that "the geographic Ukraine" is the "Ruthenian territory par excellence."[6] The bureaucracy of the Russian Empire did not regard Ukrainians as a nation, but as an ethnic group with close cultural and linguistic affinities to Russians. The Ems Ukaz of 1876, which remained in force until the revolution of 1905, forbade

der Ukraine, ed. Golczewski, 126–57, and John-Paul Himka, *Socialism in Galicia: The Emergence of Polish Social Democracy and Ukrainian Radicalism (1860–1890)* (Cambridge: Harvard Ukrainian Research Institute, 1983), 47, 50, 52.

4 For the influence of West European and East European culture and the division of Ukraine into West and East in pre-modern times, see Ihor Shevchenko, *Ukraine between East and West: Essays on Cultural History to the Early Eighteen Century* (Edmonton: Canadian Institute of Ukrainian Studies Press, 1996). On the cultural heterogeneity of Ukraine, see Hagen, Revisiting the Histories of Ukraine; Kappeler, From an Ethnonational to a Multiethnic.

5 Natalia Yakovenko, "Choice of Name versus Choice of Path: The Names of Ukrainian Territories from the Late Sixteenth to the Late Seventeenth Century," in *A Laboratory of Transnational History*, ed. Kasianov, 117–41.

6 Stanislau von Smolka, *Die Reussische Welt: Historisch-Politische Studien: Vergangenheit und Gegenwart* (Vienna: Zentral-Verlagsbüro des obersten polnischen Nationalkomitees: 1916), 13. In the original "*Ukraine*, ein ruthenisches Gebiet." Cf. Smolka, *Die Reussische Welt*, 6.

Map 1. Galicia 1914. *YIVO Encyclopedia*, 2:565.

not only printing in Ukrainian and importing literature in Ukrainian into the Russian Empire but even the use of the terms "Ukraine" and "Ukrainian." The Ukaz caused the emigration of many Ukrainian intellectuals to Galicia, where they could publish in Ukrainian.[7]

Although the Galician Ruthenians differed from the Russian Ukrainians culturally and politically in many respects, they were similar to each other in that they lived mainly in the countryside and were under-represented in the cities and industrial regions. During the nineteenth century and the first half of the twentieth, Ukrainians in Lviv numbered between 15 and 20 percent.[8] In Kiev, 60 percent of the inhabitants spoke Ukrainian in 1864; but by 1917, only 16 percent.[9]

One group of Galician Ruthenians, known as Russophiles, further complicated the process of creating a Ukrainian nation. The origins of this movement can be traced back to the 1830s and 1840s, although it did not expand until after 1848. The Russophiles claimed to be a separate brand of Russians, although their concept of Russia was ambiguous and varied in relation to the context, between Russia as an empire, eastern Christianity, and eastern Slavs. The Russophile movement was created by Russian political activists, and by the local Ruthenian intelligentsia who were disappointed by the pro-Polish policies of the Habsburg Empire, especially in

7 Jobst, Die Ukrainische Nationalbewegung bis 1917, 161, 168; Hrytsak, *Narys istorii Ukraïny*, 70–71.

8 Yaroslav Hrytsak and Victor Susak, "Constructing a National City: Case of L'viv," in *Composing Urban History and the Constitution of Civic Identities*, ed. John Czaplicka, Blair A. Ruble, and Lauren Crabtree (Washington: Johns Hopkins University Press, 2003), 142–43; Peter Fäßler, Thomas Held, and Dirk Sawitzki, ed., *Lemberg—Lwow—L'viv: Eine Stadt im Schnittpunkt europäischer Kulturen* (Köln: Böhlau 1995), 183.

9 Bihl, Aufgegangen in Großreichen, 151.

Map 2. Eastern Europe 1815. *YIVO Encyclopedia*, 2:2144.

the late 1860s. The Russophiles identified themselves with Russia, partly because of the Russian belief that Ukrainian culture was a peasant culture without a tradition of statehood. Identifying with Russia, they could divest themselves of their feelings of inferiority in relation to their Polish Galician fellow-citizens who, like the Russians, possessed a "high culture" and a tradition of statehood.[10]

Galician Ukrainian culture was for centuries deeply influenced by Polish culture, while eastern Ukrainian culture was strongly influenced by Russian culture. As a result of long-standing coexistence, cultural and linguistic differences between Ukrainians and Poles on the one side became blurred, as they did between Ukrainians and Russians on the other. The differences between the western and eastern Ukrainians were evident. The Galician dialect of Ukrainian differed substantially from the Ukrainian language in Russian Ukraine. Such political, social, and cultural differences made a difficult starting point for a weak national movement that sought to establish a single nation, which was planned to be culturally different from and independent of its stronger neighbors.[11]

10 Himka, *Socialism in Galicia*, 40–41. On Russophiles in Galicia, see Anna Veronika Wendland, *Die Russophilen in Galizien: Ukrainische Konservative zwischen Österreich und Russland, 1848–1915* (Vienna: Verlag der österreichischen Akademie der Wissenschaften, 2001).

11 Iaroslav Hrytsak, *Narys istorii Ukraïny: Formuvannia modernoï ukraïns'koï natsiï XIX–XX stolittia* (Kiev: Heneza, 2000), 81–82.

The western part of the Ukrainian territories was dominated by Polish culture from 1340 onwards, when King Casimir III the Great annexed Red Ruthenia (*Russia Rubra*), with a break between 1772 and 1867, during which Austrian politicians dominated and controlled politics in Galicia. Motivated by material and political considerations, the Ukrainian boyars and nobles had already become Catholics in pre-modern times and had adopted the Polish language. The Polonization of their upper classes left Ukrainians without an aristocratic stratum and rendered them an ethnic group with a huge proportion of peasants. Polish language and culture were associated with the governing stratum, while the Ukrainian equivalents were associated with the stratum of peasants. There were many exceptions to both propositions. For example, the Greek Catholic priests might be classified as Ukrainian intelligentsia, while there were numerous Polish peasants. However, the difference between the "dominant Poles" and the "dominated Ukrainians" caused tensions between them and, as a result of a nationalist interpretation of history, caused a strong feeling of inferiority on the part of the Ukrainians.

Until 1848, Ukrainian and Polish peasants in Galicia were serfs of their Polish landlords. They were forced to work without pay from three to six days a week on their landlords' estates. In addition they were often humiliated and mistreated by the landowners.[12] Even when serfdom was ended in 1848, the socio-economic situation of the Galician peasants did not significantly improve for many decades. In eastern Galicia, where the majority of the peasants were Ukrainians (Ruthenians) and almost all the landlords were Poles, serfdom had a significant psychological impact on the Ukrainian national movement.[13]

The Greek Catholic Church had strongly shaped the identity of Galician Ukrainians and had influenced Galician Ukrainian nationalism from its very beginnings. The Church was originally a product of the Polish-Lithuanian Commonwealth. As the direct result of the Union of Brest of 1595–1596, the Greek Catholic Church severed relations with the Patriarch of Constantinople and accepted the superiority of the Vatican. It did not, however, change its Orthodox or Byzantine liturgical tradition. When the Russian Empire absorbed the greatest part of the Polish-Lithuanian Commonwealth between 1772 and 1795, it dissolved the Greek Catholic Church in the incorporated territories and replaced it with the Orthodox Church. The Ukrainian Greek Catholic Church continued to function only in Habsburg Galicia, where it became a Ukrainian national church and an important component of Galician Ukrainian identity.[14]

Especially in the early stage of its existence, the Ukrainian national movement in Galicia was greatly influenced by the Greek Catholic Church. The secular intelligentsia in eastern Galicia who took part in the national movement emerged to a large extent from the families of Greek Catholic priests. Many fanatical Ukrainian activists in the nationalist cause, including Stepan Bandera himself, were the sons of priests. Furthermore, it was only with the help of the Greek Catholic priests present in every

12 John-Paul Himka, *Galician Villagers and the Ukrainian National Movement in the Nineteenth Century* (Basingstoke: Macmillan, 1998), 10–16.

13 For the memory of serfdom in eastern Galicia and its impact on Ukrainian collective consciousness and memory, see John-Paul Himka, "Serfdom in Galicia," *Journal of Ukrainian Studies* Vol. 9, No. 2 (1984): 26–28.

14 Bociurkiw, *Ukraïns'ka Hreko-Katolyts'ka*, 4–6.

eastern Galician village that the activists of the Ukrainian national movement could reach the predominantly illiterate peasants. This situation changed only in the late nineteenth century, when such educational organizations as Prosvita established reading-rooms in villages. In these institutions the peasants could read newspapers and other publications that disseminated the idea of a secular Ukrainian nationalism.[15] However, even after a slight emancipation from the Greek Catholic Church, the Galician brand of Ukrainian nationalism was steeped in mysticism and had strong religious overtones. The Greek Catholic religion was an important symbolic foundation of the ideology of Ukrainian nationalism, although not the only one.

Modern Ukrainian nationalism, as manifested in the late nineteenth and early twentieth centuries in Galicia, became increasingly hostile to Poles, Jews, and Russians. The hostility to Poles was related to the nationalist interpretation of their socio-economic circumstances, as well as the feeling that the Poles had occupied the Ukrainian territories and had deprived the Ukrainians of a nobility and an intelligentsia. The nationalist hostility to Jews was related to the fact that many Jews were merchants, and to the fact that some of them worked as agents of the Polish landowners. The Ukrainians felt that the Jews supported the Poles and exploited the Ukrainian peasants. The resentment toward Russians was related to the government by the Russian Empire of a huge part of the territories that the Ukrainian national movement claimed to be Ukrainian. While the Jews in Galicia were seen as agents of the Polish landowners, Jews in eastern Ukraine were frequently perceived to be agents of the Russian Empire. The stereotype of Jews supporting both Poles and Russians, and exploiting Ukrainians by means of trade or bureaucracy, became a significant image in the Ukrainian nationalist discourse.

Ukrainian nationalism thrived in eastern Galicia rather than in eastern Ukraine where the activities of the Ukrainian nationalists were suppressed by the Russian Empire. The political liberalism of the Habsburg Empire, as it developed after 1867, made Galician Ukrainians more nationalist, populist, and mystical than eastern Ukrainians. During the second half of the nineteenth century, the systematic policy of Russification in eastern Ukraine made the national distinction between Ukrainians and Russians increasingly meaningless. Most eastern Ukrainians understood Ukraine to be a region of Russia, and considered themselves to be a people akin to Russians.[16]

Because of the nationalist discourse that took place in eastern Galicia, the province was labeled as the Ukrainian "Piedmont." Because of their loyalty to the Habsburg Empire, Galician Ukrainians were known as the "Tyroleans of the East." In Russian Ukraine, on the other hand, the majority of the political and intellectual stratum assimilated into Russian culture and did not pay attention to Ukrainian nationalism. "Although I was born a Ukrainian, I am more Russian than anybody else," claimed Viktor Kochubei (1768–1834), a statesman of the Russian Empire with

15 John-Paul Himka, "Priest and Peasants: The Greek Catholic Church and the Ukrainian National Movement in Austria, 1867–1900," in *The Greek Catholic Church and Ukrainian Society in Austrian Galicia*, ed. John-Paul Himka (Cambridge and Massachusetts: Harvard University Ukrainian Studies Fund, 1986), 1–5, 9, 12–14.

16 John-Paul Himka, "The Galician Triangle: Poles, Ukrainians, and Jews under Austrian Rule," *Cross Current: A Yearbook of Central European Culture* 12 (1993): 143; Himka, *Socialism in Galicia*, 50.

Ukrainian origins.[17] Nikolai Gogol' (1809–1852), born near Poltava in a family with Ukrainian traditions, described Cossack life in his novel *Taras Bulba* in a humorous, satirical, and grotesque way. His books appeared in elegant Russian, which included Ukrainian elements, and were written without national pathos. In 1844 Gogol' wrote in a letter: "I myself do not know whether my soul is Ukrainian [*khokhlatskaia*] or Russian [*russkaia*]. I know only that on no account would I give priority to the Little Russian [*malorosiianinu*] before the Russian [*russkim*], or the Russian before the Little Russian."[18]

The Beginnings of Ukrainian "Heroic Modernity"

Ukrainian heroic modernity found expression for the first time in the writings of the nationalist extremist Mykola Mikhnovs'kyi (1873–1924), although it derives from the thoughts of such activists as Mykhailo Hrushevs'kyi, Mykhailo Drahomanov, and Ivan Franko. The most influential of these was Hrushevs'kyi, a historian and politician. In the nineteenth century, thinkers such as Georg Wilhelm Friedrich Hegel and Friedrich Engels elaborated on the popular problem of "historical" and "non-historical" nations, to which Hrushevs'kyi responded. Starting from ancient times, Hrushevs'kyi rewrote the history of the Eastern Slavs, displaying bias in favor of the Ukrainian national movement and regarding the Russian and Polish national movements with disfavor. In his voluminous *History of Ukraine-Rus'*, he separated Ukrainian history from Russian history, claiming that the Ukrainian people had ancient origins. He thereby "resolved" the problem of the "non-historical" Ukrainian people, making it as historical and as rich in tradition as the Polish and Russian peoples. This was one of the most significant late nineteenth-century "academic" contributions to the creation of a national Ukrainian identity.[19]

In his historical writings, Hrushevs'kyi did not insist that the Slavs or Ukrainians were a pure race or had to be viewed as a race. Nevertheless he used the term "race" in the context of anthropology. Writing about the ancient peoples living in the territory of contemporary Ukraine, he mentioned "dolichocephalic" (long-headed) and "brachycephalic" (short-headed) types of people inhabiting the Ukrainian territories in ancient times. He argued that "the Slavs of today are predominantly short-headed" but racially not uniform. The brachycephalic type "is still the dominant type among Ukrainians, but among the Poles and Russians this type vies with the mesaticephalic [medium headed], with a significant admixture of the dolichocephalic."[20] Looking for the origins of the Ukrainian people among ancient peoples, Hrushevs'kyi concluded

17 Bihl, Aufgegangen in Großreichen, 146.

18 Letter from Gogol' to his long-time friend Alexandra Smirnova, 24 December 1844, in N.V. Gogol', *Sobranie sochinenii* (Moscow: Russkaia kniga, 1994), 10:276, quoted in Andrew Wilson, *The Ukrainians: Unexpected Nation* (New Haven: Yale University Press, 2009), 88.

19 Serhii Plokhy, *Unmaking Imperial Russia: Mykhailo Hrushevskyi and the Writing of Ukrainian History* (Toronto: University of Toronto Press, 2005), 92–95; Timothy Snyder, *The Reconstruction of Nations: Poland, Ukraine, Lithuania, Belarus, 1569–1999* (New Haven: Yale University Press, 2003), 128–29; Kappeler, From an Ethnonational to a Multiethnic, 57.

20 Mykhailo Hrushevs'kyi, *Istoriia Ukraïny-Rusy* (Kiev: Persha spilka, 1913), 1:64–65. For English translation, see Mykhailo Hrushevs'kyi, *History of Ukraine—Rus'. From prehistory to the eleventh century*, ed. Andrzej Poppe and Frank Sysyn, trans. Marta Skorupsky (Edmonton: Canadian Institute of Ukrainian Studies Press, 1997), 1:46–47.

that the "Ukrainian tribes" originated from the Antes: "The Antes were almost certainly the ancestors of the Ukrainian tribes."[21] While analyzing ancient and medieval descriptions of people living at that time in the Ukrainian territories, he pondered about the ideal type of a historical Ukrainian and wrote that Ukrainians were "blond-haired, ruddy-skinned, and tall" and "very dirty" people.[22]

Mikhnovs'kyi, much more radical than Hrushevs'kyi, was the pioneer of extreme Ukrainian nationalism. He lived in Russian Ukraine, mainly in Kharkiv. Because he died in 1924 he did not come into contact with the radical Ukrainian nationalists from the UVO or OUN, but his writings inspired the younger generation.[23] Mikhnovs'kyi politicized the ethnicity of Ukrainians and demanded a "Ukraine for Ukrainians" (*Ukraïna dlia ukraïntsiv*). He might have been inspired by Hrushevs'kyi's historization of contemporary Ukrainians and by contemporary European discourses that combined nationalism with racism. Although Mikhnovs'kyi's concept of ethnicity was based on language, his main aim was a biological and racial marking of the Ukrainian territories or the "living space" of the Ukrainians. He claimed the territory "from the Carpathian Mountains to the Caucasus" for a Ukrainian state without foes. By "foes" Mikhnovs'kyi meant "Russians, Poles, Magyars, Romanians, and Jews ... as long as they rule over us and exploit us."[24]

Mikhnovs'kyi went so far in his ethno-biological concept as to demand, in one of "The Ten Commandments of the UNP," which he wrote for the Ukrainian National Party (*Ukraïns'ka Narodna Partia*, UNP), cofounded by him in 1904: "Do not marry a foreign woman because your children will be your enemies, do not be on friendly terms with the enemies of our nation, because you make them stronger and braver, do not deal with our oppressors, because you will be a traitor."[25]

Mikhnovs'kyi's concept of Ukraine was directed not only against people who might be considered to be foreigners but also against the majority of Ukrainians, who spoke Russian or a dialect that was neither Russian nor Ukrainian, or who were contaminated through marriage or friendship with a non-Ukrainian. This was the case of many Ukrainians after centuries of coexistence with Poles, Russians, Jews, and other ethnic groups. It was also not a political or cultural program with which the nationally non-conscious Ukrainians could have been transformed through education into nationally conscious Ukrainians. It was rather a social Darwinist concept based on the assumption that there exists a Ukrainian race, which must struggle for its survival against Russians, Poles, Jews, and other non-Ukrainian inhabitants of Ukrainian territories. Mikhnovs'kyi understood this concept as the historical destiny

21 Hrushevs'kyi, *Istoriia Ukraïny-Rusy*, 1:177; Hrushevs'kyi, *History of Ukraine*—Rus', 1:134.

22 Hrushevs'kyi, *Istoriia Ukraïny-Rusy*, 1:307, 310; Hrushevs'kyi, *History of Ukraine*—Rus', 1: 234, 236.

23 For Bandera studying Mikhnovs'kyi's writings, see Mirchuk, *Stepan Bandera*, 14.

24 The second commandment of "The Ten Commandments of the UNP" said "All people are your brothers, but Russians, Poles, Magyars, Romanians, and Jews are the enemies of our nation, as long as they rule over us and exploit us" (Usi liudy—tvoï brattia, ale moskali, liakhy, uhry, rumuny ta zhydy—tse vorohy nashoho narodu, poky vony panuiut' nad namy i vyzyskuiut' nas). Cf. Roman Koval, "Heroi, shcho ne zmih vriatuvaty Bat'kivshchyny," in *Samostiina Ukraïna*, ed. Roman Koval (Kiev: Diokor, 2003), 9. For the interrelation between racism and nationalism, see George L. Mosse, "Racism and Nationalism," in *The Fascist Revolution: Toward a General Theory of Fascism*, ed. George L. Mosse (New York: Howard Fertig, 2000), 55–68.

25 Koval, Heroi, shcho ne zmih, 9. In Ukrainian: "Ne bery sobi druzhyny z chuzhyntsiv, bo tvoï dity budut' tobi vorohamy, ne pryiateliui z vorohamy nashoho narodu, bo ty dodaiesh ïm syly i vidvahy, ne nakladai ukupi z hnobyteliamy nashymy, bo zradnykom budesh."

of the Ukrainian people and stressed that there was no alternative: "Either we will win in the fight or we will die."[26] This early Ukrainian extremist also demanded: "Ukraine for Ukrainians, and as long as even one alien enemy remains on our territory, we are not allowed to lay down our arms. And we should remember that glory and victory are the destiny of fighters for the national cause."[27]

The Lost Struggle for Ukrainian Statehood

The changes to the map of Europe after the First World War served as a very convenient opportunity for the establishment of several new national states on the ruins of the Russian and Habsburg empires. However, this scenario did not work in the case of the Ukrainians and some other nations, such as the Croats and Slovaks. The war revealed how heterogeneous were the Ukrainian people and how ambiguous was the concept of a Ukrainian state at this time. Like many other East Central European nationalities, Ukrainians fought on both sides of the Eastern Front and, like some other peoples, established their own armies to struggle for a nation state. Yet in the case of Ukraine, they struggled rather for two different states than for one and the same.

On 20 November 1917 in Kiev, an assembly of various political parties, known as the Tsentral'na Rada, or Central Council, proclaimed the Ukrainian People's Republic (*Ukraïns'ka Narodna Respublika*, UNR). On 25 January 1918, the same political body declared the UNR to be a "Free Sovereign State of the Ukrainian People." The UNR thereby declared its independence from the Bolsheviks, who had in November 1917 taken over power in the Russian Empire, but it was still dependent on the Germans who were occupying Kiev. On 9 February 1918, representatives of the Tsentral'na Rada signed the Brest-Litovsk treaty, as a result of which the UNR was officially recognized by the Central Powers (the German, Austro-Hungarian, Ottoman empires, and Kingdom of Bulgaria) and by the Bolshevik government of the Russian Soviet Federated Socialist Republic (Russian SFSR), but not by the Western Allies (United Kingdom, France, and so forth).[28]

Between 1918 and 1921, power changed hands in Kiev several times. The first new authority, the Tsentral'na Rada, was unsure whether a Ukrainian state could exist outside the Russian Federation without the help of the Central Powers. The second authority, established on 29 April 1918 around Hetman Pavlo Skoropads'kyi, was a puppet government installed and controlled by the Germans. Skoropads'kyi left Kiev with the German army in December 1918 and at the same time, a group of Austrian and Ukrainian politicians tried and failed to establish the Austrian Ukrainophile Wilhelm von Habsburg as a replacement for Skoropads'kyi. The Directorate, a provisional state committee of the UNR, which replaced Skoropads'kyi in late 1918, was soon forced

26 Mykola Mikhnovs'kyi, "Samostiina Ukraïna," in *Samostiina Ukraïna*, ed. Roman Koval (Kiev: Diokor, 2003), 43.

27 Ibid., 43.

28 Rudolf A. Mark, "Die gescheiterten Staatsversuche," in *Geschichte der Ukraine*, ed. Golczewski, 177–79; Golczewski, *Deutsche und Ukrainer*, 240, 264, 270–71.

by the Soviet army to withdraw from Kiev. Most territories claimed by the Ukrainian authorities in Kiev to be part of their state were not under their control.[29]

On 1 November 1918 in Lviv—capital of eastern Galicia—the West Ukrainian National Republic (*Zakhidno-Ukraïns'ka Narodna Respublika*, ZUNR) was proclaimed. After a few weeks, the leaders of the ZUNR were forced to leave Lviv by the local Poles and by units of the Polish army under the command of Michał Karaszewicz-Tokarzewski. The ZUNR continued its existence in Stanyslaviv (Stanisławów), a provincial city of Galicia. On 22 January 1919, the ZUNR united with the UNR, which had been forced by the Bolsheviks to leave Kiev for the west. However, this unification of the two Ukrainian states was mainly symbolic.[30]

The military forces of the UNR: the Ukrainian People's Army (*Armia Ukraïns'koï Narodnoï Respubliky*, AUNR), and of the ZUNR: the Ukrainian Galician Army (*Ukraïns'ka Halyts'ka Armiia*, UHA) consisted of many different military formations. The most disciplined and best trained among them were the Sich Riflemen (*Sichovi Stril'tsi*), whose soldiers were recruited from Ukrainians in the Austro-Hungarian army. The armies of the ZUNR and UNR were too weak to resist the Polish and Bolshevik armies. As the result of the various complicated alliances, each Ukrainian force found itself in the camp of its enemies and felt betrayed accordingly. By 2 December 1919, while threatened by the Bolshevik army, the UNR had signed an agreement with Poland. The UNR politicians agreed to allow Poland to incorporate the territory of the ZUNR, if Poland would help to protect their state against the Bolsheviks. Ievhen Petrushevych, head of the ZUNR, on the other hand, had already decided on 17 November 1919 that the UHA would join the White Army of Anton Denikin, which was at odds with the UNR. In February 1920, the majority of the UHA soldiers deserted from the Whites and allied themselves with the Bolsheviks because the latter were at war with both the Poles and the AUNR. In these circumstances it was hardly surprising that some Ukrainian politicians, for example Osyp Nazaruk, voiced the opinion that the Galician Ukrainians were a different nation from the eastern Ukrainians.[31]

Although a group of Ukrainian politicians visited the Paris Peace Conference in 1919, they were too inexperienced and too badly prepared to successfully represent the Ukrainian cause at such a gathering, where the new geopolitical shape of Europe was being determined. They also bore the stigma of having supported the Central Powers, who were blamed for the war by the victorious Allies. The Polish Endecja politician Roman Dmowski portrayed the Ukrainians in Paris as anarchistic "bandits," the Ukrainian state as a German intrigue, and the Ruthenians from the Habsburg Empire as Ruthenians who had nothing in common with Ukrainians. Other Polish politicians at the conference, such as Stanisław Grabski and Ignacy Paderewski, characterized Ukrainians in a similar manner and thereby weakened the chances of a Ukrainian state.[32]

29 Golczewski, Deutsche und Ukrainer, 279–81, 346; Mark, Die gescheiterten Staatsversuche, 178–88; Timothy Snyder, *The Red Prince: The Fall of the Dynasty and the Rise of Modern Europe* (London: The Bodley Head, 2008), 99–120.

30 Golczewski, *Deutsche und Ukrainer*, 362–63, 383–84.

31 Ibid., 383–90, 466.

32 Ibid., 344, 347, 366–69.

Other participants at the conference were also reluctant to support the idea of a Ukrainian state, partially because of the Ukrainian alliance with the Central Powers, and partially because they did not know much about Ukraine and Ukrainians. They were confused as to whether the Greek Catholic Ruthenians from the Habsburg Empire, as portrayed by the Polish delegates, were the same people as the Orthodox Ukrainians from the Russian Empire. David Lloyd George, Prime Minister of the United Kingdom, stated: "I only saw a Ukrainian once. It is the last Ukrainian I have seen, and I am not sure that I want to see any more."[33] By the Treaty of Riga on 18 March 1921, the borders of the Ukrainian territories were settled between Poland, Soviet Russia, and Soviet Ukraine, to the disadvantage of the UNR and ZUNR. The Allied Powers and many other states recognized this state of affairs, thereby confirming the nonexistence of the various Ukrainian states for which many Ukrainians had struggled between 1917 and 1921.[34]

During the revolutionary struggles, many pogroms took place in central and eastern Ukraine, especially in the provinces of Kiev, Podolia, and Volhynia, which were controlled by the Directorate, the Whites, and anarchist peasant bands. The troops of the Directorate and the Whites not only permitted the anti-Jewish violence but also participated in it. The pogroms only ceased with the coming of the Red Army. Nakhum Gergel, a former deputy minister of Jewish affairs in the Ukrainian government, recorded 1,182 pogroms and 50,000 to 60,000 victims. This scale of anti-Jewish violence was much greater than that of the pogroms of 1881–1884 and 1903–1907. Only during the Khmel'nyts'kyi Uprising in 1648 did anti-Jewish violence at a comparable level take place in the Ukrainian territories: according to Antony Polonsky, at least 13,000 Jews were killed by the Cossacks commanded by Bohdan Khmel'nyts'kyi.[35]

The Lack of a Ukrainian State and the Polish-Ukrainian Conflict

Between the First and Second World Wars, Ukrainians lived in four different states. About 26 million lived in the Ukrainian Soviet Socialist Republic (*Ukraïns'ka Sotsiialistychna Radians'ka Respublika*, Ukrainian SRR), 5 million in the Second Polish Republic (*II Rzeczpospolita Polska*), 0.5 million in the Czechoslovak Republic (Czech: *Československá Republika*, Slovak: *Republika Česko-Slovenská*), and 0.8 million in Greater Romania (*România Mare*).[36]

33 Quoted in Margaret MacMillan, *Peacemakers: Six Months That Changed the World* (London: John Murray, 2003), 236.

34 Hrytsak, *Narys istorii Ukraïny*, 111–59; Golczewski, *Deutsche und Ukrainer*, 414–21.

35 Antony Polonsky, *The Jews in Poland and Russia, 1350–1880*, (Oxford: The Littman Library of Jewish Civilization, 2010), 1:137; Antony Polonsky, *The Jews in Poland and Russia, 1914–2008*, (Oxford: The Littman Library of Jewish Civilization, 2010), 3:32–43.

36 Jarosław Hrycak, *Historia Ukrainy 1772–1999: Narodziny nowoczesnego narodu* (Lublin: Agencja "Wschód," 2000), 173, 188; Of the 31 or 32 million inhabitants of the Ukrainian SSR 26 million were Ukrainians. Cf. Volodymyr Kosyk, *Ukraïna i Nimechchyna u Druhii svitovii viini* (Lviv: Naukove tovarystvo im. Shevchenka, 1993), 36.

Map 3. Eastern Europe 1923. *YIVO Encyclopedia*, 2:2145.

During the 1920s the Ukrainians in Soviet Ukraine were exposed to the policy of Ukrainization, which strengthened the use of the Ukrainian language and promoted Ukrainian culture in public life. With the beginning of Sovietization in the early 1930s, this policy changed entirely. The collectivization of agriculture in the Soviet Union was the major cause of an artificial famine, resulting in the deaths of 2.5–3.9 million people in Soviet Ukraine in 1932–1933. In terms of national consciousness, the Soviet authorities tried to turn Ukrainians into loyal Soviet citizens, causing the unformed Ukrainian identity of the former Russian Ukrainians to blur further with Russian and Soviet identity.[37] Of all the states where Ukrainians lived, it was in Czechoslovakia that the small Ukrainian minority enjoyed the most liberal treatment. The authorities there allowed various Ukrainian schools, and three postsecondary colleges: the Ukrainian Husbandry Academy and the Ukrainian Technical and Husbandry Institute in Poděbrady, and the Ukrainian Free University in Prague. This was an unusually liberal policy toward a minority in Eastern Europe at this time. In Romania and Poland, Ukrainians were exposed to a policy of assimilation—a common

37 Hrytsak, *Narys istorii Ukraïny*, 166–86; Yekelchyk, *Stalin's Empire of Memory*, 13–18. On the question of how many people died in the famine, see John-Paul Himka, "How Many Perished in the Famine and Why Does It Matter?" in *BRAMA*, 2 February 2008, http://www.brama.com/news/press/2008/02/080202himka_famine.html (accessed 24 September 2010).

phenomenon in the new, unstable, and predominantly authoritarian Eastern European states.[38]

Because the political myth of Stepan Bandera first manifested itself in the Second Polish Republic, it is imperative to elaborate on the political circumstances in this state, in particular on the complicated relationship between Poles and Ukrainians. It is also crucial to describe the role played by the OUN in Polish-Ukrainian relations, particularly when it was led by Stepan Bandera, who thereby became the symbol of the Ukrainian struggle for independence.

In 1918 Poland was established as the Second Polish Republic. Its founders regarded this state as a successor to the Polish-Lithuanian Commonwealth (1569–1795), which they referred to as the First Polish Republic. The Polish-Lithuanian Commonwealth was a premodern and very heterogeneous state ruled by the Polish nobility. During the last three decades of the eighteenth century, it was partitioned by the Habsburg Empire, the Kingdom of Prussia, and the Russian Empire, consequently disappearing from the map of Europe. The territory of the Second Republic was smaller than that of the Polish-Lithuanian Commonwealth, but its population was still very heterogeneous. Ethnic Poles constituted up to 65 percent of the population of the Second Republic, and the remainder consisted of national minorities, including Ukrainians, Jews, Germans, Lithuanians, Byelorussians, and Russians. Both the Little Treaty of Versailles—signed between minor powers and the League of Nations in 1919—and the constitutions adopted in Poland in 1921 and 1935, guaranteed all citizens of Poland the same rights and treated them as equal before the law. In reality, however, the national minorities in the Second Republic were frequently discriminated against, at political, social, educational, administrative, and cultural levels, or were even treated as second class citizens.[39]

The Ukrainian nationalists and their illegal organizations were not the only Ukrainian political bodies in the Second Republic, but they gained increasing support during the interwar period. The major Ukrainian political party in Poland was the Ukrainian National Democratic Alliance (*Ukraïns'ke Natsional'no-Demokratychne Ob"iednannia*, UNDO), which was founded in 1925. The UNDO considered Polish rule over western Ukraine to be illegitimate, but it participated in the parliamentary elections, respected the rules of democracy, and its leader Vasyl' Mudryi was the deputy speaker of the Polish Sejm between 1935 and 1939. The UNDO wanted to establish a Ukrainian state but rejected terror and illegal subversive activities for that purpose. It supported the Ukrainian cooperative movement and wanted to improve the cultural, political, and social situation of Ukrainians in Poland. In terms of ideology it combined democracy with nationalism and cooperated with the political parties of other national minorities. Its main Ukrainian rival was the Ukrainian Socialist Radical Party (*Ukraïns'ka Sotsialistychno-Radykalna Partiia*, USRP).[40]

Poland was a predominantly rural country, whose political situation was unstable. Parliamentary democracy was endangered by various populist and authoritarian

38 Hrycak, *Historia Ukrainy*, 189–90, 193–94.

39 Szymon Rudnicki, "Anti-Jewish Legislation in Interwar Poland," in *Antisemitism and its Opponents in Modern Poland*, ed. Robert Blobaum (Ithaca: Cornell University Press, 2005), 148–88; Motyka, *Tak było w Bieszczadach*, 36–41; Tomaszewski, *Ojczyzna nie tylko Polaków*, 181–82.

40 Mirosław Szumiło, *Ukraińska Reprezentacja Parlamentarna w Sejmie i Senacie RP (1928–1939)* (Warsaw: Neriton, 2007), 21–51, 193–240.

parties, such as the nationalist and antisemitic Endecja. Because of the threat of this movement, Józef Piłsudski—one of the main founding fathers of the state, and leader of the Sanacja (sanation) movement—seized power in May 1926 by means of a coup d'état. He introduced a military dictatorship, combining socialism with romantic traditions and the type of moderate nationalism known in Poland as patriotism. Piłsudski stayed in power until his death in 1935, after which the regime moved to the right.[41]

Polish officials and politicians frequently treated the national minorities in Poland as inferior citizens or even as enemies. This only strengthened the nationalism of the Ukrainians and other national minorities in the Second Republic and exacerbated the political situation and interethnic relations.[42] As the Ministry of Foreign Affairs put it in an analytical paper, the Ukrainians were perceived as a huge problem to the Polish state: "The Ukrainian question is not as difficult to solve as the Jewish one, it is not as dangerous as the German one, but it is the oldest one, and it is the most important one because the Ukrainian population is the largest national minority in the state."[43]

With about 5 million people, constituting about 16 percent of the entire population, the Ukrainians were the largest minority in the Second Republic. In the south-eastern part of the country, the Ukrainians constituted the majority, with about 3.5 million in the formerly Habsburg eastern Galicia, and about 1.5 million in the formerly Russian Volhynia. Some 90 percent of Ukrainians lived in villages and small towns. Cities in south-eastern Poland were mainly inhabited by Jews and Poles.[44]

The Sanacja and Endecja movements developed two separate policies toward the Ukrainians and other minorities in the Second Republic. The Sanacja followed the principle of state assimilation (*asymilacja państwowa*); and the Endecja, national assimilation (*asymilacja narodowa*). National assimilation required the minorities to become Polish and to give up their language and culture. State assimilation did not expect such cultural surrender but required loyalty to the Polish state. Such loyalty was against the interests of Galician and Volhynian Ukrainians, who neither wanted to become Polish nor to be loyal to the Polish state. As a result, even liberal and left-wing Polish politicians of the Sanacja movement, who tried to improve Polish-Ukrainian relations, never gave up the notion of teaching Ukrainians loyalty to the Polish state, in order to maintain the status quo of the Second Republic.[45]

The Little Treaty of Versailles, which obliged the Polish authorities to guarantee all its citizens equal treatment, was perceived by the majority of Polish society as an unjust interference in the affairs of the Polish state and an affront to Poland's sovereignty. The treaty was eventually renounced by Józef Beck, the Polish minister of

41 Włodzimierz Borodziej, *Geschichte Polens im 20. Jahrhundert* (Munich: C. H. Beck, 2010), 124–76; Rafał Pankowski, *The Populist Radical Right in Poland: The Patriots* (New York: Routledge, 2010), 15–21.

42 Tomaszewski, *Ojczyzna nie tylko Polaków*, 194–98.

43 "Zarys historyczny Ukrainy, organizacje i działacze," AAN, MSZ, 9377, 1.

44 Tomaszewski, *Ojczyzna nie tylko Polaków*, 12–14, 52–53.

45 Cornelia Schenke, *Nationalstaat und Nationale Frage: Polen und die Ukrainer 1921–1939* (Hamburg: Dölling und Galitz Verlag, 2004), 226–30; Andrzej Chojnowski, *Koncepcje polityki narodowościowej rządów polskich w latach 1921–1939* (Wrocław: Ossolineum, 1979), 18–19.

foreign affairs, on 13 September 1934 before the League of Nations.[46] On the return of Beck from the meeting of the League in Geneva, a "triumphal greeting ceremony" took place. Musicians played the Polish anthem "Poland Is Not Yet Lost" and children handed flowers to Beck, while a crowd celebrated his "triumphal act in Geneva."[47]

Because of the comparatively liberal atmosphere of the former Habsburg Empire, the Ukrainians in Galicia had become more nationalist and rebellious than the Volhynian Ukrainians of the former Russian Empire. The Polish authorities therefore tried to isolate eastern Galicia from Volhynia. The governor of Volhynia in 1928–1938, Henryk Józewski, was sympathetic toward Ukrainian culture. He tried to win the loyalty of the Ukrainians by introducing policies that were liberal in respect of Ukrainian culture, allowing Ukrainians to celebrate Ukrainian national holidays and to Ukrainize the Orthodox Church, which the Russian Empire had used in the nineteenth century as a tool of Russification. Simultaneously, Józewski was combating all individuals and movements that were not loyal to the Polish authorities. Such policies had the unwanted effect of arousing Ukrainian awareness among Volhynian Ukrainians and stimulated the growth of hidden hatred against the Polish state. The policy of teaching Ukrainians loyalty to the Polish state, while allowing Ukrainian patriotism, strengthened the collective wish to live in a Ukrainian state without Polish paternalism. Unlike the nationalists in Galicia, the radical Ukrainian elements in Volhynia during the interwar period were united by communism and organized in the Communist Party of Western Ukraine (*Komunistychna partiia Zakhidnoï Ukraïny*, or KPZU).[48]

Ukrainians regarded the Polish state as an occupier, rather than as a legitimate authority. They not only withdrew their loyalty but also developed feelings of hatred toward Poland and Poles. Polish politicians frequently tried to induce loyalty to Poland by repressing Ukrainian national aspirations. Polish schools and the teaching of Polish patriotism were intended as important tools for the enforcement of loyalty to the Polish state among the national minorities. The "Lex Grabski," an educational act of 1924, which was named after the Polish education minister Stanisław Grabski, dissolved many Ukrainian schools and transformed some of them into bilingual Polish-Ukrainian schools (*szkoły utrakwistyczne*). The number of Ukrainian secondary schools in eastern Galicia was reduced from 2,426 in 1912, to 352 in 1927, and to 144 in 1939. In eastern Galicia there was only one high school (gymnasium) for every 16,000 Poles; but at the same time, there was only one for every 230,000 Ukrainians. The number of bilingual schools—with which neither side was content—grew from 1,926 to 2,710.[49]

In 1923 Stanisław Sobiński, chief education officer for the Lviv, Stanyslaviv, and Ternopil' (Tarnopol) voivodeships, which covered the territory of eastern Galicia, introduced a regulation forbidding the use of the term "Ukrainian," and allowing only

46 Paweł Korzec, "Polen und der Minderheitenvertrag (1918–1934)," *Jahrbücher für Geschichte Osteuropas* Vol. 22, No. 4 (1975), 523, 540–41; Golczewski, *Deutsche und Ukrainer*, 396.

47 "Tryumfalne powitanie Ministra Becka," *Gazeta Lwowska*, 2 October 1934, 1.

48 Timothy Snyder, *Sketches from a Secret War: A Polish Artist's Mission to Liberate Soviet Ukraine* (New Haven: Yale University Press, 2005), 67, 136–37, 142–44, 166–67, 190; Schenke, *Nationalstaat und nationale Frage*, 243–44, 460; Borodziej, *Geschichte Polens*, 158.

49 Mick, *Kriegserfahrungen*, 301–303; Grzegorz Mazur, *Życie polityczne polskiego Lwowa 1918–1939* (Cracow: Księgarnia Akademicka, 2007), 149.

the use of "Ruthenian" (*ruski*) even in private Ukrainian high schools. Ukrainians regarded this regulation as a serious insult. On 19 October 1926 Sobiński was shot by UVO members Roman Shukhevych and Bohdan Pidhainyi.[50]

Between 1918 and 1919, the Ukrainian language was abandoned at Lviv University as a language of instruction, and all Ukrainian chairs were suspended. After 14 August 1919, only applicants who declared that they were Polish citizens could enroll at the university. For this and other reasons, many Ukrainian students boycotted Lviv University. The Polish authorities would have allowed a Ukrainian university but not in Lviv, the main city of western Ukraine. In July 1921, a secret Ukrainian university was founded. It existed until 1925 and was financed by Ukrainian organizations and the Ukrainian diaspora. Between 1922 and 1923, the secret Ukrainian university had 1,014 students and sixty-five chairs. A Ukrainian Scientific Institute (*Ukraiński Instytut Naukowy*) was opened in 1930 in Warsaw. It was only in 1936 that a chair in the Ukrainian language was established at Lviv University.[51]

The Ukrainian nationalists used this situation. They portrayed Polish schools as an instrument for Polonizing the Ukrainians, and turning them into "traitors to the Ukrainian nation." An OUN leaflet explained:

> The Poles want by means of schools and teachers to make you into faithful slaves, obedient and obsequious citizens of Poland; they want to teach you to hate everything Ukrainian and love everything Polish. They want to make you into traitors of the Ukrainian Nation. ... Therefore do not allow the enemies to make you into Janissaries! Do not allow Poles [liakhy] to turn you into their obedient slaves! You should be the knights and fighters for the freedom of Ukraine! There is a great holy war before you.[52]

Similarly, Polish teachers were perceived as instruments of Polonization. Some of them were even shot at, as was the case in the village of Dubshche (Dubszcze) where a Polish teacher had replaced a Ukrainian.[53] Another popular gesture was the profanation of Polish state or national symbols, for instance flags, or portraits of such politicians and political idols of the Second Republic as Piłsudski. Such conduct sometimes provoked further violence, as at the school building in Berezhany (Brzezany) where OUN members tore down a Polish flag and threw it into a toilet. A local Ukrainian who criticized this act was found dead shortly afterwards. "Patriotic" demonstrations and other gatherings also resulted in casualties. In 1939 in Berezhany, Polish high school students organized a "funeral of Ukraine," marching through the town with a coffin marked "Ukraine is dead." After a few days, the bodies of two Poles who had taken part in the "funeral" were found in a river in a suburb.[54]

50 Mazur, *Życie polityczne*, 119–20, 148.

51 Ibid., 140–41, 144–46, 151.

52 Quoted in Mykola Posivnych, "Molodist' Stepana Bandery," in *Stepan Bandera*, ed. Posivnych, 2006, 15.

53 Shimon Redlich, *Together and Apart in Brzezany: Poles, Jews and Ukrainians 1919–1945* (Bloomington: Indiana University Press, 2002), 56. For another attack on a Polish teacher, see Jan Rogowski, *Lwów pod znakiem swastyki. Pamiętnik z lat 1941–1942*, ZNiO, syg. 16710/II, 15–16.

54 For demolition of portraits, see "Raport dzienny Nr. 272 z dn. 24 października 1934 r.," DALO f. 121, op. 2, spr. 134, 66. For destruction of a Polish flag, see Redlich, *Together and Apart*, 69. For the "funeral of Ukraine," see Redlich, *Together and Apart*, 57. For further attacks on teachers, see "Komunikat Nr. 7 o działalności Organizacji Ukraińskich Nacjonalistów w latach 1932–1933 i 1934. Część III. Działalność O.U.N. w 1934 r.," AAN, MSZ, syg. 5316, 108.

Although Poles made up only about 30 percent of the population of eastern Galicia and Volhynia, they still possessed more land there than the Ukrainians. In addition, settlers (Pol. *osadnicy*), many of them veterans of the First World War, received land in the eastern parts of the country with the objective of strengthening the Polish element in those regions. This irritated the Ukrainian peasantry, most of whom possessed little land despite their efforts for decades to obtain more.[55]

In general, Ukrainians had very good reasons to resent their Polish rulers. Even in regions with a predominantly Ukrainian population, Ukrainian civil servants were rare. The Ukrainian language was regarded by Polish officials as a substandard variety of Polish, and Ukrainian culture was perceived as inferior to Polish culture. By way of reaction to Polish nationalism and restrictions, Ukrainians withdrew from public life and formed their own organizations and cooperatives. Having completed their degrees, Ukrainians were often unable to make a career in public institutions or to find other employment, because of their ethnicity. Such people frequently ended up working for Ukrainian agricultural companies that hired only Ukrainians. To some extent the situation in the former eastern Galicia was similar to a state within a state.[56]

Every year on 1 November, clashes between Poles and Ukrainians erupted in Lviv and in many other places in western Ukraine. On this date, Ukrainians commemorated the proclamation of the ZUNR, which organization had been defeated by the Poles.[57] On the night of 31 October–1 November 1928, a few weeks after Bandera moved to Lviv, the UVO tried to destroy two monuments devoted to Polish "defenders" of Lviv. In this incident, one policeman was wounded by gunshot. Ukrainian flags with the inscription "UVO" were hoisted at the university building, at the city council, and at the Union of Lublin Mound.[58] On 1 November 1928 Ukrainian nationalists also hung a banner with the letters "UVO" above the Saint George Cathedral while a *panakhyda* (memorial service) was being celebrated inside. After the service, a crowd tried to march to the city center and there was a shootout with the police. In revenge, Polish youth demolished the buildings of several Ukrainian institutions, such as the Ukrainian Student House and the printing office of the newspaper *Dilo*.[59]

55 Tomaszewski, *Ojczyzna nie tylko Polaków*, 64–66; Motyka, *Tak było w Bieszczadach*, 36–37; Janina Stobniak-Smogorzewska, *Kresowe osadnictwo wojskowe 1920–1945* (Warsaw: Oficyna Wydawnicza RYTM, 2003), 58, 101, 217–19. The number of settlers is hard to determine. Statiev claims 200,000 settlers, following Rusnachenko, who, however, does not provide a source for this claim. Cf. Statiev, *The Soviet Counterinsurgency*, 36; Anatolii Rusnachenko, *Narod zburenyi: Natsional'no-vyzvol'nyi rukh v Ukraïni i natsional'ni rukhy oporu v Bilorusiï, Lytvi, Estniï u 1940–50-xh rokakh* (Kiev: Pul'sary, 2002), 140. Stobniak-Smogorzewska, *Kresowe osadnictwo*, 118, estimates that before the Second World War the settlers and their families numbered 50,000.

56 Tomaszewski, *Ojczyzna nie tylko Polaków*, 62–63, 71–72. The incomes of Ukrainians with university degrees were much lower than the incomes of the predominantly Polish workers in public institutions. At a time when a Ukrainian with a degree earned 50–60 złotys in an agricultural company, a teacher in a public high school earned 500 złotys. Cf. Bohdan Chaikivs'kyi, *"Fama": Reklamna firma Romana Shukhevycha* (Lviv: Mc, 2005), 36.

57 Christoph Mick, "Kto bronił Lwowa w listopadzie 1918r.? Pamięć o zmarłych, znaczenie wojny i tożsamość narodowa wieloetnicznego miasta," in *Tematy polsko-ukraińskie*, ed. Robert Traba (Olsztyn: Wspólnota Kulturowa Borussia, 2001), 65–71.

58 The Union of Lublin Mound is an artificial hill erected on the summit of Lviv High Castle, which is located in the area of the city. The Mound was created between 1869 and 1890 by Polish inhabitants of Lviv, to commemorate the 300th anniversary of the Union of Lublin, and was a symbolically important place.

59 Mazur, *Życie polityczne*, 123; Mirchuk, *Narys istoriï OUN*, 51.

The second half of the 1930s was especially unfavorable for Polish-Ukrainian relations. It was not so much the renunciation of the Little Treaty of Versailles, or the assassination of the Polish interior minister Bronisław Wilhelm Pieracki by the OUN, both in 1934, but the political changes after Piłsudski's death that intensified the Polish-Ukrainian conflict. After his death, Polish and Ukrainian politicians who worked to normalize Polish-Ukrainian relations were marginalized, and Polish policies toward the Ukrainians became more and more repressive. In these circumstances the competition between Ukrainian and Polish nationalism increased. In October 1938 the Polish police prevented demonstrations in favor of a Ukrainian Carpathian state. In response Ukrainian agricultural companies refused to deliver butter to Lviv and other cities, and Ukrainian nationalists set several Polish farms on fire. The Polish government reacted with collective punishment, conducting punitive expeditions against Ukrainian villagers and making mass arrests. Ukrainian politicians estimated that in late 1938 about 30,000 Ukrainians sat in Polish jails.[60]

In 1939 local Polish politicians in Lublin were talking about the "extermination" of Ukrainians.[61] A German journalist who travelled to the area in the spring of that year observed that the Ukrainian population hoped that "Uncle Führer" would bring order to the area and solve the problem of the Poles.[62] In the last months before the Second World War, more and more Ukrainians participated in nationalist ceremonies. On 23 May 1939, about 500 people came to the Saint George Cathedral to take part in a panakhyda for Konovalets'. Five days later, 4,000 came to a panakhyda at the graves of Sich Riflemen, where Ivan Hryn'okh delivered a sermon. Shortly after that, another panakhyda was organized at the graves of three famous nationalists—Vasyl' Bilas, Dmytro Danylyshyn, and Ol'ha Basarab—of whom two were executed for killing a Polish politician and one was believed to have been murdered by Polish interrogators.[63]

During the second half of the 1930s, more and more Ukrainians ceased to view the OUN as an alien and dangerous political body. At that time the UNDO and some other Ukrainian non-nationalistic parties ceased to mistrust the OUN, although they had condemned the terrorist methods of the UVO and the OUN since the early 1920s. In the late 1930s the majority of Ukrainians living in Poland began to consider Nazi Germany as a possible liberator and ally, as the OUN had done since the early 1920s. After 1939 even democratic politicians such as Vasyl' Mudryi or Kost' Pan'kivs'kyi, who until then had condemned violence, fascism, and nationalist hatred, began to collaborate with Nazi Germany and to view the OUN as an important "liberation force."[64] In his memoirs, OUN member Ievhen Stakhiv observed that all Ukrainian movements and organizations, both in exile and in the Second Polish Republic, were orienting themselves toward Nazi Germany in the years leading up to the Second World War. They

60 Mick, *Kriegserfahrungen*, 413. On 17 September 1939 there were 4,500 Ukrainian prisoners in the Bereza Kartuska detention camp alone. Cf. Ireneusz Polit, *Miejsce odosobnienia w Berezie Kartuskiej* (Toruń: Wydawnictwo Adam Marszałek, 2003), 120.

61 Golczewski, *Deutsche und Ukrainer*, 954.

62 Ibid., 932.

63 Mazur, *Życie polityczne*, 139.

64 Mudryi had been leader of the UNDO since 1935. Pankivs'kyi was a UNDO member who before the First World War had even served as a deputy in the Imperial Council of Austria, as a member of the conservative-democratic Ukrainian National-Democratic Party (Ukraïns'ka Natsional'no-Demokratychna Partia, UNDP). See Golczewski, *Deutsche und Ukrainer*, 1010–11; Szumiło, *Ukraińska Reprezentacja*, 17.

hoped that Germany would smash Poland and give Ukrainians a chance to establish a state. They saw nothing wrong in cooperating with Nazi Germany and were convinced that this might help them achieve their goals.[65] After the Munich Agreement on 29 September 1938, the Ukrainians tried to establish a Carpatho-Ukrainian state, in territories that had belonged to Czechoslovakia and were inhabited by Ruthenians (*Rusyny*), people ethnically related to the Ukrainians. The Germans ignored the requests of the Ukrainian nationalists to recognize and support the state and allowed Hungary to occupy these territories; but the disappointment of Ukrainian nationalists concerning the proposed Carpathian-Ukrainian state did not change their attitude toward Nazi Germany.[66]

The OUN: Racism, Fascism, Revolution, Violence, and the Struggle for a Ukrainian State

In 1920 Ukrainian veterans of the Sich Riflemen, such as Ievhen Konovalets', Andrii Mel'nyk, and Roman Sushko, founded the UVO in Prague. Its object was to continue the struggle for a Ukrainian state, but it became a terrorist organization. It financed itself by carrying out espionage-related tasks for other countries and did not play any important political role among Ukrainian parties. This situation changed, however, a few years later when the UVO leaders realized that, in order to become a dominant political force, they needed to incorporate other right-wing political organizations and to include youth in its ranks. For that purpose they founded the OUN at the First Congress of Ukrainian Nationalists, which was held in Vienna between 28 January and 3 February 1929. Throughout the 1930s the OUN was composed of a leadership in exile, and a homeland executive in Poland.[67]

The main political goal of both the UVO in the 1920s and the OUN in the 1930s was to mobilize the "Ukrainian masses" for a revolution, as a result of which a violent conflict between Ukrainians and their "occupiers" would be triggered. The OUN believed that "only a national revolution can liberate a nation from slavery" and allow it to "achieve independence and statehood."[68] In referring to their "occupiers" the Ukrainian nationalists primarily meant Poland and the Soviet Union. Their foes were all non-Ukrainians who lived in the "Ukrainian ethnic territories," particularly Jews, Poles, and Russians. Ukrainians who did not support the OUN's vision of an ethnically pure state and ultranationalist revolutionary policies were also perceived and persecuted as enemies, especially if they cooperated with the Polish authorities. One of these enemies was the UNDO, the largest Ukrainian party in the Second Republic, which aimed to achieve a Ukrainian state by legal means. Nevertheless, we should not forget that there was informal cooperation between the OUN and the right-wing faction of the UNDO.[69]

65 Stakhiv, *Kriz' tiurmy*, 55–56.
66 Golczewski, *Deutsche und Ukrainer*, 891–905, 932–33, 940.
67 Ibid., 547–57.
68 "Nasza walka, jej cele drogi i metody," July 1931, TsDIAL f. 205, op. 46, spr. 1033, 13.
69 For the Ukrainian enemies, see "Khto nam voroh?" *Surma*, August-September 1928, 1–2. For UNDO, its relationship to the OUN, and the relationship of Sheptyts'kyi to the OUN, see Szumiło, *Ukraińska Reprezentacja*, 30, 32–33, 43, 104, 177, 184–85. For the cooperation between the OUN and UNDO, see Andrzej A. Zięba, *Lobbing dla Ukrainy w Europie międzywojennej: Ukraińskie Biuro Prasowe w*

To further its political aims, the OUN adopted two concepts of revolution: "permanent revolution" and "national revolution." The two notions were interrelated but were not identical. In general, the "permanent revolution" was a process of preparing the Ukrainian people for the "national revolution," which was intended to become an uprising or a revolutionary act, as a result of which the OUN would defeat their enemies and establish a Ukrainian state.[70] By planning the revolution, the OUN combined many different elements that could help it seize power. It modeled itself on the Polish and Russian insurgents and revolutionaries in the nineteenth and twentieth centuries, and on the contemporary fascist and ultranationalist revolutionaries. After taking power in the "ethnic Ukrainian territories" the OUN would subordinate all non-loyal elements and establish a one-party system. The new authority would represent all social strata of Ukrainians, whose loyalty to the OUN would be enforced. The state the OUN planned to establish after the revolution would be dictatorial. Democracy was, for the OUN, a hostile and dangerous political system, distrusted by OUN members because of its non-nationalist nature.[71]

The immediate target of UVO and OUN activities was the Second Polish Republic, which they perceived as an illegitimate "enemy-occupier" of the "ethnic Ukrainian territories."[72] Czechoslovakia and Romania were not regarded by the OUN as significant enemies. Neither the UVO nor the OUN operated in Soviet Ukraine but they regarded the Soviet Union as the most dangerous enemy of the Ukrainians and the main occupier of Ukrainian territory. During the interwar period, the Soviet authorities only became the target of OUN terror when OUN member Mykola Lemyk attempted to assassinate the Soviet consul in Lviv on 22 October 1933, but murdered the secretary of the consulate, Aleksei Mailov, by mistake.[73] In various European countries, many UVO and OUN members living there were infiltrated by the Polish intelligence service and its informers.[74]

The UVO and the OUN propagated a very western Ukrainian or Galician form of nationalism and they believed that Ukrainians in Soviet Ukraine would approve of its plans for "liberating Ukraine." During the Second World War this belief would cause the OUN considerable problems, when the organization would be confronted for the first time with eastern Ukrainians and their dislike for ethnic nationalism, racism and fascism. The western Ukrainian or Galician form of nationalism was also not

Londynie oraz jego konkurenci polityczni (do roku 1932) (Cracow, Księgarnia Akademicka, 2010), 359–61.

70 For the concept of permanent revolution, see "Permanentna revolutsiia," *Surma* 37, No. 10 (1930): 4–7. For the concept of national revolution, see Mykola Stsibors'kyi, "Peredposylka natsional'noi revoliutsii," *Rozbudova natsiï* 54–55, No. 7–8 (1932): 161–69.

71 For the concept of permanent revolution, revolutionary plans, orientation on Polish nineteenth-century insurgents, and the eclectic style of the OUN, see "Permanentna revoliutsiia," *Surma*, 37, No. 10 (1930): 4–7. For fascist, antisemitic, and racist components of OUN ideology as well as for the natural and authentic quality of the nation, see Golczewski, *Deutsche und Ukrainer*, 571–603; Bruder, *"Den ukrainischen Staat*, 39–47; Carynnyk, Foes of Our Rebirth.

72 Osyp Boidunyk, "Iak diishlo do stvorennia Orhanizatsiï Ukraïns'kykh Natsionalistiv," in *Ievhen Konovalets' ta ioho doba*, ed. Iurii Boïko (Munich: Druckgenossenschaft CICERO, 1974), 359.

73 Władysław Żeleński, *Akt oskarżenia przeciwko Stefanowi Banderze, Mikołajowi Łebedowi, Darji Hnatkiwskiej, Jarosławowi Karpyncowi, Mikołajowi Klymyszynowi, Bohdanowi Pidhajnemu, Iwanowi Malucy, Jakóbowi Czornijowi, Eugenjuszowi Kaczmarskiemu, Romanowi Myhalowi, Katerzynie Zaryckiej, oraz Jarosławowi Rakowi*, Warsaw, 2 October 1935 (published as a booklet), 83.

74 For informers in the OUN, see "Proces o zamordowanie ministra Pierackiego. Zeznania komisarza Dugiełło," *Gazeta Polska*, 4 December 1935, 7. One of the main important informers in the OUN was Iaroslav Baranovs'kyi. Cf. Golczewski, *Deutsche und Ukrainer*, 566.

entirely compatible with the mentality of Volhynian Ukrainians, who found it very difficult to comprehend the mystical nationalism of the Galician type.[75]

The Generation Gap and the Transformation into a Mass Movement

From the very beginning the OUN was divided into two generations: the older one born around 1890 and the younger one around 1910. The generations were divided by many factors, of which the most important seems to be the violence and brutality experienced by the older group during the First World War. The younger generation were not exposed to this experience, had a more romantic image of war, and were more eager to use violence. The older generation consisted of people such as Ievhen Konovalets' (1891–1938), Andrii Mel'nyk (1890–1964), and Riko Iaryi (1898–1969). They had received their military training in the Austro-Hungarian army, had fought during and after the First World War in various armies and had tried to establish and preserve a Ukrainian state. As the result of pressure from the Polish authorities, or of their own choice, some of them emigrated from Poland after the First World War, to countries such as Germany, Czechoslovakia, Italy, and Lithuania.[76] The most important representatives of the OUN outside the Ukrainian area were Riko Iaryi in Berlin, Ievhen Onats'kyi in Italy, Ivan Reviuk-Bartovych in Lithuania, and Andrii Fedyna in Gdańsk (Danzig).[77]

The younger generation of the OUN consisted of such people as Stepan Bandera, Iaroslav Stets'ko (1912–1986), Stepan Lenkavs'kyi (1904–1977), Volodymyr Ianiv (1908–1991), and Roman Shukhevych (1907–1950). Their life in the 1920s and 1930s was different from that of the older generation, who lived in more comfortable circumstances in exile.[78] The younger generation, later referred to as the "Bandera generation,"[79] was too young to fight in the First World War or to assist in the foundation of the UVO. The UVO and the OUN were for them fascinating secret organizations that could be joined only by brave Ukrainians who were ready to die for independence. This generation idealized the war much more than the older one. It believed that it had missed a war and hoped to fight another one. Leading individuals of this generation grew up in patriotic and religious western Ukrainian families. During their time at high school and university in the 1920s, they were active in the Organization of the Upper Grades of the Ukrainian High Schools (*Orhanizatsiia Vyshchykh Klias Ukraïns'kykh Himnazii*, OVKUH) and the Union of Ukrainian Nationalistic Youth (*Soiuz ukraïns'koï natsionalistychnoï molodi*, SUNM). These organizations cooperated with the UVO and later the OUN, and together with them or alone, organized various nationalist and religious commemorative events and demonstrations.[80]

The process of opening the UVO to Galician youth, and transforming it into a Ukrainian nationalist mass movement, began in the second half of the 1920s. For this pur-

75 Danylo Shumuk, *Za skhidnim obriiem* (Paris: Smoloskyp, 1974), 12–24.
76 R. Lisovyi, *Rozlam v OUN: Krytychni narysy z nahody dvatsiatylittia zasnuvannia OUN* (n.p.: Vydavnytsvo Ukraïna, 1949), 38–40; Golczewski, Die Kollaboration in der Ukraine, 162.
77 Golczewski, *Deutsche und Ukrainer*, 561.
78 For the life of the UVO members in Berlin, see Golczewski, *Deutsche und Ukrainer*, 448, 745–46.
79 Klymyshyn, *V pokhodi*, 1:22.
80 Mirchuk, *Narys istoriï OUN*, 49–50; Golczewski, *Deutsche und Ukrainer*, 456; Bohdan Kazanivs'kyi, *Shliakhom Legendy: Spomyny* (London: Ukraïns'ka Vydavnycha Spilka, 1975), 15–20.

pose, the older generation, on the one hand, tried to win young Ukrainians from the OVKUH, SUNM, and other youthful organizations operating in the Second Republic.[81] The UVO leaders also established the paramilitary organization Dorost for children aged eight to fifteen, and the Iunatstvo for youth between fifteen and twenty-five.[82] On the other hand, the UVO leaders tried to include other parties and political organizations. At the First Conference of Ukrainian Nationalists from 3 to 7 November 1927 in Berlin, the UVO leaders established the Leadership of the Ukrainian Nationalists (*Provid Ukraïns'kykh Natsionalistiv*, PUN) and asked other organizations and parties such as the Legion of Ukrainian Nationalists (*Lehiia Ukraïns'kykh Natsionalistiv*, LUN) and the UNDO to merge and to hand over their leadership to the PUN. This plan did not work because no group or party was really willing to give up its sovereignty and to subordinate itself to the PUN. The situation changed, however, after the OUN was founded. At this stage of the creation of a Ukrainian nationalist mass movement, a number of organizations, including the LUN, OVKUH, and SUNM, agreed to merge and to be represented by the PUN. The PUN consisted of leading OUN members and became a kind of synonym for the leadership in exile of the OUN. Konovalets', the leader of the OUN, was the leader of the PUN.[83]

The UVO did not disappear immediately after the foundation of the OUN but existed simultaneously with it for a few years, serving as a military arm of the OUN. The most active and vigorous new members came to the OUN from the OVKUH and SUNM. Zynovii Knysh characterized these individuals as ambitious, zealous, idealistic, and willing to make sacrifices, but without any political experience.[84] Among the organizations whose members went over to the OUN was the League of Ukrainian Fascists (*Soiuz ukraïns'kykh fashystiv*, SUF), which invented the fascist greeting "Glory to Ukraine!" (*Slava Ukraïni!*).[85]

Ukrainian youth was also divided. Not all young Ukrainians supported the extreme version of Ukrainian nationalism represented by the OUN. The SUNM, for example, was divided into a radical branch, which consisted of OUN activists or sympathizers, and a moderate one, which sympathized with the UNDO. Relations between these two branches were so tense that students who belonged to the moderate branch of the SUNM, and who lived in the Ukrainian Academic House in Lviv, used an external canteen elsewhere, in order to avoid eating together with the fascistized nationalists.[86]

The younger generation began to control the homeland executive of the OUN in 1931–1932. This political body was subordinated to the leadership in exile but it was in charge of OUN policy in eastern Galicia and Volhynia. Stepan Okhrymovych, an SUNM member, became the leader of the homeland executive in 1931. He entrusted its propaganda apparatus to his friend, schoolmate, and fellow-member of Plast, Stepan Ban-

81 Interrogation of Iaroslav Makarushka, 25 February 1935, TsDIAL, f. 371, op. 1, spr. 8, ed. 76, 145–46.

82 For the integration of children at the age of eight into the OUN, see "Proces o zamordowanie ś. p. ministra Br. Pierackiego," *Gazeta Polska*, 20 November 1935, 6.

83 Mirchuk, *Narys istoriï OUN*, 85–86; Golzewski, *Deutsche und Ukrainer*, 550–61, 564–68, 677.

84 Zynovii Knysh, *Dukh, shcho tilo rve do boiu* (Winnipeg: O. D. U., 1951), 193–94.

85 For the League of Ukrainian Fascists, see Oleksandr Panchenko, *Mykola Lebed': Zhyttia, diial'nist', derzhavno-pravovi pohliady* (Kobeliaky: Kobeliaky, 2001), 15. For the greeting, see Sviatoslav Lypovets'kyi, *Orhanizatsiia Ukraïns'kykh Natsionalistiv (banderivtsi): Frahmenty diial'nosti ta borot'by* (Kiev: Ukraïns'ka Vydavnycha Spilka, 2010), 14.

86 Interrogation of Iaroslav Makarushka, 25 February 1935, TsDIAL, f. 371, op. 1, spr. 8, ed. 76, 145–46.

dera. According to Mirchuk, Okhrymovych and Bandera had studied Mikhnovs'kyi's *Samostiina Ukraïna* together during their high school years in Stryi (Stryj).[87]

In May 1932, Bohdan Kordiuk became the new *Providnyk* of the homeland executive; Bandera became the deputy leader; Volodymyr Ianiv became the head of the political-ideological apparatus; Iaroslav Stets'ko, Ianiv's deputy; Roman Shukhevych, the head of the military apparatus.[88] The younger generation, although formally dependent on the leadership in exile, attempted to formulate its own policies. In so doing, they soon proved themselves even more radical than the older generation. They were more willing to make sacrifices, to use terror as a political means, and to kill OUN members and other Ukrainians accused of working for the Polish police, and of other forms of betrayal. This difference manifested itself in particular after Bandera became the leader of the OUN's homeland executive in June 1933.[89]

Although the younger generation was generally more radical and fanatical, it did not necessarily adopt ideas that were more fascist in nature than those of the older generation. In the late 1920s and 1930s the main propagators of fascism in the OUN were Mykola Stsibors'kyi and Ievhen Onats'kyi. Like Dontsov, these men worked on a Ukrainian concept of fascism. Andrii Mel'nyk, who succeeded Konovalets' as leader of the OUN, seems also to have been an adherent of fascism. In a letter to Joachim von Ribbentrop on 2 May 1938, Mel'nyk claimed that the OUN was "ideologically akin to similar movements in Europe, especially to National Socialism in Germany and Fascism in Italy."[90] At the Second General Congress of the OUN in August 1939 in Rome, the title of *Vozhd'* was used officially for the first time in the history of the organization and was bestowed upon Mel'nyk.[91] The younger generation, on the other hand, had adopted various fascist principles, such as the Führerprinzip, mainly thanks to their favorite writer Dontsov. In leaflets that were obviously produced by them for Pentecost 1934, Konovalets' was characterized as the "leader of the Ukrainian nation and the national revolution."[92]

The younger OUN members committed spectacular acts of terror and were encouraged to do so by older members of the leadership in exile, who used the publicity for the purpose of collecting funds from Ukrainians living in North America. They advertised terror as a patriotic struggle against the occupiers. Trials after assassinations were used to inform the global community about the Ukrainian question. At a conference in June 1933 in Berlin, Konovalets' did not formally approve Bandera's proposal to use terror, but he did not try to stop the terrorist acts of the younger generation.[93]

After Pieracki's assassination, the mass arrests conducted in June 1934 caused chaos in the OUN. Bandera, as the leader of the homeland executive, was succeeded by Osyp Mashchak, who, after his arrest on 20 December 1934, was followed by the more moderate Lev Rebet. After Bandera's arrest, the homeland executive put a stop to the

87 Mirchuk, *Stepan Bandera*, 14, 18; Golczewski, *Deutsche und Ukrainer*, 560.

88 Golczewski, *Deutsche und Ukrainer*, 564–65.

89 Lisovyi, *Rozlam v OUN*, 38–40; Golczewski, *Deutsche und Ukrainer*, 567–68; Żeleński, *Akt oskarżenia*, 96–100.

90 Andrij Mel'nyk, "An Seine Excellenz Reichsaussenminister von Ribbentrop," 2 May 1939, R 104430/1–2, PAAA. See also Golczewski, *Deutsche und Ukrainer*, 934.

91 Golczewski, *Deutsche und Ukrainer*, 943–44.

92 "Komunikat Nr. 7," AAN, MSZ, syg. 5316, 76.

93 Golczewski, *Deutsche und Ukrainer*, 567–68; Ievhen Vrets'ona, "Moï zustrichi z polkovnykom," in *Ievhen Konovalets'*, ed. Boïko, 476.

assassinations and other spectacular propagandist actions and concentrated on strengthening the structure of the movement in Volhynia. More and more Ukrainians became involved in the movement. Shortly before the beginning of the Second World War, the OUN counted between 8,000 and 20,000 members and had several thousand sympathizers.[94]

Ethnic and Political Violence

During the interwar period the UVO and the OUN tried to assassinate a number of Poles, Ukrainians, Jews, and Russians, but not always successfully. Some of the Polish potential victims such as Józef Piłsudski were regarded as the founders or important statesmen of an "occupying power." Others such as Tadeusz Hołówko, head of the Department for Eastern Affairs in the Ministry of Foreign Affairs, and Henryk Józewski, governor of Volhynia, were committed to Polish-Ukrainian reconciliation. Ukrainians such as high school director Ivan Babii and the journalist and political activist Sydir Tverdokhlib did not approve of the measures of the OUN and cooperated with the Polish authorities. After Bandera became the leader of the homeland executive, a number of OUN members, such as Iakiv Bachyns'kyi and Maria Kovaliukivna, were murdered by the organization. In addition to carrying out political assassinations, the OUN killed a number of people in the course of armed robberies of banks, post offices, police stations, and private households.[95]

The OUN regarded terror as a propaganda tool that would draw international attention to the situation of Ukrainians in Poland and Soviet Ukraine, and also to its "struggle for liberation." In terms of publicity, assassinations were the most powerful type of terror acts. In reaction to some Ukrainian mass terror acts, the Polish authorities reacted with counter-terror. Between 12 July and 24 September 1930 for example, with the help of its youthful associates, the OUN set fire to Polish crops and farm buildings, and destroyed railway tracks and telecommunication lines. On 16 September 1930, in order to put an end to this violence, the Polish authorities began a campaign, euphemistically called pacification (Pol. *pacyfikacja*), which lasted until 30 November 1930. For the purpose of suppressing the OUN terror, the Polish authorities used the army and police. A number of Ukrainians accused of supporting the OUN were arrested, humiliated, beaten, and otherwise mistreated. A few were killed. The scouting organization Plast was banned, and the three Ukrainian high schools were closed. It is not known whether the OUN conducted the arson and sabotage in order

94 Wysocki, *Organizacja*, 301–11, 314, 326–28, 332–37.

95 For attempts and acts of assassination, see "Wyrok," TsDIAL, f. 205, spr. 3125, 33–35; Żeleński, *Akt oskarżenia*, 54–56; Snyder, *Sketches from a Secret War*, 157; Alexander J. Motyl, "Ukrainian Nationalist Political Violence in Inter-War Poland, 1921–1939," *East European Quarterly* Vol. XIX, No. 1 (1985): 50, 55; Mirchuk, *Narys istoriï OUN*, 28, 32; Golczewski, *Deutsche und Ukrainer*, 441, 444–45. For the assassination of Polish and Ukrainian politicians and political activists, see "Ukraińska Organizacja Wojskowa. Warszawa 30.11.1934," AAN, MSZ, syg. 9377, 30–31. For the assassination of Ivan Babii, see "Komunikat Nr. 7," AAN, MSZ, syg. 5316, 95–97; "Proces o zamordowanie ś. p. ministra Br. Pierackiego," *Gazeta Polska*, 20 November 1935, 6. For details of the attempt to assassinate Henryk Józewski, see Stepan Shukhevych, *Moie zhyttia: Spohady* (London: Ukrainian Publishers, 1991), 460–61. For the murder of the OUN member Maria Kovaliukivna and the law student Volodymyr Mel'nyk, see Kost' Pan'kivs'kyi, *Roky nimets'koï okupatsiï* (New York: Zhyttia i mysli, 1965), 141. For the murder of Bachyns'yki, see Interrogation of Roman Myhal', 21 December 1934, TsDIAL, f. 371, op. 1, spr. 8, ed. 76, 274–75, 283–84, 287–88.

to spark off an uprising, to provoke a bloody reaction, or to prevent negotiations between Polish and Ukrainian politicians. The pacification did, however, give the OUN and a number of other political Ukrainian organizations grounds for complaint to the League of Nations, concerning the policies of the Polish government and the situation of Ukrainians in Poland. The attention of several international newspapers was also drawn to the mistreatment of Ukrainians in Poland.[96]

It is difficult to establish how many people the UVO and OUN killed between 1921 and 1939. Relying on information supplied by Petro Mirchuk, Alexander Motyl estimated that the UVO and OUN attempted to kill sixty-three persons between 1921 and 1939: thirty-six Ukrainians, twenty-five Poles, one Russian, and one Jew. It should be noted that Mirchuk was an OUN member and the head of a division of the propaganda apparatus in the national executive in 1939. After the Second World War, he extolled the UVO, OUN, and UPA in his numerous publications, whitewashing a substantial number of their crimes. Motyl added correctly that, in his opinion, the actual number of persons killed by the UVO and OUN may well have been higher.[97] Maksym Hon, a specialist on the subject of Jewish-Ukrainian relations, proved that Mirchuk's suggestion, that only one Jew was killed by the OUN, was false.[98] The application of common sense and the use of historical literature and archival documents also cast doubt on Mirchuk's estimates. This is particularly apparent when we consider that the UVO and OUN had many members in the villages and smaller towns of eastern Galicia and Volhynia, where they killed people not only for political but also for economic and other reasons. By 1922 the UVO had already set 2,200 Polish farms on fire.[99] In 1937 alone, the OUN carried out 830 violent acts against Polish citizens or their property. Of these offences, 540 were classified by the Security Service of the Polish Interior Ministry as anti-Polish, 242 as anti-Jewish, sixty-seven as anti-Ukrainian, and seventeen as anti-Communist.[100] Unfortunately, no comprehensive study of this question has been carried out, and we can therefore only estimate that the number of victims killed by the UVO and OUN in the interwar period was at least several hundred.

Cooperation, Exile, and Funding

Countries such as Germany and Lithuania supported OUN newspapers and journals, provided the organization with passports, and arranged military courses for their members. With the help of the Humboldt-Stiftung, the Germans also supported Ukrainian nationalist student organizations at the University of Technology in Gdańsk (Danzig) and at other universities. The UVO and the OUN were therefore dependent on Germany and Lithuania and provided them with espionage services in return. Germany and Lithuania also supported the Ukrainian nationalists because

96 Potocki, *Polityka państwa*, 68–95; Motyka, *Ukraińska partyzantka*, 56–57; Golczewski, *Deutsche und Ukrainer*, 435, 561–63; Zięba, *Lobbing dla Ukrainy*, 368–86, 638.

97 Motyl, Ukrainian Nationalist Political Violence, 50. For Mirchuk see chapter 9, and in particular page 443 et seq.

98 Maksym Hon, *Iz kryvdoiu na samoti: Ukraïns'ko-ievreis'ki vzaiemyny na zakhidnoukraïns'kykh zemliakh u skladi Pol'shchi (1935–1939)* (Rivne: Volyns'ki oberehy, 2005), 154.

99 Golczewski, *Deutsche und Ukrainer*, 434–35.

100 "Sprawozdanie z przejawów ruchu nielegalnego /UWO-OUN/ w Małopolsce Wschodniej i na Wołyniu za rok 1937," 9 June 1938, CAW, MSW, Wydział Bezpieczeństwa, Referat Ukraiński, VIII.72.1., quoted in Snyder, The Life and Death, 83–84.

they regarded Poland as their countries' enemy, and like the Ukrainians, they laid claim to parts of Polish territories. Some UVO and OUN politicians, such as Osyp Dumin, were willing to collaborate with the Soviet Union, but it is not clear whether the Soviet authorities actually financed the UVO or the OUN. According to the Polish Intelligence Service, the OUN also collaborated with the British Secret Intelligence Service. The relationships between the UVO-OUN and these supporting states were frequently based on cooperation between the OUN and a particular institution—in Germany, for example, the *Abwehr* (military intelligence). In official statements however, the OUN denied that it cooperated with other countries, and it claimed to be financially and politically independent. Ukrainian emigrants, particularly those living in North America, also provided a further source of income for the OUN. For example, the Ukrainian War Veterans' Association and the Ukrainian National Federation raised $40,000 for the UVO combat fund and the OUN liberation fund between 1928 and 1939. In addition, the robbery of banks, post offices, and private persons in Poland provided the OUN with supplementary income.[101]

One important reason why the OUN collaborated with Germany was the political order established by the Treaty of Versailles. after the First World War. Because Germany had lost many territories, it intended to reverse the geopolitical order established by the Allies. At the same time, the Ukrainians were, in an even worse situation than Germany was. The Treaty of Versailles left them without a state and made Germany their most important partner. Two events that affected—but did not interrupt—the cooperation between the OUN and Germany and Lithuania were the German-Polish non-aggression pact signed on 26 January 1934 and the assassination of Minister Pieracki by the OUN on 15 June 1934. On the day of Pieracki's murder, the German minister of propaganda was on an official visit to Warsaw. Mykola Lebed', who was suspected of carrying out Pieracki's assassination, fled shortly afterwards to Germany. Despite friendly German-Ukrainian relations, he was then expelled to Poland at the request of Józef Lipski, the Polish ambassador in Berlin. After the German-Polish non-aggression pact, German politicians promised not to cooperate with the OUN. Nevertheless, both the Abwehr and Lithuanian politicians continued to collaborate with the OUN during the second half of the 1930s.[102]

101 For the finances of the UVO and OUN, see "Proces o zamordowanie ... Fundusze organizacji," *Gazeta Polska*, Warsaw, 13 December 1935, 6; Żeleński, *Akt oskarżenia*, 58, 61–63; Wysocki, *Organizacja*, 272–77. For collaboration with Lithuania, see "Dokumenty dotyczące działalności OUN i UWO wśród ludności ukraińskiej w USA i Kanadzie, oraz pomocy udzielanej przez Rząd litewski terrorystom ukraińskim," AAN, MSZ, syg. 5317, 8–21; "Społeczeństwo ukraińskie wobec mordesrstwa ministra Pierackiego," AAN, MSZ, syg. 5317, 48–49; Władysław Żeleński, *Zabójstwo ministra Pierackiego* (Paris: Instytut Literacki, 1973), 36–39. For collaboration with Czechoslovakia, see "Społeczeństwo ukraińskie wobec mordesrstwa ministra Pierackiego," AAN, MSZ, syg. 5317, 51–52; Żeleński, *Zabójstwo ministra*, 39. For collaboration with Germany (Abwehr) and OUN's sources of income, see Golczewski, *Deutsche und Ukrainer*, 438–54, 610, 623–28, 632, 661–67, 694–96, 700, 740–44, 767–70. For the UWVA and UNF, see Orest T. Martynovych, "Sympathy for the Devil: The Attitude of Ukrainian War Veterans in Canada to Nazi Germany and the Jews, 1933–1939," in *Re-imaging Ukrainian Canadians: History, Politics, and Identity*, ed. Rhonda L. Hinther and Jim Mochoruk (Toronto: University of Toronto Press, 2010), 181. For cooperation with British intelligence, see Report of an unknown spy from Italy, 5. 11. 1936, RGVA f. 308, op. 3, del. 379, 82; Kim Philby, *My Silent War* (St. Albans: Panther, 1973), 145.

102 Golczewski, *Deutsche und Ukrainer*, 688–90, 740–44, 752–54, 763, 767–70, 772–73; Polit, *Miejsce odosobnienia*,17; "Min. Goebbels w grodzie podwawelskim," *Illustrowany Kurier Codzienny*, 17 June 1934, 1.

Mussolini's Italy was another important partner of the OUN, as was the Croatian Ustaša, which was founded in 1929. Similarly to the OUN, the Ustaša operated until the Second World War as an ultranationalist terrorist organization. Like the OUN, it fought for an independent state against its "occupiers" and against its ethnic and political enemies in Croatia. Contact with Ustaša leader Ante Pavelić was established in late 1933 or early 1934 in Berlin, where Pavelić met with Iaryi and Lebed'. After this meeting the two OUN members visited the Ustaša camp in Italy.[103] During the course of the cooperation between the two organizations, some OUN members were trained together with Ustaša activists in paramilitary camps in Italy, which were established and sponsored by Mussolini. A leading OUN member, Mykhailo Kolodzins'kyi, gave military courses in this camp. He also began work there on "The War Doctrine of the Ukrainian Nationalists," an important OUN document in which he planned a Ukrainian uprising, propagated the cult of war, and presented a Ukrainian version of imperialism, which was intended to protect "our own race" and to extend the Ukrainian territories.[104] Kolodzins'kyi argued in "The War Doctrine" that during a national uprising, the western Ukrainian territories should be fully "cleansed" of Poles, and also that "the more Jews killed during the uprising, the better for the Ukrainian state."[105] OUN member Zynovii Knysh characterized the relationship between the Ukrainian and Croatian revolutionary nationalists as very warm:

> The Organization of Ukrainian Nationalists had good relations with the leading circles of the revolutionary Croatian organization Ustaša. These relations, between the two Leaderships, became even closer in exile, outside the borders of Croatia. ... In general, Croatians—and in particular Croatian students—respected the OUN, trusted their members, regarded the Ukrainian nationalists as more experienced in matters of revolutionary struggle, and invited them to their discussions, meetings, and congresses.[106]

The relationship between Italy and the Ukrainian and Croatian revolutionary nationalists was complicated by the assassination of Pieracki by the OUN, and the assassination of King Alexander I of Yugoslavia and French foreign minister Louis Barthou in Marseilles on 9 October 1934 by the Internal Macedonian Revolutionary Organization (*Vnatrešna makedonska revolucionerna organizacija*, VMRO). During the Pieracki trial, it was revealed that Mussolini supported the Ustaša, which was also involved in the assassination in Marseilles. The revelation of the cooperation of Italy with the OUN and Ustaša was very inconvenient for Mussolini. The simultaneous trials in respect of

103 For Lebed' visiting Pavelić and the Ustaša camp in Italy, see Interrogation of Ivan Maliutsa, 15 December 1934, TsDIAL, f. 371, op. 1, spr. 8, ed. 76, 164. For the paramilitary training camp for the OUN and the Ustaša in Sicily, see Golczewski, *Deutsche und Ukrainer*, 580–81, 741. For the meeting in Berlin, see Lucyna Kulińska, *Działalność terrorystyczna i sabotażowa nacjonalistycznych organizacji ukraińskich w Polsce w latach 1922–1939* (Cracow: Księgarnia Akademicka, 2009), 149.

104 "Defiliada v Moskvi ta Varshavi: 'Voienna doktryna ukraïns'kykh nationalistiv' Mykhailo Kolodzins'koho," Ukraïna moderna, 6 October 2012, http://www.uamoderna.com/event/186 (accessed 14 December 2012).

105 Oleksandr Zaitsev, "Viina iak prodovzhennia polityky. Posivnych Mykola. Voienno-politychna ial'nist' OUN u 1929–1939 rokakh. Lviv, 2010," *Ukraïna Moderna* 18 (2010): 239.

106 Zynovii Knysh, *Pered pokhodom na skhid: Spokhady i materialy do diialnnia Orhanizatsiï Ukraïns'kykh Natsionalistiv u 1939–1941 rokakh* (Toronto: Sribna surma, 1959), 63.

the killings of Alexander I and of Pieracki further complicated the situation.[107] As the facts became known, Mussolini decided to detain the OUN and Ustaša members in two separate localities in Sicily. The OUN stayed in the village of Tortorici until June 1937. Among the OUN members recruited by Mussolini was Stepan Bandera's brother Oleksandr, who had come to Italy in early 1933 as a student together with three other young Ukrainians. Oleksandr lived at first in Rome on a grant from the Italian government. After coming to Rome and beginning his studies in political science, Oleksandr and two other Ukrainian students in Rome joined the Italian student fascist group, *Gruppi universitari fascisti*, in order to establish contact with Italian fascist youth. In Rome, they also founded the Ukrainian student organization Zaravo, to familiarize Ukrainian students there with nationalist politics.[108]

As already indicated, the OUN became very popular among Ukrainian emigrants, especially in the second half of the 1930s. Two other influential groups uniting Ukrainian émigrés were the conservative group led by Hetman Skoropads'kyi, and the Ukrainian National Association (*Ukraïns'ke Natsional'ne Obiednannia*, UNO). The OUN competed for German funding, particularly with the Hetmanite group, which controlled the Ukrainian Scientific Institute (*Ukrainisches Wissenschaftliches Institut*, UWI) in Berlin. The OUN, however, had significant influence on Ukrainian student organizations in Germany, such as Zarevo, Osnova, and Sich. In the second half of the 1930s, the OUN also began to take control of the UNO and some other émigré organizations, which, like the OUN, developed an interest in cooperation with Germany and began to regard Ukrainian nationalism as a movement belonging to the family of European fascist movements.[109] These groups, like the OUN, began emphasizing that Ukrainian nationalism was equal to National Socialism and other fascist and nationalist movements, and states, which anticipated the opportunity to combat communism and to change the geopolitical order in Europe:

> The future Ukrainian state will be a state that is based on National Socialist fundamental principles. Ukrainians use the word "nationalism" in the sense of "National Socialism" or "Fascism." Ukrainians are on cordial terms with other contemporary nationalistic states and nations because they see in them healthy forces that will combat Bolshevism.[110]

107 For cooperation between the OUN and the Ustaša, see Interrogation of Ivan Maliutsa, 15 December 1934, TsDIAL, f. 371 (Shukhevych Stepan), op. 1, spr. 8, ed. 76, 162; "Proces o zamordowanie ... Kontakt z terorytsami chorwackimi," *Gazeta Polska*, 4 December 1935, 6. For simultaneous reporting about the two processes, see "Protses khorvats'kykh revoliutsioneriv," *Dilo*, 20 November 1935, 1, and "Zahal'ni vrazhinnia nashoho korespondenta," *Dilo*, 20 November 1935, 7. For the assassination of Alexander I and Louis Barthou, see Arnd Bauerkämper, *Der Faschismus in Europa 1918–1945* (Stuttgart: Reclam, 2006), 160; Payne, *A History of Fascism*, 406.

108 For Bandera's brother and other Ukrainian students in Rome, see Report of an unknown spy from Italy, 20. 1. 1936, RGVA f. 308, op. 3, del. 379, 2, 7; "Załącznik do pisma Nr. P. III. 851-b/55/36 do Ambasady R.P. w Rzymie," AAN, MSZ, Ambasada w Rzymie, 131–33; Stepan Bandera, "Moï zhyttiepysni dani," in *Perspektyvy ukraïns'koï revoliutsiï*, ed. Vasyl' Ivanyshyn (Drohobych: Vidrodzhennia, 1999), 11. For Oleksandr and Sicily, see Vasyl' Iashan, "Polkovnyk Mykhailo Kolodzins'kyi," in *Horodenshchyna: Istorychno-memuarnyi zbirnyk*, ed. Mykhailo H. Marunchak (New York: Shevchenko Scientific Society, 1978), 636–38.

109 Golczewski, *Deutsche und Ukrainer*, 520–41, 728–58, 777–84, 787, 791.

110 "Iak balakaty z chuzhyntsiamy pro Ukraïnu?" *Ukraïns'kyi vistnyk* 11, 3 (1938), 4–5, quoted in Golczewski, *Deutsche und Ukrainer*, 783.

Ukrainian students in Canada were convinced, like their colleagues in Europe, that Hitler, Mussolini, and Franco were doing good work. A significant number of Ukrainian First World War veterans in Canada, who were united in the Ukrainian National Federation (UNF), supported the OUN and its racial plans for Ukraine. Like the OUN, they regarded parliamentary democracy as a sham. In 1933 the Ukrainian Canadian newspaper *Novyi shliakh*, which was controlled by the Ukrainian War Veteran's Association (UWVA), compared Konovalets' to Hitler and Mussolini.[111] According to Karol Grünberg and Bolesław Sprengel, Konovalets' met Hitler in 1933. After the meeting, the leader of the OUN appealed to Ukrainians to support the *Führer* because he would "open the doors to the East."[112]

Ideology

The ideology of Ukrainian nationalism provided the OUN with orientation, united its members, and allowed them to avoid qualms of conscience when acting in criminal or ethically unacceptable ways. The main ideologist of this radical form of Ukrainian nationalism was Dmytro Dontsov, a spiritual father of the OUN, who, however, never formally belonged to the organization. Dontsov and other leading ideologists of the OUN—such as Mykola Stsibors'kyi, Ievhen Onats'kyi, Volodymyr Martynets', and Iaroslav Orshan—regarded Ukrainian nationalism as one of the European fascist movements. Ideology was also for Dontsov a "secular religion." In order to be effective, it ought not be contaminated or questioned. Believers in the ideology of Ukrainian nationalism were, according to him, expected to "maintain the purity of one's own ideology, clear in content and active of will, as well as a faith that knows no doubts. If we lose this ideology, then the most heroic efforts of the nation will be branded as banditry. If we maintain it, then we will attain everything."[113]

The OUN leaders in exile respected Dontsov and regarded him as their main ideologist and intellectual guide. On several occasions, they tried to persuade him to join the organization and to become the head of its ideological department, but he never accepted. Because he lived in Poland he might have feared arrest had he joined the OUN. For the same reasons he did not direct his criticism against the Poles and the Second Republic. Another reason why Dontsov did not join the organization was to keep his distance from the older OUN members. Dontsov did not regard that generation as the "new type of man" he was interested in creating. By the same token, he was more enthusiastic about the younger generation, encouraging them to break with Ukrainian traditions and the existing political Ukrainian parties and to create their own new revolutionary fascist movement. Many young Ukrainians of the Bandera generation followed him.[114]

111 Martynowych, Sympathy for the Devil, 177–78, 181, 199.

112 Karol Grünberg and Bolesław Sprengel, *Trudne sąsiedztwo: Stosunki polsko-ukraińskie w X–XX wieku* (Warsaw: Książka i Wiedza, 2005), 355, 392–93.

113 Dmytro Dontsov, "Nashi tsili," *Literaturno-naukovyi vistnyk*, 1, 1 (1922): 4, quoted in Motyl, *The Turn to the Right*, 70.

114 Mykhailo Sosnovs'kyi, *Dmytro Dontsov: Politychnyi portret* (New York: Trident International, 1974), 167–68, 236–39, 375–80; Motyl, *Turn to the Right*, 78. For Lenkavs'kyi and the OUN Decalogue, see Golczewski, *Deutsche und Ukrainer*, 597.

For his ideological purposes, Dontsov simplified and vulgarized the writings of such philosophers as Friedrich Nietzsche, Johann Gottlieb Fichte, and Jean-Jacques Rousseau. Because of this philosophical undertone, his texts were not comprehensible to all, but they were particularly popular among high school and university youth. Members of the OVKUH and the SUNM read them eagerly, felt enchanted by them, and encouraged other young Ukrainians to study them. In his ideology, Dontsov sought to reverse the common or universal system of values and morality. The fundamental concepts of his ideology included romanticism, dogmatism, fanaticism, and also amorality (*amoral'nist'*). Dontsov argued that all deeds that would help Ukrainians to achieve a Ukrainian state, regardless of their nature, were moral and right. He thereby encouraged the younger generation to reject "common ethics" and to embrace fanaticism because, as he claimed, only fanaticism could change history and enable the Ukrainians to establish a state. Dontsov's new system of morality was obviously problematic, because it justified all kinds of crimes and violence as long as they were conducted for the good of the nation, or in order to achieve statehood. In general, the ideologist of the Bandera generation copied many of his ideas from other European far-right and fascist discourses, in particular German and Italian.[115]

Dontsov also tried to break with the moderate and past-orientated nationalism that such people as Drahomanov, Hrushevs'kyi, and Franko had shaped. The Ukrainian radical right ideologist blamed these thinkers for their interest in socialism, their preference for universal rather than national morality, and for being moderate, rational, and eager to make compromises. He called the earlier thinkers *drahomanivtsi*, after Drahomanov, whose thinking was influenced by the nineteenth-century socialist discourses.[116] Dontsov claimed that the drahomanivtsi were responsible for the lack of a state and for the weakness of Ukrainian nationalism.[117] Like the ideologists of the OUN, he also vehemently disapproved of democracy and liberalism.[118]

Dontsov began to admire fascism in late 1922. By 1926 he had already translated parts of Hitler's *Mein Kampf* into Ukrainian and had published them. For Dontsov, Hitler was the ideal of a fascist leader. The Ukrainian ideologist compared the *Führer* to Jesus and to Saint Joan of Arc. In addition to extreme nationalism and fascism, Dontsov also popularized antisemitism. In the late 1930s, he opted for the racist kind of antisemitism preached and practiced by the National Socialists in the German Reich.[119] Nazi Germany was for him the ideal fascist state, although it was the Italian Fascists who first drew his attention to the phenomenon of fascism. In 1932 Dontsov translated Mussolini's *The Doctrine of Fascism* (*La Dottrina Del Fascismo*) into Ukrainian and published it.[120] In 1934 a biography of Mussolini by Mykhailo Ostroverkha appeared as the first volume of the *Knyhozbirnia Vistnyka* (library of *Vistnyk*), which was edited by

115 For Dontsov's concept of amorality, see Dmytro Dontsov, *Natsionalizm* (Lviv: Nove Zhyttia, 1926), 194–200. In general for Dontsov's ideology, see Motyl, *The Turn to the Right*, 61–85; Stryjek, *Ukraińska idea narodowa*, 110–90.

116 Dontsov, *Natsionalizm*, 11.

117 Motyl, *The Turn to the Right*, 76.

118 Dontsov, *Natsionalizm*, 28, 33.

119 Taras Kurylo and John-Paul Himka, "Iak OUN stavylasia do ievreïv? Rozdumy nad knyzhkoiu Volodymyra V"iatrovycha," Ukraïna Moderna Vol. 13, No. 2 (2008): 264. See also Stryjek, *Ukraińska idea narodowa*, 118–19, 132, 139–40, 143–51; Motyl, *The Turn to the Right*, 68, 71–85.

120 Shekhovtsov, By Cross and Sword, 274. Parts of *The Doctrine of Fascism* were ghost-written by Giovanni Gentile for Mussolini.

Dontsov. In the same year, *Knyhozbirnia Vistnyka* published a biography of Hitler by Rostyslav Iendyk. Both biographies were written in the genre of hagiography and far-right propaganda, and both began with an apologetic introduction by Dontsov. Mussolini and Hitler were presented as modern, trendsetting politicians and as the embodiments of movements that guaranteed order and peace in Europe. These biographies familiarized Ukrainians with the concept of a fascist leader who rules by virtue of the will of the nation and symbolizes the nation. In addition, *Vistnyk* published writings by such Nazi ideologists as Joseph Goebbels and Alfred Rosenberg.[121] According to the memoirs of Lev Rebet, leader of the homeland executive from 1934 until 1938, Ukrainian nationalist youth read *Vistnyk* very enthusiastically, and their ideas were extensively shaped by this journal.[122]

Dontsov regarded the interwar Ukrainian nationalism as a form of fascism. He radicalized and modified Ukrainian nationalism in order to integrate it into the family of European fascist movements. His attempts to familiarize western Ukrainian youth with this political phenomenon were quite successful. In 1934, the same year in which Hitler's and Mussolini's biographies were published by *Knyhozbirnia Vistnyka*, Volodymyr Levyns'kyi observed: "Oh, how widespread is the cult of Mussolini, Hitler, and other fascist strongmen among Ukrainian students! How many little Mussolinis and Hitlers have sprung up under the influence of Dontsov's writings!"[123]

Many Ukrainian students and high school pupils dreamed of being a *Führer* or a *Duce*. There were debates among Ukrainian nationalists about the two fascist leaders, the systems they represented, and the states they ruled. Because of his fundamental antisemitism and anticommunism, and the way he seized power in Germany, Hitler was more popular than Mussolini among many Ukrainian nationalists. In 1935, Ihor Virlyi wrote that Hitler fascinated western Ukrainians, because he "wrote on his banners: Perish, Jew!—because the Jews were propagators of the communist pattern, and he was striking at the foundations of communism."[124] The teacher Sofiia Rusova noticed that, when her grandson joined the scouting organization Plast, which, according to him, was full of nationalists, he began to take a great interest in nationalism, Mussolini, and Hitler.[125]

The verdict of not guilty in the trial of Sholom Schwartzbard—who had murdered Symon Petliura in Paris on 25 May 1926—had a significant influence on Dontsov's attitude to Jews. Schwartzbard was found not guilty, having claimed that he had killed Petliura to avenge the pogroms that Petliura's army had committed in Ukraine.[126] The verdict had a strong impact on Ukrainian nationalists who, after the trial, ceased to veil their antisemitism. Dontsov became one of the main propagators of antisemit-

121 Mykhailo Ostroverkha, *Mussolini. Liudyna i chyn* (Lviv: Knyhozbirnia Vistnyka, 1934); Rostyslav Iendyk, *Adolf Hitler* (Lviv: Knyhozbirnia Vistnyka, 1934). In 1937 the library of Vistnyk published the biography of Francisco Franco. Cf. R. Kerch, *Franko – vozhd' espantsiv* (Lviv: Knyhozbirnia Vistnyka, 1934). See also Golczewski, *Deutsche und Ukrainer*, 582–84.

122 Lev Rebet, *Svitla i tini OUN* (Munich: Ukraïns'kyi samostiinyk, 1964), 47.

123 Volodymyr Levyns'kyi, *Ideol'og fashyzmu* (Lviv: 1934), 28. See also Carynnyk, Foes of Our Rebirth, 318.

124 Ihor Virlyi, *Nashi chasy* (Lviv: Nakladom V. Kunantsia, 1935), 16–17, quoted in Hon, *Iz kryvdoiu*, 119.

125 A. V. Kentii, *Narys istoriï Orhanizatsiï Ukraïns'kykh Natsionalistiv (1929–1941)* (Kiev: Instytut Istoriï Ukraïny, 1998), 30.

126 Petliura's personal responsibility for the numerous pogroms committed by the troops of which he was in command seems to be limited. Cf. Henry Abramson, *A Prayer for the Government: Ukrainians and Jews in Revolutionary Times, 1917–1920* (Cambridge: Harvard University Press, 1999), 134–39.

ism among the Ukrainian ideologists. On the one hand, he attacked Jews as a "race." On the other hand, he adapted antisemitism to the Ukrainian political situation by associating Jews with the Soviet Union, which he viewed as the main "occupier" of Ukrainian territory and the main enemy of Ukrainians. For Dontsov, the Jews were guilty for many reasons, but not as guilty as the Russians who were the actual "occupiers" of Ukraine. In reaction to the Schwartzbard trial, Dontsov claimed that the Russian and the Jewish problem were interwoven and that the Ukrainians must solve the Russian problem in order to be able to solve the Jewish question:

> This murder is an act of revenge by an agent of Russian imperialism against a person who became a symbol of the national struggle against Russian oppression. It does not matter that in this case a Jew became an agent of Russian imperialism. ... We have to and we will fight against the aspiration of Jewry to play the inappropriate role of lords in Ukraine. ... No other government took as many Jews into its service as did the Bolsheviks, and one might expect that like Pilate the Russians will wash their hands and say to the oppressed nations, "The Jew is guilty of everything."
>
> Jews are guilty, terribly guilty, because they helped consolidate Russian rule in Ukraine, but "the Jew is not guilty of everything." Russian imperialism is guilty of everything. Only when Russia falls in Ukraine will we be able to settle the Jewish question in our country in a way that suits the interest of the Ukrainian people.[127]

The younger generation in the OUN adopted Dontsov's characterization of Jews and repeated it in the resolutions of the Second Great Congress, held by the OUN-B in April 1941 in Cracow.[128] When, on 7 June 1936, the OUN commemorated the death of Symon Petliura, OUN activists distributed leaflets with the message: "Attention, kill and beat the Jews for our Ukrainian leader Symon Petliura, the Jews should be removed from Ukraine, long live the Ukrainian state."[129]

The modern kind of antisemitism, which defined Jews as a race and not as a religious group, became popular among Ukrainian nationalists, especially in the 1930s. This antisemitism was popularized in publications such as *The Jewish Problem in Ukraine,* a brochure written by OUN member and ideologist Volodymyr Martynets', who was fascinated by the Nuremberg Laws of 1935. Unlike Dontsov, who claimed that the Jews were the helpers of the Russian imperialists and were pillars of the Soviet Union, Martynets' adapted the antisemitic discourse of the National Socialists in Germany. Like them, he defined the "Jewish problem" as a "racial issue." And like the Nazis, he claimed that the Ukrainian nation was the victim of the Jews, on which they preyed. For Martynets', the "Jewish problem" in Ukraine was more difficult than in other European countries, because there were more Jews in Ukraine than elsewhere in Europe. Particularly problematic were the cities, which were inhabited more by Jews than by Ukrainians. Martynets' claimed that it was necessary to "cleanse" the cities of Jews, and thus solve the "vital problem of the [Ukrainian] nation." The first step to solve the "Jewish problem" would be to isolate them from Ukrainians. Marty-

127 Dmytro Dontsov, "Symon Petliura", in *Literaturno Naukoyi Vistnyk* Vol. 7–8, No. 5, (1926), 326–28, quoted in Carynnyk, Foes of Our Rebirth, 319.

128 Golczewski, *Deutsche und Ukrainer*, 504. For the resolution, see "Postanovy II. Velykoho Zboru Orhanizatsiï Ukraïns'kykh Natsionalistiv," TsDAHO f. 1, op. 23, spr. 926, 192–93.

129 "Komunikat informacyjny Nr. 19 o działalności O.U.N.–U.W.O. za czas od 3 do 13 .VI. 1936r.," AAN, MSZ, syg. 5318, 265; Hon, *Iz kryvdoiu*, 103.

nets' argued that the Jews would otherwise corrupt the psychology and the blood of the Ukrainian race, and contaminate the Ukrainian nation. Every kind of direct coexistence with Jews was therefore undesirable. In order to prevent the interrelation between the two "races," Jews were to have their own schools, newspapers, restaurants, cafes, theatres, brothels, and cabarets, and were to be forbidden the use of the Ukrainian equivalents. Intermarriage between Jews and Ukrainians had to be forbidden, as in Germany.[130]

The OUN actively put the antisemitic components of the ideology of Ukrainian nationalism into practice. In 1935 OUN activists conducted an operation, during which they smashed windows in Jewish houses in the Zhydachiv (Żydaczów), Kalush (Kałusz), Stanyslaviv, and Stryi districts.[131] At a meeting in July 1936 in Volhynia, the OUN in the Kostopil' (Kostopol) *raion* (district) concluded that "Jews are harmful to the Ukrainian nation." Soon afterwards, OUN activists in the Kostopil' raion set several Jewish houses on fire. Approximately one hundred Jewish families were left without a roof over their heads as a result of this arson.[132]

Of the Ukrainians living in the Second Republic, it was not only Ukrainian nationalists who were obsessed with "Jewish Bolshevism." This antisemitic stereotype was also widespread among the so-called Ukrainian democratic parties. The UNDO claimed in autumn 1936 that "Jews are the most faithful and almost sole propagators of communism."[133] While antisemitism was thriving in the 1930s, western Ukrainians denied their antisemitism and made fun of the fact that others perceived them as antisemites (Fig. 1).

Related to antisemitism was the OUN's fascination with fascism. After promoting the UVO and OUN in the United States, OUN member Ievhen Liakhovych was staying in London and tried to meet with Sir Oswald Mosley, Britain's leading fascist politician. Instead, he was able to meet with the chief of the propaganda department and his deputy. During this talk, Liakhovych explained the nature of Ukrainian antisemitism to his fascist counterpart: "Antisemitism is an irrational and unjustifiable hatred. ... We [the OUN] are combating the Jews because they have always done us harm." His interlocutor agreed with him that the situation was similar in England.[134]

In *Natsiokratiia*, a treatise written in 1935, leading OUN member and ideologist Mykola Stsibors'kyi condemned democracy, socialism, and communism; at the same time, he praised fascism and dictatorship. He introduced a political system that he called natsiokratiia—the "dictatorship of the nation"—and proposed that it would become the political system of the state that the OUN would establish in the course of a national revolution. Stsibors'kyi himself could not decide whether natsiokratiia was fascist or not. On the one hand, he claimed that the "Ukrainian state will be neither fascist nor National Socialist," that Ukrainian nationalism was a singular and independent movement, and that it was only their foes who accused Ukrainian nationalists of being fascists. On the other hand, however, he claimed that "fascism itself is first of all nationalism: the love of one's own motherland, patriotic feeling brought to the level

130 Volodymyr Martynets', *Zhydivs'ka probliema v Ukraïni* (London, 1938), 2, 8, 10, 11, 13–15.
131 Hon, *Iz kryvdoiu*, 152.
132 Ibid., 102, 152.
133 Ibid., 97, 157. The UNDO claimed it in the newspaper *Svoboda*, 18 October 1936, 12.
134 Carynnyk, Foes of Our Rebirth, 321–22.

Fig. 1. The front page of the satirical magazine *Komar*, 15 February 1934.

of self-sacrifice, and the cult of self-sacrificing fanaticism." More important than Stsibors'kyi's indecision and ambiguity is the fact that natsiokratiia was modeled on fascism. According to natsiokratiia, the Ukrainian state would be ruled by the "Leader of the Nation [*Vozhd' Natsiï*], the greatest of the great sons of the nation who, due to the general trust of the nation and to his own integral attributes, will hold in his hand the power of the state."[135]

135 Mykola Stsibors'kyi, *Natsiokratiia* (Paris, 1935), 56, 72–73, 82, 105, 107, 109, 114, 116.

After Germany attacked Poland on 1 September 1939, Mel'nyk asked Stsibors'kyi to write a constitution for a Ukrainian state. According to Stsibors'kyi's draft, natsiokratiia would be the official political system of the Ukrainian state, as he had proposed in his 1935 treatise. According to the draft constitution, the Ukrainian state was to be based on the totalitarian dictatorship of a nation that would be defined in a nationalist and racial sense and would therefore guarantee rights to ethnic Ukrainians alone. Other than the OUN, all political groups, parties, and other such organizations would be forbidden. As in natsiokratiia, the leader of the OUN would be the "Head of the State–The Leader of the Nation [*Holova Derzhavy-Vozhd' Natsiï*]," whose period of office would be unlimited. In this sense, all aspects of political, social, and cultural life would be controlled by the OUN, the only legal party and organization in the state.[136]

According to the OUN's concept of fascism, the nation would be represented by and subordinated to the leader (*Vozhd'* or *Providnyk*), who would be the head of the OUN. This was the same absolute authority of the leader that the Nazis called Führerprinzip. Within the OUN, the Führerprinzip concept was officially introduced at the Second Great Congress of the Ukrainian Nationalists on 27 August 1939 in Rome, but the idea had already manifested itself previously, as for example in *Natsiokratiia* in 1935, and in the behavior of the OUN members during their trials in Warsaw and Lviv in 1935 and 1936.[137]

Fascism became very popular among Ukrainian nationalists during the 1930s. The OUN was its main but not its only promoter in Ukraine. Two other important persons who sympathized with fascism were Dmytro Paliïv, founder of the Front of National Unity (*Front natsional'noï iednosti*, FNIe) and of the newspaper *Novyi Chas*, and the Ukrainophile, Wilhelm von Habsburg.[138] In the 1930s a group of young people in Przemyśl, set up a Society of Fascist Studies (*Tovarystvo fashyzmoznavstva*). In a letter to Dontsov they stated that "Fascism is a universal phenomenon, because it is not a political doctrine but an entire worldview of indestructible principles based on religion and morality." Further they asked Dontsov to contribute to their journal, to give them leadership and guidance. They finished their letter with this statement: "Fascism, as a worldview, completely corresponds with the historical traditions and the present-day Ukrainian ideological currents whose initiator and propagator is Dr. Dmytro Dontsov."[139]

Racism, in the Ukrainian context, was very much related to the idea of independence (*samostiinist'*). Racist thinkers argued that Ukraine should become an independent state because it was inhabited by a particular race, which needed an independent nation state to develop all of its features. The OUN's racism can be traced back to Mikhnovs'kyi's appeal, "Do not marry a foreign woman because your children will be your enemies," which OUN members took literally.[140]

136 "Narys proiektu osnovnykh zakoniv konstytutsiï Ukraïns'koï derzhavy," TsDAVOV, f. 3833, op. 1, spr. 7, 2, 2v, 7, 7v.

137 Mirchuk, *Narys istoriï OUN*, 447–53; Golczewski, *Deutsche und Ukrainer*, 943–44. For the trials, see chapter 3 below.

138 Snyder, *The Red Prince*, 194–201. On Paliïv, see Oleh Kupchyns'kyi, ed., *Dmytro Paliïv: Zhyttia i diial'nist'* (Lviv: Naukove tovarystvo im. Shevchenka, 2007).

139 Letter of the Society of Fascist Studies (Tovarystvo fashyzmoznavstva) to Dmytro Dontsov, December 1935, Dmytro Dontsov Archives (Archiwum Dmitra Doncowa), BN, Mf 82672, 412.

140 Koval, Heroi, shcho ne zmih, 9.

The Ukrainian geographer Stepan Rudnyts'kyi (1887–1937) was another important Ukrainian intellectual who popularized racism and eugenics in the Ukrainian nationalist discourse. Rudnyts'kyi worked together with Hrushevs'kyi on the origins of the Ukrainian nation. He provided Hrushevs'kyi's historical theory with an essential geographical component, defining the "natural territory" or the "living space" (Ger. *Lebensraum*) of the Ukrainian people.[141] In his book *Ukraine. The Land and Its People*, published in 1910, Rudnyts'kyi claimed that "for one thousand two hundred years, the Ukrainian race has resided in this region, and has been able, not only to preserve its boundaries, but, after heavy losses, to regain and even to pass beyond them."[142] He described the Ukrainian "race" as of "tall stature, with long legs and broad shoulders, strongly pigmented complexion, dark, rich, curly hair, rounded head and long face with a high broad brow, dark eyes, straight nose, strongly developed elongated lower part of the face, medium mouth and small ears."[143] One important reason for such a racialist characterization of Ukrainians was the wish to distinguish them from Poles and Russians. Rudnyts'kyi stated that "anthropological differences of the Ukrainians from their neighbors, especially from the Poles, White Russians and Russians, are very clearly marked."[144] To him, an independent nation meant an independent race. It was a "*large community of people, the shape of whose bodies is similar to that of each other, but different from those of other nations.*"[145] In addition, he praised the science of eugenics and argued that: "On the one hand, we should enable as many healthy and racially full-fledged exemplars of the nation as possible to marry and breed. On the other hand, we should not allow sick or racially less valuable exemplars to do that."[146] Rudnyts'kyi's racist thinking had a significant impact on OUN ideology and the UPA's genocidal policy.

Mykola Sukhovers'kyi, an OUN member who lived in Chernivtsi, a city in Bukovina inhabited by Jews, Germans, Poles, Romanians, Ukrainians and others, recalled in his memoirs:

> In the "Zaporozhe" [a student fraternity] there was a decision that a member was not allowed to marry an alien girl—a non-Ukrainian. That decision was made on the basis of Mykola Mikhnovs'kyi's *Decalogue*, which was printed in *Samostiina Ukraïna* and which stated: "Do not marry a foreigner because your children will become your enemies." It needs to be recognized that Ukrainians who married Romanian girls ceased of course to be good Ukrainians, and their children directly came to belong to Romanian culture. ... I came up with two suggestions: 1) if we want to preserve our order, then no aliens are to be invited to our parties or dance classes and 2) we should invite Ukrainian girls only from peasant homes, from the surrounding areas.[147]

141 Oleh Shablii, "Peredmova," in Stepan Rudnyts'kyi, *Chomu my khochemo samostiinoï Ukraïny*, ed. L. M. Harbachuk (Lviv: Svit, 1994), 8.

142 Stepan Rudnyts'kyi, *Ukraine: The Land and Its People: An Introduction to Its Geography* (New York: Ukrainian Alliance of America, 1918), 12.

143 Rudnyts'kyi, *Ukraine: The Land and Its People*, 161–62.

144 Ibid., 162.

145 Rudnyts'kyi, *Chomu my khochemo*, ed. Harbarchuk, 39. Emphasis in the original.

146 Stepan Rudnyts'kyi, "Do osnov ukraïns'koho natsionalizmu," *Chomu my khochemo*, ed. Harbarchuk, 299.

147 Mykola Sukhovers'kyi, *Moï spohady* (Kiev: Smoloskyp, 1997), 50.

Socialism had been popular in the nineteenth-century Ukrainian national discourse but was condemned by a number of Ukrainian thinkers after the First World War. One of its most eager critics was Dontsov, who had been a Marxist before the First World War. Socialism was branded as communism and was associated with the Soviet Union. Ukrainian nationalism therefore became detached from socialism and drifted in the direction of extreme nationalism and fascism.[148] Simultaneously, Jews were increasingly perceived as agents of communism. In July 1936, many OUN members and other nationalists commemorated the Sich Riflemen in the city of Skoliv. One of the celebrants, Petro Mirchuk, recalled that communist activists disturbed the commemoration, whereupon the nationalists killed two of the communists, one of whom Mirchuk referred to as an "insolent communist Jew photographer." After the ceremony, the nationalists smashed windows in many "communist houses." Mirchuk saw these actions as legitimate ways of dealing with communists and Jews.[149]

Dislike of communism did not prevent Ukrainian nationalists from using communist symbols or adding nationalist meaning to such communist holidays as 1 May. The effect was bizarre. The nationalist elements did not entirely suppress the communist ones and instead merged with them. In effect these new images resembled German National Socialist aesthetics.[150] The attempt to integrate May Day into Ukrainian nationalist life also illustrates that, like the National Socialists and the Italian Fascists, the Ukrainian nationalists tried to attract workers to their movement. Nevertheless, because Galicia was predominantly an agrarian region, and Ukrainians largely lived and worked in the countryside as peasants or to a limited extent as farmers, it is not surprising that the OUN did not pay as much attention to the "working masses" as the National Socialists did in Germany, or the Fascists in Italy. It was more logical for the Ukrainian nationalists to concentrate on the rural population and to emphasize folkloristic and populist features. This was not very different from the program of other East Central European fascist movements, such as the Iron Guard in Romania, the Hlinka Party in Slovakia, the Arrow Cross Party in Hungary, and the Ustaša in Croatia.[151]

Religion was another important element of the ideology of Ukrainian nationalism, although relations between the Greek Catholic Church and the OUN were complex. Ukrainian nationalism and the Greek Catholic Church both opposed materialism and communism. The majority of OUN members from Galicia were Greek Catholics. Many of the leading OUN members, such as Bandera, Lenkavs'kyi, Stets'ko, and Matviieiko, were the sons of Greek Catholic priests. In 1931, Andrei Sheptyts'kyi, head of the Greek Catholic Church and a Ukrainian moral authority, initiated the Ukrainian Catholic Union (*Ukraïns'kyi Katolyts'kyi Soiuz*, UKU), which cooperated with the Ukrainian nationalists. The same year, the UKU founded the Catholic Action of Ukrainian Youth (*Katolyts'ka aktsiia ukraïns'koï molodi*, KAUM), the leader of which was Andrii Mel'nyk, manager of Sheptyts'kyi's estates. "Christian nationalism"

148 Golczewski, *Deutsche und Ukrainer*, 544; Christopher Gilley, *A simple question of 'pragmatism'?: Sovietophilism in the West Ukrainian emigration in the 1920s* (Koszalin: Koszalin Institute of Comparative European Studies, 2006), 4.

149 Mirchuk, *Narys istoriï OUN*, 344.

150 See the cover of the newspaper *Homin Kraiu* in Mirchuk, *Narys istoriï OUN*, 365.

151 See "Borot'ba khorvativ za voliu," *Surma* 75–76, No. 1–2 (1934): 7–9.

became the official ideology of the KAUM.[152] Ukrainian nationalism and the Greek Catholic Church shared the same main enemies, communism and the Soviet Union. Like the nationalists, Greek Catholic priests frequently demonized communism. M. Cherneha, for example, described communism as the "red demon."[153]

Sheptyts'kyi generally supported Ukrainian nationalism but was skeptical about the radicalization of the younger generation, which blamed its fathers for having failed to establish a Ukrainian state. In a pastoral letter addressed to Ukrainian youth in 1932, he condemned "violence and blind terror," breaking with tradition, hastiness, the radicalization of Ukrainian patriotism, and the fascination with fascism.[154]

During the interwar period, the question of loyalty toward the Polish state was an important matter separating the Greek Catholic Church from Ukrainian nationalism. When the Greek Catholic Church demonstrated its loyalty to the Second Republic, for example in the festival "Youth for Christ," the OUN distanced itself from such actions.[155] Another problem was the conflict between religious and nationalist priorities. The Greek Catholic clerics regarded God as the most essential value; and Ukrainian nationalists, the nation.[156] On a practical level, however, the Ukrainian nationalists used religious symbols and aesthetics to sacralize their political values, heroes, and aims. Furthermore, the ideology of Ukrainian nationalism and the Greek Catholic religion were the two most significant components of Galician Ukrainian identity. This can be illustrated by the brochure *Nationalism and Catholicism*, written by Mykola Konrad, professor at the Theological Academy of Lviv University, and published in 1934 by the UKU:

> O God, let these two idealisms—the Catholic "I believe" and the nationalist "I want"—as the two clear tones of the Ukrainian soul, merge harmoniously into one accord and awaken our withered hearts. Then a new era of faith, love, and power, a mighty national unity and a unified invincible front will come.[157]

The young generation in the OUN used religion as a foundation for its ideological orientation. In 1929 Stepan Lenkavs'kyi, SUNM leader, OUN member, and Bandera's lifelong friend, drafted "The Ten Commandments of a Ukrainian Nationalist," known also as "The Decalogue of a Ukrainian Nationalist" or "The Decalogue of the OUN." Lenkavs'kyi's Decalogue blurred the boundaries between ideology and religion and undermined religious morality with ideological immorality. The OUN called it the "new religion, the religion of Ukrainian nationalism."[158]

Even if not every young OUN member came from a priest's family, as did Bandera, Galician youth grew up in a religious society, for which religion was an unchallengeable system of values. Using religion as a foundation and structure for ideology, blurring the boundaries between religion and nationalism, and using ideology to undermine religion were effective ways of changing the morality of an entire religious group. In

152 Shekhovtsov, By Cross and Sword, 276–79; Pan'kivs'kyi, *Roky nimets'koï*, 140.
153 Shekhovtsov, By Cross and Sword, 279.
154 Mytropolyt Andrei Sheptyts'kyi, "Slovo do Ukraïns'koï molodi," Lviv 1932, in *Tvory moral'no-pastoral'ni* (Rome: Vydannia Ukraïns'koho Katolyts'koho Universytetu im. sv. Klymenta Papy, 1978), 104–108.
155 "Proces o zamordowanie ... Pytania adwk. Horbowyja," *Gazeta Polska*, 13 December 1935, 6.
156 Shekhovtsov, By Cross and Sword, 280.
157 Mykola Konrad, *Natsionalizm i katolytsyzm* (Lviv: Meta, 1934), 45.
158 Golczewski, *Deutsche und Ukrainer*, 598; Pan'kivs'kyi, *Roky nimets'koï*, 142.

its original version, the seventh commandment of Lenkavs'kyi's Decalogue read: "You should not hesitate to commit the greatest crime if the good of the cause requires it." Later, the words "the greatest crime" (*naibil'shyi zlochyn*) were replaced with "the most dangerous task."[159] The first commandment of the Decalogue, "Attain a Ukrainian state or die in the struggle for it," was derived from Mikhnovs'kyi's *Samostiina Ukraïna*, in which he wrote: "either we will win the fight or we will die." Lenkavs'kyi's Decalogue made the lives of the Ukrainian nationalists and their "enemies" unimportant. Murder for the sake of the nation or for the "right reason" was moral and desirable.[160]

Other lists of rules and principles that were intended to complement the Decalogue were "The Twelve Character Attributes of a Ukrainian Nationalist," and "The Forty-Four Rules of Life of a Ukrainian Nationalist." The "Twelve Character Attributes" listed such descriptions of Ukrainian nationalists as honest (*chesnyi*) and brave (*vidvazhnyi*). The characteristic "cautious" (*oberezhnyi*) meant that a Ukrainian nationalist "will always apply the principle of conspiracy." The "Forty-Four Rules" were written by Zenon Kossak, in jail. Rule 14 spoke to the conscience of its recipients and said, "You should know that you are jointly responsible for the fate of your nation." In rule 40, Kossak strengthened his nationalist argumentation, with racism: "Treasure motherhood as the source of the continuation of life. Make your family an ark of covenant of the purity of your race and nation."[161]

Another important feature of Ukrainian nationalist ideology was the cult of war and death, including the conviction that political problems can and should be solved by war. Ukrainian nationalists believed that, having failed to establish a state after the First World War, they had nothing to lose and everything to gain. On the one hand, every OUN member killed by "enemies" or "occupiers" died as a martyr for Ukrainian independence and could become a national hero. On the other hand, the killing of enemies was gallant, right, and heroic, because it was done for the liberation of Ukraine. The main functions of the cult of war and death were to integrate violence into everyday life and to dissipate the fear of dying while conducting such dangerous activities as assassinations or robberies. The song "March of the Fighters" illustrates OUN's attitude to war, death, and heroism, and how it was related to the "pain of losing Ukraine":

We were born in a great time. After the fires of war and the flame of fires We were raised on the pain of losing Ukraine We were fed by revolt and rage against enemies.	Zrodylys' my velykoï hodyny Z pozhezh viiny i z polum"ia vohniv Plekav nas bil' po vtrati Ukraïny Kormyv nas bunt i hniv na vorohiv.
Now we are marching toward the vital fight Strong, hard, indestructible as granite, Because no one has gained freedom by weeping, And those who fight can gain a world.	I os' idem u boiu zhyttievomu Mitsni, tverdi, nezlomni mov granit, Bo plach ne dav svobody shche nikomu, A khto borets', toi zdobuvaie svit.

159 Golczewski, *Deutsche und Ukrainer*, 598.
160 Mikhnovs'kyi, Samostiina Ukraïna, 43.
161 Golczewski, *Deutsche und Ukrainer*, 598–99; Mirchuk, *Narys istoriï OUN*, 106–109.

We want neither glory nor reward. Our reward is the delight of struggle; It's sweeter for us to die in fight Than to live like mute slaves in chains.	Ne khochemo ni slavy, ni zaplaty. Zaplatoiu nam rozkish borot'by; Solodshe nam u boiu umyraty Nizh v putakh zhyty mov nimi raby.
Enough of damage and discord; Brother dares not fight against brother. Under the blue-yellow flag of independence, We will unite our great nation.	Dovoli nam ruïny i nezhody; Ne smiie brat na brata ity u bii. Pid syn'ozhovtym praporom svobody Ziednaiem ves' velykyi narid svii.
Our proud call to the nation carries A great truth for all: Be faithful till death to your fatherland For us Ukraine is above all!	Velyku pravdu dlia usikh iedynu Nash hordyi klych narodovi nese: Bat'kivshchyni bud' virnyi do zahynu Nam Ukraïna vyshcha ponad vse!
The glory of the fallen fighters leads us into battle. Our most important law and command: A united Ukrainian state Strong and united from the San to the Caucasus.	Vede nas v bii bortsiv upavshykh slava. Dlia nas zakon naivyshchyi ta prykaz: Sobornaia Ukraïns'ka Derzhava Mitsna i odna vid Sianu po Kavkaz.[162]

Propagandists and ideologists of the UVO and OUN—among them Stepan Bandera in his position as the director of propaganda of the homeland executive and later as its head—frequently instrumentalized and sacralized the dead nationalists in order to negate the fear of sacrificing one's life and to evoke the feeling of revenge. Such instrumentalization of dead fighters was typical of many fundamentalist and fanatical movements.[163] The first nationalist to become a famous martyr and hero was Ol'ha Basarab, a UVO member who, on the night of 12 February 1924, either hanged herself in a prison cell or died because of mistreatment during her interrogation. In the Ukrainian heroic narrative, she hanged herself in order not to reveal organizational secrets under torture by Polish interrogators. Naturally, the narrative did not mention that Basarab had been carrying out espionage tasks for the Abwehr.[164] *Surma* and *Rozbudova natsiï*, the official periodicals of the UVO and later the OUN, commemorated the death of Basarab every year, praising her in prose and verse for her heroism and willingness to make sacrifices.[165] The cult of Basarab, like many other cults of dead nationalists, was not limited to OUN propaganda. Large crowds attended church services for Basarab. Such slogans as "Long live the Ukrainian revolution! Away with the Polish occupation! Long live Basarab!" appeared in public places.[166]

The two most popular martyrs in the interwar period were Vasyl' Bilas and Dmytro Danylyshyn. Together with ten other OUN members, they took part in the

162 "Marsh boievikiv," *Surma* 28–29, 1–2 (1930): 1. For the cult of war and death policy, see "Viina, voiennyi stan i iedynyi provid," *Surma* 47, No. 8 (1931): 1–2; "Ne vbyvaite boiovoho dukha Natsiï," *Surma* 74, No. 12 (1933): 1–4.

163 On the notion of heroes and martyrs, see Laleh Khalili, *Heroes and Martyrs of Palestine: The Politics of National Commemoration* (Cambridge: Cambridge University Press, 2007).

164 Shukhevych, *Moie zhyttia. Spohady*, 322–26; Golczewski, *Deutsche und Ukrainer*, 438–40.

165 For heroic celebrations of Basarab's willingness to make sacrifices, see for example: "Pamiaty Ol'hy Basarabovoï," *Surma* 17–18, No. 2–3 (1929): 7; "U shostu richnytsiu," *Surma* 30, No. 3 (1930): 1; "V semu richnytsiu," *Surma* 42, No. 3 (1931): 1–2.

166 For a church service for Olha Basarab at the St. George Cathedral in Lviv attended by about 2,000 people on 12 February 1933, see "Raporty sledstvennogo otdela o deiatelnosti politicheskikh partii i organizatsii, a takzhe ob ugololovnykh prestupleniakh za 1933 g.," DALO f. 121, op. 3, spr. 844, 68.

robbery of a post office in Horodok Iahailons'kyi (Gródek Jagielloński) on 30 November 1932. The OUN wounded eight persons in the course of this operation, one of them fatally. Five of the robbers were wounded, and two other nationalists—Iurii Berezyns'kyi and Volodymyr Staryk—were mistakenly shot dead by other OUN members. Danylyshyn and Bilas escaped from the scene. While fleeing, Danylyshyn killed a policeman who had asked to check his papers. The police spread a rumor to the effect that those who had escaped were Poles who had robbed a Ukrainian cooperative and had killed the manager. When Bilas and Danylyshyn were captured by Ukrainian peasants, they were beaten severely until they finally succeeded in persuading their captors that they were Ukrainians.[167]

Both robbers were arrested. A speedy trial took place from 17 to 21 December 1932, during the course of which Bilas and Danylyshyn admitted to killing the politician Tadeusz Hołówko on 29 August 1931. The two young Ukrainians—Bilas was twenty-one and Danylyshyn twenty-five—were sentenced to death. The outcome of this trial enraged many Ukrainians in the Second Republic. At the moment of the execution of Bilas and Danylyshyn on 22 December 1932, churches in Lviv and many other places rang their bells. The bell-ringing was organized by the propaganda apparatus of the homeland executive, headed by Bandera. During the following days, church services in memory of the two young Ukrainians took place, and the OUN set up a mourning period of three months. Priests who did not agree to conduct services in honor of Bilas and Danylyshyn were threatened, or were forced to do so. In countless leaflets and posters, the OUN represented Bilas and Danylyshyn as martyrs and heroes who had died for Ukraine.[168]

The last important feature of OUN ideology to be mentioned here is spiritualism. On 16 February 1933, in the eastern Galician provincial city of Truskavets' (Truskawiec), a group of OUN members and sympathizers organized a séance, during which they believed they came into contact with the ghost of the Ukrainian poet Taras Shevchenko. They apparently asked the ghost when Ukraine would become free. The reply was that this would happen in five years, but only on condition that all Ukrainians continued to further the struggle for independence. The news spread quickly among Ukrainians associated with the OUN and other nationalist and patriotic organizations. On 5 May 1933, a great session devoted to the Ukrainian national poet was organized by Ukrainian nationalists, who tried to convince as many people as possible to continue the struggle.[169]

167 "Boievyky!" (Obituary) and "Horodok Iahailons'kyi," *Surma* 62, No. 12 (1932): 1–8; Żeleński, *Zabójstwo ministra Pierackiego*, 40; Wysocki, *Organizacja*, 286–89; Mirchuk, *Narys istorii OUN*, 232–35.

168 "Raporty sledshevshego otdela o deiatelnosti politicheskikh partii i organizatsii, a takzhe ob ugololovnykh prestupleniakh za 1933 g.," DALO f. 121, op. 3, spr 844, 8, 11, 13, 47, 74–75, 77, 97; Ostap Hrytsai, "Dva khloptsi hynut' za Ukraïnu," *Rozbudova natsiï* 60–61, No. 1–2 (1933): 1–3; "Iz Ukraïns'koï Golgoty," *Surma* 67, No. 5, 1933: 1; Wysocki, *Organizacja*, 289. For OUN threats against Greek-Catholic priests, see Żeleński, *Akt oskarżenia*, 53.

169 "Raporty sledshevshego ..." DALO f. 121, op. 3, spr. 844, 100.

Conclusion

Ukraine was influenced through the centuries by various cultures, religions, and political movements, and was at the beginning of the twentieth century a very heterogeneous territory. Until the First World War Ukrainians lived in the Habsburg Empire together with such groups as Poles, Jews, and Romanians, and in the Russian Empire with Russians, Jews, and Poles. The Ukrainian national movement, which was rooted in eastern Galicia, was weaker than the Polish and Russian ones. After the First World War, Ukrainians failed in their efforts to establish a state and lived in the interwar period in Soviet Ukraine, Poland, Romania, and Czechoslovakia. In 1920, a group of Ukrainian veterans founded the UVO, which became a terrorist organization without much political significance. The situation only changed a decade later when the OUN entered the stage, involved the youth, and became a nationalist mass movement similar to the Ustaša, Hlinka Party, and Iron Guard. The OUN members lived only in Poland and in exile and had no impact on the political situation in Soviet Ukraine. Although the OUN emphasized its national, patriotic and romantic nature, it was essentially a typical East Central European fascist movement. It attempted to take power in the Ukrainian territories and to establish a state with a fascist dictatorship.

The OUN was composed of two generations: one born around 1890 and one around 1910. The older generation created the UVO and lived in exile. The younger generation controlled the homeland executive of the OUN, which was subordinated to the leadership in exile. Especially after Bandera became the leader of the homeland executive the younger generation proved to be more radical than the older one. Nevertheless, both generations were open to and fascinated with fascism. The OUN ideology combined ultranationalism with racism, mysticism, antisemitism, a cult of war and violence, anticommunism, hostility to democracy, communism and socialism. The younger generation was shaped especially by Dmytro Dontsov, who before the First World War had been a Marxist and after the war argued that Ukrainian nationalism was one of the European fascist movements. Nevertheless, he reminded Ukrainians to avoid using the term "fascism," in order not to be perceived as a part of an international movement. The democratic Ukrainian parties in the Second Republic such as the UNDO were fragile and the political situation in Poland was not favorable to them.

Chapter 2

FORMATIVE YEARS

Family, Education, Appearance, and Political Commitment

It was New Year's Day 1909 when the second child, Stepan, was born to Andrii Bandera (1882–1941), a Greek Catholic priest of Staryi Uhryniv, and his wife Myroslava (1890–1921), the daughter of Volodymyr Hlodzins'kyi, another Greek Catholic priest of Staryi Uhryniv and the nearby village Berezhnytsia. Myroslava died at the age of thirty-one from tuberculosis of the throat. She left behind three daughters: Marta (1907–1982), Volodymyra (1913–2001), and Oksana (1917–2008), and four sons: Stepan (1909–1959), Oleksandr (1911–1942), Vasyl' (1915–1942), and Bohdan (1919–1944). Her fourth daughter, Myroslava, named after her, died as a baby. Stepan's father had obtained his education at a high school in Stryi and later at the theological faculty of Lviv University. He and his family lived in Staryi Uhryniv until 1933, when they moved to Volia Zaderevats'ka. Four years later his family moved again to the village of Trostianets', to which Andrii had already been relocated in 1934. He raised his children in the spirit of patriotism and religion.[1]

During and after the First World War, Andrii took part in the struggle for a Ukrainian state. He organized local Ukrainians into military units, and in November 1918 he was engaged in the struggle for power in the regional capital of Kalush. Andrii was a deputy from the Kalush region in the ZUNR. In 1919–1920 he served as a chaplain in the UHA.[2] In biographical data compiled for visa purposes in April 1959 for the United States consulate in Munich, to which we will refer as a brief autobiography, Stepan emphasized that events relating to the attempt to establish a Ukrainian state—and the lost war against the Poles, which followed—had a substantial impact on him.[3] In addition to his patriotic and religious upbringing, these factors might have resulted in his enduring compulsion to continue the interrupted struggle for a Ukrainian state, in which his father had engaged and for which he had been persecuted by the Polish authorities after the First World War.

Stepan did not attend a primary school, because the teacher in Staryi Uhryniv was drafted into the army in 1914. He and his siblings were taught at home by their parents. Between 1919 and 1927, he attended a Ukrainian high school in the town of Stryi, about eighty kilometers from Staryi Uhryniv, living at his grandfather's. While

1 Petro Arsenych and Taras Fedoriv, *Rodyna Banderiv: Do 90-richchia vid dnia narodzhennia ta 40-richchia trahichnoï smerti providnyka OUN Stepana Bandery (1909–1959)* (Ivano-Frankivs'k: Nova Zoria, 1998), 5, 7, 10–11, 18–20. It is not clear exactly when and under which circumstances Bohdan died. He was most likely killed between 1941 and 1944.

2 Arsenych, *Rodyna Banderiv,* 7; Bandera, Moï zhyttiepysni dani, 2.

3 Bandera, Moï zhyttiepysni dani, 1–2.

Fig. 2. Bandera as a high school pupil. Poltava, Zhyttia Stepana Bandery, 13.

at high school, Bandera was actively engaged in a number of youth organizations, to which Ukrainian patriotic education was displaced after the Polish authorities restricted it in Ukrainian schools. Two of these associations were Plast, a scouting organization, and Sokil, an athletic youth organization. In Plast, Bandera was in the Chervona kalyna (Guelder Rose) troop together with people such as Okhrymovych, who would invite him a few years later to engage in the OUN. Bandera stayed in Plast until September 1930, when the Polish authorities banned the organization in Galicia, two years after prohibiting it in Volhynia. During his time at high school, Bandera was also involved in the OVKUH, which, as explained in chapter 1, included in its membership a number of other future leading OUN members, such as Shukhevych, Lenkavs'kyi, and Stets'ko. After graduating from high school, the OVKUH members met again in the SUNM. Both the SUNM and the OVKUH took care of "patriotic upbringing" in Plast, Sokil, and also Luh. The latter was a gymnastic and fire-fighting organization, which, as the result of nationalist indoctrination, occasionally refused to put out a blaze in non-Ukrainian houses. In 1927 Bandera also joined the UVO, for which he performed reconnaissance work.[4]

4 Bandera, Moï zhyttiepysni dani, 3. For the OVKUH and the SUNM, see Mirchuk, *Narys istoriï OUN*, 49–50; Golczewski, *Deutsche und Ukrainer*, 552–53; "Proces o zamordowanie ... Płast i Łuch," *Gazeta Polska*, 17 December 1935, 6. For Okhrymovych in *Chervona kalyna*, see Posivnych, *Stepan Bandera—zhyttia, prysviachene svobodi*, 17. On Bandera in the SUNM, see Mirchuk, *Stepan*, 16. For Plast, see Wysocki, *Organizacja*, 133. For Bandera joining the UVO, see Paul Stepan Pirie, "Unraveling the Banner: A Biographical Study of Stepan Bandera," MA thesis, University of Alberta, 1993, 23; Bandera, Moï zhyttiepysni dani, 5–6.

Fig. 3. Bandera as a student. Posivnych, *Stepan Bandera: Dokumenty i materialy*, 107.

Bandera sang in a choir in Kalush. His friend Mykola Klymyshyn—from the village of Mostyshche, not far from Staryi Uhryniv—often stayed next to him during rehearsals, because Bandera was adept at reading music and had a very good ear. Mykola Klymyshyn's brother, who once visited the Bandera family, told him that they sang together at home, accompanied by one of Bandera's sisters at the piano.[5] In addition to singing in a choir, Bandera also played the guitar and mandolin. In his brief autobiography, he wrote that his favorite sports included hiking, jogging, swimming, ice skating, and basketball. He also mentioned that he liked to play chess in his free time, and he emphasized that he neither smoke nor drank.[6]

After graduating from high school in 1927, Bandera planned to attend the Ukrainian Husbandry Academy in Poděbrady in Czechoslovakia, but did not do so, either because he did not get a passport, as he stated in his brief autobiography, or because the Academy in Poděbrady informed him that it was closed, as he stated during an interrogation on 26 June 1936.[7] Bandera therefore applied to study at the Agricultural and Forestry Department of the Lviv Polytechnic and its branch in Dubliany, near Lviv, the former Agricultural Academy of Dubliany.[8] He began his studies in Lviv in September 1928,

4 Pirie, *Unraveling the Banner*, 23; Bandera, Moï zhyttiepysni dani, 5–6.

5 Klymyshyn, *V pokhodi*, 1:108.

6 Bandera, Moï zhyttiepysni dani, 5.

7 Bandera, Moï zhyttiepysni dani, 4; Interrogation of Stepan Bandera, 27 September 1934, TsDIAL, f. 371, op. 1, spr. 8, ed. 76, 35–36.

8 For Bandera at the agricultural academy in Dubliany, see Iurii Tokars'kyi, *Dubliany: Istoriia ahrarnykh studii 1856–1946* (Lviv: Instytut Ukraïnoznavstva im. I. Kryp"iakevycha, 1996), 312.

but never completed them, because of his involvement in the OUN, which he officially joined in February 1929. During the academic years 1928–1929 and 1929–1930, Bandera lived in private apartments in Lviv with Osyp Tiushka, Iurii Levyts'kyi, and other colleagues, and also at the Ukrainian Student House in Supińskiego Street (Mykhaila Kotsiubyns'koho Street), the center of OUN activism in Lviv.[9] In the academic year 1930–1931, Bandera lived in Dubliany, first in a private house and then at the student residence of the Agricultural Academy. In February 1932 he moved to Lviv again and lived together with Stets'ko in lodgings in Lwowskich Dzieci Street (Turhenieva Street) until he was arrested in March 1932. After his release from prison in June, Bandera returned to his father in Staryi Uhryniv. As a result of his arrest, he lost one academic year at the university. In October 1932 he moved back to Lviv. He lodged with different people until March 1934 when he moved back to the Ukrainian Student House, in which he shared room number 56 with Ivan Ravlyk, until Bandera was arrested on 14 June 1934. During his university life in Lviv, Bandera frequently went back to his family in Staryi Uhryniv for vacations.[10] Studying was not Bandera's main concern, as he stated in his brief autobiography:

> I invested most of my time and energy during my student years in revolutionary national-liberation activities. They captivated me more and more and pushed the completion of my studies into second place.[11]

As indicated in chapter 1, Bandera was arrested several times for nationalist activism in the late 1920s and early 1930s. The first occasion was on 14 November 1928, ten days after he and his father conducted a tenth anniversary celebration of the proclamation of the ZUNR, in the village of Berezhnytsia Shliakhets'ka. The Polish authorities regarded this event as subversive propaganda, and illegal. During the commemoration, Andrii Bandera conducted divine service at the graves of Ukrainian soldiers, during which, according to Arsenych, he described the Poles as "temporary occupiers who oppress Ukrainians and therefore should be promptly expelled from the mother territories."[12] He also reminded the participants about Ukrainians who had fallen in the struggle for a Ukrainian state, and those who were suffering in Polish prisons because of their involvement in the struggle for national liberation. During this service, Stepan Bandera distributed leaflets with content similar to his father's speech. The next time Andrii and Stepan Bandera were arrested together was in 1930. In 1932–1933 Stepan Bandera was arrested six times for matters such as an illegal crossing of the Polish-Czechoslovak border, smuggling illegal OUN journals to Poland, meeting with OUN members from the leadership in exile, and in connection with the killing of Constable Omelian Czechowski, who led an investigation against the OUN. The longest period Bandera spent in prison at that time was three months from March to June 1932, after Iurii Berezyns'kyi killed Czechowski.[13]

9 Interrogation of Stepan Bandera, 27 September 1934, TsDIAL, f. 371, op. 1, spr. 8, ed. 76, 34.

10 Interrogation of Stepan Bandera, 26 September 1934 and 10 January 1935, TsDIAL, f. 371, op. 1, spr. 8, ed. 76, 33–34, 36, 48.

11 Bandera, Moï zhyttiepysni dani, 5.

12 Arsenych, *Rodyna Banderiv*, 7.

13 Arsenych, *Rodyna Banderiv*, 7–8; Posivnych, Providnyk OUN, 18–19; Żeleński, *Akt oskarżenia*, 81–82; Golczewski, *Deutsche und Ukrainer*, 565.

Fig. 4. Bandera in a folkloristic Cossack costume. Poltava, *Zhyttia Stepana Bandery,* 8.

Bandera seems to have been a fanatical nationalist in his early adolescence. As a teenager he was said to have slid pins under his nails in order to harden himself for future torture by Polish prosecutors. He was said to have done this to himself in response to a story about the famous female nationalist Basarab who, according to the heroic victimization narrative, had hanged herself in a prison cell, in order not to reveal UVO secrets while being tortured by Polish interrogators. As a university student, Bandera was reported to have continued torturing himself, by scorching his fingers on an oil lamp and by crushing them between a door and doorframe. During the self-torturing sessions, he told himself: "Admit Stepan!" and answered "No, I don't admit!" Bandera also beat his bare back with a belt and said to himself, "If you don't improve, you'll be beaten again, Stepan!"[14]

In his youth, according to his close friend Hryhor Mel'nyk, Bandera felt contempt for fellow-students who were not involved in the nationalist movement. Bandera demonstrated this once in public, when he met a colleague who had previously remarked that he did not support any political camp. While this person was shaking hands with other colleagues, Bandera refused to greet him, turning away and leaving his hands

14 For sliding pins under nails, see Ivan Kul'chyts'kyi, "Zamolodu hotuvavsia do naivazhchykh vyprobuvan,'" in *Stepan Bandera*, ed. Posivnych, 2006, 52–53. For the self-torture observed by his roommate in Dubliany, see Roman Rudnyts'kyi, "Tak hartuvavsia Vin," *The Way to Victory*, 7 January 1960, 3. Another roommate of Stepan Bandera in Dubliany, Hryhor Mel'nyk, did not mention in his memoirs that Bandera tortured himself. Cf. Hryhor Mel'nyk, "Stepan Bandera: Prychynky do kharakterystyky osoby," in *Spomyny ta rozdumy*, ed. Volodymyr Makar (Toronto-Kiev: Afisha, 2001), 3:122–24.

in his pockets. He was, however, very friendly with colleagues who fulfilled his political expectations. Those who worked with him in the OUN praised his humor, determination, organizational abilities, oratory, and a disposition to sing.[15] Klymyshyn commented on Bandera's behavior in his memoirs:

> During our meetings Bandera behaved in two ways. When we discussed organizational matters he talked very seriously, factually, and earnestly. But when the discussion about organizational matters was finished, he became cheerful, talkative, and humorous, and he liked [it] if his interlocutor behaved similarly. He could very [easily] twist or split a word and pronounce it in such a way that it became a funny pun.[16]

Another friend of Bandera's, Volodymyr Ianiv, remembered him walking in the Carpathian Mountains, talking to birds and praying to trees. Ianiv considered it amusing behavior and a sign of Bandera's love and respect for nature.[17] Hryhor Mel'nyk mentioned in his memoirs that, during a hike with Plast, Bandera put on a blanket and climbed up a tree. From the tree, he then delivered a fiery speech with "exotic" gestures, pretending to be Mohandas K. Gandhi. Another young nationalist, Lev Senyshyn, climbed behind Bandera onto the same tree and pretended to be a gorilla, eating its own fleas. He also threw some of them on "Gandhi." Other Plast members found the conduct of the two scouts very amusing.[18]

Fig. 5. Bandera in the Plast uniform, first on the right. Poltava, *Zhyttia Stepana Bandery*, 9.

15 Mel'nyk, Stepan Bandera, 117–19; Klymyshyn, *V pokhodi*, 1:112–13.
16 Klymyshyn, *V pokhodi*, 1:112.
17 Volodymyr Ianiv, "Zustrich z polk. Ievhenom Konoval'tsem na tli nastroïv doby," in *Ievhen Konovalets'*, ed. Boïko, 453.
18 Mel'nyk, Stepan Bandera, 120.

In his youth, Bandera was small and slim. In photographs from his high school years and university time, Bandera appears to be a head shorter than the majority of his colleagues. As an adolescent, he was 1.60 m (5'3") in height and usually had a short haircut. With the exception of his rather small size, Bandera possessed an unremarkable physique and physiognomy. He was left-handed and had blue eyes. In his adult years he was partly bald, and his face was slightly oval. By the age of twenty-one, he already lacked three teeth, and four by the age of twenty-seven. His most popular nickname was *baba* (woman), either because he was broad in the beam, or because he went through Lviv dressed as a woman, when on undercover duty for the OUN. Among his other aliases were: *lys* (fox), *malyi* (the little), *siryi* (grey), and Stepanko (little Stepan). As a child, Bandera had suffered from rheumatism of the knee joint, after which he could not walk at times, causing him to join the Plast two years late, by when he was able to attempt it.[19] Hryhor Mel'nyk wrote in his memoirs that Bandera looked very ordinary and inconspicuous and that he behaved like a typical student. Nobody seeing him would therefore guess that he was the leader of the homeland executive of the OUN.[20]

During the late 1920s and early 1930s Rebet noticed that Bandera had "an organizational knack and a realistic approach to matters that distinguished him from the general young and romantic environment of the OUN."[21] Mel'nyk remembered Bandera as a very devoted nationalist, concerned about other OUN members and the welfare of the organization.[22] If anybody, however, disappointed Bandera—particularly someone from the OUN—he became angry or irritable. On trial in Warsaw in 1935–1936 he raged and lost control of himself when some OUN members decided to testify in Polish.[23] Bandera also "became mad" and had to take a tranquilizer to calm down, when he learned that Hryhorii Matseiko, before leaving for Warsaw to assassinate Pieracki, had left a note for his relatives, informing them that he was going on a trip from which he would not return.[24]

Bandera's physical attributes were scarcely charismatic. However this did not deter the Ukrainian "charismatic community" from assigning charisma to him as early as the 1930s. His skills as an orator, his unpredictable temper, his fanatical determination and devotion to the "holy nationalist matter" no doubt contributed to the process of charismatization. Lev Shankovs'kyi remembered Bandera as a "student and dogged

19 For physiognomy and problems with knees, see Stepan Mudryk-Mechnyk *Spohad pro Stepana Banderu* (Lviv: Halyts'ka Vydavnycha Spilka, 1999), 27; Posivnych, Providnyk OUN, 13. For left-handedness, see "Chief of Base, Munich to Chief, Sr., 12 November 1959," NARA, RG 263, E ZZ-18, Stepan Bandera Name File, 2, 2v. For teeth, see Bogdan Cybulski, "Stepan Bandera w więzieniach II Rzeczypospolitej i próby uwolnienia go przez OUN," *Acta Universitatis Wratislaviensis* 1033 (1989): 78. For Bandera's height, see "Record of Bandera's post-mortem examination, 16 October 1959," Bayerisches Hauptstaatsarchiv (BayHStA), Landeskriminalamt 272. For height, teeth and eyes, see "Dovidka pro utrymannia Stepana Bandery v Stanislavivs'kii tiurmi, 22–28.12.1928," in *Zhyttia i diial'nist'*, ed. Posivnych, 2011, 264. The alias *baba* and Bandera's broad beam were reported to me by Irena Kozak in an interview on 16 February 2008 in Munich. For walking through Lviv dressed as a woman, see Roman Rudnyts'kyi, "Tak hartuvavsia Vin," *The Way to Victory*, 7 January 1960, 3.

20 Mel'nyk, Stepan Bandera, 128.

21 Rebet, *Svitla i tini OUN*, 59.

22 Mel'nyk, Stepan Bandera, 126.

23 See chapter 3 below.

24 Interrogation of Bohdan Pidhainyi, 27 December 1934, TsDIAL, f. 371, op. 1, spr. 8, ed. 77, 63–64; "Proces o zamordowanie ... Grzegorza Maciejko," *Gazeta Polska*, 31 December 1935, 8.

Fig. 6. 1929. Members of the Plast troop *Chervona kalyna*. Bandera third to the right. Poltava, *Zhyttia Stepana Bandery,* 15.

nationalist" who, "already in the beginning of his young years, his formative years, which he devoted totally to the matter, presented all the character traits that raised him to the post of the leader of Ukrainian nationalism."[25] Prison chaplain Osyp Kladochnyi, who confessed Bandera during his imprisonment, characterized Bandera as the *Übermensch*, or the Ukrainian superhuman. He wrote, "From him [Bandera] radiated the strength of willpower and the determination to get his own way. If there is an Übermensch [superhuman] then he was actually such a rare type of man—Übermensch, and he was the man who placed Ukraine above all."[26] Looking back on Bandera, Hryhor Mel'nyk commented:

> We, his closest comrades-in-arms, had much more opportunity to feel the greatness of an extraordinary personality—our Leader [*Providnyk*]—and to be proud of him. For us it was the model of a certain pattern of people with great character, of people who decided the historical deeds of their nations. Such people have already appeared in previous epochs of our history, in critical moments for the existence of the nation. In our times [they] were—Banderas, Kolodzins'kyis, Shukhevychs, Hasyns, Kossaks, Hrytsaïs, and many others. Using their brilliant model, exemplary character, braveness, persistence, agility, and sacrifice of their entire lives, they brought up whole generations of fighters, who went with and behind them to fight for their nation and, if it was necessary, accepted pain and sorrow for Ukraine's liberty and for her honor and glory.[27]

25 "Lyst Leva Shankovs'koho do Oracha [Iaroslava Stets'ka] vid 2.11.1959 r.," quoted in Posivnych, Providnyk OUN, 18.

26 Petro Shkarbiuk, *Vynohradnyk Hospodnii: Istoriia zhyttia o. d-ra Iosypa Kladochnoho* (Lviv: Instytut ukraïnoznastva im. I. Krypiakevycha PAN, 1995), 69, quoted in Posivnych, Providnyk OUN, 40.

27 Mel'nyk, Stepan Bandera, 133.

Career in the OUN

After joining the OUN in 1929 Bandera rapidly rose through the ranks. This happened partly because of his organizational and conspiratorial abilities and partly because of the change of generations in the OUN. His friendship with those members of the OVKUH and SUNM who were rising in the ranks of the OUN, in particular Okhrymovych, helped Bandera on the road to promotion. In 1930 Bandera headed the section of the propaganda apparatus of the homeland executive of the OUN that was responsible for the distribution of illegal publications in eastern Galicia. In 1931 he took over a section that imported them from abroad, mainly from Czechoslovakia and Gdańsk. In the same year he became director of the propaganda apparatus of the homeland executive. This position was proposed to him by Okhrymovych, head of the homeland executive and his schoolmate from Stryi. Okhrymovych died in 1931 after his release from prison where, according to the OUN, he was tortured. Okhrymovych's successor, Ivan Habrusevych, fled from Poland to Germany because the police were looking for him. Habrusevych proposed to nominate Bandera as his successor but the latter could not accept the position because he was in prison from the end of March until June 1932. After his release, however, Bandera became deputy leader of the homeland executive. From January 1933 he was de facto leader of the homeland executive, although he was not officially appointed to this position until a conference in Berlin from 3 to 6 June 1933. Bandera succeeded Bohdan Kordiuk, who had to give up his post because he was responsible for the failure of the post-office robbery in Horodok Iahailons'kyi on 30 November 1932, as the result of which Bilas and Danylyshyn were executed.[28]

In the act of indictment presented in the Warsaw trial after Pieracki's assassination, the prosecutor Żeleński wrote that, according to OUN member Roman Myhal', Bandera became the leader of the homeland executive through a coup. He radicalized the OUN and changed its attitude to terror, making the UVO a superfluous organization that soon disappeared. He also removed many people from leading positions and demanded from local branches of the OUN that they submit to him the names of people who were capable of carrying out terrorist acts.[29] According to Iaroslav Makarushka, training in the OUN changed after Bandera became the leader of the homeland executive; every person who joined the OUN was obliged to attend military, ideological, and conspiracy courses. OUN members who had attended military courses in Gdańsk (Danzig) and Berlin passed on their knowledge to other members during military courses in eastern Galicia.[30]

According to Żeleński and the OUN member Pidhainyi, Bandera received an order from the leadership in exile to organize new "combat deeds," which might have included the assassinations of Pieracki, Babii, and others. When Bandera organized these "combat deeds" he assumed that the Polish authorities would respond by opening concentration camps for Ukrainians. In order to avoid mass arrests, the homeland

28 Interrogation of Stepan Bandera, 27 September 1934, TsDIAL, f. 371, op. 1, spr. 8, ed. 76, 36; Ianiv, "Zustrich z polk. Ievhenom," 459, 461; Wysocki, *Organizacja*, 247–49; Bandera, Moï zhyttiepysni dani, 6; Mirchuk, *Stepan Bandera*, 22; Żeleński, *Akt oskarżenia*, 81, 97; Mirchuk, *Narys istoriï OUN*, 248–49.

29 Żeleński, *Akt oskarżenia*, 81–82.

30 Interrogation of Iaroslav Makarushka, 21 January 1935, TsDIAL, f. 371, op. 1, spr. 8, ed. 76, 142.

executive planned to send the Ukrainian youth into the forests, where they would organize a partisan movement and conduct an uprising or revolution.[31] During an investigation, Makarushka also stated that in February 1934 the homeland executive considered ordering Ukrainians who had been spotted by the Polish intelligence service, or who might be sent to concentration camps because of terrorist activities, to hide in the forests and organize a partisan movement or "green cadres" that would fight against the Polish state.[32] According to Pidhainyi, Bandera argued that it was "better to die from a bullet than behind wires in a concentration camp."[33]

The OUN became more radical and more "effective" after Bandera took over the leading posts. After he became the propaganda director of the homeland executive, the number and size of mass propaganda campaigns grew and the number of terrorist acts increased. However, these increases can be explained only to some extent by Bandera's determination, leadership abilities, and strength of character. Additional factors to be considered are the role of other fanatical nationalists from the Bandera generation, and Bandera's formal subordination to the leadership in exile.[34]

Because of the limitations of documentary evidence, and the fact that the OUN used conspiratorial methods, not every killing ordered by Bandera and not every detail concerning Bandera's role in the assassinations can be clarified. Nevertheless, it is known that Bandera himself chose assassins from among potential candidates, carried out the detailed preparations for some assassinations, and occasionally decided who would be assassinated.[35] There is documentary evidence that Bandera induced Matseiko to kill Pieracki, and Lemyk to kill the Soviet consul, and that Bandera ordered the killing of Bachyns'kyi and Ivan Babii. It was also Bandera who gave orders to prepare the assassinations of editor Antin Krushel'nyts'kyi; Henryk Józewski; the inspector of the prison guards in Lviv, Władysław Kossobudzki; the education welfare officer Stanisław Gadomski; and a pupil of the seventh grade of the Ukrainian high school, Korolyshyn—although none of these was carried out, due to organizational problems.[36] Bandera also ordered that Stakhiv, editor of the Ukrainian newspapers *Pratsia* and *Rada*, be beaten. When this plan did not work, he ordered that a bomb be left in the newspapers' editorial offices.[37] In addition Bandera gave poison to OUN members who were to carry out assassinations and instructed them to kill themselves if they were arrested.[38] When OUN members who were ordered to

31 Żeleński, *Akt oskarżenia*, 32; Interrogation of Bohdan Pidhainyi, 27 December 1934, TsDIAL, f. 371, op. 1, spr. 8, ed. 77, 60.

32 Interrogation of Iaroslav Makarushka, 21 January 1935, TsDIAL, f. 371, op. 1, spr. 8, ed. 76, 141–42; Mirchuk, *Narys istorii OUN*, 252; Żeleński, *Akt oskarżenia*, 80.

33 Interrogation of Bohdan Pidhainyi, 27 December 1934, TsDIAL, f. 371, op. 1, spr. 8, ed. 77, 60.

34 "Rozprava za ... Prokurator pro roliu Bandery," *Dilo*, 2 January 1935, 3.

35 According to a survey carried out by Bandera, 75 percent of OUN members who were questioned were ready to conduct an act of assassination. Cf. Żeleński, *Akt oskarżenia*, 84. For Bandera's agency in the homeland executive in terms of terrorist acts and assassinations, see: "Proces o zamordowanie ... Ustrój O.U.N.," *Gazeta Polska*, 4 December 1935, 6. For Bandera's obligations and responsibilities toward the leadership in exile, see "Sprawozdanie stenograficzne procesu Bandery," TsDIAL, f. 371, op. 1, spr. 8, ed. 75, 96.

36 "Wyrok," TsDIAL, f. 205, spr. 3125, 60; Interrogation of Bohdan Pidhainyi, 29 December 1934, TsDIAL, f. 371, op. 1, spr. 8, ed. 77, 76.

37 Interrogation of Bohdan Pidhainyi, 28 December 1934, TsDIAL, f. 371, op. 1, spr. 8, ed. 77, 69–70; Żeleński, *Akt oskarżenia*, 2, 83–91.

38 Interrogation of Bohdan Pidhainyi, 28 December 1934, TsDIAL, f. 371, op. 1, spr. 8, ed. 77, 72; Żeleński, *Akt oskarżenia*, 89.

kill other Ukrainians, including OUN members, expressed their objections, Bandera insisted that these murders should be carried out because he believed that the Ukrainians to be assassinated were "traitors" or "informers."[39]

When analyzing Bandera's role, we should keep in mind, however, that he acted within the framework of an organization and that his conduct was therefore influenced both by his superiors and by other members. In his speech on 26 June 1936 at the trial in Lviv, Bandera clarified that he personally, without consulting other authorities, ordered the killing of Pieracki, Józewski, and Kossobudzki. He stated however that decisions to kill Ukrainians were made by the "revolutionary tribunal."[40] According to OUN member Maliutsa, Konovalets' was concerned about "some of the methods" used by the homeland executive, although we do not know whether he was referring to the assassinations of Polish politicians or to Ukrainians accused of "betrayal."[41] Prosecutor Żeleński, who investigated Pieracki's assassination, came to the conclusion that it had been "decided and organized" by the leadership in exile, to improve the financial situation of the organization.[42] As a source for this information, Żeleński quoted a document from the Senyk archives, which did not survive the Second World War.[43] Żeleński's deduction might have been motivated, wholly or in part, by the wish to capture Konovalets' and other OUN leaders living outside Poland, which the Polish authorities could not achieve without the help of other states. However, a more plausible theory would be that Pieracki's assassination was planned by both the homeland executive and the leadership in exile, and that Bandera's and also Lebed's roles in this deed were significant.[44]

Because the OUN was already composed of many extreme elements when Bandera became the leader of the homeland executive, there might have been a reciprocal process of radicalization between Bandera and such zealous nationalists as Shukhevych, Lenkavs'kyi, Lebed', and Stets'ko, who all came into the homeland executive at about the same time as Bandera and had been with him in the OVKUH and the SUNM. Spectacular murders or bank robberies had taken place before Bandera became the head of the homeland executive. In August 1931 for example, Bilas and Danylyshyn killed Tadeusz Hołówko. In March 1932 Shukhevych's brother-in-law, Berezyns'kyi, killed the Ukrainian policeman Czechowski.[45]

When Bandera was variously its propaganda director (1931–1933) and its leader (1933–1934), the homeland executive conducted a range of propaganda campaigns and terrorist acts. Shortly after he became the leader of the homeland executive, the *Bulletin of the Homeland Executive of the OUN in the Western Ukrainian Territories* claimed: "Terror acts against the most prominent representatives of the occupying

39 Interrogation of Bohdan Pidhainyi, 28 December 1934, TsDIAL, f. 371, op. 1, spr. 8, ed. 77, 72. On Bachyns'yki, see Interrogation of Roman Myhal', 21 December 1934, TsDIAL, f. 371, op. 1, spr. 8, ed. 76, 274–75, 283–84, 287–88.

40 "Sprawozdanie stenograficzne," 26 June 1936, TsDIAL, f. 371, op. 1, spr. 8, od. 75, 175–76.

41 "Proces. Maluca potępia działalność O.U.N.," *Gazeta Polska*, 4 December 1935, 6; "Nespodivanyi vystup Maliutsy. Trynatsiatyi den' rozpravy," *Novyi chas*, 5 December 1935, 4.

42 Żeleński, *Akt oskarżenia*, 96–100. See also "Proces o zamordowanie ś. p. ministra Br. Pierackiego," *Gazeta Polska*, 20 November 1935, 8; "Khto dav nakaz vykonaty atentat?," *Dilo*, 18 January 1936, 3–4; "Przedsiębiorstwo ludzkiej rzeźni. Dno Ohydy," *Gazeta Polska*, 3 January 1936, 7.

43 For the Senyk archives see page 131.

44 For Bandera's role in other assassinations, see "Sprawozdanie stenograficzne procesu Bandery," TsDIAL, f. 371, op. 1, spr. 8, ed. 75, 171–72, 175.

45 Golczewski, *Deutsche und Ukrainer*, 565.

power are the typical actions that hold [ideological] impact and political-propagandist capital. ... They steer the attention of the masses to the direct fight that brings closer the moment of the final uprising."[46]

The first propaganda operation by which the homeland executive succeeded in attracting the attention of the masses was the mourning for Bilas and Danylyshyn in late December 1932 and early 1933. At this time, Bandera occupied the position of propaganda director of the homeland executive; informally, he was also the head of the homeland executive after Kordiuk left eastern Galicia in January. As propaganda director, Bandera knew how to transform his dead fellows into powerful symbols, in order to propagate feelings of revenge and to strengthen the collective unity of Ukrainians. The rite of transforming dead nationalists into heroes and martyrs had existed before Bandera became the director of propaganda. Bandera's main contribution to this campaign, as well as to those that followed, was that he understood how to popularize the death of Bilas and Danylyshyn among the "Ukrainian masses" by means of the OUN propaganda apparatus.[47]

Another activity that took on a mass character while Bandera was leading the homeland executive was the raising of mourning mounds for fallen soldiers. This operation, in which the homeland executive tried to involve the "village masses," took place in autumn 1933 and spring 1934.[48] The commemoration of fallen soldiers had occurred before Bandera led the OUN, but only at actual burial sites. Under Bandera's leadership the homeland executive motivated the "Ukrainian masses" to build symbolic mounds even in places where no fallen soldiers were buried. Ukrainians were thereby able to commemorate their fallen soldiers in every place.[49]

A mound was usually built by villagers and sanctified by a priest. If the Polish authorities did not destroy it, the mound could later be used to conduct commemorative services for fallen Ukrainian soldiers or for organizing political demonstrations on 1 November, Pentecost, and other feast days. Such commemorations frequently began with a panakhyda. The Polish authorities tended to destroy the mounds as symbols of Ukrainian nationalism and as insubordination to the Polish state. Ukrainian villagers, armed mainly with hoes and pitchforks, would therefore protect the mounds. This caused casualties on both sides. During one of these ceremonies, in Trostianets' between 6 and 8 June 1934, the ringing of church bells informed the villagers that the police were coming. A thousand or more people assembled to protect the mound from the armed policemen. "This is Ukrainian soil!" the villagers shouted.[50]

After the police had demolished a mound, the local people would often rebuild it. The repetitive and widespread demolishing and rebuilding of burial mounds led to many clashes and to casualties on both sides. In autumn 1933 and spring 1934 the OUN stirred up the "Ukrainian masses" and coordinated the actions of building the mounds. The conflict surrounding them resembled a civil war in some regions of

46 Quoted in Mirchuk, *Narys istorii OUN*, 250.
47 Wysocki, *Organizacja*, 243; Mirchuk, *Stepan Bandera*, 21–22.
48 "Komunikat Nr. 7," AAN, MSZ syg. 5316, 65.
49 Mirchuk, *Narys istorii OUN*, 251.
50 "Komunikat Nr. 7," AAN, MSZ syg. 5316, 77.

eastern Galicia. In revenge, Ukrainians sometimes took the initiative and demolished the tombs and graves of Polish soldiers and policemen.[51]

Another propaganda operation organized in the summer of 1933, when Bandera was leading the homeland executive, used an anti-alcohol campaign by the organization Vidrodzhennia. The OUN provided the anti-alcohol campaign with an ideological dimension that it originally did not possess.[52] The aim was to mobilize Ukrainians not to buy spirits and tobacco, because they were produced by the Polish state. According to the OUN's logic, the Poles suppressed Ukrainians by maintaining a monopoly on spirits and tobacco. During this operation, OUN activists urged Ukrainians to publicly pledge that they would not drink alcohol or smoke cigarettes. Drinkers who could not resist buying alcohol were beaten up. Taverns were demolished, especially those owned by Jews, and antisemitic boycotts took place.[53]

The next mass action of the homeland executive, conducted simultaneously with the anti-alcohol campaign, was directed against the Polish school system. The OUN tried to convince Ukrainian pupils to refuse to use the Polish language during lectures, to destroy such signs of the Polish state as the Polish emblem or the portraits of Polish kings in schools, to smash windowpanes in school buildings, to destroy school library books that praised Poland, and to march through the village, chanting such slogans as "Away with Polish teachers!" (*Het' z uchyteliamy-liakhamy!*) When the teacher came into the classroom in the morning, a representative of the class was to deliver a speech, informing the teacher that "in the Ukrainian territories Ukrainian pupils should be taught by a Ukrainian teacher in the Ukrainian language about Ukraine." The other pupils would duly applaud. For the sake of this campaign the OUN produced 92,000 leaflets and 9,000 booklets and distributed them in the schools. An attempt by OUN member Severyn Mada to murder the education welfare officer Gadomski, on Bandera's order, was also a part of the anti-school campaign.[54]

Acts of opposition to the Polish schools took place more frequently after the reform of education in 1924, but like the building of mounds, they did not occur on a mass scale until June 1933.[55] It is important to bear in mind that Bandera and other members of the homeland executive had already learned, in their high-school days in the 1920s, how to remove the Polish emblem during a school assembly and how to interrupt a patriotic school celebration by throwing a bomb containing irritant gas.[56] Organizing the mass anti-school operation with a strong political character in the summer of 1933, they drew on their school experience and their activities in the OVKUH and SUNM.

On 22 October 1933 in another famous operation coordinated by Bandera with a strong propagandist background, OUN member Mykola Lemyk tried to kill the Soviet consul in Lviv. The act was organized as a protest against the famine in the Soviet

51 For demolition and rebuilding of grave mounds, see "Komunikat Nr. 7," AAN, MSZ, syg. 5316, 63–71; Wysocki, *Organizacja*, 237–39. For demolition of tombs of Polish soldiers and policemen, see Redlich, *Together and Apart*, 57.

52 Mirchuk, *Stepan Bandera*, 22.

53 "Het' z liats'kymy monopoliiamy!" *Surma* 67, No. 5 (1933): 5; Bandera, Moï zhyttiepysni dani, 6–7; Mirchuk, *Narys istoriï OUN*, 257–58; Golczewski, *Deutsche und Ukrainer*, 633–34. For the pledge not to drink and smoke, see "Raport dzienny Nr. 43 z dn. 16.11.1933 r.," DALO f. 121, op. 3, spr., 75.

54 Mirchuk, *Narys istoriï OUN*, 254–56; "Komunikat Nr. 7," AAN, MSZ, syg. 5316, 56; Żeleński, *Akt oskarzenia*, 54–55; "Rozprava za ... Prokurator pro roliu Bandery," *Dilo*, 2 January 1935, 3.

55 Mirchuk, *Stepan Bandera*, 21.

56 Ibid., 12.

Ukraine. According to Pidhainyi, the OUN attempted this because it wanted to outpace the UNDO, which was planning a legal protest against the famine.[57] Bandera's role in the action was significant. He chose the assassin, explained to him the nature of the assignment, gave him a gun, and even gave him money in advance to buy new shoes and clothing for the trial that would follow the assassination. At the consulate, Lemyk confused the consul with Aleksei Mailov, the secretary of the consulate who received him, and whom Lemyk shot dead. After killing Mailov, Lemyk tried to escape and, in the process, wounded the custodian Jan Dżugai.[58]

The murder of the secretary of the consulate was enough for the OUN to celebrate a moral victory and for Lemyk to receive a life sentence.[59] Although the Polish authorities did not allow the trial to be turned into an anti-Soviet demonstration, the OUN used both the killing and the trial for propaganda purposes. Bandera had met with Konovalets' several times in 1933, and it might have been Konovalets' who urged him to organize this operation. According to his sister Volodymyra, Bandera was also motivated by relatives who had escaped from the famine to Staryi Uhryniv.[60] In another anti-Soviet operation, a bomb was left in the editorial office of the newspaper *Pratsia* on 12 May 1934 by Kateryna Zaryts'ka, not only because of the communist profile of the newspaper but also as a protest against the famine in Soviet Ukraine.[61]

Worldview

Matters that could have cast a poor light on Stepan Bandera seem to have been "forgotten" or never written down by his comrades-in-arms and admirers, and some relevant documents may have been purged or hidden. This conduct seems to be related to the larger process of collective amnesia concerning the darker side of the OUN and UPA on the part of veterans of this movement. In order to make some observations about Bandera's personality and his worldview, we need to analyze the groups, institutions, and ideologies that shaped him in his formative years, and to describe the ideological atmosphere of Bandera's youth.

As previously mentioned, Bandera grew up in a religious and patriotic family. His worldview and interests were first molded by his father, Andrii Bandera, a Greek Catholic priest who tried to combine the ideology of Ukrainian nationalism with the Greek Catholic religion.[62] OUN member Lev Shankovs'kyi characterized Andrii as the "true revolutionary who passed to his Son [*sic*] his entire passionate love to the Ukrainian nation and the question of its liberation."[63] After the primary school in Staryi Uhryniv was closed in 1914, Andrii provided Stepan with a primary education.[64] Religion was

57 Żeleński, *Akt oskarżenia*, 83.
58 Ibid., 83.
59 Żeleński, *Akt oskarżenia*, 84; Volodymyr Makar, "Postril v oboroni mil'ioniv," in *Spomyny ta rozdumy*, ed. Volodymyr Makar (Toronto-Kiev: Afisha, 2001), 2:258–59.
60 Mirchuk, *Narys istoriï OUN*, 258. For Volodymyra, see Pirie, *Unraveling the Banner*, 21. For meeting Konovalets', see Posivnych, Providnyk OUN, 24.
61 Posivnych, Providnyk OUN, 26.
62 Mirchuk, *Stepan Bandera*, 7.
63 "Lyst Leva Shankovs'koho do Oracha [Iaroslava Stets'ka] vid 2.11.1959 r.," quoted in Posivnych, Providnyk OUN, 18.
64 Pirie, *Unraveling the Banner*, 16–17; Bandera, Moï zhyttiepysni dani, 3.

for Stepan an important value but, unlike for his father, it was not more important than nationalism. During his student years, when Stepan once visited the family at Christmas, his father became angry with him because Stepan's friends came up to him in church and he left the service before it had ended. In reaction to his father's fury, Bandera answered: "First the nation, and then God!"[65] Nevertheless, the nation and God were blurred in Bandera's mind. Looking back in 1954, Bandera wrote about nationalism and religion:

> Without a doubt, the Ukrainian nationalist liberating-revolutionary movement, as directed and formed by the OUN, is a Christian movement. Its deepest roots are Christian and not merely not contradictory to Christianity. In terms of worldview, Ukrainian nationalism considers spirituality and the worldview of the Ukrainian nation as its springs. And this spirituality and worldview are very Christian as they were shaped under the thousand-year-long influence of the Christian religion.[66]

The element of religion was integrated into the political activities that Bandera organized together with his father, and later in the SUNM with other young Galician Ukrainians. Similarly, some events that Bandera coordinated, while he was propaganda director in the homeland executive, combined nationalism with religion. Priests were involved in ceremonies organized by the SUNM, and later by the homeland executive of the OUN. During the commemorations on the burial mounds for the fallen soldiers, priests were expected to conduct a panakhyda and to provide the ceremony with an aura of holiness. They were thereby involved in the process of sanctifying the ideological motives of the organizers. As already explained, after the execution of Bilas and Danylyshyn, Bandera's propaganda apparatus organized numerous services for these two executed young revolutionaries. The OUN needed the Greek Catholic Church in order to transform the dead nationalists into heroes and martyrs.

As a boy, Bandera was also influenced by the First World War, the subsequent Polish-Ukrainian war, and especially by the attempts to establish a Ukrainian state. The Austrian-Russian front divided Staryi Uhryniv for two weeks, as a result of which the Bandera house was partially destroyed. In 1936 Bandera stated that although he was only eight years old at that time, he understood that Ukrainians were on both sides of the front and had to fight against each other.[67] He also saw his father take an active part in the struggle for a Ukrainian state and was aware of his father's attempt to assert the power of the ZUNR in the Kalush region in 1918 with the help of armed Ukrainians who even stayed for some time in the family's backyard, before they left for Kalush.[68] In his short autobiography of 1959, Bandera recalled that he was especially influenced by the "celebrations and the spirituality due to the merging of the ZUNR with the UNR into one state in January 1919," which in fact was only a symbolic act without any political impact.[69] As the Polish army expelled the Ukrainian army into the east, Bandera's father left Kalush with the army for several months. After his return,

65 Pirie, *Unraveling the Banner*, 20.
66 Stepan Bandera, "Proty fal'shuvannia vyzvol'nykh pozytsii," in *Perspektyvy ukraïns'koï revoliutsiï*, ed. Vasyl' Ivanyshyn (Drohobych: Vidrodzhennia, 1999), 323–24.
67 "Sprawozdanie stenograficzne procesu Bandery," 5 June 1936, TsDIAL, f. 371, op. 1, spr. 8, ed. 75, 97.
68 Ibid., 97.
69 Bandera, Moï zhyttiepysni dani, 2; Golczewski, *Deutsche und Ukrainer*, 383–84.

Andrii Bandera's accounts of the war also made a powerful impact on young Stepan.[70]

In his youth Bandera accepted only radical parties, respected only radical nationalists, and rejected all streams that were leftist, democratic, or moderately national. Hryhor Mel'nyk reported on Bandera's contempt for the national-democratic UNDO and on his antisemitic perception of this party. Around 1924, according to Mel'nyk, when Bandera was only about sixteen, he viewed the UNDO as a party "with Jews" or "Grimbavm's party." It was a party to be combated because it worked against Ukrainian radical nationalism, which was for Bandera the only legitimate political movement. The term "Grimbavm's party" was derived from the Jewish politician Izaak Grünbaum who, in 1922, founded the Bloc of National Minorities (*Blok Mniejszości Narodowych*, *Blok fon Nashonal Minorities*, *Blok Natsional'nykh Menshyn*, or *Block der Nationalen Minderheiten*, BMN), a political party representing a coalition of various ethnic minorities living in the Second Polish Republic. The UNDO joined the BMN in 1927.[71]

Bandera's bias in favor of nationalism and the "traditional antisemitism" came from his environment, his family, and the tension inherent in Polish-Ukrainian relations during his formative years. Bandera seems to have perceived the world in bipolar or black-and-white nationalist categories as early as his high school years. His fascination with fascism as a set of ideas began either when he was in high school, joined the OVKUH, and studied Dontsov; or during his student years when he joined the OUN. Dontsov, and OUN ideologists such as Onats'kyi, familiarized the young Ukrainian nationalists in eastern Galicia with the concept of the leader, the party, and the masses. These ideologists inspired the Bandera generation to admire Mussolini and Hitler and to hate communism, Marxism, Jews, and democracy.[72]

Strongly identifying himself with the nationalist interpretation of the history of the Ukrainian people, Bandera no doubt understood himself in his high school years to be a member of a nation that had been occupied, exploited, and oppressed for centuries, mainly by Jews, Poles, and Russians. Dontsov portrayed Russians and the Soviet Union as the main enemies of Ukraine. Bandera had almost no contact with Russian and other Soviet citizens, whom the Ukrainian nationalists frequently called "Muscovites." He knew them only as an abstract, demonized enemy. We cannot tell whether, in his youth, Bandera knew how different, especially in terms of culture and mentality, eastern Ukrainians were from Galician Ukrainians.

Other important enemies of the young Stepan Bandera were the Jews. Ukrainian nationalism based its attitude toward Jews on two streams. The first one was traditional Ukrainian antisemitism, which regarded Jews as agents of the Poles and as the exploiters of Ukrainians. According to this notion, Jews exploited Ukrainian peasants economically, addicted them to alcohol, and supported Polish and Russian rule in Ukraine. Traditional Ukrainian antisemitism manifested itself in such poems as Taras Shevchenko's "Haidamaky," in which Jews are the agents of Polish landowners, and the brigands who kill Jews are Ukrainian national heroes.[73]

70 "Sprawozdanie stenograficzne procesu Bandery," 5 June 1936, TsDIAL, f. 371, op. 1, spr. 8, ed. 75, 97.

71 Mel'nyk, Stepan Bandera, 119; Szumiło, *Ukraińska Reprezentacja*, 28–29, 44, 49.

72 The OVKUH, in which Bandera was active in the 1920s, encouraged Ukrainian pupils to read Dontsov, see Mirchuk, *Narys istorii OUN*, 49.

73 Golczewski, *Deutsche und Ukrainer*, 599.

Modern racial antisemitism was the second stream of antisemitism on which Ukrainian nationalism was based. According to this kind of antisemitism, race and not religion is the main identifying mark of the Jews. The racial component, for example in Martynets's brochure *The Jewish Problem in Ukraine*, entered Ukrainian nationalism in the 1930s.[74] Dontsov and the OUN periodicals *Surma* and *Rozbudova natsiï* also propagated the racial kind of antisemitism. In addition, Dontsov frequently linked Jews with Russian imperialism and communism. In so doing, he spread the stereotype of "Jewish Bolshevism" according to which Jews were pillars of the Soviet system. After the OUN-B split from the OUN in 1940 the young nationalists who were organized around Bandera demonstrated that they had internalized Dontsov's concept of antisemitism. In the booklet "Resolutions of the Second Great Assembly of the OUN," they repeated Dontsov's remarks about Jews as pillars of the Soviet Union, almost verbatim.[75]

Deeply embedded in Ukrainian nationalism, both types of antisemitism must have reached Bandera's consciousness in his youth. Either in his high school years in the 1920s or in his student life in the first half of the 1930s, the ideology of Ukrainian nationalism made Bandera aware of the "Jewish problem" in Ukraine, the different and alien nature of the Jewish race, and the intrinsic link between Jews and communism. After the Second World War and the Holocaust, both Bandera and his admirers were embarrassed by the vehement antisemitic component of their interwar political views and denied it systematically.[76]

The two main OUN journals, *Surma* and *Rozbudova natsiï*, also significantly influenced Bandera. *Surma* began appearing in 1927 in Berlin. In 1928 it moved to Kovno where it was printed by the Lithuanian government press. From 1928 *Rozbudova natsiï* was published in Prague. *Surma* was smuggled to Poland from Gdańsk by train, or from Berlin and Prague through the Polish-Czechoslovakian border. Both ceased to appear after the assassination of Pieracki in June 1934. The chief editor of *Rozbudova natsiï*, Martynets', stated that this paper was an "ideological-programmatic laboratory of the PUN." Articles for *Rozbudova natsiï* were discussed intensively before they were published. After publication they became doctrines that all OUN members were expected to accept.[77]

As a high-ranking OUN member, Bandera must have read every issue of *Surma* and *Rozbudova natsiï*, but it is not known whether he published his articles in these journals or in other journals that appeared clandestinely in Galicia, including *Biuleten' KE OUN na ZUZ*, *Iunatstvo*, and *Iunak*. In order to avoid repercussions, OUN members who lived in Poland published articles anonymously. Because *Surma* and *Rozbudova natsiï* were printed abroad, and the articles in them were usually written by older

74 Martynets', *Zhydivs'ka probliema*. For the racial antisemitism of Martynets', see page 80 et seq.

75 "Postanovy II. Velykoho Zboru Orhanizatstiï Ukraïns'kykh Natsionalistiv," TsDAHO f. 1, op. 23, spr. 926, 180–208. For the resolution about Jews as pillars of the Soviet Union see folios 192–93. For Dontsov's attitude to Russia, Jews, his understanding of antisemitism, and the use of these ideas by the OUN in 1941, the time of the "Ukrainian Revolution," see Golczewski, *Deutsche und Ukrainer*, 503–504.

76 On the attitude of the OUN to Jews in the interwar period, see Bruder, "*Den Ukrainischen Staat,* 99–101; Carynnyk, Foes of Our Rebirth, 315–25. On antisemitism and Ukrainian nationalists after 1945, see Rossoliński-Liebe, Erinnerungslücke Holocaust, 397–430 and also chapters 9 and 10 below.

77 Wysocki, *Organizacja*, 200–202.

nationalists, it is more likely that Bandera published articles only in journals that appeared in Galicia.[78]

In particular *Surma* and *Rozbudova natsiï* followed the trend of the European radical right and fascist movements. These periodicals frequently published articles propagating antisemitism, fascism, and the cult of war. They also justified ethnic and political violence, and terror conducted in the name of the nation. Other motifs appearing in these journals were the heroism of the Ukrainian nation, and the viciousness, immorality, and insidiousness of Ukraine's "occupiers" and "enemies."

In an article in *Rozbudova Natsiï* about the Jews and Ukrainians, Iurii Mylianych wrote that "in the Ukrainian territories live more than two million Jews who are an alien and many of them even a hostile element of the Ukrainian national organism." Mylianych defined this as a problem and complained that Ukrainian politicians were not preparing to deal with it. He insisted that this problem "*must* be solved," and clarified that the Jews were, in addition to the "occupiers," a further enemy of Ukrainians. According to Mylianych, the Ukrainian Jew always supported aggressors against Ukraine, whether such aggressors were Poles, Russians, Germans, or Bolsheviks.[79]

Surma and *Rozbudova natsiï* familiarized Bandera not only with the current debate about Jews and antisemitism but also about fascism. Articles published in these two journals make it clear that, in the late 1920s and early 1930s, the OUN was already adopting many patterns typical of fascist and far-right movements, although not all contributors to the OUN journals were certain whether Ukrainians could and should became fascists. The more cautious attitude to fascism was represented by authors like Oleksandr Mytsiuk, who emphasized the traditional elements of Ukrainian nationalism and the aspirations of the Ukrainian nationalists for autonomy and claimed that there could not be a Ukrainian fascism because Ukrainians did not have a state in which they could practice it. Mytsiuk also argued that fascism was an Italian phenomenon that could exist only there.[80]

Ievhen Onats'kyi, the OUN representative in Rome and a significant contributor to the OUN journals, developed a more open and more affirmative attitude to fascism. In his first articles about fascism in *Rozbudova natsiï* he argued, similarly to Mytsiuk, that Italian Fascism and Ukrainian nationalism had their radical nationalist nature in common but that they were not the same, because Italian Fascism had a state in which it could exist and the Ukrainian nationalist movement did not. He stated that "fascism is a nationalism of a nation state." He therefore argued that the Ukrainian nationalists needed to establish a state in order to become fascists.[81]

Some months later however, having further contemplated the nature of fascism, in the article "We and Fascism" Onats'kyi changed his understanding of the relationship between fascism and Ukrainian nationalism. He ceased to emphasize that fascism was a political system that could only exist in a state and pointed out the unifying and revolutionary features of fascism. He also drew a parallel between Italy and Ukraine, implying that a country in crisis needed a group of brave and powerful men, like the

78 Mirchuk, *Stepan Bandera*, 16–18.

79 Iurii Mylianych, "Zhydy, sionizm i Ukraïna," *Rozbudova Natsiï* 20–21, No. 8–9 (1929): 271, 276. Emphasis in the original.

80 O. Mytsiuk, "Fashyzm (Dyskusiina stattia)," *Rozbudova Natsiï* 20–21, No. 8–9 (1929): 262–270; O. Mytsiuk, "Fashyzm (Dyskusiina stattia)," *Rozbudova Natsiï* 22–23, No. 10–11 (1929): 328–37.

81 Ievhen Onats'kyi, "Lysty z Italiï I. Deshcho pro fashyzm," *Rozbudova natsiï* 3 (1928): 95.

fascists in Italy who could conduct a revolution in order to overcome the crisis and make the country great and powerful like Italy:

> Fascism—means first of all *unity*. This is its first and main meaning and it is indicated by the etymology of the word "fascism," which is derived from "fascio"—bundle, bunch.
>
> At this point in time, when a country descended into chaos, when political and national enmity began reaching its peak, when all acquainted with the Russian and Ukrainian revolution became frightened due to the inevitable catastrophe ... at exactly that time a group of people emerged and called for unity in order to rebuild the "Great Italy."[82]

In this article Onats'kyi implied that fascism is not specifically Italian, although it first appeared in Italy. He argued that it was rather a group of people who, at the right time, did the right thing in Italy. According to him a similar fascist revolution, which he understood as the rebuilding of the great past, could equally have happened elsewhere.[83]

In addition to familiarizing Ukrainian youth with fascism, Onats'kyi also acquainted them with the Führerprinzip and the role of a leader in the history of a nation. He explained the role of the fascist leader, using the example of Mussolini:

> Fascism is Mussolini. Nowhere else among the idealistic movement is the anthropomorphic necessity as essential as in fascism. Everything of it is almost the result of the personal activity of Benito Mussolini. Only due to him did fascism become its particular shape. The fascists of the first times consisted first of all of diverse political remainders, defectors from diverse parties and organizations, and of people who never belonged to a political party. It was necessary to unite and inspire them with one idea and one will.
>
> Mussolini was in the beginning the dictator of a small bunch of his political friends and supporters, then of the party and then of the whole of Italy.[84]

Onats'kyi described the leader also in a more abstract way. This allowed Ukrainians to better comprehend that the leader of a fascist nation can exist not only in Italy but actually everywhere and especially in "countries in crisis" that are likely to undergo a revolution:

> He appeared when the political and social chaos of the country indeed needed a strong man, a dictator. Italy's luck was that it found her dictator in the right moment. It was not only luck but also merit. Two necessary preconditions are essential to have a leader like Mussolini emerging ... : 1) that a person, who the country needs, is called in the *right moment*, and 2) that the country is *morally able to give birth to such a person. ...*
>
> The national dictator is truly the representative of energy and the lively vitality of the nation. The crisis helps him to emerge and to present his potentials and his

82 Ievhen Onats'kyi, "Fashyzm i my (Z pryvodu statti prof. Mytsiuka)," *Rozbudova natsiï* 12 (1929): 397. Emphasis in the original.
83 Ibid., 397.
84 Ibid., 399.

> strengths but he makes himself noticeable only because the society and the very nation strive after order and life.
>
> The man of dictatorship, the man of the crisis is first of all determined by character, will, and nothing else than character singles him out from ordinary ambitious men. Like an ambitious man without the necessary intellect so an intelligent person without a strong character will not elevate to the role of leader [*providnyk*].
>
> He realizes very soon that his own interests and the nation's interests melt together and become one. He cannot compromise them [the nation's interests] in any way. Therefore the nation looks to him with trust and hope. He loves favorites. Further, he loves the brave and it does not matter to him whether somebody breaks the law or not. A dictator becomes a hero, an object of cult and emulation.[85]

Toward the end of his article about fascism, Onats'kyi came to the conclusion:

> We, the representatives of a hitherto defeated nation, see in fascism, in particular in its first stateless phase—another example to follow—the example of idealism. And we cannot be content with the enforced 'fate' [of not being independent] and need to overcome it. And we will overcome![86]

In terms of the name of the movement, Onats'kyi argued that Ukrainians would not steal the name of "fascism" from the Italians and that it would be "Ukrainian nationalism" that would unite Ukrainians and fulfill functions similar to those of fascism in Italy. Thus, like Dontsov, Onats'kyi did not insist on using the term "fascism." Instead he argued that "Ukrainian nationalism" is a form of fascism consisting of people without a state.[87] He also warned Ukrainians to be careful about presenting themselves and acting as fascists. In a brief to Iaroslav Pelenskyi from 20 January 1930 he stated that "we sympathize with the fascist ideology and share in many points its sociopolitical program" but we should not insist to be fascist because we would thereby "arm against us everyone and everything."[88]

Similarly to Dontsov, Onats'kyi believed that Ukrainian nationalism, like Italian Fascism, depended on youth.[89] And like Dontsov, he expressed the wish for a "new man," a feature typical not only of fascism but also of other totalitarian movements and ideologies in the first half of the twentieth century. One of the main tasks of the OUN was to erase from the Ukrainian population the mentality of "slaves" or "subjects" of other states, and to foster a new "heroic" mentality. This process would transform Ukrainians into heroic and fearless "Ukrainian masses" that the OUN could lead into the fight against their enemies. For Onats'kyi, fascism was therefore both a tool for obtaining a state, and a political system that the OUN would establish in the state.[90] Antisemitism for Onats'kyi was an integral part of fascism, as he justified Italian antisemitic legislation in 1938.[91]

85 Ibid., 399–400.
86 Ibid., 401.
87 Ibid., 401.
88 Ievhen Onats'kyi, *U vichnomu misti: Zapysky ukraïns'koho zhurnalista rik 1930* (Buenos Aires: Vydavnytstvo Mykoly Denysiuka, 1954), 43–44.
89 Ievhen Onats'kyi, "Lysty z Italiï I. Deshcho pro fashyzm," *Rozbudova natsiï* 1 (1928): 96.
90 Onats'kyi, "Fashyzm i my (Spryvodu statti prof. Mytsiuka)," *Rozbudova natsiï* 12 (1929): 387, 401.
91 Martynowych, Sympathy for the Devil, 191.

Onats'kyi's articles evaluating and popularizing fascism, and his polemics with Mytsiuk, appeared in the late 1920s and early 1930s. In the late 1930s skepticism relating to fascism as a non-genuine Ukrainian phenomenon disappeared in Ukrainian nationalist circles almost completely. At that time the majority of Ukrainian nationalists did not consider Ukrainian nationalism and fascism to be mutually exclusive and did not object to being identified as members of a fascist movement. In 1938 another OUN ideologist, Iaroslav Orshan, wrote: "Fascism, National Socialism, Ukrainian nationalism, etc., are different national expressions of the same spirit."[92]

As already outlined in chapter 1, other ideologists of Ukrainian nationalism including Dontsov and Stsibors'kyi developed a similar understanding of fascism to Onats'kyi's. On the one hand, they understood Ukrainian nationalism as a form of fascism, and on the other hand they emphasized the uniqueness of Ukrainian nationalism and argued that it was politically more convenient for the Ukrainian nationalists not to present themselves as fascists. Stsibors'kyi wrote about the complicated relationship between fascism, nationalism, and nation:

> Fascism concentrates all its idealism and voluntarism on one center: the very nation. The nation is its greatest value to which everything else is subordinated. Counter to democracy, which has the tendency to regard the nation as a mechanical set of a certain number of individuals, bound together first of all by real interests, *fascism regards the nation as the highest historical, spiritual, traditional and real community, within which occur the processes of existence and creativity of entire generations—the dead, living, and so far unborn—all are bound together inseparably.*[93]

Two other important ideological notions, which, in addition to nationalism and fascism, formed the young Bandera, were racism and eugenics. As already mentioned, racism as a component of nationalism was present in Mikhnovys'kyi's writing. According to Mirchuk, Bandera was fascinated by Mikhnovs'kyi's ideas and studied them during his time at high school.[94] In the early 1940s he even made them the ideological foundation of the OUN.[95] Dontsov, Martynets', and Rudnyts'kyi also spread racist ideas and popularized eugenics in Ukraine. Their thinking was influenced by the European and global discourses about racism and eugenics. In Ukrainian nationalism, racism and eugenics appeared in the context of purifying the Ukrainian nation, culture, and language of foreign—in particular, Polish, Russian and Jewish—influences, in order to obtain a pure Ukrainian "race." This kind of racism was typical of radical right movements rooted in nations that for centuries were provinces of foreign empires, or were substantially influenced by other cultures. Ukraine and Croatia were two examples of such nations.[96]

92 Iaroslav Orshan, *Doba natsionalizmu* (Paris, 1938), 29.
93 Stsibors'kyi, *Natsiokratiia*, 50–51.
94 Mirchuk, *Stepan Bandera*, 14, 18.
95 "Postanovy II. Velykoho Zboru Orhanizatsiï Ukraïns'kykh Natsionalistiv," TsDAHO f. 1, op. 23, spr. 926, 182.
96 For Rudnyts'kyi and racism in the Ukrainian national discourse, see page 84 et seq. For the Ustaša, see Goran Miljan, *Fascist Thought in Twentieth Century Europe: Case Study of Ante Pavelić*, MA thesis, Central European University, 2009, 37–38.

The terrorist acts that the homeland executive conducted in 1933 and 1934, when Bandera was successively its propaganda director, deputy leader, and leader, confirm that he and other OUN members internalized far-right nationalist ethics and also Dontsov's concept of amorality. As explained in chapter 1, the homeland executive used terror for propaganda purposes and also as a tool for the preparation of the "national revolution." The purpose of the revolution was to take over power with the help of the masses and to establish a dictatorial state. This resembled the use of terror in other fascist movements, including the German National Socialists, Italian Fascists, and the Croatian Ustaša. The main difference between the OUN and the Ustaša on the one hand, and the fascist movements within nation states including Italy and Germany on the other hand, was that the former needed first to establish a state, and the latter could directly take over power from existing governments.

Bandera spent the last five years before the Second World War in prison, where he was to some extent detached from official OUN discourses. Nevertheless, this period was very important in the development of his worldview and self-awareness. At this time, Bandera began to shape his own policies while representing the OUN at the trials in Warsaw and Lviv. The performance of fascist rituals by Bandera and other defendants during the trials suggests that Bandera's self-awareness, as the *Providnyk* of a movement that planned to establish a state with a fascist dictatorship, was already formed at that time.[97] While in prison after the trial, Bandera was able to read books and subscribe to Ukrainian and other newspapers and periodicals. He was therefore not entirely isolated from Ukrainian and European political discourses during this period. After his escape from prison in September 1939, he felt secure in his position as the *Providnyk* of the young Ukrainian revolutionary nationalists and aspired to become the leader of the entire OUN.[98]

Other ideas that influenced young Bandera and should be briefly discussed here were the concepts of "permanent revolution" and "national revolution." The term "permanent revolution" can be traced back to Karl Marx, but it was popularized by Leon Trotsky, who saw revolution as a political and social process of transforming society.[99] In the context of Ukrainian nationalism, "permanent revolution" retained the notion of permanent revolutionary transformation but anticipated very different results from those foreseen by Marx and Trotsky. It was based on the conviction that the Ukrainian nation would die if it did not succeed in getting rid of "occupiers" and "enemies" and in establishing its own state. The "permanent revolution" was intended to prepare the "Ukrainian masses" for a revolutionary act—the "national revolution"—during which the nationalists would take power, establish a dictatorial state, and expel or annihilate ethnic enemies and political opponents. For this purpose the OUN tried to re-educate Ukrainians, to change them from people with "souls of slaves to people with souls of masters, and from people with souls of defenders to people with souls of aggressors."[100] The OUN also tried to establish a dense network of members in every city, town, and village in the "Ukrainian ethnic territory." This required the involvement of Ukrainian

97 For fascist rituals during the trials, see chapter 3 below.
98 See chapter 3 below.
99 Leon Trotsky, *The Permanent Revolution, and Results and Prospects* (New York, Merit Publishers, 1969).
100 "Rolia boievoho instynktu u vyzvol'nykh zmahanniakh," *Surma* 69, No. 7 (1933): 1.

youth in the "national liberation struggle." The UVO and OUN did this by infiltrating such youth groups as the scouting organization Plast and other youth organizations.[101]

The OUN believed that, among the Ukrainian movements, parties, and organizations, only the OUN could conduct the revolution and thereby prevent the nation from dying. Other Ukrainian movements, according to the OUN, were not only incapable of conducting the revolution but were also foes of the movement, and thus opponents of the revolution. They were a target of the OUN's revolutionary terror, especially if they cooperated in any manner with the "occupiers." In practice, however, the OUN considered cooperation with some other Ukrainian parties, in order to get more support from the population during the revolution. Because the success of the "national revolution" was, in the understanding of the OUN, a matter of life or death for the entire nation, they considered it proper to use any means, including war and ethnic and political violence.[102]

Bandera internalized the concepts of "permanent revolution" and "national revolution" at the latest in the 1930s and gave special attention to the latter. This is clear from the conduct of the homeland executive in 1933–1934 with Bandera as its *Providnyk* and from the actions in the summer of 1941 when the OUN organized the "Ukrainian National Revolution."[103] Furthermore, the texts written by Bandera after the Second World War confirm that he preferred the concept of "national revolution," apparently because it was more radical than "permanent revolution." After the Second World War, Bandera would adapt this concept to the climate of the Cold War and use it to organize a revolution against the Soviet Union. Important in Bandera's understanding of the revolution were the masses and, in terms of 1941, the fascist leader (*Providnyk* or *Vozhd'*), whose role Bandera was expected to play.[104]

Related to the concept of the "national revolution" was Bandera's interest in nineteenth- and twentieth-century secret organizations. As a boy, according to his sister Volodymyra, Bandera was more interested in secret organizations, revolutionaries, and terrorists than he was in warfare or weapons. He read about and was fascinated by the nineteenth-century Russian nihilists and the more contemporary Bolsheviks. According to Volodymyra, Lenin was Stepan's favorite revolutionary. Under the influence of Dontsov, Bandera's fascination with Lenin was later transformed into a hatred of Bolshevism. His interest in the revolutionaries was apparently evoked by his father Andrii who, according to Bandera's sister, told his children stories about Petliura, Skoropads'kyi, and Trotskii.[105]

Like many other OUN activists of his generation, Bandera was also greatly influenced by Polish national culture and by Józef Piłsudski's authoritarian regime.

101 "Proces o zamordowanie ... Płast i Łuch," *Gazeta Polska*, 17 December 1935, 6.

102 For a detailed characterization of the concept of "national revolution," see for example Mykola Stsibors'kyi, "Peredposylka natsional'noï revoliutsiï," *Rozbudova natsiï* 54–55, No. 7–8 (1932): 161–69. For the concept of "permanent revolution," see "Permanentna revoliutsiia," *Surma* 37, No. 10 (1930): 4–7. For Trotsky, see Leon Trotsky, *The Permanent Revolution, and Results and Prospects* (New York, Merit Publishers, 1969).

103 For the "Ukrainian National Revolution" in summer 1941, see chapter 4, and Rossoliński-Liebe, "'Ukrainian National Revolution,'" 83–114.

104 For Bandera's understanding of revolution after the Second World War, see chapter 7 below, and Stepan Bandera, "Do zasad nashoï vyzvol'noï polityky," in *Perspektyvy*, ed. Ivanyshyn, 51–52. For Bandera's understanding of the masses, see Stepan Bandera, "Znachennia shyrokykh mas ta ïkh okhoplennia," in *Perspektyvy*, ed. Ivanyshyn, 14.

105 Pirie, *Unraveling the Banner*, 16–18, 21.

Although the OUN combated the Polish state as an "occupier," the Bandera generation was not only fluent in Polish and familiar with Polish culture but also learned from Polish history how a nation can achieve statehood. Thus Bandera both admired and hated eighteenth-century insurgents such as Tadeusz Kościuszko and twentieth-century revolutionaries such as Józef Piłsudski. Volodymyr Ianiv, an OUN activist with a realm of experience similar to that of Bandera, wrote about his experiences with Polish teachers:

> Of course, these Polish patriots tried to teach their [Ukrainian] pupils the Polish history and culture in the best light, but something unbelievable happened here: they became the best teachers of *Ukrainian patriotism*. As they talked with enthusiasm about the Polish uprisings or about the main poets, we automatically transferred it to the Ukrainian circumstances.[106]

Although Dontsov familiarized this generation with the cults of other charismatic leaders, most young Galician Ukrainians never directly experienced them. Piłsudski, on the other hand, was present in almost every sphere of life. He was on every second page in the newspapers. His portraits hung in every room of official buildings, for example in the classrooms of the high school that Bandera attended. Piłsudski's visits to other countries, his political speeches, and his health were the subject of daily talks and radio broadcasts.[107] Like some other OUN members, Bandera might even have read Piłsudski's diaries and admired his national revolutionary activities, much as he admired Lenin and other revolutionaries.[108] Simultaneously, Bandera probably hated Piłsudski as the leader of the nation that "occupied" Ukraine. The interwar period was full of diverse cults of charismatic authoritarian, fascist, and military leaders. The young Ukrainian revolutionary nationalists did not resist the temptation to invent their own.

106 Ianiv, Zustrich z polk. Ievhenom, 430. Emphasis in the original.

107 For the omnipresence of Piłsudski in everyday life in the Second Polish Republic, see Janis Augsberger, "Ein anti-analythisches Bedürfnis: Bruno Schulz im Grenzbereich zwischen Poetik und Politik," in *Politische Mythen im 19. und 20. Jahrhundert in Mittel- und Osteuropa*, ed. Heidi Hein-Kircher and Hans Hahn (Marburg: Herder Institut, 2006), 26–29. For the Piłsudski cult in the Second Polish Republic, see Hein, *Der Piłsudski-Kult*. For an exhibition entitled *Marszałek Józef Piłsudski we Lwowie*, exhibited in Lviv in 1935, see "Wystawa Marszałel Piłsudski we Lwowie," AAN, MSZ, syg. 8679, 1–5.

108 For Bandera reading diaries of Polish and German politicians, see Mudryk-Mechnyk, *Spohad pro Stepana Banderu*, 27. For other OUN members reading and admiring Piłsudski, see Polit, *Miejsce odosobnienia*, 121.

Conclusion

Stepan Bandera was raised by a Greek Catholic priest who struggled for a Ukrainian state, and who inspired his son to continue the fight. For Stepan, unlike his father, nationalism was more important than religion. In his high school years Bandera read such nationalist and racist writers as Mikhnovs'kyi and Dontsov. In 1928 he began to study in Lviv but on account of his political and terrorist activities never completed his studies. He rapidly rose through the ranks of the OUN, and in June 1933 became the official leader of the homeland executive of the OUN. As the head of the propaganda apparatus, Bandera had already demonstrated himself to be a talented organizer and a very dedicated nationalist. The policies of the homeland executive radicalized during his leadership; more and more people, amongst them Ukrainians and OUN members accused of betrayal, were executed, frequently on Bandera's initiative.

Bandera's worldview can be reconstructed from the books and papers that he read, the groups and organizations to which he belonged, the acts which he conducted, and the speeches which he delivered. This analysis shows that Bandera must have internalized the ideology of the OUN, and of Dontsov and other contemporary fascist and far-right thinkers. Bandera's worldview was shaped by numerous far-right values and concepts including ultranationalism, fascism, racism, and antisemitism; by fascination with violence; by the belief that only war could establish a Ukrainian state; and by hostility to democracy, communism, and socialism. Like other young Ukrainian nationalists he combined extremism with religion and used religion to sacralize politics and violence.

Chapter 3

PIERACKI'S ASSASSINATION AND THE WARSAW AND LVIV TRIALS

Pieracki's Assassination

On the morning of 15 June 1934, Polish Interior Minister Bronisław Pieracki said goodbye to German Propaganda Minister Joseph Goebbels, who continued his official visit to Poland by flying from Warsaw to Cracow. Pieracki then returned to his office in the Ministry of Interior Affairs at 69 Nowy Świat Street. After work, he left for the Klub Towarzyski, a restaurant and meeting place for politicians, located at 3 Foksal Street. The minister arrived at Foksal Street at about 3:40 p.m. and told his chauffeur to return at 5:30 p.m. Pieracki started walking toward the restaurant without his bodyguards. At this point, Hryhorii Matseiko, a twenty-one-year-old OUN member, began to approach him, shaking a parcel wrapped in paper from the Gajewski confectionery. The parcel contained a makeshift bomb that Matseiko was trying to detonate. The bomb, however, did not explode. Its activation required a vigorous push on the detonator, a T-shaped metal piston, which was designed to crush a glass tube containing nitric acid. If Matseiko had pushed a little harder, the tube would have broken and detonated the bomb, killing the government minister and his assailant. Once Matseiko realized that he could not blow up both the minister and himself, he pulled a gun from his coat and ran toward Pieracki, who had already passed him and was in the entrance of the restaurant. Catching up with him, Matseiko shot twice at the back of Pieracki's head. When the minister sank to the ground, Matseiko fired a third shot but missed. The young assassin fled the scene, firing several times at his pursuers, and wounding a policeman in the hand.[1]

After escaping from the scene of the crime, Matseiko disposed of the murder weapon. He did not return to the hostel, where he had been living under the name of Włodzimierz Olszański. Instead, he went to Lublin, where he stayed for a few days with a Ukrainian student by the name of Iakiv Chornii. Matseiko then travelled to Lviv and went into hiding, assisted by three OUN members: Ivan Maliutsa, Roman Myhal', and Ievhen Kachmars'kyi. On 5 August, armed with a gun and supplied with money, Matseiko crossed into Czechoslovakia with the help of Kateryna Zaryts'ka and other OUN members, and later travelled on a Lithuanian passport to Argentina, where he lived under the name Petro Knysh. He married a Ukrainian woman in Argentina but

1 Żeleński, *Akt oskarżenia*, 5, 9; Żeleński, *Zabójstwo ministra*, 4–7, 63; "Zamordowanie ministra spraw wewnętrznych Bronisława Pierackiego. Przebieg zamachu," *Gazeta Polska*, 16 June 1934, 2; "Polska w żałobie. Skrytobójstwo na ul. Foksal," *Ilustrowany Express Poranny*, 18 June 1934, 1; "Min. Goebbels w grodzie podwawelskim," *Ilustrowany Kuryer Codzienny*, 17 June 1934, 1.

could not get used to the climate; he turned to drink, suffered from mental problems, and died in 1966.[2]

How Matseiko had come to join the OUN was somewhat fortuitous. On 19 November 1931, as he was walking along a street in Lviv, where he had moved from the small town of Shchyrets (Szczerzec) two years before, he heard a shot and then a crowd calling out "Catch the murderer," pointing at a man who was running toward Matseiko. Matseiko caught him. It was subsequently revealed that the fugitive was Ivan Mytsyk, an OUN member, who, a few minutes earlier, had killed a Ukrainian high school student, Ievhen Bereznyts'kyi. In order to atone for catching Mystyk, Matseiko decided to join the OUN. Before the attack on Pieracki, the homeland executive had commissioned Matseiko to kill other people, but he had not succeeded in doing so. Pieracki was his first victim.[3]

Pieracki was a Polish patriot who had engaged in the struggle for a Polish state during and after the First World War. Since 22 June 1931, he had been the interior minister of the Second Republic. As a politician Pieracki was loyal to Piłsudski and the Sanacja government.[4] He was opposed to every kind of extremism that threatened the Polish state. *Gazeta Polska* and politicians from the Sanacja depicted Pieracki as a Polish patriot who, like Tadeusz Hołówko and Henryk Józewski, espoused Polish-Ukrainian reconciliation.[5] A more critical and open-minded observer than the Sanacja politicians and the journalists from *Gazeta Polska*, the writer Maria Dąbrowska characterized Pieracki differently:

> Now Pieracki has been killed. He was a repulsive figure, clerical and overly pious ... a social parasite—I know about him because St. [Stanisław Stempowski, Dąbrowska's life partner] had troubles with him that outraged him. The government is now making him into a great national hero: It has ordered a week of mourning for the officials and is writing panegyrics. Bishop Gawlina delivered an odious speech at the funeral. I put it into [my] "museum of dirtiness."[6]

Dąbrowska's waspishly presented dislike for Pieracki might not have been unjustified, although it was certainly influenced by the problematic relations between her life partner and Pieracki, and by the lavish religious-nationalist commemorations of Pieracki after his death.

The OUN chose to kill Pieracki because he was a well-known Polish politician and because he could be blamed for the pacification of Ukrainian villages in the autumn of 1930. In October 1934, the OUN announced in its bulletin: "On 15 June in Warsaw, a UVO fighter assassinated one of the hangmen of the Ukrainian nation. The UVO fighter killed Bronisław Pieracki, interior minister of the government occupying the western Ukrainian land."[7] The place of the assassination was especially significant. Pieracki was killed not in the south-eastern territories of the Second Republic, which the OUN

2 For Matseiko's escape and subsequent life, see Żeleński, *Zabójstwo ministra Pierackiego*, 21–22, 100–101; Żeleński, *Akt oskarżenia*, 10–12, 21–22, 36–38.
3 "Proces. Grzegorz Maciejko," *Gazeta Polska*, 31 December 1935, 8.
4 Polit, Miejsce odosobnienia, 26.
5 "Proces," *Gazeta Polska*, 18 December 1935, 6.
6 Maria Dąbrowska, *Dzienniki 1933–1945* (Warsaw: Czytelnik, 1988), 50–51.
7 *Biuleten' KE OUN na ZUZ*, 4–7 (1934), quoted in "Wyrok," TsDIAL, f. 205, spr. 3125, 12–13. See also Żeleński, *Zabójstwo ministra Pierackiego*, 23, and "Komunikat Nr. 7," AAN, MSZ, syg. 5316, 89.

understood as "the western Ukrainian land" and which he visited shortly prior to his assassination (between 3 and 9 June 1934), but in the center of Warsaw, the capital of Poland.[8]

In the first moments after the crime, the police did not suspect the OUN, to which Matseiko belonged, and at whose behest he had killed the minister, but the Polish National Radical Camp (*Obóz Narodowo-Radykalny*, ONR). The ONR was also a threat to the government and was more active in Warsaw than were Ukrainian nationalists. In the first instance, the police arrested more ONR than OUN members. The escaping Matseiko, however, left behind important evidence, namely the parcel that contained the undetonated bomb. He also left his hat, and his coat in which the police found a blue-and-yellow ribbon, the colors of the Ukrainian flag. This evidence indicated that the assassin might be Ukrainian, unless it was a non-Ukrainian who had left it deliberately in order to steer the investigation in the wrong direction.

Bandera was arrested a day prior to the assassination. He was apprehended together with twenty other young OUN members, at about 5:30 a.m. on 14 June 1934, in the student residence in Lviv. When arresting Bandera, the police did not know that they had apprehended the head of the homeland executive of the OUN.[9] During the same night, the police also arrested Karpynets' and discovered a chemical laboratory in his apartment at Rynek Dębnicki 13, in Cracow. On 17 June 1934, the police took the bomb left at the crime scene in Warsaw to Karpynets' laboratory where they found materials employed in its manufacture.[10] This discovery convinced the police of the identity of those responsible for Pieracki's assassination and caused further mass arrests of Ukrainian nationalists. In June 1934 a total of about 800 OUN members were apprehended in different Polish towns and cities; the majority on 14, 17, and 18 June.[11]

In the longer term, the OUN provoked mass arrests by the increase of propaganda and terrorist acts in 1933–1934, when Bandera took over the leadership of the homeland executive. The arrests were also the result of longer observation and infiltration conducted by the investigation department in Cracow, which was interested mainly in the illegal transportation of OUN propaganda and explosive materials from Czechoslovakia through the Czech-Polish town of Těšín (Cieszyn). The arrests occurred independently of the assassination, at least until 17 June, when the police established that the bomb left at the crime scene was prepared by the OUN. However, the OUN's decision to assassinate Pieracki on 15 June did not occur independently of the arrests. The assassination was rescheduled for 15 June because the police had begun arresting

8 For Pieracki's visit to south-east Poland between 3 and 9 June 1934 see "Komunikat Nr. 7," AAN, MSZ, syg. 5316, 88; Żeleński, *Akt oskarżenia*, 102. Independent of the fact that the OUN made Pieracki responsible for the pacification in 1930, he might have been in charge of this action. It was, however, ordered by Piłsudski himself. Thus, in addition to Pieracki many other people were involved in preparing and carrying out this action. Cf. Bruder, "*Den ukrainischen Staat*, 102; Chojnowski, *Koncepcje polityki*, 158.

9 "Komunikat Nr. 7," AAN, MSZ, syg. 5316, 83.

10 For the arrest of Karpynets' on 14 June 1934 in Cracow, see "Komunikat Nr. 7," AAN, MSZ, syg. 5316, 84. For the arrests of OUN members, see "Komunikat Nr. 7," AAN, MSZ, syg. 5316, 80–87; "Po zamordowaniu ministra spraw wewnętrznych Bronisława Pierackiego," *Gazeta Polska*, 17 June 1934, 8; Polit, *Miejsce odosobnienia*, 115. For the visit to the laboratory on 17 June, see Żeleński, *Zabójstwo ministra Pierackiego*, 7. In the indictment Żeleński wrote that it was only on 20 June that the police technicians proved that the bomb was produced in Karpynets' laboratory. Cf. Żeleński, *Akt oskarżenia*, 38.

11 "Komunikat Nr. 7," AAN, MSZ, syg. 5316, 40, 84.

OUN members on 14 June in Lviv and Cracow, having discovered, during the night of 13–14 June, the laboratory in which the bomb had been prepared.[12] Although the police already knew on 17 June who was behind Pieracki's assassination, it was only on 10 July that they announced it. This delay—in conjunction with propagandistic and ideological mourning campaigns with a strong patriotic background for the assassinated interior minister—provoked the media to extensive speculation that stoked public anger against the unknown assassin.[13]

The Ideological Dimension of Pieracki's Assassination

The first stage of the political cult of Stepan Bandera came about as a result of the politically and ideologically steered emotions released by Pieracki's assassination and by the two great trials against members of the OUN, from 18 November 1935 to 13 January 1936 in Warsaw, and from 25 May to 27 June 1936 in Lviv. Immediately after the assassination, the Polish media, especially that connected to the Sanacja movement, portrayed Pieracki as a martyr and hero and tried to set up a political myth around him. Although this effort was unsuccessful, the Polish propaganda apparatus stirred up collective anger, which struck against the OUN, once the authorities had announced who, in the capital of Poland, had killed a Polish minister and fighter for Polish independence.

On 15 June 1934, the evening newspapers were already portraying the death of Pieracki as a national tragedy. *Gazeta Polska*, a semi-official paper of the leading parliamentary group Sanacja, was at the head of the campaign. On 16 June, in the center of the front page, the newspaper printed a photograph of Pieracki looking sadly and seriously into the eyes of the readers. A dark frame made the photograph look like a huge obituary notice. Above it, a massive headline reported the "assassination of the interior minister yesterday at about 3.15 p.m." A second headline informed readers about the place of the assassination and reported Pieracki's death as having occurred at 5:05 p.m., in the hospital. It further informed readers that the killer had not yet been caught.[14] The text below Pieracki's photograph raised anger against the unknown group that was responsible for the crime. After "finding out where the roots of this crime are ... this sick part of the social organism should be burned away with a white iron," the newspaper declared. "The time of non-responsibility in Polish history is over. The criminal is responsible for both the physical crime and the political one." The article argued that Pieracki did not die for nothing, but sacrificed his life for the glory of Poland. It also implied that the minister was killed by an enemy who was cowardly and cunning enough to murder him from behind, and not in front of his eyes as an enemy on a battlefield would.[15]

12 For the observation and infiltration of the OUN by the Polish authorities, see Żeleński, *Zabójstwo ministra Pierackiego*, 11. For bringing forward the day of assassination, see Żeleński, *Zabójstwo ministra Pierackiego*, 23–24; Żeleński, *Akt oskarżenia*, 38. For the arrests on 14 June in Lviv and Cracow, see Żeleński, *Akt oskarżenia*, 9–10, 65. For the discovery of the laboratory during the night of 13–14 June, see "Zbrodnia nie ujdzie bezkarnie. Wywiad u p. Ministra Sprawiedliwości," *Gazeta Polska*, 10 July 1934, 1.

13 "Zbrodnia nie ujdzie bezkarnie. Wywiad u p. Ministra Sprawiedliwości," *Gazeta Polska*, 10 July 1934, 1.

14 *Gazeta Polska*, 16 June 1934, 1.

15 Ibid., 1.

The second page of the issue of the *Gazeta Polska* for 16 June 1934 informed readers about the details of the crime, Pieracki's death in hospital, the unsuccessful pursuit of the assassin, and the impact of the crime on society. According to this report, the news about Pieracki's assassination had spread as fast as lightning throughout the city and had caused genuine sorrow everywhere. As a sign of mourning, cinemas, restaurants, and taverns were closed. On the sidewalks, people read the special evening editions of the newspapers, which kept them informed about the crime and provoked discussion. Flags were hung on many public and private buildings. The Legion of the Young (*Legion Młodych*), a youth organization associated with the Sanacja movement, marched from the hospital where Pieracki had died, to the Belweder, the palace where Marshal Piłsudski lived. During the procession, fights with the Polish fascist organization ONR occurred. Similar emotional reactions and manifestations of sorrow emerged in Lviv, Cracow, Lublin, Łódź, Vilna, Białystok, and Toruń. *Gazeta Polska* reported that such capitals as Paris, London, and Bucharest had expressed condolences, and feelings of disgust for the unknown murderer.[16]

The crime took on the shape of a national tragedy. Pro-government media used the ceremonies of mourning, grief, and anger to elaborate a collective desire for revenge and justice. On the next day, 17 June 1934, *Gazeta Polska* devoted the entire front page to turning Pieracki into a martyr and hero. This time too, the first page bore a black frame that made it look like an obituary, but no photograph of Pieracki appeared in the frame. Instead, the name Bronisław Pieracki was printed in large letters with a cross above it, and the letters *Ś* and *P*, the abbreviation for "Of holy memory." Below, in smaller but large enough letters, Pieracki's titles, posts, honors, and medals, such as "Interior Minister," "Delegate of Sejm," and "Holder of the Virtuti Militari Medal," were listed. One of these honors was "Brigadier General," a military rank with which Marshal Piłsudski had honored Pieracki, the day after his death. Below this enumeration, the readers were informed that Pieracki had fallen while "standing on guard," and that the mourning service would take place on Monday, 18 June at the Church of the Holy Cross. After the service the coffin would be taken to the main railway station, whence it would be transported to Nowy Sącz, the city where Pieracki's family lived.[17]

On the second page, *Gazeta Polska* reported a special mourning gathering of the council of ministers at 10:00 a.m. on the day after the assassination, during which Prime Minister Leon Kozłowski announced that the "punishing hand" should catch not only the direct, but also the indirect perpetrators of the crime. The government stated that, until the day of the funeral, flags would be hung at half-mast, and that black ribbons would be affixed to them at all public buildings. The president of Warsaw—equivalent to mayor—Marian Zyndram-Kościałkowski appealed to Varsovians to decorate all private houses with flags. Government offices were obliged to mourn for eight days. The Ministry of Interior Affairs and its branch offices would mourn for twenty-eight days. The appeal requested the cancellation of ceremonies and festivities during the

16 "Zamordowanie ministra spraw wewnętrznych Bronisława Pierackiego," *Gazeta Polska*, 16 June 1934, 2. For the mourning ceremonies in Cracow, see *Ilustrowany Kuryer Codzienny*, 19 June 1934, 1. For the mourning ceremonies in Lviv, see "Manifestacja żałobna we Lwowie," *Ilustrowany Kuryer Codzienny*, 19 June 1934, 2.

17 *Gazeta Polska*, 17 June 1934, 1. For honoring Pieracki with the rank of brigadier general, see "Po zamordowaniu ministra spaw wewnętrznych Bronisława Pierackiego," *Gazeta Polska*, 17 June 1934, 2.

mourning period, and obliged all officials to wear mourning ribbons. In all towns and cities in Poland, as well as in all places outside Poland where Poles were living, mourning services were to be held. On the day of the funeral, all performances in theatres and cinemas were cancelled. Polish radio was required to broadcast special programs.[18]

Condolences from such prominent persons as Primate August Hlond, ambassadors of numerous countries to Warsaw, and organizations such as workers' associations were published on the second page. A personal decision of Marshal Piłsudski to organize a military-style funeral was announced, as was a huge mourning march, which began the same day at 12:00 on Marshal Piłsudski Square, and was attended by 100,000 people. *Gazeta Polska* also announced that Pieracki's mother had fainted when she heard on the radio about the death of her son. The Ministry of Internal Affairs offered a reward of 100,000 złotys to the person who helped catch the killer.[19] On the third page, *Gazeta Polska* published an article entitled "A Soldier's Death." It depicted Pieracki as a very respected and patriotic Pole, a faithful servant of the Polish state, as well as a representative of his generation, who, during and after the First World War, fought for Polish independence and who was engaged after the war in rebuilding the state. Pieracki's assassination was presented as a blow against all patriotic Poles and was used to evoke a desire for revenge.[20] This was strengthened by the observation that the bullet that hit Pieracki during the struggle for independence in 1915 had not prevented him from serving the state, but an assassin's bullet had. The political group that fired the bullet therefore had to be smashed.[21]

The day after his assassination, the street in which Pieracki was killed was renamed Bronisław Pieracki Street. Military, social, and workers' associations and organizations, as well as leading politicians, came to the ceremony. The renaming ceremony was conducted by the president of Warsaw, Zyndram-Kościałkowski, who stressed the tragedy of the loss with the words: "The minister of the Polish Republic, the colonel of the Polish Army, the soldier of Marshal Piłsudski was murdered! God was desecrated through the killing of a man, the fatherland was desecrated through the killing of a minister of the Republic"[22] The speaker further indicated that the street should be renamed, in order to commemorate the efforts that Pieracki had invested in the fatherland, and "to remember that everyone should live and work hard ... according to the order of the Leader of the Nation (*Wódz Narodu*) [Józef Piłsudski] to elaborate a Poland as He [the Leader of the Nation] wants to see, and for which we, His soldiers, fought."[23] Zyndram-Kościałkowski depicted Pieracki as a faithful servant of the state, in which everything happens for the glory of the leader, and always as the leader wishes. He also indicated that the loss of Pieracki harmed the whole of society, because it

18 "Po zamordowaniu ministra spaw wewnętrznych Bronisława Pierackiego," *Gazeta Polska*, 17 June 1934, 2, 4. For the special mourning gathering of the council of ministers, see also "Żałobne posiedzenie Rady Ministrów," *Ilustrowany Kuryer Codzienny*, 18 June 1934, 2; *Ilustrowany Express Poranny*, 18 June 1934, 1.

19 "Po zamordowaniu ministra spaw wewnętrznych Bronisława Pierackiego," *Gazeta Polska*, 17 June 1934, 2, 4; "Manifestacja żałobna na pl. Józefa Piłsudskiego," *Gazeta Polska*, 18 June 1934, 1.

20 "Żołnierska śmierć," *Gazeta Polska*, 17 June 1934, 3.

21 Pieracki was wounded during the battle in Jastków between 31 July and 3 September 1915. For the instrumentalization of this fact, see "Szlusuj," *Gazeta Polska*, 18 June 1934, 1.

22 "Po zamordowaniu ministra spaw wewnętrznych Bronisława Pierackiego. Stolica w hołdzie," *Gazeta Polska*, 17 June 1934, 4, 8.

23 Ibid., 8.

harmed the leader. Other Polish cities followed this example and renamed streets after Pieracki. The municipal council of Chrzanów decided to do so on 18 July 1934, and the one in Kowel followed suit on 20 July.[24]

Pieracki's assassination was also used to legitimize the establishment of the previously mentioned first Polish detention camp in Bereza Kartuska and to repudiate the Little Treaty of Versailles. Both the detention camp and the repudiation of the treaty had been planned for some time, but were carried out only after the assassination.[25] *Gazeta Polska* and *Ilustrowany Kuryer Codzienny* depicted the creation of the camp as a necessary response to the assassination.[26]

On 18 June 1934, next to a number of other condolences from various organizations and offices, *Gazeta Polska* published the first condolences from Ukrainian associations in Volhynia.[27] It reported that a large demonstration had taken place on 17 June 1934 in Lviv, and that in all other cities of the Lviv, Ternopil', and Stanyslaviv voievodeships—all three mainly inhabited by Ukrainians—mourning ceremonies took place, and resolutions condemning the assassin were passed.[28] On the front page of their 17 June issue, *Ilustrowany Kuryer Codzienny* printed a long article titled "Bloody Hands ..." The article was a response to the discovery of the OUN laboratory in Cracow and to the mass arrests of OUN members on 14 June. The author of the article exposed the violent and criminal nature of the OUN, condemned the Greek Catholic Church for sanctifying the OUN, and called on the church to distance itself from the OUN. The writer did not state that the OUN had committed the crime against Pieracki, but he described the OUN as a terrorist and criminal organization that might have carried it out.[29]

On 18 June 1934, Pieracki's corpse was transported from Warsaw to Nowy Sącz, a small city in Małopolska (Little Poland) where Pieracki's family lived and where he was to be buried on 19 June. For this journey a special "mourning train" (*pociąg żałobny*) was prepared. It consisted of a carriage with Pieracki's body inside, another carriage which was full of wreaths, and eight carriages for relatives, government members, and representatives of various organizations and government bodies. Before the train departed, Prime Minister Kozłowski delivered a speech in which he stressed that the murder of Pieracki "defamed the honor of our country, it insulted our instinct of justice and public morality."[30]

24 "Ul. Pierackiego w Chrzanowie," *Gazeta Polska*, 19 June 1934, 4; "Ulica B. Pierackiego w Kowlu," *Gazeta Polska*, 21 June 1934, 2.

25 The detention camp was established on 17 June 1934 by a decree of Ignacy Mościcki, the president of the Second Republic. Cf. Polit, *Miejsce odosobnienia*, 31. For Piłsudski's approval of the establishment of the camp, see Polit, *Miejsce odosobnienia*, 37. For regulations concerning incarceration, see Polit, *Miejsce odosobnienia*, 40. Ukrainians made up a significant number of the prisoners at Bereza Kartuska. On 17 September 1939 there were 7,000 prisoners in the camp, of whom 4,500 were Ukrainians. Cf. Polit, *Miejsce odosobnienia*, 120. For the repudiation of the treaty, see Korzec, Polen und der Minderheitenvertrag, 523, 540–41.

26 "Obozy izolacyjne," *Gazeta Polska*, 18 June 1934, 1; "Nowy okres w polskiej polityce wewnętrznej," *Ilustrowany Kuryer Codzienny*, 21 czerwca 1934, 1–2.

27 "Kondolencje reprezentacji ukraińskiej," *Gazeta Polska*, 18 June 1934, 2.

28 "Wielka manifestacja we Lwowie," *Gazeta Polska*, 18 June 1934, 2.

29 *Ilustrowany Kuryer Codzienny*, 17 czerwca 1934, 1.

30 "Żołnierz i mąż stanu. Przemówienie pana premiera L. Kozłowskiego," *Gazeta Polska*, 19 June 1934, 1.

GAZETA LWOWSKA

wychodzi każdego powszedniego dnia popołudniu.

Ceny prenumeraty:
We Lwowie bez doręczenia do domu . mies. zł. 2·—, kwart. 6·—
z dostawą do domu . mies. zł. 2·40, kwart. 7·—
Na prowincji z przesyłką pocztową . mies. zł. 2·40, kwart. 7·—
Za granicą . . . . mies. zł. 5·—, kwart. 15·—

Numer telefonu REDAKCJI I ADMINISTRACJI 21-17.
Konto PKO Lwów № 504.044

ADRES REDAKCJI I ADMINISTRACJI: LWÓW, UL. ZIMOROWICZA 15 I. p.

Listy należy frankować. — Reklamacje otwarte wolne od opłaty.
Rękopisów nadesłanych nie zwraca się.

CENA NUMERU 10 gr.

Ceny ogłoszeń:

Ś. P.

BRONISŁAW

Pieracki

generał brygady

Minister Spraw Wewnętrznych

poseł na Sejm

Kawaler Orderu Orła Białego, Virtuti Militari, Krzyża Niepodległości, Krzyża Walecznych, Polonia Restituta, Złotego Krzyża Zasługi

padł na posterunku z ręki skrytobójcy, w dniu 15 czerwca 1934. Zwłoki zostaną pochowane w N. Sączu

Ministerstwo Spraw Wewnętrznych.

Fig. 7. The front page of *Gazeta Lwowska*, 19 June 1934.

The "mourning train" left Warsaw at 1:00 p.m. On the way to Nowy Sącz, it paused for ten to thirty minutes in each of the seven main cities, allowing their delegations and the crowds who came to see the train to pay homage to the dead minister. So many wreaths were brought to the train on the way to Nowy Sącz that a second carriage had to be added for wreaths. Where the train did not stop, it was greeted with the ringing of church bells and was pelted with flowers. Airplanes escorted the train for a time. In Tarnów, crowds with torches gathered on both sides of the train, and peasant girls genuflected and prayed with outstretched hands.[31]

After three and a half days of collective mourning, the funeral itself took on a very ceremonial shape, as promised by the *Wódz*, Marshal Piłsudski, the most revered person in the state. Enchanted by nationalism and patriotism, Polish society did not notice the ideological nature of the process that transformed Pieracki into a hero and martyr. At the mourning service in Nowy Sącz, Bishop Lisowski delivered a sermon that made members of the government, and "old, battle-hardened soldiers" who had fought for the independence of Poland, weep.[32] Mounted on a gun carriage, Pieracki's coffin was then transported to the cemetery. During the funeral, Stanisław Car, deputy marshal of the Sejm, like many speakers before him, characterized Pieracki as a faithful servant of Piłsudski—the "genius and Leader of the Nation"—and expressed the hope that the hand of justice would finally catch the murderer.[33]

Newspapers, radio stations, and the educational ministry participated in these political mourning carnivals. Even if they did not all politicize the mourning rituals as extensively as *Gazeta Polska*, the semi-official paper of the Sanacja government, they did help to initiate the new political myth of the brave Pieracki who fell for his country. Polish radio (*Radjofonja Polska*), for example, canceled many scheduled programs in order to broadcast mourning services from churches in Warsaw and Nowy Sącz, and speeches from various other ceremonies. It also reported the journey of the "mourning train" in detail and broadcast programs that discussed the assassination and its repercussions.[34] The education minister ordered that every class in every school devote one hour to a discussion of Pieracki's passing.[35] *Gazeta Lwowska* transformed the whole first page of its issue for 19 June into a huge obituary (Fig. 7).[36]

The collective ideological work on the new political myth of Pieracki culminated in a book entitled *Bronisław Pieracki: Brigadier General, Interior Minister, Deputy of Sejm, Soldier, Statesman, Human Being*, published by the Creative State Propaganda Institute in late 1934.[37] The aim of the publication was to characterize Pieracki as a faithful servant of his fatherland and "his Leader [Piłsudski], who liberated Poland from enslavement." The publication placed Pieracki in the pantheon of Polish heroes,

31 "Po zamordowaniu ministra spaw wewnętrznych Bronisława Pierackiego. Ceremoniał pogrzebowy," *Gazeta Polska*, 17 June 1934, 2; "Na dworcu głównym," *Gazeta Polska*, 19 June 1934, 2; "W drodze do Nowego Sącza," *Gazeta Polska*, 19 June 1934, 4.

32 "Szloch zahartowanych żołnierzy," *Ilustrowany Express Poranny*, 21 June 1934, 1.

33 "Pogrzeb ś. p. ministra Broniława Pierackiego w Nowym Sączu," *Gazeta Polska*, 20 June 1934, 1. For Pieracki's corpse transported on a gun carriage, see *Ilustrowany Kuryer Codzienny*, 21 June 1934, 3.

34 "Radjofonja Polska ku czci ś. p. Bronisława Pierackiego," *Gazeta Polska*, 25 June 1934, 5.

35 "W szkołach o ś. p. min. Pierackim," *Gazeta Polska*, 5 July 1934, 2.

36 *Gazeta Lwowska*, 19 June 1934, 1.

37 *Bronisław Pieracki: Generał brygady, minister spaw wewnętrznych, poseł na Sejm, mąż stanu, człowiek* (Warsaw: Instytut Propagandy Państwowo-Twórczej, 1934).

martyrs, and statesmen.[38] For this purpose, the captivating and harrowing information about the assassination, the escape of the assassin, the death of Pieracki in hospital, his mother's fainting on hearing the news, the condolences from around the world, the mourning ceremonies in all Polish cities, the funeral, and the funeral orations by various politicians were ordered in a hagiographical narrative.[39]

The two main Ukrainian newspapers that appeared in the Second Polish Republic, *Dilo* and *Novyi chas,* were much more restrained about the highly stylized mourning of the Polish interior minister and did not participate in the collective elaboration of the Pieracki myth. *Dilo* limited itself to publishing factual information about the assassination and the mourning ceremonies, together with reports on the reactions of other newspapers.[40] It also published the condolences of the Ukrainian Parliamentary Representation, and reported the mass arrests of the OUN, which diverted the attention of its readers from the mourning ceremonies.[41]

At the same time, *Dilo* kept its readers informed about local trials of OUN members. During the mourning period and the following months, three such trials occurred. They were understood as political and were depicted as such by the press. At a trial in Ternopil', four OUN members were prosecuted for killing a policemen and for belonging to the OUN. The article in *Dilo* on the subject was entitled "Huge Political Trial in Ternopil' for Belonging to OUN and Murdering Police Officer."[42] In this trial, two of the OUN members were sentenced to death, one received a life sentence, and one was released.[43]

Novyi chas was even more reluctant than *Dilo* to comment on Pieracki's assassination. On 16 June 1934, the first day after the assassination, *Novyi chas* preferred to use the front page for information about one of the local trials of OUN members, rather than information about the assassination.[44] It kept to this policy in the following two issues, devoting the front and many other pages to reports about trials of OUN members in Stanyslaviv and Sambir (Sambór) and omitting any information about Pieracki's death.[45] Indeed, *Novyi chas* did not announce the assassination until 20 June 1934, the day after Pieracki's funeral, when it started the announcement with the government's decision to establish a detention camp for people endangering the state.[46]

On 10 July 1934, almost a month after the assassination, *Gazeta Polska* published an interview with Justice Minister Czesław Michałkowski. The minister explained that

38 *Bronisław Pieracki*, 9, 97.

39 Ibid., 27–109.

40 "Pislia vbyvstva min. Pierats'koho," *Dilo*, 17 June 1934, 8; "Pislia vbyvstva min. Pierats'koho," *Dilo*, 18 June 1934, 6; "Pislia vbyvstva min. Pierats'koho," *Dilo*, 20 June 1934, 3; "Varshavs'kyi zamakh," *Dilo*, 21 June 1934, 1, 4; "Varshavs'ki nastroï po krivavim atentati," *Dilo*, 24 June 1934, 2.

41 "Pislia vbyvstva min. Pierats'koho," *Dilo*, 20 June 1934, 3; "Revizii ta areshtuvannia sered ukraïntsiv u Krakovi," *Dilo*, 17 June 1934, 1; "Masovi areshtovannia u L'vovi," *Dilo*, 20 June 1934, 4; "Masovi areshtovannia u Halychyni," *Dilo*, 21 June 1934, 1.

42 "Velykyi politychnyi protses u Ternopoli," *Dilo*, 20 June 1934, 4.

43 "Prysud u ternopil's'komu protsesi," *Dilo*, 22 June 1934, 3. For a trial in Stanyslaviv, see "Velykyi politychnyi protses u Stanislavovi," *Dilo*, 22 July 1934, 4. For another trial for planning the assassination of education officer Gadomski, see "Novyi politychnyi protses u L'vovi. Za plianovane vbyvstvo kuratora Gadoms'koho," *Dilo*, 22 June 1934, 6. For the assassination of Ivan Babii, see "Dyrektor Ivan Babii zastrilenyi," *Dilo*, 27 July 1934, 1.

44 "Pered velykym protsesom O.U.N. v Stanislavovi," "Za prynalezhnist' do O.U.N." and "Politychnyi protses u Ternopoli," *Novyi chas*, 16 June 1934, 1, 2.

45 Cf. the two issues of *Novyi chas* for 17 and 18 June 1934.

46 "Pislia zamakhu," *Novyi chas*, 20 June 1934, 1.

investigators had determined that the OUN had planned and conducted the assassination, and that three people involved in the assassination had been arrested. The assassin himself was not arrested. He had escaped from Poland, although the Polish authorities had tried diligently to capture him. The names of the assassin and the people under arrest were not revealed.[47] But the interview had left no doubt as to which organization was responsible for the assassination of the exemplary Polish patriot, statesman, hero, and martyr. Polish society was outraged at that time by the assassination, and exhausted by the exaggerated and politicized mourning rituals.

After the justice minister's announcement of the results of the investigation, the UNDO, in a short resolution released on 13 July 1934 condemned the OUN, its terrorist nature, and its pernicious influence on Ukrainian youth.[48] *Novyi shliakh*, a Ukrainian newspaper published in Canada, reacted with a condemnation of UNDO and characterized its leaders as people who "signed a document that means to declare war on Ukrainian revolutionary nationalism and the OUN."[49]

Ukrainian newspapers changed their method of reporting on and judging the OUN and its terrorist acts only on 25 July 1934 when the OUN killed Ivan Babii, the director of and a teacher at a Ukrainian high school in Lviv. Before he was shot to death, Babii had already been beaten up on two occasions by OUN operatives, once on 11 November and again on 23 November 1932.[50] Having killed Babii and realizing that he could not escape, the young assassin and OUN member Mykhailo Tsar shot himself in the head and died some hours later in hospital. The assassination of Ivan Babii provoked a completely different reaction from the editors of *Novyi chas*, who had been reluctant a few days earlier to inform their readers about Pieracki's assassination but now printed an article entitled "Horrible Assassination" on the front page. A number of other articles devoted to this topic followed.[51]

Dilo also reported feverishly about the murder of Babii and the desperate assassin's suicide.[52] The assassination provoked *Dilo* to take a critical position toward the OUN and to condemn its politics again. Shortly after the assassination, an anonymous journalist for *Dilo* pointed out: "This latest murder is the result of a tragic misunderstanding. Because of a tragic misunderstanding, members of the same nation kill each other."[53] On 5 August, ten days after the murder of Babii, Metropolitan Andrei Sheptyts'kyi, the head of the Greek Catholic Church, also condemned the deed in *Dilo*. He called Babii's assassins "Ukrainian terrorists" and "enemies of the [Ukrainian] nation."[54] According to another source, Sheptyts'kyi stated in reaction to Babii's assassination: "If you want to treacherously kill all those who oppose your

47 "Zbrodnia nie ujdzie ..." *Gazeta Polska*, 10 July 1934, 1.

48 Zynovii Knysh, *Varshavs'kyi protses OUN: Na pidlozhi pol's'ko-ukraïns'kykh vidnosyn tiieï doby* (Toronto: Sribna Surma, 1986), 285–87.

49 Knysh, *Varshavs'kyi protses*, 287.

50 "Wyrok," TsDIAL, f. 205, spr. 3125, 61.; Żeleński, *Akt oskarżenia*, 55.

51 "Zhakhlyvyi atentat," *Novyi chas*, 27 July 1934, 1. For other articles see the issues of *Novyi chas* for 29 and 30 June 1934.

52 "Dyrektor Ivan Babii zastrilenyi" and "Trahedia dyrektora," *Dilo*, 27 July 1934, 1; "Pislia trahichnoï smerty dyr. Ivana Babiia," *Dilo*, 28 July 1934, 3–4. Babii was assassinated by OUN member Mykhailo Tsar. The assassination was prepared by Maliutsa, Pidhainyi, Kachmars'kyi, Myhal', and others. The assassination was ordered by Bandera before his arrest on 14 June. Cf. Żeleński, *Akt oskarżenia*, 90–91.

53 "Pislia trahichnoï smerty dyr. Ivana Babiia," *Dilo*, 28 July 1934, 4.

54 "Holos Mytropolyta," *Dilo*, 5 August 1934, 3.

work, you will have to kill all teachers and professors who work for the Ukrainian youth, all fathers and mothers of Ukrainian children."[55] The assassination of Pieracki, on the other hand, had not provoked a similar reaction on the part of Sheptyts'kyi.

More than a year later, in the second half of October 1935, the first commemorative celebration of Pieracki's death took place in Nowy Sącz. Delegations from various social, political, and cultural organizations, together with military and police units from around the country arranged to participate. According to the schedule of events, Pieracki's coffin was carried at 7 p.m. on 19 October from the new cemetery to a chapel in the old cemetery. On the morning of Sunday 20 October, Franciszek Lisowski, a bishop from Ternopil', conducted a memorial service in the chapel. During the service, members of Pieracki's family were accompanied by the First Regiment of the Riflemen from Podhale, representatives of the Polish government, of organizations from different parts of Poland, and of the local population. After the memorial service Pieracki's coffin was located in a simple military-style mausoleum. The placing of Pieracki's coffin in the mausoleum was accompanied by the military song "We, the First Brigade" (*My, Pierwsza Brygada*) performed by the riflemen. Following this ceremony, a cornerstone was set for a future riflemen's house (*dom strzelecki*) in Nowy Sącz, which was named after Pieracki. Bishop Lisowski blessed the cornerstone, and Prime Minister Marian Zyndram-Kościałkowski delivered a speech.[56] A month later, the long trial of the OUN members, who had organized Pieracki's assassination, began.

The First Trial of OUN Members in Warsaw

In a trial lasting from 18 November 1935 to 13 January 1936, twelve OUN members—Stepan Bandera, Daria Hnatkivs'ka, Iaroslav Karpynets', Ievhen Kachmars'kyi, Mykola Klymyshyn, Mykola Lebed', Ivan Maliutsa, Bohdan Pidhainyi, Roman Myhal', Iaroslav Rak, Iakiv Chornii, and Kateryna Zaryts'ka—were accused either of organizing and conducting the assassination of Pieracki, or of helping the assassin to escape. In addition, all of them were accused of "being active in the OUN, which tried to separate from the Polish state its south-eastern voivodeships." Especially the latter accusation made the trial a political one. The authorities used it to "show justice," but they did not intend to stage a show trial. On the one hand, the prosecutors investigated the crime in depth and scrupulously presented their results to the public. On the other hand, the trial was used to demonstrate how the authorities would proceed against individuals or groups who attacked or harmed the Polish state, questioned its existence or tried to separate any of its territory.[57]

55 Quoted in John-Paul Himka, "Christianity and Radical Nationalism: Metropolitan Andrei Sheptytsky and the Bandera Movement," in *State Secularism and Live Religion in Soviet Russia and Ukraine*, ed. Catherine Wanner (New York: Oxford University Press, 2012), 97.

56 "Program uroczystości ku czci ś. p. min. Bronisława Pierackiego w Nowym Sączu," *Gazeta Polska*, 18 October 1935, 2.

57 Żeleński, *Akt oskarżenia*, 2–4. The trial in Warsaw was the only trial dedicated to Pieracki's assassination, but it was followed by another massive trial in Lviv from 25 May to 27 June 1936. The Lviv trial dealt with several other crimes that were committed, in part by the OUN members who had been on trial in Warsaw, and in part by others. The numerous other OUN members who were arrested in the summer of 1934 were tried in local courts, if they did not qualify for the Warsaw or Lviv trials.

Fig. 8. OUN leaflet with the defendants from the Warsaw trail.
Poltava, *Zhyttia Stepana Bandery*, 18.

Before the Warsaw trial began, the twelve OUN members involved in Pieracki's assassination had been interrogated for about a year. For the first time since his arrest, Bandera was interrogated on 16 June 1934. During this interrogation Bandera denied that he belonged to the OUN. He informed the investigating officer, who wanted to interrogate him in Polish, that he knew Polish but would only answer in Ukrainian. Due to the "impossibility to communicate," the interrogation was postponed until 26

June.[58] On 12 November 1934, Bandera again denied belonging to the OUN. He also claimed that he did not know Lebed' and could not recognize him on a photograph. On 16 November 1934, he said that not only did he not belong to the OUN but that he had nothing in common with it.[59] On 10 January 1935, Bandera denied that he had suspected Bachyns'kyi of being an informer, denied that he had ordered his murder, and denied that he had ordered the disposal of his corpse. He would only confirm that he knew Bachyns'kyi from the Ukrainian Student House.[60] During the same interrogation he denied knowing Lemyk and ordering him to kill the Soviet consul and denied knowing Matseiko and ordering him to kill Pieracki.[61] In a similar manner, Bandera denied several dozen criminal deeds.[62]

The protocols of the interrogation between 16 June and 26 September 1934 are missing. According a protocol dated 27 September, Bandera claimed that he was interrogated without interruption from 9 a.m. on 6 August, to 8 p.m. on 11 August. Although he had already signed a protocol on 7 August at about 8 p.m., the interrogators continued to interrogate him for four more days. They did not allow him to sleep or even rest, and they informed him that they would not stop until he gave them further information. In order to interrupt the interrogation, Bandera informed them on Saturday 11 August that he would give them further statements on Monday 13 August, and would also prepare a statement about his views on the OUN for the newspapers. He was taken to his cell, from where he informed other OUN prisoners about the circumstances of the interrogation, shouting through an open window: "[It's] Bandera! I testified [*sic*]; the police keep interrogating without interruption, all day and night, and demand other statements. I was interrogated from Monday till Saturday, and on Monday they will interrogate me further." On Monday 13 August, Bandera told the interrogators that he would not do as he had promised on Saturday, and that he had only made the promise in order to interrupt the interrogation and to inform other OUN prisoners about the conduct of the interrogators.[63] Another OUN prisoner, Klymyshyn, did not mention such interrogation methods in his memoirs, but, unlike Bandera, he decided from the very beginning not to make any statement or answer any questions.[64]

Several other arrested OUN members, for example Stets'ko and Ianiv, consistently denied everything, like Bandera. Roman Shukhevych even stated that he "does not agree with the ideology of the OUN because it does not lead to the aim."[65] Nevertheless, the interrogating officers obtained a huge amount of information about the structure of the OUN and Bandera's role in the organization from other sources. One of the sources consisted of the OUN members Ivan Maliutsa, Roman Myhal', Bohdan Pidhainyi, and

58 Interrogation of Stepan Bandera, 16 June 1934, TsDIAL, f. 371, op. 1, spr. 8, od. 76, 35.

59 Interrogation of Stepan Bandera, 12 November 1934, TsDIAL, f. 371, op. 1, spr. 8, od. 76, 38.

60 Interrogation of Stepan Bandera, 10 January 1935, TsDIAL, f. 371, op. 1, spr. 8, od. 76, 39, 41. For the suggestion that Bandera ordered the burial of Bachyns'kyi's corpse, see Interrogation of Bohdan Pidhainyi, 28 December 1934, TSDIAL, f. 371, op. 1, spr. 8, od. 77, 67.

61 Interrogation of Stepan Bandera, 10 January 1935, TsDIAL, f. 371, op. 1, spr. 8, od. 76, 46–48.

62 TSDIAL, f. 371, op. 1, spr. 8, od. 76, 33–54.

63 TsDIAL, f. 371, op. 1, spr. 8, od. 76, 37, quoted in *Zhyttia i diial'nist'*, ed. Posivnych, 2011, 281–82. When I worked in TsDIAL in 2008 the file with Bandera's interrogation did not contain folio number 37. I discovered it only reading Posivnych's publication from 2011, in which the document is reprinted.

64 Klymyshyn, *V pokhodi*, 1.

65 TsDIAL, f. 371, op. 1, spr. 8, od. 77, 179. For Stets'ko and Ianiv, see Interrogation of Iaroslav Stets'ko, 18 February 1935 and 1 August 1935, TsDIAL, f. 371, op. 1, spr. 8, od. 77, 163–66; Interrogation of Volodymyr Ianiv, 7 February 1935 and 28 July 1935, TsDIAL, f. 371, op. 1, spr. 8, od. 77, 202–205.

Ievhen Kachmars'kyi, who began to reveal the secrets of the organization during their interrogations.[66]

Myhal' and Maliutsa decided to testify because they had "qualms of conscience" about their deeds. Both were involved in the murder of Ivan Babii on 25 July 1934, and Myhal' was also involved in the murder of OUN member Bachyns'kyi on 31 March 1934. Both Bachyns'kyi and Babii were killed on Bandera's order. Babii was accused by Bandera of supporting the Polish authorities and of suppressing Ukrainian nationalism. Bachyns'kyi was murdered because Bandera suspected him of collaborating with the Polish intelligence service.[67] Myhal', and Sen'kiv invited Bachyns'kyi, for a drink on 9 May 1934. They felt that they had to get drunk before shooting him, because they had an amicable relationship with him.[68] After murdering Bachyns'kyi, Myhal' fell into a deep depression, and the OUN sought to "liquidate" him.[69] Of the four individuals who informed on their comrades, only Pidhainyi later tried to withdraw his testimony on the grounds that it was made under duress.[70]

Another major source of information was the Senyk archives, an important collection of about 2,500 OUN documents that were confiscated in Prague in 1933 from the house of OUN member Omelian Senyk. The Czechoslovak intelligence service made these documents available to the Polish service.[71] The contents of the Senyk archives helped the investigators to persuade some of the defendants to testify.[72] Together with the contents of the Senyk archives, their evidence enabled Prosecutor Żeleński to write a detailed act of indictment, containing much information about the structure, deeds, and financing of the OUN.[73] In the course of the investigation, Żeleński prepared twenty-four volumes of investigation records for the Warsaw trial.[74]

According to the evidence given during the investigation, Bandera's role in Pieracki's assassination was significant. He was accused of persuading Matseiko to murder Pieracki and of providing him with the gun. He was accused of supplying Lebed' with money, for the purpose of observing Pieracki in Warsaw, and was also accused of other aspects of the crime.[75] According to prosecutor Żeleński, however, it was not Bandera who made the initial decision to kill Pieracki, but the leadership in exile, or the PUN. In

66 Interrogations of Ievhen Kachmars'kyi TsDIAL, f. 371, op. 1, spr. 8, od. 76, 77–119; Żeleński, *Zabójstwo ministra Pierackiego*, 69–70. Ivan Maliutsa was arrested on 10 August 1934, Roman Myhal' on 24 September 1934, and Bohdan Pidhainyi on 14 June 1934.

67 Interrogation of Roman Myhal, 21 December 1934, TsDIAL, f. 371, op. 1, spr. 8, od. 76, 277, 279; Żeleński, *Zabójstwo ministra Pierackiego*, 18–20; Żeleński, *Akt oskarżenia*, 2, 87–92.

68 Interrogation of Roman Myhal, 31 December 1935, TsDIAL, f. 371, op. 1, spr. 8, od. 76, 287–88; Interrogation of Roman Senkiv, 3 January 1935, TSDIAL, f. 371, op. 1, spr. 8, od. 77, 129; "Proces. Zeznania zabójcy Baczyńskiego. Pytania Myhala," *Gazeta Polska*, 12 December 1935, 4.

69 Żeleński, *Zabójstwo ministra Pierackiego*, 18–20; Żeleński, *Akt oskarżenia*, 2, 87–92.

70 Żeleński, *Zabójstwo Ministra Pierackiego*, 25–27.

71 The Polish intelligence service received 418 original and 2,055 photographed documents from the Czechoslovak intelligence service. Cf. Wyrok," TsDIAL, f. 205, spr. 3125, 14; "Proces o zamordowanie ś. p. ministra Br. Pierackiego," *Gazeta Polska*, 20 November 1935, 6; Posivnych, *Varshavs'kyi akt*, 168–69.

72 Klymyshyn, *V pokhodi*, 1:123–25.

73 For the act of indictment, see Władysław Żeleński, *Akt oskarżenia*.

74 "Proces," *Gazeta Polska*, 19 November 1935, 4. During my research I did not find the twenty-four volumes, which were very likely lost during the Second World War. Klymyshyn mentions "more than forty-five volumes," see Klymyshyn, *V pokhodi*, 1:123.

75 Żeleński, *Akt oskarżenia*, 2–3.

particular, it was alleged that Konovalets', Iaryi, and Senyk had issued the order and instructed Bandera and other members to organize and carry out the assassination.[76]

Stepan Shukhevych and Volodymyr Starosol's'kyi, two lawyers who had previously acted for the OUN, were called as witnesses for the prosecution. This made it impossible for them to act as defending lawyers in this trial, despite the request of the families of the defendants. The two lawyers were therefore replaced by Volodymyr Horbovyi, Stanislav Shlapak, Lev Hankevych, and Lev Pavents'kyi, all of them less experienced in this kind of trial than Shukhevych and Starosol's'kyi.[77] According to Stepan Shukhevych, who had not only defended OUN members at several trials but was also connected with the OUN through family ties, Konovalets' intended to admit at the beginning of the trial that the OUN had killed Pieracki, but Hankevych had changed the meaning of the message before passing it on to the other three defense lawyers.[78]

Just as the OUN regarded assassination as a means of propaganda, so they also used trials as political stages. A trial was an opportunity to propagate the cause of Ukrainian nationalism and to draw international attention to the situation of the Ukrainians in Poland. This frequently came about as the result of an unwritten agreement with elements of the Ukrainian press, which would depict trials of OUN members as political, even if they were accused of a robbery or killing a policeman. All trials of OUN members in the Second Republic were in fact political, because, in addition to the crimes that they had committed, the defendants were inevitably accused of belonging to the OUN.

The Warsaw trial of the OUN members, like Pieracki's funeral some months before, became a political spectacle for the media. Throughout the trial, almost all Polish and Ukrainian newspapers published detailed reports on the proceedings. Some of them, for example *Express Poranny* from Lviv and *Ilustrowany Kurier Codzienny* from Cracow, published sensational articles. Polish tabloid newspapers mobilized their readers' emotions, publishing front page articles with large headlines such as "Huge Revelations about Pieracki's Murders," "Leaders and Fighters of OUN Paid by Lithuania: Unbelievable Revelations at Trial in Warsaw," or "Amazing Confessions of Witnesses and Devious Strategy of Defense."[79] During the trial, the *Ilustrowany Kurier Codzienny* published detailed reports of the crime, and grief-inducing pictures of Pieracki's assassination, of the mourning ceremonies in June 1934, of Pieracki's body in a coffin on a catafalque, and of Pieracki's mausoleum in Nowy Sącz.[80]

The main Ukrainian newspaper *Dilo* published less sensational and more factual reports from the courtroom. It also printed parts of the indictment, translated into Ukrainian.[81] *Novyi chas*, another major Ukrainian newspaper, chose a more

76 Ibid., 99; Golczewski, *Deutsche und Ukrainer*, 697; "Proces o zamordowanie ś. p. ministra Br. Pierackiego," *Gazeta Polska*, 20 November 1935, 8.

77 Shukhevych, *Moie zhyttia*, 511–12; "Proces. Bandera," *Gazeta Polska*, 3 January 1936, 6.

78 Shukhevych, *Moie zhyttia*, 515.

79 "Wielkie rewelacje o mordach min. Pierackiego. Pierwszy dzień procesu w Warszawie," *Express Poranny*, 20 November 1935, 1; "Wodzowie i Bojownicy O.U.N. na żołdzie Litwy. Niesłychane rewelacje w procesie warszawskim," *Express Poranny*, 21 November 1935, 1; "Rewelacyjne zeznania świadków i podstępna taktyka obroany," *Ilustrowany Kurier Codzienny*, 14 December 1935, 13.

80 *Ilustrowany Kurier Codzienny*, 19 November 1935, 1, 16; 20 November 1935, 3, 4.

81 The indictment was published in Ukrainian as "Akt obvynuvachennia," in *Dilo*, 19 November 1935, 3–11; 20 November 1935, 3–6; 21 November 1935, 3–7. *Dilo*'s reporter complained that it was more restricted by censorship than Polish newspapers. Cf. "Zahal'ni vrazhinnia nashoho korespondenta," *Dilo*, 20 November 1935, 7.

sensational path of reporting. It published huge headlines on the first pages, such as "12 Ukrainians Accused of Complicity in the Murder of Minister Pieracki before the Court in Warsaw" and "Fighter of the Ukrainian Underground before the Court in Warsaw. The Huge Political Trial in Consequence of the Murder of Minister Pieracki."[82] On the first page of *Novyi chas*, readers could not miss the pictures of the "Croatian Insurgents," which appeared next to the articles about the OUN revolutionaries. The Ustaša was involved in the assassination of King Alexander I of Yugoslavia and French foreign minister Louis Barthou in Marseilles on 9 October 1934, and their trial took place at the same time as the trial in Warsaw.[83]

The trial began on 18 November 1935, in the eighth penal division of the regional court in Warsaw. For security reasons, the courtroom was separated from other parts of the building. Without special tickets, members of the public were excluded from the courtroom. Apart from the lawyers, security people, and other court staff, the well of the court was therefore occupied only by journalists and by relatives of the accused.[84] On a long table placed before the court, exhibits, such as weapons, and numerous bottles and flasks from Karpynets's laboratory were arranged. In addition, twenty-four thick volumes of the investigation record were stacked up.[85]

Observing Bandera, who was sitting near the exhibits, an unidentified reporter from *Gazeta Polska* characterized him as

> the leader of all the other [defendants] and the superior in the ranks of the terrorist organization ... who coordinated the terrorist action in the entire territory of Poland and who was in contact with the leading members abroad. Bandera, the ace of the terrorist organization, looks inconspicuous. Small, thin, puny, looks not older than twenty or twenty-two, receding chin, sharp features, unpleasant physiognomy, darting eyes with a small squint, nervous movements, small pinched mouth, laughs quite often, revealing uneven teeth, talks to his defending lawyers with vibrant gestures.[86]

The trial began at 10 a.m. and was soon transformed into a power struggle. After a short and formal statement concerning juridical formalities, the chairman of the court, Władysław Posemkiewicz, began to question the defendants as to their personal details—the first, in alphabetical order, being Bandera. He answered the chairman's first question, about his name, with a resonant "Stepan." This differed from the Polish equivalent "Stefan," which appeared in the indictment, and which the chairman expected to hear. Bandera then gave the names of his parents and his date of birth, in Ukrainian. The chairman reminded Bandera that the official language of the court was Polish, to which Bandera replied in Ukrainian, "I will answer only in Ukrainian [*Budu vidpovidaty til'ky po-ukraïns'ky*]." The chairman asked Bandera if he knew Polish. Bandera answered with "Tak," which means "yes" in both Ukrainian and Polish. At this point, Bandera's lawyer Horbovyi stood up, but the chairman did not allow him to

82 *Novyi chas*, 19 November 1935, 1, 20 November 1935, 1.
83 *Novyi chas*, 23 November 1935, 1.
84 "Proces o zamordowanie ś. p. ministra Br. Pierackiego," *Gazeta Polska*, 19 November 1935, 4; "Proces morderców śp. ministra Pierackiego rozpoczęty," *Ilustrowany Kurier Codzienny*, 20 November 1935, 3; "Zamachowcy ukraińscy na ławie oskarżonych," *Kurjer Bydgoski*, 20 November 1935, 1.
85 "Proces," *Gazeta Polska*, 19 November 1935, 4.
86 "Proces," *Gazeta Polska*, 19 November 1935, 4.

speak and immediately reminded the court that he would not permit any discussion of the question of language because it was regulated by a law that allowed the use of Ukrainian in trials held exclusively in the south-eastern voivodeships of Poland.[87]

The next two defendants questioned, Lebed' and Hnatkivs'ka, applied the same tactics regarding language and behavior in the courtroom as had Bandera. Karpynets', the student of chemistry and constructor of the bomb that did not explode, when reminded to speak Polish, boomed: "The prestige of the Organization of Ukrainian Nationalists enjoins me to speak Ukrainian!" Prosecutor Żeleński then applied to the court for the appointment of an interpreter, in case defendants such as Karpynets' wanted to reveal important evidence. The chairman replied that the court would consider the question later but would not take note meanwhile of any testimony in a "non-Polish language" and would regard it as a refusal to testify. Bandera immediately shouted in Ukrainian, "I want to testify!" The chairman answered in Polish, "The court will take notice of testimony only in Polish," and explained that, because the defendants had not followed his instructions, he would read out their personal details.[88]

When Bandera's lawyer Horbovyi asked for the trial to be postponed on the grounds that he had not had enough time to study the voluminous investigation record, and because five defendants had not yet managed to retain counsel, Bandera stood up, and shouted in Ukrainian, "Because not all the defendants have a defending lawyer, I abandon my defense lawyer!" The chairman stated that he had not asked Bandera to take the floor and refused all of Horbovyi's requests. The defending lawyers then tried to postpone the trial, using the argument that the defendant Chornii was under psychiatric observation during the investigation and might be mentally disordered, whereas this was not mentioned in the indictment. Prosecutor Żeleński protested that psychiatrists had examined Chornii and had determined that he was not insane. Bandera jumped up again and informed the court in a resonant voice that he was abandoning his lawyer. The chairman again requested Bandera to remain silent, unless he had been asked to speak, and informed him and the other defendants that anyone who interrupted the proceedings would be removed from the courtroom. Surprised by Bandera's capricious move to abandon his lawyer, the latter asked the court for a recess in order to confer with his client, which was granted.[89] After the break, Horbovyi informed the court that Bandera had withdrawn his request to do without defense counsel. The chairman read out part of the indictment, which gave details of the preparation and execution of Pieracki's assassination.[90]

87 "Proces," *Gazeta Polska*, 19 November 1935, 4; "Roprava za vbystvo ministra Pierats'koho," *Dilo*, 19 November 1935, 1.

88 "Proces," *Gazeta Polska*, 19 November 1935, 4; "Roprava za vbystvo ministra Pierats'koho," *Dilo*, 19 November 1935, 1.

89 "Proces," *Gazeta Polska*, 19 November 1935, 4; "Rozprava za vbystvo ministra Pierats'koho," *Dilo*, 19 November 1935, 1.

90 "Proces," *Gazeta Polska*, 19 November 1935, 4–7.

Fig. 9. OUN leaflet released after the announcement of Bandera's sentence in Warsaw. Inscription under the picture "'Die but Do not Betray!', 'Iron and Blood Will Judge Us!' (STEPAN BANDERA. OUN member, sentenced to life imprisonment in the Warsaw trial). Posivnych, *Stepan Bandera: Dokumenty i materialy*, 66.

At 10 a.m. the following day, the trial recommenced with the reading of the remainder of the indictment. With the exception of Karpynets', the defendants' demeanor was listless. Vasyl' Mudryi, UNDO politician and deputy speaker of the Sejm, came to the courtroom. Leon Jarosławski, a specialist in the Ukrainian language, was admitted as an expert but not as an interpreter.[91] The part of the indictment that was read out gave details of other assassinations and terror acts performed by the OUN. It started with the unsuccessful attempt of the UVO—forerunner of the OUN—to kill the "Leader of the Nation," Józef Piłsudski, on 25 October 1921 in Lviv and ended with the assassinations of the Ukrainians Bachyns'kyi and Babii. The latter was murdered after

91 "Proces," *Gazeta Polska*, 20 November 1935, 6.

almost all the leading OUN members were taken into custody during the arrests in June 1934.[92]

The observers at the trial also learned that some OUN members such as Spol's'kyi, Makarushka, and Myhal', whose statements during interrogations were read out in the courtroom, experienced moral problems about some OUN orders, especially concerning the murder of Ukrainians. Either during the investigation or already prior to their arrest, their attitude toward the OUN had changed. Spol's'kyi, an OUN member who was not among the defendants, stated during the investigation that he was revealing information that would enable the security authorities to "liquidate the OUN, whose activities he considers to be very harmful for the Ukrainian nation." Makarushka asserted that the OUN was making young Ukrainians "pessimistic, dogged, simple-minded, unsociable, and treacherous."[93] Myhal' stated that he was ready to die for his evidence, if it contributed to the liquidation of the OUN.[94] After the chairman finished reading the act of indictment at 4.30 p.m. on the second day of the trial, and the members of the court had left the courtroom, Lebed' jumped up and tried to shout something, but he was prevented by a guard and also by Karpynets', who shouted at him to sit down.[95]

An unidentified correspondent of *Gazeta Polska* wrote that the text of the indictment revealed astounding information about "the activities of the OUN in Poland and other countries, as well as about the help that the Ukrainian terrorists received from the Lithuanian government."[96] Other newspapers discovered especially interesting and significant information as to such collaboration and advertised it with huge headlines, frequently on the front page, such as "Lithuania Abets the Murderers from the O.U.N.!" "When Ministers Liaise with Murderers ..." and "Leaders and Fighters of the OUN Were Paid by Lithuania: Unbelievable Revelations in Trial in Warsaw."[97]

On 20 November 1935, the third day of the trial, a reporter for *Gazeta Polska* spotted a Yugoslav journalist, probably interested to hear about the connections between the OUN and the Ustaša. The Polish reporter also mentioned that Lebed's mother, whom he characterized as a plain peasant woman, had appeared in the courtroom. The chairman Posemkiewicz addressed the defendants, starting with Bandera. He read from the indictment, and asked Bandera whether he pleaded guilty. Bandera started to answer in Ukrainian: "For me as a Ukrainian . . . [*Meni iako ukraïns'komu . . .*]" According to Prosecutor Żeleński, Bandera informed the court that he was a Ukrainian citizen and therefore not subject to the Polish law. The chairman interrupted him, reminding him to speak Polish. Bandera continued in Ukrainian with a resonant voice, explaining once more that Polish law did not apply to him. The chairman informed the defendant that if he spoke a "non-Polish language" the court would regard it as a

92 Ibid., 6–8. For Piłsudski as the "Leader of the Nation," see "Po zamordowaniu ministra spaw wewnętrznych Bronisława Pierackiego. Stolica w hołdzie," *Gazeta Polska*, 17 June 1934, 8; "Mordy i sabotaże," *Kurjer Lwowski*, 20 November 1935, 1.

93 "Proces," *Gazeta Polska*, 20 November 1935, 8.

94 "Akt obvynuvachennia," *Dilo*, 20 November 1935, 7.

95 Ibid., 9.

96 "Proces," *Gazeta Polska*, 20 November 1935, 6.

97 "Litwa współdziała z mordercami z O.U.N.!" *Ilustrowany Kurier Codzienny*, 21 November 1935, 3; "Gdy ministrowie rokują z mordercami," *Ilustrowany Kurier Codzienny*, 21 November 1935, 1; "Wodzowie i Bojownicy O.U.N. na żołdzie Litwy. Niesłychane rewelacje w procesie warszawskim," *Ilustrowany Express Poranny*, 21 November 1935, 1.

refusal to testify, he would be removed from the courtroom, and relevant information concerning him would be read out from the interrogation record. Bandera answered in Ukrainian, "I want to explain . . . [*Ia khochu vyiasniaty . . .*]" The chairman told him that if he did not stop shouting he would be removed. Bandera did not lower his voice, and the chairman ordered him removed.[98] Żeleński commented on this scene in his memoirs: "Bandera resisted and so the police removed him by force. The convulsive waving of the hands and legs of this little man appeared rather comical. But there came from him unbelievable energy and fantastic strength." He also added that everybody in the courtroom understood that Bandera was indeed the leader of the defendants and carried authority.[99] A reporter from the popular newspaper *Ilustrowany Express Poranny*, on the other hand, who also observed the scene, wrote that Bandera wanted to deliver a prepared speech. He perceived Bandera as being nervous and angry. His short speech was slurred, and it was difficult to understand him.[100]

Once Bandera had been removed from the courtroom, the chairman read out Bandera's evidence from the lengthy interrogation. According to the correspondent of *Gazeta Polska*, Bandera had originally denied belonging to the OUN, planning Pieracki's assassination, and other terrorist acts. When asked by interrogators about a journey to Gdańsk, Bandera told them that the purpose was not to meet other OUN members but to invite a cousin to the wedding of his sister. While there, he went swimming in the Baltic Sea, caught a cold, was confined to bed for a week, and missed his sister's wedding. After some weeks in custody, however, Bandera ceased to deny his membership of the OUN, assured the interrogators that he wanted to give honest evidence, and declared his wish to appeal to Ukrainian youth with a publication of some sort that described the true state of affairs, calling upon Ukrainian youth to oppose the terrorist acts of the OUN and to prevent more bloodshed. When asked by the investigating officer about his original denial, Bandera claimed that he had lied in the first instance. During subsequent investigations, however, he refused to write a statement about the OUN and said that he had lied in order to put an end to the interrogation, and in order to inform his colleagues in other cells that he had not admitted anything. During succeeding interrogations, Bandera had returned to his claim that he did not belong to the OUN. When he was confronted with the evidence of Pidhainyi and Maliutsa, who had revealed Bandera's role in the OUN and his involvement in terrorist activity, Bandera had expressed his wish to say nothing. The chairman said that when the results of the investigation were presented to Bandera, he said that all of the accusations were groundless.[101]

Lebed' applied the same tactics concerning language as had Bandera, which caused a dispute between the defense and prosecution. Prosecutor Kazimierz Rudnicki explained that, if the defendants did not know Polish, the court would have asked an interpreter to translate their testimony, as it would for any other non-Polish speakers, regardless of their nationality, but because the defendants had studied at Polish

98 "Proces," *Gazeta Polska*, 21 November 1935, 6; Żeleński, *Zabójstwo ministra*, 69.

99 Żeleński, *Zabójstwo ministra*, 69.

100 "Zdenerwowanie wodza O.U.N.," *Ilustrowany Express Poranny*, 22 November 1935, 1; Żeleński, *Zabójstwo ministra*, 69.

101 "Proces," *Gazeta Polska*, 21 November 1935, 6. The *Ilustrowany Kurier Codzienny* commented that Bandera's testimonies during the interrogations were evasive and deceitful. Cf. "Wykręty i kłamliwe zeznania Bandery w śledztwie," *Ilustrowany Kurier Codzienny*, 22 November 1935, 13.

universities and knew Polish very well, it was apparent that they chose to speak Ukrainian with the intention of making a political demonstration, which the court would not tolerate. Defense lawyer Hankevych protested that Lebed' had not studied at a Polish university as had the other defendants and that he had refused to speak Polish in order not to mangle the language. Prosecutor Żeleński objected that Lebed' knew Polish from high school. At this point, Lebed' asked to speak in Polish. The chairman allowed him to speak but Lebed' continued in Ukrainian. The chairman interrupted him and read out his evidence from the interrogation record.[102]

Speaking in Ukrainian, the next defendant Hnatkivs'ka also denied belonging to the OUN and informed the chairman that she would only testify in this language. He allowed her to sit down, and he then read out her evidence from the investigation.[103] Karpynets', Pidhainyi, Maliutsa, Kachmars'kyi, Zaryts'ka, and Rak behaved in a similar fashion. The chairman responded by interrupting the defendants in turn and reading out their evidence from the investigation record.[104] Klymyshyn responded to every question with silence, as he had during the entire interrogation.[105] Some of the defendants had applied the language ploy during the investigations. For example, Bandera had stated during the interrogations that he "can speak and write Polish but refuses to use this language."[106] Other defendants also claimed that they knew Polish but would not use it, because it was the language of their "enemies" and "occupiers."[107] *Ilustrowany Kurier Codzienny* reported these linguistic contentions in a sensationally written article entitled, "The Defendants Provocatively Do Not Want to Testify in Polish!"[108]

The first defendant to testify in Polish was Myhal'. He legitimized his decision by observing that Warsaw did not lie on Ukrainian territory and that he was therefore not harming the Ukrainian nation by testifying in Polish.[109] He pleaded guilty and stated that he wanted to recount all his crimes, such as shooting Bachyns'kyi. Then he spoke about crimes committed by other defendants, as he had already described during the interrogation.[110] Nevertheless, he did not reveal all of them, and, by providing false or incomplete information, he tried to avoid incriminating some OUN members.[111] Asked by the defense lawyer Hankevych, "How would you explain that you are stressing your guilt with such pleasure, because I do not understand how somebody can push himself in such a way under the guillotine?" Myhal' replied that he wanted to right a wrong—the

102 "Proces," *Gazeta Polska*, 21 November 1935, 6.

103 Ibid., 6.

104 For Karpynets', see "Proces," *Gazeta Polska*, 21 November 1935, 7. For Pidhainyi, see "Proces," *Gazeta Polska*, 23 November 1935, 4. For Maliutsa, see "Proces," *Gazeta Polska*, 23 November 1935, 4. For Kachmars'kyi, see "Proces," *Gazeta Polska*, 26 November 1935, 6. In answer to the chairman's first question, Kachmars'kyi did not deny belonging to the OUN and stated that he pleaded "not guilty." He answered the question as many other defendants in Ukrainian. For Zaryts'ka, see "Proces," *Gazeta Polska*, 26 November 1935, 6. For Rak, see "Proces," *Gazeta Polska*, 26 November 1935, 6.

105 "Proces," *Gazeta Polska*, 23 November 1935, 4.

106 "Prowokacje osk. Bandery," *Kurjer Lwowski*, 21 November 1935, 1.

107 "Mowa prokuratora Rudnickiego w procesie o zamordowania ś. p. ministra Pierackiego," *Gazeta Polska*, 28 December 1935, 6.

108 "Oskarżeni prowokacyjnie nie chcą zeznawać *po polsku!*"*Ilustrowany Kurier Codzienny*, 22 November 1935, 13. Emphasis in the original.

109 "Rozprava za ... Myhal' hovoryt' po pol'sky," *Dilo*, 24 November 1935, 4.

110 "Osk. Myhal przemawia po polsku i przyznaje się do winy," *Ilustrowany Kurier Codzienny*, 25 November 1935, 13–15.

111 "Proces Oskarżeni," *Gazeta Polska*, 31 December 1935, 8.

death of Bachyns'kyi and Babii.[112] When his testimony was read out in the courtroom on the next day, 26 November 1935, other defendants appeared astonished, perplexed, and nervous. Two days later, the newspaper *Express Ilustrowany* published an article entitled "Impressive Revelations by Myhal': Prosecuted Ukrainians Listen with Bated Breath."[113]

The majority of the OUN members who were called as witnesses refused to testify in Polish, just as most of the defendants had done. The court regarded their behavior as a political demonstration. Those who knew Polish but refused to testify in that language were punished with a fine, or imprisonment in default. The witness Irena Khomiak was punished with a fine of 100 złotys or ten days imprisonment, for speaking Ukrainian.[114] Romana Chorna, Roman Shukhevych, Oleksandr Pashkevych, Osyp Mashchak, Dmytro Myron, and Osyp Nydza were punished with 200 złotys or ten days imprisonment.[115] On 5 December 1935, Olena Chaikivs'ka was punished with 300 złotys or ten days imprisonment, and on the order of the chairman, was removed by force from the courtroom, as she would not stop speaking in Ukrainian to him. The next day, however, she decided to testify in Polish.[116] The witness Adriian Hornyts'kyi claimed that during the interrogation he was forced to give evidence against his colleagues, by being kept outside in freezing weather for hours. Despite the attempts of the prosecutor to calm him down, Hornyts'kyi said that he venerated the OUN and stressed that he "belonged to the OUN and will belong." For this political statement he was sentenced to two days in a dark cell. Prosecutor Żeleński established that Hornyts'kyi was interrogated on 7 and 8 September. Prosecutor Rudnicki commented that on 7 and 8 September there "may or may not have been good weather, but certainly not frost," and initiated a separate investigation against Hornyts'kyi for giving false testimony.[117]

The most spectacular witness that day was the young OUN member Vira Svientsits'ka. As many other OUN witnesses before her had done, she informed the court in Ukrainian that she spoke Polish but was prepared to testify only in Ukrainian. For this statement, the chairman punished her with a fine of 200 złotys or ten days imprisonment and ordered the guards to lead her out. As Svientsits'ka was passing the dock, she went toward the defendants, raised her right arm, and shouted, "Slava Ukraïni!" The defendant Karpynets' stood up, raised his arm, and answered, "Slava Ukraïni!" This is apparently the first recorded fascist salute that OUN members performed in public. For

112 "Samoobvynuvachennia pids. Myhala," *Novyi chas*, 26 November 1935, 2.

113 "Wrażenia rewelacyj Myhala. Oskarżeni Ukraińcy słuchają z zapartym tchem ..." *Express Ilustrowany*, 28 November 1935, 2. See also "Proces," *Gazeta Polska*, 27 November 1935, 6.

114 "Rozprava za ... 100 zol. Kary na svidka za ziznannia po ukraïns'ky," *Dilo*, 30 November 1935, 3.

115 For Chorna, see "Proces," *Gazeta Polska*, 7 December 1935, 8. For Shukhevych, see "Proces," *Gazeta Polska*, 7 December 1935, 8. For Pashkevych, see "Proces," *Gazeta Polska*, 7 December 1935, 8. For Mashchak, see "Proces," *Gazeta Polska*, 7 December 1935, 8. For Myron, see "Proces," *Gazeta Polska*, 12 December 1935, 4. For Nydza, see "Proces," *Gazeta Polska*, 12 December 1935, 4.

116 "Proces. Dalsze zeznania świadków," *Gazeta Polska*, 6 December 1935, 8; "Rozprava za ... 300 zol. kary i areshtuvannia svidka," *Dilo*, 7 December 1935, 3; "Areshtuvannia svidka," *Novyi chas*, 7 December 1935, 4. For Chaikovs'ka changing her mind and testifying in Polish, see "Proces," *Gazeta Polska*, 7 December 1935, 8.

117 "Proces. Próba demonstracji na sali sądowej," *Gazeta Polska*, 10 December 1935, 7; "Rozprava za ... Cherhova kara 200 zol.," *Dilo*, 10 December 1935, 3.

performing a fascist salute in court, Svientsits'ka was punished with one day in a dark cell.[118]

On 29 November 1935, Prison Warden Wojciech Żygała, who was questioned by the chairman as a prosecution witness, delivered some interesting information about Bandera's behavior in the Brygidki prison in Lviv. Żygała discovered on a mess tin, in which Bandera had received his lunch, the inscription in Ukrainian "Die but do not betray," signed in Bandera's name. In the evening, he discovered the same inscription on another mess tin, in which Bandera had been served his supper. A few days later, Żygała heard how Bandera tried to communicate with other prisoners by tapping on the wall in Morse code. Żygała answered him and Bandera asked by tapping on the wall, "Who is in the neighboring cells? Give me the names." Żygała did not answer but went to Bandera's cell and said to him, "Mr. Bandera, please do not tap. I know Morse code and understand what you are tapping and will inform the prosecutor about it." Bandera answered: "I was just tapping around."[119]

When Antoni Fic—one of the officers who had interrogated Bandera—testified before the court, Bandera's lawyer Hankevych asked him whether it was true that Bandera was interrogated continuously without interruption from 6 to 11 September, and from 13 to 16 September 1934. Fic answered that he had interrogated Bandera only in the daytime and that he did not know whether other officers had also interrogated him during the night.[120] The OUN member Iaroslav Spol's'kyi also implied that prosecution officers used force in the interrogation. When the chairman asked him why his testimony in the courtroom differed from what he had said during the interrogation, Spol's'kyi answered that an officer had beaten him. This statement annoyed Prosecutor Żeleński, who demanded to know if Spol's'kyi had any witnesses for his claim, by whom, with what object, and on which part of his body he had been beaten, and why he had not informed anybody about this sooner. Spol's'kyi did not deliver a plausible answer to any of these questions. The prosecutor maintained that Spol's'kyi chose to change his evidence because he was afraid of OUN reprisals against him for incriminating other defendants. Żeleński further asked the court to summon Łączyński, the chief officer from the prison in Lviv, in order to clarify this incident, as Spol's'kyi had claimed that Łączyński was responsible for the beating.[121] The next day 3 December 1935, Łączyński appeared before the court and stated that he had not beaten Spol's'kyi but had sent him to a dark cell for two days as a punishment for engraving his name on a spoon during a hunger strike. Spol's'kyi confirmed this version of events.[122]

118 "Proces. Próba demonstracji na sali sądowej," *Gazeta Polska*, 10 December 1935, 7; "Rozprava za ... 200 zol. kary ta odyn den' temnytsi za ziznannia po ukraïns'y," *Dilo*, 10 December 1935, 3; "'Slava Ukraïni,'" *Novyi chas*, 11 December 1935, 5. The greeting *Slava Ukraïni* was first used by the LUN, which included the SUF, and it might therefore have been invented by the SUF. Cf. Lypovets'kyi, *Orhanizatsiia Ukraïns'kykh*, 14.

119 "Proces. Jak zachowywał się Bandera w więzieniu," *Gazeta Polska*, 30 November 1935, 6; "Rozprava za ... Myhal' hovoryt' po pol's'ky," *Dilo*, 30 November 1935, 3.

120 "Proces. Jak zachowywał się Bandera w więzieniu," *Gazeta Polska*, 30 November 1935, 6; "Dva tyzhni protsesu," *Novyi chas*, 1 December 1935, 4.

121 "Dvanatsiatyiden'. Chlen Kraïevoi Ekzekutyvy Spol's'kyi ziznaie ..." *Novyichas*, 4 December 1935, 3–4; "Proces," *Gazeta Polska*, 4 December 1935, 6.

122 "Proces," *Gazeta Polska*, 4 December 1935, 7; "Rozprava za ... Konfrontatsiianachal'nykaviaznytsi zi sv. Spol's'kym," *Dilo*, 5 December 1935, 3. Iaroslav Makarushka, against whom a separate prosecution was also initiated, testified at the trial relating to Pieracki's murder, that the investigating officers in

An even more bewildering incident occurred when the court came into session at 10:30 a.m. on the thirteenth day of the trial. The defendant Maliutsa, who was director of organizational matters in the homeland executive of the OUN, stood up and declared that, on account of Spol's'kyi's testimony the day before, and his own doubts since the beginning of the trial about his own behavior and the nature of the OUN, he wanted to testify in Polish. The court immediately removed the other defendants from the courtroom and allowed him to testify. Maliutsa gave even more details than had Myhal' before him, supplying a range of crucial information, including the names of many OUN members. This testimony overlapped with that of Myhal' and with information that Pidhainyi had revealed during the investigation. When Maliutsa finished, the defense lawyer Shlapak asked him why he had changed his mind and decided to testify. Maliutsa answered, "I came to the conclusion that the methods that the OUN applies are not good for the Ukrainian nation. We shot not only at Poles but also at our people. Director Babii was shot in this manner, and as I just learned, so was my closest colleague Maria Kovaliukivna."[123] Once the OUN applied terror to persons who were close to him, Maliutsa, like Myhal', had decided to break with the OUN strategy of denying the terror. Maliutsa further testified that Konovalets' had confided to him, in a face-to-face talk in Prague, that he also had doubts about some of the methods used by the homeland executive of the OUN. This suggests that the main instigators of terror against fellow-Ukrainians were Bandera and other young people in the homeland executive.[124]

The thirteenth day of the trial featured another significant moment. The witness Inspector Dugiełło mentioned an unnamed informer as a source of information. Defense lawyer Hankevych asked him to reveal the name of the informer in order to "reconcile the Polish and Ukrainian nations."[125] Dugiełło could not reveal the name as it was an official secret. Hankevych's comment outraged Prosecutor Żeleński so much that he delivered a short speech concerning political matters which, until then, he had scrupulously kept out of the trial:

> The court condescended to be the witness of an appeal that I address to the Ukrainian defending lawyers. You gentlemen ought not introduce political matters into the trial, and thereby upset the ambiance. This trial is not directed against Ukrainian society, and nobody should even for a moment understand it as such. There is no right yet to presume that this trial is even only indirectly directed against Ukrainian society. We are accusing here only certain people and a certain organization which, as we heard from the defendants themselves, is a misfortune of Ukrainian society.[126]

the prison in Lviv forced OUN members to testify, by pouring water on the floor of the cells in winter. Cf. "Proces. Zeznania kierownika wywiadu," *Gazeta Polska*, 7 December 1935, 8.

123 "Proces. Maluca potępia działalność O.U.N.," *Gazeta Polska*, 4 December 1935, 6; "Rozprava za ... Myhal' hovoryt' po pol's'ky," *Dilo*, 4 December 1935, 3–4.

124 "Proces. Maluca potępia działalność O.U.N.," *Gazeta Polska*, 4 December 1935, 6; "Nespodivanyi vystup Maliutsy," *Novyi chas*, 5 December 1935, 4.

125 "Proces. Zeznania komisarza Dugiełło," *Gazeta Polska*, 4 December 1935, 7.

126 "Proces. To nie jest proces przeciw społeczeństwu ukraińskiemu," *Gazeta Polska*, 4 December 1935, 7; "Rozprava za ... Vazhlyva politychna zaiava prokuratora," *Dilo*, 5 December 1935, 4.

The fourteenth day of the trial, 5 December 1935, began with the chairman's remark that, on the previous day, Karpynets' had behaved badly toward the officer escorting him from the courtroom. The chairman admonished all the defendants to behave appropriately and not to force him to use special security measures. He then read out Maliutsa's testimony from the previous day and informed the other defendants that they were free to introduce clarifications. Bandera suddenly jumped up and shouted sternly in Ukrainian what was reported as a "horrible accusation against the defendant Maliutsa."[127] The chairman asked him to be quiet, but Bandera lost control of himself and became more and more tense and agitated. The chairman ordered the guards to remove the outraged Bandera from the courtroom but he would not cooperate, so they used force and carried him out. The chairman then ordered a pause in the proceedings, after which Karpynets' stood up and spoke loudly in Ukrainian, with the result that he was also removed. After these incidents the chairman ordered the separation of the defendants from one another and from the defending lawyers, by having policemen sit between them, as at the beginning of the trial.[128]

The accusation of torture by the interrogating officers during the investigation surfaced again on 11 December 1935, when the witness Iaroslav Shtoiko—an OUN member sentenced to five years in prison—tried to withdraw his previous statements, with the claim that, by means of long interrogations that weakened him, he had been forced to speak about matters that had never occurred. In direct response to this claim and indirectly to some previous ones, Prosecutor Żeleński said that the more somebody "rats" on his colleagues and the more somebody reveals the activities of the OUN before the court, the more this person feels that he has the right to vilify the whole trial and to accuse the police and even the prosecutor of tormenting him and forcing him to give evidence.[129]

It is difficult to ascertain whether OUN members were indeed tortured during the interrogation. The OUN used trials for political goals and frequently made claims that aroused attention. Torture certainly belonged to these. But it was also in order to avoid punishment from the OUN, that some of the defendants who revealed information about the organization stated later that they did so under the pressure of torture. Investigating officers were instructed not to break the law by causing pain to the defendants in order to obtain information. However, they apparently interrogated OUN members such as Bandera, who maintained their denials, for several days at a time. This was obviously against the ethics of an interrogation and almost tantamount to torture, because the interrogated, as some of them claimed, were not allowed to sleep or even rest for several days.[130]

The chairman and especially Prosecutor Żeleński made continual efforts during the trial to prevent the defendants and their lawyers propagating the ideology of Ukrainian nationalism and transforming the trial into a political one. Rudnicki, the second prosecutor, however, understood his role differently. On 27 December 1935, in a long

127 "Rozprava za ... Vrazhinnia nashoho korespondenta," *Dilo*, 6 December 1935, 4.

128 "Proces. Wydalenie z sali Bandery i Karpyńca," *Gazeta Polska*, 6 December 1935, 8; "Rozprava za ..." *Dilo*, 6 December 1935, 3–4.

129 "Proces. Kłamliwe zeznania członków O.U.N.," *Gazeta Polska*, 12 December 1935, 4; "Rozprava za ..." *Dilo*, 12 December 1935, 3–4.

130 Żeleński also confirmed that some defendants, among them Bandera, were interrogated for several days without interruption. Cf. Żeleński, *Zabójstwo ministra*, 71.

speech in which he summarized the trial and announced the recent parliamentary resolution to abolish capital punishment, he became very political. His speech circled around the problem of Polish-Ukrainian coexistence in the Second Republic. At one point, for example, he allowed himself to compare the Poles in the Russian Empire with the Ukrainians in the Second Republic:

> However, there is a huge difference between Polish society in 1863 [the time of the January uprising against the Russian Empire] and Ukrainian society in 1918 and 1933: in 1915 only a handful of retired Russian estate custodians, some hundreds of Polonized officials, and some Russian symbols remained [in the territory claimed by the Poles]. In some hours they could be easily removed from the Polish territories. They passed by just as water flows from a granite stone. Nothing was left of them on Polish soil. However, we [the Poles] cannot go away from the territories that the OUN claims, because we are not colonizers, we have lived there for 600 years. If the Polish army and administration left, the Polish peasant and educated persons as well as the Polish intellectual and literary contributions would still remain. I do not say thereby that Ukrainian culture should not develop, but this country is the country of Polish culture, Polish and Ukrainian population. ... If we went and left the Polish population there, it would become a national minority although an important minority since it would make up to 50 percent. We know that the OUN declares that the prosperity and life of one nation depends on the destruction and death of another. Therefore we cannot leave so many Poles in the lurch and relinquish their lives.[131]

Rudnicki's reasons why the Polish state should not give up Volhynia and eastern Galicia are remarkable. Apart from the questions of national pride and cultural investment on the part of Poland, he also mentioned people's fear of the OUN. Toward the end of the speech Rudnicki characterized the OUN activists as mentally ill:

> We realize here that the thinking of these people is sick and because it is sick we are in the courtroom today. A sick mind has to be cured in a madhouse. For sick thinking we have no other help than legal punishment. I have a feeling of relief in my soul that the gallantry and generosity of my nation removed from this trial the specter of the gallows. It was right that the Polish nation granted executive clemency before the judgment was certificated. The judgment must be and will be very harsh.[132]

Rudnicki's speech was followed by Żeleński's three-day speech, which was less political and more analytical, although moderately polemical. Żeleński listed all the criminal deeds conducted by the OUN. He argued that Bandera, as the leader of the homeland executive, was the most responsible for them of all the defendants: "All this is Bandera's work."[133] On the one hand, Żeleński called Bandera a "twenty-three-year-old semi-child ... almost pathological"[134] and on the other, he argued that Ban-

131 "Mowa prokuratora Rudnickiego w procesie o zamordowania ś. p. ministra Pierackiego," *Gazeta Polska*, 28 December 1935, 6.
132 Ibid., 7.
133 "Proces. Bandera," *Gazeta Polska*, 1 January 1936, 11.
134 "Rozprava za... Prokurator pro roliu Bandery," *Dilo*, 2 January 1936, 3.

dera "has led all the defendants until this moment, as he did in prison, inscribing orders for them on spoons and mess tins."[135] He also added that "This is not only the leader [*prowidnyk*], but also one of the main culprits of Pieracki's assassination; he is the one who assembled the entire organization, and contributed to making it work superbly and accomplishing its purpose."[136]

Żeleński then characterized the other defendants and explained their culpability. He also spoke about persons who were not in the courtroom but who, like the defendants, were involved in Pieracki's assassination and other terror acts:

> There is here [in the dock] still a place for some other persons. I see in the dock neither Anna Chemeryns'ka, nor Fedyna, nor Iaroslav Baranovs'kyi, nor Senyk, nor Iaryi, nor Konovalets'. Where are you, generals of the organization, at the moment when your subordinates are judged, at the moment when the assassination of Minister Pieracki is on trial? They have been, are, and will stay in a safe place. We do not have in Poland a default judgment but we can ascertain the guilty by default. ... Although you will not sentence them, you will judge them, because you cannot leave them out, since you will be unfair not only toward them but also toward those in the dock.[137]

As to the question of Lithuanian collaboration with the OUN, Żeleński pointed out that although Lithuania was a small and impoverished country, which could not even afford to maintain a representative at the League of Nations in Geneva, it paid the OUN about $1000 a month.[138] This observation implied that Lithuania, which did not have its own terrorist organization, was interested in supporting a foreign one that combated the common enemy, the Second Republic. Vilnius, which Lithuania claimed to be its capital, had been incorporated into Poland in 1922 just like Lviv. Żeleński warned all countries in the world to be careful with Lithuanian passports because Lithuania issued fakes that were used to organize crimes. Finally, he stressed that Lithuania had supported the OUN not only before but also after Pieracki's assassination.[139]

Ultimately, Żeleński characterized the OUN as a "company" that murdered in order to make money. He stressed that murder, and spying for other countries were the main sources of income for the OUN. It sent its representatives to North America, on Lithuanian passports, to "sell" assassinations as patriotic deeds to the Ukrainian diaspora. Żeleński argued that, according to Konovalets's letter to Senyk, which had been found in the Senyk archives, Konovalets' decided to kill Pieracki because the OUN was close to "bankruptcy." He decided to murder Pieracki "not only to demonstrate the power of the organization but also to enlarge its finance capital." Żeleński pointed out that such a motive was "the lowest point of hideousness."[140] In conclusion, the prosecutor asked the judges for a verdict that would sentence Chornii, Zaryts'ka, and Rak to at least ten years, and Klymyshyn and Pidhainyi to life imprisonment. As for Bandera, Lebed', and Karpynets', although parliament had banned capital punishment on 2 January 1936,

135 "Proces. Bandera," *Gazeta Polska*, 1 January 1936, 11.

136 Ibid., 11.

137 "Proces," *Gazeta Polska*, 3 January 1936, 6.

138 "Proces. Pomoc pieniężna Litwy," *Gazeta Polska*, 3 January 1936, 6. For details of the collaboration of the OUN with the Lithuanian government, see "Wyrok," TsDIAL, f. 205, spr. 3125, 44–50.

139 "Proces. Fałszywe paszporty Litewskie," *Gazeta Polska*, 3 January 1936, 6.

140 "Proces. Przedsiębiorstwo ludzkiej rzeźni. Dno Ohydy," *Gazeta Polska*, 3 January 1936, 7.

the prosecutor asked that they be sentenced to death because, as he put it, this is "a sentence that the Polish State demands strongly from you." [141]

The correspondent for *Novyi chas* perceived Żeleński's speech as an "outpouring of aggressiveness against the defending lawyers, the defendants, and some imprisoned witnesses."[142] This observation might refer among others to the fact that Żeleński showed the court such surprising documents as a letter from the confiscated Senyk archives, in which Bandera in July 1933 had rebuked the OUN member Horbovyi, his lawyer in the Warsaw trial, for neglecting "organizational work."[143] The correspondent also observed that Żeleński illustrated his speech by raising his voice and making abrupt gestures with his hands and that the defendants listened attentively as he pointed his finger at them.[144]

After the four days of prosecution speeches, Bandera's lawyer Horbovyi began his speech with the observation that crimes such as Pieracki's assassination "have always been regarded as political crimes and not as common crimes. In theory a political crime is an attempt to introduce an illegal change into the current social relations and legal system ... in the case of a successful change of power, the act ceases to be a crime."[145] When he began talking about the Polish-Ukrainian conflict in 1918, the chairman interrupted him with the argument that such matters had nothing to do with the trial. Afterwards Horbovyi was similarly interrupted when he tried to introduce Bandera's views on the question of language in the trial.[146] Realizing that the court would not tolerate historical or politico-linguistic argument, Horbovyi asked the rhetorical question: "What connects my clients to the act?" He answered by saying, "In brief, nothing." He argued that the defendants were innocent and had been arrested and put in the dock to satisfy public opinion. The accusation was, according to him, based on unreliable material such as information received from informers whose names had not been revealed. As he began to speak about freedom as "a man's greatest treasure" he was interrupted again.[147] Toward the end of his speech, Horbovyi tried to convince the judges that they should not believe Maliutsa and should not consider his testimony, because this defendant had suffered a breakdown and therefore could not be relied upon to speak the truth.[148] Finally, he tried to challenge the allegation that Matseiko had killed Pieracki, by referring to the bits of tobacco that were found in the coat which the killer had left behind. According to Horbovyi, Matseiko did not smoke because the OUN forbade it and also because he was sick with tuberculosis. Therefore, according to him, Matseiko could not have assassinated Pieracki.[149]

The most absurd moment in Horbovyi's speech, however, occurred when he claimed that the OUN had not killed Pieracki, a crime to which the OUN had already

141 "Proces. Wniosek o wyrok skazujący," *Gazeta Polska*, 3 January 1936, 7.
142 "Promova avtora aktu obvynuvachennia," *Novyi chas*, 2 Janury 1936, 3.
143 "Shcho prokurator zakydaie d-rovi Horbovomu," *Dilo*, 31 December 1935, 4. Horbovyi was indeed an OUN member subordinated to Bandera. Cf. Danylo Shumuk, *Za skhidnim obriiem* (Paris: Smoloskyp, 1974), 429.
144 "Promova avtora aktu obvynuvachennia," *Novyi chas*, 2 Janury 1936, 3.
145 "Proces. Mowa adwokata Horbowego," *Gazeta Polska*, 4 January 1936, 6.
146 Ibid., 6.
147 "Proces. Usiłowanie podważenia ustawy oskarżenia," *Gazeta Polska*, 4 January 1936, 6.
148 "Proces. Atak na Maliucę," *Gazeta Polska*, 4 January 1936, 6.
149 "Proces. Świadkowie w oświetleniu obrony," *Gazeta Polska*, 4 January 1936, 6.

confessed in October 1934. Yet, according to Horbovyi, if the OUN had killed the minister, then Bandera, who knew that he would be sentenced to death not only in this but also in the upcoming trial in Lviv, would "have manifested his national feeling" and revealed the motives for the crime, instead of remaining silent.[150] He also argued that the OUN could not have committed the crime, because it had never committed murder outside the "ethnographic Ukrainian territories."[151] Horbovyi finished his speech with a plea to acquit all his clients, with two exceptions. Kachmars'kyi clearly belonged to the OUN and there were "circumstances that reassure the court that Bandera belonged to the OUN." However, he asked for a very mild sentence for Bandera because his client had not pleaded guilty.[152]

Shlapak, the next defense lawyer to speak, tried to develop an even more peculiar argument than Horbovyi's. First, he said that a "strange fate [*dziwne fatum*], which had haunted Ukrainians for ages, brought these twelve people into the courtroom."[153] Then he stated that "if as a result of a disaster everything would get lost and only the acts of this trial would remain, then from their content it would be possible to reconstruct the history of several years of independent Poland."[154] For this observation he was fined 300 złotys. After that, he claimed that the twelve defendants were in the courtroom because they wanted to establish a Ukrainian state. According to Shlapak, they had devoted their "youth, freedom, and even life" to this cause. When Shlapak started to quote the Polish poet Juliusz Słowacki, he was interrupted again and requested to come to the actual case.[155] Further, he insinuated that Karpynets' did not have the skills and facilities for constructing the bomb that was found by the police, and he argued that Prosecutor Żeleński knew where the bomb had been actually manufactured, but was withholding this information. For this insult he was again fined 300 złotys.[156]

Speaking on behalf of Klymyshyn and Zaryts'ka, Pavents'kyi seized on Rudnicki's observation that the thinking of the OUN members was sick. He did not disagree with the comment but thought that if that were the case, then the defendants should be hospitalized and not punished.[157] Unlike Horbovyi and Shlapak, in the rest of his speech Pavents'kyi remained factual. He admitted some of the deeds of his clients, such as smuggling illegal newspapers from Czechoslovakia, and pleaded for a mild sentence because, as he stated, there was no evidence that his clients had acted deliberately. According to Pavents'kyi, Zaryts'ka helped Matseiko escape from Poland to Czechoslovakia without knowing that she was helping Pieracki's murderer.[158] Pavents'kyi was the only defending lawyer who received congratulations on his speech from Prosecutor Żeleński.[159]

The next lawyer defending the OUN in Warsaw, Hankevych, argued that Matseiko had not killed Pieracki. He claimed that such a "powerful and prosperous organization,

150 "Proces. O.U.N. nie wykonała zamachu," *Gazeta Polska*, 4 January 1936, 6.
151 Ibid., 6.
152 "Proces. Adw. Horbowyj wnosi o uniewinnienie swoich klijentów," *Gazeta Polska*, 4 January 1936, 6.
153 "Proces. Mowa adwokata Szłapaka," *Gazeta Polska*, 4 January 1936, 6.
154 Ibid., 6.
155 Ibid., 6.
156 "Proces. Niedopuszczalne oświadczenie oborńcy," *Gazeta Polska*, 5 January 1936, 6.
157 "Proces. Mowa adwokata Pawenckiego," *Gazeta Polska*, 5 January 1936, 6.
158 Ibid., 6.
159 "Vrazhinnia nashoho korespondenta," *Novyi chas*, 5 January 1936, 17.

which was supported by some other countries," would not use an "inexperienced semi-intelligent boy" like Matseiko.[160] According to Hankevych, it was only because Matseiko was hungry and did not have anywhere to go, that he told Myhal' that he had killed Pieracki. Matseiko knew that the OUN would help him if he claimed that he had killed the Polish minister.[161]

When it came to Lebed', Hankevych stated that the reason his client stayed in Warsaw from 15 May to 15 June 1934 was his love for Hnatkivs'ka. "These young people walked through the city, did sightseeing, read."[162] The fact that Hnatkivs'ka and Lebed' gave a completely different account of the day on which Pieracki was assassinated, and which they spent together, Hankevych explained by saying that Lebed' lied because he wanted to protect his lover.[163] The lawyer described Hnatkivs'ka as an innocent victim who had never belonged to the OUN and who was in the dock because she loved Lebed', for which they were both paying the price, because love, according to him, was a "gypsy child [*cygańskie dziecię*]." Like Horbovyi, he then argued that the OUN did not kill Pieracki and that there was no evidence to prove that it did. He also argued that it was wrong to omit from the indictment the fact that "strong emotions caused by political motives ... even caused psychosis" and motivated the defendants to commit the crime. Hankevych finished his speech with the words, "Your hearts, my lords, should caution you against a judicial mistake."[164]

When the defense lawyers had finished their speeches, the chairman offered the defendants an opportunity to say their last words. Of the two defendants who decided to speak Polish at the trial, only Myhal' accepted the offer and delivered a speech in which he explained why he had broken down after killing Bachyns'kyi. He began his speech with the date of 1 November 1919, on which his schoolteacher asked her pupils never to forget this date, the anniversary of the establishment of the ZUNR, and to swear always to love their homeland. Myhal' said that he had always remained faithful to this oath. But something changed in him, when he realized that Bachyns'kyi was not a police informer as the OUN had told him. He had had a dream in which he saw himself as a pupil writing the text of the oath on 1 November 1919, and close to him were Bachyns'kyi's body and Babii's crying children.[165]

On 13 January 1936, the chairman announced the verdict. All the defendants were found guilty of belonging to the OUN and of either co-organizing the assassination or of helping the assassin escape. Bandera, Lebed', and Karpynets' were sentenced to death. However, because of the resolution adopted by the Polish parliament on 2 January 1936 to abolish capital punishment, their sentences were reduced to life imprisonment. They were also disenfranchised and deprived of some other civil rights. Klymyshyn and Pidhainyi were given life imprisonment and were disenfranchised for the rest of their lives. Hnatkivs'ka received fifteen years' imprisonment and was disenfranchised for ten years. Maliutsa, Myhal', and Kachmars'kyi were given twelve years' imprisonment and were disenfranchised for ten

160 "Proces. Mowa adwokata Hankiewicza," *Gazeta Polska*, 10 January 1936, 6.
161 Ibid., 6.
162 Ibid., 6.
163 Ibid., 6.
164 Ibid., 6.
165 "Proces. Mowa oskarżonego Myhala," *Gazeta Polska*, 10 January 1936, 6.

years. Zaryts'ka was given eight years' imprisonment and was disenfranchised for ten years. Rak and Chornii were given seven years' imprisonment and were disenfranchised for ten years.[166]

After the chairman finished reading the verdict, Bandera and Lebed' stood up, raised their right arms slightly to the right, just above their heads—as they had learned from Italian and other fascists—and called out "Slava Ukraïni!" For this gesture, which interrupted the final moments of the proceedings, both young men were removed from the courtroom.[167]

The trial had a political character but it was not a show trial. The defendants tried to use the trial as a political stage to promote the idea of their "liberation struggle" and to draw international attention to the situation of Ukrainians in Poland. These attempts were rigorously restricted by the judges and the prosecutors, who used the trial to show the destructive, harmful, and terrorist nature of the OUN. They allowed those OUN members who wanted to testify about the OUN crimes to speak at length and prevented those who attempted to defend the organization or legitimize its aims. Pieracki's assassin Hryhorii Matseiko was not sentenced because he was not apprehended. Instead a number of leading OUN members involved in the assassination were punished harshly. The three death sentences in particular appeared to fulfill a political function. The Polish authorities and judicial system used the trial to smash the leadership of the OUN in Poland and to demonstrate that it would not tolerate and would harshly punish any activities directed against the state.

Membership of the OUN was a crime in the Second Republic, a violation of articles 93 and 97 of the Criminal Code. *Gazeta Polska* wrote that belonging to the OUN was a crime because the OUN aimed to split away "Eastern Little Poland [*Małopolska Wschodnia*], Volhynia, the Chełm region, Polesia—all these territories, we have to stress having for ages been inseparably tied to the Polish Republic and inhabited by a mixed population, Polish and Ruthenian, both brought up by the Polish culture and civilization and both always attracted to Polishness."[168]

In addition to the judgment delivered orally in court, there were also "Grounds of Judgment," which were subsequently delivered in writing. The judges wrote that "emotions did not influence the defendants because they planned the murder for a longer time and prepared and conducted the murder with malice afterthought."[169] Bandera figured in the grounds of the judgment as the "spirit of the conspiracy."[170] He was an "eminent member of the OUN" who received the order from the leadership in exile to kill Pieracki, and on whose order Matseiko had done so.[171] In an article entitled "The Spirit and Notion of a Criminal Act: Stepan Bandera," which appeared in *Ilustrowany Kurier Codzienny* after Żeleński's final speech, Bandera

166 "Wyrok w procesie o zamordowanie," *Gazeta Polska*, 14 January 1936, 1, 6. The text of the judgment and of the grounds of the judgment is located in "Wyrok," TsDIAL, f. 205, spr. 3125.

167 "Oklyky pidsudnykh," *Novyi chas*, 16 January 1936, 3.

168 "Wyrok w procesie o zamordowanie," *Gazeta Polska*, 14 January 1936, 7.

169 "Wyrok," TsDIAL, f. 205, spr. 3125, 113.

170 "Wyrok w procesie o zamordowanie ... Bandera duszą spisku," *Gazeta Polska*, 14 January 1936, 7.

171 Ibid., 7.

was portrayed in a similar spirit.[172] *Dziennik Polski* introduced Bandera in the article "The List of Bandera's Crimes" as the embodiment of the OUN and its crimes.[173]

In the article "After the Trial ... Ruthenian Society Should Abandon the Politics of Hate and Crimes," the newspaper *Ilustrowany Kuryer Codzienny* blamed Ukrainian society alone for the existence and terrorist activities of the OUN. While explaining the question of Ukrainians in Poland it explicitly ignored how Polish politics and the European state of affairs contributed to the radicalization of the Ukrainian nationalism:

> The longstanding tactics of the so-called "moderate" parts of Ruthenian society proved to be disastrous. Ostensibly they condemned the OUN but simultaneously they praised the "heroic patriotism" of its members, for whom everything was forgiven, as for "gallant although confused young people." The Greek Catholic clergy conducted services for the terrorists who were executed as a result of legal judgments, their portraits appeared in Ruthenian papers and the legal press of the Ukrainian parties, such as the legal political groups who maintained a discreet silence about the OUN but daily attacked the Polish authorities that liquidated the OUN. Ukrainian educators have an enormous guilt on their conscience.[174]

Novyi chas announced the verdict on the front page with an oversized headline: "Two Death Penalties, Three Life Imprisonments, and 198 Years of Imprisonment in the Trial of the OUN." The way of presenting the verdict implied a collective punishment and must have struck readers even more than the misstatement of the number of death penalties.[175] *Dilo* stated in the article "Consequences of the Verdict" that, despite the attempts of the court and the prosecutors not to make the trial a political one, it was political and would have political implications. The newspaper equated the OUN with Ukrainian society and stressed that the trial was not only against the OUN but against the whole Ukrainian nation: "[In terms of] the fate of the twelve young Ukrainian men and women, there is no division into the 'mass' and the 'we.' The mass and we are, in this case, one and the same: the same nation, the same grief for the fate of the Ukrainian youth, the same understanding of the tragedy. The mass and we experienced the verdict on Monday in a similar—or to be more precise—the same way."[176] Furthermore, *Dilo* commented on the pointed article "After the Trial ..." in *Ilustrowany Kuryer Codzienny*. It wrote that the lords (*pany*) from the *Ilustrowany Kuryer Codzienny* deliberately called Ukrainians "Ruthenians" in order to insult them, as had happened in the "good old days" when Ruthenians were classified as subhuman.[177]

The *Biuletyn Polsko-Ukraiński* was glad that the trial had finally ended after eight weeks, and it hoped that "with the last words in the courtroom, the period marked by blood has ended, and that it has hopefully made it possible to open a period without

172 "Dusza i myśl zbrodniczego czynu: Stefan Bandera," *Ilustrowany Kuryer Codzienny*, 2 January 1936, 16.
173 "Lista zbrodni Bandera," *Dziennik Polski*, 1 January 1936, 1.
174 "Po wyroku ... Społeczeństwo ruskie powinno odgrodzić się od polityki nienawiści i zbrodni," *Ilustrowany Kuryer Codzienny*, 16 January 1936, 1.
175 "Dva prysudy smerty," *Novyi chas*, 14 January 1936, 1.
176 "Naslidky prysudu," *Dilo*, 16 January 1936, 2.
177 Ibid., 2.

bloodshed." It also pointed out that both societies needed reforms that would be an alternative to gunshots and verdicts.[178]

The brothers and Polish intellectuals Mieczysław and Ksawery Pruszyński published articles about the trial and Polish-Ukrainian relations, in which they romanticized the OUN. Both articles appeared in *Wiadomości Literackie*. Mieczysław began his article with the observation that about five million Ukrainians lived in the Polish state and that "Polish racists denied [them] even ... the name."[179] He wrote that there was an analogy between the Polish nation before 1914 and the Ukrainian one after 1914. He also criticized Polish attempts to Polonize the Ukrainians, claiming that this turned the Ukrainian population into an uneducated and a poor one. He compared Polish-Ukrainian relations with British-Irish and Spanish-Catalonian relations, and he pleaded in favor of a Ukrainian autonomy in the Polish state. This would benefit not only Ukrainians but also Poles. It would guarantee Ukrainians their own institutions and equal status. It would strengthen the moderate political Ukrainian parties and those organizations not hostile to Poles. It would weaken the radical, fanatical, and terrorist groups that were hostile to everyone else.[180]

Ksawery's article "People and Crime" was written more literally but presented similar opinions. He emphasized that because of the trial:

> Everybody in Poland knows which one of the girls was not only a member of the conspiracy but who was also the fiancée of a member whom she visited and dated. We hear the testimonies of their fathers and aunts. We know how they spent their childhood and school days, we know against whom they were fighting and whom they loved, where they lived, how much money they had. We know more about them than about dozens of our friends. We speak about them as people we know on the streetcar, at the theatre, and at home. It is really difficult to believe that these people, whom we saw, had killed. These people killed because they wanted to serve their nation. We do not think that they served well. They are doing it well only now: three quarters of the Polish press, which for seventeen years did not want to know the word "Ukrainian," learned it in the two weeks [of the trial].[181]

Mieczysław and Ksawery Pruszyński correctly criticized Polish nationalist politics toward Ukrainians in the Second Republic and made a few good suggestions for improvement, but they miscalculated the violent and destructive nature of the OUN while romanticizing this fascist movement. Ksawery pointed out the OUN nationalists' hatred toward the Polish language and state, but he did not comment on the crimes they had committed and the violent and ultranationalist ideology they believed in: "Now these people [defendants and witnesses], although they know Polish, do not want to speak Polish. Their hatred for the Polish state, the minister, and the policeman has extended to the Polish language."[182]

178 "Po procesie," *Biuletyn Polsko-Ukraiński*, Warsaw 19 January 1936, Vol. 5, No. 3 (142), 1.
179 Mieczysław Pruszyński, "Zagadnienie Ukraińskie w Polsce," *Wiadomości Literackie*, 15 December 1935, 1.
180 Ibid., 1.
181 Ksawery Pruszyński, "Ludzie i zbrodnia," *Wiadomości Literackie*, 15 December 1935, 7.
182 Ibid., 7.

Because all the defendants appealed the verdict, appeal proceedings took place between 28 and 30 April 1936. Bandera's appeal stated that the motivation for his acts was the desire to establish a Ukrainian state and that, "according to the ethics of the grouping which Bandera represents, belonging to the OUN is an act that is free of all criminal features."[183] When the chairman asked Bandera whether he pleaded guilty and wanted to give an explanation, Bandera began to answer in Ukrainian. The chairman interrupted him and said that Bandera did not want to avail himself of the right to give explanations.[184] As a result of the appeal, Chornii's sentence was reduced from seven years to four, Zaryts'ka's from eight to two, and Rak's from seven to four. Chornii was acquitted of the charge of belonging to the OUN. The other sentences remained unchanged.[185] Horbovyi, the defending lawyer, submitted to the court a request to allow Lebed' and Hnatkivs'ka to be married in the prison church.[186] Klymyshyn wrote in his memoirs that, toward the end of the proceedings when the defendants were allowed to have their last say, Bandera shouted: "Iron and blood will decide between us," and all defendants called "Slava Ukraïni!"[187]

The Second OUN Trial (in Lviv)

The second great trial, this time of twenty-three OUN members—of whom six had already been sentenced in Warsaw—began on 25 May 1936 in Lviv. In addition to Bandera, the following were in the dock: Roman Shukhevych, Iaroslav Makarushka, Oleksandr Pashkevych, Iaroslav Spol's'kyi, Volodymyr Ianiv, Iaroslav Stets'ko, Bohdan Hnatevych, Volodymyr Kotsiumbas, Bohdan Pidhainyi, Ivan Maliutsa, Osyp Mashchak, Ievhen Kachmars'kyi, Ivan Iarosh, Roman Myhal', Roman Sen'kiv, Kateryna Zaryts'ka, Vira Svientsits'ka, Anna Daria Fedak, Osyp Fenyk, Volodymyr Ivasyk, Semen Rachun, and Ivan Ravlyk. All of them were accused of belonging to the OUN, twelve were accused of involvement in the murder of Bachyns'kyi, the murder of Ivan Babii, the planning of the murders of Antin Krushel'nyts'kyi, Władysław Kossobudzki, Henryk Józewski, the Soviet consul in Lviv, the murder of the pupil of the seventh grade of the Ukrainian high school Korolyshyn, and of placing a bomb in the office of the newspaper *Pratsia*. In addition to the defending lawyers from the Warsaw trial, Stepan Shukhevych, Semen Shevchuk, Pylyp Ievyn, and Volodymyr Zahaikevych defended the twenty-three OUN members.[188] Because of the location, the defendants and their lawyers were allowed to speak Ukrainian. Taking advantage of this regulation, some of the defendants testified at great length, and put questions to the witnesses. The most eager questioner and talker was Bandera.

The building where the trial took place, on Batory Street in Lviv, was under strong police protection. Only persons with a special pass, altogether about seventy, were allowed into the courtroom. The last defendant to enter the courtroom, shortly before

183 "Proces. Wywody apelacji oskarżonych," *Gazeta Polska*, 28 April 1936, 6.
184 Ibid., 6.
185 "Proces," *Gazeta Polska*, 1 May 1936, 4.
186 "Proces. Ślub Łebeda z Hnatkiwską," *Gazeta Polska*, 30 April 1936, 6.
187 In his memoirs Knysh does not mention that they performed the fascist salute while calling "Slava Ukraïni!" Cf. Klmyshyn, *V pokhodi*, 1:194.
188 "Sprawozdanie stenograficzne," 25 May 1936, TsDIAL, f. 371, op. 1, spr. 8, od. 75, 1.

the trial began, was Bandera. As he entered, he performed a fascist salute, raising his right arm and shouting "Slava!" or "Slava Ukraïni!" All the defendants in the courtroom answered him in the same manner.[189] Shortly after this gesture the trial was opened.[190]

Chairman Dysiewicz tried to put on record the personal details of the defendants. All of them stated that they were of Ukrainian nationality. With the exception of the Orthodox Svientsits'ka, they were all Greek Catholics. Bandera, Mashchak, Spol's'kyi, Ianiv, and Stets'ko stated, moreover, that they had Ukrainian citizenship. Makarushka stated that he was "basically a Ukrainian citizen but temporarily a Polish one." When the chairman informed the defendants that a Ukrainian state did not exist and asked them if they wished to record their citizenship as Soviet Ukrainian, they replied that they were by no means Soviet. Spol's'kyi said that before he answered any questions he wanted to say that the police "chained him, choked him by the neck, twisted his arms, and kicked and beat him." Stets'ko also remarked that he had been bound in chains. Bandera answered the question as to whether he had been conscripted by saying, "Yes, into the Ukrainian Military Organization." When the chairman wanted to read out the indictment, Stets'ko, Mashchak, and Bandera demanded that this be done in Ukrainian. The chairman refused their demand, on the grounds that they had not asked for an indictment in Ukrainian and that it was now too late to prepare one.[191]

Bandera, Ianiv, Stets'ko, Makarushka, and Pashkevych had decided before the trial that all the defendants should admit their delinquencies and crimes, and that they should explain that they had committed them as a result of the difficult situation that the Polish nation imposed on the Ukrainian people.[192] On the third day of the trial, 27 May 1936, as Ianiv was being questioned, he tried to implement this plan. He began with polemics against the chairman. In response to the chairman's statement that he was accused of belonging to the OUN, Ianiv replied that he was being accused only "on the basis of subjective facts and the 'unofficial' will of the Ukrainian nation."[193]

Stets'ko, who was questioned the same day, began in a similar fashion. At the very beginning, he wanted to explain why he was a member of the OUN, and why he had announced that he had Ukrainian citizenship. He stated that, during the investigation, he had admitted to belonging to the OUN, because he had been tortured for three days. He also said that he had joined the OUN because he thought "that at this moment the duty of every Ukrainian is to attempt to establish an independent Ukrainian state." This statement was interrupted by the prosecutor. The defense lawyer Starosols'kyi claimed that, since Stets'ko was accused of attempting to separate a portion of territory from the Polish state, he should be free to explain why he wanted to do

189 "Hitlerowskie powitanie oskarżonych," *Ilustrowany Express Poranny*, 27 May 1936, 16. The unidentified correspondent of the *Ilustrowany Express* wrote in the article "Slava!" and not "Slava Ukraïni!" which was usually used by the OUN. For using "Slava Ukraïni!" and not "Slava!" in the process in Warsaw, see "'Slava Ukraïni,'" *Novyi chas*, 11 December 1935, 5.

190 "Hitlerowskie powitanie oskarżonych," *Ilustrowany Express Poranny*, 27 May 1936, 16; "Sprawozdanie stenograficzne," 25 May 1936, TsDIAL, f. 371, op. 1, spr. 8, od. 75, 1; "Velykyi politychnyi protses OUN u L'vovi," *Novyi chas*, 26 May 1936, 2.

191 "Sprawozdanie stenograficzne," 25 May 1936, TsDIAL, f. 371, op. 1, spr. 8, od. 75, 2–3; "Za vbyvstvo dyr. I Babiia," *Dilo*, 26 May 1936, 3.

192 Shukhevych, *Moie zhyttia*, 526.

193 "Sprawozdanie stenograficzne," 27 May 1936, TsDIAL, f. 371, op. 1, spr. 8, od. 75, 18.

so. The prosecutor replied that Stets'ko wanted to separate it because he belonged to the OUN, and further explanation was unnecessary.[194]

When Stets'ko used the phrase "western Ukraine," the chairman warned him that he would throw him out if he did so again. Stets'ko then tried to explain why the OUN was carrying out the campaign directed against the schools, and why it chose a revolutionary way, but the chairman again interrupted him. He allowed Stets'ko to explain whether the OUN fought against the Soviet Union, but when Stets'ko stated that the struggle "in eastern Ukraine is going on exactly as here," the chairman had him removed from the courtroom. Close to the exit, Stets'ko turned back to the public, raised his right arm, and called out, "Slava Ukraïni!" The prosecutor said that this was the third time that a defendant had performed a demonstrative act, and that he was requesting that journalists and other observers be removed from the courtroom. The defense lawyers objected, but the court rejected the objection and warned the defendants that if this occurred again, the court would reconsider the matter. For his fascist gesture, Stets'ko was punished with twenty-four hours in a dark room.[195]

The next defendant questioned by the chairman was Ivasyk. His testimony in the courtroom differed from his evidence during the interrogation. When he was asked why this was so, Ivasyk replied that the previous evidence was forced. He said that he had had to sit on a stool for nine days and eight nights, which made him agree to everything the interrogators wanted him to say. The chairman stated that, although evidence might be forced, it was not necessarily wrong, which was a clear approval of the violation of interrogation ethics. He further compared the interrogating officers to a father who hits his child because it did something wrong and does not want to admit it.[196] After the chairman finished, Prosecutor Juliusz Prachtel-Morawiański asked Ivasyk a few detailed questions concerning the torture. From Ivasyk's answers it became obvious that he might have exaggerated. However, the prosecutor did not get to the bottom of the problem as Żeleński had done in the Warsaw trial with every such claim.[197]

The last defendant to testify on 27 May 1936 was Spol's'kyi. His evidence was brief. When the chairman stated that the defendant was accused of belonging to the OUN, Spol's'kyi answered: "I admit that the assumptions in the indictment concerning my person are, with a few exceptions, correct. I admit that I belonged to the OUN but I don't consider my belonging to the OUN to be a fault, because I consider that the legal status which was created by the act of the Ukrainian state from the year one thousand . . ." At this moment, Spol's'kyi was interrupted and he was removed from the courtroom. He was probably about to refer to the proclamation of the Ukrainian state in 1918.[198]

194 Ibid., 19.

195 Ibid., 20. The censorship deleted references to Stets'ko's fascist gesture in some Ukrainian newspapers, for example in *Dilo*. Cf. "Velykyi protses OUN u L'vovi," *Dilo*, 28 May 1936, 3. At a press conference, a government representative announced that the newspapers were required not to report the defendants' demonstrations, because they constituted anti-government propaganda. Any issues, which, despite the government's warning, reported the anti-government fascist greeting, would be confiscated. Cf. "Presova konferentsiia u spravi l'vivs'koho protsesu OUN," *Dilo*, 29 May 1936, 4.

196 "Sprawozdanie stenograficzne," 27 May 1936, TsDIAL, f. 371, op. 1, spr. 8, od. 75, 21.

197 Ibid., 22.

198 Ibid., 25.

On the next day of the trial, the defendant Mashchak tried to defend his actions with the simple fact that he belonged to the OUN. He understood this as a patriotic duty and assumed that it transformed his activities into non-culpable and even admirable deeds. From the first, he stated that he was a Ukrainian nationalist. Then he explained that Babii was a traitor and that sentencing him to death was correct. He answered defense lawyer Zahaikevych's question about "the task of his life" by saying "Serving the nation with all vigor. I could do this only in the OUN, which I joined." The defense lawyer completed this statement with the argument that Mashchak did not choose private welfare but the welfare of the nation, and asked him why he chose the OUN. Mashchak replied, "I consider the OUN ideology to be the only one that can achieve the aim of liberating the nation." In response to this statement, the prosecutor protested and said that "belonging to the OUN is specifically a crime."[199] Makarushka continued: "I admit that I belonged to the OUN and held the position of intelligence officer, but I do not admit that it was my fault. My activity was legal in the light of Ukrainian acts and laws," he said. At this point the chairman interrupted him with the comment, "We, however, judge from the position of the law that is in force here."[200]

Roman Shukhevych was explicitly advised by his lawyer and relative, Stepan Shukhevych, to provide false testimony and to make patriotic statements, which, according to the lawyer, might reach the conscience of the judges and diminish the punishment.[201] The chairman informed Shukhevych that he was accused of belonging to the OUN, and of persuading Lemyk to kill the Soviet consul, which relied on Pidhainyi's testimony. On the advice of his lawyer, the defendant declared pathetically: "I admit to belonging to the OUN. The reason why I joined the OUN was the request of my heart, but I do not admit that I ordered Lemyk to kill the Soviet consul."[202] Further, the defendant lied by saying that he had nothing to do with the war department of the homeland executive, and that he had lost contact with the OUN around 1928. He testified that he rejoined the OUN at the official request of some OUN members, only in 1933 and only as a mediator, to help solve a conflict between radical and less radical factions in the OUN.[203]

The defendant Pidhainyi, was also a client and relative of the lawyer Stepan Shukhevych, who induced him to give false testimony, in order to provide Roman Shukhevych's testimony with credibility. Pidhainyi claimed that he was the director of the war department of the homeland executive, thereby intending to relieve the real director of the war department, Roman Shukhevych, of responsibility.[204] Pidhainyi also testified that he gave Lemyk the gun with which he killed Mailov, and that neither Shukhevych nor Bandera could have done so.[205] In addition to this "act of generosity" toward Shukhevych, Pidhainyi, like a number of other defendants, claimed that he was in the

199 "Sprawozdanie stenograficzne," 28 May 1936, TsDIAL, f. 371, op. 1, spr. 8, od. 75, 26; "Chetvertyi den' protsesu OUN u L'vovi," *Novyi chas*, 29 May 1936, 8.
200 "Sprawozdanie stenograficzne," 28 May 1936, TsDIAL, f. 371, op. 1, spr. 8, od. 75, 27.
201 Shukhevych, *Moie zhyttia*, 527–30.
202 Shukhevych, *Moie zhyttia*, 527; TsDIAL, f. 371, op. 1, spr. 8, od. 75, 31.
203 "Sprawozdanie stenograficzne," 29 May 1936, TsDIAL, f. 371, op. 1, spr. 8, od. 75, 31; "Piatyi den' protsesu OUN u L'vovi," *Novyi chas*, 30 May 1936, 4.
204 "Sprawozdanie stenograficzne," 29 May 1936, TsDIAL, f. 371, op. 1, spr. 8, od. 75, 35.
205 "Sprawozdanie stenograficzne," 30 May 1936, TsDIAL, f. 371, op. 1, spr. 8, od. 75, 44.

OUN but could not be guilty of anything, because being in the OUN was a patriotic duty.[206]

Bandera testified on 5 June 1936. He spoke at greater length than the other defendants, probably because the chairman allowed him to do so without interrupting each item of propaganda, as he was interested in hearing what the leader of the homeland executive had to say. After the chairman had familiarized Bandera with the charges against him, the defendant said, "I do not confess to any guilt and do not plead guilty, because all my revolutionary activities were the fulfillment of my duty." Then he asked the chairman to allow him to elucidate all the "facts, circumstances, and motivations" in detail.[207] The chairman asked Bandera if his motive was to split Eastern Little Poland from the Polish state. Bandera responded by saying, "The general motive [of the OUN] is the preparation of a rebirth and the organization of an independent Ukrainian state ... also in the Ukrainian territories that belong today to the Polish state."[208]

Continuing his testimony, Bandera called himself "the leader of the OUN in the western Ukrainian territories, and the commandant of the UVO." This irritated the chairman.[209] Bandera admitted that he had ordered the killing of Bachyns'kyi because an investigation conducted by the OUN had established that Bachyns'kyi was an informer.[210] He further testified that Babii was sentenced to death by an OUN court for "the crime of betraying the nation." He said that Babii, "as the director of a branch of a Ukrainian high school, tried to educate the youth at the school in a spirit of subservience to the Polish state ... persecuted Ukrainian nationalism, and went so far as to play the role of a police agent. He once caught a Ukrainian student distributing OUN leaflets, not on the premises of the high school [but in church during a service], and called the police."[211] Bandera explained that he was angry with Babii because he taught his pupils that Ukrainian patriotism required loyalty to the Polish state. Bandera personally disliked Babii, because Babii had caught Bandera helping a fellow high-school student cheat in an examination, and he had taken Bandera's identity card and given it to the police.[212]

Bandera also testified in detail about the attempts to assassinate the Soviet consul and the newspaper editor Antin Krushel'nytskyi, and about the bomb in the office of the newspaper *Pratsia*. He stressed his crucial role in these deeds, saying that he ordered Lemyk to kill the Soviet consul.[213] This version was confirmed by Lemyk's testimony.[214] Bandera also claimed that an "action against the Bolsheviks" was necessary because

206 Pidhainyi had been sentenced to life imprisonment at the Warsaw trial, therefore nothing worse could have happened to him in the Lviv trial, even if he had taken all the crimes of the OUN on his shoulders. "Sprawozdanie stenograficzne," 29 May 1936, TsDIAL, f. 371, op. 1, spr. 8, od. 75, 34–35.

207 "Sprawozdanie stenograficzne," 5 June 1936, TsDIAL, f. 371, op. 1, spr. 8, od. 75, 91.

208 Ibid., 91.

209 Ibid., 91.

210 Ibid., 91–92.

211 Ibid., 93.

212 Ibid., 93–94.

213 Ibid., 95. Although both Bandera and Lemyk testified that Bandera prepared the assassination of the Soviet consul and personally gave the order to Lemyk, the police investigation does not seem to confirm this claim. Roman Shukhevych may have been as much involved in the preparation of the assassination as Bandera. Shukhevych distanced himself in the trial from the OUN. Other defendants helped him in this regard, giving false testimony and taking Shukhevych's criminal actions on themselves. Cf. "Sprawozdanie stenograficzne," 24 June 1936, TsDIAL, f. 371, op. 1, spr. 8, od. 75, 179–80, and Shukhevych, *Moie zhyttia*, 527–30.

214 "Sprawozdanie stenograficzne," 16 June 1936, TsDIAL, f. 371, op. 1, spr. 8, od. 75, 147.

"Bolshevism is a figure and system with which Moscow afflicts Ukraine," and because "communism is a movement that is extremely contradictory to nationalism." He further argued that, in the "eastern Ukrainian territories, a brutal fight for everything is taking place since the Bolsheviks destroyed the Ukrainian territories." According to Bandera, nobody knew about this fight because "Soviet Ukraine is divided from the civilized world, not only by a Chinese wall, but also by a zone of Communists, Cheka officers, and Red Army soldiers."[215] Speaking further about the Communists, Bandera argued that: "Because the Bolsheviks use physical methods of fighting, we should also apply these methods toward them."[216]

Bandera also proudly announced that he had issued the order to kill Kossobudzki because, "as an inspector of the prison guards in [Brygidki prison] in Lviv, he persecuted and oppressed the Ukrainian political prisoners." The leader of the homeland executive had also ordered Józewski to be killed because "he was a representative of the Polish state ... and an actual leader of Polish politics in Volhynia."[217] The defense lawyer Horbovyi tried to help Bandera testify about deeds of which Bandera was not accused, such as the anti-school campaign in summer 1933. This was probably at Bandera's or the OUN's request, in order to hit the headlines and inform as many people as possible about the "liberation struggle" of the OUN.[218] Similarly, Horbovyi asked Bandera to "introduce his biography, and the moments that shaped his worldview."[219] In his statements, Horbovyi did not rule out the possibility that revenge might have motivated his client to issue some orders to kill.[220]

The problem of fascist greetings in the courtroom appeared again on 16 June 1936, the sixteenth day of the trial, when some OUN members were called as witnesses. The first was Lebed', who naturally did not admit belonging to the OUN. Leaving the courtroom, he raised his right arm toward the defendants and called out, "Slava Ukraïni!" Stets'ko and Ianiv answered him with the same fascist salute.[221] The next one was Lemyk, Mailov's assassin. When Lemyk had finished testifying and was leaving the courtroom, he greeted the other defendants with the raised arm and the words "Slava Ukraïni!" The last witness on this day was Oleksandr Kuts. After Kuts used the same Ukrainian fascist salute as Lebed' and Lemyk before him, the prosecutor again proposed that the trial be closed to the public, but the court rejected his application.[222] References to the fascist greetings were again deleted by the censorship from the newspaper reports.[223]

On 24 June 1936, the twenty-first day of the trial, Prosecutor Prachtel-Morawiański delivered his speech. Referring to *Konspiracja*, an OUN brochure in Polish translation from 1929, he stated that the OUN did not always hide its criminal deeds but sometimes

215 "Sprawozdanie stenograficzne," 5 June 1936, TsDIAL, f. 371, op. 1, spr. 8, od. 75, 94.
216 Ibid., 95.
217 Ibid., 97.
218 Ibid., 98.
219 Ibid., 97.
220 Ibid., 98.
221 "Sprawozdanie stenograficzne," 16 June 1936, TsDIAL, f. 371, op. 1, spr. 8, od. 75, 145; "Velykyi protses OUN u L'vovi," *Novyi chas*, 18 June 1936, 3. The record of the trial contains "Slava" and not "Slava Ukraïni!" It is more likely however that the defendants shouted "Slava Ukraïni!" and not "Slava!" For using "Slava Ukraïni!" in the Warsaw trial, see "'Slava Ukraïni,'" *Novyi chas*, 11 December 1935, 5.
222 "Sprawozdanie stenograficzne," 16 June 1936, TsDIAL, f. 371, op. 1, spr. 8, od. 75, 147.
223 See for example "Velykyi protses OUN u L'vovi," *Novyi chas*, 18 June 1936, 3.

exposed them during proceedings, in order to attract publicity, as the OUN was doing at this trial.[224] He further asked whom did such members of the OUN as Shukhevych and Bandera represent, and answered by saying, "They are only members of a terrorist organization and do not represent the Ukrainian nation. The OUN cannot represent it because it is condemned by the majority of that society, which is right about this matter."[225] Prachtel-Morawiański stated that the relatives of the defendants to whom he had spoken also had no sympathy for the organization but only regret (about its nature). Finally, he said that the defendants may have been motivated to commit crimes for political reasons, but "this is Poland and the Polish law that is in force here does not allow the eulogization of crimes."[226]

On 26 June 1936, the defendants were allowed to respond to Prachtel-Morawiański's speech, which had been interrupted for this purpose. The defendant Maliutsa said that "every idea has to overcome the examination of death. The OUN did, I did not. In the Warsaw trial, I acted reprehensibly, but I did so because of my breakdown, not because the idea was corrupted."[227] Stets'ko said that "the aim of his life was a free Ukraine, and that he would not leave this path, even if he were tortured."[228] Ianiv stated that he acted deliberately and that he was sure that there was only one path before him. His point of view, he said, was determined by faith. Referring to Oswald Spengler, he said that the moment was coming when Ukraine would need a new religion, which was Ukrainian nationalism. Only this religion, according to Ianiv, could enable Ukrainians to survive the threat of communism and other disasters.[229]

After that Bandera delivered a speech. On the one hand, he portrayed himself as a Robin Hood who protected poor Ukrainians from the mean Poles and Soviet Russians. On the other hand, he announced that he was the fascist leader of an enslaved nation, and the *Providnyk* of all Ukrainians united by nationalism and the fight for independence, according to the principle that the OUN represented the Ukrainian nation, and Bandera represented the OUN. This speech was one of Bandera's most important oratorical performances. It has excited Ukrainian nationalists down to the present day and has also been regarded as Bandera's major intellectual achievement. Bandera began by declaring, "The prosecutor said that a group of Ukrainian terrorists and their main headquarters [personnel] took their places in the dock. I want to say that we OUN members are not terrorists, because the OUN deals with all branches of political activities and national life."[230] Then he complained that he was never allowed to speak about the "entire program of the organization or about [his] entire activity." This restriction might make him look like a terrorist, whereas he did not regard himself as one. He also announced that he would confine himself "only to those facts and fragments of the revolutionary activity of the OUN that are a subject of this trial."[231]

Bandera began the factual part of his speech with Kossobudzki. He said that, in autumn 1933, he had received information from colleagues who were in the Brygidki

224 "Sprawozdanie stenograficzne," 24 June 1936, TsDIAL, f. 371, op. 1, spr. 8, od. 75, 166.
225 Ibid., 167.
226 Ibid., 167.
227 "Sprawozdanie stenograficzne," 26 June 1936, TsDIAL, f. 371, op. 1, spr. 8, od. 75, 174.
228 Ibid., 174.
229 Ibid., 175.
230 Ibid., 175.
231 Ibid., 175.

prison that "special methods of bullying and repression" were being applied to Ukrainian political prisoners. Then he stated that he had ordered an investigation and had concluded that Kossobudzki was responsible for bullying and repressing Ukrainian prisoners.[232] Bandera added that he had forbidden the political prisoners to organize a hunger strike, because:

> Revenge would later fall on the backs of colleagues who are defenseless, and with whom the administration of the prison can do anything it pleases. I considered that the organization should take charge of these comrades, and I therefore ordered the assassination of Kossobudzki. There was no trial. I have already said that organizational trials dealt only with Ukrainians and not with Poles, because we believe that there is a struggle between Ukraine and Poland, and that there is still military law, and that revolutionary struggle by means of physical methods is a moment of the struggle that has continued forever.[233]

Bandera further claimed that he had personally ordered the killing of Gadomski, Pieracki, and Józewski. He probably said this in order to stress his role in the OUN and to present himself as the brave leader of a ruthless "liberation movement," rather than to inform the court how decisions to undertake assassinations were made. He claimed that he had issued the orders to kill Gadomski and Pieracki as "representatives of the Polish state," and Józewski because he wanted to reconcile two nations, which was against the concept of the OUN's "permanent revolution."[234] Decisions to kill such Ukrainians as Babii or Bachyns'kyi for "crimes of national betrayal" were made, according to Bandera, not by him in person but by the "revolutionary tribunal."[235] The tribunal sentenced them to death because, as he elaborated, "It is the duty of all Ukrainians to subordinate their personal life to the good of the nation, and if somebody voluntarily and consciously cooperates with the enemy. ... Then we take the view that this degree of national betrayal should be punished only with death."[236]

Toward the end of his speech, Bandera mixed fanaticism, martyrdom, nationalism, fascism, and sentimentalism, and produced lines that Ukrainian nationalists have learnt by heart for decades, just as they memorized the "Decalogue of a Ukrainian Nationalist":

> Because in this trial the question of assassinations of many persons organized by the OUN was investigated, it might appear that the organization does not cherish human life, either of other persons or of its members. I will respond to this very briefly, that people who are aware that they can lose their life at any moment in their job can appreciate the merit of life. We know the value of our and other lives, but our idea, as we understand it, is so huge that, as it comes to its realization, not hundreds but thousands of human lives have to be sacrificed in order to carry it out. ...
>
> Since I have lived for a year with the certainty that I will lose my life, I know what a person who has before him the perspective of losing his greatest treasure, which is life, endures. Yet even so, throughout this period, I did not feel what I

232 Ibid., 175.
233 Ibid., 175.
234 Ibid., 175–76.
235 Ibid., 176.
236 Ibid., 176.

> felt when I sent other members to certain death, when I sent Lemyk to the consulate, or the one who assassinated Minister Pieracki. The measure of our idea is not that we were prepared to sacrifice our lives, but that we were prepared to sacrifice the lives of others.[237]

Remarkable in this speech is the antifactual and ideologically structured narrative, which aimed to mobilize the emotions and demobilize the mind, something that will remain in Bandera's speeches and writings until his death and will make his followers regard him as a leader of the Ukrainian "liberation movement," or even a demigod. Classic propaganda, Bandera's speech was full of untrue but powerful statements. He stated, for example, that sending Matseiko to his death was painful, whereas he actually disliked Matseiko for helping the police catch the OUN member Mytsyk, and also for "dealing unprofessionally" with Pieracki's murder.[238]

The most remarkable point in Bandera's speech is that "our idea, in our understanding, is so huge that, as it comes to its realization, not hundreds but thousands of human lives have to be sacrificed in order to carry it out." This claim is a continuation of Mikhnovs'kyi's misanthropic and paranoid ideology, strengthened by Dontsov's extreme nationalism, and the OUN's commitment to the ethnic and political mass violence that was an integral part of the "permanent" or "national revolution" and was euphemized as "the liberation struggle."

After Bandera's speech, Prosecutor Prachtel-Morawiański continued his speech. He finished it with a patriotic appeal to the jurors "to demonstrate to the parents of Bachyns'kyi and the family of Babii—victims of the Ukrainian organization—that Poles do not approve of the wrongs that the organization did to them and to Ukrainian society."[239]

When Prachtel-Morawiański had finished his speech, the defending lawyers began theirs. Horbovyi, an OUN member who was defending Bandera not only as his client but also as his *Providnyk*, said that "love for the motherland was the motive that guided the defendant and his activities." Then he stated that, because Bandera admitted the deeds that he was accused of and pleaded not guilty, he could not be guilty.[240] Further the OUN member Horbovyi, who was defending his *Providnyk*, argued that Bandera could not be guilty, because he was not pursuing his private interests but a national mission that was embedded in Ukrainian tradition.[241]

On 27 June 1936, after the other defending lawyers had finished their speeches, the verdict was announced. Bandera and Myhal' were sentenced to life imprisonment, Pidhainyi, Maliutsa, Kachmars'kyi, Sen'kiv, and Mashchak to fifteen years, Spol's'kyi to four years and eight months, Makarushka to four years, Zaryts'ka, Pashkevych, Ianiv, Stets'ko, Iarosh, Fenyk, Ivasyk, and Ravlyk to two years and six months, Shukhevych, Hnatevych, and Kotsiumbas to two years. Fedak, Svientsits'ka, and Rachun were acquitted.[242]

237 Ibid., 176–77.
238 "Proces ... Grzegorz Maciejko," *Gazeta Polska*, 31 December 1935, 8. On Matseiko and Bandera, see also chapter 2 above.
239 "Sprawozdanie stenograficzne," 24 June 1936, TsDIAL, f. 371, op. 1, spr. 8, od. 75, 185.
240 Ibid., 186.
241 Ibid., 187.
242 "Sprawozdanie stenograficzne," 26 June 1936," TsDIAL, f. 371, op. 1, spr. 8, od. 75, 216.

The Lviv trial, similarly to the earlier one in Warsaw, was intended both to destroy the structure of the OUN and to put its leading members in prison. Unlike the first one, it did not attempt to show the public, with the help of the media, how the authorities would punish individuals or organizations that attacked the state, conspired against it, or murdered people for political reasons. The Lviv trial, similar to the Warsaw one, was riddled with political motives and exemplified how difficult Polish-Ukrainian relations were. The defendants tried to challenge the court, the judicial system, and the Polish authorities, while insisting that they were not citizens of Poland, that Polish law did not apply to them, and that they had the right to kill people who were involved in the political system that "occupied" Ukraine. The right to speak Ukrainian allowed them to feel more comfortable and to articulate their beliefs and plans more clearly than in Warsaw, although the judges and prosecutors prevented many such attempts.

Bandera and the Aftermath of the Trials

The trials in Warsaw and Lviv made Bandera famous among Ukrainians in Poland and the diaspora. Both trials transformed the leader of the homeland executive of an ultranationalist terrorist organization into an important symbol of the Ukrainian "liberation movement." Young Ukrainians in the Second Polish Republic followed every day of the trial and admired Bandera while reading the reports in the newspapers in groups and discussing them. Bandera became known as a national revolutionary who fought for Ukrainian independence. Fascism, which the OUN had already adopted in the early 1930s, became an important element of the "liberation struggle." By the performance of fascist salutes and the treatment of Bandera as the leader of a movement that sought to "liberate" the nation and establish a state, the defendants suggested that, after "liberation," the Ukrainian state would become a fascist dictatorship. In his speech, Bandera pointed out that the OUN was determined to sacrifice "thousands of human lives" to realize the aims of the movement. The idea of being ready to sacrifice "thousands of human lives" and to exercise mass violence became integral elements of the agenda of the movement.[243]

For the creation of the Bandera cult, both trials were very significant. Neither trial was a show trial but they were political trials, during which several political issues were discussed by proxy, such as to which state the mixed territories (Volhynia and eastern Galicia) should belong, and the role of the OUN in Polish-Ukrainian relations. The Warsaw trial, due to the extensive and vivid reports in almost all Polish and Ukrainian newspapers, drew considerable attention to the Ukrainian situation in Poland, and to the young nationalist terrorists who attempted to "liberate" their nation. Its echoes were heard in many other countries, including Germany, Italy, Lithuania, and Czechoslovakia, whose governments either supported the OUN financially or co-operated with it.[244] The reports about the Lviv trial in such Polish newspapers as *Gazeta Polska* were less extensive and sensational, but the Ukrainian and Polish papers in Lviv, such as the *Lwowski Ilustrowany Express*, also published some striking articles

243 Ivan Ravliuk, "Bandera vyvodyv nas na chysti vody," in *Stepan Bandera ta ioho rodyna v narodnykh pisniakh, perekazakh ta spohadakh*, ed. Hryhorii Dem"ian (Lviv: Afisha, 2006), 367.

244 Cf. for example "Poselstwo RP w Bukareszcie," AAN, MSZ 5188, 18.

like "The Tactics of the OUN 'Bigwigs'" or "Drunken Party from OUN Funds as Encouragement and then as Award for the Murder of Bachyns'kyi."[245] Some scenes from the Lviv trial made a strong impact on contemporary Ukrainian nationalist discourses. These included Bandera's speech on 26 June 1936, the fascist salutes, and the moment when Bandera entered the courtroom, in which all the public allegedly rose to their feet, emulating the behavior of the defendants, who had stood up to greet their *Providnyk*.[246] In an article that appeared on 21 June 1936 in *Ukraïns'ke slovo*, the OUN ideologist Stsibors'kyi called the young OUN members on trial "bandery [Banderites]."[247] The trials also entered Ukrainian folk culture, which at this time was very popular among Galician Ukrainians. One of the songs about Bandera said:

Nineteen thirty five is passing, We went through it When the verdict was announced In the court in Warsaw	Trydtsiat' p'iatyi rik mynaie, my ioho mynaly Iak v Varshavi v trybunali prysud vidchytaly
Where twelve Ukrainians, Great heroes, Who wanted to attain Freedom for Ukraine.	De dvanadtsiat' ukraïntsiv, Velykykh heroïv, Shcho khotily zdobuvaty Ukraïni voliu.
Among these heroes Are also women, Hnatkivs'ka and brave Unwavering Zaryts'ka.	Pomizh tymy heroiamy Ie takozh divchata, Ie Hnatkivs'ka i Zaryts'ka, Vidvazhna, zavziata.
The first hero is Bandera. The second is called Lebed', They are not afraid of handcuffs, They are laughing at handcuffs.	Pershyi heroi—to Bandera, Druhyi Lebid' zvet'sia, Vony kaidaniv ne boiat'sia, Z kaidaniv smiiut'sia.
The twelve were sentenced By the cursed Poles. They will be followed by other Unwavering heroes.	Tykh dvanadtsiat' zasudyly Poliaky prokliati. Na ïkh mistse pryidut' inshi Heroï zavziati.[248]

245 "Taktyka 'grubych ryb' OUN," *Lwowski Ilustrowany Express*, 30 May 1936, 1858, 5; "Libacja z funduszów dyspozycyjnych OUN jako zachęta, a potem jako nagroda za zamordowanie Baczyńskiego," *Lwowski Ilustrowany Express*, 3 June 1936, 3.

246 See, for example, Shukhevych, *Moie zhyttia*, 529. Because Shukhevych and other reporters of this event do not provide a date, this story might refer to the first day of the trial, when Bandera entered the courtroom as the last defendant and raised his right arm while shouting "Slava Ukraïni!" to which other defendants responded with the same fascist salute. See "Hitlerowskie powitanie oskarżonych," *Ilustrowany Express Poranny*, 27 May 1936, 16.

247 Mykola Stsibors'kyi, "Klonim holovy," in *Stepan Bandera*, ed. Posivnych, 2006, 133–34.

248 Dem"ian, *Stepan Bandera ta ioho rodyna*, 37–38, 59–60. Dem"ian might have replaced the pejorative and politically incorrect but common word "liakhy" with the politically correct "poliaky." For other versions of the song see Ievhen Lun'o, "Iavorishchyna pro Stepana Banderu: Providnyk OUN u pisennomu fol'klori," *Narodoznavchi zoshyty* Vol. 25, No. 1 (1999): 35–36.

Bandera in Polish Prisons

After his arrest on 14 June 1934, Bandera remained in Polish prisons until 13 September 1939. According to his autobiography, he conducted three hunger strikes during this period. One lasted nine days; another, thirteen days; the third one, sixteen days.[249] According to Klymyshyn, after Bandera's arrest on the morning of 14 June 1934 he was transported together with Stets'ko and some other OUN activists to a prison in Cracow, in which Klymyshyn was already detained since the same morning. After ten days, Klymyshyn and Karpynets' were taken to the Warsaw prison at 7 Daniłowiczowska Street. In his memoirs, Klymyshyn did not say whether Bandera was also taken to this penal institution.[250] Wojciech Żygała, warden in the Lviv Brygdiki prison, testified in the Warsaw trial that Bandera was kept in this penitentiary, but he did not specify exactly when.[251] In April 1935, Klymyshyn was taken to another Warsaw prison, the Mokotów Prison at 37 Rakowiecka Street, where he and other OUN prisoners, among them Bandera, Lebed', and Pidhainyi, were held in more comfortable one-person cells, which had running water and flush toilets. They could also use the prison library, which had over 12,000 books, and some of them did so extensively. Klymyshyn could not establish contact with Bandera, who was in a cell in the opposite corner of the prison until the Warsaw trial. When Klymshyn saw Bandera once in the corridor, he was wearing ordinary clothes but was handcuffed.[252]

After the announcement of the verdict in the Warsaw trial, Bandera was also kept in the Mokotów Prison for a few weeks. It is not known whether he had been in the same prison during the Warsaw trial, or in the prison at 24 Dzielna Street.[253] After the trial finished, Bandera was allowed to meet and talk with other OUN prisoners who were in the Mokotów Prison. On a "beautiful winter day" a few weeks after the end of the Warsaw trial, Bandera was taken, together with Pidhainyi, Karpynets', Kachmars'kyi, Lebed', and Klymyshyn, to the Święty Krzyż prison near Kielce, one of the most harsh and uncomfortable prisons in the Second Republic.[254] The Święty Krzyż prison was located in a former monastery and possessed only thirty-five cells for between 600 and 1,000 prisoners. The outlying location made it inconvenient for visitors. Most prisoners in this penal institution were recognized as dangerous.[255]

After their arrival in the Święty Krzyż prison, the *Providnyk* and other OUN inmates were given a haircut. They received cumbersome wooden shoes, and prison clothes full of holes. According to Klymyshyn, Bandera in particular looked horrible after this procedure:

> Bandera suffered the most. He came to the cell the last. He waited the longest in order to be "accommodated" and froze while waiting for his turn. He got broad trousers and very big blouse, and everything so horrible, ragged and holey, that it was difficult to look at him. And they also cut his hair! Since I remember him, he

249 Bandera, Moï zhyttiepysni dani, 8.
250 Klymyshyn, *V pokhodi*, 1:114–15.
251 "Proces. Jak zachowywał się Bandera w więzieniu," *Gazeta Polska*, 30 November 1935, 6; "Rozprava za ... Myhal' hovoryt' po pol's'ky," *Dilo*, 30 November 1935, 3.
252 Klymyshyn, *V pokhodi*, 1: 118–19, 121.
253 Cybulski, Stepan Bandera w więzieniach, 73.
254 Klymyshyn, *V pokhodi*, 1:150, Cybulski, Stepan Bandera w więzieniach, 76.
255 Cybulski, Stepan Bandera w więzieniach, 76

> always has had nice light brown hair, combed to the side. And now they poured scorn on him. They horribly disfigured him. It was the look of a horrible, humiliated person. But we took it easy, with humor.[256]

The new five OUN prisoners exchanged their new clothes among each other, so that they fitted better. They first stayed in a quarantine cell without beds. They were promised that, once they learned the rules of the prison, they would be moved to the actual prison cells and provided with beds and better clothes. However, they received better clothes and blankets much sooner, from a Ukrainian guard who was asked to do so by a Ukrainian who had been imprisoned there since the end of the First World War. Due to the lack of running water and items such as toilet paper, sanitary circumstances in the prison were horrible. In addition to an extremely malodorous toilet in the corridor, every cell had a container for feces and urine, which was emptied in the morning by two inmates. Outside the cell, the prisoners always had to walk with their hands behind their back and to look down in front of their feet, which they perceived as inconvenient and humiliating. The prisoners were woken by the religious song "When the Morning Lights Arise" (Pol. *Kiedy ranne wstają zorze*) written by the Polish poet Franciszek Karpiński and performed in Święty Krzyż by other prisoners. Bandera's OUN co-prisoner Knysh remembered that it was "very sad to listen to this slavery singing."[257]

On the prisoners' tenth day in the quarantine cell, the chief officer of the prison entered, together with a hunting dog and a few guards. Knysh remembered him saying, "The student period and the times when we played 'heroes' are finished once and forever. Now we have to stay until death in his lockup. Everything depends how we will behave. If we will be proper prisoners he will treat us as intelligent people and not like ordinary thieves, and if not, then our faces will be smashed in, smashed in again, and we will be put in quarantine."[258]

After hearing this speech, Bandera was moved to a cell in which he stayed with Lebed' and a number of other prisoners, but not the rest of the OUN group. The usual cells held about fifteen to twenty prisoners with different backgrounds, characters, and interests. These differences and the narrow living-space led to conflicts, and sometimes even fights.[259] On 25 or 26 April 1936, Bandera was transported to Warsaw for the appeal. He stayed together with Lebed' and Klymyshyn in the Pawiak Prison at 24–26 Dzielna Street. After the appeal, which finished on 30 April, it is not known whether Bandera was taken back to Święty Krzyż, or held in the Pawiak Prison, or immediately taken to the prison in Kazimierza Wielkiego Street in Lviv, where he was held during the Lviv trial, from 24 May until 2 July 1936.[260] On 2 July, after the Lviv trial, the chief officer of the Lviv prison ordered that Bandera be taken to the Mokotów Prison in Warsaw again, because he feared that Bandera and other prisoners might be rescued. On the next day, they were moved again to the Święty Krzyż prison where, since April, the chief officer had been instructed to improve security measures and to transfer a number of Ukrainian prisoners, who might be connected with the OUN, to other prisons.[261]

256 Klymyshyn, *V pokhodi*, 1:153.
257 Ibid., 1:154, 156, 158, 170.
258 Ibid., 1:161–62.
259 Ibid., 1:162–89.
260 Ibid., 1:194; Cybulski, Stepan Bandera w więzieniach, 78.
261 Cybulski, Stepan Bandera w więzieniach, 78–79.

After Bandera's return to the Święty Krzyż, he, Pidhainyi, Karpynets', Kachmars'kyi, Lebed', and Klymyshyn were, on Bandera's initiative, placed in the same cell, number 21, in which they stayed with three other OUN members: Hryhorii Perehiniak, Iurii Batih, and Lutsyniak. They could read their own books—three volumes of the General Ukrainian Encyclopedia belonging to Bandera, and Ukrainian newspapers subscribed to by Bandera and Lebed'. In the cell there were also two illiterate Ukrainians and another two with only rudimentary education. The OUN prisoners taught them and the other OUN members to read and write, and otherwise educated them. Klymyshyn offered courses in grammar and literature, Pidhainyi in mathematics, physics, and chemistry, and Bandera in history and ideology. The most talented Ukrainian—taught by Klymyshyn, Pidhainyi and Bandera—was Hryhorii Perehiniak, a blacksmith born in Staryi Uhryniv, where in March 1935 he killed Vasyl' Ilkiv, for which he was sentenced to life imprisonment, six months later. In prison he became especially close to the leader of the homeland executive. Bandera's courses in history and ideology must have significantly influenced Perehiniak, who would play an important role in the process of establishing the UPA in Volhynia during the Second World War, and in initiating the ethnic cleansing against the Polish population.[262]

In the same cell there were also prisoners who did not belong to the OUN, among them some Poles. One of them, Wójcicki, was an informer. Although everyone in the cell knew it, nobody mentioned or discussed it. Once a week the prisoners ate *kapuśniak*, a soup from sauerkraut or cabbage, popular in Poland, Ukraine, and some other East Central European countries. Once, while waiting in line for the soup, Bandera stood behind Wójcicki. There was silence in the cell, which Bandera interrupted with the word "kapuś" (Pol. snitch) to which he soon added "niaczek."[263]

Before Christmas 1937, Osyp Kladochnyi, chaplain of the Ukrainian political prisoners, visited Bandera and other OUN prisoners. After three years imprisonment, this was their first opportunity to make confession. Knysh wrote in his memoirs that the confessions took a long time, which suggests that the prisoners did not live without sin in the prison, or that they discussed other subjects with the chaplain. Afterwards, Kladochnyi conducted a service. The OUN prisoners were also allowed choir practice for Christmas. The choir was conducted by Bandera, the most talented vocalist among the OUN prisoners. Klymyshyn remembered Christmas 1937 as "extraordinarily spiritual."[264]

After Christmas, however, the OUN inmates were again distributed among different cells. Bandera was very likely moved with Lebed' to the same cell as before, where he tried to establish contact with other OUN prisoners. He succeeded in doing so by leaving a scrap of paper under the toilet bowl, which he informed a prisoner from Klymyshyn's cell about. Using this method of exchanging information, the OUN prisoners organized a hunger strike. It lasted for fifteen days, but from the eighth day they were force-fed with mash, through a tube in the nose. Toward the end of the hunger

262 Klymyshyn, *V pokhodi*, 1:195–97, 199; "Bandera i chotyry tovaryshi u chesnokhrests'ki tiurmi," *Novyi chas*, 16 January 1936, 3. For Hryhorii Perehiniak and the UPA, see page 269. For the murder of Vasyl' Ilkiv, see Grzegorz Motyka, *Cień Kłyma Sawura. Polsko-ukraiński konflikt pamięci* (Gdańsk: Oskar, 2013), 22.

263 Klymyshyn, *V pokhodi*, 1:197–99.

264 Ibid., 1:203–5. The OUN prisoners celebrated Christmas Eve on 6 January, and Christmas on 7 January 1937, according to the Julian calendar.

strike, Bandera became very thin and weak; he leaned against the walls as he walked. After the hunger strike, the OUN members were moved to the same cell again and stayed there for about three months. They were then moved to other cells, and finally other prisons.[265]

Although Święty Krzyż had high security standards, the administration feared attempts to free Bandera. They invested a substantial amount of money in safety measures to prevent a potential escape. The chief officer, in particular, was very much afraid of such an attempt. He even supposed that the prison might be besieged and that if the telephone line were cut, they would not be able to summon help. For this reason he decided to build four watchtowers, which were intended to prevent Ukrainian nationalists and other armed groups from liberating Bandera. A group of about twenty OUN activists indeed planned to free Bandera from Święty Krzyż. They communicated with Bandera with the help of his former lawyer Horbovyi, and in letters which were, however, read by the prison officers. The chaplain Kladochnyi, who confessed Bandera "an hour and longer," might also have been involved in the attempt to release the *Providnyk*. The OUN planned to send two members disguised as monks to the monastery located next to the prison. The disguised OUN members planned to extricate Bandera through the monastery and escape with him into the forest. However, the prison guards and police, with the help of their informers, uncovered the plan and adopted the measures necessary to stop the rescue operation at an early stage, without drawing public attention to the incident. Nevertheless, the chief officer did not feel comfortable with the *Providnyk* in his prison. Bandera was relocated, in late 1937 or early 1938, from Święty Krzyż to the prison in Wronki, in western Poland.[266]

Shortly after Bandera's relocation, the OUN leader Konovalets' was assassinated on 23 May 1938, in Rotterdam. We do not know how Bandera reacted to this news. His close friend Klymyshyn was deeply moved and wrote a poem.[267] The Wronki prison had higher security measures and was further away from the usual area of OUN activities than the Święty Krzyż prison. This did not, however, thwart the OUN from planning another attempt to liberate Bandera in August and September 1938. The second attempt to rescue Bandera may have been related to the Konovalets' assassination, after which a number of younger OUN members wanted Bandera to become the leader of the OUN leadership in exile, or of the PUN. After rescue, Bandera was to be transported to Germany, the border of which was only ten kilometers from the prison. The PUN did not object to the idea of Bandera's escape but was reluctant to support the attempt. Nor did the homeland executive support it, and it remained a more or less private initiative of a group of OUN fighters. The initiators were Ivan Ravlyk, Roman Shukhevych, and Mykhailo Kuspis', a former prisoner of Wronki. Zenon Kossak, another former prisoner of Wronki, helped them. For this operation the OUN allegedly received a substantial amount of money from the Ukrainian diaspora in order to bribe the prison guards.[268]

265 Ibid., 1:207–13.
266 Cybulski, Stepan Bandera w więzieniach, 74, 79, 81, 83–86; Shukhevych, *Moie zhyttia*, 537–39.
267 Klymyshyn, *V pokhodi*, 1:219.
268 Rebet, *Svitla i tini*, 77–78; Zynovii Knysh, *Rozbrat: Spohady i materiialy do rozkolu OUN u 1940–1941 rokakh* (Toronto: Sribna Surma, 1960), 48.

Kuspis' bribed a former guard by the name of Piotr Zaborowski to help him approach a current prison guard, who agreed to release Bandera for money. Another person agreed to help Bandera and Kuspis' cross the German-Polish border.[269] The escape was prepared for 7 September 1938 but it is not clear why the operation was not carried out. According to Kuspis', the OUN decided, at the very last moment, that it should not be.[270] One reason might be that the OUN did not trust the bribed guards and feared a trap, in which Bandera would be killed. It might also be that the OUN did not receive enough money to pay their helpers or were afraid that Bandera's escape would worsen the situation of other Ukrainian prisoners in Polish prisons.[271] In September, the police arrested eleven persons, because Zaborowski entrusted the details of the proposed attempt to a friend, who reported them to the police.[272] One of the arrested persons, Maria Bielecka, committed suicide in a prison cell. As with the first release operation, the police proceeded very carefully to avoid attracting public attention and to protect the police informers within the OUN. Kuspis' was sentenced to eight years, Zaborowski to three. From the prison in Wronki, Bandera was taken in early 1939 to a penal institution in Brest (Brześć), in eastern Poland. According to his brief autobiography, he escaped on 13 September 1939, during the turmoil of the Second World War, with the help of Ukrainian prisoners.[273]

Conclusion

The assassination of the Polish Interior Minister Bronisław Pieracki was the most important terrorist act that the OUN performed during the interwar period. This assassination and the two subsequent trials in Warsaw and Lviv significantly contributed to the formation of the Bandera cult. The Warsaw trial drew international attention to the situation of Ukrainians in Poland. At both trials the OUN presented itself as a fascist movement which attempted to liberate Ukraine. The defendants performed fascist salutes and treated Bandera as their *Providnyk*. In doing so they implied that for them Bandera was the leader of the Ukrainian people and that he should become the leader of the Ukrainian state. Even Polish intellectuals began to romanticize the behavior of the young revolutionary idealists who were ready to die for their country. From the day of his arrest on 14 June 1936, Bandera remained in custody until the beginning of the Second World War. The attempt to rescue him demonstrated that, after Konovalets' assassination, a faction of the OUN wanted to make him the leader of the movement.

269 Rebet, *Svitla i tini*, 77; Knysh, *Rozbrat*, 58.
270 Knysh, *Rozbrat*, 60.
271 Rebet, *Svitla i tini*, 77–78; Knysh, *Rozbrat*, 68.
272 Knysh, *Rozbrat*, 60.
273 Cybulski, Stepan Bandera w więzieniach, 85–93; Bandera, Moï zhyttiepysni dani, 8.

Chapter 4

THE "UKRAINIAN NATIONAL REVOLUTION": MASS VIOLENCE AND POLITICAL DISASTER

Revolution was one of the most significant concepts of OUN ideology. The Ukrainian nationalists believed that they could create a state only in the course of a revolution, which they sometimes called an uprising. During the interwar period, the OUN occupied itself with "permanent revolution," while preparing Ukrainians in the Second Polish Republic for the final act—the "national revolution." In order to start the latter, however, the OUN needed a convenient opportunity, such as a war or other international conflict between their "occupiers." When Germany attacked Poland in September 1939, some of the OUN leaders were unsure whether the right moment for the "bloody uprising" had arrived. They were disappointed by the political changes, but Germany—especially the Abwehr—involved them in its next major expansion eastward, the war against the Soviet Union, which the OUN hoped would present the opportunity to start the "bloody uprising" and to establish an authoritarian state of a fascist type. The conflicts and splits within the movement did not prevent the Ukrainian nationalists from elaborating new revolutionary plans. The most efficient and detailed plan for a revolution was manufactured by the OUN-B and called the "Ukrainian National Revolution." Its architects adjusted it to the ethos of the "New Europe," with its fascist and racist political order.[1]

The Beginning of the Second World War

On 13 September 1939, thirteen days after Nazi Germany attacked Poland, Stepan Bandera escaped from the prison in Brest. Together with other Ukrainian ex-prisoners, he made his way to Lviv, where he allegedly stayed in the buildings of St. George's Cathedral and met with Sheptyts'kyi. On 17 September, the Soviet Union attacked Poland from the east. The German and Soviet attack on Poland was brought about by the Treaty of Nonaggression signed in Moscow on 23 August 1939 by the German and Soviet Ministers of Foreign Affairs, Joachim von Ribbentrop and Viacheslav Molotov. After a few days in Lviv, Bandera, realizing that eastern Galicia would remain in the Soviet sphere of influence, left the city for the area of Poland that was occupied by Germany, and which became known as the General Government. With him went a few other OUN members, including his brother Vasyl', who had escaped from

1 The term "Ukrainian National Revolution" is a propaganda term that the OUN-B used in 1940–1941 to describe its plans for the Ukrainian territories after the outbreak of the conflict between Nazi Germany and the Soviet Union. For this reason, in this book, it is placed within quotation marks. For use of this term by the OUN-B, see "Postanovy II. Velykoho Zboru Orhanizatsiï Ukraïns'kykh Natsionalistiv," TsDAHO f. 1, op. 23, spr. 926, 188, 193. For the alternative "Ukrainian Revolution," see "Borot'ba i diial'nist' OUN pidchas viiny," TsDAVOV f. 3833, op. 2, spr. 1, 17.

the Polish concentration camp in Bereza Kartuska. They crossed the German-Soviet border that divided the territory of the now non-existent Second Republic, and went to Cracow.[2]

In the short period of time between the German attack on Poland and the Soviet invasion, there was chaos and a political vacuum in western Ukraine. Before the Soviet army came to western Ukraine, some German units entered this territory and stayed for about two weeks. At that time, the OUN was considering whether to conduct its "national revolution." In some locations it established a militia, which attacked and killed Jews, Poles, and Ukrainian political opponents.[3] However, once the OUN realized that it was insufficiently prepared and that the political situation on account of the German-Soviet Nonaggression Pact was not favorable for such an event, the leadership decided not to attempt to take power in the territory or to establish a state. In this short period of time, the OUN killed approximately 2,000 Poles in eastern Galicia, about 1,000 in Volhynia, and an unknown number of Jews and political opponents.[4]

At that time, Polish soldiers killed an unknown number of Ukrainians in response to the OUN violence and also because some Ukrainians welcomed the Soviet army, erected triumphal arches for them, and sang "communist songs mixed with religious hymns."[5] Jews became the victims of both sides during this period.[6] In Iavoriv (Jaworów), a small town about fifty kilometers west of Lviv, for example, German troops, together with Ukrainian militiamen who were wearing yellow-and-blue armlets, destroyed the local synagogue and humiliated, tortured, beat, murdered, and otherwise mistreated the Jews.[7] Bandera, whose visits overlapped with the first violent acts conducted by the OUN, never mentioned them in his writings, just as he did not mention the greater atrocities that the OUN and UPA later committed, during and after Second World War. In his brief autobiography from 1959 Bandera stated that in September 1939 the OUN "began to establish partisan units that concerned themselves with the protection of the Ukrainian population and took possession of weapons and other military equipment for a future struggle."[8]

2 Bandera, Moï zhyttiepysni dani, 14; Hryhorii Prokuda, "Zustrich zi Stepanom Banderoiu," in *Narodoznavchi zoshyty* Vol. 25, No. 1 (1999): 84; Posivnych, Providnyk OUN, 43. Klymyshyn wrote that the door of Bandera's cell was opened on 10 September 1939. Cf. Klymyshyn, *V pokhodi*, 1:266.

3 For militia in Iavoriv, see AŻIH 301/1912, Izrael Manber, 2–3; AŻIH 301/1612, Nadel Chaim, 1–2; AŻIH 301/1614, Jakub Sauerbrunn, 1.

4 For the murder of Poles, see Motyka, *Ukraińska partyzantka 1942–1960*, 70, 72; Władysław Siemaszko and Ewa Siemaszko, *Ludobójstwo dokonane przez nacjonalistów ukraińskich na ludności polskiej Wołynia 1939–1945* (Warsaw: Wydawnictwo von borowiecky, 2000), 2:1034–37.

5 Motyka, *Ukraińska partyzantka*, 71; Grzegorz Motyka, "Postawy wobec konfliktu polsko-ukraińskiego w latach 1939–1953 w zależności od przynależności etnicznej, państwowej i religijnej," in *Tygiel Narodów: Stosunki społeczne i etniczne na dawnych ziemiach wschodnich Rzeczypospolitej 1939–1953*, ed. Krzysztof Jasiewicz (Warsaw: Rytm, 2002), 286–87. For the triumphal arches and the singing of communist songs to the Soviet army, see Jan Tomasz Gross, *Revolution from Abroad: The Soviet Conquest of Poland's Western Ukraine and Western Belorussia* (Princeton: Princeton University Press, 2002), 20, 39–40, 262.

6 Bruder, *"Den Ukrainischen Staat*, 140; Gross, *Revolution from Abroad*, 19–20.

7 AŻIH 301/1912, Izrael Manber, 2–3; AŻIH 301/1612, Nadel Chaim, 1–2; AŻIH 301/1614, Jakub Sauerbrunn, 1.

8 Bandera, Moï zhyttiepysni dani, 9.

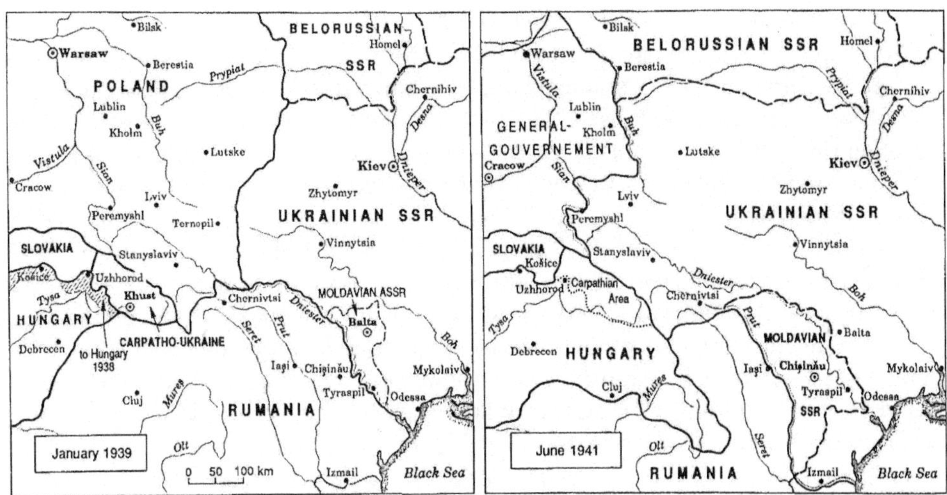

Map 4. The Second World War in Ukraine, January 1939 – June 1944.
Encyclopedia of Ukraine, 5:726.

In Cracow, Bandera met many of his comrades-in-arms. At that time, the city became the main center for Ukrainian nationalists. Nearly 30,000 Ukrainians, many of them young nationalists like Bandera, fled to the General Government in order to avoid a confrontation with the Soviet regime.[9] In addition, many Ukrainians released from Polish prisons and the Bereza Kartuska detention camp were staying in Cracow and other places in the General Government. The OUN was, at this time, the most popular Ukrainian organization, which, owing to the Soviet occupation of Ukraine, "nourished everybody's hope," as Klymyshyn wrote in his memoirs.[10] While staying in Cracow, OUN members observed an anti-Jewish pogrom, which took place in the city in December 1939.[11]

In Cracow, the Germans established the Ukrainian Central Committee (*Ukraïns'kyi Tsentral'nyi Komitet*, UTsK), a welfare and relief agency, which set up a network of Ukrainian cooperatives, schools, and youth organizations in the General Government. The UTsK was headed by Volodymyr Kubiiovych, a geographer, who was not a member of the OUN but empathized with its older generation. Like many other Ukrainians, he had experienced ethnic discrimination in the Second Polish Republic and regarded Germany as the most important partner of the Ukrainians, sharing with the Nazis many political convictions, including antisemitism and other racism. On 18 April 1941, he petitioned General Governor Hans Frank to purge "Polish and Jewish elements" from the ethnic Ukrainian territories within the General Government.[12]

While in Cracow, Bandera first lived in one of the five camps erected for Ukrainians on Loretańska Street. He later moved into an apartment on Straszewskiego

9 Kost' Pan'kivs'kyi, *Roky nimets'koï okupatsiï* (New York and Toronto: Zhyttia i mysli, 1965), 145; Finder, Collaboration in Eastern Galicia, 98.

10 Klymyshyn, *V pokhodi*, 1:267.

11 Roman Rosdolsky, "The Jewish Orphanage in Cracow," The Online Publication Series of the Center for Urban History of East Central Europe, 4, http://www.lvivcenter.org/en/publications/ (accessed 26 May 2010): 2–4.

12 Golczewski, Shades of Grey, 126–27.

Street together with his brothers Vasyl' and Bohdan.[13] At a military course in Cracow in late September, Klymyshyn met Bandera for the first time since his escape from prison. Bandera looked thin and had longer hair than usual. According to Klymyshyn, Bandera was dressed in clothes that he had taken from the prison. They went shopping together the next day between the market square and the university. Bandera bought a grey suit, and Klymyshyn a black one. Grey was Bandera's favorite color of cloth and was also one of his aliases.[14]

During his stay in Cracow, Bandera met the female OUN member Iaroslava Oparivs'ka (1917–1977) who had studied at the Lviv Polytechnic before the war.[15] Bandera married her either on 3 June 1940 in Cracow or on 5 June in Sanok.[16] Klymshyn remarked in his memoirs that the wedding ceremony was very modest; no more than ten people were present.[17] Iaroslava took on Stepan's surname and became Iaroslava Bandera. In late 1940 they moved to Warsaw, where they lived until early 1941 for security reasons, in an apartment arranged by Lebed'.[18] Their first child Natalia was born on 26 May 1941 in Sanok. In 1939 or 1941 Bandera had an operation on his nose in Berlin. His nasal septum was either broken or damaged when he was force-fed through the nose during the hunger strike in the Święty Krzyż prison.[19]

The Split in the OUN

Bandera wrote in his autobiography that in November 1939 he went for a cure for two weeks to a spa in Piešťany in Slovakia, where he met several other OUN members.[20] He went from there to Vienna, where he met more comrades-in-arms, among them Volodymyr Tymchii (Lopatyns'kyi), the current leader of the homeland executive of the OUN. Bandera and Lopatyns'kyi agreed on a joint visit to Rome, in order to hold a discussion with the new leader of the OUN and PUN, Andrii Mel'nyk. The problems to be discussed included misunderstandings and lack of cooperation between the homeland executive and the leadership in exile, and between the OUN in Ukraine and the PUN, as these organizations were called at this time. Having arrived in Rome

13 Klymyshyn, *V pokhodi*, 1:269; Interrogation of Fedor Davidiuk, 20 June 1945, HDA SBU f. 65, spr. 19127, vol. 1, 146–51, in *Stepan Bandera*, ed. Serhiichuk, 1:338. In 1956 Bandera testified that he used the name Burkut at this time. Cf. "Vernehmungsniederschrift Stefan Popel, 07.02.1956," StM, Pol. Dir. München 9281, 85.

14 Klymyshyn, *V pokhodi*, 1:269.

15 "Lyst nachalnika, 29.08.1951," HDA SBU f. 2, op. 98, spr. 12, vol. 3, 70–71, *Stepan Bandera*, ed. Serhiichuk, 3:130.

16 Iaroslava stated during interrogation that she had married Stepan on 5 June 1940 in Sanok. Cf. Interrogation of Iaroslava Bandera, BayHStA, LKA 272, 4. Stepan Bandera stated in an investigation that he had married Iaroslava in Cracow. Cf. "Vernehmungsniederschrift Stefan Popel, 07.02.1956," StM, Pol. Dir. München 9281, 85. See also Posivnych, Providnyk OUN, 11. In the same year, Stepan's brother Vasyl' married Mariia Vozniak. Cf. HDA SBU, f. 63, spr. S-9079, vol. 8, 1–3, *Stepan Bandera*, ed. Serhiichuk, 1:628.

17 Klymyshyn, *V pokhodi*, 1:273.

18 Arsenych, Rodyna Banderiv, 49–50; Dem"ian, *Stepan Bandera*, 186; Iaroslav Stets'ko, *30 chervnia 1941: Proholoshennia vidnovlennia derzhavnosty Ukraïny* (Toronto: Liga Vyzvolennia Ukraïny, 1967), 131–32.

19 Interrogation of Iaroslava Bandera, 17.10.1959, BayHStA, LKA 272, 4, 30. Iaroslava Bandera first mentioned 1939 and later 1941 as the date of the operation.

20 In a document from 9 April 1940, Mel'nyk mentions that Bandera was in Berlin in November 1939. Cf. "Zaklyk Andriia Mel'nyka do chleniv VZUN i PUN," in Volodymyr Kosyk, *Rozkol OUN (1939–1940): Zbirnyk dokumentiv* (Lviv: L'vivs'kyi natsional'nyi universytet, 1999), 41.

Fig. 10. Bandera in the 1940s. Poltava, *Zhyttia Stepana Bandery*, 25.

during the first half of January 1940, Bandera met his brother Oleksandr, who had been living in Rome since 1933 and had completed a doctorate in political economy.[21]

The negotiations with Mel'nyk did not lead to a compromise. Bandera demanded that Mel'nyk remove Iaroslav Baranovs'kyi and Omelian Senyk from the leadership. Bandera suspected the former of cooperation with the Poles.[22] Furthermore, he demanded that Mel'nyk include in the leadership new members he had proposed. Bandera and Lopatyns'kyi also asked the current OUN leader to leave for Switzerland and stay there. The motive behind this request was to marginalize Mel'nyk's role within the OUN.[23]

In his autobiography from 1959, Bandera also wrote that he demanded that the policies of the OUN should be less dependent on outside factors, by which he meant cooperation with Nazi Germany.[24] This claim from 1959, however, corresponds neither with the OUN-B's actions in 1940–1941, nor with what Bandera expressed in an

21 Bandera, Moï zhyttiepysni dani, 10–11.

22 According to Grzegorz Motyka, Bandera competed with Baranovs'kyi for the sympathy of Anna Chemeryns'ka. Cf. Motyka, *Ukraińska partyzantka*, 78.

23 Motyka, *Ukraińska partyzantka*, 77–78.

24 Bandera, Moï zhyttiepysni dani, 10–11.

undated letter to Mel'nyk, written in August 1940, when he was outraged at the rumor spread by Baranovs'kyi that Bandera was hostile to Nazi Germany.[25]

Mel'nyk did not agree with Bandera's demands and assumptions. He offered Bandera the post of an adviser to the leadership and requested absolute obedience from Lopatyns'kyi. In reaction, Bandera, and other OUN members such as Stets'ko, Ianiv, Lenkavs'kyi, and Shukhevych—members of the homeland executive in 1933–1934 when Bandera was its leader—gathered in Cracow on 10 February 1940 and proclaimed a Revolutionary Leadership (*revoliutsiinyi provid*). Bandera became the leader of this new political body.[26] This faction subsequently became known as the OUN-B (for Bandera) in order to distinguish itself from the older or actual OUN, which was known as the OUN-M (for Mel'nyk) from this point on. Lopatyns'kyi took this news to Ukraine but was killed on the German-Soviet border by Soviet guards.[27]

Until Bandera met with Mel'nyk again on 5 April 1940, the two groups hoped to arrive at an agreement. On that day, however, Bandera and Stets'ko gave Mel'nyk their own letters, which informed him about the existence of the Revolutionary Leadership of the OUN.[28] The letters must have outraged Mel'nyk, because he put Bandera and Stets'ko before the Revolutionary Tribunal on 8 April. The same day, Bandera and Stets'ko published an announcement in which they informed all OUN members that the Revolutionary Leadership had decided that Mel'nyk was no longer the leader of the organization, and that the new leader of the OUN was Stepan Bandera.[29] On 27 September, the Revolutionary Tribunal removed Bandera from the OUN.[30] Stets'ko stated in retrospect that Mel'nyk ordered the assassination of Bandera and himself, which was the reason why they moved temporarily to Warsaw.[31]

The details of the split reveal interesting information as to how Bandera and his comrades dealt with opponents. In a longer letter to Mel'nyk from 10 September 1940, Bandera informed the leader of the PUN and leadership in exile that, on 10 February, he "had to regulate the matters in the leadership because those who were responsible for it did nothing."[32] Bandera argued that he had had to do it, not for his own personal sake but because nationalists who honored his name expected it from him.[33] He claimed that Mel'nyk did not listen to people who tried to give him constructive advice, but justified his decisions with the authority of his position. Bandera implied that Mel'nyk was a puppet in the hands of Senyk and Baranovs'kyi, both of whom Bandera regarded as traitors. As a result, "the atmosphere of denial, duplicity, falsehood and suspicion remains in the leadership."[34] Furthermore, Bandera informed Mel'nyk that the late Lopatyns'kyi had refused to use the fascist salute "Glory to the Leader!" (*Vozhdevi*

25 Letter from Bandera to Mel'nyk, TsDAVOV f. 3833, op. 1, spr. 71, 19.
26 "Rishennia narady providnykiv 10 liutoho 1940 roku," in Kosyk, *Rozkol OUN*, 30.
27 Motyka, *Ukraińska partyzantka*, 78.
28 Ibid., 78. For Bandera's letter to Mel'nyk, see "Lyst Stepana Bandery do Andriia Mel'nyka," in Kosyk, *Rozkol OUN*, 32; "Bila knyha OUN: Pro dyversiu-bunt Iary-Bandera," PAA, ACC. 85.191/64, 3.
29 In another letter Mel'nyk informed Bandera about his decision on 7 April. Cf. "Bila knyha OUN: Pro dyversiu-bunt Iary-Bandera," PAA, ACC. 85.191/64, 6–9; "Komunikat Revoliutsiinoho Provodu," in Kosyk, *Rozkol OUN*, 35, 106.
30 Motyka, *Ukraińska partyzantka*, 78; Kosyk, *Rozkol OUN*, 35, 106.
31 Stets'ko, *30 chervnia 1941*, 129–30, 255.
32 Letter from Bandera to Mel'nyk, TsDAVOV f. 3833, op. 1, spr. 71, 4. For the date of the letter, see Kosyk, *Rozkol OUN*, 55.
33 Ibid., 4.
34 Ibid., 8, 10–11.

Slava!), because he was disappointed by Mel'nyk and argued that the OUN did not have a leader. The greeting "Glory to the Leader!" had been mandatory since the Second Great Congress in Rome on 27 August 1939.[35]

In the letter to Mel'nyk, Bandera also explained that on 10 February 1940 the Revolutionary Leadership of the OUN "ceased discussing and began to act," because Mel'nyk did not want to cleanse the PUN, that is to remove Senyk and Baranovs'kyi. The Revolutionary Leadership knew that it did not have the reputation and authority of the PUN, but it had on its side "truth, pure cause [*chysta sprava*], faith, and the indestructible will to lead the matter to a successful end."[36] Writing about Stsibors'kyi, who remained in the OUN-M, Bandera used antisemitic arguments to discredit this leading member of the OUN. He claimed that Stsibors'kyi had to be excluded from the OUN, because he was living with a "suspicious Russian Jewish woman" and because he was "a traitor and a Bolshevik agent."[37]

According to Bandera, Mel'nyk was surrounded by traitors such as Baranovs'kyi, and "treacherous Bolshevik agents" such as Stsibors'kyi, and did not do anything to demonstrate that he was the appropriate leader. Mel'nyk had become a leader because he inherited the position from Konovalets', which was arranged by the PUN. Bandera argued that Mel'nyk and the PUN expected that everyone would accept Mel'nyk in this position. This did not come about, however, because the traitors Baranovs'kyi and Senyk made Mel'nyk into a puppet, which meant according to Bandera's logic that the organization was controlled by "enemies" and "Bolshevik agents."[38] Logically, Bandera felt that this obliged him to take over control of the OUN and "cleanse" it of "traitors" and "enemies."[39]

As indicated in chapter 1, the split of the OUN into OUN-B and OUN-M was the result of a disagreement between two generations. It was determined by the difference in experience and expectations of the two generations and by the nomination of Mel'nyk to the leadership of the OUN and the PUN at the Second Great Congress in Rome on 27 August 1939, as a result of a will allegedly left behind by Konovalets'. The nomination of Mel'nyk for the position of leader was the sign for the younger generation to seize power in the organization. Mel'nyk did not have the authority of Konovalets' and was less vigorous than him. In the 1930s he had worked as manager of Sheptyts'kyi's estate and was barely known in the OUN. According to Knysh, some days after the beginning of Second World War, Ivan Harbusevych and Riko Iaryi, financial officer of the leadership in exile, had discussed the plan to take power in the OUN, with Bandera, Shukhevych, Lebed', and Stets'ko.[40] After the split the OUN-B soon became much more powerful than the OUN-M, because its leaders had better connections to the OUN underground in eastern Galicia and Volhynia. The numerous young Ukrainians who had escaped to Cracow, after the German attack on the Soviet Union, decided to join the OUN-B.[41]

35 Ibid., 9.
36 Ibid., 9.
37 Ibid., 20, 21.
38 Ibid., 12–13.
39 Ibid., 14–15.
40 Knysh, *Rozbrat*, 71.
41 For Bandera's attitude to Mel'nyk and other members of the leadership, see Klymyshyn, *V pokhodi*, 1:277–78.

In terms of extreme nationalism, violence, fascism, and antisemitism, the two factions did not differ greatly from each other. During an interrogation in 1948, OUN-B member Volodymyr Porendovs'kyi stated that, at the time of the German invasion of Poland, the Ukrainian nationalists were "true fascists whose gods were Hitler, Mussolini, Dontsov, and similar personalities."[42] In an article published on 8 May 1939, the leading OUN-B member Stets'ko claimed that Jews were "nomads and parasites," a nation of "swindlers, materialists, and egoists ... devoid of heroism, and lacking an idea that could inspire them to sacrifice." They were only interested in "personal profit" and were determined "to corrupt the heroic culture of warrior nations." Stets'ko stated that Ukrainians had therefore separated themselves from the Jews centuries ago in order to achieve "the purity of their spirituality and culture."[43]

The split of the OUN into the OUN-B and OUN-M was also the next significant step in the rise of the political cult and myth of Stepan Bandera. The majority of OUN members, mainly young Ukrainians, joined the OUN-B faction. They were called Banderites after their leader Bandera. The word was in use at least from late 1940 onward.[44] Members of the OUN-M were called Melnykites.[45] This kind of identification with the leader of an organization or party was common in East Central European political and military movements. In Poland, for example, the adherents of Marshal Piłsudski were called *piłsudczycy*. A word derived from "Bandera" was used in several languages (Ukr. *banderivtsi*, Pol. *banderowcy*, Rus. *banderovtsy*, Ger. *Bandera-Leute* or *Banderowzi*). The OUN-B members were not only called by others Banderites but also called themselves Banderites. The Ukrainian teacher Oleksandr Povshuk wrote in his diary on 5 October 1941:

> Now we have war. Our leadership split into two groups, Banderites and Melnykites, and each does harm to the other. The nation becomes split into two parts. Banderites—this is the OUN under the leadership of Stepan Bandera, and Melnykites—who have not defined themselves till now—under the leadership of Mel'nyk.[46]

Although the term "Banderites" became popular only after the split of the OUN in 1940, it had existed since the trials in Warsaw and Lviv at the latest. The NKVD agent Sierov used the term "Banderites" in his reports from 1940 to refer not only to the OUN-B in 1940 but also to those OUN members who had opposed Konovalets' in 1935, by whom Sierov meant the young generation in the OUN.[47] In connection with the young OUN members, Stsibors'kyi used the term "bandery" in an article on 21 June 1936 in *Ukraïns'ke slovo* about the defendants in the Warsaw and Lviv trials.[48]

42 Interrogation of Volodymyr Porendovs'kyi, 15 February 1948, HDA SBU f. 13, spr. 372, vol. 2, 193.

43 Zynovii Karbovych (Iaroslav Stets'ko), "Zhydivstvo i my," *Novyi shliakh*, 8 May 1939, 3.

44 See for example "I. Sierov's report about the agent 'Ukrainets' to Khrushchev, 3 December 1940," HDA SBU, f. 16, op. 33, spr. 36, 14–33, in *Stepan Bandera*, ed. Serhiichuk, 1:60–61. For use of the word "Banderites" in an OUN-M leaflet from 10 September 1941 concerning the murder of Mykola Stsibors'kyi and Omelian Senyk, see "Natsionalisty!" TsDAVOV f. 3833, op. 1, spr. 74, 19.

45 For the use of the term Melnykites in an OUN-B document in autumn 1941, see for example Ivan Klymiv's report to the leadership of the OUN, TsDAVOV f. 3833, op. 1, spr. 45, 2.

46 Cf. "Dennyk Povshuka Oleksandra vid 17/IX. 1939 r.," TsDAHO f. 57, op. 4, spr. 344, 3.

47 "I. Sierov's report about the agent 'Ukrainets' to Khrushchev, 3 December 1940," HDA SBU, f. 16, op. 33, spr. 36, 14–33, in Serhiichuk, *Stepan Bandera*, 1:60–61.

48 Stsibors'kyi, "Klonim holovy," in *Stepan Bandera*, ed. Posivnych, 2006, 133–34.

Because the term "Banderites" was colloquial rather than official, and because of the violence employed by OUN-B, the term soon acquired a negative connotation, especially among Jews and Poles. OUN-B members used it less regularly than its victims or opponents did.

After the split, the two factions fought against and vehemently discredited each other. In autumn 1940, the OUN-M published a "White Book of the OUN: About the Diversion-Revolt Bandera-Iaryi" in which it explained how Bandera, Iaryi, and Stets'ko illegally tried to seize power in the organization, and how Mel'nyk and other leading OUN-M members tried to prevent this, thereby protecting the organization against such vicious individuals with low morality as the authors of the "White Book" characterized the "rebels."[49] The editor of the "White Book" was Stsibors'kyi.[50]

The OUN-B responded to this publication in May 1941. Stets'ko wrote a longer piece, entitled "Why the Purge in the OUN Was Necessary." He legitimized the OUN-B decision to split from the OUN, whose leadership, according to Stets'ko, was full of traitors, did not care about the organization, and was not able to organize a revolution. Stets'ko also protected Iaryi, whom the OUN-M called a "Mongolian Jewish crossbreed" and a "Soviet agent." The OUN-M claimed that the best proof for this was the fact that Iaryi was married to a Jewish woman. Furthermore, Stets'ko applied the same antisemitic strategy as the OUN-M to discredit Stsibors'kyi. He claimed that the author of the "White Book" was a traitor to the cause because he was married to a Jewish woman.[51] In June or July 1941, in response to Stets'ko's publication, the OUN-M published "The Black Book of the Revolt: Iaryi-Bandera-Horbovyi." The OUN-M depicted the OUN-B as "Bolshevik agents" who were preparing a "Marxist Jewish revolution." It claimed that Iaryi "and his Jewish wife are living on our money."[52]

Stsibors'kyi, and other OUN-M members whom Bandera accused of betrayal or relationships with Jews, were murdered during the war, in all likelihood by the OUN-B; Stsibors'kyi and Senyk on 30 August 1941 in Zhytomyr, Baranovs'kyi on 11 May 1943 in Lviv.[53]

49 *Bila knyha OUN: Pro dyversiiu-bunt Iary-Bandera*, PAA, ACC 85.191/64, 35. The "White Book" was published not earlier than 11 October 1940.

50 Chaikivs'kyi, *"Fama,"* 74.

51 "Chomu bula potribna chystka v OUN" consists of three parts: 1. "Z kym idemo i z kym ne idemo" (With whom we are going and with whom not), 2. "V im"ia pravdy" (In the name of truth), 3. "Druhyi arkhiv Senyka" (Senyk's Second Archive). Cf. PAA, ACC 85.191/64, 1–32, 1–66, 1–34. For Iaryi, see "Bila knyha OUN," PAA, ACC 85.191/64, 88–89. For Stsibors'kyi, see "Chomu bula potribna chystka v OUN," 3, 17.

52 "Chorna knyha buntu: Iary-Bandera-Horbovyi," RGASPI f. 17, op. 125, del. 337, 159–61, 164, 170. For the OUN-B reaction to the "Black Book" during the "Ukrainian National Revolution," see "Vyïmky z orhanizatsiinykh zvitiv," TsDAVO f. 3833, op. 1, spr. 12, 38.

53 The OUN-B member Il'ia Tkachuk testified that Stsibors'kyi, Senyk, and Baranovs'kyi were all killed by the OUN-B. See Interrogation of Il'ia Tkachuk, 23 February 1944, HDA SBU f. 13, spr. 372, vol. 6, 56. Taras Bul'ba-Borovets' wrote that the "Banderite Kuzii" killed Senyk and Stsibors'kyi "by shooting them in the back on an open street." See Taras Bul'ba-Borovets', *Armiia bez derzhavy: Slava i trahediia ukrains'koho povstans'koho rukhu: Spohady* (Kiev: Knyha Rodu, 2008), 154.

The Second Great Congress of the Ukrainian Nationalists (in Cracow)

From 31 March to 3 April 1941 in Cracow, the OUN-B held the Second Great Congress of the Ukrainian Nationalists, at which it "legalized" itself and "delegalized" the OUN-M. The OUN-B gave its congress exactly the same name as the older generation had called the congress on 27 August 1939 in Rome—the "Second Great Congress of the Ukrainian Nationalists." The resolutions passed at the congress in Cracow were documented in the booklet "Resolutions of the Second Great Congress of the Organization of Ukrainian Nationalists."[54] The argument in the booklet in terms of the split resembles very much the one in Bandera's letter to Mel'nyk. It begins with the statement that "the factual control of the OUN abroad drifted, after the death of Colonel Ievhen Konovalets', into the hands of people who harmed the OUN." This was, for the authors of the booklet, a "danger for the Ukrainian National Movement." It was therefore necessary to "cure the organization," because Mel'nyk did not do so, and thereby not only "demonstrated a complete inability to lead the revolutionary movement," but also "openly took the side of traitors to and destroyers of the organization."[55]

With this in mind, the authors of the "Resolutions" booklet decided that "Colonel Mel'nyk became the leader of the OUN in an unlawful way" and the "Congress of Ukrainian Nationalists that took place on 27 August 1939 did not correspond with the requirements of the principles of the OUN."[56] Furthermore, they claimed that the testament of the Leader (*Vozhd'*) Konovalets', which nominated Mel'nyk to the leadership of the OUN, was an "invention of Iaroslav Baranovs'kyi" and that the act of 10 February 1940, which established the Revolutionary Leadership of the OUN, was a "historical necessity." This act and the Second Great Congress in 1941 rescued the organization from "opportunism and decomposition" and "the danger of decay of the Organization." All members who took part in Mel'nyk's activities against the Revolutionary Leadership were traitors who would be excluded from the OUN.[57] Finally, the authors of the booklet forbade Mel'nyk to carry out any actions under the name of the OUN and urged all nationalists to leave the OUN-M and join the "ranks of the revolutionary liberation movement of the OUN under the leadership of Stepan Bandera."[58]

The "Resolutions" also reveal important information as to how the OUN-B perceived itself. In the first paragraph, the organizers of the congress in Cracow wrote: "the idea of an Independent United Ukrainian State became, in our century, the notion of the new Ukrainian worldview and the new political movement, the *nationalist* movement, which, in the fire of the fight against the occupiers, took the shape of the political organization—the organization of Ukrainian Nationalists."[59] They were thereby pointing out that nationalism was the only tolerable Ukrainian political movement and that the OUN was the only Ukrainian organization to embody this movement. This approach to politics was an essential principle of fascist systems. It

54 "Postanovy II. Velykoho Zboru Orhanizatsiï Ukraïns'kykh Natsionalistiv," TsDAHO f. 1, op. 23, spr. 926, 180–208.
55 Ibid., 200.
56 Ibid., 200.
57 Ibid., 185, 201.
58 Ibid., 202.
59 Ibid., 182. Emphasis in the original.

stipulated that one nation can be governed only by one radical nationalist party, which is represented by only one person, who symbolizes the whole nation, for instance, the *Führer* in Germany, the *Duce* in Italy, and the *Caudillo* in Spain. In another document from this time, the OUN-B wrote: "Odyn narid, odyn provid, odna vlada," a Ukrainian version of the concept of "One nation, one party, one leader" (*Ein Volk, ein Reich, ein Führer*).[60]

In the second paragraph of the booklet, the authors introduced their own history. First, they referred to Mikhnovs'kyi as the father of the kind of nationalism that they would like to have in their state. The authors obviously did not state that Mikhnovs'kyi provided them with ideas such as "Do not marry a foreign woman, because your children will be your enemies,"[61] just as they never referred to themselves as fascists or racists, always emphasizing the national, patriotic, local, and heroic side of their movement. They referred to Konovalets', the UVO, and the First Congress of the Ukrainian Nationalists in Vienna, and not to the Second Great Congress of the Ukrainian Nationalists in Rome.[62] They introduced themselves as the "new generation of nationalist revolutionaries" who grew up in "enemy prisons and partisan forests" and "in the midst of successes and failures of the revolutionary struggle against the enemies of Ukraine."[63] Nevertheless, they were honest enough to state that their struggle against the Soviet Union had been, due to outside factors, less successful than against Poland.[64] But they denied that the tradition of Konovalets' included any kind of collaboration with non-Ukrainian organizations or countries, and argued that the OUN "counted on the strengths of the Ukrainian nation and refused, in principle, orientation on foreign powers."[65]

Concerning the resolutions of the congress, the authors of the booklet wrote that "the struggle for the strength and the good of the Ukrainian nation is the basis of our worldview" and that "only on the path of revolutionary struggle against the invaders will the Ukrainian nation achieve its state." In the part concerning the social order in the future OUN state, they claimed that the OUN struggles for "the equality of all Ukrainians in terms of rights and obligations toward the nation and the state." The non-Ukrainians in the "Ukrainian territories," where the OUN state would be established, were not mentioned, but it is known from other documents that the OUN planned to expel or kill them.[66] However, the authors specified that "the Ukrainian Nation and its State" would become "the owner of all ground and waters, under and over earth resources, industry, and communication roads." They also regulated what belongs to whom: "The Ukrainian land is for Ukrainian peasants, the factories and plants for the Ukrainian workers, Ukrainian bread for the Ukrainian people." They did not however explain in this official document what would happen to the hundreds of thousands of Jews, Poles, Russians, and many other non-Ukrainians,

60 "Borot'ba i diial'nist' OUN pidchas viiny," TsDAVOV f. 3833, op. 2, spr. 1, 85.
61 Koval', "Heroi, shcho," 9.
62 "Postanovy II. Velykoho Zboru," TsDAHO f. 1, op. 23, spr. 926, 181–82.
63 Ibid., 182.
64 Ibid., 183.
65 Ibid., 183.
66 See next subsection "Practical Preparations for the 'Ukrainian National Revolution.'"

who were owners of land and factories and conducted trade in Ukraine or ate "Ukrainian bread."[67]

Emulating the Nazis and other racist movements, the authors used the category of race. Exactly as in Nazi ideology, the OUN wanted to have a strong and healthy "Ukrainian race": "The OUN struggles for a systematic organization of the national health by the Ukrainian state authority, and the growth and strength of the Ukrainian race." As in every proper *völkisch* state, the "Ukrainian race" should be protected by its organization "against the communist worldview, against internationalism and capitalism, and against all thoughts and structures that weaken the vital forces of the nation." To establish this state, the OUN-B claimed to struggle "for a destruction of the slavery, for the decay of the Moscow prison of nations, for the decay of the entire communist system" and "the freedom of all nations that are enslaved by Moscow and their right to life in their own state." For this purpose, the OUN-B wanted to "unite all Ukrainians in one liberating front of the "Ukrainian National Revolution," which could conduct a military uprising, achieve a Ukrainian state, and rule it." In terms of tradition, it argued that it is "going to fight to realize the legacy of the Great Prophet of Ukraine Taras Shevchenko, following the *revolutionary path of Konovalets*.'"[68]

Confident that it had the spirits of Bohdan Khmel'nyts'kyi, Taras Shevchenko, Mykola Mikhnovs'kyi, and Ievhen Konovalets' on its side, the OUN-B wanted not only to found a state for the "Ukrainian race" but also to struggle for other "nations of Eastern Europe and Asia enslaved by Moscow, for a new order on the ruins of the Moscow Empire, the USSR." For this reason, the "Ukrainian National Revolution" was planned to take place not only in the "living space" of the "Ukrainian race." The OUN-B also wanted to inspire a number of other "nations enslaved by Moscow" and involve them in the "liberation struggle" against the Soviet Union. This was to take place under the slogan: "Freedom for the Nations and the Individual!"[69]

Because the OUN-B knew that it would be too weak to combat the Soviet Union alone, it wanted to ally itself with other similar movements. This idea goes back at least to Stsibors'kyi's *Natsiokratiia* from 1935.[70] The collaboration with radical right movements that were rooted in other republics of the USSR, and with states that were threatened by the USSR, was strategically very profitable for the Ukrainian nationalists because it weakened their main enemy. The OUN-B was particularly interested in cooperation with "Lithuania, Latvia, Estonia, Finland, and Byelorussia."[71] When the Soviet Union would be defeated, the OUN-B expected other nations to establish right-wing dictatorships in which, as in the OUN-B state, the particular movements would "take hold of ... all parts of social life."[72]

Additionally, the authors gave assurances that they would combat and destroy all Ukrainian democratic parties and organizations, which they called "opportunistic."[73] These parties were expected to disappear, just as the non-Ukrainian inhabitants of the "Ukrainian territories" were expected to vanish. The OUN-B hoped that some-

67 Ibid., 186.
68 Ibid., 188. Emphasis in the original.
69 Ibid., 189.
70 Stsibors'kyi, *Natsiokratiia*, 57–58.
71 "Postanovy II. Velykoho Zboru," TsDAHO f. 1, op. 23, spr. 926, 188–89.
72 Ibid., 190.
73 Ibid., 193.

thing similar would happen in other states involved, under the leadership of the OUN, in the revolutionary struggle against the Soviet Union.[74] Therefore, the OUN planned to invent propaganda for Ukrainians and for all other "states enslaved and threatened by Moscow" that were expected to participate in the revolution.[75] The OUN-B leadership hoped that its propaganda would "control all Ukrainian groups ... in particular youth in the Red Army, and workers," and "show the nations enslaved by Moscow common interests with Ukraine."[76]

The destruction of collective farms, the promise to provide the peasants with their own land, and the "alteration of the Bolshevik slavery economy into a free economy of the Ukrainian nation" were important arguments, which could mobilize the "Ukrainian masses" for the revolution. They would also awaken in them the wish to live in a Ukrainian state, ruled by the OUN, with Bandera as *Providnyk*.[77] These messages and lures, according to the authors of the booklet, were designed to reach the minds of the Ukrainian soldiers and soldiers from the "enslaved countries" who were serving in the Red Army, as well as the minds of peasants and factory workers, and to make them fight against the Soviet Union, on the side of the OUN-B and the Germans.[78]

The authors of the booklet borrowed from Dmytro Dontsov—their main teacher of extreme nationalism, antisemitism, and hatred of Russia—two interrelated antisemitic concepts. The first was that "the Jews in the USSR are the main pillar of the Bolshevik regime, and the avant-garde of the Moscow imperialism in Ukraine." The second stated that the OUN "combats Jews as a pillar of the Moscow-Bolshevik regime."[79] In the same paragraph of the "Resolutions" they denied the violent nature of Ukrainian nationalism and the fact that antisemitism was an integral element of this movement, while blaming the Soviet Union and Russia for the antisemitism in Ukraine and in the OUN: "The Moscow-Bolshevik government exploits the anti-Jewish sentiments of the Ukrainian masses, in order to divert their attention from the real perpetrator of evil, and in order to channel them, in times of uprising, into pogroms of Jews."[80]

They similarly introduced a range of fascist principles and rituals, which became obligatory for all members of the movement, and which, after the establishment of the Ukrainian state, were to become obligatory for all citizens. The red-and-black flag, which symbolizes blood and soil (Ger. *Blut und Boden*), was one of them.[81] These colors referred to the racist and proto-fascist German blood and soil ideology, which suggests the inseparability of a people (*Rasse* or *Volk*) and their "living space" (*Lebensraum*) as well as an attraction to the "soil," which acquired spiritual and mythological connotations. Furthermore, the OUN-B employed the fascist salute of raising the right arm "slightly to the right, slightly above the peak of the head" while calling "Glory to Ukraine!" (*Slava Ukraïni!*), the response to which was "Glory to the Heroes!"

74 Ibid., 193.
75 Ibid., 196.
76 Ibid., 197.
77 Ibid., 190–91.
78 Ibid.,192.
79 Ibid., 189, 192.
80 Ibid., 192.
81 Ibid., 199.

(*Heroiam Slava!*).[82] The greeting "Glory to the Leader!" (*Vozhdevi Slava!*) had already been applied to Mel'nyk since the earlier Second Great Congress of the OUN in Rome.[83]

Obligatory holidays were also proclaimed: Unification Day on 22 January, the Day of the Revolutionary Heroes on 23 March, and the Day of Struggle on 31 August.[84] The Führerprinzip was established on the notion of a *Providnyk* and not a *Vozhd'* because the term "Vozhd'" had been reserved for Mel'nyk, since the congress in Rome.[85] At the congress in Cracow, Stepan Bandera, leader of the Banderites, was naturally and unanimously chosen to be the *Providnyk* of the OUN.[86] According to Danylo Shumuk, it was Myron Orlyk who proposed Bandera as *Providnyk* at the Cracow congress in March–April 1941.[87] The OUN-B in Ukraine, under the leadership of Lopatyns'kyi's follower Ivan Klymiv, were not informed that the leadership had decided to use the sole title of *Providnyk* in relation to Bandera. During the "Ukrainian National Revolution" the OUN-B would print and display posters with Bandera titled as a *Vozhd'*.[88]

The young OUN-B members who officially elected Bandera as leader of the OUN-B—and thus of the future Ukrainian state they planned to establish—perceived him as a charismatic personality. However, this should not suggest that Bandera was a charismatic person in himself. It was rather the expectation of the "charismatic movement" or a "charismatic community" that perceived Bandera as a charismatic leader or that charismatized him. One should not however overlook Bandera's oratorical abilities. OUN member Mykhailo Bilan, who met Bandera a few times in England in the 1950s, confessed in an interview that Bandera "could hypnotize a man. Everything that he said was interesting. You could not stop listening to him."[89]

The OUN-B's fascistization and positive attitude to Nazi Germany in 1940 and the first half of 1941 was very much affected by the proclamation of a Slovak state in March 1939, and a Croatian state in April 1941. Both states were led by organizations similar to the OUN: Hlinka's Slovak People's Party (*Hlinkova slovenská ľudová strana*, HSLS or Hlinka's Party) and the Croatian Revolutionary Organization (*Hrvatska revolucionarna organizacija*, HRO), known as the Ustaša. Kost' Pan'kivs'kyi, a contemporary observer of the OUN, commented in retrospect: "Of all the 'independent' nations, the fate of the Slovaks and Croatians was closest to ours. And we thought at that time that they were in a much better position, because both Hitler and Mussolini not only

82 Ibid., 199. During the "Ukrainian National Revolution" all OUN members were obliged to use only this greeting. Cf. "Instruktsiia propahandy ch. 1," TsDAVOV f. 4620, op. 3, spr. 379, 34. The greeting "Slava Ukraïni" was first introduced by the LUN, which incorporated the SUF. Cf. Golczewski, *Deutsche und Ukrainer*, 550.

83 Letter from Bandera to Mel'nyk, TsDAVOV f. 3833, op. 1, spr. 71, 9.

84 TsDAHO f. 1, op. 23, spr. 926, 199.

85 "Postanovy II. Velykoho Zboru," TsDAHO f. 1, op. 23, spr. 926, 204. The term was also used in the Soviet Union to honor Stalin.

86 Ibid., 207.

87 Shumuk heard it from Horbovyi, in a Gulag after the war. Cf. Shumuk, *Za skhidnim obriiem*, 429–30.

88 "Ukraïns'kyi Narode!" "Hromadiany!" TsDAVOV f. 3822, op. 1, spr. 63, 12–13, 181; "Ukraïns'kyi Narode!" TsDAVOV f. 3822, op. 1, spr. 41, 1–2; "Hromadiany!" TsDAVOV f. 4620, op. 3, spr. 378, 39.

89 OUN member Mykhailo Bilan, interviewed by author, London, 10 July 2008. On the charismatic fascist European leaders, see Eatwell, ed., *Charisma and Fascism*. On the European leaders in general, see Ennker, ed., *Der Führer im Europa*.

'recognized,' but—to tell the truth—granted them 'independence.' Neither the first nor the second could achieve it by their own strengths."[90]

After the Ustaša proclaimed the Independent State of Croatia (*Nezavisna Država Hrvatska*, NDH) on 10 April 1941, the leadership of the OUN-B in Cracow was very excited. It immediately sent a telegram of congratulations to Pavelić, the Croatian *Poglavnik*. The OUN-B politicians understood it as evidence that it might be possible to proclaim and establish a Ukrainian state. They believed or hoped that the "New Europe"—under the aegis of Nazi Germany—would need an independent Ukraine, just as it needed an independent Croatia and Slovakia.[91]

Practical Preparations for the "Ukrainian National Revolution"

The closer the German attack against the Soviet Union approached, the more specific were the OUN-B's plans for the establishment of a Ukrainian state. The Ukrainian state was planned to come into being as a result of the "Ukrainian National Revolution," under the leadership of the OUN-B. In May 1941, as part of the preparation for the revolution, the OUN-B completed a very important document called "The Struggle and Activities of the OUN in Wartime," further referred to here as "Struggle and Activities," on which OUN-B leaders Bandera, Lenkavs'kyi, Shukhevych, and Stets'ko had been working for several weeks.[92] The document was intended to provide the revolutionaries with orientation and specific information concerning the development of the revolution. According to the document, the OUN-B planned to use a "favorable situation" of a "war between Moscow and other states," in order to conduct the revolution, to which the OUN-B sought to mobilize the whole Ukrainian nation.[93] The goal of the revolution was to establish the "totalitarian power of the Ukrainian nation in the Ukrainian territories," which would need a "strong political and military organization in all Ukrainian territories," that is to say the OUN-B.[94]

A huge challenge for the OUN-B revolution and state were the minorities. The authors of "Struggle and Activities" divided them into: "a) our friends, i.e. the members of the enslaved nations [and] b) our enemies, Muscovites, Poles, and Jews." Since the first group was expected to help the OUN conduct the revolution against the Soviet Union, they were to "have the same rights as Ukrainians" in the future Ukrainian OUN-B state. The second group would be "destroyed in the struggle, in particular those who protect the regime" of their country. This corresponded with the principle: "Our power should be horrible for its opponents. Terror for enemy aliens and our traitors."[95] There was to be no mercy for Ukrainians who disagreed with the

90 Pan'kivs'kyi, *Roky nimets'koï okupatsiï*, 178.

91 Borys Levyts'kyi, "Natsional'nyi rukh pid chas Druhoï svitovoï viiny: Interv"iu z B. Levyts'kym," *Dialoh* 2 (1979): 15.

92 "Borot'ba i diial'nist' OUN pidchas viiny," TsDAVOV f. 3833, op. 2, spr. 1, 15–89. One part of this document called "Propahandyvni vkazivky na peredvoiennyi chas, na chas viiny i revoliutsiï ta na pochatkovi dni derzhavnoho budivnytstva" (Instructions for the Prewar Period, the Time of War and Revolution, and the First Days of State Building) is located in TsDAVOV f. 3833, op. 1, spr. 69, 23–47. For the authors of the document, see Stets'ko, *30 chervnia 1941*, 50; Carynnyk, Foes of Our Rebirth, 329.

93 "Borot'ba i diial'nist' OUN pidchas viiny," TsDAVOV f. 3833, op. 2, spr. 1, 15.

94 Ibid., 16.

95 Ibid., 38–39.

politics of the OUN-B. The Ukrainian people would have to understand that the OUN-B was the only power in Ukraine. To convince the masses of this, OUN-B members tried to frighten the resistant parts of the nation by assuring them that they would be punished.[96]

After the start of the revolution, revolutionaries coming to Ukraine from the General Government were intended to get in touch with the OUN underground and to take control of radio stations for the purpose of mobilizing the masses.[97] A very important point contained in "Struggle and Activities" was to concentrate on the ideological, propagandistic, and theatrical parts, and not to waste energy fighting, which should be limited to fighting for such crucial points as radio stations or industrial areas.[98] If possible, the OUN was not to fight against the Red Army[99] or NKVD units[100] and was to actively prevent all Ukrainians from doing so,[101] probably because the OUN-B expected the Germans to do it for them. Using the political vacuum, that would follow the withdrawal of the Soviet authorities, was, for the OUN-B, more important than warfare. While taking advantage of the political vacuum, the OUN-B would establish the organs of the state. The officials of the state and ordinary citizens would welcome the incoming German army and express a wish to collaborate with Nazi Germany:

> We treat the coming German army as the army of allies. We try before their coming to put life in order, *on our own* as it should be. We inform them that the Ukrainian authority is already established, it is under the control of the OUN under the leadership of Stepan Bandera; all matters are regulated by the OUN, and the local authorities are ready to establish friendly relations with the army, in order to fight together against Moscow and collaborate [with Nazi Germany].[102]

When greeting the arriving German troops, OUN members were to inform them that they had already cleared the terrain of Soviet troops and were ready for further struggle, alongside the Germans, against the Soviet Union.[103] Since the Jews, according to the resolution of the Second Great Congress, were the "main pillar of the Bolshevik regime, and the avant-garde of Russian imperialism in Ukraine," they were, for the OUN-B activists, as for the Germans, synonymous with agents of the Soviet Union.[104] In 1941, the stereotype of "Jewish Bolshevism" was prevalent in the OUN-B. Jews blurred with "Soviets" in the minds of the Ukrainian nationalists and, like the "Soviet occupiers," were to be removed from the "Ukrainian territories."

96 "Propahandyvni vkazivky," TsDAVOV f. 3833, op. 1, spr. 69, 27. For details of how the OUN-B wanted to control the political situation in the Ukrainian state, see "Borot'ba i diial'nist' OUN pidchas viiny," TsDAVOV f. 3833, op. 2, spr. 1, 44–45.

97 "Borot'ba i diial'nist' OUN pidchas viiny," TsDAVOV f. 3833, op. 2, spr. 1, 16.

98 Ibid., 17.

99 Ibid., 16–17.

100 Ibid., 32. Some OUN-B forces did fight sporadically after the beginning of the German-Soviet war. Cf. Internal telegram of the OUN, 31 July 1941, TsDAVOV f. 3833, op. 1, spr. 15, 7.

101 "Borot'ba i diial'nist' OUN pidchas viiny," TsDAVOV f. 3833, op. 2, spr. 1, 16. For very similar suggestions concerning proper relations with the Germans, see ibid., 32.

102 Ibid., 23. Emphasis in the original.

103 Ibid., 32, 83.

104 "Postanovy II. Velykoho" TsDAHO f. 1, op. 23, spr. 926, 192.

While taking over power and establishing a dictatorial regime, the OUN-B were to nominate new officials as village, city, and town presidents, administration staff, militiamen, and so forth. All these officials were obliged to swear an oath to Stepan Bandera.[105] All important posts were to remain in the hands of OUN members.[106]

Another important aim of the revolutionary propaganda was to convince the Ukrainian people that the proclamation or the "rebirth" of the state was real and was a very important act. For this purpose, OUN-B-members were to organize meetings in all possible villages, towns, and cities, and read out their manifesto about the "renewal of the Ukrainian state."[107] The standardized text of this manifesto was:

> In the name of all Ukraine, the Organization of Ukrainian Nationalists under the leadership of Stepan Bandera proclaims the Ukrainian state, for which entire generations of the best sons of Ukraine have given their lives. The Organization of Ukrainian Nationalists, which, under the leadership of its Creator and Leader Ievhen Konovalets' conducted an intense struggle for freedom in the last decades of Muscovite-Bolshevik oppression, calls upon the whole Ukrainian nation not to lay down its arms until there is sovereign Ukrainian authority over all Ukrainian lands.
>
> Sovereign Ukrainian authority will guarantee the Ukrainian people law and order, the universal development of all its forces, and the satisfaction of all its needs.[108]

All the people gathered, including women and children, were to commit themselves to the leadership of Stepan Bandera, and to swear an oath of loyalty to the Ukrainian state. They were expected to swear that they would serve the Ukrainian state with their lives, defending it to the last drop of their blood. At the end of the proclamation, every Ukrainian fit for service was to be inducted into the "Ukrainian National Army," and mobilized for immediate deployment in the area.[109]

One task of the recruited militiamen and soldiers, who had already sworn an oath to Bandera, was to take "disturbing persons" and survivals from the enemy side (*marodery, nedobytky*) from their place of residence to a "hidden and inaccessible place (forests, mountains etc.), where particular liquidation actions" were to be conducted.[110] The OUN-B members, and in particular the OUN-B militiamen were advised to follow the rule: "During the time of chaos and confusion, it is permissible to liquidate undesirable Polish, Muscovite [Russian or Soviet], and Jewish activists."[111] Moreover, the Ukrainian insurgents were obliged to compile blacklists with personal data of "all important Poles ... NKVD people, informers, provocateurs ... all important Ukrainians who, in the critical time, would try to make 'their politics' and thereby threaten the decisive mind-set of the Ukrainian nation."[112]

105 "Borot'ba i diial'nist' OUN pidchas viiny," TsDAVOV f. 3833, op. 2, spr. 1, 30. For the text of this oath, see ibid., 41. For militia, see ibid., 60.
106 Ibid., 44.
107 "Propahandyvni vkazivky," TsDAVOV f. 3833, op. 1, spr. 69, 26.
108 Ibid., 43.
109 Ibid., 26.
110 "Borot'ba i diial'nist' OUN pidchas viiny," TsDAVOV f. 3833, op. 2, spr. 1, 30.
111 Ibid., 32.
112 Ibid., 58.

The part of the document concerning the Security Service (*Sluzhba Bezpeky*, SB) of the OUN-B was also unambiguous about what to do with non-Ukrainians:

> We have to remember that these existing elements have to be, as the main pillar of the NKVD and the Soviet authority in Ukraine, exterminated while [we are] establishing the new revolutionary order in Ukraine. These elements are:
>
> 1. Muscovites [*Moskali*], sent to the Ukrainian territories in order to strengthen the Moscow power in Ukraine.
> 2. Jews [*Zhydy*], as individuals as well as a national group.
> 3. Aliens [*Chuzhyntsi*], especially various Asians with whom Moscow colonized Ukraine ...
> 4. Poles [*Poliaky*] in the western Ukrainian territories, who have not ceased dreaming about the reconstruction of a Greater Poland.[113]

The OUN-B used similar standards to define the "enemies of the Ukrainian nation" in the eastern Ukrainian collective farms. In this regard, the OUN-B classified as enemies "all the strangers who came to the collectives to oversee the exploitation of the collectivized villages," "Jews, working in the collectives, as the implementers of Bolshevik power," "all the representatives of the Bolshevik power," and informers.[114]

During the revolution, however, the crucial role of destroying the enemies of the OUN and establishing the new authority was to be played, not by the SB, but by the National Militia (*Narodnia Militsiia*). All men between the ages of eighteen and fifty and capable of bearing arms were to be included in the militia.[115] Because the OUN-B had no uniforms for the militia, every militiaman was to wear either a yellow-and-blue armband, or a white armband with the inscription "National Militia."[116] The leader of a militia unit should be a "known nationalist," loyal to the OUN-B.[117] The building in which the militia station would be established was to have a yellow-and-blue Ukrainian flag on it.[118] For the purpose of establishing the militia, the OUN-B was wary of "provincial cities that are inhabited with foreign-national elements." In such cases, the Ukrainian militiamen were to be recruited from adjacent villages.[119] The Ukrainian militiamen from villages were expected to establish "order [*lad i*

113 Ibid., 60.

114 Ibid., 66.

115 Ibid., 62, 64. All Ukrainian men between eighteen and fifty who were obliged to join the militia were to be divided into professional militiamen who were employed full time, and reserve forces ("volunteer members"—chleny-dobrovol'tsi), who earned a living otherwise, but could be mobilized at any time.

116 Ibid., 62; Landesarchiv Nordrhein-Westfalen (LN-W), Bonn, Rep. 350, vol. 5, 16. In 1941, the OUN-B used yellow-and-blue and not blue-and-yellow flags. Cf. "Borot'ba i diial'nist' OUN pidchas viiny," TsDAVOV f. 3833, op. 2, spr. 1, 83; Roman Volchuk, *Spomyny z peredvoiennoho L'vova ta voiennoho Vidnia* (Kiev: Krytyka, 2002), 89. At that time, the OUN-M used blue-and-yellow flags, see Taras Kurylo, "Syla ta slabkist' ukraïns'koho natsionalizmu v Kyievi pid chas nimets'koï okupatsiï (1941–1943)," *Ukraïna Moderna* Vol. 13, No. 2 (2008): 117.

117 "Borot'ba i diial'nist' OUN pidchas viiny," TsDAVOV f. 3833, op. 2, spr. 1, 62. Testimonies of Holocaust survivors from small communities—in which people did not live in anonymity—confirm that the leaders of the militia were "well-known" local Ukrainian nationalists. See, for example, AŻIH, 301/3983, Anna Złatkies, 1.

118 "Borot'ba i diial'nist' OUN pidchas viiny," TsDAVOV f. 3833, op. 2, spr. 1, 64.

119 Ibid., 68.

poriadok]" in the cities and to "cleanse" them of "Soviet intelligence, counter-insurgency, etc. officials, Muscovites, Jews, and others."[120]

The act of registering all Jews by the militia was related to the plan to exterminate or remove them from Ukraine after establishing the state. In view of the number of Jews in the Ukrainian territories, this could happen only step by step.[121] During the first phase of the revolution, the registration would simplify the act of detaining the Jews in concentration camps together with "asocial elements and wounded."[122] Citizens of the OUN-B state were expected to provide the militia with information about "Red Army soldiers, NKVD men, Jews [*zhydiv* (*evreïv*)], and informers—in short, everyone who does not belong to the village community."[123]

Propaganda would also play an important role during the revolution because, as the authors of the text knew, it could mobilize the masses to revolutionary action. The OUN-B activists were obliged to employ all kinds of propaganda, from spreading rumors to singing revolutionary songs, printing and distributing booklets and newspapers, and broadcasting "national revolutionary" propaganda by radio.[124] The main content of the propaganda was the "renewal" of the Ukrainian state by the OUN-B, and the necessary war against the "Muscovite-Jews" and other enemies of the Ukrainians.[125] Very popular was the slogan "Kill the enemies among you—Jews and informers."[126]

Slogans that the OUN-B leadership invented for the Ukrainian soldiers in the Red Army contained many antisemitic and nationalist expressions. To motivate the soldiers to change sides, the inventors of the slogans frequently used the stereotype of "Jewish Bolshevism." Some of them were: "Death to Muscovite-Jewish Communism!" "Stalin's and Jewish Commissars—the First Enemy of the Nation!" "Marxism—a Jewish Creation!" "Muscovite-Jewish Communism—the Enemy of the Nation!" "Without the Muscovite-Jewish Commune Everyone Will Be an Owner," "Kill the Enemies among You, the Jews and Informers!" In addition to antisemitic slogans, the OUN-B invented numerous radical nationalist, populist, and racist ones, such as "Ukraine for Ukrainians!" "In the Ukrainian Territory—Ukrainian Rule!" "Ukrainian Property into Ukrainian Hands," "Death to the Exploiters of Ukraine!" "It is Better to Destroy National Property than to Give it to the Muscovite Stealers!" "Ukrainian Bread and Gold Only for Ukrainians!" "With the Nation—Against the Enemies of the Nation."[127] The slogans from "Struggle and Activities" appeared, among others, in the leaflets prepared for the "Ukrainian National Revolution." The illustrations in these leaflets mixed nationalism with antisemitism (Figs. 11–12).

120 Ibid., 72.
121 Ibid., 62.
122 Ibid., 69.
123 Ibid., 62.
124 "Propahandyvni vkazivky," TsDAVOV f. 3833, op. 1, spr. 69, 23, 25–28. The OUN-B modified, for example, "The Internationale" to use it for the "national revolution." Cf. Ibid., 25.
125 Ibid., 24.
126 "Borot'ba i diial'nist' OUN pidchas viiny," TsDAVOV f. 3833, op. 2, spr. 1, 80. In Ukrainian: *Vbyvaite vorohiv, shcho mizh vamy—zhydi, i seksotiv*. This slogan was developed for factory workers.
127 "Borot'ba i diial'nist' OUN pidchas viiny," TsDAVOV f. 3833, op. 2, spr. 1, 77–78, 80.

Fig. 11. OUN-B leaflet, 1941, TsDAVOV f. 3822, op. 1, spr. 63, 219.

The Ukrainian nationalist anxiety about the cities—and the belief that they had nothing in common with the Ukrainian culture that was deeply ingrained in the villages—manifested itself in slogans such as "Peasant Ukraine Conquers Cities and Kills the Enemies of Ukraine."[128] The OUN leaders planned to mobilize the Ukrainian villages against the cosmopolitan cities in which, according to the authors of "Struggle and Activities," most of the foes of the Ukrainians lived.[129]

Spreading rumors about the death of Stalin or the start of a revolution in Moscow was also intended to become an important activity of OUN-B activists during the "Ukrainian National Revolution,"[130] as were putting up yellow-and-blue and red-and-black flags at every administrative building, painting tridents in black on buildings, printing posters, hanging them in public spaces, prompting the population to par-

128 Ibid., 80.
129 "Propahandyvni vkazivky," TsDAVOV f. 3833, op. 1, spr. 69, 26.
130 "Borot'ba i diial'nist'diial'nist' OUN pidchas viiny," TsDAVOV f. 3833, op. 2, spr. 1, 80.

ticipate in parades, greeting OUN-B members from the area of the General Government, cheering and greeting the German troops in the name of the Leader Stepan Bandera, organizing propagandist funerals for dead revolutionaries, and so on.[131] In addition, the OUN-B revolutionaries were to motivate the population to refuse to help wounded enemies. They were also expected to inform everybody in the revolutionary territories that there would be no mercy for those who did not follow the rules and orders of the OUN.[132]

The text of "Struggle and Activities" also contains detailed information as to how the leaders of the OUN-B imagined ruling the Ukrainian state. A necessary precondition for establishing state institutions was a political and ethnic "cleansing." Once OUN territory was "cleansed" of "hostile elements," then "militia, paramilitary organizations, stable military units, and all other institutions that are necessary for normal life ... will be established."[133] Bandera and other authors of the document took as the starting point for their political plans the principle "The power of the Nation—entirely in the ORGANIZATION."[134] As in the resolutions of the Second Great Congress of the Ukrainian Nationalists in Cracow, they thereby equated the state and the nation with the organization:

> In the Ukrainian State, the OUN should become the only political organization of the Ukrainian nation. All who want to work for the good of the Ukrainian nation and remain in the realm of legality which the OUN applies to its members—should join the OUN.[135]
>
> In other words, "The Ukrainian Nation is the OUN—the OUN is the Ukrainian Nation! All people under the banner of the OUN!"[136]

Bandera and other authors of "Struggle and Activities" were concerned about eastern Ukrainians, who, they assumed, did not know the OUN.[137] On the one hand, the authors stated that they could subordinate themselves to an eastern Ukrainian "independent center"—if such a political body would emerge and consolidate power in eastern and central Ukraine.[138] On the other, they wanted to implement a "one-party system" in eastern Ukraine, which would force eastern Ukrainian organizations and parties to subordinate themselves to the OUN. The young Ukrainian radical nationalist revolutionaries felt that it was their responsibility to introduce the "one-party system," because the "multi-party system ... demonstrated its harmfulness in Ukraine and in other countries. Therefore, the OUN rejects and combats this system." As in every authoritarian state, not the "principle of parties but one of authority" should be applied: "the Head of the Ukrainian State should be a person who has the authority and the trust of the whole nation." The members of the nation would be educated by the organization to love and admire the *Providnyk*: "The

131 Ibid., 80–83.
132 Ibid., 82.
133 Ibid., 21.
134 Ibid., 22. Emphasis in the original.
135 Ibid., 54.
136 "Propahandyvni vkazivky," TsDAVOV f. 3833, op. 1, spr. 68, 26.
137 "Borot'ba i diial'nist' OUN pidchas viiny," TsDAVOV f. 3833, op. 2, spr. 1, 18.
138 Ibid., 19.

Fig. 12. OUN-B leaflet, 1941, PAAA, R 105191.

Organization of Ukrainian Nationalists takes over the task of controlling Ukrainian political thought, the education and training of the leading cadres, and the upbringing of the whole nation."[139]

"Struggle and Activities" also emphasized the "upbringing and organization of the entire student, worker, and peasant youth."[140] Although the authors occasionally mentioned non-military organizations, the establishment of military and paramilitary formations was to have the highest priority in the OUN-B state.[141] The OUN-B wanted to recruit its new members and the future citizens of the state with the help of the youth organization Iunatstvo, which would take care of every child from the age of six. At that age, children would join the Virliata; at the age of ten the Stepovi Orly; at fourteen Plastuny; at eighteen Zaporozhtsi. At the age of twenty-one, after

139 Ibid., 19.
140 Ibid., 22.
141 Ibid., 22.

fifteen years of nationalist brainwashing and paramilitary training, they would be ready to join the OUN. For those young Ukrainians who decided not to join the OUN, it had other paramilitary, sport, and cultural organizations, all controlled by the OUN.[142] This system would allow the OUN to reproduce itself during future generations. The OUN would thereby control the Ukrainian state, not only during the lifetime of their revolutionary leaders but as long as it educated and disciplined Ukrainian youth and recruited its future cadres. This political situation would ideally endure for the unlimited future, especially if the OUN reached the point at which every citizen of the Ukrainian state would be a member. The boundary between Ukrainian society and the OUN would blur and society would consist only of "FIGHTERS AND FANATICS."[143]

In the Ukrainian state controlled by the OUN-B, one of the main tasks of the court system would be to punish "not only enemies, traitors of the nation, but also all thieves of government property, speculators etc., with death."[144] Generally, however, leaders of the OUN-B did not want to replace the Soviet justice system with a more democratic one. It was easier and more effective for them to replace the term "class" with "nation" and retain the Soviet system:

> Because the existing [Soviet] law was written from the perspective of class struggle, of destroying the class enemy and exterminating Ukrainians as a nation, it may be possible to replace the terms and to use all these [methods], all these shootings and the Cheka against the enemies for everything that harms Ukraine.[145]

The OUN-B further planned to restore the Church and to use it in building the state. Freedom of speech would be "permitted as long as it corresponds with the good of the state," which would mean that it did not hurt the good name of the OUN. In particular, the "newspapers ... radio, theatre, films etc. ... can be only nationalistic. ... All popular publications in which nationalistic ideas and slogans are not popularized have to be forbidden." In the schools the "teaching should be only about liberation, revolution, the history of Ukraine ... the true Ukraine, Her Heroes, the dignity of the man, the OUN."[146]

In addition to preparing the revolution on paper and developing plans for the future Ukrainian state, the OUN-B also made a range of preparations with the Abwehr in the General Government, and in Soviet western Ukraine where it controlled the nationalist underground. In the General Government, the OUN-B collaborated with such Abwehr officers as Wilhelm Canaris,[147] Theodor Oberländer,[148] Hans

142 Ibid., 57.
143 Ibid., 23. Emphasis in the original.
144 Ibid., 37.
145 Ibid., 38.
146 Ibid., 38.
147 Rolf-Dieter Müller, *An der Seite der Wehrmacht: Hitlers ausländische Helfer beim "Kreuzzug gegen den Bolschewismus" 1941–1945* (Berlin: Links, 2007), 194; Alexander Dallin, *German Rule in Russia 1941–1945: A Study of Occupation Policies* (London: Macmillan, 1957), 115.
148 Andreas Kappeler, "Hans Koch (1894–1959), "in *Osteuropäische Geschichte in Wien: 100 Jahre Forschung und Lehre an der Universität*, ed. Arnold Suppan, Marija Wakounig, Georg Kastner (Innsbruck: Studien Verlag, 2007), 243; Philipp-Christian Wachs, *Der Fall Theodor Oberländer (1909–1998): Ein Lehrstück deutscher Geschichte* (Frankfurt: Campus Verlag, 2000), 55–71.

Koch,[149] and Alfred Bisanz.[150] The Abwehr provided the OUN-B with resources to train and arm its members in the General Government and in the underground in Ukraine. The Germans expected the latter to attack the Soviet army from the rear, after the beginning of Barbarossa.[151] Further, the military collaboration resulted in, among other things, the formation of the Abwehr battalions, Nachtigall with 350 soldiers, and Roland with 330. Both were made up of Ukrainian soldiers, led by German and Ukrainian officers. The Ukrainians called the battalions Brotherhoods of Ukrainian Nationalists (*Druzhyny Ukraïns'kykh Natsionalistiv*).[152] The OUN-B also provided an espionage service for the Abwehr, using its organizational structure in western Ukraine and working as soldiers, spies, and translators in the Abwehr.[153] The OUN-B was associated with the Security Police School in Zakopane, at which Ukrainian policemen and the Security Service, or SB (*Sluzhba Bezpeky*) of the OUN-B, were trained. The OUN-B was also associated with other police academies in Cracow, Chełm, and Rabka, at which Ukrainian police forces were recruited.[154]

Those OUN-B-members who did not join the Nachtigall and Roland battalions received military training for three or four months at the Ievhen Konovalets' military school in Cracow and were engaged in the task forces (*pokhidni hrupy*).[155] These units most likely included 800 OUN-B members.[156] The task forces consisted of small groups, whose role was to follow the German army and, together with OUN members from the underground, to organize the administration in the liberated territories and to familiarize the local communities with OUN-B-propaganda. Month-long military courses were also organized by the Abwehr in the General Government for OUN members who came from eastern Galicia and Volhynia, which had been absorbed

149 Kappeler, Hans Koch, 243; Ray Brandon, "Hans Koch," in *Handbuch der völkischen Wissenschaften*, ed. Ingo Haar and Michael Fahlbusch (Munich: K. G. Saur, 2008), 329–32.

150 Klymyshyn, *V pokhodi*, 1:293–94.

151 "Pokazaniia byvshego nachal'nika otdela abvera Berlinskogo okruga polkovnika Ervina Shtol'tse, 29. 05. 1945," Aleksandr Diukov, *Vtorostepennyi vrag: OUN, UPA i reshenie "evreiskogo voprosa"* (Moscow: Regnum, 2008), 124; "Protokol dopytu zaareshtovanoho nimets'koho polkovnyka Ervina Shtol'tse shchodo kontaktiv z OUN," HDA SBU f. 10876, spr. 372, vol. 1, 134, 144–50 in *Stepan Bandera*, ed. Serhiichuk, 1:320–21. According to Stolze, Bandera deposited a considerable part of the money that he received from the Abwehr in a Swiss account.

152 Armstrong, *Ukrainian Nationalism*, 74; Patryliak, *Viis'kova diial'nist'*, 274–88.

153 Klymyshyn, for example, mentions meeting such a Ukrainian soldier working in the Abwehr. See Klymyshyn, *V pokhodi*, 1:322–23. For the recruitment of Ukrainians for the Abwehr, see Andrii Bolianovs'kyi, *Ukraïns'ki viis'kovi formuvannia v zbroinykh sylakh Nimechchyny (1939–1945)* (Lviv: L'vivs'kyi natsional'nyi universytet im. Ivana Franka, 2003), 53–54.

154 For Shukhevych, see Berkhoff, *Harvest of Despair*, 289, 298. The Security Police school in Zakopane was established in December 1939, the academies in Cracow, Chełmn, and Rabka in mid-1940, in Chełmn in December 1940. Cf. Finder, Collaboration in Eastern Galicia, 103. For the SB, see Stephen Dorril, *MI6: Inside the Covert World of Her Majesty's Secret Intelligence Service* (New York: Simon & Schuster, 2002), 226.

155 Motyka, *Ukraińska partyzantka*, 81; Klymyshyn, *V pokhodi*, 1:297–301; Interrogation of Anton Bodnar, 5–8.03.1945, HDA SBU f. 13, spr. 372, vol. 4, 155.

156 The OUN-B activist Tymish Semchyshyn provided the number of about 800 during an interrogation. Cf. Interrogation of Tymish Semchyshyn, 28 October 1944, HDA SBU f. 13, spr. 372, vol. 1, 145. Grzegorz Motyka estimated 750 to 1,200 members in the task forces. Cf. Motyka, *Ukraińska partyzantka*, 93. Roman Ilnytzkyi, a historian who was in the OUN-B, claimed that there were 4,000 people in the task forces after the OUN-B activists and sympathizers in Ukraine had joined them. See Roman Ilnytzkyi, *Deutschland und die Ukraine 1934–1945: Tatsachen europäischer Politik* (Munich: UNI, 1958), 2:143. Vasyl' Shchehliuk, who published the memoirs of the OUN-B member Luka Pavlyshyn wrote that there were 9,000 people in the task forces. Cf. Vasyl' Shchehliuk, *"Iak rosa na sontsi": Politychnyi roman-khronika, napysanyi na osnovi spohadiv kolyshn'oho diiacha OUN-UPA L. S. Pavlyshyna* (Lviv: Feniks, 1992), 50.

into Soviet Ukraine. After a course they would return to Ukraine and remained there in the underground. Because the OUN members from Soviet Ukraine tried to cross the German-Soviet border in large and armed groups, many of them were detected and killed by the Soviet border guards. Soviet documents speak about the detection of thirty-eight groups, a total of 486 people.[157]

The underground OUN-B forces in Ukraine were more numerous than in the General Government. According to Ivan Klymiv's estimate, prepared for OUN-B leaders close to the start of the revolution, these forces numbered about 20,000 members in 3,300 locations.[158] Of these members, 5,000 were in Volhynia, 13,000 in eastern Galicia, and 1,200 in Lviv.[159] In addition, the OUN-B youth group Iunatstvo counted 7,000 members in the underground in April 1941, and an unknown group of sympathizers.[160]

The OUN had an average of six members in each locality, and substantially more in Lviv than in any other city. All in all, this was enough to mobilize the population for the "Ukrainian National Revolution," to seize power in many of the western Ukrainian localities, and to motivate the population to ethnic and political violence. In eastern Ukraine the structure of the OUN-B ranged from weak to non-existent. In early May 1941, Bandera's courier brought Klymiv ten copies of "Struggle and Activities." This document provided Klymiv and other leading OUN-B members in eastern Galicia and Volhynia with a set of detailed and comprehensive directives for the coming uprising.[161] Klymiv finished nominating candidates for the regional revolutionary administrations (*Oblasni Ukraïns'ki Natsional'ni Revoliutsiini Provody*) and the district revolutionary administrations (*Raionni Ukraïns'ki Natsional'ni Revoliutsiini Provody*) as early as 20 March 1941.[162] On 7 June 1941, Bandera's courier informed Klymiv exactly when the German invasion of the USSR would begin.[163]

Shortly before OUN-B member Bohdan Kazanivs'kyi left for Ukraine, he met with Bandera in the General Government. Kazanivs'kyi noticed that his superior possessed the aura of the Ukrainian *Providnyk*, and that he was a living propaganda weapon:

> There was no solace in his [Bandera's] words and no promises of a comfortable life in the underground. ... Although the outlook was not rosy, the order of the Leader [*Providnyk*] was holy for us, and we were prepared to walk into a fire for the great idea of liberating Ukraine. The words of the Leader [*Providnyk*]: "I believe you will not disappoint my expectations toward you!" were for us a sign and enabled us later to hold out a lot.[164]

Kazanivs'kyi remembered that he was never before in his life as impressed by someone as he was in that moment by the *Providnyk*. Another OUN-B member Luka

157 Motyka, *Ukraińska partyzantka*, 81–82.
158 "Zahal'nyi ohliad," not earlier than August 1941, TsDAVOV f. 3833, op. 1, spr. 45, 1–2.
159 Ibid., 1.
160 Patryliak, *Viis'kova*, 181.
161 Interrogation of Shymon Turchanovych, 21 October 1944, HDA SBU f. 13, spr. 372, vol. 1, 84
162 TsDAVOV f. 3833, op. 1, spr. 45, 2.
163 Ibid., 2.
164 Bohdan Kazanivs'kyi, *Shliakhom Legendy: Spomyny* (London: Ukraïns'ka Vydavnycha Spilka, 1975), 118.

Pavlyshyn noticed at about the same time that even the high-ranking OUN-B member Riko Iaryi addressed Bandera as "Vozhd'" and did not dare to sit next to him while talking to him. According to Pavlyshyn, Iaryi once said to Bandera:

> We need to create a strong and disciplined national organization that would "keep Ukraine in its hands." ... Ukrainians are inherently anarchists, prone to Cossack freedom [*vol'nytsia*], and with such people you cannot build an independent nation. We need an "authoritarian leader [*avtorytarnyi vozhd'*]" and self-sacrificing "executors of the leader's will."[165]

Bandera was pleased with the idea that the German attack on the Soviet Union might allow the OUN-B to create a Ukrainian state and thus enable him to become its leader. In conversation with other OUN-B members at that time, he expressed the idea that "war is the continuation of politics by other means."[166]

During the period when the OUN-B was preparing for the "Ukrainian National Revolution," western Ukraine was exposed for twenty-one months to Sovietization on all cultural, political, and social levels. The Soviet power legitimized its occupation with the idea that western Ukraine had been liberated from Polish occupation. The Soviet authorities established a congress of the people and, with the help of fake elections held on 22 October 1939, unified western Ukraine with the Ukrainian SSR.[167] Soviet politicians thereby achieved what the Ukrainian nationalists called *sobornist'* (unification) and had failed to achieve from the very beginning of their existence. The Soviet authorities replaced numerous Polish and Catholic emblems in schools and offices, such as the portraits of Piłsudski, and crucifixes, with portraits of Lenin and Stalin. Ukrainian nationalists hated the new portraits no less than the previous ones.[168]

Soviet politics were class oriented but class was interlinked with ethnicity. The Sovietization of western Ukraine was accompanied by Ukrainization. After September 1939, Ukrainian became the official language at Lviv University. The number of Ukrainian and Jewish students and Ukrainian professors increased and the number of Polish students and professors declined. Newcomers from Soviet Ukraine, local Ukrainians and Jews, and Jews who had fled from German-occupied territory replaced Poles in administration and other profitable positions. In 1940, the Lviv city soviet counted 476 members, including 252 Ukrainians, 121 Poles, seventy-six Jews, and twenty-seven members of other nationalities.[169]

Sovietization relied on terror and repression, directed against various social, political, economic, and ethnic groups, such as the former Polish political elite, Polish military settlers, Jewish refugees from Polish territories occupied by the Germans, Jewish Bundists and Zionists, and Polish and Ukrainian nationalists.[170] As a

165 Shchehliuk, *"Iak rosa*, 48.

166 Ibid., 47.

167 Mick, *Kriegserfahrungen*, 437; Gross, *Revolution from Abroad*, 71; Timothy Snyder, *Bloodlands: Europe between Hitler and Stalin* (New York: Basic Books, 2010), 128.

168 Gross, *Revolution from Abroad*, 63, 127.

169 Mick, Incompatible Experiences, 341. For the Lviv University, see Jan Draus, *Uniwersytet Jana Kazimierza we Lwowie 1918–1946: Portret kresowej uczelni* (Cracow: Księgarnia Akademicka, 2007), 75–88. For the Lviv city soviet, see Yones, *Smoke in the Sand*, 48.

170 Mick, "Incompatible Experiences," 341.

result of three major deportations into the interior of the USSR in 1940, and one in 1941, between 309,000 and 327,000 people were deported in freight cars from the eastern parts of the previous territory of the Second Republic. Of those, at least 140,000 were deported from eastern Galicia, including 95,000 permanent inhabitants of eastern Galicia (80 percent Poles, 10 to 15 percent Ukrainians, and 5 to 10 percent Jews), and 45,000 Jewish refugees from central or western Poland. In addition, the Soviet authorities arrested between 45,000 and 50,000 people in eastern Galicia.[171] After arrest, many of them were tortured during their investigation, sometimes until they lost consciousness.[172] Eastern Ukrainians, on the other hand, had experienced the harshness of the Soviet policies already before. In 1932–1933 they suffered under the artificial famine, and in 1937–1938 many were killed during the Great Terror.[173]

After the attack by Nazi Germany on the Soviet Union on 22 June 1941, the NKVD carried out further mass arrests of political opponents in western Ukraine. Because the German army was moving fast, the Soviet authorities could not evacuate these prisoners and decided to kill them. According to Soviet documents, 8,789 prisoners were executed in the Ukrainian SSR,[174] 2,800 of these in Lviv.[175] The order to execute them was issued by Lavrentii Beriia, the chief of the People's Commissariat for Internal Affairs (*Narodnyi komissariat vnutrennikh del*, NKVD).[176] On the morning of 24 June 1941, the NKVD chief in Lviv received it in the form of a radio telegram from Nikita Khrushchev, the first secretary of the Communist Party of Ukraine.[177]

The Ukrainian nationalists, in particular the OUN, were an important enemy of the Soviet Union. In western Ukraine, the policies of the Soviet authorities forced the Ukrainian nationalists to become an underground movement. Between October 1939 and December 1940 alone, the Soviet authorities arrested 4,435 nationalists, killed 352 of them, and confiscated hundreds of rifles, which had belonged to the nationalists. In order to frighten the Ukrainian population and to discourage it from supporting the OUN, the Soviet authorities organized trials of OUN members. In the first trial, which was held in November 1940, ten of the eleven OUN members who were tried, among them leaders from the homeland executive, were sentenced to death and executed. In January 1941 in Lviv, forty-two nationalists, out of fifty-nine on trial, were sentenced to death. Among them were eleven women. Of the forty-two sentenced to death, twenty were actually executed. The remainder were sent to Gu-

171 Gross, *Revolution from Abroad*, xiv; Mick, *Kriegserfahrungen*, 441, 444. For more details based on NKVD documents about the number of deported persons, see http://www.sciesielski.republika.pl/sov-dep/polacy/liczdep.html (accessed 7 September 2010).

172 Depositions of Leo Fedoruk, Omelian Matla, Nadia Koraltowycz, Bogdan Kazaniwskyj, Bundesarchiv-Militärarchiv Freiburg (BA-MA), RW 2/148, 331–34, 342–45, 353–54, 355–60.

173 Snyder, *Bloodlands*, 21–118.

174 Berkhoff, *Harvest of Despair*, 14.

175 Johann Druschbach, a professor from Kiev who worked with the NKVD in Lviv, heard this number as he was escaping from Lviv to Kiev in an NKVD airplane on 28 June, together with thirteen high Soviet officials. Cf. Interrogation of Johann Druschbach, LN-W, Gerichte Rep. 350, vol. 2, 72. The German authorities estimated 3,000 corpses and shortly afterward, 3,500. Cf. Hans Heer, "Einübung in den Holocaust: Lemberg Juni/Juli 1941," *Zeitschrift für Geschichtswissenschaft* Vol. 49, No. 5 (2001): 410.

176 Gross, *Revolution from Abroad*, xiv, 170–76, 178–86.

177 Johann Druschbach, who was sent by Khrushchev in May 1941 from Kiev to Lviv where he stayed in the "palace" of the chief of the NKVD, testified to this in the Oberländer investigation. Cf. LN-W, Gerichte Rep. 350, vol. 2, 71.

lag. Among those sent to the Gulag was Dmytro Kliachkivs'kyi, who would play a very significant role in 1943 in preparing and conducting the ethnic cleansing against Poles in Volhynia. In Drohobych, sixty-two people were brought to trial, of whom twenty were executed. On another occasion in Drohobych, thirty-nine people were brought to trial.[178]

The Soviet terror also affected the Bandera family. On 23 March 1941, the Soviet police arrested Stepan's father Andrii and his daughters Marta and Oksana, either simply because they were related to Stepan Bandera or because OUN member Stefanyshyn, who was wanted by the Soviet authorities, was hiding in the house. The Soviet regime had detailed information about Bandera's father from the NKVD agent "Ukrainets," who spied on the OUN-B in the General Government. Andrii Bandera was placed in a prison in Stanislaviv for five days and then transported to a prison in Kiev, where a military tribunal sentenced him to death on 8 July 1941. He was shot two days later. Marta and Oksana were deported to Siberia.[179]

In the final weeks before the German attack on the Soviet Union, there was no consensus amongst Ukrainian politicians in the General Government concerning the possible creation of a Ukrainian state. Hitler and other leading German politicians did not permit the OUN-B or any other Ukrainian group to establish a state in the territories which would be released from the Soviet occupation. The Abwehr might have discussed such political issues with the OUN-B or the OUN-M but it was not empowered to allow such plans. In a document concerning the activities of the Ukrainian politicians from 21 June 1941, the Gestapo (*Geheime Staatspolizei*, Secret State Police) noticed that the Ukrainian emigrants in the General Government tried to unite themselves and to establish a council which could become the basis for a future Ukrainian government. Ukrainian emigrants were, however, according to the Germans, divided into at least two camps: one around Volodymyr Kubiiovych, the head of the UTsK, who leaned toward the views of Mel'nyk and the OUN-M, and one surrounding Bandera. The Germans considered Kubiiovych to be more loyal to them and thus more appropriate for a Ukrainian leader, but Kubiiovych considered Mel'nyk to be the right personality for a Ukrainian leader. Regarding Bandera, they did not know if he would accept German superiority. In order to avoid political complications in the territories that they would occupy after 22 June 1941, the Gestapo took measures to prevent the departure of the leading Ukrainian politicians from the General Government to the "newly occupied territories" and forbade some of them including Bandera to go there.[180]

178 Motyka, *Ukraińska partyzantka*, 85–86; Rusnachenko, *Narod zburenyi*, 209–10.

179 Arsenych, *Rodyna Banderiv*, 11–12, 18, 65–66; "Spetsial'noe sobshchennie," HDA SBU, f. 16, op. 33, spr. 36, 14–33, in *Stepan Bandera*, ed. Serhiichuk, 1: 63. The NKVD shot at least 473 prisoners in Kiev. Cf. Berkhoff, *Harvest of Despair*, 16. About the NKVD agent "Ukrainets," see "Spetsial'noe soobshchenie," HDA SBU, f. 16, op. 33, spr. 36, 14–33, in *Stepan Bandera*, ed. Serhiichuk, 1:58–64.

180 "Der Chef der Sicherheitspolizei und des SD, Schnellbrief, Berlin, den 21. Juni 1941," PAAA, R 104151, 455483–455487. See also "Ereignismeldung UdSSR, Nr. 11, 03.07.1941," BAB R58/214, 59.

The "Ukrainian National Revolution"

The "Ukrainian National Revolution" began simultaneously with Operation Barbarossa, in the early hours of 22 June 1941, when Nazi Germany—supported by troops from Finland, Hungary, Italy, Romania, and Slovakia—attacked the Soviet Union. About 800 OUN-B activists in four task forces, which were divided into groups of five to twelve members, followed the German army eastward through the Ukrainian territories. Bandera did not go to Ukraine but stayed in the General Government, close to the border of the "newly occupied territories," and, with the help of couriers, coordinated the activities of the task forces.[181] The alleged 20,000 OUN-B activists who had remained underground in western Ukraine began to seize power, together with the activists from the task forces, just as "Struggle and Activities" had instructed them. Klymiv, who called himself the commander-in-chief of the Ukrainian National Revolutionary Army, also acted according to the directives elaborated by Bandera, Lenkavs'kyi, Shukhevych, and Stets'ko in "Struggle and Activities." One of the orders issued by Klymiv, shortly before or after the German attack on the Soviet Union said, "I am introducing mass (family and national) responsibility for all offences against the Ukrainian State, the Ukrainian Army, and the OUN." Given the OUN-B understanding of "offences against the Ukrainian State" at that time, this and similar orders must be interpreted as direct incitements to ethnic and political violence, which, during the "Ukrainian National Revolution," took mainly the shape of anti-Jewish pogroms.[182]

After 22 June 1941, the OUN-B activists sporadically harassed the withdrawing Soviet forces, shooting at them from ambush, for example in Lviv on 25 June.[183] More frequently however, they waited until the Soviet soldiers had left, and they then took control. They organized meetings, at which they familiarized the local population with their aims and proclaimed statehood, reading the proclamation and making the assembled population swear an oath of loyalty to the Ukrainian state and the *Providnyk*, Stepan Bandera.[184] They carried with them portraits of Stepan Bandera and distributed them among Ukrainians during the propaganda meetings.[185]

While organizing the administration of the state, the OUN-B activists also organized units of the Ukrainian National Militia, which were to protect the established administrative organs and to kill the "undesirable Polish, Muscovite [Russian or Soviet], and Jewish activists" who were on the blacklists compiled before the outbreak of the "revolution."[186] Like Operation Barbarossa, the "Ukrainian National Revolution" soon became an event of mass violence, in particular anti-Jewish violence. To incite the population to engage in pogroms, German soldiers and OUN-

181 Stets'ko, *30 chervnia 1941*, 158. Bandera stayed somewhere close to the former German-Soviet border. Lebed said in his biographical sketch for the CIA from 1952 that it was in Kholmshchyna. Cf. Mykola Lebed, Biographic Data, 18 May 1952, RG 263, ZZ-18, Box#80, NN3-263-02-008, Mykola Lebed Name File, vol. 1, 42.

182 Carynnyk, Foes of Our Rebirth, 332.

183 On 25 June 1941 the OUN-B activists attempted an insurrection, which was suppressed by the Soviet army. Cf. "Ereignismeldung UdSSR, Nr. 10, 02.07.1941," BAB R58/214, 53; Investigation record of Emanuel Brand, 27 June 1960, LN-W, Gerichte Rep. 350, vol. 3, 129.

184 "Propahandyvni vkazivky," TsDAVOV f. 3833, op. 1, spr. 69, 26.

185 Mykola S.-Chartoryis'kyi, *Vid Sianu po Krym: Spomyny uchasnyka III pokhidnoï hrupy Pivden'* (New York: Hoverlia, 1951), 145.

186 "Borot'ba i diial'nist' OUN pid chas viiny," TsDAVOV f. 3833, op. 2, spr. 1, 32, 58.

B activists used the bodies of prisoners killed by the NKVD units and left in the prison cells or buried in mass graves next to the prison buildings. The local Jews were held responsible for the NKVD massacres. The organization of the state and the pogroms overlapped. On the way to Lviv in a task force on 25 June 1941, Iaroslav Stets'ko, strongly antisemitic at the time of the revolution, wrote to Stepan Bandera from the village of Mlyny: "We are setting up a militia that will help to remove the Jews and protect the population," and continued "Father Lev Sohor has already organized a militia and has a written mandate from the OUN for this, and the village has accepted this. So have them [the Jews] come here to meet the militia, and it will eliminate those Jews and so forth."[187]

Stets'ko's message to Bandera confirms that the OUN-B was acting according to "Struggle and Activities" and suggests that the militia would be used to incite and conduct anti-Jewish violence. On 17 June 1941, Reinhard Heydrich, Director of the Reich Security Main Office (*Reichssicherheitshauptamt*, RSHA), gave instructions concerning the encouragement of "self-cleansing actions [*Selbstreinigungsaktionen*]" to dozens of SS and police personnel. On 29 June, he sent his instructions to the leaders of the *Einsatzgruppen*, who were to use *Vorkommandos* (advance units) to effect the "self-cleansing actions."[188] Günther Hermann, a commander of *Sonderkommando* IV, received, according to Erwin Schulz, the leader of *Einsatzkommando* 5 of Einsatzgruppe C, an order from Otto Rasch, the commander of the Einsatzgruppe C, to support the Ukrainian militia.[189] Even if these measures were not coordinated with the OUN both groups shared similar intentions toward the Jews and developed similar plans concerning their annihilation.

Pogroms, Proclamations, and National Celebrations in Lviv

For the OUN-B, the first and most important step was the proclamation of statehood. The leadership decided not to wait until the German troops reached the Ukrainian capital Kiev, but to proclaim the state in Lviv, the largest city of western Ukraine. The OUN-B might have decided to proclaim the state in Lviv because it wanted to preempt the OUN-M, which anticipated a similar plan, or because it wanted to see how the Germans would react, or because Lviv was more familiar to the OUN-B than Kiev and eastern Ukraine in general. The proclamation in Lviv was not as impressive as it would have been in Kiev but was significant enough to be taken seriously by the Germans and by the western Ukrainian population.[190]

187 Iaroslav Stets'ko to Stepan Bandera, No. 13, 25 June 1941, TsDAVOV f. 3833, op. 1, spr. 12, 10. On the antisemitism of the OUN-B leader Iaroslav Stets'ko, see Berkhoff, Organization of Ukrainian Nationalists, 149–84; Martynovych, "Sympathy for the Devil," 189. For the activities of the Ukrainian militia, see Pohl, *Nationalsozialistische*, 46.

188 BA, R 70 Sowjetunion/32, 391, in Peter Longerich and Dieter Pohl ed., *Die Ermordung der europäischen Juden: Eine Umfassende Dokumentation des Holocausts* (Munich: Piper, 1989), 118–19. See also Tomasz Szarota, *U progu Zagłady: Zajścia antyżydowskie i pogromy w okupowanej Europie; Warszawa, Paryż, Amsterdam, Antwerpia, Kowno* (Warsaw: Wydawnictwo Sic!, 2000), 210–14.

189 Sandkühler, *"Endlösung" in Galizien*, 116.

190 According to German documents, the OUN-B also sent a group of 30 persons to Kiev with the task of proclaiming the OUN-B state there and announcing it on the radio. Cf. "Ereignismeldung UdSSR, Nr. 20, 12.07.1941," BAB R 58/214, 131.

In deciding to proclaim the state after seizure of the territory by German troops, the OUN-B followed the examples of the Hlinka Party in Slovakia, and their clerical fascist leader Father Jozef Tiso, and the Croatian Ustaša. The HSLS had proclaimed a Slovak state on 14 March 1939, after Nazi Germany had dismantled Czechoslovakia. The Ustaša had proclaimed theirs on 10 April 1941, four days after the Wehrmacht entered Yugoslavia. Both states were recognized by Germany and other Axis powers. They were not independent states, as the Hlinka Party and Ustaša claimed, but satellite states of Germany. In both states, other political parties were banned, and Jews and other groups, such as Gypsies, were denied rights. Like the OUN-B, both the Hlinka Party and the Ustaša were devoted to the notion of "ethnic" purity, which they wanted to introduce in the multi-ethnic territories that they claimed as theirs. Just as the OUN-B regarded Poles and Russians as the occupiers of Ukraine, so the Hlinka Party regarded the Czechs as the occupiers of Slovakia, and the Ustaša regarded the Serbs as the occupiers of Croatia. All three movements regarded the Germans as liberators and allies. The Slovak example inspired the Ustaša, just as both of them inspired the OUN-B. They caused the OUN-B to believe and hope that Germany would accept the Ukrainian state proclaimed by the OUN-B, just as it had accepted the Slovak and Croatian states. The OUN-B leadership was aware that Ukraine was different from Slovakia and Croatia, but they believed that Ukraine was no less important for the "New Europe" than the other two new states, and that Germany would accept its independence.[191] The OUN-B member Volodymyr Stakhiv wrote in an official memorandum, which he sent on 23 July 1941 to Hitler:

> Since 1938, two new states have appeared in Europe: Slovakia and Croatia. Notwithstanding the difference in area and size of the population of these countries, the Ukrainian problem has a much greater significance, because to solve it, fundamental changes will be realized in the political and economic structure of the European continent, and in the raising of a problem of intercontinental significance. And the further course of German-Ukrainian relations will not only depend on the ultimate resolution of the problem, but also on the methods that will be applied at the outset.[192]

Kost' Pan'kivs'kyi, an older Ukrainian politician, who collaborated with the Germans during the Second World War but was not a nationalist extremist, wrote that, at the time of the "Ukrainian National Revolution," the OUN activists appeared as:

> people who for years had had contacts with the Germans, who were ideologically linked with fascism and Nazism, who in word and in print and in deed had for years been preaching totalitarianism and an orientation toward Berlin and Rome.

191 For Slovakia, see Yeshayahu Jelinek, *The Parish Republic: Hlinka's Slovak People's Party, 1939–1945* (New York: Columbia University Press, 1976), 30, 46, 48. On Croatia, see Sabrina P. Ramet, "The NDH—An Introduction," *Totalitarian Movement and Political Religions*, Vol. 7, No. 4 (2006): 399–406; Stanley G. Payne, "The NDH State in Comparative Perspective," in *Totalitarian Movement and Political Religions*, Vol. 7, No. 4 (2006), 410–15.

192 Volodymyr Stakhiv, "Seiner Exzellenz dem Herrn Deutschen Reichskanzler. Denkschrift der Organisation Ukrainischer Nationalisten zur Lösung der Ukrainischen Frage," Bundesarchiv Koblenz (BAK), R 43 II /1500, 76.

... Those whom our community regarded as German partners and potential leaders of the national life.[193]

When the Germans and Ukrainian nationalists entered Lviv on 30 June, there were 160,000 Jews in the city, 140,000 Poles, and 70,000 Ukrainians. The number of Jews in Lviv had increased significantly after the beginning of Operation Barbarossa, as Jewish refuges escaped from the territories of the Second Republic occupied by Germans, to those occupied by the Soviet Union.[194] Among the German units entering the city was the Ukrainian Nachtigall battalion, which formed part of the 1st. Battalion of the special command regiment Brandenburg 800.[195] When they marched into Lviv, the soldiers of this battalion shouted “Slava Ukraïni!” to the local people who welcomed them enthusiastically.[196] Ukrainians in Lviv were very excited at the sight of the Ukrainians in German uniform. When the battalion marched into the market square, people not only welcomed the soldiers with flowers but also genuflected and prayed.[197] In the ecstasy of the “Ukrainian National Revolution,” Ukrainians called the Nachtigall battalion the “Stepan Bandera battalion.”[198]

Statehood was proclaimed at eight o'clock in the evening on 30 June 1941, in a meeting room in the building of the Prosvita Society. The meeting was announced as a liberation ceremony.[199] The OUN-B had wanted to deliver the proclamation in the state theater, a more imposing building, but it had already been requisitioned by the German army.[200] Stepan Bandera, the most important figure in the revolution, was not able to proclaim statehood himself. Bandera, according to Stets'ko, had been “confined” by the Germans on 29 June 1941.[201] Shortly before the beginning of Operation Barbarossa the RSHA released directives to prevent Bandera from entering the “newly occupied territories.”[202]

After the Second World War, Lebed' stated that Bandera had stayed in Kholmshchyna, the region of Chełm (Kholm), and had coordinated the “Ukrainian National

193 Pan'kivs'kyi, *Roky nimets'koï okupatsiï*, 13.

194 Mick, *Kriegserfahrungen*, 499. In 1931, 198,000 Polish speakers (63.5 percent) lived in Lviv, along with 75,300 (24.1 percent) Yiddish and Hebrew speakers, and 35,100 Ukrainian speakers (11.3 percent). The actual number of Jews and Ukrainians was higher than that of the Yiddish, Hebrew, and Ukrainian speakers because many Jews and Ukrainians spoke Polish. Grzegorz Mazur, who compared several estimates, came to the conclusion that in the interwar period 50 to 52 percent of Lviv inhabitants were Polish, 30 to 34 percent Jewish, and 12 to 16 percent Ukrainian. Cf. Mazur, *Życie polityczne*, 23.

195 The Brandenburg 800 regiment was part of the Abwehr, which belonged to the Wehrmacht.

196 Kazanivs'kyi, *Shliakhom Legendy*, 209.

197 Interrogation of Friedrich Wilhelm Heinz, LN-W, Gerichte Rep. 350, vol. 2, 190.

198 Cf. “Zvit ch. 5,” TsDAVOV f. 3833, op. 1, spr. 12, 13; TsDAHO f. 57, op. 4, spr. 341, 3; Kurt Lewin, *Przeżyłem: Saga Świętego Jura w roku 1946* (Warsaw: Zeszyty Literackie, 2006), 61; Lucyna Kulińska and Adam Roliński, *Kwestia ukraińska i eksterminacja ludności polskiej w Małopolsce Wschodniej w świetle dokumentów Polskiego Państwa Podziemnego 1943–1944* (Cracow: Księgarnia Akademicka, 2004), 207.

199 “Aufzeichnungen des Vortragenden Legationsrats Großkopf,” in *Akten zur deutschen Auswärtigen Politik 1918–1945*, Serie D, Band XIII, ed. Walter Bußmann (Göttingen: Vandenhoeck & Ruprecht, 1970), 167.

200 Armstrong, *Ukrainian Nationalism*, 79–80.

201 “Komunikat,” TsDAVOV f. 3833, op. 1, spr. 6, 2.

202 “Der Chef der Sicherheitspolizei und des SD, Schnellbrief, Berlin, den 21. Juni 1941,” PAAA, R 104151, 455487.

Revolution" from there.[203] Statehood was therefore proclaimed by Bandera's representative, Iaroslav Stets'ko, who tried to represent both the national will and German interests. During the meeting in the Prosvita hall, after saluting the absent Bandera, Stets'ko read the formal statement:

> In accordance with the will of the Ukrainian people, the Organization of Ukrainian Nationalists under the leadership of Stepan Bandera declares the reestablishment of the Ukrainian State, for which entire generations of the best sons of Ukraine have sacrificed themselves.[204]

The declaration further stated that the independent Ukrainian authority would guarantee order to the Ukrainian people, that the Ukrainian state coming into being in western Ukraine would later be subordinated to the authority in Kiev, and that the Ukrainian state would closely cooperate with the "National Socialist Great Germany, which, under the leadership of Adolf Hitler, is creating a new order in Europe and the world, and is helping the Ukrainian nation liberate itself from Muscovite occupation."[205]

The text of the OUN-B proclamation resembled the one used by the Ustaša on 10 April 1941. Like the OUN-B state, the Ustaša state was proclaimed by the deputy-leader, the *Doglavnik* Slavko Kvaternik, and not by the *Poglavnik* Pavelić in person. Kvaternik, however, had not gone as far as Stets'ko and had not introduced Hitler into the proclamation text. He referred only to "the will of our allies." The Ustaša proclamation text said:

> People of Croatia! The providence of God, the will of our allies, the century-old struggle of the Croatian people, our self-sacrificing Leader [*Poglavnik*] Ante Pavelić and the Ustaša movement, within and outside the country, has decided that we today, on the eve of the resurrection of the son of God, will also witness the resurrection of our Croatian state.[206]

According to the minutes of the meeting on 30 June 1941 in the Prosvita hall, after the reading of the declaration by Stets'ko, people in the hall broke into applause several times. The Greek Catholic Church was represented at the gathering by Iosyf Slipyi. Another clergyman, Dr. Ivan Hryn'okh in Abwehr uniform, represented the Nachtigall battalion. The gathering finished with salutes addressed to Stepan Bandera, Adolf Hitler, and Metropolitan Andrei Sheptyts'kyi, and with the singing of the national anthem "Ukraine has not yet perished" (*Shche ne vmerla Ukraïna*).[207]

Two German officers, Hans Koch and Wilhelm Ernst zu Eikern, also came to the meeting, although they arrived late. Koch said that he welcomed the meeting, but only for celebrating the liberation from the Bolsheviks, not for proclaiming statehood. The officers reminded those assembled that the war was not over, and that this

203 Mykola Lebed, Biographic Data, 18 May 1952, RG 263, ZZ-18, Box#80, NN3-263-02-008, Mykola Lebed Name File, vol. 1, 42.

204 "Akt proholoshennia ukraïns'koï derzhavy, 30.06.1941," TsDAVOV f. 3833, op. 1, spr. 5, 3.

205 Ibid., 3.

206 Slavko Vukčević, *Zločini na jugoslovenskim prostorima u prvom i drugom svetskom ratu: Zločini Nezavisne Države Hrvatske, 1941–45*, vol 1. (Belgrade: Vojnoistorijski institut, 1993), document 3 (the declaration). I am grateful to Per Rudling and Tomislac Dulić for this reference.

207 Minutes of the proclamation ceremony on 30 June 1941, TsDAVOV f. 3833, op. 1, spr. 4, 6, 7.

was not an appropriate time to proclaim statehood. They also stated that the only person who could decide whether a Ukrainian state would come into existence was Adolf Hitler.[208] After the proclamation ceremony and also at 11.00 a.m. the next morning, OUN-B activists made use of a radio station which, after the retreat of the Soviet troops, was occupied by the Nachtigall battalion and renamed the "Ievhen Konovalets' Station."[209] They broadcasted, both in Ukrainian and German, about the proclamation ceremony and the existence of the Ukrainian state. A soldier spoke emotionally about his arrival in Lviv and about the fraternal relations between the German and Ukrainian sides, especially their leaders. He also sang German and Ukrainian songs and informed listeners of the existence of the "Ukrainian Wehrmacht."[210] The OUN-B also familiarized radio listeners with a pastoral letter written by the head of the Greek Catholic Church, Sheptyts'kyi, who announced that Stets'ko's government and the Ukrainian state had come into being by the will of God, and that "we welcome the German army as an army which liberated us from the enemy." In the same letter to the "Ukrainian nation" Sheptyts'kyi also suggested that he supported the OUN-B's plans for statehood, but not ethnic violence: "We expect from the government established by him [Stets'ko] wise, just leadership, and measures that would take into consideration the needs and welfare of all citizens who inhabit our land, without regard to what faith, nationality, and social stratum they belong."[211] One of the OUN-B radio speakers on 1 July 1941 was Hryn'okh. On 30 June, he had visited Sheptyts'kyi together with Stets'ko and had obtained the Metropolitan's "consent and blessing" for the declaration of the state.[212]

On 1 July 1941, while Hryn'okh and other soldiers from the "Stepan Bandera battalion" were singing German and Ukrainian military and revolutionary songs on the radio, a pogrom took place in the city. Germans and the Ukrainian militia, established and controlled by the OUN-B, were killing Jews en masse and inciting the local population to do the same.[213] The militia in Lviv had been formed on 30 June 1941 in the courtyard of the Metropolitan's palace on St. George's Hill, by Ivan Rav-

208 "Aufzeichnungen des Vortragenden Legationsrats Großkopf," in *Akten zur deutschen Auswärtigen Politik 1918–1945*, 167–68. See also "Rücksprache mit Prof. Dr. Koch am 10.07.1941," BA Berlin-Lichterfelde, R 6 /150, 4–5; Kost' Pan'kivs'kyi, *Vid derzhavy do komitetu* (New York and Toronto: Zhyttia i Mysli, 1957), 30–32.

209 Myroslav Kal'ba, *U lavakh druzhynnykiv* (Denver: Vydannia Druzhyn Ukrains'kykh Natsionalistiv, 1982), 9–10; Information leaflet No. 1, 1 July 1941, BAB, NS 26/1198, 1.

210 "Niederschrift über die Rücksprache mit den Mitgliedern des ukrainischen Nationalkomitees und Stepan Bandera vom 3. Juli 1941," BAB, NS 26/1198, 1, 2, 12. For Iaroslav Starukh, see "Protokol doprosa obviniaemogo Vasiliia Okhrymovicha Ostapovicha, 06.01.1953," HDA SBU f. 5, spr. 445, vol. 5, 12–16, in *Stepan Bandera*, ed. Serhiichuk, 3:388–89.

211 "Niederschrift über die Rücksprache mit den Mitgliedern des ukrainischen Nationalkomitees und Stepan Bandera vom 3. Juli 1941," BAB, NS 26/1198, 1–3. For Sheptyts'kyi's pastoral letter, see "Pastyrs'kyi lyst mytropolyta A. Sheptyts'koho z nahody vidnovlennia Ukraïns'koi derzhavy," in *Ukraïns'ke derzhavotvorennia. Akt 30 chervnia 1941. Zbirnyk dokumentiv i materialiv*, ed. Orest Dziuban (Lviv, Kiev: Piramida, 2001), 126.

212 Interrogation of Ivan Hryn'okh, LN-W, Gerichte Rep. 350, vol. 2, 23; Hansjakob Stehle, "Sheptyts'kyi and the German Regime," in *Morality and Reality: The Life and Times of Andrei Sheptyts'kyi*, ed. Paul Robert Magocsi (Edmonton: Canadian Institute of Ukrainian Studies, University of Alberta, 1989), 127.

213 At the time of the revolution there were at least 1,200 OUN-B members in Lviv who could have been included in the militia. Cf. "Zahal'nyi ohliad," written not earlier than August 1941, TsDAVOV f. 3833, op. 1, spr. 45, 1. The eyewitness Alfred Monaster commented that the Ukrainian militiamen "sprang up like mushrooms" in Lviv. Cf. AŻIH, 302/58, Alfred Monaster, 2.

lyk, who came to Lviv together with Stets'ko in the second task force, and by local OUN-B members.[214] During the first days, Bohdan Kazanivs'kyi and Omelian Matla played an important role in the militia.[215] Both of them had been imprisoned and tortured by the NKVD.[216] In his post-war memoirs, Kazanivs'kyi wrote that while under torture by the NKVD he thought about Bandera who, "chained to the wall in a dark cell [of a Polish prison] for a year, without sleep, did not surrender."[217] Shukhevych, the Ukrainian commander of the Nachtigall battalion, was also involved in appointing the militia leadership. In the morning of 30 June, he went with his division of the Nachtigall battalion to the Saint George Cathedral where he, together with Kazanivs'kyi, inspired those present to "revolutionary deeds" while informing them publicly that the OUN-B will proclaim the Ukrainian state.[218] After 2 July, the militia in Lviv was, according to Hans Joachim Beyer, a high official of the SD and an adviser to the Einsatzgruppe C, subordinated to the SS and was thereafter known as the Ukrainian police.[219] Stets'ko, however, still regarded the police as the militia of the Ukrainian government.[220] The first head of the militia was the OUN-B member Ievhen Vrets'ona, replaced some weeks later by Volodymyr Pitulei.[221]

In accordance with "Struggle and Activities," the militiamen were to wear either a yellow-and-blue armlet, or a white armlet with the inscription "National Militia." However, a number of the militiamen were acting clandestinely and therefore did not wear them.[222] The historian Jeffrey Burds, who compared photographs of the pogrom with the photographs in the identification cards of the Ukrainian militiamen, noticed that some of the pogromists could be identified (Figs. 13–16). Because of their armlets, others were recognized as militiamen by many victims, survivors, and bystanders, not only in Lviv but also in other cities, towns, and villages where pogroms occurred.[223] Some Ukrainian militiamen in Lviv put on olive-green

214 For Ravlyk, see Stets'ko, *30 chervnia 1941*, 181–82. For recruitment, see Dmytro Honta, "Drukarstvo Zakhidnoï Ukraïny pidchas okupatsiï," Konkurs na spohady, Oseredok Ukrainian Cultural and Educational Centre Winnipeg, 13–14. For the second OUN-B task force, which stayed in Lviv from 30 June to 11–12 July, see Bruder, *"Den Ukrainischen Staat*, 149.

215 Kazanivs'kyi, *Shliakhom Legendy*, 212–14.

216 Depositions of Omelian Matla and Bogdan Kazaniwskyj; BA-MA, RW 2/148, 342–44, 355–60.

217 Kazanivs'kyi, *Shliakhom Legendy*, 179.

218 Ibid., 212–13.

219 "Podiï na zakhidn'o-ukrains'kykh. Interviu z dots[entom]. d[okto]rom H.I. Baierom, Krakiv 5.7.1941," in *Ukraïns'ke derzhavotvorennia*, ed. Dziuban, 153; Pan'kivs'kyi, *Roky nimetskoï okupatsiï*, 401.

220 Stets'ko, *30 chervnia 1941*, 256.

221 "Podiï na zakhidn'o-ukrains'kykh," in *Ukraïns'ke derzhavotvorennia*, ed. Dziuban, 153; Pan'kivs'kyi, *Roky nimetskoï okupatsiï*, 403. See also Rossoliński-Liebe, Der Verlauf und die Täter, 223.

222 "Borot'ba i diial'nist' OUN pid chas viiny," TsDAVOV f. 3833, op. 2, spr. 1, 62; Ivan Hymka (John-Paul Himka), "Dostovirnist' svidchennia: reliatsia Ruzi Vagner pro L'vivskyi pohrom vlitku 1941," *Holokost i suchasnist'* 2, 4 (2008): 63–64.

223 For yellow-and-blue armlets on the militiamen beating and murdering Jews, see Eliyahu Yones, *Die Straße nach Lemberg: Zwangsarbeit und Widerstand in Ostgalizien 1941–1944*, ed. Susanne Heim (Frankfurt am Main: Fischer Taschenbuch Verlag, 1999), 18–19; AŻIH, 301/4654, Henryk Szyper, 6; AŻIH, 301/1809, Janisław Korczyński, 1; AŻIH, 301/1864, Salomon Goldman, 1; AŻIH 229/22, Maurycy Allerhand, 1; AŻIH 301/3774, Salomon Hirschberg, 1; AŻIH, 301/1181, Lilith Stern, 2–3; Testimony of Joanna H. in Bogdan Musiał, *»Kontrrevolutionäre Elemente sind zu erschießen«: Brutalisierung des deutsch-sowjetischen Krieges im Sommer 1941* (Berlin: Propyläen, 2000), 176; Moritz Grünbart, "Das Blutbad von Lemberg. Ein Erlebnisbericht von Moritz Grünbart," *Der Spiegel*, 11, 1960, 20–21; Interrogation of Moritz Grünbart, LN-W, Gerichte Rep. 350, vol. 2, 180–81.

Fig. 13. Ukrainian militiamen with one of their victims during the Lviv pogrom. Wiener Library.

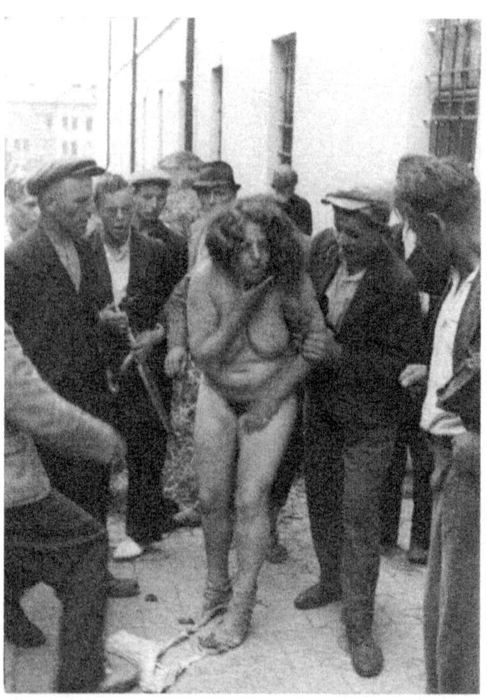

Fig. 14. Ukrainian militiamen with one of their victims during the Lviv pogrom. Wiener Library.

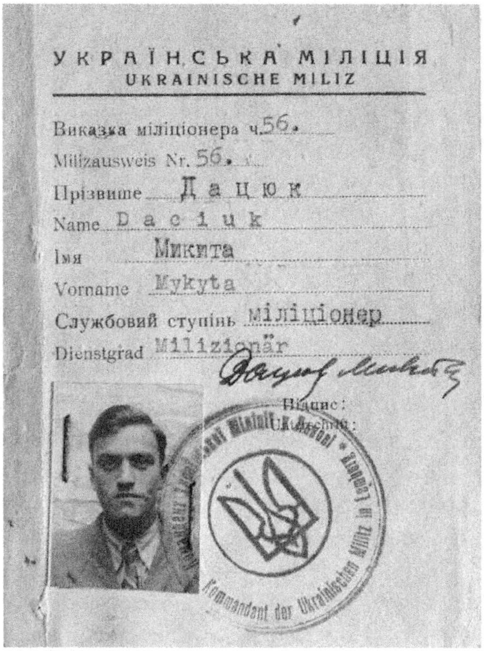

УКРАЇНСЬКА МІЛІЦІЯ
UKRAINISCHE MILIZ

Виказка міліціонера ч. 56.
Milizausweis Nr. 56.
Прізвище Дацюк
Name Daciuk
Імя Микита
Vorname Mykyta
Службовий ступінь міліціонер
Dienstgrad Milizionär
Підпис:
Unterschrift:

Fig. 15. A militia ID of a militiaman on figure 13. DALO, f. R12, op. 1, spr. 130, 1. Courtesy of David Alan Rich.

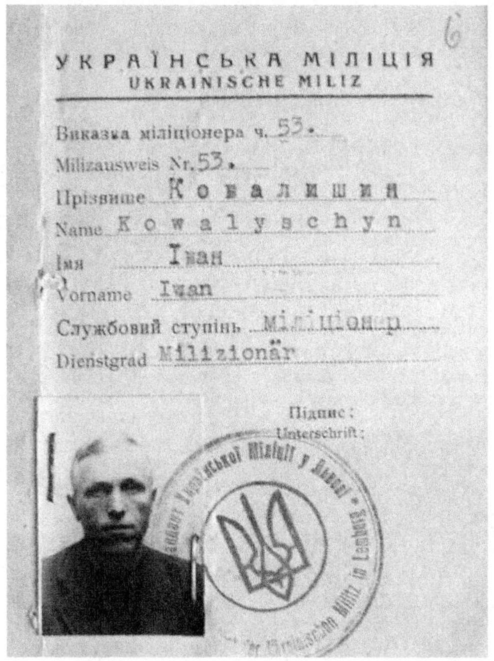
6

УКРАЇНСЬКА МІЛІЦІЯ
UKRAINISCHE MILIZ

Виказка міліціонера ч. 53.
Milizausweis Nr. 53.
Прізвище Ковалишин
Name Kowalyschyn
Імя Іван
Vorname Iwan
Службовий ступінь Міліціонер
Dienstgrad Milizionär
Підпис:
Unterschrift:

Fig. 16. A militia ID of a militiaman on figure 14 and 13. DALO, f. R12, op. 1, spr. 130, 6. Courtesy of David Alan Rich.

uniforms, which had previously been used by the Soviet militia. They removed the Soviet emblems from these uniforms and wore them with the yellow-and-blue armlets and mazepynka caps.[224] The OUN-B tried to eliminate elements from the militia that were not loyal to the organization.[225] During their recruitment, the militiamen received ethical training, which included swearing an oath to Stepan Bandera and independent Ukraine.[226]

As already mentioned, in the morning of 30 June 1941, German and Ukrainian troops discovered numerous bodies of prisoners who had been murdered by the NKVD. The corpses were in the cells of four prisons, and in mass graves in the prison yards. Estimates of the number of corpses ranged from 2,800[227] to 4,000;[228] the lower figure seems more likely. The majority of the NKVD victims were apparently Ukrainians, about a quarter of the victims were Poles, and there was an unknown number of Jews.[229] A few prisoners, who survived the NKVD massacre in the prisons, had escaped after the Soviet army left and before the Germans came in.[230] Rumors about the massacres and tortures in the prisons had circulated even before the Germans arrived on 30 June, inspected the prisons, forced Jews to exhume bodies, and to bring out the first corpses from the cells.[231] According to Dr. Georg Saeltzer and a German officer, some of the bodies showed signs of torture.[232]

As early as 28 June 1941, two Ukrainian defectors informed the German Army that "two days ago there were riots in Lviv, during which Jews and communists were murdered."[233] However, no other documents confirm that riots took place in Lviv before 30 June. According to Erwin Schulz, leader of Einsatzkommando 5, Hitler ordered a reprisal action against Lviv Jews for the NKVD massacre, but it is not clear whether the pogrom was organized on account of this order.[234] On 30 June, the Germans and OUN-B activists began using the corpses of the NKVD victims to provoke

224 Interrogation of Cornelius von Hovora, 29 February 1960, LN-W, Gerichte Rep. 350, vol. 2, 215; Interrogation of Emanuel Brand, 27 June 1960, LN-W, Gerichte Rep. 350, vol. 3, 129; "Der Oberstaatsanwalt," LN-W, Gerichte Rep. 350, vol. 5, 16.

225 The report of Mykola Mostovych from 31 September 1941, TsDAVOV f. 3833, op. 1, spr. 15, 71.

226 See for example the recruitment of Volodymyr Panasiuk, a Volhynian who was trained as a militiaman by Ukrainian nationalists from Galicia, in Upravlinnia Sluzhby Bezpeky Ukraïny v Rivens'kii oblasti (USB v Rivens'kii oblasti), No. 19090, t. 3, 3, 3v, 100, 101, or USHMM, RG, 31.018M, reel 20. On the militia, see also Pohl, *Nationalsozialistische*, 46.

227 Interrogation of Johann Druschbach, LN-W, Gerichte Rep. 350, vol. 2, 72. Druschbach heard this number from senior NKVD officers with whom he flew from Lviv to Kiev on 28 June 1941.

228 "Wahrnehmung über die bolschewistischen Bluttaten in Lemberg vom 7.7.1941," BA-MA, RH 26/454/6b, 2. Other documents mention 4,000. Cf. "Das Ukrainische Rote Kreuz, 7.7.1941," BA-MA, RW 2/148, 373.

229 Mick, *Kriegserfahrungen*, 469.

230 Depositions of Leo Fedoruk, Omelian Matla, Josefa Soziada, Ludwik Pisarek, Bogdan Kazaniwskyj, Anna Domin, Edward Chruslicki, Rosalie Sobonkiewicz, Richard Eckl, BA-MA, RW 2/148, 331–34, 342–45, 346–49, 355–66, 367–69.

231 Interrogation of Dr. Georg Saeltzer, BA-MA, RW 2/148, 340; AŻIH, 301/54, Rózia Wagner, 1.

232 "Darstellung der Ereignisse 30.06.1941, 15 Uhr," BA-MA, RH/24/49/8, 174; Interrogation of Dr. Georg Saeltzer on 6. July 1941," BA-MA, RW 2/148, 339; Heer, Einübung in den Holocaust, 410. On this question, see also Sandkühler, *"Endlösung" in Galizien*, 303. Zygmunt Albert, assistant of a Polish physician, did not see signs of torture on the corpses in Lviv. Cf. Hryciuk, *Polacy we Lwowie 1939–1944: Życie codzienne* (Warsaw: Książka i Wiedza, 2000), 190.

233 "Vernehmung von zwei ukrainischen Überläufern, 28. Juni 1941," BA-MA RH 26/100/36, 111.

234 Interrogation of Erwin Schulz, 1 August 1958, LN-W, Gerichte Rep. 350, vol. 4, 124; "Der Oberstaatsanwalt," LN-W, Gerichte Rep. 350, vol. 5, 44.

violence. This resulted in the pogrom, but the most brutal and humiliating events took place the next day and continued on 2 July.[235]

On 30 June 1941, the Secret Field Police (*Geheime Feldpolizei*) noted that the people of Lviv were enthusiastic about the coming of the German troops and were bitter about the "infamous action of the Bolshevists" and the "Jews who live in the city and who collaborated with the Bolsheviks."[236] A German officer wrote to his wife on 30 June: "The Russians and Jews ruled over others cruelly and carried out massacres in the prisons." He also noted that the Ukrainians were in a mood that could easily become a pogrom.[237] In the yard of the Brygidki prison, company commander Hans Schmidt watched how "crowds of Jews or maybe other inhabitants of Lviv" carried corpses from the prison basements and placed them in the yard. Later the same day and in the same prison, he observed how the Jews were mistreated and beaten. He was told that the Jews "draw on themselves the hate of the people because they collaborated with the Russians and denounced the victims."[238]

The powerful stereotype of "Jewish Bolshevism" was an important element of both OUN-B and Nazi propaganda. It made the Ukrainian population—at whom the OUN-B propaganda was directed—believe that it was the Jews who were responsible for the atrocities of the Soviet regime, in particular the mass killings of prisoners after 22 June 1941.[239] That Jews were among the victims of the NKVD, that they were not substantially overrepresented in the NKVD, and that they did not profit more or suffer less than other ethnic groups under the Soviet occupation did not impress the nationalists, who blamed the Jews for the NKVD murders and believed that the Jews ruled the Soviet Union and were responsible for the famine in 1932–1933.[240]

In connection with the "Jewish Bolshevism" stereotype and the events of 1 July 1941, Kurt Lewin, a survivor of the pogrom, made the following observation, which he included in his memoirs in 1945, "A young representative of the Herrenvolk [master race] with an intelligent physiognomy—but disfigured with a mischievous smile—came to us and said: 'Nu, Juden die Rache ist süss. [So, Jews, revenge is sweet.]' I just didn't know what the revenge was for."[241]

235 For the course of the Lviv pogrom, see Himka, The Lviv Pogrom of 1941, 209–43; Rossoliński-Liebe, Der Verlauf und die Täter, 207–43

236 "Wahrnehmung über die bolschewistischen Bluttaten in Lemberg vom 7.7.1941," BA-MA, RH 26/454/6b, 1; "Darstellung der Ereignisse 30.06.1941," BA-MA, RH 24/49/8, 176.

237 "Feldpostbrief Eugen Meyding, 30.06.1941," LG Fulda 20 283/59, quoted in Heer, "Einübung in den Holocaust," 411.

238 Interrogation of Hans Schmidt, 29 June 1960, LN-W, Gerichte Rep. 350, Bd. 2, 209–10.

239 The Secret Field Police noticed in Lviv on 30 June that Ukrainians claimed that the dead prisoners were martyrs who suffered for Ukraine and should be avenged. They were offended by the proposal to investigate this crime. Cf. "Wahrnehmung über die bolschewistischen Bluttaten in Lemberg vom 7.7.1941," BA-MA, RH 26/454, 6b.

240 For the number of Jews in the top ranks of the Soviet NKVD, see N. V. Petrov and K. V. Skorkin ed., *Kto rukovodil NKVD 1934–1941* (Moscow: Zvenia, 1999), 495. On 1 October 1936, the leadership group of the NKVD included 33 Russians (30 percent of the total), 43 Jews (39 percent), 6 Ukrainians (5 percent). On 1 September 1938 there were 85 Russians (57 percent), 32 Jews (21 percent), 10 Ukrainians (7 percent). On 26 February 1941 there were 118 Russians (65 percent), 10 Jews (5 percent), 28 Ukrainians (15 percent). For Jews in the NKVD prisons, see Interrogation of Moritz Grünbart, LN-W, Gerichte Rep. 350, vol. 2, 177–78.

241 Lewin, *Przeżyłem*, 60–61.

Stefan Szende (Adolf Folkman), another Jewish survivor, wrote in his memoirs in March 1944 that, on 1 July 1941:

> German posters and Polish and Ukrainian leaflets based on the German posters appeared in the city. The German military commando used them to inform the Ukrainian and Polish populations that, in the prisons, corpses of thousands of Ukrainians and Poles were found. All were killed by the Jewish Bolsheviks. Public feeling was agitated by horrible accusations against the Jews. The agitation fell on fruitful ground. In the whole city, robbing and looting hordes roamed. The Jews were equated with the Bolsheviks, actually only the Jews were deemed to be Bolsheviks. We were outlawed [*vogelfrei*]. ... Hundreds of Jews were dragged from their houses, thrashed, kicked, murdered. Other thousands were herded together to the prison on Zamarstynowska Street.[242]

In the early hours of 1 July 1941, by when the OUN-B state had already been proclaimed, Ukrainian militiamen forced their way into Jewish apartments. They frequently seized male Jews, and occasionally the whole family, and took them by force to the yards of the three prisons where the corpses of the NKVD's victims had been found. Other militiamen seized Jews in the streets, while checking identity cards. One prison to which Jews were taken was on Zamarstynowska (Zamarstynivs'ka) Street, another was the Brygidki prison on Kazimierzowska (Horodots'ka) Street, and the third was on Łąckiego (Briullov) Street, close to the citadel. The Brygidki prison and the prison on Zamarstynowska Street were in the Jewish quarter. On the way to the prisons, the Jews were beaten by a furious crowd of both men and women, with fists, cudgels, canes, and other implements. Some of the Jews were forced to crawl on their knees.[243] Before the gate to the prison, pogromists stood in two rows and beat the Jews who had to go between the rows into the yards. When the Jews arrived in the yards, they were forced to carry the already-decomposing corpses from the cells in the basement and to put them in rows in the prison yards. Sometimes, after the Jewish men had carried them outside, Jewish women were compelled to wash the corpses and kiss their hands[244] in order to demonstrate to the crowds that the Jews were responsible for Soviet crimes and should now pay for it.

The Jews who carried the corpses from the cells were beaten, frequently to death, by Germans and Ukrainians, with rifle butts, metal bars, cudgels, spades, and other objects. During the pogrom, Ukrainian militiamen collected more and more Jews and drove them to the prison yards. There they replaced those already beaten to death, whose corpses were piled at the edge of the prison yard, next to those of the prisoners killed by the NKVD. Kurt Lewin, who was forced to work in the Brygidki

242 Stefan Szende, *Der letzte Jude aus Polen* (Zürich: Europa Verlag, 1945), 179.

243 Murdered prisoners were also found in a fourth prison on Jachowicza Street (Akademika Romana Kuchera Street). For Ukrainian militiamen with cudgels intruding into a Jewish house, forcing the whole family outside, and transporting Jews to prisons, while beating and mistreating them, see Interrogation of Fritz Spod, LN-W, Gerichte Rep. 350, vol. 2, 39. For taking Jews to the Brygidki prison, see Lewin, *Przeżyłem*, 57–58. For forcing Jews to crawl, see Hryciuk, *Polacy we Lwowie*, 204. For herding Jews together to the prison in Łąckiego Street, see Rogowski, "Lwów pod znakiem swastyki," ZNiO, syg. 16710/II, 56–57. For Ukrainian militia taking Jews to the Brygidki prison, see AŻIH, 301/4626, Anna Maria Peiper, 1. For stopping Jews in the streets, see AŻIH, 229/54, Teka Lwowska, Gold, 2; Yones, *Die Straße nach Lemberg*, 18–19.

244 On being forced to wash the corpses and kiss their hands, see Hryciuk, *Polacy we Lwowie*, 204.

prison, was especially afraid of an elegantly dressed man in a beautiful embroidered shirt, frequently worn by Ukrainian patriots, who

> beat with an ironclad cane. After a while, he beat only against the heads. With every hit he wrenched off strips of skin. He put some people's eyes out, wrenched off ears. When the cane broke, he immediately took a large charred piece of wood and smashed my neighbor's skull. The skull broke and the brain splattered in all directions, also on my face and clothes.[245]

The man in the embroidered shirt seems to have been a typical "victim" of the ideology of Ukrainian nationalism and the stereotype of "Jewish Bolshevism." Herman Kac, who was also forced to work in the yard of the Brygidki prison, recalled in 1947 that "Germans and Ukrainians mistreated us horribly and blamed us for the NKVD murders. They lined the Jews up to be shot." Kac recalled being the forty-eighth in line. As a German soldier was taking aim at him, a German officer came and said "Enough for today."[246]

The Jews were forced to work in the Brygidki prison until about 9 p.m. Lewin estimated that of the approximately 2,000 Jews crowded into the Brygidki prison on 1 June, about eighty survived. Before the Germans allowed them to go home, soldiers of the Nachtigall battalion came to the yard and mistreated the remaining Jews for a while. A German soldier threw a grenade against a group of Jews, and German soldiers continued killing the wounded victims in the yard. Before the survivors were allowed to leave the yard, they were told to come back the next day, at 4 a.m.[247]

In the two other prisons, Jews were treated a similar way. Stefania Cang-Schutzman saw how the Jews in the Łąckiego Street prison were beaten and otherwise mistreated, how women were undressed, and how pregnant women were beaten in the stomach. The Ukrainians ordered the Jews to give up jewels, money, and all other valuable objects that they possessed.[248] Another survivor from the Łąckiego Street prison remembered that a German officer interrupted the violence of the crowd with the comment: "We are not Bolsheviks." People watching the mistreatment of the Jews from the roofs demanded, however, that the Jews in the prison yard be killed.[249] Alfred Monaster wrote in his testimony that on 1 July, in the prison on Łąckiego Street, beautiful Jewish women were selected, raped, and killed.[250]

Zygmunt Tune and his brother were taken by Ukrainian militiamen from their apartment to the prison on Zamarstynowska Street. Before the entrance, they were beaten by a crowd of angry people, and later in the prison yard by some Nachtigall battalion soldiers. They were forced to give away all valuable objects. A group of Ukrainians then beat them with sticks. Afterwards they were forced to clean the yard with their bare hands. All the time, more and more Jews, in poorer and poorer health, were forced into the yard. At about 2 p.m. some Germans brought a machine-gun in order to shoot the Jews but were prevented by an officer of the Gestapo. At

245 Lewin, *Przeżyłem*, 58–59.
246 AŻIH, 301/2299, Herman Kac, 1. Kac was mistaken in his recollection of the date of the event. He thought it was on 20 July 1941. His narrative suggests that it was 1 July 1941.
247 Lewin, *Przeżyłem*, 59–62.
248 AŻIH, 301/1794, Stefania Cang-Schutzman, 1–2.
249 AŻIH, 229/54, Teka Lwowska, Gold, 4.
250 AŻIH, 302/58, Alfred Monaster, 13–14.

about 8 p.m., the Jews who had survived until then were allowed to leave the yard. A German soldier told them that he could not protect them from the Ukrainians and suggested that they hid in the woods.[251]

Jews were beaten and killed not only in the three prison yards but also on the way there and in many other places in the city. They were forced to clean the streets, exactly as in Vienna in March 1938, and in several places in Poland after September 1939.[252] Company commander Hans Schmidt observed how "Jewish women, on their knees, had to pick splinters of glass from the sidewalk with their [bare] hands."[253] Izydor Ferber saw how Jews in the market square were forced to clean the paving-stones with their handkerchiefs, and how they were beaten severely.[254] Kazimiera Poraj was in the market square when "Ukrainian-speaking German soldiers" forced a group of Jews, among them her mother, to clean the toilets with their own clothes. At the same time, they were beaten mercilessly with cables. A group of Jews had to pick splinters of glass from the streets and put them into two carts, also while being beaten with cables.[255] German officers saw a group of women being mistreated by the

Fig. 17. One of the victims of the Lviv pogrom. Wiener Library.

251 AŻIH, 301/2242, Zygmunt Tune, 1–2. See also AŻIH, 301/54, Rózia Wagner, 3.
252 Interrogation of Irena Feinsilber, 29 June 1960, LN-W, Gerichte Rep. 350, vol. 3, 157.
253 Interrogation of Hans Schmidt, 29 June 1960, LN-W, Gerichte Rep. 350, vol. 2, 211. See also Hryciuk, *Polacy we Lwowie*, 204–5.
254 Yad Vashem Archives (YVA)-O.33/251, Izydor Ferber, 1–3, in Witold Mędykowski, "Pogromy 1941 roku na terytorium byłej okupacji sowieckiej (Bukowina, wschodnie województwa RP, państwa bałtyckie) w relacjach żydowskich," in *Świat nie pożegnany*, ed. Krzysztof Jasiewicz (Warsaw: Instytut Studiów Politycznych, 2004), 783.
255 AŻIH, 302/217, Kazimiera Poraj, 3.

Ukrainian militiamen in the market square.[256] A man was forced to clean horse manure from the street, by putting it in his hat.[257] A group of Jews were made to crawl on hands and knees through the streets.[258] Jews were thrown into the street from the windows of their apartments.[259] In one yard, the German soldier Hermann Teske saw a group of Jews with bloody noses. A pogromist told him that it was customary during pogroms to mark Jews by twisting their noses so hard that they broke. The soldier then witnessed how a pogromist did so.[260] Jacob Gerstenfeld observed from an apartment house window:

> Old people, children and women [in a bomb crater] were forced, under a hail of blows, to wrench out the paving stones with their bare hands, and to move the dirt of the street from one place to another. One woman was tied to a man working nearby and they were forced by blows to run in opposite directions. A teenage boy fainted under blows, and others were called to bury the apparent corpse alive. In this one place, I saw four or five people murdered. About 60 people were involved. Throughout the violence on the street, life went on in its usual routine. The passers-by stopped for a moment or two, some to laugh at the "ridiculous" look of the victims and went calmly on.[261]

The Nachtigall battalion, which was celebrated by the pogromists as the Stepan Bandera battalion, did not play a major role in the pogrom but some members were involved. After marching into Lviv on 30 June 1941, the battalion secured the radio station and the three prisons in which the NKVD left the corpses.[262] One soldier from the battalion declared that "some soldiers [from his battalion] committed excesses" on this day, after they were welcomed with flowers.[263] On the same day, Roman Shukhevych—the Ukrainian commander of the battalion—learned that his brother Iurii had been killed in one of the NKVD prisons. The next day, Iurii's funeral took place.[264]

On 1 July 1941, a number of survivors saw Nachtigall soldiers beating Jews in front of and inside the yard of the prison on Zamarstynowska Street.[265] In Łąckiego Street and in the Brygidki prison on Kazimierzowska Street, Ukrainian-speaking soldiers in Wehrmacht uniforms were seen doing the same.[266] However, there is no absolute certainty that all the Ukrainians in German uniforms who were seen mistreating and killing Jews in the prison yards belonged to the Nachtigall. There were

256 Interrogation of Friedrich Brüggemann and Cornelius von Hovora, LN-W, Gerichte Rep. 350, vol. 2, 85, 216.

257 AŻIH, 301/3510, Felicja Heller, 1.

258 YVA-O.33/251, Izydor Ferber, 1–3, in Mędykowski, Pogromy 1941, 783.

259 Interrogation of Friedrich Brüggemann, LN-W, Gerichte Rep. 350, vol. 2, 85.

260 Interrogation of Hermann Teske, LN-W, Gerichte Rep. 350, vol. 2, 4.

261 Jacob Gerstenfeld-Maltiel, *My Private War: One Man's Struggle to Survive the Soviets and the Nazis* (London: Mitchell, 1993), 54.

262 Heer, Einübung in den Holocaust, 419.

263 Autobiographies of well-known OUN members, TsDAVOV f. 3833, op. 1, spr. 57, 16.

264 Interrogation of Friedrich Midellhauve, Ivan Hryn'okh, Otto Rogenbuck, Theodor Oberländer, LN-W, Gerichte Rep. 350, vol. 2, 14, 22, 77, 223.

265 For the testimonies identifying *Nachtigall*, see AŻIH, 301/2242, Zygmunt Tune, 1; Lewin, *Przeżyłem*, 61.

266 For Łąckiego Street, see Interrogation of Abraham Goldberg, 28 June 1960, LN-W, Gerichte Rep. 350, vol. 3, 139. For Brygidki, see Interrogation of Maurycy Reiss, 30 June 1960, LN-W, Gerichte Rep. 350, vol. 3, 169; Interrogation of Eliyahu Jones, 28 June 1960, LN-W, Gerichte Rep. 350, vol. 3, 150.

Ukrainians in German uniforms from other units in Lviv at that time, and also Ukrainian interpreters with the Wehrmacht, who were hostile to Jews and Poles, just like the Nachtigall soldiers.[267] On the way from Lviv to Vinnytsia, the Nachtigall battalion, according to the soldier Viktor Khar'kiv ("Khmara"), "shot all the Jews he met in two villages."[268]

In 1960, a criminal investigation against the officer of the battalion, Theodor Oberländer, took place in the German Federal Republic. During the investigation, Oberländer confirmed that he saw soldiers from the Nachtigall battalion in front of a prison, who "encouraged the population to display the corpses outside." He also testified that the Nachtigall soldiers from one company had a day off duty, but he did not mention that the soldiers mistreated and killed Jews.[269] Other German officers of the Nachtigall battalion testified similarly to Oberländer.[270] After a careful investigation of the pogrom and the participation of the Nachtigall battalion in this atrocity, the German state prosecutor (*Oberstaatsanwalt*) came to the conclusion that soldiers from the second company of the battalion "in all probability" participated in the pogrom and were "guilty of the murder of numerous Jews."[271] The prosecutor, however, closed the proceedings against Oberländer, because he did not find any evidence that Oberländer issued an order to the Nachtigall soldiers to kill Jews. Nor did the prosecutor initiate any proceeding against Nachtigall veterans, because he was not able to identify exactly which soldiers committed crimes.[272]

Hryn'okh, OUN-B member and chaplain of the Nachtigall battalion, was also interrogated during the same investigation against Oberländer. Like many other nationalists, he not only denied the involvement of the battalion in anti-Jewish violence but also stated that he did not notice that a pogrom took place in Lviv at all. As to whether there were anti-Jewish riots in Lviv, Hryn'okh answered as follows: "I did not see anything like this, although during my stay in Lviv, I repeatedly walked and drove through the streets. I can also state with all certainty that nothing was reported to me." After he heard the testimonies of other witnesses who described the pogrom, he stated: "I cannot exclude that something like this happened. I myself, however, as I have already said, did not see anything and did not hear anything."[273]

Wilek Markiewicz watched from a window how some pogromists in Franciszek Smołka (Hryhorenko) Square competed to find more and more sophisticated tortures. He also noticed young Ukrainian peasant women who were more brutal than the men. One of the men forced a Jew to carry him on his shoulders, while beating him on the head with a cudgel, until the victim fell on the ground. He heard a woman scream: "People, let me go please. I haven't done anything bad to anybody." A number of male voices countered: "Don't listen to her! Kill her immediately!"[274]

267 "Abschrift aus dem Bericht der Gruppe GFP 711, Juli 1941," BA-MA, RW 2/148, 379.

268 Autobiographies of well-known OUN members, TsDAVOV f. 3833, op. 1, spr. 57, 17; Bruder, *"Den Ukrainischen Staat*, 150. This soldier was Viktor Khar'kiv "Khmara," see Patryliak, *Viis'kova*, 361–62.

269 Interrogation of Theodor Oberländer, LN-W, Gerichte Rep. 350, vol. 2, 223.

270 See for example Interrogation of Friedrich Wilhelm Heinz, LN-W, Gerichte Rep. 350, vol. 2, 192.

271 "Der Oberstaatsanwalt," LN-W, Gerichte Rep. 350, vol. 5, 42; "Der leitende Oberstaatsanwalt," LN-W, Gerichte Rep. 350, vol. 14, 181–82. The second company of the *Nachtigall* received the order to secure the prisons. Cf. "Der Oberstaatsanwalt," LN-W, Gerichte Rep. 350, vol. 5, 39–40.

272 "Der leitende Oberstaatsanwalt," LN-W, Gerichte Rep. 350, vol. 14, 181–82.

273 Interrogation of Ivan Hryn'okh, LN-W, Gerichte Rep. 350, vol. 2, 23.

274 AŻIH, 301/1737, Wilek Markiewicz, 2.

The pogromists also enjoyed making Jews perform "Bolshevik" rituals. Some were made to walk, singing Russian marching songs, and shouting praise to Stalin.[275] A crowd surrounded a group of 200 to 300 young Jewish men and women who, with raised hands, were forced to sing "the Russian communist song 'My Moscow.'"[276] Near the citadel, Ukrainians escorted about a hundred men, their hands in the air, who were made to shout, "We want Stalin!" According to the survivor Kazimiera Poraj, all of them were killed.[277]

The films and photographs made by German soldiers during the pogrom contain very much the same information as the testimonies of the survivors. They show that women were kicked and were beaten in the face and elsewhere with sticks and tools. They were pulled by the hair and tossed from one pogromist to another. Many of the women were stripped naked and exposed to the mob, which made fun of them and mistreated them. Some were chased through the streets.[278] What the films do not show—but which we know from testimonies of survivors—is that women were raped, and pregnant women were hit and kicked in the stomach.[279]

As already mentioned, the most violent day of the pogrom was 1 July 1941 but the pogrom continued in many parts of the city on 2 July and lasted until the evening of that day. According to Monaster, the pogrom began in the Jewish quarter and spread the next day to other parts of the city.[280] On 2 July, an unknown number of Jews were assembled by the militiamen and members of the Einsatzkommandos in a sports field on Pełczyńska (Dmytra Vitovs'koho) Street. Of the assembled Jews, 2,500–3,000 were shot in the forests around Lviv by Einsatzkommandos 5 and 6 of Einsatzgruppe C, under the leadership of Otto Rasch. Felix Landau, member of an Einsatzkommando, wrote in his diary that the first Jews were shot on 2 July. On 3 July he wrote that "500 Jews came to be shot. 800 people were killed here in Lviv."[281]

On 3 July 1941, Lejb Wieliczkier and his brother and father were taken from their apartment by Ukrainian militiamen, "to work." They were led to the militia building. A group of Jews were already standing before the building, when the family arrived. The militiamen selected young Jews, took them to the basement, and beat them there with iron bars. Some of them did not stand up again. The rest were taken to the sports field on Pełczyńska Street. They were beaten and otherwise mistreated by the militiamen on the way. In front of the sports field, the Germans selected skilled craftsmen from among the Jews and sent them home. The rest were to enter the

275 Musiał, *Konterrevolutionäre Elemente,* 177.

276 Alizia Rachel Hadar, *The Princess Elnasari* (Heinemann: London, 1963), 16.

277 AŻIH, 302/217, Kazimiera Poraj, 6.

278 The movies that show the violent scenes of the pogrom are Deutsche Wochenschau—No. 566/29, 10.07.1941 and USHMM Film Archive, tape 402, RG-60.0441. I am grateful to John-Paul Himka for showing me these movies. The collection of the photographs is in the possession of the Wiener Library. Some of them were published in Ivan Khymka (Himka), "Dostovirnist' svidchennia," 53–60. See also the Interrogation of Horst Haimer Sternberger, LN-W, Gerichte Rep. 350, vol. 2, 123; Interrogation of Irena Feinsilber, 29 June 1960, LN-W, Gerichte Rep. 350, vol. 3, 158.

279 For rapes, see AŻIH, 302/58, Alfred Monaster, 13–14. Cang-Schutzman's sister, five months pregnant, was kicked in the stomach and lost the child. Cf. AŻIH, 301/1794, Stefania Cang-Schutzman, 2. Another woman, six months pregnant, died after mistreatment. Cf. Interrogation of Irena Feinsilber, 29 June 1960, LN-W, Gerichte Rep. 350, vol. 3, 158.

280 AŻIH, 302/58, Alfred Monaster, 14–15.

281 For Felix Landau, see Felix Landau's diary, LN-W, Gerichte Rep. 350, vol. 12, 29–30. See also Pohl, *Nationalsozialistische,* 68–69; Heer, Einübung in den Holocaust, 424–25; Sandkühler, *"Endlösung" in Galizien,* 117–18.

sports field, where they remained for two days without food and drink. During these two days, the Germans and Ukrainian militiamen frequently tortured, beat, and generally mistreated them. Lejb and his father watched as Jews were repeatedly loaded on trucks. Together with some other Jews, however, father and son were released two days later.[282]

On 4 July 1941 Simon Wiesenthal was one of about forty Jews who were arrested, taken to a prison, ordered to stand in a row with their faces against the wall, and waited to be executed. Unlike many others however, he did not die. Shortly before Wiesenthal was to have been shot, a superior ordered the executioner to leave off work for the day (*Schluß für heute. Feierabend!*). Imprisoned overnight and awaiting execution the next day, Wiesenthal was rescued by a Ukrainian militiaman who knew him from before the war.[283] On 7 July 1941, German soldiers seized Eliyahu Yones, together with other Jews in hiding, and ordered them to spread lime on the earth in one of the yards of the Brygidki prison. On arrival, Yones was overwhelmed by the extreme stench of decomposing corpses. He noticed that the ground under his feet was as soft as gum, had cracks five centimeters (two inches) wide, and could not absorb the number of corpses that were buried in the yard.[284]

After the pogrom, the Jews in Lviv had no rights and were *vogelfrei*. Their apartments were frequently looted while they were still living there. They were allowed to go into the streets to buy food and other products, only two days a week.[285] According to Henryk Szyper this rule was introduced by Iurii Polians'kyi, who was appointed mayor of Lviv by the Stets'ko government. German and Ukrainian police regularly arrested Jews in their apartments or in the streets and took them to perform various public works. Although the organized violence ceased in the evening of 2 June, Jews were further mistreated and killed on numerous occasions.[286]

The number of victims of the first pogrom, from 30 June to 2 July 1941, is hard to estimate. The Judenrat estimated that 2,000 Jews were killed during the first days of occupation in Lviv.[287] A German security report from 16 July said that "police captured and shot 7,000 Jews."[288] Historians Dieter Pohl and Eliyahu Yones, who studied the pogrom, came to the conclusion that 4,000 Jews lost their lives,[289] while Christoph Mick, another historian who investigated this event, concluded that 7,000 to 8,000 Jews were killed.[290]

A reconstruction of the course of the pogrom shows that it was a well-organized action. The Ukrainian militia established by the OUN-B collaborated closely with German formations, which included units of the Sicherheitspolizei and the Sicherheitsdienst (SD), and the Einsatzkommandos of Einsatzgruppe C. The Germans must

282 AŻIH, 302/26, Lejb Wieliczkier, 8–12; 301/1864, Salomon Goldman, 1–5; AŻIH, 301/230, Jakub Dentel, 2. Dentel misdated the events in his 1945 written testimony.

283 Maria Sporrerand Herbert Steiner, eds., *Simon Wiesenthal: Ein unbequemer Zeitgenosse* (Vienna: Orac, 1992), 34; ShoahFoundation, 36104 Simon Wiesenthal, 141.

284 Yones, *Die Straße nach Lemberg*, 24–25.

285 Hryciuk, *Polacy we Lwowie*, 205.

286 AŻIH, 301/4654, Henryk Szyper, 12–3; AŻIH, 302/26, Lejb Wieliczkier, 13–21; Yones, *Smoke in the Sand*, 81–84; AŻIH, 301/230, Jakub Dentel, 2.

287 Gerstenfeld-Maltiel, *My Private War*, 54.

288 Yones, *Smoke in the Sand*, 83.

289 Pohl, *Nationalsozialistische*, 61; Yones, *Smoke in the Sand*, 81.

290 Mick, *Kriegserfahrungen*, 473.

have coordinated the pogrom with the OUN-B, at the latest in the evening of 30 June 1941, shortly after they realized how popular and powerful the OUN-B in Lviv was and how they could manipulate the rage of the locals by means of the corpses left by the NKVD. Although the German and Ukrainian perpetrators did not leave any written documents concerning such preparations, other sources suggest otherwise. For example, according to one of the witnesses of the pogrom, a Ukrainian militiaman warned a Jewish woman, with whom he was in love, as to the danger. He did so on 1 July at 5 a.m., that is to say, a few hours before the main pogrom started.[291]

The behavior of individual German soldiers varied. Some of them filmed the pogrom. One reason for doing so was to place the blame for the violence on the local population.[292] Some Wehrmacht officers showed remorse. One gave a loaf of bread to a Jew.[293] Other German soldiers, humiliated, tortured, shot, or otherwise mistreated Jews, or explained to them that they were responsible for the pogrom.[294] Eliyahu Yones, who was forced to work in the Brygidki prison, commented on one German officer:

> After the action [carrying out the corpses from the cells] a German officer came to us, took off his gas mask [which he carried because of the stench of the corpses] and delivered a speech to us, in which he said that, because of us, the Jews, "the whole world is bleeding," that we instigated this war and because of us thousands of victims would fall in the battlefields. "Look what you did!" He shouted and pointed to the huge mass grave in the prison yard. We stood apathetically, we didn't hear his words, and did not understand what he wanted from us.[295]

Another important group of perpetrators in the Lviv pogrom was the crowd. It consisted mainly of Ukrainians but also included Poles. Ukrainians were a minority in Lviv but, unlike Poles, they were not threatened by the OUN-B and were encouraged by Ukrainian propaganda to support the process of establishing the state and to take revenge on the Jews. Some Ukrainian pogromists came to Lviv from the villages and towns around the city. In addition to ideology, they were motivated by the opportunity to steal Jewish property, which was permitted during the pogrom.[296] Many young Ukrainians, students in particular, participated in the pogrom. Among the pogromists, Emanuel Brand recognized a Ukrainian student with whom he had studied at the Institute of Pedagogy in Lviv.[297] Dmytro Honta, a veteran of the First World War who wanted to join the OUN-B militia in Lviv, mentioned in his memoir that students volunteered for it.[298]

Poles also participated in the pogrom and were not just passive bystanders. However, they participated to a lesser extent than Ukrainians, although they outnumbered the Ukrainians in Lviv. Like the Ukrainians, the Poles found bodies of their

291 AŻIH, 302/58, Alfred Monaster, 9.
292 Szarota, *U progu Zagłady*, 31–32.
293 Musiał, *Kontrrevolutionäre Elemente*, 244.
294 Yones, *Die Straße nach Lemberg*, 20–21; Lewin, *Przeżyłem*, 58–61; AŻIH, 301/1737, Markiewicz Wilek, 2.
295 Yones, *Die Straße nach Lemberg*, 20–21.
296 See for example AŻIH, 301/770, Markus Auschheim, 1. Also the testimony of Salomon Hirschberg for the pogrom in Ternopil' AŻIH 301/3774, Salomon Hirschberg, 1.
297 Interrogation of Emanuel Brand, LN-W, Gerichte Rep. 350, vol. 3, 15.
298 Honta, Drukarstvo Zakhidnoï Ukraïny, 13–14.

relatives amongst the NKVD's victims. Jews in Lviv noticed Poles among the pogromists and perceived them as dangerous, although not as dangerous as Ukrainians.[299] Maksymilian Boruchowicz remembered that Ukrainians were aggressive and that Poles were very distanced from Jews.[300] At one place in Lviv, Alizia Rachel Hader noticed that the mob mistreating Jews "seemed to be composed mainly of Ukrainians, but ... included some Poles."[301] Kost' Pan'kivs'kyi and Jozef Szrager also noticed Poles among the pogromists.[302] Ievhen Nakonechnyi remembered that some Poles donned yellow-and-blue armbands, but he did not remember Ukrainians participating in the pogrom, and he claimed that linking the OUN-B to the pogroms was anti-Ukrainian propaganda.[303] Jan Rogowski, a Polish high school teacher, remembered a Pole laughing about Jews who were beaten by Ukrainian militiamen.[304] In contrast to the pogrom of 1918 in Lviv, and the pogroms in the summer of 1941 in north-eastern Poland, Poles did not play a major role in the Lviv pogrom of 1941, because they were afraid of the Ukrainian militiamen and OUN-B activists. They were also less favored by the Germans than Ukrainians were.[305] During the night of 3–4 July 1941 in Lviv, a German security force, composed of members of the SD, SS, and the Einsatzkommando 4a, shot twenty-five Polish professors and seventeen members of their families.[306] The Germans obtained the names and addresses of the professors from the OUN-B. Mykola Lebed' was in charge of this operation.[307]

Because the pogrom in Lviv took place at the same time as the proclamation of the Ukrainian state, the city was full of yellow-and-blue and swastika flags, and posters blaming the Jews for the murder of the prisoners, or celebrating Stepan Bandera and Adolf Hitler with slogans such as "Long Live Stepan Bandera, Long Live Adolf Hitler." The "Great German Army," the OUN, and the war against "Jewish communists" were also celebrated on posters, under which fell the bodies of murdered Jews. One of the posters said:

> To stop this Jewish-communist brigandage, to help Ukraine liberate itself, Adolf Hitler, the great leader of the German people, has ordered the steel-clad columns of the invincible German army to set off into battle and to destroy the bloody lair of the Jewish-Bolshevik commune once and for all. The German soldiers have

299 AŻIH, 301/230, Jakub Dentel, 1.

300 AŻIH, 301/98, Maksymilian Boruchowicz, 3–4.

301 Hadar, *The Princess Elnasari*, 16.

302 Pan'kivs'kyi, *Vid derzhavy*, 35; For Jozef Szrager, see Yones, *Smoke in the Sand*, 80, quoting Jozef Szrager, YVA, o-3/4013.

303 Ievhen Nakonechnyi, *"Shoa" u L'vovi* (Lviv: Piramida, 2006), 112–13, 115.

304 Rogowski, "Lwów pod znakiem swastyki," ZNiO, syg. 16710/II, 56.

305 On Polish pogromists, see also Mick, *Kriegserfahrungen*, 470. On the pogrom in 1918, see William W. Hagen, "The Moral Economy of Ethnic Violence: The Pogrom in Lwów, November 1918," *Geschichte und Gesellschaft* Vol. 31, No. 2 (2005): 203–26. On the pogroms in north-eastern Poland in 1941, see Andrzej Żbikowski, "Pogroms in Northeastern Poland—Spontaneous Reaction and German Instigation," in *Shared History—Divided Memory: Jews and Others in Soviet-Occupied Poland, 1939–1941*, ed. Elazar Barkan, Elizabeth A. Cole, and Kai Struve (Leipzig: Leipziger Universitätsverlag, 2007), 315–54.

306 Zygmunt Albert, ed., *Kaźń profesorów lwowskich lipiec 1941* (Wrocław: Wydawnictwo Uniwersytetu Wrocławskiego, 1989), 48–52; LN-W, Gerichte Rep. 350, vol. 5, 46–47; Draus, *Uniwersytet Jana Kazimierza*, 110, 118. Several hundred Polish students were also arrested and held at the headquarters of the Ukrainian militia and in a prison under German administration. About a hundred of them were murdered. See Hryciuk, *Polacy we Lwowie*, 193.

307 Volchuk, *Spomyny*, 89–90.

come to us as our friends. In our towns and villages Ukrainians are welcoming them as their liberators.[308]

Posters with slogans such as "Ukraine for the Ukrainians" were based on Mikhnovs'kyi's racist nationalism. They informed their readers as to whom the territory in which they lived should belong, and who should and should not be allowed to live in it.[309] Many of the posters and other revolutionary propaganda materials linked the idea of founding a Ukrainian state with killing the Jews. One such poster "To the Ukrainian Nation! [*Ukraïns'kyi Narode!*]" read: "Know! Moscow, Hungarians, Jews [*Zhydova*]—are your enemies, Kill them, do not forget! Your leadership is the leadership of the Ukrainian Nationalists OUN, your leader is Stepan Bandera, your aim is an Independent United Ukrainian State"[310] On 30 June 1941, a group of about ten Jews was forced to print the OUN-B posters and other propaganda material that motivated the crowd to kill the Jews.[311]

Ukrainian nationalists and beautifully dressed Ukrainian patriots, who came to Lviv to welcome the Germans, greeted each other with the official OUN-B salute, calling "Glory to Ukraine!" and responding "Glory to the Heroes!" According to Alfred Monaster, some of them used also the German Nazi salute.[312] Militiamen forced Jews to perform the Ukrainian fascist salute, in order to humiliate them. On 30 June 1941, when J. Berman, a Jewish teacher of German, raised his left instead of his right arm, he was beaten and kicked by a Ukrainian militiaman. Then he had to salute three times with his right arm while calling out "Glory to Ukraine!" Afterwards he was beaten again but was eventually released.[313]

On 2 July 1941, Kurt Lewin decided to go into the streets because he felt that his apartment was not safe. He put on a blue shirt and a yellow tie. This kept the Ukrainian militiamen and Germans at a distance and allowed him to move through the city.[314] A Jewish woman who needed to leave her apartment building stuck to her jacket a small yellow-and-blue ribbon, such as boys were distributing in the streets during the pogrom. This allowed her to go untouched through the city.[315] Szende wrote in his memoirs that he and some other Jews "were protected by the authority of a Greek Catholic priest and the Greek Catholic church in the vicinity."[316]

OUN-B propaganda presented Bandera as the *Providnyk* of the OUN. The survivor Lewin wrote in his memoirs in 1946 that on 2 July 1941 "the city was full of yellow-and-blue banners. ... In the streets, the proclamations of Stepan Bandera were posted—the leader of the Ukrainians was calling for murder and conflagration."[317]

308 "Ukraïntsi! Seliany! Robitnyky!," L'vivs'ka Natsional'na Biblioteka (LNB), 299, 421s, 1, quoted in Carynnyk, Foes of Our Rebirth, 341.

309 Some of the posters are in the collection of TsDAVOV. See TsDAVOV f. 3822, op. 1, spr. 63, 12–13, 112–14. See also Eliyahu Jones, *Żydzi Lwowscy w okresie okucpacji 1939–1945* (Łódź: Oficyna Bibliofilów, 1999), 46.

310 "Ukraïns'kyi Narode!" TsDAVOV f. 3833, op. 1, spr. 1, 181.

311 Honta, Drukarstvo Zakhidnoï Ukraïny, 14–16.

312 AŻIH, 302/58, Alfred Monaster, 2, 6.

313 Before he was forced to salute he was also beaten severely in an "interrogation" by two militiamen. Cf. AŻIH, 229/26, J. Berman, 4.

314 Lewin, *Przeżyłem*, 64–65.

315 AŻIH, 302/58, Alfred Monaster, 21–22.

316 Szende, *Der letzte Jude*, 180.

317 Lewin, *Przeżyłem*, 64–65.

Jan Rogowski, a teacher at a grammar school in Lviv, also saw the yellow-and-blue flags hanging together with swastika flags on the city hall, and posters with the slogans that appeared in "Struggle and Activities."[318] In his memoirs, Rogowski wrote that "Bandera was supposed to be the Ukrainian leader [*ukraiński Führer*] who wanted to style himself on Hitler."[319] The OUN member Roman Volchuk remembered "proclamations, which ended with 'Long Live Stepan Bandera and Adolf Hitler,' posted around the city."[320]

Szyper noticed that, after German troops came to Lviv, German and Ukrainian flags were hung out everywhere, and the Ukrainians expected that a Ukrainian "state of a fascist kind" would be established. He also heard a speech by the mayor of Lviv, Polians'kyi, in which the speaker expressed loyalty to Hitler.[321] Writing in December 1941, an anonymous witness had noticed the yellow-and-blue flags next to the swastikas, overcrowded Greek Catholic churches, and "everywhere the announcements with the signature of the leader of the Ukrainian Nationalists Bandera: 'Ukraine for the Ukrainians.'"[322] Yones noticed the slogan "Long live Adolf Hitler and Stepan Bandera. Death to the Jews and communists."[323] In his memoirs, he described how a Ukrainian militiaman with a yellow-and-blue armlet came to examine his passport when he wandered near the OUN posters. After the militiaman realized that Yones was a Jew, he hit him with his fist so solidly in the face that Yones needed about an hour before he could stand up.[324]

After the proclamation of statehood and at the time of the most violent moments of the pogrom, Stets'ko, leader of the new Ukrainian government, was writing letters in German, the lingua franca of the "New Europe," to leaders of other European fascist states. He informed the *Poglavnik* Pavelić that, "as a result of a centuries-long struggle of the Ukrainian people for their sovereignty, the Ukrainian state was proclaimed in Lviv on 30 June 1941." He stated his firm belief that "both revolutionary nations [Ukrainian and Croatian], hardened in battle, will guarantee the establishment of healthy circumstances in the Europe of the new order." A similar aspiration for "creative collaboration" between the Spanish and Ukrainian nations was aired in Stets'ko's letter to the *Caudillo*. Meanwhile Mussolini was informed that the Ukrainian state had been re-established in the territories "liberated from Muscovite-Jewish occupation ... according to the will of the Ukrainian people that finds its expression in the Organization of Ukrainian Nationalists under the leadership of Stepan Bandera." Stets'ko also sent the *Duce* his warm greetings, wished a speedy victory to his brave nation, and expressed his conviction that Ukraine would be part of the "new fascist order that must replace the Versailles system."[325]

318 "Borot'ba i diial'nist' OUN pidchas viiny," TsDAVOV f. 3833, op. 2, spr. 1, 77–80.

319 Rogowski, "Lwów pod znakiem swastyki," ZNiO, syg. 16710/II, 10.

320 Volchuk, *Spomyny*, 90.

321 AŻIH, 301/4654, Henryk Szyper, 6–7. For Polians'kyi, see Andrzej Żbikowski ed., *Archiwum Ringelbluma: Relacje z Kresów*, (Warsaw: ANTA, 2000), 3:507.

322 An anonymous report of a refugee from Warsaw about the murder of Jews in Lviv, 8 December 1941, Żbikowski, *Archiwum*, 3:721.

323 "Der Oberstaatsanwalt," Staatsanwaltschaft Bonn, LN-W, Rep 350. vol. 5, 15.

324 Yones, *Die Straße nach Lemberg*, 18–19.

325 Letter to the Führer [sic] of Fascist Italy Benito Mussolini in Rome, 3 July 1941, Letter to General Francisco Franco, 3 July 1941, Letter to the Poglavnik of the Independent Croatian State Dr. Ante

In a letter to Hitler, Stets'ko offered his congratulations. "In the name of the Ukrainian people and its government" he expressed the desire that the German leader would "crown the struggle with an eternal triumph." The premier of the Ukrainian state also wrote that the victories of the German army would allow Hitler to expand the "New Europe" to its eastern parts. "In this way you [Hitler] have allowed the Ukrainian people, as one of the fully entitled and free members of the European family of peoples, in its sovereign Ukrainian state, to play an active part in the grand plan."[326] Besides these official letters, the self-proclaimed premier planned to send representatives of the OUN-B government to Slovakia, Romania, Japan, Croatia, Germany, and probably other member states of the "New Europe."[327]

In sending the letters to the leaders of European fascist states, Stets'ko behaved similar to his Croatian counterpart, Kvaternik, who proclaimed the NDH on 10 April 1941. Shortly after the proclamation, Kvaternik sent a letter to Hitler, in which he thanked the *Führer* "in the name of the Croatian people, for the protection the German army has given the Croat national rebellion, and [to] request your recognition of the Independent State of Croatia by the Greater German Reich." He finished the letter with "Long live the Führer of the German people!"[328]

The government that Stets'ko was trying to announce in his letters was called the Ukrainian State Administration (*Ukraïns'ke Derzhavne Pravlinnia*).[329] It was not comprised solely of OUN-B members but also some other Ukrainian politicians. Such cooperation with other parties or political camps was quite typical of some of the fascist movements, which needed to consolidate their power. The National Socialists, for example, cooperated with other political blocs, mainly with conservatives and national conservatives before they established their regime and eliminated other political parties. The head of the Ukrainian State Administration was Stets'ko. His deputy was Lev Rebet. Other well-known OUN members in this government were Mykola Lebed', Roman Shukhevych, Roman Ilnytzkyi, Iaroslav Starukh, Volodymyr Horbovyi, and Ivan Klymiv.[330] A few days after its formation, the Ukrainian State Administration was banned by the Germans and ceased to function, but it established a Council of Elders (*Rada Sen'ioriv)* to carry on as a body that would represent the Ukrainians, under the control of the OUN-B. The OUN-B wanted to make Dmytro Dontsov the leader of the Council of Elders, but the position finally went to Kost' Levyts'kyi and Andrei Sheptyts'kyi. The Ukrainian State Administration and the Council of Elders were to have performed the function of a parliament in the OUN-B state. They expressed a desire to hold their meetings in the impressive building of the University of Lviv, which had been used by the Galician parliament

Pavelić, 3 July 1941, Letter to the Führer and Reichskanzler des Grossdeutschen Reiches Adolf Hitler, TsDAVOV f. 3833, op. 1, spr. 22, 1–3, 8–9.

326 TsDAVOV f. 3833, op. 3, spr. 7, 26. The letter arrived on 27 July 1941. Cf. BAK, R 43 II/1500, E292958.

327 List of deputies of the Ukrainian government abroad, TsDAVOV f. 3833, op. 1, spr. 10, 4.

328 *Zločini Nezavisne Države Hrvatske, 1941–45* (Belgrade: Vojnoistorijski institut, 1993), document 4 (the telegram). I am grateful to Per Rudling and Tomislac Dulić for information about the letter from Kvaternik to Hitler.

329 "Postanova ch." 1 signed by Iaroslav Stets'ko, TsDAVOV f. 3833, op. 1, spr. 6, 1.

330 "Sklad Ukraïns'koho Derzhavnoho Pravlinnia," TsDAVOV f. 3833, op. 1, spr. 10, 1–2.

until 1918.[331] Members of the Council of Elders swore "to be faithful till death, to the great Idea." The text of the oath finished with "Glory to the Unified Independent Ukraine! Glory to the OUN and its Providnyk Stepan Bandera!"[332]

From fragments of the minutes of sessions of either the government or the Council of Elders or the State Administration, we know that one of these institutions was discussing how to solve the "Jewish problem" in Ukraine.[333] The participants in the discussion did not specify exactly how this "annihilation action" was to be conducted. One participant, the writer Oleksa Hai-Holovko, claimed that the ethnic question in Ukraine was to be solved in the "German way." He meant that the Jews "have to be treated very harshly" and that we "must finish them off" because "Jews are very insolent." The OUN-B member Lenkavs'kyi stated that "regarding the Jews, we will adopt any methods that lead to their destruction." Furthermore, the participants very enthusiastically discussed a kind of Ukrainian Generalplan Ost. All non-Ukrainians living in Ukraine were to be evacuated or annihilated, and all Ukrainians living outside "ethnic Ukrainian territory" were to be resettled in "ethnic Ukrainian territory," or the territories in which these Ukrainians lived were to be incorporated into the Ukrainian state. For example, all the Ukrainians from Moscow and Leningrad were to be resettled in Ukraine.[334]

The absence of Bandera, and later of Stets'ko, who was placed under *Ehrenhaft* (honorable captivity) on 9 July 1941, did not interrupt the "Ukrainian National Revolution," which had been going on for several weeks.[335] Probably to improve German-Ukrainian relations, which had deteriorated after the tensions surrounding the proclamation of the state on 30 June, Ukrainians were allowed to organize a second huge pogrom in Lviv. This pogrom started on 25 July and lasted until 28 July. It was called the "Petliura days" and was organized to avenge the acquittal of Schwartzbard by the French court who had killed Petliura on 25 May 1926.[336]

During the "Petliura days," as in the first pogrom, the Ukrainian militiamen seized Jews in streets or in their apartments and brought them to the prison on Łąckiego Street and the Gestapo building on Pełczyńska Street. There the Jews were humiliated, beaten, and killed. Peasants from local villages came to Lviv and were seen humiliating, beating, raping, killing, and robbing Jews.[337] Gerstenfeld noticed

331 "Ereignismeldungen UdSSR, Nr. 12, 04.07.1941," BAB R58/214, 69. On the Council of Elders, see also "Zvit, 22.7.1941," TsDAVOV f. 3833, op. 1, spr. 15, 3; Pan'kivs'kyi, *Vid derzhavy*, 41; Interrogation of Mykhailo Stepaniak, GARF f. R-9478, op. 1, del. 136, 36–38.

332 "Prysiaha Ukraïns'koï Rady Sen'ioriv u L'vovi adresovana Stepanovi Banderi, 22.7.1941," HDA SBU, spr. 10876, vol. 4, 40–41, in *Stepan Bandera*, ed. Serhiichuk, 1:148–50.

333 The archivists called the document "Copy of the minutes of the meeting of the Administration of Ukraine." Cf. TsDAVOV f. 3833, op. 1, spr. 9, 1–12. Marco Carynnyk believes it was the Council of Elders. Cf. Carynnyk, Foes of Our Rebirth, 338. The date of the document confirms the assumption that it may have been the Council of Elders.

334 Copy of the minutes of the meeting of the Ukrainian State Administration, TsDAVOV f. 3833, op. 1, spr. 9, 1–4.

334 Ibid., 1. For a very similar statement about dealing with the "non-Ukrainians" in "Ukraine," see "Borot'ba i diial'nist' OUN pidchas viiny," TsDAVOV f. 3833, op. 1, spr. 69, 36.

335 "Komunikat," TsDAVOV f. 3833, op. 1, spr. 6, 2.

336 Petliura's personal responsibility for the pogroms committed by the troops of which he was in charge seems to be limited. Cf. Abramson, *A Prayer for*, 139.

337 AŻIH, 301/230, Jakub Dentel, 2.; AŻIH, 301/1864, Salomon Goldman, 5; AŻIH, 301/4654, Henryk Szyper, 14; AŻIH, 301/1584, Izak Weiser, 1; AŻIH, 302/26, Lejb Wieliczkier, 21; AŻIH, 301/4944, Jan

that "crowds in the streets" during the Petliura days "were full of numbers of youths in embroidered Ukrainian shirts."[338] Wehrmacht soldiers participated "in the most disgusting way" in this pogrom, which outraged their superior, General Karl von Roques.[339] The number of victims of the "Petliura days" is hard to estimate. Yones estimated it at 1,500.[340]

Pogroms and Nationalist Celebrations in Other Western Ukrainian Localities

The greatest pogrom in western Ukraine was staged in Lviv, but several thousand Jews were killed in pogroms in many other places. Andrzej Żbikowski identified thirty-five pogroms in western Ukraine; Aharon Weiss, fifty-eight; Jeffrey Kopfstein, 124, and Kai Struve up to 140.[341] Dieter Pohl estimated that the number of victims of all pogroms ranged between 13,000 and 35,000.[342] Alexander Kruglov estimated the number of Jewish victims of shootings and pogroms in July 1941 in western Ukraine, at between 38,000 and 39,000.[343]

Two other major pogroms in eastern Galicia occurred in Ternopil' and Zolochiv (Złoczów). In both cases Ukrainian militias cooperated with German troops. On 2 July 1941 in Zolochiv, Jews were beaten, murdered, and otherwise mistreated by militiamen and other pogromists, who asked the Germans for permission to take revenge. On 3 July, male Jews were forced by the Ukrainian militia and the German troops to exhume corpses of the NKVD victims from a mass grave in the yard of the castle in Zolochiv. When they had finished, they were shot by the Germans. More and more Jews were then brought to this grave and shot, so that the grave from which the Jews were forced to remove the NKVD victims was filled with bodies of murdered Jews. Altogether, 3,000 Jews were killed in Zolochiv by the Germans and local people, inspired by the OUN-B. As in Lviv, the OUN-B put up posters and distributed leaflets in which it welcomed the Germans as allies and liberators.[344]

Badian, 1–6; AŻIH, 301/1117, Leonard Zimmerman, 1; AŻIH, 301/1801, Henryk Baldinger, 1–4; AŻIH, 301/2278, Lucyna Halbersberg, 1; AŻIH, 301/18, Ryszard Rydner, 1.

338 Gerstenfeld-Maltiel, *My Private War*, 60.

339 "Kriegs-Erinnerungen des General der Infanterie Karl von Roques aus der ersten Zeit des Ostfeldzuges 1941, I. Teil" BA-MA, N 152/10, 10.

340 Jones, *Żydzi Lwowscy*, 53. Jacob Gerstenfeld-Maltiel wrote that, according to Judenrat documents, 18,000 to 20,000 Jews disappeared by the end of the "Petliura days." Cf. Gerstenfeld-Maltiel, *My Private War*, 61. Ryszard Rydner mentioned 15,000 victims. See AŻIH, 301/18, Ryszard Rydner, 1.

341 Andzej Żbikowski, "Lokalne pogromy Żydów w czerwcu i lipcu 1941 r. na wschodnich rubieżach II Rzeczypospolitej," *Biuletyn Żydowskiego Instytutu Historycznego* Vol. 162–163, No. 2–3 (1992): 12–13; Aharon Weiss, "The Holocaust and the Ukrainian Victims," in *A Mosaic of Victims. Non-Jews Persecuted and Murdered by the Nazis*, ed. Michael Berenbaum (New York: New York University Press, 1990), 110; Jeffrey Kopstein, Draft paper prepared for the Experts Roundtable on the Second World War in Ukraine, organized by the Ukrainian Jewish Encounter Initiative in partnership with the Konrad-Adenauer-Stiftung, held in Potsdam (Cecilienhof) and Berlin, June 27–30, 2011, 1; Kai Struve, "Rites of Violence? The Pogroms of Summer 1941," *Polin. Studies in Polish Jewry* 24 (2012): 268.

342 Dieter Pohl, "Anti-Jewish Pogroms in Western Ukraine," in *Shared History*, ed. Barkan, 306. For pogroms in Volhynia, see Berkhoff, *Harvest of Despair*, 56–57; Snyder, The Life and Death, 90–93.

343 Alexander Kruglov, "Jewish Losses in Ukraine, 1941–1944," in *Shoah in Ukraine*, ed. Brandon, 274.

344 Shlomo Wolkowicz, *Das Grab bei Zloczow: Geschichte meines Überlebens: Galizien 1939–1945* (Berlin: Wichern-Verlag, 1996), 41–52; Bernd Boll, "Zloczow, Juli 1941: Die Wehrmacht und der Beginn des Holocaust in Galizien," *Zeitschrift für Geschichtswissenschaft* Vol. 50 (2002): 905–14;

German troops arrived in Ternopil' on 2 July 1941. The following day, corpses of the NKVD's victims were found in the prison, and several Jews were beaten, robbed, and generally mistreated. The actual pogrom started on the morning of 4 July and continued until 6 July.[345] In Ternopil' the main perpetrators were the Waffen-SS Wiking division together with local OUN-B activists, in particular militiamen, assisted by numerous other pogromists from the town and nearby villages. One survivor of this pogrom mentioned that a Ukrainian woman let her know that, at a meeting on 3 July, Ukrainians demanded permission from the Germans to take revenge on Jews.[346]

During the pogrom, Ukrainians pointed out Jewish houses to the Germans, from which they seized Jewish men, who were forced to clean cars in the market square, and were then shot in the basements and in the cemetery.[347] Some Waffen-SS soldiers raped Jewish women.[348] Others forced Jews to carry out corpses from a courthouse and wash them. Afterwards about 1,000 Jews were killed with cudgels and spades, as a soldier informed his parents in Vienna.[349] A survivor, Salomon Hirschberg, stressed the role of the Ukrainian militia with the yellow-and-blue armlets, "recruited from the local elements as well as from adjacent villages" and mentioned that Ukrainians also used local radio to propagate violence.[350] According to the records of a Ukrainian health organization, more than 4,000 Jews were killed in this pogrom.[351] In the cemetery on 7 July, the Ukrainian militiamen shot a group of Jews without the assistance of the SS.[352]

As well as in Lviv, Ternopil' and Zlochiv, smaller pogroms occurred in many other localities. Some of the smaller anti-Jewish massacres seemed to have had a more spontaneous character; others were incited by the OUN-B and the Germans. During these pogroms Jews were killed by peasants or local residents armed with iron bars, sticks, spades, pitchforks, cudgels, scythes, or hammers, and their apartments were afterwards looted, sometimes by their neighbors. In a few places Jews were burned in barns, as in Jedwabne.[353] In many places in which the pogroms took place, the OUN-B had established militias similar to those in Lviv. These militiamen carried out instructions similar to those suggested in "Struggle and Activities" and did not behave differently from their comrades in Lviv. As in Lviv, in many other Galician and Volhynian locations, the pogroms overlapped with the proclamation of statehood. On 3 July 1941 in Ternopil', one day before the pogrom, portraits of Bandera, Hitler, and Konovalets' were exhibited at a meeting where OUN-B members greeted

Marco Carynnyk, "Zolochiv movchyt'," *Krytyka* Vol. 96, No. 10 (2005): 14–17. For the OUN-B posters and leaflets, see "Ereignismeldung UdSSR, 16.07.1941," BAB R58/214, 195.

345 Cf. the testimony of Basar Zwi AŻIH, 301/1038, Basar Zwi, 1. Another survivor, Salomon Hirschberg, mentions ten days. Cf. AŻIH, 301/3774, Salomon Hirschberg, 6.

346 AŻIH, 301/3551, Sara Frydman, 1–2. Salomon Hirschberg also mentions this meeting. Cf. AŻIH, 301/3774, Salomon Hirschberg, 1.

347 AŻIH, 301/3551, Sara Frydman, 2–3.

348 Ibid., 2.

349 Franzl's letter from Ternopil' to his parents in Vienna written on 6 July 1941, BA-MA, RW4/442a.

350 AŻIH, 301/3774, Salomon Hirschberg, 1–2.

351 Salomon Hirschberg mentions the list, see AŻIH, 301/3774, Salomon Hirschberg, 6. Basar Zwi mentions 5,000 killed by shooting during the pogrom. Cf. AŻIH, 301/1038, Basar Zwi, 1.

352 Sandkühler, *"Endlösung" in Galizien*, 120.

353 For burning Jews in barns, see AŻIH, 301/176, Gina Wieser, 2. For Jedwabne, see Gross, *Neighbors*.

the Germans, celebrated the liberation from "Jewish Bolshevism," and proclaimed statehood (Fig. 18).[354]

Fig. 18. Celebrations in Ternopil' on 3 July 1941. On the placards behind the speakers: Stepan Bandera, Adolf Hitler, and Ievhen Konovalets'. Cherednychenko, *Natsionalizm proty natsiï*, 93.

To welcome the Germans and signalize support for the new Ukrainian state, the OUN-B instructed local Ukrainians to erect triumphal arches.[355] During the "Ukrainian National Revolution," triumphal arches of various kinds were indeed erected in numerous villages, towns, and cities. They were decorated with the Ukrainian and German flags and such inscriptions as "Glory to Ukraine—Glory to Bandera!" "Long Live the German Army!" "Long Live the Leader of the German Nation Adolf Hitler!" "Freedom for Ukraine—Death to Moscow!" "Glory to Our Leader [*Providnyk*] Stepan Bandera!" (Figs. 19–20).[356] In Volhynia, the triumphal arches were ubiquitous, and mainly bore the inscriptions "Heil Hitler!" and "Glory to Ukraine!"[357] The OUN-B member Mykola Chartoryis'kyi, who went from the General Government to Ukraine in the third task force, commented on this kind of propaganda: "Everywhere in villages and cities, at the entrance gates, among other slogans hang huge inscriptions: *Glory to Ukraine!—Glory to the Heroes! Long Live the OUN Providnyk Stepan Bandera! Long Live the Independent United Ukrainian State!*"[358]

Michał Sobków remembered that the new administration in Koropets' (Koropec) renamed one street as Bandera Street and another as Senyk Street, and that the

354 For establishing the militia in other localities by the local OUN-B members, see Chartoryis'kyi, *Vid Sianu po Krym*, 48. The picture of a German officer and two men in plain clothes at the podium is printed in Vitalii Cherednychenko, *Natsionalizm proty natsiï* (Kiev: Politvydav Ukraïny, 1970), 93. For the date and the course of this event, see "Rezoliutsiï," TsDAVOV f. 3833, op. 1, spr. 15, 15. For a picture of a Nazi officer and a Ukrainian nationalist making a fascist salute on the platform, see Sabrin, *Alliance for Murder*, 168.

355 "Propaganda Instruction No. 1," TsDAVOV f. 4620, op. 3, spr. 379, 34.

356 "Instruktsiia propahandy ch. 1," TsDAVOV f. 4620, op. 3, spr. 379, 34. For pictures and descriptions of triumphal arches, see Grelka, *Die ukrainische Nationalbewegung*, 256; Testimony of Jerzy Krasowski, KAW, II/737, 25; Cherednychenko, *Natsionalizm*, 93; the cover of Diukov, *Vtorostepennyi vrag*; Testimony of Jerzy Krasowski, KAW, II/737, 25.

357 "Volynshchyna i Rivenshchyna," TsDAVOV f. 3833, op. 1, spr. 15, 72.

358 Chartoryis'kyi, *Vid Sianu po Krym*, 42. Emphasis in the original.

Ukrainian militiamen greeted one another with the fascist salute and the words, "Glory to Ukraine!" to which the response was: "Glory to the Heroes!" He also noticed that, after some time, ordinary Ukrainians ceased greeting one another with the traditional "Glory to Jesus Christ" (*Slava Isusu Khrystu*) and, like the OUN-B revolutionaries, adopted the fascist salute and the OUN-B slogans.[359]

Another important element of the revolution was the solemn welcoming of the German troops. For this purpose, the local population dressed in folk costumes and carried the traditional bread and salt. The OUN-B's mechanical, repetitive, and theatrical re-enactment of the proclamation of the Ukrainian state, in numerous towns and cities, was soon noticed by German troops.[360] The OUN-B also encouraged the Ukrainian population to display Ukrainian and German flags on their houses. It demanded that all communist books and portraits be brought to the main square of the village and burnt. At the same time, the village population was expected to assemble for a propaganda speech. After the burning of portraits of Soviet leaders, the portraits of Stepan Bandera and other nationalist heroes were to be displayed.

Fig. 19. Triumphal arch in Zhovkva. Inscription on the arch: "Heil Hitler!, Glory to Hitler! Glory to Bandera! Long Live the Independent United Ukrainian State. Long live the Vozhd' Stepan Bandera." Courtesy of Marco Carynnyk.

359 Michał Sobków, "Rozdroże narodów. W Koropcu," *Karta. Niezależne Pismo Historyczne* 16 (1995): 79–80.

360 "Ereignismeldungen UdSSR, Berlin, 17.07.1941, Nr. 25," BAB R58/214, 202.

Fig. 20. Triumphal arch with the inscription: "Glory to Ukraine! Glory to Bandera! Es lebe die deutsche Armee! Heil Hitler!"

The graves of OUN activists and German soldiers were to be decorated with flowers. When passing the graves, people were expected to raise their right arm in order to honor the dead heroes with the fascist salute.[361]

The OUN-B instructions were taken seriously and carried out in numerous localities. For example, in the village of Perevoloka, after conducting a pogrom, OUN-B activists organized an event at which they forced "Soviet activists" to burn Soviet books and portraits of Soviet leaders. They also prepared a blacklist, as "Struggle and Activities"—written by Bandera and other OUN-B leaders—instructed them, and they killed about twenty-five people who were on the list.[362] Regional leader Levko Zakhidnyi forbade greeting Jews and shaking hands with them.[363] OUN-B member Stepan Mechnyk noticed that, during the OUN-B revolution, Ukrainians erected mounds for soldiers, with the inscription "Fallen for the Freedom of Ukraine," priests conducted memorial services at these mounds, and OUN-B revolutionaries delivered patriotic speeches.[364]

Some patriotic teachers also agreed with the OUN-B agenda. A group of them addressed a leaflet to their colleagues with the statement:

> We were forced to poison children's minds with Jewish internationalism, love for everything Russian, and contempt for our own country, language, literature, and culture. ... Yet we, the great army of Ukrainian culture, did not even for a minute forget, even in the terrible bondage of serfish Bolshevism, that we are the heirs to Cossack glory, that we are the most resilient people, whose name is the Ukrainians. Even during the fiercest torture imposed on us by the invaders from the Russian-Bolshevik Empire, and the Jews, that Judas tribe the whole world curses,

361 "Instruktsiia propahandy ch. 1," TsDAVOV f. 4620, op. 3, spr. 379, 34.

362 Interrogation of Pavlo Andreevich Luchko, 21 January 1947, USHMM RG-31.018M, reel 31, HDA SB f. 5, spr. 26874, 184, 187.

363 "Nakaz, ch. 3, 1.8.1941," TsDAVOV f. 3833, op. 2, spr. 3, 12.

364 Stepan Mechnyk, *Pochatok nevidomoho: Spohady 1945–1954* (Munich: Ukraïns'ke vydavnytstvo, 1984), 14.

we preserved the purity and transparency of our language, the melodiousness of our famous Ukrainian songs. ... Let us welcome the German army, the most civilized army in the world, which is expelling the Jewish Communist swine from our land. Let us help the Organization of Ukrainian Nationalists under the leadership of Stepan Bandera build a great Independent Ukrainian State.[365]

During the first weeks after the German attack on the Soviet Union, the conduct of Metropolitan Sheptyts'kyi was ambiguous, just as it was in the last part of the war. At the beginning, the head of the Greek Catholic Church was enthusiastic about the "Ukrainian National Revolution" and in particular the attempts of the OUN-B to found a Ukrainian state. For this reason, as already indicated, he supported the OUN-B state in a pastoral letter, but not OUN-B policies toward ethnic minorities.[366] On 1 June 1941, however, when Rabbi Jecheskiel Lewin asked Sheptyts'kyi to appease the pogromists, Sheptyts'kyi offered shelter to Lewin and his family but did not intervene.[367] The Holocaust survivor Edmund Kessler wrote in his diary, which he kept from 1942 to 1944, about Sheptyts'kyi during the pogrom: "The Ukrainian archbishop preaches a sermon in which, instead of calming the excited mood and taming their barbarous instincts, he demagogically incites the mobs, and in the name of their sacred religion, calling upon the population to retaliate against the Jews for their supposed bestial murder of political prisoners, even though these prisoners included some Jews too."[368] According to the OUN-B, Sheptyts'kyi ordered all Greek Catholic priests to decorate their churches with German flags and to obey the German and the new Ukrainian authorities.[369] He was concerned about the conflict within the OUN and, for this reason, advised Mel'nyk to become reconciled with Bandera and Stets'ko.[370] Sheptyts'kyi criticized the OUN for the greeting "Glory to the Heroes!"—"Glory to Ukraine!" because it replaced the religious greeting "Glory to Jesus Christ!"[371] In the aftermath of the "Ukrainian National Revolution," he was, according to the agency of the Polish government-in-exile, disappointed by the OUN-B and called its members "unserious people" and "snot-nosed kids [*smarkachi*]."[372] The Metropolitan rescued and helped to rescue more than a hundred Jews during the Holocaust, hiding them in Greek-Catholic monasteries, churches, and also his

365 "Uchyteli Ukraïntsi!," TsDAHOU f. 57, op. 4, spr. 370, 25, quoted in Carynnyk, Foes of Our Rebirth, 341.

366 Dziuban, ed., *Ukraïns'ke derzhavotvorennia*, 126.

367 Lewin, *Przeżyłem*, 28.

368 Renata Kessler, ed., *The Wartime Diary of Edmund Kessler* (Boston: Academic Studies Press, 2010), 34.

369 "Zvit pro robotu v spravi orhanizatsiï derzhavnoï administratsiï na tereni Zakhidnykh Oblastei Ukraïny," TsDAVOV f. 3833, op. 1, spr. 15, 4.

370 "Lyst Mytr. Andreia Sheptyts'koho do p. Polkovnyka Andryia Mel'nyka," in *Rohatyns'ke slovo*, Rohatyn, 26 July 1941, 3.

371 Zhanna Kovba, ed., *Mytropolyt Andrei Sheptyts'kyi: Dokumenty i materialy 1941–1944* (Kiev: Dukh i Litera, 2003), 38.

372 "Sprawozdanie Sytuacyjne z Ziem Wschodnich za pierwszy kwartał 1943 r.," in *Ziemie Wschodnie: Raporty Biura Wschodniego Delegatury Rządu na Kraj 1943–1944*, ed. Mieczysław Adamczyk, Janusz Gmitruk and Adam Koseski (Warsaw: Muzeum Historii Polskiego Ruchu Ludowego, 2005), 45.

residence.[373] People who were rescued by Sheptyts'kyi remembered him as a very kind and noble man.[374]

The behavior of Greek Catholic priests varied during the revolution. For example, the priest Gavdunyk from Nezvys'ko (Niezwiska) was one of the main organizers of a pogrom on 2 and 3 July 1941, in which Jews from several adjacent villages were killed.[375] A priest in Luka, close to Nezvys'ko, agreed to help a Jewish couple on condition that they would agree to be christened.[376] The priest in Bolekhiv (Bolechów), according to the survivor Matylda Gelerntner, said at a meeting that "Jews are a damned nation, of damned origin, a harmful element, and thus they should be destroyed."[377] In her testimony, Ellen Pressler, another survivor of Bolekhiv, mentioned priests who incited peasants to violence. However, she also remembered a priest who invited the local nationalist leaders to a meeting and tried to convince them to stop the anti-Jewish violence. Because they did not listen to him and continued the pogrom, he removed the Ukrainian flag from his church.[378] In a sermon in Koropets' shortly after the German invasion of the Soviet Union, the Greek Catholic priest Skorokhid condemned the murder and imprisonment of Poles by Ukrainian militiamen. When the service ended, militiamen were waiting for him in front of the church. After a short talk, Skorokhid took the first train and left Koropets'. In his place came another priest who equated Poles with Russians in his sermons and called both peoples the "enemies of the Ukrainian nation."[379]

The report of a OUN-B task force—Iaroslav Stets'ko, Lev Rebet, Iaroslav Starukh, and others—written on 29 July 1941, shows how a particular group of OUN-B activists acted during the "Ukrainian National Revolution" in the town of Iavoriv.[380] Other documents such as the testimonies from Jewish survivors held in the AŻIH allow us to look at the events in Iavoriv in a broader context.[381]

In Iavoriv during the two-week occupation in September 1939, Ukrainian militiamen with yellow-and-blue armlets assisted the German troops, who, in a variety of ways, humiliated, tortured, beat, murdered, and otherwise mistreated the Jews, and destroyed the synagogue.[382] This incident stuck in the minds of the Jews from this provincial town, located close to the German-Soviet border. As the German attack on the Soviet Union began, many Jews suspected what awaited them and decided to escape from the town. This possibly prevented the German troops who had entered

373 For Sheptyts'kyi, see Szymon Redlich, "Moralność i rzeczywistość: Metropolita Andriej Szeptycki i Żydzi w czasach Holokaustu i II wojny światowej," *Zagłada Żydów. Studia i materiały* 4 (2008): 241–59.

374 Lewin, *Przeżyłem*, 27, 118–19.

375 AŻIH 302/105, Markus Willbach, 22–23; AŻIH 301/1434, Izak Plat and Sabina Charasz, 2–3.

376 AŻIH 302/105, Markus Willbach, 24.

377 AŻIH, 301/2145, Matylda Gelerntner, 1.

378 AŻIH, 301/2146, Ellen Pressler, 1–3.

379 Sobków, Rozdroże narodów, 78.

380 "Zvit, ch. 5," TsDAVOV f. 3833, op. 1, spr. 12, 13. For Rebet and Starukh in this group, see Motyka, *Ukraińska partyzantka*, 89.

381 AŻIH 301/1612, Nadel Chaim, 1–2; AŻIH 301/1613, Rachela Scheer, 1; 301/1614, Jakub Sauerbrunn, 1. AŻIH 301/1912, Izrael Manber, 1–3.

382 AŻIH 301/1912, Izrael Manber, 2–3; AŻIH 301/1612, Nadel Chaim, 1–2; AŻIH 301/1614, Jakub Sauerbrunn, 1.

Iavoriv on 25 June 1941, and the local OUN-B activists, from organizing a pogrom.[383] In this sense, Iavoriv was an exception. In general, only a few Jews escaped from western Ukraine to Soviet territory before the coming of the Germans.[384]

The local Ukrainian population of Iavoriv welcomed the German army with flowers.[385] The task force arrived in Iavoriv on 28 June 1941 from Krakovets', where it had established an administration and militia under the "leadership of Stepan Bandera."[386] After the Germans' arrival in Iavoriv, an OUN-B activist first called a meeting of local OUN members and sympathizers, which elected "in the name of the OUN and the Providnyk Stepan Bandera," the head of the militia and the heads of the regional and town administration. All of them had to swear an oath, as provided for in "Struggle and Activities." They then went to the German commandant in the town, and bid welcome to him and the "great German army ... in the name of the OUN, the new administration, and the whole Ukrainian nation." The German commandant authorized the town administration, but added one Pole. Although this irritated the OUN-B activists, they did not protest but decided to deal with the problem later.[387]

At 4 p.m. on 28 June 1941, they organized a meeting of—as the report claims—all citizens of Iavoriv, at which they wanted to familiarize the local Ukrainians with the new authorities and ask them to swear an oath to Stepan Bandera, as "Struggle and Activities" prescribed. But at that moment, the news arrived that the Stepan Bandera battalion, that is the Nachtigall battalion, would soon march into the town. They therefore interrupted the preparations for the meeting and erected a triumphal arch with the inscription "Glory to Ukraine—Glory to Bandera" and waited for the battalion, with flowers in their hands. Because the battalion did not arrive, they started the gathering, for which they had meanwhile decorated a room in the town hall. According to the report, the room was filled with people and flowers. The new officials, who were elected by the OUN-B activists, delivered speeches, which were interrupted by applause. The OUN-B activists endorsed the elected officials in front of the gathered people, who began to venerate Stepan Bandera and Ukraine with loud shouts and sang the national anthem. Afterwards, they "put into motion the whole [administrative] apparatus to get the entire raion going."[388]

The OUN-B task forces proceeded in a similar fashion in many other locations. In some cases they not only organized a militia but also arranged a church service for the new authorities, or organized paramilitary youth organizations named after Stepan Bandera.[389] The German army and Adolf Hitler were celebrated and venerated

383 AŻIH 301/1616, Jonas Beer, Włodzimierz Hochberg, 1; AŻIH 301/1613, Rachela Scheer, 1. Other survivors remembered 26 June as the day when the Germans came to Iavoriv, see AŻIH 301/1912, Izrael Manber, 4. Some of the Jews who left Iavoriv to escape from the Germans came back after a few days.

384 Shmuel Spector estimated that about 12,000 to 13,000 Jews, or only about 5 percent of the Jewish population, escaped from Volhynia. Cf. Spector, *The Holocaust of Volhynian Jews*, 55. Probably even fewer Jews fled from eastern Galicia. See Yehuda Bauer, *The Death of the Shtetl* (New Haven: Yale University Press, 2009), 61.

385 AŻIH 301/1616, Jonas Beer, Włodzimierz Hochberg, 1; AŻIH 301/1912, Izrael Manber, 4.

386 "Zvit, ch. 5," TsDAVOV f. 3833, op. 1, spr. 12, 5, 13.

387 Ibid., 13.

388 Ibid., 13.

389 "Zvit Ostapa Dotsmana," "Druzhe Verhun," TsDAVOV f. 3833, op. 1, spr. 12, 14–15; Interrogation of Vladymyr Lohvynovych, 4 July 1944, HDA SBU f. 13, spr. 372, vol. 1, 3.

by the revolutionary masses in all revolutionary territories. General Karl von Roques observed on 30 June in Dobromyl (Dobromil):

> About 4.00 p.m. I reached my accommodation in Dobromyl. Already on the way there, Ukrainian children threw flowers under our feet. In Dobromyl, a dressed-up crowd was waiting for me in front of our building. When the car stopped, a dozen Ukrainian women in colorful national dresses surrounded me. Everyone gave me a bouquet; in the state building, the mayor and a representative of the national Ukrainian movement delivered a longer speech (both in tolerably good German). I was celebrated as conqueror and liberator from the Bolshevik yoke. ...
>
> Pleasure and excitement was given highest expression the next day, during a meeting of all the inhabitants in front of the town hall. When I came back from a trip to the front, in the oilfields around Drohobych, in the evening shortly after 8 p.m., I saw the gathering. I got out and went to the balcony of the town hall where several officers were already assembled. The crowd of many thousands, dressed up, in the middle all the clergy in robes, next to them all the girls in their traditional costumes with the long pearl necklace encircled several times around their neck and shoulder were a very colorful picture. After several speeches I also had to deliver a speech. A translator translated every sentence into Ukrainian. Every time the name "Adolf Hitler" was mentioned the people became delirious and clapped. During all my trips in these days my car was showered with flowers in all localities.[390]

In Olszanica, the local population welcomed the Germans as liberators and organized church services. Attracted by the religious chants, two German soldiers looked inside a church; the priest interrupted his sermon, expressed thanks in German to the two officers for the liberation, and began to pray in German together with the congregation, for Germany and its army.[391]

In some places, representatives of villages came to the raion center to participate in the proclamation ceremony, as in the town of Radekhiv (Radziechów) in the Lviv *oblast*, where on 13 July 1941 the OUN-B organized a celebration in which 6,000 people took part. The celebration began with a church service, in which representatives of all villages in the Radekhiv raion allegedly participated. After the service, Stets'ko's proclamation was reread in an administrative building. Participants in the meeting hoped that the militia that had already been established would soon grow into a Ukrainian army.[392]

In Zhuravno (Żurawno) a group of thirty young people dressed in festive clothes carried the Ukrainian yellow-and-blue flag and shouted: "Death to the Jews and communists." Later, after the Ukrainians took power and established a militia, "fanatical Ukrainians rounded up dozens of Jews, forced them all into some damp cellars and beat them with great cruelty."[393]

390 "Kriegs-Erinnerungen des General der Infanterie Karl von Roques aus der ersten Zeit des Ostfeldzuges 1941, I. Teil," BA-MA Freiburg, N 152/10, 4–5.

391 "Tagesmeldung, 2.7.1941," BA-MA, RH 26/454/6a, 1–2.

392 Mechnyk, *Pochatok*, 12–13.

393 Haim Tal, *The Fields of Ukraine: A 17-Year-Old's Survival of Nazi Occupation: The Story of Yosef Laufer* (Denver: Dallci Press, 2009), 4.

In Stanislaviv, which was liberated by Hungarian troops, the celebration took place on 12 July 1941. It began with a church service and was attended by representatives of the Hungarian authorities. From a podium, the engineer Semianchuk read the OUN-B proclamation, which the crowd frequently interrupted with shouts like "Glory to the Ukrainian State!" "Glory to Stepan Bandera!" "Glory to the OUN!" "Glory to Adolf Hitler!" "Glory to the Allied Hungarian Army!" Then everybody stood up and the orchestra played the national anthem. Afterwards, OUN activist Rybchuk informed the crowd that the OUN had completed the first stage of the fight against the "occupiers of Ukrainian territories," who had "tortured [thousands of victims] to death in prisons and camps in the Solovetsky Islands after deportation." The victims were honored with a moment of silence. Then the crowd was informed that "now the organization under the leadership of Stepan Bandera is in the second stage [of the fight], in which it will establish a Ukrainian state."[394]

The ceremony was also attended by Ukrainian militiamen in mazepynka caps who, shortly before the celebrations, were prevented by the Hungarian army from organizing a huge pogrom in Stanislaviv, although they did organize a small one. The OUN-B complained about this incident in its reports.[395] In the hall of the Ivan Franko theatre in Stanislaviv, another ceremony took place. Professor Hamers'kyi announced in his speech to the audience:

> We live now in important historical days. The German army under the leadership of Adolf Hitler creates a new hope for the world and helps us to build a Ukrainian state that will collaborate with National-Socialist Great Germany. The Organization of Ukrainian Nationalists, which, under the leadership of Ievhen Konovalets', its deceased founder and leader, and Stepan Bandera, its current leader, is waging a heroic battle against the horrible oppression of the Ukrainian nation and is emerging from underground to create Ukrainian independence.[396]

In Rivne on 27 July 1941, 10,000 people attended a "Celebration of Ukrainian Independence" in the square of the old castle. The main attraction of the celebration was the First Battalion (*kurin'*) of the "Ukrainian Army." Many OUN groups arrived with banners that displayed slogans such as "Long Live Our Vozhd' Bandera" and "We Struggle for the State of Volodymyr the Great." While the local OUN leaders were delivering speeches, the crowd performed the fascist salute, calling once "Glory to the Heroes!" and responding three times "Glory to Ukraine!" At other times, the crowd shouted "Long Live Stepan Bandera!" "Long Live Stets'ko's Government!" and "Long Live Adolf Hitler!" Finally, after the speeches, the First Battalion swore an oath, and the numerous flags, among them the red-and-black flag of the battalion,

394 "Sviato proholoshennia Ukraïns'koï Derzhavy v Stanislavovi, 12 i 13 VII 1941 r.," TsDAVOV f. 3833, op. 1, spr. 15, 45.

395 For the militiamen at the ceremony, see ibid., 45. On the OUN complaining about the friendly attitude of the Hungarian army to Poles and Jews, see "Vidnosyny na Hutsul'shchyni!" TsDAVOV f. 3833, op. 1, spr. 15, 74. On preventing pogroms by the Hungarian army, see Pohl, *Nationalsozialistische*, 65–66; Mędykowski, *W cieniu gigantów*, 283–86. For a small pogrom in Stanislaviv, see AŻIH, 302/135, Julian Feuerman, 2. For the OUN-B also complaining about the Slovaks who did not discriminate against Poles and Jews as the OUN-B demanded, see "Vid povitovoho OUN v Mykolaïvi," TsDAVOV f. 3833, op. 1, spr. 12, 23.

396 "Sviato proholoshennia," TsDAVOV f. 3833, op. 1, spr. 15, 45.

which was also the OUN-B flag, and one with the inscription "Freedom for Ukraine or Death," were blessed.[397]

As well as organizing and performing nationalist celebrations, and exercising ethnic and political violence, the OUN-B released a few newspapers, which praised the revolution and the leaders of the revolution. The newspaper *Samostiina Ukraïna*, in Stanyslaviv oblast, printed OUN-B propaganda from 7 July 1941 onward. On 10 July, it reprinted the text of the proclamation on the front page, with a photograph of the protagonist of this event, Iaroslav Stets'ko (Fig. 21). On 24 July, *Ukraïns'ke slovo* printed a photograph of the *Providnyk* Stepan Bandera, together with articles about the "Ukrainian-German-Hungarian war" against the "NKVD and its villains who tortured the Ukrainian nation" (Fig. 22).[398]

Letters and Leaders

Because Bandera and Stets'ko had been arrested by the Germans and were not with the revolutionary masses during the "Ukrainian National Revolution," the OUN-B tried to have them released, and permitted to return to Ukraine. For this purpose, OUN-B activists began to collect "plenipotentiary letters" that they wanted to send to Hitler. The "plenipotentiary letters" were often signed by numerous Ukrainians at the local proclamation ceremonies. For this reason, the content of the standardized text from the "Struggle and Activities" was modified. Here is an example of one of these standard documents:

> We, citizens of the village Rudnyky, were called to a ceremonial assembly at which the Independent Ukrainian State was proclaimed. We listened to the text of the proclamation act with inexpressible pleasure: We are proud to have such a leader [*providnyk*] of the OUN and of the whole Ukrainian Nation as *STEPAN BANDERA*. We are very grateful to the invincible Allied German Army and to its leader [*vozhd'*] Adolf Hitler, who helps to liberate the Ukrainian people from Jewish-Muscovite slavery [*z-pid zhydivs'ko-moskovs'koï nevoli*].
>
> Long live Great National Socialist Germany and its leader Adolf Hitler.
>
> Long live the Independent Ukrainian United State.
>
> Long live the leader of the *OUN* and of the whole Ukrainian Nation *STEPAN BANDERA*.[399]

Some of the letters began with the heading "declaration" (*zaiava*),[400] others with "resolution" (*rezoliutsiia*),[401] and still others were addressed directly, without any

397 "Zvit z pivnichno-zakhidnykh ukraïns'kykh zemel," TsDAVOV f. 3833, op. 1, spr. 15, 7v. Similar manifestations took place in other localities. Cf. TsDAVOV f. 3833, op. 1, spr. 15, 7. For a similar manifestation in Lublin, see "Ereignismeldung UdSSR, Nr. 20, 12.07.1941," BAB R58/214, 131.

398 "Akt prohloshennia Ukrains'koi derzhavy," *Samostiina Ukraina*, 10 July 1941, 1; "Sviatochna akademiia," *Ukrains'ke slovo*, 24 July 1941, 1.

399 TsDAVOV f. 3833, op. 1, spr. 29, 1. Emphasis in the original. The text of the letter from the village of Rudnyky was used with small modifications in letters from such places as Omel'no, Kulikovychi, Iavlon'ka, Raznyi, and Tel'chi. See TsDAVOV f. 3833, op. 1, spr. 29, 1, 4–5.

400 "Zaiava do Uriadu Iaroslava Stets'ka," TsDAVOV f. 3833, op. 1, spr. 31, 1.

401 Resolution from the village of Elblanivka, 13 July 1941, TsDAVOV f. 3833, op. 1, spr. 29, 2–3.

Бог і Україна!

САМОСТІЙНА УКРАЇНА

Редакція і Адміністрація: Станиславів, вул. Карпінського ч. 7, І поверх, ч. тел. 22.
Ціна 50 коп. або 5 нім. фенігів

Рік І. Станиславів, 10 липня 1941. Ч. 3.

АКТ ПРОГОЛОШЕННЯ УКРАЇНСЬКОЇ ДЕРЖАВИ

1. Волею Українського народу, Організація Націоналістів під проводом Степана БАНДЕРИ проголошує створення Української Держави, за яку поклали свої голови цілі покоління найкращих синів України.

Організація Українських Націоналістів, яка під проводом її Творця й Вождя Евгена КОНОВАЛЬЦЯ вела в останніх десятиліттях кривавого московсько-большевицького поневолення завзяту боротьбу за свободу, взиває весь український нарід не скласти зброї так довго, доки на всіх українських землях не буде створена Суверенна Українська Влада.

Суверенна Українська Влада запевнить Українському народові лад і порядок, всесторонній розвиток усіх його сил та заспокоєння всіх його потреб.

2. На західніх землях України твориться Українська Влада, яка підпорядкується українському Національному Урядові, що створиться у столиці України — КИЇВІ.

3. Новоповстаюча Українська держава буде тісно співдіяти з Націонал-Соціялістичною Великою Німеччиною, що під проводом свойого Вожда Адольфа ГІТЛЄРА творить новий лад в Европі і в світі та допомагає Українському Народові визволитися з підмосковської окупації.

Українська Національна Революційна Армія, що твориться на українській землі, боротиметься дальше з СОЮЗНОЮ НІМЕЦЬКОЮ АРМІЄЮ проти московської окупації за Суверенну Соборну Державу і новий лад у цілому світі.

Хай живе Українська Суверенна Соборна Держава! Хай живе Організація Українських Націоналістів! Хай живе провідник Організації Українських націоналістів й Українського Народу СТЕПАН БАНДЕРА!

СЛАВА УКРАЇНІ!

Пастирські листи Князів Церкви у велику хвилину

З Волі Всемогучого і Всемилостивого Бога в Тройці Єдиного почалася Нова Епоха в житті Державної Соборної Самостійної України.

Народні Збори, що відбулися вчорашнього дня, ствердили і проголосили ту Історичну Подію.

Повідомляючи Тебе, Український Народе, про таке вислухання наших благальних молитов, взиваю Тебе до вияву вдячності для Всевишнього, вірності для Його Церкви і послуху для Влади.

Воєнні часи вимагатимуть ще многих жертв, але діло розпочате в імя Боже і з Божою Благодаттю буде доведене до успішного кінця.

Жертви, яких конечно потреба до осягнення нашої цілі, полягатимуть передусім на послушньому віддаванні справедливим Божим законам, непротивним розказам Влади.

Український Нарід мусить в тій Історичній Хвилі показати, що має досить почуття авторитету, солідарності і життєвої сили, щоб заслужити на таке положення серед народів Европи, в якім би міг розвинути усі Богом собі дані сили.

Карністю, солідарністю, совісним сповненням обовязків докажіть, що Ви дозріли до Державного Життя.

Побідоносну Німецьку Армію витаємо як освободительку від ворога. Установленій владі віддаємо належний послух. Узнаємо Головою Краєвого Правління Західних Областей України Пана Ярослава СТЕЦЬКА.

Голова Управління Ярослав Стецько

Від Уряду Нам покликаного до життя очікуємо мудрого, справедливого проводу та заряджень, які узгляднювали б потреби і добро всіх замешкуючих Наш Край громадян, без огляду на це, до якого віроісповідання, народності і суспільної верстви належать. Бог нехай благословить усі Твої праці, Український Народе, і нехай дасть усім нашим Провідникам Святу Мудрість з Неба.

Дано у Львові при Арх. Храмі Св. Юра 1. VII. 1941.

(—) + АНДРЕЙ.

Благословлю Українську Самостійну Державу. Дякую Всевишньому в глибині душі за вислухання наших благальних молитов і молю Бога, щоб Українська Держава сперта на Божому Законі, забезпечила щастя, добробут і спокійне життя всім громадянам української землі без огляду на різниці віроісповідні, національні і суспільні.

Станиславів, 6 липня 1941 р.

+ ГРИГОРІЙ,
Єпископ.

Всі творчі сили українського народу обєднуються в одному спільному фронті будови власного державного життя

Дня 6. VII. 1941 р. відбулася у Львові нарада чільних представників українського громадянства в справі консолідації всіх сил довкола ідеї відбудови української державності.

Присутні вислухали звіти про консолідацію, переведену з ініціятиви О. У. Н. під проводом Степана Бандери серед української еміграції та її великий успіх серед усіх віддомів української суспільності з виїмком відосібненої групи інж. Андрія Мельника.

Дискусія виявила повну одностайність усього українського громадянства, яке прагне цілою душею з'єднання всіх сил для спільної нам, єдиної, великої і святої справи.

По дискусії принято одноголосно такі резолюції:

Представники українського львівського громадянства, зібрані в дні 6. VII 1941 р. вітають непереможні німецькі війська під проводом великого вождя Адольфа Гітлера, що несуть українському народові визволення від большевицького ярма та дають йому змогу відбудувати самостійну українську державу.

Зібрані [illegible] актом консолідації українського громадянства на [illegible]

Fig. 21. *Samostiina Ukraina*, 10 July 1941, 1.

УКРАЇНСЬКЕ СЛОВО

ВИХОДИТЬ ЩО ДРУГИЙ ДЕНЬ

Рік I. Станиславів, четвер 24 липня 1941. Ч. 2.

СВЯТОЧНА АКАДЕМІЯ

О. ОЛЕСЬ

Крики... Усміхи привітні...
Прапори... пісні...
— Будьте мужні, непохитні,
Єдністю міцні!

Свято волі... скрізь бенкети...
Мрій, надій рої...
— Зброю в руки! за мушкети!
Будуть ще бої!...

Де ділись пута, грати...
Люде, як брати...
— Вартові, вночі не спати!
Пильно стерегти!

Розчинилися темниці...
Друзі серед нас...
— Будьте тверді, як із криці
Боятись не час!

Скільки сонця і блакиті —
В небі, на землі!...
— Чи рушниці всі набиті?
Гострені шаблі?

Гей, стрільці, як слід влучати
І назад не йти!
— Вартові, вночі не спати!
Пильно стерегти!

Незабутні дні

Провідник Степан БАНДЕРА

Fig. 22. *Ukrains'ke slovo*, 24 July 1941, 1.

heading, to the "leader of the Organization of Ukrainian Nationalists Stepan Bandera"[402] or to the "leader of the German people Adolf Hitler"[403] or to the "head of the government of the Ukrainian state Iaroslav Stets'ko."[404] In some letters, a plea to Hitler to release Bandera and Stets'ko and let them come to Ukraine was added, as in the one from Ksaverivka, which was probably drafted by a local person with a strong affiliation to the OUN-B. The letter is composed in a very simple style. It includes numerous grammatical errors that suggest the author was a peasant with a weak grasp of the written language:

> To the leader of the Organization of Ukrainian Nationalists Stepan Bandera.
>
> Announcement
>
> We, the citizens of the village Ksaverivka, assembled on Sunday, 19 July 1941, in the square to demonstrate before the world that the Ukrainian Nation fights for its rights and for an Independent Ukrainian State.
>
> We are firmly subordinated to the Ukrainian Government that was proclaimed in Lviv and we will faithfully carry out all the orders that will be given us. We ask the leader of the German Nation to confirm the temporary council of the village.
>
> We are grateful to the German Army and its Leaders. First of all we are grateful to Chancellor Adolf Hitler for his command to his heroic Army to drive out the Bolshevik Jewish bandit and Polish treason, which oppressed the Ukrainian People in jails and camps. We met the German Army with great happiness because it drove out the bandit army from our Ukraine and liberated us.
>
> We believe that Germany will not desire to enslave the Ukrainian Nation and that it will once and for all make the Ukrainian People a Nation of will and deed, which will join the fight against Jewish Communism [*zhydo komuna*] and all oppressors of the Ukrainian people who oppressed the Ukrainian People, and severely opposed Germany and Hitler.
>
> We ask Adolf Hitler, the great Genius of the German People, to release for us our OUN Leader Stepan Bandera who led the Ukrainian people many years under the terror of Poland and Moscow and we believe that he will now also lead us on the right path as he has so far. The Ukrainian people and the Organization of Ukrainian Nationalists believe in his forces and also that only he as the Leader of the Ukrainian Nationalists is able to lead us and to put a stop to the whole communist diversion and to make collaboration with great Germany possible.
>
> Glory to the German Army
>
> Glory to the Führer [*firerovi*] of the German Nation Adolf Hitler
>
> Glory to Ukraine
>
> Glory to the Heroes.[405]

This letter is reasonably representative of the other letters addressed to Bandera, Hitler, and Stets'ko. It provides important evidence about the OUN-B, as well as

402 Letter from the village of Ksaverivka, 19 July 1941, TsDAVOV f. 3833, op. 1, spr. 29, 13.

403 Letter from Steniatyn to Adolf Hitler, 19 July 1941, TsDAVOV f. 3833, op. 1, spr. 31, 36.

404 Letter from the village Ksaverivka to Iaroslav Stets'ko, 18 July 1941, TsDAVOV f. 3833, op. 1, spr. 29, 9.

405 TsDAVOV f. 3833, op. 1, spr. 29, 13–14. A list of eighty signatures is affixed to the letter. The same letter was also addressed to Iaroslav Stets'ko and signed by seventy-five people. See TsDAVOV f. 3833, op. 1, spr. 29, 9–12.

about the mental and political state into which it was trying to push the revolutionary Ukrainian masses. The disdain for Jews and communists, who in popular opinion became one and the same, was sometimes expressed more vividly than in the quoted letter. In the village of Steniatyn, for example, three elaborate letters were written to Bandera, Hitler, and Stets'ko.[406] The authors of this correspondence called themselves "peasants and intelligentsia." They expressed deep gratitude to and admiration for the German *Führer* and his army. They believed that the "Great Leader of the German Nation ... has destroyed forever the enemies of our nation, and the communist threat to the civilized world."[407] Hitler had delivered them from communist barbarity, thus allowing them to re-join the "civilized world." That Nazi morality made this "civilized world" one of modern barbarity did not influence their expressed desire to become a part of it. In this and other letters, the writers admired Hitler for his "invincible world-famous army," his "fairness," and his will to liberate the Ukrainian people from the "yoke of the Jewish-Muscovite and Polish Bolshevist subhuman beings, the hangmen of the Ukrainian people."[408]

However fair and glorious Hitler may have seemed to the "revolutionary masses," he had arrested and imprisoned Bandera in Berlin. Some letters were open in expressing the desire to have Bandera come home. The OUN-B must have informed the writers and signatories of the leader's arrest and convinced them that only Bandera could lead the Ukrainian nation to independence. These authors hoped that the "fraternal German nation" would understand the crucial importance of their leader.[409]

Bandera was the most admired object of the revolution. Some authors stated that words were inadequate to express the strength of their admiration for the *Providnyk* and that their love for him was immeasurable. A few specified that they loved Bandera with "pure peasant hearts [*sertsia chysto selians'ki*]"—the highest form of love. Their only wish was to be the "faithful servants of their *Providnyk* and their nation." They wanted to be like him and other great heroes of the Ukrainian nation.[410]

In a leaflet published by the homeland executive of the OUN "To the Ukrainian Nation," which circulated during the revolution, Bandera was depicted as the telos of the Ukrainian nation. He was placed at the summit of Ukrainian history as the *Vozhd'* of all Ukrainians. Ukrainian history was reduced to a glorious past, which ended when vicious strangers destroyed the magnificent Ukrainian medieval state and enslaved the Ukrainians. Then followed centuries of revolutionary struggle for independence, of which the last stage was the revolutionary struggle of the OUN under the leadership of Bandera. The text ended with "Glory to Ukraine," "Glory to the Heroes," "Glory to the vozhd.'"[411]

406 "Do Vysokopovazhanoho Stepana Bandery," "Do Holovy Uriadu Ukraïns'koï Derzhavy Stets'ka Iaroslava," "Do Firera Nimetskoho Narodu Adol'fa Hitlera," TsDAVOV f. 3833, op. 1, spr. 31, 29–32, 36–37.

407 "Do Firera Nimetskoho Narodu Adol'fa Hitlera," TsDAVOV f. 3833, op. 1, spr. 31, 36. In another part of the same letter the enemies are called "bestial asiatics" (*zizvirili aziaty*).

408 Ibid., 36.

409 "Do Firera Nimets'koho Narodu Adol'fa Hitlera," TsDAVOV f. 3833, op. 1, spr. 31, 36.

410 "Do Vysokopovazhanoho Stepana Bandery," TsDAVOV f. 3833, op. 1, spr. 31, 29.

411 "Ukraïns'kyi Narode," TsDAVOV f. 3833, op. 1, spr. 41, 1–2.

Throughout the "Ukrainian National Revolution," Stepan Bandera, the embodiment of the revolution, was not to be found in the revolutionary territories. His person was controlled by the Germans, first in Cracow and then in Berlin. But the spirit and the charisma of the *Providnyk* were with the revolutionary masses. Bandera's presence was palpable in the proclamation ceremonies and in all the letters addressed to Hitler, Bandera, and Stets'ko. Ivan Klymiv wrote to Stepan Bandera that he had immediately known where to place his loyalties after the split in the OUN, because he and other fellow OUN-members "saw Bandera twice under the gallows, unconquerable and loyal to the idea."[412] It was obvious to them that Bandera was the true Ukrainian *Providnyk* and that, during the "Ukrainian National Revolution," the whole revolutionary territory should be covered with posters and leaflets extolling Bandera.[413]

The last object of admiration, Iaroslav Stets'ko, was depicted in the letters as a famous freedom fighter and leading figure in the OUN. The writers greeted Stets'ko with a nationalist salute. Stets'ko was for them the person who had proclaimed statehood in Lviv and thus performed the most revolutionary of deeds, a model now acted out in villages, towns, and cities across Ukraine. As the main hero of 30 June 1941 Stets'ko evoked almost the same admiration and filial love as the *Providnyk* did.[414]

Result of the "Ukrainian National Revolution"

According to Klymiv, the OUN-B tried to establish statehood in 213 districts (raions) across Ukraine, 187 in western Ukraine and twenty-six in eastern Ukraine.[415] In the Zolochiv district, the OUN-B found 8,000 supporters.[416] This suggests that the OUN-B might have persuaded a total of more than 1.5 million people to back its project. Considering the short time in which the OUN-B was working to establish statehood, the "Ukrainian National Revolution" of the OUN-B evidently spread quickly, but it ended abruptly due to conflicts with the Germans. In contrast, according to Klymiv, the OUN-M proclaimed statehood in only two districts.[417]

A violent nationalist "uprising," to some extent similar to the "Ukrainian National Revolution," occurred in Lithuania after Germany attacked the Soviet Union on 22 June 1941. It was organized by the Lithuanian Activist Front (*Lietuvos aktyvistų frontas*, LAF), which had constituted itself in November 1940 in Berlin and was composed of radical-right and national conservative politicians who had left Lithuania after the Soviet Union occupied their country in June 1940. Headed by Kazys

412 "Zahal'nyi ohliad," not earlier than August 1941, TsDAVOV f. 3833, op. 1, spr. 45, 3. By claiming that he "saw Bandera twice under the gallows unconquerable and loyal to the idea," Klymiv meant the trials against the OUN in 1935–1936 in Warsaw and in 1936 in Lviv.

413 Ibid., 3. For posters and leaflets distributed by the OUN-B in Kiev and the south-eastern city Mykolaïv, see PAAA, R 105182, 218925–218928.

414 "Do Holovy Uriadu Ukraïns'koï Derzhavy Stets'ka Iaroslava," TsDAVOV f. 3833, op. 1, spr. 31, 31.

415 "Zahal'nyi ohliad," not earlier than August 1941, TsDAVOV f. 3833, op. 1, spr. 45, 1–2. See also the document "Zvit pro robotu v spravi orhanizatsiï derzhavnoï administratsiï na tereni Zakhidnykh Oblastei Ukraïny" in TsDAVOV f. 3833, op. 1, spr. 15, 1–4.

416 Report from the meeting of Ukrainian citizens of the Zolochiv district, TsDAVOV f. 3833, op. 1, spr. 34, 40.

417 "Zahal'nyi ohliad," not earlier than August 1941, TsDAVOV f. 3833, op. 1, spr. 45, 2.

Škirpa, the LAF established a few commissions that were intended to become the Lithuanian government after the German attack on the Soviet Union. On 23 June 1941, Lithuanian nationalists seized a radio station in Kaunas, over which Leonas Prapuolenis announced that an independent Lithuanian state with a provisional government had been created. As in Ukraine, the government was not accepted by the Germans and existed only for a few days. The process of establishing the state went along with a number of pogroms, as a result of which several hundred Jews were killed by locals, the LAF, other Lithuanian groups, and Germans.[418]

In addition to those in Lithuania and western Ukraine, pogroms also took place after 22 June 1941 in other territories occupied by Germany, including north-eastern Poland and Latvia, and to a lesser extent in Belarus and Estonia.[419] After the beginning of Operation München on 2 July, very bloody pogroms occurred in Bessarabia and northern Bukovina, which were invaded and occupied by Romanian troops.[420] This indicates that the German invasion and the NKVD massacres were an important trigger for the pogroms. In western Ukraine, however, pogroms also took place in localities where the Germans were not present at the time of pogrom, or where the Hungarians had invaded, or in which there were no prisons with NKVD victims. These facts and also the OUN-B complaints about the Hungarian army and the Slovaks, who restricted the OUN-B's anti-Jewish activities, or were "too friendly" toward Jews and Poles, indicate that a certain number of pogroms were organized and carried out by the OUN-B activists or the local population, without any encouragement or help from the Germans.[421]

Ellen Pressler, for example, noticed that power in Bolekhiv was taken over by local Ukrainian nationalists, who formed the militia and organized a pogrom before

418 Christoph Dieckmann, "Lithuania in Summer 1941. The German Invasion and the Kaunas Pogrom," in *Shared History*, ed. Barkan, 370–85; Siegfried Gasparaitis, "'Verrätern wird nur dann vergeben, wenn sie wirklich beweisen können, daß sie mindestans einen Juden liquidiert haben.' Die 'Front Litauischer Aktivisten' (LAF) und die antisowjetischen Aufstände 1941," *Zeitschrift für Geschichtswissenschaft* Vol. 49 (2001): 889–90, 897–904.

419 For pogroms in north-eastern Poland, see Żbikowski, Pogroms in Northeastern Poland, 315–54; Mędykowski, *W cieniu gigantów*, 217–29. For pogroms in Lithuania, see Dieckmann, Lithuania in Summer 1941, 355–85. For Latvia, see Katrin Reichelt, *Lettland unter deutscher Besatzung 1941–1944* (Berlin: Metropol, 2011), 84–94. For Lithuania, Latvia, and Estonia, see Mędykowski, *W cieniu gigantów*, 196–213. For Latvia and Estonia, see "Ereignismeldung UdSSR, Nr. 40, 01.08.1941," BA R58/215, 134. During the pogroms in Belarus, Jews were mainly robbed but not killed. Cf. Mędykowski, *W cieniu gigantów*, 230–40, 336.

420 On Bessarabia and Bukovina, see Vladimir Solonari, "Patterns of Violence. The Local Population and the Mass Murder of Jews in Bessarabia and Northern Bukovina, July-August 1941," *Kritika: Explorations in Russian and Eurasian History* Vol. 8, No. 4 (2007): 749–87; Simon Geissbühler, *Blutiger Juli. Rumäniens Vernichtungskrieg und der vergessene Massenmord an den Juden 1941* (Padeborn: Schöningh, 2013).

421 On Stanislaviv, see AŻIH, 302/135, Mędykowski, *Pogromy 1941*, 793. On Kalush, see AŻIH, 301/4928, Mundek Kramer, 1. On Otyniia close to Stanislaviv, see AŻIH, 301/4897, Bodiner, 1–2. On Terebovlia, see Sabrin, *Alliance for Murder*, 5. On Kremenets', see Lower, Pogroms, Mob Violence, 224. On Tuchyn, see AŻIH, 301/397, Jakub and Esia Zylberger, Hersz and Doba Mełamed, 1. On Kolomyia, see Żbikowski, *Archiwum*, 3: 906–907. See also Golczewski, Shades of Grey, 131–32, 137; Andzej Żbikowski, "Anti-Jewish Pogroms in Occupied Territories of Eastern Poland, June–July 1941," in *The Holocaust in the Soviet Union: Studies and Sources on the Destruction of the Jews in the Nazi-Occupied Territories of the USSR, 1941–1945*, ed. Lucjan Dobroszycki and Jeffrey S. Gurock (Armonk: M. E. Sharpe, 1993), 178–79; Żbikowski, Lokalne Pogromy, 16. On the OUN and the Hungarian army, see "Vidnosyny na Hutsul'shchyni!" TsDAVOV f. 3833, op. 1, spr. 15, 74; Pohl, *Nationalsozialistische*, 65–66. For the OUN-B and the Slovaks, see "Vid povitovoho OUN v Mykolaïvi," TsDAVOV f. 3833, op. 1, spr. 12, 23.

the Hungarian army came to the town.[422] Matylda Gelerntner, another survivor of Bolekhiv, noticed that the Ukrainians were heavily armed, and claimed that they were "Germans" in order to convince the Hungarian troops that they had more right to rule in Bolekhiv.[423] In Khotymyr (Chocimierz) a troop of Hungarian soldiers would not allow a band of Ukrainian pogromists to drown a group of Jews from Tlumach (Tłumacz), in the Dniester river.[424] On the way from Ternopil' to Lviv, Uri Lichter observed "murderers with axes and scythes," long before he saw a German.[425] Izio Wachtel reported that, after the Soviet soldiers retreated from his town of Chortkiv and "before the Germans entered, the Ukrainians arrived in the town with ... axes and scythes and other instruments, and slaughtered and killed and robbed the Jews. With the arrival of the Germans, the wild killing ceased and the murder by orders began."[426]

The vast majority of pogroms in Ukraine occurred in eastern Galicia and in Volhynia.[427] After the German attack on the Soviet Union, in territories to the east of Galicia and Volhynia, Jews were killed in mass shootings. Alexander Kruglov estimated that, in July 1941, 38,000 to 39,000 Jews died as a result of pogroms and mass shootings. In August, between 61,000 and 62,000 Jews were shot in Ukraine, and in September between 136,000 and 137,000.[428] An Einsatzgruppe C report from September 1941, when the German army was in eastern Ukraine, complained about the difficulty of persuading Ukrainians "to take active steps against the Jews."[429]

Although this study concentrates on Bandera and the OUN and explores their role in the pogroms and other events, it is also important to briefly outline the whole spectrum of perpetrators and motives. As already indicated, the pogromists in western Ukraine can be divided into three groups: the Germans, the OUN-B, and the local population.[430] The Germans enabled the anti-Jewish violence, by attacking and conquering the Soviet Union. They also triggered pogroms in several places, but not all, and coordinated their execution. The OUN-B organized a militia, which both collaborated with the Germans and killed Jews independently. It also incited the local population to anti-Jewish violence, by spreading antisemitic propaganda and advocating, together with Germans, revenge on the Jews for the NKVD murders. The local population was driven to anti-Jewish violence by the German and OUN-B propaganda, especially by the instrumentalization of the NKVD murders. The local perpetrators came from different social groups and acted with different reasons, of which antisemitism, nationalism, racism, and fascism were important, but not the only ones.

422 AŻIH, 301/2146, Ellen Pressler, 1–3.

423 AŻIH, 301/2145, Matylda Gelerntner, 1.

424 Mędykowski, *W cieniu gigantów*, 283. The drowning of Jews in the Dniester was a popular pogrom method in this part of eastern Galicia, see Mędykowski, *W cieniu gigantów*, 171–73, 175, 176, 283–85.

425 Uri Lichter observed on the way from Ternopil' to Lviv "murderers with axes and scythes" long before he saw a German. See AŻIH, 302/61, Uri Lichter, 3.

426 Quoted in Bartov, Wartime Lies, 493.

427 Some pogroms organized by the OUN-M also took place in Bukovina. A small pogrom also occurred in Kiev. For Bukovina, see Solonari, Patterns of Violence. For Kiev, see Oleksandr Mel'nyk, "Anti-Jewish Violence in Kyiv's Podil District in September 1941 through the Prism of Soviet Investigative Documents," *Jahrbücher für Geschichte Osteuropas* Vol. 61, No. 2 (2013): 223.

428 Alexander Kruglov, Jewish Losses in Ukraine, 1941–1944, 274–75.

429 Reuben Ainsztein, *Jewish Resistance in Nazi-Occupied Eastern Europe* (London: Paul Elek, 1974), 251.

430 See also Himka, The Lviv Pogrom of 1941, 243; Rossoliński-Liebe, Der Verlauf und die Täter, 242–43.

Other important motives were, as already indicated, connected with the economy and the perpetrators wish to enrich themselves. Thus, Jewish houses were also plundered by peasants who came to the towns and cities with carts for the purpose. Philip Friedman, survivor of the Holocaust in Galicia, and an early Holocaust historian, wrote that, among the perpetrators, one could find all kinds of people: peasants, teachers, municipal administrators, pharmacists, school inspectors, priests, judges, students, high-school pupils, and women.[431]

Bandera's Agency and Responsibility

Although it is not an easy task to explain in which sense and to what extent Bandera was responsible for the pogroms and other forms of ethnic and political violence in western Ukraine in summer 1941, this study requires to look for a nuanced, complex, and adequate answer to this difficult question.

First, it is important to remember that the Gestapo advised Bandera not go to the "newly occupied territories." He was, therefore, not present in Lviv when Ukrainian statehood was proclaimed, when the local OUN-B members and the task forces spread antisemitic propaganda, or when they organized the militia, which became one of the main perpetrators of the pogrom in Lviv and many other places. However, Bandera's physical absence from Lviv, and many other localities in which the pogroms took place, does not exonerate him of the responsibility for the crimes committed by the OUN-B, because he had prepared the "Ukrainian National Revolution," which anticipated establishing a state and eliminating the political and ethnic "enemies" of this state. The preparation included writing "Struggle and Activities," together with Stets'ko, Shukhevych, and Lenkavs'kyi, and, with the help of this and other documents, informing the underground in Ukraine how to act after the beginning of the German attack on the Soviet Union. "Struggle and Activities" was unambiguous about what the Ukrainian nationalists should do with Jews, Poles, Soviets, and Ukrainian opponents. Klymiv, leader of the OUN-B in Ukraine, received "Struggle and Activities" in early May 1941 and was guided by it when he organized and conducted the violent uprising. "Struggle and Activities" consisted of a series of general and specific instructions to Klymiv, and to the OUN-B in Ukraine, which committed numerous war crimes during the "Ukrainian National Revolution," while following the instructions included in this document.

Second, it is not known whether Bandera issued direct orders after 22 June 1941 to conduct or support anti-Jewish violence, nor how much he knew about the run of events. The fact that he was the *Providnyk* of the organization suggests that he must have been consulted by his underlings about the course of events. Stets'ko wrote that Bandera did not go to Ukraine but stayed in the General Government, close to the former German-Soviet border, to coordinate the actions of the task forces with the help of couriers. The OUN-B task forces, as already mentioned, organized the militia and other organs of the state. After 22 June, Stets'ko stayed in contact with the *Providnyk* by sending him telegrams. He also received telegrams from Bandera but,

431 Friedman, Ukrainian-Jewish Relations, 199–200, footnote 30. See also Wendy Lower, Pogroms, Mob Violence, 222; Sandkühler, *"Endlösung" in Galizien*, 303.

unlike Stets'ko's correspondence, Bandera's telegrams have not remained in the archives. The Germans, according to Stets'ko, confined Bandera on 29 June. But it is not clear if and how they limited Bandera's actions. The Germans might have forbidden him to go to Lviv, but they did not arrest him at that time. This allowed him to continue coordinating the task forces and having an impact on the course of the uprising. The fact that he arrived late at a meeting organized by Ernst Kundt on 3 July 1941 in Cracow suggests that Bandera was not staying in Cracow but was coordinating the task forces from somewhere closer to the Ukrainian territories. Lebed specified in 1952 that it was somewhere in Kholmshchyna.[432]

Third, Bandera was the *Providnyk* or *Vozhd'* of the OUN-B, and thus he was the leader of the Ukrainian nationalist and genocidal movement, which organized and conducted the "Ukrainian National Revolution." The OUN-B, like a number of other fascist and authoritarian movements, implemented the Führerprinzip and officially elected Bandera as its *Providnyk*. Bandera did not disagree with this decision, nor did he indicate that he disagreed with the general line of OUN-B policies. On the contrary, he was proud to be the *Providnyk* of the movement, actively engaged in the "revolutionary deeds," and hoped to become the leader of the Ukrainian state and all Ukrainians. In this sense, Bandera bears political responsibility for the deeds of his organization, in a similar manner to Hitler, Pavelić, Antonescu, and other leaders of violent movements. Yet we should not overlook the fact that Bandera's agency and power were more limited than Hitler's, Pavelić's, or Antonescu's, especially after Bandera was arrested on 5 July 1941.

Considering all these factors, we may conclude that Bandera was responsible for the ethnic and political mass violence in the summer of 1941, although his responsibility certainly differed from Hitler's, Pavelić's, Antonescu's and other leaders whose movements committed war crimes or were involved in atrocities. To estimate Bandera's responsibility we should differentiate between a legal moral, ethical, and political responsibility and explain if Bandera was guilty of any of them. Because the Germans did not allow Bandera to go to the "newly occupied territories," confined him on 29 June, when he might have tried to go to Lviv, and took him into honorary arrest on 5 July, the spectrum of his involvement in atrocities after 22 June 1941 was limited. We also do not know what kind of orders (if any), he issued after 22 June 1941, although we know that he participated in the uprising while coordinating the task forces with the help of couriers, and that thereby his actions may have impacted the general course of events. If he was indeed only a "passive personality," a national or international court of justice may have convicted him by means of the principle of "universal jurisdiction" over crimes against humanity as happened to Adolf Eichmann in Jerusalem in 1962.[433] More solid evidence for Bandera's legal involvement is in the document "Struggle and Activities," which he prepared together with other leading OUN-B members prior to the uprising. This document clearly

432 Stets'ko, *30 chervnia 1941*, 151, 158; "Niederschrift über die Rücksprache mit Mitgliedern des ukrainischen Nationalkomitees und Stepan Bandera, 3.7.1941," BAB NS 26/1198, 1–5, 10. See also Shumuk, *Za skhidnim obriiem*, 431; Mykola Lebed, Biographic Data, 18 May 1952, RG 263, ZZ-18, Box#80, NN3-263-02-008, Mykola Lebed Name File, vol. 1, 42.

433 For "passive personality" and "universal jurisdiction," see Leora Bilsky, "The Eichmann Trial and the Legacy of Jurisdiction," in *Politics in Dark Times: Encounters with Hannah Arendt*, ed. Seyla Benhabib, Roy Thomas Tsao, Peter J. Verovšek (Cambridge: Cambridge University Press, 2010), 202.

included ethnic and political mass violence as a means of revolution and was, as already mentioned, a line of general and specific instruction to the underground in Ukraine, which fulfilled it. Had a Ukrainian court, which was interested in the transformation of Ukrainian society toward democracy, considered this document and applied the notion of transnational justice, it would have convicted Bandera and several other OUN-B leaders involved in the preparation and conduct of the "Ukrainian National Revolution," in order to provide recognition to the victims and promote civic trust and democracy in Ukraine.[434]

Bandera's moral, ethical, and political responsibility, on the other hand, seems to be more evident. It resulted from the fact that he prepared the "Ukrainian National Revolution," and wanted to realize its goals. Furthermore, Bandera never condemned the results of the "Ukrainian National Revolution" nor suggested that he disagreed with them. After the National Ukrainian Revolution, the OUN-B published Bandera's letter from 15 July 1941 to Ivan Klymiv, the leader of the OUN-B in Ukraine, in which the *Providnyk* gave thanks to Klymiv and other "Friends-Heroes" for what they had done. Before publishing the letter, Stets'ko must have given Bandera details of the revolutionary events in person.[435]

Unlike Bandera, his three brothers—Bohdan, Vasyl', and Oleksandr—were not prevented from participating in the "Ukrainian National Revolution" in the "newly occupied territories." Bohdan and Vasyl' arrived in Ukraine from the General Government, and Oleksandr from Rome. Vasyl' organized a meeting in Stanislaviv, and Bohdan in Kalush, at which they announced the proclamation of the OUN-B state as "Struggle and Activities" and other documents instructed them.[436] According to testimonies of Jewish survivors, in addition to these "revolutionary" activities, either Vasyl' or Oleksandr organized pogroms around Bolekhiv, not far from their home village of Staryi Uhryniv.[437]

434 On transnational justice, see Pablo De Greiff, "Theorizing Transnational Justice," in *Transnational Justice*, ed. Melissa S. Williams, Rosenmary Nagy, and Jon Elster (New York: New York University Press, 2012), 42–44; Ruti Teitel, *Transitional Justice* (Oxford: Oxford University Press, 2000), 13.

435 "Druhovi Ivanovi Klymovomu Liehendi, Kraievomu Providnykovi OUN na MUZ, Chlenovi Provodu OUN," TsDAVOV f. 3833, op. 1, spr. 44, 4.

436 HDA SBU f. 65, spr. 19127, vol. 1, 146–51, in *Stepan Bandera*, ed. Serhiichuk, 1:336, 338–39. For Oleksandr, see Interrogation of Fedor Davidiuk, 13 June 1941, HDA SBU f. 65, spr. 19127, vol. 1, 135–56, in *Stepan Bandera*, ed. Serhiichuk, 1:331.

437 Ellen Pressler mentiones in her testimony that one of Bandera's brothers organized pogroms around Bolekhiv. See AŻIH, 301/2146, Ellen Pressler, 1. On pogroms around Kalush, see AŻIH, 301/4928, Mundek Kramer, 1. Franziska Bruder identified Vasyl' Bandera as the organizer of the pogroms. See Bruder, *"Den Ukrainischen Staat*, 146. It could, however, have been either Vasyl' or Bohdan, or even both, because at the beginning of July they both visited Teodor Davidiuk in Holyn', who was married to their sister Volodymyra. Holyn' is in the vicinity of Bolekhiv. Cf. HDA SBU f. 65, spr. 19127, vol. 1, 146–51, in *Stepan Bandera*, ed. Serhiichuk, 1:336, 338–39. OUN-B member Mykola Chartoryis'kyi met one of the Bandera brothers in Stryi, see Chartoryis'kyi, *Vid Sianu po Krym*, 51.

Conclusion

The Second World War set Bandera free. He went to Lviv but soon left for Cracow because the OUN realized that the international situation did not lend itself to conducting a national revolution. The conflict between the generations led to a split of the OUN in 1940 into the Bandera and Mel'nyk factions. The OUN-B in collaboration with the Nazis prepared itself for Operation Barbarossa and the "Ukrainian National Revolution." It attempted to establish a Ukrainian state after the German attack on the Soviet Union and hoped that the Germans would approve of it, as they had accepted the states established by the Hlinka Party and the Ustaša. After the German attack on the Soviet Union on 22 June 1941, the OUN-B task forces assisted the German troops and together with them and the local Ukrainians organized a number of pogroms in western Ukraine as the result of which several thousand Jews were murdered, robbed, or otherwise mistreated. Bandera's responsibility for these acts of mass violence is a question that can only be answered in a nuanced and complex way because his agency was restricted by the Germans.

A few hours after the outbreak of the pogroms in Lviv on 30 June 1941, the OUN-B proclaimed Ukrainian statehood. In the following days, Stets'ko wrote letters to Hitler, Mussolini, Pavelić, and Franco and asked them to accept the new Ukrainian state, but the leading Nazi politicians did not give their approval. They had plans for Ukraine and the Baltic states that were different from those for Croatia and Slovakia. The Germans arrested some members of the OUN-B leadership, among them Bandera and Stets'ko, and took them to Berlin. Some Ukrainians, motivated by the OUN-B, tried in numerous letters to convince Hitler to release Bandera and Stets'ko and allow them to rule a Ukrainian state. They hoped that Bandera would be allowed to be their *Providnyk* and would be able to rule a state apparatus that would transform Ukraine into a purely Ukrainian country.

Chapter 5

RESISTANCE, COLLABORATION, AND GENOCIDAL ASPIRATIONS

During the Second World War, Ukrainians were both victims and perpetrators. They fought both willingly and under coercion on the side of Stalin against Hitler, and on the side of Hitler against Stalin.[1] According to estimates by historians, 6,850,000 people (16.3 percent of the population), were killed in Ukraine during the Second World War, of whom 5,200,000 were civilians of various nationalities.[2] When Nazi Germany attacked the Soviet Union on 22 June 1941, about 2.7 million Jews lived in the territory of present-day Ukraine, or 2.47 million within the borders of the Ukrainian SSR of 1941. During the German occupation of Ukraine, which lasted for some two years in its western territories, and for some three years in its eastern ones, the Germans, with the help of their accomplices, killed more than 1.6 million Ukrainian Jews. Half of them were annihilated in eastern Galicia and Volhynia, whose united territory was much smaller than the rest of the country. Among the 900,000 Ukrainian Jews who saved themselves by escaping with the Soviet Army, there was only a very small number from western Ukraine. The number of survivors in western Ukraine was also low. Whereas 97 percent of the Jews in the Ternopil' oblast did not survive the Holocaust, 91 percent of the Jews in the Kharkiv oblast survived. In general, among the 100,000 Jews who survived the war in Ukraine in hiding or in Nazi slave labor camps, there were less than 20,000 from eastern Galicia and Volhynia.[3]

In eastern Galicia 570,000 Jews and in Volhynia 250,000 were annihilated in four stages. The first stage was the pogroms, which cost about 30,000 Jewish lives in both regions, and which were analyzed in the previous chapter in connection with the "Ukrainian National Revolution." In the second stage, which began during the pogroms and lasted until the end of 1941, Einsatzgruppe C shot about 50,000 Jews in eastern Galicia and 25,000 in Volhynia. The third stage differed between eastern Galicia and Volhynia. About 200,000 Jews in Volhynia were shot close to the ghet-

1 More than 4.5 million Ukrainians served in the Red Army during the Second World War, and there were also more than 2,000 partisan groups with some 200,000 fighters in Ukraine. At the same time, up to one million soldiers, many of them Ukrainians, served in various German formations. Cf. Bohdan Krawchenko, "Soviet Ukraine under Nazi Occupation, 1941–44," in *Ukraine during World War II: History and its Aftermath*, ed. Yury Boshyk (Edmonton: Canadian Institute of Ukrainian Studies, University of Alberta 1986): 30–31; Mykhailo Koval, *Ukraïna v Druhii svitovii i Velykii Vitchyznianii viinakh (1939–1945)* (Kiev, Al'ternatyvy 1999), 270; Mark R. Elliott, "Soviet Military Collaborators during world War II," in: *Ukraine during World War II*, ed. Boshyk, 98. For the Ukrainian police and the Waffen-SS Galizien, see this chapter.

2 Vadim Erlikhman, Poteri narodonaseleniia v XX veke: spravochnik (Moscow: Russkaia panorama, 2004), 33–35. See also Ray Brandon and Wendy Lower, "Introduction," in *Shoah in Ukraine*, ed. Brandon, 11.

3 Kruglov, Jewish Losses in Ukraine, 273, 284; Polonsky, *The Jews in Poland and Russia*, 3:569. For the total number of Jews in Ukraine in June 1940, see also Brandon, "Introduction," 17.

toes or in the local fields and forests. The Einsatzkommandos and Sicherheitspolizei (Security Police), who were assisted by the Ukrainian police, finished the murder of Volhynian Jews in late 1942. In eastern Galicia, more than 200,000 Jews were sent to the Bełżec annihilation camp, 150,000 were shot, and 80,000 were killed or died in the ghettos and labor camps. The extermination of the majority of eastern Galician Jews was completed in the summer of 1943. In the fourth stage, about 10 percent (80,000) of all western Ukrainian Jews fought for their lives while hiding in the woods, countryside, towns and cities. Ukrainian nationalists were involved in different ways in all four stages of the murder of the western Ukrainian Jews and committed other massacres of civilians, while pursuing their revolutionary and genocidal ideas.[4]

The OUN-M and the Question of Eastern Ukraine

During the first weeks after the onset of the German invasion of the Soviet Union, the OUN-M, like the OUN-B, also sent task forces to organize a state in Ukraine. Although the OUN-M task forces in western Ukraine were less of a presence and less effective than the OUN-B's, the OUN-M managed to establish the Ukrainian National Council (*Ukraïns'ka Natsional'na Rada*, UNR) in Kiev, an administrative organ dissolved by the Germans on 17 November 1941.[5] In Bukovina, OUN-M members staged pogroms in towns and villages around Chernivtsi.[6] The OUN-M leader Andrii Mel'nyk was no less eager than Bandera to collaborate with the Germans. On 26 July 1941, the newspaper *Rohatyns'ke slovo* republished Mel'nyk's article "Ukraine and the New Order in Europe" including:

> We collaborate closely with Germany and invest everything in this collaboration: our heart, feelings, all of our creativeness, life and blood. Because we believe that Adolf Hitler's new order in Europe is the real order, and that Ukraine is one of the avant-gardes in Eastern Europe, and perhaps the most important factor in strengthening this new order. And, what is also very important, Ukraine is the natural ally of Germany.[7]

Both before and after the German attack on the Soviet Union, there was ruthless conflict between the OUN-B and the OUN-M. The OUN-M activists Omelian Senyk and Mykola Stsibors'kyi were murdered on 30 August 1941 in Zhytomyr, in all probability by the OUN-B.[8] According to OUN-B member Myron Matviieiko, his fellow-member Mykola Klymyshyn organized the assassinations.[9] Taras Bul'ba-Borovets' wrote that the "Banderite Kuzii" killed Senyk and Stsibors'kyi "by shooting them in

4 Kruglov, Jewish Losses in Ukraine, 278–88; Pohl, *Nationalsozialistische*, 43–44, 139–262, 385; Spector, *Holocaust of Volhynian Jews*, 11; Snyder, The Life and Death, 92, 96–97.

5 Berkhoff, *Harvest of Despair*, 51–52; Motyka, *Ukraińska partyzantka*, 94.

6 Solonari, Patterns of Violence, 766–69; Diukov, *Vtorostepennyi vrag*, 77.

7 "Ukraïna i novyi lad v Evropi," *Rohatyns'ke slovo*, 26 July 1941, 3.

8 The OUN-B member Il'ia Tkachuk testified that Stsibors'kyi, Senyk, and Baranovs'kyi were killed by the OUN-B. Cf. Interrogation of Il'ia Tkachuk, 23 February 1944, HDA SBU f. 13, spr. 372, vol. 6, 56. See also Motyka, *Ukraińska partyzantka*, 94.

9 "Protokol doprosa parashiutysta po klichke 'Miron,' 16 July 1951," HDA SBU f. 6, op. 37, spr. 56232, 27–72, in *Stepan Bandera*, ed. Serhiichuk, 3:83.

the back on an open street."[10] The OUN-M used the murders to discredit the OUN-B, claiming that the two OUN-M members were killed by "Cain's murderous hand from the ranks of the Banderite communist diversion."[11] In turn, the OUN-B blamed the Germans.[12] The RSHA, however, arrested a number of OUN-B members for this killing and established a homicide division in Lviv, headed by Kurt Fähnrich, which investigated the murder. This suggests that the Germans did not kill the two OUN-M activists.[13] According to German documents, the Ukrainian intelligentsia was outraged by the murders and demanded prosecution of the OUN-B.[14]

The Germans realized that not all Ukrainians supported the OUN-B's "Ukrainian National Revolution."[15] However, they also noticed that OUN-B activists organized meetings in many parts of Ukraine, collected signatures on appeals to release Bandera, and had a huge influence on the militia, mayors, and administration.[16] The OUN-B was certainly popular in eastern Galicia and Volhynia, but it was unknown and sometimes even unwelcome in eastern Ukraine.[17] Eastern Ukrainians were not interested in the ultranationalist, antisemitic, and racist ideology and identity that the OUN-B and other western Ukrainian nationalists propagated. The OUN-B activists who went with the task forces to eastern Ukraine were overwhelmed by the difference in the mentality of eastern Ukrainians. Some of them said that eastern Ukraine was beautiful but that it was not their homeland. They frequently romanticized eastern Ukraine in order to rationalize and accept it. One woman from an OUN-B task force claimed that "the theories of Marxism-Leninism destroyed the soul of the [eastern Ukrainian] nation" and observed that eastern Ukrainians were astonished when they saw OUN-B members praying in a group.[18] The OUN-B's posters, which propagated the political ideas of the organization, alarmed the Ukrainians in Kiev.[19]

Many eastern Ukrainians did not speak Ukrainian. They spoke Russian or a mixture of Russian and Ukrainian. Many of them considered the Russian language to be more civilized than Ukrainian. When the OUN-B activists from the task forces came to central and eastern Ukraine, the population sometimes wondered about the language used by the OUN-B. Eastern Ukrainians preferred reading newspapers in

10 Cf. Bul'ba-Borovets', *Armiia*, 154.

11 "Natsionalisty!, 10 September 1941," TsDAVOV f. 3833, op. 1, spr. 74, 19.

12 "Ereignismeldung UdSSR, Nr. 96, 27.09.1941," BAB R58/217, 357.

13 "RSHA IVD3a-2893/41g, Schnellbrief!, 13.09.1941," BStU, MfS HA IX/11, ZR 920 A. 142, 26–27.

14 "Ereignismeldung UdSSR, Nr. 79, 10.09.1941," BAB R58/217, 9.

15 "Ereignismeldung UdSSR Nr. 25, 17.07.1941," BAB R58/214, 201. Especially the "older intelligentsia" was against the OUN-B. Cf. "Ereignismeldung UdSSR, Nr. 96, 27.09.1941," BAB R58/217, 357; "Ereignismeldung UdSSR, Nr. 99, 30.09.1941," BAB R58/217, 445.

16 Germans reported in early August that OUN-B activists in Lviv were still organizing manifestations, celebrating, and demonstrating the power of the OUN-B militia. Cf. "Ereignismeldung UdSSR, Nr. 44, 06.08.1941," BAB R58/215, 192. On 12 August Germans reported that the militia and mayors in Volhynia were under the strong influence of the OUN-B. Cf. "Ereignismeldung UdSSR, Nr. 50, 12.08.1941," "Ereignismeldung UdSSR, Nr. 51, 13.08.1941," BAB R58/215, 261. For reports about the OUN-B activities in Khmel'nyts'kyi, Berdychiv, Vinnytsia, see BAB R58/216, 20. On 18 August it was reported that the Ukrainian militia was still looting and that the OUN-B was collecting letters in which it demanded that Bandera come to Ukraine. Cf. "Ereignismeldung UdSSR, Nr. 56, 18.08.1941," BAB R58/216, 76–77. In September the OUN-B collected signatures in Staryi Uhryniv and other places for the release of Bandera. Cf. "Ereignismeldung UdSSR, Nr. 78, 09.09.1941," BAB R58/216, 355; "Ereignismeldung UdSSR, Nr. 79, 10.09.1941," BAB R58/217, 10.

17 "Zvit, Zhytomyr 20-27.07.1941," TsDAVOV f. 3833, op. 1, spr. 14, 47.

18 "Spomyny uchasnyka pokhodu III. pivdennoï hrupy," TsDAVOV f. 3833, op. 2, spr. 16, 15.

19 Berkhoff, *Harvest of Despair*, 193.

Russian rather than in Ukrainian. *Nove ukraïns'ke slovo* was the only daily Ukrainian newspaper in the Reichskommissariat and sold poorly. Its forerunner *Ukraïns'ke slovo* had appeared without German censorship until 10 December 1941 and was more popular.[20] Eastern Ukrainians sometimes mistook the OUN-B activists for Polish-speaking Germans. The OUN-B activists felt the need to convince the eastern Ukrainians that the OUN-B were also Ukrainians. This happened, for example, to Chartoryis'kyi from the third task force in the Podolian town of Fel'shtyn:

> "We're not Germans!" I explain. "We are your brothers, Ukrainians from the western lands—from Galicia," I add to be on the safe side. ... "We've come to visit you and to see if there's anything we can help you with ..."
>
> "So there haven't been any Germans here?" I ask again.
>
> "No, only you ..."
>
> "But we're not Germans! We're just like you. ... Can't you tell by our language?" I asked.
>
> "Yes, it looks like even Germans can talk like us!" one of them answers.[21]

The document "Instructions for Work with Workers from SUZ [Eastern Ukrainian Territories]," which was drawn up for the task forces that would go to eastern Ukraine, included the information that the eastern Ukrainians were not a different race. It also claimed that "it is difficult to draw a line that would mark where in [eastern] Ukraine a Ukrainian begins and a Muscovite ends" and that eastern Ukrainians had a "psychological Muscovite complex."[22] Ievhen Stakhiv went with a task force to eastern Ukraine to mobilize the masses for the "Ukrainian National Revolution." He informed me in an interview in 2008 that he had realized that eastern Ukrainians were skeptical about and resistant to the OUN-B and its plans for a fascist and authoritarian state, and that it was impossible to win them over.[23] On the other hand, Chartoryis'kyi of the third task force recalled in his post-war memoirs that some Ukrainians in villages close to Vinnytsia accepted the portraits of Stepan Bandera that the OUN-B members distributed at the propaganda meetings, and that some local Ukrainians even reproduced them.[24] OUN-B member Pavlyshyn remembered that the local Ukrainians in one village near Zhytomyr thought at first that the OUN-B were Soviet partisans. The village teacher then warned the local people against the OUN-B task force: "Do you know who is standing before you, children? A remnant of Petliura's army, a German agent. Our Budyonnyi's army beat them, but didn't finish them off. Get out of here!"[25] The Germans noticed that eastern Ukrainians were different from western Ukrainians. They reported that the eastern Ukrainians did not understand "racist or idealistic antisemitism" because they "lack the leaders and the 'spiritual drive [der geistige Schwung].'"[26]

After Germany attacked the Soviet Union, another organization that tried to establish a state and applied terror toward Jews and other non-Ukrainians was the

20 Berkhoff, *Harvest of Despair*, 193; Kurylo, Syla ta slabkist', 119.

21 Chartoryis'kyi, *Vid Sianu po Krym*, 113–14.

22 "Instructions for the Work with Workers from SUZ," TsDAVOV f. 3833, op. 1, spr. 85, 128.

23 Ievhen Stakhiv, telephone interview by author, Berlin/New Jersey, 11 November 2008.

24 Chartoryis'kyi, *Vid Sianu po Krym*, 145.

25 Shchehliuk, *"Iak rosa,"* 52.

26 "Ereignismeldung UdSSR, Nr. 112, 13.10.1941," BA R58/218, 158; PAAA, R 105182, 219821.

Polis'ka Sich, a paramilitary formation of Ukrainian nationalists under the leadership of Taras Bul'ba-Borovets'. This movement set up a "republic" in Olevs'k, a district center in the Zhytomyr region. The "republic" existed until November 1941, when Germans took over the administration. The streets in the area controlled by the Polis'ka Sich were renamed: one became "Polis'ka Sich Street"; another, "Otaman Taras Bul'ba Street."[27] The attitude of the Polis'ka Sich to Jews did not differ substantially from that of the OUN. They mistreated Jews and conducted pogroms during the summer of 1941. Together with local Ukrainian policemen and a German Einsatzkommando, some members of the Polis'ka Sich killed many Jews in Olevs'k in a mass shooting on 19–20 November 1941.[28]

After the "Ukrainian National Revolution" ended and the situation in Ukraine stabilized, the OUN-M took a different path from that of the OUN-B. The Germans did not ban it or persecute its members. On the contrary, it was the murder of OUN-M members Stsibors'kyi and Senyk that deteriorated the relations between the Germans and the OUN-B.[29] Although the OUN-M tried not to worsen its relations with the Germans, a number of OUN-M activists were arrested, particularly in Kiev.[30] The OUN-M did not organize an underground or an army like the OUN-B but tried to integrate its members into the administration. They were active in the UTsK and engaged in the organization of the Waffen-SS Galizien division.[31] Mel'nyk, the leader of the OUN-M, and a number of other leading OUN-M members were arrested only in early 1944 when they tried to establish relations with the Allies.[32]

Disagreement

The OUN-B proclaimed a state, and a significant number of western Ukrainians would have agreed to live in such a collaborationist state with Stepan Bandera as their *Providnyk* or *Vozhd'*, but Adolf Hitler, and some other Nazi leaders had other plans. In order to win their support for the fight against the Soviet Union, Alfred Rosenberg, Reich Minister for the Occupied Eastern Territories, wanted to give the non-Russians some degree of self-government, but Reichskommissar of Ukraine Erich Koch and several other high ranking Nazis, including General Governor Hans Frank, were against Rosenberg's propositions.[33] In the longer term the fate of Ukraine was to be regulated according to Generalplan Ost: Germans would be settled in Ukrainian territories, some Ukrainians would be enslaved, and the remainder

27 Bul'ba-Borovets', *Armiia*, 153.

28 Motyka, *Ukraińska partyzantka*, 106; Jared McBride, "Ukrainian Neighbors: The Holocaust in Olevs'k" presented at the workshop, *Sixty-Five Years Later: New Research and Conceptualization of the Second World War in Europe*, Stanford University, October 2010.

29 "RSHA IVD3a-2893/41g, Schnellbrief!, 13.09.1941," BStU, MfS HA IX/11, ZR 920 A. 142, 26–27.

30 Kurylo, Syla ta slabkist', 124.

31 "Dopovidna ahenta NKVS pro diial'nist' ounivtsiv na okupovanii hitlerivtsiamy terytorii̇ Ukraïny, 22.07.1944," HDA SBU, f. 65, spr. 9079, vol. 2, 288–95, 300–6, 324 in *Stepan Bandera*, ed. Serhiichuk, 1:190; Statiev, *Soviet Counterinsurgency*, 106.

32 Motyka, *Ukraińska partyzantka*, 129.

33 Brandon, "Introduction," 18. On Rosenberg, see Rudolf A. Mark, "The Ukrainians as Seen by Hitler, Rosenberg and Koch," in *Ukraine: The Challenges of World War II*, ed. Taras Hunczak and Dmytro Shtohryn (Lanham: University Press of America 2003), 23–36; Armstrong, *Ukrainian Nationalism*, 104–5, 113, 117; Dallin, *German Rule in Russia 1941–1945*, 46–58, 84–89.

"eliminated."[34] In practical terms the Germans were, however, dependent on the collaboration of the local population in order to control the occupied territories and to annihilate the Jews.

After Germany's attack on the Soviet Union, the Germans forbade Bandera to leave Cracow for Lviv. Ernst Kundt, under-secretary of state in the General Government, organized a meeting in Cracow on 3 July 1941, in which Bandera and four other politicians from his newly proclaimed government took part. Bandera's German was not fluent. Horbovyi—Bandera's lawyer from the Warsaw and Lviv trials—was one of the four politicians and translated for him. Kundt informed his guests that the Ukrainians might feel like allies of the Germans, but they were not. The Germans were the "conquerors" of Soviet territory, and Ukrainian politicians should not behave in an irrational manner by attempting to establish a state before the war against the Soviet Union had ended. Kundt said that he understood the Ukrainians' hatred toward the Poles and Russians, and the Ukrainians' eagerness to build a state with a proper army. But if they wanted to remain on good terms with Germany and not to compromise themselves in the eyes of the Ukrainian people, they should "stop doing things" and wait for Hitler's decision.[35]

Bandera, who arrived late at the meeting, emphasized that, in the battle against the Soviet Union, the Ukrainian nationalists were "not passive observers, but active members, in the form that the German side allows them." He explained that he had issued orders to his people to fight alongside the Germans and to establish a Ukrainian administration and government in German-occupied territory. Bandera tried to convince Kundt that the authority of the leader of the Ukrainian people came from the OUN, which was the organization that ruled and represented the Ukrainian people. He had tried to clear his policy with Abwehr officers, but they were not competent to resolve political questions of this nature. Kundt replied that only the Wehrmacht and the *Führer* were empowered to establish a Ukrainian government. Bandera conceded that such higher sanction had not been received, but a Ukrainian government was already in existence and its goal was cooperation with the Germans. He was not able to provide any evidence whatsoever of German approval and therefore emphasized that Ukrainian military chaplain Dr. Ivan Hryn'okh was present in a German uniform at the proclamation meeting on 30 June 1941 in Lviv.[36]

The meeting ended with short monologues from each side. Kundt repeated that the proclamation of Ukrainian statehood was not in the German interest and reminded the Ukrainians that only the *Führer* could decide whether, and in what form, a Ukrainian state and government could come into being. The fact that the OUN-B

[34] The Generalplan Ost would affect 64% of Ukrainians, 75% of Byelorussians, and 85% of Poles, see Czesław Madajczyk, ed., *Vom Generalplan Ost zum Generalsiedlungsplan* (Munich: Saur, 1994), 61, 64, 66. For the Generalplan Ost in general, see also Czesław Madajczyk, "Vom 'Generalplan Ost' zum 'Generalumsiedlungsplan,'" in *Der "Generalplan Ost": Hauptlinien der nationalsozialistischen Planungs- und Vernichtungspolitik*, ed. Mechtild Rössler and Sabine Schleiermacher (Berlin: Akademie-Verlag, 1993), VII. For Hitler's attitude toward Eastern Europeans and Ukraine, see Madajczyk, *Vom Generalplan*, 23–25; Henry Picker, *Hitlers Tischgespräche: Im Führerhauptquartier 1941–1942* (Bonn: Athenäum Verlag, 1951), 50–51, 69, 115–16.

[35] "Niederschrift über die Rücksprache mit Mitgliedern des ukrainischen Nationalkomitees und Stepan Bandera, 3.7.1941," BAB NS 26/1198, 1–5, 10. See also Shumuk, *Za skhidnim obriiem*, 431.

[36] "Niederschrift über die Rücksprache mit Mitgliedern des ukrainischen Nationalkomitees und Stepan Bandera, 3.7.1941," BAB NS 26/1198, 9–12.

had informed the German side of its intentions did not mean that the OUN-B had been allowed to proceed.[37] Bandera admitted that he was acting with authority received from the Ukrainian people, but without the approval of the German side. Seeking reconciliation with Kundt, Bandera finally stated that he believed that only Ukrainians could rebuild their own life and establish their own state, but they could do so only with German agreement.[38]

On 5 July 1941, Bandera was taken to Berlin and was placed in Ehrenhaft (honorable captivity), the following day.[39] Stets'ko wrote to Bandera from Lviv, asking what he should do and whether he should inform the masses that the *Providnyk* had been imprisoned. He also encouraged Bandera to negotiate with the Nazis. Stets'ko survived an assassination attempt on 8 July but was arrested the following day. On the night of 11 July, Abwehr officer Alfons Paulus escorted him by train from Cracow to Berlin. Stets'ko was released from arrest on 12 July, as was Bandera on 14 July, both on condition that they report regularly to the police.[40] They stayed together in an apartment house on Dahlmannstrasse in Berlin-Charlottenburg.[41] In Berlin, Stets'ko wrote an autobiography for his interrogators, in which he repeated a point that he had made in his article "We and Jewry" in May 1939:

> Although I consider Moscow, which in fact held Ukraine in captivity, and not Jewry, to be the main and decisive enemy, I nonetheless fully appreciate the undeniably harmful and hostile role of the Jews, who are helping Moscow to enslave Ukraine. I therefore support the destruction of the Jews and the expedience of bringing German methods of exterminating Jewry to Ukraine, barring their assimilation and the like.[42]

While in Berlin, Stets'ko, the premier of the non-existent Ukrainian state, met the prime minister of the provisional government of Lithuania, Kazys Škirpa, who was brought to the German capital for reasons similar to those for Stets'ko's arrival. On two occasions Stets'ko also met with the Japanese ambassador Ōshima Hiroshi. He was also allowed to go to Cracow, where he met Lebed', and he was visited in Berlin

37 On 23 June 1941 the OUN-B member Volodymyr Stakhiv sent Hitler an official letter in which he wrote that the OUN believed that the Jewish-Bolshevik impact on Europe would soon be checked and that the "recreation of an independent national Ukrainian state in the terms of the Brest-Litovsk peace treaty will stabilize the national (*völkisch*) New Order." In the name of Bandera, Stakhiv also sent out the memorandum "Denkschrift der OUN zur Lösung der ukrainischen Frage," in which the OUN expressed its friendly relationship to Nazi Germany and tried to persuade the Nazis to a political collaboration, by applying historical and economic factors. See BAK R 43 II/1500, 61; the whole memorandum is on folios 63–77. The OUN-B member Riko Iaryi also sent a telegram from Vienna to Berlin. He assured Hitler of the OUN-B's loyalty, its readiness to struggle together with the "glorious German Wehrmacht" against "Muscovite Bolshevism," and its willingness to mobilize more Ukrainians living in Germany who could fight for the "liberation of Ukraine" and "finish with the chaos in Eastern Europe." Cf. TsDAVOV f. 3833, op. 1, spr. 22, 10.

38 "Niederschrift," BAB NS 26/1198, 12–14.

39 "Ereignismeldung UdSSR Nr. 13, 05.07.1941," BAB R58/214, 75; "Ereignismeldung UdSSR, Nr. 15, 07.07.1941," BAB R58/214, 90; "Ereignismeldung UdSSR, Nr. 11, 03.07.1941," BAB R58/214, 59.

40 "Komunikat Iaroslav Stet'sko," TsDAVOV f. 3833, op. 1, spr. 6, 2; "Zhyttiepys," TsDAVOV f. 3833, op. 3, spr. 7, 9; "Stet'sko's letter to Bandera," TsDAVOV f. 3833, op. 1, spr. 20, 5; Bruder, *"Den Ukrainischen Staat*, 135; Investigation of Alfons Paulus, 24 September 1945, HDA SBU f. 13, spr. 372, vol. 37, 197–214, in *Stepan Bandera*, ed. Serhiichuk,1:356; Pan'kivs'kyi, *Roky nimets'koï okupatsiï*, 146–47.

41 Stets'ko, *30 chervnia 1941*, 271; Stakhiv, *Kriz' tiurmy*, 98.

42 "Mii zhyttiepys," TsDAVOV f. 3833, op. 3, spr. 7, 6; Zynovii Karbovych, "Zhydivstvo i my," *Novyi shliakh*, 8 May 1939, 3. See also Berkhoff, Organization of Ukrainian Nationalists, 162.

by the OUN-B member Ivan Ravlyk.[43] Bandera—the *Providnyk* of the non-existent state—stayed in Berlin, with identification papers from the RSHA, and a gun to defend himself. He could move in Berlin but was not allowed to leave the city.[44]

In accordance with an order from Heydrich on 13 September 1941, a number of leading OUN-B members, including Bandera and Stets'ko, were arrested on 15 September, the reason for which was the assassination of Stsibors'kyi and Senyk on 30 August in Zhytomyr. This act had entirely changed the attitude of the Nazis to the OUN-B, who, according to the RSHA, "encouraged the Ukrainian population in Galicia and in the operative area [of the Germans] with extensive propaganda not only to resist the directives of German offices, but also to liquidate political enemies. Until now, over ten members of the Organization of Ukrainian Nationalists under the leadership of Andrii Mel'nyk have been killed."[45] According to Lebed' the Germans had the names and addresses of the leading OUN-B members from the OUN-M.[46] Following their arrest, Bandera, Volodymyr Stakhiv, and other OUN-B members were first held by the Gestapo at their premises on Prinz-Albrecht-Strasse,[47] and Stets'ko at the Alexanderplatz prison.[48]

At a meeting organized by Koch on 12 July 1941 in Lviv, all Ukrainian groups except for the OUN-B expressed loyalty to the German authorities. The OUN-B activists came to the meeting and wanted to discuss the questions of Ukrainian sovereignty and the release of their *Providnyk*. Koch informed them that only the *Führer* could decide these issues.[49] According to Lebed's autobiographical sketch from 1952, he, Iaryi, Shukhevych and Klymiv met with five German officers of the Wehrmacht, a few days after Stets'ko's arrest. The German officers proposed to the OUN-B members to "improve cooperation on the basis of a transfer of administrative power [to the OUN-B] on the territory occupied by the Wehrmacht" if the OUN-B withdraws the "Declaration of Independence." The OUN-B refused this proposition.[50]

As early as the second half of July 1941, the Germans were trying to prevent the printing and distribution of OUN-B papers and other propaganda material.[51] In late July, the OUN-B leaders in Galicia assured the German side that they were prepared to collaborate, although they were not pleased with the political situation.[52] In August 1941, Klymiv reminded OUN-B members that the organization was not

43 Stets'ko, *30 chervnia 1941*, 272–73, 276; Armstrong, *Ukrainian Nationalism*, 38.

44 Information collected by the Soviet secret police about Ukrainian nationalists, TsDAHO f. 57, op. 4, spr. 340, 67; "Vernehmungsniederschrift Stefan Popel," 7 February 1956, StM. Pol. Dir. München 9281, 84.

45 "RSHA IVD3a-2893/41g, Schnellbrief! 13.09.1941," BStU, MfS HA IX/11, ZR 920 A. 142, 23–24. In 1944 the OUN-M claimed that the OUN-B killed a total of 1,500 OUN-M members. Cf. "Dopovidna ahenta NKVS pro diial'nist' ounivtsiv na okupovanii hitlierivtsiamy terytorii Ukraïny, 22.07.1944," HDA SBU, f. 65, spr. 9079, vol. 2, 288–95, 300–6, 324, in *Stepan Bandera*, ed. Serhiichuk, 1: 186.

46 Mykola Lebed, Biographic Data, 18 May 1952, RG 263, ZZ-18, Box#80, NN3-263-02-008, Mykola Lebed Name File, vol. 1, 45.

47 For detention by the Gestapo in the Prinz-Albrecht-Strasse, see "Vernehmungsniederschrift Stefan Popel," 7 February 1956, StM. Pol. Dir. München 9281, 84; Stets'ko, *30 chervnia 1941*, 319. According to Luka Pavlyshyn, Bandera was also detained in the Berlin-Moabit prison (Zellengefängnis Lehrter Straße 1–5), see Shchehliuk, "*Iak rosa*," 54.

48 Stets'ko, *30 chervnia 1941*, 160, 319.

49 "Ereignismeldung UdSSR, 15.07.1941," BAB R58/214, 173.

50 Mykola Lebed, Biographic Data, 18 May 1952, RG 263, ZZ-18, Box#80, NN3-263-02-008, Mykola Lebed Name File, vol. 1, 38–39.

51 "Ereignismeldung UdSSR, 17.07.1941," BA R58/214, 200.

52 "Ereignismeldung UdSSR, Nr. 38, 30.07.1941," BAB R58/215, 105.

fighting against the Germans but was trying to improve relations with them, a statement that was reported to Berlin.[53] At about the same time, the Germans discovered an inscription in Kovel': "Away with Foreign Authority! Long Live Stepan Bandera!" This indicates that some sections of the OUN-B were ambiguous about Germany and that Bandera was becoming a symbol of opposition to the Germans, even if he himself wanted to collaborate with them.[54] The German authorities dissolved the OUN-B militia and parts of the OUN-B administration and established a new administration, which, however, still included many OUN-B members.[55]

On 19 July 1941, Hitler decided to incorporate eastern Galicia as Distrikt Galizien into the General Government. A direction to this effect was given on 1 August 1941.[56] Karl Lasch became the governor of Distrikt Galizien; Otto Wächter replaced him in January 1942. Volhynia and most of pre-1939 Soviet Ukraine became Reichskommissariat Ukraine, and were governed by Reichskommissar Erich Koch. Hitler's decision of 19 July disappointed and frustrated many Ukrainian nationalists who had hoped that all Ukrainian territories would remain united in one political body (Map 5). They interpreted the incorporation of eastern Galicia into the General Government as incorporation into Poland. Bandera and Stets'ko protested in official letters to "Your Excellency Adolf Hitler." The *Providnyk* asked the *Führer* to reverse the division and explained the situation by comparing the Ukrainian nationalists to the National Socialists from the eastern homeland (*ostmärkische Heimat*).[57] Stets'ko informed Hitler that he hoped that this administrative division was only temporary. He claimed that the division pained the Ukrainian people, and he asked the *Führer* to "make up for the pain."[58] Sheptyts'kyi also objected,[59] and Polians'kyi, OUN-B mayor of Lviv, even wanted to commit suicide.[60]

Relations between the OUN-B and the Nazis were ambiguous until the assassination of Stsibors'kyi and Senyk on 30 August 1941. It was only after the assassination that the Nazis began arresting and shooting OUN-B members,[61] and that the Gestapo closed the OUN-B offices in Vienna and at Mecklenburgische Strasse 73 in Berlin.[62] In early October 1941 in Zboiska (near Lviv), Lebed' organized the first conference of

53 "Zaiava," TsDAVOV f. 3833, op. 1, spr. 63, 8; "Ereignismeldung UdSSR, Nr. 60, 22.08.1941," BAB R58/216, 132.

54 On 9 September, Germans reported OUN-B "independence propaganda" in Volhynia but also cooperation between the OUN-B and the Wehrmacht. Cf. "Ereignismeldung UdSSR, Nr. 78, 09.09.1941," BAB R58/216, 354–55. On 27 September, Germans reported about the ambiguity of the OUN-B. Cf. "Ereignismeldung UdSSR, Nr. 96, 27.09.1941," BAB R58/217, 357.

55 "Ereignismeldung UdSSR, Nr. 34, 26.07.1941," BAB R58/215, 56. On 18 August Germans reported that the Ukrainian militia was still looting, making anti-German statements, disobeying German orders, and demanding that Poles should wear armbands like Jews. Cf. "Ereignismeldung UdSSR, Nr. 56, 18.08.1941," BAB R58/216, 76–77.

56 "Ereignismeldung UdSSR, Nr. 44, 06.08.1941," BA R58/215, 191; "Ereignismeldung UdSSR, Nr. 40, 01.08.1941," BAB R58/215, 119.

57 "An Seine Exzellenz den Herrn Deutschen Reichskanzler Adolf Hitler," 3 August 1941, BAK R 43 II/685, 22–23.

58 Ibid., 7–8.

59 For Sheptyts'kyi, see "Ereignismeldung UdSSR, Nr. 32, 24.07.1941," BAB R58/215, 19.

60 On the mayor, see "Ereignismeldung UdSSR, Nr. 38, 30.07.1941," BAB R58/215, 104.

61 "RSHA IVD3a-2893/41g, Schnellbrief!, 13.09.1941," BStU, MfS HA IX/11, ZR 920 A. 142, 22–27; Berkhoff, *Harvest of Despair*, 52; Armstrong, *Ukrainian Nationalism*, 96–97.

62 "RSHA IVD3a-2893/41g, Schnellbrief! 13.09.1941," BStU, MfS HA IX/11, ZR 920 A. 142, 26.

Map 5. The Second World War in Ukraine, January 1942 – October 1945.
Encyclopedia of Ukraine, 5:726.

the OUN-B. The participants were impressed by the military successes of the Wehrmacht and were certain that Germany would win the war. They therefore decided that the OUN-B should not oppose the Germans but should go underground.[63]

On 28 October 1941, a group of OUN-B members sent a letter to the Gestapo in Lviv. They stated that Hitler had deceived Ukraine and that America, England, and Russia would allow an independent Ukraine to arise, from the San to the Black Sea. "Long live a great independent Ukraine without Jews, Poles, and Germans," they wrote and added: "Poles across the San, Germans to Berlin, Jews on the hook." Finally, the authors stated that Germany needed Ukraine to win the war, and they demanded the release of imprisoned comrades.[64] After 25 November 1941, the official policy of the Einsatzgruppen was to shoot OUN-B members in secret as looters, and a number of OUN-B members were killed by the Germans in various circumstances.[65] In

63 GARF R-9478, op. 1, del. 136, 45–48; Motyka, *Ukraińska partyzantka*, 100.
64 "Ereignismeldung UdSSR, Nr. 126, 29.10.1941," BAB R58/218, 323.
65 Berkhoff, *Harvest of Despair*, 52; Motyka, *Ukraińska partyzantka*, 110.

December 1941 the OUN-B announced that the Nazis had arrested 1,500 of their members.[66]

In July and August 1942, 48 OUN-B members, among them Bandera's brothers Vasyl' and Oleksandr, were delivered to the concentration camp at Auschwitz. In October 1943, a further 130 OUN-B members were delivered to Auschwitz from Lviv. In the camp, they had the rank of political prisoners. They stayed in KZ Auschwitz I and worked where the chances of survival were good, such as the kitchen, bakery, tailor's workshop, and storerooms for objects confiscated from new arrivals. They also received food parcels from the Ukrainian Red Cross. Some OUN-B members at Auschwitz were released in December 1944. Some were evacuated in January 1945 to other camps. Of the 48 delivered in 1942, 16 did not survive the camp. In total, more than 30 of the approximately 200 OUN-B members delivered to Auschwitz did not survive, including Bandera's brothers, Vasyl' and Oleksandr. The testimonies of the prisoners who survived the camp are ambiguous about the circumstances surrounding the death of Bandera's brothers.[67]

According to the OUN-B prisoner Petro Mirchuk, Vasyl' and Oleksandr died as a result of mistreatment by a Polish *Vorarbeiter* (foreman) Franciszek Podkulski, and Oberkapo Józef Kral, a few days after being delivered to Auschwitz. Both of Stepan Bandera's brothers were mistreated because of their name, which was known to Podkulski and Kral from the Warsaw and Lviv trials.[68] The Polish doctor Jerzy Tabeau, however, who worked as a nurse in Auschwitz, testified on 12 July 1964 at the Frankfurt Auschwitz Trial that one of the Bandera brothers—he did not remember which one—died of diarrhea in the hospital for the prisoners in Auschwitz.[69] Stepan's third brother Bohdan was not arrested by the Germans. He apparently died in unknown circumstances in eastern Ukraine, where he had gone with an OUN-B task force after the German attack on the Soviet Union on 22 June 1941.[70]

A few months before arresting the leading members of the OUN-B, the Germans had detained more than 300 members of the Romanian Iron Guard. The Romanian fascist movement, known as the Iron Guard, was founded in 1927 and first led by Corneliu Zelea Codreanu (1899–1938). His follower Horia Sima (1907–1993) allied

66 *Prolom* 1941, No. 1, 23–24, quoted in *Ukraïns'ke derzhavotvorennia*, ed. Dziuban, 442–43.

67 Adam Cyra, "Banderowcy w KL Auschwitz," *Studia nad faszyzmem i zbrodniami hitlerowskimi* 30 (2008): 388–402; Bruder, *"Den Ukrainischen Staat*, 137. Franziska Bruder, "'Der Gerechtigkeit dienen.' Die ukrainischen Nationalisten als Zeugen im Auschwitz-Prozess," in *Im Labyrinth der Schuld: Täter–Opfer–Ankläger*, ed. Irmtrud Wojak and Susanne Meinl (Frankfurt: Campus Verlag, 2003), 138–54; V-K., A.-T., *Chomu svit movchyt'* (Kiev, 1946), 39; For arrest of OUN-B activists in October in Mykolaïv, see "Ereignismeldung UdSSR, 18.10.1941," BAB R58/218, 213; Pohl, *Nationalsozialistische*, 325.

68 According to Mirchuk, Oleksandr was an Italian citizen. While staying in Rome from 1933, he married a relative of Galeazzo Ciano—Benito Mussolini's son-in-law and the Italian Minister of Foreign Affairs. After Vasyl's and Oleksandr's death, other OUN-B prisoners informed the UTsK in Cracow about this incident. The UTsK contacted Oleksandr's wife and she in turn, Galeazzo Ciano, who approached Himmler. The administration at Auschwitz was ordered to launch an investigation of this incident, which Podkulski did not survive. Oleksandr's wife was informed that her husband had died of diarrhea. See Petro Mirchuk, *In the German Mills of Death 1941–1945* (New York: Vantage Press, 1976), 43–45, 50–52. Mirchuk also mentioned the same during the Auschwitz Trial in 1964, see Bruder, Der Gerechtigkeit dienen, 146. According to Dem'ian, the name of Oleksandr's wife was Mariia, see Dem"ian, *Stepan Bandera ta*, 491.

69 Bruder, Der Gerechtigkeit dienen, 142.

70 "Protokol doprosa zaderzhannogo Davidiuka Fedora Ivanovicha, 20.07.1945," HAD SBU f. 65, spr. 19127, vol. 1, 146–51, in *Stepan Bandera*, ed. Serhiichuk, 1:340; Arsenych, *Rodyna Banderiv*, 59–60.

himself with General Antonescu and for a short period of time they ruled Romania together, after King Carol II abdicated in September 1940. In January 1941 the conflict between Antonescu and Sima escalated. The Iron Guard legionaries tried to take over power but failed. Hitler decided to support Antonescu in order to secure Romanian support for the war. Over 300 legionaries fled to Germany where the Sicherheitspolizei detained and supervised them. In Romania about 9,000 legionaries were arrested at that time. When Sima fled to Italy in December 1942 from a camp in Berkenbrück near Berlin and asked Mussolini to support the Iron Guard, Hitler was so angry that, according to Goebbels, he first considered sentencing Sima to death. From early 1943 on, Romanian legionaries were detained in concentration camps in Fichtenhain, Dachau, Ravensbrück, and Sachsenhausen.[71]

After being taken to Berlin in early July 1941, Bandera and Stets'ko offered much less resistance to the Nazis than nationalist historiography and Ukrainian nationalist propaganda portrayed. They tried to repair the relationship with the Germans, encouraged Ukrainians to collaborate with Germany, and tried to persuade the Germans that they needed and should keep the government established by Stets'ko. In an open letter dated 4 August 1941, Stets'ko encouraged Ukrainians to help the German army in its struggle against the Soviet Union and hoped that the Nazis would accept the Ukrainian state, when they eventually controlled all Ukrainian territories.[72] On 14 August 1941, Bandera wrote to Alfred Rosenberg, Reich Minister for the Occupied Eastern Territories, explaining that he was prepared to discuss the German demand to dissolve the government proclaimed on 30 June 1941.[73] On 9 December 1941, Bandera wrote in a memorandum to Rosenberg: "The Ukrainian nationalists believe that German and Ukrainian interests in Eastern Europe are identical. For both sides, it is a vital necessity to consolidate (normalize) Ukraine in the best and fastest way and to include it into the European spiritual, economic, and political system." He again proposed collaboration and argued that the Nazis needed the Ukrainian nationalists, because only they could help the Nazis to "bring the Ukrainian masses spiritually close to contemporary Germany." According to Bandera, the Ukrainian nationalists were predisposed to help the Nazis, because they were "shaped in a spirit similar to the National Socialist ideas." Bandera also offered that the Ukrainian nationalists would "spiritually cure the Ukrainian youth" who lived in the Soviet Union.[74]

In spite of Bandera's propositions, Rosenberg and other leading Nazi politicians were not interested in discussing this and other related issues with him. Meanwhile, the Germans had begun to cooperate with other groups and individuals who were as eager as Bandera to help them. The OUN-B member Stakhiv wrote in his memoirs

71 Heinen, *Die Legion "Erzengel Michael" in Rumänien*, 428–33, 447–53, 460–63, 518–21; Martin Broszat, "Die Eiserne Garde und das Dritte Reich. Zum Problem des Faschismus in Ostmitteleuropa," *Politische Studien* 9 (1958): 628; Payne, *A History of Fascism*, 396; Koop, *In Hitlers Hand*, 190–96. For Goebbels, see 1 January 1943, *Die Tagebücher von Joseph Goebbels*, ed. Elke Fröhlich, Part II (Munich: K.G. Saur, 1993), 7:29–30.

72 "Komunikat, 04.08.1941," TsDAVOV f. 3833, op. 1, spr. 6, 3.

73 "Stepan Bandera an Reichsminister Alfred Rosenberg. Berlin, den 14. August 1941," in Bußmann, *Akten zur deutschen*, 261–62.

74 Bandera's memorandum to Alfred Rosenberg, Berlin 9 December 1941, in *OUN v 1941 rotsi: Dokumenty chastyna 1*, ed. Stanislav Kul'chyts'kyi (Kiev: Instytut istoriï Ukraïny NAN Ukraïny, 2006), 564.

that when he visited Berlin in December 1941, Bandera gave him a message for Mykola Lebed', his deputy in Ukraine, informing him that the OUN-B should not fight against the Germans but should try instead to repair German-Ukrainian relations.[75]

Ukraine without Bandera

The Nazis did not want to collaborate with the hot-headed OUN-B but were interested in working with more moderate Ukrainian nationalists. In contrast to Jews and Poles, Ukrainians were a privileged ethnic group in the General Government. Unlike the Roman Catholic Church, the Greek Catholic Church in the General Government was not oppressed. The Ukrainian intelligentsia thrived in the General Government, where seventy Ukrainian periodicals existed, a government-sponsored school system became reality, and from where students were sent to study at German universities. The Ukrainian politicians tried to "entirely Ukrainianize" the Polish scholarly institute Ossolineum and the Technical University in Lviv. They thereby continued the Ukrainization that had already begun under Soviet occupation. The main cause of Ukrainian discontent in the General Government was the German drive for manpower for farms and factories in Germany. But the UTsK—the most important Ukrainian collaborationist institution—took care of it and convinced Ukrainians to support the German war effort and to work for the common cause.[76]

Because the Germans wanted to win their loyalty, they applied liberal politics toward Ukrainians in the General Government and played them off against the Poles. Ukraine did not become an independent state as the Ukrainian nationalists wanted, but life for Ukrainians in Galicia under German occupation was not very different from the life of collaborating national groups in states like Slovakia or Croatia. In contrast, the policies toward Ukrainians in Reichskommissariat Ukraine were much harsher. The Nazis treated the Reichskommissariat as a colony and the Ukrainians there were simply to supply the Reich with grain.[77] All universities were closed down and education was limited to four years of primary school.[78] In two decades, Himmler planned to have a system of exclusively German cities at the intersections of highways and railroads in the Reichskommissariat.[79] Because the Ukrainian territories were to be settled with Germans and some Ukrainians were to be enslaved and others "eliminated," the Nazis regarded the eastern Ukrainians simply as a labor force. If they were not productive or became "superfluous," they could be starved to death or shot. Erich Koch, head of the Reichskommissariat, claimed that "if this people works ten hours daily, it will have to work eight hours for us."[80] Apart from work, Hitler

75 Stakhiv, *Kriz' tiurmy*, 99–100.

76 "Ereignismeldung UdSSR, Nr. 39, 31.07.1941," R58/215, 114; Mick, *Kriegserfahrungen*, 494. The Ukrainization of Lviv University and other institutions had begun during the Soviet occupation of western Ukraine after September 1939, see Mick, *Kriegserfahrungen*, 432–39; Golczewski, Shades of Grey, 134–35.

77 Berkhoff, *Harvest of Despair*, 114–63, 187.

78 Golczewski, Shades of Grey, 134.

79 Berkhoff, *Harvest of Despair*, 45, 165.

80 Quoted in Berkhoff, *Harvest of Despair*, 47.

said that he would allow only music for the masses and religious life in Reichskommissariat Ukraine.[81]

From April 1940 until January 1945, the head of the UTsK, the most important Ukrainian collaborationist institution in the General Government, was Volodymyr Kubiiovych. Prior to the Second World War, Kubiiovych had socialized with members of the OUN in Berlin.[82] Their goals and political views did not differ greatly but he was more cautious and diplomatic. In April 1941, Kubiiovych asked Hans Frank, head of the General Government, to set up an ethnically pure Ukrainian enclave there, free from Jews and Poles.[83] In July 1941, on the initiative of the OUN, Kubiiovych asked Frank for a "Ukrainian National Army" or Ukrainian Wehrmacht, which would fight alongside the German Wehrmacht against the Red Army and the "Jewified English-American plutocracy" (*verjudete englisch-amerikanische Plutokratie*).[84] In August 1941, Kubiiovych asked Frank to have "a very significant part of confiscated Jewish wealth turned over to the Ukrainian people." It belonged to Ukrainians and had ended up in Jewish hands "only through a ruthless breach of law on the part of the Jews, and their exploitation of members of the Ukrainian people."[85] He thereby used arguments similar to those of Father Jozef Tiso and Marshal Ion Antonescu.[86] The UTsK was obviously pressing for aryanization at all administrative levels.[87]

The UTsK was associated with the collaborationist newspaper *Krakivs'ki visti*, which not only republished German propaganda but also encouraged Ukrainian intellectuals to express antisemitic views. In 1943 Bohdan Osadczuk and Ivan Rudnyts'kyi, who would become prominent Ukrainian intellectuals after the Second World War, published articles in *Krakivs'ki visti* on the NKVD massacres in Vinnytsia in 1937–1938. The campaign in *Krakivs'ki visti* instrumentalized the Ukrainian victims of the Soviet terror in Vinnytsia in order to mobilize Ukrainians to fight against the Soviet Union. Osadczuk, who covered the German, Ustaša, and other press for *Krakivs'ki visti*, wrote in August 1943: "The mass graves in Vinnytsia, *Hrvatski Narod* states, are new proof of the politics of destruction that the Jews from the Kremlin have conducted among the Ukrainian people. The murdered Ukrainians again throw guilt on Stalin and his Jewish collaborators and summon the world to an implacable struggle against the Jewish-Bolshevik threat, which would like to bring

81 Berkhoff, *Harvest of Despair*, 35.

82 Golczewski, Die Kollaboration in der Ukraine, 160.

83 Jan T. Gross, *Polish Society under German Occupation: The Generalgouvernement, 1939–1944* (Princeton: Princeton University Press, 1979), 186.

84 Kubiiovych to Frank, 7 July 1941, in Wasyl Veryha, *The Correspondence of the Ukrainian Central Committee in Cracow and Lviv with the German Authorities, 1939–1944* (Edmonton: CIUS, 2000), 1:317–18.

85 Kubiiovych to Frank, 29 August 1941, quoted in Golczewski, Shades of Grey, 133–34. The document also appears in Veryha, *Correspondence*, 342.

86 Tatjana Tönsmeyer, "Kollaboration als handlungsleitendes Motiv? Die slowakische Elite und das NS-Regime," in *Kooperation und Verbrechen*, ed. Dieckmann, 51.

87 In Drohobych, for example, Ukrainians were forcing Jews to move out of their apartments because they "did not want to live together with them." Ukrainians cut off the electricity and gas to the Jewish apartments. The UTsK in Drohobych aryanized the property of Jewish craftsmen. Cf. "Betr. Judenangelegenheiten," DALO, f. R-1928, op. 1, spr. 4, USHMM RG 1995.A.1086, reel 31.

upon Europe the same fate that the defenseless victims in Vinnytsia met."[88] Rudnyts'yi called the victims of the Soviet terror the "real martyrs for the Ukrainian national idea."[89]

During the entire period of German occupation, antisemitism was popular in Ukraine, not only in the "anti-German" nationalist underground but also among many organizations and intellectual circles. In 1941 the brochure "Ukraine in the Claws of Jews" was published. This unsigned German-Ukrainian production contained all kinds of antisemitic stereotypes that were applied to the Ukrainian situation.[90] In June 1944, Kubiiovych was invited to take part in an anti-Jewish congress planned by Hans Frank.[91]

In early 1943, Himmler ordered the establishment of a Waffen-SS Galizien division, made up of Ukrainian soldiers, but forbade it to be called Ukrainian. In a speech on 16 May 1944, Himmler claimed that he had called it Galician "according to the name of your beautiful homeland." He also made comments such as "I know if I ordered the Division to exterminate the Poles in this area or that area, I would be a very popular man." Hitler justified the Ukrainian division with the assumption that Galician Ukrainians were "interrelated" with Austrians because they had lived for a long time in the Habsburg Empire. The full name of the Waffen-SS Galizien division was the 14th Waffen Grenadier Division of the SS (*14. Waffen-Grenadier-Division der SS*). Of the 80,000 Ukrainians who volunteered for it, only 8,000 were recruited. After Ukrainians from police battalions and other units joined the division, the Waffen-SS Galizien grew to 14,000 soldiers. A significant number of the men who joined the Waffen-SS Galizien had served in Schutzmannschaft battalions 201, 204, and 206, of which at least battalion 201 almost certainly perpetrated atrocities against civilians in "anti-partisan operations" in Belarus. Other recruits had served in the German security police in western Ukraine. Ukrainians in the Waffen-SS Galizien were trained and indoctrinated by Himmler's SS. They had two hours of education in National Socialist Weltanschauung every week. In August 1943, the soldiers of the Waffen-SS Galizien received blood group tattoos in their left armpits, and 140 men of the division were given additional training in the vicinity of Dachau concentration camp. The soldiers of the Waffen-SS Galizien took the oath: "I swear by God this holy oath, that in the struggle against Bolshevism, I will give absolute obedience to the Commander-in-Chief of the German Armed Forces, Adolf Hitler, and if it be his will, I will always be prepared as a fearless soldier, to lay down my life for this oath."[92] It was as late as February 1945 that Pavlo Shandruk, the Ukrainian general of the division, asked the Germans to allow an amendment to the text of the oath. He proposed to add "and the Ukrainian people" but he did not ask to have Hitler's name removed.[93]

88 Cf. B[ohdan] O[sadchuk], "Kryvava propahanda Ukrainy: Vynnytsia v evropeis'kii presi," *Krakivs'ki visti*, 7 August 1943.

89 For Rudnyts'kyi, see Ivan Lysiak [P.H.], "Nad vidkrytymy mohylamy u Vynnytsi," *Krakivs'ki visti*, 13 July 1943, 1–2.

90 "Ukraïna v zhydivs'kykh labetakh," TsDAVOV f. 3833, op. 2, spr. 74.

91 Hans Frank, *Das Diensttagebuch des deutschen Generalgouverneurs in Polen 1939–1945* (Stuttgart: Deutsch Vergals-Anstalt, 1975), 864.

92 "An den Reichsführer, 05.2.1945" BAB Berlin NS 19/544, 89.

93 For the question of the oath, see "An den Reichsführer, 05.2.1945" BAB Berlin NS 19/544, 87–89. For Himmler's speech, see Heinrich Himmler, "Rede des Reichsführers-SS am 16.5.44 vor dem Führerkorps der 14.Galizischen SS-Freiw. Division," "Informatyvna sluzhba, VI, Postii, dnia 17.05.44,"

The establishment of the division was supported by Sheptyts'kyi. At its first parade, Frank and Kubiiovych took the first salute, and Bishop Iosyf Slipyi performed a religious service. In his speech, Kubiiovych appealed to the division to protect Ukraine against communism, as part of the "New Europe." Vasyl' Veryha, a veteran of this division, mentioned in his memoirs that Ukrainian policemen greeted the Waffen-SS Galizien soldiers with "Heil Hitler!" and that the response was "Glory to Ukraine!" (*Slava Ukraïni!*). He did not specify whether the soldiers and policemen raised their right arms. The Waffen-SS Galizien was established to fight against the Soviet army and did so near Brody in July 1944. Shortly before it was officially included in the division, members of the fourth SS police regiment, which consisted of Ukrainians, had murdered several hundred Polish civilians in Huta Pieniacka on 28 February 1944. According to testimony by UPA partisans, the SS police regiment was supported by UPA freedom fighters when they exterminated the Polish village population. In Slovakia, where the Waffen-SS Galizien helped the Germans to suppress the Slovak National Uprising, individuals from the Waffen-SS Galizien may have committed crimes against civilians as well. Two days after the end of the Second World War 1945, the division surrendered to the British Army. On the grounds that they were Polish citizens and with the intervention of the Vatican, soldiers from the division were not handed over to the Soviet Union, as Vlasov's Russian Liberation Army (*Russkaia osvoboditelnaia armiia*, ROA) soldiers were.[94]

The Ukrainian Police and the OUN-B

In accordance with a directive from Himmler in July 1941, the Ukrainian militia, which had been established by the OUN-B after the German invasion of the Soviet Union, was redeployed in August and September 1941 as a Ukrainian police force, known as *Hilfspolizei* and *Schutzmannschaften*.[95] The Germans generally tried to purge the police of OUN-B members, because they needed people who would carry out orders without pursuing their own political purposes. Nevertheless, many OUN members remained in the police, concealing their association with the OUN-B. Volodymyr Pitulei, commander of the Ukrainian police retained many OUN members in the police force, despite the German order to replace them. Some local German

TsDAVOV, f. 4620, op. 3, spr. 378, 1–9. For recruitment in Dachau, see Vasyl' Veryha, *Pid krylamy vyzvol'nykh dum: Spomyny pidkhorunzhoho dyvizii 'Halychyna'* (Kiev: Vydavnytsvo imeni Oleny Telihy, 2007), 26–27. For education in National Socialist *Weltanschauung*, see Michael James Melnyk, *To Battle: The Formation and History of the 14*[th] *Galician Waffen-SS Division* (Solihull: Helion, 2002), 57. For the SS blood group tattoos, see Melnyk, *To Battle*, 57. For other questions, see Golczewski, Die Kollaboration in der Ukraine, 178–79; Golczewski, Shades of Grey, 136; Himka, A Central European Diaspora, 24; Howard Margolian, *Unauthorized Entry: The Truth about Nazi War Criminals in Canada, 1946–1956* (Toronto: University of Toronto Press, 2000), 133–34.

94 For Sheptyts'kyi, see Yones, *Smoke in the Sand*, 94–95. For using German and Ukrainian fascist greetings in public, see Veryha, *Pid krylamy*, 26–27. For Kubiiovych, see Mick, *Kriegserfahrungen*, 509–10. For Huta Pieniacka, collaboration with the UPA during the massacre in Huta Pieniacka, and related questions, see "Vytiah iz ahenturnoï spravy NKVD URSR 'Zviri' pro podiï v Huti Peniats'kii," *Poliaky ta ukraïntsi mizh dvoma totalitarnymy systemamy 1942–1945*, ed. Serhii Bohunov (Warsaw: Instytut Pamięci Narodowej, 2005), 4:976–80; Motyka, *Ukraińska partyzantka*, 181; Margolian, *Unauthorized Entry*, 133–34; Tönsmeyer, Kollaboration, 25.

95 Golczewski, Die Kollaboration in der Ukraine, 172; Kulińska, *Kwestia ukraińska*, 210; Finder, Collaboration in Eastern Galicia, 104–105.

officials transferred additional OUN-B militiamen to the Hilfspolizei, not knowing that they were members of or sympathizers with the OUN, or for practical reasons. As a result many OUN-B and also OUN-M members remained in the police and in the course of the following weeks and months many more joined it. According to the OUN-B member Bohdan Kazanivs'kyi there were even many OUN-B members among the commandants of the police school in Lviv in which new policemen were recruited.[96] In March 1942, the OUN-B local leaders issued orders to their members to join the police en masse. They tried to have at least one OUN-B member in every police unit, in order to control the police force.[97] The OUN-B also tried to replace OUN-M members in the Schutzmannschaften with its own people.[98] In early 1943, the "Eastern Bureau" of the Polish government-in-exile reported that "the main organizational core [of the OUN-B] in Volhynia is the approximately 200 police stations."[99] The influence of the OUN-B on some of the Ukrainian police was also noted by the Germans.[100] Eliyahu Yones, who worked in the slave-labor camp Kurowice, wrote in his memoirs that the Ukrainian policemen at his camp were Ukrainian nationalists who were proud to wear blue uniforms and Ukrainian caps.[101]

In spring 1942, there were over 4,000 Ukrainian policemen in the General Government.[102] In 1942 in Volhynia, there were 12,000 Ukrainian policemen and only 1,400 Germans.[103] In terms of violence and antisemitism, the new Ukrainian policemen in the General Government and Volhynia were not very different from the previous Ukrainian militiamen. Eliyahu Yones was seized on 12 November 1941 by Ukrainian policemen in Lviv. After he was beaten and robbed by them, a German officer asked him some questions concerning his occupation. Together with other Jews, Yones then had to stay with his face to the wall, and hands on the wall, for several hours. During this time, the Jews were further beaten and humiliated. After several hours they were driven by truck to a bathhouse, where they had to hand over the rest of their belongings and then:

> In the evening, the light was switched on [in a hall of the bathhouse]. Suddenly, we received a new order: "sing."
>
> In the middle of the hall, many Ukrainian men gathered and later, Ukrainian women also came. They took delight in the singing and it was obvious that they looked forward to the upcoming events.

96 Finder, Collaboration in Eastern Galicia, 105; Interrogation of Volodymyr Porendovs'kyi, 15 February 1948, HDA SBU f. 13, spr. 372, vol. 2, 197; Mick, *Kriegserfahrungen*, 483; For Volodymyr Pitulei, see Kazanivs'kyi, *Shliakhom Legendy*, 263–66.

97 "Instruktsiï," TsDAVOV f. 3833, op. 1, spr. 46, 1; "Selected Records of Former Soviet Archives of the Communist Party of Ukraine, 1919–1937, 1941–1962 and 1965," USHMM RG 31.026M, reel 7, 37. For the connection between the OUN and police, see Shumuk, *Za skhidnim obriiem*, 12. For a UPA partisan who, as a policeman, before joining the UPA, helped the Germans to escort Jews to mass graves, see Interrogation of Vladimir Lohvinovich, 4 July 1944, HAD SBU f. 13, spr. 372, vol. 1, 3.

98 "Meldungen aus den besetzen Ostgebieten, Nr. 4, 22.07.1942," BAB R58/697, 63.

99 "Sprawozdanie Sytuacyjne z Ziem Wschodnich za pierwszy kwartał 1943 r.," Adamczyk, *Ziemie Wschodnie*, 22.

100 "Meldungen aus den besetzen Ostgebieten, Nr. 14, 31.06.1942," BAB Berlin R58/698, 83; "Meldungen aus den besetzen Ostgebieten, Nr. 33, 11.12.1942," BAB Berlin R58/698, 147, 154.

101 Yones, *Die Straße nach Lemberg*, 85–86.

102 Finder, Collaboration in Eastern Galicia, 105–106.

103 Timothy Snyder, "The Causes of Ukrainian-Polish Ethnic Cleansing 1943," *Past and Present* 179 (2003): 210.

> The Ukrainians mistreated us until the morning hours. Their disgraceful deeds culminated in their taking an old Jew from the row, who kept a big book in his hand, a Gemarah, which he read. They ordered him to put the book on the floor, to step on it, and to dance a Chasidic dance on it. At first he refused, but finally they forced him, while heavily beating him. He began dancing when the Ukrainians around him beat him; they accompanied his dance with cheers.
>
> Then they sat him on the floor and lit his beard, but the beard did not burn. While some Ukrainians experimented with his beard, others took six Jews with beards from our rows, put them next to the old one and also lit their beards. At first the beards burned, but then the fire sprang on the clothes, and the Jews burned to death in front of us. ...
>
> The Ukrainians continued their mistreatment. They took from our row a deaf Jew who was bald. His head was their target. They threw against him bath devices made from metal and wood. The competition finished soon, as the head of the deaf man was shot into two parts and his brain flew on his clothes and the floor.
>
> There was a Jew with a crooked foot. The Ukrainians tried to straighten it by force. The Jew screamed loudly, but they did not succeed. They were busy with the straightening of this foot until they broke it. The Jew did not stand up again, probably because his heart was broken as well.
>
> Trembling, we were forced to accompany these mistreatments with singing, and as a reward, we were beaten terribly. ...
>
> We were beaten the whole night. In the morning I was one of the twenty-three who survived of a group of about 300 who had come here the previous day. Most were killed by uninterrupted beating.[104]

Of the twenty-three survivors, twenty died during the following hours and days on account of the injuries they obtained during the night in the bathhouse.[105] This description of the deeds of the Ukrainian policemen represents only a very small part of what they did to the Jews while patrolling the ghettos and assisting the Germans with deportations, raids, and shootings. In rural areas, there were few if any German policemen and authority was almost entirely in the hands of the Ukrainian police and the local Ukrainian administration.[106] Holocaust survivor Rena Guz remembered how Ukrainian policemen in the Povorsk (Powórsk) region in Volhynia severely beat Jews, forced them to dance naked, and escorted a group of Jews from the ghetto to the forest, where they made them dig a grave, and then shot them.[107] Bohdan Stashyns'kyi, from the town of Borshchovychi (Barszczowice), close to Lviv, witnessed the prominent role of the Ukrainian Hilfspolizei in the shooting of Jews in his district on several occasions.[108] Like the Polish Kripo (criminal investigation department),

104 Yones, *Die Straße nach Lemberg*, 32–36.

105 Ibid., 36–37. The German administration complained in March 1942 that in the Lviv ghetto Ukrainian policemen frequently mistreated Jews without reason. Cf. "Lviv Oblast" f. 12, op. 1, del. 112, USHMM: RG Acc 1995 A 1086, 43.

106 For the role of the Ukrainian administration in the Holocaust in Kamianets'-Podil's'kyi in Podolia, see Markus Eikel and Valentina Sivaieva, "City Mayors, Raion Chiefs and Village Elders in Ukraine, 1941–4: How Local Administrators Co-operated with the German Occupation Authorities," *Contemporary European History* Vol. 23, No. 3 (2014): 405–28.

107 AŻIH, 301/5737, Guz Rena, 3–4.

108 "Voruntersuchung gegen Bogdan Staschynskij, 22.05.1962," BAK B 362/10137, 282.

the Ukrainian Hilfspolizei was responsible for hunting down and killing Jews who escaped from the ghettos and were hiding in the forests. In western Ukraine, the Ukrainian police shot hundreds or perhaps thousands of Jews who tried to survive in the forest or who hid in the villages.[109]

Many Jews were murdered in Ukraine during the second half of 1942 in particular, as the ghettos were dissolved at that time. Some of the Jews in eastern Galicia (Distrikt Galizien of the General Government) were deported to the Bełżec extermination camp in the course of the Aktion Reinhardt; others were shot. In Volhynia (Reichskomissariat Ukraine) the Jews were shot by units composed of the Sicherheitspolizei (Security Police) and Sicherheitsdienst (Security Service) near the ghettos or in local forests and fields; they were buried in mass graves dug by Soviet POWs (Prisoners of War), local peasants, Ukrainian policemen, or the Jewish victims themselves. The annihilation of the largest number of Volhynian Jews finished in December 1942, and of eastern Galician Jews in July 1943. Dissolving the ghettoes and assisting the Germans by shootings, the Ukrainian policemen seem to have been, in general, no less brutal and eager than the German police or Gestapo officers. For example, during a mass deportation of Jews from the Lviv ghetto in August 1942, a Ukrainian officer of the Hilfspolizei complained that members of Organization Todt obstructed him in completing his duties.[110]

The role of the Ukrainian police in mass shootings was also a significant one. They helped the Germans identify the Jews with the help of lists that had sometimes been prepared by the local Ukrainian administration or by ordinary Ukrainians—frequently their former neighbors. Then the Ukrainian policemen escorted the Jewish victims to the mass graves, and ensured that the Jews did not escape from the execution site, where they were usually shot by Germans and occasionally by Ukrainian policemen.[111] In his study on the Holocaust in Volhynia Shmuel Spector cited the description of one of the numerous shootings which happened before the Jews had been moved to the ghettos. The description was left by a survivor who had lost her relatives during this massacre. On the afternoon of 12 August 1941,

> Two truckloads of Ukrainian policemen and the Gestapo murderers entered the townlet [of Horokiv in Volhynia]. Within minutes all the Ukrainian youth, which probably had prepared itself in advance, enlisted itself to assist them. For about two hours some 300 men, including children aged 14, were seized in the streets or driven from their homes. In searching for and finding the Jews, the Ukrainian youths demonstrated such diligence and energy that no description can do justice to the ignominy of this people.

109 Pohl, *Nationalsozialistische*, 372–73; Snyder, The Life and Death, 94–97.

110 For the complaint, see Pohl, *Nationalsozialistische*, 218. For the deportation action in August 1942, see Pohl, *Nationalsozialistische*, 216–18. For the situation in Volhynia, see Spector, *The Holocaust of Volhynian Jews*, 172–87. For the Ukrainian police generally, see Finder, Collaboration in Eastern Galicia, 100–12; Golczewski, Die Kollaboration in der Ukraine, 173–74; Pohl, *Nationalsozialistische*, 277–78, 289–91, 311–12.

111 For Ukrainian police conducting a mass execution of Jews, see AŻIH, 301/1510, Fefer Bajla, 2. The Ukrainian auxiliaries of the Einsatzgruppe C also carried out shootings. Cf. Dieter Pohl, "The Murder of Ukraine's Jews under German Military Administration and in the Reich Commissariat Ukraine," *Shoah in Ukraine*, ed. Brandon, 55. See also Pohl, *Nationalsozialistische*, 278.

> The Germans did not take part in the abductions. This was carried out with clear conscience by our Ukrainian neighbors who had lived side by side with the Jews for generations. High school students, sons of the nation of murderers, came to drag out their fellow Jewish students. Within minutes, neighbors who for many years had lived next to a Jewish house, became beasts of prey pouncing on their Jewish neighbors. Within a short time the unfortunate victims, my husband, my brother and my brother-in-law, were assembled in the yard of the militia post where they were kept for several hours.
>
> In the meantime a group of men was led to the Park where they were ordered to dig up a large pit. As soon as the digging was completed, they began bringing the unfortunate victims in groups. They were not yet aware of what awaited them. The Ukrainian militia performed its job splendidly. No one among the unfortunates managed to get away. The job of shooting was performed by the German murderers, whose superior training prepared them for it. At six o'clock in the evening the whole thing was over.[112]

In some places, however, the Ukrainian police did not only escort and watch but also participated in the shooting. On 6 September 1941 in Radomyshl', the Ukrainian police assisted Sonderkommando 4a, which shot 1,107 adult Jews. The Ukrainian police themselves shot 561 Jewish youths.[113] During an NKVD interrogation in July 1944, Iakov Ostrovs'kyi stated that, during two shootings, 3,300 Jews were annihilated. Of these, 1,800 were killed by the Germans and 1,500 by the Ukrainian police.[114] According to Stanisław Błażejewski, the Ukrainian policeman Andryk Dobrowolski from Małe Sadki in Volhynia boasted that he personally killed 300 Jews.[115] Joachim Mincer wrote in his diary in 1943 that the "executions in the prison yard" were conducted "mainly by Ukrainian policemen." He identified the main persecutor as a policeman by the name of Bandrowski who "liked to shoot Jews on the street."[116]

From the German attack on the Soviet Union in June 1941 until the summer of 1943, the Ukrainian militiamen and later the Ukrainian policemen learned how to annihilate an entire ethnic group in a relatively short time. Some of them made practical use of this knowledge when they joined the UPA at the request of the OUN-B, in spring 1943.[117] In March 1943, the Polish Home Army (*Armia Krajowa*, AK) observed that Ukrainian policemen in Volhynia sang the words, "We have finished the Jews, now we will do the same with the Poles" and that their economic situation improved during the process of helping the Germans kill the Jews of Volhynia.

112 NCD IP (Nazi Crimes Department, Israeli Police), *pei-ayin* 01273, quoted in Spector, *The Holocaust of Volhynian Jews*, 74–75.
113 "Ereignismeldung UdSSR, Nr. 88, 17.09.1941," BAB R58/217, 164.
114 Interrogation of Iakov Ostrovs'kyi, 7 July 1944, USHMM, RG-31-018M, reel 29, 87.
115 Testimony of Stanisław Błażejewski, KAW, II/36, 10.
116 Quoted in Bartov, Wartime Lies and Other Testimonies, 493.
117 Pohl, Ukrainische Hilfskräfte, 208, 215–216.

The OUN-B in 1942

In April 1942, the Second Conference of the OUN-B took place. At this time, the leaders of the OUN-B considered that the Germans would win the war in the East against the Soviet Union but lose against the Allies in the West. In these circumstances they hoped that the Nazis might change their minds and establish a Ukrainian state with Bandera and Stets'ko as its leaders. Officially however, they wanted to distance themselves from the Germans, so as not to jeopardize relations with the Allies.[118] The leadership of the OUN-B declared that it did not intend to "take part in anti-Jewish actions, in order to avoid becoming a blind tool in alien hands." Yet, in the same resolution, the OUN-B stated that it regarded "Jews as a tool of Russian Bolshevik imperialism," which means that it had not changed its attitude toward them.[119] Other OUN-B documents from 1942 also confirm that the OUN-B did not revise its attitude toward the Jews, and that it took the "Jewish Bolshevism" stereotype for reality. One OUN-B leaflet stated "We do not want to work for Moscow, for the Jews, the Germans, or other strangers, but for ourselves."[120]

In 1942 the Nazis regarded the OUN-B as a "predominantly anti-German, illegal organization."[121] In leaflets distributed in Poltava in the same year, the OUN-B declared its intention to establish a Ukrainian army that would fight against the Wehrmacht.[122] In the Horokhiv region in Volhynia in September 1942, the Germans found a slip of paper attached to a barn, calling on Ukrainians to free themselves from the Germans. The slip was signed in Stepan Bandera's name.[123]

Although in 1941 and 1942, the Gestapo arrested a number of leading OUN-B members in Ukraine and in Germany, several of whom were sent to concentration camps, these measures did not destroy the organization or even substantially affect it.[124] The OUN-B quickly recovered, and more members were recruited for the underground. Bandera, as the legendary *Providnyk* of the movement, did not disappear from the universe of OUN-B activists after the Germans took him to Berlin in early July 1941. For example, the recruitment of new OUN-B members included an oath on Stepan Bandera, Christ, Christ's wounds, wounds of the heroes of the OUN, and a range of historical Ukrainian heroes like Khmel'nyts'kyi. The oath had to be performed under portraits of Bandera and Konovalets' on each side of a trident, and under yellow-and-blue, and red-and-black flags.[125]

Preparing in 1942 for the first anniversary of the proclamation of 30 June 1941, the OUN-B stressed that it wanted to "tie the Nation much more strongly to the Organization and to Providnyk Stepan Bandera." For this purpose, OUN-B activists

118 Motyka, *Ukraińska partyzantka*, 108–109.
119 "Nepovnyi tekst postanov II-oï Konferentsiï," TsDAHO f. 57, op. 4, spr. 346, 14.
120 "Meldungen aus den besetzen Ostgebieten, Nr. 17, 20.08.1942," BAB R58/223, 19.
121 "Ereignismeldung UdSSR Nr. 191, 10.08.1942," BAB R58/221, 288.
122 Ibid., 315–16.
123 "Ereignismeldung UdSSR Nr. 22, 25.09.1942," BAB R58/222, 103.
124 For arrests, see "Meldungen aus den besetzen Ostgebieten, Nr. 30, 20.11.1942," BAB R58/223, 50–51, 57–60. The Gestapo arrested altogether 210 OUN-B members who lived in Germany.
125 "Prysiaha!, n.d.," TsDAVOV f. 3833, op. 1, spr. 37, 5ab; "Meldungen aus den besetzen Ostgebieten, Nr. 4, 22.05,1942," BAB R58/697, 63–64.

delivered speeches and organized church services.[126] Portraits of Bandera and Stets'ko appeared on the first page of the OUN-B *Biuleten'* from June–July 1942.[127] In April 1942, the Germans arrested a group of OUN-B members. The Nazis characterized them as young people without occupation, who spread nationalistic propaganda among peasants and frequently carried "holy medallions and chauvinistic prayers" and "banners with the inscription 'Heil Hitler!'"[128]

The UPA—Mass Violence and "Democratization"

The decision of the OUN-B to found an army was taken at a conference in November 1942 and a meeting in December 1942. The first units of the army were formed in February 1943 in Volhynia, where the OUN-B was headed by Dmytro Kliachkivs'kyi (Klym Savur). In the first instance, the OUN-B called its army the Ukrainian Liberation Army (*Ukraïns'ke Vyzvol'ne Viis'ko*, UVV) but after April-May 1943 the name "Ukrainian Insurgent Army" (*Ukraïns'ka Povstans'ka Armiia*, UPA) became prevalent. This name was previously used by an army headed by Taras Bul'ba-Borovets', who had never recognized the OUN-B proclamation of a state on 30 June 1941. After the OUN-B took over the name of the original UPA, Bul'ba-Borovets' renamed his army as the Ukrainian People's Revolutionary Army (*Ukraïns'ka Narodno-Revoliutsiina Armiia*, UNRA). At the same time, the OUN-B terrorized Bul'ba-Borovets' and his troops, killing his wife and several of his closest officers. Bul'ba-Borovets' proposed collaboration with the Germans but was arrested by them on 1 December 1943 in Warsaw and sent to the Sachsenhausen concentration camp for political prisoners.[129]

Between 19 March and 14 April 1943 alone, about 5,000 out of a total of 12,000 Ukrainian policemen in Volhynia deserted the police force and joined the UPA at the behest of the OUN-B.[130] Other Ukrainians who joined the UPA, with experience in the mass killing of civilians, were soldiers from Schutzmannschaft battalion 201, which was disbanded on 31 December 1942. This battalion had been formed from the Nachtigall and Roland battalions in late 1941 and was sent to Belarus in 1942 to combat partisans. The majority of the people killed in Belarus by this and other Schutzmannschaft battalions were not partisans but civilians.[131] Some individuals from this battalion, such as Roman Shukhevych and Vasyl' Sydor, occupied leading positions in the UPA. After the disbandment of the battalion, a significant number of its members also joined the Waffen-SS Galizien division.[132] An unknown number of Ukrainians deserted from the Waffen-SS Galizien division and joined the UPA. Some of

126 "Instruktsiia v spravi sviatkuvannia 30 chervnia," TsDAVOV f. 3833, op. 1, spr. 85, 2; "Meldungen aus den besetzen Ostgebieten, Nr. 15, 7.08.1942," BAB R58/698, 110–11.

127 *Biuleten'*, No. 6–7, June-July 1942: 1, RGASPI f. 17, op. 125, spr. 337, 27.

128 "Ereignismeldung UdSSR Nr. 191, 10.08.1942," BA R58/221, 305; "Meldungen aus den besetzen Ostgebieten, Nr. 4, 22.05.1942," BAB R58/697, 64.

129 Motyka, *Ukraińska partyzantka*, 112–14, 118, 120–21; Bul'ba-Borovets', *Armiia*, 250–67.

130 Grzegorz Motyka, "Polski policjant na Wołyniu," *Karta* 24 (1998): 126; Motyka, *Ukraińska partyzantka*, 194; Snyder, Causes of Ukrainian-Polish, 211–12; Finder, Collaboration in Eastern Galicia, 108.

131 Snyder, *Bloodlands*, 250–51.

132 Motyka, *Ukraińska partyzantka*, 115. According to Mykhailo Stepaniak, the OUN-B in November 1942 issued the order that Ukrainians from Schuma 201 should not prolong their contracts with the Germans. Cf. GARF R-9478, op. 1, del. 136, 105.

them deserted before the division was defeated by the Red Army near Brody in July 1944; some, after the defeat.[133] Ivan Katchanovski estimated that 46 percent of the OUN and UPA leaders had served in the local Ukrainian police, in Schutzmannschaft battalion 201, or in the Waffen-SS Galizien division, or had been recruited in German-sponsored military or intelligence schools.[134]

The UPA partisans were recruited by OUN-B revolutionaries. Like the OUN-B, they used the greeting "Glory to Ukraine!"—"Glory to the Heroes!" but they abandoned the fascist raising of the arm "slightly to the right, slightly above the peak of the head." They received a thorough ideological education, which was "steeped in the spirit of fanaticism," as the UPA partisan Danylo Shumuk remembered. In their ideology lessons, they learned by heart the "Decalogue of a Ukrainian Nationalist," "The Forty-Four Rules of Life of a Ukrainian Nationalist," and hymns like "O Lord, Almighty and Only" (*Bozhe Velykyi Iedynyi*), and other ideological and religious pieces. They were not allowed to discuss anything and were expected to accept everything that the OUN-B ideologists taught them. Shumuk noticed that this kind of ideological-religious education enabled the UPA insurgents to reconcile the mass murders with their own consciences. They were taught to believe that they could commit mass murders against other ethnic groups, because these groups had harmed "Ukrainians" in the past.[135] In 1944 the UPA counted between 25,000 and 30,000 partisans, who were grouped in more than 100 battalions. It could mobilize up to 100,000 people. After late 1944 and early 1945 the number of partisans declined.[136]

Like the OUN-B activists, the UPA leaders had serious difficulties in cooperating with eastern Ukrainians, for whom nationalist and racist ideology was strange. The UPA leaders frequently mistrusted eastern Ukrainians and did not regard them as "their people." Shukhevych, according to the SB officer Ivan Pan'kiv, ordered eastern Ukrainians killed "on shaky grounds or without any grounds and even contemplated their total extermination, including even OUN and UPA members."[137]

The UPA was divided into UPA-West, UPA-South, and UPA-North. Most UPA partisans were no older than thirty, the majority were under twenty-five, and many were even younger than twenty. The leaders of the UPA, who were leading OUN-B members, were no older than forty. Kliachkivs'kyi, the first colonel of the UPA and the commanding officer of UPA-North, was thirty-two in 1943. His follower Lytvynchuk was twenty-eight in 1945, when he headed UPA-North. Shukhevych, who replaced Kliachkivs'kyi as commander-in-chief of the UPA in August 1943, was thirty-six. The UPA was policed by the Security Service (*Sluzhba Bezpeky*, SB) of the OUN-B, which used draconian measures, including murder and torture, to keep partisans from deserting or defecting. During one month from mid-September to mid-October 1943, the SB executed 110 persons, of whom sixty-eight were Ukrainians. In Novem-

133 "Kontakty UPA s vermakhtom, 21.08.1944," KAW, M/II/30/2, 152.
134 Katchanovski studied biographies of 118 OUN and UPA leaders. Cf. Ivan Katchanovski, "Terrorists or National Heroes," Paper presented at the Annual Conference of the Canadian Political Science Association, Concordia University, Montreal, Canada, 1–3 June 2010. The biographies that Katchanovski studied are in Petro Sodol', *Ukraïns'ka povstans'ka armiia, 1943–49: Dovidnyk* (New York: Proloh, 1994), 63–136.
135 Shumuk, *Za skhidnim obriiem*, 15, 20, 24, 34.
136 Motyka, *Ukraińska partyzantka*, 424.
137 Statiev, *Soviet Counterinsurgency*, 126.

ber 1943, it shot twenty-four deserters from a single company during the course of a day. Despite these harsh measures, many Ukrainians deserted from the UPA. On 8 November 1943 for example, a whole company defected to the Red Army.[138] Some joined the UPA, not for patriotic or ideological reasons, but to avoid forced labor in Germany, or because they were policemen and feared Soviet retribution, or because their friends were in the UPA, or for other reasons.[139] Women in the UPA played an important role as nurses or SB agents.[140]

Between 17 and 21 February 1943, the OUN-B organized the Third OUN Conference. The leadership of the OUN-B thought that Germany would lose the war, and that Ukrainians would have to struggle for independence against the Soviet and Polish armies. Germans were not an essential enemy of the OUN-B or the UPA, because they fought the Soviet Union and might eventually withdraw from Ukraine. However, for the sake of eventual cooperation with the Allies, the leadership of the OUN-B emphasized that it was struggling against two imperialisms: Nazi Germany and the Soviet Union.[141] For the same reason, the OUN-B decided to break away from fascism and to "democratize" itself, but the term "democracy" still had a very negative meaning among the OUN-B and UPA leaders. As at the First Great Assembly in April 1941, the OUN-B also wanted to mobilize other European "enslaved nations" in order to cooperate with them in the struggle against the Soviet Union. The OUN-B condemned all Ukrainians who would collaborate with the Nazis or Soviet authorities. In so doing, the OUN-B and UPA leaders condemned 80 percent of all Ukrainians, as eastern Ukrainians were frequently loyal to the Soviet Union and regarded the UPA as an alien and enemy-like army. The OUN-B preserved the idea of the "Ukrainian National Revolution" of 1941 but it abandoned the right-arm fascist salute.[142] In May 1943, the OUN-B theoretically abandoned the Führerprinzip and established a triumvirate of Zinovii Matla, Dmytro Maïvs'kyi, and Roman Shukhevych. In reality, the triumvirate was dominated by Shukhevych and did not essentially deviate from the Führerprinzip.[143]

Between 21 and 25 August 1943, the OUN-B organized the Third Extraordinary Great Assembly. The participants decided to give Bandera the opportunity to become the leader of the OUN whenever he would be able to resume the position.[144] In official documents, the OUN-B was now manifesting even more hostility against "German Hitlerism and Muscovite Bolshevism"[145] and "international and fascist-national-socialist concepts,"[146] than it had at the Third Conference in February. It stated that it did not want to live in the "New Europe" for which it had yearned in 1941,[147] but it

138 Statiev, *Soviet Counterinsurgency*, 84, 107.
139 Shumuk, *Za skhidnim obriiem*, 26.
140 For women in the nationalist movement, see Burds, Gender and Policing, 289–90.
141 Stepaniak, a participant in this conference, said in an interrogation that the "anti-German declarations were never implemented." Cf. "Protokoly doprosa chlena tsentral'nogo provoda OUN Stepaniak M. D, 20.08.1944," GARF R-9478, op. 1, del. 136, 107.
142 *OUN v svitli*, 76–77, 81–82, 89; Motyka, *Ukraińska partyzantka*, 116–17.
143 Interrogation of Mykhailo Stepaniak, 25 August 1944, HDA SBU f. 13, spr. 372, vol. 1, 40–44; Motyka, *Ukraińska partyzantka*, 116–17.
144 Interrogation of Mykhailo Stepaniak, 25 August 1944, HDA SBU f. 13, spr. 372, vol. 1, 57.
145 *OUN v svitli*, 91.
146 Ibid., 107.
147 Ibid., 114.

based its political concepts on Mikhnovs'kyi and his racist Ukrainian nationalism.[148] With the concept of "Freedom for the Nations and the Person" the OUN-B wanted to break up the Soviet Union into several states. This slogan became the main concept of the Conference of Enslaved Nations of Eastern Europe and Asia, which took place on 21–22 November 1943 near Zhytomyr. The conference, attended by thirty-nine delegates from thirteen countries, was allegedly organized in cooperation with Rosenberg. The conference must have been a disaster for the OUN-B, as they destroyed the minutes and afterwards killed several of its delegates.[149]

In official documents released after the Third Extraordinary Great Assembly, the OUN-B guaranteed the "equality of all citizens of Ukraine" and the rights of minorities, at least those that were "aware of a common fate with the Ukrainian nation" and would "fight together with it for a Ukrainian state."[150] The reason for these statements and considerations was the desire to collaborate with the Allies and to win over the eastern Ukrainians. At this time, the OUN-B was sure that Britain and the United States, both democratic states, would win the war and could help the OUN-B in the fight against the Soviet Union. The OUN-B sent its representatives to Sweden, Italy, and Switzerland, to make contact with the Allies. It also began negotiations with the Home Army (*Armia Krajowa*, AK). It hoped that the AK, which was in contact with the Polish government in London, would help it to contact the Allies. The AK, however, was reluctant to agree to the OUN-B's request, because of the ethnic cleansing conducted by the UPA against the Polish population at this time.[151] In July 1944, for the sake of a "democratic" image and eventual cooperation with Britain and the United States, the OUN and UPA established the Ukrainian Supreme Liberation Council (*Ukraïns'ka Holovna Vyzvol'na Rada*, UHVR).[152]

The UPA and Mass Violence against Poles

At the same time as the OUN-B leadership was discussing how to "democratize" or renew itself and to guarantee rights to national minorities, the UPA in Volhynia under the leadership of Kliachkivs'kyi was conducting an ethnic cleansing, in which they murdered several dozen to several hundred Poles a day. The OUN-B and UPA leadership knew about this ethnic cleansing from the outset. It discussed it and approved it at the Third Extraordinary Great Assembly, which Kliachkivs'kyi attended. From participants, we know that this decision was deliberately not recorded in the official documents.[153] The first systematic mass murders of Poles began in March 1943, when the Ukrainian policemen joined the UPA, but the OUN-B had already killed several hundred Poles in January and February 1943. During these first experimental mass killings, the OUN-B realized that the Poles would not leave the "Ukrainian territories" as the OUN-B demanded, and might try to resist the attacks.

148 Ibid., 91–92.
149 Motyka, *Ukraińska partyzantka*, 126–27; Dorril, *MI6*, 229.
150 *OUN v svitli*, 112, 115, 118.
151 Motyka, *Ukraińska partyzantka*, 622; Dorril, *MI6*, 230–31. For Sweden, see "Protokoly doprosa chlena tsentral'nogo provoda OUN Stepaniak M. D, 30.08.1944," GARF R-9478, op. 1, del. 136, 135.
152 Motyka, *Ukraińska partyzantka*, 130–35.
153 Interrogation of Mykhailo Stepaniak, 25 August 1944, SBU f. 13, spr. 372, vol. 1, 56; Motyka, *Ukraińska partyzantka*, 116.

Therefore, the only way to remove them would be to annihilate them.[154] According to reports of the Polish underground, one of the UPA leaders stated: "On 1 March 1943 we begin an armed uprising. It is a military operation, and as such it is directed against the occupier. The current occupier [the Germans] is however temporary and we should not lose strength fighting against them. When it comes to the Polish question, this is not a military but a minority question. We will solve it as Hitler solved the Jewish question. Unless [the Poles] remove themselves [from the 'Ukrainian territories']."[155]

The Poles who lived in Volhynia and Galicia did not understand why they should leave their homes and did not know where they could go. With the exception of the military settlers who had come after the First World War, Poles had lived in Volhynia and eastern Galicia for centuries and considered it their homeland. Ukrainians were their immediate neighbors. After centuries-long coexistence, the cultural differences between Poles and Ukrainians, especially in the villages, had blurred and were not essential. In 1943 however, the Polish inhabitants of villages became the main target of the UPA, which barely existed in urban areas and was at home in the villages and forests. The annihilation of the Jews in Ukraine, in which the Ukrainian police were involved, had a significant influence on the OUN-B's decision to annihilate the Poles, as it demonstrated that a relatively small number of people could annihilate an entire ethnic group in a relatively short period.[156]

Officially, the OUN-B and UPA euphemized the mass murder of Poles as an "anti-Polish action" but in internal documents the term "cleansing" (*chystka*) was common.[157] UPA orders even specified the date by which a particular territory had to be "cleansed" of Poles. These documents frequently ended with the greeting "Weapons ready—Death to Poles" (*Zbroia na verkh—Smert' poliakam*).[158] The OUN-B justified the "cleansing" by citing both proven and alleged collaboration of Poles with the German and Soviet authorities. Another excuse for the murder of Poles was the position of the Polish government in London, which considered Volhynia and Galicia as territories that would be included in the Polish state after the war. Furthermore, the OUN-B assumed that the Poles living in the "Ukrainian territories" were guilty of centuries-long suppression of Ukraine, and that this justified their death at the hands of the UPA and other Ukrainians. In July 1943, which was one of the most violent months of the ethnic cleansing, the OUN-B distributed a leaflet in which it blamed Poles for triggering the conflict and provoked the UPA to murder them.[159] The OUN-B and UPA encouraged Ukrainians to take the land and property of Poles and offered them "ideology and protection from Polish revenge."[160]

154 For killing Poles in January and February 1943, see Motyka, *Ukraińska partyzantka*, 194, 311–12, and Statiev, *Soviet Counterinsurgency*, 85.

155 "Relacja mjr. T. Klimowskiego," Studium Polski Podziemnej (SPP), collection 13, vol. 61, quoted in Motyka, *Ukraińska partyzantka*, 307.

156 Motyka, *Ukraińska partyzantka*, 309.

157 Compare, for example, the order of 9 April 1943 from Mykola Lebed' to the leadership of the UPA, in Petro Balei, *Fronda Stepana Bandery v OUN 1940 roku* (Kiev: Tekna, 1996), 141. For this order see also Snyder, Causes of Ukrainian-Polish, 202.

158 "Nadzvychaine zariadzhennia, 06.04.1944," KAW, M/II/30/2, 3.

159 Motyka, *Ukraińska partyzantka*, 310, 365.

160 Snyder, Causes of Ukrainian-Polish, 227–28.

In its propaganda, the OUN-B considered it important to depict the ethnic cleansing as an action provoked by Poles, and for which Poles were responsible. It also blamed Germany, the Soviet Union, and the war in general for the mass murder.[161] However, in unofficial talks and documents, it referred to mass murder as "ethnic cleansing" and debated whether it was favorable for Ukraine or not. According to Stepaniak, he and Lebed' argued at the Third Extraordinary Great Assembly that the "UPA compromised itself with its bandit deeds against the Polish population," just as the OUN-B had compromised itself through collaboration with the Germans. During an NKVD interrogation, Stepaniak stated that the majority of the OUN-B leaders were against his and Lebed's alleged position.[162] Yet it is not clear whether Lebed' and Stepaniak indeed opposed the terror of the UPA at the Third Extraordinary Great Assembly, or if Stepaniak only stated this under interrogation, in order not to incriminate himself. Another OUN member, Oleksandr Luts'kyi, confirmed Stepaniak's version of the events of the Third Extraordinary Great Assembly.[163] In April 1943 however, according to Petro Balei, Lebed' had already issued orders concerning the annihilation of Poles in Volhynia. This suggests that Lebed' did not oppose the "cleansing," at least in its first stage.[164] After Shukhevych inspected Volhynia, the leadership of the OUN-B and UPA decided to conduct a similar ethnic cleansing the following year in eastern Galicia. The mass murder of Poles in eastern Galicia began in early 1944 and lasted until spring 1945. Although it was no less cruel than the murders in Volhynia, fewer Poles were killed in eastern Galicia.[165]

Some OUN-B activists and UPA partisans did not agree with the policy of killing Poles, sometimes for personal reasons, but orders required them to carry it out.[166] Not only did the UPA partisans and OUN-B activists personally kill Poles but they also involved the Ukrainian population in the killings. Many Ukrainians in Volhynia and eastern Galicia did not oppose this policy. The OUN-B and the UPA motivated Ukrainians with nationalist and racist slogans and promised them the land of the Polish peasants and an opportunity to enrich themselves. Many of the victims were killed with instruments like axes or pitchforks, which made the mass murders brutal and cruel.[167] Probably because of the shortage of cartridges, the aggressors sometimes preferred to use axes or knives, even when they possessed firearms.[168] Ordinary Ukrainians sometimes murdered their immediate Polish neighbors or were involved in their murder.[169]

161 Motyka, *Ukraińska partyzantka*, 380.

162 Interrogation of Mykhailo Stepaniak, 25 August 1944, SBU f. 13, spr. 372, vol. 1, 56. See also Motyka, *Ukraińska partyzantka*, 366.

163 Interrogation of Oleksandr Luts'kyi, 19–20 July 1945, SBU f. 13, spr. 372, vol. 1, 336.

164 Balei, *Fronda Stepana Bandery*, 141. See also Snyder, Causes of Ukrainian-Polish, 202; Bul'ba-Borovets', *Armiia*, 250–66.

165 Motyka, *Ukraińska partyzantka*, 367, 379, 408.

166 Ibid., 308.

167 Ibid., 310, 315, 332, 334, 336. Klym Savur (Kliachkivs'kyi), the main advocate and promoter of the "cleansing," promised Ukrainians the land of Polish peasants. Cf. "Rozporiadzhennia, 15.7.1943," TsDAVOV f. 3833, op. 1, spr. 48, 1.

168 Motyka, *Ukraińska partyzantka*, 381.

169 See for example Testimony of Katarzyna Ograbek, KAW, II/2541/4. For other testimonies concerning Poles murdered by the UPA see the collection Siemaszko, *Ludobójstwo dokonane*. The archives of the Karta Institute in Warsaw hold a large collection of testimonies by Polish survivors of the UPA "cleansing."

The OUN-B and UPA were prepared to murder all Poles who would not leave the "Ukrainian territories," including women and children. They frequently returned on the second or third day after an attack and looked for survivors in order to slaughter them. The UPA regularly demanded that Ukrainians in mixed marriages kill their spouses and children.[170] Poles had lived in Volhynia and eastern Galicia for decades and centuries, and were often bilingual. The UPA partisans frequently could not identify Poles by language. If they could not learn from local Ukrainians who was Polish, they asked the suspect to pray in Ukrainian.[171] The idea of annihilating the "non-Ukrainian" partner in a mixed marriage goes back to the racist roots of OUN-B ideology. In "The Nation as a Species," an undated brochure published perhaps in 1944, the OUN came to the conclusion that a mixed marriage was a crime that should be punished: "The Ukrainian nation is against mixed marriage and regards it as a crime. ... The substance of our families must be Ukrainian (father, mother, and children). The family is the most important organic unity, the highest cell of the national collective, and thus we have to keep it purely Ukrainian."[172]

Elsewhere in the brochure, we read that all nations are races and that the Ukrainian nation is a unique race, the purity of which should be protected by law, because it is natural for every nation to protect itself against weaker races. To substantiate its racist arguments, the authors of the brochure referred to the Ukrainian geographer Rudnyts'kyi:

> Professor Dr. St. Rudnyts'kyi, in his book *On the Basis of Ukrainian Nationalism* writes that "mixed marriages with our neighboring peoples are disadvantageous," as they lead to the denationalization of many and the degeneration of others. ... Our neighbors played a very sad role in mixed marriages because they are much weaker physically, culturally, and racially, which impacts us in a negative way. ... The reflex against mixed marriages is natural, as it rises out of the instinct of self-preservation and growth of the Nation. It is typical for all national societies. Nations in the process of expansion strictly adhere to this law. For instance, in Germany racial laws determine the destiny of the people and of the individual throughout his entire life. (The same is true for Italians and others.)[173]

The UPA was the army that the OUN-B leaders expected to "cleanse" the Ukrainian race. Perhaps as a result of this conviction, acts of pathological sadism occurred frequently. In May 1943 in the village Kolonia Grada, for example, UPA partisans killed two families who could not escape as all the others had, after they realized that the UPA was attacking the neighboring village of Kolonia Łamane. The partisans killed all the members of these two families, cut open the belly of a pregnant woman, took the fetus and her innards from her, and hung them on a bush,

170 Motyka, *Ukraińska partyzantka*, 346–47. Sometimes neighbors of the dead "Poles" wondered why the particular persons were killed, since nobody considered them as Poles. Cf. Motyka, *Ukraińska partyzantka*, 347.

171 This happened to Ambroży Wreszczyński on 3 August 1943 in the village Zielony Dąb. Cf. Motyka, *Ukraińska partyzantka*, 341.

172 "Orhanizatsiia Ukraïns'kykh Natsionalistiv. Natsiia iak spetsies. Rodyna v systemi orhanizovanoho ukraïns'koho natsionalizmu," HDA SBU, f, 13, spr. 376, vol. 6, 6v. Undated brochure, not earlier than 1943. I am grateful to Per Anders Rudling for drawing my attention to it.

173 Ibid., 6v. The author of the brochure was referring to Stepan Rudnyts'kyi, *Do osnov ukraïns'koho natsionalizmu* (Vienna, 1923). For Rudnyts'kyi see page 84.

probably to leave a message for other Poles who had escaped the attack and might come back to the village.[174] Some of these murders were conducted under the leadership of Hryhorii Perehiniak, who before the war was imprisoned in Święty Krzyż in the same cell as Bandera and other OUN activists. Bandera taught Perehiniak history and ideology and stayed on good terms with him, not least because they came from neighboring villages.[175]

For the purpose of killing Poles, some UPA units used methods similar to those used by the Germans to annihilate Jews in Ukraine. This knowledge was based on the experience of OUN-B activists in the Ukrainian police. The UPA partisans would sometimes give candy to Polish children and be very polite to the population generally, in order to calm them. They would ask the Poles to go to a meeting, and then they would either take small groups from the meeting and shoot them, or they would burn the entire Polish population of a village, in a barn or other building. They would attack on Sundays, when the Polish villagers were gathered for a service in church, and would either throw grenades into the church, burn it down, or enter and murder everyone inside. They would dig a large grave, take groups of Poles to it, and either shoot the Poles or murder them with sharp implements, either beside the grave or in it. When the grave was full of corpses, they would cover it with earth, almost exactly as the Einsatzkommandos had done with the Jews. After murdering the population in one place, these UPA units could move quickly from one locality to another, in order to surprise the population and prevent it from escaping. The UPA partisans could also attack several villages on the same day, as happened on 11 July 1943 for example, when the UPA attacked ninety-six localities. In July 1943, one of the bloodiest months of the "cleansing," the UPA attacked 520 localities and killed between 10,000 and 11,000 Poles.[176] On 11 and 12 July 1943, the UPA murdered about 4,330 Poles.[177] Ivan Vasiuk, a nineteen-year-old UPA member captured by the Soviet police, stated that his company exterminated 1,500 Poles in three villages in 1943. He himself killed nineteen persons, including eight men, six women, and five children.[178] In addition to the ethnic cleansing of Poles in 1943–1944, the OUN-UPA also annihilated an unknown number of Ukrainians who were Roman Catholics, or had close relationships with Poles, or did not support the ethnic cleansing, or for other reasons.[179]

In July 1943, the AK reported that Ukrainian peasants were saying that, after the Jews, "the Poles are next in line." That month the AK noticed that the slogan "Death

174 Motyka, *Ukraińska partyzantka*, 323; Siemaszko, *Ludobójstwo dokonane*, 1:621.

175 For the murders that were committed by the UPA unit under the leadership of Perehiniak, see Motyka, *Ukraińska partyzantka*, 190. For Bandera teaching Perehiniak history and ideology in the prison cell, see Klymyshyn, *V pokhodi*, 199. Klymyshyn, who was also in the same prison cell, described Perehiniak as a very gifted student. See also page 164 et seq., above.

176 Motyka, *Ukraińska partyzantka*, 328–29, 331, 334, 337–40.

177 Ewa Siemaszko, "Ludobójcze akcje OUN-UPA w lipcu 1943 roku na Wołyniu," in *Antypolska akcja OUN-UPA 1943–1944: Fakty i interpretacje*, ed. Grzegorz Motyka and Dariusz Libionka (Warsaw: Instytut Pamięci Narodowej, 2002), 67.

178 Interrogation of I. N. Vasiuk, 9 January 1945, TsDAHOU, f. 1, op. 70, spr. 237, 2, 3, quoted in Statiev, *Soviet Counterinsurgency*, 86.

179 For a UPA order to kill Ukrainians, see "Document, No. 44: Dovidka UShPR pro posylennia vyshkolu kadriv UPA, aktyvizatsiu diial'nosti zahoniv ukraïns'kykh povstantsiv proty partyzaniv i poliakiv," in *Litopys UPA*, vol. 4, ed. P. Sokhan (Kiev: Afisha, 2002), 126. The document is located in TsDAHO, f. 1, op. 22, spr. 75, 94–95.

to the Poles" (*Smert' liakham*) became so popular among Ukrainians in Lviv, that it was even used as an everyday greeting. In July 1943, the AK in Stanislaviv observed that Ukrainians used the greeting "Death to the Poles" while answering "Glory to Ukraine."[180] Janina Kwiatkowska was travelling in January 1945 with two sisters from Ternopil' to Chortkiv. They had to stay overnight in the provincial town of Terebovlia and did not want to remain at the railway station. In Ukrainian, which they spoke as fluently as Polish, they asked a Ukrainian woman to allow them to stay in her house. The woman took them for Ukrainians and agreed. When they asked her where her husband was, the woman answered carelessly, "He went to murder Polacks and will soon be back." Kwiatkowska referred to the man as a Banderite in her testimony.[181]

The mass murder carried out by the OUN-B astounded the Polish population in Volhynia. Poles in Volhynia—and later, even more so in eastern Galicia—tried to defend themselves against the murderous units of the UPA. The Polish Home Army (*Armia Krajowa*, AK) tried to help the Poles in Volhynia to defend themselves but because the number of UPA partisans and mobilized Ukrainians was much greater than that of the AK and other Poles, they met with limited success. The AK, which was connected with the Polish government in London, held the opinion that Poles should not leave the territories, and that the Polish state should retain the same eastern border after the Second World War. This geopolitical idea clashed totally with that of the OUN-UPA, which considered Volhynia and eastern Galicia to be Ukrainian territories and part of a future Ukrainian state. The AK frequently encouraged the Polish population not to leave when the UPA demanded that it leave immediately.[182] Poles sought to escape from the UPA terror by moving to towns or villages with facilities for self-defense. Those who survived were repatriated to the territories of eastern Germany that became the western part of the People's Republic of Poland (*Polska Rzeczpospolita Ludowa*, PRL), a state established on 22 June 1944 in Lublin and ruled by Communists. The Germans who lived in these territories were repatriated to the territory of contemporary Germany.[183]

After some Ukrainian policemen deserted in March 1943, Poles joined the German police and later, when the Soviet army arrived, the local Soviet militia and the Soviet destruction battalions (*istrebitel'nye batal'ony*). In 1943, 5,000 to 7,000 Poles joined the Soviet partisans.[184] Soviet partisans and Soviet soldiers in Volhynia and eastern Galicia appeared to the Poles to be allies, and indeed they sometimes prevented UPA attacks against Poles.[185] Poles in German or Soviet battalions or in the AK, in particular those who had experienced the UPA terror or whose families were killed by the UPA, not only defended themselves but also sought revenge by

180 Kulińska, *Kwestia ukraińska*, 10, 16, 20.

181 Testimony of Janina Kwiatkowska, KAW, II/1352, 8.

182 Ryszard Torzecki, *Polacy i Ukraińcy: Sprawa ukraińska w czasie II wojny światowej na terenie II Rzeczypospolitej* (Warsaw: Wydawnictwo Naukowe PWN, 1993), 32.

183 Stefan Meyer, *Zwischen Ideologie und Pragmatismus: Die Legitimationsstrategien der Polnischen Arbeiterpartei 1944–1948* (Berlin: Wissenschaftlicher Verlag, 2008), 59.

184 Snyder, Causes of Ukrainian-Polish, 221; Adamczyk, *Ziemie Wschodnie*, 139–40.

185 Motyka, *Ukraińska partyzantka*, 405.

murdering Ukrainian civilians.[186] Poles in the AK, Peasants' Battalions (*Bataliony Chłopskie*, BCh), Schutzmannschaft battalion 202, and other units committed numerous war crimes against the Ukrainian civilian population. In some villages, Pavlokoma, for example, they applied annihilation methods resembling those of the UPA in Volhynia and eastern Galicia.[187]

During the period 1943–1945, the OUN and UPA, together with other mobilized Ukrainians, killed a total of between 70,000 and 100,000 Poles. Grzegorz Motyka, a specialist on this subject, estimated that the number might be closer to 100,000 than to 70,000. In different circumstances, Poles killed between 10,000 and 20,000 Ukrainians, of whom the majority were not killed in Volhynia and eastern Galicia, where the OUN and UPA conducted the ethnic cleansing, but in territories that were mainly inhabited by Poles and not Ukrainians, and now belong to Poland.[188]

Some Orthodox and Greek Catholic priests supported the perpetrators. Orthodox priests blessed the axes, pitchforks, scythes, sickles, knives, and sticks, which Ukrainian perpetrators, among them peasants mobilized by the UPA or the OUN-B, used to slaughter Poles.[189] On 15 August 1943 Sheptyts'kyi published a pastoral letter in which he condemned murder by "young people" with "good intentions." He was not as much concerned about the victims as about the good name of the nation: "We have even been witnesses of terrible murders committed by our young people, perhaps even with good intentions, but with pernicious consequences for the nation." In the same letter he also asked "fathers" to "warn your sons against crime" and to "remember that you will achieve nothing good through actions that are opposed to God's law."[190] In November 1943, he released a pastoral letter signed by the entire Ukrainian episcopate. He again condemned murder in powerful words but spoke about "bands" and, as before, did not specify which murders he was condemning.[191] Bolesław Twardowski, Roman Catholic archbishop of Lviv, asked Sheptyts'kyi to intervene in order to stop the murder of Roman Catholic priests. In a letter dated 15 November 1943, Sheptyts'kyi denied that the ethnic cleansing of Poles was happening, claiming that Roman Catholic priests were murdered, not for political reasons, but because they were rich: "In the complete chaos of the present moment, all the worst elements rise to the surface and run wild. Regarding murder statistics, I think that murders connected with robbery occupy a very important place—and Roman

186 Ibid., 317, 327, 350, 399–400. Motyka, Polski policjant, 127, 138; Snyder, Causes of Ukrainian-Polish, 223.

187 Grzegorz Motyka, "Polska reakcja na działania UPA—skala i przebieg akcji odwetowych," in *Antypolska akcja*, ed. Motyka, 81–85; Motyka, *Ukraińska partyzantka*, 578; Motyka, *Tak było w Bieszczadach*, 238–45, 252–56; Petro Potichnyi, *Pavlokoma, 1441–1945: Istoriia sela* (Toronto: Fundatsiia Pavlokoma, 2001).

188 In Volhynia, Ukrainians killed 50,000 to 60,000 Poles, and Poles killed 2,000 to 3,000 Ukrainians. In eastern Galicia, Ukrainians killed 20,000 to 25,000 Poles, and Poles killed 1,000 to 5,000. In the territories of today's Poland, Poles murdered 8,000 to 12,000 Ukrainians, and Ukrainians killed 6,000 to 8,000 Poles. Cf. Motyka, *Ukraińska partyzantka*, 410–12. In Volhynia, the UPA also killed about 350 Czechs. See Motyka, *Ukraińska partyzantka*, 284.

189 Berkhoff, *Harvest of Despair*, 292; Żur, *Mój wołyński epos*, 58.

190 "List pasterski metropolity Szeptyckiego do duchowieństwa i wiernych," Adamczyk, *Ziemie Wschodnie*, 102, 104.

191 Andrei Sheptyts'kyi, *Pys'ma-poslannia Mytropolyta Andreia Sheptyts'koho ChSVV z chasiv nimets'koï okupatsiï* (Yorkton: Redeemer's Voice Press, 1969), 419–20, 422–23.

Catholic priests have in general a reputation of being rich people."[192] He further claimed that they were not murdered by the OUN-UPA but by "Bolshevik partisans, Jewish bands, and agitators of revolutionary Polish organizations from Warsaw, who even boast in their publications about murdering Poles."[193] In the first draft of his letter to Twardowski however, Sheptyts'kyi did not deny that Ukrainians were killing Poles but wrote: "The Ukrainian parties of Bandera and Mel'nyk deny responsibility for the murders; they steadfastly maintain that they have forbidden their members to kill Poles." This suggests that he knew what the OUN and UPA were doing but decided to blame others for the actions of the Ukrainian nationalists.[194]

The UPA and the Murdering of Jews

In addition to conducting the ethnic cleansing of the Polish population, the UPA, together with the OUN-B and especially the SB of the OUN-B, murdered Jews. The majority of the Jews killed in 1943 and 1944 by the Ukrainian nationalists had escaped from the ghettos in order to avoid the transports to Bełżec or being shot in front of mass graves. They hid in bunkers, or camps in the woods, or in peasant houses. Some of these Jews were killed as the UPA murdered Poles and destroyed their houses.[195] The survivors of these attacks frequently described the perpetrators as "Banderites" and considered them to be Ukrainian nationalists. The OUN and UPA documents and other sources disclose that the "Banderites" were members of the SB of the OUN-B, OUN-B activists, UPA partisans, and sometimes Ukrainian peasants or bandits. The Ukrainian police were not usually described as Banderites, but as policemen, because of their uniforms.[196] Antisemitism in the UPA was common and the UPA partisans, like the OUN activists, took the stereotype of "Jewish Bolshevism" for reality. The UPA partisan Fedir Vozniuk stated during an interrogation that UPA leaders in 1943 and 1944 issued orders to their members to kill Poles and Jews.[197] According to a Polish witness, UPA partisans passing through Głęboczyce, Volhynia in 1943 sang: "We slaughtered the Jews, we will slaughter the Poles, old and young, every one; we will slaughter the Poles, we will build Ukraine."[198] Under the UPA terror, relations between Poles and Jews improved, and the two groups were sometimes allied against their common aggressor. For the same reason, Poles and Jews also allied themselves with Soviet partisans.[199]

192 Józef Wołczański, "Korespondencja arcybiskupa Bolesława Twardowskiego z arcybiskupem Andrzejem Szeptyckim w latach 1943–1944," *Przegląd Wschodni* Vol. 2, No. 2 (6) (1992–1993): 482.

193 Wołczański, Korespondencja, 482.

194 Wołczański, Korespondencja, 479. See also Himka, Christianity and Radical Nationalism, 109.

195 For murdering Jews while murdering Poles, see AŻIH, 301/2896, Tabacznik (translation from Yiddish); AŻIH, 301/74, Rozenblat M. (translation from Yiddish); In Hanaczów Jews and Poles defended themselves, see AŻIH, 301/808, Edmund Adler, 2–3. See also the testimonies collected in Siemaszko, *Ludobójstwo dokonane*, 1:91–92, 189, 191, 216, 277.

196 For the term "Banderites" see the next subsection.

197 "Vytiahy iz protokolu dopytu Fedora Vozniuka vid 23 travnia 1944 r," Bohunov, *Poliaky ta Ukraïntsi*, 894.

198 Siemaszko, *Ludobójstwo dokonane*, 1:872. Ukr. "Vyrizaly my zhydiv, vyrizhemo i liakhiv, i staroho, i maloho do iednoho; Poliakiv vyrezhem, Ukrainu zbuduiem."

199 Bruder, *"Den Ukrainischen Staat*, 168.

Mania Leider, who escaped from a train on its way to Bełżec and hid in a forest in Peremyshliany region, was protected by Polish and Jewish partisans.[200] In July 1943, the UPA attacked the village of Medwedówka. The invaders killed fifty-seven Poles and four Jews.[201] In the village of Nowiny Czeskie in 1943 and 1944 the UPA murdered a number of Jews, Poles, and Czechs.[202] On 30 August 1943 in the village of Myślina, Ukrainians under the leadership of Fedor Hałuszko killed a number of Poles and four Jewish families, including three children.[203] In March 1944, a group of 500 Jews who were hiding in a forest in the Peremyshliany region escaped to a Polish village, Hanaczów, after they were warned by a Banderite. The next day, when Ukrainian nationalists attacked the village, Poles and Jews defended themselves together against the invaders. The Banderites killed seventy Poles and two Jewish families. At Easter, the UPA attacked the village again and killed sixty Poles and an unknown number of Jews.[204] In the military colony Bortnica, in the Dubno region, fifteen Poles and eight Jews organized self-defense. In autumn 1943, Ukrainians attacked them and killed twenty people. At Christmas 1943, they attacked again, killing eight Poles and three Jews.[205]

Some of the Jews who tried to survive with the Soviet partisans fought with them against the UPA and the Germans.[206] Szlojme Katz joined a Soviet partisan group in the Zhytomyr region in May 1943. He took part in a number of battles against the Germans and the UPA and testified to having killed six Banderites and twelve Germans.[207] Jankel Fanger, who hid in the woods in the Peremyshliany area, decided to avenge two Jews who were delivered to the Germans by a Ukrainian peasant, shortly before the arrival of the Soviet army. The peasant had done so because the Jews had run out of money to pay him. Fenger went to the peasant's house and informed him that he was from the Ukrainian underground and had come to punish him for hiding "enemies of the Ukrainian people." After the peasant showed him the bottle of vodka and a bag of salt, which he had received from the Germans for delivering the Jews, Fanger killed the peasant and his wife, but not their children.[208]

Many Jews hid in bunkers and camps in the forests. If they were discovered by OUN or UPA nationalists, twenty to hundred or even more Jews could be murdered at once.[209] Izraela and Barbara Lissak testified that Banderites discovered three Jewish bunkers. They threw a shell into one and fired at Jews who escaped from the others. The Lissaks also reported that the Banderites, attacking three Polish families,

200 AŻIH, 301/843, Mania Leider, 3–4.
201 Siemaszko, *Ludobójstwo dokonane*, 1:270.
202 Ibid., 1:91–92.
203 Ibid., 1:367.
204 AŻIH, 301/808, Edmund Adler, 2–3.
205 Siemaszko, *Ludobójstwo dokonane*, 1:60.
206 According to Shmuel Spector there were at the end of 1943 between 1,700 and 1,900 Jewish partisans in Volhynia. Cf. Spector, *The Holocaust of Volhynian Jews*, 323.
207 AŻIH, 301/589, Szlojme Katz, 1–2. For other Jews in partisan units, see AŻIH, 301/1488, Józef Sapożnik, 1; AŻIH, 301/926, Samuel Melchior, 1–3.
208 Yones, *Die Straße nach Lemberg*, 128.
209 AŻIH, 301/1222, Izraela and Barbara Lissak, 6–7; AŻIH, 301/2193, Ignacy Goldwasser, 9–13; AŻIH, 301/808, Edmund Adler, 2; AŻIH, 301/1136, Lipa Stricker, 4; AŻIH, 301/3359, Edzia Szpeicher, 5; AŻIH, 301/6012, Leon Hejnysz, 2–4; AŻIH, 301/198, Leon Knebel, 5; AŻIH, 301/879, Kin Mojżesz, 2–4; Pohl, *Nationalsozialistische*, 377.

killed twelve Jews and ten Poles.[210] Ignacy Goldwasser hid with his mother and other Jews in bunkers around Boryslav. Shortly before the arrival of the Soviet Army, Banderites began killing the Jews hiding in the bunkers.[211] Of the hundred people who hid together with Lipa Stricker, only about ten survived. On 2 March 1944, Stricker observed from a hiding-place in the bushes how a group of Ukrainians went to a bunker. Using knives, they slaughtered all the people in the bunker, among them his family.[212] Edzia Szpeicher hid in a bunker close to Drohobych with twenty other Jews. One day, some Banderites introduced themselves as Soviet partisans and invited the Jews hiding in the bunker to join their unit. After they emerged, the Banderites ordered them to undress and killed them.[213] In March 1944, the UPA forced a Pole who was supplying food for sixty-five Jews hiding in a bunker in a forest near Naraiv, Berezhany region, to show them where the Jews were hiding. They then killed fifty-one of them.[214] Leon Knebel, who hid in the woods near Boryslav, remembered the Banderites as much more cruel than the "Waldschutzpolizei," who also looked for Jews in the woods. On one occasion the nationalists killed twenty-four Jews, among them a young woman. The Banderites cut off her hands and strips of skin from her body.[215]

The OUN-B and UPA did not intend to kill all the Jews who were hiding in the forest immediately, but offered some of them "protection." The OUN-B registered these Jews, kept them in "camps," and forced them to work for the OUN-B and UPA. The "camps" were frequently farms or houses of murdered Poles. Most of such Jews were killed by the nationalists before the Red Army arrived in western Ukraine.[216] The leadership of the OUN-B and UPA had no interest in letting the Jews survive the war, because they suspected that the Jews might join the Red Army, support the Soviet authorities, or provide information about the Ukrainian nationalist partisans to their Soviet enemies.

An unknown number of Jewish doctors, dentists, and nurses agreed or were forced to treat UPA insurgents. During their period with the UPA, they were usually frightened of the partisans and OUN-B activists and tried to escape.[217] Like the Jews "employed" by the OUN-UPA in collective farms or camps, the majority were killed shortly before the Red Army came to western Ukraine. Holocaust survivor and early Holocaust historian Philip Friedman commented on this question:

> Ukrainian sources speak of a considerable number of Jewish physicians, dentists, and hospital attendants who served in the ranks of the UPA. The question is: Why did only a small number of them remain alive? The Bandera groups also utilized other Jewish skilled workers. According to Lew Shankowsky, practically every UPA group had a Jewish physician or pharmacist, as well as Jewish tailors, shoe-

210 AŻIH, 301/1222, Izraela and Barbara Lissak, 6–7.
211 AŻIH, 301/2193, Ignacy Goldwasser, 9–13.
212 AŻIH, 301/1136, Lipa Stricker, 4.
213 AŻIH, 301/3359, Edzia Szpeicher, 5.
214 AŻIH, 301/879, Kin Mojżesz, 2–4.
215 AŻIH, 301/679, Leon Knebel, 5.
216 AŻIH, 301/1510, Fefer Bajla, 2–3; AŻIH, 301/397, Jakub and Esia Zylberger, Hersz and Doba Mełamed, 12–14; Siemaszko, *Ludobójstwo dokonane*, 1:405; Bruder, *"Den Ukrainischen Staat*, 219; Bartov, Wartime Lies and Other Testimonies, 496–97.
217 AŻIH, 301/74, Rozenblat M. (translation from Yiddish).

makers, barbers, and the like. Again the question arises: What happened to these hundreds of thousands of Jewish professionals and skilled workers? Betty Eisenstein states that in the spring of 1943 the Bandera groups began to imitate the German tactics of "selection." Only the skilled workers were left alive, and they were concentrated in special camps, where they worked at their trades or on the farms. One such camp, established in April 1943 near Poryck, Volhynia, contained more than 100 Jews. A second camp, which had some 400 Jews, was located in Kudrynki, nearly 20 miles from Tuczyn, Volhynia. Eisenstein reports that at the approach of the Soviet army the Bandera groups liquidated the Jews of the camps.[218]

The few Jews who escaped to the Red Army confirmed that the UPA killed its Jewish doctors shortly before the Red Army arrived in western Ukraine.[219] The total number of Jews who survived their period with the UPA seems to be low and is difficult to estimate.[220] Lea Goldberg managed to survive, working as a nurse. The Banderites first wanted to kill her but then decided that she could stay because she was useful and could be murdered any time later. She was with a UPA group of about 400 partisans and frequently feared for her life. She heard how the nationalists cursed the Jews, Poles, and Soviet partisans, and said that they needed to kill the Jews for the sake of Ukraine and had to attack and wipe out Polish villages. While at the UPA camp she observed several times how the UPA partisans tortured and murdered Soviet partisans, Poles, and Jewish children. After a UPA partisan tried to kill her, she escaped to the Soviet partisans and remained with them until the Red Army arrived.[221]

One of the orders to murder the Jews in the UPA collective farms and work camps came from the SB of the OUN-B, an entity that might have killed more Jews than the UPA partisans. "All non-professional Jews [serving in the UPA] should be secretly eliminated so that neither [other] Jews nor our people will know," the order said. "The rumor should be spread that they went to the Bolsheviks."[222] During an NKVD interrogation, Ivan Kutkovets' stated that the SB of the OUN-B issued an order in 1943 to "physically exterminate Jews who were hiding in the villages."[223] In the Rivne region, the Ukrainian nationalists "literally hunted for Jews, organizing round-ups and combing the forest paths, ravines, etc."[224]

218 Friedman, Ukrainian-Jewish Relations, 188–89. This article was first published in YIVO Annual of Jewish Social Science 12 (1958–1959), 259–63. On this question, see also Spector, *Holocaust of Volhynian Jews*, 270–72.

219 Yones, *Die Straße nach Lemberg*, 111–12.

220 For one case, see Redlich, *Together and Apart*, 127–28. For four others, see Volodymyr V"iatrovych, Stavlennia OUN do ievreïv: Formuvannia pozytsiï na tli katastrofy (Lviv: MS, 2006), 78–81. Ukrainian historians and OUN-UPA veterans have frequently mentioned that the UPA rescued Jews. This assumption, however, is not confirmed by the testimonies of Jewish survivors and other documents.

221 AŻIH, 301/1011, Lea Goldberg (translation from Yiddish).

222 "Document, No. 44: Dovidka YShPR pro posylennia vyshkolu kadriv UPA, aktyvizatsiu diial'nosti zahoniv ukraïns'kykh povstantsiv proty partyzaniv i poliakiv," in *Litopys UPA*, vol. 4, ed. P. Sokhan (Kiev: Afisha, 2002), 126; Statiev, *Soviet Counterinsurgency*, 85.

223 TsDAHOU, f. 57, op. 4, d. 351, 52, quoted in Weiner, *Making Sense of War*, 264.

224 Interrogation of Vladimir Solov'ev TsDAHOU, f. 57, op. 4, d. 351, 10, quoted in Weiner, *Making Sense of War*, 263.

In the last few months before the Red Army arrived in western Ukraine, Jews occasionally fled from forests and bunkers where they were hiding, to seek protection in German work camps. The survivor Hilary Koenigsberg testified in 1948:

> With the beginning of 1944 the Banderite bands multiplied, began tracking Jewish bunkers in the woods and in the villages, killing all in a cruel way. Peasants revealed the bunkers. Sometimes they brought the Jews to the police with an axe in hand. Then happened what might seem to be unbelievable. The Jews fled from woods and bunkers to the camps. The [remainder] of the Jewish police and the administrators of the local estates made profit [from] it. Under the pretext that they could not take any more Jews into the camps they demanded bribes in money or items. The Banderite bands and the local nationalists raided every night, decimating the Jews. Jews sheltered in the camps where Germans were stationed, fearing an attack by Banderites. Some German soldiers were brought to protect the camps and thereby also the Jews.[225]

The survivor Edzia Spielberg-Flitman, her six-year-old brother, and her mother were rescued by a local German officer. Edzia remembered that "80 percent [of my family] were killed by the Ukrainians who were our friends" and that the Ukrainians "were worse than the Germans."[226] Mojżesz Szpigiel testified in 1948 that several members of his family were killed by Ukrainian peasants and Ukrainian policemen. Describing the murder of 120 Jews on a farm by the Ukrainian police, he wrote: "It is important to state that this killing was not a German action, that it was performed by Ukrainian policemen and bandits." When Ukrainian policemen attacked the last Jews in a farm, a German "major ... went [there] with his aide and hit one [Ukrainian] policeman on the head with his revolver ... and ordered them to leave immediately."[227]

As the Red Army came closer to western Ukraine in spring 1944, the interests of the UPA and the Germans began to overlap, and as a result many UPA units began to collaborate with the Germans again.[228] At a conference in Lviv in October 1943, the leadership of the OUN had already decided that, like the UPA, Polish troops in Ukrainian territory should not fight against German troops, and they passed on this resolution to the Polish underground.[229] One UPA partisan stated during an interrogation that fighting Germans made no sense for the UPA.[230] Members of the UPA occasionally shot Jews at the Germans' request. According to a Wehrmacht intelligence report, "The UPA has successfully taken up pursuit of the Jewish gangsters and up to now shot almost a hundred."[231] In March or April 1944, the UPA informed the Germans that it would cleanse the Chełm (Kholm)—Rawa-Ruska (Rava Rus'ka)

225 AŻIH, 301/3337, Hilary Koenigsberg, 14.

226 Edzia Spielberg-Flitman, Shoah Foundation videotaped testimony, 14 March 1995, Skokie, Illinois, transcribed by Joshua Tobias, quoted in Bartov, Wartime Lies and Other Testimonies, 496.

227 Mojżesz Szpigiel, USHMM, reel 37 301/3492, Łódź, 10 March 1948, quoted in Bartov, Wartime Lies and Other Testimonies, 496–97.

228 Golczewski, Die Kollaboration in der Ukraine, 177.

229 "Protokol doprosa obviniaemogo Vasylia Okhrymovicha Ostapovicha, 27.12.1952," HDA SBU f. 5, spr. 445, vol. 4, 271–78, in *Stepan Bandera*, ed. Serhiichuk, 3:368–69.

230 Interrogation of Anton Bodnar, 5–8 March 1945, HDA SBU f. 13, spr. 372, vol. 4, 188.

231 Staatsanwaltschaft Dortmund, 45 Js 24/62, "Reste von Gutachten und Dokumenten aus dem Bestand des Pz. AOK4," quoted in Golczewski, Shades of Grey, 143.

region of "Poles, bandits, and Jews."[232] Dontsov insisted in 1944 that the "struggle against Jewry is in the interest and in the traditions of the Ukrainian nation."[233]

It is difficult to estimate how many Jews the OUN-B and the UPA actually killed in 1943 and the first half of 1944. Given the clandestine nature of this mass murder, we might never be able to establish an accurate number. The analyses done for this and previous research conducted by other historians suggest that in 1943 and 1944 the OUN-B and UPA killed hundreds or even thousands of Jews in Volhynia and eastern Galicia, but the actual number is difficult to determine. Grzegorz Motyka, who studied the anti-Polish violence of the UPA in depth, with the anti-Jewish angle as only a minor part of his study, estimated that the UPA killed between 1,000 and 2,000 Jews.[234] Shmuel Spector, who investigated the Holocaust in Volhynia, wrote that "thousands of survivors of the German liquidation Aktionen were slaughtered by Ukrainian nationalist partisans." According to him only 3,500 Jews (1.5 percent) survived the Holocaust in Volhynia. Of the 40,000 Jews who fled from ghettos and hid in forested areas, villages, or other hiding spots only 9 percent survived.[235] Ewa and Władysław Siemaszko, who like Motyka concentrated on the anti-Polish violence of the UPA, came to conclusions similar to that of Spector.[236]

Nobody has calculated how many Jews in eastern Galicia escaped from the ghettos, slave labor camps, or transports to extermination camps and tried to survive in the forest or in other hideouts. Eastern Galicia offered less space for organized survivor camps than Volhynia because it was less forested. However, there were more than twice as many Jews in eastern Galicia than in Volhynia, and thus the number might be as high as in Volhynia or even higher. Only 2 to 3 percent, or 10,000 to 15,000 Jews, survived the Holocaust in eastern Galicia.[237] Therefore the number of Jews in Volhynia and eastern Galicia who hid in forests and other hideouts but did not survive seems to be between 60,000 and 80,000.[238] The current state of research does not allow for a close specification as to how many of these Jews were killed by the OUN and UPA, the local population, the Ukrainian police, or the Germans, or who died from causes such as disease or hunger while hiding.

The Ukrainian police were certainly involved in the murder of more Jews than the OUN-B and UPA combined had killed. The police themselves may also have killed more Jews than the OUN-B and UPA, because the police helped the Germans during mass shootings, patrolled the ghettoes, hunted for Jews in the woods, and transported them to the extermination camps. However, the police seem to have killed

232 Pohl, *Nationalsozialistische*, 376.

233 Quoted in Statiev, *Soviet Counterinsurgency*, 85.

234 Motyka, *Ukraińska partyzantka*, 296.

235 Spector, *The Holocaust of Volhynian Jews*, 199–200, 256, 357–58.

236 Siemaszko, *Ludobójstwo dokonane*, 2:1079–80.

237 Pohl, *Nationalsozialistische*, 385.

238 Two other realistic estimations suggest a similar and a higher number. First, if we assume that 10 percent (82,000) of the Volhynian and eastern Galician Jews (820,000) tried to survive in the woods or in the countryside, and that 13,500 to 18,500 of them managed to survive, as Spector and Pohl determined, it would mean that between 63,500 and 68,500 were murdered or died of other causes. Second, if we assume that in eastern Galicia 14 percent (80,000) of all the Jews who had lived there in June 1941 did not survive their time of hiding, as Spector estimated for Volhynia, then in eastern Galicia and Volhynia together, 115,000 would not have survived this period of the Holocaust. Because of the different Nazi extermination policies in Volhynia and eastern Galicia the first number appears to be more credible.

fewer of the Jews who tried to survive in the woods or in other hideouts than the OUN-B and UPA did, because the UPA controlled the woods and large parts of the countryside. Furthermore, the police were infiltrated by the OUN-B, and many Ukrainian policemen involved in the murder of Jews deserted in the spring of 1943 for the UPA. As already mentioned, they brought with them the skills and methods of exterminating a large number of people in a relatively short time.[239]

The role of the local population in the Holocaust in Volhynia and eastern Galicia was also significant. Some of the local Ukrainians helped the Jews to survive, while many others were indifferent and some actively helped the Germans, the Ukrainian police, and the UPA hunt for and kill the Jews. The peasants knew that the Jews were outlawed (*vogelfrei*) and that nobody would prosecute them for robbing or murdering the Jews. On the contrary, hiding or helping the Jews was risky because one's neighbors might have reported them to the police or to the Germans. The disappearance of the Jews from villages and towns was also a long-standing goal of the moderate Ukrainian national movement, which had dominated Ukrainian politics before the formation of the OUN. Some peasants had more trust in the moderate form of Ukrainian nationalism than in the fascistized and extreme form of OUN nationalism.[240] Finally, religion, in which many peasants found a justification for the genocide of the Jews, also played a role in these mass murders. One peasant in Volhynia said to his Jewish acquaintance who had escaped from the ghetto: "Hitler has conquered almost the whole world and he is going to slaughter all the Jews because they had crucified our Jesus. You think you can escape from this fate? You shouldn't run away from the ghetto; at least you would have rested in the same grave with your family. Now who knows where you're going to die. My advice for you is to return to the ghetto."[241]

As in the case of "democratization" and the ethnic cleansing of Poles, the OUN-B began to falsify its immediate past with regard to anti-Jewish mass violence. In late October 1943, the UPA ordered the preparation of statements that the Germans had persecuted Jews in 1941 without any help from the Ukrainian police:

> c. Lists that would confirm that the Germans carried out anti-Jewish pogroms and liquidations by themselves, without the participation or help of the Ukrainian police, and instead, before carrying out the executions, urged the Jewish committee or the rogues themselves to confirm with their signatures the presence of the Ukrainian police and its involvement in the actions.

239 On this question, see the subsection "The Ukrainian police and the OUN-B" and "The UPA and the Mass Violence against Civilians" in this chapter.

240 On the long-standing goal of the Ukrainian national movement, see John-Paul Himka, "The Reception of the Holocaust in Postcommunist Ukraine," in *Bringing the Dark Past to Light: The Reception of the Holocaust in Postcommunist Europe*, ed. John-Paul Himka and Joanna Beata Michlic (Lincoln: University of Nebraska Press, 2013), 630.

241 Spector, *The Holocaust of Volhynian Jews 1941–1944*, 241.

d. Material that would clearly confirm that Poles had initiated and taken part in anti-Jewish pogroms and at the same time that they had served as the hirelings and agents of the Germans in their struggle with Ukrainians.[242]

At the same time as hunting, murdering, and exploiting Jews, the OUN-B guaranteed them, in official and propaganda documents, equality and minority rights. This very much resembled its attitude to Poles.[243] On 1 November 1943, the leadership of the UPA announced "that we tolerate all nationalities—also Jews, who work in favor of the Ukrainian state. They will be regarded as Ukrainian citizens with full civic rights. We have to inform Jewish doctors and other professionals who are part of our effort about this."[244]

The attitude of the OUN-B and the UPA to the Jews was related to their attitude to Poles, Russians, and other minorities, and it was determined by the fact that many Ukrainian policemen, who in 1942 were involved in the destruction of the Volhynian and Galician Jews, deserted in spring 1943 for the UPA. Nevertheless, one should not forget that the OUN-B and UPA consisted of various kinds of people, and that it would inappropriate to portray it as a monolith, composed of only racist fanatics and war criminals. Examining the social composition of the UPA, we would find people of different classes, with different educational backgrounds, and of both genders. As already mentioned, some joined the UPA voluntarily and supported it willingly. Others, however, were forced to join by the OUN-B or UPA members, or did so to avoid German or Soviet repression, or for other reasons. Some of the UPA partisans were communists or disapproved of nationalism for other reasons, before they were forced to join. While in the UPA, however, some of them adjusted or changed their views over a period of time, adopting the nationalist, racist, and antisemitic agenda of the movement. Oleksandr Povshuk, for example, a Volhynian Ukrainian who was skeptical about the Ukrainian nationalists, was forcibly enlisted in the UPA in summer 1943. He at first criticized the OUN in his diary, for collaboration with the Germans, the annihilation of Poles, and several other aspects. After a year, he changed his views and made nationalism and antisemitism important aspects of his identity.[245]

The ethnic and political mass violence conducted by the UPA in 1943 and 1944 cannot be explained solely by the nationalist and racist ideology of the OUN-B. As a set of rules that approved of killing the "enemies of the Ukrainian nation," this ideology was certainly sufficient to turn ordinary men and women into murderers, but the question is how and why this ideology came into being and in what political and military context it was put into practice. This leads us to four factors: first, to the social and political situation of Ukrainians in the interwar period or even before; second, to the military aims and strategies of the UPA; third, the tone that the Nazi

242 "Nakaz Ch. 2/43, Oblasnym, okruzhnym i povitovym providnykam do vykonannia," TsDAVOV f. 3833, op. 1, spr. 43, 9. The translation is from Carynnyk, Foes of Our Rebirth, 345; Bruder, *"Den Ukrainischen Staat*, 222; Motyka, *Ukraińska partyzantka*, 290; Rusnachenko, *Narod zburenyi*, 136.

243 Motyka, *Ukraińska partyzantka*, 295–96.

244 Iurii Kyrychuk, *Ukraïns'kyi natsional'nyi rukh 40–50 rokiv XX stolittiia: Ideolohia ta praktyka* (Lviv: Dobra sprava, 2003), 145.

245 "Dennyk Povshuka Oleksandra vid 17/IX. 1939 r.," TsDAHO f. 57, op. 4, spr. 344, 28, 38–41, 51–54. See also John-Paul Himka, "Refleksje żołnierza Ukraińskiej Powstańczej Armii: Pamiętnik Ołeksandra Powszuka (1943–1944)," in *Prawda historyczna a prawda polityczna w badaniach naukowych*, ed. Bogusław Paź (Wrocław: Wydawnictwo Uniwersytetu Wrocławskiego, 2011), 182–89.

occupation and Nazi ideology had set; and fourth, the fact that there was no strong administration in these territories at a time when the front was changing.

As explained in previous chapters, the Ukrainians did not succeed in retaining a state after the First World War. In the interwar period, they were discriminated against in Poland and therefore had good reasons to dislike and oppose the Polish authorities. Because of the famine and Stalin's repressions, the fate of Ukrainians in the Soviet Ukraine in the 1930s was even worse. This experience certainly had an impact on the motives and aims of the OUN-B and UPA. During the Second World War, the leadership of the OUN-B was afraid that the situation after the First World War would be repeated and that once again the Ukrainians would be unable to establish a Ukrainian state. The Polish government-in-exile insisted on the inclusion of the contested territories in the Polish state, thereby confirming the fears of the Ukrainian nationalists. Furthermore, Soviet leaders made no secret of the fact that they would include all Ukrainian territories in the Soviet Union and would detain or execute all political opponents. In order to mobilize peasants to violence, the OUN and UPA promised them a Ukrainian state, and land belonging to Poles. The prospect of acquiring Polish or Jewish houses and their contents was another important motive for the conduct of ethnic violence. It would be incorrect to state that only OUN-B members and UPA partisans, or peasants motivated by Ukrainian genocidal nationalism hunted for Jews in the forests in 1943 and 1944. In addition, other types of Ukrainians, including robbers and peasants who were motivated primarily by non-nationalist motives or a mixture of ideological and economic motives, killed Jews.[246] Finally, we should mention that some Ukrainians helped Jews and Poles survive the war, by hiding them, providing them with food, warning them of the approach of their enemies, and in other ways. In so doing they endangered themselves and their families.[247]

Bandera and Banderites

While the OUN-B and the UPA were conducting the ethnic cleansing of the Poles and hunting Jews, Bandera was not in Ukraine. He remained confined in Berlin and Sachsenhausen. The leadership of the OUN-B and the UPA were in contact with Bandera through his wife, and through other channels. Bandera might therefore have been informed about OUN-B and UPA policies, but we do not know to what extent, or what his opinion was concerning the ethnic cleansing in Volhynia and eastern Galicia, and other forms of ethnic and political violence at that time. I did not find any documents confirming that Bandera approved or disapproved of the ethnic

246 On the politics of the Second Republic toward minorities, see Tomaszewski, *Ojczyzna nie tylko Polaków*, 194–98; Włodzimierz Mędrzecki, "Polityka narodowościowa II Rzeczypospolitej a antypolska akcja UPA w latach 1943–1944," in *Antypolska akcja OUN–UPA*, ed. Motyka, 14–18. On the politics of the Polish government in exile, see Ihor Iliushyn, "Kwestia ukarińska w planach polskiego rządu emigracyjnego i polskiego podziemia w latach drugiej wojny światowej," in *Antypolska akcja OUN–UPA*, ed. Motyka, 118–20.

247 Until 10 July 2014 Yad Vashem honored 2472 Ukrainians as Righteous Among the Nations. Cf. http://www.yadvashem.org/yv/en/righteous/statistics.asp (accessed 10 July 2014). On Poles rescued by Ukrainians, see Romuald Niedzielko ed., *Kresowa księga sprawiedliwych 1939–1945: O Ukraińcach ratujących Polaków poddanych eksterminacji przez OUN i UPA* (Warsaw: Instytut Pamięci Narodowej, 2007).

cleansing, or the murder of the Jews and other minorities. After the war, he never condemned the ethnic cleansing or pogroms or even admitted that they happened. Such conduct was rather typical of the leaders and members of the movement, and of its sympathizers. The ethnic and political violence conducted by the OUN and UPA during the Second World War was certainly not against Bandera's pre-war beliefs and convictions, which he expressed at the Lviv trial for example, when he argued: "Our idea, as we understand it, is so great that, as it comes to its realization, not hundreds but thousands of human lives [will] have to be sacrificed in order to carry it out."[248] Similarly, Bandera's planning and preparation of the "Ukrainian National Revolution" in 1940–1941, which included mass violence against ethnic minorities and political opponents, also suggest that the violence conducted by the OUN-B and UPA in 1942–1944 might not have been against Bandera's political views and expectations.

Although Bandera was not involved in the mass violence of 1942, 1943, and 1944, and although his personal, as opposed to moral, responsibility for those murders was either very limited or non-existent, the killing of thousands of Poles and several hundreds or even thousands of Jews by the OUN-B and UPA in 1943–1944 contributed to the formation of his political myth and affected his political image. This happened because the OUN-B activists and the UPA partisans were known to their victims as Banderites, or Bandera's people. The term "Banderites" goes back to the split of the OUN into the OUN-M and OUN-B, in 1940. It existed in June and July 1941 but was not commonly used at that time by the victims of the pogroms. Two years later however, the word "Banderites" was known to everyone in western Ukraine and was frequently used to describe the OUN-B activists, UPA partisans, and apparently, other Ukrainian perpetrators. In his written testimony in German from 28 April 1945, Moses Brüh, who survived the war in western Ukraine, used the term "Banderisten" to describe the UPA partisans who killed Poles in Volhynia and raided the Jews who hid in the bunkers.[249] In their collective testimony written in Polish in 1945, Jakub and Esia Zylberger, and Hersz and Doba Melamed described as *banderowcy* or Banderites the UPA partisans who murdered the Poles, hunted the Jews in the woods, kept them in work camps, and tried to annihilate them before the coming of the Soviets. They did not label as Banderites those perpetrators whom they perceived as peasants, who hunted the Jews, or as the militiamen who killed the Jews during the pogrom in Tuchyn (Tuczyn) in 1941.[250] Dozens of other survivor testimonies collected by the CŻKH between 1944 and 1948 depict the Banderites similarly to Zylberger and the Melameds.[251]

248 For contact between the OUN-B, UPA, and Bandera, see Interrogation of Mykhail Polevoi, 13 January 1946, HDA SBU f. 13, spr. 372, vol. 4, 235. For Bandera's convictions, see chapter 3 above. Bandera said these words on 26 June 1935 during the Lviv trial, when he was explaining the aims of the OUN.

249 AŻIH, 301/4971: Moses Brüh, 7.

250 AŻIH, 301/397, Jakub and Esia Zylberger, Hersz and Doba Melamed, 1, 10, 12–14.

251 On Banderites murdering Jews and Poles, see for example AŻIH, 301/1222, Izraela and Barbara Lissak, 6–9; AŻIH, 301/2193, Ignacy Goldwasser, 10–12; AŻIH, 301/3359, Szpeicher Edzia, 5; AŻIH, 301/4680, Marek Lessing, 12–14; AŻIH, 301/6012, Leon Hejnysz, 2–4 (testimony written down in 1964); AŻIH, 301/1510, Fefer Bajla, 2; AŻIH, 301/2888, Grinzajd Mina (translation from Yiddish); AŻIH, 301/3337, Hilary Koenigsberg, 12, 14–15. Koenigsberg speaks of "bands of Banderites"; AŻIH, 301/305, Jakub Grinsberg, 2; AŻIH, 301/808, Edmund Adler, 2–3; AŻIH, 301/198, Rafał Szleger, 5; AŻIH, 301/198, Leon Knebel, 5; AŻIH, 301/879, Kin Mojżesz, 2–4; AŻIH, 301/803, Munio Inslicht, 2; AŻIH, 301/589, Szlojme Katz, 1.

Among Poles and Jews between 1943 and 1945, the term had a practical meaning, referring to people who might arrive at any time and commit murder. The term was colloquial and was used to identify Ukrainian nationalist insurgents, in particular OUN-B activists and UPA partisans. Its users undoubtedly employed it on occasion to refer to bandits who did not belong to the OUN-B or the UPA and committed murder for other reasons. Nevertheless, the general use of the term was to describe the Ukrainian nationalists. It was not used with reference to the Ukrainian police, who were referred to as such.[252] The soldiers of Taras Bul'ba-Borovets', who also murdered Jews but did not belong to the OUN-B or UPA, were identified not as Banderites but as "bul'bivtsi" or "bulbowcy" or "bul'bovtsy."[253] Because Jews and Poles used the term "Banderites" to describe people who murdered them and conducted other atrocities against them on a daily basis, the term acquired a strongly pejorative meaning in these communities. It basically meant bandits, villains, or murderers.

The AK used the term "Banderites" in its documents in 1942 and more frequently in 1943 and 1944 to describe the OUN-B and the UPA, or sometimes Ukrainian villagers who raided and murdered Poles. The AK in western Ukraine explained in its documents that the term appeared after the split of the OUN into the OUN-M and the OUN-B.[254] Soviet or pro-Soviet partisan units in western Ukraine, consisting of Russians, Ukrainians, Poles, Jews, and other ethnic groups, also used the term "Banderites" to describe the UPA and possibly also other nationalist partisan formations.[255] The Soviet secret service, Soviet partisans, and politicians started to use the term "Banderites" more frequently at about the same time as the AK did in 1942, and in 1943 they often used it to describe the OUN and the UPA. The term "Banderites" had appeared in Soviet secret documents for the first time in late 1940 when the conflict between Bandera and Mel'nyk broke out.[256] One Soviet document explained that "the Banderites now use the name UPA."[257] The UPA also referred to itself as Banderites and meant thereby a patriotic, anti-Soviet movement that struggled for the independence of Ukraine.[258] The German military referred to the OUN-B activists as the *Bandera-Gruppe* (Bandera group) or *Bandera-Bewegung* (Bandera movement) and sometimes described them as a band.[259]

252 AŻIH, 301/1205, Iza Lauer, 8–9.

253 AŻIH, 301/1046, Lazar Bromberg, 2–3.

254 Compare the collections of AK documents from 1942–1944: Kulińska, *Kwestia ukraińska*, 19–20, 28, 30–31, 35, 54, 186, 192–93, 202, 206, 209, 232–33. The AK documents also used such other colloquial terms as "band" (*banda*) or "Ukrainian band" (*ukraińska banda*) when they referred to a group of Ukrainians who raided neighboring villages. Cf. 87 105, 107, 135, 146. Other terms—"UPA bands" (*bandy UPA*), "Ukrainian bandits" (*bandyci ukraińscy*)—were also in use. Cf. 145, 150.

255 AŻIH, 301/589, Szlojme Katz, 1–2. Katz testified that he joined a Soviet partisan group in the Zhytomyr region in May 1943 and killed six Banderites and twelve Germans; AŻIH, 301/1488, Józef Sapożnik, 2.

256 "Selected Records of Former Soviet Archives of the Communist Party of Ukraine, 1919–1937, 1941–1962 and 1965," USHMM RG 31.026M, reel 7, 6; "Dokladnaia zapiska o deiatel'nosti ukrainskikh natsionalistov, 5 December 1942," TsDAHO f. 1, op. 22, spr. 75, 6; TsDAHO f. 1, op. 22, spr. 75, 5–6, 75–78. For use in 1940 see I. Sierov's report about the agent "Ukrainets to Khrushchev, 3.12.1940," HDA SBU, f. 16, op. 33, spr. 36, 14–33, in *Stepan Bandera*, ed. Serhiichuk, 1:60–61.

257 GARF R-9478, op. 1, del. 132, 469.

258 A leaflet to the soldiers in the Red Army, RGASPI f. 17, op. 125, del. 338, 9.

259 The term "Bandera-Gruppe" already appears on 2 July 1941 in German military documents, see "Ereignismeldung UdSSR, Nr. 10, 02.06.1941," BAB R58/214, 53. The name "Bandera" was also frequently used in German as an adjective, see "Ereignismeldung UdSSR, 15.07.1941," BAB R58/214, 171; "Ereignismeldung UdSSR Nr. 25, 17.07.1941," BAB R58/214, 201–202. For *Bandera-Bewegung*,

At the Third Extraordinary Great Assembly in August 1943, the OUN-B leadership distanced itself from the pogroms of 1941 and the movement's identification with fascism and fascistization, but Bandera did not disappear entirely from the minds of OUN-B activists and UPA partisans. Many sources suggest that the UPA partisans identified themselves with him. During the negotiations with Bul'ba-Borovets' in 1943, the OUN claimed that Bandera was the only leader of Ukraine.[260] In "What We Are Fighting for," a leaflet from 1943, the OUN introduced Bandera as a sufferer for the cause.[261] The brochure "Our Leaders: Symon Petliura, Ievhen Konovalets', Stepan Bandera," apparently printed in 1943, introduced Bandera as the ideal figure of a revolutionary fighter who spent many years in prison for his commitment to liberation.[262] On 30 June 1943, Bandera was acclaimed by the OUN-B activists and UPA partisans as the most important person connected with the proclamation of a Ukrainian state on 30 June 1941. The OUN-B text that explained how to celebrate the proclamation ended with "Long Live the Leader of the Organization of Ukrainian Nationalists and of the Ukrainian Nation, Stepan Bandera!!! Glory to Ukraine—Glory to the Heroes!!!"[263]

Resistance, Further Collaboration, and the Reactivation of Bandera

In addition to conducting the ethnic cleansing against the Polish population in Volhynia and eastern Galicia, and hunting the Jewish survivors in the woods, the UPA struggled against Soviet partisans and later, to a lesser extent, against the Red Army and the Polish AK, and to a much lesser extent against the Germans. In Volhynia the UPA mainly attacked the Germans when they left the towns and cities in which they usually stayed, and which they left only in groups, for safety reasons.[264] UPA attacks on Germans were mainly to obtain their weapons and equipment, or to prevent them from taking food from the population. The UPA generally avoided attacking German troops however, because it knew that the Germans were losing the war and would withdraw from Ukraine.[265] In Galicia where relations between Ukrainians and Germans were much better than in Volhynia, attacks against Germans were even less frequent.[266]

see "Ereignismeldung UdSSR Nr. 191, 10.08.1942," BAB R58/221, 288. In 1943 Germans were somewhat confused about the structure of the OUN-B in Ukraine and regarded the troops of Bul'ba-Borovets' as *Bandera-Bande* (Bandera band), see "Meldungen aus den besetzten Ostgebieten, Nr. 46, 19.03.1943," BAB R58/224, 42.

260 "Do chleniv provodu Organizatsiï Ukraïns'kykh Natsionalistiv pid provodom Stepana Bandery," TsDAHO f. 57, op. 4, spr. 338, 432.

261 "Neskol'ko slov o natsionalistakh," TsDAHO f. 1, op. 22, spr. 61, 49.

262 "Nashi Providnyky: Symon Petliura, Ievhen Konovalets', Stepan Bandera," TsDAVOV f. 3833, op. 1, spr. 36, 30–31.

263 "Materialy na sviatkuvannia sviata ukraïns'koï derzhavnosti den' 30 chervnia," TsDAVOV f. 3833, op. 1, spr. 85, 4.

264 Motyka, *Ukraińska partyzantka*, 189–91, 201, 207. On the problem of collaboration and resistance of the UPA, see Franziska Bruder, "Kollaboration oder Widerstand? Die ukrainischen Nationalisten während des Zweiten Weltkrieges," *Zeitschrift für Geschichtswissenschaft* Vol. 54 (2006): 20–44. On fighting against Soviet partisans, see Gogun, *Partyzanci Stalina na Ukrainie*, 128–52.

265 Motyka, *Ukraińska partyzantka*, 220.

266 Ibid., 224–25.

Because the Soviet Union was their common enemy, the UPA and the Germans concluded local agreements in 1943 and 1944 and tried to avoid fighting one other.[267] On 28 September 1943 the leadership of the OUN in Ukraine warned Otto Wächter, the Governor of Distrikt Galizien, that the Soviets were preparing to assassinate him. "We are not adherents of the German policies in the East ..." they wrote, but "the Bolshevists are for us the number-one enemy ..." and "Dr. Otto Wächter is by the way, a quite decent man. ... We have allowed ourselves to take over the protection of your person, Mr. Governor, through our men."[268] For the sake of collaboration with the Allies however, the OUN-B and UPA kept the collaboration with the Germans a secret, portrayed itself as the enemy of "Nazi imperialism," and applied in this matter a propaganda strategy similar to that regarding the ethnic cleansing of Poles and the murder of Jews.[269] The Germans also kept the cooperation with the OUN-UPA a secret. When they withdrew from Ukraine, they left the OUN-UPA tons of arms and ammunition. The German army regarded this cooperation as a good investment in the war against the Soviet Union.[270]

During negotiations with German troops on 2 April 1944, "Okhrim," the leader of the UPA in Volhynia, demanded the release of Stepan Bandera and other political prisoners.[271] The Greek Catholic priest and OUN-B member Ivan Hryn'okh asked the SS and German police in the General Government on 28 March 1944 to allow him to see Bandera. He argued that Bandera's release would improve relations between the UPA and Nazi Germany. The Germans responded to this proposal only several weeks later, after the next Soviet offensive began. They took Hryn'okh to Berlin and allowed him to meet with Bandera.[272]

When Hryn'okh came to the German capital to visit the *Providnyk*, Bandera was detained in Zellenbau, a building in the Sachsenhausen concentration camp near Berlin, where the RSHA kept special political prisoners (Sonderhäftlinge and Ehrenhäftlinge).[273] It is difficult to reconstruct the exact date from which Bandera was kept in Zellenbau. The divergent accounts suggest that he was moved from Berlin to Sachsenhausen several times. Stets'ko wrote in 1967 that Bandera came to Zellenbau in January 1942.[274] In an interview in 1950, Bandera said that he was held

267 Ibid., 229–37.

268 "OUN an Herrn Otto Wächter, Lemberg den 28.9.1943," Archives of Horst A. von Wächter, 2. I am grateful to John-Paul Himka for this reference.

269 Ibid., 128.

270 According to Simpson, the Nazis gave the operation for cooperation with the OUN-UPA in 1944 the name *Sonnenblume* (Sunflower). Cf. Christopher Simpson, *Blowback: America's Recruitment of Nazis and Its Effects on the Cold War* (London: Weidenfeld & Nicolson, 1988), 162.

271 In negotiations with the Germans in May 1943 Bul'ba-Borovets had asked, probably at the request of the OUN-B, for the release of Ukrainian political prisoners. Cf. "Meldungen aus den besetzten Ostgebieten, Nr. 55, 21.05.1943," BAB R58/224, 187.

272 "Sovershenno sekretno, spetsial'noe soobshchenie, 09.04.1945," HAD SBU f. 13, spr. 372, vol. 372, 245–47, in *Stepan Bandera,* ed. Serhiichuk, 1:279; Motyka, *Ukraińska partyzantka*, 231–34; "Translation of a collaboration proposal," BA-MA RH2/2544, 3; UPA's contacts with Wehrmacht, 21.04.1944, KAW, M/II/30/2, 152–53.

273 Sonderhäftlinge and Ehrenhäftlinge were important political prisoners who received special treatment. Some, such as Kurt Schuschnigg lived with their families in one-family houses; others, such as Bandera, were imprisoned in solitary cells. Cf. Koop, *In Hitlers Hand*, 7–12.

274 Stets'ko, *30 chervnia 1941*, 320.

in Berlin by the Gestapo until 1943 and was then moved to Zellenbau.[275] In an interrogation in 1956 in Munich, he stated that he was relocated from Berlin to Sachsenhausen in the winter of 1942–1943.[276] Bandera's prisoner number 72192 was assigned to him in October 1943. His prison card shows that he was released on 28 September 1944.[277] Kurt Eccarius, an SS-Hauptscharführer who was in charge of Zellenbau, stated in an interrogation in August 1946 that Bandera, with six other OUN members, was already located in Zellenbau in late 1941. According to Eccarius, a Gestapo officer "Schultze" visited Bandera in his cell in Zellenbau and took him to Berlin several times for negotiations.[278]

Bandera was detained in Zellenbau together with other prominent politicians such as the Romanian fascist Horia Sima, who, together with six other members of the Iron Guard, was there from early 1943 until August 1944.[279] Gottfried Graf von Bismarck-Schönhausen, a grandson of Otto von Bismarck; Stalin's son Iakov Dzhugashvili; Fritz Thyssen, a German industrial magnate; and Stefan Grot-Rowecki, the leader of the Polish Home Army were also imprisoned in Zellenbau. Kurt Schuschnigg, chancellor of Austria between 1934 and 1938, lived with his family in a house in a special area of the camp.[280] For the entire period of his imprisonment in Sachsenhausen, Bandera had the status of Sonderhäftling or Ehrenhäftling, and enjoyed much better treatment than an average political prisoner in a German concentration camp.[281] Bandera's wife Iaroslava, who lived with her daughter Natalia in an apartment in Berlin-Charlottenburg, could send parcels of food, underwear, clothes, and other items to him every two weeks. They could also visit him.[282]

Zellenbau had eighty cells. Like the other prisoners, Bandera had his own cell, number 73. Several other Ukrainians, such as Stets'ko, Bul'ba-Borovets', and later Mel'nyk, were also imprisoned in Zellenbau. They were assembled there in order to begin negotiations about renewed collaboration between the Ukrainians and Germans. Bandera could read newspapers and did communicate with other prisoners, although the communication must have been secret. According to Mel'nyk, at least

275 Stepan Bandera, "Pershe interviu providnyka OUN, Stepana Bandery z chuzhynnymy zhurnalistamy," Perspektyvy, ed. Ivanyshyn, 636.

276 "Vernehmungsniederschrift Stefan Popel," 7 February 1956, StM. Pol. Dir. München 9281, 84. Ievhen Stakhiv visited Bandera in December 1941 at the prison in the Prinz-Albrecht-Strasse, see Stakhiv, *Kriz' tiurmy*, 99. According to Luka Pavlyshyn, Bandera was also detained in the Berlin-Moabit prison (Zellengefängnis Lehrter Straße 1–5), see Shchehliuk, "Iak rosa," 54.

277 Stepan Bandera's prison card FSB-Archiv, Moscow N-19092/Tom 100, 233. Bandera confirmed this date in an interview in 1950. Cf. Stepan Bandera, "Pershe interviu providnyka OUN, Stepana Bandery z chuzhynnymy zhurnalistamy," *Perspektyvy*, ed. Ivanyshyn, 636. See also Interrogation of Vasyl' Diachuk-Chyzhevs'kyi, perhaps 1946, HDA SBU f. 13, spr. 372, vol. 6, 21.

278 "Vernehmungsprotokoll, Berlin 22. August 1946," FSB-Archiv, N 19092, vol. 25, AGMS, JSU 1, vol. 25, 38.

279 Heinen, *Die Legion "Erzengel Michael" in Rumänien*, 461, 522.

280 Koop, *In Hitlers Hand*, 7–15, 95–109, 178–207; Tomasz Szarota, *Stefan Rowecki "GROT"* (Warsaw: Państwowe Wydawnictwo Naukowe, 1985), 245–46.

281 "Vernehmungsprotokoll, Berlin 22. August 1946," FSB-Archiv, N 19092, vol. 25, AGMS, JSU 1, vol. 25, 38.

282 [Name withheld], interview by author, Munich, 17 February 2008; "Protokol doprosa zaderzhannogo Davidiuk Fedora Ivanovicha, 13.06.1945," HAD SBU f. 65, spr. 19127, vol. 1, 135–56, in *Stepan Bandera*, ed. Serhiichuk, 1:327–28.

one OUN member, Oleh Kandyba, died or was killed in the camp, which Mel'nyk learned about from Bandera.[283]

Bandera was not entirely cut off from politics and the activities of the OUN-UPA. The OUN-B knew that Bandera's wife visited him, and they used her to forward letters in both directions. Contact with Bandera could not have been difficult, because in 1943 the OUN-B in Ukraine bought cloth of the best quality, to be conveyed to Bandera by his wife, for a suit. According to the testimony of OUN-B member Mykhailo Polevoi, other people also had access to the *Providnyk*.[284] Although the OUN-B knew of Bandera's circumstances in Berlin and Sachsenhausen, it portrayed him as a sufferer and martyr. One leaflet from 1942 claimed that Bandera "suffers for our idea in the cellar rooms of prisons."[285] A leaflet from 1943 said, "Stepan Bandera—the best son of Ukraine, and the fighter for its liberty, has been tortured by the Germans for two years in a prison."[286]

The *Providnyk* was released from Zellenbau on 28 September 1944, and was kept in Berlin under house arrest. Shortly afterwards, the Germans also released Stets'ko, Mel'nyk, Bul'ba-Borovets', and about 300 other OUN members who had been held in different camps. While under house arrest Bandera could move about the city and meet other people.[287] In a bulletin on 14 November the OUN announced that "the Leader Stepan Bandera is free."[288] The Nazis had released Bandera and some other special political prisoners from Zellenbau because Germany was losing the war and wanted to organize Russians, Ukrainians, and other Eastern Europeans for the last struggle against the Red Army. Sima and other legionaries had already been released at the end of August 1944, following which they established a Romanian government in Vienna. This was intended to motivate Romanians to support Hitler and to mobilize them to fight against the Soviet Union.[289]

On 5 October 1944, Bandera asked to speak to the German authorities, which resulted in a meeting with SS-Obergruppenführer Gottlob Berger. Berger reported to Himmler that he had suggested that Bandera cooperate with Andrei Vlasov, leader of the ROA, which was established in the autumn of 1944 to fight alongside the Germans against the Red Army. Bandera turned down the proposal because he thought that "through this cooperation he would lose his supporters in Ukraine." He claimed that his movement in Ukraine had become so strong that Stalin would not succeed in defeating it. At the end of his letter to Himmler, Berger briefly characterized Bandera

283 Bul'ba-Borovets', *Armiia*, 277; Andrii Mel'nyk, "Pam"iati vpavshykh za voliu i velych Ukraïny," in *Orhanizatsiia Ukraïns'kyh Natsionalistiv 1929–1954* (Paris 1955), 31.

284 Interrogation of Mykhail Polevoi, 13.01.1946, HDA SBU f. 13, spr. 372, vol. 4, 235; Interrogation of Vasyl' D'iachuk-Chyzhevs'kyi, HDA SBU f. 13, spr. 372, vol. 6, 3. See also Iaroslava Stets'ko-Muzyka, "Z ideiamy Stepana Bandery," in *Zhyttia i diial'nist'*, ed. Posivnych, 2008, 184.

285 "Meldungen aus den besetzten Ostgebieten, Nr. 10, 03.07.1942," BAB R58/698, 7.

286 TsDAHO f. 1, op. 22, spr. 61, 49.

287 Interrogation of Oleksandr Luts'kyi, 19 and 20 July 1945, HDA SBU f. 13, spr. 372, vol. 1, 333; [name withheld], interview by author, Munich, 17 February 2008; Interrogation of Vasyl' Diachuk-Chyzhevs'kyi, apparently 1946, HDA SBU f. 13, spr. 372, vol. 6, 4.

288 "Sovershenno sekretno, spetsial'noe soobshchenie," 9 April 1945, HDA SBU f. 13, spr. 372, vol. 372, 245–47, in *Stepan Bandera*, ed. Serhiichuk, 1:279.

289 Heinen, *Die Legion "Erzengel Michael" in Rumänien*, 461–63; Broszat, Die Eiserne Garde und das Dritte Reich, 636; "Eiserne Garde," in *Enzyklopädie des Holocaust: Die Verfolgung und Ermordung der europäischen Juden*, ed. Israel Gutman (Munich: Piper, 1993), 1: 404; Payne, *A History of Fascism*, 396.

and wrote that he was at that moment very important for them but might later become dangerous, and that he hated both Russians and Germans. Berger finished his letter with the comment that he was proposing to make use of Bandera's movement.[290]

Negotiating with Berger and other Nazi politicians, Bandera was not as much against collaboration with Germany, which was at war with the Soviet Union, as he was against collaboration with Vlasov, who was for him a Russian imperialist. Other Ukrainian and several other non-Russian politicians representing countries formerly in the Soviet Union took a similar position. In order to separate "imperialists" from "nationalists," the Germans organized national committees for Ukrainians and other non-Russian people.[291]

On 14 November 1944 in Prague, Vlasov was appointed leader of the Committee for the Liberation of the Peoples of Russia (*Komitet Osvobodzheniia Narodov Rossii*, KONR). At about the same time, arrangements began for a similar institution for Ukrainians. On 23 February 1945 Rosenberg assigned Shandruk to establish the Ukrainian National Committee (*Ukraïns'kyi Natsional'nyi Komitet*, UNK) in Weimar, and officially recognized it on 12 March 1945. Apart from Shandruk and Bandera, Volodymyr Kubiiovych, Oleksandr Semenko, Andrii Mel'nyk, and Pavlo Skoropads'kyi were involved in establishing the UNK and became its leaders. On 17 March 1945 the UNK appointed Shandruk as head of the Ukrainian National Army (*Ukraïns'ka Natsional'na Armiia*, UNA). The UNK tried to mobilize Ukrainians, of whom about two million were in German-held territory, for the UNA. The Waffen-SS Galizien was renamed the First Division of the UNA, but the Germans used the old name until the end of war.[292]

The task of Bandera, Mel'nyk, and Skoropads'kyi was to convince their political supporters to continue fighting against the Soviet Union. In December 1944, the Abwehr took Bandera and Stets'ko to Cracow, where they helped Abwehrkommando 202 prepare a Ukrainian unit for parachuting into the hilly surroundings of Lviv. The Germans gave the unit a million roubles, stolen in Russia, which sum the troop was to transport to Shukhevych. Bandera, Stets'ko, and Lebed' gave the courier Iurii Lopatyns'kyi letters to Shukhevych. Bandera instructed the courier to give the UPA the order to fight the Soviet army from the rear. He also stated that he was prepared to return to Ukraine. Stets'ko asked the courier to inform the OUN-B and UPA leaders in Ukraine that he still regarded himself as prime minister of Ukraine.[293]

On 6 January 1945, Bandera celebrated the Greek Catholic Christmas in Lehnin, a village about forty kilometers south-west of Berlin.[294] He then went with his family and some of his followers to Weimar, and stayed there for three weeks.[295] According

290 "Besprechung mit Bandera," BAB NS/19, 1513, 1–3.

291 Bul'ba-Borovets', *Armiia*, 300.

292 "Informationsdienst Ost, 21.03.1945," BAB, R6/597, 21–22; Golczewski, Die Ukraine im Zweiten Weltkrieg, 259–60; Bruder, *"Den Ukrainischen Staat*, 228–29.

293 Interrogation of Siegfried Müller, 15 September 1946, HDA SBU f. 13, spr. 372, vol. 39, 125–138, in *Stepan Bandera*, ed. Serhiichuk, 1:528–29; TsDAHO f. 57, op. 4, spr. 340, 68; "Interrogation of Vasyl' Diachuk-Chyzhevskyi, apparently 1946, HDA SBU f. 13, spr. 372, vol. 6, 4; Interrogation of Vasyl' Diachuk-Chyzhevs'kyi, apparently 1946, HDA SBU f. 13, spr. 372, vol. 6, 22; Interrogation of Oleksandr Luts'kyi, 19 and 20 July 1945, HDA SBU f. 13, spr. 372, vol. 1, 333–34; Motyka, *Ukraińska partyzantka*, 429.

294 [Name withheld], interview by author, Munich, 17 February 2008.

295 "Vernehmungsniederschrift Stefan Popel, 07.02.1956," StM, Pol. Dir. München 9281, 84–85.

to Shandruk, during meetings of the UNK in Weimar, Mel'nyk remained cautious about the idea of the proposed last crusade against the Soviet Union. In contrast, Bandera argued for "full support to the end, whatever it may be."[296] Two other witnesses, OUN-B member Ievhen Stakhiv and the Abwehr officer Siegfried Müller, confirmed that, while in Weimar, Bandera mobilized Ukrainians for an army that would support the Nazis in their fight against the Soviet Union.[297] Later, however, Bandera informed OUN members and the CIA that he had not supported the UNK or the Third Reich after his release from Sachsenhausen.[298]

In late January or early February 1945, Bandera and his wife and daughter went to Berlin. In early February, they "escaped" from Berlin and travelled, with the help of Lebed' and Matviieiko, to Vienna. There the OUN-B organized a conference in which several leading OUN members participated. Bandera was elected representative of the leadership of the Foreign Units of the OUN (*Zakordonni Chastyny OUN*, ZCh OUN). When the Red Army approached Vienna, Bandera went to Prague, and from there to Innsbruck.[299]

At a meeting of the leadership of the OUN in Ukraine on 5–6 February 1945, Bandera was re-elected leader of the entire OUN. Shukhevych had resigned from this position and became the leader of the OUN in Ukraine alone. The leadership in Ukraine further decided that Bandera should not return to Ukraine but stay abroad, where he could, as a former prisoner in a Nazi concentration camp and a symbol of Ukrainian nationalism, make propaganda for the national cause.[300]

At about the time as Bandera was suggesting "full support to the end, whatever it may be," Shimon Redlich, a Jew who had survived the three years of German occupation in eastern Galicia, observed the "most dramatic event in Brzezany during that single year after liberation":

> I stood near a window facing the Rynek [market square]. With me in that room were several people. One of them was Bela ... who sat at the piano. Out there, in the far end of the Rynek was a small crowd. It was snowing. A truck appeared and stopped in the middle of the crowd. On its platform were a few people. One of them seemed to read something from a piece of paper. After a few minutes the truck moved with those standing on the platform. Except one. That man re-

296 Pavlo Shandruk, *Arms of Valor* (New York: Robert Speller & Sons Publishers, 1959), 230. Shandruk did not write the date of the meeting at which Bandera argued for "full support to the end, whatever it may be." It must have happened before Bandera went from Berlin to Vienna, in late January or early February 1945.

297 Stakhiv, *Kriz' tiurmy*, 196; Interrogation of Siegfried Müller, 15 September 1946, HDA SBU f. 13, spr. 372, vol. 39, 125–38, in *Stepan Bandera*, ed. Serhiichuk, 1:532–33.

298 "Spetssoobshchenie o formirovanii tak nazyvaemogo Ukrainskogo Natsional'nogo komiteta, 27.04.1945," HDA SBU f. 13, spr. 372, vol. 39, 257–59, in *Stepan Bandera*, ed. Serhiichuk,1:281–82. Bandera and Stets'ko informed the CIA that they did not support the UNK. Cf. Richard Breitman and Norman J. W. Goda, *Hitler's Shadow: Nazi War Criminals, U.S. Intelligence, and the Cold War* (Washington: National Archives, 2010), 76.

299 "Protokol doprosa parashiutysta po klichke 'Miron', 16.07.1951," HDA SBU f. 6, op. 37, spr. 56232, 27–72, in *Stepan Bandera*, ed. Serhiichuk, 3:77–79; "Protokol doprosa obviniaemogo Okhrimovicha Vasiliia Ostapovicha, 21.10.1952," HDA SBU f. 5, spr. 445, vol. 1, 216–25, in *Stepan Bandera*, ed. Serhiichuk, 3:270–71; Interrogation of Vasyl' Diachuk-Chyzhevs'kyi, perhaps 1946, SBU f. 13, spr. 372, vol. 6, 4. For Bandera in Vienna, see also Halyna Hordasevych, *Stepan Bandera: Liudyna i mif* (Lviv: Literaturna ahentsiia Piramida, 2001), 106–107.

300 Motyka, *Ukraińska partyzantka*, 429–30.

> mained, hanging, his body dangling from side to side. Bela was playing Chopin's mourning march [*sic*]. I was told that the man who was hanged was a *banderovits*, a Ukrainian nationalist. People were talking about atrocities committed by the *banderovtsi* against the Soviets.[301]

The fate of the Banderites in Ukraine changed dramatically after the Red Army took control of western Ukraine in summer 1944. The OUN-B and UPA continued to murder Poles who were still in Ukraine and began to murder those Ukrainians whom they accused of supporting the new Soviet regime. The Soviet authorities, for their part, started to eliminate the Banderites, in which category they included OUN members, UPA insurgents and its supporters, and also Ukrainian civilians accused of supporting the Ukrainian nationalists or of being Banderites.

301 Redlich, *Together and Apart*, 142.

Conclusion

After their detention in Germany, Bandera and Stets'ko attempted reconciliation with the Nazi leaders but the latter found other, more reliable Ukrainian partners for collaboration, such as Volodymyr Kubiiovych. In late July 1941 Hitler decided to include eastern Galicia into the General Government and to create the Reichskommissariat Ukraine from the rest of the conquered Ukrainian territories. This decision disappointed the OUN-B who had hoped that Hitler would allow them to unite the Ukrainian territories. In addition, several hundred OUN-B members were arrested in Ukraine and Germany and confined in different concentration camps as political prisoners. As a result of the conflict with the OUN-B the Germans dissolved the Ukrainian militia, which had been established by the OUN-B, and set up the Ukrainian police. Nevertheless, the OUN-B members tried to remain in the police while concealing their affiliation with the organization. In the following months the OUN-B sent more and more members to the police with the purpose of infiltrating and controlling it. The Ukrainian policemen significantly outnumbered the Germans and were deeply involved in the annihilation of the Jews. In spring 1943, about 5,000 out of a total of 12,000 Ukrainian policemen in Volhynia deserted the police and joined the UPA, which the OUN-B had formed a few months before.

From early 1943 on, the UPA conducted an ethnic cleansing against the Polish population in Volhynia and eastern Galicia, killing between 70,000 and 100,000 civilians. At the same time, the OUN-B, UPA, the Ukrainian police and Ukrainian peasants killed several thousand Jews who had escaped from the ghettos and hid in the forests. During these massacres Bandera was imprisoned in Berlin and in Zellenbau, a building for special political prisoners in the Sachsenhausen concentration camp. During this period he had only limited contact with the leadership of the OUN and UPA. Nevertheless, the killing of thousands of civilians by the OUN and UPA strengthened the Bandera myth, because the murderers were frequently perceived by their victims as Banderites and also identified themselves with Bandera. In view of their dire situation on the eastern front, the Germans renewed their collaboration with the OUN-B in the spring of 1944, as they had done with the Iron Guard and some other nationalist and fascist movements. Bandera and other Ukrainian leaders were released in autumn 1944 in order to mobilize the Ukrainians for the fight against the Soviet Union, which Bandera, according to Shandruk, took very seriously. In early February 1945, Bandera went to Vienna with his family. He was reelected as the leader of the OUN and decided to stay in exile to make propaganda for the national cause.

Chapter 6

THIRD WORLD WAR AND THE GLOBALIZATION OF UKRAINIAN NATIONALISM

On 8 May 1945 in Berlin-Karlshorst, Fieldmarshal Wilhelm Keitel signed an instrument of surrender on behalf of the German armed forces, officially bringing active operations to a close. The Second World War, the greatest political catastrophe in the history of mankind, had cost some forty-five million human lives and seen many cities, towns, and villages razed to the ground. While millions of people not only in Europe but across the world were breathing a sigh of relief, the OUN and UPA were yearning for the outbreak of a third world war. The OUN leaders hoped that, after the defeat of Germany, the Western Allies would attack the Soviet Union, enabling the OUN to establish an independent state. Although until at least 1951 the intelligence services of the United States and the United Kingdom did not rule out a Soviet attack against the West, the Western governments were much more reluctant than the OUN leadership to spark off another war. Instead, the ideological conflict between the Soviet Union and the Western powers resulted in the Cold War, which divided the world, apart from the non-aligned nations, into Eastern and Western blocs until 1991.[1]

Once the Red Army had pushed the Wehrmacht westwards in the spring and summer of 1944, the Soviet authorities began to reestablish their power in western Ukraine. It was clear to Stalin by this time, and after the Yalta conference of 4–11 February 1945 also to the Allies, that western Ukraine would remain in Soviet hands after the war. On 9 September 1944, an agreement was signed between the Polish Committee of National Liberation (*Polski Komitet Wyzwolenia Narodowego*, PKWN) and the government of the Ukrainian SSR, regulating the resettlement of Poles from Ukraine and of Ukrainians from Poland. Between 1944 and 1946, 700,000 Poles, survivors of the massacres in Volhynia and eastern Galicia, were resettled in Poland from the Ukrainian SSR, and 488,000 Ukrainians from newly-communist Poland were resettled in the Ukrainian SSR. During Operation Vistula (Pol. *Akcja Wisła*) in 1947, 140,000 Ukrainians who had remained in south-east Poland were forcibly resettled in the northern and western territories of Poland. The Polish army used very cruel methods against the Ukrainian population, and numerous Ukrainian civilians were killed, robbed, raped, and otherwise mistreated during the resettlement. After these ethnic relocations the Polish-Ukrainian

1 According to Motyka the Soviet Union took the threat of a third world war seriously and prepared for it. Cf. Motyka, *Ukraińska partyzantka*, 503. Western intelligence services also saw a war against the Soviet Union, especially in 1948, as imminent. Cf. Harry Rositzke, *The CIA's Secret Operations: Espionage, Counterespionage and Covert Action* (Boulder: Westview Press, 1988), 1. For the OUN-UPA and third world war, see Burds, AGENTURA, 99.

Map 6. Eastern Europe 1945. *YIVO Encyclopedia*, 2:2146.

borderland was ethnically separated for the first time in centuries.[2]

Between 1941 and 1944, almost all the Jews of western Ukraine were annihilated by the Germans, with the help of the Ukrainian police and local people, and also by the OUN and UPA, both on their own and in collaboration with the Germans. In June 1941, before the Germans invaded the Soviet Union, about 250,000 Jews lived in Volhynia and about 570,000 in eastern Galicia (Distrikt Galizien). Of these, only about 1.5 percent survived the German occupation in Volhynia and only 2 to 3 percent in eastern Galicia.[3] The only enemies of the OUN and UPA remaining after the Second World War in western Ukraine were the Soviet authorities, who, ironically enough, implemented some of the main goals of the Ukrainian nationalists. By the incorporation of western Ukraine into the Ukrainian SSR, the Soviet rulers had achieved the *sobornist'*, or unification of Ukrainian territories in one state, and, by resettling the Poles and other nationalities, they had made Ukraine more homogenous than it had ever been before.

2 Boeckh, *Stalinismus*, 371–91; Grzegorz Motyka, "Konflikt polsko-ukraiński w latach 1943–1948: Aktualny stan badań," *Warszawskie Zeszyty Historyczne* 8–9 (1999): 323–25; Motyka, *Tak było w Bieszczadach*, 405–13; Bruder, *"Den Ukrainischen Staat*, 234.

3 For Volhynia, see Spector, *Holocaust of Volhynian Jews*, 11. For eastern Galicia, see Pohl, *Nationalsozialistische*, 43–44, 385. In June 1941, 160,000 Jews resided in Lviv. By October 1944, only 1,689 Jews were registered in this city. See also Kruglov, Jewish Losses in Ukraine, 284. See also page 277, and 242 et seq.

In general, many Soviet policies bore striking similarities to those of the OUN-B. Both were totalitarian and authoritarian in nature and both used ethnic violence to solve political problems. Bandera was the ultranationalist or fascist alternative to Stalin and Khrushchev. Though the OUN-B frequently claimed after the Second World War that the UPA was fighting against the totalitarian Soviet Union for a nationalist democratic Ukraine, the reference to democracy was nothing more than a pretence, intended to persuade the United Kingdom and the United States to provide support for the insurgent movement.

The Subordination of the Greek Catholic Church

After the Red Army arrived in western Ukraine in the summer of 1944, the Soviet authorities renewed the policy of Sovietization they had begun in 1939. One item of this policy was to subordinate the Greek Catholic Church, a very important component of eastern Galician identity and of Ukrainian nationalism. The body of the Greek Catholic Church consisted in 1939 of 4,200,000 believers, 2,950 priests, 1,090 nuns, 520 monks, 3,400 parishes, and 4,400 churches.[4]

In 1943–1944 the Soviet government was ready to compromise with the Greek Catholic Church and also tried to establish relations with the Vatican.[5] Sheptyts'kyi and his follower, Bishop Slipyi, also tried to negotiate with the Soviet Union. Together with Bishop Hryhorii Khomyshyn in late 1944, they called on the UPA to "return from the wrong path." Sheptyts'kyi prepared emissaries to go to Kiev and Moscow and to welcome the Soviet authorities and Stalin. After Sheptyts'kyi's death in November 1944, Slipyi sent a delegation to Moscow to assure the Soviet government of the loyalty of the Church. In late 1944, the Soviet authorities treated the Greek Catholic Church as equal to other churches but were disappointed by the positive attitude of many Greek Catholic priests to the OUN-UPA underground. The Soviet leaders were also troubled by the anticommunism of the Vatican, to which the Greek Catholic Church was subordinate. In January 1945, the Orthodox Church referred to the Vatican as an enemy. Shortly afterwards in early spring 1945, the attitude of the Soviet authorities to the Greek Catholic Church changed entirely.[6]

In March 1945, Stalin ordered the incorporation of the Greek Catholic Church into the Russian Orthodox Church. On 8 April 1945, the newspaper *Vil'na Ukraïna* published Iaroslav Halan's article "With Cross or Knife?" which accused the church of collaborating with the Germans, supporting the OUN-UPA, and betraying the Ukrainian nation.[7] In April, Slipyi and thirty-three other clergymen were arrested. Slipyi, accused of being a "Vatican agent" and an "accomplice of the Germans and the Bandera underground," was sentenced to eight years in a labor camp, and it was only in 1963 that he was released and allowed to leave the Soviet Union. After Slipyi's arrest, the church was coordinated by an "Initiative Group" organized by the Soviet

4 Boeckh, *Stalinismus*, 498.
5 Statiev, *Soviet Counterinsurgency*, 263.
6 Ibid., 265–66; Boeckh, *Stalinismus*, 500.
7 Volodymyr Rasovych, "Z khrestom chy z nozhem?," *Vil'na Ukraïna*, 8 April 1945, 5–6. Halan published the article under the pseudonym Volodymyr Rasovych. Cf. Motyka, *Ukraińska partyzantka*, 420.

authorities and headed by the Greek Catholic priest Havryïl Kostel'nyk. The task of the group was to unite priests who wanted to dissolve the union of 1596 with the Vatican and to join the Russian Orthodox Church.[8]

During the following months, under ruthless pressure from the Soviet authorities, more than 70 percent of the Greek Catholic priests joined the Initiative Group. The majority of priests did not do so out of conviction but because they were afraid of being repressed or deported.[9] Those who resisted were arrested as "Vatican agents," "Bandera agents," "Nazi collaborators," or "bourgeois nationalists." In late September 1945, 78 clergymen were arrested in the Lviv region alone.[10] According to church statements, between 500 and 800 priests were in prison in western Ukraine in 1946.[11] According to official statistics, by 8 March 1946 when the Greek Catholic Church was officially dissolved, 908 priests had joined the Initiative Group and 251 stayed out of it. Bohdan Bociurkiw, an expert on the Greek Catholic Church, concludes that as 1,684 priests were registered in September 1945, there is a discrepancy of 525 priests between that figure and the 1,159 who either joined or refused to join the Russian Orthodox Church. However, it is hard to estimate how many of these 525 priests were arrested, deported, or killed by the Soviet authorities, because some of them had left with the Germans in 1944 and others had left the church, or gone underground, or had simply died. The number of monks and nuns declined significantly as a result of Soviet repression.[12]

In addition to being terrorized by the Soviet police, many Greek Catholic priests, particularly those who collaborated with the Soviet authorities, were attacked and executed by the OUN-UPA. The OUN announced in summer 1946 that those priests who joined the Russian Orthodox Church should publicly conceal their transfer, or they would be killed or otherwise punished. Kostel'nyk, head of the Initiative Group, was killed on 20 September 1948.[13]

The act of dissolving the Brest Union of 1596 with the Vatican and joining the Russian Orthodox Church was a farce. The synod, in which 216 clergymen and nineteen laymen participated, took place on 8 March 1946 under the auspices of the Soviet authorities and was filmed for propaganda purposes. The Initiative Group was represented by Kostel'nyk, Antonii Pel'vets'kyi, and Mykhailo Mel'nyk. Pel'vets'kyi said in his speech that "the great Soviet Union liberated us from German fascist slavery." Kostel'nyk stated that "the union [with the Vatican] is a declaration of religious war against the entire Orthodox world for the glory of Rome." On 31 March Kostel'nyk, Pel'vets'kyi, and Mel'nyk went to Kiev, where they met with Khrushchev and watched a film about the synod. Two days later, they continued to Moscow where Kostel'nyk asked Patriarch Alexy to "admit us to the All-Russian Orthodox Church." When interviewed, Kostel'nyk denied that there had been mass arrests of Greek Catholic priests and stated that only the leaders of the church, such as Slipyi, were

8 Statiev, *Soviet Counterinsurgency*, 266–67; Boeckh, *Stalinismus*, 508; Bociurkiw, *Ukraïns'ka*, 100.
9 Statiev, *Soviet Counterinsurgency*, 267.
10 Bociurkiw, *Ukraïns'ka*, 120.
11 Boeckh, *Stalinismus*, 516.
12 Bociurkiw, *Ukraïns'ka*, 145–46, 161, 168–70.
13 Ibid., 179–81.

arrested for “active treacherous activity as accessories to the advantage of the German occupiers, and [that] their indictments were passed to the Military Tribunal.”[14]

The Conflict between the OUN-UPA and the Soviet Authorities

In addition to the total destruction of the Jewish population and the resettlement of the Polish population, Ukraine experienced another human tragedy caused by the brutal conflict between the OUN-UPA and the Soviet regime. In the first half of 1944, 120,000 western Ukrainians, among them many collaborators, left Ukraine with the Germans in order to escape Soviet persecution.[15] In the following years, several thousand Ukrainians loyal to the Soviet regime were sent from eastern Ukraine to the western regions as teachers, nurses, physicians, engineers, and so forth. In 1946 drought and confiscation of crops from the collective farms in eastern Ukraine caused a famine in which 800,000 to 1,000,000 people died.[16] By 1950, 1,850,000 Ukrainians who had worked during the war in Germany as forced laborers returned to Ukraine. Many of them were branded as “traitors” but were not sent to the Gulag, as historians during the Cold War believed. The majority of them, 58 percent, were sent to their places of origin, 19 percent were conscripted into the Red Army, 14 percent were enlisted in working battalions of the People’s Commissariat of Defense, 6.5 percent ended up in NKVD spetskontingents (workers in the Gulag administered by the NKVD chief administration), and 2 percent were sent to camps as reserve units.[17]

The greatest challenge to the plan for Sovietizing western Ukraine was the OUN-UPA underground. At the zenith of its strength in 1944, the UPA numbered 25,000 to 30,000 partisans and could mobilize up to 100,000 people.[18] To prevent young people from joining the UPA, the Soviet regime conscripted the astonishingly high number of 700,000 people in western Ukraine into the Red Army, in the period between its arrival in the summer of 1944 and the end of 1945.[19] The new authorities also tried, by means of an extensive and intensive ideological repertoire, to Sovietize young people’s minds, through schools, youth and debating clubs, libraries, and cinemas. The OUN and UPA were frequently depicted in the darkest propagandist colors: They were “German-Ukrainian nationalists,” “traitors,” “bandits,” and the “enemies of the Ukrainian and Soviet people.” Several hundred agitators were sent to western Ukraine in order to persuade the population to accept the Soviet idea. In November and December 1944, 4,000 propaganda meetings were organized in the Drohobych district alone. In May 1945, 170 newspapers propagating the Soviet idea appeared in western Ukraine.[20]

In order to mobilize local people against the OUN and UPA, the Soviet authorities organized destruction battalions (*istrebitel’nye batal’ony*) under the command of the central NKVD Destruction Battalion Headquarters, which from 1 December 1944 was

14 Bociurkiw, *Ukraïns’ka*, 143–47, 155–56.
15 Boeckh, *Stalinismus*, 293.
16 Motyka, *Ukraińska partyzantka*, 504–505.
17 Boeckh, *Stalinismus*, 296–303, 309–11.
18 Motyka, *Ukraińska partyzantka*, 424, 428.
19 Ibid., 416. Statiev provides the number 750,000. Altogether 3,184,726 Ukrainians were enlisted in the Red Army. Cf. Statiev, *Soviet Counterinsurgency*, 78.
20 Motyka, *Ukraińska partyzantka*, 418.

controlled by the Head of the NKVD Directorate for the Struggle against Banditry. The battalions in western Ukraine had 100–159 men at first. When the tactics of the guerrillas changed, the battalions were dispersed in platoons of 25–50, or even in sections with 10–12 men. To a great extent, the militia recruited the members of the destruction battalions from people who were threatened by the OUN-UPA. At the outset, service in the destruction battalions was unpaid, but many local people joined in order to protect themselves and their relatives. The recruits included peasants, relatives of Red Army soldiers, demobilized Red Army soldiers, amnestied OUN-UPA members, people from eastern Ukraine, those whose relatives had been killed by the OUN-UPA, and ethnic minorities, in particular Poles. In the Drohobych region, Poles constituted up to 40 percent of the destruction battalions. The Soviet authorities also recruited neighborhood watch units (*gruppy sodeistviia istrebitel'nym batal'onam*), groups of lightly armed village activists, which supported the destruction battalions. On 1 January 1945, the destruction battalions in western Ukraine counted 23,906 members, and the watch units 24,025. On 1 January 1946, the destruction battalions counted 39,727 members, and the watch units 26,000—more in total than the number of OUN-UPA partisans at that time.[21]

The situation in western Ukraine in the first years after the Second World War resembled a civil war. In addition to protecting the local population against the OUN-UPA and banditry, the destruction battalions committed numerous criminal acts, frequently as a result of greed or a desire to exact revenge for OUN-UPA crimes. The UPA, on the other hand, regarded the destruction battalions as its armory and frequently attacked them. Between 1 January and 30 March 1946 in the Stanislaviv region alone, the UPA disarmed forty militia units totaling 700 men and captured 605 weapons. Because the destruction battalions and district police were infiltrated by the nationalist underground, the Soviet authorities purged almost half their members in July 1946. Subsequently the militiamen were better screened and received more thorough indoctrination and training than the members of the destruction battalions. In 1948, when the OUN-UPA consisted of no more than a few hundred members, there were 85,421 people in the militia in western Ukraine.[22]

A very powerful measure used to halt support for and cooperation with the UPA, to diminish its size, and to persuade the rebellious parts of the population to adopt the Soviet idea, was deportation. OUN-B member Burian already complained on 13 November 1944: "The whole population is losing spirit. ... The attitude of the population has changed considerably in comparison with a month ago. People have been powerfully intimidated by arrest and exile to Siberia. Now in general they don't want to take [anyone] into their apartments, because they are afraid of denunciations."[23]

Another OUN-B member stated: "The population looks at us as if we're sentenced to death. They sympathize with us but don't believe in our success and don't want to tie their own fate to ours."[24] As a result of deportations and other measures, Ukrainians began in late 1944 not only to doubt the OUN propaganda and to with-

21 Statiev, *Soviet Counterinsurgency*, 211, 215, 218, 220; Motyka, *Ukraińska partyzantka*, 424.
22 Statiev, *Soviet Counterinsurgency*, 222–24, 227.
23 DALO, f. 3, op. 1, d. 70, 2, quoted in Burds, AGENTURA, 101.
24 Report of raion rebel chief, Lviv region, dated March 1947. DALO, f. 3, op. 2, d. 121, 108–13, quoted in Burds, AGENTURA, 102.

draw their support from the UPA but also to help the Soviet authorities combat the nationalist insurgents.[25]

The first secretary of the Party Committee in Lviv stated that "the most sensitive point of the bandits is their family."[26] By February 1944, Khrushchev had already proposed the deportation of the families of people active in the underground. The first deportation of 2,000 people started on 7 May 1944. On account of the very difficult conditions, many people, especially children, died during the deportations. Western Ukrainians were deported to the Komi Republic, the Irkutsk region, and other distant places in the interior of the USSR, where they worked in forestry or coal mines. In 1944, 12,762 people were deported; in 1945, 17,497.[27] The largest deportations took place in 1947 (77,791 people), 1949 (25,527 people), and 1950 (41,149).[28] Altogether, the Soviet regime deported about 203,000 people from western Ukraine,[29] of whom 171,000 were accused of belonging to or supporting the OUN-UPA or of being the kin of an OUN-UPA member.[30] The majority of the deportees were women and children whose OUN-UPA husbands and fathers were either hiding in the forests or had died in the struggle against the Soviet regime. Families could take up to 500 kilograms of belongings with them, and the rest of their property was confiscated. They were deported for periods ranging from five to twenty-five years.[31]

Deportation was a regular Soviet method of resolving political problems and caused a great deal of sorrow. Thousands of western Ukrainians were deported because their relatives were in the OUN-UPA, or because they were accused of helping and supporting the OUN-UPA, which they might have done under duress, or of which they might have been entirely innocent. Because of the crimes committed by the OUN and UPA, however, the deportations released very different emotions in western Ukrainian society. On 21 October 1947, a woman waiting for the deportation train began to lament. Another woman, who was not being deported, asked:

> Why are you screaming now? You should have screamed earlier. Then, you were certainly laughing. Then, when your son was murdering my husband, and I wept close to the bed of a child bereft of its father, I knew that you would pay twofold, and I was not wrong. You and only you are responsible for our suffering, for the tears of orphaned children, widows ... whose fathers and husbands died at the hands of your son and other bandits.[32]

Another measure related to the deportations, and which weakened the UPA, was the collectivization of farms. By this means, the Soviet authorities intended to change the organization of agriculture and to halt the supply of food to the insurgents. Two-

25 Burds, AGENTURA, 101.

26 Motyka, *Ukraińska partyzantka*, 478.

27 Stanisław Ciesielski, Grzegorz Hryciuk, and Aleksander Srebrakowski, *Masowe deportacje ludności w Związku radzieckim* (Toruń: Adam Marszałek, 2003), 281, 291; Motyka, *Ukraińska partyzantka*, 479.

28 In 1946, 6,350 persons; in 1948, 817; in 1951, 18,523; and in 1952, 3,229 persons were deported from western Ukraine. Cf. Ciesielski, *Masowe deportacje*, 291, 294; Motyka, *Ukraińska partyzantka*, 533–37.

29 Ciesielski, *Masowe deportacje*, 291, 294; Motyka, *Ukraińska partyzantka*, 536–37, 649.

30 Boeckh, *Stalinismus*, 349.

31 Ciesielski, *Masowe deportacje*, 291, 294; Motyka, *Ukraińska partyzantka*, 536–37, 649; Boeckh, *Stalinismus*, 349.

32 TsDAHO f. 1, op. 23, spr. 4963, 34, quoted in Motyka, *Ukraińska partyzantka*, 537.

thirds of the 77,791 persons deported in 1947 after the beginning of collectivization were people from *seredniak* and *kulak* families, that is, according to Soviet standards, medium-rich and rich families.[33] The collectivization in western Ukraine was completed earlier than in Belarus, which suggests that the conflict with the OUN and UPA accelerated it. In 1950, 98.7 percent of all western Ukrainian farms were collective. In general, peasants did not join the *kolkhozes* (collective farms) voluntarily, but out of fear and necessity.[34] Those peasants who joined the collectives were terrorized by the UPA and constituted a substantial portion of their victims. After a while, the local residents turned their backs on the insurgents and denounced them.[35] According to Statiev, during the early Sovietization of western Ukraine, the UPA leader Shukhevych claimed: "Not a single village should recognize Soviet authority. The OUN should destroy all those who recognize Soviet authority. Not intimidate but destroy. We should not be concerned that people might damn us for brutality. Nothing horrible would happen if only half of the forty million Ukrainians survived."[36]

Another effective method of eradicating support for the OUN-UPA was terror against real and alleged UPA helpers and sympathizers. Although it was officially forbidden, the NKVD (from 1946 the MVD) and the NKGB (from 1946 MGB) frequently killed or otherwise mistreated people who did not belong to the OUN-UPA or had not committed any crime.[37] This happened because the NKVD regarded all western Ukrainians as "bandits" or "nationalists," and also so that they could report progress in defeating the "bandits." Random individuals or the entire families of suspects were killed quite regularly, sometimes by drunken policemen, and sometimes for sadistic reasons. Rape of female prisoners was common and dozens of women who resisted rape were killed by the NKVD police. The NKVD officers usually reported these victims as "bandits," "nationalists," or "Banderites" and were rarely made to face justice for their actions.[38] In March 1946, for example, an NKVD unit, consisting mainly of Ukrainian soldiers, was sent to the Ukrainian village of Rodarychi:

> Before going on the mission, [Lieutenant] Iliubaev, [Sergeant] Rezin and Private Saiko drank a liter of moonshine. ... Having searched the house of Kutovik and found nothing suspicious, Iliubaev and his section walked to the neighboring house, that of Maria Fedorovna Kul'chitskaia. ... At that time, Anna Kutovik ran out of her house toward the village council, shouting that she had been robbed. ... Private Saiko beat her up with a submachine gun and then shot her dead in the street. On hearing the shots, a local resident, 50-year-old Stanislav Ivanovich Tovbukh, ran out of his house. ... Saiko took Tovbukh 100 meters away and shot him. ... After that, Iluibaev ordered that everyone in [Kul'chitskaia's] house be

33 Serhyi Kudelia, "Choosing Violence in Irregular Wars: The Case of Anti-Soviet Insurgency in Western Ukraine," *East European Politics and Societies and Cultures*, 26 November 2012: 14–15.

34 Motyka, *Ukraińska partyzantka*, 542.

35 Kudelia, Choosing Violence in Irregular Wars, 23–25.

36 Statiev, *Soviet Counterinsurgency*, 131.

37 For the structure and functioning of the NKVD and NKGB in Soviet Ukraine, see Boeckh, *Stalinismus*, 182–97.

38 Statiev, *Soviet Counterinsurgency*, 283. Statiev quotes Timofei Strokach, "Dokladnaia zapiska o narusheniiakh sovetskoi zakonnosti v organakh NKVD-NKGB," 2 June 1945, TsDAHO, f. 1, op. 23, spr. 2410, 102, 103. See also Burds, Gender and Policing, 317.

> shot. ... Saiko, Soloviev and Khalitov lined up 21-year-old Emilia Kul'chitskaia, 13-year-old Ekaterina Kul'chitskaia, and a disabled man, 76-year-old Ivan Priima, into a single row by the bed. The teenager wept and begged them not to kill her, while the disabled Priima fell to his knees and asked them to spare him. But Saiko, Solov'ev and Khalitov shot the girls dead, while Priima feigned death and thus survived. ... Iliubaev reported to the Battalion commander, Captain Shtefanov, that he had liquidated five bandits.[39]

As during the first occupation of western Ukraine in 1939–1941, the NKVD frequently mistreated and tortured people during interrogations. Although beating was the primary method of obtaining information, the NKVD also electrocuted suspects and burned them with cigarettes.[40]

In 1944 the Soviet authorities arrested Iurii Stel'mashchuk, an important OUN and UPA leader. With his help, they were able to track down and kill "Klym Savur" (Dmytro Kliachkivs'kyi) on 12 February 1945, the first OUN-B leader of the UPA and the main organizer of the ethnic cleansing in Volhynia in early 1943. Savur's killing outraged many OUN-UPA members and deteriorated the mood of many UPA partisans. The NKVD also used Stel'mashchuk to identify, arrest, and kill several other nationalist insurgents and, with his help at meetings, to propagate the Soviet idea. In late 1945, Stel'mashchuk was sentenced to death and executed.[41]

The Soviet regime practiced public executions from at least 1943 until 1951.[42] In Ukraine, the idea of hanging "bandits" publicly was popularized by Khrushchev. "In order to intimidate the bandits," he wrote in a letter to Stalin on 15 November 1944, "those sentenced to death ... should be hanged rather than shot. The trials should be open and the local population should be invited. ... The execution of the sentence pronounced by a tribunal should be carried out publicly in the village where the sentenced committed the crime. This will sober the bandits."[43] In mid-December 1944 in the village of Dobrosyn in the Zhovkva district, the NKVD hanged the local commander of the SB, while about fifty people looked on. In late December 1944, three people were hanged in the square in the town of Bus'k. Placards with the inscription "For the Betrayal of the Ukrainian Nation" were hung on their chests. Sometimes the Soviet executioners left the bodies to hang for several days, in order to observe the reaction of passers-by and determine thereby who was related to the dead nationalists.[44] Shimon Redlich, who observed the hanging in Berezhany, noticed that the victims were referred to as Banderites.[45] Janina Kwiatkowska remembered that the Soviets hanged Banderites in public places in Chortkiv, in order to frighten the

39 Loburenko, deputy minister of internal affairs of Ukraine, to Korotchenko, "Soobshchenie," 31 March 1946, TsDIAL f. 3. op. 1, spr. 424, quoted in Statiev, *Soviet Counterinsurgency*, 283.

40 Motyka, *Ukraińska partyzantka*, 484–88, 528–29. "Physical methods of coercion" were legal in the USSR, although some police officers were punished for using a "medieval method," as in the case of two, who, in March 1945 in Ternopil', were sentenced to ten years, for grilling the foot of a woman under interrogation, on a stove. Torture remained a common interrogation method at least until the end of Stalinism. Cf. Statiev, *Soviet Counterinsurgency*, 247–48.

41 Motyka, *Ukraińska partyzantka*, 499; Bruder, *"Den Ukrainischen Staat*, 231; Statiev, *Soviet Counterinsurgency*, 205.

42 Statiev, *Soviet Counterinsurgency*, 251.

43 Rusnachenko, *Narod zburenyi*, 254; Statiev, *Soviet Counterinsurgency*, 250.

44 Motyka, *Ukraińska partyzantka*, 480–81.

45 Redlich, *Together and Apart*, 142.

population, end its support of the OUN and UPA, and to demonstrate that the Banderites were "bandits" and "traitors."[46] The number of people hanged in public by the NKVD is hard to estimate. Toward the end of 1944 in the Stanislaviv district alone, the Soviet authorities publicly executed twenty-eight people.[47]

In order to enable OUN-UPA members to return to society and thereby weaken the structure of the underground, the Soviet authorities announced several amnesties. The first was declared on 12 February 1944,[48] another in November 1944, and a third in May 1945. Between 1946 and 1949 four further amnesties were announced. The first did not persuade many partisans to surrender. Nevertheless, the winter and difficult conditions in the underground discouraged a substantial number of them, including peasants without much patriotic enthusiasm, from hiding any longer in the forests and from resisting the Soviet authorities.[49] The amnesties helped such people return home. Up to July 1946, a total of 111,809 fugitives surrendered in western Ukraine, of whom 62,357 claimed to be draft evaders.[50] The OUN-UPA leadership regarded surrender as betrayal, and the SB of the OUN frequently punished surrender with death.[51] The general attitude of the Soviet authorities toward OUN-UPA members who surrendered was different from their attitude toward those who were captured. In general, the Soviet authorities did not kill those who surrendered. The sporadic shooting of those who had surrendered was regarded as a violation of "socialist legality" and punished accordingly.[52]

The UPA partisans who surrendered were usually used by the Soviet authorities for two purposes: propaganda, and the detection of members of the underground. The life of such ex-partisans depended on these requirements and on new loyalty to the Soviet authorities. They were allowed to speak at public meetings and were expected to explain why they had gone underground, how they had killed people, and how they realized that joining the "bourgeois nationalists" was a mistake. This was intended to make a strong impression on the audience. The authorities also expected the former UPA partisans to persuade their relatives to leave the underground and to work in the police force or destruction battalions. Those who had surrendered were regarded by the SB of the OUN as traitors and were frequently killed by them.[53]

Some of the nationalists who surrendered under the amnesties, and who confessed their crimes, were tried and sentenced only after the elapse of several years. In the 1980s a number of such trials took place. One defendant was Iakov Ostrovs'kyi, who during the first Soviet occupation of western Ukraine had denounced the Ukrainian nationalists, and who had served in the Ukrainian police during the German occupation, remaining in contact with the OUN. In March 1943 he left the police, and in July 1943 he joined the UPA, in which he remained until July 1944, when he surrendered to the Soviet authorities. During an NKVD interrogation

46 Janina Kwiatkowska, KAW, II/1352, 7.
47 Motyka, *Ukraińska partyzantka*, 480.
48 TsDAHO f. 57, op. 4, spr. 37, 266–67.
49 Bruder, *"Den Ukrainischen Staat*, 232; Motyka, *Ukraińska partyzantka*, 435, 475.
50 Statiev, *Soviet Counterinsurgency*, 202.
51 For OUN threats to murder the family of a surrendered UPA partisan, see the interrogation of Vasyl' Pchelians'kyi, 9 August 1944, HDA SBU f. 13, spr. 372, vol. 4, 88.
52 Statiev, *Soviet Counterinsurgency*, 205.
53 Ibid., 203–205.

Ostrovs'kyi confessed to murdering "only twenty-five to thirty" people. Although the Extraordinary State Commission[54] found a witness to Ostrovs'kyi's crimes, he was not prosecuted at the time, possibly because he had given himself up. His case was reopened only in 1981. On the basis of his own testimony and other evidence, Ostrovs'kyi was sentenced to death and executed in 1983.[55]

The attitude of local Ukrainians to the OUN-UPA changed, not only due to the deportations, collectivization, and the Soviet terror but also as a result of the terror of the OUN-UPA against the local population, and the fanatical fight of the OUN-UPA against an enemy they could not defeat. The OUN-UPA was fairly popular between early 1943 and mid-1944. At that time, it could count on support from a substantial part of the western Ukrainian population. During the war, western Ukrainians were exposed to a different kind of foreign terror, and many of them believed that the UPA could liberate Ukraine. Bunkers and hideouts in which the rebels could hide were very widespread in western Ukraine. In 1945 the Soviet police found such hideouts in every fourth peasant cottage in the Lviv region, and many remained undiscovered. Some of the bunkers were designed to function as hospitals, libraries, archives, or warehouses. One bunker was so large that it could hold 200 people. In the two-year period 1945–1946 alone, Soviet forces in western Ukraine uncovered 28,986 hideouts.[56]

As the local population began to have doubts about the nationalist underground movement and to withdraw its support, the OUN-UPA started terrorizing the local Ukrainians, enforcing assistance, and spreading frightening propaganda. A very popular rumor was that Stalin would resettle all western Ukrainians in Siberia, and that only the OUN-UPA could prevent this, or that "the western Ukrainians will be exterminated [by the Soviets], exactly as the Jews were destroyed by the Germans."[57] One UPA leaflet claimed that the Soviet authorities began collectivization in order to annihilate the Ukrainians by famine, as in Soviet Ukraine in 1932–1933.[58] The insurgents also tried to strengthen their popularity by spreading a belief about the imminent outbreak of a third world war, in which the OUN-UPA, together with American and British troops, would defeat the Soviet Union and establish a Ukrainian state.[59]

At least since 1945, an increasing number of western Ukrainians ceased to believe the insurgents' propaganda rumors, as a result of which the OUN leadership was compelled to conscript Ukrainians into the UPA by force. Similarly, individuals in the

54 The commission was established on 2 November 1942 by the Presidium of the Supreme Soviet. Its full name was: The Extraordinary State Commission for ascertaining and investigating crimes perpetrated by the German-Fascist invaders and their accomplices and the damage inflicted by them on citizens, collective farms, social organizations, state enterprises and institutions of the USSR (*Chrezychainaia gosudarstvennaia komissiia po ustanovleniiu i rassledovaniiu zlodeianii nemetsko-fashistskikh zakhvatnikov i ikh soobshchnikov i prichinennogo imi ushcherba grazhdanam, kolkhozam, obshchestvennym organizatsiiam, gosudarstvennym predpriiatiiam i uchrezhdeniiam SSSR*). For the Extraordinary State Commission, see Marina Sorokina, "People and Procedures. Toward a History of the Investigation of Nazi Crimes in the USSR," in *The Holocaust in the East: Local Perpetrators and Soviet Responses*, ed. Michael David-Fox, Peter Holquist, and Alexander M. Martin (Pittsburgh: University of Pittsburgh Press, 2014), 118–41.

55 John-Paul Himka, "'Skazhytie, mnogo liudei vy rozsstrelialy' 'Net, ne mnogo—chelovek 25–30,'" 4 July 2012, http://www.uamoderna.com/md/173, *Ukraïna Moderna* (accessed, 7 November 2012).

56 Burds, AGENTURA, 94; Statiev, *Soviet Counterinsurgency*, 231.

57 Statiev, *Soviet Counterinsurgency*, 105.

58 HDA SBU, spr. 372, vol. 51, 195–98, quoted in Kudelia, Choosing Violence in Irregular Wars, 18.

59 Statiev, *Soviet Counterinsurgency*, 89; Burds, Early Cold War, 22.

OUN-UPA who did not believe that the OUN-UPA could defeat the Soviet Union, and who spoke out in favor of surrender, were killed by the SB of the OUN.[60] The SB killed hundreds of OUN members and UPA partisans whom it suspected of betrayal or of being *seksoty* (informers).[61] In 1945 in Volhynia alone, the SB killed about 1000 UPA partisans.[62] From 1 January to 1 April 1945, the SB investigated 938 OUN members, of whom they murdered 889 for "collaboration with the Soviets."[63] Like the NKVD, the SB applied the principle of collective responsibility, and frequently punished not only "unfaithful" individuals but also their families, with death. As a result, more and more ordinary Ukrainians regarded the insurgents as bandits and denounced them to the NKVD.[64] Sometimes even the families of OUN-UPA members refused to help their relatives and advised them to give themselves up.[65] If peasants delayed or failed to deliver food supplies, the SB regarded them as foes.[66] As early as August 1944 one OUN leader believed that 90 percent of the peasants desired to remain neutral in the conflict between the OUN-UPA and the Soviet authorities. Another leader reported: "The masses are disappointed to such a degree that they refuse to give shelter or food even to those [UPA partisans] they know."[67] In 1948 one OUN member testified that "the local population stopped supporting bandits [OUN-UPA]; we have to take supplies by force or under threat of weapons. When we come to houses the dwellers say directly: 'Go away, otherwise we'll go to Siberia because of you.'"[68]

In general, people in western Ukraine were in a very difficult situation. They had to navigate survival in the face of two brutal and cruel regimes which were in combat with each other, and each of which demanded their loyalty. Supporting the Soviet power meant death at the hands of the OUN-UPA. Supporting the OUN-UPA meant either death or deportation at the hands of the NKVD. In the autumn of 1946, when the Soviet authorities tried to raise grain requisitions, the OUN-UPA left the message: "Soon the Bolsheviks will conduct the grain levy. Anyone among you who brings grain to the collection points will be killed like a dog, and your entire family butchered."[69]

The elections to the Supreme Soviet on 10 February 1946 became a bilateral demonstration of power. The OUN-UPA tried to persuade Ukrainians not to take part, in order to delegitimize Soviet power, at least symbolically. The Soviet authorities forced the Ukrainians to vote, frequently convoying entire groups to the polling stations or visiting the resistant individuals at home with a ballot box and "asking" them to vote.[70] On 30 June 1946 in villages near Kolomyia, the OUN-UPA hung up eight "nationalistic flags" that "they secured with mines." Four people died when the Soviet

60 HDA SBU f. 13, spr. 372, vol. 4, 176–78; Motyka, *Ukraińska partyzantka*, 436.
61 Burds, "AGENTURA," 102.
62 Motyka, *Ukraińska partyzantka*, 433.
63 Rusnachenko, *Narod zburenyi*, 319; Statiev, *Soviet Counterinsurgency*, 129.
64 Motyka, *Ukraińska partyzantka*, 435.
65 Ibid., 538, 542.
66 Statiev, *Soviet Counterinsurgency*, 129.
67 Ibid., 127.
68 Motyka, *Ukraińska partyzantka*, 546.
69 TsDAHO, f. 1, op. 23, spr. 1741, 48, quoted in Burds, AGENTURA, 109.
70 Motyka, *Ukraińska partyzantka*, 510.

police forced peasants to take them down.[71] On 27 May 1947, OUN activists blew up a Lenin monument in Iavoriv.[72] The nationalist insurgents destroyed several trucks with equipment that the Soviet officials were using to show propaganda movies.[73]

In 1944 and 1945, the UPA fought several battles with the Red Army and other Soviet troops but in general, it tried to avoid open confrontation with the Red Army, which was much stronger and better armed.[74] The main victims of the OUN-UPA were informers, people accused of supporting Soviet power or who joined the kolkhozes, and people transferred from eastern Ukraine to western Ukraine and who worked as teachers or administrative staff. The UPA frequently burned the houses of peasants who joined the collectives. They also killed village chairmen, collective-farm directors, and individuals who "betrayed the nation" or "contributed to the establishment of Soviet power," together with their entire families. The methods employed by the OUN-UPA were sometimes very cruel and sadistic, and the corpses were used for propaganda purposes. The OUN-UPA developed an entire spectrum of rituals to mutilate the corpses. One instruction included: "Liquidation of informers [seksoty] with all possible methods, firing, hanging, and also quartering with the inscription on the chest 'For collaboration with the NKVD.'"[75]

In the center of a village in the Rivne region in June 1944, the OUN-UPA hanged a local peasant suspected of collaboration. They then "hacked the corpse of the hanged bandit to pieces with an axe." In the Lviv region in August 1944, OUN-UPA members gouged out the eyes of members of two whole families, one by one in front of the others, and then hacked them to pieces in front of the villagers.[76] On 3 May 1946 in the village of Mil's'k, the perpetrators tortured two officials to death, "taking out their eyes, cutting them with knives, burning their bodies with iron, hitting them with a ramrod."[77] They frequently used axes, hatchets, and other tools, as they had during the ethnic cleansing in 1943 in Volhynia and in 1944 in eastern Galicia. In the town of Sernyky in the Rivne region, five people from the family of a collective farm were slaughtered with a hatchet in 1948.[78]

The nationalist insurgents frequently worked with texts and symbols. On 3 September 1944 in Staryi Lysets', six people were killed. A sign was posted on a fence: "For the betrayal of the Ukrainian nation, all will die in the same way."[79] On 11 September 1944, a couple named Marżenko and their four-year-old daughter were killed. The culprits left a letter: "Death to the informers of the NKVD—the enemies of the working people. Death to the Bolshevik fascists, imperialists, and capitalists."[80] On

71 Ibid., 517.
72 Ibid., 518.
73 Ibid., 523–24.
74 Ibid., 440–50, 489–99.
75 GARF, 9478, op. 1. t. 126, 226–28, quoted in Motyka, *Ukraińska partyzantka*, 472. For similar instructions, see Burds, AGENTURA, 104–105.
76 Burds, AGENTURA, 106.
77 Motyka, *Ukraińska partyzantka*, 517.
78 Ibid., 549.
79 The NKVD stated in its documents that Marżenko did not work for them. Cf. Motyka, *Ukraińska partyzantka*, 472. The OUN-UPA was particularly brutal to Poles who were suspected of collaborating with the Soviet authorities. Poles frequently regarded the Soviet Union as a force that could help them survive the OUN-UPA terror and were willing to help the Soviet authorities. Cf. Burds, AGENTURA, 117–19.
80 Motyka, *Ukraińska partyzantka*, 473.

24 December 1944 in Volia Vysots'ka, eighteen families were killed. The inscription "For the betrayal of the Ukrainian nation. Death to the NKVD informers" was left on the bodies.[81] On 31 July 1944, about twenty bandits raided the village of Verbovets'. They went to the house of Teodor Protsiuk. He was not at home but the bandits found his wife, and four children between the ages of four and thirteen. They killed all the children and fatally wounded the wife. They then went to the adjacent house of Ivan Ulin, strangled him, and left the inscription on his corpse: "All traitors and NKVD employees will die such a dog's death," which they signed with "The Revolutionary Army." They next went to the home of Ivan Kuchera, another member of the village administration, and asked him to give them a ride to the next village. They killed him 300 meters from the village and left the same inscription on his corpse as they had on Ulin's.[82]

Alexander Statiev, who studied the conflict between the OUN-UPA and the Soviet regime in depth, pointed out that the "list of deeds that the UPA regarded as treason was endless." In Pisochne in Volhynia, the UPA killed eight boys and four girls whose fathers had reported to the Red Army for mobilization. The UPA regarded even peasants who joined a collective farm under coercion as "communist traitors."[83] In Pidzvirynets' on 27 May 1947, the UPA killed twelve persons and injured two. Among the victims were members of the village council, the family of its members, the school principal, and two women from eastern Ukraine.[84] On 28 March 1946 in Molotkiv, four former OUN members, who had legalized themselves under an amnesty, decided to re-join the OUN. They disarmed fifty-four members of a unit of the destruction battalion, killed four of them, went to the house of another, and murdered his entire family of five people.[85] On the night of 15 to 16 May 1948 in the village of Vychivka, all six members of the family of a fighter with a destruction battalion were killed.[86]

On the night of 21 November 1944, forty Ukrainian nationalist insurgents raided the village of Dubechno. They shot the head of the village soviet in front of the villagers and fastened a note to his back: "The person who has been shot is the head of the village soviet, and if anyone takes his place, the same fate will befall him." They then went to the village soviet, where they killed the armed guard, and a peasant, on whose back they fastened a note with a bayonet driven into his spine: "This corpse is a traitor to the Ukrainian people who defended the Soviets. If anyone comes to work in his place, he will perish in the same way." In the same premises, the nationalists glued anti-Soviet slogans to the walls, tore up portraits of party and state leaders, and smeared the faces on the portraits with the victims' blood.[87]

The homes of the accused were frequently burned down. The OUN-UPA sometimes killed entire groups of people accused of loyalty to the Soviet regime or who had come as teachers or administrative staff from eastern Ukraine. In the village of

81 Ibid., 473.
82 GARF f. 9478, op. 1, d. 131, 293.
83 Statiev, *Soviet Counterinsurgency*, 130–31.
84 Motyka, *Ukraińska partyzantka*, 518.
85 Ibid., 519–20. The OUN-UPA disarmed destruction battalions in many other places. Cf. Ibid., 520.
86 Ibid., 549.
87 GARF, f. R-9478, op.1, d. 381, 60, quoted in Burds, AGENTURA, 107.

Shchepiatyn', for example, eighty-seven people from eastern Ukraine were killed.[88] On 15 December 1948, the OUN-UPA member B. Baryliak returned to his home in Semykhiv. After learning that his parents had joined the collective farm, he shot his seventy-year-old father and badly injured his sixty-three-year-old mother.[89] OUN-UPA members also killed themselves and their colleagues, in order to prevent the disclosure of information about fellow partisans.[90]

It took the Soviet authorities more than five years to destroy the nationalist underground in western Ukraine. Among the most important factors that strengthened the nationalist resistance were revolutionary idealism, fanaticism, vehement hatred of the Soviet Union, and sacralized suicidal nationalism. A set of instructions in 1947 declared, "The enemy has an advantage in numbers, weaponry, and military technology, but we surpass him in our sacred idea."[91] The Soviets killed the majority of the OUN-UPA members in 1944 and 1945, but they could not destroy the OUN-UPA hard core, which went underground and became undetectable. In 1946 the Soviet authorities realized that they had to change their methods in order to liquidate the nationalist underground. In February 1947, they decided to proceed against the OUN-UPA with small specialized security forces, instead of army units, and to work more and more with the help of agents and informers (*agentura*). Because the OUN-B tried to turn the NKVD agents, parallel agentura networks appeared.[92] But with time, the NKVD system emerged victorious. By 1948 the OUN member Ruslan wrote: "The Bolsheviks try to take us from within, through the agentura. And this is a horrifying and terrible method [because] you can never know directly in whose hands you will find yourself. At every step you can expect [an enemy] agent. From such a network of spies, whole teams are often penetrated."[93]

In addition to using the agentura, the NKVD conducted practical psychological warfare. If a captured OUN-UPA member did not reveal the whereabouts of fellow members, even under torture, NKVD agents, disguised as SB officers or OUN-UPA members, would pretend to rescue him, in order to get the information. In one such case, the NKVD obtained names of 600 OUN members, of whom ninety-nine were arrested and 123 killed.[94]

In July 1946, the OUN-UPA leadership decided to dissolve the UPA battalions and replace them with small OUN and SB units that were harder to detect. In 1948 there were very few UPA units, hiding mainly in the Carpathian Mountains, but the idea of a third world war was still alive in them.[95] In 1949 there were only two UPA units.[96] The number of OUN-UPA anti-Soviet actions dropped in 1947 to 2,068, and in 1948 to 1,387. They were directed mainly against employees of collective farms

88 Motyka, *Ukraińska partyzantka*, 472–73.

89 Ibid., 549.

90 Ibid., 573.

91 "Ternovym providnykam, komandyram viddiliv UPA, usim chlenam OUN i povstantsyam do vidoma," 1 May 1947, Potichnyj Collection, box 80, vol. 3, f. 6, quoted in Kudelia, Choosing Violence in Irregular Wars, 8.

92 Burds, Early Cold War, 37; Statiev, *Soviet Counterinsurgency*, 234.

93 DALO, f. 3, op. 2, d. 456, 190, quoted in Burds, AGENTURA, 126–27; Bruder, *"Den Ukrainischen Staat*, 232; Motyka, *Ukraińska partyzantka*, 532.

94 Statiev, *Soviet Counterinsurgency*, 244–45.

95 Motyka, *Ukraińska partyzantka*, 512–14.

96 Ibid., 543.

and Soviet activists. Between 1 January and 30 April 1950, the OUN-UPA killed twenty chairmen of village councils, nineteen directors of collective farms, and thirty regional militia auxiliaries in the Stanislaviv region.[97] Many OUN-UPA members lived in bunkers dug in forests, under the houses of peasants, or under buildings that were only seldom controlled by the NKVD, such as schools and collective farms. The nationalist insurgents usually left the bunkers only at night, disguised as peasants. In winter, they tried not to leave their bunkers for entire months. Usually they had four to five associates in every village who informed them about what was happening in the region.[98]

On 5 March 1950, the UPA commander-in-chief, Roman Shukhevych, shot himself during an attempt to arrest him in the village of Bilohorshcha near Lviv, in order to avoid being arrested. The OUN-UPA in Ukraine continued to exist for another few years, but their membership was reduced to several dozen individuals. They were unable to wage a struggle against Soviet troops, but they did not surrender and continued to kill civilians whom they accused of "betraying Ukraine." They regarded the beginning of the Korean War on 25 July 1950 as the herald of a third world war. According to incomplete data, there were 647 OUN-UPA members in Ukraine in 1952. Communications between OUN-UPA units was often poor. The OUN-UPA partisans usually knew only about OUN-UPA units in the immediate vicinity. Vasyl' Kuk, the last commander of the UPA, was arrested on 24 May 1954. In 1955 the Soviet authorities were still looking for 475 OUN-UPA members, of whom fifty were still conducting "anti-Soviet acts." In 1955 the OUN-UPA conducted thirty-five operations in which ten or fifteen people were killed. The last OUN-B unit, consisting of three people, was arrested in 1960. A small number allegedly hid in bunkers with the help of their relatives until the collapse of the Soviet Union in 1990.[99]

Outside western Ukraine, the UPA underground functioned in the Polish, Czechoslovak, and Belarusian territories that bordered on Ukraine. In 1944–1946 the UPA tried to stop the resettlement of Ukrainians from Poland to Ukraine, by attacking the Polish troops who were conducting it, and by blowing up railway tracks and destroying Polish villages.[100] The UPA also organized several raids into Czechoslovakia. During one of the first raids, from 2 to 13 December 1945, UPA partisans stole cattle, robbed shops, and killed eighteen "communists and Jews," eleven of them Jews in Kolbasov. This was probably one of the last pogroms that the OUN-UPA organized. Some of the UPA troops who came to Czechoslovakia later crossed the border to Poland, or to Austria and later Bavaria, where they surrendered to the Americans and sought out Ukrainians who had remained in Germany after the war.[101] In Belarus, the structure of the OUN-UPA existed in the territories that Ukrainian nationalists claimed to be Ukrainian. As in Ukraine, the OUN-UPA killed people suspected of loyalty to the Soviet regime, and they destroyed collective farm property. Between 1944 and 1947, the Ukrainian underground killed 1,225 people in Belarus. As in Ukraine, Poland, and

97 Ibid., 549.
98 Ibid., 546–47.
99 Ibid., 575–76, 608–10, 637, 641, 647–49.
100 Ibid., 581–89.
101 Ibid., 592–97.

Czechoslovakia, the OUN-UPA in Belarus was liquidated in the late 1940s and early 1950s.[102]

The OUN-UPA had eliminated extreme antisemitism from their propaganda in 1942 and 1943 but the question of the Jews did not entirely vanish in OUN-UPA brochures, even though there were almost no Jews in Ukraine. In 1950 the OUN distributed a brochure addressed to "Jews—Citizens of Ukraine" and signed "Ukrainian Insurgents." Although the authors sought reconciliation with the Jewish population, they threatened them:

> If anyone should, you Jews should treat the entire national-liberation struggle of the Ukrainian nation with respect and sympathy. ...
>
> Remember that you are on Ukrainian land and that it is in your own interest to live in complete harmony with its rightful owners—the Ukrainians. Stop being an instrument in the hands of Muscovite-Bolshevik imperialists. The moment is soon coming when the times of Khmel'nyts'kyi will be repeated, but this time we would prefer that they were without anti-Jewish pogroms.[103]

Some of the OUN activists and UPA partisans who were deported to the Gulag set up organizational structures there. This helped to protect them against organized crime in the camps and enabled them to organize or participate in uprisings and strikes. It seems that the OUN-UPA members, like the underground in the Baltic republics, played an important role in these uprisings, although it is difficult to estimate how significant it was. The largest uprising occurred after Stalin's death on 5 March 1953, in the camps in Noril'sk, Vorkuta, and Kengir. Aleksandr Solzhenitsyn, who spent eight years in the Gulag as a prisoner, wrote: "in our camp it began with the arrival of the Dubovka transport—mainly western Ukrainians, OUN members. The movement everywhere owed a lot to these people, and indeed it was they who set the wheels in motion. The Dubovka transport brought us the bacillus of rebellion."[104] Yet Solzhenitsyn also explains that the OUN members brought with them a new law for the killing of "traitors":

> Murders now followed one another in quicker succession than escapes in the best period. They were carried out confidently and anonymously: no one went with a blood-stained knife to give himself up; they saved themselves and their knives for another deed. At their favorite time—when a single warder was unlocking huts one after another, and while nearly all the prisoners were still sleeping—the masked avengers entered a particular section, went up to a particular bunk, and unhesitatingly killed the traitor, who might be awake and howling in terror or might be still asleep. When they had made sure that he was dead, they walked swiftly away. ... And so murder (although as yet there had been fewer than a dozen) became *the rule,* became a normal occurrence. "Anybody been killed

102 Ibid., 604–607.

103 Volodymyr V"iatrovych, *Stavlennia OUN do ievreiv: Formuvannia pozytsii na tli katastrofy* (Lviv: Vydavnytstvo Ms, 2006), 137, 139.

104 Aleksandr I. Solzhenitsyn, *The Gulag Archipelago 1918–1956: An Experiment in Literary Investigation* (New York: Harper & Row, 1974–1978), 3: 235.

today?" prisoners would ask each other when they went to wash or collect their morning rations.[105]

According to Soviet documents and estimates by historians, during the conflict with the OUN-UPA the Soviet authorities killed a total of 153,000 people, arrested another 134,000, and deported 203,000,[106] mainly in 1944–1945.[107] A much greater proportion of the population was killed or persecuted in western Ukraine than in other Ukrainian territories. One important reason for the extensive Soviet terror in western Ukraine was the strengthening of Soviet power and loyalty to Soviet Union in the "rebellious" territory that had not belonged to the Soviet Union before 1939. It is impossible to say how many western Ukrainians who were arrested, sentenced, or killed were actual members of the OUN or UPA, or were simply accused of being "Ukrainian nationalists." That one was a "Ukrainian nationalist" was a very serious accusation. It meant that one either murdered "Soviet people" or "betrayed" the "Soviet Ukrainian fatherland" by collaborating with the Nazis, even if only by cooking meals for them under constraint, for example. For some Soviet judges and persecutors "it was worse to be a Ukrainian nationalist than to participate in the murder of hundreds of Jews."[108] Nevertheless, a number of the Ukrainians sentenced as "Ukrainian nationalists" or "Banderites" were not only "traitors to the Soviet Ukrainian fatherland" but actual war criminals who had killed civilians.

During the conflict with the Soviet authorities, the OUN-UPA murdered more than 20,000 civilians and killed less than 10,000 Soviet soldiers, members of the destruction battalions, and NKVD staff. The majority of the civilian victims of the OUN-UPA were workers at the kolkhozes, and peasants accused of supporting the Soviet authorities.[109] By 1953 about 490,000 western Ukrainians had suffered murder, arrest, or deportation, as the result of the Soviet repressions.[110] The severity of the Soviet terror in western Ukraine cannot be explained solely by the "rebellious" activities of the OUN and UPA. Other, more important factors that inflated this conflict were the policies of Stalinism, the strengthening of Soviet power and of loyalty to the Soviet authorities, and matters such as local revenge or conflicts between neighbors. There is no doubt, however, that fanatical Ukrainian nationalism, which

105 Solzhenitsyn, *Gulag Archipelago*, 3:236.

106 Motyka, *Ukraińska partyzantka*, 649; Boeckh, *Stalinismus*, 366–67. Of the 134,000 arrested, 103,003 were accused of belonging to the anti-Soviet nationalist underground, and 31,434 were accused of other anti-Soviet acts, such as espionage, agitation, or terrorism. Of the 103,003, 82,930 and of the 31,464, 26,787 were imprisoned or sent to Gulag. Cf. Boeckh, *Stalinismus*, 367.

107 During 1944–45 the Soviets killed 103,313 OUN-UPA members and arrested 110,785. A further 50,058 OUN-UPA members came out of hiding, and 13,704 deserters from the Red Army were arrested along with 83,284 western Ukrainians who refused to be conscripted. Cf. Motyka, *Ukraińska partyzantka*, 502. In 1946 the Soviets killed 10,774 "bandits," arrested 9,541, and 6,120 came out of hiding, see Motyka, *Ukraińska partyzantka*, 528.

108 Penter, Collaboration on Trial, 787.

109 According to a KGB report from 1973, the OUN-UPA killed 30,676 people between 1944 and 1953. Among them were 8,340 NKGB-MGB, NKVD, Red Army soldiers, and soldiers from destruction battalions; 1,454 members of village councils; 314 chairmen of kolkhozes; 15,355 peasants and workers at kolkhozes; 676 other workers; 1,931 members of the intelligentsia; 50 priests; 860 children, old people, housewives; and other groups. Cf. Motyka, *Ukraińska partyzantka*, 650. Between February 1944 and December 1946 the OUN-UPA killed 11,725 people. Among them were 6,250 civilians or, if we include the members of the destruction battalions, 6,980. Cf. Burds, AGENTURA, 109.

110 153,000 were killed, 134,000 arrested, 203,000 deported. Cf. Motyka, *Ukraińska partyzantka*, 657. Boeckh mentions 500,000. Cf. Boeckh, *Stalinismus*, 366.

blinded the leaders of the OUN and UPA, escalated the bloody conflict, and cost the lives of many Ukrainian civilians.

Operation Rollback

During the second half of 1944, the leadership of the OUN-B and the UHVR sent a task force, including Lebed', Hryn'okh, and Myroslav Prokop, to establish contact with the Western allies. The task force went to Croatia and Italy; Vrets'ona was also sent to Switzerland. The first attempts to establish contact were not successful.[111] Nevertheless, OUN-B activists and UPA partisans in Ukraine soon began to disseminate rumors about their successful collaboration with the American and British armies. One rumor spread in 1944 said that an army of 8,000 Ukrainian Canadians was to invade the Soviet Union. Another said that 200,000 American Ukrainians were marching to Ukraine from Italy.[112] Other rumors said that America and England would help the OUN-UPA to defeat the Soviets and establish a Ukrainian state, when they finished the war against Germany.[113] The main purpose of the rumors was to enhance the OUN-UPA's reputation among Ukrainians and to give them hope of liberation from the Soviet regime:

> At the end of June [1945] in village Lyshnevychi in Brody raion, rebels convened a village assembly, [using their] weapons to force local peasants into the meeting. The chairman of the village soviet was led into the meeting [at the point of] two tommy guns and seated at the presidium. ... Speaking at the meeting, a rebel whose name was not given said: "You, peasants. The Bolsheviks and the NKVD men, who want to build a Belomor canal with the bones of the Ukrainian people, say that the war [with the Germans] is over. And this is true, but this does not concern us because we are only just beginning the true war for 'the independence of Ukraine.' England and America will help us. Our representatives have already agreed with England on this question, and even the Bolshevik Manul's'kyi has agreed to it. You should not fulfill the demands of the Soviets because anyone who works [for them] will be hanged as a traitor to the Ukrainian land. We have more power, you can see that for yourselves. Soon the Bolsheviks will conduct a grain levy. If anyone of you carries grain to the stations, then we will kill you like a dog, and your family will be hanged and cut to pieces. That should be understandable enough. And if you understand, then get back to your homes."[114]

In a village assembly in the Kamianets'-Podil's'kyi region in December 1945, another OUN member announced: "War between the Soviet Union and the Anglo-Americans is inevitable. The start of the war is planned for spring or autumn 1946."[115]

111 RG 263, ZZ-18, Box#80, NN3-263-02-008, Mykola Lebed Name File, vol. 1, 50–51; Motyka, *Ukraińska partyzantka*, 622; Dorril, *MI6*, 230–31; Statiev, *Soviet Counterinsurgency*, 106. Contact between the OUN and the British intelligence service very likely existed before the Second World War. Cf. Philby, *My Silent War*, 145; Dorril, *MI6*, 224. See also chapter 1 above.

112 Statiev, *Soviet Counterinsurgency*, 89.

113 Burds, Early Cold War, 22.

114 Report of I. Bogorodchenko to Shamberg (Moscow) and Zlepko (Kiev), DALO, f. 3, op. 1, spr. 212, 165–66, quoted in Burds, Early Cold War, 21.

115 Quoted in Burds, Early Cold War, 26.

Similarly, rumors about Bandera were spread. One said that he was seen in early September 1944 in Bolekhiv and other villages in the Stanislaviv region, in a jeep with eight American soldiers.[116]

Churchill's "Iron Curtain Speech" of 5 March 1946, which made it clear how tense were relations between the Eastern and Western blocs, had an enormous influence on the OUN-UPA. In his speech, Churchill stated: "From what I have seen of our Russian friends and allies during the war, I am convinced that there is nothing for which they have less respect than for weakness, especially military weakness. For that reason, the old doctrine of a balance of power is unsound."[117] His speech distressed the Soviet leaders and, in an interview a few days after the speech, Stalin called Churchill a "firebrand of war." "I do not know whether Mr. Churchill and his friends will succeed in organizing ... a new crusade against 'Eastern Europe,'" Stalin said. "But if they succeed in this ... one may confidently say they will be beaten just as they were beaten twenty-six years ago."[118]

Ukrainian nationalists regularly exploited Churchill's speech. In order to nourish hope and assert their position, OUN activists and UPA partisans in Ukraine repeated phrases like "If not today, then tomorrow England will declare war on the USSR" or "There will be a war and Ukraine will be made independent, under the protection of America." In the twelve months following Churchill's speech, the activity of the OUN-UPA increased by more than 300 percent.[119] On 17 December 1946, V. S. Riasnoi, deputy director of the Ministry of Internal Affairs (*Ministerstvo Vnutrennikh Del*, MVD) of the Ukrainian SSR, wrote in a document to his director, Timofei Strokach: "Notify all operations personnel in the organs of the MVD that work in the struggle against OUN rebels is simultaneously a struggle against agents of foreign intelligence services."[120] In January 1947, as a result of the alleged and real cooperation between the OUN-UPA and the American and British intelligence services, the Soviet authorities changed their tactics for combating the OUN-UPA. The Soviet apparatus began to regard the OUN-UPA not only as internal enemies but also as foreign enemies, and the Soviet counter-insurgency apparatus was transferred from the Ministry of Internal Affairs (MVD, before 1946 NKVD) to the Ministry of State Security (MGB, before 1946 NKGB).[121]

Even if the actual support from the United States and the United Kingdom was much smaller than that presented in nationalist propaganda, assumptions about cooperation with foreign intelligence services were not baseless. In 1946 some American politicians like George Kennan and Allan Dulles, later director of the American Central Intelligence Agency (CIA), initiated Operation Rollback, which was officially adopted in 1948. The operation was not in the hands of the CIA but the innocuous-sounding Office of Policy Coordination (OPC). The operation was financed by Marshall Plan funds, up to $100 million a year by 1951.[122]

116 "Raport nachel'nyka," HDA SBU spr. 10876, vol. 2, 552, in *Stepan Bandera*, ed. Serhiichuk, 1:211.
117 Quoted in Burds, Early Cold War, 24.
118 Quoted in Burds, Early Cold War, 25.
119 Burds, Early Cold War, 27.
120 Ibid., 34.
121 Ibid., 36–37.
122 Ibid., 6. Christopher Simpson calls the operation Bloodstone, but he has Rollback in mind. Cf. Simpson, *Blowback: America's Recruitment*, 99–102.

The aim of the operation was the "rollback of communism" in Eastern Europe. This was intended to come about through the strengthening of Eastern European nationalist movements that would destroy the Soviet Union from within. One goal of the operation, according to a document from 30 August 1948, was to "establish contact with the various national underground representatives in free countries and through these intermediaries pass on assistance and guidance to the resistance movements behind the iron curtain."[123] To some extent, the plan resembled the OUN plan to involve nations located in the Soviet Union in a multi-nationalist revolution that would disintegrate the Soviet Union. In this matter, the expectations of the OPC toward Eastern Europe overlapped with the plans of the OUN-B. Such personalities as Bandera, Stets'ko, and Lebed' appeared as anti-Soviet experts in this field. The OUN-UPA, still active behind the Iron Curtain, was a brilliant example of a guerrilla movement that Operation Rollback was meant to support. The main goal was psychological support, as a consequence of which, the operation heated up the atmosphere of the Cold War and turned a third world war into a subject that neither the Western nor the Eastern bloc could exclude. "The political warfare initiative was the greatest mistake I ever made," Kennan, the architect of Operation Rollback, admitted in 1975. "It did not work out at all the way I had conceived it."[124]

Toward the end of the Second World War, the CIA and the British Secret Intelligence Service (SIS), also known as MI6, were looking for people and organizations that could provide them with intelligence about the Soviet Union, in order to "get any early warning of a Soviet attack on Western Europe."[125] In this regard also, the Ukrainian nationalist underground was attractive to them. Evan Thomas claimed that Frank Wisner, the director of the OPC, "sought to learn the lessons of the German defeat in the East—a defeat he felt was due in large measures because the Nazis failed to capitalize on the anticommunist sentiment of the Russian people."[126] Furthermore, there were many Ukrainian political émigrés in the West who could have been recruited as Cold War soldiers and agents. Randolph F. Carroll, an agent of the Counter Intelligence Corps (CIC), stated in 1947, "Ukrainian emigration in the territory of Germany, Austria, France, Italy, in the greatest majority is a healthy, uncompromising element in the fight against the Bolsheviks. In case of war, there can be recruited a minimum of 130,000 good, idealistically inclined soldiers with an experienced cadre of young officers."[127]

Displaced Persons

After the Second World War, of the 8 million displaced persons (DPs) in German territory, about 2.5 million were Ukrainians. The majority of the Ukrainian DPs had been deported to Germany during the war as forced laborers (*Ostarbeiter*). By 1950,

123 Peter Grose, *Operation Rollback: America's Secret War behind the Iron Curtain* (Boston: Houghton Mifflin, 2000), 98; Burds, Early Cold War, 6.

124 Grose, *Operation Rollback*, 98; Burds, Early Cold War, 6.

125 Quoted in Burds, Early Cold War, 8.

126 Evan Thomas, *The Very Best Men: Four who Dared: The Early Years of the CIA* (New York: Simon & Schuster, 1995), 355–56, note 6.

127 CIC Special Agent Randolph F. Carroll, European Theater, Region III, 1947, quoted in Burds, Early Cold War, 11.

1,850,000 persons had returned to the Ukrainian SSR; the majority of them in the first two years after the war. They were not deported to the Gulag or Siberia as many people in the West believed during the Cold War, but were mainly sent to their places of origin. At home, however, they frequently faced discrimination. In 1947 about 200,000 Ukrainians remained in West Germany and about 50,000 in Austria and Italy. They lived mainly in DP camps. Among these 250,000 Ukrainians, there were 120,000 who had left Ukraine with the retreating German army in the summer of 1944 because they were afraid of the consequences of their collaboration with the Germans or had other reasons for avoiding a confrontation with the Soviet authorities. Among them were almost all the radical right intellectuals who, in the 1930s and 1940s, had regarded fascism and antisemitism as progressive European politics.[128]

The Soviet authorities demanded that all its citizens return home, but a number of Ukrainian DPs organized an anti-repatriation movement. They faked their identities, boycotted screenings, and wrote memoranda to the British and American governments, in which they protested against screenings, especially if screening measures were assisted by Soviet officials. Sometimes, the Ukrainians rendered screening impossible. For example, when a Soviet repatriation mission wanted to enter a camp in Mittenwald, the Ukrainians attacked it with bricks. According to OUN-B activist Mechnyk, the mobilization of Ukrainian DPs against the repatriation was an important activity of the OUN. One avoidance strategy was to organize a church service and remain there when the officials came to the camp. The resistance of Ukrainian and other DPs jeopardized the image of the Soviet Union. The Soviet secret service kidnapped a number of individuals and repatriated them by force. Many of them were later tortured during investigations, died in prisons, or were sent to the Gulag. The United Nations Relief and Rehabilitation Administration (UNRRA), which was responsible for the DP camps, assumed that Ukrainians tried to avoid screening because many of them were former Nazi collaborators. A popular method of avoiding repatriation among western Ukrainians was to insist that they were not Soviet citizens, because they had lived in Poland before the Second World War and therefore should not be repatriated to Soviet Ukraine.[129] In July 1947, UNRRA was replaced by the International Refugee Organization, or IRO, which in general was more sympathetic to DP anticommunism and reluctance to return to the Soviet Union.[130]

The Ukrainian DPs lived mainly in the American and British occupation zones. They gave their camps Ukrainian names like Orlyk and Lysenko. Between 3,000 and 5,000 people lived in each camp. Ukrainian DPs organized schools for their children and relocated the Ukrainian Free University (*Ukraïns'kyi Vil'nyi Universytet*, UVU) from Prague to Munich. In addition, the Ukrainian Technical and Husbandry Insti-

128 Vic Satzewich, *Ukrainian Diaspora* (London: Routledge, 2002), 93–97. Up to 1950, 1,850,000 *Ostarbeiter* came back to the Ukrainian SSR. Cf. Boeckh, *Stalinismus*, 293, 296, 303; Julia Lalande, *"Building a Home Abroad"–A Comparative Study of Ukrainian Migration, Immigration Policy and Diaspora Formation in Canada and Germany after the World War II* (Dissertation at the University of Hamburg, 2006), 40. For the 120,000 who left Ukraine in 1944 with the Germans, see Boeckh, *Stalinismus*, 293.

129 Lalande, *"Building*, 50–55; Mechnyk, *Pochatok*, 60, 62.

130 Anna Holian, "Anticommunism in the Streets: Refugee Politics in Cold War Germany," *Journal of Contemporary History* Vol. 45, No. 1 (2010): 152.

tute in Regensburg, the Ukrainian Higher School of Economics in Munich, and the Ukrainian Theological Seminary were founded. The scouting organization Plast was recreated. In 1946 the ZCh OUN—consisting of OUN-B members who left Ukraine with the Germans in 1944 or were released from the concentration camps—set up the scouting organization Ukrainian Youth Organization (*Spilka Ukraïns'koï Molodi*, SUM) in Augsburg.[131] The ZCh OUN had a network of its representatives in all DP camps in the American, British, and French occupation zones. It also recruited new members for its cadres and penetrated the DP camps. The general anticommunist and anti-Soviet attitude of Ukrainians made the ZCh OUN an attractive organization. In 1948 the ZCh OUN had 5,000 members in Western Europe, of whom 70 percent lived in DP camps.[132] US intelligence officials estimated in 1948 that up to 80 percent of all Ukrainian DPs from eastern Galicia were loyal to Bandera.[133]

Life in post-war Germany was difficult and chaotic for both the Germans and the DPs. The DPs were viewed by the German public as a social and economic problem. Apart from the Ukrainians, there were Jews, Latvians, Lithuanians, Poles, Russians, and other national groups in the DP camps. There was not much interaction between the different groups, although some were united by anticommunism. In addition, there were also cultural and political divisions within the national groups. The German police frequently raided the camps and mistreated the DPs because of real or alleged involvement in the black market and other criminal activities. When Shmuel Danziger, a concentration camp survivor, was shot to death in March 1946 by a German policeman, the situation changed slightly. After this incident, the American military authorities forbade the German police to enter the camps unless accompanied by American military police.[134]

Resistance against deportations strengthened nationalism among the DPs, and hatred toward the Soviet Union.[135] The DPs organized anticommunist demonstrations and rallies outside the camps. One such demonstration took place on 10 April 1949 in Munich, the capital of Bavaria. Several thousand DPs assembled to protest against religious persecution in the Soviet Union.[136] Because the authorities did not allow a political demonstration, the Ukrainian organizers assured them that it would be a religious gathering. But in reality it became an event at which the distinction between religious and nationalist elements became entirely blurred. The demonstration began with a multi-denominational religious service, including Roman Catholics, Greek Catholics, Orthodox, and Protestants. The Greek Catholic Church presented as martyrs people such as the Roman Catholic Archbishop Aloysius Viktor Stepinac of Croatia, who had collaborated with the Ustaša regime during the war and who was later sentenced by the Yugoslav authorities to sixteen years imprisonment. Representatives of Ukrainians, Belarusians, Lithuanians, Latvians, Estonians, Slovaks,

131 Lalande, "*Building*, 62, 65–68, 70, 72, 83–84, 86.

132 "Dokladnaia zapiska," November 1951, HDA SBU f. 13, spr. 372, vol. 43, 1–47, in *Stepan Bandera*, ed. Serhiichuk, 3:144–46; Mechnyk, *Pochatok*, 69–71; Dorril, *MI6*, 234.

133 Breitman, *Hitler's Shadow*, 78.

134 Anna Holian, *Between National Socialism and Soviet Communism: Displaced Persons in Postwar Germany* (Ann Arbor: University of Michigan Press, 2011), 45–47, 268.

135 Lalande, "*Building*, 139.

136 Some accounts suggested 3,000 to 4,000, others 10,000. Cf. Holian, Anticommunism, 152. Mechnyk, *Pochatok*, 145, also calculated 10,000.

Cossacks, and Turkestanis gave speeches, in which they condemned the lack of religious freedom in their homelands, and introduced the history of their national "liberation movements."[137] The OUN-B member Petro Mirchuk spoke on behalf of the Anti-Bolshevik Bloc of Nations (ABN) but was interrupted when someone cut the microphone cable. Another OUN-B activist recognized the saboteur as a "German communist and a Muscovite."[138] When the demonstrators began marching toward the former headquarters of the Soviet mission, the German police and American military forces tried to stop the crowd with tear gas and bayonets.[139]

The demonstration in April 1949 took place at a time when DPs were leaving Germany, but it was not the last anticommunist demonstration in Germany that the ABN and the OUN staged. They would hold several hundred more in the countries in which they would be resettled. Among the Ukrainian DPs who were resettled were OUN members, many of whom did not change their revolutionary, ultranationalist, or fascist convictions after 1945. The anti-Soviet and anticommunist climate of the Cold War made it possible to adjust their far-right worldviews to the new situation, without revising it substantially. The resettlement of the DPs therefore resulted in the internalization and globalization of Ukrainian nationalism, with all its fascist and radical right facets.[140]

After the end of the Second World War, Ukrainian communities in countries such as Canada and the United States began to lobby their governments to allow the displaced Ukrainians to settle there, and not to return them to the Soviet Union. The most popular and convincing argument that the Ukrainian lobbyists used was the "anticommunist" character of the Ukrainian DPs. One Ukrainian lobbying group in Canada wrote: "These people are anticommunist, and are representatives of every walk of life. ... These displaced persons, if assisted to settle in Canada, would spearhead the movement and combat Communism since they are victims of its menace."[141]

The soldiers of the Waffen-SS Galizien shared the fate of the DPs. Before the Waffen-SS Galizien surrendered to the British in Austria on 10 May 1945, the division was renamed the First Division of the Ukrainian National Army (*Ukraïns'ka Natsional'na Armiia*, UNA). The UNA had been established on 17 March 1945, in accordance with a proposal of Rosenberg's, under the command of General Shandruk. Until the very end of the war however, the German High Command continued to list it as the Ukrainian 14th SS Grenadier Division, in its order of battle. After surrender, the Waffen-SS Galizien soldiers avoided repatriation, with the help of the Vatican. As Shandruk, head of the UNA, wrote: "The Archbishop [Ivan Buchko] had pleaded with His Holiness Pope Pius XII to intercede for soldiers of the Division, who are the flower of the Ukrainian nation."[142] Negotiating with the British, Shan-

137 Holian, Anticommunism, 155–56. Stepinac's attitude to the Ustaša regime was ambiguous. On the one hand, he did not approve of the Ustaša terror. On the other, he did not denounce its crimes, probably because he was a supporter of an independent Croatian state. Cf. Mark Binodich, "Controversies surrounding the Catholic Church in Wartime Croatia, 1941–45," *Totalitarian Movement and Political Religions* Vol. 7, No. 4 (2006): 450, 452.

138 Mechnyk, *Pochatok*, 145.

139 Holian, Anticommunism, 159; Mechnyk, *Pochatok*, 146–47.

140 Mechnyk, *Pochatok*, 165.

141 "Admission to Canada, Resolution, 24 May 1948" LAC (Library and Archives Canada), RG 26 (Department of Citizenship and Emigration) vol. 130, quoted in Lalande, "*Building*, 148.

142 Quoted in Simpson, *Blowback*, 180.

druk also used the argument that, unlike the soldiers of the Vlasov army, the Ukrainian soldiers were Polish citizens.[143] Ukrainian soldiers from the Waffen-SS Galizien who surrendered to the British in Austria were detained in a camp in Rimini.[144]

The British changed the status of the Waffen-SS Galizien soldiers from that of prisoners of war to that of surrendered enemy personnel and wanted to distribute them throughout the Commonwealth. However, some countries, including Canada, were not pleased with this idea. The Canadian government only changed its attitude after persistent lobbying by Ukrainian institutions, which bombarded Ottawa with letters, in which they portrayed the soldiers from the Waffen-SS Galizien as "western minded, religious, democratic, good, strong, and healthy workers" and as "valuable and desirable citizens." The lobby praised the "anti-Soviet" and "anticommunist" views of the Waffen-SS Galizien Ukrainians and argued that they had been conscripted only because of their patriotism. Other arguments the lobby used were that the Waffen-SS Galizien soldiers had never fought against Western armies, and that they had not fought for Nazi Germany, but for an independent Ukraine.[145]

On 13 July 1948, the British government sent a secret telegram to all Commonwealth governments, including a proposal to end Nazi war crime trials in the British zone of Germany, which would accelerate the resettlement. The screening process undergone by the DPs could not be effective in any event, due to the lack of access to documents. These were either in the possession of the Soviet Union, which regarded all DPs as war criminals, or in the possession of the American and British intelligence services, which were preoccupied with looking for "dangerous" communists and were not paying much attention to war criminals. Officials undertaking the screening process were inexperienced and had little knowledge about the Nazi regime or the situation in Ukraine during the Second World War. More important for them was whether the particular individual could work hard, than whether he had been involved in war crimes or had been indoctrinated by Himmler's SS. They also failed to make any physical search for SS tattoos. The Soviet Union, which again and again made the ridiculous claim that all DPs were war criminals, motivated the screening officials to regard all Ukrainians as victims of Soviet accusations.[146]

In December 1952, when the resettlement was almost finished, the British SIS intervened with the Canadian government on behalf of individuals who did not meet normal security requirements. The Canadian government set up a committee on defectors and allowed these individuals to enter with this status. The governments of Canada, Britain, and the United States made the decision that information about these "defectors" could be revealed only with the agreement of all three governments. The term "defector" became a synonym for former Nazis or Nazi collaborators posing as anticommunists.[147] Eventually, about 90 percent of the 250,000 Ukrainian DPs moved between 1947 and 1955 from Germany and Austria to Argentina, Australia, Belgium, Brazil, Britain, Canada, France, the United States, and Venezuela. The

143 Golczewski, Die Kollaboration in der Ukraine, 179.
144 Margolian, *Unauthorized Entry*, 135.
145 Lalande, "*Building*, 149–53; Satzewich, *Ukrainian Diaspora*, 101.
146 Dorril, *MI6*, 240–41; Lalande, "*Building*, 164–65. Margolian estimates that about 2,000 war criminals and collaborators entered Canada. Cf. Margolian, *Unauthorized Entry*, 3–4.
147 Dorril, *MI6*, 241.

majority went to the United States and Canada.[148] Of the 11,000 Waffen-SS Galizien Ukrainians who surrendered to the British, 3,000 were returned to the Ukrainian SSR. The rest were admitted to Britain in 1947. The Canadian government agreed to admit the Waffen-SS Galizien veterans despite protests from the Canadian Jewish Congress. In total, between 1,200 and 2,000 of them moved to Canada.[149]

Conclusion

During the Second World War the ethnic configuration of people in the western Ukrainian territories changed entirely. The Germans, Ukrainian policemen, OUN and UPA, and local population killed almost all the Jews there. Those Poles who survived the ethnic cleansing conducted by the UPA were resettled in Poland, and Ukrainians from Poland were resettled in Ukraine. The Greek Catholic Church, a very important component of the identity of western Ukrainians, was dissolved by the Soviet authorities who, after their coming to power in western Ukraine in the spring and summer of 1944, also began to liquidate the nationalist underground. The UPA resisted the Soviet authorities until the early 1950s. The local population suffered severely during this conflict from both sides. The UPA killed over 20,000 civilians and close to 10,000 Soviet soldiers, members of the destruction battalions, and NKVD staff. According to Soviet documents, the Soviet authorities killed 153,000 Ukrainians, arrested 134,000 and deported 203,000. Among the Soviet victims were many civilians who neither belonged to the nationalist underground nor supported it.

In 1944 about 120,000 Ukrainians left Ukraine together with the Germans in order to avoid a confrontation with the Soviet authorities. After the war they stayed in DP camps together with some OUN members and other elements of Ukrainian society, who during the war had been confined in concentration camps and did not want to return to Soviet Ukraine. Both within and outside Ukraine the OUN hoped that a third world war would break out between the Soviet Union and the Western states and that this would help them liberate Ukraine. Although this did not come about, the Cold War enabled Bandera and other OUN members to ally with the British and American intelligence services. The American Central Intelligence Agency, which aimed for the "rollback of communism" in Eastern Europe, was willing to collaborate with émigrés who had contacts with movements such as the UPA. At the same time, the OUN-B continued to kill its opponents and also tried to control those Ukrainian DPs who resisted resettlement to the Soviet Union. By 1955, 250,000 Ukrainians had moved from German and Austrian DP camps to different Western countries around the globe; among them were numerous Bandera adherents.

148 80,000 moved to the United States, 38,000 to Canada, 21,000 to Australia, 10,000 to each of Britain, France, and Belgium. Cf. Satzewich, *Ukrainian Diaspora*, 89.

149 Margolian, *Unauthorized Entry*, 131–32, 135, 146; Lalande, "*Building*, 149–53.

Chapter 7

THE *PROVIDNYK* IN EXILE

The Opponents and Victims of Nazi Germany

In May 1945, the leadership of the OUN issued an official statement, in which it denied its engagement in fascist politics before and during the Second World War: "The Ukrainian liberating-revolutionary movement was not and is not a term equivalent to Italian Fascism and German National-Socialism."[1] Shortly before the statement was published Bandera had left Vienna for Innsbruck, in the French occupation zone of Austria. On 18 April 1945 Bandera met Ievhen Stakhiv there and ordered him to go to Zagreb, to find Lebed' and return him to Austria. Lebed' had gone to Croatia as the representative of the OUN-B and the UHVR, in order to establish contact with Allied troops. Stakhiv accepted the order but asked Bandera to find somebody to take care of his wife and baby, but his *Providnyk* refused to do so. Bandera's lack of empathy angered Stakhiv, but with the help of a friend he carried out his order.[2]

When Bandera came to Innsbruck, the city was filled with Ukrainian émigrés, in particular OUN-B members. In the summer of 1945, Bandera attended the wedding of Natalia Kovalivs'ka and Osyp Tiushka, with whom he lived together in an apartment during his student days in Lviv. Vienna was controlled at that time by all four Allies and, because of the presence of Soviet troops, was not safe for Ukrainian political émigrés. In the second half of 1945, Bandera moved to the Tyrol, to the alpine resort of Seefeld, which was, close to the German border. He rented the whole floor of a villa, where he lived for several months with his security guard Mykhailo Andriiuk, his driver Miklosh, and his secretary Marichka.[3] One of the names Bandera used at this time was Karpiak, under which he was registered in Innsbruck and Seefeld.[4]

In 1945 the ZCh OUN began to organize its new center in Munich, the capital of Bavaria, which was located in the American occupation zone of Germany.[5] Munich became the heart of Ukrainian émigré activity after the Second World War. Ukrainian social and political organizations were based in a two-story building at Dachauer Strasse 9. The first floor was occupied by a Ukrainian church, and the second by such organizations as the ABN, the editorial office of *Ukraïns'kyi samostiinyk*, the League of Political Prisoners, the Ukrainian Red Cross, Plast, and the ZCh

1 "Dekliaratsiia provodu Orhanizatsiï Ukraïns'kykh Natsionalistiv pislia zakinchennia druhoï svitovoï vyiny v Evropi," in *OUN v svitli*, 122.
2 Stakhiv, *Kriz' tiurmy*, 196–98.
3 Stakhiv, *Kriz' tiurmy*, 203, 216; Motyka, *Ukraińska partyzantka*, 622.
4 "Vernehmungsniederschrift Stefan Popel," 7 February 1956, StM, Pol. Dir. München 9281, 85.
5 HDA SBU f. 13, spr. 372, t. 6, 4, 8.

OUN.[6] For a time, the office of the ZCh OUN was at Lindwurmstrasse 205. In 1954 the ZCh OUN and the ABN moved to Zeppelinstrasse 67. The ZCh OUN opened a publishing house in the basement of this building and began to issue its newspaper, *Shliakh peremohy*. The basement and an apartment in the house would belong to the OUN at least until the time of writing this book.[7]

After the war, Bandera and his family moved several times. He had more than one address at a time, and frequently changed his place of residence. In August 1945, he came to Munich without his family to organize the ZCh OUN center. He registered himself under the name Michael Kasper, at Franz-Niessl-Strasse 14. In February 1946, his wife and daughter moved from Innsbruck to his apartment in Munich and also registered themselves under the name Kasper. When Bandera learned that Soviet intelligence had seized a courier he had sent to Ukraine, he moved in May 1946 to Söcking, a village about thirty kilometers from Munich, close to the town of Starnberg. He lodged with Mrs. Schwandtner at Hanfelder Strasse 1 and registered himself under the name Stefan Popel. Although he was registered at Hanfelder Strasse 1, he also lived with his family in a house that was hidden in the forest, close to Starnberg.[8] While living in Söcking, Bandera frequently went to Munich and sometimes stayed overnight in an apartment which he rented or had at his disposal, possibly from the American authorities.[9] Bandera lived in the house in the woods until 1950.[10] From late 1949 until May 1950, his family stayed in a DP camp in Mittenwald. At this time, Bandera hid in various places because the MVD was looking for him.[11] From mid-1950 to 1954, he lived in Breitbrunn, a village by Lake Ammersee, about thirty-five kilometers from Munich. During this period, his daughter Natalia attended high school in the nearby town of Herrsching.[12] While living outside Munich, Bandera traveled to work by car. He had a motor accident in 1953 but was not injured.[13] In 1952 Bandera's family lived in Oberau for some months, close to Garmisch-Partenkirchen, a village in the Alpine region.[14] In summer

6 "Protokol doprosa parashiutista po klichke 'Miron,'" 16 July 1951, HDA SBU f. 6, op. 37, spr. 56232, 27–72, in *Stepan Bandera*, ed. Serhiichuk, 3:92; Mechnyk, *Pochatok*, 57.

7 Vasyl' Sushko, *Zavdannia vykonav* (Lviv: Misioner, 1999), 133; The OUN member Andrii Kutsan, interview by author, Munich, 14 February 2008.

8 "Vernehmungsniederschrift Stefan Popel," 7 February 1956, StM, Pol. Dir. München 9281, 85–86; Interrogation of Iaroslava Bandera, BayHStA, Landeskriminalamt 272, 4; Danylo Chaikovs'kyi, *Moskovs'ki vbyvtsi Bandery pered sudom* (Munich: Cicero, 1965), 8. In 1978 Söcking was incorporated into Starnberg.

9 "Protokol doprosa parashiutista po klichke 'Miron,'" 16 July 1951, HDA SBU f. 6, op. 37, spr. 56232, 27–72, in *Stepan Bandera*, ed. Serhiichuk, 3:94; Bruder, *"Den Ukrainischen Staat*, 248. Bandera, Stets'ko, and several other people from the ZCh OUN frequently lived at addresses where they were not registered, see Slava Stets'ko-Muzyka, Z ideiamy Stepana Bandery, 179.

10 "Vernehmungsniederschrift Stefan Popel," 7 February 1956, StM, Pol. Dir. München 9281, 86; Chaikovs'kyi, *Moskovs'ki vbyvtsi*, 8. According to Vasyl' Shushko, Bandera rented the house at least until 1954, see Sushko, *Zavdannia vykonav*, 144.

11 "Vernehmungsniederschrift Stefan Popel," 7 February 1956, StM, Pol. Dir. München 9281, 86.

12 Stets'ko-Muzyka, Z ideiamy Stepana, 179; "Protokol doprosa parashiutista po klichke 'Miron,'" 16 July 1951, HDA SBU f. 6, op. 37, spr. 56232, 27–72, in *Stepan Bandera*, ed. Serhiichuk, 3:90; Sushko, *Zavdannia vykonav*, 145.

13 Interrogation of Iaroslava Bandera, BayHStA, Landeskriminalamt 272, 4.

14 "Slovo Natalky Bandery," in Chaikovs'kyi, *Moskovs'ki vbyvtsi*, 306. Natalia Bandera also stated that the Bandera family lived in Hildesheim, but she did not specify when.

1954, he moved with his family to Munich, where he lived at Rosenbuschstrasse 6 until 1956, and then at Kreittmayrstrasse 7.[15]

False documents obtained by Bandera helped him to expunge his ambiguous relationship with the Nazis. On 6 June 1945, for example, he received an ID card bearing the name "Stefan Popel" from the Camp Committee (*Lagerkomitee*) and the commandant (*Lagerkommandant*) of the Mauthausen concentration camp. According to this document Bandera was a person "who was kept from 15.9.1941 to 6.5.1945 in Nazi-German concentration camps and was liberated from the concentration camp at Mauthausen"—where he was never a prisoner. (Fig. 23).[16]

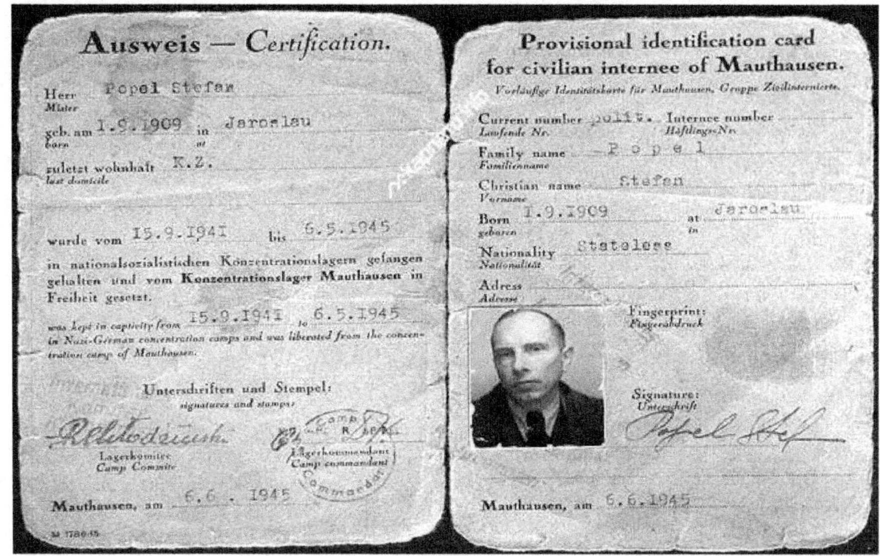

Ausweis — *Certification.*

Herr / *Mister* Popel Stefan

geb. am / *born* 1.9.1909 in / *at* Jaroslau

zuletzt wohnhaft / *last domicile* K.Z.

wurde vom 15.9.1941 bis 6.5.1945 in nationalsozialistischen Konzentrationslagern gefangen gehalten und vom Konzentrationslager Mauthausen in Freiheit gesetzt.

was kept in captivity from 15.9.1941 *to* 6.5.1945 *in Nazi-German concentration camps and was liberated from the concentration camp of Mauthausen.*

Unterschriften und Stempel: / *signatures and stamps:*

Lagerkomitee / *Camp Committe*

Lagerkommandant / *Camp commandant*

Mauthausen, am 6.6.1945

Provisional identification card for civilian internee of Mauthausen.

Vorläufige Identitätskarte für Mauthausen, Gruppe Zivilinternierte.

Current number / *Laufende Nr.* polit. Internee number / *Häftlings-Nr.*

Family name / *Familienname* Popel

Christian name / *Vorname* Stefan

Born / *geboren* 1.9.1909 at / *in* Jaroslau

Nationality / *Nationalität* Stateless

Adress / *Adresse*

Fingerprint: / *Fingerabdruck*

Signature: / *Unterschrift*

Mauthausen, am 6.6.1945

Fig. 23. Stepan Bandera's ID from the IRO. Stepan Bandera Museum in Staryi Uhryniv.

Ukrainian emigrants in Germany often used pseudonyms at this time, in order to avoid deportation to Soviet Ukraine. "Popel" means snot in German and very likely caused laughter among the officials. It is not entirely clear whether Bandera adopted the pseudonym from the Ukrainian word "popil," which means "ashes," or used the passport of the Ukrainian chess player Stepan Popel', which was allegedly stolen from his apartment in Paris in 1944.[17]

Bandera also used a number of press cards. One, from 15 October 1950, confirmed that he was a correspondent of the newspaper *Ukrainian Independist*, living in Söcking. Another from 12 February 1955 was from the French newspaper

15 "Vernehmungsniederschrift Stefan Popel," 7 February 1956, StM, Pol. Dir. München 9281, 87. The ZCh OUN commission established in 1959 to investigate Bandera's death wrote that Bandera moved in 1955 to Kreittmayrstrasse 7. See the report of the investigating commission at the Archive of the Stepan Bandera Museum in London (ASBML), 3113, 2.

16 Cf. Bandera's registration card (Ausweis-Certification) from Mauthausen in the exhibition of the Stepan Bandera Historical Memorial Museum in Staryi Uhryniv.

17 See Bruder, *"Den Ukrainischen Staat*, 248; Ivan Iaremko, "Romantyk Shakhiv," *L'vivska hazeta*, 17 July 2007, http://www.gazeta.lviv.ua/articles/2007/08/17/25619/ (accessed 22 August 2010).

L'Ukrainien. In 1947 Bandera used a journalist's pass issued by *Ukraïns'ka trybuna*.[18]

In addition to using false documents, Bandera was protected by the American, British, and later, the West German intelligence services. The American and British intelligence services were already taking an interest in Nazis and Nazi collaborators, before the end of the war. They were also interested in people and organizations, such as the German Military Intelligence on the Eastern Front (*Fremde Heere Ost*, FHO), and the various Eastern European far-right movements, including the OUN, who could provide them with information about the Soviet Union or who possessed other valuable knowledge. With the help of the CIA, Reinhard Gehlen, former head of the FHO, established the Federal Intelligence Service (*Bundesnachrichtendienst*, BND), the intelligence service of West Germany. American intelligence protected Gehlen and his advisers.[19]

People such as Bandera, who could either provide information about the Soviet Union or mobilize the émigré communities with anticommunist propaganda or had contact with underground organizations behind the Iron Curtain, were of special interest to the American, British, and German intelligence services. Besides Ukrainians, there were also Croatians, Slovaks, Russians, Poles, Lithuanians, Latvians, Estonians, Romanians, and Hungarians who worked for Western intelligence services. That some of them had collaborated with the Nazis and were involved in war crimes did not matter, as long as they were useful for the Cold War. American and British intelligence possessed knowledge, although not always very accurate, about the people with whom they worked.[20] Harry Rositzke, former head of the CIA, commented in 1985: "It was a visceral business of using any bastard as long as he was anticommunist ... [and] the eagerness or desire to enlist collaborators meant that sure, you didn't look at their credentials too closely."[21]

The Ukrainian émigrés understood this situation and tried to benefit from it as much as possible. Collaborating with Western intelligence services meant protection for the OUN from legal proceedings and gained it support for its struggle against the Soviet Union. After Lebed' returned from Zagreb, he went to Rome, where he claimed to represent the interests of Ukraine as the "foreign minister" of the UHVR, which presented itself as a kind of Ukrainian government-in-exile. Father Ivan Hryn'okh, who was awarded the Iron Cross by the Germans for his work in the Nachtigall battalion, accompanied him. Together with Bishop Ivan Buchko, they negotiated with the Americans and British how to prevent the repatriation of the Waffen-SS Galizien soldiers. In the spring of 1945, Lebed' established contact with the Office of Strategic Services (OSS) in Berne, the forerunner of the CIA, and to which Vrets'ona, the former Abwehr agent and chief of the German-Ukrainian police in Lviv, offered his services. Volodymyr Stakhiv, minister of foreign affairs in

18 Both are in the possession of the Stepan Bandera Historical Memorial Museum in Staryi Uhryniv. For *Ukraïns'ka trybuna*, see Chaikovs'kyi, *Moskovs'ki vbyvtsi*, 7.

19 Mary Ellen Reese, *Organisation Gehlen: Der Kalte Krieg und der Aufbau des deutschen Geheimdienstes* (Berlin: Rowohlt, 1992), 92; Burds, Early Cold War, 12. On the protection of Nazis by American intelligence in general, see Breitman, *Hitler's Shadow*, 35–66.

20 Simpson, *Blowback*; Breitman, *Hitler's Shadow*, 73–91.

21 Simpson, *Blowback*, 159.

Stets'ko's government from 1941, did the same in Munich.[22] Almost simultaneously, the Soviet Ukrainian writer and poet Mykola Bazhan demanded, at the assembly of the United Nations in London on 6 February 1946, that Ukrainian collaborators be handed over to the Soviet authorities.[23]

Bandera had met with officials of the British Secret Intelligence Service (known as MI6), in the British zone at the end of the war. MI6 regarded Bandera as potentially useful for Cold War purposes, and therefore decided to help him.[24] The American Counter Intelligence Corps (CIC) in Munich also protected Bandera from Soviet intelligence, although it was more interested in cooperation with the UHVR, which began to compete with the ZCh OUN after the war. The CIC concluded that Bandera's extradition would "imply to the Ukrainians that we as an organization are unable to protect them, i.e., we have no authority. In such a case, there is not any reason or sense for them to cooperate with us."[25] In a secret memorandum to the Immigration and Naturalization Service, Frank Wisner, director of the Office of Policy Coordination (OPC), commented on the role of the United States in protecting Bandera and other Ukrainian nationalists in the American occupation zone:

> At the end of the last war many members of the OUN came to Western Europe to avoid capture by the advancing Soviets. The OUN re-formed in Western Europe with its headquarters in Munich. It first came to the attention of American authorities when the Russians demanded extradition of Bandera and many other anti-Soviet Ukrainian nationalists as war criminals. Luckily the [Soviet] attempt to locate these anti-Soviet Ukrainians was sabotaged by a few far-sighted Americans who warned the persons concerned to go into hiding.[26]

In June 1946, a special MGB task force entered the American occupation zone, in order to kidnap Bandera. The task force consisted of five people in two cars. Before the operation started, negotiations between the Soviet and American officials had taken place. The chief of the CIC, General Edwin Silbert, promised the MVD chief of the Berlin operational sector, Major General Aleksei Sidnev, to help apprehend Bandera in the American occupation zone. Bandera, however, had been under Silbert's protection since summer 1945, and the negotiations with Soviet intelligence were mere camouflage. Using the Polish alias "Stanislau Sitkowski," Bandera hid in the complex that housed the Gehlen Organization. The MGB task force did not find him, although it visited several places in several cities where it was informed by the CIC that Bandera might be hiding.[27]

22 Dorril, *MI6*, 232; "Protokol doprosa zakhvachennogo parashiutista Matviieiko Mirona Vasil'evicha," 14–15 July 1951, HDA SBU f. 13, spr. 372, vol. 42, 237–49, in *Stepan Bandera*, ed. Serhiichuk, 3:115, 119–20.

23 H. Dmytrenko, "Novi khaziaï ukraïns'ko-nimets'kykh natsionalistiv," *Vil'na Ukraïna,* 19 June 1946, 7; Chaikovs'kyi, *Moskovs'ki vbyvtsi*, 7; Mstyslavets', "Liudoïd," *Vil'na Ukraïna*, 31 July 1946, 5.

24 Dorril, *MI6*, 231.

25 "Source Kilkenny," an attachment to SC Washington to SS Amzon, 20.11.1946, RG 263, E ZZ-18, NARA, Stepan Bandera Name File, 1v. See also AB-51 to AB-43, 28.10.1946, NARA, RG 263, E ZZ-18, Stepan Bandera Name File, 1v.

26 John Loftus, *The Belarus Secret: The Nazi Connection in America* (New York: Knopf, 1982), 102–3, quoted in Burds, Early Cold War, 14.

27 Burds, Early Cold War, 12–13. Sacharow and Filippovych write that the operation to apprehend Bandera in the American occupation zone began only in September 1946, see Vladimir Vladimirovič Sacharow, Dmitrij Nikolaievič Filippovych, and Michael Kubina, "Tschekisten in Deutschland:

Bandera was protected and supported by the Gehlen Organization and also received help from members of such organizations as the former Hitler Youth (*Hitlerjugend*), the SS, and other individuals and organizations in situations similar to that of Bandera. The CIC noted that an underground organization of former Nazis helped Bandera to cross the border between the American and French occupation zones several times.[28] In 1947 American intelligence described Bandera's bodyguards as ready to "do away with any person who may be dangerous to [Bandera] or his party"[29] and as "ruthless killers who intercept and liquidate persons who attempt to apprehend *Bandera*."[30] In 1950 he was seen with nine bodyguards.[31]

In the long run, Lebed', who became Bandera's rival after the Second World War, succeeded in cooperating much more successfully with American intelligence than Bandera did. This was so, even though the CIA described Lebed' as a "well-known sadist and collaborator of the Germans."[32] Afraid that OUN-UPA war crimes would cause him and other Ukrainian émigrés problems, Lebed' wrote a book entitled *UPA: Ukrainian Insurgent Army*, which was published in 1946 by the Publishing Office of the UHVR. In this publication, the former leader of the OUN-B and the SB of the OUN-B depicted the OUN and UPA as anti-Soviet and anti-German freedom fighters and denied or ignored all war crimes on their part. Lebed' seems to have been especially afraid that the West would find out about his involvement in the murder of Jews and in the ethnic cleansing in Volhynia in 1943.[33] Lebed's book was perhaps the first comprehensive post-war publication that not only denied the OUN and UPA atrocities but also argued that the UPA helped ethnic minorities in Ukraine, in particular Jews. Lebed' wrote that Jews remained in the UPA, even though they had the opportunity to join the Soviets, and that many of them "died a hero's death protecting the ideals for which the whole Ukrainian nation was fighting."[34] He also transformed the Poles into aggressors who threatened and provoked the UPA: "We issued the order to the Poles to leave the territories that were important for UPA actions. When that had no effect, their resistance was liquidated by force."[35]

Organisation, Aufgaben und Aspekte der Tätigkeit der sowjetischen Sicherheitsapparate in der sowjetischen Besatzungszone Deutschland (1945–1949)," in *Anatomie der Parteizentrale: Die KPD/SPD auf dem Weg zur Macht*, ed. Manfred Wilke (Berlin: Akademie Verlag, 1998), 323–24. See also Dorril, *MI6*, 232; "Protokol doprosa zakhvachennogo parashiutista Matviieiko Mirona Vasil'evicha," 14–15 July 1951, HDA SBU f. 13, spr. 372, vol. 42, 237–49, in *Stepan Bandera*, ed. Serhiichuk, 3:119.

28 Burds, Early Cold War, 13.

29 Breitman, *Hitler's Shadow*, 79.

30 Burds, Early Cold War, 13.

31 "Ukrainian Rebel Hides Again. After Brief Talk in Germany," *Christian Science Monitor*, 21 April 1950, NARA, RG 263, E ZZ-18, Stepan Bandera Name File, 1. According to another interview Bandera was protected by a "squad of husky armed bodyguards." Cf. *News Review*, 13 April 1950, NARA, RG 263, E ZZ-18, Stepan Bandera Name File, 1.

32 Card Ref. D 82270, July 22, 1947, NARA, RG 319, E 134B, B 757, Mykola Lebed IRR Personal File, Box 757, quoted in Breitman, Hitler's Shadow, 86.

33 Mykola Lebed', *Ukraïns'ka Povstans'ka Armiia: Ïï heneza, rist i diï u vyzvol'niï borotbi ukraïns'koho narodu za ukraïns'ku samostiinu sobornu derzhavu* (Presove biuro UHVR, 1946).

34 Mykola Lebed', *UPA,Ukraïns'ka Povstans'ka Armiia* (Munich: Suchasnist', 1987), 69.

35 Lebed', *Ukraïns'ka Povstans'ka Armiia*, 89. Presenting victims as aggressors was a common practice among Nazis during the Final Solution. Cf. Snyder, *Bloodlands*, 214.

Bandera and Conflicts in the Organization

The conflict between the UHVR, or Lebed's group of the ZCh OUN, and Bandera, the leader of the ZCh OUN, interfered with the cooperation between the Western intelligence services and the Ukrainian nationalists and complicated the relationship with the OUN-UPA underground in western Ukraine. When Bandera and Lebed' met in late December 1945, they had a long discussion about politics within the OUN in exile. Both were unhappy with the result of their conversation. The main subject of their discussion was the question whether the ZCh OUN should subordinate itself to the UHVR as Lebed' suggested, or whether the UHVR should be subordinate to the ZCh OUN, as Bandera argued.[36] This conflict between two new OUN factions had already manifested itself after Bandera's release from Zellenbau. Bandera and several other ZCh OUN members, including at least Iaroslav Stets'ko, Stepan Lenkavs'kyi, Bohdan Pidhainyi, Mykola Klymyshyn, Ivan Kashuba, Myron Matviieiko, Osyp Tiushka, Ievhen Lozyns'kyi, Petro Mirchuk, and Ivan Vovchuk, did not accept the supremacy of the UHVR and objected to the rejection, at the Third Extraordinary Grand Assembly in 1943, of the Führerprinzip and other fascist ideas. Bandera's faction wanted to reintroduce the Führerprinzip and make Bandera the *Providnyk* of all Ukrainian émigré organizations. Many of Bandera's post-war supporters had been detained in prisons or concentration camps from the second half of 1941 onward, to the end of 1944 or the beginning of 1945, and had been isolated from what was happening in the OUN-UPA at that time. The opposition to the "fascist faction" was formed by people such as Lev Rebet, Daria Rebet, Mykola Lebed', Volodymyr and Ievhen Stakhiv, Vasyl' Okhrymovych, Roman Ilnytzkyi, Ivan Hryn'okh, Ivan Butnovs'kyi, Zenon Matsiuk, Myroslav Prokop, Ievhen Vrets'ona, and Vasyl' Potishko.[37]

At a meeting of the OUN-B in December 1944 in Cracow, and later at a conference in Vienna in February 1945, at which he was elected representative of the leadership of the ZCh OUN, Bandera expressed his concerns about the changes introduced at the grand assembly in 1943. He believed that they were redundant and that he should remain the *Providnyk* of the movement. He understood the rejection of fascism, or as it was called later "democratization," as "Soviet principles" that damaged the real nature of the OUN.[38]

In February 1946 in Munich, Bandera's cohorts declared the ZCh OUN to be their own organization, independent of the UHVR. Bandera's opponents called themselves the Foreign Representation (*Zakordonne Predstavnytsvo*, ZP) of the UHVR, or ZP UHVR. Both organizations claimed to represent the OUN and UPA in Ukraine. For a few years there was no clear boundary between the two groups, and the split was not definite. Lebed', for example, was active in both groups until 1948, when he finally dissociated himself from the ZCh OUN and remained in the ZP UHVR. On 16 April 1946, the ZCh OUN founded the Anti-Bolshevik Bloc of Nations, or ABN, whose

36 Stakhiv, *Kriz' tiurmy*, 217; "Dokladnaia zapiska," November 1951, HDA SBU f. 13, spr. 372, t. 43, 1–47, in *Stepan Bandera*, ed. Serhiichuk, 3:138–39.

37 Stakhiv, *Kriz' tiurmy*, 228.

38 "Protokol doprosa obviniaemogo Vasylia Okhrymovicha Ostapovicha," 16 December 1952, HDA SBU f. 5, spr. 445, vol. 4, 102–14, in *Stepan Bandera*, ed. Serhiichuk, 3:353; "Protokol doprosa obviniaemogo Okhrimovicha Vasiliia Ostapovicha," 21 October 1952, HDA SBU f. 5, spr. 445, vol. 1, 216–225, in *Stepan Bandera*, ed. Serhiichuk, 3:270–71.

leader became Stets'ko.[39] Like the ZCh OUN, the ABN was financed by MI6, which used Vatican intermediaries in order to conceal the source.[40] The OUN-UPA in Ukraine knew about the ABN and had great hopes for it.[41]

The ABN united the representatives of several Eastern European "enslaved nations." Some of them, for instance Ferdinand Ďurčanský, former minister for internal and foreign affairs in Jozef Tiso's clerical fascist Slovakia, had collaborated with the Nazis and had been deeply involved in the persecution and annihilation of Jews and in other war crimes. Similarly to Stets'ko and Lenkavs'kyi in relation to Ukraine shortly before the beginning of the Second World War, Ďurčanský had talked about "solving the Jewish Question [in Slovakia] 'as in Germany.'" During the war Ďurčanský supported the anti-Jewish policies of Tiso's government, which led to the destruction of several thousand Slovak Jews. After the war he was tried in absentia and sentenced to death by the same court that condemned Tiso to the death-penalty. Unlike his *Vodca*, Ďurčanský was never arrested and died a natural death in 1974. Some other members of the ABN were former Nazis, or veterans of movements such as the Ustaša and the Romanian Legionaries, which had cooperated with the OUN before and during the Second World War. The ABN regarded the Soviet Union as a "prison of nations" and like the OUN-B during the war, and the ZCh OUN after the war, wanted to separate this multinational empire into nation states with far-right authoritarian governments. In the ABN's plans for a post-Soviet Eastern Europe, there was no place for Jews, Russians, or other minorities who did not live in their "own ethnic territories."[42]

In January 1947, conflict between the ZCh OUN and the ZP UHVR escalated. Ievhen Stakhiv wrote in his memoirs that the ZP UHVR was "democratic," and the ZCh OUN "totalitarian." Although the two factions certainly differed in their attitude toward democracy, the ZP UHVR and the "democratic" factions of the OUN émigrés who cooperated with it did not have much in common with the principles of democracy. They ignored and denied the war crimes of the OUN and UPA and falsified the history of the movement, similarly to the ZCh OUN. Antisemitism and nationalism pervaded both groups.[43] In 1947 Bandera became extremely angry with the "democratic" émigrés who refused to subordinate themselves to him and who refused to accept the supremacy of the ZCh OUN. He used the SB of the ZCh OUN to intimidate and liquidate opponents whom he regarded as traitors and foes. The *Providnyk* ordered the head of the SB of the ZCh OUN, Matviieiko, to conduct a range of

39 Stakhiv, *Kriz' tiurmy*, 220–23; Motyka, *Ukraińska partyzantka*, 622–24; Mechnyk, *Pochatok*, 205.

40 Dorril, *MI6*, 233, 238–39; Bishop Ivan Buchko helped to transfer money. Cf. "Agenturnoe donesenie," 29 November 1949, HDA SBU f. 2, op. 37, spr. 65, 226–237, in *Stepan Bandera*, ed. Serhiichuk, 2:342; "Protokol doprosa zakhvachennogo parashiutista Matviieiko Mirona Vasil'evicha," 12 July 1951, HDA SBU f. 6, op. 37, spr. 56232, 16–26, in *Stepan Bandera*, ed. Serhiichuk, 3:40.

41 "Informatsiia pro diiu i orhanizatsiini spravy ABN," in *Informatsinyi biuleten'*, No. 1 (1948): 4–6.

42 Holian, Anticommunism, 145–48. For Ferdinand Ďurčanský, see Jelinek, *The Parish Republic*, 19, 20, 28, 35–37, 43–44. For Ďurčanský, see James Mace Ward, *Priest, Politician, Collaborator: Jozef Tiso and the Making of Fascist Slovakia* (Ithaca: Cornell University Press, 2013), 164, 265. For former Nazis and successors of the Ustaša and the Romanian Legionaries, see Rudling, Return of the Ukrainian Far Right, 230.

43 Stakhiv, *Kriz' tiurmy*, 228. For nationalism and antisemitism in the ZP UHVR, see Ilnytzkyi, *Deutschland und die Ukraine*, 2:144. In his dissertation, Roman Ilnytzkyi quoted antisemitic OUN-B documents from 1941 without commenting on them. He did not even comment on slogans like "fight against Jews and communists." His PhD supervisor was the former Abwehr officer Hans Koch.

assassinations, targeting among them Lev and Daria Rebet.[44] Not all these "death sentences" were carried out. In the case of the Rebets, the SB officers refused to execute the order, because it meant killing people they had known for many years. Nevertheless, members of the "democratic" faction were frightened, and some began to carry weapons.[45] During one dispute in March 1947, Lebed' either fired a pistol at Bandera or threatened him with it, after which Bandera ordered Matviieiko to kill Lebed'.[46]

The ZCh OUN in Bavaria applied terror toward opponents and "traitors," as the OUN-UPA did in western Ukraine, although not on the same scale. It is not clear how many people the ZCh OUN killed after the Second World War. The police department in Munich noted that Ukrainians in DP camps, particularly in the Mittenwald camp, talked about a hundred people who had been killed by the SB of the ZCh OUN, and also about the cremation of the corpses. The Bavarian police assumed that these incidents were not reported because the Ukrainian emigrants were intimidated by the perpetrators. The police were unable to bring any charges for these murders. In general, they were confused and overwhelmed by the conflicts among the Ukrainian émigrés and by the intrigues of the MGB, from 1954 the Committee for State Security (*Komitet gosudarstvennoi bezopasnosti*, KGB). It may be that some of the crimes were concealed by American and British intelligence, or even committed in cooperation with them, as these services had assigned the ZCh OUN to spy on the "Bolsheviks" and "communists" among the DPs.[47]

Stephen Dorril, a historian specializing in the subject of secret services, states that the SB killed more than one hundred people in total in West Germany after the Second World War, and that it cooperated with the CIA by liquidating individuals suspected of communism or of cooperation with the Soviet Union. According to Dorril, the bodies of some of the victims were cremated by the SB and the CIC in the Mittenwald DP camp.[48] Ukrainian émigré Borys Levyts'kyi, who privately investigated SB crimes in West Germany, estimated the number of the SB's victims at between thirty and forty, some of them his friends.[49] In addition, about twenty OUN-M members were killed by the OUN-B after the war in Bavaria.[50] Only a few ZCh OUN activists were put on trial, such as the three Ukrainian nationalists who tried to kill their political opponent Diomed Gulay, on 15 November 1951 in the Schliessheim

44 Andrii Rebet, interview by author, Munich, 22 February 2008; "Protokol doprosa parashiutista po klichke 'Miron,'" 16 July 1951, HDA SBU f. 6, op. 37, spr. 56232, 27–72, in *Stepan Bandera*, ed. Serhiichuk, 3:82–83; Stakhiv, *Kriz' tiurmy*, 229.

45 Stakhiv, *Kriz' tiurmy*, 229.

46 For the version with firing, see Burds, Early Cold War, 16. For the version with threatening, see "Informatsiia nachal'nika," HDA SBU f. 3, op.37, spr. 65, 109, in *Stepan Bandera*, ed. Serhiichuk, 1:609–10. For Bandera's order to liquidate Lebed', see "Protokol doprosa parashiutista po klichke 'Miron,'" 16 July 1951, HDA SBU f. 6, op. 37, spr. 56232, 27–72, in *Stepan Bandera*, ed. Serhiichuk, 3:71.

47 Document about the OUN in Bavaria written by inspector Adrian Fuchs, 13 September 1960, StM, Staatsanwaltschaften 34887, vol. 1, 59; "Schlussbericht der Untersuchung zu vier vermissten ukrainischen Personen," StM, Staatsanwaltschaften 34887, vol. 2, 52; Bruder, *"Den Ukrainischen Staat*, 249.

48 Dorril, *MI6*, 234–45. According to Dorril the action had the name Ohio. Lebed', Stets'ko, Lenkavs'kyi, Hryn'okh, and Bandera directed it. Cf. Dorril, *MI6*, 234–45; Simpson, *Blowback*, 151.

49 "Bundeskriminalamt, Besprechungsbericht,"27 April 1962, BAK, B 362/1080, 255.

50 Motyka, *Ukraińska partyzantka*, 624.

DP camp.[51] Furthermore, only a few people had the courage to report that their relatives had disappeared.[52]

Ukrainians living in the DP camps spoke about OUN torture cellars, in which people disappeared.[53] In 1962 the western Ukrainian KGB agent Stashyns'kyi, who was informed by infiltrators into the ZCh OUN about the criminal side of the ZCh OUN, stated to West German investigators that the SB had a bunker close to Munich, in which it interrogated, tortured, and "let disappear" Ukrainian émigrés who were accused of being traitors or of cooperating with the Soviet Union. Stashyns'kyi said that the methods used by the SB were very similar to those he knew from the KGB, and that both secret services rendered homage to the slogan "We have no prisons."[54] The last documented violent act of the OUN was planned to take place in Canada in 1974, where the OUN, according to the Royal Canadian Mounted Police (RCMP), was "planning a violent act—possibly the kidnapping of a Soviet diplomat."[55]

In addition to killing opponents, the ZCh OUN intimidated journalists who did not write about Bandera and the organization in a way that his followers thought appropriate. For example, in an article in the *Süddeutsche Zeitung*, a reporter named Hart described the paramilitary training programs of Bandera and the Banderites in Germany.[56] After the publication of his article, a "Committee of Ukrainians in Munich" invited Hart to Dachauerstrasse 9, where the ZCh OUN had its office. The journalist went there with two policemen. The committee told Hart that he had published incorrect information and that it would sue him for libel. He explained to the angry nationalists how they could initiate proceedings. During the meeting, one of the policemen perceived "hidden threats in the words and gestures of the Ukrainians."[57]

Shukhevych, leader of the UPA and OUN in Ukraine, supported the ZP UHVR rather than the ZCh OUN. In September 1947, he wrote a letter to OUN émigrés, emphasizing that the UHVR had the right to represent the UPA, while acknowledging that the UPA had been founded by the OUN-B. He also appealed to the émigrés to stop fighting each other and to concentrate on the struggle against the common enemy.[58] In an announcement on the fifth anniversary of the founding of the UPA in October 1947, Shukhevych emphasized once more that the UHVR represented the UPA, and he did not mention the ZCh OUN or Bandera.[59]

51 The perpetrators stabbed Gulay with a knife several times but did not kill him. Cf. "Ukrainische Attentäter vor Gericht," "Mordanschlag auf den Kosakengeneral," "Drei gegen den Kosaken," StM, Staatsanwaltschaften 34887, vol. 2.

52 "Schlussbericht der Untersuchung zu vier vermissten ukrainischen Personen," StM, Staatsanwaltschaften 34887, vol. 2, 45–52.

53 Bruder, *"Den Ukrainischen Staat*, 249.

54 "Voruntersuchung gegen Bogdan Staschynskij," 22 May 1962, BAK, B 362/10137, 272.

55 Inquiry 74WLO-2S-83, "Re: Acts of aggression against the Soviet Union in Canada"—inquiry from the RCMP Liaison Office, Washington D.C. to CIA, Washington, DC, December 9, 1974, NARA, RG 263, E ZZ-18, Stepan Bandera Name File.

56 "Politische Banden werden aktiv. Faschistische Emigranten im Untergrundkampf," *Süddeutsche Zeitung*, 14 November 1950, StM. Pol. Dir. München 9281, l.

57 K.-7-B 195/50, München 27 January 1950, Stadt Archiv München, Pol. Oir. 843.

58 "Zaiava holovnoho komanduvannia Ukraïns'koï Povstans'koï Armiï," 25 September 1947, HDA SBU f. 13, spr. 372, vol. 44, 189–90, in *Stepan Bandera*, ed. Serhiichuk, 1:601–604.

59 "Sviatochnyi nakaz," 14 October 1947, HDA SBU f. 13, spr. 372, vol. 44, 188–89, in *Stepan Bandera*, ed. Serhiichuk, 1:606–609.

Bandera's relationship with the American intelligence agencies began to deteriorate in the late 1940s. The CIA changed its attitude to the ZCh OUN because of Bandera's conflict with Lebed' and the ZP UHVR, which was the main Ukrainian partner of the CIA. In 1947 Bandera still believed that a third world war would break out no later than 1950. He considered that he needed good relations with the United States in order to liberate Ukraine with its help. He also attempted reconciliation with Mel'nyk and the OUN-M.[60] Bandera met with Mel'nyk in January 1948 and apparently later as well. Their discussion in 1948 included some very sensitive matters, such as the murder of OUN-M members by the OUN-B during and after the war. On 10 February 1948, Bandera published an official announcement on this subject to all OUN members, in which he declared that the OUN-B had never murdered any OUN-M members. It is hardly surprising that the OUN-M and OUN-B were never reconciled.[61]

From 28 to 31 August 1948, the Second Extraordinary Conference of the ZCh OUN took place in Mittenwald. The two factions again discussed whether they could come to an agreement. Bandera demanded the full subordination of all ZCh OUN members, which the "democratic" faction again refused, stressing the supremacy of the UHVR. Rebet openly criticized the Führerprinzip and Bandera's fascination with fascism. According to Ievhen Stakhiv, Bandera slammed his fists on the table and shouted: "There will be no compromise. Either they subordinate to me or they can leave." After the conference, the individuals from the "democratic" faction officially left the ZCh OUN. Their decision was strengthened by an open letter, in which the older OUN member Vrets'ona informed Bandera that he might intimidate ZCh OUN members and extort full subordination from them, but that he could not do so from the ZP UHVR. Bandera again called all Ukrainian emigrants who were not loyal to him "traitors" and "communists." In letters to the leadership of the OUN in Ukraine, he described the ZP UHVR as a "sick phenomenon [*khoroblyve iavyshche*]" that was costing him half his energy. After the official split, the ZCh OUN continued to compete with the ZP UHVR, which included the "democratic" faction of the ZCh OUN, for the loyalty of the leadership of the OUN and UPA in Ukraine. Contact with the nationalist underground in Soviet Ukraine was essential for the collaboration with the American, British, and other intelligence services on which the ZCh OUN and the ZP UHVR were financially dependent.[62]

After the split in August 1948, Bandera even wanted to go to Ukraine in person, but his supporters Klymyshyn and Tiushka apparently dissuaded him.[63] MI6 refused

60 "Vypiska iz protokola doprosa Dyshkanta," 30 November 1947 HDA SBU f. 13, spr. 372, vol. 43, 322–34, in *Stepan Bandera*, ed. Serhiichuk, 1:622–25.

61 "Spetsial'noie soobshchenie," 23 April 1948, HDA SBU f. 2, op. 37, spr. 65, 176–77, in *Stepan Bandera*, ed. Serhiichuk, 2:41–44; "Komunikat, "10 February 1948, HDA SBU f. 2, op. 37, spr. 65, 179–81, in *Stepan Bandera*, ed. Serhiichuk, 2:44–47; "Vypiska iz protokola obvyniaiemogo Khamuliak T. V.," HDA SBU f. 65, spr. S-9079, vol. 6, 27–29, in *Stepan Bandera*, ed. Serhiichuk, 2:54; Sushko, *Zavdannia vykonav*, 170.

62 Stakhiv, *Kriz' tiurmy*, 246–51; Kyrychuk, *Ukraïns'kyi natsional'nyi rukh*, 357; "Protokol doprosa," 24–27 November 1948, HDA SBU spr. 10876, vol. 1, 38–42, in *Stepan Bandera*, ed. Serhiichuk, 2:77; "Lyst Stepana Bandery," spring 1951, HDA SBU f. 13, spr. 372, t. 41, 389–423, in *Stepan Bandera*, ed. Serhiichuk, 2:582, 595; Mechnyk, *Pochatok*, 125–28.

63 Stakhiv, *Kriz' tiurmy*, 248; Mudryk-Mechnyk, *Spohad pro Stepana Banderu*, 14; interrogation of Ivan Kashuba, Munich, 12 November 1959, Stepan Bandera Museum in London (ASBML), 3094, 4.

to parachute Bandera into Ukraine, because it thought that the Soviet Union might not interpret this as intelligence gathering but as a political step.[64] During the competition for the loyalty of the leadership of the OUN-UPA in Ukraine, each faction sent several members to Soviet western Ukraine. The most important emissary from the ZCh OUN was Myron Matviieiko, who was dropped, together with five other people, from a plane under the orders of MI6 on the night of 14–15 May 1951. The ZP UHVR sent Vasyl' Okhrymovych with three other people in a CIA plane four days later. It seems that only the ZP UHVR succeeded in contacting the leadership in Ukraine.[65]

The leaders of the OUN and UPA in Ukraine continually appealed to the émigrés to stop quarrelling. They confirmed that the ZP UHVR was the main representative of the OUN-UPA and claimed that the ZCh OUN should subordinate itself to the UHVR, which had been established to represent all Ukrainian nationalist organizations.[66] Neither Shukhevych, nor Kuk, the last leader of the UPA, had much sympathy with the conflicts within the émigré community, with Bandera's dictatorial and terroristic management of the ZCh OUN, or with his sustained fascination with fascism and authoritarianism.[67]

In 1950, in order to end the conflict with the ZP UHVR, Bandera resigned from his position as leader of the ZCh OUN. Lenkavs'kyi became the new leader of the ZCh OUN, followed, at the Third Conference of the ZCh OUN in Munich in April 1951, by Stets'ko.[68] On 22 August 1952, Bandera also resigned as leader of the entire OUN but, after he realized that his resignation did not improve matters between the ZCh OUN and the ZP UHVR, he decided to resume the leadership of both the OUN and the ZCh OUN. The ZCh OUN and the ZP UHVR continued to compete bitterly for the loyalty of the OUN-UPA leadership in Ukraine, until the last Ukrainian nationalist insurgents were killed by the Soviet authorities.[69]

In 1953 the Fourth Conference of the ZCh OUN took place in London. It was decided at this conference that the OUN leadership in Ukraine had the decisive word in the conflict between the ZCh OUN and the ZP UHVR. Bandera was sure that the conflict would be resolved in his favor because Matviieiko, who in the meantime had been caught by the MGB and was working for them, sent him a telegram that confirmed Bandera's supremacy in the OUN. However, the ZP UHVR received also a radiogram from Vasyl' Kuk, in which Bandera was blamed for not applying the resolutions of the Third Extraordinary Grand Assembly of the OUN-B in August 1943. After the receipt of these two communications, a committee—consisting of Lev Rebet, Zinovii Matla, and Stepan Bandera—was appointed as the leadership of the OUN. Bandera agreed to this but announced a week later that the radiogram from

64 "Protokol doprosa parashiutista po klichke 'Miron,'" 16 July 1951, HDA SBU f. 6, op. 37, spr. 56232, 27–72, in *Stepan Bandera*, ed. Serhiichuk, 3:96.

65 Motyka, *Ukraińska partyzantka*, 628, 630.

66 "Otnoshenie provoda OUN," 6 February 1951, HDA SBU f. 13, spr. 372, vol. 41, 179–84, in *Stepan Bandera*, ed. Serhiichuk, 2:426.

67 Motyka, *Ukraińska partyzantka*, 611, 625–26.

68 "Handbuch der Emigration. Teil: Ukrainer," 1 July 1953, BAK, B 206/1080, 14; Mechnyk, *Pochatok*, 206.

69 "Zaiavlenie ob ukhode s posta predstavitelia 'provoda' OUN," 22 September 1952, HDA SBU f. 13, spr. 379, 179–83, in *Stepan Bandera*, ed. Serhiichuk, 3:188; "Stepan Bandera Resigns His Post ..." 30 September 1952 NARA, RG 263, E ZZ-18, Stepan Bandera Name File, 1.

Kuk to the ZP UHVR was a Soviet falsification. After this incident, Rebet and Matla established the OUN-abroad (*OUN-za kordonom*, OUN-z), with Rebet as its leader. Lebed', on the other hand, had lived in the United States since 1949, where he headed the CIA-controlled Cold War propaganda-for-profit enterprise Prolog Research Cooperation, which published newspapers, booklets, and books, and prepared radio programs for Ukraine, the Ukrainian émigré communities, and eventually other countries behind the Iron Curtain.[70]

Because the Rebet-Matla faction had taken over the newspaper *Ukraïns'kyi samostiinyk*, the ZCh OUN opened its own newspaper *Shliakh peremohy* in 1954, which was printed in the new publishing house Cicero at Zeppelinstrasse 67, Munich.[71] The conflict between the two factions was so vicious that in February 1954 the Munich police had to intervene. The Rebet faction reported to the police that after Bandera had lost the publishing house of *Ukraïns'kyi samostiinyk*, he sent his people to destroy some of the Rebet faction's printing facilities. When preparing to oppose the operation, the police assumed that the angry Banderites might be armed.[72]

The conflict between the two factions remained virulent until the very end of their existence and was to some extent inflamed by the KGB. The OUN-z was permanently afraid of the ZCh OUN, which referred to the OUN-z as "communists," "traitors," and "democrats." The visit of Volodymyr Kurovets' to Munich illustrates the climate of the time. Kurovets' arrived in Munich from England on 7 January 1956. He visited Pidhainyi and celebrated the Greek Catholic Christmas with him. Kurovets' had belonged to the ZCh OUN until 1953 and had worked as a courier between Munich and western Ukraine, which suggests that he might have been turned by the KGB. Pidhainyi had been close to Bandera for a long time. Like Bandera, he was sentenced to life imprisonment at the Warsaw trial and was with Bandera in prison. He left the ZCh OUN in 1952. In Munich on 8 January 1956, Kurovets' told Pidhainyi that he would go to the ZCh OUN office the next day, to celebrate Stepan Bandera's name day. On 9 January, he left Pidhainyi's apartment and disappeared. Pidhainyi immediately presumed that the ZCh OUN had killed Kurovets'. As the ZCh OUN could not explain what had happened to his friend, Pidhainyi went to the Munich police and reported his disappearance.[73] But Bandera had an alibi: he had not been in Munich from 8 to 10 January but in the Tyrol with his family.[74] The police could not solve the disappearance of Kurovets', just as it could not solve the mysterious disappearance of many other Ukrainian emigrants.[75]

The ZCh OUN was attacked several times by other émigré organizations and by the intelligence services of the Eastern bloc. On the night of 6–7 March 1957 an in-

70 Motyka, *Ukraińska partyzantka*, 631–32; Mechnyk, *Pochatok*, 210; Stakhiv, *Kriz' tiurmy*, 262. For Lebed', see Breitman and Goda, *Hitler's Shadow*, 88–90.

71 A14-493, Notes from the foreign language press, 21.04.1954, NARA, RG 263, E ZZ-18, Stepan Bandera Name File, 1.

72 "Betreff: Druckerei Cicero," 16 February 1954, StM, Pol. Dir. München 9281.

73 "Vernehmungsschrift Bohdan Pidhainyj," 14 January 1956, StM, Pol. Dir. München 9281, 5–11.

74 "Vorführungsnote Stefan Popel," 20 January 1956, StM, Pol. Dir. München 9281, 48; "Vernehmungsniederschrift Stefan Popel," 8 February 1956, StM, Pol. Dir. München 9281, 61.

75 In summer 1967 the Munich police routinely asked the police in London about Kurovets'. They learned that he never came back to London from Munich and, according to émigré information, was shot there in June 1956. Cf. KA II-147/68, 14.02.1968, StM. Pol. Dir. München 9281, 48.

truder broke into the office of the ZCh OUN and searched for documents.[76] Although the police suspected Stefan Lippolz (Liebholz), a KGB agent who infiltrated the Ukrainian nationalists in Munich, they could not prove this.[77] On 18 April 1958, the ZCh OUN received a parcel containing explosive materials, which was intended as a threat and not to kill, although the explosion was strong enough to blacken the person who opened the parcel. The ZCh OUN most likely received it from the KGB rather than from the National Alliance of Russian Solidarists (*Natsional'no Trudovoi Soiuz*, NTS), a radical-right Russian émigré organization with which the ZCh OUN was in conflict, and which also received parcels containing explosive materials.[78] In July 1958, people living close to the office of the ZCh OUN at Zeppelinstrasse 67 received letters from a "Group of Ukrainian Emigrants," accusing Bandera and other members of his organizations of killing several people named in the letters and of committing other crimes. One ZCh OUN member was accused of raping a female who lived in the building in which the ZCh OUN had its office.[79] In a letter sent to the police on 2 June 1958, Bandera's people were accused of raping German women and poisoning Rebet.[80] The police investigated the allegation of rape and determined that it was unfounded. They concluded that the letter had been prepared in the intelligence office in Karlshorst in East Berlin, and they closed the investigation of Bandera and the ZCh OUN.[81]

Bandera and Western Intelligence Services

As early as 1945, American military intelligence had helped Bandera to establish an intelligence school. It was located a few kilometers from Munich, apparently in the Mittenwald DP camp. Courses in "infiltration into installations, explosives, codes, ciphers, courier systems, organizing of informant nets, etc." were taught there.[82] Also in 1945, the MGB began to "turn" ZCh OUN operatives. Demyd Chyzhevs'kyi and Iaroslav Moroz, two of the first ZCh OUN members who were sent to Ukraine in 1946 and 1947 as couriers, came back to Germany as Soviet agents. Chyzhevs'kyi's task was to split the OUN, and Moroz's to kill Bandera, Stets'ko, Lebed', and Hryn'okh.[83]

In 1947 or 1948, Bandera ordered UPA commander Petro Mykolenko-Baida, who had come with a UPA unit from Ukraine to Bavaria and was living in a DP camp in

76 Commissar Adrian Fuchs of the Munich criminal police could not clarify who broke in, and did not exclude the possibility that the ZCh OUN had staged this burglary. Cf. "Strafanzeige," 8 March 1957, StM, Pol. Dir. München 9281.

77 "Anzeige Tgb. Nr. 1020/57 v. 8.3.57, 09.03.1957; 1 a Js 640/57," 11 April 1957, StM, Pol. Dir. München 9281.

78 "Von: Der Oberstaatsanwalt dem Landgericht München I (Schönberger) An: Herrn-Generalstaatsanwalt bei dem Oberlandsgericht, Herrn Generalstaatsanwalt Dr. Hechtel persönlich in München, München 31. Juli 1958," StM, Staatsanwaltschaften 34887, vol. 3, 1. Another document mentions that the ZCh OUN received the parcel on 20 August. Cf. "Instruktion Nr. 6.," StM, Staatsanwaltschaften 34887, vol. 2, 71–72.

79 "Handakten zu der Strafsache gegen Bandera Stepan wegen Mord," StM, Staatsanwaltschaften 34887, vol. 3, 1, 3–4.

80 "Letter to police in Munich," 2 June 1958, StM, Staatsanwaltschaften 34887, vol. 3.

81 "Schreiben Aktenzeichen: 1 a Js 2540/58; Tgb. Nr. 35/38 VS-Vertr.," 1 December 1958, StM, Staatsanwaltschaften 34887, vol. 3, 12–13.

82 Burds, Early Cold War, 14.

83 "Handbuch der Emigration. Teil IV: Ukrainer," 1 July 1953, BAK, B 206/1080, 43, 46, 49; Chaikovs'kyi, *Moskovs'ki vbyvtsi*, 8.

Regensburg, to organize a Ukrainian partisan movement in the forests of Bavaria. This idea surprised Mykolenko-Baida, who believed that a partisan movement could be established only in Ukraine. Nevertheless, following Bandera's order, Baida and a few other OUN-UPA members, recruited several Ukrainians from the DP camps, for training in the Bavarian forests. During the course of this training, Bandera informed the recruits that they would go back to the Soviet Union and fight for an independent Ukraine. The same recruits later attended espionage courses in the Mittenwald DP camp and were sent to the Soviet Union.[84]

Bandera's insistence on dominating the OUN as its sole leader, and his wish to retain the fascist structure of the OUN-B in the ZCh OUN, which led to fierce conflicts with other Ukrainian organizations, caused his relationship with American intelligence to deteriorate. The CIA preferred to cooperate with Lebed' and the ZP UHVR, because it regarded them as more professional, efficient, and reliable than Bandera and the ZCh OUN. In 1951 a CIA agent infiltrated the ZCh OUN. At about the same time, when Bandera tried to penetrate the CIA with his agents, the CIA concluded that Bandera had become "anti-American" and put an end to its cooperation with him.[85]

MI6 had trained Bandera's agents in Munich and London and had parachuted them into western Ukraine since 1949. The CIA did the same with ZP UHVR people and warned MI6 that Bandera had no support from the OUN leadership in Ukraine. This, however, did not convince MI6, which claimed that the CIA underestimated the importance of the leader of the "strongest Ukrainian organization abroad."[86] MI6 perceived Bandera as "a professional underground worker with a terrorist background and ruthless notions about the rules of the game. ... A banditry type if you like, with a burning patriotism, which provides an ethical background and a justification for his banditry. No better and no worse than others of his kind."[87]

Several ZCh OUN agents were trained in MI6 facilities in London. At a course in April 1951, Bandera taught the recruits that Britain and the United States would soon attack the Soviet Union and help Ukraine gain independence. Stets'ko taught them about the ABN, and Lenkavs'kyi instructed them about the activities of the OUN in exile. The agents were to be flown to Malta, from where the plane to Ukraine was to take off. One day before the flight, Bandera, Stets'ko, and Lenkavs'kyi bid farewell to the agents and reminded them to establish contact with the OUN in Ukraine. In Malta, Pidhainyi, the main connection between the ZCh OUN and MI6, gave the agents capsules of potassium cyanide to take if they were arrested by the Soviet authorities. The poison was handed to the agents on the initiative of the ZCh OUN. The agents were equipped with a rifle, two pistols, forged Soviet documents, and radios with which they were to establish contact with London and Munich.[88]

84 Balei, *Fronda Stepana Bandery*, 14–15; "Dokladnaia zapiska," November 1951, HDA SBU f. 13, spr. 372, vol. 43, 1–47, in *Stepan Bandera*, ed. Serhiichuk, 3:148–49.

85 Breitman, *Hitler's Shadow*, 81; EGMA-19914, Chief of Base, Munich to Chief SR, 29.03.1956, NARA, RG 263, E ZZ-18, Stepan Bandera Name File, 1v; Attachment B to EGMA-19914, Subject: Stefan Bandera's Anti-American Activities, 29.03.1956, NARA, RG 263, E ZZ-18, Stepan Bandera Name File, 1v.

86 Breitman, *Hitler's Shadow*, 82.

87 Ibid., 81.

88 "Protokol doprosa zakhvachennogo parashiutista Pidgirnogo Evgeniia Ivanovicha," 10 June1951, HDA SBU f. 7, op. 76, spr. 1, vol. 2, 1–16, in *Stepan Bandera*, ed. Serhiichuk, 3:21–24, 27–28, 31, 37–

The ZCh OUN was so badly infiltrated that the group accompanying Matviieiko included an MGB agent by the name of "Slavko." Matviieiko was captured on 6 June 1951, three weeks after his parachuting. By the end of June, he had switched sides and agreed to work for the MGB. The ZP UHVR member Okhrymovych, who was parachuted into Ukraine four days after Matviieiko, was caught on 6 October 1952. From both of them the MGB obtained crucial information about the ZP UHVR and the ZCh OUN in Munich. Okhrymovych refused to cooperate and was executed on 19 May 1954. Matviieiko, head of the SB of the ZCh OUN however, began his second career as an intelligence officer—with the MGB. He soon became an important agent with whose help the MGB liquidated the last OUN-UPA troops in Ukraine. He also deceived the ZCh OUN for several years by sending fake radio telegrams. On 19 June 1958, the Presidium of the Supreme Soviet of the Ukrainian SSR forgave Matviieiko all his offences.[89]

Between 1949 and 1954, a total of seventy-five ZCh OUN and ZP UHVR agents were parachuted into Ukraine. With Czech wartime pilots at the controls, the planes evaded Soviet radar screens by flying at 200 feet (61 meters) across the Soviet border and climbing at the last moment to 500 feet (152 meters), the minimum height for a safe parachute drop. In May 1952, one group was sent by submarine. In 1953 two groups used hot-air balloons that lifted from British and West German ships close to the Polish coast. Other groups tried to reach Ukraine on foot. Ukrainian MI6 and CIA agents did not realize that very few of their missions could meet with success, because of infiltration by Soviet intelligence. In particular, the ZCh OUN was heavily infiltrated. In 1948 Leon Łapiński alias "Zenon," director of OUN SB in the Lublin region of south-east Poland, began to work for the Polish Department of Security (*Urząd Bezpieczeństwa*, UB) and the Soviet MGB. The two intelligence services launched a joint operation, "C1," which lasted until 1954. With the help of "Zenon" the UB built up an entirely fictitious network of OUN members. In late 1948 and early 1949, "Zenon" established contact with the ZCh OUN in Munich. Thereafter, the UB controlled the ZCh OUN agents and couriers who went through Poland to western Ukraine. The UB also established its agents in West Germany. In addition, MI6 agent and Soviet spy Kim Philby, among others, kept Soviet intelligence informed about the parachuting of ZCh OUN agents. Bohdan Pidhainyi, who was responsible in the ZCh OUN for the connection between Munich and Ukraine, realized in 1952 that the agent network of the ZCh OUN was entirely controlled by the UB and MGB. He left the ZCh OUN and joined the ZP UHVR, which was also compromised. Only in 1955 did the leadership of the ZCh OUN recognize and admit that their agent networks in West Germany and Vienna were deeply infiltrated.[90]

38; "Protokol doprosa parashiutista po klichke 'Miron,'" 16 July 1951, HDA SBU f. 6, op. 37, spr. 56232, 27–72, in *Stepan Bandera*, ed. Serhiichuk, 3:98.

89 Motyka, *Ukraińska partyzantka*, 628–31.

90 Philby, *My Silent War*, 145; Motyka, *Ukraińska partyzantka*, 627–32; Motyka, *Tak było w Bieszczadach*, 467–76; Stakhiv, *Kriz' tiurmy*, 261; Richard J. Aldrich, *The Hidden Hand: Britain, America and the Cold War Secret Intelligence* (Woodstock: Overlook Press, 2002), 170–71. For details concerning the agent "Zenon" and the network established by the UB, see Igor Hałagida, *Prowokacja "Zenona": Geneza, przebieg i skutki operacji MBP o kryptomimie "C1" przeciwko banderowskiej frakcji OUN i wywiadowi brytyjskiemu, 1950–1954* (Warsaw: EFEKT, 2005). For the recognition of the infiltration in 1955, see KGB's Operation "Karmen" Against Ukrainian Groups: 1, 5, 07 June 1955, NARA, RG 263, E ZZ-18, Stepan Bandera Name File, 1v. For avoiding radar and parachuting, see

MI6 realized that the ZCh OUN was heavily infiltrated and that its rival, the ZP UHVR, controlled the "entire Ukrainian liberation movement in Ukraine," in 1953. At this time, American and British officials tried to reconcile Bandera with Lebed', but Bandera opposed these attempts. In February 1954, MI6 ended its cooperation with Bandera, ceased to train agents loyal to him, and informed Lebed' that it "would not resume [its] relationship with Bandera under any circumstances."[91] Bandera then tried to establish his own intelligence service, which he financed in part with counterfeit money. The ZCh OUN had been forging American dollars since 1948. As a result, several of Bandera's couriers were arrested. Matviieiko and his wife had to hide in France from the American authorities, for almost a year.[92]

For the purpose of training its own agents, the ZCh OUN even bought a farm. Stets'ko, however, tried to dissuade Bandera from training teams and sending them to Ukraine. He argued that they would be captured by the MGB, but Bandera continued these operations because he believed that they strengthened the reputation of the ZCh OUN. Otherwise, Bandera thought, the ZCh OUN would become merely an émigré organization without connections to its country and would cease to be of interest to the intelligence services that financed it.[93] In general however, Bandera was much less successful with intelligence work than he was as the symbol of Ukrainian nationalism. In 1957 the CIA and MI6 concluded that all the agents Bandera had sent to Ukraine were under Soviet control. The CIA and MI6 wanted to "silence" Bandera because his unprofessional intelligence work only disturbed their plans for the Soviet Union. At the same time, they tried to prevent Soviet intelligence from kidnapping or killing the legendary Ukrainian *Providnyk*, which would have turned him into a martyr.[94]

After MI6 ceased to cooperate with Bandera, the ZCh OUN leader began to search for new sponsors and alliances. In 1955 Bandera and Stets'ko went to Paris, to negotiate with French intelligence. There is no evidence that they were successful, even though the OUN had cooperated with French intelligence in 1946.[95] After MI6, no other intelligence service parachuted Bandera's people into Ukraine, but sponsorship of the ZCh OUN and other Ukrainian émigré groups by secret services continued. For

Dorril, *MI6*, 242–43; Simpson, *Blowback*, 173. For Secret Intelligence Service (SIS) couriers, see "Protokol doprosa zakhvachennogo parashiutista Matviieiko Mirona Vasil'evicha," 12 July 1951, HDA SBU f. 6, op. 37, spr. 56232, 16–26, in *Stepan Bandera*, ed. Serhiichuk, 3:44. The majority of parachuted Ukrainian MI6 and CIA agents were caught by the Soviet authorities. According to Mykhailo Klymchuk, an OUN-UPA member and former Waffen-SS soldier who remained in the United Kingdom after the war, only three Ukrainians returned from Soviet Ukraine after parachuting—interview by author, London, 14 May 2008. For infiltration of the ZP UHVR, see "Anklageschrift gegen Bogdan Staschynskij," 24 March 1962, BAK, B 362/10137, 190b.

91 Breitman, *Hitler's Shadow*, 82–83.

92 "Stenograma: Protokol doprosa Matviieiko Mirona Vasil'evicha," 9 December 1952, HDA SBU f. 6, spr. 56232, 173–79, in *Stepan Bandera*, ed. Serhiichuk, 3:339; "Protokol doprosa Matviieiko Mirona Vasil'evicha," 10 December 1952, HDA SBU f. 6, spr. 56232, 180–87, in *Stepan Bandera*, ed. Serhiichuk, 3:341; ASBML, 3094, 4–5.

93 Sushko, *Zavdannia vykonav*, 144, 146, 167.

94 Breitman, *Hitler's Shadow*, 83; Dorril, *MI6*, 247.

95 For 1955, see E-36, Natalie C. Grant to Jacob D. Beam, 29 April 1956, NARA, RG 263, E ZZ-18, Stepan Bandera Name File, 1. The OUN-B member Zenon Matla established contact with French intelligence in 1946. Cf. "Protokol doprosa zakhvachennogo parashiutista Matviieiko Mirona Vasil'evicha," 14–15 July 1951, HDA SBU f. 13, spr. 372, vol. 42, 237–49, in *Stepan Bandera*, ed. Serhiichuk, 3:126. For Lebed' and French intelligence in 1946, see also Snyder, *The Red Prince*, 233–34.

example, the Belgian and very likely the Canadian intelligence services sponsored nationalist anti-Soviet propaganda through particular newspapers and radio stations.[96]

In 1956 the Italian Military Intelligence (*Servizio Informazioni Forze Armate*, SIFAR) sponsored Bandera for a short time, apparently not realizing that all Bandera's connections to Ukraine were infiltrated. The only intelligence service that did not cease to support Bandera was the German BND.[97] Bandera's personal contact in the BND was Heinz-Danko Herre, who, during the Second World War, had been Chief of Staff of Vlasov's ROA, and Gehlen's deputy in FHO, German Military Intelligence on the Eastern Front.

Although the CIA and MI6 informed the BND that the ZCh OUN had been infiltrated by the Soviet intelligence and had no contact with Ukraine, Herre did not change his attitude toward Bandera. In April 1959, when Bandera again asked the BND for support, Herre simply pointed to Bandera's popularity and to the continuity between the BND and the pre-war Abwehr: "Bandera has been known to us for about twenty years. ... Within and without Germany he has over half a million followers."[98] Herre believed that Bandera supplied him with "good reports on the Soviet Union." "Due to political overtones," he did not inform the West German government about the cooperation with Bandera, and kept it secret even within the BND.[99]

Bandera also maintained contacts with Franco's post-fascist regime in Spain. Vasyl' Sushko, Bandera's guard and close friend, pointed out that, of all the countries in the world, it was with Franco's Spain that the ZCh OUN had the best relationship, where Stets'ko was still treated as the prime minister of Ukraine.[100] In 1950 Bishop Buchko went to Spain and met with Franco on Bandera's behalf. Buchko persuaded Franco to admit UPA partisans and Waffen-SS Galizien veterans to his military academy. Later that year, the *Providnyk* and Stets'ko went together to Madrid to discuss this and related questions, in person with the *Caudillo*. One result of this cooperation was the institution of Ukrainian nationalist broadcasting from Madrid, three times a week.[101] In 1956 Franco invited Bandera to settle in Spain, where, after the Second World War, several other far-right leaders from various countries, such as Ante Pavelić and Juan Perón, found shelter. Bandera considered this generous proposal while visiting Spain again and taking a closer look at the country. In the end, however, he did not accept the offer, probably because his organization was deeply entrenched in Munich.[102]

Contact with the Spanish leader led to a dispute between the *Providnyk* and Stets'ko', who had been "premier" of the OUN-B "government" in 1941. Bandera was jealous of Stets'ko's excellent relationship with the *Caudillo*. Together with Bandera's unlimited appetite for power, this led to conflict with his closest ally. Stets'ko' always

96 "Protokol doprosa zakhvachennogo parashiutista Matviieiko Mirona Vasil'evicha," 14–15 July 1951, HDA SBU f. 13, spr. 372, vol. 42, 237–49, in *Stepan Bandera*, ed. Serhiichuk, 3:127–28.

97 Breitman, *Hitler's Shadow*, 83.

98 Ibid., 84.

99 Ibid., 84.

100 Sushko, *Zavdannia vykonav*, 165.

101 "Protokol doprosa zakhvachennogo parashiutista Matviieiko Mirona Vasil'evicha," 14–15 July 1951, HDA SBU f. 13, spr. 372, vol. 42, 237–49, in *Stepan Bandera*, ed. Serhiichuk, 3:128–29.

102 Sushko, *Zavdannia vykonav*, 165.

regarded Bandera as his *Providnyk* and obeyed him in accordance with his political beliefs. Democracy was for Stets'ko as great an evil as it was for Bandera. They both believed that only a national revolutionary power could combat the totalitarian Soviet Union. They cooperated with democratic states like the United Kingdom and the United States for pragmatic and strategic reasons, and not because they believed in or valued democracy. The ABN, headed by Stets'ko, was financially dependent on Bandera's ZCh OUN. In 1955 Bandera decided that he would finance only half the ABN's costs (DM 100,000 per year). This step forced Stets'ko to dismiss personnel and to look for funds elsewhere. Bandera stated that he had cut funding because he believed that other nations represented in the ABN should cover the other half of the ABN's expenses, but his move also had psychological ramifications and was related to Stets'ko's political prestige in international far-right circles. In particular, Stets'ko's pilgrimage to Franco and a visit to Chiang Kai-shek in Taiwan in 1955–1956 made Bandera envious.[103]

In addition to protection by the intelligence services, Bandera was protected by other institutions in Germany and by networks of former Nazis. In 1956 the Bavarian state government considered proceedings against Bandera in connection with such illegal activities as kidnapping, murder, and counterfeiting money. Early that year, the Munich police interrogated Bandera about the confusion surrounding his name, the disappearance of Kurovets', and related questions. However, Bandera was, at that time, protected by the West German official Gerhard von Mende, of the Office for Displaced Persons (*Büro für heimatvertriebene Ausländer*). During the Second World War, von Mende had headed the section for the Caucasus and Turkistan in Alfred Rosenberg's *Ostministerium*, recruiting Soviet Muslims from Central Asia to fight against the Soviet Union. He occasionally acted as liaison between the Germans and the Ukrainian nationalists. After the war, von Mende cooperated with American intelligence and was associated with former Nazi officials, several of whom occupied influential positions. One of them, Theodor Oberländer, even served in Adenauer's government between 1953 and 1960, as the federal minister for displaced persons, refugees, and war victims. On behalf of Bandera, von Mende interceded with the Bavarian government in 1956 and earlier, in respect of residence permits and other matters. As a result of such interventions, some police files concerning Bandera were closed.[104]

103 Sprava Myroslava Styranky, 30.12.1955, NARA, RG 263, E ZZ-18, Stepan Bandera Name File, 1v. For Stets'ko's visits to Spain and Taiwan, see Slava Stetzko, "A.B.N. Ideas assert themselves: The 20th Anniversary of the Anti-Bolshevik Bloc of Nations (A.B.N.), 1943–1963," *Ukrainian Review*, 3 (1963): 9.

104 Munich to Director, MUCO 033, 5 September 1956, NARA, RG 263, E ZZ-19, B 11, Aerodynamic: Operations, 14, 1v; Breitman, *Hitler's Shadow*, 83–84. For Bandera's connection to von Mende, see also "Vorführungsnote Stefan Popel," 20 January 1956, StM, Pol. Dir. München 9281, 47. For von Mende's connections with American intelligence, see Ian Johnson, *A Mosque in Munich: Nazis, the CIA, and the Muslim Brotherhood in the West* (Boston: Houghton Mifflin Harcourt, 2010), 53–57. For the Munich police proceeding against Bandera, see "Vorführungsnote Stefan Popel," 20 January 1956, StM, Pol. Dir. München 9281, 45–48; "Vernehmungsniederschrift Stefan Popel," 7 February 1956, StM, Pol. Dir. München 9281, 81–90. For von Mende and Ukrainian nationalists during the Second World War, see John-Paul Himka, "Introduction," *Engels and the 'Nonhistoric' Peoples: The National Question in the Revolution of 1848*, Roman Rosdolsky, ed. John-Paul Himka (Glasgow: Critique Books, 1986), 2–3.

After the Second World War, Bandera visited Ukrainian communities in Austria, Belgium, Canada, the United Kingdom, Holland, and Italy.[105] In Canada, Bandera probably visited the main pre-war ideologue of Ukrainian nationalism, Dmytro Dontsov, who had been teaching Ukrainian literature at the Université de Montréal.[106] In 1953 Bandera invited Dontsov to become the editor of a ZCh OUN newspaper. Dontsov turned down the offer, as he had done before the war in a similar case.[107] The only country that Bandera attempted to visit, but to which he was never admitted, was the United States. In his visa application from 1955, Bandera asserted that he wanted to visit his family, but the American officials did not trust him: "Bandera and his organization are widely disliked by émigrés of many persuasions and nationalities. It is believed that Bandera wishes to come to this country to conduct political agitation against legitimate political organizations with ties with Ukrainian groups abroad, which the Agency supports [like the ZP UHVR] or upon which it looks with favor."[108] Bandera's applications were rejected until October 1959. Only shortly before his assassination, the officials in Munich recommended that he be granted a visa.[109] He never made the trip, but his speeches were recorded, and sent to the United States, where Bandera adherents listened to them at gatherings.[110]

Bandera's Private Life

It is difficult to provide an accurate description of Bandera's private life after the Second World War because memoirs and testimonies, of people who were related to him, worked for him, or were his friends, differ substantially from each other and leave a very ambiguous impression. This is caused, on the one hand, by the ideologization of perception and memory, especially by people such as Iaroslava Stets'ko and Vasyl' Sushko, for whom Bandera was the *Providnyk* and a hero. On the other hand, Bandera's inconsistent character and personality left different impressions on different people. Bandera was a loving father who could tenderly play with his children but then hit them if they did something against his wishes, such as going to a festival at which folklore groups from the Soviet Union danced or sang. In public, he appeared to be a good husband especially when he was among his friends, but he could hit his wife Iaroslava when he was angry with her. He apparently did not abuse alcohol and

105 EGMA-18250, Chief of Base Munich to Chief, SR, 15.01.1956, NARA, RG 263, E ZZ-18, Stepan Bandera Name File, 1v. Dorril claims that Bandera secretly visited Washington in 1950 to establish better relations with American intelligence. Cf. Dorril, *MI6*, 244. For a picture of Bandera in Canada, see Mudryk-Mechnyk, *Spohad pro Stepana Banderu*, 18.

106 "Otnoshenie provoda OUN," 6 February 1951, HDA SBU f. 13, spr. 372, vol. 41, 179–84, in *Stepan Bandera*, ed. Serhiichuk, 2:418–19.

107 Sosnovskyi, *Dmytro*, 198–99, 379–80.

108 "Subject: Stefan Bandera," 19.01.1956, NARA, RG 263, E ZZ-18, Stepan Bandera Name File, 1v.

109 EGMA-18250, Chief of Base Munich to Chief, SR, 15.01.1956 and Action SR6, from Munich to Director, 30.12.1955, NARA, RG 263, E ZZ-18, Stepan Bandera Name File, 1v.

110 Stepan Bandera, "Promova na p"iatu zustrich ukraïntsiv ZSA i Kanady 1954 roku," in *Perspektyvy ukraïns'koï revoliutsiï*, ed. Vasyl' Ivanyshyn (Drohobych: Vidrodzhennia, 1999), 617–22.

remained very religious, although he had some extra-marital affairs. In addition to the Greek Catholic church, he sometimes attended a German Catholic one.[111]

Bandera's private life was known to his SB bodyguards, such as Matviieiko, Kashuba, and Shushko, who spent much time with Bandera while protecting him and his family. From Matviieiko's and Kashuba's statements, we know that the *Providnyk* used his position and sometimes his "charisma" for private purposes. When Matviieiko was interrogated by the MGB, he might have exaggerated in his descriptions of Bandera's private life, but Kashuba did not have any reason to manipulate his evidence. Matviieiko's and Kashuba's statements about Bandera overlap on his obsession with women and on his extramarital affairs. According to Matviieiko, Bandera proposed an affair to Ievhen Harabach's wife Maria Metsyk, who looked fifteen years younger than Bandera's wife Iaroslava. Harabach overlooked the affair because, as the financial officer in the ZCh OUN, he was involved in fraud relating to the organization's funds. This allowed Bandera to intimidate him and to demand that he ignore the adulterous relationship with his wife. Bandera also tried to develop a sexual relationship with a female servant, who was subsequently dismissed by his wife.[112] According to Kashuba, Bandera also had an affair with the "German female au pair" of a "Jewish family" in the house where he lived in Munich after 1954. The affair was known to Iaroslava, who was frequently angry with her husband.[113]

Two more children were born to Bandera after the war. The first was a son born on 16 May 1946 in Munich and registered under the name Andrii Popel, and the second was a daughter born on 27 August 1947 in Regensburg and registered as Alexandra Popel.[114] When Bandera's wife went to hospital for the birth of their third child, Lesia, the wife of one of Bandera's security guards, Mykhailo Banias, took care of Bandera's children. According to Matviieiko, Bandera tried to rape her during the night. When her husband noticed traces of violence on his wife's body in the morning and learned from her what had happened, he became so angry that, at first, he wanted to shoot Bandera. Finally he decided to report the matter to his superior, Matviieiko, head of the SB. After this incident, Banias ceased to work for the SB.[115]

According to Matviieiko, although Iaroslava loved Stepan, he frequently hit and kicked her. He even kicked her in the belly when she was pregnant. In general, Iaroslava was unhappy with her marriage after 1945. She probably stayed with Stepan because she had no other choice and was intimidated by him. Some of Bandera's

111 "Protokol doprosa parashiutista po klichke 'Miron,'" 16 July 1951, HDA SBU f. 6, op. 37, spr. 56232, 27–72, in *Stepan Bandera*, ed. Serhiichuk, 3:85–86.

112 *Stepan Bandera*, ed. Serhiichuk, 3:83–84, 86, 87. According to Matviieiko, Harabach's predecessor Mykola Klymyshyn was also involved in fraud, because of which he left for the United States.

113 Attachment D to Egma 48874, 7.01.1960, NARA, RG 263, E ZZ-18, Stepan Bandera Name File, 2v.; Sprava: Ivan Kashuba pro ostanni momenty v zhyttiu Bandera, 04.01.1960; NARA, RG 263, E ZZ-18, Stepan Bandera Name File, 1v. After Bandera's assassination this affair was wrongly linked to his death.

114 "Vernehmungsniederschrift Stefan Popel," 7 February 1956, StM, Pol. Dir. München 9281, 90.

115 "Protokol doprosa parashiutista po klichke 'Miron,'" 16 July 1951, HDA SBU f. 6, op. 37, spr. 56232, 27–72, in *Stepan Bandera*, ed. Serhiichuk, 3:71–72.

Fig. 24. Bandera 1958. Posivnych, *Stepan Bandera—zhyttia, prysviachene svobodi*, 5.

friends did not like to visit the family.[116] Bandera was sometimes rude to and severe with his three children. He hit them, and forbade them to participate in events in which Russian, Polish, or Jewish children participated.[117] Several people refused to work with Bandera on account of his difficult character. His attitude to his wife also repelled people.[118]

Although the American and British intelligence services protected Bandera after the war, his way of life was determined by the danger of being killed or kidnapped by Soviet intelligence. Bandera and his family had to hide when the MGB or KGB were looking for them. His children grew up with the family name Popel and were not aware of their real family name until the death of their father.[119] Details concerning his financial status are not known, but he presumably had at his disposal a considerable amount of money, received from the intelligence services and from OUN members living around the world, who sponsored his fight against the "red devil." In addition Bandera counterfeited American dollars, and received non-monetary gifts from the intelligence services. In 1950, for example, MI6 presented him with a new car on St. Nicolas Day. All this allowed him to lead quite a comfortable life.[120]

116 "Protokol doprosa parashiutista po klichke 'Miron,'" 16 July 1951, HDA SBU f. 6, op. 37, spr. 56232, 27–72, in *Stepan Bandera*, ed. Serhiichuk, 3:72, 86.

117 Ibid., 87; Mudryk-Mechnyk, *Spohad pro Stepana Banderu*, 14; Irena Kozak, interview by author, Munich, 16 February 2008.

118 "Protokol doprosa parashiutista po klichke 'Miron,'" 16 July 1951, HDA SBU f. 6, op. 37, spr. 56232, 27–72, in *Stepan Bandera*, ed. Serhiichuk, 3:81–82.

119 Stets'ko-Muzyka, Z ideiamy Stepana, 179.

120 "Protokol doprosa parashiutista po klichke 'Miron'," 16 July 1951, HDA SBU f. 6, op. 37, spr. 56232, 27–72, in Serhiichuk, *Stepan Bandera*, 3: 85–86.

Photographs of Bandera's private life reveal that he appeared in public as a good and loving father and husband.[121] This image is strengthened by the memoirs of people such as Iaroslava Stets'ko and Vasyl' Sushko. Yet for Stets'ko, Bandera was the *Providnyk* and "such a great person that it is not easy to talk about him." Although Iaroslava Stets'ko's memories are structured in a clearly propagandist way to "praise the wisdom and strength" of her *Providnyk*, they have to be considered in this brief analysis of Bandera's personality. They show us, on the one hand, how Bandera's admirers perceived him and, on the other hand, how he might have behaved in the presence of his followers and friends. According to Stets'ko, Bandera was a very good father who took care of his family and friends. He liked to laugh and frequently joked. One of his hobbies was developing photographs. Others were hiking and skiing.[122]

After his death, Bandera's widow Iaroslava stated that he had loved his children very much, and that his children had loved him. "Although I was often mournful and sad at home, my husband was very fun-loving," she stated. "He could play with our children as a child." He was empathetic toward people from his organization. The sickness of an employee could make him sad.[123] Dmytro Myskiv, who was close to Bandera's family and spent weekends and holidays with them from about 1954, also remembered that Bandera had a good relationship with his children and wife, and that he was very religious. On Sundays, they always went to church and only afterwards, out for a trip.[124]

The memoirs of Vasyl' Sushko, one of Bandera's security guards, are interesting but also problematic. Like Stets'ko, Sushko regarded Bandera as his *Providnyk*, a hero, and a father figure. His memoirs therefore lack information that would contradict his image of the *Providnyk*. Sushko went as far as to claim that Bandera respected his political opponents, omitting the fact that Bandera had ordered several of them to be assassinated. Yet despite the ideological nature of Sushko's memoirs, they do complement the picture of Bandera's private life. According to Sushko, Bandera liked to exercise and encouraged his friends and employees to do so, because he wanted to have a strong and healthy organization. He enjoyed swimming, skiing, and jogging. While exercising with Sushko, Bandera made comments like, "Vasyl', we have to be healthy because Ukraine needs people with healthy bodies and spirits." Like Stets'ko, Sushko also claimed that Bandera was a good father and had a harmonious family life. However, he substantiated this claim with observations that Bandera gave his daughter Natalia flowers on her birthday, because Iaroslava refused to celebrate it. Sushko wrote that he and Bandera stayed in a hotel only once during their business trips. They usually slept either in a tent or in the apartment of an OUN member, in order to save organizational funds.[125]

After Bandera's assassination, Iaroslava and her three children moved to Toronto. This was made possible by the financial help of the ZCh OUN, which opened a fund

121 For pictures of Bandera in private life after the Second World War, see *Zhyttia i diial'nist'*, ed. Posivnych, 2008, 157, 181, 191; Sushko, *Zavdannia*, l.

122 Stets'ko-Muzyka, Z ideiamy Stepana, 179–80, 185–86.

123 Interrogation of Iaroslava Bandera, 17 October 1959, BayHStA, Landeskriminalamt 272, 32–33.

124 Interrogation of Dmytro Myskiv, 19 October 1959, BayHStA, Landeskriminalamt 272, 36.

125 Sushko, *Zavdannia*, 137–38, 169, 170–71.

to provide support and bought a house for the family in Toronto. Natalka Bandera married OUN-B member Andrii Kutsan and lived with him from 1970 until her death in Munich in 1985.[126] Bandera's sisters Marta and Oksana had been deported in 1942 to Krasnoyarsk Krai, where they lived and worked on several collective farms. Volodymyra was arrested, sentenced to ten years detention and banishment, and was deported to Kazakhstan in 1946. According to the MGB, they received financial help from the OUN-UPA underground. After Stalin's death in 1953, they were taken to Moscow for two months. According to Arsenych, the MGB proposed that they could remain in Moscow if they would appeal on the radio for OUN-UPA partisans to emerge from the underground. The sisters apparently refused and were returned to where they had lived before coming to Moscow. Volodymyra was released and returned to Ukraine in 1956. Marta and Oksana were officially released in 1960 but were not allowed to return to Ukraine. They were made to work at jobs such as house building, woodcutting, and labor in kolkhozes. They were moved from one place to another, apparently every two or three months. Marta died in 1982 in Krasnoyarsk Krai, and Oksana returned to Ukraine in August 1989 to her sister Volodymyra, but was allowed to stay permanently in Ukraine only in 1991, after the collapse of the Soviet Union.[127]

Bandera's Worldview after the Second World War

After the Second World War, Bandera published a range of articles. He also gave several interviews, which were broadcast or were published in newspapers. After his death, his articles and interviews were collected and republished by the ZCh OUN.[128] While awaiting the third world war and continuing to work on the Ukrainian national revolution, Bandera visited Ukrainian communities in Austria, Belgium, Canada, England, the Netherlands, Italy, and Spain. During his visits, Bandera made speeches, in which he encouraged Ukrainian émigrés not to give up the fight against the Soviet Union, to support the "Ukrainian liberation movement," and not to stop "fighting for freedom." In all his articles, interviews, and speeches, Bandera either ignored or denied the atrocities the OUN-B and the UPA had committed during and after the Second World War. He wrote his articles in solemn, monotonous, pathetic language, which resembled the writings of Soviet officials, although he used vocabulary typical of far-right thinkers. His main subjects were "liberation" and the "struggle for independence." All other matters, including the well-being of entire nations or the human dignity, were subordinated to these "noble" concepts.

Bandera's early post-war writing did not differ much from the OUN-B ideology of 1940 and 1941, when he essentially shaped the line of the OUN-B's convictions. After the war Bandera avoided several words and expressions popular in 1941, but he

126 Andrii Kutsan, interview by author, Munich, 14 February 2008.

127 Arsenych, *Rodyna Banderiv*, 65–68, 72. For financial help, see *Stepan Bandera*, ed. Serhiichuk, 1:101. For Oksana Bandera in 1989 onward in Ukraine, see page 340 below.

128 Bandera's articles appeared in various Ukrainian nationalist newspapers. They were collected and republished in 1978 in Stepan Bandera, *Perspektyvy ukraïns'koï revoliutsiï*, ed. Stepan Lenkas'kyi (Munich: Vydannia Orhanizatsiï Ukraïns'kykh Natsionalistiv, 1978). The volume was reprinted in 1993 by the Vidrodzhennia publishing house. See Stepan Bandera, *Perspektyvy ukraïns'koï revoliutsiï*, ed. Vasyl' Ivanyshyn (Drohobych: Vidrodzhennia, 1999).

propagated similar values to those of 1941, such as the cult of war, and heroic death. As before the German attack on the Soviet Union, he wanted to control and use the masses to achieve his nationalist ends. In a letter to Shukhevych in November 1945, Bandera wrote: "Our struggle is first of all a struggle for the soul of the human being, for the masses, for access to them and influence over them."[129]

Bandera's first postwar article appeared in January 1946 under the pseudonym S. Siryi, in the newspaper *Vyzvol'na polityka*. In this article Bandera expressed his wish to continue the revolution that had failed in summer 1941, but he used different rhetoric to describe his plans. In particular, he avoided antisemitic and fascist phrases but maintained the ultranationalist far-right core of his argument. As in the letter to Shukhevych in November 1945, Bandera concentrated on the question of mobilizing the masses. He regarded them as a weapon, a tool to achieve his sacred aim: "In our fight, the mass is an important factor; as a conglomeration of individuals, we incorporate and unite it."[130]

In an article "To the Principles of Our Liberation Policy" from November 1946, Bandera returned to the idea of the "Ukrainian National Revolution" from 1941. He began by announcing: "The Ukrainian national revolution is the struggle for the life and liberty of the nation and the individual." Unlike in 1941, he did not identify Jews and Poles as enemies, because they had been killed during the war or resettled afterwards and had thus ceased to be a problem for him and other nationalists. He also changed the tone or adjusted it to the early Cold War situation, replacing the 1941 notion of "Jewish Bolshevism" with "Russian Bolshevik imperialism" but left the ultranationalist and populist core of his argumentation unchanged: "Russian Bolshevik imperialism ... tries to rule the whole world and, with this aim, it subordinates, exploits, and causes the deterioration of nations and individuals."[131]

Bolshevism and communism were, for Bandera, the same as Russian imperialism and nationalism: "The Russian nation tied its fate to Bolshevism. Decisive for it was Russian imperialism, which went into the blood of the whole Russian nation and the sympathy for Bolshevism."[132] He wrote in another article: "Communism—this is the most important form of hidden Moscow imperialism."[133] Bandera's desire to conduct a revolution against the Soviet Union, together with other nationalist movements, goes back to the 1940–1941 concept of a multi-nationalist revolution, in which the OUN-B had planned to involve many other far-right movements rooted in other Soviet republics. In 1946 Bandera wrote: "We put an equals sign between the Ukrainian revolution and the liberation of all nations oppressed by Bolshevism."[134] For this purpose, the ZCh OUN wanted to mobilize the masses not only in Ukraine but also in other republics of the Soviet Union. The multi-nationalist revolution would begin "when in the consciousness of the masses of all [revolutionary] nations occurs the

129 "Lyst Stepana Bandery," 18 November 1945, HDA SBU spr. 10876, vol. 1, 154–63, in *Stepan Bandera*, ed. Serhiichuk, 1:383.
130 S. Siryi, "Znachennia shyrokykh mas ta ïkh okhoplennia," in *Perspektyvy*, ed. Ivanyshyn, 15.
131 Ibid., 45.
132 S. Siryi, "Plianovist' revoliutsiinoï borot'by v kraiu," in *Perspektyvy*, ed. Ivanyshyn, 59.
133 Stepan Bandera, "Perspektyvy ukraïns'koï natsional'no-vyzvol'noï revoliutsiï," in *Perspektyvy*, ed. Ivanyshyn, 509.
134 Siryi, "Do zasad nashoï vyzvol'noï polityky," in *Perspektyvy*, ed. Ivanyshyn, 52.

understanding for the idea that the struggle of every nation is our common struggle."[135]

In a paper, "A Word to The Ukrainian Nationalists-Revolutionaries Abroad," which was intended to be distributed in 1948 in western Ukraine as a brochure, Bandera explicitly denied that the OUN-B had any sympathy for Nazi Germany in 1941:

> Some reproach [the OUN-B] for using phrases and gestures in a sympathetic tone toward Germany in the act of 30 June 1941. In this matter, it is time to state some open words because our truth is unambiguous and clear and we should stop the erroneous labeling of reality. We always stress the independence of Ukrainian policy, which concentrates only on the Ukrainian matter and not flirtation (an ineffective one!) with foreign powers.[136]

In the same article, Bandera omitted several other facts that could have compromised the movement. He did not mention that Stets'ko sent letters in 1941 to the leaders of the European fascist states, or that the OUN-B wanted its state to become a part of the "New Europe," although he admitted that the interests of the OUN-B coincided with those of Germany. His apologetic narrative concealed the fact that in 1941 the Ukrainian nationalists resembled the Nazis in many essential matters, such as their common interest in the annihilation of the Jews in Ukraine, whom both groups saw as communists, parasites, and an alien race.[137] In the same piece Bandera encouraged the Ukrainian insurgents to persist in fighting, and ordinary Ukrainians to continue sacrificing their lives: "In all parts of the national struggle, in all its forms, the Ukrainian nation established hecatombs of victims, of its best children. But not in vain. They all [the sacrificed Ukrainians] protect the spirit of the Ukrainian nation."[138] He encouraged them to fight and die, despite the fact that the OUN-UPA could not win against the Soviet Union, being much weaker, unable to produce any weapons or equipment, having no hospitals, and so forth. This indicates that the *Providnyk* did not respect human life and regarded the people living in Ukraine as a means to achieve his sacred aims.

After 1945 Bandera developed two ways of using the term "democracy." On the one hand, he claimed that democracy was a betrayal of Ukrainian nationalism. His opponents from the ZP UHVR and the OUN-z were for him communists and Bolsheviks, because they claimed to be democrats. The statements of the Lebed' group, OUN-z, and the ZP UHVR, that they were democratic and anti-totalitarian, angered Bandera. This was for him an "expression of socio-political primitivism and the egoism of a clique."[139] Democracy was for Bandera a betrayal of his sacred revolutionary and nationalist ideals. It blurred the boundaries between communism and nationalism and was therefore a Bolshevik provocation. On the other hand, he felt resentful if someone from outside the organization called the ZCh OUN undemocratic. Then he

135 Ibid., 53.

136 Stepan Bandera, "Slovo do Ukraïns'kykh natsionalistiv-revoliutsioneriv za kordonom," in *Perspektyvy*, ed. Ivanyshyn, 88. For the original brochure from 1948, see Stepan Bandera, *Slovo do Ukraïns'kykh natsionalistiv-revoliutsioneriv za kordonom* (1948), 17.

137 Bandera, Slovo do Ukraïns'kykh, 88.

138 Ibid., 94.

139 Ibid., 126.

argued that only "opponents of the Ukrainian national movement" would state that the ZCh OUN was undemocratic, totalitarian, or fascist.[140]

It was clear to Bandera that there was nothing wrong with the ultranationalist and criminal nature of the OUN and UPA. He believed that only such a movement could fight effectively against the Soviet Union. Therefore, people who demanded "democratization" of the OUN and UPA were traitors and communists.[141] In a similar spirit Bandera protested against the "international boycott" of Spain and Franco. He claimed that reproaching Franco was a gesture of Bolshevism, not democracy. In short, Bandera never had a problem recognizing the totalitarian nature of the Soviet Union but found it difficult to criticize states such as Fascist Italy, Nazi Germany, or Franco's Spain. For Bandera, fascism and far-right authoritarianism were legitimate state systems, superior to democracy because they were more distanced from communism than democracy was. Nazi Germany was not evil because it had annihilated European Jewry and killed millions of other civilians, but because it was imperialistic and did not allow the OUN-B to establish a Ukrainian state.[142]

Materialism, which Bandera saw as the "product of a completely alien foreign spirit," was no less an evil for him than communism or democracy. According to Bandera, "the materialistic world view was introduced in Ukrainian life, partly by foreign colonization of Ukraine, and partly by socialism." It was introduced in Ukraine by communists "to destroy the soul, entity, and idiosyncrasy of the Ukrainian people, to turn the Ukrainian nation and the Ukrainian individual into a subservient object that accommodates Moscow's goals."[143]

In the spirit of Dontsov, Bandera placed emphasis in his writings on the power of ideology and "Ukrainian power of liberation."[144] For him, the ideology of Ukrainian nationalism was closely related to God and religion: "Huge, clear idea of Ukrainian nation, the struggle for the freedom of Ukraine and for God's Truth in the Ukrainian territory—this is the inexhaustible source of power of our movement. ... God sanctifies and supports our struggle for the truth against Satan's red kingdom."[145]

Bandera's concept of nation was based on ontology and racial theory. He not only repeatedly stressed the "idiosyncrasy of the Ukrainian nation" but regarded it as an organism or human being. He believed that the destruction of communism and the foundation of a Ukrainian state would enable its citizens to develop "their own social order, adequate to the whole Ukrainian nation's needs and wishes, which would guarantee the Ukrainian nation the best development, and all citizens of Ukraine unmeasured liberty, justice, and wealth."[146]

Bandera's critique of the Soviet Union had not only an ideological and propagandistic but also a ritualistic character. He repeated the same or slightly modified

140 Stepan Bandera, "Ukraïns'ka Natsional'na Revolutsiia, a ne tilky protyrezhymnyi rezystans" in *Perspektyvy*, ed. Ivanyshyn, 151–52, 159–60. The article was first published in *Ukraïns'kyi samostiinyk* in 1950, No. 4, 5, 7, 8, 10–13, and 15.

141 Stepan Bandera, "Proty ideinoho rozbroiuvannia vyzvol'noï borot'by," in *Perspektyvy*, ed. Ivanyshyn, 244.

142 Ibid., 248–49.

143 Bandera, Ukraïns'ka Natsional'na Revolutsiia, 140.

144 Ibid., 130.

145 Ibid., 131.

146 Ibid., 143.

anti-Soviet phrases over and over again. In his propagandist crusades against the Soviet Union Bandera was certainly correct in condemning its totalitarian character, but the deeply antidemocratic nature of his critique did not allow him to articulate that the Soviet Union was a totalitarian state that arrested, deported, and killed millions of innocent people and continually violated human rights. Instead, like a Greek Catholic priest, he divided the universe into good and bad, or black and white. Communism, the Soviet Union, the Communist Party, Soviet ideology, materialism, and the Soviet people were on the dark side. The revolutionary Ukrainian nationalism, its followers, and other forms of radical right activism that could destroy the Soviet Union and "liberate" the people living in it were white. Democracy was black, rather than grey. On these grounds, Bandera's worldview was no less problematic and antidemocratic than that of the Soviet leaders. His orthodox nationalism did not allow him to level any democratic or constructive criticism at the Soviet Union.

Because of his nationalist and far-right worldview and his dislike for democracy, it is difficult to classify Bandera as a dissident, even if he was a vehement opponent of the Soviet regime ruling Ukraine. When the *Providnyk* criticized the suppression of the Hungarian Revolution of 1956, he wrote that the Soviet Union applied the "Moscow-Bolshevik strategy of pogroms," but he never admitted the Ukrainian involvement in the anti-Jewish pogroms in 1941.[147] Similarly, he never took a stand for democracy in the republics and satellite states of the Soviet Union. In accordance with Bandera's post-war writings, it seems reasonable to believe that he would have introduced some kind of far-right or neo-fascist autocracy in Ukraine, had there been such a possibility. Such a Ukrainian state would have been, in terms of democracy, no better than the Soviet Union and would have needed a real antitotalitarian opposition to turn it into a democracy.

Religion never ceased to play a crucial role in Bandera's political essays. He believed that the Greek Catholic Church was the foundation of Ukrainian nationalism. He frequently stressed that Christianity was a significant component of Ukrainian identity and that religion gave Ukrainians the power to resist the Soviet Union: "Faith tremendously strengthens the powers of the soul. A true and deep faith in God, the Redeemer, gives every man and the whole nation the possibility to take as much power as the soul can accommodate."[148] By the same token, he feared that communism would deprive Ukrainians of Christianity and thereby undo the "Ukrainian people."[149] The *Providnyk* equated the physical destruction of people in the Soviet Union with the politics of atheism and thus believed and argued that atheism could physically annihilate people. Human beings without religion and nationality were dead for Bandera, even if they were in the best physical and intellectual condition.[150]

Bandera's fascination with war, and his wish to fight another one, was enormous. Until his death he did not stop hoping that a third world war would break out soon

147 Stepan Bandera, "Nezminna stratehiia Moskvy," in *Perspektyvy*, ed. Ivanyshyn, 393. First published in *Shliakh peremohy*, 18 November 1956.

148 Stepan Bandera, "Z nevycherpnoho dzherela," in *Perspektyvy*, ed. Ivanyshyn, 413. First published in *Shliakh peremohy*, 7 January 1957.

149 Stepan Bandera, "Proty fal'shuvannia," in *Perspektyvy*, ed. Ivanyshyn, 323–24.

150 Stepan Bandera, "Khoch iaki velyki zhertvy—borot'ba konechna," in *Perspektyvy*, ed. Ivanyshyn, 357. First published in *Shliakh peremohy*, No. 2–3, 1956; Bandera, Z nevycherpnoho dzherela, 410.

and enable Ukrainians and other peoples to combat the Soviet Union and to establish national states. In an interview in 1950, Bandera said that people in Ukraine knew that a war would break out, because the Soviet Union was preparing itself for one and would start it soon.[151] In a letter in 1951 to the leadership of the OUN in Ukraine, he argued that the Western countries were preparing themselves for a war against the Soviet Union and needed two more years to produce enough weapons to begin one.[152] When Dwight Eisenhower visited Germany in 1951, Bandera prepared himself for a meeting with the NATO commander. He wanted to discuss the role of the OUN in a third world war and to ask him for financial help in preparing soldiers for this huge liberation event.[153] In 1958 Bandera still claimed that "The Third World War would shake up the whole structure of world powers even more than the last two wars."[154] The number of victims that such a war would create did not matter to the *Providnyk*, because nationalist independence was more important than human life:

> A war between the USSR and other states would certainly cause a great number of victims to the Ukrainian nation, and also probably great destruction of the country. Nevertheless, such a war would be welcomed not only by active fighters-revolutionaries, but also by the whole nation, if it would give some hope of destroying Bolshevik suppression and achieving national independence.[155]

Bandera was against the reduction of nuclear weapons and claimed that the "fear of nuclear war" in the West was groundless. He argued that the West did not understand the true nature of the Soviet Union and was too afraid of a nuclear war. According to him, the politics of appeasement toward the Soviet Union was a mistake. The West should understand that it was threatened by the Soviet Union's nuclear power and should have demonstrated its own power.[156]

Although Bandera and the ZCh OUN cooperated with MI6, the BND, and to a lesser extent with the CIA and other intelligence agencies, Bandera never ceased to depict Ukrainian nationalists as brave, autonomous, and self-sufficient fighters. Similarly, he argued that Ukrainians could achieve independence only on their own: "A nation that is suppressed by a foreign state can achieve its real and durable liberation only by its own struggle."[157] In addition, he propagated the message that Ukrainian nationalism was a romantic insurgent movement that had nothing in common with fascism, violence, antisemitism, and ethnic politics:

151 Stepan Bandera, "Pershe interviu providnyka OUN, Stepana Bandery z chuzhynnymy zhurnalistamy" in *Perspektyvy*, ed. Ivanyshyn, 637. In 1951 Stalin was indeed afraid of a war with Western Europe and ordered the East European satellites to build up their armies. Cf. Snyder, *Bloodlands*, 362.

152 "Lyst Stepana Bandery," spring 1951, HDA SBU f. 13, spr. 372, vol. 41, 389–423, in *Stepan Bandera*, ed. Serhiichuk, 2:568.

153 "Protokol doprosa zakhvachennogo parashiutista Matviieiko Mirona Vasil'evicha," 12 July 1951, HDA SBU f. 6, op. 37, spr. 56232, 16–26, in *Stepan Bandera*, ed. Serhiichuk, 3:42.

154 Bandera, *Perspektyvy ukraïns'koï*, 512.

155 Ibid., 515.

156 Cf. Stepan Bandera, "Na pivmeti," in *Perspektyvy*, ed. Ivanyshyn, 604–609. First published in *Shliakh peremohy*, 3 May 1959. For the Ukrainian nationalists and the role of nuclear weapons in the struggle against the Soviet Union, see Rossoliński-Liebe, Erinnerungslücke Holocaust, 409, 415–16.

157 Stepan Bandera, "Tretia svitova viina i vyzvol'na borot'ba," in *Perspektyvy*, ed. Ivanyshyn, 226–27. First published in *Surma*, No. 22–24, 1950.

> The terms "Ukrainian nationalist" and "nationalist movement" have a completely different meaning from similar terms in the West. The Ukrainian nationalist movement has nothing in common with Nazism, Fascism, or National Socialism. Ukrainian nationalism struggles against imperialism, totalitarianism, racism, and every kind of dictatorship or application of violence.
>
> The name "Ukrainian nationalist" is equal to "Ukrainian patriot," one who is ready to struggle for the liberty of his own nation and to sacrifice for his nation everything that he possesses, even life.[158]

The climate of the Cold War provided Bandera's thinking with enough legitimacy to keep his self-presentations from being challenged. The atrocities committed by the OUN-UPA, and Bandera's role in them were hardly known, and if some information on these subjects appeared, it was rebuffed as groundless anti-Ukrainian Soviet propaganda. In radio interviews Bandera claimed that the OUN could not have been involved in any kind of war crime because it was a "liberation movement" that "fought for freedom." In the 1950s, he stated that his organization still had contact with the OUN-UPA underground in Ukraine and that he frequently sent his best "fighters for independence" to Soviet Ukraine.[159] Such statements must have made a considerable impression on his audience who would have perceived him as a real, important, devoted, and admirable anticommunist freedom fighter. Although Bandera must have known that the OUN-B was not popular in eastern Ukraine, he argued that all Ukrainians supported him and his organization: "The bright masses of the Ukrainian nation provide this movement [OUN-UPA] with the fullest possible support and follow its leadership," he stated in a radio interview in 1954.[160]

Although Bandera's speeches and writings touched upon various political subjects such as the Soviet Union, a third world war, and nuclear weapons, they were all about "liberation," "freedom," and "independence." They combined the monotony of a Soviet official with the fanaticism of a far-right activist and the futurist, revolutionary enthusiasm of a fascist. The "liberation" of Ukraine was Bandera's life goal and he was ready to sacrifice the well-being of entire nations to achieve it. He ignored and concealed the atrocities committed by the OUN and UPA during and after the war because he believed that the Ukrainian nationalists had the right to kill thousands of civilians in order to achieve their aims. His writings suggest that he did not feel any empathy for people murdered in the name of "liberation" or "independence." He portrayed himself and the OUN and UPA as victims of Nazi Germany and the Soviet Union, because this was the only way to could continue the struggle for independence. Admitting the atrocities committed by the movement and its extensive fascistization would compromise him, other émigrés, and the very idea of "liberation" and "independence."

158 Stepan Bandera, "Interviu nimets'koï radiostatsiï v Kel'ni zi Stepanom Banderoiu," in *Perspektyvy*, ed. Ivanyshyn, 616. First published in *Shliakh peremohy*, No. 43–44, 1954.

159 Bandera, Interviu nimets'koï radiostatsiï, 612.

160 Ibid., 612.

Stashyns'kyi, Oberländer, Lippolz, and the Assassination of Bandera

The MGB, and from 1954 the KGB, tried several times to kidnap or assassinate Bandera.[161] Assassinations and more often the seizure of Ukrainians who engaged in the nationalist underground were common after the Second World War in countries such as Germany and Austria. For example, the OUN-B member Volodymyr Horbovyi, a Bandera's defense lawyer during the trials in Warsaw and Lviv in 1935–1936, was apprehended in Prague in 1946. He was interrogated first in Poland, then in the Soviet Union. During the interrogations, he was beaten and otherwise mistreated. Finally, he spent twenty-five years in the Gulag.[162] Similarly, the Ukrainian patriot Wilhelm von Habsburg, who had helped the OUN to establish contacts with the Allies after the war, was seized in Vienna on 26 August 1947. He was sentenced to twenty-five years but died of tuberculosis a year after he was seized, or more precisely as the result of catastrophic conditions in Soviet prisons and the withholding of medical help.[163]

According to OUN-B historiography, Iaroslav Moroz prepared the first attempt to assassinate Bandera in 1947. He intended to leave the impression that Bandera was killed by his Ukrainian émigré opponents.[164] Although the OUN-B historiographers did not mention it, Moroz was an OUN-B courier who arrived in Ukraine from Bavaria in 1946 and was turned into an MGB agent. When he went back to Munich in order to assassinate Bandera, the SB killed Moroz in June 1947.[165] According to OUN-B historiography, the next attempt was prepared by Volodymyr Stel'mashchuk, who was identified by OUN-B historiographers as a Polish agent of the MGB, with the position of captain in the AK. Although Stel'mashchuk had several helpers, the SB uncovered his identity and he failed to murder Bandera.[166] It might be that he arrived in Bavaria without the intention of assassinating Bandera, but in order to capture him or to infiltrate the ZCh OUN. Like Moroz, Stel'mashchuk was executed by the SB in May 1949.[167] In 1950 the OUN-B found that two agents from Prague were preparing to assassinate Bandera. They failed because he was warned and went into hiding. His family moved at that time to the DP camp in Mittenwald. Next, two agents from East Berlin came to Munich in 1952 but were arrested by Western intel-

161 The NKVD-KGB documents concerning Bandera's assassination and attempts to assassinate Bandera are still classified. In response to my e-mail request, the FSB archive in Moscow informed me by letter dated 18 July 2006 that it does not possess any documents concerning Bandera's assassination.

162 Stakhiv, *Kriz' tiurmy*, 217–18; Shumuk, *Za skhidnim obriiem*, 429–33; Horbovyi's interrogation in Poland 9 August 1947, see HDA SBU f. 6, spr. 70138, vol. 1, 179–84, in *Stepan Bandera*, ed. Serhiichuk,1:596–601.

163 Snyder, *The Red Prince*, 242–45.

164 Chaikovs'kyi, *Moskovs'ki vbyvtsi*, 8.

165 "Handbuch der Emigration. Teil IV: Ukrainer," 1 July 1953, BAK, B 206/1080, 46. For a KGB investigation record of Moroz, see "Protokol doprosa zaderzhannoho Moroz T. T.," 7 July 1946, HDA SBU f. 9, spr. 106, t. 3, 5–7, in *Stepan Bandera*, ed. Serhiichuk, 1:495–515.

166 Chaikovs'kyi, *Moskovs'ki vbyvtsi*, 8. Similarly to the OUN, the AK was persecuted by the MGB. Therefore Stel'mashchuk was almost certainly not an AK member when he worked for the MGB. Cf. "Handbuch der Emigration. Teil: Ukrainer," 1 July 1953, BAK, B 206/1080, 47.

167 "Handbuch der Emigration. Teil: Ukrainer," 1 July 1953, BAK, B 206/1080, 47. The document does not say who exactly executed Stel'mashchuk, but OUN-B historians claimed that "Stel'mashchuk disappeared from West Germany." Cf. Chaikovs'kyi, *Moskovs'ki vbyvtsi*, 9.

ligence services and released after two years.[168] In 1953 the agent Stepan Lippolz appeared in Munich and infiltrated the ZCh OUN.[169] In 1955 Bandera received a letter from Vienna, in which he was warned that the KGB was organizing an assassination attempt against him from East Berlin.[170]

The actual assassination took place on 15 October 1959. Iaroslava Bandera was sunbathing on the balcony of her apartment when, at about 1 p.m., a car drove into the courtyard of the building at Kreittmayrstrasse 7. Hearing its arrival, she looked down from the balcony and recognized the vehicle as her husband's. From his apartment on the first floor, Melach Gamse heard someone scream and fall to the ground in the stairwell. He opened the door of his apartment and discovered his neighbor from the third floor, whom he knew as Stefan Popel, lying between his apartment and the one opposite, with his head against the wall. Bandera's mouth and nose were bleeding slightly. He could not speak and was gasping for air. Magdalena Winklmann, who had also opened her door when she heard someone gasping in the stairwell, testified that Bandera's last utterance was "Ui." After a while, Iaroslava Bandera heard Melach and Chaja Gamse screaming to her from the stairwell and went down to see what happened. Melach Gamse called an ambulance which took Bandera to a hospital at about 1:20. The *Providnyk* died on the way.[171] At the hospital, a pistol was found on Bandera, in a shoulder-holster.[172]

Before the ambulance arrived, Iaroslava called the office of the ZCh OUN at Zeppelinstrasse 67. Iaroslav Bentsal', Kashuba, and Lenkavs'kyi drove to Bandera's house, where they learned from Natalia that her father had been taken to hospital. Kashuba and Lenkavs'kyi spoke to the Gamses, who explained what had happened. They remembered the Gamses as a "Jewish family."[173] Four months later, during the investigation of Bandera's death, Kashuba stressed that both families who found Bandera in the stairwell were Jewish.[174] During the investigation, Iaroslava Bandera also testified that both families were Jewish. According to her, the Gamses had lived in Vilna before the Second World War and had come to Munich in 1955 from Israel. They and the Bandera family were on good terms. Natalia gave private lessons to Mr. and Mrs. Gamse's son. The Weiner family came to Munich, according to Iaroslava, from Israel or Belgium.[175]

The fact that both families who found the dying Bandera were Jewish did not leave the community of Ukrainian nationalists in peace. The Ukrainian commission

168 Chaikovs'kyi, *Moskovs'ki vbyvtsi*, 9; "Vernehmungsniederschrift Stefan Popel," 7 February 1956, StM. Pol. Dir. München 9281, 86–87.

169 Chaikovs'kyi, *Moskovs'ki vbyvtsi*, 8–9; KGB's Operation "Karmen" Against Ukrainian Groups, 5–6, 07.06.1955, NARA, RG 263, E ZZ-18, Stepan Bandera Name File, 1v.

170 "Vernehmungsniederschrift Stefan Popel," 7 February 1956, StM. Pol. Dir. München 9281; KGB's Operation "Karmen" Against Ukrainian Groups: 3–4, 7 June 1955, NARA, RG 263, E ZZ-18, Stepan Bandera Name File, 1v. The Ukrainian commission of ZCh OUN activists established to investigate Bandera's death also mentions several attempts to assassinate Bandera: one in 1946 organized by Moroz, one in 1948 organized by Zabs'kyi, and one in 1951–1952 organized by Leguda and Lemian. Cf. Report of the investigating commission, ASBML, 3113, 2.

171 Investigation of Iaroslava Bandera, Melach and Chaja Gamse, Magdalena Winkelmann, 16 October 1959 BayHStA, Landeskriminalamt 272, 2, 4, 8, 9.

172 "Sicherstellung einer Schußwaffe," BayHStA, Landeskriminalamt 272, 1, 42.

173 Interrogation of Iaroslav Bentsal', 16 October 1959, BayHStA, Landeskriminalamt 272, 13.

174 Sprava: Ivan Kashuba pro ostanni momenty v zhyttiu Bandera, 4 January 1960; NARA, RG 263, E ZZ-18, Stepan Bandera Name File, 1v.

175 "Informatsiï Pani Slavy," 5 November 1959, ASBML, 3100, 3.

to investigate Bandera's death, established in 1959 by the ZCh OUN, interrogated a number of OUN and ABN émigrés. Reading the protocols of the investigations makes it clear that the Ukrainians who were questioned frequently connected Bandera's death to Jews, apparently because the stereotype of "Jewish Bolshevism" still persisted in this community. When interrogated, the ZCh OUN members, spoke very ill of Ukrainian émigrés who had a relationship with a Jew, and did not want such people to work for the OUN-B's newspaper.[176]

After Bandera's death, the ZCh OUN and Bandera's relatives suspected, or insisted—as did Stets'ko—that the *Providnyk* had been murdered, and they demanded a post-mortem. The autopsy was conducted on 16 October 1959 and the results were announced on 19 October. Bandera had died as the result of contamination with potassium cyanide. Dr. Laves, who conducted the post-mortem, attended by other doctors, determined the cause of death by a bitter almond oil smell from the brain, and by traces of cyanide in the stomach.[177]

The Bavarian police, the Ukrainian commission of five ZCh OUN activists investigating Bandera's death, and private investigators from the Yorkshire Detective Bureau, hired by the ZCh OUN, determined that either Bandera was poisoned when he ate something that contained cyanide, or that cyanide was forced into his mouth immediately before his death. Another theory was that he had swallowed the poison in order to end his life. Yet nobody could ascertain how the cyanide actually found its way into Bandera's body, and whether it did so by "enemy hand" as the ZCh OUN and other Ukrainian organizations suggested. Bavarian police officer Adrian Fuchs, who investigated the case, did not exclude this theory, but he found it more likely that Bandera had ended his life himself, which the Ukrainian émigrés found unacceptable. The Yorkshire Detective Bureau came to the conclusion that Bandera was murdered, but they could not establish exactly how.[178]

At about noon on the day in question, Bandera had driven from the building of the ZCh OUN organization on Zeppelinstrasse, with Eugenia Mack in his car, to a marketplace where he bought a box of grapes, a box of plums, and a small basket of tomatoes. He drove Mack back to the building and then drove without a bodyguard to his house for lunch. When Mack had suggested that he call a bodyguard, Bandera had said that he did not need one.[179] Bandera was usually picked up in the morning by a bodyguard and accompanied by one on his way home. On 15 October, it was Osyp Ferlewycz who came to Bandera's house by moped at 7:40 a.m. and accompanied Bandera in the car in which Bandera drove his son Andrii and a friend to school, and which he then drove to work. Bandera planned to eat lunch all that week in the

176 "Ziznannia plastuna. Do spravy Liudmyly Stapenko," ASBML, 3120, 4; "Ziznannia plastuna. Chleny provodu ZCh OUN rivnozh reahuvaly na tse," ASBML, 3120, 5; "Ziznannia druha Shuma," ASBML, 3142, 1.

177 Record of Bandera's dissection, 16 October 1959, BayHStA, Landeskriminalamt 272; Chaikovs'kyi, *Moskovs'ki vbyvtsi*, 26.

178 For the ZCh OUN five-man investigating commission and the private investigators from Bradford, see Chaikovs'kyi, *Moskovs'ki vbyvtsi*, 37, 40; Investigation into the Death of Stepan Bandera, 24 June 1960, ASBML, 3158, 1.

179 Interrogation of Eugenia Mack, 17 October 1959, BayHStA, Landeskriminalamt 272, 23.

canteen of the organization and therefore noted in the schedule for his security personnel that he did not need security at lunchtime.[180]

Between noon and 12:30 Bandera ate a piece of apple and half a plum in the market hall, but the police ruled out the possibility that the poison arrived in his stomach with these items, as other people ate the fruit without problems.[181] A day before his death, Bandera had lunch with two BND officials in the Ewige Lampe restaurant.[182] Because of the secret nature of such meetings, the police could not ascertain who were the people with whom Bandera had lunched, but they ruled out the possibility that poison was given to Bandera during this meal, because cyanide kills immediately. There was a possibility, however, that Bandera might have swallowed the cyanide in a slow-dissolving capsule, which would cause death after delay, but there was no evidence to support this idea. Investigating officer Fuchs considered that the most plausible theory was that Bandera took his own life on account of family problems, in particular, conflict with his wife concerning an alleged affair with the neighbor's au pair.[183]

The Soviet Union immediately connected Bandera's assassination with Theodor Oberländer, the federal minister for displaced persons, refugees, and war victims in Adenauer's government. On 21 October 1959, *Radians'ka Ukraïna*, and a day later, *Komsomol'skaia pravda* insinuated that Oberländer murdered Bandera because he knew too much about the minister's role in the pogroms in Lviv in 1941.[184] In May 1960, KGB agent Stefan Lippolz tried to convince the journalist Gösta von Uexküll and the Munich police that Bandera was killed by ZCh OUN member Dmytro Myskiv. Lippolz lived in Munich from 1953 until 1956 and owned the Stephansklause restaurant, which ZCh OUN activists regularly visited. He was a KGB agent and spied on Ukrainian émigrés in Munich. Von Uexküll lived in Hamburg and worked for *Die Welt,* in which he had a newspaper column that dealt with the Ukrainian nationalists.[185] Von Uexküll informed the police about Lippolz's suggestions but, as Myskiv was not in Munich at the time of Bandera's death, the police did not pay much attention to them.[186]

In 1956, the CIC had arrested Kostiantyn Kapustyns'kyi, a KGB agent, in Munich. After nine months of investigations, they handed him over to German authorities, who sentenced him to fifteen months imprisonment. After his release, Kapustyns'kyi

180 Interrogation of Roman Debryckyj and Osyp Ferelycz, 17 October 1959, BayHStA, Landeskriminalamt 272, 19, 22.

181 Document signed by Dr. Berg and Dr. Thoma, 2 December 1959, BayHStA, Landeskriminalamt 272.

182 Attachment A to Egma 48874, 14.07.1960, NARA, RG 263, E ZZ-18, 4, Stepan Bandera Name File, 2v; Interrogation of Iaroslav Bentsal', 16 October 1959, BayHStA, Landeskriminalamt 272, 13.

183 Attachment C to Egma 48874, 4 January 1960, NARA, RG 263, E ZZ-18, 2–3, Stepan Bandera Name File, 2v; From Chief of Base Munich to Chief SR, 2 May 1960, NARA, RG 263, E ZZ-18, Stepan Bandera Name File, 1v; Attachment A to Egma 48874, 14 July 1960, NARA, RG 263, E ZZ-18, 15–16, Stepan Bandera Name File, 2v.

184 I. Brechak, "Smert' na bonns'kii psarni," *Radians'ka Ukraïna*, 21 October 1959, 4; B. Aleksandrov, "Neschastnyi sluchai ili ubiistvo?" *Komsomol'skaia pravda*, 22 October 1959, 3.

185 Stephan Liebholz to Gösta von Uexküll, 12 May 1960, BayHStA, Landeskriminalamt 272, 4; Interrogation of Gösta von Uexküll, 9 November 1961, BAK, B 362/10142, 349; "Ermittlungsbericht," 19 October 1961, BAK, B 362/10142, 253–56.

186 On 12 October 1959 Myskiv went to Rome and returned to Munich on 16 October. Cf. "Anklageschrift gegen Bogdan Staschynskij," 24 March 1962, BAK, B 362/10137, 198b–99; Chaikovs'kyi, *Moskovs'ki vbyvtsi*, 53; "Strafsache gegen Bogdan Staschynskij, 9 StE 4/62," 19 October 1062, BAK, B 362/10139, 562b.

no longer wanted to work for the KGB, but was forcibly recruited again. According to OUN-B sources, Kapustyns'kyi defected to the West in May 1960 and informed the German police who had killed Bandera. Kapustyns'kyi's alleged disclosure in May 1960 did not make any impact on the investigation.[187] On 8 October 1960, the ZCh OUN received a letter from the Bavarian police, to the effect that it had closed the investigation because it had no indication as to who might have poisoned Bandera.[188]

Everything changed when Bohdan Stashyns'kyi entered the building of the police station at the Tempelhofer Damm in West Berlin on 12 August 1961. The handsome thirty-year-old man with an East European accent informed the police that he was a Soviet intelligence agent and that he wanted to talk to the Americans. After forty-five minutes he and his wife were picked up by an American intelligence officer. The next day, Stashyns'kyi was flown to Frankfurt am Main. He originally stayed in a private community of houses used only by the CIA or the American army and was interrogated several times by American intelligence officers. On 1 September, the Americans handed him over to the German authorities. Stashyns'kyi revealed first to the CIC and later to the BND and the West German police, how he had killed Lev Rebet, leader of the OUN-z, on 12 October 1957 in Munich, and then how he had killed Bandera in the same city almost exactly two years later. He also explained why he had decided to give himself up to the West Berlin police. His story seemed so incredible that he had to make a great effort to convince the investigating officers, and later the court, to believe him.[189]

Stashyns'kyi revealed to his investigators that he was born in 1931 in the village of Borshchovychi, about twenty kilometers from Lviv. In autumn 1948, he began to study pedagogy at Lviv University. He was arrested in 1950 for travelling as a student without a valid ticket. An officer proposed that he work for the Soviet authorities and implied that the MGB was aware of his family's connection to the nationalist underground. Concerned about the fate of his family, he agreed to cooperate.[190]

Stashyns'kyi's first task was to find the murderer of the Ukrainian communist writer Iaroslav Halan who had been killed with a hatchet in his apartment in Lviv on 24 October 1949. In order to smuggle Stashyns'kyi into the OUN-UPA underground, the MGB pretended to be searching for Stashyns'kyi in Borshchovychi and Lviv in late March and early April 1951. This convinced the local OUN-UPA activists that Stashyns'kyi was hiding from the MGB, and enabled him to join the underground. After about two months with the OUN-UPA, Stashyns'kyi reported to the KGB that he had discovered Halan's assassin and had left the underground. After three months the alleged assassin, Mykhailo Stakhur, was caught and executed.[191]

After this operation, Stashyns'kyi could not continue to study in Lviv. He worked for the MGB in the Lviv region until the summer of 1952, arresting OUN-UPA activists who were in hiding. He was then trained for two years in Kiev, to work as an MGB agent abroad. In addition to practical training, he learned German and at-

187 Chaikovs'kyi, *Moskovs'ki vbyvtsi*, 45–46, 594–95.
188 Chaikovs'kyi, *Moskovs'ki vbyvtsi*, 37.
189 BAK, B 362/10551, 107.
190 Interrogation of Bohdan Stashyns'kyi, 6 September 1961, BAK, B 362/10141, 34–37.
191 Interrogations of Bohdan Stashyns'kyi, 6 September 1961, 7 September 1961, BAK, B 362/10141, 38–39, 41–43. For Mykhailo Stakhur and Halan's assassination, see chapter 8 below, subsection "Halan—Soviet Martyr and Heroic Intellectual."

tended ideological courses to strengthen his Soviet patriotism. In July 1954, he moved to Poland and four months later to the German Democratic Republic (*Deutsche Demokratische Republik*, DDR) where the KGB provided him with papers under the name "Joseph Lehmann." Stashyns'kyi posed as an ethnic German repatriate.[192] In 1956 his supervisor "Sergej" explained to him that the leaders of the Ukrainian nationalist organizations in West Germany were harming the Soviet Union. Their anti-Soviet propaganda damaged the Soviet image and discouraged many Ukrainian émigrés from returning home. "Sergej" informed Bohdan that the first leader he was to assassinate would be Lev Rebet.[193]

The method used to kill Rebet was to fire a jet of poison gas at his face from a spray gun, in which a cyanide capsule had been crushed. The gun was small and flat, and it could easily be hidden from view, if wrapped in a newspaper, for example. The cyanide would narrow the blood vessels of the victim and cause death. After a while, they would enlarge and return to their normal size. The inhaled cyanide would evaporate after ten minutes, which would make it impossible to ascertain that the person died a violent death as the result of inhaling poison. The assassin would swallow a pill before the assassination and inhale an antidote shortly after it, in case he himself had inhaled some of the poison. To calm his nerves he would take a sedative half an hour before the assassination.[194]

After spying on Rebet and other Ukrainian émigrés in Munich for several weeks and preparing the assassination, Stashyns'kyi found a convenient moment on 12 October 1957. He fired the poison toward Rebet's face with the spray gun wrapped in a newspaper, at a distance of about forty centimeters (sixteen inches), in the stairwell of the house at Karlsplatz 8, where Rebet had his office. Rebet was found dead on the second floor of the stairwell at 10:40 a.m. Stashyns'kyi flew to East Berlin the next day and reported on 14 October that he had accomplished his task. The doctor who conducted the post-mortem examination of Rebet found no evidence of a violent death and concluded that he probably died of a heart attack.[195]

In May 1958, Stashyns'kyi was sent to Rotterdam, where the twentieth anniversary of the death of Ievhen Konovalets' was to be commemorated. He photographed the ceremony on 25 May at the graveside. The KGB had planned to disturb the ceremony, having planted a stink bomb, which did not explode. In the first instance, the KGB had even thought about detonating a real bomb, but changed their minds when they realized that the explosion would kill not only the Ukrainian nationalists but also a number of random bystanders (Figs. 25 and 26).[196]

192 Interrogation of Bohdan Stashyns'kyi, 7 August 1961, BAK , B 362/10141, 43; Interrogation of Bohdan Stashyns'kyi, 1 September 1961, BAK, B 362/10136, 4; Karl Anders, *Mord auf Befehl: Der Fall Stachynskij* (Tübingen: Fritz Schlichtenmayer, 1963), 17–19.

193 Interrogations of Bohdan Stashyns'kyi, 7 September 1961, BAK, B 362/10141, 55–56; "Voruntersuchung gegen Bogdan Staschynskij," 22 May 1962, BAK, B 362/10137, 274.

194 Interrogation of Bohdan Stashyns'kyi, 7 September 1961, BAK, B 362/10141, 59.The pill was later analyzed by West German technicians. It was not an antidote, as the KGB informed Stashyns'kyi, but a kind of tranquilizer. See "Svidchennia profesora doktora Miullera," in Chaikovs'kyi, *Moskovs'ki vbyvtsi*, 247–48.

195 "Anklageschrift gegen Bogdan Staschynskij," 24 March 1962, BAK, B 362/10137, 194v–95.

196 Interrogation of Bohdan Stashyns'kyi, 6 December 1961, BAK, B 362/10143, 408–12; Documents from 4 and 6 December 1961 concerning the bomb at the grave of Konovalets', BAK, B 362/10136, 116–17. Konovalets' was assassinated on 23 and not 25 May 1938.

Fig. 25. Bandera's speech at the twentieth anniversary of Ievhen Konovalets' assassination. Chaikovs'kyi, *Moskovs'ki vbyvtsi Bandery pered sudom*, 711.

Fig. 26. The twentieth anniversary of Ievhen Konovalets' assassination at Konovalets's grave in Rotterdam: Stepan Lenkavs'kyi, Stepan Bandera, Andrii Mel'nyk. Posivnych, *Stepan Bandera—zhyttia, prysviachene svobodi*, 78.

In January 1959 Stashyns'kyi was ordered to Munich to keep track of Stepan Bandera alias Stefan Popel. He flew to Moscow in April and was informed that his next task would be to assassinate Bandera. Because Stashyns'kyi claimed that there was always a bodyguard at Bandera's side, KGB technicians prepared a spray gun with two barrels, each holding a cyanide capsule that could be fired separately. One capsule was for the bodyguard, the other for Bandera. In May 1959, Stashyns'kyi flew from Berlin to Munich. On the second or third day after his arrival, he found a convenient moment when he saw Bandera alone in his garage. Nevertheless, he did not proceed to fire at Bandera, probably because he was at odds with himself, as he later confessed. He threw the weapon away and tried to open the door of Bandera's apartment building with special keys prepared by KGB technicians, but without success. Stashyns'kyi returned to Berlin then flew to Munich with new keys. He found the right one, but postponed Bandera's assassination. During the summer, he spent some days in Borshchovychi with his parents and came back to Munich on 14 October 1959 with a similar weapon. The next day, he went to Bandera's apartment building at Kreittmayrstrasse 7, and in the stairwell, in the vicinity of the front door, fired the poison from both barrels at Bandera's face. The second barrel had been reserved for Bandera's bodyguard, who was not accompanying the *Providnyk* that day. Stashyns'kyi stated that he was too nervous to control this step and instead of firing only one capsule of cyanide, he fired both. The quantity of cyanide that reached Bandera's mouth was so large that the *Providnyk* swallowed some drops. This enabled the experts to identify the poison during the post-mortem.[197]

For Bandera's assassination, KGB head Alexander Shelepin rewarded Stashyns'kyi, on 5 or 6 December 1959 in Moscow, with the Order of the Red Banner. He also gave him permission to marry Inge Pohl, whom he had met in a Berlin casino in April 1957. Shelepin's permission was necessary because KGB personnel did not usually marry people from outside the Soviet Union. After Bandera's assassination, the KGB kept Stashyns'kyi in Moscow in order to improve his skills and bring him into other operations.[198]

During the investigations in Germany, Stashyns'kyi disclosed that his relationship with Inge Pohl had changed him. He said that when he saw a newsreel in autumn 1959 he understood that he had killed two human beings, and not two enemies of the Soviet Union. The newsreel showed Bandera's funeral, the corpse in the coffin, and the mourning relatives and friends. Stashyns'kyi had obviously known that firing poison with the spray gun into his victims' faces would kill them, but he meant that the weapon was so subtle that he felt that he "acted only theoretically."[199]

At the beginning of her relationship with Stashyns'kyi, Inge noticed that he was a "convinced communist" and that he "praised everything that was related to Russia and communist ideology."[200] She stated that she did not share his fascination with the Soviet Union and that they often had disputes about this issue. She knew him as

197 "Anklageschrift gegen Bogdan Staschynskij," 24 March 1962, BAK, B 362/10137, 195v–97v.
198 Ibid., 198–98v.
199 Psychiatric opinion, Aktenzeichen BVU 7/61, 9 BJs 561/61, 5 March 1962, BAK, B 362/10137, 209, 214; Interrogation of Inge Pohl, 11 September 1961, BAK, B 362/10141, 64.
200 Interrogation of Inge Pohl, 11 September 1961, BAK, B 362/10141, 64.

Joseph Lehmann, an ethnic German repatriate who had to learn German because he grew up in Poland. Inge's vehement criticism of the Soviet Union pained him but they otherwise understood each other very well. They become engaged in April 1959. In autumn 1959, Stashyns'kyi informed Inge that he would be transferred to Poland for a year and could not take her with him. Then at Christmas, he unexpectedly visited her in East Berlin and unveiled his true identity and occupation. Inge was not only surprised but shocked; nevertheless, she went along with it. She followed Bohdan to Moscow and stayed there for eight weeks. He warned her to be polite and not to criticize the Soviet Union, because the KGB was not used to criticism. After Bandera's assassination, Bohdan informed Inge that she was the first foreign woman a KGB agent had been allowed to marry. In late March, Inge and Bohdan came to East Berlin, where they contracted a civil and church marriage on 23 April 1960. Soon afterwards, they were back in Moscow. At this time Inge noticed that her husband underwent a transformation. According to her, Bohdan understood, during his travels to Germany and his contact with her, that what he had been taught at university and by the KGB about the West and the Soviet Union was erroneous.[201]

Stashyns'kyi also realized that he had lost the trust of his KGB superiors after he married Inge. On one occasion, Bohdan and Inge discovered the wires of a bugging device in their apartment. This, and the delivery of opened letters from East Berlin, strengthened Stashyns'kyi's disappointment in the Soviet Union and in his occupation. Inge became pregnant in summer 1960. Even before Bohdan informed "Sergej", his superior already knew about it. The KGB suggested an abortion, which Inge and Bohdan refused. They wanted Inge and Bohdan to stay in Moscow for the next few years. At this time, Bohdan confided in Inge about his involvement in the assassinations in 1957 and 1959, although he was officially forbidden to do so. He also told Inge that if anything happened to him, she should reveal to American intelligence how Rebet and Bandera had died. In January 1961, Inge went to her family in East Berlin. During the following weeks, the KGB put pressure on Inge to return to Moscow but she refused and tried to convince the KGB to allow Bohdan to come to Berlin. Finally, Inge was allowed to give birth in East Berlin but Bohdan was not permitted to join her.[202]

Bohdan's and Inge's son Peter was born a month prematurely on 31 March 1961. When Inge returned home with Peter, she tried to contact American intelligence with the help of a friend, but that did not work. She then decided to join Bohdan in Moscow, which pleased the KGB. With the help of KGB agents, Inge packed her belongings to fly to Moscow in early August, but on 6 August Peter became ill, and he died of pneumonia two days later in the hospital.[203]

After Peter's death, the KGB allowed Bohdan to visit his wife in Berlin. Before takeoff from Moscow, Bohdan's escort implied that either Inge or a Western intelligence agent had killed Peter in order to bring Bohdan to Berlin. This remark in-

201 Ibid., 68–70; Psychiatric opinion, Aktenzeichen BVU 7/61, 9 BJs 561/61, 05.03.1962, BAK, B 362/10137, 220.

202 Interrogation of Inge Pohl, 11 September 1961, BAK, B 362/10141, 68–76.

203 In the hospital in Berlin, Bohdan learned that the baby did not die of pneumonia but choked on food he had vomited. A babysitter was responsible for this neglect. Cf. "Voruntersuchung gegen Bogdan Staschinskij," 24 January 1962, BAK, B 362/10143, 558; Interrogation of Inge Pohl, 11 September 1961, BAK, B 362/10141, 76–78.

furiated him. The first night in Berlin, 10–11 August 1961, Bohdan spent with Inge in the KGB complex in Berlin-Karlshorst. Inge and Bohdan planned to escape to West Berlin after the funeral, which was arranged for 13 August. On 15 or 16 August they were due to fly to Moscow. They knew that the escape would be difficult because they were permanently under observation. They used a convenient moment, one day prior to the funeral. After losing their "escort" they went from Dallgow, where they visited Inge's father, to Falkensee. There they took a taxi to the Friedrichstrasse station in East Berlin, where they went on by another taxi to the Schönhauser Allee station and from there by commuter train to West Berlin, where they reached the police station in Tempelhofer Damm.[204]

Stashyns'kyi's escape from East Berlin put the KGB and the Communist Party of the Soviet Union in a very uncomfortable position. On 13 October 1961, the press office of the Council of Ministers of the DDR organized an international press conference in East Berlin, at which—with the help of Stefan Lippolz—it explained who, they claimed, had killed Stepan Bandera, how, and why. About 130 journalists attended the conference, after which Lippolz gave an interview to Moscow radio.[205] The conference was opened by Kurt Blecha, chairman of the Council of Ministers of the DDR, who informed the audience that "Bonn intelligence [BND] is the immediate successor of Nazi intelligence." He then introduced Lippolz as a person who "was pursued by Bonn intelligence and threatened with death," and who had saved himself by escaping to East Germany.[206] When Blecha had finished, Gerhard Kehl, a lieutenant colonel of the Ministry for State Security (*Ministerium für Staatssicherheit*, MfS), the East German intelligence service known as the Stasi, stated that his colleague Blecha was right when he called Bonn intelligence the immediate successor of Nazi intelligence. He spoke about the OUN and its leader, "the well-known bandit and mass-murderer Bandera." Kehl stated that Bandera was not killed "as a consequence of his crimes but in order to prevent the crimes of the bloody General Gehlen and his contemporary intelligence becoming known."[207]

Only after these introductory speeches did Lippolz reveal his biography to the audience. He said that he was born in Aleksandrowka in Volhynia, had worked for the Abwehr during the Second World War, was captured by the Red Army in 1945, and remained in Soviet captivity until 1952. In 1953 he moved to Munich, where he took over the Stephansklause restaurant, which became the favorite eating place of Ukrainian émigrés. He said that ZCh OUN member Iaroslav Sulima, who worked for the BND, introduced him in 1955 to BND agent Peter Wander, alias Dr. Weber, who persuaded him to work for the BND. His job was to infiltrate the ZCh OUN. In 1957 Dr. Weber gave him a white powder, with which he was to poison Bandera. Lippolz responded that he could not do it and proposed the ZCh OUN member Myskiv for the task, in whom Bandera had complete trust. Afraid of the BND, Lippolz left Munich for Austria, where he heard that Bandera had been murdered. When he returned to Munich, Myskiv informed him that the BND had forced him to poison

204 Interrogation of Inge Pohl, 11 September 1961, BAK, B 362/10141, 78–80. Inge described their escape slightly differently during the trial. Cf. Chaikovs'kyi, *Moskovs'ki vbyvtsi*, 238–39.
205 "Bericht, GVS 160-7/71," BStU, AK 2832/76, vol. 1l, 122–24.
206 "Stenografische Niederschrift," 2, BStU, MfS ZAIG 10591, vol. 1.
207 "Stenografische Niederschrift," 3–4, BStU, MfS ZAIG 10591.

Bandera. Afterwards, Lippolz left Germany again but corresponded with Myskiv who, fearing that the BND would kill him, also wanted to leave West Germany. Lippolz hid from the BND in Norway and several other European countries, until he finally found safety in the DDR. Then he found out that Myskiv was dead.[208] This story might have sounded convincing to the journalists at the conference but it would not have impressed anybody, had Lippolz mentioned that Myskiv had not been in Munich between 12 and 16 October 1959, and that he was not killed, but died of natural causes on the night of 26–27 March 1960 after drinking home-made vodka and having sex in his Munich apartment with Maria Konczak, twenty-eight years younger than he was, an employee of Bandera's neo-fascist newspaper *Shliakh peremokhy*.[209]

On 17 November 1961, at President Kennedy's request, West German Chancellor Adenauer informed the public how Stashyns'kyi had escaped in August from East to West Berlin and had revealed that he had killed Rebet and Bandera.[210] The next day, Lippolz told the press that he had never heard of Stashyns'kyi and thought that he must be a "paid element" whose job was to persuade the public that the BND had nothing to do with Bandera's assassination.[211]

The controversy between the Federal Republic of Germany (*Bundesrepublik Deutschland*, BRD) and the DDR concerning Bandera's murder was, from the very beginning, embedded in the Soviet campaign against Theodor Oberländer, minister for displaced persons, refugees, and war victims in the federal government. Oberländer had studied agricultural science in the 1920s and had worked in this position at several German universities and institutes. He joined the NSDAP in 1933 and combined his scientific work with party politics. In 1941 he was one of the German officers of the Ukrainian Nachtigall battalion. The DDR, and several other satellite states and republics of the Soviet Union, including Russia and Ukraine, used the fact that Oberländer was an officer in the Nachtigall battalion to conduct a propaganda campaign against him in order to discredit the Adenauer government.[212]

The campaign against Oberländer began in spring 1959 and was probably inspired by Erich Koch who stated during a trial in Warsaw in March 1959, "I completely do not understand why I stand here, fourteen years after the war, in front of this court, when my former head of the regional administration in the NSDAP administration of East Prussia, SA-Hauptsturmführer Theodor Oberländer, is today a minister in Bonn!"[213]

During the following months, Oberländer became the object of hate and condemnation and the subject of communist "antifascist" rituals performed by several politicians from Soviet republics and satellite states. In July 1959, Władysław Gomułka, leader of the Polish United Workers' Party (*Polska Zjednoczona Partia Robotnicza*,

208 BStU, AK 13460/86, vol. 3, 238–52.

209 "Anklageschrift gegen Bogdan Staschynskij," 24 March 1962, BAK, B 362/10137, 198v–89; Chaikovs'kyi, *Moskovs'ki vbyvtsi*, 53; "Strafsache gegen Bogdan Staschynskij, 9 StE 4/62," 19 October 1962, BAK, B 362/10139, 562v; Document of the Munich Police considering Lippolz's letters to Gösta von Uexküll, 14 June 1960, Munich, BayHStA, Landeskriminalamt 272. For Myskiv, see Opinion of Kriminal Oberamtmann Schmitt, 14 June 1960 Munich, BayHStA, Landeskriminalamt 272.

210 Chaikovs'kyi, *Moskovs'ki vbyvtsi*, 55–56; "Bart ab," *Der Spiegel*, 29 November 1961, 32–34.

211 BStU, MfS ZAIG 9677, vol. 1; BStU, MfS HA IX/11, AK 2832/76, vol. 1.

212 For Nachtigall battalion, see page 190 above, et seq.

213 Wachs, *Der Fall*, 206.

PZPR), initiated the campaign against the minister and the Nachtigall battalion, stating that Oberländer was responsible for the murder of the Polish professors in Lviv during the night of 3–4 July 1941.[214] Soviet propaganda repeated this statement many times. During the following months, the Polish newspaper *Trybuna Ludu*, the Hungarian *Népszabadság,* and other newspapers connected the battalion and Oberländer with further massacres, such as the shooting of 12,000 Jews in Kam"ianets'-Podil's'kyi, and 34,000 Jews in Babi Yar, in which the battalion was not involved. The battalion's actual war crimes, such as the shooting of Jews in two villages on the way to Vinnytsia, were not mentioned during the campaign.[215]

On 31 July 1959, the Society of People Persecuted by the Nazi Regime (*Vereinigung der Verfolgten des Naziregimes*, VNN) submitted a charge against Oberländer and the battalion of murdering "310,000 Poles, Jews, and communists in the time between 30 June 1941 and 20 November 1943," to the Federal State Administration of Justice Department in Ludwigsburg, West Germany. The VNN was a political organization founded in 1947 and based in West Germany. It frequently published lists of politicians who had worked with the National Socialists or were considered to have been involved in compromising activities. The Nachtigall battalion was described in the charge as a unit that had committed several war crimes, and Oberländer, together with other German officers of the battalion, as a person who was responsible for these crimes.[216] The West German authorities began an investigation of this case and ended it in 1960. The investigators did not find any evidence that Oberländer or any other officers had issued an order to kill Jews, but they did not exclude the possibility that Ukrainian soldiers from the battalion had participated in the pogrom and committed war crimes.[217] In reaction to these accusations Oberländer claimed at a conference on 30 September 1959 in Bonn that, although he was in Lviv between 1 and 7 July 1941 and was always moving about, he did not see any violence or excesses at all—which was obviously a lie.[218]

The investigation in the BRD led to developments in the DDR. Albert Norden, professor at the Humboldt University and prominent member of the Central Committee of the Socialist Unity Party of Germany (*Sozialistische Einheitspartei Deutschlands*, SED), became Oberländer's main opponent. At a conference in East Berlin on 22 October 1959, Norden presented some documents to the journalists and claimed that a trial against Oberländer was necessary because Oberländer was a "Nazi putschist against the Weimar Republic, one of the people most responsible for the preparation of the Second World War, and the hangman of Slavic intelligentsia and Jews."[219] Oberländer's show trial *in absentia* in the DDR began on 20 April 1960, the seventy-first anniversary of Adolf Hitler's birth, and ended on 29 April. The subject of Bandera was an important element of the DDR trial against the BRD minister. Bandera was referred to as the leader of the Ukrainian nationalists, and Oberländer

214 For the killing of Polish professors, see page 214 above.

215 For propaganda, see Wachs, *Der Fall*, 207–208. For the annihilation of the Jewish population by Nachtigall, cf. TsDAVOV f. 3833, op. 1, spr. 57, 17; Bruder, *"Den Ukrainischen Staat*, 150.

216 LN-W: Gerichte Rep. 350, vol. 1, 6–8.

217 LN-W: Gerichte Rep. 350, vol. 5, 42; LN-W: Gerichte Rep. 350, vol. 14, 181–82. See also chapter 4 above. For VNN, see Wachs, *Der Fall*, 212–13.

218 Wachs, *Der Fall*, 219.

219 Ibid., 226.

as the person who supported the terrorist and murderous activities of Bandera's people. Oberländer was accused of recruiting young Ukrainians for the Nachtigall battalion and ordering them to annihilate hundreds of thousands of innocent people.[220]

Because Bandera died in the middle of the campaign against Oberländer, the Eastern bloc politicians used his death to support the theory that Oberländer, in cooperation with Gehlen, had killed the leader of the Ukrainian nationalists because he could have revealed more incriminating facts about the minister. Immediately after Bandera's assassination, cartoons depicting Bandera, Gehlen, and Oberländer appeared in the newspapers. The most popular cartoon showed Oberländer standing and weeping, close to a coffin containing Bandera's corpse. The caption said: "He was such a good man. It is a great pity that he knew too much about me."[221]

The lavish measures of the propaganda apparatus of the various republics and satellite states of the Soviet Union did not influence the investigation and trial of Stashyns'kyi. The trial for the murder of Rebet and Bandera took place in the Federal Court of Justice (*Bundesgerichtshof*) in Karlsruhe from 8 to 15 October 1962. The verdict was announced on 19 October. During the trial, Stashyns'kyi explained in detail how he came to work for the KGB, how he killed Rebet and Bandera, how he met Inge Pohl, and how his attitude toward the KGB and his criminal deeds had changed. The psychologist Joachim Rauch certified that Stashyns'kyi was accountable for his actions and explained the change in Stashyns'kyi's attitude. The defendant's version of the assassination was confirmed by experts. The judges believed Stashyns'kyi and his narrative, parts of which the defendant might have polished slightly, in order not to incriminate himself even more.[222]

Acting on behalf of Daria Rebet, Dr. Mira appealed for a mild sentence for Stashyns'kyi. He stressed that Mrs. Rebet did not hold a grudge against Stashyns'kyi and that she considered that the Central Committee of the Communist Party of the Soviet Union (*Kommunisticheskaia Partiia Sovetskogo Soiuza*, KPSS) was responsible for the murder of Lev Rebet.[223] Daria Rebet spoke in a similar tone. She stressed that she could not blame Stashyns'kyi but only the "Soviet system."[224] Natalia Bandera, on behalf of her absent mother, began her speech with the claim that "almost the whole family of my deceased father and my mother died at the hands of enemies." She talked about her own suffering and the suffering of her family and stressed that her father "was a deeply religious man" who "died for God and an independent, free Ukraine—for the freedom of the whole world."[225] Before Iaroslava Bandera's lawyer began his speech, the American politician Charles J. Kersten, whom the Bandera family had asked to speak, encouraged the judge to call the Soviet government to account. He stressed that this was the wish of Iaroslava Bandera.[226] Like Natalia

220 Ibid., 267, 276.

221 *Radians'ka Ukraïna* 21 October 1959, 4; *Komsomol'skaia pravda* 22 October 1959, 3. The same caricature was printed in several other newspapers, for example in *Neues Deutschland* on 19 October 1959. Cf. Wachs, *Der Fall*, 223.

222 The minutes of the trial are in Chaikovs'kyi, *Moskovs'ki vbyvtsi*, 120–271.

223 "Promova d-ra Mira," in Chaikovs'kyi, *Moskovs'ki vbyvtsi*, 297–303.

224 "Slovo Pani Dariï Rebet," in Chaikovs'kyi, *Moskovs'ki vbyvtsi*, 303–304.

225 "Slovo Natalky Bandery," in Chaikovs'kyi, *Moskovs'ki vbyvtsi*, 305–307.

226 "Promova Charl'za Dzh. Kerstena," in Chaikovs'kyi, *Moskovs'ki vbyvtsi*, 311.

Bandera, Dr. Iaroslav Padokh, the attorney for Iaroslava Bandera, appealed to God and claimed that "Bandera's and Rebet's death and this unbelievable trial, conducted in front of the highest court of Germany ... helps not only the Ukrainian people but all freedom-loving nations to achieve victory in their hard struggle against violence."[227]

Stashyns'kyi's lawyer, Dr. Helmut Seydel, argued that "the defendant is not the doer of the crime but only the helper of the perpetrator" and that "he was only an instrument of the KGB."[228] The judge, Heinrich Jagusch, agreed with this explanation. He stated that "the defendant was in both cases [Rebet's and Bandera's] not the murderer, although he himself conducted the acts of murder, but only an instrument, a helper." That Stashyns'kyi admitted his guilt and claimed to regret it was taken into consideration, and he was sentenced to only eight years imprisonment, in which the time already spent in prison was included.[229]

The tribunal's decision implied that the real murderer was not Stashyns'kyi but his superiors. The judge mentioned Shelepin and Khrushchev but did not blame them personally. The tribunal gave Stashyns'kyi a mild sentence because it considered him a mere cog in the greater totalitarian Soviet system. The trial therefore appeared to be a political one; the Soviet leaders, not Stashyns'kyi, became its main defendants even if they were not in the court. Jagusch—in the spirit of the Cold War—compared the Soviet Union to Nazi Germany and Stashyns'kyi to Adolf Eichmann, whose trial in Jerusalem was taking place almost simultaneously.[230] Jagusch's rhetoric and the court's sentence suggest that the impact of the Cold War on Stashyns'kyi's trial was strong. In 1963 Inge Pohl and Stashyns'kyi's defending lawyer Seydel pleaded for a reduction of the sentence or an early discharge.[231] Stashyns'kyi was released on 31 December 1966, after serving two-thirds of his sentence.[232] Bohdan and Inge's relationship did not survive the turbulence; she divorced him.[233]

Shelepin, head of the KGB, together with KGB personnel in Moscow, Kiev, and East Berlin, was deeply involved in the assassinations of Rebet and Bandera. Whether Khrushchev personally issued the order to assassinate Bandera cannot be proved, as long as the documents concerning the case remain classified. The same applies to several details concerning Stashyns'kyi's defection and his fate after the trial. Yet the fact is that the KGB received the orders from the Central Committee of the KPSS. Khrushchev, the first secretary of the KPSS at the time of Rebet's and Bandera's deaths, did not hide his attitude toward anti-Soviet émigrés: "There are times when security services should physically eliminate the leaders of the counter-revolution in exile," he remarked to Fidel Castro in May 1963.[234]

227 "Promova d-ra Iaroslava Padokha," in Chaikovs'kyi, *Moskovs'ki vbyvtsi*, 316.

228 "Promova oborontsia Stashyns'koho advokata d-ra Zaidelia," in Chaikovs'kyi, *Moskovs'ki vbyvtsi*, 323.

229 "Usne obgruntovannia vyroku," Chaikovs'kyi, *Moskovs'ki vbyvtsi*, 338, 340.

230 Ibid., 329, 334, 339.

231 Letter from Dr. Helmuth Seydel to Generalbundesanwalt, 14 October 1964, BAK, B 362/10557, 5; Letter from Inge Pohl, 29 November 1964, BAK, B 362/10557, 65–66.

232 Letter from Dr. Recken to Peter Stähle, 6 February 1969, BAK, B 362/10140, 979.

233 BAK, B 362/10557, 5; BAK, B 362/10557, 65–66.

234 Quoted in William Taubman, *Khrushchev: The Man and His Era* (London: Free Press, 2005), 598. See also Aleksandr Fursenko and Timothy Naftali, *'One Hell of a Gamble': Khrushchev, Castro, Kennedy and the Cuban Missile Crisis 1958–1964* (London: John Murray, 1998), 334, 401.

The ZCh OUN was disappointed with the lenient sentence imposed on Stashyns'kyi for killing their *Providnyk.* Stets'ko and other Ukrainian nationalist émigrés used the trial to support their political campaign against the Soviet Union.[235] During and after the Stashyns'kyi trial in Karlsruhe, the ZCh OUN's conduct, however, did not differ greatly from that of the Central Committee of the KPSS. After Stashyns'kyi's trial, the ZCh OUN organized a press conference on 10 October 1962, in order to contradict some aspects of Stashyns'kyi's testimony. In particular they were concerned about the evidence relating to the OUN-UPA's murder of Poles during the Second World War, which the defendant witnessed in his youth. The ZCh OUN leaders denied it and claimed that it was only "Stashyns'kyi's false depiction of the struggle of the Ukrainian underground."[236]

235 For the ideological dimension of Bandera's assassination, see chapter 9.
236 Chaikovs'kyi, *Moskovs'ki vbyvtsi*, 341.

Conclusion

The end of the Second World War made it necessary for the Ukrainian nationalists to falsify their own past in order to stay in Western countries and promote the struggle for the independence of Ukraine. The leadership of the OUN and UPA had already begun the process of whitewashing its past in late 1943 when it ordered the collection and destruction of documents that connected the leadership to the pogroms and other forms of ethnic violence. After the war the OUN émigrés began to deny the involvement of the OUN and UPA in the Holocaust, collaboration with the Nazis, the ethnic cleansing of the Poles, the fascistization of the movement, the plans to establish a fascist collaborationist state, and a number of other matters that cast a poor light on the movement. Instead they presented the OUN and UPA as an idealistic and heroic anti-German and anti-Soviet resistance movement. The Western intelligence services collaborated with OUN émigrés despite their knowledge about the crimes committed by their movement. The competition for the resources from the intelligence services and the ideological dissimilarities between the OUN émigrés caused another split in the organization.

The Second World War did not change Bandera's far-right views, but the *Providnyk* adapted them to the realities of the Cold War in order to collaborate with the British and American intelligence services. He attempted to reintroduce a leader principle into the organization, which would make him once again the sole leader of the entire movement. Like other OUN members Bandera never condemned or even admitted the atrocities committed by the OUN and UPA during the Second World War. In his writings he did not mention Jews and Poles as the "enemies of the Ukrainian nation," because they no longer lived in Ukraine in substantial numbers. Bandera was skeptical of democracy, defended Franco's policies, and believed that only a far-right militaristic organization could liberate Ukraine and rule it in an appropriate way. Despite Franco's invitations Bandera decided to stay in Munich where he established a center, at which he was protected by former Nazis such as Gerhard von Mende and American intelligence. He visited Ukrainian communities in several Western countries, but not the United States, whose consulate in Munich did not recommend a visa until it was too late for him to visit. His family life seems to have been harmonious although there is evidence to suggest that he mistreated his wife. He was obsessed with women and apparently tried to rape one victim. Soviet intelligence made several attempts to kidnap or assassinate him over the years, thereby affecting his life and also the well-being of his family. Bandera's assassination came about during the campaign against Theodor Oberländer and caused much international speculation.

Chapter 8

BANDERA AND SOVIET PROPAGANDA

The examination of the impact of Soviet propaganda on the Bandera cult is a significant feature of this study. Although Soviet propaganda was intended to undo the Bandera cult and myth, it significantly strengthened them in the long term. The Soviet propaganda apparatus reacted to Bandera and the OUN-B for the first time in July 1941, shortly after the beginning of Operation Barbarossa and the "Ukrainian National Revolution." Soviet intelligence had already infiltrated the OUN in the early 1930s. In 1940, the agent "Ukrainets" established himself within the OUN-B, and provided the Soviet intelligence with detailed information about the OUN, its split into two factions, and its leading members.[1]

In the first issue of the military newspaper *Za radians'ku Ukraïnu* on 31 July 1941 Oleksandr Korniichuk published the article: "Death to the Traitors of Ukraine!" "Hitler asked the traitors of the Ukrainian people—Petliurites, OUN members, Hetmanites, the yellow and blue dirt—for help," Korniichuk wrote. The "yellow and blue" was a reference to the colors of the national flag, used by the OUN-B, other Ukrainian nationalist and fascist organizations, and before them the Ukrainian national movement, the UNR, and the Ukrainian national democrats. Bandera was the only person, apart from Hitler and Stalin, whom Korniichuk mentioned by name: "For the lies, provocations, and murder of our freedom-loving people, we will respond to the yellow-and-blue band and its leader Stepan Bandera with only one word—death!" (Fig. 27).[2]

After the Soviet army withdrew from western Ukraine in autumn 1941, the "yellow-and-blue" became only a marginal target of Soviet propaganda. Until the Red Army came back to Ukraine in late 1943 Soviet Ukrainian newspapers mentioned the Ukrainian nationalists only sporadically and portrayed them as "traitors" or "Nazi henchmen." Bandera and his adherents (*bandery* or *banderivtsi*) were introduced next to other groups of Ukrainian nationalists, such as *skoropads'ki* or *mel'nyky*, as Hitler's agents.[3]

In 1942 the twenty-fifth anniversary of the Ukrainian SSR was celebrated in Moscow. The Communist Party of Ukraine brought out a leaflet devoted to Stalin and one to Nikita Khrushchev, the first secretary of the KPU. Stalin was addressed as the Leader (*Vozhd'*) or "Our Dear Josef Vissarionovich! [*Dorohyi nash, ridnyi Iosyf Visarionovych!*]" or "dear father comrade Stalin [*bat'ko ridnyi tovarysh Stalin*]." The emotional admiration of Stalin resembled to some extent the admiration of

1 "Spetsial'noe soobshchenie," HDA SBU, f. 16, op. 33, spr. 36, 14–33, in *Stepan Bandera*, ed. Serhiichuk, 1:58–75.

2 Oleksandr Korniichuk, "Smert' zradnykam Ukraïny!" *Za radians'ku Ukraïnu*, 31 July 1941. This article was already noticed by the OUN in August 1941. Cf. TsDAVOV f. 3833, op. 1, spr. 42, 19.

3 See for example "Zvernennia do naselennia okupovanykh raioniv Ukraïny," *Radians'ka Ukraïna*, 5 June 1943, 1–2.

Bandera during the "Ukrainian National Revolution." Bandera, however, was not usually depicted as the father of Ukrainians but as the *Providnyk* or *Vozhd'*. Because the word *Vozhd'* means leader in both Russian and Ukrainian, Bandera and Stalin shared the same title. In this sense, the concept of Stalin as the leader of Soviet Ukraine competed with the concept of Bandera as the leader of a Ukrainian authoritarian state of a fascist type.[4]

Fig. 27. Inscription under the picture "OUN fascist motorization."
Za radiansku Ukraïnu, 5 August 1941.

At the sixth session of the Ukrainian Supreme Soviet in Kiev on 1 March 1944, Nikita Khrushchev delivered a speech entitled "Liberation of the Ukrainian territory from German invaders and the current tasks concerning the rebuilding of the national economy in Soviet Ukraine."[5] Khrushchev extolled Stalin, the Soviet Union, Soviet partisans, and the Red Army, which was "destroying the fascist invaders and cleansing the Soviet territory from them."[6] He stressed that the Soviet people had suffered considerably during the previous three years, and he mentioned several atrocities that Nazi Germany had committed in Ukraine, such as the massacres at

4 For the leaflet, see RGASPI f. 17, op. 125, del. 145, 13. The leaflet for Khrushchev is on folio 14.

5 Nikita Khrushchev, *Osvobozhdenie ukrainskikh zemel' ot nemetskikh zakhvatchikov i ocherednye zadachi vosstanovleniia narodnogo khoziaistva Sovetskoi Ukrainy* (Moscow: Pravda, 1944).

6 Khrushchev, *Osvobozhdenie ukrainskikh zemel'*, 6.

Babi Yar, Dnipropetrovs'k, and Kharkiv. Khrushchev did not mention that the majority of the victims in these massacres were Jews, in order to evoke the impression that the main victims of Nazi terror were the Soviet people in general.[7] This kind of approach to the Second World War became standard in the Soviet Union and continued until its very end. It was a part of Soviet nationalism that was intended to strengthen Soviet identity. It negated the Holocaust as genocide against Jews and claimed that Soviet citizens were the group that suffered most.[8] Khrushchev also appealed to Ukrainian patriotism. He pointed out that "the Ukrainian people are faithful to the great Union of Soviet Socialist Republics."[9] Furthermore, he stressed that the Ukrainian people would try to include in the Ukrainian Soviet state as many of the Ukrainian territories as possible and would oppose the plans of the Polish government in London, "which does not represent the interests of the Polish people but of lords [*pany*] and wants not only to include western Ukraine ... but dreams also about a great Polish state from the Dnieper to the Black Sea."[10]

The first secretary of the Communist Party of Ukraine devoted one section of his speech to the "Ukrainian-German nationalists—Hitler's henchmen, the worst enemies of the Ukrainian people."[11] He said that the "Ukrainian-German nationalists did everything ... to enable Germans to enslave our Ukrainian people," and thus were traitors.[12] Khrushchev did not point to Bandera but mentioned "Melnykites, Banderites, Bulbites."[13] He emphasized that the "Ukrainian-German nationalists" went underground and developed anti-German slogans after they realized that nobody in Ukraine supported them. He also stressed that the nationalists "were fighting only against the Soviet partisans and the Red Army and terrorized the population."[14] Toward the end of the speech, Khrushchev stated that "we should contend with them as we did with the German intruders ... as enemies of our homeland."[15]

German-Ukrainian Nationalists

After the Germans left the western Ukrainian territories in early summer 1944, Soviet propaganda frequently labeled the OUN and UPA as the "Ukrainian-German nationalists" or "German-Ukrainian nationalists." It thereby suggested that the Ukrainian nationalist underground was an integral part of the Nazi empire, which was to be defeated like its masters who had meanwhile withdrawn from Ukraine but had left their accomplices. This propaganda campaign was intended to help defeat

7 Ibid., 20–21.

8 On the problem of dealing with the Holocaust in the Soviet Union, see Weiner, *Making Sense of War*, 209–16, Johan Dietsch, *Making Sense of Suffering: Holocaust and Holodomor in Ukrainian Historical Culture* (Lund: Lund University, 2006), 101.

9 Khrushchev, *Osvobozhdenie ukrainskikh zemel'*, 6.

10 Ibid., 10.

11 This is also the title of the second part of the speech. Cf. Khrushchev, *Osvobozhdenie ukrainskikh zemel'*, 15.

12 Ibid., 15.

13 Ibid., 16. In a script that is based on Khrushchev's speech or is perhaps even transcript of the speech, the name Bandera and the term Banderites frequently appear dissimilarly from the published version of the speech. Cf. RGASPI f. 17, op. 125, del. 336, 2–31.

14 Khrushchev, *Osvobozhdenie ukrainskikh zemel'*, 16.

15 Ibid., 16. Khrushchev informed Stalin about the "Ukrainian-German nationalists" in a letter of 15 November 1944. Cf. "Tovarishchu Stalinu, I. V.," TsDAHO f. 1, op. 23, spr. 1060, 1–5.

the nationalist underground and was therefore interwoven with the terror campaign against the OUN-UPA and against members of the western Ukrainian population who either supported the nationalist underground or were accused of doing so. A very popular and drastic method used in this campaign was the public hanging of Banderites and "collaborators."[16] The bodies of the hanged individuals were sometimes left for several days in public with inscriptions such as "Banderite," "Ukrainian-German Nationalist," or "For the Betrayal of the Ukrainian Nation." Sometimes the Soviet executioners removed trousers and underwear from the hanged "bandits" to humiliate them even more and to strengthen the propaganda effect. Local people, sometimes entire groups of school children, were forced to watch these executions.[17] Sometimes, the authorities herded up to 8,000 peasants from several villages to attend a public trial.[18] UPA partisans or OUN activists were frequently hanged without trial. The suspicion that a person belonged to or had helped the OUN-UPA was enough to hang that person in public as a Banderite. Sometimes a rumor was spread shortly before the execution that the Banderite possessed cut-off ears of several dozen people when he was apprehended.[19] The public hanging of Banderites took place almost everywhere in western Ukraine.[20]

In 1944 and 1945, western Ukraine was bombarded with propaganda material that aimed to persuade OUN activists and UPA partisans to surrender. Many of the leaflets used a national-religious narrative that resembled OUN rhetoric. Soviet material portrayed the OUN and UPA as traitors to the Ukrainian people and as henchmen of the Nazis. On the one hand, Soviet propaganda promised to do no harm to those "Ukrainian-German nationalists" who threw away their weapons and left the forests. On the other, it intimidated those who did not submit to the authorities. In a leaflet from 12 February 1944 we read: "Leave the OUN bands! Break off all connection with the German-Ukrainian nationalists! ... They misled you into betraying the Ukrainian people, brought dishonor and death on you—take revenge on them! ... Leave the forests! Give your weapons to the Red Army! Go back to your villages, to honest, peaceful work for the well-being of our nation!"[21] The leaflet ended with a guarantee to "forgive all misdeeds committed against the Fatherland" if the recipients broke off their connections with the OUN and UPA.[22]

On 20 July 1945, *Radians'ka Ukraïna* reported that several Ukrainian nationalists had accepted the government's offer of amnesty. They had been forgiven and were now living in peace but many "bandits" were still in hiding and were terrorizing the population. A caricature printed beside the announcement demonstrated what

16 On this question, see also the subsection "The Conflict between the OUN-UPA and the Soviet Authorities" in chapter 6, page 295 above,

17 Motyka, *Ukraińska partyzantka*, 481.

18 Statiev, *Soviet Counterinsurgency*, 250.

19 Ibid., 480.

20 For hanging in villages, see Weiner, *Making Sense of War*, 177. For hanging in cities and towns, see Motyka, *Ukraińska partyzantka*, 480–81; Redlich, *Together and Apart*, 142; "Testimony of Janina Kwiatkowska," KAW, II/1352, 7.

21 "Do uchasnykiv tak zvanykh 'UPA' ta 'UNR', 12 February 1944, Kiev," (leaflet signed by Khrushchev), TsDAHO f. 57, op. 4, spr. 37, 267.

22 Ibid, 267. By 1950 at least six further amnesties addressed to the UPA partisans were published. See Bruder, "*Den Ukrainischen Staat*, 232; Motyka, *Ukraińska partyzantka*, 435, 475. See also page 300 above.

happened to those "Ukrainian-German nationalists" who refused to submit to the authorities. The caricature shows an oversized fist, which emerges from the sleeve of an embroidered shirt, a symbol of Ukrainian folklore and nationalism, and smashes a bandit. The newspaper informs us that the fist stands for the "forty-million-strong free Ukrainian people." Just above the fist, we read "20 July," and see that the bandit has dropped a pistol with an engraved swastika from the blow of the fist. His hat, decorated with a trident, another symbol used by Ukrainian nationalists, flies off his head. As in numerous other Soviet caricatures from this time, the swastika, trident, and yellow-and-blue are symbols of the "Ukrainian-German nationalists" (Fig. 28).[23]

Fig. 28. "20 July." *Radians'ka Ukraïna*, 20 July 1944.

After the amnesty expired on 20 July 1945, the strategy of Soviet propaganda toward Ukrainian nationalists changed. "The people forgave those who dropped their weapons and surrendered to the Soviet authorities," we read in an article of that date, "but those who continue the notorious cause of Cain will die a dog's death in their Hitlerite garbage. ... This is the will of the people. It will be carried out as soon as possible. Those who prevent us from building up a happy life in our free, united Soviet Ukraine, in our Soviet Motherland, must and will be annihilated!"[24]

23 "Sorokamilionnyi ukraïns'kyi vil'nyi narod ne dozvolyt', shchob iakas' mizerna kupka bandytiv pereshkodzhala iomu myrno pratsiuvaty," *Radians'ka Ukraïna*, 20 July 1944, 3.

24 "Ostatochno dobyty reshtky ukraïns'ko-nimets'kykh natsionalistiv," *Vil'na Ukraïna*, 24 July 1945, 1.

For several months prior to the amnesty of 20 July 1945, Soviet propaganda let the Ukrainian nationalists themselves speak, in order to demonstrate the felonious nature of the OUN-UPA and to encourage their members to surrender. The Ukrainian nationalists were described in the Soviet press as if they had understood that they were deluded by their leaders and were enemies of the Ukrainian people. On 6 February 1945, *Vil'na Ukraïna* printed a report "Our Country! Soviet Country!" by Ostap Vyshnia about Peremyshliany, a provincial town in the Lviv oblast. Vyshnia described a speech, by a man aged about thirty-five, to his fellow citizens:

> Citizens! You know me. I was in command of the Banderite station in our district. I requested you to fight against the Soviet authorities, not to surrender, to kill Soviet people, and asked you to hide in "bunkers" and forests. I ordered you to kill those who defected to the Soviet authorities and to kill not only them but also their parents, wives, and children. ... But now I regret what I and my comrades did. Now I understand how much misery and calamity we caused with our work. Now it is clear in my mind where our leaders and Bandera were leading us. It is no secret that Bandera—and with him all we Banderites—worked according to the advice of the Gestapo, and it is right to call us German-Ukrainian nationalists. I call on all those who were following me to go to the representatives of Soviet power and to give up their weapons. ... You see, I am alive; the Soviet authorities did not do anything bad to me. I beg you once more, let us end our miserable doings, let us cooperate with the Soviet authorities.[25]

After the speech, according to Vyshnia, people who had lost relatives at the hands of the OUN-UPA wept. To change the attitude of the population toward the OUN-UPA, the speakers frequently introduced murders committed by the local nationalists against people who were known to the community. At the same time, they omitted Soviet crimes committed toward the same local population.

On 18 February 1945, *Vil'na Ukraïna* published "To All Deceived Who Are in Forests and Bunkers—Our Appeal" written by a group of Banderites who had left the underground. The signatures of the defectors and a group photograph appeared. The authors of the article confessed their crimes and tried to encourage the nationalists in hiding to leave the underground. "We were in forests and bunkers for a long time, we carried out the will of German imperialists, Hitlerites," the defectors claimed:

> We deceived our peasants, our youth, we spread different hostile rumors, we claimed that we were fighting for a "free Ukrainian independent state," but in reality we were murdering our village men and faithfully serving the Germans.
>
> But when we read the appeal of the government of Soviet Ukraine we understood that our deeds are against the people—we broke with our dark past life and we approach a new path, the path of honest labor and activity. ...
>
> We were intimidated several times with the idea that if we surrendered to the Soviet authorities we would be killed, tortured, or deported to Siberia. In reality,

25 Ostap Vyshnia, "Nasha zemlia! Radians'ka zemlia!" *Vil'na Ukraïna*, 6 February 1945, 5. For a similar case, see Mykhailo Han'kovych, "Chomu ia porvav z banderivtsiamy," *Vil'na Ukraïna*, 15 May 1945, 7.

this is a lie, an invention. Having come back from the forests, we are free and are not under any pressure.[26]

Similarly, in the issue of *Radians'ka Ukraïna* for 20 July 1945, a member of the SB OUN reported that he was deceived by his leaders: "I, Borys Ivan, joined the OUN in 1942 and worked as the sub-district commander of the SB. The leaders ... deluded us. They ordered us to help the Germans in the struggle against the Soviet Union; they ordered us to kill innocent people. They told us that we would achieve our Ukraine in this way but we see that the leaders of the OUN deceived us."[27]

In its early phase, the campaign against the OUN-UPA was embedded in the hate campaign against Nazi Germany which did not distinguish between Nazis and Germans. Killing a German was equal to killing a Nazi and was an expression of Soviet patriotism and bravery. "If you haven't killed a German in the course of the day, your day has been wasted. ... If you have killed one German, kill another: nothing gives us so much joy as German corpses," wrote Ilya Ehrenburg, one of the leading Soviet writers.[28] Similarly, the campaign against Ukrainian nationalists was, from the very beginning, embedded in an ideological campaign to strengthen Soviet patriotism in Ukraine, especially in the western regions. The Ukrainian nationalists were introduced as the negation of the Soviet ideal of patriotism and as traitors to the Ukrainian SSR, who helped the Germans to enslave the motherland.[29] During the campaign against the Germans, *Radians'ka Ukraïna*, *Vil'na Ukraïna*, and many other Soviet Ukrainian newspapers published reports of the Extraordinary State Commission that investigated Nazi crimes in Ukraine. The reports were presented in a furious, accusatory, and vengeful narrative.[30]

On 29 October 1944, *Radians'ka Ukraïna* announced that, because western Ukraine had been in the Soviet Union for less than two years, the policy of Sovietization should be introduced scrupulously: "Especially here in the western oblasts, the mass political and ideological work should be developed on a particularly wide scale, and with particular scope, and should be conducted with particular knowledge." The article further introduced the Ukrainian nationalists as "Ukrainian-German nationalists, all these Banderites, Bulbites etc." It explained that these "Banderites and Bulbites" had betrayed their motherland, the Soviet Union:

> Here, in the western oblasts they conducted their Cain's work with a particular determination—they spread national hatred and tried to sever the friendship of

26 "Do vsikh obdurenykh, shcho perebuvaly u lisakh i skhronakh—nash zaklyk," Vil'na Ukraïna, 18 February 1945, 4.

27 Ie. Ch. Hrushko, "Ïkh zhde rozplata," *Radians'ka Ukraïna*, 20 July 1944, 3.

28 Quoted in Anatol Goldberg, *Ilya Ehrenburg: Writing, Politics and the Art of Survival* (London: Weidenfeld and Nicolson, 1984), 197.

29 For an article on Soviet patriotism in Ukraine, see Mykola Tykhonov, "Patriotyzm ukrains'koho narodu," *Radians'ka Ukraïna*, 12 December 1944, 2, or S. Kolesnikova, "Lenin i Stalin pro radians'kyi patriotyzm," *Radians'ka Ukraïna*, 18 February 1945.

30 See for example "Povidomlennia nadzvychainoï Derzhavnoï Komisiï pro ruinuvannia, hrabezhi ta zlochynstva nimets'ko-fashysts'kykh zaharbnykiv ta ïkh spil'nykiv u misti Rivne ta Rovens'kii oblasti," *Radians'ka Ukraïna*, 9 May 1944, 3; "Povidomlennia nadzvychainoï Derzhavnoï Komisiï pro zlodiiania nimtsiv na terytoriï L'vivskoï oblasti," *Vil'na Ukraïna*, 29 December 1944, 2–4; "Pomsta i smert' fashysts'kym zaharbnykam! Povidomlennia nadzvychainoï Derzhavnoï Komisiï pro zlodiiania nimtsiv na terytoriï L'vivs'koï oblasti—hriznyi obvynuval'nyi akt fashysts'kym zlochyntsiam," *Vil'na Ukraïna*, 5 January 1945, 3. For the Extraordinary State Commission, see Sorokina, People and Proceedures.

> the Ukrainian people with the great Russian people and other peoples of the Soviet Union, they lied and dishonored. They did everything to weaken the Ukrainian people and in this manner they helped the Hitlerites to conduct the Germanization of Ukraine, to turn it into a German colony.[31]

In the same article the anonymous author argued that the "Ukrainian-German dogs of Hitler" were not only the OUN-B and the UPA but also all other Ukrainian nationalists and collaborators, including the OUN-M, the Waffen-SS Galizien, the UTsK headed by Kubiiovych, and people working in the collaborationist newspapers and administration. They appeared in Soviet propaganda as a homogenous group that, with the help of Nazi Germany, harmed the Ukrainian people. The worst or most vicious elements of this group were the OUN and UPA. Unlike many others, they did not leave with the Germans but stayed in the underground and prolonged the German terror, continuing to murder peaceful Soviet citizens.[32]

Fig. 29. "The Independent Garbage." *Radians'ka Ukraïna*, 27 March 1945.

31 "Posylyty ideino-politychnu robotu v zakhidnykh oblastiakh," *Radians'ka Ukraïna*, 29 October 1944, 1.

32 Ibid., 1. This article was reprinted in other newspapers. See for example *Vil'na Ukraïna*, 3 November 1944, 2.

On 17 November 1944, one of the first articles about the Ukrainian nationalists by the prominent Ukrainian communist writer Iaroslav Halan appeared in *Radians'ka Ukraïna*. The article was titled "In the Black Pit of Betrayal and Crimes." At the beginning, Halan stated: "In terms of crimes, the Banderite bandits are not inferior to their hosts—Hitlerite masters. They burn people alive. Cut off arms and legs. Bury people alive. This is the German school. The Gestapo is the teacher of crime for the Banderites, Bulbites, and Melnykites." Halan wrote that the Ukrainian nationalists printed anti-German leaflets in a German printing plant in Luts'k, but that not one "German perished from the Banderite leaflets, and the Banderites' bullets flew not against German troops but against the bodies of Ukrainian and Polish peasants, their mothers, wives and children, and against partisans."[33] Caricatures printed next to articles written by Halan and other Soviet writers frequently made fun of the proclamation of 30 June 1941, Stets'ko's government, and the idea of an independent Ukrainian state (Figs. 29 and 30).

Fig. 30. "The Independents." *Radians'ka Ukraïna*, 14 April 1945.

33 Iaroslav Halan, "V chornii iami zrady i zlochyniv," *Radians'ka Ukraïna*, 17 November 1944, 2.

Volodymyr Beliaiev, another writer for *Radians'ka Ukraïna*, published an article in December 1944 about the killing of Polish professors in Lviv on the night of 3–4 July 1941. Unlike later Soviet commentators, he did not connect this fact to the Nachtigall battalion.[34] In an article "Ukrainian-German Nationalists—the Worst Enemies of the Ukrainian Nation," O. Kasymenko denounced the OUN-UPA because the Ukrainian nationalists wanted to separate Ukraine from the Soviet Union. Kasymenko, and later several other authors, made a connection between the OUN and politicians such as Petliura and Vynnychenko, who had tried to establish a Ukrainian state during the First World War. What made Petliura the forerunner of the OUN, according to Kasymenko, was that he wanted to separate Ukraine from Russia and that he collaborated with the Germans. Kasymenko, like Halan and several other Soviet writers, mixed facts with completely false information, in order to strengthen the propagandist impact of his writing. Also like Halan, he tried to portray the OUN-UPA as an alien body: "Who are they, the Ukrainian-German nationalists? This is a small band of devious traitors isolated from the nation." Finishing his article, the author stressed that the Ukrainian nation was consolidated "around the great leader comrade Stalin and will always be faithful to the great idea of the friendship of Soviet peoples."[35]

Professor Vasyl' Osichyns'kyi of Lviv University explained the Soviet interpretation of Ukrainian nationalism in greater detail. He began with the Sich Riflemen who were for him nothing more than an instrument of German politics and who betrayed the Ukrainian nation. According to Osichyns'kyi, only the Soviet Union gave Ukrainians the possibility to establish their "own state—the Ukrainian SSR." From the very beginning, the Sich Riflemen represented the "Ukrainian nationalistic counterrevolution." The main activist of this counterrevolution was the Tsentral'na Rada, the assembly of Ukrainian politicians that in 1917 proclaimed the Ukrainian National Republic, supported the imperialistic policies of the German Empire, and thereby "jeopardized the eternal wish of the Ukrainian nation to live in union with the fraternal Russian people." Petliura, according to Osichyns'kyi, was an early Ukrainian nationalist who betrayed the Ukrainian nation by making an alliance with Poland and offering it the western Ukrainian territories. After the First World War, the Ukrainian nationalists escaped from Ukraine and worked for the intelligence services of such countries as Poland, Romania, and Germany. During the interwar period, "all these traitors gathered mainly in fascist Germany" where the Gestapo "made them into tools of German imperial fascism. On this ground, contemporary Ukrainian-German nationalism grew up, which was an integral part of the German-fascist system." Osichyns'kyi introduced Konovalets' as "Hitler's personal friend" who was killed by the Gestapo in 1938 "through some misunderstanding between lords and mercenaries." According to Osichyns'kyi, Bandera became the leader of the OUN because the Gestapo did not like Mel'nyk. During the Second World War, the

34 Volodymyr Beliaiev, "Bahattia fashysts'koï inkvizytsiï," *Radians'ka Ukraïna*, 8 December 1944, 3.

35 O. Kasymenko, "Ukraïns'ko-nimets'ki natsionalisty—nailiutishi vorohy ukraïns'koho narodu," *Radians'ka Ukraïna*, 10 December 1944. The article was reprinted in other newspapers, for example in *Vil'na Ukraïna*, 13 December 1944, 2–3. Another author who connected the OUN-UPA with Ukrainian nationalists from First World War was P. Lisovyi, "Nimets'ki fashysty—khaziaï ukraïns'kykh natsionalistychnykh zaprodantsiv," *Vil'na Ukraïna*, 20 February 1945, 4.

"Ukrainian-German nationalists" helped the Nazis to exploit Ukraine. The Banderites went underground at the Germans' request in order to give the impression that they were fighting against the occupiers, but in reality they were still serving the Germans. Melnykites did not go underground and openly collaborated with the Germans; they mobilized Ukrainians for work in Germany and established the Waffen-SS Galizien. Osichyns'kyi concluded his article with the words: "Their lords—the German fascists—are perishing under the blows of the Red Army. They, too, will perish."[36]

Iaroslav Halan put the Soviet description of Banderites and the "Ukrainian-German nationalists" in a nutshell in his pamphlet *Vampires*: "Thus, the Hitlerites [*hitlery*] left; the Banderites [*bandery*] remained. Allied with fascism and its regime not by life but by death, they kept operating by inertia even after their Mecca, Nazi Berlin, lay in ashes. ... Banderites have been lucky enough to avoid the gallows, and they operate according to all the rules of fascist policy."[37]

The term "fascism" appeared in early Soviet propaganda very frequently, its meaning completely distorted and politicized. It was used as a political swearword. The Soviet propaganda apparatus identified all opponents of the Soviet Union as fascists. Some of them, such as Bandera, Mel'nyk, and Croatian politicians such as Pavelić, did adopt fascism but a number did not. One example is the depiction of the Polish AK and Polish politicians such as Józef Beck and Edward Rydz-Śmigły as fascists.[38] Although some Polish politicians were sympathetic toward Nazi Germany prior to the Second World War, and some units of the AK collaborated with the Germans, these politicians and the AK did not adopt fascism. They were introduced in the Soviet narrative as fascists because they did not fight against Nazi Germany on the Soviet side, did not accept Soviet supremacy in Poland, and fought against the Polish communist authorities.[39] In addition, Soviet propaganda used the term "fascist" as a catchphrase and a weapon and applied it during the Cold War to democratic states from the Western bloc.[40]

Long before the Red Army came to western Ukraine in spring and summer 1944, Soviet leaders such as Khrushchev had been informed about the murder of Poles and Jews by the OUN and UPA, and their fighting against and killing Soviet partisans. When the Red Army reached western Ukraine, the OUN-UPA was still conducting ethnic cleansing against the Poles in eastern Galicia and murdering Jews who hid in the forests. The Soviet authorities did not invent these atrocities but depicted them in a distorted, simplistic, and propagandist manner, paying no attention to the nature

36 Vasyl' Osichyns'kyi, "Pidli z pidlykh," *Radians'ka Ukraïna*, 6 February 1945, 3.

37 Iaroslav Halan, *Liudy bez bat'kivshchyny* (Kiev: Dnipro, 1967), 94.

38 "Pokinchymo z vorohamy pol's'koho narodu," *Radians'ka Ukraïna*, 7 February 1945, 4.

39 "Pol's'ko-fashysts'ki bandyty pid maskoiu demokrativ," *Radians'ka Ukraïna*, 21 June 1945. For collaboration by the AK with the Germans, see Tadeusz Piotrowski, *Poland's Holocaust: Ethnic Strife, Collaboration with Occupying Forces and Genocide in the Second Republic, 1918–1947* (Jefferson, NC: McFarland, 1998), 88–89. For nationalism and antisemitism in the AK, see Frank Golczewski, "Die Heimatarmee und die Juden," in *Die polnische Heimatarmee: Geschichte und Mythos der Armia Krajowa seit dem Zweiten Weltkrieg*, ed. Bernhard Chiari (Munich: Oldenbourg Wissenschaftsverlag, 2003), 635–76, especially 664.

40 Wippermann, *Faschismus: Eine Weltgeschichte*, 9.

of the crimes, and stripping the victims of the OUN and UPA mass violence of their national identities, by depicting them simply as Soviet people.[41]

One of the main distortions on the part of Soviet propaganda in the early phase was the identification of the OUN and UPA as an integral part of the Nazi empire. Banderites were not depicted as human beings but either as beasts or the limbs of a beast that was Nazi Germany. One caricature printed in *Radians'ka Ukraïna* showed a poisonous snake with a trident on its cap and another on its black skin, crawling out of a coffin, which, with a helmet with a swastika on it, symbolized defeated Nazi Germany (Fig. 31).[42]

Fig. 31. *Radians'ka Ukraïna,* 15 March 1945.

From late 1944, *Vil'na Ukraïna* published several speeches by representatives of Ukrainian peasants, workers, and intelligentsia. All of them argued in support of Soviet power and condemned the "Ukrainian-German nationalists." On 12 November 1944, speeches by peasant representatives of the Lviv oblast appeared. Ivan Mekh, head of the village council of Sukhovil, said:

41 See Amar, *A Disturbed Silence*, 158–84.

42 *Radians'ka Ukraïna*, 16 March 1945; *Vil'na Ukraïna*, 20 March 1945.

> We suffered cruel treatment for three years under the German predators, they tortured and murdered us for three years, they wanted to turn us into slaves. But they did not succeed.
>
> At the request of the great Stalin the whole Soviet people supported the Great Patriotic War and began a fervent fight against the Hitlerite oppressors. Our peasants did not believe the Germans and their assistants, the German-Ukrainian nationalists, and we harmed the enemy as much as we could.[43]

Ivan Turok from the village of Nahachiv said in his speech:

> The Germans killed our people and burned our villages. The Banderite bandits did the same.
>
> Our nation cursed them, they did so much harm!
>
> We liquidated the remains of the fascist rule, we rebuilt the economy, and the Banderites tried to disturb us from doing so. Death to the Banderites! (Applause, calls: "Shame on the Banderites! Death to them!")
>
> Comrades! How long will we tolerate the Ukrainian-German nationalists? We have to grapple with them as soon as possible.
>
> From the first days of the liberation of our village, more than 300 people joined the Red Army. They are now combating the enemy on his own territory; they protect the honor of the Soviet motherland. And here some remnants mumble that they love Ukraine and that they fight for it.
>
> Nothing of the kind! Banderites are the same fascists as the German bandits. They were hired by Hitler to kill the Ukrainian people. We have to come together to wipe out the fascist lickspittles. Enough hate for them has accumulated in us. We will wipe out the Ukrainian-German nationalists. (Applause.) Comrades! The Red Army is pushing the enemy further and further. We read with great pleasure in Comrade Stalin's speech that the fascist beast will soon be killed in its own lair and that the flag of victory will soon be planted over Berlin. (Applause.)[44]

M. H. Trehuba, head of the oblast health authority, stated: "These agents of the German fascists, the German-Ukrainian nationalists, tried to slow down our work. They mumble something about 'independent Ukraine' but in reality they are the worst enemies of Ukraine and the Ukrainian people. They dream about making the Ukrainian people slaves of fascist Germany again."[45]

Ol'ha Sobol', a school-teacher in Zolochiv, described how people suffered under German occupation and how they were now rebuilding the social structures with the help of the Soviet authorities. Then she explained that "our work would be even more effective if the scum of society, the German-Ukrainian nationalists, did not bother us.

43 Ivan Mekh, "Khlibom ta koshtamy my b"iem voroha," *Vil'na Ukraïna*, 12 November 1944, 3.

44 Ivan Turok, "Znyshchymo bandytiv banderivtsiv," *Vil'na Ukraïna*, 12 November 1944, 3.

45 M. H. Trehuba, "Povnistiu znyshchyty fashysts'kykh bliudolyziv—ukraïns'ko-nimets'kykh natsionalistiv," *Vil'na Ukraïna*, 2 December 1944, 3.

Fig. 32. Banderite Murderer. Himmler: "Bravo, bravo! You've learned my lessons well."
Vil'na Ukraïna, 24 January 1945.

Now we have to accumulate all our strength, to liquidate as soon as possible the remains of the fascist occupation, the Banderites, to pull out and destroy this dirt by the roots."[46]

An important aspect of the Soviet propagandist approach to the OUN and UPA was the exposure of their war crimes. In contrast, the war crimes of the Red Army or the NKVD were never mentioned. Soviet propaganda frequently introduced Bandera in the context of the crimes of the OUN and UPA. Halan, for example, began one of his articles with the description of a fourteen-year-old girl who could not look at meat because one of the "bandits" who broke into her parents' house decided not to kill her "to the glory of Stepan Bandera" but killed her parents in her presence and told her that this was her food.[47]

46 Ol'ha Sobol', "Vyrvaty z korinniamy banderivs'ku nechyst'!" *Vil'na Ukraïna*, 3 December 1944, 3.

47 Iaroslav Halan, "Chomu nemaie imennia," *Vil'na Ukraïna*, 19 November 1944.

In early 1945, Soviet propaganda began to refer to the OUN-UPA and other Ukrainian nationalists as "bourgeois."[48] This is not surprising if we bear in mind that in Soviet ideology fascism was nothing other than deformed capitalism.[49] As early as the 1920s Communist thinkers had linked fascism with capitalism and had described the Italian Fascists as petit bourgeois nationalists.[50] The Ukrainian nationalists were enemies of the Soviet Union not only because they collaborated with Nazi Germany and betrayed the Soviet people but also because they were bourgeois. They were a product of such class enemies as the *kurkul*, or affluent peasant, and helped such "bourgeois" states as Nazi Germany. According to D. Z. Manuïl's'kyi, who delivered a speech on 6 January 1945 to western Ukrainian teachers, the kurkul was the class that contributed to the development of the OUN and other Ukrainian nationalists. Because the kurkul class had already been liquidated in Soviet Ukraine in the early 1930s, the OUN developed only in "the reactionary Polish state" and later under the occupation of "Hitlerite Germany" with which the kurkul class, according to Manuïl's'kyi, also collaborated.[51]

On 2 February 1945, a group of Ukrainian academics stated in *Vil'na Ukraïna* that Banderites were both kurkuls and "Hitler's agents." At Hitler's behest and to maintain their "bourgeois" property, they had killed Poles, and those Ukrainians whom they accused of being communists.[52] V. Kolisnyk characterized Bandera as a "son of a kurkul near Stanislaviv."[53] Another author argued that kurkuls are the "pillar of Ukrainian fascists" and used the term "Banderite-kurkul vampires" (*banderivs'ko-kurkul's'ki upyri*).[54]

Presenting the Ukrainian nationalists as a small group of traitors and enemies of the Ukrainian people was another important aspect of Soviet propaganda. Manuïl's'kyi in his speech on 6 January 1945 emphasized that the Ukrainian nationalists had nothing in common with the Ukrainians whom they murdered en masse. To substantiate this claim he described the Ukrainian nationalists as "cursed by their people, their parents, without kin, tribe, or motherland" and "armed by Germans, with German Marks in their pockets, with German rifles in their hands, in German coats and trousers, defending the German cause." Logically they could not be Ukrainian or represent the interests of Ukrainians.[55]

Describing the "slaughter in villages ... in the Rivne oblast in summer 1943" Manuïl's'kyi presented Ukrainians, and not Poles, as the main victims of this anti-Polish ethnic cleansing. This resembles the Soviet representation of the Holocaust, the main victims of which were not Jews but Soviet people. Manuïl's'kyi also pointed out that the Ukrainian nationalists sometimes shouted "Glory to Bandera!" while

48 D. Z. Manuïl's'kyi, "Ukraïns'ko-nimets'ki natsionalisty na sluzhbi u fashysts'koï Nimechchyny," *Vil'na Ukraïna*, 13 January 1945, 4.

49 Snyder, *Bloodlands*, 115.

50 Payne, *A History of Fascism 1914–1915*, 124.

51 Manuïl's'kyi, "Ukraïns'ko-nimets'ki natsionalisty," *Vil'na Ukraïna*, 13 January 1945, 5. For the *kurkuls* as a pillar of the "German-Ukrainian nationalists" in Soviet ideology, see also Pavlo Zhyvotenko, "Kaïnove plem"ia," *Vil'na Ukraïna*, 14 September 1946, 3.

52 "Povertaitesia do myrnoï pratsi, znyshchuite prodazhnykh ahentiv Hitlera—banderivtsiv!" *Vil'na Ukraïna*, 2 February 1945, 4.

53 V. Kolisnyk, "'Pid chuzhymy praporamy," *Vil'na Ukraïna*, 30 August 1947, 6.

54 Pavlo Zhyvotenko, "Kurkuli—liuti vorohy trudovoho selianstva," *Vil'na Ukraïna* 19 October 1947, 3.

55 Manuïl's'kyi, "Ukraïns'ko-nimets'ki natsionalisty," *Vil'na Ukraïna*, 13 January 1945, 5.

they were burning small children in houses and barns. He described several methods the Banderites used to murder Ukrainians and came to the conclusion that the Ukrainian people could write its own "Red Book about perfidious extermination, terrible crimes, torturing and killing conducted by Banderites." Then he began to legitimize the NKVD terror: "And these beasts dare to say that the organs of Soviet power apply terror toward them. Holy is the sword that hacks off the heads of such perpetrators!"[56]

After explaining that the OUN was advised by the Germans to unleash terror against civilians, and challenging the meaning of the "Ukrainian underground," Manuïl's'kyi depicted the Ukrainian nationalists as a homogenous group without any divisions and factions: "All this 'underground' army carried black coats of German cloth, with yellow armbands, on which was written: 'Bandera.'" Bandera, wrote Manuïl's'kyi, was arrested by the Germans only after he agreed to be arrested.[57] Ivan Hrushets'kyi, leader of the Lviv oblast Communist Party (Bolsheviks) of Ukraine (*Komunistychna Partiia (bil'shovykiv) Ukraïny*, KP(b)U) wrote in a similar tone on 15 January 1945. He appealed to Ukrainians not to believe the Banderites, because they were still "trying to turn Ukraine into a colony of fascist Germany." Then he stressed that, except for the fact that Banderites spoke Ukrainian, there was no difference between them and Nazis. In order to help the Nazis, according to Hrushets'kyi, Banderites blew up Soviet trains, which were on their way through Ukraine toward the front, and they killed peasants because they did not want them to attend schools where the Soviet authorities would teach them in Ukrainian. Hrushets'kyi also stressed that the leadership of the OUN consisted of kurkuls who exploited poor Ukrainian peasants.[58]

In this early Soviet discourse, Bandera, as the main symbol of the "Ukrainian-German nationalists," also became a traitor and deceiver. As such, he deceived thousands of Ukrainians who were named Banderites after him, believed in him, trusted him, and fought for an "independent Ukraine." In an article titled "Letter to a Dupe" a group of "Ukrainian Soviet writers" wrote:

> Do you think that Stepan Bandera calls you to fight 'for Ukraine'? This is the same Judas who has been eating German bread and drinking German beer for fifteen years. Does he lead the struggle for an 'independent' Ukraine from Prague, occupied by Germans, where he sits in the office of the head of the Gestapo? Ha, this scallywag is really a good fighter—only not for Ukraine but for German black profit.[59]

In a similar manner, the same Soviet writers explained what the OUN, UPA, and UHVR meant:

56 Ibid., 5. Manuïl's'kyi's words about the holy sword were later quoted as the words of a poet by other participants in the anti-OUN discourse. See, for example, Volodymyr Konvisar, "Slovo pro tykh, shcho pidnialy mech sviashchennyi," *Vil'na Ukraïna*, 24 March 1945, 6.

57 Ibid., 5–6.

58 Ivan Hrushets'kyi, "Do kintsia znyshchymo naimytiv Hitlera—bandy ukraïns'ko-nimets'kykh natsionalistiv," *Vil'na Ukraïna*, 16 January 1945, 3.

59 "Lyst do zadurenoho," *Vil'na Ukraïna*, 10 February 1945, 5.

> They invented names for their bands: OUN, UPA. And recently, in order to change colors—something like UHVR. Do you want to know what this dog's growling means? I will tell you in my simple human language: OUN means Horde of Extraordinary Killers [*Orda Ubyvts' Nesamovytykh*], UPA means Mongrels of the Mangy Adolf [*Ubliudky Parshyvoho Adol'fa*], and UHVR—this is very simple Kill-Steal-Hang-Cut [*Ubyvai-Hrabui-Vishai-Rizh*]. This is the program of these Cains and Judases.[60]

Like the Ukrainian nationalists, the Greek Catholic Church was also portrayed as a traitorous institution and an enemy of the Soviet people. On 8 April 1945, using the pseudonym Volodymyr Rasovych, Iaroslav Halan published an article in *Vil'na Ukraïna*, entitled "With Cross or Knife?"—in which he referred to the Greek Catholic Church as an agent of the Vatican, the German Empire, and Nazi Germany. Halan claimed that Andrei Sheptyts'kyi was financed by the German Empire, the Habsburg Empire, and the Vatican in order to be used for Germany's colonial plans for Eastern Europe. According to Halan, Sheptyts'kyi used the church to separate the Galician Ukrainians culturally from other Ukrainians. The Ukrainian communist writer explained that Sheptyts'kyi's plan was to unite all Orthodox churches with the Vatican, with which the Greek Catholic Church had been united since the late sixteenth century. This would make Sheptyts'kyi the head of all Orthodox churches in Ukraine and Russia, from the Zbruch River to Vladivostok. During the First World War, Sheptyts'kyi failed because the Habsburg and German empires lost the war. After Hitler became chancellor of Germany, Sheptyts'kyi naturally began to orient himself toward Germany in order to accomplish his earlier plans. He finished his article with the conclusion: "These enemies of the Ukrainian people, dressed in the cassocks of Greek Catholic priests, are the organizers of the bands of German-Ukrainian nationalists and the agents of German occupiers."[61]

According to another author, Kost' Huslystyi, the very foundation of the Greek Catholic Church was a betrayal of the Ukrainian people. Huslystyi celebrated as heroes the few nobles who opposed the Union of Brest of 1596, an agreement between the Vatican and the Orthodox Church in the Polish-Lithuanian Commonwealth. For the same reason Huslystyi presented the Cossacks as heroes because they never accepted the Greek Catholic Church and had fought the Polish Catholic nobility. The Orthodox priests and nobles who accepted the union were traitors and enemies of the Ukrainian people. In the Soviet discourse, to be a Banderite frequently implied membership not only of the OUN or UPA but also of the Greek Catholic Church.[62]

The UTsK and its directors Volodymyr Kubiiovych and Kost' Pan'kivs'kyi were also introduced by Soviet propaganda as enemies of the Soviet Ukrainian people. Volodymyr Konvisar called Kubiiovych and Pan'kivs'kyi "professor-bandits," "dogs with tridents," or "dogs that howl on command from the hangman Hitler." He neither explained nor even mentioned how and why the UTsK collaborated with the

60 Ibid., 5.

61 Volodymyr Rasovych, "Z khrestom chy z nozhem?", *Vil'na Ukraïna*, 8 April 1945, 5–6. For Halan's pseudonym, see Motyka, *Ukraińska partyzantka*, 420.

62 Cf. Kost' Huslystyi, "Z istoriï borot'by ukraïns'koho narodu proty tserkovnoï uniï," *Vil'na Ukraïna*, 7 July 1945, 4–5.

Germans, aryanized Jewish property, spread antisemitic propaganda, supported the setting up of the Waffen-SS Galizien, and so forth. Such facts seem to have been less important for the Soviet regime than emotional phrases.[63]

Dontsov attracted particular attention from Soviet propaganda. He was characterized as a person who attacked Russian culture and socialist intellectuals, like Drahomanov, who did not support the Ukrainian separatist movement. Soviet ideology claimed that Dontsov spread the "cult of betrayal" among the Ukrainian youth. He was like Hetman Ivan Mazepa, whom Russian national history and Soviet ideology regarded as the Ukrainian traitor par excellence, because he changed sides in 1708 and allied himself with the Swedish king Charles XII, the main enemy of Peter the Great in the Great Northern War. Soviet propaganda condemned Dontsov as the main "ideologist of Ukrainian-German nationalism," whose publications were "riddled with hostility to mankind." Osyp Mstyslavets', who published one of the first articles condemning Dontsov, was well informed about the main ideologist of Ukrainian fascist ideology. He knew that Dontsov published Hitler's and Mussolini's biographies and edited the newspaper *Vistnyk*, and he was aware of many other important facts concerning Dontsov's life. In his article, Mstyslavets' established a direct link between the crimes of the OUN and UPA, whose victims he saw for himself in 1944, and the ideology of Dontsov. According to Mstyslavets', nothing was more responsible for OUN and UPA crimes than Dontsov's ideology.[64]

The instrumentalization of Kubiiovych, Dontsov, and the Greek Catholic Church did not play a major role at local assemblies, however, where peasants cursed the Banderites and their masters—the Nazis. Especially after the capitulation of Nazi Germany on 8–9 May 1945, the "Ukrainian-German nationalists" were understood to be the last rump of German fascism and the greatest shame for the Soviet Union because the actual enemy, Nazi Germany, was already defeated. On 23 May 1945, *Vil'na Ukraïna* filled an entire page with excerpts from speeches at an assembly in the village of Zboïs'ka, and with a photograph of peasants listening to a speech by a Soviet activist. The picture and the excerpts from the speeches appear to be a representation of an ideal village meeting, which other villages were expected to emulate. Andrii Mel'nyk, one of the peasants who spoke at the assembly, said: "The Banderites' hands are covered with the blood of their own people. They are responsible for many innocent victims. Therefore, they are afraid to leave their dog's lairs; they are afraid of a severe punishment."[65] A peasant, Mariia Ponchyn, claimed to speak on behalf of all "the women of the western oblasts of Ukraine," who would, according to her, "help the organs of Soviet power to detect the remains of the German accomplices, Ukrainian-German nationalists who do not leave their bunkers in the woods and prolong their sordid doings."[66] The head of the village council wondered with whom the "Ukrainian-German nationalists" would collaborate, now that Nazi Germany had been defeated. He also asked when they would finally understand that they had been deceived, and he hoped that this would happen soon,

63 Volodymyr Konvisar, "Providnyky do prirvy," *Vil'na Ukraïna*, 13 April 1945, 6.
64 Osyp Mstyslavets', "Liudoïd Dontsov ta inshi ..." *Vil'na Ukraïna*, 19 June 1946, 5.
65 Andrii Mel'nyk, "Nekhai skhamenut'sia, poky ne pizno," *Vil'na Ukraïna*, 23 May 1945, 5.
66 Mariia Ponchyn, "Dopomozhemo vykryty vorohiv," *Vil'na Ukraïna*, 23 May 1945, 5.

because the Soviet authorities did not want to shed blood.[67] Mar'ian Khmarnyi, secretary of the village council, said that the Banderites had been "deceived by the German fascists" and had continued the work of their masters like faithful dogs, although their masters were already dead.[68]

The next issue of *Vil'na Ukraïna* printed the words of other peasants, as well as workers and holders of other positions in the Lviv oblast. The peasant Hryts'ko Koval' argued that the "German mercenaries—Banderites" would not prevent Ukrainians from rebuilding Ukraine.[69] Dmytro Stan'ko, a school director in Lavrykiv said:

> Deceived by fascist propaganda, the Ukrainian-German nationalists continue to carry out the orders of Hitlerites, they conduct criminal work directed against the Ukrainian people. ... If the bandits do not obey the Soviet government and the Communist Party, they will all, as will all those who help them, be held accountable for betraying our Motherland. ...
>
> I, as the school director, will try with all my strength and knowledge to raise children to be honest and devoted patriots of our Soviet state. ... And how do the bandits from the forests contribute to our well-being? They, as Hitlerites, destroy cultural facilities and kill honest people. They show their faces to the people and now if they will not rethink and show regret, they will be annihilated. We will contribute to this endeavor. Our conversation with the bandits will be short. Weeds and thistles will grow on their graves, and our children will curse them.[70]

Shortly after the defeat of Nazi Germany, the Banderites became an important subject at a conference of women from the Lviv oblast. Oleksandra Pastushna stated:

> The Hitlerite hordes, which intruded into our country in 1941, took all rights from women and men. Only those who killed and robbed Soviet people—together with the Germans—thrived. These were the Ukrainian-German nationalists. These people, these cursed Banderites, killed my husband. Why? Because he liked life on a collective farm.[71]

A. M. Ahalakova said at the same conference that the "fascist mercenaries—Banderite bandits" burned down her mother's house because she dated a Soviet officer.[72] I. P. Senta characterized the OUN-UPA as "forest bandits—Ukrainian-German nationalists" and appealed to all women "to work harder and to conduct a more severe struggle against Banderites."[73] Olena Mykytenko, an activist of the KP(b)U committee of the Bibrka region, said:

> The Germans' friends—the Ukrainian-German nationalists intimidate first of all the women, they try to turn them against the Soviet power. Yet the women saw clearly and see now that Banderites are friends of the Germans, that they are the enemies of the Ukrainian people. Attacking our people, they have no mercy for

67 Mykhailo Hirchuk, "Banderivtsi v us'omu dopomahaly nimtsiam," *Vil'na Ukraïna*, 23 May 1945, 5.
68 Mar'ian Khmarnyi, "Vitaiemo zvernennia Radians'koho uriadu," *Vil'na Ukraïna*, 23 May 1945, 5.
69 Hryts'ko Koval', "Dopomozhemo vykryvaty bandytiv," *Vil'na Ukraïna*, 25 May 1945, 3.
70 Dmytro Stan'ko, "Vykhod'te z lisiv!," *Vil'na Ukraïna*, 25 May 1945, 3.
71 Oleksandra Pastushna, "My, zhinky—velyka syla!" *Vil'na Ukraïna*, 1 June 1945, 3.
72 A. M. Ahalakova, "Ia stala traktorystkoiu," *Vil'na Ukraïna*, 1 June 1945, 3.
73 I. P. Senta, "Za rozkvit nashoho radians'koho zhyttia," *Vil'na Ukraïna*, 1 June 1945, 4.

women or children. Recently these beasts hanged the activist Mykolaieva, only because she spread the words of Bolshevik truth among the people. Thereby, the Banderites make themselves more and more unpopular. That's nothing. Soon they will all be destroyed.[74]

The heroization of Stalin and the Red Army was another very important part of the propaganda directed against "Ukrainian-German nationalists" and Banderites. Dozens, perhaps even hundreds, of articles about Stalin and his speeches to the Ukrainian people appeared in Soviet Ukrainian newspapers at the same time as the public condemnation of the Banderites.[75] At many meetings praise of Stalin was closely related to the condemnation of the "Ukrainian-German nationalists."[76] In July 1945 in Lviv, a huge triumphal arch was erected to honor Red Army units that were returning from Germany. Pictures of Red Army trucks with enormous portraits of Stalin driving through the arch appeared in the newspapers.[77]

Fig. 33. Stalin, Zhukov, Khrushchev, and the Ukrainian people. *Vilna Ukraïna* 27 July 1945.

For the first anniversary of the liberation of Lviv by the Red Army, the stage in the opera house was decorated with a huge portrait of Stalin.[78] Shortly afterwards, on 27 July 1945, *Vil'na Ukraïna* published a black-and-white drawing of Stalin with Marshal of the Soviet Army Georgii Zhukov on his right and Khrushchev on his left,

74 Olena Mykytenko, "Staranno pidhotuvatys' i provesty zhnyva," *Vil'na Ukraïna*, 2 June 1945, 4.

75 See, for example, "V den' vsenarodnoho torzhestva—Sviata Peremohy nashe spasybi ridnomu Stalinu!" *Vil'na Ukraïna*, 9 May 1945, 3; "Narod slavyt' vozhdia," *Vil'na Ukraïna*, 28 July 1945, 1; F. Polkunov, "Tovarysh Stalin—Velykyi vozhd' radians'koho narodu," *Vil'na Ukraïna*, 12 October 1947, 2.

76 See, for example, "100—tysiachnyi mitynh u L'vovi," *Vil'na Ukraïna*, 4 May 1945, 6.

77 *Vil'na Ukraïna*, 24 July 1945, 5.

78 *Vil'na Ukraïna*, 31 July 1945, 1.

standing in a place that seems to be the market square in Lviv (Fig. 33). The happy crowd around the three Soviet leaders smiles at them. A man dressed in peasant clothing holds bread and salt. A little girl of about five hands flowers to Stalin and leans her head against him. The *Vozhd'* puts his left hand on her head. A huge red banner with the coat of arms of Soviet Ukraine waves above the three Soviet leaders. Another one waves from the tower of the town hall. The simple black-and-white picture with two red elements was a perfect explanation of who held power in western Ukraine at the end of the Second World War.[79]

The International Military Tribunal at Nuremberg, during which such names as Bandera, Mel'nyk, and Kubiiovych were mentioned, again drew the attention of the Soviet propaganda apparatus to the question of Ukrainian radical nationalism. The Soviet Ukrainian press began to demand that the OUN leaders and other Ukrainian politicians be put in the dock. The real defendants at Nuremberg were, however, only Germans. No Croatian, Hungarian, Lithuanian, Romanian, Slovak, or Ukrainian collaborators or war criminals were prosecuted there. Some other leaders such as Ion Antonescu, Jozef Tiso, and Ferenc Szálasi were convicted in their respective countries. Others, such as Pavelić, Sima, and Bandera were not prosecuted, because they distorted and concealed the crimes committed by their movements, or because there was not enough evidence to put them on trial, or they were protected by Western intelligence, or disappeared.[80]

Bourgeois Nationalists

The stormy campaign against the "Ukrainian-German nationalists" ended in early 1947. The timing seems to be related to the fact that, in December 1946, the Soviet authorities realized that the OUN and UPA were not only an insurgent movement rooted in western Ukraine but also an organization that was attacking the Soviet Union from outside with the help of Western intelligence.[81] At about the same time, Soviet propaganda began to refer to the OUN and UPA underground in Ukraine, the ZCh OUN, UHVR, and other Ukrainian nationalist organizations, as "Ukrainian bourgeois nationalists." The campaign against the "bourgeois nationalists," unlike the previous one, stressed from the outset the relationship between Ukrainian nationalism and capitalism or capitalist states such as the United States, the United Kingdom, and West Germany. Fascism was still an important component of the campaign directed against the Ukrainian genocidal nationalists but, in the course of the Cold War, the main enemy of the Soviet Union became capitalism, which Soviet ideology considered to be a deformed variant of fascism.[82]

On 24 January 1948, *Radians'ka Ukraïna* published what was probably the most complex caricature of Ukrainian nationalism (Fig. 34 and 35).[83] The cartoon portrays

79 *Vil'na Ukraïna*, 27 July 1945, 1.

80 For articles about the Nuremberg trials and Bandera, see "Do suvoroï i spravedlyvoï kary klyche nevynna krov," *Vil'na Ukraïna*, 22 February 1946, 4; Petro Karmans'kyi, "Pok护lademo kinets'!" *Vil'na Ukraïna*, 22 February 1946, 4; V. M. Pan'kiv, "Zradnykiv na sud narodu!" *Vil'na Ukraïna*, 6 March 1946, 5.

81 See chapter 6 above, subsection "Operation Rollback," page 309.

82 Snyder, *Bloodlands*, 115.

83 *Radians'ka Ukraïna*, 24 January 1948, 4.

Fig. 34. "The hope of restoring capitalism in Ukraine." *Radians'ka Ukraïna* 24 January 1948.

Fig. 35. "The hope of restoring capitalism in Ukraine." *Radians'ka Ukraïna* 24 January 1948.

the funeral of the "hope of restoring capitalism in Ukraine." It illustrates very well how Soviet propaganda at that time shaped the image of Ukrainian nationalism in Soviet Ukrainian media. The cartoon is more abstract than the usual Soviet cartoons of that period. It depicts the Ukrainian nationalists in unusual roles among western politicians and thereby explains what the Ukrainian nationalist leaders were doing outside Ukraine. Bandera, portrayed as the widow of the late economic and political system, is located at the very center of the cartoon. He has large breasts, wears a mourning dress and a veil. His sorrow is represented by the huge tears that he wipes away with a white handkerchief. He is accompanied on his left by British Foreign Secretary Ernest Bevin, who says, "Don't pester me, Mr. Bandera. I can barely stay on my feet. Try to get support from Marshall." He walks immediately behind the hearse, on which two crows are perched. "There seems to be no corpse, but even so it reeks of carrion," one says to the other.

George C. Marshall, the American military leader for whom the economic plan for rebuilding Europe was named, is walking directly behind the widow and holding Bandera's right hand. Bandera looks so sad and stunned that he obviously needs this help. Marshall's eyes are closed; his head tilted up as if he were trying not to see what is going on and to stay calm. A woman and two men in mourning dress march behind Marshall. The woman is Lady Astor, the first woman to take up her seat in House of Commons, and a firm critic of communism and Stalin. One of the men next to Lady Astor might be Clement Attlee, British prime minister from 1945 to 1951.

A funeral band—a conductor, two men with tubas, and one with a drum—marches behind Lady Astor and the two gentlemen. The conductor is labeled as "Kherst" and is William Randolph Hearst, owner of a chain of American anticommunist newspapers who had sympathized with National Socialism and Italian Fascism in the 1930s. Four ducks sit in the tubas. Two of them hold a poster with the inscription "Hearst—McCormick and Co.," which refers to another anticommunist newspaper chain, owned by Robert R. McCormick. The drummer is the pan-Turk politician Aydin Yalcin, another enemy of the Soviet Union. A long file of war veterans, who resemble bandits more than soldiers, marches behind the orchestra. One of them holds a ragged banner with the inscription "SS Galicia Division" and a swastika under it. Another carries a poster with the inscription, "Who Said That We Are Bandits? We Are Insurgents!" One of the veterans is holding a pistol and is about to shoot Yalcin, but another veteran tries to restrain him by saying, "This is our man." Behind the Waffen-SS Galizien veterans march two dapper men. The sign they are carrying reads, "Ukrainian Canadian Committee." Behind them march the DPs who have followed them to Canada.

On the left of the cartoon, a cameraman is filming the procession while standing on a car. It is labeled "Hollywood." The dollar sign on its hood emphasizes the commercial nature of this institution. Next to the car, Alex Birns, a Jewish-American mobster and racketeer, looks at the veteran who is about to shoot Yalcin. "Frankly speaking, this fighter won't bring in capital for our company," Birns says. Like Hearst and KUK, he symbolizes the new continent and its capitalist nature. The introduction of a Jewish-American mobster as a symbol of criminality interwoven with capitalism might be a sign of the antisemitism that existed in the Soviet Union after the Second World War.[84] The long row of Waffen-SS Galizien veterans and other nationalists in the procession indicates their emigration to capitalist countries which, according to the cartoon, were no less criminal than the Ukrainian nationalists themselves.

Lower down, to the left of the procession, the poet Ievhen Malaniuk sits and recites a poem while playing a hurdy-gurdy. Malaniuk was published in the 1930s in *Vistnyk*, a newspaper edited by Dontsov. His traditional Cossack-style haircut, known as a *khokhol*, makes him unrecognizable. Only the caption on the leg of his shabby pants reveals his identity. The poet has put his hat out in the hope of getting some coins. One unidentified man stands behind Malaniuk, another one beside him. Like the poet, both keep their eyes down. One of them holds his hand out for alms.

To the right of the funeral crowd, Stanisław Mikołajczyk, prime minister of the Polish government-in-exile, walks beside Ferenc Nagy, prime minister of Hungary between February 1946 and May 1947, who resigned under duress and left for the United States. Mikołajczyk has a flask in his coat pocket and is holding a small cup. Nagy asks Mikołajczyk what's wrong. "I myself don't feel well," Mikołajczyk answers. An older woman asks a policeman "Who is being buried?" and gets the harsh answer that they are burying a person who needs to be buried.

A horse is pulling the hearse, in which a vase is standing on a box. An inscription says, "The Hope of Restoration of Capitalism in Ukraine." The horse that is pulling the hearse says, "My carriage is the most suitable one for this crowd!" Kubiiovych, former head of the UTsK who, as General Secretary of the Shevchenko Scientific Society after the war, became an important émigré politician, is leading the horse. Dontsov, the ideologist who radicalized and fascistized Ukrainian nationalism, marches on the other side of the horse. The position of Kubiiovych and Dontsov in front of the hearse suggests the continuity of political orientation among Ukrainian émigrés. A man labeled as "Bully" (John Bull) and a man captioned as "Earl" are marching on one side of the hearse. Both are carrying torches. On the other side, Winston Churchill with his characteristic cigar is carrying a torch and shedding a tear.

Six men and a boy are leading the procession. Franco, one of the last European dictators, is marching at the very front. He is carrying a pillow with a scepter and looking at Charles de Gaulle, the French general and statesman who led the Free French Forces during the war. De Gaulle is holding a pillow with a trident, the symbol of Ukraine as introduced by the Ukrainian national movement in the late nineteenth century. The small and stout Franco looks at the tall and thin de Gaulle and asks, "Tell me, General, who is the man in the black mask?"—referring to a man behind them wearing a top hat and with a mask over his eyes. "A president who wants to stay anonymous," de Gaulle answers.

The man with the mask is Harry Truman, president of the USA. He carries a wreath with a black ribbon with the inscription "From Wall Street." On his right, marches Father Vasyl' Laba, a chaplain of the Waffen-SS Galizien. Laba, carrying a wreath from Pope Pius XII, is shedding a tear. To the left of Truman in the caricature, marches Władysław Anders, the Polish general who, after the war, was

84 For antisemitism in the Soviet Union, see Snyder, *Bloodlands*, 339–77.

associated with the Polish anticommunist government-in-exile in London. Anders is carrying a wreath with the inscription "From Forest Colleagues" referring to the Polish nationalist underground (Pol. *leśni ludzie*), which fought against the communists after the Second World War. Randolph Churchill, a small man with a cigar in his mouth, marches in front of the president of the USA. He holds his head high and seems to enjoy himself in the role of an important personality. The identity of the son of the most famous twentieth-century British politician is indicated not only by his cigar but also by the inscription on the ribbon of his wreath: "From Father and Me, R. Churchill." Besides him marches an archetype of a German Nazi, a mixture of Hitler and a conservative general. The plaster on his cheek symbolizes that he is already defeated, but the *Spitzhaube*, or Prussian army helmet, which he carries on a pillow over his head, indicates pride and a will to continue. On the pillow, lower than the Spitzhaube we read "Tsentral'na Rada," the assembly of Ukrainian politicians during the First World War, which collaborated with and depended on the German Empire. The inscription on the banner above the funeral procession reads, "Hopes and Dreams Have Been Shattered." The message is strengthened by a swastika at one end of the banner and by a trident at the other. The inscription under the cartoon says, "They are sad because we are happy."

All in all, the cartoon provided the Soviet audience with a range of messages. It informed its recipients that the Ukrainian nationalists were working with western capitalists who were allied with fascists and continued their anti-Soviet policies in a slightly modified version. The connection between fascism and capitalism was indicated, among other ways, by the prominent positioning of Franco at the very head of the funeral procession, the depiction of Hearst, who sympathized with National Socialism and Italian Fascism in the 1930s, and by several other symbols such as the archetype of a German Nazi mentioned. It also indicated that there was no real difference between fascism and capitalism. Capitalism appeared as a kind of successor to fascism, which had to be replaced after Nazi Germany and fascist Italy were defeated. The cartoon not only marginalized the significance of democracy in the Western bloc after 1945 but also introduced representatives of democratic states as enemies of the Soviet Union, marching along with Nazis. Finally, the cartoon informed its recipients that Ukrainian nationalists had already lost the battle and would not seize power in Ukraine or establish capitalism there but would continue attacking the Soviet Union with the help of "fascists" and "capitalists."

The Reaction of the Nationalist Underground to Soviet Propaganda

The OUN in Ukraine reacted to the Soviet propaganda and began to protect its image. One significant publication that defended the OUN and Bandera was the brochure *Who Are the Banderites and What Are They Fighting For*. The Russian version appeared in 1948, the Ukrainian one in 1950.[85] The Ukrainian version was

85 *Kto takie banderovtsy i za chto oni boriutsia* (OUN pod rukovodstvom Stepana Bandery, 1948); *Khto taki banderivtsi ta za shcho vony boruts'sia* (Kiev, Lviv: OUN, 1950).

Fig. 36. Nil Khasevych. Bandera's woodcut portrait.

published with illustrations by the artist Nil Khasevych, among them Bandera's woodcut portrait. The Russian version appeared without illustrations. Both editions were published anonymously but their author was Petro Fedun, alias Poltava, a member of the OUN, UPA, and UHVR who, unlike Bandera, claimed the supremacy of the UHVR over the OUN. A few years after the publication, Poltava and Khasevych were killed by the NKVD: Poltava in December 1951, Khasevych in March 1952.

One important point in Poltava's brochure was his definition of Banderites:

> Banderites is a popular term for all members of the insurgent and underground struggle that the Ukrainian nation began during the German occupation. ... This term comes from the name of the famous son of the Ukrainian nation, a longstanding revolutionary fighter for the freedom and state independence of Ukraine, the Leader of the revolutionary Organization of Ukrainian Nationalists (OUN)—Stepan Bandera. ... Thus, according to their organization or party membership Banderites are either a) members of the OUN, led by S. Bandera, or b) Ukrainian patriots without a party affiliation who struggle for the freedom and state independence of Ukraine either in the Ukrainian Insurgent Army (UPA) or in the revolutionary underground.[86]

[86] *Khto taki banderivtsi*, 5–6.

Poltava provided a common understanding of the term that would change slightly over time and had a very different meaning in other discourses, in particular the Soviet one. Elsewhere, Poltava added that "deep patriotism" is another important characteristic of Banderites. One proof for the "deep patriotism" of Banderites was the argument that they did not surrender to enemies but shot themselves with their last bullets.[87]

According to Poltava there was nobody in the entire Soviet Union who had not heard about Banderites. Yet the majority of people did not know the truth about them, because they believed Soviet propaganda and therefore thought that Banderites were "'Ukrainian-German nationalists,' that is Hitlerites, or in accordance with the more recent Bolshevik lie, English-American agents, or real 'kurkuls' or 'bourgeois', or real 'bandits.'"[88] Then Poltava claimed that all Soviet propaganda was a lie and that the task of the brochure was therefore "to tell the Soviet people a short truth about us, Banderites, about our revolutionary liberation movement."[89] Thereby, Poltava used Soviet propaganda, which obviously distorted the OUN and the nationalist underground, in order to present his distorted image of the OUN-UPA as a true one. Like many other ideologists in Ukraine and in the diaspora at that time, he depicted the OUN-UPA as a "revolutionary liberation movement," composed of "freedom-loving patriots" and "idealistic romantics" who did not commit any war crimes but only fought for justice, liberty, and independence.

With the help of Soviet propaganda, Poltava also denied collaboration with Germany: "In particular we Banderites have never collaborated with Germans as the Bolshevik enemies of the nation lie about us."[90] Similarly, the author denied the OUN-UPA's terror against Jews, Poles, and Ukrainians and claimed that, because of the Banderites' "famous and heroic" past, the "nation loves and support us."[91] Banderites were for him a group that would rescue not only Ukrainians but all non-Russian nations from the Soviet regime: "We Banderites fight against Bolsheviks because they conduct policies of severe national suppression and economic exploitation of Ukraine and all the other non-Russian nations of the USSR."[92] Poltava also claimed that Bolsheviks "burn alive Ukrainian patriots," by whom he meant Banderites, or sent them to Siberia "for our love for Ukraine." He enumerated several dreadful crimes and stated that Bolsheviks committed them against Ukrainian patriots.[93]

Introducing the program and political aims of the Banderites, Poltava claimed that they were trying to establish "an independent Ukrainian national state in the Ukrainian ethnographic territory." At the same time, he believed that the "Banderite revolutionary movement had nothing in common either with fascism or with Hitlerism" and that only "Bolshevik enemies of the nation connect us with fascism."[94] He also introduced the ABN, which, together with the OUN-UPA, was trying to mobilize

87 Ibid., 27.
88 Ibid., 4.
89 Ibid., 5.
90 Ibid., 9.
91 Ibid., 11.
92 Ibid, 11.
93 Ibid., 16.
94 Ibid., 18, 21.

other nations of the Soviet Union for a struggle against the Soviet regime and stressed that the ABN would be glad if the Russian nation would join their revolutionary struggle.[95]

In addition to his denial of crimes against Jews and Poles, Poltava denied the crimes by the OUN and UPA against those civilians whom the nationalists accused of being communists or supporters of the Soviet regime, and of whom they killed more than 20,000 civilians, including women and children from the families of the "communist traitors": "We do not fight against the Soviet national masses. ... We liquidate only the leading representatives of the party, MVD and MGB agents, and all those collaborating venal elements who actively oppose our movement and are hostile to the Ukrainian nation."[96]

Fig. 37. Nil Khasevych. UPA partisans and a child.

In his brochure, Poltava tried to establish an image of the OUN-UPA that contradicted Soviet propaganda. This nationalist image was no less problematic than the Soviet one. With the destruction of the OUN-UPA in the early 1950s the romanticized image of the national revolutionaries continued to exist in western Ukraine, mainly at the family level or in informal circles. This image was passed from generation to generation, for example, through songs that parents sang to their children, fairy

95 Ibid., 22, 23.
96 Ibid., 25.

tales, or romantic stories about the OUN, UPA, Bandera and Shukhevych, who had heroically fought against the Soviet oppressors for a free Ukraine and died the death of martyrs. “My mother sang me Ukrainian insurgent songs to put me to bed. And we were not an unusual family. Thus the cult of Bandera and the Banderites was very strong among us, already before the fall of communism,” the leading Ukrainian historian Iaroslav Hrytsak, born in 1960, said in an interview in early 2013.[97]

Because romanticizing or expressing admiration for Bandera or the OUN-UPA was punishable, and anyone who did so in public could be accused of counter-revolutionary propaganda, the *Providnyk* became, over time, a symbol of resistance. Simultaneously every black spot on the image of the OUN-UPA and Bandera was whitewashed. The nationalist propaganda that came to Ukraine from abroad was limited but also had some impact on the Bandera image. At their publishing house Cicero, at Zeppelinstrasse 67 in Munich, the ZCh OUN reprinted Bandera’s *Perspectives of the Ukrainian Revolution*, bound with the cover of *From the History of the Collectivization of Agriculture in the Western Oblasts of the Ukrainian SSR*, and smuggled it to Soviet Ukraine, where it was introduced into library catalogues.[98]

Halan—Soviet Martyr and Heroic Intellectual

An interesting question related to the Soviet occupation of western Ukraine and the Bandera myth was the person and cult of the Ukrainian communist writer, Iaroslav Halan, who was born in Dynów in 1902, attended a high school in Przemyśl (Peremyshl’), and joined the KPZU in 1924. Between 1923 and 1928, Halan studied in Vienna and Cracow. He subsequently worked as a teacher of Polish in a Ukrainian high school in Luts’k (Łuck), from which he was soon dismissed because of his communist affiliation, and from then on he earned his living as a journalist. He was arrested in 1936 and 1937. His wife studied in Kharkiv and was killed during one of Stalin’s purges. This, however, did not change Halan’s attitude to the Soviet Union and communism. The most important phase of his career began toward the end of the Second World War and accelerated afterwards when he worked for the newspaper *Radians’ka Ukraïna* as a journalist, and in particular as a correspondent at the Nuremberg trial.[99]

Halan wrote a range of articles, essays, and short stories, which condemned Ukrainian nationalism and the Greek Catholic Church. In that way he attacked the two most important components of western Ukrainian or Galician Ukrainian

97 Masha Mishchenko, “Superechlyvyi heroi Bandera: pysav zukhvali lysty Hitleru i zbytkuvavsia z Handi,” 2 January 2013, http://maxpark.com/community/ukraine/content/1742683 (accessed, 23 February 2013).

98 P. S. Honcharuk, *Z istoriï kolektyvizatsiï sil’s’koho hospodarstva zakhidnykh oblastei Ukraïns’koï RSR* (Kiev: Naukova Dumka, 1976). The publication can be found in several libraries in Ukraine and other countries. Other ZCh OUN books published inside Soviet covers were, for example, the resolutions of the Fifth Great Congress of the OUN with the cover of *Materialy XXV z’ïzdu komunistychnoï partiï Ukrainy* (Kiev: Politvydav Ukrainy, 1976), and a collection of articles by Iaroslav Stets’ko, Ievhen Orlovs’kyi, Oleh Dniprovskyi, and others, with the cover of *Pereiaslav-Khmel’nyts’kyi i ioho istorychni pamiatky* (Kiev: Vydavnytstvo Akademiï Nauk Ukraïns’koï RSR, 1972).

99 Motyka, *Ukraińska partyzantka*, 560; Iurii Mel’nychuk, *Iaroslav Halan: Literaturno-krytychnyi narys* (Kiev: Radians’kyi pys’mennyk, 1951), 14–15; Vitalii Maslovs’kyi, *Zbroia Iaroslava Halana* (Lviv: Kameniar, 1982), 8–15.

identity. At the same time, the Ukrainian communist writer legitimized the Soviet occupation of Ukraine, the Soviet terror against civilians, and the dissolution of the Greek Catholic Church. Because of his talent and the ideological usefulness of his writing, Halan became perhaps the most important western Ukrainian writer and intellectual after the war. His works frequently appeared first as newspaper articles or pamphlets and were then collected and published as brochures or in anthologies.[100] Although Halan was a convinced communist and believed in the Soviet Union and "Moscow's civilizing mission," he criticized some aspects of Soviet policies in western Ukraine, for example the superiority of the Russian language and the destruction of cultural artifacts. The Soviet authorities regarded him as a person who "cannot be trusted blindly."[101]

On 24 October 1949, Halan was murdered at the desk in his apartment by means of a hatchet. After the killing, a wave of repression was directed against the Lviv intelligentsia. Many students were dismissed from the universities.[102] According to Stashyns'kyi, who was slipped into the UPA underground by the MGB to find Halan's murderer, Halan was killed by Mykhailo Stakhur. The UPA partisan came to Halan's apartment together with Ilarii Lukashevych, a student who visited the writer regularly. The guards, who were permanently stationed at the entrance to Halan's apartment building, admitted Stakhur because of his companion. Stakhur was arrested in July 1951 and at the end of a trial on 15 and 16 October 1951, he was sentenced to death and executed on the same day.[103]

Stakhur's trial was a typical Soviet show trial. Several Soviet Ukrainian newspapers published the identical reports of the trial, which confirmed the common Soviet bias concerning Ukrainian nationalism.[104] According to the Soviet Ukrainian press, the judge came to the conclusion that the assassination was organized "on instructions from the Vatican." Stakhur was ordered by his superiors to kill the communist writer because Halan "spoke out against the Vatican and, during the Nuremberg trial, demanded that Stepan Bandera be extradited and put on trial." Stakhur also admitted that he collected secret information for "Stepan Bandera, who passed them to Anglo-American intelligence." The prosecutor demanded "only one judgment, one punishment—death on the gallows [because] a rabid dog should be destroyed."[105]

100 Some of Halan's most important publications are "Z khrestom chy z nozhem?", published under the pseudonym Volodymyr Rasovych in *Vil'na Ukraïna*, 8 April 1945, 5; *Liudy bez bat'kivshchyny* (Kiev: Derzhavne vydavnytsvo khudozhn'oï Literatury, 1952); *Na sluzhbi u Satany* (Kiev: Derzhavne vydavnytsvo khudozhn'oï Literatury, 1952); *Lytsari nasyl'stva i zrady* (Kiev: Radians'kyi pys'mennyk, 1973).

101 Motyka, *Ukraińska partyzantka*, 562.

102 Ibid., 562.

103 "Interrogations of Bohdan Stashyns'kyi," 6 and 7 September 1961, BAK B 362/10141, 38–39, 41–43; Motyka, *Ukraińska partyzantka*, 564–66. For the name of Lukashevych, see "Sudovyi protses u spravi uchasnyka ounivs'koï bandy Stakhura—vbyvtsi pys'mennyka Iaroslava Halana," *Lenins'ka molod'*, 18 October 1951, 1.

104 *Lenins'ka molod'*, 18 October 1951, 1–2; *L'vovskaia pravda*, 16 October 1951, 3–4; *Vil'na Ukraïna*, 16 October 1959, 3; *Vil'na Ukraïna*, 17 October 1959, 3.

105 "Sudovyi protses u spravi uchasnyka ounivs'koï bandy Stakhura—vbyvtsi pys'mennyka Iaroslava Halana," *Lenins'ka molod'*, 18 October 1951, 1–2; "Sudebnyi protsess po delu uchastnika ounovskoi bandy Stakhura—ubiitsy pisatelia Iaroslava Galana," *L'vovskaia pravda* 16 October 1951, 3.

After his death Halan became a Soviet martyr, even more popular than during his life. From 1951 onward, several biographies of Halan appeared.[106] His publications were reprinted many times. Volumes with propagandistic pamphlets, essays, and poems, directed against the "Ukrainian bourgeois nationalists," honored Halan in their titles.[107] In Lviv, Kiev, Kharkiv, and other cities, streets were named after him. In 1954 the film *We Cannot Forget This* appeared, which told the story of a writer named Alexander Garmash and was based on Halan's life.[108] In 1973 the film *Until the Last Minute* also portrayed Halan's "heroic" life.[109] On 24 October 1960, a museum devoted to Halan was opened in the four-room apartment at 18 Hvardiis'ka Street, in which the writer was murdered. In 1972 a monument to Halan was unveiled in Lviv.[110]

The museum familiarized visitors with the writer's life, writings, political activism, and devotion to the idea of communism, with the help of such items as his signature, manuscripts, pictures, letters, illustrations from his publications, personal belongings, and furniture. Each room in the four-room museum apartment was devoted to a different period of Halan's life. The furniture and smaller objects stood, according to the museum-guide booklet, exactly as they had when Halan lived in the apartment. One of the most important items was Halan's desk, at which he was murdered by a "Vatican agent," as the museum-guide booklet informed visitors. The newspapers *Pravda* and *L'vovskaia pravda* and the manuscript of his last work, *The Greatness of a Liberated Person* (*Velych vyzvolenoï liudyny*), lay on the desk. They bore three spots of Halan's blood, which, according to the museum booklet, fell on them when Halan was hit with a hatchet on 24 October 1949.[111]

Exhibits in the fifth room of the museum were collected according to the motto "The Writer Prolongs His Struggle." The museum booklet described it as follows:

> Although Ia. Halan died, his fervent artistic word lives and operates. In Ukraine alone Halan's works were republished fifty times, altogether more than two million copies. They are popular not only in the Soviet Union but also abroad. In addition to his many publications that had already appeared in the fraternal republics of our Motherland, the writer's works appeared in German, Romanian, Hungarian, Czech, and other languages of the countries of the socialist camp.[112]

106 Some of the biographies and historical or literary publications devoted to Halan are Iurii Mel'nychuk, *Iaroslav Halan: Literaturno-krytychnyi narys* (Kiev: Radians'kyi pys'mennyk, 1951); Antolii Elkin, *Iaroslav Galan* (Moscow: Sovietskii pisatel', 1955); Hryhorii Kulinchyk, *Iaroslav Halan* (Kiev: Dnipro, 1965); Vladimir Beliaev and Antolii Elkin, *Iaroslav Galan* (Moscow: Molodaia gvardiia, 1971); *Iaroslav Halan u fotohrafiiakh* (Lviv: Kameniar, 1977); L. A. Dashkivs'ka, *Iaroslav Halan i teatr* (Kiev: Naukova dumka, 1978); Vitalii Maslovs'kyi, *Zbroia Iaroslava Halana* (Lviv: Kameniar, 1982).

107 B. Vasylevych, *Post Iaroslava Halana* (Lviv: Kameniar, 1967).

108 Leonid Lukov (film director), *Ob etom zabyt' nel'zia*, Kinostudia im. Gor'koho, 1954.

109 Valerii Isakov (film director), *Do poslednei minuty*, Odesskaia Kinostudiia, 1973.

110 Grzegorz Rossoliński-Liebe, "Der Raum der Stadt Lemberg in den Schichten seiner politischen Denkmäler" *Kakanien Revisited*, 20 December 2009: 7.

111 Iakiv Tsehel'nyk and Iurii Skrypchenko, *Literaturno-memorial'nyi muzei Iaroslava Halana* (Lviv: Knyzhkovo-zhurnal'ne vydavnytsvo: 1996), 3–36. See also D. Sapiga, *Literaturno-memorial'nyi muzei Iaroslava Galana* (Lviv: Kameniar, 1975), 5–15.

112 Tsehel'nyk, *Literaturno-memorial'nyi muzei*, 36. In 1975 the museum guide booklet stated that Halan's works were republished seventy times in two and a half million copies. Cf. Sapiga, *Literaturno-memorial'nyi muzei*, 15.

Soviet Heroes and Monuments to the Victims of the OUN-UPA

Like the OUN and UPA, Soviet propaganda presented victims of their political opponents as heroes and martyrs. "Having learnt the practice of burning people alive from the German camps," Pavlo Zhytenko wrote, "Banderites tied an old forester to a tree, brought a bunch of dry branches, set them on fire, and the unfortunate victim of the Banderite hangmen died the death of a national martyr."[113] Though the account may have been true, since the OUN and UPA often applied sadistic methods to kill people, one should differentiate between the description of an event and the narrative stylization of their victims. In a sense, all Red Army soldiers who died in the struggle against Nazi Germany or the OUN-UPA were represented by Soviet propaganda as heroes and martyrs. Their death was used to legitimize the Stalinist system and the incorporation of Ukraine in the Soviet Union. Similarly, some NKVD personnel who died while taking action against the nationalist underground were commemorated as martyrs or heroes.

The two best-known individuals turned into Soviet heroes and martyrs in postwar Ukraine were the Red Army general Nikolai Vatutin and the Soviet intelligence agent and partisan Nikolai Kuznetsov. Vatutin died in a hospital in Kiev six weeks after he was injured by a UPA partisan on 28 February 1944. Kuznetsov was killed on 9 March 1944 in a fight against UPA partisans. Not only were several streets, schools, museums, and theatres named after Vatutin and Kuznetsov but also two cities: one founded in 1947 in Cherkasy oblast and known as Vatutine and one founded in 1973 in the Rivne oblast and known as Kuznetsovsk. A monument dedicated to Vatutin was unveiled in Kiev in 1948; one to Kuznetsov in Lviv, in 1962.[114]

In western Ukraine, as in other parts of the Soviet Union, graveyards for the fallen soldiers of the Red Army were established, as were monuments, and memorial complexes in their honor, in almost every city, town, and village. Several were erected in cities such as Lviv. The most popular image of a Soviet politician, present in every Ukrainian town, city, and many villages, was that of Lenin. The local authorities took care of monuments devoted to Soviet politicians and the Red Army. Annual memorial celebrations were organized at the monuments, for example on 9 May, Victory Day. It was however forbidden to commemorate the OUN members and UPA partisans who were killed by the Red Army, the destruction battalions, and the NKVD. According to Soviet ideology, the OUN activists and UPA partisans were killed as bandits and enemies of the Soviet people.[115] The same policies were applied to civilians killed by the NKVD who were not in the OUN-UPA but who either helped the OUN-UPA because the Ukrainian nationalists intimidated them, or who did not help the OUN-UPA at all but were accused of belonging to or helping them. Regardless of their actual status, all such victims of NKVD and other Soviet terror were presented by Soviet propaganda as Banderites, fascists, collaborators, bourgeois

113 Pavlo Zhytenko, "Smert' i vichne prokliattia bandytam!" *Vil'na Ukraïna*, 16 June 1946, 6.

114 David Marples, *Heroes and Villains. Creating National History in Contemporary Ukraine* (Budapest: Central European University Press, 2007), 155, 158; Rossoliński-Liebe, Der Raum der Stadt, 7.

115 On 30 December 1952 the Ministry of Culture of the Ukrainian SSR forbade the erection of monuments without the approval of the authorities. See K. Krepkyi, head of the propaganda section in the Oblast Committee of the KPU to M. K. Lazurenko, Secretary of the Oblast Committee of the KPU, March 1957, DALO, f. 3, op. 6. spr. 97, 40.

nationalists, capitalists, kulaks, and essentially as enemies of the Soviet Union and therefore the Ukrainian people.

In western Ukraine, the KPU built not only monuments that heroized the Red Army and thus indirectly condemned the OUN-UPA but also monuments to the victims of the OUN-UPA or to those who died in the struggle against them. Such monuments were erected in western Ukraine from the early 1950s. In March 1957, as the fortieth anniversary of the October Revolution approached, K. Krepkyi, head of the propaganda section of the Lviv Oblast Committee of the KPU, wrote to M. K. Lazurenko, secretary of the Oblast Committee of the KPU that in the entire Lviv oblast there were only six monuments to "combatants of the Great Patriotic War and Soviet activists who died in the struggle against the Ukrainian bourgeois nationalists."[116] After this complaint, hundreds of relevant monuments were erected.

A number of monuments to people who were killed by the OUN-UPA had plaques with inscriptions such as "Eternal glory to the heroes who gave their lives for the glory and independence of our motherland."[117] Other monuments named the "Ukrainian bourgeois nationalists" as responsible for the killings. Depending on the district, monuments in the Lviv oblast that were explicitly or implicitly devoted to the victims of the OUN-UPA constituted between 10 and 80 percent of all monuments in the late 1960s. In most districts, however, they did not exceed 20 percent.[118]

In the village of Strilkiv, Stryi district, the unveiling of a monument with the inscription "In memory of our fellow-villagers who died in the struggle against the Ukrainian bourgeois nationalists and German-fascist occupiers" was planned for 9 May 1967. The monument was devoted to people from the villages of Strilkiv, Berezhnytsia, Lotatnyky, Slobidka, and Mertiuky who "were murdered by the Ukrainian bourgeois nationalists at the time of establishing Soviet authorities and kolkhoz structures" or who had "died on the fronts of the Great Patriotic War (1941–1945)." In Holobutiv, Stryi district, a monument "in honor of the first kolkhoz chairman who was murdered by Ukrainian bourgeois nationalists" was erected in 1957. In the village of Bratkivtsi, Stryi district, a similar monument devoted to Mykola Dubyk, the first kolkhoz chairman, was unveiled in the same year. In 1961 in the village of Dubliany, Sambir district, a three-meter-high (ten-foot) figure of a combatant was erected for those who were "murdered by the Ukrainian bourgeois nationalists." In the village of Sukhodoly, Brody district, a monument with the inscription "Evstakhii Petrovych Ostrovs'kyi 1928–1945. To the faithful Komsomol member who was murdered by Ukrainian bourgeois nationalists" was erected in the cemetery in 1965. In the village of Kornychi, Sambir district, a concrete pyramid-like monument two and a half meters (eight feet) high "in the memory of those who were murdered by German fascist occupiers and Ukrainian bourgeois nationalists" was erected in 1963.[119]

116 DALO, f. 3, op. 6, spr. 97, 39–40.
117 DALO, f. 3, op. 10, spr. 111, 22.
118 I considered only districts of the Lviv oblast. Monuments devoted explicitly to the Red Army were not included in this estimate, cf. DALO, f. 3, op. 10. spr. 111, 7–82. The statistics relating to relevant monuments in other oblasts of western Ukraine may not follow the same pattern.
119 DALO, f. 3, op. 10, spr. 111, 7, 8, 9, 24, 25, 45.

For the fiftieth anniversary of the October Revolution, the erection of a monument to the "teacher Iosyp Hryhorovych Karl, murdered by Ukrainian bourgeois nationalists" was planned for the village of Zaluzhany, Sambir region. In the town of Turka, Lviv oblast, a four-meter-high (thirteen-foot) obelisk was erected in 1959. A plaque with names of "members of the Komsomol from the Turka district who died in the fight against the Ukrainian bourgeois nationalists" was affixed to the monument. In the Turka district, monuments to the "glorious soldiers-compatriots, who died at the front during the Great Patriotic War in 1941–1945 and also those who died in the struggle against OUN members," were erected in the villages of Bitlia in 1965, Hnyla in 1966, Husne in 1966, Verkhne in 1965, Krivka in 1966. In Pustomyty, a district center in the Lviv oblast, a monument devoted to those who died in the struggle against the "German fascists and Ukrainian nationalists between 1941 and 1948" was erected in 1955. Another monument in Pustomyty, devoted to these who "struggled for the establishment of Soviet power and who were killed by Ukrainian bourgeois nationalist bands" was planned for 1967. At the cemetery in Stryi a monument devoted to "the Hero of the Soviet Union who was killed by Ukrainian bourgeois nationalists" was erected in 1966. A monument was planned to be erected by 1 June 1967 in Skole, in honor of Mykhailo Pon, a "martyred" member of the KPZU, who was "murdered by Ukrainian bourgeois nationalists" on the Makivka mountain in 1933. At the Vasyl' Stefanyk collective farm in Iaseniv, Brody district, and the Taras Shevchenko collective farm in Leshniv, also in the Brody district, monuments were erected to "fellow villagers who died in the Great Patriotic War or were murdered by Ukrainian bourgeois nationalists." In the village of Velykyi Liubin', Horodok district, a memorial plaque was unveiled in 1966 with the inscription "In this place on 26 April 1945 Stepan Hryhorovych, the first head of the village council of Velykyi Liubin', was murdered by Ukrainian bourgeois nationalists. Eternal Glory to the faithful son of the people." In the village of Zvertiv, Nesterov (Zhovkva) district, a three-meter-high (ten-foot) statue of "woman-mother" was unveiled in 1965. The monument was devoted to the "party and Soviet activists who were murdered by Ukrainian bourgeois nationalists." In the village of Turynka, district Nesterov, one monument to "fellow villagers murdered by the Ukrainian bourgeois nationalists" was unveiled in 1962 and another one in 1967. In Pidbuzh, Drohobych district, a monument to soldiers "fallen during the liberation of the village" was erected in 1951. Another one to "fallen activists murdered by the Ukrainian bourgeois nationalists" was erected close to the cultural center and unveiled on 9 May 1967. In the village of Volia, Drohobych district, a 2.7-meter-high (nine-foot) obelisk was erected and unveiled in 1955 at the grave of the "secretary of the Komsomol organization, Mariia Svyshch, who was martyred by Ukrainian bourgeois nationalists."[120]

Between 1965 and 1967, monuments to individuals who were "murdered by Ukrainian bourgeois nationalists" were unveiled in thirty-five villages of the Drohobych district. In the village of Kustyn, Radekhiv district, a statue of "Mother-

120 Ibid., 9, 13–14, 16–17, 18, 20, 36, 46, 49, 52, 56, 57. The plaque on the monument in Pustomyty did not explicitly mention "Ukrainian nationalists," but the secretary of the CPU in Pustomyty district claimed that the monument was dedicated to the victims of the "German fascists and Ukrainian nationalists."

Motherland" (*maty bat'kivshchyna*) who is holding a wounded soldier in her lap was unveiled in March 1966. The monument bore a plaque with names of "fourteen people who in 1941–1945 were killed by the Ukrainian bourgeois nationalists." In the Iavoriv district, the KPU planned to erect six obelisks and one monument on the occasion of the fiftieth anniversary of the October Revolution, to those who "had fallen in the struggle against the German-fascist occupiers and the Ukrainian bourgeois nationalists." In Mykolaïv, a monument to the "glory of the soldiers who fell during the liberation of the town during the Great Patriotic War and for the Soviet activists who were murdered by the Ukrainian bourgeois nationalists during the struggle for the establishment of the Soviet power" was erected in 1946. In the Zolochiv district, six monuments in different villages for "soldiers and fellow villagers who fell in the Great Patriotic War or were murdered by Ukrainian bourgeois nationalists" were erected in 1965 and in 1967. In Boryslav a monument to "soldiers who were murdered by Ukrainian bourgeois nationalists" was erected in 1968.[121]

This enumeration of monuments, which could be prolonged, illustrates that the Soviet authorities tried hard, particularly in villages and small towns, to convince the local residents that the OUN and UPA murdered local civilians and that nationalist insurgents were "traitors" and "enemies of the Ukrainian people." Local Ukrainians exposed to this propaganda knew from their own experience that the nationalist insurgents terrorized the local communities and killed civilians. However, they also remembered the Soviet terror, which was at times even harsher than the nationalist one. Unlike the nationalists' crimes, those of the Soviets were completely absent from the official memory discourse. In reaction to this, western Ukrainians launched an informal anti-Soviet rebellious discourse on the subject of the OUN-UPA. This discourse transformed the OUN-UPA into a symbol of resistance. With time, the criminal, authoritarian, and deeply antidemocratic nature of the Ukrainian nationalist movement was buried in oblivion, and the Ukrainian nationalists reappeared, especially in the late 1980s, as anti-Soviet freedom fighters.[122]

Bandera in the Late Soviet Discourse

From early 1950 onward, an increasing number of monographs and essay collections on Bandera and related subjects appeared, written by historians, journalists, political activists, and members of the Communist Party. There were also joint publications by academics and famous authors, for example Mykhailo Rudnyts'kyi, a professor at Lviv University, with Stalin Prize laureate Vladimir Beliaev. This trend continued until the late 1980s. All official publications in the Soviet Union about Banderites and Ukrainian nationalists were written to extol the Soviet Union and to condemn the Banderites and other enemies. The content and meaning of the publications was monitored by the Soviet censorship.[123]

121 Ibid., 57–59, 63, 65, 66, 69, 82.
122 For a complete list of monuments in the Lviv Oblast, see DALO, f. 3, op. 10, spr. 111, 7–82.
123 For the joint publication, see Vladimir Beliaiev and Mikhail Rudnitskii, *Pod chuzhimi znamenami* (Moscow: Krasnoe znamia, 1954).

Some Soviet Ukrainian historians and writers read and commented on publications from the Ukrainian diaspora such as the newspapers *Svoboda*, *Shliakh peremohy*, and *Nova dumka*. They also mocked the political actions of such diaspora organizations as the Ukrainian Congress Committee of America (*Ukraïns'kyi Kongresovyi Komitet Ameryky*, UKKA) and the Ukrainian Canadian Congress (*Kongres Ukraïntsiv Kanady*, UCC).[124]

Authors in the Soviet Union who wrote political pamphlets frequently claimed that they presented only pure and self-evident facts. The majority of the publications, however, did not quote any sources and did not follow academic rules. The Ukrainian Soviet author and most popular victim of the Ukrainian nationalists, Halan, was the intellectual guru of several Soviet writers and historians. Klym Dmytruk for example, a prolific Soviet writer, ended his essay collection *Without Homeland*, which was translated into English, by citing Halan: "No matter how Stets'ko, Slipyi, Pobihushchyi and other such traitors go out of their way to impede progress, they will never succeed. The renegades should remember the words addressed to them by Yaroslav Halan: 'They will die like traitors at some foreign back door.'"[125]

Soviet historians and writers had access to the archives and were familiar with such crucial documents as "The Struggle and Activities of the OUN in Wartime." For example, Beliaev knew about the blacklists that the OUN-B activists prepared before the beginning of the "Ukrainian National Revolution."[126] Soviet ideology, however, had absolute priority over knowledge of history. The only archival documents quoted by historians were those that did not clash with ideological standards and did not challenge Soviet dogma. One of the most popular Soviet dogmas in the Bandera problematic was the labeling of Theodor Oberländer and the Nachtigall battalion as the killers of the Polish professors in Lviv on the night of 3–4 July 1941. They were also accused of being the main perpetrators of the Lviv pogrom, as well as participants in numerous other massacres after the German invasion of the Soviet Union commenced on 22 June 1941. After Gomułka's speech in 1959, Oberländer appeared frequently in Soviet publications as a "professional killer." Some publications stated that Oberländer killed the Polish professors himself, others that Bandera persuaded Oberländer and the Gestapo to kill the Polish professors, or that Hryn'okh, the battalion chaplain, forgave the soldiers their sin of killing the professors.[127]

Despite the censorship and the obligatory ideological structure, the quality of the Soviet publications about Banderites and Ukrainian nationalists varied. In the 1970s and 1980s a few studies appeared that did not completely ignore the factual side of history. Among their authors were historians such as Vitalii Cherednychenko and V. P. Troshchyns'kyi, who worked in the archives and read English, German, and Polish

124 See, for example, Ievhen Sheremet, *Ukraïntsi za fakhom* (Kiev: Tovarystvo "Ukraïna," 1980), 4; Klim Dmitruk, *Without Homeland* (Kiev: Dnipro Publishers, 1984), 101.

125 Dmitruk, *Without Homeland*, 126.

126 Vladimir Beliaev, *Formula iada* (Moscow: Sovetskii pisatel', 1972), 42. For the document, see page 181 et seq. above, and TsDAVOV f. 3833, op. 2, spr. 1, 15–89. For the blacklists, see TsDAVOV f. 3833, op. 2, spr. 1, 58.

127 Dmitruk, *Without Homeland*, 48; Beliaiev, *Pod chuzhimi znamenami*, 39–40; Vladimir Beliaev, *Ia obviniiaiu!* (Moscow: Izdatel'stvo politicheskoi literatury, 1978), 57; Dieter Schenk, *Der Lemberger Professorenmord und der Holocaust in Ostgalizien* (Bonn: Dietz, 2007), 255; Wachs, *Der Fall*, 207–208.

publications about the Ukrainian nationalists by John Armstrong, Roman Ilnytzkyi, and Ryszard Torzecki. However, even studies written by Cherednychenko, Troshchyns'kyi, and other Soviet historians who did not completely ignore reality are unreliable. In general, their authors mixed Soviet ideology with historical facts. A speech by a communist politician was for them a more reliable source than an original archival document. For example, Cherednychenko quoted Albert Norden, a member of the Central Committee of the SED, as a source to prove that the Nachtigall battalion under the leadership of Oberländer killed 3,000 Poles and Jews in Lviv between 1 and 6 July 1941. And a quotation from Lenin was even better evidence for any claim.[128]

A very important feature of Soviet propagandist writings was the use of emotional and offensive language. Soviet writers and journalists such as Polikarp Shafeta, Klym Dmytruk, and Vladimir Beliaev wrote stories about Banderites with the simple intention of spreading hatred against the nationalist "enemies of the people." Describing the Ukrainian nationalists, Soviet writers used a range of derogatory terms. For example, the OUN was called the "criminal OUN gang"; the Banderites, "Banderite hangmen"; Bandera, a "Führer" and not a *Providnyk* or *Vozhd'* as he called himself and was known among his admirers. Stets'ko was called a "doddering dandy" or "insolent mini-führer." Soviet writers also alleged that the OUN-UPA leaders were rapists and that Shukhevych received medical treatment for a "social disease."[129]

Some of the Soviet publications published in English instrumentalized the war crimes committed by the Ukrainian nationalists and condemned the Western bloc for helping war criminals. One of them concerned Dmytro Sachkovs'kyi,

> a former police commandant in the town of Kolki, Volin Region, [who] found shelter in Winnipeg, Canada. The fascists greatly evaluated his sadistic skills and commissioned him personally to annihilate the Jewish population. For Sachkovski this was the greatest of joys and satisfaction. One summer day in 1941 he sounded the alarm and with his police band organized a round-up in the town. Having driven several dozen people, women, old men and children to the meadow, he commanded. "Down on your knees!"
>
> The people fearing something horrible to come began to sink to the ground.
>
> "And now graze, chew the grass," shouted the police commandant and struck everyone in a row with his ramrod.
>
> The children began to cry, the women and old men were asking for pity. But the commandant was just getting into his role.
>
> "You've had your feed, Jewish cattle," shouted Sachkovski in glee. "Now off you go to the river to drink."

128 For Troshchyns'kyi see, for example, V. P. Troshchyns'kyi, *Naimantsi fashyzmu: Ukraïns'ki burzhuazni natsionalisty na sluzhbi hitlerivtsiv u mizhvoiennyi period 1921–1939 rr.* (Kiev: Naukova dumka, 1981). For Cherednychenko see, for example, Vitalii Cherednychenko, *Natsionalizm proty natsiï* (Kiev: Vydavnytstvo politychnoï literatury Ukraïny, 1970), and *Anatomiia zrady: Ukraïns'kyi burzhuaznyi natsionalizm—znariaddia antyradians'koï polityky imperializmu* (Kiev: Vydavnytstvo politychnoï literatury Ukraïny, 1978). For quoting Norden as a source, see Cherednychenko, *Natsionalizm*, 94.

129 Dmitruk, *Without Homeland*, 52, 83, 99, 104; Beliaiev, *Pod chuzhymy znamenamy*, 41.

They drove them into the Styr river, water up to their necks and a hail of blows from above. The people, exhausted by all this, began falling into the river.

"Serves you right!" smiled the commandant with satisfaction, overjoyed that he could at least make some fun of human misery. Then everybody was forced out of the water and driven on. Bentsion Stanker was 80 years old and from the horrible torture lost his last strength and could not walk. Sachkovski fired a shot. The old man fell, grasped his chest and began writhing in the sandy road.

"End my misery," he asked weakly.

"Want an easy death Jew!" sneered Sachkovski. "By evening you'll die anyway."

The people from the neighboring villages remember even today how this fascist hanger-on killed a boy from the Jewish family Kalman, who hid from the bandits in the chimney. He kissed the boots of Sachkovski, and asked him to hire him as a herdsman, but not to kill him. The killer was inexorable. Hearing the cries of the child, a woman ran out of the house and began to plead for him. Sachkovski killed her too.

So as you see, another Kovalchuk has escaped overseas from national punishment.[130]

Banderites such as Sachkovs'kyi were depicted as sadists who killed for pleasure. In Soviet publications, Banderites and other Ukrainian nationalists normally murdered Soviet people, but in English translations, they frequently killed Jews. This allowed Western readers to follow the stories more easily and find them more credible, and it was sometimes a more appropriate description of the event in question. Jewish policemen who collaborated with the Nazis were described as Zionists who served the Germans in order to "save their own skin." In Soviet publications, Zionists were allied with Ukrainian nationalists. Dmytruk called this alliance a "malignant partnership of the Magen David and the nationalist trident." Zionists were cruel like the Banderites and killed Jews and other Soviet people in the same way as the Nazis did.[131] Although antisemitism was officially forbidden in the Soviet Union, in reality it did exist on many levels. In the 1960s, the anti-Zionist campaign directed against Israel presented Zionists and Jews as Nazi collaborators, and Zionism as a "world threat."[132]

Soviet Ukrainian movies were another medium that featured Bandera. The leader of the Banderites appeared especially in films about the OUN-UPA, Ukrainian nationalism, and the Second World War. Examples were *The Nation Blames*,[133] *Since We Remember*,[134] *The Killer Is Known*,[135] *They Did Not Come Back from the Route*,[136]

130 P. Shafeta, *People and Cains: Essays, Articles, Pamphlets* (Kiev: Politvidav Ukraini Publishers, 1982), 79–80.

131 Dmitruk, *Without Homeland*, 63–65. For equating Nazism with Zionism in Soviet history, see Dietsch, *Making sense*, 109.

132 Per Anders Rudling, "Anti-Semitism and the Extreme Right in Contemporary Ukraine," *Mapping the Extreme Right in Contemporary Europe: From Local to Transnational*, ed. Andrea Mammone, Emmanuel Godin, and Brian Jenkins (London: Routledge, 2012), 191–92; Snyder, *Bloodlands*, 348–49.

133 V. Sychevs'kyi (film director), *Narod zvynuvachuie*, Ukrainokhroniky 1959.

134 A. Fedoriv (film director), *Vidkoly pam"iataie istoriia*, Ukrainokhroniky 1969.

135 L. Udovenko (film director), *Vbyvtsia vidomyi*, Ukrainokhroniky 1972.

136 F. Karpins'kyi (film director), *Z marshruta ne vernulys'*, Ukrainokhroniky 1975.

and *Militant Atheists*.[137] The films frequently addressed the subject of the murder of civilians by Ukrainian nationalists during and after the Second World War. Similarly to the Soviet writers, the film directors used the actual atrocities committed by the OUN-UPA and other Ukrainian nationalist formations to spread hatred against all opponents of the Soviet Union who could be denounced as Banderites. They frequently showed people without arms or legs and claimed that they were the victims of the Ukrainian nationalists. Other popular themes in these films included the exhumation of mass graves, and the trials of OUN members or UPA partisans who confessed to killing "Soviet people" on orders from Bandera, Shukhevych, or Kubiiovych.

Banderites also became a popular subject for historical novels and films in communist Poland and Czechoslovakia.[138] In Poland, fifty-eight academic and popular historical works, fifty autobiographies, and sixty novels about the OUN-UPA and Ukrainian nationalism appeared.[139] Like the books and films in the Ukrainian SSR, they omitted many central facts that contradicted the official line. A few of them introduced entirely fabricated events. One of the most popular publications in Poland was *Fiery Glow in the Bieszczady Mountains* by Jan Gerhard (Wiktor Lew Bardach).[140] It appeared in 1959, was reprinted twelve times, and a total of 500,000 copies were distributed in Poland. In 1961 Ewa Patelska and Czesław Patelski filmed the novel as *Artillery Sergeant Kalen*, which was frequently screened on television.[141] The subject of the novel and the film was the defeat of the OUN-UPA and Polish anticommunist armies by Polish Communist troops in the Bieszczady Mountains during the first two years after the Second World War. As in other communist productions, there was enormous polarization between good and brave communists and bad and cruel nationalists. The execution of Polish soldiers taken prisoner is presented in the movie as a ritual execution with a huge hatchet, during which a crowd of UPA partisans screams, "Bandera, Bandera, Bandera!"[142]

The word "Banderites" was an important component of the Soviet propaganda discourse, at least since 1944. All kinds of people who opposed Soviet policies in some way, or were accused of opposing them, could be classified as Banderites, especially if they had some sympathy for nationalism, or if they or their relatives were in the OUN or the UPA. The word "Banderites" had a very derogatory meaning and basically meant a traitor of the Ukrainian nation, a Nazi collaborator, a fascist, an enemy of the Soviet Union, a murderer with blood on his hands, or a spy for Western intelligence services. The word was frequently used to discredit anti-Soviet dissidents

137 Ie. Tatarets' (film director), *Voiovnychi ateïsty*, Ukrainokhroniky 1985.

138 For publications on the OUN-UPA in Czechoslovakia, see Michal Šmigeľ, *Banderovci na Slovensku 1945–1947: Niektoré aspekty pôsobenia jednotiek Ukrajinskej povstaleckej armády na území krajiny* (Banská Bystrica: Katedra histórie Fakulty humanitných vied Univerzity Mateja Béla, 2008), 9–43.

139 Grzegorz Motyka, "Obraz Ukraińca w literaturze Polski Ludowej," in *Problemy Ukraińców w Polsce po wysiedleńczej akcji "Wisła" 1947 roku*, ed. Włodzimierz Mokry (Cracow: Szwajpolt Fiol, 1997), 216.

140 Jan Gerhard, *Łuny w Bieszczadach* (Warsaw: Wydawnictwo Ministerstwa Obrony Narodowej, 1959). For the real name, see Grzegorz Motyka, "'Łuny w Bieszczadach' Jana Gerharda a prawda historyczna," Problemy Ukraińców, ed. Mokry, 161.

141 Ewa Patelska and Czesław Patelski, *Ogniomistrz Kaleń*, Zespół Filmowy Studio, 1961.

142 *Ogniomistrz Kaleń*. Other popular novels were Henryk Cybulski, *Czerwone noce* (Warsaw: Wydawnictwo Ministerstwa Obrony Narodowej, 1969), and Tadeusz Kruk, *Karabin i menazka* (Warsaw: Czytelnik, 1964).

and other political opponents. With time, the term "Banderite" or sometimes just "bandera" became popular not only in Soviet Ukraine but also in other republics and satellite states of the Soviet Union. Danylo Shumuk—who had spent forty-five years in total in Polish, German, and Soviet prisons and camps—was, after his release in 1970, described by a local man in a streetcar in Odessa as a "bandera" because he spoke Ukrainian.[143]

The eponym Bandera, as in Banderite (*banderivets'* or *bandera*) in the singular and Banderites (*banderivtsi*) in the plural, was omnipresent in Soviet publications about Ukrainian nationalism. All OUN members, UPA partisans, and frequently all Ukrainian nationalists were described as Banderites. The person Stepan Bandera was also introduced in almost every publication on the Second World War and Ukrainian nationalism but did not have as prominent a role as the eponym. Bandera as a person and politician did not receive much more attention than such prominent "Banderites" as Konovalets', Stets'ko, and Bul'ba-Borovets'. It is also of interest that there were very few Soviet publications devoted to Stepan Bandera alone.

The prolific Soviet Ukrainian writer Iurii Mel'nychuk claimed about Banderites:

> Banderites is an ugly word. It became a synonym for betrayal, selling out, fratricide. Any honest person who has to pronounce the word gets a feeling of outrage, hate, and repulsion toward the hideous monsters. This is a very appropriate feeling because when we talk about Banderites we mean the Ukrainian bourgeois nationalists, their betrayal and selling out, snakelike ferocity, and hostility toward the Ukrainian people.
>
> Go to the villages of the western Ukrainian oblasts and ask children in the presence of whom the Banderite villains killed their parents; ask old grandmothers who saw Banderites shoot their sons, daughters, grandchildren with German parabellums; go to those villages where Banderites burnt national property, and ask, "Who are the Banderites?" You will hear from old and young the answer, "Bloody killers, fascist brutes, bandits." ...
>
> The great Soviet people routed the German fascist hordes. Soviet Ukraine liberated itself from the fascist occupation; the people began a peaceful, creative life. And the pitiful remnants, the Ukrainian-German nationalists, the Banderites, went to the forest and emerged from their caves only in the dark nights to kill, hang, burn, rob, to disturb the peaceful life and the socialistic construction. But the people with its angry hand destroyed, crushed the national-fascist Banderite beast.
>
> There are no Banderites anymore. The collective farmer, worker, teacher, and Komsomol member now work peacefully. However, we have no right to stop being careful and alert, we should detect and liquidate every kind of alien propaganda because our repulsive enemies—the Anglo-American imperialists—do not like the peaceful life and creative success of the Soviet people.[144]

143 Shumuk, *Za skhidnim obriiem*, 441.

144 Iurii Mel'nychuk, "Banderivs'kykh holovoriziv pokarano," in *Sluhy zhovtoho diiavola*, ed. Iurii Mel'nychuk (Lviv: Knyzhkovo-zhurnal'ne vydavnytsvo, 1957), 36–37.

Shortly after Bandera's assassination, the same Ukrainian Soviet writer wrote the pamphlet *At Foreign Thresholds*, in which he rewrote the story of Bandera's life, including the complicated collaboration with the Germans and the Western bloc, and compared him to a dog. The story begins with the dog biting its master, a priest who has taken care of it since it was a pup. The angry master sends the dog away, and it lives on garbage, but after some time the master feels sorry for his dog and takes it in again. However, the Bandera dog and another villainous dog begin raiding and terrorizing the neighborhood, as a result of which the neighbors organize themselves and beat the dog so hard that it barely survives. Other people drive it from the village. Living alone, the dog attacks people and bites them, which it considers to be heroism. Villainous dogs join him. A foreign master lures him with a bone. He calls him by shouting "Wo ist mein Hund? [Where is my dog?]," and the Bandera dog barks "Heil Hitler!" to the master. After some time, the new master begins a war and takes his dog with him. The war is in the territory where the dog grew up, so he "runs ahead of his master, shows him the way, warns him about dangers, guards his peace and life ... snaps at the throats of his countrymen." On one occasion, the new master shoes a horse. The Bandera dog, very proud of his achievements, comes to him, stretches out his paw, and wants to be shod like the horse. This makes the master so angry that he punishes the dog. When the war ends with dog's master losing, the dog finds a new master for whom it has to change the tone of its barking, but not to stop barking for another war. After some time, however, the dog irritates the new master, who hits it. One day, on the way to his apartment the dog falls from the steps and dies. Following this fable, Mel'nychuk informed his readers that Stepan Bandera—the "villain of a Ukrainian fascist"—had recently died, and that his fall from the steps was a secret murder, carried out on the orders of Theodor Oberländer, whom Bandera was blackmailing. The author then insinuated, while introducing the term "banderivshchyna" (Bandera movement) that Bandera was the person responsible for the death of 310,000 persons in Lviv after the German attack on the Soviet Union. The same number appeared in the charge against the Nachtigall battalion and Oberländer, which the VNN filed on 31 July 1959 by the Federal State Administration of Justice Department in Ludwigsburg. Mel'nychuk finished his pamphlet with the saying "A dog's death for a dog."[145]

[145] Iurii Mel'nychuk, "Pid chuzhym porohom," in *Prodai-dushi*, ed. Iurii Mel'nychuk (Lviv: Kameniar, 1967), 164–71. For the charge, see LN-W: Gerichte Rep. 350, vol. 1, 6–9, and chapter 7 above.

Conclusion

Soviet propaganda took notice of Bandera and the OUN-B in the summer of 1941, but it only started a campaign against the Ukrainian nationalists in early 1944. As a result of various cultural, social and political processes, Soviet propaganda made Bandera into one of the most significant symbols of Ukrainian nationalism. Khrushchev and other Soviet politicians used the term "Banderites" to label all kinds of political opponents. This entirely changed the meaning of the term, which had originally been used by the victims of OUN-UPA mass violence to define its perpetrators. During the early conflict with the Ukrainian nationalists, the Soviet authorities used violence for propaganda purposes. Many "Banderites" were publicly hanged by the NKVD, while rumors were spread that they were in the possession of severed human ears at the time of arrest. The first major propaganda campaign against the Ukrainian nationalists branded the OUN and UPA as "German-Ukrainian nationalists." It portrayed the Ukrainian nationalist movement as an integral part of the German Empire which continued to fight and terrorize the population even after the defeat of its master. In early 1947 Soviet propaganda began to call the OUN and UPA "bourgeois nationalists" and to emphasize the cooperation of the Ukrainian nationalists with Western countries. Because capitalism in the Soviet discourse was considered to be a deformed variant of fascism, these countries were frequently also labeled as "fascist." Furthermore Bandera and his movement were depicted as people who had betrayed Ukraine, just as Vlasov, in the Soviet propaganda, had betrayed Russia.

Soviet propaganda turned everybody, including Soviet soldiers and NKVD officers, killed by the Ukrainian nationalists or Germans, into heroes and martyrs. One of the most famous Soviet martyrs killed by the Ukrainian nationalists was the western Ukrainian communist writer Iaroslav Halan. After his assassination a memorial museum was erected in his apartment and monuments were devoted to him. Likewise the Soviet authorities named cities after Soviet generals and partisans who had been killed by the Ukrainian nationalists. They also erected numerous monuments to all kinds of the OUN and UPA victims. The victory over the Ukrainian nationalists became a significant component of the Ukrainian Soviet myth. Together with the denial of Soviet mass violence against the Ukrainian civilians it did not allow for many Ukrainians to mourn their relatives. It thereby impacted upon the memory of the atrocities committed by the Ukrainian nationalists, who in these circumstances were turned by ordinary western Ukrainians into martyrs and anti-Soviet heroes.

Chapter 9

THE REVIVAL OF THE CULT

Bandera's Death and the Funeral

Bandera's assassination transformed him into a martyr and reinforced his political cult and myth. Immediately after the killing, factions of the Ukrainian diaspora turned his death into one of the greatest catastrophes in Ukrainian history. They triggered a plethora of deeply politicized and ritualized mourning commemorations that went on for several weeks. In this way, the diaspora communities revitalized the cult of the *Providnyk* and turned themselves once more into a "charismatic community." After his death, Bandera was commemorated in several countries including Argentina, Australia, Belgium, Brazil, Britain, Canada, France, the United Kingdom, the United States, and Venezuela. The globalization of the Bandera cult would not have been possible without the relocation of the DPs in the late 1940s and early 1950s. The most enthusiastic émigré element that commemorated Bandera consisted of those Ukrainians who left Ukraine in 1944 with the retreating German army, and the Waffen-SS Galizien veterans who surrendered to the British army. Some of these émigrés were already admirers of Bandera during the trials in Warsaw and Lviv in 1935–1936, regarded him as their *Providnyk* during the "Ukrainian National Revolution" in the summer of 1941, or knew him as the legendary leader of the revolutionary movement when they fought in the UPA.

The Munich *Shliakh peremohy*, one of the main newspapers controlled by the ZCh OUN, for which Bandera had officially worked as a journalist, turned the front page of 18 October 1959 into a huge obituary with Bandera's photograph placed in the center (Fig. 39). Although at this time it was neither known who had killed Bandera nor whether he had actually been assassinated, the editors stated in oversized letters above the portrait and under a cross in a military style: "With great sadness and pain we inform the members of the OUN and Ukrainian society that, at 1.00 p.m. on 15 October 1959, STEPAN BANDERA, the Great Son of the Ukrainian Nation and the longstanding leader of the revolutionary fight for the state independence of Ukraine, Head of the Leadership of the Foreign Units of the Organization of Ukrainian Nationalists, was killed by an enemy's hand." On both sides of the picture, the editors provided some biographical background: "a longstanding prisoner of Polish jails who was sentenced by a Polish court to a death sentence, which was changed to a life sentence, and who was a prisoner in German jails and concentration camps from 1941 to 1944." The front page also informed readers that after a church service at 9.00 a.m. on 20 October 1959, Bandera's funeral and a panakhyda would take

Fig. 38. Bandera's corpse in the coffin. Poltava, *Zhyttia Stepana Bandery*, 51.

place at 3.30 p.m. at the Waldfriedhof in Munich and that the mourning period for the *Providnyk* would last from 15 October until 15 December.[1]

Other nationalist newspapers published in the Ukrainian diaspora, such as the Toronto *Homin Ukraïny* and the London *Ukraïns'ka dumka* addressed Bandera's death in a similar manner. *Homin Ukraïny* turned the front page of the issue for 24 October 1959 into a huge obituary with Bandera's photograph featured in the middle. The headline consisted of the inscription: "Of bright memory" (*sl. p*) and the name "STEPAN BANDERA." Introductions to two articles, which continued on page 6, were printed on either side of the photograph. One article was entitled "Fighter, Leader, and Symbol," while the second was entitled "In Deep Sadness." They informed readers that the death of Bandera "shocked the entire Ukrainian diaspora on this side of the ocean" and that he was killed by an enemy of the Ukrainians. Readers were advised that, in the person of Bandera, a symbol of both the general Ukrainian struggle and of an entire epoch in the struggle for independence had passed away.[2]

1 *Shliakh peremohy*, 18 October 1959, 1.
2 "Borets', Providnyk i Symvol," "U hlybokomu smutku...," *Homin Ukraïny*, 24 October 1959, 1, 6.

ШЛЯХ ПЕРЕМОГИ

Der Weg zum Sieg
Ukrainische Wochenschrift

The Way to Victory
Ukrainian Weekly

„SCHLACH PEREMOHY"

43 (296) Неділя 18. жовтня 1959 р. Рік видання VI.

З великим смутком і болем повідомляємо Членство ОУН і Українське Громадянство, що 15. жовтня 1959 р. о 1. год. дня загинув з ворожої руки Великий Син Українського Народу і довголітній керівник революційної боротьби за державну незалежність України, Голова Проводу Закордонних Частин Організації Українських Націоналістів

СТЕПАН БАНДЕРА

Член Української Військової Організації з 1927 р.

Член Організації Українських Націоналістів з 1929 р.

Член Крайової Екзекутиви ОУН з 1931 р., а згодом до 1934 р. її Провідник і одночасно Крайовий Комендант УВО, та з 1933 р.

Член Проводу Організації Українських Націоналістів.

Похорони відбудуться в Мюнхені у вівторок 20. жовтня 1959 року в такому порядку: о 9. год. Заупокійна Служба Божа в церкві св. Івана Хрестителя; о 15.30 год. — Панахида й похорон на кладовищі Вальдфрідгоф.

Голова Проводу Організації Українських Націоналістів з 1940 р.

Голова Бюра Проводу всієї ОУН з 1945 р.

Довголітній в'язень польських тюрем, засуджений польським судом на кару смерти, замінену на досмертну тюрму, та в'язень німецьких тюрем і концтаборів з 1941 до 1944 р.

Жалоба триватиме два місяці — з 15. жовтня по 15. грудня 1959 року.

* 1. 1. 1909. † 15. 10. 1959.

Вічна й славна Йому пам'ять!

Провід Закордонних Частин
Організації Українських Націоналістів

Fig. 39. *Shliakh peremohy*, 18 October 1959, 1.

On the front page of 22 October 1959, instead of an obituary, *Ukraïns'ka dumka* published a photograph of Bandera's bust and a long, lamenting, and apologetic article that began with: "Stepan Bandera does not live! Stepan Bandera was killed by an enemy's hand." The bust had been prepared in a DP camp in Bavaria in 1948 in two copies, one wooden and one of gypsum, by Mykhailo Chereshn'ovs'kyi, a UPA partisan who had arrived in Bavaria from Ukraine in 1947. It showed Bandera some twenty years before his death, perhaps in the early 1940s, when the OUN-B was conducting the "Ukrainian National Revolution."[3] The article claimed that the news about Bandera's death reached "not only Ukrainian society but all patriots of all other nationalities" with lightning speed and saddened them. Readers were informed that 15 October would "remain forever a day of mourning for the whole Ukrainian nation, exactly like the anniversaries of the deaths of Symon Petliura, Ievhen Konovalets', and Taras Chuprynka [Roman Shukhevych]." The article also claimed that with "the moment of Bandera's death came the time when all Ukrainian patriots, without exception, were obliged to ... value Bandera as a revolutionary and politician." It ended with the assertion that Bandera's death should not be understood as an end. On the contrary, it should inspire the faithful revolutionary émigré nationalists to further struggle:

> The name of Stepan Bandera was, during his lifetime, a militant banner for the whole Ukrainian nation and it remains such after the death of the Providnyk of the Ukrainian national liberation revolution, until our Fatherland definitively, once and for all, by the blood of the Heroes of the sanctified land, rids itself of every enemy and foe.[4]

The obituaries and mourning articles referred to Bandera as a true patriot and a national hero, and depicted him as a fearless opponent of Nazi Germany and the Soviet Union. Especially after his death, to mention that he was a fanatic, a radical nationalist fascinated with fascism, or a Nazi collaborator, was regarded as Soviet propaganda, or as a Jewish or Polish provocation. The OUN members, veterans of the UPA and the Waffen-SS Galizien, and other Ukrainian nationalists, who identified themselves with Bandera, were especially irritated by articles about Bandera that described the war crimes committed by the OUN or UPA. In reaction to such articles, the nationalist émigrés frequently blamed the author for spreading anti-Ukrainian propaganda and described how the NKVD, Poles, or Germans killed Ukrainians.[5]

On 5 November 1959, *Ukraïns'ka dumka* reprimanded Juliusz Sokolnicki for committing a "disgraceful act." Sokolnicki had published an article in the *Daily Telegraph*, in which he connected Bandera with the UPA's ethnic violence against the Polish population in 1943–1944. The editors of *Ukraïns'ka dumka* demanded an apology. The Association of Ukrainians in Great Britain (*Soiuz ukraïntsiv u Velykii*

3 Dmytro Stepovyk, *Skul'ptor Mykhailo Chereshn'ovs'kyi: Zhyttia i tvorchist'* (Kiev: Vydavnytstvo imeni Olehy Telihy, 2000), 89.

4 "Stepan Bandera," *Ukraïns'ka dumka*, 22 October 1959, 1–2.

5 For pride in being Banderites, see "Pered maiestatom smerty sv. p. Stepana Bandery," *Ukraïns'ka dumka*, 19 October 1959, 3. For annoyance at connecting Bandera with the OUN-UPA's war crimes and for emphasizing Soviet, Polish, or German atrocities against Ukrainians, see "Hanebnyi vchynok poliaka," *Ukraïns'ka dumka*, 5 November 1959, 1.

Brytanii, SUB) tried to publish a letter of protest in the *Daily Telegraph* and, when it was not accepted, published it in *Ukraïns'ka dumka*. In the letter the SUB activists claimed that they were shocked by Sokolnicki, who was "misinformed concerning the life and career of Mr. Bandera." They emphasized that Bandera was imprisoned from July 1941 until April 1945 and that "therefore he cannot be held responsible for anything that happened in Ukraine in 1944, particularly from 1943 onwards." Similarly, they claimed that "it was the troops of [the Soviet partisan leader Sydir] Kovpak who carried out the atrocities [and who] had been sent to wipe out [the Ukrainian nationalist freedom fighters] under orders from Moscow." They described the "persecutions that the inhabitants of West Ukraine suffered under the Polish occupation" and added that "in face of our common enemy—Russian Communism—there should be cooperation between our two nations."[6] The incorrect dating of Bandera's imprisonment suggests that the *Providnyk's* admirers did not know much about him. More interesting, however, is how they whitewashed the war crimes of the OUN and UPA, with the help of a victimized and instrumentalized image of Bandera. Such denial of the OUN and UPA atrocities would continue for over half a century. His critics, on the other hand, would make Bandera personally responsible for crimes which were committed by his movement and not by him in person.

Given the number of religious and political commemorations that Bandera's admirers performed in October and November 1959, reprimanding people who mentioned OUN-UPA atrocities was only a marginal activity. The commemorations were organized among the Ukrainian diaspora around the globe, in countries such as Argentina, Australia, Austria, Belgium, Brazil, Canada, France, West Germany, New Zealand, the United Kingdom, and the United States.[7] Religion and politics blurred in these deeply ritualized ceremonies. During the panakhydas, the priests frequently introduced political motifs, mainly hatred against the Soviet Union and Russia, and sometimes also against the Jews and Poles. The gatherings and demonstrations after the panakhydas frequently became orgies of political hatred against the "red devil." Like the panakhydas, they mingled politics with religion.[8]

The Bandera family and the ZCh OUN received several hundred letters of condolence from individuals, mainly diaspora Ukrainians including schoolchildren, and from several dozen organizations such as the UPA, Waffen-SS Galizien veterans, and Ukrainian nationalist student and religious organizations.[9] Various nationalist celebrations that had been planned before 15 October 1959 were renamed to honor Stepan Bandera, for instance the UPA celebration organized by the association of

6 "Stepan Bandera i ioho ochorniuvachi," *Ukraïns'ka dumka*, 12 November 1959, 1; "Hanebnyi vchynok poliaka," *Ukraïns'ka dumka*, 5 November 1959, 1.

7 The list of localities, in which the Bandera commemorations took place in 1959, included Amberg, Amsterdam, Boston, Brantford, Buenos Aires, Buffalo, Calgary, Chatham, Chicago, Cleveland, Curitiba, Denver, Detroit, Düsseldorf, Edinburgh, Edmonton, Flin Flon, Frankfurt, Hamilton, Innsbruck, Jersey City, Klagenfurt, Landshut, Lightbridge, Liège, London, Manchester, Mons, Montreal, Munich, New York, Nottingham, Osnabrück, Ottawa, Paris, Philadelphia, Pittsburgh, Port Arthur, Port William, Regensburg, Regina, São Paulo, Saskatoon, Sudbury, Toronto, Vancouver, Vienna, Wellington, Winnipeg.

8 "Pomynal'ni Bohosluzhenia v tserkvakh Toronta," *Homin Ukraïny*, 24 October 1959, 6; "U poshanu providnykovi," *Homin Ukraïny*, Toronto, 31 October 1959, 7; *Homin Ukraïny*, 7 November 1959, 3; *Homin Ukraïny*, 14 November 1959, 5–6; Chaikovs'kyi, *Moskovs'ki vbyvtsi*, 512–30.

9 Chaikovs'kyi, *Moskovs'ki vbyvtsi*, 504–12.

former UPA soldiers in Canada on 18 October in Toronto.[10] In some cities, including London, the celebrants repeated the Bandera commemorations in late 1959.[11]

All Ukrainian newspapers, not only those controlled by the ZCh OUN but many others, for example the New Jersey *Svoboda*, the main newspaper of the Ukrainian diaspora, reported on Bandera's funeral. On its front page on 31 October 1959, the *Homin Ukraïny* featured an article entitled "The Final Journey of the Providnyk Bandera." The authors glorified "the final 500-meter journey of Bandera" during which time he was accompanied by ten priests and 1,500 mourners. Admirers came from all around the world to bid farewell to their *Providnyk*, who "perished on the forefront of a bloody, lingering war against the cruel, deceitful, villainous enemy." *Svoboda* and *Ukraïns'ka dumka* claimed that over 2,000 people attended the funeral. To show readers the seriousness of the tragedy that had struck Ukrainians, newspapers printed several photographs from the funeral. *Homin Ukraïny* published a photograph showing Bandera's coffin carried by four men, with the funeral procession following it. Marching alongside the coffin in the center of the photograph are a man in a suit and four uniformed young women, apparently members of the SUM. The faces of the man and all four uniformed teenagers appear to be filled with sorrow and concern. One of the women is looking down at the ground and weeping. The eyes of the man in the suit are focused on the final 500 meters of his *Providnyk's* journey. His face is not only sad but also appears pensive and seemingly irritated. The facial expressions of all the people in the picture communicate the same message—that of the loss of an irreplaceable personality.[12]

During the funeral, Stets'ko delivered a speech, which later appeared in several newspapers. The leader of the ABN claimed that Bandera's name was the symbol of the contemporary anti-Moscow struggle of Ukraine for independent statehood and personal freedom, and that Bandera's phenomenon grew outside the frame of the revolutionary OUN, becoming common Ukrainian property, representative of the whole fighting nation. In another part of the speech, Stets'ko praised Bandera's piety as a motivation for struggle: "Christianity was an indivisible part of His spirituality, faith in God, and Christian morality—a principle of His dealing, His strong patriotism. His nationalism was integrally linked with Christianity. He knew that we can struggle successfully against Moscow, the center of combative godlessness and tyranny, only if, next time, Ukraine proves its historical role in Eastern Europe." And this would be a "struggle for the Christ against the Antichrist-Moscow." Toward the end of his speech, Stets'ko became spiritual and metaphysical: "Today we separate from Bandera's physical remains, but he will live in our hearts, in the souls of the Ukrainian nation, and THAT STEPAN BANDERA will be not seized from us by any brutal, physical, barbaric Moscow's strength."[13]

10 "Sviato UPA pid znakom smerty sl. p. S. Bandery;" *Homin Ukraïny*, 24 October 1959, 7.

11 "Zhalobna akademiia v pam"iat' Stepana Bandery, 13.12.1959," ASBML, 1638.

12 "Ostannia doroha providnyka Bandery," *Homin Ukraïny*, 31 October 1959, 1. See also the pictures in *Homin Ukraïny*, 31 October 1959, 1; *Svoboda*, 31 October 1959, 1; *Ukraïns'ka dumka*, 29 October 1959, 1.

13 "Slovo Iaroslava Stets'ka nad vidkrytoiu mohyloiu sl. p. Stepana Bandery," *Ukraïns'ka dumka*, 22 October 1959, 1–2; "Slovo Iaroslava Stets'ka nad mohyloiu S. Bandery," *Shliakh peremohy*, 25 October 1959, 1. Emphasis in the original.

Fig. 40. Bandera's Funeral Munich, 20 October 1959. TShLA.

Those diaspora Ukrainians who could not attend the funeral in Munich mourned Bandera in their above-mentioned locations. In Edmonton, the Organizations of the Liberation Front (*Orhanizatsiï Vyzvol'noho Frontu*, OVF) started to prepare for commemorations on 15 October 1959, the day of Bandera's death. On 20 October, the day of Bandera's funeral in Munich, memorial services were organized in almost all Ukrainian churches in Edmonton. On 25 October, a panakhyda was organized at the St. Josaphat Ukrainian Catholic Cathedral at 7 p.m., with six priests officiating. Members of the SUM and the Plast Scout Organization appeared in their uniforms and presented their banners. Members of the LVU were also in attendance. The cathedral was full of people, both uniformed and in plain clothes. After the male choir of the Ukrainian National Home (*Ukraïns'kyi Narodnyi Dim*) enriched the atmosphere in the church with its vocal performances, the parish priest delivered a sermon, in which he praised Bandera's love, commitment, and labor for Ukraine. The blue-and-yellow flag of Ukraine and the red-and-black flag of the OUN were flown at the entrance to the church, where young girls distributed black ribbons.[14]

After the church service, the celebration continued at the Ukrainian National Home, which had also been decorated with flags. It was there that the mourning assembly (*zhalibna akademiia*) took place. The hall could not accommodate the crowd that had gathered to mourn Bandera's death, and some people were turned away. The commemorative gathering opened with Chopin's "Funeral March." A person referred to as "D. M." read a poem entitled "Immortal Son" (*Bezsmertnyi syn*), which he had written for Bandera, then the male voice choir of the Ukrainian

14 "U pokloni Providnykovi," *Homin Ukraïny*, 7 November 1959, 3.

National Home sang several religious and nationalist songs. Bandera's portrait was central to the stage decoration and had been prepared especially for the occasion by the renowned Ukrainian artist Professor Iuliian Butsmaniuk. The portrait hung on a black wall in the background, with Bandera's dates of birth and death on either side, with a huge wreath and a trident, the symbol of Ukraine, as well as two baskets with red roses placed underneath.[15]

In Ottawa, Ukrainians formed a committee of LVU and SUM members. At 5:30 on 25 October 1959, V. Shevchuk conducted a panakhyda in the Greek Catholic church, during which the SUM choir in uniform sang several nationalist and religious songs. Toward the end of the panakhyda, the priest introduced the person of the "deceased Providnyk and Vozhd' of the Ukrainian nation" in "touching words." After the panakhyda a commemorative gathering took place, apparently attended by Ukrainians with various political views.[16]

In Cleveland, all festivities and dancing in the Ukrainian community were cancelled as a result of the sad news. The SUM ballet group, which was to have performed at a Democratic Party event, refused to dance. On 20 October 1959, the Greek Catholic church was filled with uniformed SUM and Plast members. In the Ukrainian Orthodox church, the priest characterized Bandera as a patriot and defender of Ukraine and drew an analogy between him and George C. Marshall, who was buried on the same day in Washington. After the church services, the mourners went to the SUM building where they performed the political part of the commemoration with the help of a symbolic coffin of the *Providnyk*.[17]

On 1 November 1959, Ol'ha Lus'ka published one of the first poems relating to Stepan Bandera.[18] Leonid Poltava (Leonid Parkhomovych) published another on 7 November.[19] During the following weeks, months, and years, a number of other poems devoted to the *Providnyk* appeared, in Ukrainian, German, and English.[20] On 14 November, *Homin Ukraïny* reported that Radio Prague broadcast the news about Bandera's death one hour before he actually died.[21] Photographs of Bandera's bust were printed next to eulogistic articles that were supposed to make his demise look more pathetic and magnificent.[22]

15 Ibid., 3.

16 "U pokloni Providnykovi," *Homin Ukraïny*, 14 November 1959, 5.

17 Ibid., 6.

18 Ol'ha Lus'ka, "Stepanovi Bandery," *Shliakh peremohy*, 1 November 1959, 1.

19 Leonid Poltava, "Na smert' Stepana Bandery," *Homin Ukraïny: Literatura i mystetsvo*, 7 November 1959, 2.

20 Chaikovs'kyi, *Moskovs'ki vbyvtsi*, 570–81.

21 "Praha zradyla ubyvtsiv," *Homin Ukraïny: Literatura i mystetsvo*, 7 November 1959, 2.

22 See for example *Homin Ukraïny*, 14 November 1959, 1. The newspapers controlled by the ZCh OUN also published photographs of other OUN-UPA leaders. For a photograph of the bust of Roman Shukhevych, see for example *Homin Ukraïny*, 5 March 1960, 1.

Fig. 41. Commemorative gathering, United Kingdom 1959. TShLA.

Dmytro Dontsov, who after the Second World War had been teaching Ukrainian literature at the University of Montreal, published an article about Bandera on 14 November 1959. Dontsov reminded the mourning Ukrainians that Bandera was not a democrat and that he was killed like Petliura and Konovalets', by which he meant that Bandera was assassinated by the Soviet Union or by Jews. Dontsov concluded that Bandera was assassinated because of his name, which "could become a banner under which all brave and honest Ukrainians unite in a critical hour."[23]

The death of another Eastern European fascist leader, Ante Pavelić, the *Poglavnik* of the NDH, on 28 December 1959 in Madrid, caused the same elements of the Ukrainian diaspora that had mourned Bandera to mourn Pavelić. The Croatian leader had survived an assassination attempt in El Palomar near Buenos Aires on 10 April 1957, the sixteenth anniversary of the founding of the Ustaša state. He moved to Madrid in November 1957 but died several months later as a result of the attack, which was apparently carried out by the Yugoslav intelligence service. The OUN paper *Homin Ukraïny* claimed that Pavelić was a "great proponent of Ukraine and other nations enslaved by Moscow." In a eulogy for Pavelić, *Homin Ukraïny* honored the *Poglavnik* as a "great patriot" and "fighter for independence" exactly as it had with Bandera a few weeks before. The OUN newspaper based in Toronto further emphasized that the ABN and the OUN participated in Pavelić's funeral and placed wreaths beside his coffin.[24] Volodymyr Pastushchuk, the second OUN and ABN speaker at Pavelić's funeral, bade the Croatian *Poglavnik* farewell in Spanish:

23 Dmytro Dontsov, "Im"ia-symvol," *Homin Ukraïny*, 14 November 1959, 2.
24 "Pomer Ante Pavelich," *Homin Ukraïny*, 23 January 1960, 7.

> In a few minutes, the Spanish earth will cover the body of the greatest among Croats. The Red murderers killed his body, but his spirit and his liberating ideas and national pride will live among us. Ante Pavelić taught us to love our motherlands and to be faithful to our national ideas. He gave his life for his brothers and fellows, which is evidence of the greatest love. ... We Ukrainians understand the sorrow of our brother Croats because, only two months ago, we sorrowed for the loss of the *Providnyk* of our liberation movement, the unforgettable Stepan Bandera of blessed memory, killed by the same criminal communist hand. With the death of Pavelić, the Croatian nation has lost its great leader; and our family of enslaved nations, one of the best strategists of the anticommunist struggle.[25]

Anticommunist Celebrations, Demonstrations, and Rituals

The fifteenth day of October became an important date in the calendar of the nationalist factions of the Ukrainian diaspora, which commemorated Bandera's death every year until the collapse of the Soviet Union. In a number of places, such commemorations continued until at least 2009. Bandera became an important symbol of anticommunist struggle among Ukrainians and other "enslaved nations." His "charismatic communities" propagated various nationalist, far-right, and neo-fascist ideas during his many commemorations. His death symbolized the suffering of Ukraine and all Ukrainians. It was misused to deny the atrocities committed by the OUN and UPA. The fact that Bandera was murdered by the KGB reassured the commemorating factions that they were engaged in a holy war against the Soviet Union for an independent Ukrainian state. The assassination also transformed Bandera into a symbol of liberation and resistance. This treatment of Bandera resembled the conduct of the Ustaša communities, and even more so of the Slovak émigrés who, during Jozef Tiso's trial and after his execution on 18 April 1947, commemorated the leader of the Slovak clerical fascist movement as a political martyr.[26]

The largest and most lavish Bandera commemorations and demonstrations took place on "round" anniversaries of his death, such as the fifth and tenth. In this subsection, only some of the most representative will be described, and more attention will be paid to cities with strong communities of Ukrainian political émigrés, such as Edmonton, Toronto, and Munich, and to capital cities—London, Washington, and Ottawa, where the largest anticommunist Bandera demonstrations took place. Cyclical commemorations—accompanied by poems or songs composed in honor of the *Providnyk* and repeatedly reproduced in newspapers and brochures or recited and sung at various gatherings—fulfilled two interrelated functions. First, they transposed Bandera into a hero and martyr. Second, they reinforced the collective disavowal of the atrocities committed by the OUN, UPA, and various Ukrainian collaborators. Commemorating the *Providnyk*, his adherents transposed themselves, with the help of his distorted and instrumentalized image, into victims, heroes, and

25 Ibid., 7.

26 Stanislava Kolková, "Das Bild von Jozef Tiso als 'Führer mit christlichem Antlitz' und 'Symbol der slowakischen Unabhängigkeit in Vergangenheit und Gegenwart—Versuch einer Annährung," in *Der Führer im Europa*, ed. Ennker, 271.

martyrs. The aggressive propaganda of the Soviet Union reassured the "charismatic communities" that they were in the right and thereby strengthened the Bandera cult among Ukrainian emigrants.

One of the first Bandera commemorations in 1960 took place in Calgary on 20 February. At this event, the participants watched a film of Bandera's funeral and listened to people who had known the *Providnyk* in person.[27] On Pentecost (*Zeleni Sviata*), 28 May 1960, 200 people gathered at Bandera's grave to participate in a panakhyda during which a priest blessed a large cross at the grave. The ZCh OUN member Iaroslav Bentsal' delivered a patriotic speech in honor of his *Providnyk*.[28]

Bandera's grave, with its large and remarkable military cross, became a popular pilgrimage site for Ukrainians from Europe, North and South America, and Australia.[29] On 15 October 1960, *Homin Ukraïny* again published a photograph of Bandera's bust on the first page and informed its readers that, "on 15 October of this year, one year passes since Moscow, the eternal enemy of the Ukrainian nation, took away the thread of the heroic life of our Providnyk," although still no evidence existed as to who might have killed Bandera.[30] On page 2 of the same issue, the editors published photographs of Bandera's funeral and a poem devoted to him. In several articles they asked their readers to continue Bandera's revolutionary struggle, which they understood as the only correct way to liberate Ukraine.[31]

In Toronto, the association of UPA veterans combined Bandera's commemoration with the Holiday of Arms (*Sviato Zbroï*), which usually took place on 14 October. On 15 October 1960, panakhydas for the "repose of the soul of Bandera of blessed memory" and "all UPA warriors who sacrificed their lives for Ukraine's freedom" were conducted in two churches. Participants included SUM and Plast members, and the male choir Prometei of the SUM sang. On 16 October, a commemorative gathering was organized in the Ukrainian Home at 83–85 Christie Street. The Prometei choir performed "The Military Song" (*Boiova Pisnia*) and a few other similar nationalist and military songs. A number of people delivered speeches, and other mourners sang religious and military songs. The stage was decorated with busts of Bandera and Shukhevych, between which a poster of Jesus and a UPA emblem were placed.[32] Similar celebrations were organized on 15 and 16 October in Boston, Chicago, Cleveland, Edmonton, London, Montreal, Munich, Ottawa, Philadelphia, and many other localities. In a number of places, Bandera's admirers erected symbolic coffins, at which SUM members and other mourners performed nationalist rituals, recited poems, and sang religious, military, or nationalist songs in honor of their *Providnyk*. Many of them decorated the stage with Bandera's portrait, under which children and

27 "Vechir spomyniv pro Stepana Banderu v Kalgarakh," *Homin Ukraïny*, 5 March 1960, 2.

28 "V Zeleni Sviata na mohylakh Heroïv," *Shliakh peremohy*, 11 May 1960, 1.

29 See for example "Rozmova z hist'my z-za okeanu," *Homin Ukraïny*, 2 December 1963, 3.

30 "Zvernennia Provodu Zakordonnykh Chastyn OUN," *Homin Ukraïny*, 15 October 1960, 1.

31 "Iedyna real'na vyzvol'na kontseptsiia," "Ioho dilo ne vmerlo nikoly," "Nevhnutomu bortsevi," *Homin Ukraïny*, 15 October 1960, 2.

32 "Sviato UPA i richnytsia smerty sl. p. S. Bandery," *Homin Ukraïny*, 22 October 1960, 1, 5.

Fig. 42. Children commemorate Bandera at a symbolic coffin of the *Providnyk* in the 1960s in Galashiels (Scotland), TShLA.

teenagers, dressed in folkloristic Cossack costumes, or SUM or other uniforms, performed various political and religious rituals.[33]

On the second anniversary of Bandera's death, an émigré institution, called the Underground Post of Ukraine, released four cinderella stamps. The first stamp showed Bandera in high school or at university age. The second featured Bandera after his release from prison in Poland. The third depicted Bandera's bust, prepared by the artist Chereshn'ovs'kyi, which showed Bandera as a statesman during the Second World War. This period was described as the time "when under [Bandera's] banners 200,000 fighters of the Ukrainian Insurgent Army and OUN cadres conducted an implacable struggle against two occupiers of Ukraine—the Hitlerites and the Muscovites." The last stamp showed Bandera after the Second World War. The stamps were distributed by SUM members, characterized by *Shliakh peremohy* as "the generation that prepares itself for taking over the banner of the struggle for the sovereignty and independence of Ukraine and is following the path that was pointed out by the great *Providnyk* Stepan Bandera." *Shliakh peremohy* encouraged its readers to put the Bandera stamps on letters when corresponding with friends. The stamps were distributed in Australia, Belgium, Canada, France, Germany, the United Kingdom, and the United States.[34]

33 "Montreal v pokloni sl. p. S. providnykovi St. Banderi," *Homin Ukraïny*, 22 October 1960, 5; "U pershu richnytsiu smerty sl. p. providnyka S. Bandery," *Homin Ukraïny*, 29 October 1960, 2; "U richnytsiu smerty sl. p. S. Bandery," *Homin Ukraïny*, 5 November 1960, 7; "U richnytsiu smerty sl. p. S. Bandery," *Homin Ukraïny*, 5 November 1960, 7; "U pokloni Providnykovi," *Homin Ukraïny*, 16 January 1961, 6; "U pershu richnytsiu smerty S. Bandery," *Homin Ukraïny*, 28 October 1960, 7; "Desiatyrichchia sumivs'koï diial'nosty v Klivlendi," *Shliakh peremohy*, 22 January 1960, 3.

34 "Nove vydannia marok Pidpil'noï Poshty Ukraïny," *Shliakh peremohy*, 15 October 1961, 2.

Fig. 43. The choir Veselka commemorates the first death anniversary of Stepan Bandera in Halifax (England), TShLA.

Like the first anniversary, the second anniversary of Bandera's death was commemorated in many localities around the globe.[35] In São Paulo the commemorations began with a panakhyda in the Greek Catholic church, in which Bandera's symbolic coffin was arranged. The coffin was decorated with flowers. Nuns put a trident made of rose petals on the coffin. During the panakhyda two young men stood with banners on each side of the coffin. After the mourning service, the participants moved to a secular building for the political part of the commemoration. There were so many people that there was only standing room for many of them. I. Sobko opened the second part of commemorations with a minute of silence, after which he said, "The enemies [of Ukraine] try to destroy us in foreign lands, but the spirit of Stepan Bandera gives us the power of victory." A children's choir under the direction of a nun performed the Brazilian national anthem. The panakhyda and the political gathering were broadcast for those Ukrainians in Brazil who did not attend the commemoration.[36]

On 17 November 1961, the day on which the German authorities revealed who had killed Bandera and how, the ZCh OUN organized a press conference, at which they

35 "U druhi rokovyny smerty Providnyka," *Shliakh peremohy*, 5 November 1961, 5; *Shliakh peremohy*, 12 November 1961, 5; *Shliakh peremohy*, 19 November 1961, 5; "Den' UPA i rokovyny smerty St. Bandery," *Homin Ukraïny*, 28 October 1961, 6; "V pokloni sl. pam. Stepanovi Banderi," *Shliakh peremohy*, 10 December 1961, 5.

36 "U druhi rokovyny smerty Providnyka," *Shliakh peremohy*, 12 November 1961, 5.

informed the journalists about the details of the assassination.[37] Ukrainian nationalist articles connected Bandera's murder with the assassinations of Petliura in 1926 and Konovalets' in 1938 and depicted the Soviet Union as a country that was continuing Stalin's policies.[38] Immediately after the identity of Bandera's assassin was officially announced, various Ukrainian associations, committees, and other organizations around the world began organizing demonstrations against the Soviet Union. On 18 November 1961, 1,500 activists attended a meeting in Bradford of the Federation of Ukrainians in Great Britain (*Ob"iednannia Ukraïntsiv u Velykii Brytaniï*, ObVB), at which they demanded that, for the assassination of their *Providnyk*, the "free world" put on trial Alexander Shelepin, the head of the KGB, Nikita Khrushchev, the first secretary of the KPSS and chairman of the Council of Ministers of the Soviet Union, in addition to the whole "Muscovite government," and the entire Central Committee of the KPSS.[39] Under a huge photograph of Bandera, *Shliakh peremohy* published Shelepin's and Stashyns'kyi's pictures on the first page and called them "the organizer of the murder" and "the executioner."[40] In the next issue, *Shliakh peremohy* reported on page 1 that Stets'ko would be the next to be assassinated. On page 3 it published Petro Kizko's poem "Not Enough Revenge," in which the author demanded "such a punishment for Moscow that a fire would burn it for ages."[41]

On Sunday 19 November 1961, anti-Soviet and anticommunist demonstrations took place in Munich, Edmonton, Derby, Port Arthur, and Port William. On Saturday 25 November, demonstrations occurred in seven localities around the globe. The next day, similar demonstrations were conducted in thirty-one localities and on Sunday 3 December, in twenty-four. Altogether, according to the ZCh OUN historiography, in the final months of 1961 and the first few months of 1962, the Ukrainian diaspora held 132 anti-Soviet and anticommunist demonstrations and meetings.[42]

At a demonstration in London on 25 and 26 November 1961, activists carried posters with inscriptions such as: "The blood of the Ukrainian Leader is on Khrushchev's hands!" "Down with Russian murderers!" "Ukraine mourns the murder of Bandera!" "Today Khrushchev kills Ukrainians, tomorrow it may be you!" "Your children's future is threatened by the oppressors of Ukraine!" "Bandera died for Ukraine's freedom," "BE AWARE! Khrushchev is out to bury you!" "Communism is another form of Russian imperialism!"[43]

A demonstration in New York took place on 2 December 1961 in front of the building used by the Soviet delegation to the United Nations. The protestors carried

37 "Bart ab," *Der Spiegel*, 29 November 1961, No. 49, 32–34; "Zaiava provodu ZCh OUN pered predstavnykamy chuzhynets'koï presy," *Shliakh peremohy*, 26 November 1961, 1.

38 "Vbyvnyk Bandery vykrytyi!" *Shliakh peremohy*, 26 November 1961, 1, 4; "Vbyvnyky v uriadi SSSR," *Shliakh peremohy*, 3 December 1961, 1.

39 "Na sud moskovs'kykh zlochyntsiv!" *Shliakh peremohy*, 3 December 1961, 1.

40 *Shliakh peremohy*, 26 November 1961, 1.

41 "Cherhovoiu zhertvoiu moskovs'koho teroru mav buty Iaroslav Stets'ko," *Shliakh peremohy*, 3 December 1961, 1; Petro Kizko, "Zamalo pomsty," *Shliakh peremohy*, 3 December 1961, 3.

42 Seventy-six demonstrations took place in Europe, fifty in Canada and the USA, three in Argentina and Brazil, and three in Australia. Cf. Chaikovs'kyi, *Moskovs'ki vbyvtsi*, 71–72, 596–98. See also "Natavrovuiemo moskovs'kykh zlochyntsiv!" *Shliakh peremohy*, 17 December 1961, 3–4; *Shliakh peremohy*, 24 December 1961, 3; *Shliakh peremohy*, 7 January 1962; *Shliakh peremohy*, 21 January 1962, 3; ASBML, 1636.

43 Chaikovs'kyi, *Moskovs'ki vbyvtsi*, 596.

Ukrainian and American flags, and caricatures of Khrushchev; they distributed leaflets, and explained the purpose of their protest to passers-by. At 5 p.m. they burned the Soviet flag and then "with huge rage" stormed the building, which they tried to enter through doors and windows. At other demonstrations, such as one in Minneapolis, Ukrainian political activists also burned Soviet flags. At some demonstrations, the protestors were joined by "freedom fighters" from Soviet republics such as Estonia, from which Waffen-SS soldiers and Nazi collaborators had also moved to North America after the Second World War.[44]

The ZCh OUN also used Bandera's death to start a fund called the Stepan Bandera Liberation Struggle Fund (*Fond vyzvol'noï borot'by im. Stepana Bandery*). Donations from individuals and associations ranged from $5 to $200, and in 1960, amounts up to $3,105 were received.[45] Funds were also collected for the trial of Stashyns'kyi. One of the arguments was "not to let the enemy triumph," as in the trial of Schwartzbard for Petliura's assassination in Paris in 1926. The organizations collected DM 197,800, the equivalent of about $50,000.[46] With the help of these funds, the ZCh OUN published historical propaganda literature such as *Russian Colonialism in Ukraine* and *Murdered by Moscow: Petliura, Konovalets, Bandera. Three Leaders of the Ukrainian National Liberation Movement Assassinated at the Orders of Stalin and Khrushchev*.[47] The second book was written by Lenkavs'kyi, author of "The Ten Commandments of a Ukrainian Nationalist," who, during the "Ukrainian National Revolution" in July 1941, had stated that "regarding the Jews we will adopt any methods that lead to their destruction."[48]

On 22 July 1962, *Shliakh peremohy* announced that the Ukrainian community close to Villa Adelina in Argentina was constructing a large hall for the community, the Stepan Bandera Ukrainian Home.[49] On the same day, a monument to the heroes of Ukraine was unveiled at the SUM camp in Ellenville, New York. The camp had been opened in June 1955 in order to "educate Ukrainian youth about their history and culture, as well as cultivating them to become active members of their Ukrainian and local communities while serving God and their Ukrainian homeland" as the heads of the SUM and the founders of the camp put it. They understood their patriotic duty as the education of Ukrainian diaspora children in the spirit of the OUN and UPA. Five similar camps—Veselka, Verkhovyna, Bilohorshcha, Karpaty, and Dibrova—were opened in North America. Some of them, for instance the Dibrova camp, were also used as a recreational center and vacation spot for diaspora Ukrainians.[50] The monument in the Ellenville camp was erected free of charge by the

44 Ibid., 70–71; "Spalyly bol'shevyts'kyi prapor," *Shliakh peremohy*, 17 December 1961, 1.

45 "Na Fond vyzvol'noï borot'by im. Stepana Bandery," *Homin Ukraïny*, 7 November 1959, 5; *Homin Ukraïny*, 5 March 1960, 5; *Homin Ukraïny*, 2 April 1960, 6.

46 Chaikovs'kyi, Moskovs'ki vbyvtsi, 76–77, 601–603.

47 Stepan Lenkavs'kyi, *Murdered by Moscow: Petlura, Konovalets, Bandera, three leaders of the Ukrainian National Liberation Movement, Assassinated at the Orders of Stalin and Khrushchov* (London: Ukrainian Publishers, 1962); *Petlura, Konowalez, Bandera: Von Moskau ermordet* (Munich: Ukrainischer Verlag, 1962); *Russischer Kolonialismus in der Ukraine: Berichte und Dokumente* (Munich: Ukrainischer Verlag, 1962).

48 For Lenkavs'kyi, see chapters 1 and 4 above.

49 "Ukraïns'kyi Narodnii Dim im. St. Bandery u Villia Adelina," *Shliakh peremohy*, 22 July 1962, 5.

50 Rossoliński-Liebe, Celebrating Fascism, 12. On Camp Veselka, see "Tabir Veselka," *Homin Ukrainy*, 17 September 1980, 11.

company owned by the former UPA partisans Mykhailo Shashkevych and Mykola Sydor. It consisted of a 12.8-meter-high (forty-two-foot) Ukrainian trident. The monument was produced by the sculptor Chereshn'ovs'kyi, a former UPA partisan, Dr. Lev Dobrianskyj, the head of the UKKA and professor of economics at Georgetown University, and the architect Zaiats'. On one side of the trident, there were busts of Petliura and Konovalets', and on the other, busts of Shukhevych and Bandera. According to the SUM, the youth movement of the OUN-B, "All of these heroes sacrificed their lives in the battle for Ukraine's sovereignty and nationhood and serve as an inspiration to all Ukrainian youth." Ukrainian diaspora children have congregated for decades in front of the monument to recite poems, sing religious, nationalist, or military OUN-UPA songs, perform folk dances, and eat Ukrainian food.[51]

The unveiling of the monument was integrated into the twentieth anniversary of the founding of the UPA, on 21 and 22 July 1962, which was attended by 5,000 people. In the evening of the first day of celebrations, a drama group from Philadelphia acted the play "The Army of Freedom UPA" (*Armiia voli UPA*) by OUN member Leonid Poltava. The second day of celebrations began with church services, after which the celebrants blessed the banner of the Roman Shukhevych UPA association. The opening ceremony was initiated by a parade of SUM and Plast members, UPA veterans, and other celebrants who, in their military-style uniforms or in plain clothes and with banners of their units in their hands, maneuvered through the area of the camp, while the leaders of the Ukrainian diaspora reviewed them from the stand. Afterwards, Dr. Dobrianskyj and other political activists delivered speeches. The leadership of the ZCh OUN and the Central Committee of the ABN sent greetings to the celebrants.[52]

On the third anniversary of Bandera's death, the radical right factions of the Ukrainian diaspora organized commemorative celebrations in a number of localities, as in the two previous years.[53] This time however, the religious and nationalist celebrations were overshadowed to some extent by the trial of Stashyns'kyi in Karlsruhe, which took place between 8 and 19 October 1962. The nationalist press reported every day of the trial in detailed articles filled with anti-Soviet phrases. At the same time, it also published the usual articles about the assassination of Konovalets' and the "heroism and tragedy" of UPA leaders.[54] According to *Shliakh peremohy*, Iaroslav Stets'ko stated at a conference after the trial: "There must be a country in the free world that, on the basis of the sentence of the Federal Court of Justice in Ger-

51 "Deshcho pro M. Chereshn'ovs'koho," *Shliakh peremohy*, 2 September 1962, 3; Stepovyk, *Skul'ptor*, 147–48; "Natsional'na manifestatsiia v Ellenvill," *Shliakh peremohy*, 5 August 1962, 1.Tania Sawa-Priatka: *A Short History of the Ukrainian American Youth Association's "Oselia" on the Occasion of Its 50th Anniversary*, http://www.cym.org/us/ellenville/Oselia50_UWarticle.asp (accessed 30 May 2011). First published in *America*, 21 May 2005.

52 "Natsional'na manifestatsiia v Ellenvill," *Shliakh peremohy*, 5 August 1962, 1.

53 "Vshanuvaly pamiat' Providnyka," *Shliakh peremohy*, 4 November 1962, 5; "V tretiu richnytsiu smerti sl. p. St. Bandery," *Shliakh peremohy*, 11 November 1962, 3; *Shliakh peremohy*, 18 November 1962, 3; "Ni na krok ne vidstupymo," *Shliakh peremohy*, 18 November 1962, 5; "U pokloni lytsariam," *Shliakh peremohy*, 2 December 1962, 5; ASBML, 1629.

54 See for example "Tak vbyla Moskva polk. Konoval'tsia," *Shliakh peremohy*, 12 October 1962, 3; "Z nakazu TsK partiï i uriadu v Moskvi Stashyns'kyi zamorduvav Providnyka OUN, sl. p. Stepana Banderu," *Shliakh peremohy*, 14 October 1962, 1, 4; "Velyki liudy velyka stratehiia," *Shliakh peremohy*, 14 October 1962, 2.

many, will bring the terrorist methods of the government of the USSR before the International Tribunal in The Hague." He further demanded to "bring the matter of the villains from Khrushchev's government" not only to the International Tribunal but also to the United Nations Commission on Human Rights and the European Court of Human Rights in Strasbourg.[55]

T. Zaryts'kyi expressed what the ZCh OUN and Ukrainian nationalists thought about Stashyns'kyi's mild sentence of eight years for the murder of their *Providnyk*. He wrote that 90 percent of the press had a tendency to belittle Stashyns'kyi's guilt, when he was actually "very perfidious, dogged, aggressive, and from his birth a criminal type." The author further claimed that Stashyns'kyi was a traitor to the Ukrainian nation and his family and was also a "Muscovite janissary."[56]

Another notable statement about the sentence came from Artur Fuhrman, perhaps the most devoted foreign admirer of the OUN and of Ukrainian nationalism in the 1960s. Fuhrman was a German who was deported to a camp in Vorkuta after the Second World War, where he spent five years together with Ukrainian nationalists. His autobiographical historical novels, *Blood and Coal* and *Under Bandera's Banner*, were published in Ukrainian by the ZCh OUN publishing houses in Munich and London. In his novels, he frequently referred to the Ukrainian nationalists as Banderites, and himself as a Banderite. Bandera was for Fuhrman not only the leader of an organization but also of the "enslaved Ukrainian people" and thus also a "synonym for Ukraine."[57] Commenting on the trial in Karlsruhe, Fuhrman called it a "good weapon in the hands of the freedom-loving Ukrainian nation, in particular in the hands of the OUN." He insisted that the OUN should never stop disseminating the court's finding that the decision to assassinate Bandera came from the Russian government. In order to make it clear how Ukrainian nationalists could profit from this decision and use Bandera's death in their campaign, Fuhrman repeated the words of Congressman Charles J. Kersten: "The verdict of the court that the Bolshevik government is the clandestine organizer of the murders will permeate the consciousness of the whole world. This fact, like the sword of the archangel Michael, will unmask the Soviet-Russian leaders and demonstrate to mankind their real faces ... and thus Bandera's death was not in vain."[58]

On the fifth anniversary of Bandera's death, the nationalist elements of the Ukrainian diaspora organized numerous commemorations and several anti-communist protest marches in various countries. At a demonstration in New York on 15 October 1964 the protesters carried banners with inscriptions like "Khrushchev and Shelepin—Bloody Murderers" and "Russians Hands off Ukraine" and distributed leaflets with the heading "We Accuse Moscow and Ask America to Be Alert." On 17 October 1964, 500 Ukrainians arrived in Washington from several American cities. They placed a wreath at the Shevchenko monument while singing nationalist songs.

55 "Khrushchova na mizhnarodnii sud!" *Shliakh peremohy*, 28 October 1962, 4.

56 T. Zaryts'kyi, "Na pochatku bula zrada," *Shliakh peremohy*, 4 November 1962, 4. For a very similar characterization, see St. Shums'kyi, "Novitnii moskovs'kyi ianychar," *Shliakh peremohy*, 18 November 1962, 2; Petro Kizko, "Chy til'ky pomichnyk," *Shliakh peremohy*, 25 November 1962, 2.

57 "Die Sache Banderas wird siegen," ASBML, 2106, 2; "Bandera ist die Ukraine," ASBML, 2113, 1. Artur Furman, *Krov i vuhillia* (Munich: Ukrainian Publishers, 1961); Artur Furman, *Pid praporom Bandery* (London: Ukrainian Publishers, 1964).

58 A. Furman "Protes v Karl'sruhe—tse zbroia," *Shliakh peremohy*, 4 November 1962, 4.

They then went to the Soviet embassy, which they picketed in heavy rain for three hours, singing "partisan songs" and holding banners with inscriptions such as "God Bless America! God Liberate Ukraine!" A group of protesters went into the embassy and informed the staff, in Ukrainian, that they were representatives of the Ukrainian Liberation Front (*Ukraïns'kyi Vyzvol'nyi Front*, UVF) and had come to deliver a memorandum, in which they condemned Moscow for killing Bandera. The protest ended with the nationalist demonstrators singing "It Is Not Time" (*Ne pora*) and the Ukrainian anthem "Ukraine has not yet perished" (*Shche ne vmerla Ukraïna*). On the same day in Ottawa, Ukrainians picketed the Soviet embassy.[59]

In 1964 in Edmonton, the Ukrainian community combined the commemoration of its leader's death with two other nationalist and religious celebrations: the first was the Feast of Saint Mary the Protectress; the second, the Weapons Holiday. As in previous years, the day of festivities started at St. Josaphat Cathedral. Afterwards, a crowd of 200 people at the Ukrainian National Home building listened to their *Providnyk's* speech, which had been recorded five years before, and which enabled them to admire his "farsightedness and political reason."[60]

Besides commemorating Bandera and organizing religious celebrations for the Ukrainian *Providnyk*, the Ukrainian diaspora nationalists followed, attended, or publicized similar events organized for other fascist leaders. In January 1967, *ABN Correspondence* announced that on 30 November 1966 a memorial service in honor of Corneliu Zelea Codreanu, the charismatic leader of the Iron Guard in Romania, had been held at the Saint Nicholas Church in Munich.[61] In the same year, Stets'ko published *30 chervnia 1941* (30 June 1941), in which he denied that the militia set up by the OUN-B was involved in any anti-Jewish violence during the "Ukrainian National Revolution" and presented the proclamation of state on that day in Lviv as an anti-German act of resistance. Stets'ko's very popular book began with a foreword by Dontsov.[62]

The tenth anniversary of Bandera's death attracted several hundred followers to Munich from various European countries and from North America. The nationalists appeared at Bandera's grave on 11 October 1969 in order to "honor the memory of the Providnyk of the Ukrainian National Revolution, and to declare the indestructible will of the Ukrainian nation to prolong the liberation struggle until the victory over Moscow."[63] The ABN organized a press conference in Munich, to which it invited journalists in order to remind them how important the struggle against the Soviet Union was. The nationalists also attended several church services devoted to the memory of their *Providnyk*, and a panakhyda at his grave, which was performed by six priests. During this event, Bishop Kyr Platon reminded the mourners that Ban-

59 "Protymoskovs'ki demonstratsiï," *Homin Ukraïny*, 31 October 1964, 2; "Vashington pid znakom Bandery," *Homin Ukraïny*, 7 November 1964, 4, 8. For the mourning gatherings see "U 5-richchia smerty Stepana Bandery," *Homin Ukraïny*, 31 October 1964, 3, 5; "Z ukraïns'koho zhyttia u sviti," *Homin Ukraïny*, 31 October 1964, 6; "U 5-richchia smerty Stepana Bandery," *Homin Ukraïny*, 7 November 1964, 3, 7.

60 "U 5-richchia smerty Stepana Bandery," *Homin Ukraïny*, 7 November 1964, 3.

61 "Memorial Service in Honour of Corneliu Codreanu," *ABN Correspondence* Vol. XVIII, No. 1 (1967): 37.

62 Stets'ko, *30 chervnia 1941*, 9–11, 182, 246.

63 "Na poshanu providnyka OUN St. Bandery," *Homin Ukraïny*, 25 October 1969, 1.

dera was a "deeply religious man and a great patriot of the Ukrainian nation." Then 200 SUM members held a parade and two female SUM members from England poured water from the Dnieper River and scattered soil at the grave, mixed with bread and the red fruit of the guelder rose, a national symbol of Ukraine and the title of the anthem of the UPA (*Chervona Kalyna*). About 1,500 mourners attended a commemorative gathering at a Munich theater, where they listened to Stets'ko's oration, and vocal performances by the Homin choir from Manchester. When the gathering ended, the participants marched to the house at Kreittmayrstrasse 7, where Bandera had been assassinated. They listened to political speeches, placed a wreath, and sang "It Is Not Time" and the Ukrainian anthem.[64]

Admirers who were unable to visit the grave of their *Providnyk* on the tenth anniversary held rallies, marches, church services, and commemorative gatherings in numerous localities around the globe.[65] In Winnipeg, which had designated Iaroslav Stets'ko an honorary citizen of the city in 1966, (Fig. 44) the commemoration of the tenth anniversary was enriched by soil from Bandera's grave in Munich. This relic had been brought to the Canadian city by Semen Ïzhyk in order to radiate an aura of "nationalist holiness" during the solemn and well-attended Bandera commemorations.[66] In London, under a Bandera portrait and OUN-B and Ukrainian national flags, young SUM members in folk costumes and uniforms recited poems.[67]

In Washington on 11 October 1969, Mykhailo Shpontak, in the company of two female SUM members, laid a wreath under the Shevchenko monument. Several anticommunist activists, among them OUN-B member Petro Mirchuk, delivered speeches while the crowd of 500 people, armed with 100 banners and 5,000 leaflets, began to walk toward the Soviet embassy. Although the police tried to prevent the demonstrators from invading the embassy, two protestors succeeded in placing at the entrance a "Wanted" poster for Shelepin, the man who had ordered the killing of Bandera.[68]

A similar demonstration was organized for the following weekend in Central Park in New York, at which SUM and Plast youth appeared in uniforms, with Bandera banners in their hands, while they stood next to older nationalists. After listening to anticommunist speeches, the protesters and mourners, armed with Hungarian, Polish, Bulgarian, Cossack, Georgian, North Caucasian, Croatian, and Estonian flags, marched to the building of the Soviet delegation to the United Nations. There, the demonstrators burned several Soviet flags. An SUM member and a woman in a

64 Ibid., 1, 4.

65 "Vshanuvannia pamiati St. Bandery," *Homin Ukraïny*, 11 October 1969, 1, 4; "U desiatu richnytsiu smerty sl. p.St. Bandery," *Homin Ukraïny*, 11 October 1969, 2, 7; "Sviatkuvannia v Montreali," "Panakhyda v Toronti," *Homin Ukraïny*, 25 October 1969, 1; "U desiaty richchia smerty S. Bandery," *Homin Ukraïny*, 15 November 1969, 3, 7, 13; "U desiatu richnytsiu smerty S. Bandery," *Homin Ukraïny*, 22 November 1969, 9.

66 "Desiati rokovyny smerty Bandery," *Ukrainian News*, 23 October 1969, 5. For designating Stets'ko an honorary citizen of Winnipeg, see "Former Prime Minister of Ukraine—Honorary Citizen of Ukraine," *ABN Correspondence*, Vol. VXIII, No. 3 (1967): 31.

67 See the picture on the cover. The image is from the collection of the TShLA.

68 "U Vashyngtoni vidznachyly manifestatsieiu 10-littia vbystva Stepana Bandery," *Homin Ukraïny*, 25 October 1969, 1.

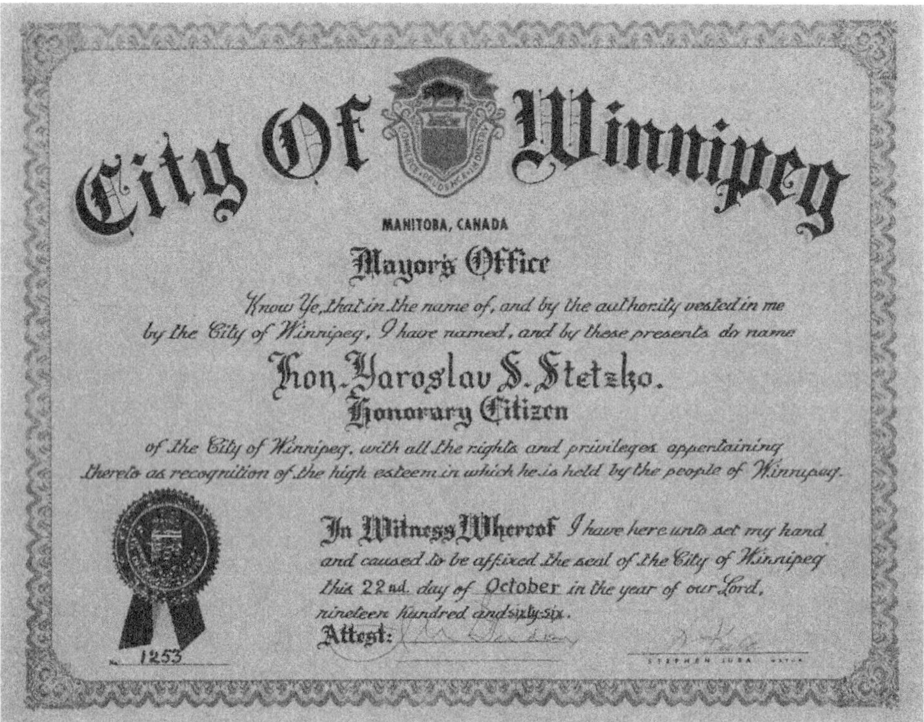

City Of Winnipeg

MANITOBA, CANADA

Mayor's Office

Know Ye, that in the name of, and by the authority vested in me by the City of Winnipeg, I have named, and by these presents do name

Hon. Yaroslav S. Stetzko.

Honorary Citizen

of the City of Winnipeg, with all the rights and privileges appertaining thereto as recognition of the high esteem in which he is held by the people of Winnipeg.

In Witness Whereof I have here unto set my hand and caused to be affixed the seal of the City of Winnipeg this 22nd. day of October in the year of our Lord, nineteen hundred and sixty-six.

Attest:

1253

Fig. 44. The document nominating Iaroslav Stets'ko as an Honorary Citizen of Winnipeg. *ABN Correspondence* No. 3 (1967): 31.

Cossack dress wanted to hand over an accusatory letter to the officials in the embassy, but nobody opened the door.[69]

The Toronto commemorative committee advertised the fifteenth anniversary of Bandera's death on the first page of *Homin Ukraïny*. The committee combined Bandera's anniversary with the Weapon Holiday and the UPA celebration. Among the attractions were performances by three choirs, and a speech by the prominent OUN-B member Mykola Klymyshyn, who, like Petro Mirchuk, had been awarded the degree of doctor of philosophy at the Munich Ukrainian Free University (*Ukraïns'kyi Vil'nyi Universytet*, UVU).[70] Ukrainians in Buenos Aires performed a panakhyda on 15 October 1974. Five days later, they gathered in the building of the Prosvita society, to perform the secular part of the commemoration, which they began with a moment of silence. One mourner then read Mykola Shcherbak's poem "15 October 1959" and older nationalists carried into the hall a wreath with a blue-and-yellow and red-and-black ribbon and handed it over to SUM members, who put it under the portrait of Bandera. This act symbolized the handing over of the revolutionary struggle to the youth. Several activists, both young and old, then recited poems devoted to the

69 "Protybol'shevyts'ka demonstratsia u N'iu-Iorku," *Homin Ukraïny*, 22 November 1969, 1, 4.
70 *Homin Ukraïny*, 12 October 1974, 1.

Providnyk and sang UPA and other military songs. At the end, all sang "Ukraine has not yet perished."[71]

The same groups that commemorated Bandera also initiated the cult of Dontsov, who died on 30 March 1973 in Montreal. The *ABN Correspondance* filled the cover of the May-June issue in 1973 with Dontsov's portrait and the inscription: "Great political thinker, champion of the idea of a common front of nations subjugated by Russian imperialism in their struggle for national independence."[72] At the fifth anniversary of Dontsov's death, *Homin Ukraïny* published a photograph of Dontsov's bust, prepared by Chereshn'ovs'kyi, who had also sculpted busts of Bandera, Shukhevych, Petliura, and others.[73] In 1983, at the hundredth anniversary of his birth and the tenth anniversary of his death, Dontsov was commemorated as a "great thinker," "revolutionary," and "philosopher."[74]

The twentieth anniversary of Bandera's death was combined with the fiftieth anniversary of the founding of the OUN. On its first page on 3 October 1979, *Homin Ukraïny* published portraits of four prominent Ukrainian nationalists—Konovalets', Bandera, Shukhevych, and Stets'ko—and announced that on 7 October nationalists would "commemorate the heroism of thousands of fallen OUN members" in Toronto.[75] On 10 October, it similarly published a large photograph of Bandera's bust, and an interview with the Ukrainian dissident Valentyn Moroz about the OUN, and explained why they were combining the fiftieth anniversary of the founding of the OUN with the twentieth anniversary of Bandera's assassination: "The name of Stepan Bandera is inseparable from the history of the OUN, during his life as well as after his heroic death. He lives in the OUN, and due to it and with it in the hearts and souls of the whole Ukrainian nation, as a symbol of the will to freedom and independence as a banner of a nation on a path of revolutionary liberation."[76] On the next page, Liubomyr Rykhtyts'kyi explained that it is "not possible to kill a historic symbol [Stepan Bandera] as it is not possible to kill an idea."[77] The Head of the UVF stressed that "Bandera's spirit is calling all of us."[78]

Excitement about the combined anniversary arose in numerous Ukrainian communities around the world, but the most lavish commemorations took place in Munich, the most important pilgrimage site for the Ukrainian nationalists.[79] A number of leading Ukrainian nationalists, including Mykola Klymyshyn and Bandera's son Andrii, came to Munich for this event. They had backed Stets'ko, the tireless leader of the ABN since 1946 and the leader of the ZCh OUN since he succeeded Bandera's follower Lenkavskyi' in this position in 1968. The politico-religious commemorations began with a conference on 11 October 1979 in the Munich Penta Hotel,

71 "Vistky z Argentiny," *Homin Ukraïny*, 16 November 1974, 7.
72 *ABN Correspondance* Vol. XXIV, No. 3 (1973).
73 "Velykyi myslytel' natsionalizmu," *Homin Ukraïny*, 29 March 1974, 3.
74 "Shliakhom velykoho myslitelia—revolutsionera," *Homin Ukraïny*, 30 March 1983, 1; "Dmytro Dontsov—philosopher, ideologist, political thinker," *Homin Ukraïny*, 30 March 1983, 2; "V 10-tu richnytsiu smerty D. Dontsova," *Homin Ukraïny*, 6 April 1983, 11; "Dmytro Dontsov—ideoloh vyzvol'noï borot'by," *Literatura i mystetsvo. Misiachnyi dodatok Homonu Ukraïny*, October 1983, 1–2.
75 "Sviatkove vidznachennia OUN," *Homin Ukraïny*, 3 October 1979, 1.
76 "Stepan Bandera—prapor ukraïns'koï revoliutsiï," *Homin Ukraïny*, 10 October 1979, 1.
77 Liubomyr Rykhtyts'kyi, "Ubyty symvol nemozhlyvo," *Homin Ukraïny*, 10 October 1979, 2.
78 "Dukh Bandery klyche vsikh nas," *Homin Ukraïny*, 10 October 1979, 3.
79 See the announcement in *Homin Ukraïny*, 19 September 1979, 1.

Fig. 45. Iaroslav Stets'ko and Andrii Bandera during the conference on 11 October 1979 in Munich. *ABN Correspondance* No. 6 (1979): 36.

where Stets'ko read the text "We Accuse Moscow and Warn the Free World." In his speech, Stets'ko, according to *Homin Ukraïny*, enumerated the "assassinations of Ukrainian fighters, informed [the audience] about the policies of enforced Russification, encouraged [them] to boycott the Olympics in 1980 in Moscow ... and called for a political-psychological counteroffensive against Moscow."[80] When Stets'ko had finished, Andrii Bandera addressed the question of Shelepin, the former head of the NKVD, and expressed his disappointment that, although the trial in Karlsruhe had declared him guilty, the German authorities had still not arrested him (Fig. 45).[81]

Several hundred older OUN and younger SUM members attended the panakhyda on 13 October 1979 in Munich. Nationalists who could not appear at the grave of their *Providnyk* sent wreaths with red-and-black or blue-and-yellow ribbons, from Australia, Belgium, Canada, France, England, and the United States. Klymyshyn and other nationalists, including SUM and ABN leaders, delivered speeches at the graveside. Representatives of Ukrainian nationalist communities in several countries saluted. The article in *Homin Ukraïny* did not clarify whether they used the original fascist OUN-B salute from 1941, which consisted of raising the right arm "slightly to the right, slightly above the top of the head" while calling out "Glory to Ukraine!" or whether it was a revised version without the fascist gesture.[82]

80 "Miunkhen u 20-littia skrytovbystva Stepana Bandery," *Homin Ukraïny*, 31 October 1979, 1,

81 Ibid., 1, 4.

82 "Miunkhen u 20-littia skrytovbystva Stepana Bandery," *Homin Ukraïny*, 31 October 1979, 4. For the original fascist version of the salute, see "Postanovy II. Velykoho Zboru," TsDAHO f. 1, op. 23, spr. 926, 199.

After the oratorical and other performances at the grave, the mourners attended a commemorative gathering at the Penta Hotel in a hall decorated with the red-and-black OUN-B and the Ukrainian blue-and-yellow flags, as well as portraits of Bandera. Stepan Mechnyk, one of Bandera's comrade-in-arms, opened the event. He informed 800 assembled nationalists about a telephone call from a secretary of Iosyf Slipyi, the Greek Catholic patriarch in Rome, who assured him that the twentieth anniversary of the death of the *Providnyk* was also solemnized in the capital of Western Christianity. During the gathering, a number of Ukrainian dance and vocal groups from several countries, including the Bandura Quartet from France, the Dibrova women's group from Munich, and the Chaban group from England, performed. A few individuals recited poems devoted to the *Providnyk*. Finally, all the performers gathered on stage and sang the Ukrainian anthem, to the glory of the *Providnyk*. The participants then marched through Munich to the apartment building at Kreittmayrstrasse 7, as they had done ten years earlier. At the head of the procession marched Stets'ko with such prominent OUN members as Klymyshyn and Mechnyk, and several young nationalists in SUM uniforms. In front of the building where Bandera was assassinated, Omelian Koval' delivered a speech, in which he called upon Ukrainian youth to prolong the struggle initiated by their parents, who were from the "Bandera generation." The young people then burned the Soviet flag (Fig. 46), and the crowd sang the Ukrainian anthem and "It Is Not Time!" Afterwards, young Ukrainians collected signatures on a petition to the Munich city council to rename Kreittmayrstrasse as Stepan-Bandera-Strasse and to erect a commemorative plaque on the building where the *Providnyk* had been assassinated.[83]

Fig. 46. Burning the Soviet flag in front of the building in the Kreittmayrstrasse 7 in Munich on 13 October 1979. *Shliakh peremohy*, 11 November 1979, 1.

83 "Miunkhen u 20-littia skrytovbystva Stepana Bandery," *Homin Ukraïny*, 31 October 1979, 4.

Fig. 47. Demonstration in London in front of the Soviet embassy on the twentieth anniversary of Bandera's assassination. *ABN Correspondance* No. 2 (1980): 19.

Similar commemorations and demonstrations took place on the twentieth anniversary of Bandera's assassination in many other cities. In London, Ukrainians demonstrated with pro-Bandera and anti-Soviet posters, in front of the Soviet embassy (Fig. 47).[84] In New York, the Ukrainian dissident Valentyn Moroz set fire to the Soviet flag at an ABN demonstration in front of the premises of the Soviet delegation to the United Nations (Fig. 48).[85] The youth journal *Avangard* published a drawing of Bandera's head growing out of a cross, which bore the inscription "The Vengeance Will Come!" (Fig. 49).[86] Bronze medals were also released on the occasion of the twentieth anniversary of Bandera's death.[87]

The Ukrainian nationalists did not usually consider how Jews might perceive the cult of the *Providnyk*, or what they thought about the ritualized denial of the atrocities and war crimes committed by the Ukrainian insurgents and police during the Second World War. But in November 1979, *Homin Ukraïny* proudly informed its leaders on the first page that, shortly before the twentieth anniversary of Bandera's death, a Committee of Ukrainian-Jewish Cooperation in Jerusalem sent a telegram with expressions of sympathy. The committee was founded in 1979 by Ukrainian Jewish émigrés and headed by Iakov Suslensky.[88]

84 *ABN Correspondence*, No. 2 (1980): 19.
85 Ibid., 7.
86 *Avangard. Zhurnal ukraïns'koï molodi*, Vol. 149, No. 6 (1979), 335.
87 *Homin Ukraïny*, 23 July1980, 5.
88 "Komitet ukraïns'ko-ievreis'koï spivpratsi v Ierusalymi skladaie spivchuttia z pryvodu 20-richchia smerty S. Bandery," *Homin Ukraïny*, 14 November 1979, 1. For the committee, see Volodymyr Ku-

Fig. 48. Valentyn Moroz setting a Soviet flag on fire in New York at an ABN demonstration on the twentieth anniversary of Bandera's assassination. *ABN Correspondance* No. 2 (1980): 7.

The period between the round-number celebrations was also filled with fascinating events. During Captive Nations Week in July 1982, for example, representatives of the UPA and other North American Ukrainian nationalist associations were invited to Washington to celebrate, with thirty Congressmen, the fortieth anniversary of the UPA. According to *Shliakh peremohy,* the UPA flag flew over the capitol on 11 July 1982. The UPA flag was the red-and-black OUN-B flag, which had been introduced at the Second Great Congress of the Ukrainian Nationalists in Cracow in March–April 1941.[89] Iosyf Slipyi, Patriarch of the Greek Catholic Church, who on 30 June 1941 attended the meeting at which Stets'ko had proclaimed the Ukrainian state, and who had lived in exile after he was released by the Soviet authorities in 1963, declared on the occasion of the fortieth anniversary of the UPA: "The Ukrainian Insurgent Army was born from the Christian awareness of the need to fight against Satan and his earthly servants."[90] A year later, on the twenty-fifth anniversary of the founding of Captive Nations and the alleged fortieth anniversary of the ABN, Stets'ko, head of the ABN and the OUN was invited to Congress. Vice President George Bush received the "last premier of a free Ukrainian state," as Stets'ko still called himself, on 18 July 1983. A day later, President Reagan received Stets'ko at the White House.[91]

biiovych and V. Markus, "Jews," *Encyclopedia of Ukraine*, ed. Volodymyr Kubiiovych (Toronto: University of Toronto Press, 1988), 2:390. On the Holocaust and Jewish-Ukrainian relations during the Cold War, see Rossoliński-Liebe, Erinnerungslücke Holocaust, 415–18.

89 "Prapor UPA na Kapitoli," *Shliakh peremohy*, 22 August 1982, 1. For the flag and the Second Great Congress of the Ukrainian Nationalists, see chapter 4 above.

90 Iosyf Slipyi, "Poslannia u 40-richchia narodzhennia UPA," *Shliakh peremohy*, 10 October 1982, 1.

91 For Stets'ko calling himself the "former Ukrainian premier," see "Captive Nations Week Observed," *Ukrainian Echo*, 31 August 1983, 1; "Ukraïna staie predmetom svitovoï polityky: u 25-littia tyzhnia

Fig. 49. "The Vengeance Will Come."
Avangard. Zhurnalukraïns'koïmolodi Vol. 149, No. 6 (1979), 335.

In 1982 the Ukrainian community in Cleveland began collecting money for a monument devoted to the UPA soldiers, which would bear the inscription: "There is no greater love than to give one's life for one's friends."[92] Before they even began collecting in Cleveland, other Ukrainian communities around the world had already erected several similar monuments. In Edmonton for example, the bust of a uniformed Roman Shukhevych by the sculptor Chereshn'ovs'kyi was unveiled in 1973 in front of a huge Ukrainian Youth Complex. The building itself was constructed between 1972 and 1974, partially funded by the Alberta provincial and Canadian federal

ponevolenykh narodiv i 40-richchia ABN," *Homin Ukraïny*, 17 August 1983, 1. For Stets'ko at the White House, see "Ukraïna staie predmetom svitovoï polityky: u 25-littia tyzhnia ponevolenykh narodiv i 40-richchia ABN," *Homin Ukraïny*, 17 August 1983, 1, 3; "Polytychnyi aspekt vidznachennia richnyts': TPN i ABN," *Homin Ukraïny*, 24 August 1983, 1, 4.

92 "Pamiatnyk voïnam UPA v Klivlendi," *Shliakh peremohy*, 22 August 1982, 1.

Fig. 50. The UPA monument in the camp Kyïv in Oakville (Ontario, Canada). *Al'manakh Homonu Ukraïny* 1991, 172.

governments as a result of the policy of multiculturalism introduced in Canada in 1971.[93] Besides erecting monuments to famous UPA leaders, the Ukrainian nationalist émigrés celebrated them in public. For example, on 22 June 1980, the thirtieth anniversary of Shukhevych's death, 6,000 Ukrainian nationalists from Chicago, Detroit, Montreal, Munich, New York, Ottawa, Pittsburgh, and several other cities gathered in Toronto to attend a religious memorial service.[94] In 1988 the association of former UPA soldiers unveiled a monument in the Kyïv camp in Oakville (Ontario, Canada), devoted to the "glorious UPA." Engraved on a piece of rock, it showed a UPA insurgent in a uniform with a huge trident behind him (Fig. 50).[95]

93 For Canadian multiculturalism and Ukrainian nationalism in Canada, see Rossoliński-Liebe, Celebrating Fascism, 12, 14–15; Rudling, Multiculturalism, 743–45.

94 "Khai slava pro velykoho komandyra prokhodyt' u viky," *Homin Ukraïny*, 2 July 1980, 3.

95 *Al'manakh Homonu Ukraïny* 1991, 172.

The act of 30 June 1941 was another significant component of the anti-Soviet commemorations performed regularly by the veterans of the OUN, UPA, Waffen-SS Galizien and their children. A modified version of the text of the state proclamation of 30 June 1941 was presented yearly in nationalist newspapers as a brave, anti-German act of the "renewal of Ukrainian statehood." The Ukrainian nationalists had removed the expressions of admiration for Hitler and the desire for close collaboration with the "National Socialist Great Germany, which, under the leadership of Adolf Hitler, is creating a new order in Europe." This adjustment allowed them to perceive the act of 30 June 1941 as a symbol of deep and sincere Ukrainian patriotism and resistance against Nazi Germany. [96]

In the early 1980s the Ukrainian diaspora, in particular the Ukrainian communities that commemorated Bandera as their *Providnyk*, or the state proclamation of 30 June 1941 as an anti-German act, developed another essential nationalist narrative, namely of the artificial famine in Soviet Ukraine of 1932–1933, which they called the "Famine Holocaust" or the "Ukrainian Holocaust." They thus drew a parallel with the destruction of European Jews during the Second World War, known since the late 1970s as the Holocaust. The term "Holodomor" became popular in Ukraine and among the diaspora especially in the late 1980s. The phonetic similarity of Holodomor to Holocaust was not a coincidence. The immediate trigger for the nationalists' famine discourse was the popular miniseries *Holocaust,* which was broadcast in 1978 by NBC and was watched by millions of North Americans. Presenting the story of one Jewish family from Berlin since the coming of the Nazis to power in 1933 until the end of the Second World War, the miniseries drew the attention of many North Americans to the destruction of European Jews. The miniseries presented Ukrainians as Nazi collaborators and Holocaust perpetrators. *Holocaust* thereby clashed with the ideological Bandera symbolism and the way that the Ukrainian diaspora dealt with its past, particularly as to the denial of Ukrainian involvement in the Holocaust and collaboration with Nazi Germany.[97]

At that time and into the 1980s, relatively little demographic research had been conducted on the subject of the famine; this made it easier to exaggerate the number of victims. The approximate number of 2.5 to 3.9 million Ukrainian victims of the famine became known only in the early 1990s. The nationalist elements of the diaspora claimed that during the "Holodomor" more Ukrainians were killed than Jews were during the Holocaust. In articles, leaflets, books and on monuments, they inflated the numbers to five, seven, eight, or 10 million Ukrainian victims of the

96 For the original text, see "Akt proholoshennia ukraïns'koï derzhavy, 30.06.1941," TsDAVOV f. 3833, op. 1, spr. 5, 3. For the falsified reprint of the text, see "Text of sovereignty proclamation," *Ukrainian Echo*, 25 June 1980, 3.

97 On the instrumentalization of the famine and the soap opera *Holocaust*, see Dietsch, *Making Sense*, 124–25. For an article calling the famine the "horrible Ukrainian holocaust" and claiming seven million Ukrainian victims, see "Zhakhlyvyi ukraïns'kyi holokost," *Homin Ukraïny*, 1 September 1982, 9. The term appeared for the first time in 1988. Cf. John-Paul Himka: "Review of Johan Dietsch, 'Making Sense of Suffering' and Stanyslav Vladyslavovych 'Kul'chyts'kyi, Holod 1932–1933 rr. v Ukraini iak henotsyd/Golod 1932–1933 gg. v Ukraine kak genotsid'" *Kritika: Explorations in Russian and Eurasian History* Vol. 8, No. 3 (Summer 2007): 684.

famine.[98] They sometimes counted Ukrainian victims between 1921 and 1956 generally, and claimed 15 million victims, which figure they presented in contrast to the 6 million Jewish victims.[99] Roman Serbyn, Professor of East European history at the University of Montreal, at which Dontsov was teaching after the Second World War, wrote: "Much has been written in recent years about the man-made famine that ravaged Ukraine in 1932–1933 and caused the deaths of seven to ten million people."[100] In an academic volume published in 1986, Marco Carynnyk compared the Ukrainian victims of the famine to the Jewish victims of the Holocaust.[101] The participants of the Holodomor discourse instrumentalized the suffering of the famine victims for various reasons, the most important of which were to draw attention to the Soviet denial of the famine and to the political situation in Soviet Ukraine, and to respond to the accusations concerning Ukrainian involvement in the Holocaust.[102]

Shortly before the twenty-fifth anniversary of Bandera's assassination, two important Ukrainian nationalist activists died: Stepan Bandera's son Andrii on 19 July 1984, and Iosyf Slipyi, charismatic head of the Greek Catholic Church and an important symbol of Ukrainian nationalism, on 7 September 1984. Ukrainian nationalist papers such as the Munich-based *Shliakh peremohy* and the Toronto-based *Homin Ukraïny* immediately began transforming both the deceased into heroes and martyrs as they had previously dealt with Bandera and several other personalities.[103]

Despite these two losses, 1984 was a special year for all Bandera admirers, as it included the twenty-fifth anniversary of the death and seventy-fifth anniversary of the birth of their *Providnyk*. Early in the year, *Shliakh peremohy* brought out a red-and-black wall calendar with Bandera's portrait and a quotation from Bandera's posthumously edited volume *Perspectives of the Ukrainian Revolution*.[104] In May *Homin Ukraïny* designated Bandera and Shukhevych as heroes of the month.[105] On 17 October, it published Bandera's portrait on the first page, together with a picture of the pro-Bandera demonstration in Munich in 1979. An article reminded its readers

98 On 23 October 1983 a famine monument was unveiled in Edmonton. At the unveiling ceremony Petro Savaryn claimed seven million victims. See Tom Barrett, "Agony of Ukraine recalled," *Edmonton Journal*, 24 October 1983, 1; Rudling, Multiculturalism, 751–52.

99 "Ukraine since the 'New Order'," "Major instance of Genocide in the 20th century," *Ukrainian Echo*, 1 June 1983, 1, 2.

100 Roman Serbyn, "The First Man-Made Famine in Soviet Ukraine 1921–1923," *Ukrainian Weekly*, 6 November 1988, 5.

101 Marco Carynnyk, "Blind Eye to Murder: Britain, the United States and the Ukrainian Famine of 1933," in *Famine in Ukraine 1932–1933*, eds. Roman Serbyn and Bohdan Krawchenko (Edmonton: Canadian Institute of Ukrainian Studies, University of Alberta, 1986), 135–36. In the 1990s Carynnyk became one of the most reliable scholars investigating the antisemitism of the OUN-UPA, and a critic of the nationalist misrepresentation of the famine. Cf. chapter 10 below.

102 In general on the famine, see Dietsch, *Making Sense*; Himka, Review of Johan Dietsch, 683–94.

103 For Andrii Bandera, see "Pokhoron sl. pam. A. Bandery," *Shliakh peremohy*, 12 August 1984, 1,2; "Zamist' kvitiv na mohylu druhovi," *Shliakh peremohy*, 19 August 1984, 2; "Sviatii pamiati Andriia Bandery," *Shliakh peremohy*, 9 September 1984, 2; "Pokhoron sl. pam. Andriia Bandery," *Homin Ukraïny*, 1 August 1984, 1; "Prysviata sl. p. Andriievi Banderi," *Homin Ukraïny*, 1 August 1984, 2; "In Memoriam of Andriy Bandera," *Ukrainian Echo*, 29 August 1984, 3, 6. For Slipyi, see "U pokloni sviatomu," *Shliakh peremohy*, 23 September 1984, 1; "Zavishchannia blazhenishoho," *Shliakh peremohy*, 23 September 1984, 1; "Budemo virni zavishchanniu Patriiarkha!" *Shliakh peremohy*, 7 October 1984, 1; "Sviatishyi Otets' Ivan-Pavlo II do ukraïns'koho narodu v Kanadi," *Shliakh peremohy*, 14 October 1984, 2; "Sv. p. Patriiarkh UKTS Iosyf I," *Homin Ukraïny*, 19 September 1984, 1–2.

104 "U 25-richchia z dnia smerty Stepana Bandery," *Shliakh peremohy*, 1984.

105 Iaroslav Sokolyk, "Heroï travnia," *Homin Ukraïny*, 13 June 1984, 2.

that the portrait showed the symbol of the Ukrainian nation.[106] The KUK summoned the "Ukrainian citizens of Canada" to commemorate Bandera as "one of the greatest twentieth-century defenders against the communist-Russian empire."[107]

One day before the anniversary, *Shliakh peremohy* published Bandera's portrait on the first page. In the article surrounding the portrait, it summarized Bandera's life in a standardized heroic and laudatory narrative, set in the "time of iron and blood."[108] On another page, it explained that the Munich émigrés frequently took their foreign visitors to Bandera's grave.[109] In the next issue, *Shliakh peremohy* published further articles about the revolutionary nature of the *Providnyk*, pictures of his funeral, and of his grave covered with wreaths.[110] A week later, it stated that October was Bandera month in Munich and informed its readers that in 1984, as in previous years, Ukrainians from numerous countries around the world would make a pilgrimage to Bandera's grave. After their arrival, the participants first attended a politicized panakhyda and then went to the hall of the Munich Conservatory for a commemorative gathering. During the ceremony, Stets'ko reminded the audience that the revolutionary struggle was not over: "Around us is the world of enemies—the post-Versailles system that legalized the occupation of Ukraine." In Cossack costumes, the Nottingham choir sang UPA songs under a huge portrait of Bandera. Finally, 800 participants marched through the city with torches and banners in their hands. Instead of walking to Kreittmayrstrasse 7 and burning a Soviet flag as in previous years, the crowd marched to the Odeonsplatz, where SUM activists had built a stand. They delivered anticommunist speeches and informed passers-by, in German and Ukrainian, about the purpose of their activism.[111]

On 20 October 1984 in London, after a church service in remembrance of the *Providnyk*, about 1,500 people walked through the city with banners, shouting anti-Soviet slogans. In the afternoon, they assembled to hear a speech by Vasyl' Oles'kiv, and anticommunist and revolutionary nationalist songs such as "We Were Born from the Blood of the Nation," performed by the Manchester choir in Cossack and folk costumes, under a huge portrait of Stepan Bandera.[112] In addition to the numerous regular locations of Bandera anniversaries, such as New York, Washington, and Winnipeg, Ukrainian nationalists performed their anticommunist rituals in honor of Bandera, in Hollywood in 1984.[113]

The next round of Bandera commemorations took place in 1989 without the OUN and ABN leader Iaroslav Stets'ko, who had died in Munich on 5 July 1986. Slava (Iaroslava) Stets'ko, the widow of the "last premier of Ukraine," became the new

106 "Stepan Bandera—symvol ukraïns'koï natsiï," *Homin Ukraïny*, 17 October 1984, 1–2. See also "Stepan Bandera: the man, the symbol" *Ukrainian Echo*, 17 October 1984, 4; "25 years later ...," *Ukrainian Echo*, 17 October 1984, 5.

107 "Zvernennia KUK," *Homin Ukraïny*, 24 October 1984, 2.

108 "Zvernenia provodu OUN u 25-richchia herois'koï smerty Stepana Bandery," *Shliakh peremohy*, 14 October 1984, 1.

109 On this page the OUN activists depicted themselves with members of the European Council of Liberation, "Konferentsiia Ievropeis'koï Rady Svobody," *Shliakh peremohy*, 14 October 1984, 5.

110 "Stepan Bandera—revoliutsyinyi providnyk," *Shliakh peremohy*, 21 October 1984, 1, 6.

111 "U pokloni Stepanovi Banderi," *Shliakh peremohy*, 28 October 1984, 1, 6; "Stepan Bandera na tli epokhy," *Shliakh peremohy*, 4 November 1984, 1, 2; Volodymyr Lenyk, "U pokloni Stepanovi Banderi," *Ukraïns'ka dumka*, 8 November 1984, 2.

112 "U pamiat' i proslavu," *Ukraïns'ka dumka*, 15 November 1984, 5.

113 "V pokloni Stepanovi Banderi," *Homin Ukraïny*, 5 December 1984, 10.

leader of the ABN. Vasyl' Oles'kiv assumed the leadership of the OUN.[114] Shortly after his death, Stets'ko also became a cult figure, although he was not admired and celebrated as intensively and lavishly as Bandera. Forty days after Stets'ko's death, an anonymous poet published a poem entitled "For the Providnyk," devoted to the legendary leader of the ABN. It praised Stets'ko's strong belief in the "Holy Truth," his willingness to make sacrifices, and his determination. It also mourned the loss of Stets'ko, which was compared to the loss of Bandera. Together with a dozen other equally pathetic and bellicose poems, the poem was recited by SUM members in their brown uniforms at a commemorative gathering in Munich on 13 August 1986.[115] Even before this commemoration, the death of Stets'ko was also officially honored in Taipei on 19 July, during a congress of the Captive Nations.[116]

Stets'ko's passing certainly affected the nationalist Ukrainian communities but it did not prevent them from prolonging the struggle against the "red devil" while staging further commemorations in honor of Bandera, and performing numerous anticommunist rituals. On 15 October 1989, *Shliakh peremohy* published a photograph of Bandera's bust on the first page, with his signature and the article "Stepan Bandera—The Maker of a New Era." As in previous years, Bandera was introduced as the first son of the nation, which was underlined by Leonid Poltava's motto "You will never forget the one who became the banner of the people!" Further, the Banderite newspaper based in Munich published a poem devoted to the *Providnyk* on the first page, and an article about the trial of Bohdan Stashyns'kyi written by Stepan Lenkavs'kyi, who had died in 1977.[117]

In 1989 the commemorations in Munich proceeded as usual. Bishop Platon and other priests performed a panakhyda at the grave, which was attended by numerous nationalists, both young and old, in uniforms or plain clothes. Many of them carried red-and-black flags. Oles'kiv, the new OUN leader, delivered a speech. Later, the nationalists went to a commemorative gathering organized by Kashuba, a former SB officer. Volodymyr Mazur delivered a speech about the "vicious enemies" and the "enormous suffering" of the Ukrainian nation. He stood at a podium covered with an embroidered cloth, and the stage behind him was decorated with a huge Bandera poster with "1959" and "1989" on either side. Various musical groups played and sang nationalist and folk pieces for the *Providnyk*. The main difference between this and all previous festivities was that similar commemorations in western Ukraine, particularly in Bandera's birthplace Staryi Uhryniv, were mentioned in the diaspora press. This was a sign of upcoming political changes.[118]

114 Lypovets'kyi, *Orhanizatsiia Ukraïns'kykh*, cover.

115 "Providnykovi," *Shliakh peremohy*, 24 August 1986, 1; "Poklin velykomu synovi Ukraïny," *Ideia i chyn.Orhan Kraiovoï Upravy Spilky Ukraïns'koï Molodi v Nimechchyni*, August 1984, 1.

116 "U Taipeï vshanuvaly sl. pam. Iaroslava Stets'ko," *Shliakh peremohy*, 24 August 1986, 1.

117 "Stepan Bander—tvorets' novoï epokhy," *Shliakh peremohy*, 15 October 1989, 1. Stepan Lenkavs'kyi, "Politychna otsinka protsesu proty vbyvtsiv sl. pam. Stepana Bandera," *Shliakh peremohy*, 15 October 1989, 1, 6; Ol'ha Lus'ka, "Stepanovi Banderi," *Shliakh peremohy*, 15 October 1989, 1.

118 "V pokloni providnykovi Stepanovi Banderi," *Shliakh peremohy*, 29 October 1989, 1, 2; "Slovo-vidkryttia zhalobnoï Akademiï Holovy Mizhkraiovoho Sviatkovoho Komitetu Ivana Kashuby," *Shliakh peremohy*, 29 October 1989, 1; "Zhalobni urochystosti v Miunkheni," *Shliakh peremohy*, 29 October 1989, 1, 2; "Stepan Bandera na tli suchasnoï doby," *Shliakh peremohy*, 29 October 1989, 1, 2.

The First Bandera Museum

The first museum devoted to Bandera was unveiled on 20 October 1962, one day after the announcement of the verdict in the trial of Bohdan Stashyns'kyi. The Stepan Bandera Museum of the Ukrainian Liberation Struggle (*Muzei Ukraïns'koï Vyzvol'noï borot'by im. Stepana Bandery*) was opened in the building of the SUB in Nottingham, England.[119] The core items in the museum were Bandera's personal belongings. The ZCh OUN regarded Britain as a safer place for these "sacred" objects than Munich.[120]

In 1978 the museum was relocated to London and reopened on 6 October 1979.[121] According to Vasyl' Oles'kiv, leader of the ZCh OUN from 1986 to 1991 and longstanding director of the museum, the idea behind the relocation was to make it more accessible for foreign visitors.[122] The museum, however, was never designed to attract the general public, but served as a pilgrimage site for Ukrainian nationalists, known only to insiders.[123] The wish of the founders of the museum was to save Bandera's personal belongings for future generations. They shipped a substantial portion of them from Bandera's office and home in Munich to Nottingham and later to London, where they were located on the first floor of the building of the OUN publishing house, Ukrainian Publishers, at 200 Liverpool Road. The entire museum has been located there ever since, in a dark, bunker-like room of about twenty-six square meters, with small windows immediately below the ceiling. The two central exhibits of the museum are Bandera's death mask and the clothes in which he was assassinated. His suit and shirt bear traces of the blood that he allegedly spat out after Stashyns'kyi fired the capsule with potassium cyanide at his face. The death mask was taken from Bandera's face in order to immortalize Bandera's physiognomy, charisma, and greatness (Fig. 51). The main purpose behind displaying the bloodstained clothes is to invoke the terrible moment of assassination, which symbolizes the extinction of Ukraine and Ukrainians by the Soviet oppressors. Other belongings of the *Providnyk* are located in his wardrobe, which stands open. Inside, visitors see Bandera's jackets, shirts, including one with a tie, dark leather gloves, a hat, briefcase, pullovers, coat, pajamas, dark leather shoes, sport shoes, walking boots, ice skates, and even a small folding spade.

Standing in the museum room between Bandera's wardrobe, radio, sofa, commode, and a large wooden desk with a huge semi-circular stamp, a wooden desk clock, and a typewriter that had belonged to Ievhen Konovalets', visitors receive the impression that they are somewhere between Bandera's office, living room, and bedroom. The impression is strengthened by the portraits of Konovalets' and Petliura that hang in the same order as they had hung in Bandera's office in Munich, on either

119 "Muzei," *Shliakh peremohy*, 12 October 1962, 3.

120 OUN member Mykhailo Bilan, interview by author, London, 10 July 2008.

121 *Muzei Ukraïns'koï Vyzvol'noï Borot'by im. Stepana Bandery*, 1979, anonymous leaflet.

122 OUN member Vasyl' Oles'kiv, telephone interview by author, Berlin/London, 27 November 2008.

123 When I visited the museum in 2008, it bore no sign. A clerk in a small shop nearby informed me that he had never heard anything about a museum in the area although he had worked in the shop for thirty years.

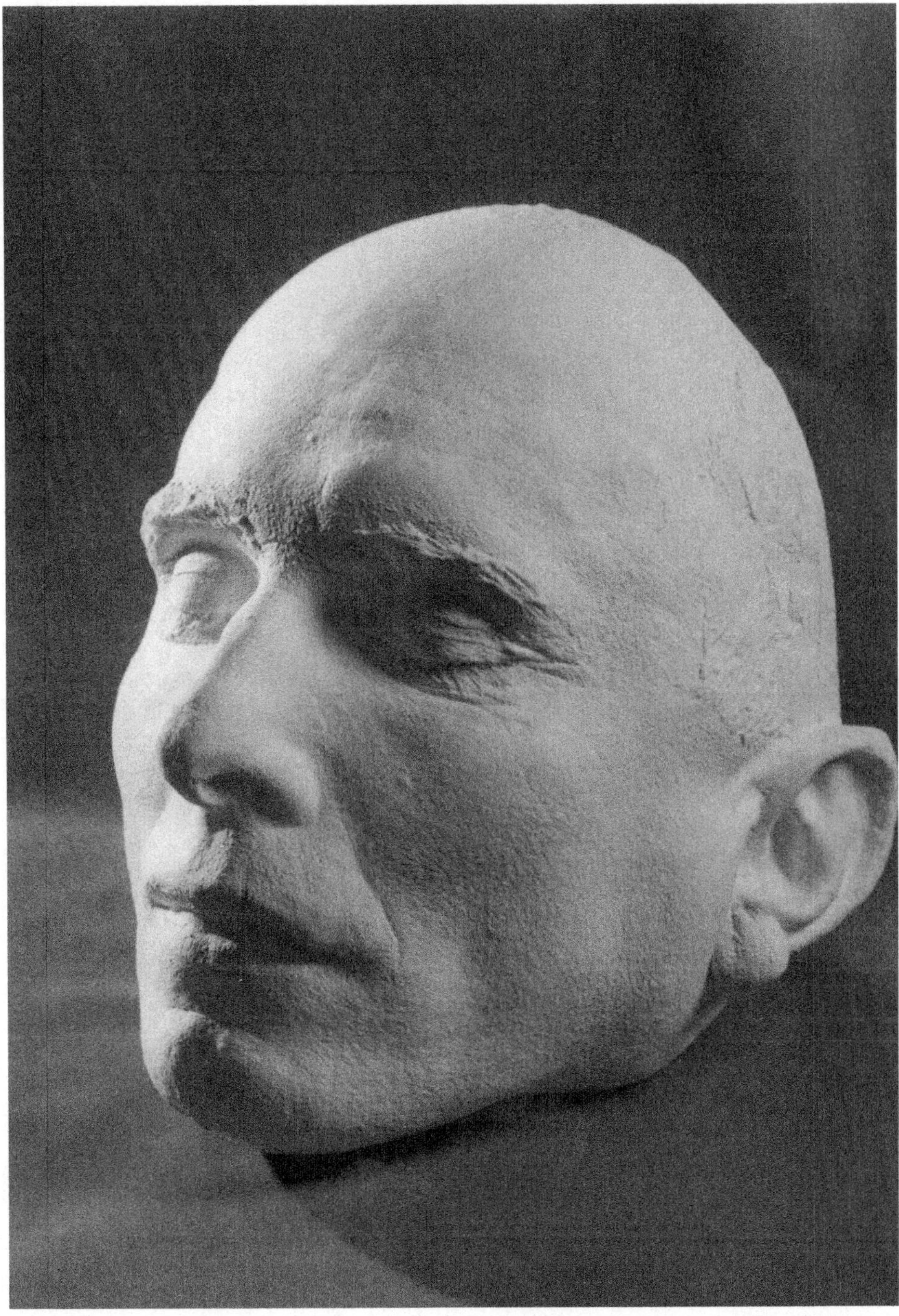

Fig. 51. Bandera's death mask in the Bandera museum London.
Lizun, *Vbyvstvo Stepana Bandery*, 80.

side of a cross, above a trident, on the wall behind the desk. Although the blood on the jacket and shirt informs the visitor about Bandera's death, the bust behind the desk, the death mask, and the dried flowers from the funeral wreaths revise the impression and suggest that the *Providnyk* is actually there among the visitors. A number of items are exhibited in six display cases and on the walls. Some of them did not belong to Bandera but conceptualize Bandera as a symbol of the OUN, UPA, and Ukrainian nationalism in general.[124]

One of such objects is Shukhevych's bust. It was prepared, like Bandera's, by Chereshn'ovs'kyi. Both busts are placed on pedestals from which they appear to look at the visitors. The collection of Bandera's articles edited posthumously by his adherents and published in 1978 under the title *The Perspectives of the Ukrainian Revolution* lies on a table covered with an embroidered cloth. It resembles a Bible on an altar. One of the display cases contains Bandera's bloody jacket, shirt, and his shoulder holster, but without the pistol that was found on him at the hospital. Another display case exhibits two leather bags of a UPA partisan who, as a small paper strip informs the visitors, arrived in Bavaria from Ukraine in 1947. The other four display cases show items of different provenance. Many of them are propaganda materials like newspapers, leaflets, and pamphlets from the 1940s and 1950s, some of them brought from Ukraine to Bavaria, others printed in the diaspora. Also included in this group are medals, OUN and UPA stickers, booklets, organizational awards, and diplomas. One display case contains a dozen embroidered cloths of different types and implies the interrelation between Ukrainian nationalism and Ukrainian folklore. Another group includes portraits of OUN and UPA leaders, several photographs of the *Providnyk* and objects related to him, such as the house in which he grew up in Staryi Uhryniv, the church where his father served, pictures from his youth, including one in a Cossack costume and with a rifle in his hands (Fig. 4, page 95), pictures of his family in Munich, and of an interview with journalists. Finally, the display cases demonstrate a collection of Bandera cinderella stamps, two postcards bearing these stamps, and some *bofons*, or bonds for the OUN combat fund, including a 100 hryvnia Bandera *bofon* (Fig. 52).[125]

The exhibits on one wall are a set of portraits of OUN members and a set of colored drawings showing Ukrainian prisoners in the Auschwitz camp. The portraits are divided into two rows. The top one displays male OUN members: Ievhen Konovalets' in the middle, Stepan Bandera and Iaroslav Stets'ko on either side of him, and then Mykhailo Soroka and Stepan Lenkavs'kyi; the row below shows the female members: Alla Hors'ka, Iryna Senyk, Oksana Popovych, Kateryna Zaryts'ka-Soroka, Halyna Dydyk, and Oksana Meshko.

The drawings with scenes from Auschwitz, which was both a concentration camp and an extermination camp, hang in a row of fifteen paintings under the portraits of the male and female OUN heroes. The author of the drawings is Petro Balei, a prisoner of the camp and the author of several books, including one about Bandera. The

124 OUN member Vasyl' Oles'kiv, telephone interview by author, Berlin/London, 27 November 2008.

125 The Bandera bofon with Iaroslav Stets'ko's signature was issued in 1982. Others were released in 1964 and 1994. Cf. Serhii Bohunov, ed., *Bofony: Hroshovi dokumenty OUN i UPA* (Kiev: Sluzhba Bezpeky Ukraïny, 2008), 164, 166, 171.

Fig. 52. A hundred hryvnia Bandera *bofon* with Iaroslav Stets'ko's inscription, 1982. ASBML.

pictures are the only exhibits in the museum that are related to the Holocaust. Yet they do not hang in the museum to explain what Auschwitz or the Holocaust were, or what people were detained and annihilated there, and why. The drawings and the inscriptions beneath them suggest to visitors that the only prisoners in Auschwitz were Ukrainians, in particular the OUN-B members, and therefore imply that the Ukrainian nationalists could not have been involved in the Holocaust.

The drawings show personalities such as Stepan Lenkavs'kyi, Lev Rebet, Mykola Klymyshyn, and Iulian Zablots'kyi in striped uniforms, lying or sitting on their beds, smoking cigarettes, stealing food, being beaten by the Kapos and Germans with cudgels and whips, standing in a row during a roll call, cleaning the barracks, or sweeping the camp. One picture shows prisoners being gassed in a gas chamber. There is no inscription that would specify who these people are. Other drawings suggest that they can only be OUN-B members. Furthermore, there is no explicit or implicit indication that there were also Jews in Auschwitz, not to mention the fact that they made up the vast majority of the victims. Moreover, nothing in the pictures or in the museum indicates that the Ukrainian prisoners of Auschwitz did not share the fate of the Jews, of whom the vast majority were killed in the camps, whereas the majority of Ukrainians survived the camp.[126]

A very similar interpretation of Ukrainians in concentration and death camps was presented in 1945 and 1946 by two anonymous authors, very likely OUN members, in the publication *Why the World Is Silent*. The authors did not mention Jews as prisoners of German camps. The only Jews in their publication are Jewish Kapos. Ukrainian prisoners are divided into traitors and patriots. The patriots are mainly Banderites, and the Ukrainian patriots are the main victims of the German concentration camps. The authors claim that Ukrainian patriots were murdered and mistreated not only by camp guards but also by other prisoners, in particular Poles,

126 The OUN members were detained in KZ Auschwitz I as political prisoners. The majority of the Jews deported to Auschwitz were annihilated in KZ Auschwitz II-Birkenau. Among the non-Jewish prisoners in Auschwitz, mainly the sick and incapable of work were killed. Cf. Mykhailo Marunchak, *Ukraïns'ki politychni v'iazni v natsysts'kykh kontsentratsyïnykh taborakh* (Winnipeg: Svitova liha ukarïns'kykh politychnykh v'iazniv), 121–24.

Russians, and Bolsheviks. The Bandera museum follows a very similar logic, turning the OUN and in particular the OUN-B, into the main victims of the Holocaust.[127]

Pictures on another wall of the Bandera museum are devoted to the UPA, which Bandera never led or even belonged to, but of which he was the spiritual leader and eventually one of its main symbols. The pictures show UPA leaders such as Rostyslav Voloshyn, Volodymyr Shchyhel's'kyi (Captain "Burlaka"), Vasyl' Sydor, and a priest with four UPA partisans in front of a collective grave of UPA partisans with a huge cross, partisans conducting a medical inspection of other partisans, a small UPA unit from 1946, and pictures that allegedly show bodies of murdered UPA partisans. Next to this collection, visitors see a poster announcing the opening of the museum on 20 October 1962 in Nottingham, and a historically stylized announcement "The Appeal of Struggling Ukraine" to the youth of the Ukrainian diaspora, which informs the young Ukrainian audience:

> In exile you have to become the avant-garde of the liberating struggle, just like us, the youth in the homeland. You have entirely devoted yourselves to the interests of struggling Ukraine ... fight next to your fellows [in Ukraine] who with arms in their hands struggle for the liberation of the nation. ... Before you, Ukrainian youth, just as before our whole emigration, lies the task of familiarizing foreigners with the liberation struggle of the Ukrainian nation. Do it on every occasion and with all resources. Use for it your personal friendships, contacts with the youth of other nations, and international youth organizations. Inspire the youth of all nations for a struggle against Bolshevism.[128]

The bottom part of the frame in a historically stylized announcement displays the first commander in chief Shukhevych reading "The Appeal of Struggling Ukraine" to Ukrainian youth, which is divided into intelligentsia listening to the UPA leader, and fighters who, with rifles in their hands and OUN banners, run into a battle against the Soviets.[129]

The Bandera museum that was opened in Nottingham and relocated to London has been a nationalist shrine rather than an educational institution. It was not created to elucidate Bandera's life, the concept of a leader, or the history of the OUN and UPA, but to worship the *Providnyk* and to deny the problematic aspects of the "liberation movement," with the help of the Bandera cult and his distorted and victimized image. Its creators were OUN members and veterans of Waffen-SS Galizien and the UPA, who had worshiped Bandera in the 1930s and 1940s and who tried to pass on the cult to their children. The museum exemplifies very well how the Ukrainian nationalists sacralized the *Providnyk* and turned him into a transcendent object of admiration. Similarly, it demonstrates how its creators heroized and victimized their collective memory of the Second World War and how they turned OUN members and UPA veterans into heroes, martyrs, and victims of the Nazis. The subject of Poles, Jews, and other victims of the Ukrainian nationalists is completely absent from the museum, although the OUN and UPA are featured extensively.

127 V-K., A.-T., *Chomu svit movchyt'* (Kiev, Paris, 1946), 4, 27, 35, 36, 39, 41, 46, 48, 51. For the OUN members in Auschwitz see page 251 et seq., above.

128 "Zvernennia voiuiuchoï Ukraïny. Ukraïns'ka Molode!"

129 Ibid.

Historians and the Bandera Cult

As well as being celebrated at numerous nationalist commemorations and anti-Soviet demonstrations and worshiped in the museum, the *Providnyk* also became a very important component of the narrative of Ukrainian history and an object of historiographical extolment. Diaspora historians represented the *Providnyk* as a national hero who sacrificed his life for Ukraine, and they omitted or denied all compromising facts about him and the OUN. They embedded him in the narrative of a "national liberation" struggle for an "independent Ukrainian state," conducted by the OUN, the UPA, and the Waffen-SS Division Galizien, all of which were whitewashed in respect of war crimes, and the Waffen-SS Galizien in respect of collaboration with Nazi Germany. This way of presenting Bandera was related to the fact that many of the historians who published on Bandera were OUN members, veterans of the Waffen-SS Galizien and the UPA, or sincere admirers of the *Providnyk* and his political ideas. This manner of explaining Ukrainian twentieth-century history impacted also on historians who were not rooted in the diaspora communities but who, due to the anticommunist Cold War narrative, the lack of archival documents, or other reasons, took over partly or entirely the narrative established and propagated by the diaspora communities.

Petro Mirchuk, Bandera's first hagiographer, was an OUN-B member and, prior to the Second World War, head of a division of the propaganda apparatus in the national executive.[130] Mirchuk was also an Auschwitz survivor, an organizer of numerous Bandera commemorations, and an advocate of Jewish-Ukrainian reconciliation—on condition that the Jews acknowledged that Ukrainians did not kill Jews during the Second World War, that the OUN and UPA rescued them, and that Ukrainians were victims of the Holocaust equally with Jews. After the Second World War, Mirchuk stayed in DP camps until 1950, when he settled in the United States. He wrote a number of publications on Ukrainian nationalism, and his works had a significant influence on the way the Ukrainian diaspora understood the OUN, the UPA, and Ukrainian nationalism in general. After the collapse of the Soviet Union, many of Mirchuk's publications were republished in Ukraine. They were regarded as important, academic, and reliable works. In his publications Mirchuk transformed Bandera into the symbol of the OUN, UPA, Waffen-SS Galizien, the "national liberation movement," and all other groups of patriotic and nationalist insurgents. Although some of Mirchuk's publications were fabricated, several of them contain valuable facts, but leave out even more, and introduce false information. The main aim of his writings was to provide the far-right narrative with credibility and to fortify the right-wing diaspora communities in their politicized self-understanding.

In the introduction to his 1961 biography, *Stepan Bandera: Symbol of Revolutionary Uncompromisingness*, Mirchuk stated that he was writing the biography in the genre of hagiography (Ukr. *zhyttia sviatykh*) because he believed that this was the only correct genre for the portrayal of the life of "one of the greatest of Ukrainian patriots, one of the greatest Ukrainian revolutionary nationalists." He argued that Ukrainians needed such a publication because it would be a "source of power, which

130 Golczewski, *Deutsche und Ukrainer*, 942.

reinforces our belief in the Ukrainian nation."[131] Mirchuk did not deny the range of assassinations conducted in 1933–1934 under the leadership of Bandera; at least not those that were already known. However, he legitimized and rationalized them by depicting them as a legitimate answer to the "Polish terror" or as patriotic deeds. Thus Bandera was introduced not as a leader of a terrorist nationalist organization but as a "patriotic revolutionary" protecting the Ukrainian nation against the Polish occupiers. Killing politicians or civilians whom the OUN accused of harming or betraying the nation was, for Mirchuk, a patriotic deed that had nothing to do with violence or terrorism. On the contrary, it was an appropriate expression of patriotic feelings.[132]

According to Mirchuk, investigating "totalitarian" and "dictatorial" tendencies in the OUN or in Bandera was illegitimate and was a frequent practice of the enemies of the OUN. Bandera was a democrat who differentiated between the "legal social-civic life and the [necessary] forms of revolutionary underground." Like every OUN member, he obeyed democratic order and respected democracy and human rights.[133] Describing Bandera after his arrest on 14 June 1934, Mirchuk condemned the torture of Ukrainian prisoners in Polish jails and delivered a detailed description. He claimed that the "handcuffed and tortured Stepan Bandera was the epitome of the mythical Prometheus," who suffered for Ukraine.[134] Describing the trial of the OUN in Warsaw in 1935–1936, Mirchuk changed the political meaning of the fascist salute "Slava Ukraïni!" which the OUN members performed several times in the courtroom. He described how the OUN members shouted "Slava Ukraïni!" but did not mention that they extended their right arms. He thereby turned this greeting into something for which Ukrainian patriots born after the Second World War could have sympathy.[135] Similarly, Mirchuk explained Bandera's and the OUN's conduct during the Second World War:

> The leadership of the revolutionary OUN under the leadership of Stepan Bandera did not delude itself and did not hope that Hitler's Germany would support rebuilding the independent Ukrainian state. ... Thus it definitely declined any kind of collaboration with Hitler's party and in particular any conjunction of the OUN's deeds with the politics of Hitler's Germany.[136]

Because it was, however, impossible to entirely deny OUN-B collaboration with Nazi Germany, Mirchuk claimed that the OUN-B "decided that it was not only possible but also necessary to make contact with the anti-Hitler circles of the German army. [This cooperation] was necessary [in order] to have Ukrainian troops in Ukrainian territory in the first weeks of the war, who would become the core of a regular Ukrainian army."[137] The questions of Jews and the Holocaust were not discussed in this section, although the pogroms took place at the time and in the location of the revolutionary actions of the OUN-B. Furthermore, the OUN-B did not

131 Mirchuk, *Stepan Bandera*, 6–7.
132 Ibid., 26–30.
133 Ibid., 37–38.
134 Ibid., 43. For torturing Ukrainian prisoners, see chapter 3 above.
135 Ibid., 45–47.
136 Ibid., 71.
137 Ibid., 75.

intend to install a fascist dictatorship in Ukraine but established a "Ukrainian National Committee" to represent all Ukrainians in the government established by the OUN-B. Moreover, the OUN-B combated Soviet and German imperialism from the very beginning of the "Ukrainian National Revolution."[138] Mirchuk confirmed that the OUN-B killed OUN-M members but only those who worked for the Gestapo or who handed over OUN-B members. The murder of Stsibors'kyi and Senyk was, however, a Soviet act and had nothing to do with Bandera or the OUN-B.[139]

Repeating the proclamation of the Ukrainian state from 30 June 1941, Mirchuk omitted all references to collaboration and friendly relations with "National Socialist Great Germany, which, under the leadership of Adolf Hitler, is creating a new order in Europe and the world, and is helping the Ukrainian nation liberate itself from Muscovite occupation," which had been mentioned in the proclamation.[140] Thus according to Bandera's first hagiographer, "on the political level, the Act of 30 June 1941 was a manifestation of the freedom of the Ukrainian nation and its attitude toward new deeds performed in front of the whole world and in front of history." And further, the act was the beginning of the "armed rising against Hitler's Germany."[141]

After his arrest by the Germans, Bandera suffered, but he did not give up, and was "not afraid of torture or death for the freedom of Ukraine as previously [he had not been] from the hands of Poles."[142] The *Providnyk* opposed the Germans until the end of the Second World War, despite the tortures of the Gestapo to which he was exposed:

> And this "No" [to the collaboration with Germany] Bandera could keep until the collapse of Hitler's Germany, although he had to suffer for it long years of hard imprisonment in German prisons and camps, being prepared every day for death. ... The moral strength of Stepan Bandera and his physical endurance against torture appeared to be more powerful than the entire physical strength of the Gestapo.[143]

The best proof for Mirchuk of Bandera's refusal to collaborate with the Germans during the Second World War was the *Providnyk's* denial of this collaboration, which can be found in several of Bandera's articles written after the Second World War.[144]

In general, Mirchuk claimed that the OUN-B was the only Ukrainian organization that opposed Hitler and Stalin. All other political bodies compromised themselves through collaboration.[145] Banderites were for Mirchuk those brave people who fought for Ukraine and never collaborated with Nazi Germany.[146] Other organizations and individuals also "worked for the nation," but in collaboration with Nazi Germany.

138 Ibid., 76–77.
139 Ibid., 89.
140 Mirchuk, *Stepan Bandera*, 77–78. For the actual text of the proclamation, see "Akt proholoshennia ukraïns'koï derzhavy, 30.06.1941," TsDAVOV f. 3833, op. 1, spr. 5, 3. See also chapter 4 above.
141 Mirchuk, *Stepan Bandera*, 83.
142 Ibid., 81.
143 Ibid., 82.
144 Ibid., 93. See chapter 7 above, subsection "Bandera's Worldview after the Second World War."
145 Ibid., 93.
146 Ibid., 97–98.

"They wrote memorials to the government of Germany, Hitler, Himmler, and other leaders of contemporary German politics."[147]

After his release from Sachsenhausen, Bandera, according to Mirchuk, "again led the revolutionary struggle of the whole Ukrainian nation against the Red Moscow occupier."[148] After the Second World War, the struggle for independence was even more difficult than before, because of those elements of the OUN and the Ukrainian diaspora who did not subordinate themselves to the *Providnyk*. As in previous parts of the biography, Mirchuk omitted here that the OUN-B killed opponents and suspects in the DP camps.[149] During the Cold War, Bandera was again for Mirchuk the sole Ukrainian politician who was prepared to collaborate only with those anti-Soviet powers that accepted his demand for an independent Ukrainian state.[150]

One of the most interesting sections of Mirchuk's biography is about the nation, the party, and democracy. In this section, Mirchuk introduces the argument that the nation must be ruled by only one organization, cites Bandera's "Word to the Ukrainian Nationalists" from 1946, and argues that the OUN did not represent a particular element of Ukrainian society but the whole nation:

> The Organization of Ukrainian Nationalists (revolutionaries) ... is not a representative of the interests of any particular part of the nation. ... The OUN is struggling for the good of the whole Ukrainian nation and all citizens of Ukraine, and not for any particular part, social strata, and the like. The OUN derives its program from the needs of the whole Ukrainian nation.[151]

On democracy, Mirchuk writes:

> Stepan Bandera never misused the words 'democracy' and 'democratic,' he never fought with phrases about democracy, because he disdained shallow demagogy. At the same time, he was always a fighter for the principles of democracy in Ukrainian political life, in the future Ukrainian state, and also in current life; and ideas propagated by him during his life, which we have already cited, substantiate this very convincingly.[152]

Logically, only enemies of the OUN-B or of the Ukrainian people spread rumors that Bandera was "antidemocratic" and "totalitarian."[153]

In another publication, *My Meetings and Discussions in Israel (Are Ukrainians "Traditionally anti-Semites"?)*, published by the "Ukrainian Survivors of the Holocaust," Mirchuk approached the problem of Jewish-Ukrainian relations and the role of the OUN-B in them.[154] The monograph begins not with an introduction but with a short biographical note about the author, from which readers learn that he is a mem-

147 Ibid., 95–96.
148 Ibid., 99.
149 Ibid., 101. For the killing of Ukrainians by the OUN-B after the Second World War see chapter 6 above.
150 Mirchuk, *Stepan Bandera*, 102.
151 Ibid.,103; Bandera, Slovo do Ukraïns'kykh, 78.
152 Mirchuk, *Stepan Bandera*, 109.
153 Ibid., 110.
154 Petro Mirchuk, *My Meetings and Discussions in Israel: Are Ukrainians "Traditionally anti-Semites"?* (New York: Ukrainian Survivors of the Holocaust, 1982).

ber of the Society for Jewish-Ukrainian Collaboration, an honorary member of the Jewish Identity Centre, and that he was a prisoner of Auschwitz from July 1942 until 19 January 1945. The biographical note also contains pictures of Mirchuk in characteristic striped prisoner's garb. What it does not contain is any clarification why he and other non-Jewish inmates of Auschwitz did not share the fate of Jews in Auschwitz, and how the OUN-B was involved in pogroms before some of its members were imprisoned in the concentration camps.[155]

The difference between a Jew and a non-Jew in Auschwitz was significant. What Stanisław Krajewski elaborated for Poles and Jews is even truer for Ukrainians:

> For "Aryans," Auschwitz was "merely" a destructive labor camp with the threat of death. Their families were frequently free. For the Jews, Auschwitz was a death camp, frequently for their whole families. Outside the camp, at large, nobody was waiting for them. Even if their later experiences were comparable with those of other inmates they did not share the same fate.
>
> The tattoo with the number on the underarm meant for a Jew a happy destination; he avoided immediate death in the gas chamber. For a Pole [or a Ukrainian] it was one of the most terrible options.[156]

Because of their political status, the OUN-B members had even greater chances of survival than an average Polish or Ukrainian prisoner, but Bandera's first hagiographer understood the matter differently. During his visit to Israel in 1981, which resulted in *My Meetings and Discussions in Israel*, Mirchuk showed his Auschwitz tattoo to a number of people. At Yad Vashem, he displayed it to a young person, mourning relatives who had been killed in Auschwitz, and informed her: "I saw it [the Auschwitz camp] with my own eyes, I personally experienced it." In the remainder of the conversation, he felt it necessary to point out that "there were [in Auschwitz] thousands like me—Ukrainians."[157]

Mirchuk also met a number of Holocaust historians in Israel, mainly directors and other employees of museums, and informed them that their perception of the Holocaust and Ukraine was completely wrong, for which he, a Ukrainian prisoner of Auschwitz with a tattoo on his arm, was the best evidence. In every conversation, he repeated that Ukrainians had never been antisemitic and that they were not involved in any kind of atrocities during the Second World War. Mirchuk's best evidence for the "misperception" of Ukrainians and "misinformation" as to the involvement of Ukrainians in the Holocaust was the anti-Ukrainian sentiment among Holocaust historians and Jews. Once he stated: "[Only] the Auschwitz 'disclosure' on my arm ... stops anti-Ukrainian assailment."[158]

In a conversation with Rabbi David Kahana, who had been saved by Sheptyts'kyi, Mirchuk could not understand why Yad Vashem was reluctant to honor Sheptyts'kyi. The evidence, that in the summer of 1941 Sheptyts'kyi reinforced Stets'ko's govern-

155 Mirchuk, *My Meetings*, 2–3. Mirchuk was, however, aware of the difference between Jewish and non-Jewish prisoners. He described it in his own memoirs of Auschwitz. Cf. Mirchuk, *In the German Mills of Death*, 60–61.

156 Stanisław Krajewski, "Auschwitz als Herausforderung," *Unbequeme Wahrheiten: Polen und sein Verhältnis zu den Juden*, ed. Helga Hirsch (Frankfurt am Main: Suhrkamp, 2008), 120.

157 Mirchuk, *My Meetings*, 25–26.

158 Ibid., 29.

ment with a pastoral letter and later supported the creation of the Waffen-SS Division Galizien, was for Mirchuk merely anti-Ukrainian propaganda. Discussing with Kahana the complicated nature of Sheptyts'ky, he repeated the OUN-B's antisemitic stereotypes of "Jewish Bolshevism" from 1941: "No Rabbi, it's the bitter truth. Jews willingly became the bulwark of the Red Russian occupation of Ukraine, the bloody Bolshevik terrorism. And very often they also became the organizers—overt and covert leaders."[159]

The subject of Ukrainian-German collaboration during the Second World War was also for Mirchuk mere anti-Ukrainian propaganda. According to him, "it was not Ukrainians, but actually Jews, who collaborated with German Nazis in the destruction of Jews. Jewish 'Judenrats,' Jewish police, Jewish informers, and the 'Sonderkommando' were composed only of young Jews in concentration camps." He was very much convinced of the truth of his understanding of the Second World War and the Holocaust. When criticized for some of his explanations, he claimed that his history was true because he would not state anything that was "untrue."[160]

In addition to denying Ukrainian involvement in the Holocaust, Mirchuk also claimed that not Jews but Ukrainians were the main victims of Nazi policy. Anyone who did not agree with Mirchuk on this matter or even worse, addressed the OUN's or UPA's war crimes, in particular the crimes against Jews, or the collaboration with Nazi Germany, was for him "anti-Ukrainian." The only way not to be "anti-Ukrainian" was to deny the OUN's war crimes and to claim that the OUN and UPA were a resistance movement, and that Ukrainians such as Stepan Bandera were national heroes and victims of Nazi policies. According to Mirchuk, only "the Bolsheviks call everyone who opposes Russian imperialism 'bandits' and 'fascists.' They even use these same labels when attacking those American presidents who oppose their aims and methods, such as President Reagan."[161]

Such a way of dealing with the subjects of Bandera, the OUN and UPA, the Holocaust, and the Second World War strongly affected the youth of the Ukrainian diaspora, who, as a result, believed in a range of political myths related to these questions. Elements of Ukrainian diaspora youth became a negative mirror image of Soviet Ukrainian youth. In 1983 a group of Ukrainian college students from the United States and Canada traveled through Europe with Professor Petro Goi and Sonia Szereg. Visiting the museum at the Dachau concentration camp, the young Ukrainians realized that "there is no mention of Ukraine or Ukrainians, yet many of the students had heard of or were personally acquainted with Ukrainians who had been prisoners in Dachau." The students decided to "take action." On 17 August at 4:00 p.m. seventeen students, two professors, and one priest came to the museum with banners and "formed a circle in the hall of nations where Ukraine is not represented." As the museum's assistant director asked them for the reason for this demonstration they explained it and declared that they were ready for a hunger strike. After the museum directorate decided to meet the demands of the protestors, one of which was to display the Ukrainian flag along with the flags of other nations,

159 Ibid., 61.
160 Ibid., 14–15.
161 Ibid., 149–50.

the students celebrated a panakhyda in the chapel in the grounds of the camp.[162] The fact that some Ukrainians from the Waffen-SS Galizien were trained in the vicinity of Dachau did not attract the attention of the students.[163]

The last publication related to Mirchuk that should be briefly described is *I Am Alive Thanks to the UPA*, a short autobiography of Stella Krentsbakh, a Jewish woman who owed her survival to the UPA but who apparently did not exist. The autobiography appeared in a volume of articles coedited by Mirchuk, and was forged by Mirchuk himself or another OUN veteran.[164] The short text begins with the words: "I attribute the fact that I am alive today, and devoting all the energy of my thirty-eight years to a free Israel, exclusively to the Almighty and the Ukrainian Insurgent Army (UPA)." The autobiography includes many expressions that come very close to antisemitic stereotypes and tells the story of a Jewish woman who was born in "the town of B., which lies seventy-five kilometers from Lviv" and who, when at a Ukrainian high school, "began to hate the enemies of Ukraine and to love its friends." During the Second World War she "became a member of the heroic UPA," survived the war among people who "do not divide people into races, only into honest people and dishonest ones." After the war she went to live in Israel.[165]

Another significant Bandera hagiographer was the poet, writer, and political activist Leonid Poltava (Leonid Parkhomovych). Poltava published not strictly historical but rather artistic publications about the *Providnyk*. He collected poems and songs about Bandera and published them together with Bandera stamps and pictures of Bandera's busts and portraits in *The Image of Stepan Bandera in Literature and Art*. Poltava's main motivation was to lay the foundations for a larger project that would honor the *Providnyk* by collecting artistic items devoted to him. In general, those collected and presented by Poltava seem to be a concoction of far-right, neo-fascist, and romantic ideas. Many of the poems mourn the loss of the *Providnyk* or *Vozhd'*. They emphasize the heroism and magnitude of the leader and stress that he did not die, because the Banderites were continuing the revolution. In one place, Poltava stated that Bandera is the banner of Ukraine because the word "bandera" means "banner" in Spanish. For Poltava, the fact that the Madrid radio station in Franco's Spain broadcasted songs about Bandera was evidence of the greatness of the Ukrainian *Providnyk*.[166]

In another publication, *The Life of Stepan Bandera*, Poltava published a range of private pictures from Bandera's youth and of his family members in order to show readers the ordinary side of the *Providnyk*. Bandera's biography was introduced as the *Providnyk* wrote it in 1959 for the United States consulate in Munich. In the main part, Poltava presented pictures of Bandera, in Cossack costume with a rifle in

162 "Ukrainian students protest in Dachau," *Homin Ukraïny*, 12 October 1983, 2.
163 Veryha, *Pid krylamy vyzvol'nykh dum*, 26–27. See also chapter 5 above.
164 Stella Krentsbakh, "Zhyvu shche zavdiaky UPA," *V riadakh UPA: Zbirka spomyniv buv. Voiakiv Ukraïns'koï Povstans'koï Armiï*, ed. Petro Mirchuk and V. Davydenko (New York: Nakladom T-va b. Voiakiv UPA v ZDA i Kanadi, 1957), 342–49. In 2009 Krentsbakh's biography was translated into English and published in Moisei Fishbein's blog http://mosesfishbein.blogspot.com/2009/10/memoirs-of-stella-krenzbach-i-am-alive.html (accessed 27 July 2011). For Fishbein, see page 478 et seq., below.
165 Krentsbakh, Zhyvu shche zavdiaky UPA, 342, 343, 345–46, 349.
166 Leonid Poltava, *Obraz Stepana Bandery v literaturi i mystetsvi* (New York: Ameryka, 1979), 7, 10 ff, 28 ff.

his hands, with other Plast members at a railway station, in the meadow and in a forest, with other students, as part of a collage from the Warsaw and Lviv trials, laughing together with other OUN members, next to a portrait of Stets'ko, in Germany after the Second World War with UPA soldiers to be sent to Ukraine, with the SUM youth in folk costumes, on vacation with his children and wife in summer and winter, and giving a speech at the grave of Konovalets' on the anniversary of his death. Poltava's comments on the pictures reinforced the idea that Bandera was both an ordinary man and extraordinary *Providnyk*.[167]

The heroic discourse on the OUN-UPA and the "liberation movement" was shaped by a number of other historians and activists, in addition to Poltava and Mirchuk.[168] Some of them were members of the OUN-B, such as Volodymyr Kosyk,[169] Ivan Hryn'okh,[170] Iaroslav Stets'ko, Mykola Klymyshyn,[171] Stepan Lenkavs'kyi,[172] Stepan Bandera himself,[173] Volodymyr Ianiv,[174] Mykola Lebed',[175] Roman Ilnytzkyi[176] and Taras Hunchak.[177] Others such as Petro Potichnyj[178] were veterans of the UPA, and still others of the Waffen-SS Galizien, such as Vasyl' Veryha,[179] Oleksa Horbatsch,[180] Roman Drazhn'ovs'kyi,[181] and Petro Savaryn.[182] A number of them, such as Ilnytzkyi, Hryn'okh, and Horbatsch worked at the Free Ukrainian University (UVU)

167 Leonid Poltava, *Zhyttia Stepana Bandery* (New York: META, 1987).

168 In addition to those already introduced, Petro Mirchuk published several other historical monographs and a vast number of articles. The most popular ones are: *Koly horiat' lisy* (n.p: Zahrava, 1947), *Akt vidnovlennia Ukraïns'koï Derzhavnosty 30 chervnia 1941 roku: Iioho geneza ta politychne i istorychne znachennia* (New York: Vydannia Holovnoï upravy Orhanizatsiï oborony chotyr'okh svobid Ukraïny, 1952), *Ukraïns'ka Povstans'ka Armiia 1942–1952* (Munich: Cicero, 1953), *Za chystotu pozytsii ukraïns'koho vyzvolnoho rukhu* (Munich: P. Mirchuk, 1955), *Mykola Mikhnovs'kyi: Apostol ukraïns'koï derzhavnosty* (Philadelphia: T-vo ukraïns'koi studiiuiuchoï molodi im. M. Mikhnovs'koho, 1960), *Stepan Bandera: Symvol revoliutsiinoï bezkompromisovosty* (New York: Orhanizatsiia oborony chotyr'okh svobid Ukraïny, 1961), *In the German mills of death, 1941–1945* (New York: Vantage Press, 1976), *Ukraïins'kaderzhavnist', 1917–1920* (Philadelphia: n.p. 1967), *Narys istoriï OUN* (Munich: Ukraïns'ke vydavnytsvo, 1968), *Revoliutsiinyi zmah za USSD: Khto taki 'banderivtsi,' 'mel'nykivtsi,' 'dviikari'* (New York: Soiuz Ukraïns'kykh Politv"iazniv, 1985).

169 Wolodymyr Kosyk published several monographs and a vast number of articles. The very selective edition of documents *L'Allemagne national-socialiste et l'Ukraine* (Paris: Publications de l'Est européen, 1986) was translated into German, English, and Ukrainian.

170 See chapters 1, 4, and 5 above.

171 Mykola Klymyshyn published two volumes of historical memoirs, see *V pokhodi do voli*, vol. 1–2 (Detroit: Ukraïns'ka Knyharnia, 1987).

172 Stepan Lenkavs'kyi, *Petlura, Konowalez, Bandera: Von Moskau ermordet* (Munich, Ukrainischer Verlag, 1962).

173 For Bandera's writings and interviews, see chapter 7 above.

174 For Ianiv's writings and worldview, see this chapter.

175 In 1946 Lebed' had already published a monograph in which he whitewashed the OUN and UPA. Cf. *Ukraïns'ka Povstans'ka Armiia: Ïi heneza, rist i diï u vyzvol'nii borotbi ukraïns'koho narodu za ukraïns'ku samostiïnu sobornu derzhavu* (N.p.: UHVR, 1946).

176 Ilnytzkyi published two volumes on Germany and Ukraine during World War II. *Deutschland und die Ukraine 1934–1945: Tatsachen europäischer Politik*. vol. 1–2 (Munich: UNI, 1958).

177 On Taras Hunchak and his brother's, sister's, and father's membership of the OUN, see Taras Hunchak, *Moi spohady – stezhky zhyttia* (Kiev: Dnipro, 2005), 16, 22, 30.

178 Potichnyj was a child soldier in the UPA. He arrived in Munich from Ukraine in 1947 in a UPA unit. Cf. Peter J. Potichnyj, *My Journey* (Toronto: Litopys UPA, 2008), 83–93.

179 On Veryha in Waffen-SS Galizien, see Vasyl' Veryha, *Pid krylamy vyzvol'nykh dum* (Kiev: Vydavnytstvo imeni Oleny Telihy, 2007).

180 On Horbatsch in the Waffen-SS Galizien, see Melnyk, *To Battle*, 335–36.

181 On Drazhn'ovs'kyi in Waffen-SS Galizien, see Andrii Bolianovs'kyi, *Dyviziia "Halychyna": Istoriia* (L'viv: A. Bolianovs'kyi, 2000), 386.

182 In his memoirs Petro Savaryn expresses pride in being a veteran of the Waffen-SS Galizien. See Petro Savaryn, *Z soboiu vzialy Ukraïnu: Vid Ternopillia do Al'berty* (Kiev: KVITs 2007), 252–53, 275, 336.

in Munich; others such as Mirchuk and Kosyk were associated with the UVU or completed PhDs at this university.[183] Ianiv was the rector of the UVU from 1968 until 1986, and Drazhn'ovs'kyi from 1993 to 1995.[184] Hunchak was a professor at Rutgers University, Potichnyj at McMaster University. Horbatsch was professor of Slavic languages at the Johann Wolfgang Goethe University of Frankfurt am Main from 1965 to 1982.[185] Petro Savaryn was chancellor of the University of Alberta from 1982 to 1986.[186] Bohdan Osadczuk, who was neither in the OUN nor the Waffen-SS Galizien but published articles in the collaborationist newspaper *Krakivs'ki visti* in 1943, was a professor at the Otto-Suhr-Institut for Political Science of the Free University of Berlin from 1966.

The falsification of documents was another well-organized and institutionalized activity related to the discourse of extolling and denying. Lebed', who had whitewashed the history of the OUN-UPA in a monograph published as early as 1946,[187] retyped a number of documents from the time of the Second World War. After his death in 1998, they were donated to the Harvard Ukrainian Research Institute. The HURI considered all the documents received from Lebed' as original, and it invited radical right historians such as Volodymyr V"iatrovych to study them and to popularize them among "patriotic" historians in post-Soviet Ukraine.[188] Only a few political activists, such as Mykola Klymyshyn, were honest enough to admit that their writings had been whitewashed at the personal request of Bandera or at their own initiative.[189] Among OUN members, apparently, only Ievhen Stakhiv tried to oppose the discourse of denial and pointed out how OUN activists such as Lebed' falsified history.[190] In his memoirs, however, even Stakhiv omitted the 1941 pogroms.[191]

At a commemorative gathering in Munich in 1950, Ianiv, OUN member and long-time rector of the UVU in Munich, characterized Shukhevych as "one of the greatest legends of mankind" whose political career began when he killed the Polish official Sobiński in 1926. When discussing the Second World War and the Ukrainian nationalists, Ianiv omitted all war crimes committed by the UPA under the leadership of Shukhevych.[192] In an interview in 1977, Ianiv proudly recalled the act of killing Sobiński and implied that reading the historical drama *Kordian*, written by

183 Hryn'okh (1909–1994) was assistant professor 1974–1977, full professor 1978–1990, and professor emeritus 1991–1994 at the UVU in Munich. Horbatch (1915–1997) was assistant professor from 1965 to 1967, full professor from 1971 to 1990, and professor emeritus from 1991 to 1997. Cf. Mykola Shafoval, ed., *Universitas Libera Ucrainensis 1921–2006* (Munich: Verlag Steinmeier, 2006), 122.

184 Shafoval, *Universitas*, 80–94, 101–3.

185 Valerii Mokienko, "Das sprachwissenschaftliche Werk Oleksa Horbatschs," *Die Ukraine in Vergangenheit und Gegenwart. Aufsätze zu Geschichte, Sprache und Literatur. Greifswalder Ukrainische Hefte*, ed. Alexander Kratochvil, Vol. 1, No. 1 (Greifswald: Ernst-Moritz-Arndt-Universität Greifswald, Lehrstuhl für Ukrainistik, 2004), 12.

186 Rossoliński-Liebe, Celebrating Fascism, 5–7.

187 See chapter 6 above, page 322.

188 On the retyping, see Himka, Iak OUN stavylasia, 260. For understanding the documents to be original, see Ksenya Kiebuzinski, "Institute Receives Lebed Papers," January 2004, http://www.huri.harvard.edu/na/lebedpapers.html (accessed 30 July 2011). For V"iatrovych, see Rossoliński-Liebe, Debating, Obfuscating and Disciplining the Holocaust, 207–8, 213–14; Rudling, The OUN, the UPA and the Holocaust, 28–31.

189 Klymyshyn, *V pokhodi*, 1:333.

190 Stakhiv, *Kriz' tiurmy*, 100.

191 Stakhiv, *Kriz' tiurmy*.

192 Volodymyr Ianiv, *Shukhevych—Chuprynka: Liudyna i symvol. Dopovid na zhalibni akademiï 19 lystopada 1950 v Miunkheni* (Munich: Molode zhyttia, 1950), 4, 8.

the Polish romantic writer and poet Juliusz Słowacki, made him rationalize this crime and consider it a noble act.[193]

In the 1970s, the Ukrainian diaspora established two major academic institutions, the Harvard Ukrainian Research Institute (HURI) in 1973 and the Canadian Institute of Ukrainian Studies (CIUS) at the University of Alberta in 1976. Neither was as massively infiltrated by OUN-B members as the UVU in Munich, and they were not as heavily involved in the denial of war atrocities and the extolment of the OUN and UPA, but both failed to come to terms with the past, particularly on the subject of the Second World War. In 1976 the CIUS together with the Shevchenko Scientific Society in Europe initiated a huge project entitled *Encyclopedia of Ukraine*. The head of this important academic project was Volodymyr Kubiiovych, one of the major Ukrainian collaborators with the Nazis, and who, after the Second World War, became the Secretary General of the Shevchenko Scientific Society. This project, on the one hand, gave rise to a useful and authoritative encyclopedia of Ukrainian history, but, on the other hand, it presented a nationalist narrative of the Second World War in Ukraine and did not even include an entry on the Holocaust.[194]

After 1945, very few Ukrainian intellectuals in the diaspora tried to rethink Ukrainian extreme nationalism or objected to the nationalist obfuscation of history. One was Ivan Lysiak-Rudnyts'kyi, a professor at the University of Alberta from 1971 until his death in 1984, who, during the Second World War, had published in the collaborationist newspaper *Krakivs'ki visti*.[195] In his postwar essays Lysiak-Rudnyts'kyi described the OUN-B's fascism as "home-grown fascism" and emphasized that the OUN had more in common with other East Central European movements than with Fascist Italy and Nazi Germany: "One should look for the nearest relatives of the Ukrainian nationalism first of all not in German National Socialism or Italian Fascism—both products of urbanized and industrialized societies but rather among parties of this kind in agrarian, backward nations of Eastern Europe: the Croatian Ustaša, the Romanian Iron Guard, the Slovak Hlinka Party, the Polish ONR (National Radical Camp) etc."[196]

Lysiak-Rudnyts'kyi was also one of very few Ukrainian émigré intellectuals who was aware of the difference between democracy and nationalism. Because he distinguished between these two political concepts, other émigré intellectuals perceived him as a leftist, which in Ukrainian intellectual émigré discourses meant communist and "traitor." Unlike many other intellectuals, Lysiak-Rudnyts'kyi understood the impact of nationalist activism on academia, and the openness of Ukrainian intellectuals to far-right thinking, as a problem. In his opinion, the most dangerous influence on Ukrainian intellectuals came from the OUN-B activists. In letters from 26 April 1974 onward to his uncle, Ivan Kedryn-Rudnyts'kyi, Lysiak-Rudnyts'kyi pointed out that the OUN-B did not change its political views after the Second World

193 Dmytro Shtohryn, "Volodymyr Ianiv—poet," in *Volodymyr Ianiv, Poeziia*, ed. Dmytro Sapiha (Lviv: Kameniar, 2009), 9, 78.

194 For Kubiiovych, see page 169, 254 above.

195 See chapter 5 above, pages 254–55.

196 Ivan Lysiak-Rudnyts'kyi, *Mezhdu istoriei i politikoi* (Moscow: Letnii Sad, 2007), 530. See also Letter from Ivan Lysiak-Rudnyts'kyi to Ivan Kedryn-Rudnyts'kyi, 26 April 1974, ASSS, Ivan Kedryn-Rudnyts'kyi Archives, 4, 23. I am grateful to Mariusz Radosław Sawa for drawing my attention to this document.

War. What changed was that the majority of the Ukrainian diaspora began to accept OUN-B far-right discourses and interpretation of history as standard scholarly explanations. According to him, the OUN-B tried to dominate the Ukrainian diaspora as it had tried to dominate Ukrainian political life in the 1930s and 1940s. It prolonged the cult of a leader, applied "mafia-conspiratorial methods" to deal with its opponents, and suppressed open debates. He understood the prolongation of the "home-grown fascist" politics by Ukrainian émigré intellectuals as very harmful or,

> the main evil in the life of the Ukrainian diaspora. It ... brings us into derision and compromises us in the eyes of the western world, isolates us from processes that take place in Ukraine, spiritually and politically paralyzes us. The hegemony of the OUN-B movement [*banderivshchyna*] desacralizes the Ukrainian national idea. What is worth this idea if "free" Ukrainians cannot oppose bolshevism with nothing better than a more primitive creation of the same bolshevism? I hold the opinion that our home-grown totalitarianists do not differ in terms of morality from Bolsheviks, they are only less intelligent than they [the Bolsheviks].[197]

The denying-extolling discourse on the OUN-UPA and Ukrainian nationalism became especially strong in the late 1970s and 1980s. It was also affected by the Cold War and the anti-Soviet and dissident nature of the 1970s and 1980s, when the anticommunist and anti-Soviet features of the OUN-UPA were highly respected by almost all Ukrainian diaspora intellectuals and equated with democratic values. Interest in a critical exploration of the role of Ukrainians or Ukrainian nationalists in the Second World War or the Holocaust was frequently regarded with suspicion, resentment, or hostility.

Authoritarian and fascist leaders, parties, and other organizations also became popular among dissidents in countries other than Ukraine at that time. In Poland for example, the anticommunist and anti-Soviet movement Solidarność revitalized the Piłsudski cult by publishing stamps, envelopes, and posters, depicting Piłsudski alone or accompanied by other politicians of the Second Republic, soldiers who fought for the Polish state in 1918, and such contemporary figures as Lech Wałęsa and Pope John-Paul II.[198]

The anticommunist discourse impacted on historians and the historical discipline as such. In 1985 David Marples published an article in *The Ukrainian Weekly*, in which he euphemized and minimized the OUN and UPA crimes against Jews, Poles, and Ukrainians, claiming that "some undisciplined actions on the part of an armed group were almost inevitable." He further claimed that the UPA was a multicultural force: "according to a Western source, the nationality groups within the [UPA's] ranks included Azerbaijanis, Uzbeks, Tatars, and Jews." Given that Marples did not investigate this subject on his own at that time and apparently had no sympathy for Ukrainian nationalism, as he argued twenty-five years later, it must have been the common political or academic discourse about the OUN, UPA, and the Second World War that, in the 1980s, shaped his understanding of the subject. After the millen-

197 Letter from Ivan Lysiak-Rudnyts'kyi to Ivan Kedryn-Rudnyts'kyi, 26 April 1974, ASSS, Ivan Kedryn-Rudnyts'kyi Archives, 4, 23–24.

198 Wolfgang Schlott, *Pilsudski-Kult: Die Wiedergeburt einer charismatischen Persönlichkeit in der Solidarność-Ära (1980 bis 1989)* (Bremen: Forschungsstelle Osteuropa, 2003), 17–30.

nium Marples began to investigate Ukrainian nationalism and to publish important and original works about the OUN and UPA, and the Second World War in Ukraine. He became a true critic of the nationalist apologists and also a nuanced and sophisticated interpreter of the difficult past.[199]

John-Paul Himka—who in the 1970s and 1980s wrote excellent books on nineteenth-century socialism, the Ukrainian peasants, and the Greek-Catholic Church—characterized the UPA, in an article published in *Labour Focus on Eastern Europe* in 1982 about the opposition in Ukraine, as "an anti-Nazi and subsequently anti-Soviet resistance force" and did not mention any atrocities committed by it or the OUN.[200] In an article "World Wars" for the *Encyclopedia of Ukraine,* he did not mention that the OUN and UPA persecuted Jews during the Second World War and stated that "in the spring of 1943 thousands of Ukrainian policemen in German service deserted to form the fighting nucleus of the UPA [in order to attack] German outposts." Similarly, he did not mention that in 1944 the OUN-UPA began collaborating once again with Nazi Germany. He asserted that the "UPA began liquidating Polish settlements in Volhynia" but omitted the fact that they also did so in eastern Galicia, and he relativized it with: "This soon escalated into full-scale Polish-Ukrainian ethnic warfare across western Ukraine."[201] In the 1990s Himka, similarly to Marples, changed his views on the OUN, UPA, and the Second World War in Ukraine.[202]

When analyzing the approach of historians to the OUN and UPA in the 1980s, it is necessary to point out that there were various reasons for extolling the OUN and UPA and for denying or euphemizing their crimes. Certainly, not all historians extolled Ukrainian nationalism or euphemized the OUN's and UPA's atrocities because they were Ukrainian nationalists or believed in the ideology of Ukrainian nationalism. Another important reason for uncritical treatment of the OUN and UPA was the lack of critical scholarly research on this subject. The archetypal monograph on the OUN and the Second World War was John Armstrong's *Ukrainian Nationalism,* first published in 1955. As already mentioned, Armstrong omitted two central events in his study: pogroms against Jews in western Ukraine in the summer of 1941 and the ethnic cleansing against the Polish population by the UPA in Volhynia and eastern Galicia in 1943–1944. There are at least four reasons for these and several other omissions from Armstrong's monograph. First, Soviet archives during the Cold War were inaccessible, as the result of which he was unable to study many important documents. Second, Armstrong obtained information about the conduct of Ukrainian nationalists during the Second World War while conducting interviews with OUN activists and UPA veterans, who gave him whitewashed self-portraits and incorrect

199 David Marples, "Ukraine During World War II: Resistance Movements and Reannexation," *The Ukrainian Weekly,* New Jersey, Vol. LIII, No. 41, 13 October 1985, 7, 13. David Marples informed me privately that he did not "recall having strong feelings about UPA one way or another at that time [when writing the article]," and that he wrote it for Radio Liberty where he worked as a Research Analyst on Ukraine. He advised me to "keep in mind [that] there was practically nothing available at that time in terms of archival material."

200 John-Paul Himka, "The Opposition in Ukraine," *Labour Focus on Eastern Europe* Vol. 5, No. 3–4 (1982): 36–37. I am grateful to John-Paul Himka for informing me about this article.

201 John-Paul Himka, "World Wars," *Encyclopedia of Ukraine,* ed. Volodymyr Kubiiovych (Toronto: University of Toronto Press, 1993), 5:724–28.

202 See chapter 10 below.

and apologetic accounts of the movement. Although Armstrong claimed to regard the interviews as "highly colored," he relied on them as primary sources. Third, he did not work with the testimonies of the Jewish, Polish, or Ukrainian survivors of the OUN and UPA atrocities which describe events in western Ukraine during the Second World War very differently from the interviews of the OUN activists and UPA veterans, and also differently from German documents, of which many did not contain any information concerning the OUN-UPA's violence. Fourth, the Cold War and the anti-Soviet and anticommunist nature of the OUN-UPA affected the perception of Ukrainian nationalism among Western scholars. Ukrainian nationalists were regarded during the Cold War as anticommunist "freedom fighters," and because they did not mention their involvement in the Holocaust and labeled any investigation as anti-Ukrainian or as Soviet propaganda, even scholars of the Second World War and Ukrainian history accepted their narrative, rather than critically investigate the subject on the basis of archival documents, including testimonies of the survivors.[203]

Although in 1987–1988 Martin Broszat and Saul Friedländer debated the question of "rational" German scholarship versus the "mythical memory" of the Holocaust victims, the testimonies of Jewish survivors were until the late 1990s not regarded as reliable documents for the study of the Holocaust and the Second World War. This approach was common, not only among Ukrainian nationalist historians but also among many professional historians. German historians, in particular, repeatedly stressed the "subjectivity" and unreliability of Holocaust survivors' testimonies and the "objectivity" and reliability of the perpetrators' documents, in particular those of the meticulous German officers. This approach enabled many German, Ukrainian, and other historians to avoid facing the horrifying reality and complexity of the Second World War and the Holocaust, but it had a disastrous impact on the process of writing the history of the Holocaust in Eastern Europe. Histories written according to this method missed many significant aspects, they did not correlate with the reality and complexity of the past, their facts cannot be empirically verified without extensive omissions, and they legitimized the nationalist memory politics popularized by the diaspora communities and national conservative historians in democratic states.

Historians such as Armstrong, who did not investigate the violence of the OUN and other similar movements and marginalized the Holocaust in general, also looked for alternatives to the term "fascism." Armstrong, the author of the first comprehensive monograph on the OUN, coined the term "integral nationalism." This concept was for him something similar to fascism, but he argued that the OUN, Ustaša, and similar movements should not be called "fascist," apparently because the term "fascism" and the concept of fascism were contested and politicized, and its use could suggest to readers that the historian in question was a communist or anti-Ukrainian, and destroy the historian's career. Soviet propaganda labeled the United States, Britain, France, West Germany, and other capitalist states and also non-fascist authoritarian regimes as fascist. Communist and other left-wing activists in Western countries used the term to discredit political enemies of various orientations. Such a use

203 Armstrong, *Ukrainian Nationalism*, 329–33. On Armstrong, see Rossoliński-Liebe, 'Ukrainian National Revolution,' 87.

of the term made it meaningless and strongly affected its meaning to scholars. The term "integral nationalism," on the other hand, naturally became very popular both among anticommunist scholars like Armstrong,[204] and among nationalist diaspora activists. "Integral nationalism" did not depict the OUN and its veterans as "fascist" but suggested that Ukrainian nationalism was a genuine, independent, self-sufficient nationalist movement, which had nothing in common with fascist ideology, other fascist movements, and especially not with Nazi Germany and the Holocaust.[205]

Bandera's hagiographer, Mirchuk, emphasized the uniqueness of Ukrainian nationalism and claimed that only "enemies of Ukraine" and "opponents of the OUN" could claim that the OUN was fascist or approved of fascism and copied it. According to him, the OUN obtained its ideas and ideological foundations exclusively from "Ukrainian spirituality and tradition" and could not be fascist because fascism was not compatible with Ukrainian traditions and history.[206] Political scientist Alexander Motyl wrote in 1980 that the OUN was a radical nationalist organization with all the features typical of fascist movements, but he added that the OUN could not have been fascist because there was no Ukrainian state in which the OUN could practice fascist politics.[207] The fact that the "stateless state" was common for East European fascist organizations, parties, and movements, and that only a few of them achieved a state attracted the attention of very few scholars at that time, including scholars of fascism.[208]

204 The Memorial Committee of the Department of Political Science at the University of Wisconsin–Madison characterized their colleague Armstrong, who died on 23 February 2010, as a "fierce opponent of Soviet regimes," who was "at odds with the liberal students and campus protests of the 1960s and 1970s," who erected a "bomb shelter ... in his home" which he "kept fully stocked and proudly displayed to their frequent dinner guests," and who taught his three daughters "how to shoot." See John Witte, David Tarr, Crawford Young, Memorial resolution for Professor Emeritus John Armstrong - 1/18/2011, http://www.polisci.wisc.edu/news/default.aspx?id=71 (accessed 13 April 2013).

205 Armstrong, *Ukrainian Nationalism*, 19–23; Armstrong, Collaborationism in World War II, 400. On the term fascism during the Cold War see Griffin, *Nature of Fascism*, 3–4; Wippermann, *Faschismus*, 9.

206 Mirchuk, *Narys istoriï OUN*, 93–94.

207 Motyl, *Turn to the Right*, 163–69.

208 For fascist movements without states, see Ursprung, Faschismus in Ostmittel- und Südosteuropa, 22. An important exception among Ukrainian historians was Ivan Lysiak-Rudnyts'kyi.

Conclusion

Bandera's assassination sincerely distressed those factions of the Ukrainian diaspora who knew him as a brave, devoted, and idealistic freedom fighter or as the legendary *Providnyk.* His loss was mourned by various Ukrainian anticommunist and far-right nationalist communities around the globe for weeks. Newspapers such as *Shliakh peremohy, Homin Ukraïny,* and *Ukraïns'ka dumka* published hundreds of mournful articles and poems, and expressed their disapproval of people who connected Bandera with the crimes committed by the OUN and the UPA, even if they understood Bandera to be the main symbol of this movement. These crimes were then denied or ascribed to the Soviet partisans, the Soviet army, and the Germans. The fifteenth of October became a very important date in the calendar of those factions of the Ukrainian diaspora who commemorated Bandera as a martyr and national hero at panakhydas, political gatherings, and anticommunist demonstrations. The first Bandera museum, unveiled in 1962, exhibited Bandera's various personal effects in addition to artifacts related to the OUN and UPA "liberation struggle," the cruelty of the Soviet occupation and the suffering of the OUN-B members at Auschwitz. The ethnic and political violence committed by the OUN and UPA during and after the Second World War was not exhibited in the museum although the movement was an integral, if not the central part of the exhibition. The OUN-B members were presented as tragic heroes and the sole inmates of Auschwitz. A similar narrative appeared in Petro Mirchuk's numerous publications about the Second World War. Mirchuk also wrote the first Bandera hagiography and paved the way for a number of post-Soviet Bandera "patriotic" biographers.

The apologetic discourses on Bandera and the OUN and UPA, along with the victimization discourses on the Ukrainian famine in 1932–1933 and the suffering of Ukrainians during and after the Second World War were so powerful, especially in the final decades of the Cold War, that even open-minded scholars such as John-Paul Himka and David Marples were also impacted by them. John Armstrong's standard monograph about the Ukrainian nationalist movement and the Second World War contained very little information about the atrocities committed by the OUN and UPA, and was therefore highly prized by the Ukrainian diaspora and its historians. Only a very few scholars at that time, such as Ivan Lysiak-Rudnyts'kyi, objected to the apologetic discourses and the use of scholarship for propagating denial and creating various nationalist myths. Nevertheless, even Lysiak-Rudnyts'kyi did not have any problems with silence about Volodymyr Kubiiovych's past, because the former head of the UTsK initiated the *Encyclopedia of Ukraine* and supported several other projects that were perceived by the Ukrainian diaspora as being very important. The climate of the Cold War and the OUN's determination to support the Western bloc in the fight against the "red devil" buried the dark moments of the OUN and UPA in oblivion. Any mention of them was perceived as Soviet, Polish, Jewish, and other forms of anti-Ukrainian propaganda.

Chapter 10

RETURN TO UKRAINE

On 24 August 1991, during the course of the dissolution of the Soviet Union, the Ukrainian parliament declared the existence of an independent Ukrainian state. The declaration was confirmed in a referendum on 1 December 1991 by 90.3 percent of the population. The collapse of the Soviet Union resulted from Mikhail Gorbachev's *perestroika* and from the 1989 revolutions in satellite states of the Soviet Union such as Poland, Hungary, East Germany, Czechoslovakia, and Bulgaria. In the longer perspective, the collapse of the Soviet empire was caused by such dissident movements as Solidarność in Poland, Charta 77 in Czechoslovakia, and the Shistdesiatnyky and Rukh in Ukraine. The contribution to the dissolution of the Soviet Union of far-right émigré organizations such as the OUN, LAF, Ustaša, Iron Guard, and Hlinka's Party—many of which were united during the Cold War in Stets'ko's ABN—was marginal. Nevertheless, the OUN and UPA returned to Ukraine in the late 1980s as anti-Soviet icons. The fallen OUN activists and UPA partisans were promoted by nationalist dissidents and right-wing politicians as a resistance movement and as the last postwar fighters against the "red devil." Their collaboration with Nazi Germany, their antisemitic and fascist ideology, and their involvement in the Holocaust and other forms of mass violence during and after the Second World War were completely forgotten.

The Bandera cult reappeared in western Ukraine, in particular in the former eastern Galicia, a few years before the official declaration of independence. It adapted to the new cultural, social, and political circumstances and has persisted until the time of writing. Except for the Ukrainian diaspora, the cult was limited to western Ukraine, with the main core in eastern Galicia, but far-right groups in central and eastern Ukrainian villages, towns, and cities began organizing and worshiping the *Providnyk* as a symbol of Ukrainian nationalism and as a martyr who died for Ukraine. In addition to politicians and radical right activists, nationalist historians also played an important role in improving, modernizing, and propagating the cult. On the one hand, their writings legitimized the agendas of far-right activists, and on the other, they blurred the difference between history and politics.

The revival of the Bandera cult in post-Soviet Ukraine demonstrated that the cult of a fascist or authoritarian leader is not a relic or an isolated phenomenon, typical only of German neo-Nazis, Italian neo-Fascists, or other far-right groups propagating racism and hatred. It can actually enchant and confuse a large part of a society, including even the most critical, reasonable, and rational intellectuals. The Bandera cult in post-Soviet Ukraine took many more varied forms than it had in the diaspora during the Cold War. In post-Soviet Ukraine, the cult was popularized by politics, historiography, museums, novels, movies, monuments, street names, political events, music festivals, pubs, food, stamps, talk shows, and other means. In order to grasp the nature of the Bandera cult there, we will analyze and explore several of its forms with the help of thick description, and will try to uncover the motives and agendas of its creators and propagators.

Double Propaganda

From 1989 to 1991, the citizens of western Ukraine were, on the one hand, exposed to established Soviet propaganda, and on the other, to reemerging Ukrainian nationalist propaganda. Soviet propaganda tried to discredit the OUN and the UPA until the very end of the existence of the Soviet Union. In the late 1980s, more articles on the Ukrainian nationalists began to appear in the Soviet Ukrainian press. Such articles generally extolled the heroism of Soviet activists and reminded their readers of the villainous side of the OUN-UPA. As in the past, they depicted the OUN activists and UPA partisans as traitors, enemies of the Ukrainian people, or "Ukrainian bourgeois nationalists." At the same time, new monuments to the Soviet heroes murdered by the OUN-UPA were erected. On 14 February 1988 for example, a monument devoted to Feodor Ulianov was unveiled in the village of Rykiv in the Turkivs'kyi region. Ulianov, in charge of an MGB unit, conducted an anti-OUN-UPA operation on 16 February 1945. Nikolai Romanchenko introduced Ulianov in *L'vovskaia pravda* as a genuine Soviet martyr. He was captured and tortured during an attempt to arrest the Banderite leader "Roman." His colleague, Sergei Zuev, took his own life with his last bullet rather than allow the Banderites to seize him. According to the article, Ulianov's last words after hours of painful torture were: "God damn you animals! Long live Communism!"[1]

OUN members were still put on trial in the late Soviet period. The main purpose of such trials was to remind the population that the OUN and UPA had committed horrible crimes and did not deserve to be rehabilitated or honored. At many trials, the defendants confessed their crimes and pleaded guilty. In August 1987 for example, the trial began of a man called R. Didukh. During the trial, the defendant revealed that he had joined the OUN in 1941, when he was recruited by Ivan Stetsiv, who ordered him to execute Soviet activists. He also pleaded guilty to having tortured two young girls, killing a young man, burning an entire family to death, and massacring twenty-one Polish families, in addition to cooperating with the German police. The court sentenced Didukh to death and applied for Stetsiv's extradition from Canada.[2]

Soviet propaganda viewed Bandera as one of the main symbols of Ukrainian nationalism and made him the central figure of late-period Soviet anti-nationalist propaganda campaigns. Soviet Ukrainian newspapers published at least three series of articles about the *Providnyk*, in August 1989, October 1990, and December 1990.

1 Nikolai Romanchenko, "Plamia," *L'vovskaia pravda*, 16 February 1988, 3. See also Marples, *Heroes and Villains*, 81. According to the article, the council of the Turkiv region had already named one street after Ulianov in 1966.

2 Marples, *Heroes and Villains*, 81–82.

Map 7. Eastern Europe 2000. *YIVO Encyclopedia*, 2:2147.

The first series was printed in *Pravda Ukrainy* under the title "Banderovshchina." The authors, V. Zarechnyi and O. Lastovets, remarked that the recent growth of national identity in Ukraine, caused by the politics of democratization and glasnost, was leading to the "rehabilitation of the bloody banderovshchina." They claimed that they wrote the article because some Ukrainians had begun to blame the Communist Party and the Soviet authorities for not making any compromises with the OUN-UPA during and after the Second World War, which would have ended the "fratricide" that occurred. The authors introduced the history of the OUN and UPA in a typical Soviet way, exposing the villainous nature of the Ukrainian nationalists, extolling Soviet power and denying or diminishing Soviet crimes in western Ukraine.[3] In October 1989, the same newspaper published the article "Bloody Traces of the Banderites," in which A. Gorban recalled Halan's murder.[4]

The second series of articles, written by the Soviet Ukrainian historian Vitalii Maslovs'kyi, appeared in October 1990 in *Radians'ka Ukraïna* under the title "Bandera: Banner or Band."[5] The date suggests that, as in the diaspora, a Bandera

3 V. Zarechnyi and O. Lastovets, "Banderovshchina," *Pravda Ukrainy*, 9 August 1989, 3; 10 August 1989, 4; 11 August 1989, 3; 12 August 1989, 3; 13 August 1989, 3; 15 August 1989, 3; 17 August 1989, 3; 18 August 1989, 3; 19 August 1989, 3.

4 A. Gorban', "Krovavye sledy banderovtsev," *Pravda Ukrainy*, 11 October 1989, 4.

5 Vitalii Maslovs'kyi, "Bandera: Prapor chy banda," *Radians'ka Ukraïna*, 14 October 1990, 3; 16 October 1990, 3; 18 October 1990, 3.

cult had begun emerging in Soviet Ukraine around the anniversary of his death on 15 October. Maslovs'kyi stated that, given the current fascination with Bandera in western Ukraine, he wanted to find whether the name Bandera was derived from the Spanish word "banner" or from the Ukrainian word "band [*banda*]." Maslovs'kyi was one of the leading Soviet experts on the OUN-UPA. He had studied the subject for several years and was acquainted with many crucial archival documents. He included some significant information in his article, such as the introduction of the fascist salute by the OUN-B at the Second Great Congress of the Ukrainian Nationalists in March-April 1941, and details of the killing of OUN-M members by the OUN-B.[6] Yet Maslovs'kyi, in a way typical of Soviet historians, diminished, omitted, and denied Soviet crimes and the totalitarian nature of the Soviet regime. He also tried to strengthen hatred against the OUN-B by offensive terminology and by providing incorrect information. For example, he introduced the Nachtigall battalion as an SS division and not as an Abwehr battalion.[7] Unlike earlier Soviet historians, however, he did not deny that Bandera was murdered by the KGB agent Stashyns'kyi.[8]

V. Dovgan', author of the third anti-Bandera series, began by observing that "destructive nationalist elements" had been "inflating" a Bandera cult in Ukraine:

> Various publications, in particular in Galicia (i.e. in Lviv, Ternopil', and Ivano-Frankivs'k oblasts) popularize his road of life and reprint his articles and speeches. Portraits and signs with his portrait grow in popularity. In July of this year in Drohobych, during a meeting of former UPA bandits, the foundation stone was laid for a future Bandera monument. And on 14 October [1990] a monument to Bandera was unveiled in the Ciscarpathian village of Uhryniv. Streets in several cities in Galicia have also been named after him. In numerous cities, particularly in Lviv and Ivano-Frankivs'k, we hear a loud "Slava!" to the honor of Bandera and appeals to the youth to follow the path that he outlined. ...
>
> Who were Stepan Bandera and the Banderites who took the name of their Providnyk? What is the banderovshchina that weighed like a horrible ghost for more than 10 years on the western Ukrainian countryside?[9]

Like Maslovs'kyi, Dovgan' was well informed about the history of the OUN and Bandera's life. He studied crucial documents such as "Struggle and Activity" and knew many details concerning Bandera's life. He reminded his readers about the OUN-B's collaboration with Nazi Germany and the ethnic violence from 1941 onward. At the same time, he omitted and denied Soviet violence, in particular the torture and killing of prisoners in 1940–1941 in western Ukraine and the brutal killing and deportation of civilians after 1944. He also ascribed a range of deeds to the Ukrainian nationalists, which they had not committed. One of them was the killing of the Polish professors by the Ukrainian Nachtigall battalion. Dovgan' also addressed the question of Bandera's collaboration with the SIS and the parachuting of ZCh OUN members into Soviet Ukraine. Although some newspapers, such as the Moscow *Megapolis-Ekspress* on 31 May 1990 and the Ukrainian nationalist *Za vil'nu*

6 Vitalii Maslovs'kyi, "Bandera: Prapor chy banda," *Radians'ka Ukraïna*, 14 October 1990, 3.
7 Ibid., 3.
8 Ibid., 3.
9 V. Dovgan', "Kem byl Bandera," *Pravda Ukrainy*, 13 December 1990, 4.

Ukraïnu on 9 August 1990, had announced that Bandera was killed by Stashyns'kyi, Dovgan' argued that it was still an open question whether Bandera had been killed by Stashyns'kyi or by Oberländer.[10]

In addition to Soviet propaganda, western Ukraine was also exposed at this time to Ukrainian nationalist propaganda. In April 1990, *Pravda Ukrainy* wrote that "Lviv emissaries" referred to Bandera at several meetings in Volhynia as the "'great son' of the Ukrainian nation."[11] On 30 June 1990 at the market square in Lviv, Ukrainian nationalists and dissidents celebrated the declaration of 30 June 1941. According to Maslovs'kyi, Oleh Vitovych, one of the leaders of the Association of Independent Ukrainian Youth (*Spilka Nezalezhnoï Ukraïns'koï Molodi*, SNUM), said in his speech: "The ideas for which Stepan Bandera was fighting are also present today. These are the ideas of the nationalism of the revolutionary movement in Ukraine. We, the young generation of nationalists, arm ourselves with these ideas."[12]

In 1990, at its twenty-eighth congress, the Communist Party of Ukraine debated whether the OUN and UPA should be rehabilitated. The decision to take up the issue was brought about by the ongoing rehabilitation of Ukrainian nationalists in western Ukraine, which manifested itself, as *Pravda Ukrainy* wrote, in "lavish celebrations, religious services, renaming of streets and squares, erection of monuments, and the placing of commemorative plaques devoted to S. Bandera, R. Shukhevych, and other leaders of the OUN-UPA." At the congress, the party called the brutal conflict between the OUN-UPA and the Soviet authorities in the 1940s and 1950s a "fratricidal war." It condemned the Stalinist terror but decided not to rehabilitate the OUN and UPA.[13]

The First Bandera Monument in Ukraine

Staryi Uhryniv, Bandera's birthplace, became a particularly turbulent place during the breakup of the Soviet Union. It was only in 1984 that the Soviets destroyed the chapel in which Andrii Bandera had performed church services. On 15 October 1989, the thirtieth anniversary of Bandera's death, seven young people, four men and three women from Stryi and Lviv, set up a bronze cross at the site, and on the same day a public meeting took place there. The KGB failed to arrest the seven young people, who were in hiding, helped by local inhabitants.[14]

On Heroes' Day, 27 May 1990, the SNUM from Ivano-Frankivs'k set up a foundation stone for a Bandera monument in front of the house in which Bandera was born. At about the same time, the chapel was rebuilt. Funds for the monument were collected at public anti-Soviet meetings, which frequently took place in western Ukraine

10 V. Dovgan', "Kem byl Bandera," *Pravda Ukrainy*, 13 December 1990, 4; 14 December 1990, 4; 16 December 1990, 4; 19 December 1990, 4; 21 December 1990, 4; 23 December 1990, 4; 25 December 1990.

11 "My obviniaem natsionalizm!" *Pravda Ukrainy*, 11 April 1990, 1.

12 Vitalii Maslovs'kyi, "Bandera: prapor chy banda," *Radians'ka Ukraïna*, 14 October 1990, 3.

13 "O popytkakh polytycheskoi reabilitatsii OUN-UPA," *Pravda Ukrainy*, 19 December 1990, 1, 3.

14 Stepan Lesiv, the Stepan Bandera Historical Memorial Museum in Staryi Uhryniv, interview by author, Staryi Uhryniv, 18 May 2008; "Nyshchennia pam"iatnykiv zapochotkuvaly za SRSR," BBC, http://www.bbc.co.uk/ukrainian/ukraine/2011/01/110112_stepan_lesiv_bandera_ek.shtml (accessed 22 August 2011).

at that time. The monument was prepared in a cement factory in Dubivtsi, Halych region and was transported piece by piece to Staryi Uhryniv by taxi. It was put together at night from 13 to 14 October, under the protection of a crowd of about one hundred people. The monument looked quite makeshift and consisted of two pillars and a bust with a bell underneath. It was unveiled on 14 October 1990, the Feast of the Protection of the Mother of God (*Sviato Pokrovy*) and the Feast of the UPA. According to Stepan Lusiv, 10,000 people attended the ceremony. *Shliakh peremohy* reported that there were 15,000. For the sake of the celebration, a sign with the inscription "Stepan Bandera Street" was placed on the house behind the monument. Some celebrants held blue-and-yellow or red-and-black flags, or portraits of Bandera, or wore folk clothes, in particular embroidered shirts. On one side of the monument, a blue-and-yellow flag, and on the other, a red-and-black one, were set up. The celebration began with a moment of silence. A UPA veteran then fired a rifle in the air, and the crowd sang the Ukrainian anthem. After the singing of the nationalist song "We Were Born in a Great Hour" (*Zrodylys' my velykoï hodyny*) Vitalii Hapovych, leader of the SNUM, asked that the blue-and-yellow cover be taken off the monument. The crowd began shouting "Glory!" Afterwards, Bandera's sister Volodymyra Davydiuk and some nationalist activists, among them OUN-B émigrés, delivered speeches. A priest then blessed the monument and performed a panakhyda.[15]

On 14 October 1990, the same day on which the Bandera monument was unveiled in Staryi Uhryniv, 10,000 people attended the opening of the first Bandera museum in Ukraine. The museum was located in the house in Volia Zaderevats'ka where Bandera's family had lived between 1933 and 1936. Among the speakers was Bandera's sister, Oksana Bandera.[16] On the same day, the Lenin monument in Lviv was dismantled, although the authorities had been protecting it at night from 13 October onward.[17] On 15 October, according to *Vyzvol'nyi shliakh*, 10,000 people came to a meeting with a panakhyda, close to the Lviv university building, to commemorate the thirty-first anniversary of Bandera's assassination. About thirty people were on the stage at the meeting, among them the Ukrainian dissident and member of the Ukrainian Helsinki Group, Ivan Kandyba.[18]

The first Bandera monument in Ukraine did not fulfill its function for long. It was blown up at about 5 or 6 a.m. on 30 December 1990, possibly in order to prevent a celebration of Bandera's birthday there on 1 January 1991. However, the monument was rebuilt and unveiled at the same place on 30 June 1991, the fiftieth anniversary of the proclamation of 30 June 1941. The rebuilt monument looked quite similar to

15 Stepan Lesiv, interview by author, Staryi Uhryniv, 18 May 2008; "Vidkryttia pershoho v Ukraïni pam"iatnyka sl. pam. Providnykovi Stepanovi Banderi," *Shliakh peremohy*, 25 November 1990, 1; "Vrochyste vshanuvannia Stepana Bandery v Ukraïni: Vidkryttia muzeiu i pam"iatnyka," *Shliakh peremohy*, 28 October 1990, 1.

16 "Vrochyste vshanuvannia Stepana Bandery v Ukraïni. Vidkryttia muzeiu i pam"iatnyka," *Shliakh peremohy*, 28 October 1990, 1; "Vrochyste vshanuvannia Stepana Bandery v Ukraïni," *Vyzvol'nyi shliakh* Vol. 514, No. 1, (January 1991): 116–17.

17 Rossoliński-Liebe, Der Raum der Stadt, 13; Walter Moßmann, Didi Danquart (film directors), *Menschen und Strassen: Lemberg—geöffnete Stadt* (1993, film company SWF and arte); "Proshchai 'vozhd'", *Za vil'nu Ukraïnu*, 15 October1990, 3; "Zdemontuvaly Lenina u L'vovi," *Vyzvol'nyi shliakh* Vol. 514, No. 1 (January 1991): 83–84.

18 "Vystup I. Kandyby na mityngu v chest' S. Bandery," *Vyzvol'nyi shliakh* 514, No. 1, (January 1991): 117.

the first one. It was a little taller and there were two tridents instead of a bell under the bust. Again 10,000 people, some of them dressed in folk garments and carrying blue-and-yellow and red-and-black flags, appeared at the unveiling. After the unveiling, the monument was guarded by SNUM activists. But it was blown up even sooner than the first one, at about 3 a.m. on 10 July. During the demolition, the perpetrators, very likely six Soviet security officers acting on orders from the Defense Department of the Soviet Union, shot and wounded one of the SNUM activists, Vasyl' Maksymchuk. The same night, the Ievhen Konovalets' monument in Zashkiv, Lviv oblast, was blown up. Five days earlier, on 5 July 1991, a monument near Brody, devoted to the Waffen-SS Galizien soldiers, had also been blown up.[19]

The third Bandera monument in Staryi Uhryniv was unveiled on 17 August 1992, in an already independent Ukraine and was guarded thereafter by the police. The unveiling was combined with the fiftieth anniversary of the UPA and was followed by three days of patriotic celebrations. The architect of the third Bandera monument was Bandera's nephew Zynovii Davydiuk, Volodymyra's son. The monument, this time a bronze statue, was recast from a Lenin statue that had been prepared for unveiling in the provincial city of Kalush.[20] Ivan Kashuba, main editor of *Shliakh peremohy* and former head of the SB of the ZCh OUN, delivered a speech at the unveiling ceremony.[21] Other leading OUN émigrés, including Mykola Lebed', also visited western Ukraine at that time.[22]

The Second Turn to the Right

After the dissolution of the Soviet Union, a number of OUN émigrés returned to Ukraine. They founded several radical right, antidemocratic parties and other organizations, which considerably impacted on Ukrainian politics, society, culture, and academia, especially in the western parts of the country, where the UPA had operated until the early 1950s. Slava Stets'ko had succeeded her husband as leader of the ABN in 1986, and Vasyl' Oles'kiv in 1991 as leader of the OUN-B. In 1992 she founded the Congress of Ukrainian Nationalists (*Kongres Ukraïns'kykh Natsionalistiv*, KUN), and in 1997 she was elected to the Ukrainian parliament, in which she served until her death in 2002.[23]

In Kiev, OUN-B émigrés set up the Stepan Bandera Centre of National Revival (*Tsentr Natsional'noho vidrodzhennia imeni Stepana Bandery*, TsNV) at 9 Iaroslaviv Val Street. The OUN leadership, the Munich-based OUN-B newspaper *Shliakh peremohy*, and the London-based OUN-B journal *Vyzvol'nyi shliakh* were

19 Stepan Lesiv, interview by author, Staryi Uhryniv, 18 May 2008; "Akty vandalizmu u Staromu Uhrynovi ta v Zhashkovi," *Shliakh peremohy*, 28 July 1991, 2; "Nyshchennia pam"iatnykiv zapochotkuvaly za SRSR," 12 January 2011, http://www.bbc.co.uk/ukrainian/ukraine/2011/01/110112_stepan_lesiv_bandera_ek.shtml (accessed 22 August 2011); Ivan Krainyi, "Pam"iatnyk Banderi pidryvalo holovne rozviduval'ne upravlinnia," *Vyzvol'nyi shliakh* Vol. 567, No. 6, (June 1995): 664–65.

20 A Shevchenko statue was also recast from the same Lenin statue; Stepan Lesiv, interview by author, Staryi Uhryniv, 18 May 2008.

21 *Vyzvol'nyi shliakh*, Vol. 534, No. 10 (October 1992): 1154; "Krupnyky vtsililoï istoriï," *Visnyk istoryko-memorial'noho muzeiu Stepana Bandery* 1 (2006): 22.

22 Maksym Skoryk, "'Karaius', muchus', ale na kaius'..." *Vysokyi Zamok*, 2 April 1992, 2.

23 Wilson, *The Ukrainians*, 180–81; Myron Jarosewich, "Slava Stetsko Visits Washington," *Ukrainian Weekly*, 17 August 1997, 2; Shekhovtsov, Pravoradikal'naia partiinaia politika, 11–12.

relocated there. In 2000, Andrii Haidamakha was elected leader of the OUN at the Ninth Great Congress. In 2009 the Twelfth Great Congress of the OUN elected Stefan Romaniw as leader of the OUN (Fig. 53). Both Haidamakha and Romaniw grew up in the diaspora and were recruited to the OUN when they were members of SUM.[24] Like many other OUN diaspora nationalists, the OUN Leader Romaniw has also been an activist of multiculturalism.[25] After his election as leader of the OUN, Romaniw stated:

> I remind myself of the words of Ievhen Konovalets', who said: "We can either be the creators of history or be its victims." The Organization of Ukrainian Nationalists has always demonstrated that it wants to create history, and the present Leadership is searching for that path. ...
>
> We are trying to create the understanding that the OUN is in fact that spark which can ignite community spirit. Today Ukraine and the Diaspora—this is a global Organization; an Organization where we complement one another, an Organization in which we need each other, and thus on the Leadership's part, we constantly remember: We are an Organization that is strewn around the world, but the purpose of our experience, our goal, is the same everywhere. That is why our task must be the education/development/raising of youth in Ukraine and in the Diaspora, because young people should know their roots, and love God and Ukraine. ...
>
> I call upon you today not only to sacrifice, I call upon you to be ready to cooperate, so that you, dear friends, young and old, will stand in the vanguard together with the Leadership of the OUN to ignite this fire in America, in Canada, in Poland, in Australia, in Great Britain, or in Ukraine.
>
> We are a global organization, our strength is our unity! I call upon you all to unite around our great ideal. ...
>
> Glory to Ukraine![26]

A number of ultranationalist and radical right parties and other organizations that claimed to stand in the tradition of the OUN-B and the UPA emerged in Ukraine after the dissolution of the Soviet Union. The Ukrainian National Assembly (*Ukraïns'ka natsional'na asambleia*, UNA) and its paramilitary wing, Ukrainian National Self-Defense (*Ukraïns'ka natsional'na samooborona*, UNSO) were founded in 1991. The UNA and UNSO based their ideology on Dontsov, Arthur de Gobineau, and Walter Darré, and modeled themselves on the National Democratic Party of Germany (*Nationaldemokratische Partei Deutschlands*, NPD). From 1991 to 1994 and again from October 2005, their leader was Iurii Shukhevych, the son of the legendary UPA leader Roman Shukhevych. Like the generation of his fathers, Iurii Shukhevych held extremist nationalist views. In an interview in 2007, for example, he said that "the ghetto was invented not by Hitler, but by the Jews themselves."

24 Lypovets'kyi, *Orhanizatsiia Ukraïns'kykh*, 75, 84.

25 For Romaniw as chairman of Multicultural Arts Victoria Inc., see http://www.multiculturalarts.com.au/events2011/givingvoice.shtml (accessed 26 September 2011). On multiculturalism and Ukrainian radical diaspora nationalism, see Rossoliński-Liebe, Celebrating Fascism, 1–16; Rudling, Multiculturalism, 733–68.

26 Lypovets'kyi, *Orhanizatsiia Ukraïns'kykh*, 87.

Following Soviet anti-Zionist dogma, he also argued that Simon Wiesenthal "was a Gestapo agent."[27]

Fig. 53. Stephan Romaniw, the leader of the OUN since 2009. Lypovets'kyi, *Orhanizatsiia*, 86.

Another major radical right party founded in 1991 was the Social-National Party of Ukraine (*Sotsial-natsional'na partiia Ukraïny*, SNPU). Its official party symbol was the Wolfsangel, or wolf's hook, used previously by various SS Divisions and far-right, fascist, and neo-fascist movements. The SNPU claimed that its ideology was derived from such writings as Stets'ko's *Two Revolutions*. In 2004 the SNPU gave birth to the All-Ukrainian Union Svoboda (Freedom), or Svoboda Party which became a member of the Alliance of European National Movements (AENM) and has been connected since 2009 with such other radical right parties as the French National Front, the Hungarian Jobbik, the Italian Tricolor Flame, the National Rebirth of Poland, and the Belgian National Front.[28] The views of the charismatic, populist, revolutionary, and ultranationalist leader of the Svoboda Party, Oleh Tiahnybok, are well illustrated by a speech that he gave in 2004, during which he said:

27 Rudling, "Anti-Semitism and the Extreme Right," 194. See also Shekhovtsov, The Creeping Resurgence, 209, 212–13; Paul Kubicek, "What Happened to the Nationalists in Ukraine?" *Nationalism & Ethnic Politics*, 5, 1 (1999): 31–32.

28 Shekhovtsov, "The Creeping Resurgence," 213–17; Rudling, Return of the Ukrainian Far Right, 239. For Stets'ko's *Two Revolutions*, see Z. Karbovych [Iaroslav Stets'ko], "Dvi revoliutsiï: Z pryvodu herois'koï smerty hen. Tarasa Chuprynky," *Surma*, 27 April 1951, 6–8. In general on radical right parties in early post-Soviet Ukraine, see Taras Kuzio, "Radical Nationalist Parties and Movements in Contemporary Ukraine before and after Independence: The Right and Its Politics, 1989–1994," *Nationalities Papers*, Vol. 25, No. 2 (1997): 211–36.

> The enemy came and took their [UPA's] Ukraine. But they [UPA fighters] were not afraid; likewise we must not be afraid. They hung their machine guns on their necks and went into the woods. They fought against the Russians, Germans, Jews, and other scum who wanted to take away our Ukrainian state! And therefore our task—for every one of you, the young, the old, the grey-headed and the youthful—is to defend our native land! ... These young men and you, the grey-headed, are the very combination that the Russian and Jewish mafia that is ruling Ukraine fears most.[29]

With the growth of nationalism after the dissolution of the Soviet Union, the OUN and UPA became a significant component of western Ukrainian identity. Similarly to Ukrainians in the diaspora during the Cold War, many people in western Ukraine began to commemorate Bandera as a national hero and freedom fighter and to deny the atrocities committed by the Ukrainian nationalists. After the Soviet Union was dissolved, it ceased to be perceived as the main enemy of Ukraine, and the hatred against it was re-directed against left-wingers, Russian-speaking eastern Ukrainians, and occasionally the European Union. Far-right nationalists began to claim that Ukraine was occupied by democrats, Russians, or Russified eastern Ukrainians who ought to be Ukrainized or Banderized. Many western Ukrainians complained that Ukraine was dependent on Russian culture, economy, politics, radio, television, and language. They also argued that people who criticized Bandera and the OUN and UPA were afflicted by *banderophobia*, which they defined as holding a hostile attitude toward Ukrainian culture.[30]

The growth of nationalism and radical right activism in Ukraine led to ethnic and political harassment and violence. It is difficult to say how many people became victims of nationalist violence but, because of it, a number of Russians and Jews left or tried to leave Ukraine. A few such cases were documented by the US Immigration and Naturalization Service (INS). Although we should be critical of these documents, because some refugees might have exaggerated in order to gain admission to the United States, we should not reject their reports as anti-Ukrainian fantasy. Irina Chtchetinin, an ethnic Russian and Jew living in Lviv, decided to leave Ukraine with her husband and three children after radical right groups attacked her Jewish-Russian neighbors. According to the historian Jeffrey Burds, who investigated the reports, Irina's neighbors were brutally tortured in their own apartment: "The husband was branded with a hot electric clothes iron, his wife's eye was ripped out of its socket, while their assailants screamed anti-Russian and anti-Semitic epithets. Ukrainian police refused even to take a report of the attack, or to follow up with an investigation of the incidents."[31] Another Jewish-Russian woman, Vera Korablina from Kiev, testified that a new ultranationalist boss fired all the Jewish workers in

29 Shekhovtsov, The Creeping Resurgence, 216.

30 On claiming that Ukraine is occupied by democrats, see Kuzio, Radical Nationalist Parties, 215–16; Andrii Parubyi, interview by author, Lviv, 12 May 2006. For Banderophobia, see *Fenomen Banderofobii v russkom soznanii* (Kiev: Ukraïns'ka Vydavnycha Spilka, 2007).

31 Jeffrey Burds, "Ukraine: The meaning of persecution. An American scholar reflects on the impact of the Ukrainian Jewish experience on international asylum law in the post-Soviet era," *Transitions online*, 2 May 2006, http://www.sovhistory.neu.edu/Burds-Transitions.pdf (accessed 6 November 2012), 1, 3.

her section in 1990, and that in 1993, nationalists beat her new employer. They demanded from him "payment of special dues for Russians and Jews who worked in Ukraine." Like her friend, she received death threats by telephone and mail. In early 1994, she was tortured by men who argued that "her Russian surname and passport could not conceal her 'Yid' origins." In September 1994, the walls and furniture in her office were painted with anti-Russian and antisemitic graffiti. Her Jewish employer disappeared soon after this incident.[32]

The Bandera Cult in Historiography

The collapse of the Soviet Union and the emergence of the Ukrainian state caused changes in the field of professional history but almost none in the field of apologetic historical writing. The process of change was determined by the opening up of Soviet archives, rediscovery of testimonies of the victims as a source to study the Holocaust and far-right movements, and the de-nationalization and de-ideologization of professional history after the end of the Cold War. Historians such as John-Paul Himka gradually ceased to regard the ideology of Ukrainian nationalism as an important narrative of Ukrainian history and began to investigate the actual history of the OUN, UPA, and the Second World War in Ukraine.[33] John Armstrong, on the other hand, the main historian during the Cold War who dealt with Ukrainian nationalism, seems to have ceased altogether to apply a critical approach to Ukrainian history, after the collapse of the Soviet Union. At a conference in Lviv in August 1993, he claimed that "the objective of the historian ... is to clarify the true position of the hero in his own time." He admired Bandera, Shukhevych, Lebed', Stets'ko, Dontsov, Kubiiovych, and Sheptyts'kyi and did not pay any attention to the atrocities committed by the Ukrainian nationalists during and after the Second World War or to their collaboration with Nazi Germany.[34]

The discourse on Bandera and the OUN-UPA in Ukraine also became nationalized and radicalized in reaction to the Soviet legacy. Historians who were socialized in Soviet Ukraine began to invent a new narrative, which defined itself through the negation of the Soviet narrative and resembled Cold War writings by OUN émigrés. The radical right sector of the Ukrainian diaspora also contributed to the radicalization of the post-Soviet historical discourse in a practical way. The OUN organized historical conferences, for example in Kiev on 28 and 29 March 1992, at which Slava Stets'ko and Volodymyr Kosyk explained to the Ukrainian historians how to write history.[35] The OUN émigrés established the Institute for the Study of the Liberation

32 Ibid., 3–4.

33 See for example John-Paul Himka, "*Krakivski visti* and the Jews, 1943: A Contribution to the History of Ukrainian-Jewish Relations during the Second World War," *Journal of Ukrainian Studies* Vol. 21, No. 1–2 (1996): 81–95. In 2007 Himka commissioned Dieter Pohl to write an entry on the Holocaust in Ukraine for the internet version of the Encyclopedia of Ukraine, which had been initiated, co-founded, and edited by Kubiiovych.

34 John A. Armstrong, "Heroes and Human: Reminiscences Concerning Ukrainian National Leaders During 1941–1944," *The Ukrainian Quarterly*, Vol. LI, No. 2–3 (1995): 213.

35 For the conference, see Mykola Shatylov, "Vpershe i na zavzhdy. Istorychna konferentsiia ukraïns'kykh natsionalistiv u Kyievi," *Vyzvol'nyi shliakh* Vol. 530, No. 5 (May 1992): 546–48. The OUN journal *Vyzvol'nyi shliakh* published articles in the early 1990s, written by historians such as Iaroslav Hrytsak, whose book *Sketch of Ukrainian History*, first published in 1996 and later republi-

Movement (*Tsentr doslidzhen' vyzvol'noho rukhu*, TsDVR),[36] whose office has been located since then in the building of the Academy of Sciences at 4 Kozel'nyts'ka Street in Lviv.[37]

The agenda of the TsDVR has been to reproduce and popularize the work of such OUN-B historians as Petro Mirchuk and Volodymyr Kosyk and to produce its own works according to the nationalist narrative initiated by the OUN émigrés. This has meant promoting the OUN as a democratic organization and the UPA as an army of liberation, and denying their ultranationalist nature and the atrocities that they had committed. The deeper purpose behind this activity was to elevate the "liberation movement" as a very important component of Ukrainian identity. The TsDVR expressed its agenda in a language that bears a striking resemblance to the language of OUN-B diaspora historians:

> The history of the struggle of liberation is the basis of the national idea of every state, the basis for its values and orientation. The past of the Ukrainian people—in particular its liberation struggle—was for many years silenced and twisted by the totalitarian regimes. Therefore, a new non-prejudiced view of the Ukrainian liberation movement is extraordinarily urgently needed. The twentieth century was the high point of the development of the Ukrainian resistance—the best example is the struggle of the Organization of Ukrainian Nationalists and the Ukrainian Insurgent Army from the 1920s to the 1950s. Unfortunately, today, the activities of those structures remain one of the least studied parts of the Ukrainian historiography. The study of the various aspects of the struggle of the Ukrainians for their national and social freedom is the main purpose of The Center for the Study of the Ukrainian Liberation Movement.[38]

The diaspora and the OUN émigrés continued to publish on the subject of Bandera and the OUN-UPA after 1991. Petro Goi, head of the branch of the Ukrainian Free University in New York, collected several hundred articles about Bandera's assassination, published them in ten thick volumes and called his monumental edition the foundation for the science about Bandera, or Banderology (*banderoznavstvo*). His wish was to enable "Ukrainian historians in the future" to "study the tragic incidents around the murder of Stepan Bandera" and to make the *Providnyk* the object of an academic cult.[39]

The new ultranationalist narrative that appeared in post-Soviet Ukraine was a negative mirror image of the Soviet one, but because it negated the Soviet narrative it appeared to historians socialized in Soviet or post-Soviet Ukraine to be critical and true. The denial-oriented publications written by the OUN émigrés were used as evidence for claims that the OUN-UPA did not conduct ethnic cleansing in 1943–

shed a few times, was extensively used at Ukrainian universities and in schools. Hrytsak was already a Doctor of Philosophy (kandydat istorychnykh nauk) when his article appeared in *Vyzvol'nyi shliakh*. Cf. Iaroslav Hrytsak, "Ukraïns'kyi natsionalizm: Mynule, suchasne, maibutnie," *Vyzvol'nyi shliakh* Vol. 530, No. 6 (June 1992): 672–73. Hrytsak, *Narys istoriï Ukraïny*.

36 Lypovets'kyi, *Orhanizatsiia Ukraïns'kykh*, 84.

37 Cf. http://cdvr.org.ua/ (accessed 27 September 2011); Kurylo, Iak OUN stavylasia do ievreïv, 252.

38 "Informatsiina dovidka of the TsDVR," http://upa.in.ua/book/?page_id=7 (accessed 27 September 2011). The translation is from Rudling, The OUN, the UPA and the Holocaust, 27.

39 Petro Goi, "Bilia dzherel banderoznavstva," *Zbirka hazetnykh i zhurnal'nykh materialiv pro vbyvstvo Stepana Bandery*, ed. Petro Goi (New York, 1999), 1:1.

1944, did not kill Jews, and that the OUN-B did not adopt fascism in the 1930s. Mykola Lebed's first monograph on the UPA from 1946 was reprinted in 1993.[40] In 1995 the Vidrodzhennia publishing house reprinted Petro Poltava's *Who Are the Banderites and What Are They Fighting For* from 1950. In 1999 it reprinted Bandera's *Perspectives of the Ukrainian Revolution*, and several other nationalist publications. Vidrodzhennia provided the reprints with nationalist introductions and added contemporary pictures of demonstrations and ceremonies conducted by paramilitary organizations, such as a photograph of a unit of the Stepan Bandera Tryzub standing in front of the Bandera monument.[41] A number of prominent Ukrainian scholars and politicians engaged in such organizations and took part in such ceremonies. Serhii Kvit, who in 2007 became the rector of the most prestigious Ukrainian university, the National University of Kiev-Mohyla Academy, had in the 1990s been the centurion (*sotnyk*) of the Stepan Bandera Tryzub and member of the KUN.[42]

Popular Biographies

The popular and academic discourse about Bandera in Ukraine was influenced by two groups. One was composed of OUN émigrés such as Mirchuk, and nationalist dissidents such as Levko Luk"ianenko, holder of an honorary Doctorate in Law from the University of Alberta, who argued that Jews controlled the Soviet Union and were responsible for a significant number of Soviet atrocities. The second group consisted of OUN and UPA veterans who lived in Soviet Ukraine and were allowed for the first time to express their opinions without Soviet censorship. Many declared themselves to be the only true sources on OUN-UPA history. Their interpretations did not differ greatly from those of such veterans and historians as Mirchuk and Potichnyi, who lived and published after the Second World War in the diaspora, without Soviet censorship.[43]

The first major post-Soviet Bandera biography, *Stepan Bandera—Symbol of the Nation*, was published by former OUN-B member and anticommunist activist Petro Duzhyi (1916–1997). Duzhyi joined the OUN in 1932 and participated in the "Ukrainian National Revolution" of 1941 as a member of an OUN-B task force. In 1944 he became the director of the propaganda department of the OUN. In June

40 For Lebed', see Mykola Lebed', *Ukraïns'ka Povstans'ka Armiia: Ïï heneza, rist i diï u vyzvol'niï borotbi ukraïns'koho narodu za ukraïns'ku samostiïnu sobornu derzhavu* (Drohobych: Vidrodzhennia, 1993).

41 Petro Poltava, *Khto taki banderivtsi ta za shcho vony boruts'sia*, ed. Iaroslav Radevych-Vynnyts'kyi (Dorohobych: Vidrodzhennia, 1995), 62; Stepan Bandera, *Perspektyvy ukraïns'koï revoliutsiï*, edited by Vasyl' Ivanyshyn (Drohobych: Vidrodzhennia, 1999); Stepan Bandera, *Perspektyvy ukraïns'koï revoliutsiï* (Kiev: Instytut Natsional'noho Derzhavoznavstva, 1999).

42 Serhii Kvit wrote his dissertation on Dmytro Dontsov and defended it at the Ukrainian Free University in Munich. See Per Anders Rudling, "Warfare or War Criminality," *Ab Imperio* 1 (2012): 359, note 18; "Serhi Kvit—sotnyk VHSPO 'Tryzub' im. S. Bandery," *Banderivets*, No. 2, 1998, http://old.banderivets.org.ua/index.php?page=pages/gazeta/1998-02 (accessed 2 December 2012).

43 On Luk"ianenko, see Per Anders Rudling, "Organized Anti-Semitism in Contemporary Ukraine: Structure, Influence and Ideology," *Canadian Slavonic Papers*, Vol. 48, No. 1–2 (2006): 90–91; Rudling, Anti-Semitism and the Extreme Right, 196.

1945, he was arrested by the NKVD and, after two years imprisonment in Kiev, he was detained in the Gulag until 1960.[44]

Like Mirchuk, the main OUN diaspora historian and Bandera hagiographer Duzhyi was not a professional historian. Archival documents and critical thinking were alien to him. He wrote and published a Bandera biography in two volumes, to confirm the nationalist interpretation of Bandera's life. Although Duzhyi's book about the *Providnyk* contained a good deal of valuable information, it was embedded in the genre of denial and apologetics. One would not learn from Duzhyi's biography anything about the influence of antisemitism and fascism on Bandera's thinking and acting, or about OUN-B collaboration with Nazi Germany, or the pogroms of July 1941. Similarly, one would not learn anything about the ethnic cleansing of Poles by the UPA, or the killing of Ukrainian and Russian civilians, although Duzhyi devoted a substantial part of his book to describing the UPA. Instead, one learns that only Bolsheviks and other foes called the OUN fascist, that Ukrainian nationalism is based on Shevchenko's poetry, and that there was nothing wrong with the assassinations organized by the OUN in the 1930s, because they were only "acts of retribution."[45]

One aspect that made Duzhyi's biography different from Mirchuk's was the very extensive incorporation of such documents as Bandera's brief autobiography, articles he wrote, and transcripts of interviews he gave. These documents were published in the diaspora after Mirchuk had finished his hagiography. Duzhyi regarded these documents as reliable sources and took everything in them for granted. Thus his biography, almost 500 pages long, is essentially an extension of Bandera's thirteen-page autobiography. Duzhyi began each of the numerous short chapters of his book with a quotation from Bandera's autobiography, or from his articles, or from pieces written by other OUN members. He then extended these quotations with his own contributions which, in terms of language and argument, did not differ greatly from the quoted documents.[46]

A very popular Bandera biography, republished at least three times, including once by the Bandera museum in Dubliany, was written by the Lviv writer Halyna Hordasevych.[47] She was not in the OUN but stated that if she had been ten years older she would have joined it and followed the *Providnyk*.[48] In the introduction, Hordasevych wrote that she intended to introduce Bandera as a human being. She was motivated by the observation that everyone in Ukraine and many people in other former Soviet republics used the term "Banderites" in the sense of "enemy of the people" but knew little or nothing about the person. She claimed that, especially in eastern Ukraine, anyone who spoke Ukrainian was labeled as a Banderite. Making an analogy between Banderites, Petliurites (derived from Symon Petliura), and Mazepites (derived from the seventeenth-century Cossack leader Ivan Mazepa), she claimed that Ukrainians accused of treason were first called Mazepites, then

44 Petro Duzhyi, *Stepan Bandera—Symvol natsiï: Eskiznyi narys pro zhyttia i diial'nist' providnyka OUN*, (Lviv: Halyts'ka Vydavnycha Spilka, 1996), 1:7, 257.

45 Duzhyi, *Stepan Bandera*, 1:124–25, 140.

46 Duzhyi, *Stepan Bandera*, vol. 1–2.

47 Halyna Hordasevych, *Stepan Bandera: liudyna i mif* (Kiev: Biblioteka ukraïntsia, 1999); Halyna Hordasevych, *Stepan Bandera: liudyna i mif* (Lviv: Spolom, 2000); Halyna Hordasevych, *Stepan Bandera: liudyna i mif* (Lviv: Piramida, 2001).

48 Halyna Hordasevych, *Stepan Bandera: liudyna i mif* (Lviv: Piramida, 2001), 9.

Petliurites, and finally Banderites. This comparison had frequently appeared in the Soviet literature. In post-Soviet Ukraine its negative meaning was turned into an element of the heroic invention of tradition and became a common motif of various affirmative Bandera biographies.[49]

In order to challenge the ideological notion of Banderites as traitors, and to present Bandera as a human being, Hordasevych studied a range of Soviet and diaspora publications about him. In her book, she signaled several times that she trusted neither the nationalist nor the Soviet historiographical genre, but she eventually arrived at the typical post-Soviet nationalist conclusion: "He was a man around whom myths have been created, which is however, a feature only of heroic personalities; therefore Stepan Bandera is the hero of Ukraine."[50] Like other post-Soviet biographers, she used Soviet propaganda to deny that Bandera collaborated with Germany and that the OUN-B and UPA were involved in ethnic and political violence. An analysis of her biography demonstrates how much of a symbol Bandera was in Soviet and post-Soviet discourses, and how difficult it was in post-Soviet Ukraine to write about the person and about the movement that the *Providnyk* represented.[51]

Ievhen Perepichka, a far-right activist and the head of the Lviv KUN, wrote another monumental and popular Bandera biography titled *The Phenomenon of Stepan Bandera*.[52] In addition to collecting documents about Bandera, Perepichka had, since the early 1990s, organized various ultranationalist and neo-fascist manifestations and celebrations, frequently with the participation of paramilitary groups.[53] Like Duzhyi and Hordasevych, Perepichka did not have any historical training, did not care about academic standards, and extensively quoted forged documents published in diaspora publications.[54] Given Perepichka's convictions and methods, it is not surprising that he regarded Bandera as

> a legendary person, what a pride, the symbol of the Ukrainian nation. The whole epoch of the national-liberating struggle and all the fighters for the liberation of Ukraine were named after him. The Muscovite occupiers called all Ukrainians Banderites and also the patriots from other nations who fought for the liberation of their homelands: Lithuanian Banderites, Latvian Banderites, Kazakh Banderites, Estonian Banderites, Kyrgyzstani Banderites.[55]

Perepichka began his Bandera biography with the Bandera family tree and finished it with that of his own family.[56] Between the two, Perepichka described all the possible deeds that the ideology of Ukrainian nationalism classifies as the "suffering of the Ukrainian nation," including the famine in Soviet Ukraine in 1932-1933. He reduced the Second World War to the killing of Ukrainians mainly by Soviet and German forces and, like Mirchuk and Duzhyi, did not analyze or even mention the

49 Ibid., 7–8.
50 Ibid., 154.
51 Ibid., 98–101.
52 Ievhen Perepichka, *Fenomen Stepana Bandery* (Lviv: Spolom, 2006).
53 Ibid., 674, 677.
54 For example, ibid., 339.
55 Ibid., 5.
56 Ibid., 12–13, 676.

atrocities committed by the OUN and UPA during and after the Second World War.[57] The only Jews who appear in Perepichka's biography are those who were rescued by Ukrainians.[58] Moreover, OUN members and UPA insurgents, not Jewish, Polish, or Ukrainian civilians, appear to have been the main victims of the atrocities committed by the German and Soviet occupiers of Ukraine. Bandera appears to be the symbol of Ukrainian suffering in general.

Ihor Tsar wrote a short but very popular Bandera biography, with the unambiguous title, *What We Love Bandera For*. He argued that it was God who sent Bandera to Ukrainians:

> Stepan Bandera is the hero of the twentieth century, a legendary person, the most prominent person in Ukrainian history. The time came to raise his name in the whole free Ukraine in order to enable every living soul to thank God that He sent us, in the darkest times of the history of mankind, such a bright personality. In particular, Bandera rescued the honor of Ukraine in the twentieth century because he could motivate the nation to a self-sacrificing struggle against Stalinist communism, fascism, and chauvinism. ... Bandera elevated the Ukrainian nationalism of love to the highest willingness to make sacrifices. His slogan was "God and Ukraine!" We love Bandera for that.[59]

Bandera and Academia

In the two decades following the collapse of the Soviet Union, no professional historian has written a critical biography of Bandera; but a number of historians, such as Omer Bartov, Karel Berkhoff, John-Paul Himka, Frank Golczewski, Grzegorz Motyka, and Dieter Pohl, were investigating such related subjects as the Second World War and the Holocaust in Ukraine, Soviet politics in Ukraine during and after the Second World War, and the OUN and UPA. The publications of these historians had almost no impact on post-Soviet historians who rather published material that stimulated nationalist activists and politicians to erect Bandera monuments and to perform various OUN and UPA commemorations. Similarly to the diaspora historians before them, the post-Soviet historians collected some important empirical data but applied nationalist interpretations and frequently did not pay much attention to academic standards.[60]

The most prolific Bandera biographer has been Mykola Posivnych. As far as 2012, Posivnych had edited three volumes, including excerpts from memoirs and documents about Bandera, republished the indictment from the Warsaw trial in 1935 in Ukrainian, and published a short Bandera biography.[61] Posivnych's three volumes

57 Cf. ibid., 191–208, 271–96.

58 Ibid., 354.

59 Ihor Tsar, *Za shcho my liubymo Banderu* (Lviv, 2000), 3.

60 Many items published by nationalist post-Soviet historians were not peer-reviewed. Because many such historians did not read English or perhaps any languages other than Ukrainian, Russian, and Polish, their isolation from international debates influenced their approach to history.

61 Mykola Posivnych, *Stepan Bandera—zhyttia, prysviachene svobodi* (Toronto: Litopys UPA, 2008); Mykola Posivnych, ed., *Stepan Bandera: Dokumenty i materialy (1920–1930 rr.)* (Lviv: Afisha, 2006); Mykola Posivnych, ed., *Zhyttia i diial'nist' Stepana Bandery: Dokumenty i materialy* (Ternopil': Aston, 2008); Mykola Posivnych ed., *Zhyttia i diial'nist' Stepana Bandery: Dokumenty i materi-*

consist partially of the same excerpts from the memoirs of OUN members and various OUN documents as those compiled by other writers. The introduction to the three volumes was written by OUN-B member and diaspora historian Volodymyr Kosyk who, in the 1950s, had been the ZCh OUN liaison to Chiang Kai-Shek's Taiwan and Franco's Spain. The three volumes include a biographical text about Bandera's youth, written by Posivnych in a narrative that does not differ greatly from Kosyk's or Mirchuk's, but which contains much more valuable empirical data.[62]

In his three volumes, Posivnych did not comment on the republished extracts of memoirs and added only brief biographical comments about their authors. Because all of them were written by OUN members, in particular OUN-B, this kind of editing is problematic, or even inadmissible. The editor republished, for example, an article about Bandera at the Lviv trial, written by Stsibors'kyi in 1936, in which he prizes Bandera's "heroic" behavior. In the biographical note for Stsibors'kyi', however, Posivnych did not mention that, in a letter to Mel'nyk, which the editor even republished in the same volume, Bandera called Stsibors'kyi a "treacherous Bolshevik agent" who was living with a "suspicious Moscow Jewish woman" or that Stsibors'kyi was killed on 30 August 1941, in all probability by the OUN-B, on Bandera's order. Similarly, Posivnych did not comment on another republished document, Bandera's letter to Mel'nyk from September 1940, which contains several nationalist and antisemitic passages. Instead of publishing original archival documents, which are accessible in Ukrainian achieves, Posivnych reprinted some documents from diaspora publications without paying attention to the fact that OUN émigrés had forged and manipulated some documents.[63] In general, Posivnych's volumes contain extracts from memoirs and documents that are significant for the understanding of Bandera, but their unprofessional editing suggests that they have a commemorative rather than a scholarly character. In addition to popularizing important sources, they also propagate the Bandera cult.[64]

In his short biography *Stepan Bandera—A Life Devoted to Freedom*, Posivnych indicated the sources on which he relied, and applied some other academic standards, but he wrote it in a narrative, which resembles the narratives that structure Mirchuk's, Duzhyi's, Hordasevych's, and Perepichka's Bandera biographies. Instead of analyzing all aspects of Bandera's life, his political activities, or the OUN's policies, Posivnych described only those features that caused Bandera and the OUN to appear as heroic and admirable elements of the Ukrainian past, and thus valuable elements

aly (Ternopil: Ason, 2011); Mykola Posivnych, *Varshavs'kyi akt obvynuvachennia Stepana Bandery ta tovaryshiv* (Lviv: Tsentr doslidzhen' vyzvol'noho rukhu, 2005). In 2010 Posivnych edited another volume on Bandera, see Mykola Posivnych and Bohdan Hordasevych, eds., *Stepan Bandera: 1909–1959–2009: Zbirnyk statei* (Lviv: Triada Plius, 2010).

62 Posivnych, Molodist' Stepana Bandery, 2006, 5–35; Mykola Posivnych, Molodist' Stepana Bandery, 2008, 9–39. For Kosyk, see Rudling, Warfare or War Criminality, 358, note 7. For a critical review of Posivnych's representation of the OUN, see Zaitsev, Viina iak prodovzhennia, 235–45.

63 For the reprinted documents, see Posivnych, ed., *Stepan Bandera*; Posivnych, ed., *Zhyttia i diial'nist'*, 2008; Posivnych, ed., *Zhyttia i diial'nist'*, 2011. For Bandera's letter to Mel'nyk from September 1941, see Posivnych, ed., *Zhyttia i diial'nist'*, 2008, 261–97. The document is located in TsDAVOV f. 3833, op. 1, spr. 71, 1–22. For Stsibors'kyi, see chapters 4 and 5 above, and Mykola Stsibors'kyi, "Klonim holovy," in *Stepan Bandera*, ed. Posivnych, 2006, 133–34.

64 Some of Posivnych's books were published by the OUN-founded TsDVR and others by the Litopys UPA, an émigré OUN publishing house. For example, Posivnych's *Varshavs'kyi akt* was published in cooperation with the TsDVR and *Stepan Bandera—zhyttia, prysviachene svobodi* by Litopys UPA.

of the Ukrainian identity. Describing the OUN before the Second World War, he justified the crimes committed by the OUN in the early 1930s as having been decided upon by the OUN court.[65] Describing the trials in Warsaw and Lviv, he wrote that the OUN used the greeting "Glory to Ukraine!" but did not point out that OUN members used it as part of a fascist salute. The omission might be the result of reliance on diaspora publications that falsified the records, or it might have been a conscious decision to deny the actual meaning of the salute.[66] Similarly, when describing the role of the OUN-B and UPA during the Second World War, Posivnych omitted the fact that they were involved in numerous atrocities.[67]

Many books on the subject of Bandera, the OUN, and the UPA have been published since 2000 by the OUN-founded TsDVR. After the election of Viktor Iushchenko to the presidency of Ukraine in 2005, the Ukrainian government began to promote the TsDVR's nationalist and selective approach to history as part of the official state history. To establish a coherent national version of Ukrainian history, the Ukrainian Institute of National Memory (*Ukraïns'kyi instytut natsional'noï pam"iati*, UINP) was established in 2006 in Kiev, and Ihor Iukhnovs'kyi, a physicist and a sympathizer with the radical right SNPU, became its director. In 2007, the director of the TsDVR, Volodymyr V"iatrovych, became the representative of the UINP in the Lviv oblast. From 2008 until the end of Iushchenko's tenure in power in early 2010, V"iatrovych worked in Kiev, first for the UINP and then as director of the archives of the Security Service of Ukraine (*Sluzhba Bezpeky Ukraïny*, SBU), the successor of the KGB. The SBU played a major role in determining on which documents the UINP should base its nationalist version of Ukrainian history and how this history should be written. From the outset, the UINP concentrated on promoting two ideologically interrelated aspects of Ukrainian history, which were intended to unite Ukrainians through victimization and heroization. The first was the promotion of the famine in Soviet Ukraine in 1932–1933 as an act of genocide against Ukrainians, in the execution of which many Jews were involved as perpetrators. The second was the extolment of the OUN and UPA and the denial of their atrocities, as practiced before by the Ukrainian diaspora and the TsDVR.[68]

Unsurprisingly, the UINP with its nationalist director Iukhnovs'kyi and the "patriotic" historian V"iatrovych had a great impact on the politics of memory in Ukraine. On 16 May 2007, at the urging of the UINP, Iushchenko ordered the organization of a series of ceremonies, honoring Iaroslav and Iaroslava Stets'ko. On 12 September 2007, he designated Shukhevych as a Hero of Ukraine, and on 20 January 2010, shortly before the end of his term in office, he did the same with

65 Posivnych, *Stepan Bandera—zhyttia*, 32.

66 Ibid., 38. See also Posivnych, *Providnyk OUN*, 31. For a very similar omission, see Olena Petrenko, "Makellose HeldInnen des Terrors. Die Organisation der Ukrainischen Nationalisten im Spannungsfeld zwischen Heroisierung und Diffamierung," *Terrorismus und Geschlecht: Politische Gewalt in Europa seit dem 19. Jahrhundert*, ed. Christine Hikel and Sylvia Schraut (Frankfurt, Main: Campus-Verlag, 2012), 200–201.

67 Posivnych, *Stepan Bandera—zhyttia*, 57–60.

68 Rudling, The OUN, the UPA and the Holocaust, 27, 30, 64, note 270.

Bandera. The latter designation unleashed a debate about the OUN-UPA, Ukrainian nationalism, and Bandera's role in Ukrainian history.[69]

The nationalist interpretation of history practiced at the TsDVR was one of the main reasons why Iushchenko promoted and relied on this institution. This kind of history allowed the Second World War to be dealt with, without paying any attention to the Ukrainian involvement in the Holocaust and other atrocities, which destabilized the process of creating a national Ukrainian collective identity. In 2006 V"iatrovych, at that time the director of the TsDVR, published a short book, *The Attitude of the OUN to the Jews*, which allows us to understand how nationalist post-Soviet historians deal with the genocide of the Jews. V"iatrovych wrote the monograph to demonstrate that the OUN was not hostile to Jews, did not murder them, and rescued a significant number.[70] John-Paul Himka and Taras Kurylo commented on V"iatrovych's method of presenting history:

> V"iatrovych manages to exonerate the OUN of charges of antisemitism and complicity in the Holocaust only by employing a series of highly dubious procedures: rejecting sources that compromise the OUN, accepting uncritically censored sources from émigré OUN circles, failing to recognize antisemitism in OUN texts, limiting the source base to official OUN proclamations and decisions, excluding Jewish memoirs, refusing to consider contextual and comparative factors, failing to consult German document collections, and ignoring the mass of historical monographs on his subject written in the English and German languages.[71]

The result of applying this method confirmed the expectation that the OUN was not hostile to Jews. In the entire book V"iatrovych introduced only one critical publication on antisemitism in the OUN, written by Berkhoff and Carynnyk, but dismissed it with the claim that it reminded him of Soviet publications.[72] Similarly, V"iatrovych argued that the OUN member and diaspora historian Taras Hunchak delivered the best research on the Jews and Ukrainian nationalism and repeated after him that the stereotype of "Judeo-Bolshevism" was not a stereotype but reality.[73] Referring to Hrytsak's article "Ukrainians in Anti-Jewish Actions in the Time of the Second World War," V"iatrovych claimed that the document from the Third Extraordinary Great Assembly in August 1943, in which the OUN-B distanced itself from anti-Jewish violence, was a falsification, because it would verify the "myth about the participation of Ukrainian nationalists in anti-Jewish actions in 1941–

69 For the designation of Shukhevych, see http://www.president.gov.ua/documents/6808.html (accessed 27 September 2011). For the designation of Iaroslav Stets'ko and Iaroslava Stets'ko, see http://www.president.gov.ua/documents/6145.html (accessed 27 September 2007). For the designation of Stepan Bandera, see http://zakon1.rada.gov.ua/cgi-bin/laws/main.cgi?nreg=46/2010 (accessed 27 September 2011). For petitioning Iushchenko, see "Instytut natsional'noï pam"iati zvernuvsia do Iushchenka, aby vin prysvoïv Romanu Shukhevychu zvannia Heroia Ukraïny," *Zik. Syla Informatsii*, July 2, 2007 (accessed 27 September 2011).

70 Volodymyr V"iatrovych, *Stavlennia OUN do ievreïv: Formovannia pozytsiï na tli katastrofy* (Lviv: Ms, 2006).

71 Kurylo, Iak OUN stavylasia do ievreïv, 265.

72 The article was Karel C. Berkhoff and Marco Carynnyk's "The Organization of Ukrainian Nationalists and Its Attitude toward Germans and Jews: Iaroslav Stets'ko's 1941 *Zhyttiepys*," *Harvard Ukrainian Studies* 23, 3/4 (1999): 149–84. Cf. V"iatrovych, *Stavlennia OUN*, 9. Later he introduced Motyka's book but dismissed it in a similar fashion. Cf. V"iatrovych, *Stavlennia OUN*, 76.

73 V"iatrovych, *Stavlennia OUN*, 11, 43. For Hunchak see page 450 above.

1943."[74] A document from July 1941, according to which OUN-B member Lenkavs'kyi stated that "regarding the Jews we will adopt any methods that lead to their destruction," was referred to by V"iatrovych as a Soviet "falsification with the purpose of provocation."[75] He explicitly denied the involvement of the OUN-B in the pogroms of July 1941 and denied the killing of Jews by the UPA.[76] In order to equate the killing of a few dozen OUN members with the killing of millions of Jews, the director of the TsDVR published, next to pictures of a mass grave containing the bodies of Jews, a picture of a row of young men who, according to the caption, were OUN members shot by the Germans.[77] Furthermore, V"iatrovych introduced the OUN and UPA as rescuers of Jews. He described the collective farms at which the UPA forced Jews to work but omitted the fact that the OUN and UPA liquidated the Jews working on these farms. Similarly, he omitted to point out that the SB of the OUN-B killed Jewish doctors and nurses who worked in the UPA. In writing about the few Jews who survived the UPA, he mentioned the fictitious biography of Stella Krentsbakh published by Mirchuk in 1957. Relying on the memoirs of Roman Shukhevych's wife Natalia Shukhevych, which were written by Vasyl' Kuk and Iurii Shukhevych, V"iatrovych wrote that she rescued a Jewish girl in 1942–1943, without mentioning Shukhevych's involvement in mass violence, and without clarifying the circumstances in which his wife allegedly rescued the girl.[78]

No less effective than V"iatrovych was the poet Moisei Fishbein who, like V"iatrovych, ignored research on the OUN, UPA, and the Holocaust in Ukraine and who, with the support of Iushchenko's government, promoted a similar interpretation of relations between Jews and Ukrainian nationalists to that of V"iatrovych. At the Conference on Ukrainian Subjects at the University of Illinois in 2009, Fishbein mentioned the names of a few Jews who allegedly survived in the UPA, and tried to persuade the audience that Ukrainian nationalists were not hostile to Jews during the Second World War:

> The claim that "the UPA engaged in anti-Jewish actions" is a provocation engineered by Moscow. It is a provocation. It is a lie that the UPA destroyed Jews. Tell me: how could the UPA have destroyed Jews, when Jews were serving members of the UPA? I knew a Jew who served in the UPA. I also knew Dr. Abraham Shtertser, who settled in Israel after the war. There was Samuel Noiman whose [UPA] codename was Maksymovych. There was Shai Varma (codename Skrypal/Violinist). There was Roman Vynnytsky whose codename was Sam.
>
> There was another distinguished figure in the UPA, a woman by the name of Stella Krenzbach, who later wrote her memoirs. She was born in Bolekhiv in the Lviv region. She was the daughter of a rabbi, she was a Zionist, and in Bolekhiv she was friends with Olia, the daughter of a [Ukrainian] Greek-Catholic priest. In

74 V"iatrovych, *Stavlennia OUN*, 16–17. For Iaroslav Hrytsak's article, see Iaroslav Hrytsak, "Ukraïntsi v antyievreis'kykh aktsiiakh u roky Druhoï svitovoï viiny," in *Strasti za natsionalizmom: Istorychni eseï*, ed. Iaroslav Hrytsak (Kiev: Krytyka, 2004), 166.

75 V"iatrovych, *Stavlennia OUN*, 62. For the document and the context of Lenkavs'kyi's statement, see page 218 above.

76 V"iatrovych, *Stavlennia OUN*, 59–61.

77 Ibid., 69, 71.

78 Ibid., 76–80. For Krentsbakh and Mirchuk, see chapter 9 above. On V"iatrovych, see also Rossoliński-Liebe, Debating, Obfuscating and Disciplining the Holocaust, 207–8.

1939 Stella Krenzbach graduated from Lviv University's Faculty of Philosophy. From 1943 she served in the UPA as a nurse and intelligence agent. In the spring of 1945 she was captured by the NKVD while meeting a courier in Rozhniativ. She was imprisoned, tortured, and sentenced to death. Later, this Jewish woman was sprung from prison by UPA soldiers. In the summer of 1945 she crossed into the Carpathian Mountains together with a group of Ukrainian insurgents, and on 1 October 1946 she reached the British Zone of Occupation in Austria. Eventually, she reached Israel. In her memoirs, Stella Krenzbach writes: "I attribute the fact that I am alive today and devoting all the strength of my thirty-eight years to a free Israel, only to God and the Ukrainian Insurgent Army. I became a member of the heroic UPA on 7 November 1943. In our group I counted twelve Jews, eight of whom were doctors."[79]

Ukrainian historians who have denied or diminished the war crimes of the OUN and UPA, and their involvement in the Holocaust, have been supported by two Russian historians, Alexander Gogun and Kirill Aleksandrov. These historians found a parallel with Bandera and the OUN-UPA, in Vlasov and the ROA. Like Bandera, Vlasov collaborated with Nazi Germany. He was executed by the Soviet regime in 1946. As in the case of Bandera, Soviet propaganda described Vlasov as a "traitor" and "enemy of the Soviet people" and like Bandera, he was rehabilitated by the post-Soviet intellectuals and presented as a democrat. Gogun stated, for example, in an article about the ROA: "The Vlasov movement was a democratic movement [*Vlasovskoe dvizhenie bylo dvizheniem demokraticheskim*]." In order to prove this, relying on Aleksandrov's publication, Gogun detected in the ROA a few non-Russian soldiers, in particular three alleged Jews.[80] In another article, "Jews in the Struggle for an Independent Ukraine," co-authored with Oleksandr Vovk, Gogun applied a similar method to the UPA. The authors omitted the anti-Jewish violence of the OUN and UPA and gave the impression that Jews served and fought willingly in the UPA "for an independent Ukraine—against Hitler and Stalin."[81] In an article about Bandera, Alexandrov argued that, as a "Muscovite historian," he could not criticize Bandera and the OUN-UPA because their nature was distorted by Soviet stereotypes. He argued that a critical investigation of Bandera and his movement was less important than the refutation of Soviet myths. Then, through the negation of the Soviet myths, he reintroduced Bandera as a hero who deserved to be honored like Vlasov.[82]

79 Moses Fishbein, "The Jewish Card in Russian Special Operations Against Ukraine: Paper delivered at the 26th Conference on Ukrainian Subjects at the University of Illinois at Urbana-Champaign, 24–27 June, 2009, http://www.vaadua.org/VaadENG/News%20eng-2009/fishbeyn2.htm (accessed 2 October 2009).

80 Alexandr Gogun, "Evrei v russkom osvoboditel'nom dvizhenii," *Korni*, No. 26 (April-June 2006): 180–88, http://lib.OUN-UPA.org.ua/gogun/pub08.html (accessed 25 September 2011). Gogun relied on Kirill Aleksandov, Ofitserskii korpus armii general-leitenanta A. A. Vlasova 1944–1945 gg. (Saint Petersburg: Russko-baltiiskii informatsionnyi tsentr BLITs, 2001).

81 Aleksandr Gogun and Aleksandr Vovk, "Evrei v bor'be za nezavisimuiu Ukrainu," *Korni*, No. 25 (January-March 2005): 133–41, http://lib.OUN-UPA.org.ua/gogun/pub07.html (accessed 1 December 2012).

82 Kirill Aleksandrov, "Bandera: postskryptum «moskal'skoho» istoryka," in *Strasti za Banderoiu*, ed. Tarik Cyril Amar, Ihor Balyns'kyi, and Iaroslav Hrytsak (Kiev: Hrani-T, 2010), 75, 77, 84–85, 88. For Gogun, see Gogun and Vovk, *"Evrei v bor'be,"* and Alexander Gogun, "Stepan Bandera—ein Freiheitskämpfer?" http://gedenkbibliothek.de/downloads/texte/vortragstexte/Dr_Alexander_Gogun (acces-

Iurii Mykhal'chyshyn, political scientist and official ideologist of the Svoboda Party, applied a rather different although no less problematical approach to the history of the OUN-UPA and Ukrainian nationalism. He did not deny the fascism of the OUN or the participation of the OUN-UPA in atrocities, nor did he claim that the UPA rescued Jews or that Jews patriotically fought for the Ukrainian state. The Svoboda ideologist approved of the OUN-UPA atrocities and OUN fascism and proudly insisted that the Holocaust was "a bright episode in European civilization."[83] After defending his PhD (*kandydat nauk*) thesis entitled "Transformation of a Political Movement into a Massive Political Party of a New Type: The Case of NSDAP and PNF (Comparative Analysis)" at the Department of Political Science at Ivan Franko University, Mykhal'chyshyn published a collection of essays on fascist ideology called *Vatra 1.0*.[84] He brought together the programs of the National Fascist Party of Italy and of the Social-National Party of Ukraine, and texts by Italian, German, and Ukrainian ideologists, such as Mykola Stsibors'kyi, Iarsolav Stets'ko, Joseph Goebbels, Ernst Röhm, and Alfred Rosenberg. On the website of the journal *Vatra: National–Revolutionary Journal*, Mykhal'chyshyn declared: "Our banner carriers and heroes [are] Ievhen Konvalets', ... Stepan Bandera, and Roman Shukhevych, Horst Wessel and Walther Stennes, Jose Antonio Primo de Rivera and Léon Degrelle, Corneliu Codreanu and Oswald Mosley, and thousands of other comrades."[85] Mykhal'chyshyn's approach to Ukrainian history confused many patriotic and "liberal" historians and intellectuals who were accustomed to deny the fascist tendencies of the OUN and atrocities committed by the OUN and UPA, or who understood Ukrainian nationalism to be a "national liberation movement."[86]

Bandera's Museums

Resurrection in Dubliany

During the academic year 1930–1931 and from the beginning of the next academic year until February 1932, Bandera lived in Dubliany, a town of about 10,000 people, very close to Lviv.[87] Sixty years later, this fact became extremely important to the citizens of this suburb of Lviv, in particular to the administration of the Lviv State Agrarian University (*L'vivs'kyi natsional'nyi ahrarnyi universytet*, LNAU). In 1993 a memorial plaque was unveiled at the student residence where Bandera lived for a short period.[88] Five years later, Petro Hots', a Lviv librarian and nationalist poet,

sed 24 October 2011). See also see Rossoliński-Liebe, Debating, Obfuscating and Disciplining the Holocaust, 209–14.

83 "Ukrainskii natsist: uchit'sua u KHAMASa terrorizmu i nenavisti k Izrailiu!" *Jewish News*, 6 June 2011, http://jn.com.ua/disasters/mikhalchishin_606.html (accessed 15 November 2011)

84 Iurii Mykhal'chyshyn, *Vatra. Versiia 1.0* (Lviv: Ievrosvit, 2010). See also Rudling, Return of the Ukrainian Far Right, 241.

85 "Nasha Vatra. Vatra. Natsional'-revoliutsiinyi chasopys" http://www.vatra.org.ua/nasha-vatra (accessed 15 November 2011).

86 See for example Taras Wosnjak, "Der Neonazismus und Swoboda," http://ukraine-nachrichten.de/neonazismus-swoboda_3361_politik?mid=51 (accessed 14 January 2012).

87 TsDIA, f. 371, op. 1, spr. 8, ed. 76, 34.

88 Petro Hots', *Muzei Stepana Bandery v Dublianakh* (Lviv: Krai, 2005), 1.

looking for a grant for the publication of his new collection of poems *The High Castle* (*Vysokyi zamok*), gave a copy of his manuscript to Volodymyr Snityns'kyi, the new director of the LNAU, a "Ukrainian patriot and a quite active, progressive person." Snityns'kyi grew up in the "nationally conscious village" of Kozivka where a Bandera bust had been unveiled in 1992.[89] In *The High Castle* the director of the LNAU discovered the poem "Stepan Bandera in Dubliany." It began with the phrases: "A student like all the rest, it seems: tempered in the village, with a village disposition ... [*Student, zdaietsia, iak i usi: Selians'kyi hart, selians'ka vdacha* ...]." The poem inspired Snityns'kyi to return Bandera's spirit to Dubliany. Snityns'kyi decided to set up a Bandera museum at the LNUA and asked Hots' to take the position of the director of this institution. He also set about erecting a Bandera monument in Dubliany on the campus of the LNAU.[90]

Hots' needed time to consider the offer because he was not a historian but a poet who had studied library science and philology and had worked for years as a librarian. He specialized in Ukrainian romantic literature and poetry and not in nationalism, fascism, antisemitism, or ethnic violence. Nevertheless, this did not prevent him from accepting the proposal and becoming director of the museum, not least because, as he wrote, "already in the third grade I was called a Banderite and nationalist."[91] He soon became involved in the subject of Bandera, although quite differently from the way a critical historian or museologist would have done. In 2003 Hots' published a small collection of poems devoted to the *Providnyk*, titled *Stepan's Birthday*.[92]

The museum was opened on 4 January 1999 and became the Stepan Bandera Museum: Centre of National-Patriotic Education (*Muzei Stepana Bandery: Tsentr natsional'no-patryiotychnoho vykhovannia*). During the opening ceremony, the museum was blessed by a priest from the Greek Catholic Church and one from the Ukrainian Autocephalous Orthodox Church. On the same day, the two priests also blessed an oblong black granite stone, which bore the inscription: "At this Place the Stepan Bandera Monument Will Be Erected." The stone was located in front of the old building of the LNAU, in the middle of a square where a monument to Lenin had stood. The opening ceremony of the museum and the blessing of the stone were attended by such personalities as Slava Stets'ko, Iurii Shukhevych, Vasyl' Kuk, and Ivan Hel', and by a group of UPA veterans with Bandera banners and blue-and-yellow and red-and-black flags.[93]

The actual monument was not unveiled until 2002. It was a statue about three and a half meters (eleven feet) high, prepared by the sculptor Iaroslav Loza, his son Volodymyr, and the architects Mykola Shpak and Volodymyr Bliusiuk. The statue

89 Bohdan Holovyn, "Sertse, spovnene liubovi, chynyt' liudiam lush dobro," *Z liuboviu do liudei: Z viroiu v Ukraïnu*, ed. Mykhailo Zubenets' (Lviv: LNAU, 2008), 87, 95–96.

90 Petro Hots', "Volodymyr Snityns'kyi—dukhovyi bat'ko muzeiu Stepana Bandery u Dublianakh," *Z liuboviu do liudei.*, ed. Zubenets', 194–95. For the poem, see Petro Hots' "Stepan Bandera u Dublianakh," *U Stepana urodyny* (Lviv: NVM PT UAD, 2003), 9.

91 Hots', Volodymyr Snityns'kyi, 196.

92 Petro Hots', *U Stepana—Urodyny: Poezii pro Stepana Banderu* (Lviv: NVM PT UAD, 2003).

93 Hots', Volodymyr Snityns'kyi, 197; Petro Hots', *Povernennia u bronzi*, brochure (Dubliany, 2001); Volodymyr Snityns'kyi, director of LNAU, interview by author, Dubliany, 2 June 2008; Hots', *Muzei Stepana Bandery*, 19.

showed Bandera wearing a suit and an unbuttoned knee-length coat. He was shown as a student in the early 1930s but in the pose of a thinker or romantic poet. His head and right leg were turned to the right, but his torso and left leg remained straight. He did not appear to be moving in the direction in which he was looking. His right hand was on his heart and he was holding a book in his left. The symbolism of the gesture suggested love for Ukraine and the Ukrainian people and a devotion to knowledge and science.[94]

At the unveiling on 5 October 2002, a number of nationalist activists appeared again in Dubliany. The monument was blessed by Greek Catholic and Orthodox priests. "It is an honor for us to unveil this monument at our academy where Stepan Bandera once studied," Snityns'kyi stated in his speech and continued:

> Not only the heroic UPA fighters who opposed the most powerful totalitarian regimes of the twentieth century, the Nazi and communist ones, were named after him but also all fighters for the independence of Ukraine in the following generations. Therefore the memory of him obliges us to self-sacrificing work in the name of the development of our state.[95]

Iurii Shukhevych stressed in his speech that, although Bandera had spent much time in Polish and German prisons, he had remained the spiritual leader of the UPA. He encouraged the gathering to remain faithful to Bandera's principles. Other prominent speakers included the leader of the Brotherhood of OUN-UPA Fighters, Oles' Humeniuk; the head of the Lviv KUN organization, Mykhailo Vovk; the head of the Lviv city council, Liubomyr Buniak; Bandera's relatives, Myroslava Shtumf and Zenovii Davydiuk, and a number of deputies, among them the radical right and populist politician Oleh Tiahnybok.[96] The artistic part of the celebration was performed by the vocal group Sokil, which recited the poem "Stepan Bandera" by Petro Hots'. The poem informed the celebrants that Bandera "was given to us by heaven as a symbol."[97] Some students were dressed in folk costumes and carried flowers to the monument. Other students lined the way to the monument. UPA veterans appeared at the ceremony in uniform, carrying blue-and-yellow and red-and-black flags, or Bandera banners.[98]

The Bandera museum opened in Dubliany in 1999 was located in two rooms in the new building of the LNAU. One room was about twelve square meters (130 square feet), the other about thirty square meters (323 square feet). According to Snityns'kyi the fundamental idea of the museum was the "personalization of [Ukrainian] history" by means of the Ukrainian *Providnyk* Stepan Bandera.[99] Hots', the director and sole employee of the museum, tried to accomplish this task by

94 Petro Hots', "Pam"iatnyk Stepanovi Banderi v Dublianakh," *Z liubov"iu do liudei*, ed. Zubenets', 221–24; Hots', *Povernennia u bronzi*.

95 "Vidkryttia pam"iatnyka Stepanovi Banderi u Dublianakh," *Visti. Hazeta L'vivs'koho Derzhavnoho Ahrarnoho Universytetu*, Dubliany, Vol. 32, No. 5 October (2002), 2.

96 Ibid, 2.

97 Hots', Pam"iatnyk Stepanovi Banderi, 226.

98 *Visti. Hazeta L'vivs'koho derzhavnoho ahrarnoho universytetu, Dubliany*, October 2002, No. 5 (32), 1, 2, 8.

99 Volodymyr Snityns'kyi, director of LNAU, Dubliany, interview by author, 2 June 2008.

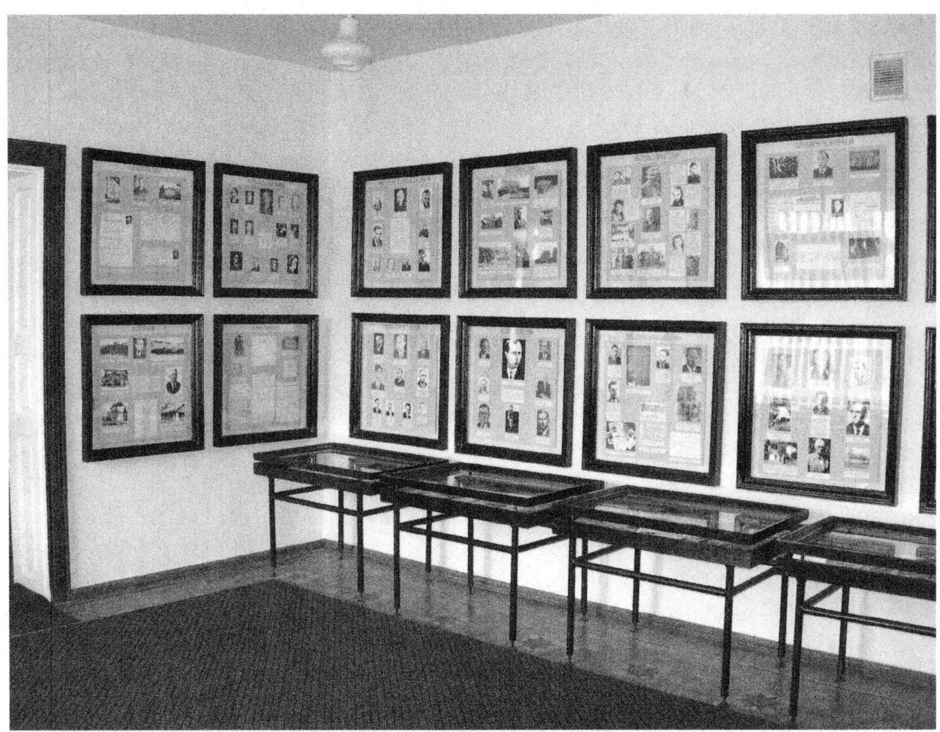

Fig. 54. Stepan Bandera Museum:
Centre of National-Patriotic Education in the LNAU in Dubliany.

embedding Bandera's biography in a narrative of Ukrainian history that was reduced to the "national-revolutionary liberation struggle for an independent Ukraine." This history was presented in the museum in twenty-four display cases, each of which contained pictures with a brief description. The majority of the pictures were photocopies of photographs printed in diaspora publications by OUN activists such as Mirchuk. The exhibition was divided into four parts: Bandera's youth and family, the student period, the OUN and UPA, and the assassination and rebirth. Each part was embedded in a narrative that characterized the Ukrainian people and the Ukrainian nationalists as victims, with the help of the history of the Bandera family. Parts of the exhibition paid special attention to the nationalists who studied in Dubliany. A descriptive analysis of the exhibition allows us to see how those who constructed it understood Bandera and intended to represent him (Fig. 54).

The first display case was devoted to Bandera's father Andrii. It depicted him as a person who lived a pious and spiritual life, struggled for Ukraine, helped shape the *Providnyk*, and died for Ukraine when he was executed by the Soviets in July 1941. It exhibited pictures of objects relating to Andrii Bandera, such as the church in which he served, and photocopies of archival documents reprinted in diaspora publications. The next display case held pictures of Bandera's three sisters and three brothers. Their pictures were located around one of the *Providnyk*. A further display case bore the inscription "The Tragic Fate of the Family" and exhibited pictures of Bandera's sisters and other relatives as well. The "tragic fate of the family" was also an essential component of guided tours through the museum. These were conducted by the director, Hots', who retired in 2007, and by his successor, Oksana Horda, a professor of Ukrainian studies at the LUAN. Like the OUN émigrés and post-Soviet nationalist historians on whom they based their knowledge, Hots' and Horda emphasized the suffering of the Bandera family in order to portray Ukrainians, and in particular Ukrainian nationalists, as victims of the Soviet and Nazi regimes. A display case titled "In the Home Village" contained pictures of the graves of Bandera's sister and mother, OUN and UPA members from Staryi Uhryniv, a village church, and Bandera among young Ukrainians in Staryi Uhryniv. Another one titled "Home Nest" indicated that, despite the "tragic fate," the Bandera family did not pass into oblivion. It held pictures of the first and third Bandera monuments in Staryi Uhryniv, a piece of the destroyed first monument, the old and rebuilt building of the Bandera museum in Staryi Uhryniv, a memorial plaque in the house of Bandera's birth, a well close to the house of Bandera's family in Staryi Uhryniv, and a rebuilt chapel close to the building.[100]

The section of the exhibition relating to Bandera's education indicated that, after Ukraine became independent, the spirit of the *Providnyk* returned to his former educational institutions. A picture of the high school in Stryi attended by Bandera in the 1920s showed a monument to the *Providnyk* in front of the building. Other pictures showed Bandera's fellow-pupils who became OUN members, such as Stepan Lenkavs'kyi, Zenon Kossak, and Stepan Okhrymovych. Another display case showed the student residence where Bandera lived in Lviv, the Polytechnic building in Lviv, and Bandera's course record books. Two further display cases, devoted to his studies in Lviv and Dubliany, showed various student residences and local houses in which Bandera lived or ate, the Bandera monument at the campus of the LNAU, and also Iosyf Tushnyts'kyi, a local resident who claimed to remember the legendary nationalist student. The director placed his poem "Stepan Bandera in Dubliany" among the pictures. All in all, this part of the exhibition made it clear that the places that were once touched by Bandera's foot were to remain special. Students were to be made aware that the young *Providnyk* and "freedom fighter" studied, lived, or dined in them.

The part of the exhibition devoted to the revolutionary struggle of the OUN began with a display case titled "Those Who Sacrificed Their Lives for Ukraine." It included Ol'ha Basarab, the first UVO member who became a famous martyr; Mykola Lemyk, who assassinated the secretary of the Soviet consulate; Hryhorii Matseiko, Pieracki's assassin, and other OUN martyrs and heroes. A further display case introduced the arrest of Bandera in 1934 and the trials in Warsaw and Lviv. It displayed a picture of the student residence where Bandera was arrested, copies of documents, and a picture of Lviv University, which it erroneously described as the "building of the district court in which many Ukrainian nationalists were sentenced." A visitor interested in learning why Bandera was arrested and sentenced or what happened during the trials in Warsaw and Lviv did not find any such information in the exhibition.

100 I attended three guided tours through the musem. Two were conducted by Petro Hots' (one in 2004 and one in 2006), and the third one by Oksana Horda on 16 May 2008.

The display case titled "The Renewal of the Ukrainian State" bore in the middle an amended version of the "Act of the Renewal of the Ukrainian State of 30 June 1941." The exhibited version omitted the phrase about close collaboration with "National Socialist Great Germany, which under the leadership of Adolf Hitler, is creating a new order in Europe."[101] Pictures of such OUN members as Stets'ko, Lebed', Shukhevych, Klymiv, and Rebet surrounded the fabricated text. The display case devoted to the OUN task forces who marched through Ukraine after the German attack on the Soviet Union showed pictures of some members of these units, such as Klymyshyn and Stakhiv. Like the previous case, it did not contain any information about the fascistization of the OUN, its collaboration with Nazi Germany, its involvement in the pogroms of July 1941, or its attempts to establish a fascist state that the OUN-B wanted to "cleanse" of non-Ukrainians.

As in the London museum, the UPA occupied an important place in the Dubliany museum, although Bandera never led or even joined this army, was only its spiritual leader, and had a rather marginal impact on its policies. In the middle of one display case devoted to the nationalist insurgents, the creator of the museum placed the portrait of UPA partisan Danylo Kuz'mins'kyi, a graduate of the Lviv Polytechnic and its branch in Dubliany. The portrait was surrounded by pictures of other UPA partisans, with very brief descriptions containing names, pseudonyms, and dates and places of birth. Another display case introduced the medical service of the UPA. It presented a number of portraits of mainly female UPA partisans who tended the wounded partisans, and a picture of a priest behind sickbeds. The picture was described as a UPA hospital. The inscriptions informed visitors how many years a particular UPA member spent in Soviet prisons or Gulag for serving in the UPA. A further display case exhibited UPA propaganda. It showed portraits of propaganda officers such as Petro Fedun, photocopies of propaganda documents, the text of the oath of a UPA partisan, and a picture of a partisan taking an oath in 1944. The last UPA display case introduced the UPA leaders, with Kliachkivs'kyi and Shukhevych in the center. The ethnic and political violence conducted by the UPA under the leadership of Kliachkivs'kyi and Shukhevych was not included in the exhibition. Unlike the OUN and UPA atrocities, the NKVD crimes were not omitted. On the contrary, this part of the exhibition contained quite a quantity of text and explained extensively how the Soviet police mistreated and killed Ukrainian civilians and destroyed the nationalist underground. The exhibition interrelated these atrocities with the assassination of Bandera, which symbolized the suffering of Ukraine and the most tragic moment in its history.

The last part of the exhibition portrayed Bandera's life in exile, his funeral, and his resurrection in independent Ukraine. One display case showed pictures of Bandera with journalists, and his journalist identification cards. Another featured pictures that presented Bandera as a father who loved his wife and children, a man who liked to joke with friends, and a devoted politician who never ceased working on the

101 For the original document, see "Akt proholoshennia ukraïns'koï derzhavy," 30 June 1941, TsDAVOV f. 3833, op. 1, spr. 5, 3.

Ukrainian revolution. The display case devoted to the assassination and funeral presented pictures of the large cross on Bandera's grave in Munich, and a picture of the *Providnyk's* death mask. The last two display cases familiarized visitors with recent history, in particular Bandera's post-Soviet rebirth. One of them contained a poem by Hots', dedicated to the *Providnyk*, titled "This Man Was an Entire Era." The poem was surrounded by pictures of Bandera monuments in Stryi, Staryi Uhryniv, Boryslav, and several other western Ukrainian locations.

The narrative of the exhibition suggested that Bandera had been resurrected in Ukraine because he led the "national liberation struggle," fell in the struggle for Ukraine's independence, and became the symbol of an entire epoch of heroes and martyrs. The selectiveness of the exhibition narrative, in particular the omission of the atrocities committed by the OUN and UPA, was necessary to portray Bandera and the "Bandera generation" as brave and tragic heroes. Bandera's family played an important part in the exhibition because many of its members suffered at the hands of the Soviet and Nazi regimes. The family history strengthened the narrative of victimization and enabled the museum visitors to identify with the OUN and UPA as victims of the two regimes.

In addition to the mounted display cases, the museum also exhibited various objects in twelve standing display cases, and on a table and a chair located in the smaller room, which was also the office of the museum director. A considerable number of the exhibited objects were nationalist publications about Bandera and the OUN and UPA, which had appeared in the diaspora or in Ukraine after 1991. Some of them lay open in the display cases and showed photographs of Shelepin and Stashyns'kyi and the order that Stashyns'kyi received from Shelepin to murder Bandera. Other items included various devotional objects, such as posters, stamps, plates, postcards, and calendars with pictures of Bandera monuments, museums, and memorial plaques. A small bust, a videotape of Oles' Ianchuk's film *Assassination: An Autumn Murder in Munich*, and a UPA uniform were another significant part of the exhibition. Issues of the newspaper *News from the Stepan Bandera Museum in Dubliany*, a portrait of the LNAU rector Snityns'kyi, pictures of some famous visitors, newspaper articles about Bandera and his family, pictures of diaspora commemorations at Bandera's grave, diaspora journals such as *Vyzvol'nyi shliakh*, brochures of such neo-fascist organizations as the "social-nationalist organization" Patriot Ukraïny, and pictures and figures of saints were located among the diaspora publications or between the display cases.

The exhibits were collected in order to refute the Soviet image of Bandera and to invent a contradictory one, which however, despite its positive nature, very much resembled the Soviet version. A closer look at the exhibition, the arrangement of exhibits, and the director's narrative suggest that some of the items such as soil, a symbol of ethnic nationalism, were regarded as particularly important. The soil—from Staryi Uhryniv, the birthplace of the *Providnyk*—was exhibited in a small bowl, which stands among pictures of Bandera's blood-stained suit, and a tape with his voice. Other very significant objects were the pictures of Bandera's grandson Stephen (Stepan) who, after 1991, became a kind of reincarnated *Providnyk* and a new star of Ukrainian nationalism. He was frequently invited as an honored guest to monument unveilings and museum openings, and other nationalist celebrations.

Fig. 55. Central Composition in the Stepan Bandera Museum: Centre of National-Patriotic Education in the LNAU in Dubliany.

The guided tour through the museum was based on the exhibits and the exhibited publications. The guides, Petro Hots' and Oksana Horda,[102] concentrated on the Bandera family and the person of Stepan Bandera, in particular on their suffering under the Soviet regime. Bandera was presented as a person who objected to alcoholism and smoking, in order to give a good example to the students of the LUAN. A typewriter used by the UPA was introduced by Horda as one on which members of the "Ukrainian national revolutionary liberation movement" wrote leaflets to discourage alcoholism and smoking, which were introduced to Ukraine by the Poles and Russians. She also pointed out that in Soviet times people believed that the OUN-UPA used typewriters to produce lists of people whom they planned to execute, but according to her, it was obviously not true. Although the OUN and UPA were an important part of the guided museum narrative, the mass violence practiced by them was

102 I attended three guided tours through the museum, the first one in 2004 and the second one in 2006 led by Petro Hots', the first director of the museum. The third one in 2008 was led by Oksana Horda, the second director. The three tours did not differ considerably.

Fig. 56. P. Zaichenko's portrait of Stepan Bandera in the Stepan Bandera Museum: Centre of National-Patriotic Education in the LNAU in Dubliany.

not mentioned during the guided tours. Only the museum booklet mentioned that Bandera was involved in "assassinations of enemies of the Ukrainian nation," without providing any details about the enemies or why they had to be killed.[103]

The religious components of the museum were noticeable not only in the pictures and figures of saints but also on the altar-like composition on the central wall of the museum (Fig. 55). The composition included a miniature of the statue at the Bandera monument in Dubliany, which stood, with flowers, on a 1.5-meter-high (five-foot) flower stand. Behind the stand, red-and-black and blue-and-yellow flags were fixed to the wall and formed a V. Between the flags, above the Bandera statue hung a portrait of a person, who to some extent resembles Bandera, but could just as well depict somebody else (Fig. 56). The museum directors and Snityns'kyi, who purchased the portrait, claimed that the portrait depicted Bandera, although the physiognomy of the person does not necessarily confirm this assumption. Also the inscription "P. Zaichenko, 1945" and Snityns'kyi's claim that Bandera posed for the portrait, being at

103 Hots', *Muzei Stepana Bandery v Dublianakh*, 11, 18; Bandera, Moï zhyttiepysni dani, 5.

Fig. 57. The scene of blessing the "foundation stone" for the Bandera monument in Dubliany by Mykola Horda.

that time in western Ukraine, do not confirm it. They rather suggest that someone else took the place of the *Providnyk* in the most symbolic part of the museum.

Another central historical painting in the museum portrayed the scene of blessing the "foundation stone" for the Bandera monument in Dubliany on 4 January 1999. Its author Mykola Horda had worked before 1991 as an artist in a Soviet factory. After 1991 he began painting various Ukrainian nationalist motifs. In 1999 he was asked by Hots', the director of the Bandera museum, whether he would be willing to prepare a historical painting for the museum. As the Bandera monument in Dubliany was under construction at that time, Hots' decided to immortalize the noble scene of blessing the black granite foundation stone. The source for the painting was a dull and unimpressive photograph of the Greek Catholic priest blessing the stone. However, with the help of Hots', Horda provided it with much symbolism and transformed it into an emotive and symbolic painting (Fig. 57).[104]

In the center of the painting, Horda placed the Greek Catholic and Orthodox priests, together with Snityns'kyi holding a microphone. On the table next to the black granite stone and in front of the priests, the painter immortalized the red fruits of the guelder rose, which is one of the most significant symbols of Ukraine, a can of earth from Bandera's home village, and a plastic bag with earth from Bandera's grave. At the sides and behind the three central figures, a number of other personalities appear, some of whom, such as the Bandera biographer Hordasevych, did not attend the ceremony but were included because of their symbolic significance. On one side of Snityns'kyi, Horda painted the head of Slava Stets'ko in a fur cap; on the other, the head of Iurii Shukhevych, one of the few who appeared in the original photograph. Between Stets'ko and the Greek Catholic priest, the painter placed Vasyl' Kuk, former commander of the UPA, and Oleksandr Semkovych, professor at the

104 Mykola Horda, interview by author, Lviv, 16 May 2008.

LNAU. Between the two priests he included the poet Oles' Angeliuk, and further to the right of the Orthodox priest, the poet Ivan Hubka, Hordasevych, and finally the poet Ivan Hnatiuk with the Black Book of Ukraine, which symbolizes the crimes of the Soviet regime and the suffering of the Ukrainian nation. Horda also immortalized the sculptor Iaroslav Loza, a few professors of the LUAN, UPA veterans, and two children, one of whom seems to be enjoying the ceremony. To the left of Snityns'kyi and Shukhevych, the artist located the museum director Hots', staring, like Stets'ko and Hordasevych, directly at the painter. With him are the nationalist dissident Ivan Hel', a boy holding the university edition of Hordasevych's *Stepan Bandera: Human and Myth*, and Anzhela Kuza, professor of Ukrainian language and literature at the LUAN, whose husband complained to the painter that his wife was really much more beautiful than in the painting and asked him to repaint her image several times.[105]

Although the museum was not located in Lviv but in a small suburb, it was not completely unnoticed. In December 2007, eight years after the opening, the museum newspaper wrote that 43,000 people had visited the museum, among them several dozen local and national politicians.[106] Every first-grade student of the LANU made a two-hour excursion to this nationalist temple.[107] The museum did not have an internet presence, but the Bandera monument was presented next to the university logo at the official website of the LANU.[108]

Volia Zaderevats'ka and Staryi Uhryniv

In addition to the museum in Dubliany, two other museums devoted to the *Providnyk* were opened in the 1990s: one in Volia Zaderevats'ka on 14 October 1990, and a second in Staryi Uhryniv in 1993.[109] The museum in Volia Zaderevats'ka was opened on 14 October 1990 in the house in which Bandera's family lived between 1933 and 1936. The house was in the immediate vicinity of the church where Bandera's father worked as a priest for a few years. The museum was established by the dissident movement Rukh and by OUN member Zynovii Krasivs'kyi. In 1995 Mykhailo Balabans'kyi, graduate of a music school, became the director. Like Hots', Balabans'kyi defined his historical education as nationalism. "There is a very strong nationalism in my soul," he said in an interview. As a child, he sewed caps for the UPA partisans and later read Soviet publications on the OUN-UPA, which infuriated him. In 1997 in front of the museum, Balabans'kyi built a Bandera monument, which consisted of an oversized head of Bandera, placed on a rock. Five years later, he built a "boulevard for the fighters for Ukraine" (*aleia bortsiv za Ukraïnu*), which leads visitors from the gate to the museum door. The boulevard consisted of six white concrete plates, each about 2.5 meters (eight feet) high. One of them held a short quotation from Petliura,

105 Mykola Horda, interview by author, Lviv, 16 May 2008.
106 "Z litopysu zhyttia muzeiu," *Visti Muzeiu Stepana Bandery v Dublianakh*, December 2007, 1.
107 Oksana Horda, interview by author, Dubliany, 14 May 2008.
108 http://lnau.lviv.ua/ (accessed 31 August 2011).
109 A further museum, which I did not inspect, was opened in early 2008 in the former premises of the high school in Stryi, attended by Bandera in the 1920s, now used by School number 7. This museum is called the Stepan Bandera Virtual Museum. See http://school7.ho.ua/virtual_museum.html (accessed 16 September 2011).

and five other concrete plates held cast bronze portraits of Petliura, Konovalets', Shukhevych, Stets'ko, and Oleksa Hasyn.[110]

The exhibit at the museum does not differ substantially from that in Dubliany. The family history was embedded in the history of the "national-revolutionary liberation movement." Among the exhibits were various OUN-UPA propaganda materials, a typewriter on which "anti-Bolshevik leaflets" were drafted, a few pieces of furniture that belonged to the Bandera family, portraits of Ukrainian nationalists, pieces of clothing that belonged to Bandera's father, uniforms of UPA partisans, and portraits of various saints. The director of the museum informed me that "people come to the museum as to a church."[111]

The main Bandera museum in Ukraine was built in Staryi Uhryniv, Bandera's birthplace. The museum was originally located in a small house with a memorial plaque: "Stepan Bandera, The Great Son of Ukraine, the Leader of the OUN, Was Born in this House." In 2000 the museum moved to a new and eye-catching three-story building built in a Carpathian style close to the old museum building and the Bandera monument. It included a café, conference room, library, and archive. The exhibition in the new museum was no less ideological than the exhibitions in Dubliany and Volia Zaderevats'ka. The main difference was the size and number of collected objects. Unlike the other two, the Staryi Uhryniv museum possessed a collection of archival documents from the 1920s and 1930s and some original personal documents of Bandera, such as his IDs from the 1940s and 1950s. The Staryi Uhryniv museum also edited its own journal, *Bandera's Country* (*Banderivs'kyi krai*), in which various academic and political articles appeared.[112]

The Bandera museums were erected in the eastern Galician part of Ukraine, to popularize the Bandera cult, promote nationalism, and strengthen the nationalist version of Ukrainian identity. Their heroic aesthetics resembled the former Soviet museums devoted to the heroes of the Soviet Union, although they opposed the former Soviet narratives. In contrast to the London museum, the Ukrainian museums paid much attention to the Bandera family and not only to the *Providnyk* and the OUN-UPA. This element was particularly important in the museum in Volia Zaderevats'ka, which was set up in the former house of the Bandera family. The museums used the family extensively as an exhibition motif, because its suffering fortified the nationalist victimization narrative. It also enabled the visitors to better identify with Bandera and the Ukrainian nationalists. The museum exhibitions, similarly to Bandera's hagiographies, did not address the question of Bandera's world view, the OUN ideology and the atrocities committed by the OUN and UPA. Religion was very visible and significant in all post-Soviet Bandera museums. It merged with nationalism and transformed the museums into shrines promoting nationalism and denial.

110 Mykhailo Balabans'kyi, *Muzei-Sadyba Stepana Bandery v seli Volia-Zaderevats'ka* (Volia Zaderevats'ka, 2000), 91.

111 Mykhailo Balabans'kyi, interview by author, Volia Zaderevats'ka, 9 May 2008.

112 I visited the museum in 2004 and 2008.

Bandera Streets, Plaques and Monuments

Renaming streets and erecting plaques and monuments in honor of Bandera has been another important form of the Bandera cult in post-Soviet Ukraine. Such streets, monuments, and plaques have been used to mark areas of public space, to indicate change in the political system, or to honor the *Providnyk*, his followers, and his revolutionary ideas. Ukrainian nationalist monuments and street names are intended to indicate that public space, after centuries of "national liberation struggle," finally belongs to the Ukrainians. They also invite Ukrainians to identify themselves with Bandera, and to understand themselves to be Banderites, even half a century after the death of the *Providnyk*. The erection of monuments and renaming of streets is also a part of the invention of a new collective identity—an anti-Soviet, anticommunist, anti-Russian, Ukrainian nationalist identity. The Soviet authorities understood this process and continued to destroy the first nationalist monuments before leaving western Ukraine.

The first Bandera monument, as already described, was erected in Staryi Uhryniv on 14 October 1990. It was prepared quickly in semi-underground conditions by local nationalist activists and dissidents. Its unveiling ceremony attracted about 10,000 people who listened to the speeches, waved blue-and-yellow or red-and-black flags and sang OUN-UPA songs. After the first monument was blown up on 30 December 1990, the next one was unveiled on 30 June 1991. The unveiling again attracted about 10,000 people and the demolition took place on 10 July 1991. The third, a bronze statue recast from a Lenin statue, was unveiled on 17 August 1992 and has remained until the time of writing this book.[113]

During the following two decades, far-right activists and local politicians unveiled a number of Bandera monuments, busts, and plaques in the three eastern Galician oblasts of Ukraine: Lviv, Ivano-Frankivs'k, and Ternopil'. Some of the locations in these three oblasts were Berezhany, Beriv, Boryslav, Chervonohrad, Drohobych, Dubliany, Hrabivka, Ivano-Frankivs'k, Kolomyia, Kozivka, Lviv, Krements, Mykytynytsi, Mostys'ka, Sambir, Stryi, Stusiv, Terebovlia, Ternopil', Volia Zaderevats'ka, and Zalishchyky. Some monuments were unveiled in 1991, as in Kolomyia, others in 1992 as in Stryi, several around 1999, the year of the ninetieth anniversary of Bandera's birth and the fortieth of his death, as in Drohobych and Dubliany, and a number were built ten years afterwards, around the hundredth anniversary of his birth and the fiftieth of his death, as in Ivano-Frankivs'k (Fig. 58), Lviv (Fig. 59), and Ternopil'. Some of them were located in symbolic places. In Drohobych, for example, the Bandera statue was constructed in the zone of the former Jewish ghetto, and in Ivano-Frankivs'k in European Square, between Bandera and Konovalets' Streets. All Bandera monuments are located in the three oblasts of Ivano-Frankivs'k, Lviv, and Ternopil', which are the territory of the former eastern Galicia. Nevertheless, cities outside these three oblasts, such as Rivne and Luts'k, Chernivtsi in Bukovina, and Kiev, also considered erecting Bandera monuments shortly before or after the

113 Stepan Lesiv, interview by author, Staryi Uhryniv, 18 May 2008. See below the subsection "The First Bandera Monument in Ukraine."

Fig. 58. The Bandera monument in Ivano-Frankivs'k unveiled on 1 January 2009.

hundredth anniversary of his birth and fiftieth of his death, in 2009. The initiative toerect Bandera monuments outside eastern Galicia frequently came from far-right organizations and parties like Tryzub and Svoboda, which, unlike in eastern Galicia, did not belong to the political mainstream.[114]

Some municipal and oblast councils, not only in eastern Ukraine, categorically dismissed proposals to erect a Bandera monument. The city council of Uzhhorod, capital of the Zakarpattia Oblast, which in the interwar period was a part of Czechoslovakia, rejected the proposal of the Council of the Ternopil' Oblast to erect a Bandera monument in Uzhhorod, with the argument that "we do not share the fascination with the personality and the attempt to idealize the citizen of the Austrian-Hungarian Empire Stepan Bandera. We are a multinational oblast and thus we consider agitation for any radical actions as outrageous."[115]

Naming streets after Bandera and other Ukrainian nationalists became a very popular activity after 1991. It was even more popular than the erection of monuments, because of the difference in cost. Western Ukrainian cities outside eastern Galicia, such as Kovel' and Volodymyr-Volyns'kyi, which did not erect monuments to the *Providnyk*, named streets after him. In some locations, a street named after him

114 For Bandera monuments, see the exhibition of the Bandera museum in Dubliany. On Drohobych, see Omer Bartov, *Erased: Vanishing Traces of Jewish Galicia in Present-Day Ukraine* (Princeton: Princeton University Press, 2007), 208. On Ivano-Frankivs'k, see "V Ivano-Frankivs'ku v urochystii obstanovtsi vidkryly pam"iatnyk providnykovi OUN Stepanu Banderi," 2 January 2009, http://vidgolos.com/623-v-ivano-frankivsku-v-urochistijj-obstanovci.html (accessed 17 October 2011).

115 "V Uzhorodi vidmovliaiut'sia stavyty pam"iatnyk Banderi, 10 April 2009, http://www.unian.net/ukr/news/news-310592.html (accessed 17 October 2011).

would lead to his monument or to another important nationalist monument. In addition to Bandera monuments, local nationalist activists also erected many monuments and plaques devoted to other OUN members and UPA partisans and named streets after them as well. Events from the history of Ukrainian nationalism, such as the Act of 30 June 1941, were displayed on plaques, for instance on the Prosvita building in the Lviv Rynok square. In Lviv, two streets were even named after the same UPA leader: one became Roman Shukhevych Street and the other General Chuprynka Street, derived from Shukhevych's nom de guerre.

Among the other Ukrainian "heroes" from the OUN or UPA who were given monuments, were war criminals such as Dmytro Kliachkivs'kyi, who initiated the ethnic cleansing in Volhynia in early 1943. One monument devoted to Kliachkivs'kyi was unveiled in Zbarazh in 1995 and another one in Rivne in 2002. In addition, a number of streets were named after him. Without permission, Ukrainian nationalists also erected monuments in the Polish Beskids in order to commemorate the UPA partisans who fell in 1947, fighting against Polish soldiers. In 2007 the Main Department for Tourism and Culture in the Administration of the Ivano-Frankivs'k Oblast released a tourist guide called *On the Paths of the Ukrainian Insurgent Army*, with the help of which one could travel for weeks, if not months, from one OUN-UPA monument to another, or from a UPA museum to a Bandera museum, or stay in towns and cities walking only through streets with nationalist names.[116]

In Munich, a memorial plaque in German and Ukrainian was unveiled in the name of President Iushchenko, on the facade of the ZCh OUN building at Zeppelinstrasse 67, in honor of Iaroslav and Iaroslava Stets'ko.[117] In 2002 the Lviv Regional State Administration established a commission to build a lane for prominent Ukrainians at the Lychakivs'kyi cemetery in Lviv, where it was planned that Bandera, Konovalets', and Mel'nyk were to be reinterred. The commission intended to complete the work by 2008 but the plan did not work out.[118] In early 2008, the Council of the Ternopil' Oblast expressed its intention to reinter Bandera in Staryi Uhryniv in 2009.[119]

The largest Bandera monument was erected in Lviv. It took several years to accomplish this task, which was initiated shortly after the collapse of the Soviet Union, when a massive grey stone with the inscription "A Monument to Stepan Bandera Will Stand Here" was placed in Kropyvnyts'kyi Square next to the neo-gothic building of the former Roman Catholic Elisabeth Church. The square lies on Horodots'ka Street, one of the main streets in Lviv, connecting the center with the railway station. On the other side of the square is Bandera Street, which has borne this name since 1992. It connects the Bandera monument with the Polytechnic, where Bandera studied in the

116 Cf. R. Handziuk, *Stezhkamy Ukraïns'koï Povstans'koï Armiï: Turystychnyi Putivnyk* (Ivano-Frankivs'k: Misto NV, 2007). For the UPA monuments in Poland, see Józef Matusz, "Nielegalnie czczą pamięć UPA," *Rzeczpospolita*, 18 October 2008, http://www.rp.pl/artykul/206382.html (accessed 15 October 2011).

117 There is a slight discrepancy between the German text, which contains the word "Freiheit" (freedom), and the Ukrainian text, which uses "samostiinist'" (independence).

118 "Na Lychakivs'komu kladovyshchi pokhovaiut' ostanky zhertv komunistychnykh represii," 23 October 2006, http://ua.korrespondent.net/ukraine/277943 (accessed 12 October 2011).

119 "Zemliaky Bandery za perekhovannia Bandery v ridnomu seli," 27 January 2008, http://h.ua/story/80500/ (accessed 17 October 2011).

early 1930s. Bandera Street also connects the monument with Ievhen Konovalets' Street and General Chuprynka Street. One reason for choosing Kropyvnyts'kyi Square as a location for a Bandera monument was, according to its planners, to signal to visitors of Lviv that they are in the "Bandera city," in Ukrainian "Bandershtat."[120]

The process of setting up the monument was initiated and conducted by the Society to Erect the Stepan Bandera Monument (*Komitet iz sporudzhennia pam"iatnyka Stepanu Banderi*, KiSPSB) whose head, from 2002 until the opening of the monument in 2007, was Andrii Parubii, one of the founders of the ultranationalist SNPU, in 2006 a deputy in the Lviv oblast council (*L'vivs'ka oblasna rada*) and, since 2007, a deputy in the Ukrainian Parliament as a member of the *Nasha Ukraïna* (Our Ukraine) Party. The KiSPSB included such organizations as the Brotherhood of OUN-UPA Fighters, the Union of Political Prisoners, Prosvita, and, according to Parubii, the "whole intelligentsia of Lviv."[121]

Unlike in other cities, the process of erecting the monument in Lviv took several years. First the KiSPSB organized seven competitions, which took ten years. It was only in 2002 that the KiSPSB chose a project by the architects Mykhailo Fedyk and Iurii Stoliarov, the sculptor Mykhailo Prosikira, and the builder Hryhorii Shevchuk. The project was not only a Bandera figure on a pedestal but a kind of complex, mixing monumental fascist and post-Soviet aesthetics. One element of the complex was a statue of Bandera, 4.2 meters (fourteen feet) high, which was placed on a granite pedestal 1.8 meters (six feet) high, with a golden inscription of the name Stepan Bandera. The second element in the monument was a "triumphal arch," 28.5 meters (ninety-four feet) high, which, according to Parubii, would "render the spirit of that [Bandera] epoch" and, according to the architect Fedyk, was "post-modern." The actual plan was to erect an arch thirty meters (ninety-eight feet) high, in order to achieve the size of the highest Soviet monument in Lviv, the Glory Monument from 1970, which honors the Red Army.[122]

As in Dubliany, the designers of the Lviv monument decided to place Bandera's right hand on his heart. His left arm hangs down with a clenched fist. Bandera appears to be about twenty-five years old. He is dressed in an open coat, a suit, and a tie. His face appears thoughtful. The wind, which moves the lower edges of his coat slightly backward and to the right, gives some dynamic to the statue. The attic of the triumphal arch bears a gold trident. The four columns of the triumphal arch symbolize four epochs in the history of the Ukrainian nation: the Kievan Rus' and the Kingdom of Galicia and Volhynia, the Cossack epoch, the 1917–1920 struggle and the short existence of the ZUNR, and finally, the period after the collapse of the Soviet Union.[123]

120 Grzegorz Rossoliński, "Bandera und Nikifor—zwei Modernen in einer Stadt: Die 'nationalbürgerliche' und die 'weltbürgerliche' Moderne in Lemberg," ed. Lutz Henke, Grzegorz Rossoliński, and Philipp Ther, *Eine neue Gesellschaft in einer alten Stadt* (Wrocław: ATUT, 2007), 116. Parubii said in an interview that the massive grey stone was placed in 1991. The paper *L'vivs'ka hazeta* wrote that it was only in 1993. See Lidiia Mel'nyk, "Monumental'ni prystrasti," *L'vivs'ka hazeta*, 25 March 2004, 5.

121 Rossoliński, Bandera und Nikifor, 115.

122 Ibid., 117–18.

123 Rossoliński, Bandera und Nikifor, 118; Lidiia Mel'nyk, "Monumental'ni Prystrasti," *L'vivs'ka Hazeta*, 25 March 2004, 5.

Bandera was placed in front of the triumphal arch with historical plaques because he was, according to Parubii and Fedyk, the most important person in Ukrainian history. Bandera's "revolutionary methods," according to Parubii, should not be condemned, because they corresponded with the epoch in which he lived. Moreover, since every nation has a right to a "liberation struggle," other nations should not interfere in the traditions, culture, and internal affairs of this particular nation but should allow this community to celebrate every kind of hero and to approve of this invention of a heroic tradition.[124]

The Lviv Bandera monument was unveiled on 13 October 2007, the sixty-fifth anniversary of the founding of the UPA. At that time, the construction of the complex was not entirely finished. The statue was on the pedestal but the triumphal arch behind the monument consisted only of a steel framework. It lacked the granite slabs and was therefore covered by two red-and-black and two blue-and-yellow pieces of cloth. Celebrants with orange flags of Our Ukraine, flags of the Svoboda Party, flags of various regional KUN branches and several other nationalist parties, organizations, and unions, and naturally blue-and-yellow and red-and-black flags, surrounded the monument. In the immediate vicinity of the celebrants stood UPA veterans in uniforms that must have been designed and sewn after 1990, as the UPA did not have standard uniforms in the 1940s. Several dozen young people in Plast uniforms and in plain clothes also came to the ceremony. Some celebrants carried Bandera banners or held books such as Tsar's Bandera hagiography, *For What We Love Bandera*. Between the speeches that were delivered, a group of men, in historical, possibly seventeenth-century outfits, fired volleys from rifles and pistols.[125]

The monument, covered with a white sheet, was unveiled by the head of the KiSPSB, Andrii Parubii; the head of the KiSPSB from 1998 till 2002, Iaroslav Pitko; the founder of the KiSPSB, Iaroslav Svatko; the head of the Brotherhood of OUN-UPA Fighters, Oles' Humeniuk, and the head of the twenty-third Stepan Bandera Plast troop, Mykola Muzala (Fig. 59). After Parubii pulled the sheet down, a military band started playing the Ukrainian anthem "Ukraine has not yet perished," the crowd began singing, and a row of six soldiers fired volleys. After the anthem, the speaker asked a representative of the Plast troop to place earth from Bandera's home village Staryi Uhryniv, and from his grave in Munich, under a slab in front of the monument. As the young celebrant was performing this symbolic act, the speaker read the "Decalogue of a Ukrainian Nationalist." He read the seventh commandment as "You will not hesitate to commit the most dangerous task if the good of the cause requires it" and not "the greatest crime" as Lenkavs'kyi, the author of the Decalogue, conceptualized it. Between the speeches and ceremonial acts, a male choir in embroidered shirts and jackets sang nationalist songs.[126]

Religion was deeply integrated in the ceremony of opening the monument. Priests of the Greek Catholic Church, the Ukrainian Orthodox Church, and the Ukrainian Autocephalous Orthodox Church prayed for several minutes. Then, a Greek Catholic

124 Rossoliński, Bandera und Nikifor, 119.

125 Documentary on the unveiling ceremony broadcast by Lviv Television on 13 October 2007; Tsar, *Za shcho*.

126 Documentary on the unveiling ceremony broadcast by Lviv Television on 13 October 2007.

Fig. 59. The singing of the Ukrainian national anthem during the unveiling ceremony of the Stepan Bandera monument on 13 October 2007 in Lviv.

priest addressed the crowd and introduced Bandera as a religious man who was not indifferent to the injustice his people suffered and who decided to liberate them. Talking about Bandera during the Second World War, the priest stressed that Bandera was arrested by the Germans and that his brothers were killed by Poles who worked for the Gestapo in Auschwitz.

The clergymen from the two other churches spoke in the same spirit, carefully omitting all elements that could cast a poor light on the *Providnyk* or his movement. One of them stated, “The Ukrainian government will only become democratic when it will act as Bandera and his fellows did.” Further, he referred to the OUN-UPA members as disciples who served the holy idea of an independent Ukraine, and finished his speech with “We pray that no intruder ever sets foot on our sacred Ukrainian soil” and shouted “Slava Ukraïni!” The crowd answered “Glory to the Heroes!”[127]

After the clergymen’s speeches, soldiers in white uniforms placed huge bouquets of blue and yellow flowers in front of the monument. Their donors were, as the speaker announced, such politicians as President Iushchenko and Andrii Sadovyi,

127 Ibid.

mayor of Lviv. Organizations like Plast and the veterans of the UPA also placed their bouquets in front of the monument. The speaker honored the "UPA fighters who died for the independence of Ukraine" and the "UPA fighters who struggled for the independence of Ukraine and are today together with us." He ended every announcement with a loud "Glory!" The crowd responded with "Glory, Glory, Glory!"[128]

Petro Oliinyk, head of the Lviv regional state administration, referred to Bandera as the *Providnyk* and claimed that he was "an example of how to serve the Ukrainian nation ... [and how to] be a patriot." He added that "we had dreamt of having a president who would recognize the UPA ... and yesterday the President of Ukraine signed an order that approved the celebration of the sixty-fifth anniversary of the UPA," which the crowd applauded. Oliinyk finished his speech with "Glory to the people who contributed to the erection of the monument! Glory to the [UPA] veterans! Glory to the best sons of Ukraine! Glory to Ukraine!" The crowd replied with "Glory to the Heroes!"

Dressed in an embroidered shirt, Myroslav Senyk, head of the Lviv oblast council, delivered an oration. He stressed the Ukrainian nature of the monument and emphasized that every village in the Lviv oblast and also such eastern Ukrainian cities as Kharkiv, Kherson, and Donetsk contributed financially to its establishment. Afterwards he stated that "we [Ukrainians] are proud to be Banderites, ... [which] means to love our nation and to struggle for a better fate for that nation."[129]

Oles' Homeniuk, who represented the UPA fighters and veterans and was dressed in a UPA uniform, addressed the crowd. He was the most excited speaker at the ceremony. Homeniuk began his speech with "Almighty God! I thank you that we fighters, former insurgents who protected Ukraine with weapons, lived to this [glorious] day." In a very emotional voice, he added that "we are extremely glad that in our medieval Lviv, the genius of the revolution will finally stand at the gate to our city." He then claimed that the Bandera monument is the "place at which the young generation of boys and girls who reach adulthood will take an oath of fraternity." The place "will provide them with the national spirituality that they need to continue our idea of independence ... and here will also come young couples after the marriage ceremony [to take wedding pictures]."[130]

Petro Franko, the head of the Society of Political Prisoners and Persons Subjected to Repressions, addressed the crowd with "Glory to Jesus Christ!" and compared Bandera to George Washington. He claimed that Bandera was a "unique personality" whose family suffered considerably. Finishing his speech, Franko called Bandera "our Vozhd', our ideologist, our Providnyk of the Ukrainian nation, who obliges us all to build together the Ukrainian nation."[131]

The poet Ivan Hubka, introduced as a "participant of the national liberation struggle," called Bandera the "genius son of Ukraine" and informed the audience that the KUK considered releasing a gold Bandera order to elevate the status of the *Providnyk*. He also called for the renaming of more streets in Lviv after the OUN-

128 Ibid.
129 Ibid.
130 Ibid. It is a tradition in Ukraine and several other Eastern European countries that pictures of the married couple are taken in the most beautiful or important places in the city.
131 Ibid.

UPA and its members and claimed that the "Banderites do not allow anybody else to be the master in our home."[132]

The poet Ihor Kalynets', head of the fund that had collected money for the monument, informed the audience that Bandera created the Ukrainian nation in practice, and not just in theory like the poet Taras Shevchenko. This had resulted in many victims and made it difficult to erect a monument to him. After fourteen years, however, the idea had been finally implemented. He pointed out that "Twenty percent of the Ukrainian nation had to die in imperialist wars to let Ukraine be the most glorious nation in Eastern Europe." He called Bandera "not only a unique personality but also a symbol of struggling Ukraine." Finally, he claimed that the "Ukrainian Revolution is not finished yet" and that Bandera will remind us to continue it. Thanking the sponsors, he also thanked the donors from the Ukrainian diaspora.[133]

The celebration ended with a poem and a parade. The poem "Banderites" was recited by Bohdan Stelmakh who, in a loud and fiery tone, repeated several times that all Ukrainians are Banderites, that they should be proud of it, and that Ukraine needs a new young and heroic Bandera. After this short but loud and deeply patriotic oratorical performance, various military units and the Stepan Bandera Plast troop conducted a parade. They marched around the Bandera monument to the music of a military band. The ceremony finished as loudly as it began.[134]

Bandera Commemorations after the Collapse of the Soviet Union

The ritual of commemorating the *Providnyk* was transplanted from the diaspora to Ukraine, but it did not evaporate in the diaspora. In contrast to the nationalist communities in the diaspora, the nationalists in Ukraine preferred to commemorate Bandera's birth on 1 January rather than on the anniversary of his assassination on 15 October. As in the diaspora, the most lavish commemorations took place on round anniversaries. They combined politics and religion and were directed against "our enemies." The post-Soviet commemorating communities were, as in the diaspora, composed of veterans, nationalist intellectuals, and also various far-right and neo-fascist groups and parties associated with other European radical right parties, such as the German NPD, the Italian Tricolor Flame, and the Polish National Rebirth. This resembled the networking provided before 1990 by the ABN. Many local "liberal" and "progressive" intellectuals legitimized the nationalist commemorations by their silence and concealed admiration.

In 1999, the celebration of the ninetieth anniversary of Bandera's birth and the fortieth anniversary of his death was rather modest, compared with that in 2009 of the hundredth anniversary of his birth and the fiftieth of his death. On 1 January 1999, a group of uniformed UPA veterans and uniformed young nationalists from paramilitary groups gathered at the Bandera monument in Staryi Uhryniv to honor their *Providnyk*.[135] On 12 January 1999, the newspaper *Za vil'nu Ukraïnu* informed its readers about a Bandera event at the Lviv opera house, without specifying the

132 Ibid.
133 Ibid.
134 Ibid.
135 "Selo Uhryniv 1 sichnia 1999 roku," *Vyzvol'nyi shliakh* Vol. 611, No. 2 (February 1999): 158.

date of the celebration. The stage was decorated with a Bandera portrait, to which the number ninety, indicating the ninetieth anniversary of his birth, was fixed. According to the published photographs, the artistic part comprised vocal groups dressed in folk and military costumes, which sang, danced, and marched on the stage. The two main speakers were Slava Stets'ko, the head of the OUN and KUN, and Ihor Nabytovych, a professor of philosophy at the Drohobych Pedagogical University. Stets'ko read out a hagiographical version of Bandera's biography and acquainted the celebrants with such ideas as "Bandera was the personification of the national liberation revolution against Moscow," and thus a model for young Ukrainians. She stressed that only the "politics of will" could deal with the economic crisis and resolve the problem of language and culture in Ukraine. Nabytovych introduced Bandera not only as a Ukrainian hero but also as a thinker and praised the universal sense enclosed in Bandera's ideas. The professor gave the impression that Bandera had been an eminent political philosopher, a Ukrainian Jean-Jacques Rousseau or John Stuart Mill, who in his writings contemplated about various kinds of liberties.[136]

The impending hundredth anniversary of Bandera's birth and the fiftieth of his death had already whipped up emotions and stirred up the political situation in Ukraine in late 2007 and early 2008, when the oblast councils of Lviv and Ivano-Frankiv'sk and the city council of Ternopil' devoted the year 2008 to the *Providnyk*. In Ternopil', the idea was initiated by KUN activists.[137] In late 2008, the Ukrainian parliament voted in favor of marking the hundredth anniversary of Bandera's birth and decided that the *Providnyk* should be celebrated at "state level."[138] Iukhnovs'kyi, head of the UINP, characterized Bandera in a ceremonial publication devoted to the Ukrainian leader as the "Vozhd' of Ukraine, Vozhd' without an army, but with the nation, Vozhd' in the hard time, when there was no wide support of the liberal Ukrainian intelligentsia." In doing so, Iukhnovs'kyi only followed Ukrainian president Iushchenko, who established the UINP and Iukhnovs'kyi as its head, and who claimed at a commemorative gathering on 22 December 2008: "Today we honor one of the leaders of the Ukrainian liberation movement, who, at the time of mortal struggle, transformed the spirit of our nation into bloom."[139] The Ukrainian Post released a stamp and an envelope with a Bandera photograph from the 1940s (Fig.

136 "Ideï i chyn Stepana Bandery—nash dorohovkaz," *Za vil'nu Ukrainu*, 12 January 1999, 2.

137 For Lviv, see "2008 rik na L'vivshchyni oholosheno rokom Stepana Bandery," 19 December 2007, http://novynar.com.ua/politics/16140 (accessed 17 October 2011). For Ternopil', see "U Ternopoli oholosheno Rik Stepana Bandery," 11 January 2008, http://www.unian.net/ukr/news/news230319.html, (accessed 14 November 2011). For Ivano-Frankivs'k, see "2008 rik na Prykarpatti bude Rokom Stepana Bandery," 28 December 2007, http://www.newsru.ua/ukraine/28dec2007/god.html (accessed 14 November 2011).

138 In the Ukrainian parliament, 236 deputies voted for decree number 3364, which regulated the official Bandera state commemorations; 226 votes were required to issue the decree. Cf. "V Ukraïni na derzhavnomu rivni vidznachatymut' 100-richchia z dnia narodzhennia Bandery," 25 December 2008, http://novynar.com.ua/politics/49008 (accessed 28 October 2011).

139 "Zemliaky Bandery za perekhovannia Bandery v ridnomu seli," 27 January 2008, http://h.ua/story/80500/ (accessed 17 October 2011); "V Ivano-Frankivs'ku v urochystii obstanovtsi vidkryly pamiatnyk providnykovi OUN Stepanu Banderi," 2 January 2009, http://vidgolos.com/623-v-ivano-frankivsku-v-urochistijj-obstanovci.html (accessed 17 October 2011); Viktor Iushchenko, "Vitannia prezydenta Ukraïny uchasnykam urochystoï akademiï z nakhody 100-richchia vid dnia narodzhennia Stepana Bandery," 22 December 2008, Ihor Iukhnovs'kyi, "2009 rik—rik Stepana Bandery," *Stepan Bandera: Zbirnyk materialiv i dokumentiv*, ed. Vladyslav Verstiuk (Kiev: Ukraïns'kyi Instytut Natsional'noï Pamiaty, 2009), 6–7.

60).[140] The SUM published a cartoon about Bandera's assassination and a Bandera coin. It also collected money for a renovation of the Petliura, Konovalets', Bandera, and Shukhevych monument in the SUM camp in Ellenville, New York.[141]

Fig. 60. Bandera stamps, released in 2008 by the Ukrainian Post.

Nadia Oleksenchuk, head of the education department of the Lviv city council, announced in August 2008 that the first lesson in 2009 in all schools in the Lviv oblast would be devoted to the *Providnyk*.[142] The Ternopil' city council announced that the same would happen in Ternopil' schools on 31 December 2009.[143] In all schools in the Ivano-Frankivs'k oblast, according to the *Plastovyi portal*, a lesson called "Stepan Bandera—Symbol of the Undefeated Nation" was taught in September

140 "Ukroposhta vydala do 100-richchia Stepana Bandery pamiatnyi convert," 30 December 2008, http://www.unian.net/ukr/news/news-292930.html (accessed 17 October 2011).

141 "Nova knyha-komiks pro natsional'no-vyzvol'ni zmahannia!" September 2009, http://www.cym.org/UA/news/comic-book_Bandera (accessed 15 October 2011); "Vidnovlennia Pamiatnykiv Heroiam na Oseli KU SUM v Ellenvilli," 4 October 2009, http://www.cym.org/US/download/Pamyatnyky_Project.pdf (accessed 15 October 2011).

142 "Pershyi urok u shkolakh L'vova rekomenduiut' prysviatyty Stepanu Banderi," 28 August 2008, http://zaxid.net/home/showSingleNews.do?pershiy_urok_u_shkolah_lvova_rekomenduyut_prisvyatiti_stepanu_banderi&objectId=1059868 (accessed 15 October 2011).

143 "31 hrudnia u shkolakh Ternopolia proide urok, prysviachenyi Banderi," 28 December 2009, http://www.unian.net/ukr/news/news-354545.html (accessed 17 October 2011).

2008.[144] The education department of the Luts'k city council announced one competition for the best academic essay by a university student on the subject "Stepan Bandera—the True Depiction of the Personality, Fighter, and Citizen," and another for schoolchildren for the best essay on "My Attitude to the OUN Providnyk Stepan Bandera." Bandera admirers in Luts'k were invited to a ceremonial concert on 26 December 2008, on the hundredth anniversary of his birth. At the same time, a similar celebration under the motto "Long Live Bandera and His State" took place in the Ivano-Frankivs'k Theater.[145] Also in Ivano-Frankivs'k, a Bandera monument was unveiled on 1 January 2009, and on 14 October a memorial plaque was devoted to Vasyl' Bandera. The plaque was located on the building in which Vasyl' Bandera and other OUN-B members were arrested on 14 and 15 October 1941.[146] The Bandera monument in Ternopil' was unveiled on 26 December 2008, five days before the hundredth anniversary of his birth.[147] The Ternopil' oblast council expressed the wish to transfer Bandera's remains from Munich to Staryi Uhryniv.[148] The celebration of the anniversary in Chernivtsi was opened by Viktor Pavliuk, deputy head of the oblast state council, who announced that "we should together conduct celebratory activities in honor of the Providnyk of the OUN, in order to dissolve the anti-Ukrainian stereotypes settled in the consciousness of the Ukrainian population by ideologists from the Communist Party."[149] In Kharkiv, a court did not allow the city council to ban Bandera commemorations.[150]

On the Feast of Saint Mary the Protectress on 14 October 2008 in Kiev, two completely opposite demonstrations were organized. The first one was at the Shevchenko monument and attracted, among others, UPA veterans, skinheads, and men and women in folk costume. Some of them carried red-and-black OUN-B flags and Bandera posters and listened to the vocal performances of men in uniform-like dark khaki suits, who stood on the stage of the Festival of Insurgent Song, behind an old automatic cannon. The other demonstration was organized by the leftwing populist Progressive Socialist Party of Ukraine (*Prohresyvna sotsialistychna partiia Ukraïny*, PSPU) in Independence Square (*Maidan Nezalezhnosti*). Its participants burned a red-and-black flag and carried Soviet anti-fascist and anti-NATO cartoons, of which

144 "Vidnovleno rodynnyi dim plastuna, providnyka OUN Stepana Bandery," 30 December 2008, http://www.plast.org.ua/news?newsid=2985 (accessed 17 October 2011).

145 "U Luts'ku zaplanovani zakhody do 100-richchia Stepana Bandery," 21 December 2008, http://www.unian.net/ukr/news/news-291322.html (accessed 17 October 2011); "'Khai zhyve Bandera i ioho derzhava...'," 28 December 2008, http://www.unian.net/ukr/news/news-292614.html (accessed 17 October 2011).

146 "V Ivano-Frankivs'ku v urochystii obstanovtsi vidkryly pam"iatnyk providnykovi OUN Stepanu Banderi," 2 January 2009, http://vidgolos.com/623-v-ivano-frankivsku-v-urochistijj-obstanovci.html (accessed 17 October 2011); "Memorial'nu doshku Vasyliu Banderi vidkryly v Ivano-Frankivs'ku,"14 October 2009, http://www.unian.net/ukr/news/news-278571.html (accessed 17 October 2011).

147 "U Ternopoli vidkryly pam"iatnyk Banderi," 26 December 2008, http://novynar.com.ua/politics/49173 (accessed 17 October 2011).

148 "Zemliaky Bandery za perekhovannia Bandery v ridnomu seli," 27 January 2008, http://h.ua/story/80500/ (accessed 17 October 2011).

149 "Nashym spil'nym zavdanniam zalyshaiet'sia poshyrennia pravdy pro UPA ta provedennia prosvitnyts'kykh zakhodiv na poshanu Providnyka OUN—Stepana Bandery," 9 January 2009, http://www.oda.cv.ua/index.php?option=com_content&task=view&id=4365&Itemid=63 (accessed 27 October 2011).

150 "Sud ne dozvolyv kharkivs'kii vladi zaboronyty vshanuvannia Bandery," 1 January 2009, http://donetsk-ua.livejournal.com/46059.html (accessed 28 October 2011).

several suggested the continuation between the Nazis and NATO, and the participation of Ukrainian nationalists in both. One older woman carried a poster with a swastika and the inscription "These are fascist movements: Lithuania, Latvia, Ukraine, and Georgia." Two men held a banner with the inscription "Eternal Glory to the Victims of the OUN-UPA Villains."[151] A year later on 14 October 2009, many more people than in 2008, perhaps several hundred, marched through the streets of Kiev with Bandera posters, red-and-black flags, and Svoboda Party banners. They shouted slogans such as "Bandera our Leader—Protection of the Mother God our Festivity!" "Glory to the Heroes, Death to the Enemies!" One older man in a UPA cap brought a machine gun, to honor the *Providnyk*.[152]

Between the events of October 2008 and October 2009, others connected with Bandera took place in the Ukrainian capital. On 23 May 2009, nationalists in folk costumes and neo-fascist outfits, holding Bandera posters and performing fascist salutes, honored the Ukrainian *Providnyk* in front of the monument to Iaroslav the Wise.[153] At 6 p.m. on 1 January 2009, 2,000 people with torches and Svoboda Party flags marched along Khreshchatyk Boulevard to Independence Square, where they held a meeting. Andrii Mokhnyk, leader of the Kiev Svoboda Party branch informed the Bandera admirers that contemporary Ukrainian politicians were not able to take responsibility for Ukraine as Bandera had done when he had ordered the killing of Mailov and Pieracki, and when he had proclaimed a Ukrainian state in 1941. He stressed that Ukraine needed a *Providnyk* like Bandera. On the same day, the Svoboda Party conducted similar Bandera rallies and demonstrations in the oblast cities Ivano-Frankivs'k, Kharkiv, Odessa, Luhans'k, Lviv, Simferopol', Volodymyr-Volyns'kyi, and Zaporizhzhia, as well as in numerous towns and villages. Some of them were prepared in collaboration with the local authorities. The celebrations in western Ukrainian villages were very well attended. In the village of Velyka Berezovytsia, inhabited by slightly more than 7,000 people, 2,000 came to the panakhyda and took part in the commemorative gathering.[154]

Bandera's grandson Stephen Bandera was very busy in 2009. As in previous years, he was invited to the unveiling of monuments to his grandfather, and to various rallies and anniversaries, both in Ukraine and in the diaspora.[155] At the unveiling

151 "Pokrovs'ki mityngy," 15 October 2008, http://novynar.com.ua/gallery/politics/402?img=1 (accessed 17 October 2009).

152 "Marsh bez hasel pro kovbasu, abo do 67-richchia UPA," 15 October 2009, http://www.unian.net/ukr/news/news-341359.html (accessed 17 October 2011).

153 "Mitynh Bratstva OUN-UPA," 25 May 2009, http://novynar.com.ua/gallery/politics/442?img=0 (accessed 15 October 2011).

154 "Marsh u Kyievi z nahody 100-richchia Stepana Bandery," 2 January 2009, http://kbulkin.wordpress.com/2009/01/02/march-kyiv-stepan-bandera-100-anniversary/ (accessed 28 October 2011); "'Svoboda' vshanuvala 100-richchia z Dnia Narodzhennia Stepana Bandery po vsii Ukraïni," 1–2 January 2009, http://www.tyahnybok.info/diyalnist/novyny/005767/ (accessed 28 October 2011); "1 sichnia u Kyievi, Kharkovi, Zaporizhzhi vidbudut'sia smoloskypni pokhody na chest' Stepana Bandery," 31 December 2008, http://sd.org.ua/news.php?id=15980 (accessed 28 October 2011); "Urochysta akademia z nahody 100-richchia vid dnia narodzhennia Stepana Bandery," 21 December 2008, http://www.Ternopil'.svoboda.org.ua/diyalnist/novyny/005661/ (accessed 28 October 2011).

155 For Stepan Bandera's oration at the unveiling ceremony of the Bandera monument in Drohobych on 14 October 2001, see "Stephen Bandera molodym postav v drohobyts'komu skveri," *Za vil'nu Ukrainu*, 16 October 1999, 2. For Stepan Bandera unveiling other Stepan Bandera monuments, see the exhibition of the Stepan Bandera Museum in Staryi Uhryniv.

Fig. 61. The Canadian SUM choir Prolisok in folk costumes at the commemorative gathering on 17 October 2009 in the hall of the Munich Anton Fingerle Education Centre. http://www.cym.org/archives/Munich2009.asp (accessed 14 October 2011).

Fig. 62. The female SUM members from the United Kingdom at the commemorative gathering on 17 October 2009 in the hall of the Munich Anton Fingerle Education Centre. http://www.cym.org/archives/Munich2009.asp (accessed 14 October 2011).

of the Bandera monument in Ternopil' on 26 December 2008, he informed the crowd that he was proud to have been born in the Bandera family and to be the grandson of a Ukrainian hero. At a rally on 1 January 2009 in Staryi Uhryniv, he reminded the celebrants that his grandfather had been the "symbol of the Ukrainian nation," thanked the organizers in the name of the Bandera family for organizing the festivity, and listened to other prominent speakers, such as the leader of the radical right Svoboda Party, Oleh Tiahnybok.[156]

On 17 and 18 October 2009, Stephen Bandera graced celebrations of his grandfather in Munich with his presence. On the first day of the Munich celebrations at about 2 p.m., several hundred Bandera enthusiasts from a number of countries, armed with red-and-black OUN-B flags and nationalist banners, including those of the radical right Svoboda Party, marched to Bandera's grave, where they laid several wreaths. Some celebrants were in uniform, for instance the female and male SUM members, and the musicians of the Baturyn orchestra from Toronto, which elevated the spirit of the commemoration with military music. At the grave, a priest performed a panakhyda, after which a number of speakers, including Bandera junior and Stefan Romaniw, head of the OUN, delivered speeches.[157]

At about 7 p.m. on the same day, the celebrants attended a commemorative gathering in the hall of the Anton Fingerle Education Center in Munich. They first listened again to the speeches of such eminent Ukrainian nationalists as Bandera, Kutsan, and Romaniw. Then, they enjoyed vocal performances by a uniformed group of female SUM members from the United Kingdom, and the Canadian SUM choir Prolisok in folk costumes (Figs. 61 and 62). Both the speeches and the performances took place on a stage decorated with an immense portrait of the *Providnyk*. Between the political and artistic performances, the Bandera family, numbering three men and five women entered the stage and smiled at the celebrants, while standing under the portrait of their famous ancestor. The next day, the celebrations were completed with a church service.[158]

Similar commemorative gatherings took place in 2009 in several other places inhabited by the Ukrainian diaspora. In Edmonton on 25 October 2009, about 400 people gathered at the Roman Shukhevych Ukrainian Youth Complex, at 9615–153 Avenue. The hall was decorated with a painting of the Virgin Mary, which was fixed upon a cross made from blue-and-yellow cloth. The background was red-and-black. The Ukrainian and Canadian flags were fixed on both sides of this decoration. On the right side of the stage, the audience could see a huge portrait of Bandera with the dates 1909–1959. A golden trident was hung from above the stage above the picture

156 "Z nahody vidznachennia 100-richchia vid Dnia narodzhennia ta provedennia v Ternopil's'kii oblasti roku Stepana Bandery, 26 hrudnia vidbulosia urochyste vidkryttia pam"iatnyka providnykovi OUN-UPA," 3 January 2009, http://www.tneu.edu.ua/ua-i-article-i-id-i-550-i-nSID-i-public_organizations-i-index.html (accessed 15 October 2011); "Iak vidznachatymut' 100-richchia Stepana Bandery," 16 December 2008, http://www.unian.net/ukr/news/news-290326.html (accessed 15 October 2011); "Na Ivano-Frankivshchyni proishlo viche do 100-richchia vid narodzhennia Bandery," 2 December 2009, http://www.unian.net/ukr/news/news-293136.html (accessed 15 October 2011).

157 "Miunkhen. U 50-richchia pidstupnoho vbyvstva Providnyka OUN, Stepana Bandery, 17-ho zhovtnia 2009," http://www.cym.org/archives/Munich2009.asp (accessed 17 October 2011); Miunkhen, 17 zhovtnia 2009 roku, vidprava do 50-richchia vbyvstva Providnyka, 21 October 2009, http://oko.if.ua/2009/10/21/3747/ (accessed 17 October 2011).

158 Ibid.

of the Virgin. The podium was covered in red-and-black cloth, and was decorated with a trident on top.[159]

The celebration began with a panakhyda, during which the participants sang dirges for Stepan Bandera and performed a wide range of religious rituals under the leadership of three priests. Nationalist rituals followed. Roman Brytan, who co-ordinated the entire event, presented a mysterious, nationalist, and martyrdom-tinged narrative of the history of Ukraine, in segments of two to three minutes each. Between the speeches, many individual artists and musical groups, in peasant blouses and Cossack costumes, sang pop, folk, and classical songs, to glorify Bandera, some of which were based on the lyrics of OUN and UPA songs. Children of the SUM, wearing light-brown uniforms and ties sang different pop songs about the OUN, the UPA, and the Orange Revolution, which took place from late November 2004 to January 2005 in Ukraine and brought President Iushchenko to power. Altogether, some fifteen performances took place.[160]

In addition to musical performances, Bohdan Tarasenko recited Bandera's 1936 speech before the Polish court in Lviv, in which Bandera explained why he had given permission for the liquidation of a number of Poles, Russians, and Ukrainians. The organizers also played back a recorded interview Bandera had given Western journalists in the 1950s, explaining the necessity of a war against the Soviet Union. The event ended with a speech by Ihor Broda, leader of the League of Ukrainian Canadians in Edmonton, during which he gave thanks to the celebrants and artists for being such a "spiritual nation," also emphasizing that the participants had helped keep the memory of Bandera alive by coming to the celebration. The speech also asserted that modern-day Ukraine is threatened by "Moscow" and that Bandera was the person who could defend Ukraine against Russia.[161]

The Bandera commemorations surrounding the hundredth anniversary of his birth and the fiftieth of his death were crowned with the designation of Stepan Bandera as a Hero of Ukraine, by President Iushchenko on 20 January 2010, and publicly announced on 22 January. At the celebration, Iushchenko handed the order to Bandera's grandson Stephen Bandera (Fig. 63). The younger Bandera announced in a short speech that this was "not only a great but an enormous honor" and that the Ukrainian state had finally acknowledged "the heroic deed of Stepan Bandera and hundreds of thousands of Ukrainian patriots who fell for this state."[162] Soon after the designation, the new Ukrainian president Viktor Ianukovych promised the Russian president Vladimir Putin to strip Bandera of the order, which the Donetsk District Administrative Court carried out in April 2010.[163]

159 Rossoliński-Liebe, Celebrating Fascism, 12.

160 Ibid., 12.

161 Ibid., 12.

162 For the designation of Stepan Bandera, see http://zakon1.rada.gov.ua/cgi-bin/laws/main.cgi?nreg=46/2010 (accessed 27 September 2011). For the ceremony, see "Stepan Bandera Hero of Ukraine," http://www.youtube.com/watch?v=Wy7eTLy2_Io (accessed 15 October 2011).

163 "Yanukovych Promised Medvedev to Take Away Rank of Hero of Ukraine from Bandera and Shukhevych," 9 March 2011, http://risu.org.ua/en/index/all_news/state/34810/ (accessed 15 November 2012); "Court strips Bandera of Hero of Ukraine title," *The Ukrainian Weekly*, 23 January 2011, 1.

Fig. 63. Stephen Bandera and President Iushchenko at the designation ceremony of Stepan Bandera as Hero of Ukraine on 20 January 2010. http://www.ucc.ca/2010/02/01/ukraines-president-recognizes-ukraines-freedom-fighters/ (accessed 10 January 2012).

The post-Soviet Bandera and OUN-UPA commemorations excited thousands of Ukrainian nationalists and enabled thousands or possibly even millions of Ukrainian patriots to believe in the greatness of the *Providnyk* and the "liberation movement." However, they were perceived very differently by people whose relatives or acquaintances had been persecuted or murdered by OUN members and UPA partisans. One such person was Bela Feld. She emigrated in 1935 from the Polish town of Brzezany to Palestine. Bela's immediate family was killed during the Second World War. In 1997 she visited the town of her youth. During this visit, she asked inhabitants of the now homogenously Ukrainian town of Berezhany for one of her childhood friends, Halyna Dydyk. At the time of her visit, the inhabitants were celebrating the anniversary of the establishment of the Ukrainian state, "dressed in their colorful peasant folk costumes." After asking for her childhood friend, Bela was immediately urged by the celebrants to visit the grave of her friend, who, during her struggle for a Ukrainian state, had become a "national hero." Hearing this and seeing the exited crowd of celebrants around her, Bela felt "like running away." She did not want to go to the grave and was "emotionally exhausted." Furthermore, she did not know how to behave, because she knew from survivors who had arrived in Israel after the war that "the Bandera people, the members of the Ukrainian underground, were the worst." She also "remembered Halyna the way she was before the war, before all that. And suddenly she turned into a hero and a martyr, associated with that name, Bandera. I knew that something was wrong, *'s'iz nisht git.'*" Then she politely refused the invitation.[164]

The Providnyk in Festivals, Pubs, Novels, and the Cinema

In post-Soviet Ukraine, the Bandera cult took even more eccentric shapes than in the diaspora. It was disseminated by the previously described historians, politicians, veterans, and nationalist activists, and in addition, by writers, film directors, journalists, organizers of bicycle trips, businessmen who opened UPA pubs, and various musical groups that sang at the alternative music festival Bandershtat, organized by the far-right National Alliance (*Natsional'nyi Al'ians*). Also, newspapers such as *Banderivets'*, published by the ultranationalist paramilitary Stepan Bandera Trident Organization from Drohobych, propagated the Bandera cult in various ways.[165]

Fig. 64. Image at the website of the festival "Bandershtat." Inscription: "Freedom or Death!" http://bandershtat.org.ua/ (accessed 14 October 2011).

Bandershtat has been organized annually since 2007, near Luts'k in Volhynia (Fig. 64). The name may have been derived from a song and music album from 1991 by the rock band Braty Hadiukiny, called "We Guys from the Bandera City." The participants in Bandershtat not only spent a few days sleeping in tents and listening to alternative music but also took part in various nationalist rituals. They dressed in UPA and NKVD uniforms and pretended to fight each other, invited UPA veterans and listened to their talks, formed a huge word BANDERA by standing behind each other and had themselves photographed from a plane, invited paramilitary and neo-

164 Redlich, *Together and Apart*, 157–59.

165 The newspaper *Banderivets': Informatsiinyi biuleten' Vseukraïns'koï orhanizatsiï "Tryzub" im. Stepana Bandery* began appearing in 2000.

fascist organizations that positioned Wolfsangel flags in front of their tents, and intended to invite Stepan Bandera's grandson Stephen Bandera. Bandershat was organized by the 2005-founded National Alliance, which specialized in organizing torch parades and paramilitary training camps. According to the Alliance, the aim of the festival was to "elevate the national idea in Ukrainian youth" and to "immortalize the image of Stepan Bandera as a national symbol."[166]

In 2007 the pub Kryïvka was opened in the Rynok square of Lviv. It was located in the cellar of a sixteenth-century tenement and was designed as a bunker of the UPA. Everyone who entered was greeted with "Glory to Ukraine!" uttered by a uniformed man with a rifle. The guest was expected to respond with "Glory to the Heroes!" The interior was decorated with nationalist and military objects. The pub commercialized a romanticized and distorted image of the UPA. On the one hand, it overlooked the violence committed by the Ukrainian partisans, and on the other, it did not inform the guests that life in a UPA bunker was painful and unbearable, as its inhabitants suffered from various diseases, wore the same underwear and clothes for weeks, and were regularly bitten by lice.[167]

In one room, a few giant posters popularized the idea of Bandera as a human being. They showed the *Providnyk* at different ages, accompanied by his family and friends, or in short pants during holidays at the seaside. The menu, as well as informing guests about dishes, the names of many of which related to the UPA, also depicted several sketches of the UPA bunkers and photographs of UPA partisans. One of the depicted partisans was the legendary UPA leader Dmytro Kliachkivs'kyi who unleashed the ethnic cleansing in Volhynia in early 1943. Kliachkivs'kyi and several UPA partisans were apparently presented in the menu to invoke the impression that they had eaten the same dishes that were served at Kryïvka. The menu listed various kinds of bacon, including kosher bacon (*kosherne salo*). One of the devices exhibited in the pub was a rifle. Every guest, including children, could pick it up and play with it. The ambience of the pub suggested that the rifle had been previously used by the UPA insurgents.[168]

Iurii Nazaruk, the manager of the pub, reasoned in an interview that Kryïvka was both a museum and a pub, intended to change the negative Soviet image of the UPA by disseminating "true knowledge about the UPA." According to him, the pub was more effective than nationalist publications and the Bandera monument in Lviv, which was too monumental and thus made modern people skeptical about the Bandera cult. According to Nazaruk, people who did not regard the UPA insurgents as heroes did not understand anything about the Ukrainian "liberation movement." Asked about antisemitism in the UPA, Nazaruk responded that there were many

166 "Bandershtat. Festyval Ukraïns'koho duhu," http://bandershtat.org.ua/pro-festyval/ideya/ (accessed 14 October 2011); "Na Volyni sostoitsia festival 'Bandershtat—2008'", 2 August 2008, http://www.unian.net/rus/news/news-265064.html (accessed 13 October 2011); "'Bandershtat-2011' sobral v Lutske deputatov, voiakov OUN-UPA i molodez'", 16 August 2011, http://censor.net.ua/photo_news/178578/bandershtat2011_sobral_v_lutske_deputatov_voyakov_ounupa_i_molodej_fotoreportaj (accessed 13 October 2011).

167 For testimonies about the life of the UPA partisans in bunkers, see Ana Boguslavskaja and Oled Schilowski (film directors), *Die Bandera-Bande: Guerilla-Kämpfer im 2. Weltkrieg.* Discovery Channel 2009.

168 http://www.kryjivka.com.ua/ (accessed 14 October 2011); *Kryïvka. Meniu*, 10. For Kliachkivs'kyi, see chapter 5 above. I inspected the pub in 2008.

Jewish physicians in the UPA, and that there may even have been a Jewish UPA unit that fought for an independent Ukrainian state. He added that even if such a unit did not exist, this myth about the UPA was true "because it is a good myth [rather than a bad Soviet myth]."[169]

In 2008 the biker club "Banderas" was opened in Chernivtsi, the main city of Bukovina. One of the symbols of the club became a UPA partisan on a motorbike. Every member of the club was obliged to display the symbol on a leather vest.[170] Vasyl' Kozhelianko, a Chernivtsi-based author, published in 2000 the counterfactual novel *Parade in Moscow*, in which Hitler accepts the proclamation of the OUN-B state on 30 June 1941 and conquers Moscow in November 1941. Kozhelianko also has Bandera take the salute of the armies of the Axis countries at the Lenin Mausoleum on Red Square in Moscow on 7 November 1941. Next to the Ukrainian *Providnyk*, Kozhelianko places Hitler, Mussolini, Antonescu, Franco, Horthy, and the "Japanese emperor."[171]

Oksana Zabuzhko, the most famous Ukrainian female writer, composed a far more pathetic book about Ukrainian nationalism than had Kozhelianko. Unlike the latter's fantasy, Zabuzhko's historical novel *The Museum of Abandoned Secrets* was rapidly translated into other languages.[172] Before writing the book, she consulted V"iatrovych who provided her with historical material and explained to her the relations between Jews and Ukrainian nationalists during the Second World War. In consequence, Zabuzhko based a significant part of her novel on Krentsbakh's fictitious memoirs, published by OUN-B historian and former head of a division of the OUN propaganda apparatus, Petro Mirchuk. Unsurprisingly, Zabuzhko depicted the UPA as an army that looked after Jews during the Second World War and did not commit any atrocities against them, allowing them to fight against the Soviet Union for an independent Ukrainian state.[173]

In 2009 the organization *Eko-Myloserdia* organized a bike trip called *Stepan Bandera's European Paths*, for nine teenagers and six adults. The trip began on 1 August 2009 in Sokal', Lviv oblast, and was planned to go through Poland and Slovakia, and to end at Bandera's grave in Munich on 24 August. Because of its name and political nature, the expedition evoked much emotion and attracted a good deal of media attention, even before it began, especially in Poland. As the bikers came to the Polish border, opponents organized a demonstration with posters like "Those Who Glorify the Fascist S. Bandera Themselves Become Fascists." The bikers were not let through the border, although they possessed valid passports and visas.[174]

169 Iurii Nazaryk, interview by author, Lviv, 15 May 2008.

170 "U Chernivtsiakh na chest' Bandery zasnuvaly baikers'kyi klub Banderas," 26 May 2008, http://novynar.com.ua/politics/28003 (accessed 14 October 2011); "Baikers'kyi klub 'Banderas' stvorenyi do 100 richchia providnyka OUN," 26 May 2008, http://www.unian.net/ukr/news/news-253248.html (accessed 14 October 2011).

171 Vasyl' Kozhelianko, *Defilada v Moskvi* (Lviv: Kal'varia, 2000), 12.

172 Oksana Zabuzhko, *Muzei pokynutykh sekretiv* (Kiev: Fakt, 2010); *Museum der Vergessenen Geheimnisse*, translated by Alexander Krathochvil (Graz: Droschl, 2010).

173 Rudling, The OUN, the UPA and the Holocaust, 33.

174 "Ukraïns'ko-pols'kyi skandal na imeni Stepana Bandery," 11 August 2009, http://www.radiosvoboda.org/content/article/1797625.html (accessed 28 October 2011); Marcin Wojciechowski, "Ukraińska Swoboda jeszcze napsuje nam krwi," 20 August 2009, http://wyborcza.pl/1,86758,6943561,Ukrainska_Swoboda_jeszcze_napsuje_nam_krwi.html (accessed 17 October 2011).

In 2007 and 2008, the Ukrainian television channel Inter prepared the talk show *Great Ukrainians*. From a hundred selected personalities, ten were chosen, including such characters as the physician Mykola Amosov, the poet Taras Shevchenko, the medieval king Iaroslav the Wise, the Cossack leader Bohdan Khmel'nyts'kyi, the philosopher Hryhorii Skorovoda, and of course, the legendary *Providnyk* Stepan Bandera. Then ten short movies about the ten Ukrainians were produced under the direction of journalists, politicians, and actors, including Leonid Kravchuk, the first president of Ukraine. The movie about Bandera was produced by journalist Vakhtang Kipiani. The movies were shown on the Inter channel, and shortly after, could be watched on the Internet. Fans chose their favorite "great Ukrainian" by sending an SMS. The show excited Ukrainian society and was the subject of daily discussions for months. People debated at home and at work who was their most admired Ukrainian and who should therefore win the contest. Many sent not one but dozens or even hundreds of SMS messages for their favorite candidate. Bandera became the "great Ukrainian" number three, after Iaroslav the Wise, and Amosov. That the *Providnyk* did not win was allegedly due to a fraud conducted by a group of political activists who wanted to prevent the division of Ukraine which, according to them, Bandera's winning would cause. Although, with the exception of Bandera, no twentieth-century extremists or communist leaders qualified for the first ten, a number of them qualified for the first hundred, including the UPA leader Shukhevych in twelfth place, Lenin in twenty-third, Konovalets' in fortieth, Brezhnev in sixty-third, and Khrushchev in ninety-third.[175]

Although Kipiani's movie about Bandera was an apologetic and uncritical advertisement for the *Providnyk*, historians and intellectuals in Ukraine accepted it rather than discussing or challenging it. The movie began with a short, pathetic talk by a young uniformed Plastun, perhaps aged twelve, with a physiognomy similar to Bandera at that age. The young patriot, sitting at a campfire in a forest, informed his older colleagues, and the film director sitting next to him, how Bandera prepared himself for future torture at enemy hands, by inserting pins under his nails.[176]

Kipiani's movie consisted of clips from black-and-white documentary films, in which the director placed his cartoon actors. Kipiani not only provided narrative but also appeared in the film as an actor, mainly among archival documents or in significant places like the prison or courthouse. He appeared as a link between the present and the past, or the audience and the *Providnyk*. He presented Bandera as a patriotic Ukrainian politician who fought, suffered, and died for Ukraine. Typically for the post-Soviet apologetic discourse he omitted all facts that could cast a poor light on the *Providnyk* and showed instead a band playing a heroic and patriotic rock song about Ukrainian partisans in the ruins of a church. In order to familiarize the audience with the *Providnyk* as a human being, Kipiani showed pictures of Bandera

175 "Velyki ukraïntsi," http://greatukrainians.com.ua/ (accessed 14 October 2011); Vasyl' Rasevych, "Velyka manipulatsiia," 17 May 2008, http://zaxid.net/blogs/showBlog.do?velika_manipulyatsiya&objected=1054002 (accessed 14 October 2011).

176 Vakhtang Kipiani, *Stepan Bandera*, 2009, http://greatukrainians.com.ua/council/ (accessed 15 October 2011). For Bandera torturing himself, see chapter 2 below, page 95.

with friends and family and let Bandera's grandson Stephen Bandera talk at length about his grandfather, his family, and himself.[177]

Several other documentary and historical feature films about Bandera were produced after 1991. On the occasion of his ninetieth birthday anniversary, the television network Vikna made the twenty-five-minute film *Stepan Bandera's Three Loves*. It began with Stephen Bandera jogging through Kiev, while being introduced as a person who bears a name "with which so many murders are associated that any Mafia don would be envious." Then director Iurii Diukanov introduced Bandera's life and the history of the OUN, by telling the story of Bandera's love for three women. Bandera appeared in the documentary as a romantic Ukrainian hero, who idealistically struggled for Ukraine and was tragically assassinated by his cruel and deceitful enemies. The link between love and nationalism was the main vibrant message of this patriotic production.[178]

Ten years later, on the hundredth anniversary of Bandera's birth, Serhii Sotnychenko, Taras Tkachenko, and Olena Nozhekina produced the documentary *The Price of Freedom* with Stephen Bandera as the central character. The young star of Ukrainian nationalism introduced the life of his grandfather, embedded in OUN and UPA history in several brief acts, in which each was followed by short speeches by such historians as Alexander Gogun, Iaroslav Hrytsak, Taras Hunchak, Grzegorz Motyka, Ivan Patryliak, Mykola Posivnych, Timothy Snyder, Iaroslav Svatko, Volodymyr V"iatrovych, and such political activists as the former OUN-B members Irena Kozak and Ievhen Stakhiv, and the OUN leader Andrii Haidamakha. Crucial matters, such as the denial of the pogroms and the rationalization of the ethnic violence, were confirmed by nationalist historians such as V"iatrovych, and nationalist activists such as the OUN leader Haidamakha, and not by critical historians like Motyka or Snyder, who in the movie confirmed only less controversial aspects. As a result Stephen Bandera became the main narrator of Ukrainian history, who introduced the main personality of Ukrainian history, his grandfather the *Providnyk*, and whose opinions are confirmed by a number of authoritative historians.[179]

The most popular movie about Bandera, *Assassination: An Autumn Murder in Munich*, was produced in 1995 by screenplay writer Vasyl' Portiak and film director Oles' Ianchuk. In addition to *Assassination*, the latter produced a number of other nationalist movies, including *Famine-33* (*Holod-33*) about the famine of 1932–1933, *The Undefeated* (*Neskorennyi*) about Roman Shukhevych, and *The Company of Heroes* (*Zalizna Sotnia*) about the UPA. In *Assassination* and *Undefeated*, the role of Stepan Bandera was played by the same actor, Iaroslav Muka. The ideological goal of *Assassination* was the romanticization and sentimentalization of the *Providnyk* and of the Ukrainian nationalists who remained in Munich after the Second World War. The historical text at the beginning of the film presented the OUN and UPA as a

177 Kipiani, *Stepan Bandera*, 2009.

178 Iurii Diukanov (film director), *Try liubovi Stepana Bandery*. Vikna, 1998. Available online at http://OUN-UPA.org.ua/video/ (accessed 28 October 2011).

179 Cf. Serhii Sotnychenko, Taras Tkachenko, and Olena Nozhekina (directors), *Tsina svobody*, Kinotur 2008.

resistance movement fighting the Germans and Soviets.[180] The post-war Bandera, as portrayed by the actor Iaroslav Muka, was not exactly a carbon copy of the original. Not only did Muka's physiognomy require considerable imagination to recognize him as Stepan Bandera but his sluggish temper did not seem to correspond with the fervent and excitable personality of the *Providnyk*. However, Muka's slow temper and subtle suggestions of absentmindedness allowed a sentimental and almost intellectual depiction of Bandera. This was often strengthened with sentimental music, particularly when Bandera was travelling by car or when he was working on the revolution. Bandera's doctrinal insistence on his absolute authority in the OUN and his demanding complete subordination from every OUN member after the war were not featured in the film, as they would have jeopardized Bandera's sentimental and intellectual portrayal. The main motif of the film was Bandera's assassination. Shortly before the tragic act, the viewer saw Stashyns'kyi as an honest and sympathetic man, being trained at KGB headquarters in Moscow and drinking a toast of champagne to Bandera's upcoming death, with two high-ranking Soviet officials. Bandera was killed on the staircase in Munich, to disconcerting and disquieting music, which immediately became sentimental and mourning in tone, as a huge obituary appeared on screen.

Post-Soviet Monuments to the Victims of the OUN-UPA

Despite vigorous attempts to fill Ukraine with nationalist monuments, commemorative plaques, and street names, many Soviet monuments and other signs in public places survived, especially in eastern Ukraine, where a few nationalist monuments were erected. In Lviv, the "capital" of western Ukraine, the Lenin monument and several other Soviet statues were removed before the dissolution of the Soviet Union, but the largest Soviet monument, the Glory Monument (*Monument Slavy*) was not. In the small spa town of Slavs'ke in the Carpathian Mountains, a statue of the Virgin Mary was installed in a monument devoted to the Red Army.[181] In eastern Ukraine, nationalist monuments devoted to the OUN-UPA or its leaders were very rarely erected. In 1992 in Kharkiv, the Popular Movement of Ukraine (*Narodnyi Rukh Ukraïny*, NRU), with the approval of the city council, unveiled a small and almost unnoticeable UPA monument in the Molodizhnyi Park. The monument was protected by guards but was vandalized on at least one occasion.[182]

The process of nationalizing Ukraine by means of OUN and UPA heroes was a reaction to the previous Sovietization of Ukraine and to the prolongation of Soviet traditions, particularly in eastern Ukraine. It is not surprising that it soon caused a counteraction, in particular in eastern Ukraine, where populist pro-Russian parties, such as the Party of Regions (*Partia rehioniv*), began erecting monuments devoted to the victims of the OUN and UPA, while further denying the atrocities of the Soviet

180 Oles' Ianchuk (film director), *Holod-33*, Kinostudia im. Dovzhenka 1991; Oles' Ianchuk (film director), *Atentat: Osinnie vbyvstvo v Miunkheni*, Oles'-film 1995; Oles' Ianchuk (film director), *Neskorenyi*, Oles'-film 2000; Oles' Ianchuk (film director), *Zalizna Sotnia*, Oles'-film 2004.

181 Andrij Portnov, "Pluralität der Erinnerung: Denkmäler und Geschichtspolitik in der Ukraine," *Osteuropa* Vol. 58, No. 6 (2008): 200.

182 Portnov, Pluralität der Erinnerung, 208.

regime and extolling its achievements. Up to the time of writing, an approach to the Ukrainian past that would not extol either the OUN-UPA or Soviet totalitarianism but would mourn the victims of both sides has not asserted itself. During the terms of office of the nationalist president Iushchenko, populist or communist parties and other organizations in eastern Ukraine unveiled at least four heroic, anti-nationalist monuments devoted to the victims of the OUN-UPA. On 14 September 2007 in Simferopol, the communist organization Homeland (*Rodina*) unveiled a monument called "Shot in the back," which showed a female figure holding a wounded man, a Soviet citizen or soldier murdered by the UPA. The Russian inscription on the monument said, "To the memory of the Soviet people's sacrifices who were killed by the helpers of the fascists—the fighters of the OUN-UPA and other collaborators."[183] Petro Symonenko, first secretary of the Communist Party of Ukraine, said at the unveiling ceremony: "The agents of this organization [OUN-UPA] supervised by fascists, shot Soviet citizens, innocent people. We came here today to commemorate everyone who liberated the Soviet Union. You went and you were underhandedly shot in the back from a corner by the helpers of the fascists."[184] Leonid Grach, the leader of the Crimean Communists, informed the participants that "more than 4,000 Crimeans, citizens of the Soviet Union, were sent to western Ukraine in order to help (heal, teach etc.), and were killed there by the helpers of the fascists."[185]

Another monument to the victims of the OUN-UPA, a 1.5-meter-high (five-foot) upright block, built into an existing monument to the soldiers of the Great Patriotic War, was unveiled on 26 June 2008 in Svatove, a district center in the Luhans'k oblast. The unveiling ceremony was attended by members of the Communist party of Ukraine and members of the communist organization *Molodaia gvardiia* (Young Guard). Like Grach in Simferopol', Mykola Sherstiuk, the mayor of Svatove, argued that the monument is devoted to local "teachers, doctors, and the military ... mostly women" who were sent to the Lviv and Ivano-Frankivs'k oblasts after the Second World War and were killed there by the nationalists.[186] Ievhen Kharin, vice-mayor of Luhansk, said in his speech: "The war is not over, the war continues. It is cruel and dirty. For the souls of our children and grandchildren whose parents and grandparents lie in graves."[187] The Luhans'k oblast council published on this occasion a book titled *We Will not Betray Victory and Truth*, with excerpts from the writings of the Soviet Ukrainian historian Maslovs'kyi, who was allegedly murdered by nationalists in Lviv in 1999.[188]

183 "V Krymu sostoialos'otkrytiie pamiatnika zhertvam OUN-UPA," 14 October 2007, http://old.kpunews.com/krim_topic11_1494.htm (accessed 11 October 2011).
184 "Simonenko otkryl v Simferopole pamiatnik zhertvam OUN-UPA," http://korrespondent.net/ukraine/events/207397-simonenko-otkryl-v-simferopole-pamyatnik-zhertvam-OUN-UPA (accessed 11 October 2011).
185 Ibid.
186 "Na Luhanshchyni vidkryly pam"iatnyi znak 'zhertvam OUN-UPA, zahyblym na L'vivschyni'," 26 June 2008, http://ua.korrespondent.net/ukraine/504706-na-luganshchini-vidkrili-pamyatnij-znak-zhertvam-OUN-UPA-zagiblim-na-lvivshchini (accessed 11 October 2011).
187 Ibid.
188 Ibid.

Fig. 65. Monument to the OUN-UPA victims unveiled in Luhans'k on 8 May 2010 by the Party of Regions.

The largest monument to the victims of the OUN-UPA was unveiled in Luhans'k on 8 May 2010 by the Party of Regions, whose candidate Viktor Ianukovych had won the presidential elections in early 2010, succeeding Iushchenko. The Party of Regions was a negative mirror image of Iushchenko's Our Ukraine. The Luhans'k monument was erected not far from the Soviet memorial of the Young Guard, a Second World War underground resistance group, who after the war became an important political myth in the Soviet Union. The monument to the victims of the OUN-UPA depicted a mother tied to something resembling a tree. Her face expressed death or unconsciousness. A man on his knees in front of her seemed to protect her and a child looking up at her face. The hands of the man were tied with a rope. The inscription beneath the figures read, "The truth should not be forgotten." A black granite plaque held the inscription "To the citizens of Luhans'k who were killed by nationalist persecutors from the OUN-UPA 1943–1956" and displayed several names beneath it (Fig. 65).[189]

189 "V Luganske otkryli pamiatnik zhertvam, pogibshim ot ruk voinov OUN-UPA," 8 May 2010, http://lugansk.comments.ua/news/2010/05/08/204843.html (accessed 11 October 2011).

The process of erecting monuments devoted to the victims of the OUN-UPA by various communist groups, veterans of the Red Army, and the Party of Regions was related to the rehabilitation of figures such as Stalin. On 5 May 2010, three days before the opening of the monument in Luhans'k, the first Stalin monument to be erected since 1953 was unveiled in the eastern Ukrainian city of Zaporizhzhia. The 2.5-meter-high (eight-foot) monument showed Stalin from the waist up on a granite block. It was located near the building with the office of the regional branch of the KPU. During the ceremony, Soviet veterans wore uniforms with medals and waved the red flag with hammer and sickle. The unveiling ceremony was picketed by a group of protesters dressed in traditional Ukrainian clothes. Some of them carried Ukrainian nationalist symbols or posters with inscriptions such as "Stalin killed my youth." On 28 December 2010, the head of the bust was removed and on 31 December the remainder of the Stalin bust was demolished.[190]

Kresowiacy, Polish Martyrology, and Bandera

Another remarkable discourse about Bandera and the OUN-UPA began a few years before the dissolution of the Soviet Union in Poland. It was initiated by the community of *kresowiacy*, composed of people resettled after the Second World War from the former Polish eastern territories, including survivors of the ethnic cleansing in Volhynia and eastern Galicia, and various Polish nationalist activists. Although not all members of the kresowiacy community were vindictive nationalists, the community as a whole invented a victimized narrative of their own past, in which Polish-Ukrainian relations, the Second World War, and the ethnic cleansing of the Polish population in Volhynia and eastern Galicia were embedded in Polish martyrology. The discourse concentrated on the suffering of Poles, denied the discriminatory policies against the Ukrainians in the Second Polish Republic, and instrumentalized the suffering of the Polish survivors in a way that was not free of a desire for vengeance.

The nature of the kresowiacy community was also determined by two other factors. The first was that the political situation between 1945 and 1990 did not allow the survivors of the ethnic cleansing to come to terms with the traumatic past and to openly mourn the loss of their relatives. The second factor consisted of the generally uncritical, multipatriotic, and multinationalist politics of reconciliation between Poland and Ukraine after 1990. This multipatriotic approach acknowledged the perpetrators on both sides as patriotic soldiers, freedom fighters, or even national heroes, and it did not pay much attention to the victims of the "national heroes."

Characterizing the kresowiacy community, one should also differentiate between the nationalist instrumentalization of history, conducted by the community activists, and the empirical research conducted by historians associated with the community. Historians such as Ewa Siemaszko and Władysław Siemaszko collected a vast num-

190 "New Stalin statue fuels tension in Ukraine," 5 May 2010, http://in.reuters.com/article/2010/05/05/idINIndia-48257020100505 (accessed 11 October 2011); "Ukrainian Communists unveil monument to Stalin amid nationalist protest," 5 May 2010, http://www.foxnews.com/world/2010/05/05/ukrainian-communists-unveil-monument-stalin-amid-nationalist-protest/ (accessed 11 October 2011); "Stalin statue blown up in Ukraine," 2 January 2011, http://www.freerepublic.com/focus/f-news/2650328/posts (accessed 11 October 2011).

ber of survivor testimonies, which are a very important source for the study of the ethnic cleansing conducted against the Poles in 1943–1944. The testimonies were frequently instrumentalized by other kresowiacy historians, who presented the ethnic cleansing as genocide (*ludobójstwo*), thereby competing in suffering with other genocides, in particular the Holocaust and the crimes of the Soviet regime. For example, Aleksander Korman described 362 "methods of physical torture, and also of psychological ones applied by the terrorists from the OUN-UPA and other Ukrainian chauvinists ... against Poles" and pointed out that Aleksandr Solzhenitsyn mentioned only fifty NKVD torture methods.[191] Similarly, the kresowiacy community regarded the investigation of Polish crimes against the Ukrainian population as a distortion and falsification of history and accused historians who investigated them, of carrying out a "top-secret instruction" from the OUN to distort the history of the ethnic cleansing against Poles.[192] No less problematic were the numerous mistakes or deliberate falsifications in the publications of this community. For example, the cover of a photograph album that documents the UPA murders of Poles shows a picture of the corpses of four children bound to a tree. The photograph, however, did not depict OUN-UPA victims but showed children killed in 1923 by a mentally ill mother.[193]

In 1999 in Wrocław, the kresowiacy community erected a memorial—the silhouette of a crucified Jesus, cut into two massive slabs of stone. The front of the monument bore a plaque with the inscription: "To the Polish citizens murdered in the south-eastern border territories in 1939–1947 by the Organization of Ukrainian Nationalists (OUN) and the Ukrainian Insurgent Army (UPA)." A second plaque fixed to the monument informed viewers that the monument held earth from 2,000 mass graves. A third one honored the Ukrainians who gave shelter to Poles (Fig. 66).[194] In addition to the one in Wrocław, the kresowiacy communities erected monuments and memorial plaques in other Polish cities, including Gdańsk, Kłodzko, and Chełm. In 2003, on the sixtieth anniversary of the ethnic cleansing in Volhynia, the Society to Commemorate the Victims of the Crimes of Ukrainian Nationalists in Wrocław (*Stowarzyszenie Upamiętnienia Ofiar Zbrodni Ukraińskich Nacjonalistów z Wrocławia*, SUOZUNzW) unveiled a monument in the military cemetery in Przemyśl, which depicted corpses of children bound to a tree with barbed wire, as in the photograph from 1923. When it became apparent that the photograph depicting the dead children was taken twenty years before the ethnic cleansing, the SUOZUNzW denied that the monument was prepared on the basis of this particular

191 Aleksander Korman, *Stosunek UPA do Polaków na ziemiach południowo-wschodnich II Rzeczypospolitej* (Wrocław: Nortom, 2002), 5, 101–13. For the instrumentalization of genocide, see Anton Weiss-Wendt, "Hostage of Politics: Raphael Lemkin on "Soviet Genocide," *Journal of Genocide Research* Vol. 7, No. 4 (2005): 551–59.

192 "Tupet 'Ukraińca' dr Grzegorza Motyki. Czy G. Motyka jest wykonawcą ściśle tajnej instrukcji—uchwały z dn. 22 czerwca 1990r. Organizacji Ukraińskich Nacjonalistów?", 25 March 2011, http://www.kresykedzierzynkozle.home.pl/page90.php, (accessed 15 November 2011).

193 Aleksander Korman, *Ludobójstwo UPA na ludności polskiej: Dokumentacja fotograficzna* (Wrocław: Nortom, 2003). On the subject of the photographs, see Ada Rutkowska and Dariusz Stola, "Fałszywy opis, prawdziwe zbrodnie," *Rzeczpospolita. Plus Minus* 19–20 May 2007, 15. Available at http://www.civitas.edu.pl/pub/mediaOnas/2007/rzeczpospolita_2007_05_19_falszywy_opis_prawdziwe_zbrodnie_pdf2%5B1%5D.pdf (accessed 9 October 2011).

194 Korman, *Ludobójstwo*, 73.

Fig. 66. Memorial in Wrocław devoted to "the Polish citizens murdered in the south-eastern border territories in 1939–1947 by the Organization of Ukrainian Nationalists (OUN) and the Ukrainian Insurgent Army (UPA)."

photograph and argued that binding children to a tree was one of the UPA's killing methods. Nevertheless, the monument was dismantled in 2008.[195] In Legnica in 2009, the city council named a street "The Boulevard of the Victims of the Genocide of the OUN-UPA" (*Aleja Ofiar Ludobójstwa OUN-UPA*).[196] In addition to their own monuments, the kresowiacy also identified themselves with the Soviet monuments erected to the victims of the OUN-UPA.[197]

In 2004 the most prolific historian of the kresowiacy community, Edward Prus, published a Bandera biography titled *Stepan Bandera (1909–1959): Symbol of Crime and Cruelty*.[198] Prus began publishing on the subject of the OUN-UPA, in the mid-1980s in communist Poland.[199] Although he accumulated an impressive amount of documentation on Ukrainian nationalism, the majority of his publications pre-

195 Mariusz Godos, "Kontrowersyjna rzeźba," 15 October 2008, http://www.zycie.pl/informacje.php?region=Przemy%B6l&nr=1035&page=1 (accessed 13 October 2011).

196 "Aleja Ofiar Ludobójstwa OUN-UPA," 3 October 2009, http://forum.gazeta.pl/forum/w,48782,101066063,101066063,_8222_Aleja_ofiar_ludobojstwa_OUN_UPA_8221_.html (accessed 10 October 2011).

197 Korman, *Ludobójstwo*, 43, 47.

198 Edward Prus, *Stepan Bandera (1909–1959): Symbol zbrodni i okrucieństwa* (Wrocław: Wydawnictwo Nortom, 2004).

199 Edward Prus, *Herosi spod znaku tryzuba: Konowalec–Bandera–Szuchewycz* (Warsaw: Instytut Wydawniczy Związków Zawodowych, 1985), *Z dziejów współpracy nacjonalistów ukraińskich z niemcami w okresie II wojny światowej i okupacji* (Katowice: Akademia Ekonomiczna im. Karola Adamieckiego, 1985), *Atamania UPA: Tragedia kresów* (Warsaw: Instytut Wydawniczy Związków Zawodowych, 1988), *Patriarcha galicyjski* (Warsaw: Instytut Wydawniczy Związków Zawodowych, 1989).

sented a victimized nationalist narrative. Prus omitted and denied atrocities committed by Polish military troops, and he inflated the atrocities of the OUN-UPA into massacres much more horrible than the Holocaust and all other major crimes against humanity. Many of his publications were written in a non-academic format without an appropriate indication of sources. As in the case of Soviet publications, this made it impossible to verify the integrity of the author's arguments. In addition to imitating offensive Soviet language, he also used propagandist articles in Soviet newspapers, and documents such as Albert Norden's speech at a press conference in 1959 as sources, exactly as the Soviet historians had done.[200] In addition, his publications were not free from factual mistakes.[201]

In the Bandera biography, relying on such Soviet writers as Beliaev, Prus stated that Bandera "in his youth strangled small cats with one hand in the presence of his colleagues, in order to 'toughen his will' and after the early 1930s, applied these methods to humans."[202] Similarly Prus characterized Bandera as "nasty and cruel. It should be emphasized strongly: in Poland and in Ukraine—in general—Bandera is a symbol of atrocities, crimes, arson, looting—all the most evil things a man can conduct. 'You bandera! [Pol. *Ty bandero!*]' is a swear word for a Ukrainian from Kiev because this term is the negation of the evangelic truth and of good."[203] In addition to denying that Ukrainians and other national minorities were discriminated against in Poland, Prus also blamed Bandera, the OUN, and Jews for the Soviet deportations of Poles during the first occupation of eastern Poland in 1939–1941. Like Soviet historians, he wrongly argued that the Nachtigall battalion was the main perpetrator of the Lviv pogrom in July 1941.[204] In general, the most prominent kresowiacy historian combined the Soviet approach to history with the Polish martyrological one, which was not free of antisemitism. Prus wrote an entire monograph on something he called the "Banderite Holocaust" but simultaneously denied Polish crimes against Jews and presented "Jewish Bolshevism" as a historical fact.[205]

The Bandera Debate

In early 2009 the online newspaper *Zaxid.net* published a series of essays about Bandera and started a debate that became more fervent a year later, when President Iushchenko designated Bandera a Hero of Ukraine. It was the first debate in which critical voices were not entirely ignored, and which challenged the apologetic narrative on Bandera, the OUN-UPA, and Ukrainian nationalism. During the debate, Ukrainian intellectuals openly discussed for the first time subjects such as Ukrainian fascism, antisemitism, and the ethnic and political atrocities conducted by the OUN

200 For Soviet articles and Norden, see Edward Prus, *Holocaust po banderowsku: Czy Żydzi byli w UPA?* (Wrocław: Wydawnictwo Nortom, 1995), 37; Prus, *Stepan Bandera*, 212.

201 For example in his Bandera biography Prus wrote that Bandera was arrested on 14 July 1934 at the Polish-Czechoslovak border and not in the Ukrainian student residence in Lviv, and that after the Second World War Bandera used the name "Stefan Popiel" instead of "Stefan Popel." Cf. Prus, *Stepan Bandera*, 93, 313.

202 Prus, *Stepan Bandera*, 17.

203 Ibid., 9.

204 Ibid., 122, 186, 212.

205 Prus, *Holocaust po banderowsku*, 130; Prus, *Stepan Bandera*, 186.

and UPA. At least three groups with different points of view manifested themselves. The first, embodied by Franziska Bruder, John-Paul Himka, David Marples, Per Anders Rudling, Timothy Snyder, and myself, represented a critical approach to Bandera and the OUN and UPA. The second group, represented by "liberal" and "progressive" Ukrainian scholars such as Iaroslav Hrytsak, Andrii Portnov, Vasyl' Rasevych, and Mykola Riabchuk; and diaspora intellectuals such as Alexander Motyl and Zenon Kohut, tried to combine a critical approach to Bandera and the OUN-UPA with post-Soviet and diaspora nationalism and defended Bandera by using various arguments. The third group, which included Volodymyr V"iatrovych, Marco Levytsky, Askold Lozynskyj, and Stephen Bandera, denied everything that Bandera critics reasoned about the *Providnyk* and OUN-UPA, and defended them by means of various strategies of omission, denial, and justification.

In early 2009, when *Zaxid.net* published the essays, it became clear that the subject of the blemishes of Bandera and his movement was still taboo. The popular and progressive internet journal published V"iatrovych's article without any comment, although he declared that OUN assassinations and murders were not terrorist acts, that the ethnic violence conducted by the OUN-UPA was a legitimate measure of the "national liberation fight," and that Bandera did not collaborate with Nazi Germany. In contrast, my own article, drawing attention to the atrocities committed by the OUN-B and criticizing the denial-oriented attitude toward such issues in today's Ukraine, drew the remark from the editors that they "do not agree with a number of the author's theses."[206]

The second debate after the designation of Bandera as a Hero of Ukraine took place, for the most part, in English-language newspapers and journals, and to a smaller extent in Ukraine. On 7 February 2010, David Marples wrote in the *Edmonton Journal* that Iushchenko "surely erred when he conferred on Bandera the title—paradoxically it sounds typically Soviet—Hero of Ukraine [because] in the 21st century, his [Bandera's] views seem archaic and dangerous. He embraced violence, terror and intolerance toward other ethnicities living on Ukrainian lands."[207] Marples' statement caused a flow of angry reactions from Ukrainian nationalists and motivated "liberal" historians to write more moderate but no less problematic articles. The debate was not so much about the person of Bandera as it was about the symbol of Ukrainian nationalism and the OUN-UPA, or more precisely about the evaluation of their deeds and their relevance for today's Ukraine.

In his article "A Fascist Hero in a Democratic Kiev" Snyder wrote that Bandera and the OUN sought "to turn Ukraine into a fascist one-party dictatorship without national minorities."[208] In an interview in March 2010, he emphasized that Bandera

206 Volodymyr V"iatrovych, "Bandera: stari ta novi mify," *zakhid.net*, 8 January 2009, http://zaxid.net/home/showSingleNews.do?bandera_stari_ta_novi_mifi&objectId=1068824 (accessed 1 November 2011); Grzegorz Rossoliński-Liebe, "Obraz Stepana Bandery v pol's'kii natsional'nii svidomosti," http://zaxid.net/news/showNews.do?obraz_stepana_banderi_v_polskiy_natsionalniy_svidomosti&objectId=1069869 (accessed 1 November 2011).

207 David Marples, "Hero of Ukraine Linked to the Murder of 4000 Jews," *Edmonton Journal*, 7 February 2010.

208 Timothy Snyder, "A Fascist Hero in Democratic Kiev," 24 February 2010, *The New York Review of Books*, http://www.nybooks.com/blogs/nyrblog/2010/feb/24/a-fascist-hero-in-democratic-kiev/ (accessed 1 November 2011).

lived in a fascist era and was very much influenced by fascism. He argued that "in the 1920's and 30's, Bandera was ideologically fascist. However these were times when many Europeans were fascists. French writers were fascists, Romanian philosophers were fascists, and the Italian government was fascist. Further, there is no doubt that fascism had a great influence on National Socialism."[209] Like Marples, Snyder condemned the violence of the OUN-UPA and criticized Bandera's designation as a hero:

> Firstly, the idea of declaring certain individuals to be heroes is a very Soviet idea, and I think that those people who approve of Bandera's actions and support declaring him (and especially Shukhevych) a hero, should pause for a moment and consider the fact that the introduction of the hero appellation is a borrowing from the Soviet Union. Both fascists and communists held the view that individuals could be heroes. ... People are arguing about who should be declared a hero, but no one is expressing any doubts as to whether there should even be such an appellation.[210]

Himka described the history of the OUN in terms similar to Snyder's, but with more details concerning OUN ideology and the war crimes committed by this movement in the name of that ideology:

> OUN was indeed a typical fascist organization as shown by many of its features: its leader principle (Führerprinzip), its aspiration to ban all other political parties and movements, its fascist-style slogan (Slava Ukraïni! Heroiam slava!), its red-and-black flag, its raised-arm salute, its xenophobia and antisemitism, its cult of violence, and its admiration of Hitler, Mussolini, and other leaders of fascist Europe. What's not fascist here?[211]

Unlike Snyder, Himka also offered a commentary on the present. He explained how apologists present fascism as patriotism, and fascists and war criminals as freedom fighters. One such historian, Kohut, termed by Himka an "ideological watch dog," had been an expert on pre-modern Ukrainian history. He neither studied Ukrainian nationalism, nor the OUN and UPA, nor published anything about these subjects, but in the debate he reproached Marples and Himka for their assessment of Bandera. Criticizing Kohut, Himka brought attention to the very important and disturbing problem of historians who were socialized in nationalist diaspora communities, identified with the political tradition of Bandera and the OUN-UPA, and had a vested and culturally determined interest in denying the war crimes of that movement.[212]

Scholars in the next group—described in this book as "progressive" and "liberal"—protected the right to have an "inconvenient hero." Many of them were not so much

209 Timothy Snyder, "Declaring People to be Heroes is a Soviet Idea," 15 March 2010, http://www.ukrainianstudies.uottawa.ca/pdf/UKL442.pdf (accessed 1 November 2011); "Profesor Snaider: proholoshennia heroiem—radians'ka ideia," 3 March 2010, BBC Mii svit, http://www.bbc.co.uk/ukrainian/ukraine/2010/03/100303_snyder_ie_it.shtml (accessed 1 November 2011).

210 Ibid. Snyder's critique of the OUN and UPA does not correspond with his more apologetic attitude to Polish history. Cf. Rossoliński-Liebe, Debating, Obfuscating and Disciplining the Holocaust, 222–24.

211 John-Paul Himka, "Should Ukrainian Studies Defend the Heritage of OUN-UPA?", 10 February 2010, http://www.ukrainianstudies.uottawa.ca/pdf/UKL441.pdf (accessed 1 November 2011).

212 Ibid.

interested in history as concerned by current politics, in particular by paragraph 20 of the resolution of the European Parliament from 25 February 2010, which "deeply deplores the decision by the outgoing President of Ukraine, Viktor Yushchenko, posthumously to award Stepan Bandera, a leader of the Organization of Ukrainian Nationalists (OUN) which collaborated with Nazi Germany, the title of 'National Hero of Ukraine'; hopes, in this regard, that the new Ukrainian leadership will reconsider such decisions and will maintain its commitment to European values."[213]

Very typical for this group were the opinions expressed by Iaroslav Hrytsak who specialized in Ukrainian nineteenth-century history but also published a few articles on Jewish-Ukrainian relations, the Second World War, and the Holocaust.[214] During the debate, Hrytsak expressed mainly political concerns about the designation of Bandera as a Hero of Ukraine, because it could jeopardize the process of the integration of Ukraine into the European Union. In an interview given on 27 January 2010, he argued that the status of Bandera, as of every national hero, is contested: "A hero for some is an anti-hero for others," and that "if we really wish to begin the process of integration with the EU, we have to be careful with the sensitivity of our neighbors—in particular those who are our only strategic partners [Poles]."[215]

In an article published a few weeks later, he stated that the Holocaust had been an important part of European self-understanding but not in Ukraine and several other countries that had been either republics or satellite states of the Soviet Union. Furthermore, he stated that small nations, in which category he included Ukrainians, should have, in terms of dealing with their own history, different rights from those of other nations and should be allowed to commemorate "inconvenient heroes," such as Bandera, as symbols of resistance:

> "Small" nations have the right to have [inconvenient heroes like Bandera], as long as they celebrate those heroes not as symbols of violence against other people, but as symbols of resistance and struggle for their own survival and their own dignity. In the case of Bandera, the issue is not whether he was a fascist—the question is whether the majority of people who celebrate him, celebrate him *as* a fascist.[216]

Alexander Motyl also responded to the resolution of the European Parliament. In his evaluation of Bandera and the Ukrainian nationalism, Motyl did not discuss such aspects as fascism in the OUN or the pogroms in 1941. He called the ethnic cleansing in 1943–44 the "Ukrainian-Polish violence in Volhynia," which, in his view, had nothing in common with ethnic violence conducted by the Ustaša and should be compared instead to the violence of the "Irish nationalists against the British." In addition to romanticizing the OUN-UPA's violence, he pointed out the Soviet

213 "European Parliament resolution of 25 February 2010 on the situation in Ukraine," http://www.europarl.europa.eu/sides/getDoc.do?type=TA&reference=P7-TA-2010-0035&language=EN&ring=B7-2010-0120 (accessed 4 November 2011).

214 For the articles, see for example Hrytsak, Ukraïntsi v antyievreis'kykh aktsiiakh. For V"iatrovych, see V"iatrovych, *Stavlennia OUN*, 16–17.

215 Iaroslav Hrytsak, "Shche raz pro Iushchenka, shche raz pro Banderu," *Zaxid.net*, 27 January 2010, http://zaxid.net/blogentry/57801/ (accessed 3 November 2011).

216 Iaroslav Hrytsak, "Klopoty z pam"iattiu," *Zaxid.net*, 8 March 2010, http://www.zaxid.net/article/60958/ (accessed 3 November 2011).

atrocities committed in Ukraine and the OUN-UPA struggle against the Soviet Union and argued that Bandera represented that struggle.[217]

In his reflections on Bandera and the EU resolution, Motyl asked, "Does conferral of Hero of Ukraine status represent a disregard for European values?" His answer was: "Viewed historically, European values include above all militarism, racism, anti-Semitism, imperialism, and chauvinism. The values of democracy and human rights are a relatively recent historical addition to the plate and, strictly speaking, are not so much European values as the officially declared values of the European Union. Worse, these EU values are violated as often as they are observed—by Europeans themselves."[218] Along these lines, he argued that the European Union and "Europeans" should not interfere in Ukrainian matters because "many nationally conscious Ukrainians—who represent the core of Ukraine's civil society and democratic movement—resent being singled out for their views of their heroes and point to double standards and European hypocrisy."[219]

Mykola Riabchuk, a popular intellectual whose publications portrayed Ukraine as a Russian colony, also explained why Ukrainians need not come to terms with their own past but should rather continue celebrating the *Providnyk*. Relying on Motyl, he argued:

> Ukraine is not just a "normal" nation, with firm identity and secure statehood, that chooses presumably between authoritarianism and democracy, i.e. in this case, between crypto-fascist legacy exemplified by Bandera and OUN and liberal-democratic values promoted by the EU. ... The real choice is to either defend the national sovereignty, dignity, and identity, or give them away to Russia and/or its 'Creole' subsidiaries. Under these circumstances, the second part of Bandera's legacy remains relevant—that of patriotism, national solidarity, self-sacrifice, idealistic commitment to common goals and values.[220]

Andrii Portnov, an ambitious and talented historian also followed similar ways of reasoning. In an article published in *Krytyka*, he was unconcerned about the heroization of Bandera and the OUN-UPA. Following Armstrong, he called the OUN-UPA "integral nationalists" and suggested that their cult would be a legitimate pursuit, and part of the de-Sovietization of Ukraine. He hesitated as to whether one solution to the problems of contemporary Ukrainian politics of memory could be a "regional pluralism of symbols," which in the Ukrainian case meant monuments to Stalin in the east and to Bandera in the west.[221]

217 Alexander Motyl, "Ukraine, Europe, and Bandera," *Cicero Foundation Great Debate Paper*, No. 10/05, March, 2010, 6–9, http://www.cicerofoundation.org/lectures/Alexander_J_Motyl_UKRAINE_EUROPE_AND_BANDERA.pdf (accessed 4 November 2010).

218 Alexander Motyl, "Ukraine, Europe, and Bandera," 12.

219 Ibid., 13. See also Per Anders Rudling, "Iushchenkiv fashyst: kult Bandery v Ukraïni ta Kanadi," *Strasti za Banderoiu*, ed. Tarik Cyryl Amar, Ihor Balyns'kyi, Iaroslav Hrytsak (Kiev: Hrani-T, 2010), 274–75.

220 Mykola Riabchuk, "Bandera's Controversy and Ukraine's Future," *Russkii vopros* No. 1, 2010 http://www.russkiivopros.com/?pag=one&id=315&kat=9&csl=46#_edn13 (accessed 3 November 2011).

221 Andrii Portnov, "Kontekstualizatsiia Stepana Bandery," *Krytyka*, 3–4 (2010), 14. See also Grzegorz Rossoliński-Liebe and Per Anders Rudling, "Review of Krytyka. Hefte 3–4; 7–8; 9–10. Kiev 2010," *H-Soz-u-Kult*, 15 June 2011, http://hsozkult.geschichte.hu-berlin.de/rezensionen/2011-2-212 (accessed 1 November 2011). After the debate Portnov seems to have changed his attitude to Bandera, the OUN,

The historian Anatolii Rusnachenko, who specialized in the OUN-UPA, took offence at Snyder's categorization of Bandera as a fascist. He set about correcting Snyder, who, according to him, "does not master the topic very well." Rusnachenko claimed that "attributing fascism to Bandera is a clear exaggeration, even if there were [fascist] tendencies." Rather than denying the OUN crimes, Rusnachenko diminished them. "True, the OUN did carry out terror (even though it was not on a significant scale), but we should not forget about the terror that the Poles carried out in occupied Eastern Galicia." Rusnachenko did not clarify how 70,000 to 100,000 Polish victims of the Ukrainian nationalist terror were not significant, but he was concerned that one who investigates the crimes of the OUN-UPA might forget the Ukrainian victims murdered by Poles during and after the Second World War. Finally, he took Snyder to task for his unwillingness to separate Bandera the fascist leader from Bandera the heroic symbol of Ukrainian patriotism. Snyder, Rusnachenko wrote, "does not want to admit that Bandera was and remains simply a symbol of the liberation movement and a personification of the idea of uncompromising struggle against all enemies of Ukraine and Ukrainianness."[222]

Vitalii Ponomar'ov insisted that both Himka's and Snyder's characterizations of the OUN as a fascist organization were wrong. His first evidence for this claim was that Soviet propaganda also described the OUN as fascist. Another was that the OUN could not possibly have been fascist because, "as the historian Iaroslav Hrytsak rightly remarked, it is contradictory to the nature of fascism to write about 'Polish,' 'Czech,' or 'Ukrainian' fascism because fascism sought a partial or total destruction of these nations."[223]

One of the participants in the debate, Niklas Bernsand, from Lund University, whose article was translated into Ukrainian and published in the leading Ukrainian journal *Krytyka*, compared the cult of Bandera to that of the Croatian general Ante Gotovina, who was sentenced by the International Criminal Tribunal for the former Yugoslavia in April 2011 to twenty-four years imprisonment for crimes against humanity. "Should the Croats," Bernsand asked, "be judged for their public expressions of sympathy for a person who is responsible for the ethnic cleansing of non-Croat cities and villages?" He answered his question in the negative and applied this logic to the Bandera cult in Ukraine: "I will not ... argue 'for' or 'against' the presidential decree about turning Bandera into a Hero of Ukraine."[224]

The Bandera radical apologists, similarly to some of the "liberal" or diaspora intellectuals, argued with Snyder, Himka, and Marples and tried to correct them. Unlike the "liberal" intellectuals, they openly and extensively used far-right propaganda and introduced erroneous information. In response to Marples' article, Marco Levytsky, the editor of *Ukrainian News* in Edmonton, suggested that the linking of

and the post-Soviet apologetic memory of mass violence. See for example Andrei Portnov, "Istoria dlia domashnego upotrebleniia," *Ab Imperio* 3 (2012): 309–38.

222 Anatolii Rusnachenko, "Symvol i ioho krytyky," *Krytyka*, 9–10 (2010), 7. See also Rossoliński-Liebe, Review of Krytyka.

223 Vitalii Ponomar'ov, "Deheroïzatsiia Oporu," *Krytyka*, 7–8 (2010), 22. See also Rossoliński-Liebe, Review of Krytyka.

224 Niklas Bernsand, "Beznevynnist' pamiaty," *Krytyka*, 7–8 (2010), 22. See also Rossoliński-Liebe, Review of Krytyka.

the OUN and Bandera to the pogroms in 1941 is "Vladimir Putin-style ex-KGB falsification." Similarly, he claimed that the Jews "had disproportionate membership" in the NKVD and blamed them for the killing of "4,000 to 8,000 civilian prisoners," who were murdered by the NKVD after 22 June 1941 in Ukrainian prisons. In addition, he claimed that the UPA did not kill Jews and he quoted Fishbein, who stated that writing about Jews killed by the UPA is a "provocation engineered by Moscow." Levytsky also enumerated all the famous Ukrainians who saved Jews.[225]

Stephen Bandera defended the honor of his grandfather, his family, and all those individuals who identified themselves with the *Providnyk*. In his response to Marples' article, the *Providnyk's* grandson argued that Marples' column was "a rehash of misinformation." He claimed that the statement about OUN involvement in the pogrom was misleading. As evidence, he offered the fact that not a single OUN member was brought to trial by the International Military Tribunal at Nuremberg. Similarly, in order to evoke the impression that no OUN members were involved in the Holocaust, he pointed out that Bandera's two brothers were killed in Auschwitz. Furthermore, he argued that "our family cleared the Bandera name before the Commission of Inquiry on War Criminals in Canada in 1985." Stephen Bandera ended his article with the argument that "if Stepan Bandera was even guilty of half the crimes of which Marples and his ilk accuse him, then he would have been swinging from the gallows at Nuremberg 65 years ago."[226]

The debate did not focus on the person of Bandera but rather on Bandera as the symbol of the OUN and UPA, or of a specific epoch of Ukrainian history, or on the movement associated with his name. During the debate, it became clear that Ukrainian historians and intellectuals were not prepared to distance themselves from difficult elements of the Ukrainian past, such as the fascist tendencies in Ukrainian history and the atrocities committed in the name of Ukrainian nationalism. A huge obstacle to rethinking or discussing the history of Ukrainian nationalism was the fact that the Holocaust was marginalized, ignored, and politically distorted in the Soviet Union, in communities of the Ukrainian diaspora, and also in post-Soviet Ukraine. Another obstacle to debating Bandera was the lack of critical research on Bandera, Ukrainian nationalism, and the involvement of Ukrainians and the OUN-UPA in the Holocaust and other kinds of ethnic and political violence. However, we should keep in mind that several articles and monographs (for example by Marco Carynnyk, Karel Berkhoff, Schmuel Spector, and Grzegorz Motyka) relating to Bandera and the OUN-UPA had already been published a decade before the debate, or even earlier. These publications were known to historians or intellectuals, at least such as Iaroslav Hrytsak, Alexander Motyl, Mykola Riabchuk, and Andrii Portnov, who read English, German, Polish, and other languages. V"iatrovych also quoted some of the

225 Marco Levytsky, "Ukrainian Nationalists Played No Part in Massacre of 4,000 Jews," *Edmonton Journal*, 9 February 2010; Marco Levytsky, "'Strong Evidence' by Per Anders Rudling and 'Dubious Documents' by John-Paul Himka," (unpublished letter to the *Edmonton Journal*), The Ukraine List #442, 15 March 2010, http://www.ukrainianstudies.uottawa.ca/pdf/UKL442.pdf (accessed 3 November 2011).

226 Stepan Bandera, "Family Name Cleared," *Edmonton Journal*, 9 February 2010. The International Military Tribunal at Nuremberg did not indict Bandera or any other leaders of East Central European nationalist, antisemitic, and fascist movements that had been involved in the Holocaust and other crimes against humanity.

publications, even if only to dismiss them as "Soviet propaganda." One should therefore not underestimate the impact of the Bandera cult on the course of the debate and on the general understanding of Bandera in post-Soviet Ukraine and in the Ukrainian diaspora.[227]

Finally, one needs to point out that the debate was not only about history but also about Ukrainian identity, which is still in the process of construction. It is difficult to predict how much time this process will take and what its results will be. The Soviet Union and the far-right factions of the Ukrainian diaspora left Ukrainian intellectuals a difficult and challenging political and intellectual heritage. Nevertheless, Ukrainian intellectuals and politicians are not obliged to preserve and protect victimized, heroized, or otherwise distorted and politicized versions of their own history. Nor do they need to behave as if they could have no control over the Bandera cult and the process of creating a new Ukrainian identity. In the end, none but they would have to rethink Bandera and the difficult part of Ukrainian history related to and associated with him.

Bandera in the Context of other Leader Cults

During the twentieth century, cults of authoritarian, fascist, nationalist, communist, military, and other leaders erupted in many countries, societies, and movements. They persisted in their original or in mutated forms for different lengths of time. Some of them, like the Bandera cult, have thrived until today. After the dissolution of the Soviet Union, the cults of communist leaders generally disappeared in East Central Europe, although we should not forget the attempts to rehabilitate Stalin in some parts of the former Soviet territories, including eastern Ukraine. At the same time, cults of former fascist, authoritarian, and other far-right leaders reappeared in several postcommunist countries, although the leaders themselves were already dead. The new cults appeared because of various reasons such as political and cultural confusion, or nostalgic identification with the romanticized forms of former movements or their ideologies. Post-Soviet leader cults have been created by various groups, including paramilitary organizations, intellectuals, restaurant managers, and vendors of wine and T-shirts. A similar kind of commercialization and diffusion of leader cults had already occurred in Italy and to a lesser extent in Germany, before the collapse of the Soviet Union.

In Poland, the cult of Roman Dmowski—the leader of the Polish Endecja, who in the 1920s and 1930s "elevated antisemitism from a historically and religiously rooted prejudice to the level of political ideology and action"—materialized in a monument to Dmowski, unveiled in 2006 in Warsaw.[228] Unlike the Bandera cult, the Dmowski cult did not impact on leading historians and intellectuals. It mainly affected or was

227 According to the TsDVR website, Ivan Patryliak, one of the leading Ukrainian historians, argued shortly after the debate: "Bandera has fulfilled the mission of a national banner and as a symbol of the banner till now. It would be logical to erect for such outstanding personalities as Bandera a Park of Glory of national heroes with monuments and memorials." Cf. "Dlia taïkh znakovykh postatei iak Bandera slid zrobyty Park Slavy natsional'nykh heroïv,– istoryk," http://cdvr.org.ua/content/для-таких-знакових-постатей-як-бандера-слід-зробити-парк-слави-національних-героїв-історик (accessed 16 July 2012).

228 Pankowski, *The Populist Radical Right in Poland*, 27.

constructed by conservative and right-wing politicians and by some confused scholars. Nevertheless, one should not underestimate the legitimizing power of academic silence around this antidemocratic phenomenon. Similarly to the Bandera cult, that of the Endecja leader was cultivated during the Cold War by factions among emigrants. Like the Bandera worshipers, Dmowski admirers have denied or diminished the antisemitic and extremist views expressed by him and the Endecja movement and have prized his patriotism and his devotion to the process of establishing a nation state. They have also propagated distorted nationalist versions of Polish history. They have denied the Polish involvement in the Holocaust and have presented the Poles as tragic but brave heroes and martyrs, and the victims of their neighbors, in particular Germans and Russians.[229]

The rehabilitation of the Romanian authoritarian leader Antonescu was related to the fact that he was convicted by a Romanian communist tribunal and executed by the communist Romanian authorities. This, as in the case of Bandera's assassination, gave him a touch of martyrdom. Unlike Bandera however, Antonescu was not imprisoned during the Second World War, during which his troops committed numerous war crimes against Jews and other people. National-communist Romanian writers and historians depicted Antonescu as a patriot and victim as early as the 1970s, but the actual rehabilitation of Antonescu took place after 1990. In postcommunist discourses, the Romanian leader was turned into an "anti-Bolshevik fighter," a "great patriot," "martyr," and a "complex personality." No mention was made of his involvement in the Holocaust, and Jews were remembered only as helpers of the Bolsheviks. Streets were named after him and a few busts were unveiled. Some officers from Antonescu's government were rehabilitated, among them Prime Minister Gheron Netta who had introduced the racial laws in 1940. It was only in the early 2000s that the Romanian government removed Antonescu monuments, renamed the Antonescu streets and introduced a law prohibiting all kinds of radical right propaganda, in order not to jeopardize Romanian integration into the European Union and NATO.[230]

In addition to the Antonescu cult, far-right Romanians did not permit the decay of the cult of Corneliu Zelea Codreanu, the charismatic founder and leader of the Legion of the Archangel Michael, known as the Iron Guard. In contrast to this cult, a cult of Codreanu's follower Horia Sima did not reemerge in Romania, either during the Cold War or after 1990. Similarly to Bandera, Sima spent a substantial part of the Second World War in German detention. In August 1944, he was released to form a Romanian government and to mobilize Romanians for further struggle against the Soviet Union. After the Second World War, Sima was not prosecuted by international war tribunals because he was not in Romania when the crimes were committed. During the Cold War, Sima lived in Austria, France, and Spain. Like Bandera he became a fervent anticommunist Cold War fighter, and a controversial leader of the far-right Romanian émigrés. Unlike Bandera, he was not assassinated, and died in Madrid in 1993. During the Cold War, veterans of the Iron Guard, living in Canada,

229 Ibid., 21–31.

230 William Totok, "Antonescu-Kult und die Rehabilitierung der Kriegsverbrecher," *Holocaust an der Peripherie: Judenpolitik und Judenmord in Rumänien und Transnistrien 1940–1941*, ed. Wolfgang Benz and Brigitte Mihok (Berlin: Metropol, 2009), 197–212.

Portugal, Spain, the United States, and several Latin American countries, prolonged the cult of Codreanu and worshiped Sima, only to a much lesser extent. After 1990, the Codreanu cult reappeared in Romania but for various reasons did not attract as much attention as the Antonescu cult.[231]

In postcommunist Slovakia, attempts to rehabilitate the clerical fascist leader Jozef Tiso came from nationalist, émigré, and Catholic circles. Tiso had already been turned into a martyr by Slovak far-right émigrés after his execution in April 1947. Afterwards he was commemorated as a hero, patriot, victim of circumstance, or a martyr. During the Cold War, Tiso's admirers lived similarly to the Ukrainian diaspora in various Western countries. They included personalities such as Ferdinand Ďurčanský, who had been sentenced *in absentia* to death in the same trial as Tiso, but was not executed, and who, during the Cold War worked together with Stets'ko in the ABN. Another far-right Slovak thinker, Milan Ďurica, a professor in Italy and a Roman Catholic priest, argued that Tiso was a democrat and an opponent of the Nazis, who saved the lives of 35,000 Jews. After the breakup of the Soviet bloc, the Slovak far-right émigrés began, similarly to Bandera's adherents in Ukraine, to play an important role in reinventing Tiso's myth in Slovakia. Nevertheless, unlike in Ukraine, some Slovak historians did not succumb to the nationalist myths of the far-right émigrés and began challenging their thesis.[232] One plaque in memory of Tiso was unveiled in July 1990 in Banovce nad Bebravou and another one in October 1991 at the house of his birth in Bytča. The attempt to install a plaque in 2000 in Žilina was cancelled due to protests from the US embassy in Bratislava and from the Jewish community of Slovakia.[233] Defending the plaques, some Slovak public figures argued that "Tiso's contribution to the nation should be separated from his responsibility for the wartime state." They thereby used arguments similar to those of the Ukrainian "liberal" historians who defended Bandera.[234] The integration of Slovakia in the EU downplayed the Tiso cult to some extent, but after Slovakia joined the EU in 2004 some far-right, populist, and clerical public figures continued to rehabilitate Tiso. In December 2006 Ján Sokol, Archbishop of Bratislava-Trnava stated that under Tiso's presidency the country "enjoyed a period of well-being." Cardinal Ján Chrisostom Korec defended Tiso five months later on television, arguing that Tiso had "very good relations with Jews."[235] The Jewish community frequently protested against such attempts to rehabilitate the Slovak *Vodca*.[236] James Mace Ward, who in 2013 published the first scholarly biography of Tiso, concluded that: "Only in a moral order

231 Constantin Iordachi, *Charisma, Politics and Violence: The Legion of the "Archangel Michael" in Inter-war Romania* (Trondheim: Program on East European Cultures and Societies, Norwegian University of Science and Technology, 2004), 148–51; Shafir, Between Denial and 'Comparative Trivialization, 11–13; "Eiserne Garde," in *Enzyklopädie des Holocaust*, 1: 404.

232 Ward, *Priest, Politician, Collaborator*, 268, 274.

233 Gila Fatran, "Holocaust and Collaboration in Slovakia in the postwar discourse," in *Collaboration with the Nazis. Public Discourse after the Holocaust*, ed. Roni Stauber (New York: Routledge, 2011), 197; Nina Paulovičová, "The 'Unmasterable Past'? Slovaks and the Holocaust: The Reception of the Holocaust in Post-communist Slovakia," in *Bringing the Dark Past to Light: The Reception of the Holocaust in Postcommunist Europe*, ed. John-Paul Himka and Joanna Beata Michlic (Lincoln: University of Nebraska Press, 2013), 561.

234 Ward, *Priest, Politician, Collaborator*, 271.

235 Paulovičová, 'Unmasterable Past'?, 561; Ward, *Priest, Politician, Collaborator*, 278–79.

236 Paulovičová, 'Unmasterable Past'?, 561.

that devaluates [the memory of the Holocaust and European values] can Tiso triumph as a martyr."[237]

Pavelić seems to have been celebrated and sacralized by Ustaša veterans and radical right sections of the Croatian diaspora, very similarly to Bandera by the far-right factions of the Ukrainian diaspora. After 1990 the Pavelić cult appeared in Croatia but it did not take as lavish and persistent form as the Bandera cult in Ukraine. Uncritical and hagiographical books on Pavelić appeared, cafes and kindergartens were named after him, but no monuments authorized by the Croatian authorities devoted to the *Poglavnik* were unveiled and no streets were named after him. The *Poglavnik* and Croatian fascism were rehabilitated to some extent by the policies of reconciliation instituted by the first government of Franjo Tuđman. These policies were intended to bring together the admirers and the opponents of the Ustaša legacy. They diminished Ustaša crimes and sought to differentiate between the good NDH (Independent State of Croatia) and the bad Ustaša. This resembled the distinction between commemorating Bandera as a fascist, or as a symbol of resistance, which was made by some Ukrainian "liberal" and "progressive" intellectuals during the Bandera debate. Radical right groups such as the Croatian Party of Rights (*Hrvatska stranka prava*, HSP) openly celebrated the *Poglavnik*, using the former Croatian fascist aesthetics and symbols. They also reintroduced fascist rituals, such as the Ustaša greeting "Ready for the Homeland!" (*Za dom spremni!*). The radical right activists argued, similarly to the nationalist and some "liberal" historians in Ukraine, that the Ustaša was not involved in the Holocaust, because several Jews survived the Second World War in the territories controlled by the Croatian fascists. An important symbol for Pavelić's admirers became Bleiburg, where Yugoslav partisans had killed Ustaša functionaries in 1945. The site has been visited by many different types of Croatian patriots and far-right activists, who commemorated the Ustaša members killed in Bleiburg as heroes and martyrs. Ustaša flags frequently waved during these commemorations, and portraits of the *Poglavnik* and other prominent Ustaša were available at stands. After 2000 the rehabilitation of the Ustaša and Pavelić became less evident, although the nationalist tendency to diminish Ustaša crimes has not evaporated in postcommunist Croatia.[238]

237 Ward, *Priest, Politician, Collaborator*, 283.

238 Ljiljana Radonic, *Krieg um die Erinnerung: Kroatische Vergangenheitspolitik zwischen Revisionismus und europäischen Standards* (Frankfurt am Main: Campus-Verlag, 2010), 158, 202, 212, 232, 256, 315, 377; Vjeran Pavlaković, "Flirting with Fascism: The Ustaša Legacy and Croatian Politics in the 1990s," The Shared History and The Second World War and National Question in ex-Yugoslavia, Conference in Seville, Spain, January /February 2008, http://www.centerforhistory.net/images/stories/pdf/flirting_with_fascism.pdf (accessed 22 December 2012).

CONCLUSION

Nationalist, fascist, and other totalitarian leaders played an important role in twentieth-century European history. They symbolized various political ideas, including genocidal ones, mobilized movements and sometimes even whole societies to fight against other people, set up political cults around themselves, and claimed to represent the pride of their nations. Stepan Bandera, the legendary *Providnyk* of the OUN-B, was one of the central figures of the revolutionary and genocidal Ukrainian nationalist movement, which resembled movements such as the Ustaša, the Iron Guard, and the Hlinka Party. As one of the most significant symbols of the OUN and UPA, Bandera has for decades occupied an important place in the Ukrainian collective memory and identity. Ukrainian patriots and nationalists have remembered him as a true national hero and anticommunist martyr who struggled and fell for Ukraine, and have worshiped him as a brave freedom fighter.

To understand Bandera, it is important to distinguish between two levels. The first level comprises the different politics of memory and collective memories that glorify Bandera and those that stigmatize him. The second level consists of the history of his life, his cult, and his movement. In order to investigate these two, not entirely separate, levels it was necessary to examine Bandera, his movement, and his cult from various perspectives but without equating the perspectives offered by different kinds of documents. To equate testimonies of the survivors of the OUN or UPA atrocities with OUN-UPA propaganda leaflets that deny the experiences recorded in such testimonies, would relativize and distort history. Similarly, one should be critical of documents such as records of NKVD coercive interrogations, and Soviet articles and pamphlets, in which Bandera and his followers were accused of crimes that they had not committed.

Bandera and his cohorts changed in the course of time. They adjusted to new political and social circumstances but they did not substantially change their far-right, essentially fascist, convictions, or abandon the idea of "liberating" Ukraine and turning it into an authoritarian nation state of a fascist type. Despite his expectations, Bandera did not become the *Providnyk* of a Ukrainian collaborationist state in 1941. This fact, as well as his detention until September 1944, helped him to avoid arrest and repression after the Second World War and enabled him to prolong the "liberation struggle" against the "enemies of the Ukrainian nation" during the Cold War. Unlike Pavelić in Croatia, who had been more "lucky" and "successful" than the *Providnyk* in 1941, Bandera did not need to ask Perón or Franco for protection after the Second World War, although the *Caudillo* invited him to settle in Spain. At that time, Bandera allied himself with some Western intelligence services and enjoyed their protection.

The OUN, as a movement rooted in western Ukraine, changed between the 1930s and the early 1950s but, similarly to Bandera, it did not give up its nationalist and ethnic orientation. The OUN was the offspring of the terrorist UVO and in the 1930s it remained a terrorist and ultranationalist organization very similar to the Ustaša, with which it closely cooperated. It began to develop in a different direction from that of the Ustaša, after Hitler did not recognize the Ukrainian state proclaimed on 30 June 1941 in Lviv, and had a number of leading OUN-B members arrested. Nevertheless, in terms of ethnic violence the OUN did not differ substantially from the Ustaša and several other East Central European fascist movements. After founding the UPA in late 1942 and early 1943, the OUN became a partisan underground movement similar to the Forest Brothers in the Baltic States but once again it did not give up its fanatical and suicidal nationalism and did not cease killing civilians en masse.

The ambiguity concerning Bandera, his movement, and his cult may be illustrated by the use of the term "Banderite," which has been employed to describe different kinds of people and concepts. People were known as Banderites or otherwise identified with Bandera at different times, for different reasons, and in different circumstances. Among "Banderites" we would find, on the one hand, war criminals, fascist revolutionaries, and people in the diaspora or in post-Soviet Ukraine, who, for various reasons, developed a positive attitude to Bandera and who commemorated and sacralized him. On the other, we would also find people who were named after Bandera because they were accused of helping the OUN-UPA, or because they spoke Ukrainian in Russian speaking parts of Ukraine, or because they were considered to be opponents of the Soviet regime. When evaluating the Bandera cult, it is important to recall these differences and to emphasize the various politicizations of the subject.

The Person, the Movement, and the Cult

It would be wrong to impose on Bandera only one political identity, and label him as a nationalist, fascist, terrorist, or opponent of the Soviet Union, or a revolutionary idealist. As this study has shown, Bandera was influenced by a number of ideologies and environments, and also by religion. Depending on the specific point in time, he was more open to fascism than to nationalism, or to terrorism than to revolutionary idealism. Beside his political career he also had a private life: he was the son of a Greek Catholic priest, a brother to three sisters and three brothers, a husband and father of three children, the friend of a large number of people, some of whom liked his sense of humor, and a father figure to some of his comrades-in-arms. He was also allegedly an unsuccessful rapist and a man obsessed with women. Conflicting ideas flowed through his mind and he engaged in various activities, but his most important achievement was to become the leader of a movement that tried to establish an authoritarian nation state of a fascist type, and that attempted to "cleanse" this state of ethnic enemies and political opponents, including Jews, Poles, Russians, "Soviets," and even communist, leftist, conservative, and democratic Ukrainians.

Bandera seems not necessarily to have had an evil, monstrous or sadistic personality, as some of his critics would argue. The main discomfort caused by his personality results from the fact that he totally subordinated himself to the idea of "liberating" Ukraine. He accepted mass violence as a means to that end and as a result, he lacked empathy toward certain kinds of people, in particular the "occupiers" and the "enemies of the nation." He regarded their elimination as a political success and was prepared to send thousands of his followers to certain death. Even if some of his ideals such as protecting the Ukrainians against Poles and Russians might appear to have been noble, the methods he and his movement used should be exposed and criticized, together with their ongoing denial and euphemization.

Bandera grew up in a patriotic and religious family and environment. His mindset was initially shaped by his father, a Greek Catholic priest and national activist who engaged in the struggle for a Ukrainian state. Religion was a very important value for Bandera but not more than nationalism. In his youth, Bandera's attitudes were influenced by the unsuccessful attempts to establish a Ukrainian state and by the Polish-Ukrainian conflict. The state proclaimed by Ukrainians in November 1918 in Lviv was destroyed by Poles. The state the Ukrainians tried to establish in Kiev, at about the same time, was destroyed by the Soviets. Ukrainians in the Second Polish Republic regarded Poles as occupiers of Ukrainian territories, while Poles often treated Ukrainians as second-class citizens. Polish authorities closed Ukrainian-language schools, forbade the use of the term "Ukrainian," and in 1934 even repudiated the Little Treaty of Versailles, which had guaranteed minority rights to Byelorussians, Jews, Lithuanians, Russians, Ukrainians, and other non-Polish citizens of the Second Republic. This state of affairs and also the situation of Ukrainians in Soviet Ukraine, in particular the famine of 1932–1933, had a substantial impact on Bandera. It convinced him and many other young Ukrainians that they had to use every method, including war and mass violence, to establish a state that would allow the Ukrainian people to "survive."

In his high-school period, Bandera studied Mikhnovs'kyi, Dontsov, and other ideologists who radicalized Ukrainian nationalism, which, in the nineteenth century, had been social and moderate rather than ethnic, racist, and aggressive. Bandera was also fascinated by various secret revolutionary and terrorist organizations such as the Russian nihilists, the Polish insurgents, the Bolsheviks, Italian Fascists, and German National Socialists. Under the influence of Dontsov, Bandera's fascination with Lenin was transformed into a hatred of communism. As head of the propaganda apparatus of and later the leader of the homeland executive, Bandera demonstrated that he had internalized the ideological notions of extreme Ukrainian nationalism and European authoritarian, fascist, and racist discourses.

Ukrainian far-right nationalism was rooted in eastern Galicia, where it became religious, populist, and mystical. Nevertheless, some of its most important ideologists, such as Mykhnovs'kyi and Dontsov, came from Russian Ukraine. Ukrainians from regions other than eastern Galicia had major difficulties comprehending the spiritualized and populist form of Galician nationalism. Galician Ukrainians understood nationalism not as an ideological or political substance but most of all as culture. They based nationalism on religion and blurred the boundaries between them, of which one good example was Lenkavs'kyi's "The Ten Commandments of a Ukrainian Nationalist." By this means the extremist Ukrainian nationalists undermined religious morality with ideological immorality and called their ideology the "new religion, the religion of Ukrainian nationalism."

The writings of Mikhnovs'kyi and Dontsov are crucial for the understanding of the worldview of the Bandera generation. Mikhnovs'kyi, an early propagator of an ethnic Ukrainian nationalism, coined the slogan "Ukraine for Ukrainians" and recommended Ukrainians not to "marry a foreign woman because your children will be your enemies." Dontsov, the main ideologist of the Bandera generation, combined various nationalist, fascist, populist, and racist motifs. Like Mussolini, he was a socialist before the First World War. After the war, he became a far-right thinker and a passionate critic of communism, socialism, and democracy. He cleared moderate and socialist components out of Ukrainian nationalism and tried to transform it into a fascist ideology which was intended to protect Ukrainians against the Soviet Union and other "enemies."

Racism and eugenics were popularized in the Ukrainian nationalist discourse both before and after the First World War by intellectuals such as Stepan Rudnyts'kyi, whose influence on Ukrainian revolutionary and genocidal nationalism should not be underestimated. Rudnyts'kyi used racist theories to emphasize cultural and political differences between Ukrainians, and Poles and Russians, who, after centuries of close coexistence in the Ukrainian territories had become culturally and also linguistically quite similar. Young Ukrainian nationalists such as Bandera and Stets'ko came together at high schools, universities, and in organizations such as Plast, Sokil, and Luh. After school they read Mikhnovs'kyi, Dontsov, and Rudnyts'kyi; they discussed politics and their favored ideologists and followed the international authoritarian and fascist discourses. The Polish authorities strengthened their fascination with racism, fascism, and authoritarianism, by forbidding almost all activities that enhanced Ukrainian culture and consciousness. Polish policy motivated young Ukrainian nationalists to engage in forbidden conspiratorial organizations, to conduct terrorist acts, and to kill the "traitors of the Ukrainian nation."

UVO, the first terrorist and nationalist organization, founded in 1920 in Prague by Ukrainian veterans of the First World War, did not play any major political role. Ukrainian nationalists became more popular and powerful only during the establishment of the OUN which absorbed other nationalist and fascist organizations and could mobilize an increasing number of Ukrainians for its ultranationalist ideas. The leaders of the OUN promised to change the stateless condition of the Ukrainian nation imposed by the Treaty of Versailles and to establish a Ukrainian state which would protect the Ukrainians. Although the OUN sometimes collaborated with right-wing factions of the UNDO, it criticized this national-democratic party and other centrist parties for their collaboration with the Polish authorities. In this manner the OUN weakened any democratic tendencies in Ukrainian society. The OUN's admiration of and orientation toward Nazi Germany, the cult of ethnic and political violence, its fascination with fascism, and its fervent hostility toward ethnic "enemies" and political opponents enabled it to win an increasing number of supporters. The nationalist policies practiced in Poland, especially after Piłsudski's death, strengthened the OUN, which promised to liberate Ukraine from its "occupiers" and to rid its territory of its ethnic foes and political opponents.

The OUN was from the very beginning divided into two generations, one born around 1890 and one around 1910. Bandera, one of the most eager and determined representatives of the younger generation, rose quickly through the ranks of the OUN. After becoming the *Providnyk* of the OUN homeland executive in 1932, Bandera essentially contributed to the radicalization of the organization, which consisted, however, of many other elements not less fanatical than him. In this sense there was a reciprocal relationship of radicalization and fanaticization between the main subject of this study and other young nationalists such as Stets'ko, Shukhevych, Lenkavs'kyi, and Lebed'. The OUN homeland executive under Bandera's leadership began killing more and more Ukrainians, among them OUN members accused of betrayal. If the executioners expressed moral doubts about killing other OUN members, who were frequently Ukrainian students or high school pupils accused of betrayal or collaboration with Polish authorities, Bandera insisted that his orders be carried out. Although Bandera in his role as the leader of the homeland executive was subordinated to Konovalets' and the leadership in exile, his contribution to the terror was significant. His eagerness and ruthlessness might have surprised his superiors, who were alarmed by the killing of other Ukrainians, especially OUN members. The plans to organize "green cadres" or a partisan movement suggest that Bandera and his homeland executive considered changing their tactics from organized terror to an underground movement, which would conduct an uprising and try to take power.

Bandera's cult emerged for the first time during the trials in Warsaw and Lviv in 1935 and 1936, after Pieracki's assassination. The propaganda apparatus of Piłsudski's Sanacja portrayed Pieracki as a martyr, implied that he died for Poland, and tried to set up a political myth around him. This campaign stirred up collective anger among the Poles, which rebounded against the OUN when the authorities announced who, in the capital of Poland, had killed the minister and fighter for Polish independence. In this manner the Pieracki campaign unintentionally contributed to the formation of the Bandera cult. In particular the Warsaw trial drew much attention to the situation of Ukrainians in Poland, and to the revolutionary struggle of the Ukrainian nationalists. During the trials the OUN tried to use the court as a political stage; the defendants presented the organization as a movement that was driven by idealism and deeply patriotic feelings and sought to liberate the Ukrainian nation from the Polish and Soviet occupation. The defendants and witnesses frequently performed fascist salutes to the words "Glory to Ukraine!" (*Slava Ukraïni!*) in front of the court and the press, for which they were punished by the court. The defendants demonstrated that they regarded Bandera as their *Providnyk* and implied that he might become the leader of the Ukrainian people after a change of political circumstances. Ukrainians followed the trials, reading reports in newspapers, discussing them, and writing folk songs about them and the brave Bandera.

The trials were political but they were not show trials. The "heroic" and patriotic conduct of the young Ukrainian idealists, who were punished for speaking their mother language, caused Polish intellectuals such as Mieczysław and Ksawery Pruszyński to romanticize the OUN and to compare Polish-Ukrainian relations to British-Irish and Spanish-Catalonian relations. The expertise of the prosecutor, Żeleński, concerning the morality of the organization, its ruthlessness toward its enemies, and the use of terror for propagandist and financial purposes, did not challenge the image of the romantic and idealistic OUN revolutionaries. Bandera's death sentence, even though commuted to life imprisonment, turned him into a hero and martyr in the eyes of many Ukrainians in the Second Republic.

Although the press reported much less about the Lviv trial than the one in Warsaw, the second trial was very significant for the formation of the Bandera cult. During the Lviv trial, the OUN mounted a ritualized propagandist spectacle. Bandera acted as the *Providnyk* of a fascist revolutionary organization that represented the Ukrainian nation and fought for the rights of the Ukrainian people. Fascist salutes were performed in Lviv even more often than in the first trial. Unlike in Warsaw, the defendants were allowed to speak in Ukrainian, which made them feel more comfortable and encouraged them to deliver political speeches. Unlike in Warsaw, during the Lviv trial Bandera did not deny his involvement in the terrorist activities of the OUN or the fact that the organization had killed the Polish minister and a number of other persons. On the contrary, he recalled the killings and proudly announced that he personally ordered many of them to be carried out. According to him, they were a part of the Ukrainian "liberation struggle," even if the majority of the victims were other Ukrainian patriots. Important for the understanding of Bandera's worldview in the 1930s was his speech on 26 June 1936 during the Lviv trial, during which he stated that "our idea in our understanding is so huge that as it comes to its realization, not hundreds but thousands of human lives have to be sacrificed in order to carry it out."

The attempts to release Bandera from Polish prisons suggest that a faction of the OUN regarded him as very significant for the movement and wanted him to become the new OUN leader after Konovalets' assassination in May 1938. However, it was only the German invasion of Poland in September 1939 that set Bandera free. It also started a new and essential period in his life and in the history of the movement. Poland disappeared from the map of Europe, and the western Ukrainian territories were included in Soviet Ukraine. Ukrainian nationalists and other Ukrainian political groups allied themselves with Nazi Germany, the main power in Europe, which they believed could help them to establish a Ukrainian state. The ideological similarities between the National Socialists and Ukrainian nationalists facilitated this cooperation, but the OUN did not have much contact with leading Nazi circles, and cooperated mainly with the Abwehr. At that time the conflict between the two generations within the OUN escalated and caused a split in the organization. The Bandera faction was better organized than the Mel'nyk group. It had better connections with the nationalist underground in western Ukraine and succeeded in incorporating more members. The two OUN factions regarded each other as enemies. After the German attack on the Soviet Union the OUN-B killed a number of OUN-M members including Mykola Stsibors'kyi, the author of *Natsiokratiia*. Before the attack Bandera complained that Stsibors'kyi had lived with a "suspicious Russian Jewish woman," and was thus "a traitor and a Bolshevik agent."

During the period of more than twenty months between the beginning of the Second World War and the German invasion of the Soviet Union, Cracow and the General Government became the center of OUN-B activities. The OUN-B collaborated with the Abwehr in the preparations for Operation Barbarossa. The Germans provided the OUN with various facilities and supported it financially. The OUN trained its members in police academies, established the Nachtigall and Roland battalions, and organized about 800 people in the task forces. According to Klymiv, head of the OUN-B in Ukraine, the OUN-B had 20,000 members and 7,000 youth members in the underground in Ukraine. OUN groups from western Ukraine crossed the German-Soviet border to undergo military training in the General Government and to stay in touch with the leadership.

In April 1941 the younger generation of OUN members organized the Second Great Congress of the Ukrainian Nationalists in Cracow. At this congress Bandera was officially elected leader of the OUN. The congress introduced the Führerprinzip and officially introduced a number of fascist principles, symbols and rituals, including the authoritarian principle "one nation, one party, one leader" (*odyn narid, odyn provid, odna vlada*), the red-and-black flag symbolizing blood and earth (*Blut und Boden*), and the fascist salute while calling "Glory to Ukraine!" (*Slava Ukraïni!*) and responding "Glory to the Heroes!" (*Heroiam Slava!*") The fascistization of the OUN reached its peak at that time.

While involved in the preparation of Operation Barbarossa, the OUN-B planned the "Ukrainian National Revolution." Bandera, together with Lenkavs'kyi, Shukhevych, and Stets'ko, composed a document called "The Struggle and Activities of the OUN in Wartime." Two main interrelated aims expressed in this document were to establish a state, which would be ruled by the OUN, and to eliminate the ethnic and political enemies of this state and introduce a fascist dictatorship. Bandera as the *Providnyk* of the OUN-B would become the *Providnyk* of this state. In preparing the "Ukrainian National Revolution," the OUN-B was inspired by the Hlinka Party and the Ustaša, which, in collaboration with Nazi Germany, had established similar states in March 1939 and April 1941 respectively. However, while planning the "Ukrainian National Revolution" and waiting for the beginning of Operation Barbarossa, the OUN-B leadership did not have much political contact with or support from the Nazi leadership. Bandera and the OUN-B seem to have simply hoped that Hitler would accept the new Ukrainian state to be proclaimed by the OUN-B, just as he had accepted Slovakia and Croatia.

After the German invasion of the Soviet Union began on 22 June 1941, the NKVD executed over 8,000 prisoners in the Ukrainian SSR, among them Bandera's father Andrii. This terror contributed to the radicalization of the political situation in Ukraine and increased the hostility toward Jews. The OUN-B activists left the underground and acted according to the instructions set out in "Struggle and Activities." Bandera did not cross the former border between Nazi Germany and the Soviet Union, possibly because the Germans did not allow him to go to the "newly occupied territories." Instead Stets'ko went to Lviv, where, in the evening of 30 June he proclaimed Ukrainian statehood. In the proclamation, Stets'ko stressed that the OUN-B wanted to closely cooperate with the "National Socialist Great Germany, which, under the leadership of Adolf Hitler, is creating a new order in Europe and the world."[1] In his brief autobiography written several days after the proclamation, Stets'ko stated that he supported the "destruction of the Jews and the expedience of bringing German methods of exterminating Jewry to Ukraine, barring their assimilation and the like."[2]

The OUN-B members in the task forces, which followed the front line during Operation Barbarossa, made similar proclamations in hundreds of places, mainly in western Ukraine. The proclamations frequently coincided with pogroms, the perpetrators of which consisted of Germans, OUN activists, and local people. The OUN-B's role in the pogroms should not be underestimated, as the OUN-B controlled the underground in many localities and indoctrinated Ukrainians with various antisemitic and racist leaflets and booklets. When considering the OUN-B's role in the pogroms, it should be noted that pogroms broke out in places that the Germans did

1 "Akt proholoshennia ukraïns'koï derzhavy, 30.06.1941," TsDAVOV f. 3833, op. 1, spr. 5, 3.

2 "Mii zhyttiepys," TsDAVOV f. 3833, op. 3, spr. 7, 6.

not invade, and also that the OUN-B activists complained about the Hungarian and Slovak troops who restricted their violent activities toward Jews and other "enemies of the Ukrainian nation." In those parts of Ukraine where the OUN was not active, pogroms did not take place or were much smaller than in eastern Galicia and in Volhynia. Germans in eastern Ukraine complained that they could not mobilize the local Ukrainians to anti-Jewish violence. Officially, however, the OUN-B regarded the Russians and not the Jews as their main enemies. "Although I consider Moscow, which in fact held Ukraine in captivity, and not Jewry, to be the main and decisive enemy, I nonetheless fully appreciate the undeniably harmful and hostile role of the Jews, who are helping Moscow to enslave Ukraine,"[3] commented Stets'ko on the OUN-B's complicated relations with Russians, Soviets and Jews. Similarly, we should not forget that the social composition of pogromists cannot be limited to OUN-B members and OUN-B sympathizers alone. The perpetrators came from different social groups and killed Jews not only for nationalist but also for economic and other reasons.

The worst pogrom in western Ukraine, which took place in Lviv, was unleashed by the Germans with the collaboration of the Ukrainian militia established by the OUN-B. The perpetrators blamed local Jews for the deaths of prisoners killed by the NKVD, and mobilized the local population to mistreat and murder the Jews. Similar cooperation between the Ukrainian militia and the German troops, including Einsatzkommandos 5 and 6, came about during the first mass shooting of Jews in Lviv. The OUN-B also helped Germans to apprehend Polish professors and their relatives, who were shot shortly after the pogrom by a German security force. The collaboration between the OUN-B militia and the units subordinated to the RSHA was not prevented by the fact that the RSHA limited the political aspirations of the leaders of the OUN-B after 22 June 1941 forbidding some of them to go to the "newly occupied territories."

At the time of the pogrom and the first mass shootings, Stets'ko wrote letters to Hitler, Mussolini, Franco, and Pavelić, in an attempt to persuade them to recognize the OUN-B state with Bandera as its *Providnyk*. Meanwhile, Bandera tried to convince Kundt in Cracow that Nazi Germany needed a Ukrainian state ruled by the OUN-B. The *Providnyk* assured the German official that the OUN-B was loyal to the Nazi leaders, was helping the German army in the struggle against the Soviet Union, wanted to collaborate closely with Hitler's Germany, and he hoped that Germany would accept his state. However, the Nazi leaders did not approve of this state, and did not plan to establish any national states in this part of Europe, although some of them, including Rosenberg, played with such ideas. A few weeks after the proclamation, eastern Galicia was included in the General Government and other Ukrainian territories became Reichskommissariat Ukraine.

After his arrest in early July 1941, Bandera spent the next three years in Berlin and Sachsenhausen. He was placed under house arrest until September 1941, when he was moved to the jail at Gestapo headquarters in Prinz-Albrecht-Strasse, Berlin. In 1942 or 1943, he was transferred to the Zellenbau barrack, a special building for special political prisoners within the Sachsenhausen concentration camp, close to

3 Ibid., 6.

Berlin, where his wife and daughter were living. During the war, a number of other OUN-B members were arrested and sent to German concentration camps where they remained with the status of political prisoners until late 1944 and early 1945. Among those who did not survive the concentration camps were Bandera's two brothers, Vasyl' and Oleksandr.

In letters to Rosenberg in August and December 1941, Bandera tried to bring about a reconciliation with Nazi Germany and to persuade the Reich Minister for the Occupied Eastern Territories that Germany needed a Ukrainian state and ought to cooperate with the OUN-B. Similarly, in December 1941, he asked his deputy Lebed' to attempt to repair German-Ukrainian relations. In an open letter dated 4 August 1941, Stets'ko, who was brought to Berlin shortly after Bandera in early July 1941, encouraged Ukrainians to help the German army in their struggle against the Soviet Union. At that time however, the Germans were not interested in further collaboration with the OUN-B. They collaborated with the UTsK and also with the OUN-M, regarding people such as Kubiiovych as more reliable partners.

Despite the arrest of the OUN-B leadership and the persecution of several less prominent OUN-B members, there was, however, unofficial collaboration between the Nazis and many OUN-B members. Although in late 1941, the OUN-B went underground, it sent its members into the Ukrainian police, which supported the Germans during the destruction of the Jewish population in Ukraine. Without their help the murder of the Jews in western Ukraine, would not have been possible. In the spring of 1943, many of the policemen deserted to the UPA, which had been formed in late 1942 by the OUN-B to "clear" the Ukrainian territory of Poles and to fight against Soviet partisans and less frequently against the Germans. Between early 1943 and mid-1945, the UPA murdered between 70,000 and 100,000 Polish civilians, and hundreds or even thousands of Jews who had escaped from the ghettos and tried to survive by hiding in the woods or in peasants' houses. The AK and other Polish troops, on the other hand, killed between 10,000 and 20,000 Ukrainian civilians, the majority of them outside the territories in which the UPA killed Poles. While in Berlin and Sachsenhausen, Bandera had some limited contact with the OUN-B and UPA leadership in Ukraine through his wife and apparently other channels, but we do not know to what extent he was informed about events in western Ukraine and whether he had any influence on them. Nevertheless, the atrocities committed by the OUN-B and UPA were not inconsistent with Bandera's pre-war beliefs, nor with his ideas expressed in "Struggle and Activities" in 1941, nor with the general attitude of the OUN-B toward the "enemies of the Ukrainian nation" when Bandera had been its *Providnyk*. After the war Bandera never condemned these crimes or admitted that they happened.

Not all young Ukrainians joined the UPA for ideological reasons. Some joined by chance, others because their friends were in the UPA, or because they were forced by the OUN-B, and still others because they were in the police and feared Soviet retribution. However, whatever the reasons why they joined the UPA, service in this movement transformed many ordinary Ukrainians into ruthless killers. The process of such a transformation was elaborated by Christopher Browning in *Ordinary Men* and Harald Welzer in *Täter* (*Perpetrators*).[4] Both scholars studied the psychological processes of German soldiers who killed civilians on a mass scale during the Holocaust.

When evaluating the involvement of Ukrainian nationalists in the annihilation of the Jews, it is important to clarify certain matters. First, 85 to 90 percent of the Jews in western Ukraine were not killed by the OUN and UPA but by the Germans and the Ukrainian police. Among the latter were members of and sympathizers with both factions of the OUN. The remaining 10 to 15 percent, who tried to survive in the woods or various hideouts in the countryside were murdered by the Germans, the Ukrainian nationalists (OUN-B, UPA, SB of the OUN-B, and other groups), Ukrainian police, and by the local Ukrainian and to a lesser extent Polish population. Second, we find among the Ukrainian perpetrators (OUN, UPA, Ukrainian police and the local population), people of different social classes, political convictions, or with different educational backgrounds, who acted for different motives, of which nationalism was only one, but in the case of the OUN and UPA, the most important one. Third, the majority of the Jews in western Ukraine were killed by the Germans with the help of the Ukrainian police before the UPA began to play an important role in the region. Ukrainians formed the majority of the police staff, especially in the countryside, and therefore played a significant part in the annihilation of the Ukrainian Jews. They assisted the Einsatzgruppen, guarded the Jews in the ghettos, hunted for refugees in the woods, and sent them from the ghettos to the extermination camps. In spring 1943 a number of these policemen deserted to the UPA. Fourth, Jews who tried to survive in the woods were hunted not only by the OUN and UPA but also by Ukrainian policemen, peasants, and bandits. Fifth, the murder of the Jews by the OUN-UPA was related to the annihilation of Poles in Volhynia and eastern Galicia. Sixth, a small number of Jews survived in the UPA, mainly because they escaped from the UPA shortly before or after the arrival of the Red Army in western Ukraine.

Important for the evaluation and understanding of the atrocities committed by the OUN and UPA during the Second World War are the testimonies of Jewish survivors. Until recently, survivor testimonies and memoirs have been regarded as unreliable and "subjective" in contrast to the reliable and "objective" documents of the Holocaust perpetrators, especially the German ones. Perpetrators were believed to be rational and to have kept clear records of their atrocities. On the other hand, historians assumed that the survivors were traumatized, that they exaggerated, and that one could not rely on their experiences and memory or use their testimonies and memoirs to study the Second World War or the Holocaust. In the first decades after the war, this approach to history fulfilled the role of a shelter. It enabled the post-war generations not to perceive many brutal and horrible features of the Holocaust, the feelings and experiences of survivors and also sometimes to preserve the good name of the nation. But this attitude to the survivors and their memory re-humiliated the victims of the Holocaust and other atrocities. Also, from a methodological point of

4 Christopher Browning, *Ordinary Men: Reserve Police Battalion 101 and the Final Solution in Poland* (New York: Harper Collins, 1992); Harald Welzer and Michaela Christ, *Täter: Wie aus ganz normalen Menschen Massenmörder werden* (Frankfurt am Main: Fischer Taschenbuch Verlag, 2007).

view, the negation of the testimonies was incorrect and led to serious misrepresentations of history. Although it is certainly true that historians should not take every detail from survivor testimony or memoirs for granted and should not write history based on this kind of document alone, one cannot write the history of the Holocaust in regions such as Volhynia and eastern Galicia while dismissing the survivor testimonies and memoirs as post-traumatic fantasy. By ignoring these documents, we miss many crucial aspects of the annihilation of the Jews, especially aspects related to the groups who persecuted the Jews at the local level. German documents do not say much about the anti-Jewish violence of the Ukrainian extreme nationalists, because the Germans did not make any records of OUN-UPA crimes, with the exception of a few cases when the nationalists boasted to have killed a group of Jews, in order to obtain new weapons or ammunition. Nor did OUN documents say much about this type of atrocity because the leadership of the OUN and UPA collected and destroyed documents that documented their war crimes. After the war the veterans propagated a heroic version of UPA history and also argued that Ukrainian nationalists had rescued Jews. There are therefore several important aspects of the Holocaust that are found only in the testimonies and memoirs of Jewish survivors.

The very popular term "liberation movement" (Ukr. *vyzvol'nyi rukh*) used to describe the OUN and UPA is misleading and was used in this study only in quotation marks because of its ideological meaning. The "liberation struggle" or "liberation war" practiced by the OUN and UPA could not have been liberation because it was not necessary to kill several thousand civilians to liberate Ukraine. The term "liberation movement" suggests that the OUN and UPA were entirely or primarily devoted to the liberation of Ukraine. The study of the movement, however, shows that the OUN and UPA were very much preoccupied with the idea of "cleansing" the Ukrainian territories of ethnic and political opponents.

The conduct of the Greek Catholic Church during and shortly after the Second World War was investigated only as a sideline in this study. It is difficult to talk about a single stream of policy of the Greek Catholic Church toward the minorities targeted by the OUN, the UPA, and the Germans, because the church consisted of various types of people. During the pogroms in 1941, Greek Catholic priests behaved in different ways toward the Jews. Some of them cursed the Jews and organized pogroms; others helped Jews in various ways. In 1943 and 1944, when the UPA conducted the ethnic cleansing in Volhynia and eastern Galicia, some Orthodox and Greek Catholic priests blessed axes, pitchforks, scythes, and other weapons used for murder, and they supported the Ukrainian nationalists in other ways. Sheptyts'kyi, the head of the Greek Catholic Church, demonstrated ambiguous behavior. On the one hand, he rescued and helped to rescue more than a hundred Jews. On the other hand, he failed to condemn the genocidal policies of the Ukrainian nationalists or condemned them only very indirectly, and refused to believe certain facts related to the mass violence conducted by Ukrainians.

In addition to conducting the ethnic cleansing of the Poles and hunting down the Jews, the UPA fought against the Soviet partisans and later the Red Army, even killing one of their generals. To a much smaller extent, the UPA had also attacked Germans before it began to collaborate with them in spring 1944. Bandera and a few dozen other OUN political prisoners were released in September 1944 because Germany was losing the war and the Nazi leaders decided to use the detained Ukrainian politicians to mobilize Ukrainians against their common enemy. Because Bandera and other Ukrainian politicians refused to cooperate with the "Russian imperialist" Vlasov, Rosenberg created the UNK, in which the Ukrainian politicians supported the Germans in their last, desperate military activities. Bandera helped the Germans until he went from Berlin to Vienna in early February 1945. A few weeks before he left for Vienna, the *Providnyk*, according to Shandruk, had opted for "full support to the end, whatever it may be."

The extent to which Bandera was responsible for atrocities committed by Ukrainian nationalists during the Second World War is a difficult and complex question, which can be answered appropriately only in a nuanced way. When planning the "Ukrainian National Revolution," Bandera prepared the OUN-B to perform ethnic and political violence, which, during the revolution, took mainly the form of pogroms. Bandera co-authored "Struggle and Activities," discussed plans with the Abwehr, and played the role of the *Providnyk* in front of the groups of OUN-B activists who arrived in the General Government from Ukraine. He encouraged them to fight against the "enemies of the Ukrainian nation" and to "liberate" Ukraine from Soviet occupation. After the German attack on the Soviet Union, Bandera did not go to the "newly occupied territories" but stayed in the General Government as the Germans had advised him. Although he did not meet Klymiv after 22 June 1941, "Struggle and Activities" gave Klymiv general and specific instructions how to act after the beginning of Operation Barbarossa and the "Ukrainian National Revolution." It is not known whether, after the German attack on the Soviet Union, Bandera issued direct orders concerning the question of ethnic and political violence. Stets'ko informed his *Providnyk* in a telegram on 25 June that "We are setting up a militia that will help to remove the Jews and protect the population." Bandera's communications to Stets'ko, however, unlike Stets'ko's telegrams to the *Providnyk*, did not find their way into the archives. As the *Providnyk* of the OUN-B, Bandera must have been well informed about the run of events in Ukraine, including the anti-Jewish violence. With the help of couriers, he also stayed in contact with the task forces. Bandera's later denial of the pogroms was typical of the behavior of other OUN-B members, such as Hryn'okh and Stets'ko, who were in Lviv during the pogrom, knew exactly what happened there, or were involved in establishing the OUN-B militia. After the war, they insisted that they did not see any anti-Jewish incidents in Lviv between 30 June and 2 July 1941 and were not aware that a pogrom in the city took place, although they confirmed in their testimonies and memoirs that they walked through the city at that time, like Hryn'okh, or controlled the Ukrainian militia, like Stets'ko.

In this context, we should also ask whether Bandera's physical absence from the "newly occupied territories" in late June and early July 1941 exonerates him of the crimes committed by the OUN and similarly of the various atrocities later committed by the UPA. No reasonable person would doubt that Hitler was politically and morally responsible for the various atrocities committed in Auschwitz or at the Eastern Front, although the *Führer* did not personally supervise the Einsatzkommandos in Poland, Ukraine, and Belarus; nor did he stand in front of the gas chambers, controlling the procedure in Auschwitz and other extermination camps. Similarly, Pavelić is considered to be responsible for the Ustaša's killings of Serbs, Jews, and Roma, although he might not have known all the details concerning the particular killings. Nevertheless, there is a difference in terms of agency between Hitler,

Pavelić, and Bandera, because Hitler and Pavelić were not detained when their forces committed war crimes and other atrocities. Thus the scope of their involvement was different from Bandera's, especially concerning the crimes committed when Bandera was either in Berlin or Sachsenhausen, and when his contact with the leadership of the OUN and UPA was limited. To hold Bandera personally responsible for the crimes committed by the UPA during the period of his arrest would be counterfactual and irrational. Nevertheless, the question of Bandera's moral responsibility is much more complex, because in terms of enthusiasm for or approval of mass violence against "enemies" or against particular ethnic group he seems not to have differed substantially from Hitler or Pavelić. Similarly, according to Hannah Arendt's concept of justice and the notions of transformative justice and of transitional justice, Bandera seems to be responsible for "crimes against humanity" because his actions in 1941 and the actions of his movement during the entire war were an attack on both human plurality and particular ethnic groups and thus on humanity as such. A court in a democratic Ukraine, interested in recognizing the victims of the OUN-B, promoting civic trust and strengthening democracy, would have convicted Bandera and other members of the OUN for their numerous violations of human rights.[5]

When discussing Bandera, the OUN and UPA, and atrocities conducted by the Ukrainian nationalists, we should also re-evaluate the ideological notion of leadership. The *Providnyk* or *Vozhd'*, like the *Führer*, *Duce*, or *Poglavnik*, was an essential practical and ideological element of a fascist movement. The *Providnyk* was an important aspect of the official propaganda of the OUN and of the worldview of its members. Bandera's followers believed in the *Providnyk*, admired him, and fought for him. In return, he encouraged and inspired them, even if many of them never met him in person. As indicated in chapters 4 and 5, Bandera was perceived as the *Providnyk* of the movement and its spiritual leader during and after his detention, although Lebed', who, however, did not enjoy the charisma established around Bandera, replaced him. After his arrest, therefore, Bandera was still referred to as the *Providnyk* in various OUN-B and UPA publications and was commemorated at the anniversaries of the proclamation of 30 June 1941. This did not change, even after Lebed' was replaced with a triumvirate in February 1943, and the OUN-B decided to break away from fascism and totalitarianism. This does not incriminate Bandera but emphasizes that many of the OUN members and UPA partisans involved in the atrocities against Jews, Poles, Ukrainians, and other ethnic groups regarded Bandera as their spiritual leader and identified with him while "cleansing" the territory of the "enemies of the Ukrainian nation."

During the Second World War, the Bandera cult and myth went through further metamorphoses. After the split of the OUN into the OUN-B and the OUN-M, Bandera's followers called themselves, and were called by others, Banderites. Although the term "Banderites" did not predominate during the "Ukrainian National Revolution" in the summer of 1941, it became one of the main terms describing the Ukrainian nationalists loyal to Bandera in 1942, and even more in 1943 and 1944. Jews

5 Hannah Arendt, *Eichmann in Jerusalem: A Report on the Banality of Evil* (New York: Penguin, 1994), 268–69; Leora Bilsky, *Transformative Justice: Israeli Identity on Trial* (Ann Arbor: University of Michigan Press, 2004), 131–32; Teitel, *Transitional Justice.*

and Poles used it to describe OUN members and UPA insurgents and sometimes other Ukrainian perpetrators, such as peasants mobilized to ethnic violence by the OUN and the UPA. The survivors used the word in a very pragmatic way. They described as "Banderites" those Ukrainian nationalists who might arrive and kill them at any time. The AK, Germans, and Soviet partisans also used "Banderites" to refer to the Ukrainian nationalists. The Soviet propaganda apparatus started to apply the term in early 1944 and radically changed the meaning of the word. "Banderites" became in the Soviet propaganda discourse an expression used to discredit the opponents of the Soviet Union. Soviet ideology transformed it into one of the most powerful and militant propaganda slogans. The extensive use of the word in the Soviet media also influenced Bandera himself, who understood it as evidence of his greatness.

In order not to be deported to the Soviet Union after the Second World War, Bandera and other Ukrainian émigrés manipulated their identity and falsified the history of the movement, in particular the anti-Jewish, anti-Polish, and anti-Ukrainian violence. One of Bandera's IDs said that he was "kept from 15.9.1941 to 6.5.1945 in Nazi-German concentration camps and was liberated from the concentration camp at Mauthausen," although Bandera never was an inmate of this camp. In 1946 Lebed' published a book about the UPA, in which he omitted or denied the participation of the OUN in the pogroms of 1941, collaboration with the Germans, plans and attempts to establish a fascist authoritarian state, the ethnic cleansing conducted by the UPA in 1943–1944 in Volhynia and eastern Galicia, and a number of other matters that could have jeopardized his new career as a CIA agent and the future of many Ukrainian OUN veterans who decided to stay in the Western bloc.

The intelligence services of the United Kingdom, the United States, and later West Germany were interested in cooperation with the anti-Soviet underground in western Ukraine and therefore worked together with Bandera, Lebed', and other émigrés. They trained OUN agents, supported the émigrés financially, and protected them against the KGB. A former officer in Rosenberg's Ostministerium, Gerhard von Mende, who after the war worked in the Office for Displaced Persons, helped Bandera to regulate his status and to solve bureaucratic and political problems. Franco offered Bandera resettlement in Spain, but Bandera refused. He felt safe in West Germany and did not want to give up the structures he had built up there.

The conflicts within the OUN did not cease after the Second World War. Former friends deeply distrusted each other, fired weapons at each other, and ordered each other's assassinations. One reason for the new conflicts was the competition for resources supplied by Western intelligence services. Another important reason was the existence of ideological differences among the factions in the ZCh OUN. Bandera and a number of his supporters insisted on leading the organization according to the Führerprinzip, as in 1941. The *Providnyk* demanded total subordination from all OUN members, but other nationalists opposed these policies, which they regarded as outdated. They wanted a more pragmatic or "democratic" organization although they never introduced radical changes such as an open and non-denial-oriented attitude to the history of the movement. Bandera's fundamental nationalism, authoritarianism, and obsession with fascism scared a number of former like-minded comrades. They took the view that Bandera had not changed since 1941 and refused to cooperate with him.

Bandera's worldview after the Second World War did not alter but rather adjusted to the reality of the Cold War. He did not mention Jews and Poles as the enemies of the Ukrainian nation, because they did not live in Ukraine any longer. The *Providnyk* directed his hatred against the Soviet Union without substantially changing his far-right convictions. Many of his post-war ideas were in harmony with anti-Soviet and anticommunist politics of that time. Bandera defended the *Caudillo* against "attacks" from the democratic states but was at the same time irritated by any suggestion that the ZCh OUN was not democratic or that Ukrainian genocidal nationalism was anti-democratic. He never admitted the crimes committed by the Ukrainian nationalists during the Second World War, and claimed that he had always opposed the German and Soviet regimes and was a victim of both. He presented himself in interviews given in the 1950s as a leader of the anti-Soviet underground movement, which had not stopped fighting against the "red devil."

While Bandera tried to dominate the ZCh OUN and planned to "liberate" Ukraine, some groups of UPA insurgents continued fighting in western Ukraine until the late 1940s and early 1950s. They continued to kill civilians en masse, but the main perpetrators at that time were the NKVD (from 1946 the MVD), and the new victims of political violence were the families of the insurgents, and Ukrainians accused of supporting the UPA or of being Ukrainian nationalists. The last category included actual war criminals and various Nazi collaborators as well as people who "betrayed the Soviet fatherland." During the ruthless conflict with the OUN-UPA the Soviets killed 153,000 people, arrested 134,000, and deported 203,000 to the Gulag and to Siberia. Altogether until 1953, about 490,000 western Ukrainians, or nearly one person in every western Ukrainian family suffered under Soviet repression. At the same time, the OUN-UPA murdered over 20,000 civilians and killed about 10,000 Soviet soldiers, members of the destruction battalions, and NKVD staff. Most of those killed by the nationalist partisans were workers from kolkhozes, teachers, nurses, and doctors resettled from eastern Ukraine. Blinded by genocidal nationalism, suicidal romanticism, anticommunism, and deluded by the stories about the upcoming third world war distributed by Bandera and other nationalist émigrés, the UPA ignored the fact that it could not win a war against the Soviet Union, which was many times stronger than the western Ukrainian insurgent groups. Under the ruthless terror of the Soviet regime, the Ukrainian population withdrew its support for the nationalist insurgents. Nevertheless, Soviet terror and Soviet propaganda substantially strengthened anti-Soviet resentment in western Ukraine, dissolved the memory of the atrocities committed by the Ukrainian nationalists, and thereby helped the Ukrainian insurgents to gradually reappear as heroic anti-Soviet icons.

When the OUN and UPA were fighting against the NKVD in Ukraine, Bandera's life in exile was overshadowed by the KGB, which tried to kidnap and kill him. Bandera, and to a lesser extent his family, had very good reasons to fear for their lives, although they were protected by the SB of the ZCh OUN and warned by the CIC about the plans of the KGB. They used other names and were forced to hide several times when the KGB was after them. The Soviet leaders assassinated the *Providnyk* fourteen years after the end of the Second World War. The assassination was prepared almost perfectly, and its details became known only when the assassin submitted himself to the West German police.

Fascism

The question whether Bandera was a fascist, or in which sense and to what extent, depends on the question of how we define fascism and at which time we consider Bandera and the OUN to have been fascist. Cold War historians such as Armstrong, some Ukrainian diaspora historians, and also historians in post-Soviet Ukraine considered the OUN to be a form of "integral nationalism." This suggestion, however, is misleading, because of the actual meaning of this concept. Furthermore, it does not allow the contextualization of the OUN, because of the absence of comparative studies on "integral nationalism." In order to correctly contextualize Bandera and the extreme, revolutionary, ethnic, and genocidal form of Ukrainian nationalism, and to comprehend the nature of this movement, we used the theoretical concepts established by scholars such as Eatwell, Griffin, Sternhell, Paxton, Kershaw, Mann, Mosse, Nolte, and Payne, and the criteria of a fascist movement, which were explained and presented in the introduction.

The OUN in the 1930s and early 1940s met all the basic criteria of a fascist movement, which were formulated in Nolte's "fascist minimum" or in the enlarged version presented in the introduction to this study. In addition, the OUN fulfilled two other crucial characteristics of a fascist movement. First, it tried to take power through a revolution and establish its own authoritarian nation state of a fascist type. Second, it anticipated the salvation and renewal of society through palingenesis, which in the Ukrainian case was related to the idea that the Ukrainian nation would die out if the OUN did not establish a state. Only a state governed by the OUN-B would allow the Ukrainians to survive, be reborn, and thrive.

In 1941 the OUN-B proclaimed a state and established a government, but it could not retain them. As demonstrated in chapter 4, this was not because of ideological differences between the Ukrainian nationalists and National Socialists or the "inability" and "naivety" of the OUN-B leaders, but because of outside factors on which the OUN-B did not have much or any influence. The Nazi leaders had plans for the Ukrainian territories that were different from those for Croatia and Slovakia, but similar to those for Lithuania.

Conflicts, even very serious ones with lethal consequences, were not unusual between fascist, authoritarian, and other far-right movements. Their ideologies made them feel related and united them against communism and democracy. But for fascist and authoritarian leaders, practical matters were in general more important than ideological similarities. A classic inter-fascist conflict prior to the Second World War occurred between the Austrofascists and the German National Socialists. Despite ideological similarities, the National Socialists killed the first Austrofascist leader Dollfuss, and after incorporating Austria in the Reich, they imprisoned his successor Schuschnigg and kept him in the same concentration camp as Bandera although under different conditions. Similarly, when the conflict in Romania between Antonescu and the Iron Guard escalated in early 1941, more than 300 legionaries fled to Germany and were detained in German camps. The leader of the Iron Guard, Horia Sima, was detained in Zellenbau, the same building for special political prisoners in which Bandera was confined.

Especially in the 1920s, its ideologists argued that the OUN could not be a typical fascist movement because of their own national traditions or matters of culture and language. These arguments, however, were typical of all small fascist movements such as the Ustaša, HSLS, and the Iron Guard. Ukrainian nationalists were independent in the sense of fighting for independence or for a state that would be independent of Poland, Russia, or the Soviet Union. However, they were dependent on Nazi Germany, without which they could not hope to establish and maintain a state. The OUN-B needed the protection of Nazi Germany and for that reason it collaborated with Germany and presented itself as a movement related to it. The model of the Ukrainian state, as elaborated by the leading OUN ideologist Stsibors'kyi in *Natsiokratiia* and by the OUN-B leadership at the Second Great Congress of the Ukrainian Nationalists in Cracow a few months before the German attack on the Soviet Union, displayed most characteristics typical of fascist states.

Because the OUN-B leadership outlined the independent Ukrainian state as an ethnic nation state or "Ukraine for Ukrainians," according to one of the OUN-B slogans, the state was to be "purified" of non-Ukrainian inhabitants. For this reason, the OUN made ethnic violence and the cult of war the central concepts of its ideology. For the same reason, the OUN-B leadership combined the proclamation of the state in 1941 with anti-Jewish violence and the killing of other ethnic and political opponents. By the same token, it "cleansed" the western Ukrainian territories of Poles, and Jews in hiding. The annihilation of the Jews by the Germans with the help of the Ukrainian police also met the expectations of the OUN-B, because it helped rid the territory of non-Ukrainian elements. It also provided the Ukrainian policemen, who in early 1943 deserted for the UPA, with practical knowledge as to how to annihilate an entire ethnic group in a region, in a relatively short period. The OUN-B leadership made extensive use of this knowledge in order to "clear" Volhynia, and later eastern Galicia, of Poles. Given the forms of violence conducted by the OUN, it belonged to the more rather than to the less violent fascist movements. Similarly, the concept of the "enemy of the Ukrainian nation" and the kind of mass violence practiced to annihilate the non-Ukrainian inhabitants of the "Ukrainian territories" suggest that the OUN belonged to the more rather than the less racist movements. The questions that arise in this context are whether and when the OUN ceased to be a typical East Central European fascist movement. Did it happen after Bandera's arrest and the German rejection of the state proclaimed by the OUN-B on 30 June 1941, or when the OUN-B formed the UPA in late 1942 and early 1943, or after the Second World War, when the UPA opposed the Soviet Union until the early 1950s, or has the OUN remained fascist until today?

When evaluating the question of fascism, we should also recall the theoretical concepts that contradict the assumption than the OUN was a typical fascist movement. Paxton, for example, suggested that fascism can only appear in a state after a period of democracy or a period of disappointment with democracy. According to this reasoning, it would only be possible to consider the OUN a fascist organization if we were to accept that there was a period of democracy in the Second Republic, in which the OUN emerged and acted prior to the Second World War. This assumption, however, would not be entirely convincing, for at least two reasons. First, the Second Republic was a multiethnic state ruled by Poles, and not a Ukrainian state with a democratic political system. Second, it is difficult to talk about democracy in the Second Polish Republic, especially after Piłsudski's coup d'état in 1926. Paxton would have classified the OUN as a fascism "created by mimicry," or as one of the movements that borrowed "elements of fascist décor in order to lend themselves an aura of force, vitality, and mass mobilization," rather than a typical fascist movement. According to his classification of five stages, the OUN would reach stage three but only for a very short period of time.[6]

The Ukrainian extreme nationalists, with the exception of a few ideologists, did not usually call themselves fascists, although they claimed to be related to other fascist movements. Between 1918 and 1945, the word "fascism" occurred in the Ukrainian far-right discourse less frequently than the terms "Ukrainian nationalism" and "revolutionary nationalism." "Ukrainian nationalism" became the official description of the OUN movement, similar to "National Socialism" and "Italian Fascism." Bandera and the OUN understood themselves as Ukrainian nationalists, spiritually related to the National Socialists, Italian Fascists, and similar movements, such as the Ustaša and Iron Guard. They did not understand "nationalism" and "fascism" to be mutually exclusive. Only after the conflict with Nazi Germany, and even more so after Germany began to lose the war, the OUN and UPA leaders started to distinguish between Ukrainian nationalism and fascism. Nevertheless, Bandera and his ZCh OUN faction did not develop any negative feelings toward fascism during and after the end of the Second World War although they publicly announced that Ukrainian nationalism had never been related to fascism and had nothing in common with it.

No fascist movement can exist without a leader. The Ukrainian language has two terms for leader, *Providnyk* and *Vozhd'*. Bandera was usually referred to as the *Providnyk*, and only less frequently, *Vozhd'*. Unlike *Providnyk*, *Vozhd'* also means leader in Russian and was used by Lenin and Stalin, among others. In Ukrainian in the 1920s and 1930s, *Vozhd'* had a more totalitarian meaning than *Providnyk*, but this distinction evaporated in the late 1930s and early 1940s. In the 1920s and 1930s, the UVO and the OUN used *Providnyk* to describe the leader of the entire organization, the leader of the homeland executive, or the leader of a combat unit. At that time, *Vozhd'* was the more appropriate translation of *Duce* or *Führer*. The term "Vozhd'" appeared in documents such as Stsibors'kyi's *Natsiokratiia*, in 1935. After Konovalets' assassination in 1938, the leadership of the OUN gave Mel'nyk the title of *Vozhd'*. In order to distinguish themselves from the older generation, the younger ultranationalists referred to their leader as the *Providnyk*, on whom they based their own Führerprinzip. The advantage of the word *Providnyk* was that it did not occur in Russian, and therefore Bandera could not have been confused with Stalin. Nevertheless, some sectors of the OUN-B, unaware of the policies of the OUN-B leadership in the General Government, referred to Bandera as *Vozhd'* during the "Ukrainian National Revolution." The OUN-B intended to make Bandera the *Providnyk* of the Ukrainian state that it succeeded in proclaiming but failed to keep. The term *Providnyk* remained in use during the Second World War. When Nazi Germany began losing the war, the OUN and UPA leadership officially distanced itself from fascism, denied ever having been fascist and replaced the Führerprinzip based on the *Providnyk*, with a triumvirate. Nevertheless, Ukrainian nationalists loyal to Bandera continued to regard him as their *Providnyk*. Similarly during the Cold War, nationalists supporting Bandera continued to call him the *Providnyk*. After Bandera's assassin-

6 Paxton, The Five Stages of Fascism, 3, 11–12.

ation, the term "Providnyk" was used to describe Bandera as the legendary leader of the movement; first by the Ukrainian diaspora and later by Bandera's admirers in post-Soviet Ukraine. While they honored Bandera as the *Providnyk*, they did not necessarily intend to do so in respect of Bandera as a fascist leader. When they used the term, they usually meant the leader of a movement that tried to liberate Ukraine from German and Soviet occupation, and they honored Bandera as the symbol of the "liberation struggle," frequently not being aware of the actual meaning of the term, and sometimes the history of the movement.

When evaluating Bandera and his cult in the context of fascism, we should also discuss the question of Ukrainian neo-fascism, or the rebirth of fascism. The epoch of fascism "officially" finished with the end of the Second World War, the collapse of Nazi Germany and Fascist Italy, and the disappearance of other fascist movements and regimes. The atrocities committed by Nazis and similar movements completely discredited fascism, but the fascists did not evaporate after 1945 or suddenly become democrats. The rise of the Bandera cult after his assassination did not transform or retransform the Ukrainian diaspora and later post-Soviet Ukrainians into fascists. Nevertheless, the communities which, during the Cold War or after the dissolution of the Soviet Union, began to glorify Bandera, his movement, or his political ideas, developed a positive form of memory of Bandera and the OUN. By commemorating and celebrating Bandera, they did not allow the epoch of fascism to pass away. Similarly, they refused to accept a critical and unapologetic dealing with the movement's past. Instead, they made Bandera and the OUN an essential component of their identity and continued to sacralize them. Paxton suggested that organizations that "imitate the exotic colored-shirts of an earlier generation" are not the most interesting phenomena today. According to him, "new functional equivalent of fascism would probably work best, as George Orwell reminded us, clad in the mainstream patriotic dress of their own place and time."[7] This apocalyptic suggestion seems to materialize in today's western Ukraine, where young admirers of Bandera, or the Waffen-SS Galizien, wear patriotic clothes, in particular embroidered shirts and other items of folk wardrobe, perform fascist salutes during their "patriotic" Bandera events, and shout various fascist and neo-fascist slogans.

The Afterlife

The two capsules of cyanide fired by the western Ukrainian KGB agent Bohdan Stashyns'kyi into Bandera's face at about 1:00 p.m. on 15 October 1959 were the beginning of the *Providnyk's* turbulent afterlife. Newspapers controlled by OUN-B émigrés, such as *Shliakh peremohy*, *Homin Ukraïny*, and *Ukraïns'ka dumka* commemorated Bandera's death for weeks, presenting him as a hero and martyr who fell for Ukraine. About 1,500 admirers attended Bandera's funeral in Munich. Others mourned the *Providnyk* in churches and at commemorative gatherings in a number of localities in Argentina, Australia, Austria, Belgium, Brazil, Canada, France, the United Kingdom, West Germany, New Zealand, and the United States. The resettlement of the DPs in the late 1940s and early 1950s was the basis for the globalization

7 Paxton, The Five Stages of Fascism, 22.

of Bandera's afterlife. The OUN, UPA, and Waffen-SS Galizien veterans passed the Bandera cult on to the younger generations. The cult did not start to disappear in the nationalist diaspora communities until the dissolution of the Soviet Union and has not even done so in some of them at the time of writing.

By commemorating Bandera, the diaspora communities—among them individuals who had admired the *Providnyk* in the 1930s and 1940s—turned themselves again into "charismatic communities." Bandera's commemorations were deeply ritualized. They were usually composed of a religious part—the panakhyda—and a political gathering. The distinction between religion and nationalism blurred during the commemorations, composing a powerful anti-Soviet mixture. The Bandera cult was also propagated during protest marches and anti-Soviet demonstrations in cities such as London, Ottawa, and Washington. In Munich, the mecca of the Banderites, members of the "charismatic community" visited the Bandera grave and burned Soviet flags in front of the apartment building in which the *Providnyk* was assassinated. In late 1959, some of the Bandera worshipers also mourned and extolled the Croatian *Poglavnik*, Pavelić, who died two months after Bandera, as the result of an assassination attempt in April 1957. The Bandera commemorations were also related to and sometimes embedded in various militaristic and religious celebrations of the Waffen-SS Galizien, UPA, Weapons Holidays, and Feast of Saint Mary the Protectress.

In addition to commemorations and demonstrations, the Bandera cult manifested itself in the Bandera museum established in Nottingham and relocated to London. The creators of this institution honored Bandera as a hero and martyr who fought and fell for Ukraine, as the spiritual leader of the OUN and UPA, and also as the symbol of the Ukrainian "liberation struggle." The museum was not established to educate visitors about Bandera's life, or Ukrainian genocidal nationalism. It was created to eulogize and sacralize the *Providnyk* and the "tragic" but "heroic" struggle of his generation. The creators of the museum created an interesting connection between Bandera and the UPA. Although Bandera never joined this army, the UPA became one of the central features of the exhibition. This was not entirely unjustified, because some of the UPA partisans had regarded Bandera as the spiritual leader of Ukrainian revolutionary nationalism and strongly identified with him. Nevertheless, the main purpose of prominently featuring the UPA in the Bandera museum seems to be the denial of UPA atrocities through Bandera's victimization and glorification. The Holocaust and the Ukrainian contribution to the Holocaust were completely ignored in the museum. The pictures of the Ukrainian prisoners at the Auschwitz concentration camp suggested that only OUN-B members were kept and annihilated in this camp. Petro Mirchuk, the first Bandera hagiographer, similarly presented the Jewish-Ukrainian relationship during the Second World War in his publications about Bandera and the Ukrainian nationalists. Mirchuk paved the way for later Bandera hagiographers and deniers of the Ukrainian contribution to the Holocaust and of other atrocities committed by the Ukrainian nationalists.

The apologetic and eulogizing narrative about Bandera and his "liberation movement" was created not only by nationalist fanatics, Bandera's hard admirers and far-right activists, but also by a number of scholars who worked at universities in Canada, Germany, France, and the United States. Some of these scholars, such as Taras Hunchak, Petro Potichnyi, and Volodymyr Kosyk were veterans of the OUN or

UPA. John Armstrong, the first professional historian who investigated the Ukrainian nationalists during the Second World War, was not entirely uncritical about his object of study but, for various reasons, he did not include in his research the pogroms in 1941, the ethnic cleansing in 1943–1944, the murder of Jews by the UPA, and several other matters that need to be considered when writing the history of Ukrainian nationalism during the Second World War. Armstrong, like many other historians at that time, worked with and relied on Ukrainian and German sources alone. He ignored the perspective and experiences of OUN and UPA victims. In addition, he seems to have been impacted by the Cold War revival of national narratives of the states on which communism had been imposed in 1944. For these and other reasons, the author of the first comprehensive monograph on Ukrainian nationalism presented a number of erroneous conclusions, which were not perceived as such at the time and by some historians even today. His study was regarded not only by Ukrainian nationalists—such as Dontsov, who quoted and praised Armstrong in his foreword to Stets'ko's book *30 chervnia 1941* (30 June 1941)—but also by politically unmotivated professional historians as a standard, academic, objective, and reliable monograph on Ukrainian nationalism during the Second World War.[8]

Ivan Lysiak-Rudnyts'kyi was not the only Galician Ukrainian who left Ukraine during the Second World War, worked at a Western university during the Cold War, and had the opportunity to rethink genocidal nationalism or to open himself toward democracy. As indicated in chapter 9, many other Ukrainian intellectuals worked during the Cold War at various universities in Canada, France, West Germany, and the United States. The majority of them however, unlike Lysiak-Rudnyts'kyi, erected ideological walls and began to protect their nationalist ideas as patriotic traditions or anticommunist convictions. They did not investigate the Second World War, Ukrainian fascism, and the Holocaust but instead, either ignored these subjects or wrote apologetic and distorted histories, which presented the Ukrainian nationalists as anti-German and anti-Soviet freedom fighters. Lysiak-Rudnyts'kyi, both a historian and contemporary witness, rethought rather than empirically investigated the OUN and the Second World War. He was critical of the OUN-B, whose members he had known from Ukraine and also from his life after emigration.

Nevertheless, Lysiak-Rudnyts'kyi seems to have had no objections concerning post-war collaboration with people such as Kubiiovych. The former UTsK leader was in his eyes a more moderate and rational individual than the banderivshchyna, not least because after the Second World War Kubiiovych initiated many valuable projects, such as the Ukrainian Encyclopedia. The question whether it was necessary to ignore what Kubiiovych had done during the Second World War in order to develop the Encyclopedia and other projects did not matter to Lysiak-Rudnyts'kyi.

Although the Bandera cult during the Cold War was a typical far-right nationalist and neo-fascist cult, the diaspora Ukrainians joined the "charismatic communities" commemorating Bandera for various reasons. Some of them commemorated Bandera because they had already admired the *Providnyk* during the trials in Warsaw and Lviv in 1935–1936, or during the "Ukrainian National Revolution" in 1941. Other Ukrainians engaged in the Bandera cult because they were Ukrainian patriots,

8 Dmytro Dontsov, "Vstupne Slovo," Stets'ko, *30 chervnia 1941*, 9–10.

or because they thought that performing Bandera rituals, or honoring the "freedom fighters" of the UPA, would be effective ways of protesting against the Soviet regime. Younger people who were raised in the diaspora communities were involved in the Bandera cult by their parents, friends, or youth organizations such as SUM and Plast. A part of the "charismatic community," at least the OUN and UPA veterans who had participated in the Holocaust or collaborated with Germans during the Second World War, were aware of the atrocities committed by the Ukrainian revolutionary nationalists, the fascistization of the movement, and the collaboration with Nazi Germany. They also understood that commemorating Bandera, or celebrating him as a Ukrainian national hero or as a victim of the Soviet regime, was a good way of denying the atrocities committed by the OUN and UPA, and other "inconvenient" moments of OUN history. Nevertheless, some other sections of the Ukrainian communities might not have been aware of the OUN and UPA atrocities, because Armstrong and other historians did not explain them in their studies or because the Bandera cult suggested that heroes and martyrs did not kill civilians and did not collaborate with Nazis.

During the Cold War, the OUN-B leaders were recognized as anticommunist "freedom fighters" not only by the far-right Ukrainian diaspora communities but also by many other anti-Soviet groups, including the leading politicians of the largest and most powerful states of the Western bloc. During the 1950s, Bandera gave interviews on the radio, in which he assured the West German audience that the OUN and UPA were composed of patriotic freedom fighters who had fought against the Nazi regime and continued the struggle against the Soviet one. Stets'ko, who in 1941 had written letters to the *Führer*, the *Duce*, the *Poglavnik*, and the *Caudillo*, asking them to accept the newly proclaimed Ukrainian state, was in 1966 designated an honorary citizen of the Canadian city of Winnipeg. In 1983 he was invited to the Capitol and the White House, where George Bush and Ronald Reagan received the "last premier of a free Ukrainian state." On 11 July 1982 during Captive Nations Week, the red-and-black flag of the OUN-B, introduced at the Second Great Congress of the Ukrainian Nationalists in 1941, flew over the United States Capitol. It symbolized freedom and democracy, and not ethnic purity and genocidal fascism. Nobody understood that it was the same flag that had flown from the Lviv city hall and other buildings, under which Jewish civilians were mistreated and killed in July 1941 by individuals who identified themselves with the flag.

Soviet propaganda, which depicted Bandera in complete contrast to the narrative of the Ukrainian diaspora, infuriated and radicalized the Ukrainian far-right diaspora communities and strengthened the Bandera cult. According to Soviet ideology, Bandera and his followers betrayed the Ukrainian nation similarly to the way Vlasov and his movement betrayed the Russian nation. Soviet propaganda provided the term "Banderites" with new connotations. The meaning of the word changed from "murderer"—as used by Poles and Jews exposed to OUN and UPA mass violence in 1943 and 1944—to "traitor," "bandit," "fascist" and "capitalist." Between 1944 and 1946, Soviet propaganda also used the term "German-Ukrainian nationalists" very frequently, to refer to UPA insurgents. It suggested that the Ukrainian nationalists were lackeys or a limb of Nazi Germany, which continued fighting against the Soviet Union even after the defeat of its master. A few years after the end of the Second

World War, Soviet propaganda started to favor the term "Ukrainian bourgeois nationalists," which condemned the Ukrainian nationalists as "capitalists."

Like the UPA, the Soviet regime understood and used violence as propaganda. The NKVD hanged UPA partisans and disfigured their bodies before the eyes of locals, including even groups of school children, while spreading rumors about human ears found in the pockets of the Banderites. Soviet ideology transformed the Ukrainian communist writer Iaroslav Halan, who denounced the Ukrainian nationalists and was allegedly killed by a UPA rebel, into a hero and martyr. In general, the Soviet discourse transformed all kinds of victims killed by the Ukrainian nationalists into martyrs and heroes of the Soviet Union. Soviet propaganda also ignored and denied the war crimes committed by the NKVD, Soviet partisans, and Red Army soldiers, and did not allow the victims' relatives to mourn their loss. In these circumstances many ordinary Ukrainians turned the OUN and UPA into anti-Soviet heroes and forgot their atrocities against Jews, Poles, and Ukrainians.

During the period of perestroika, when the Bandera cult re-emerged in western Ukraine, people there were exposed to two propagandist narratives—the Soviet and the Ukrainian nationalist. The anti-Soviet movement, composed in western Ukraine of dissidents and nationalists, used Bandera and the OUN-UPA as anticommunist icons, symbolizing freedom and independence. The first and the second Bandera monuments erected in Staryi Uhryniv, Bandera's birthplace, were demolished by a Soviet task force. The third monument of the *Providnyk* was ironically and symbolically recast from a statue of Lenin. Many monuments devoted to the victims of the Ukrainian nationalists or to the heroes of the Soviet Union were replaced by monuments devoted to Bandera and the OUN and UPA "heroes." Bandera and the Ukrainian revolutionary nationalists again became important elements of western Ukrainian identity. Not only far-right activists but also the mainstream of western Ukrainian society, including high-school teachers and university professors, considered Bandera to be a Ukrainian national hero, a freedom fighter, and a person who should be honored for his struggle against the Soviet Union. The post-Soviet memory politics in Ukraine completely ignored democratic values and did not develop any kind of non-apologetic approach to history. Nationalism became the main foundation of the collective identity in western Ukraine, and a kind of post-Soviet and pro-Russian populist communism in eastern Ukraine.

After the dissolution of the Soviet Union, OUN émigrés such as Slava Stets'ko, the widow of Iaroslav Stets'ko, returned to Ukraine, where they founded far-right political organizations such as the KUN, explained to young historians, at conferences organized by the OUN, how to write history, and facilitated the popularization of the Bandera cult in other ways. Local OUN veterans such as Petro Duzhyi, and leaders of paramilitary and far-right organizations such as Ievhen Perepicha published voluminous hagiographies of the *Providnyk*. Other OUN émigrés, such as Volodymyr Kosyk, initiated the TsDVR, which was incorporated into the Lviv Academy of Sciences. The TsDVR provided an academic foundation for the Bandera cult and has continued to whitewash the Ukrainian history of OUN and UPA atrocities. It thereby continued a process begun by OUN émigrés such as Mykola Lebed', Petro Mirchuk, and Kosyk in the early Cold War years. The director of the TsDVR, Volodymyr V"iatrovych, had a significant influence on the memory politics of the Ukrainian government during Iushchenko's presidency. This resulted in the designation of Bandera and other leaders of the OUN and UPA as heroes of Ukraine.

In addition to V"iatrovych, a number of other historians propagated and legitimized the Bandera cult. Some of them, such as Mykola Posivynch, composed hagiographic biographies; others, such as Alexander Gogun, assumed that everything that was anti-Soviet, like Bandera, the OUN-UPA, Vlasov, and the ROA, was democratic. Some historians, similarly to the far-right activists, legitimized the new post-Soviet narratives or denied the Ukrainian contribution to the Holocaust with the help of Soviet discourses and stereotypes, which they claimed to deconstruct. Edward Prus' biography of Bandera, published in 2004, appears to totally contradict these post-Soviet nationalist distortions. The kresowiacy historian combined Soviet discourses with the Polish nationalist and martyrological narrative. Although he came to completely different conclusions from those of V"iatrovych and Hunchak, Prus agreed with them that "Jewish Bolshevism" was not a stereotype or a nationalist perception of reality, but the reality.

By 2009 about thirty Bandera monuments were unveiled in western Ukraine, four Bandera museums were opened, and an unknown number of streets were renamed after him. The Bandera cult that appeared in post-Soviet Ukraine resembles that which the Ukrainian diaspora had practiced during the Cold War. The new enemies of the Banderites became Russian-speaking eastern Ukrainians, Russians, democrats, and occasionally Poles, Jews, and others. The spectrum of people who practice this cult is very wide. Among the Bandera admirers, one can find on the one hand far-right activists with shaved heads performing the fascist salute during their commemorations, and arguing that the Holocaust was the brightest episode in Ukrainian history, and on the other hand, high-school teachers and university professors. Both groups assume that Ukraine is dependent on Russia. Occasionally, they argue that Ukraine is occupied by democrats or Russified eastern Ukrainians, whom they would like to Ukrainianize or Banderize. Similarly, they perceive constructive critique or academic inquiry on the subject of Bandera or Ukrainian nationalism as a political campaign against their nation or as banderophobia.

In general, the Bandera cult in post-Soviet Ukraine took more eccentric forms than in the diaspora. Businessmen and far-right activists commercialized the cult while opening UPA pubs, and organizing Bandera music festivals. The cult was also made attractive to people who considered the Bandera monument in Lviv too monumental or did not want to belong to far-right paramilitary organizations. Similarly, the cult attracted a number of leading intellectuals and scholars into far-right organizations. One good example is Serhii Kvit, the rector of the National University of Kiev-Mohyla Academy, who, apart from writing an apologetic dissertation about Dmytro Dontsov at the Ukrainian Free University in Munich, was a member of the KUN. The process of sacralizing Bandera in western Ukraine was accompanied by erecting monuments devoted to Stalin and to the victims of the UPA, and preserving numerous monuments to Lenin and to various Soviet heroes in eastern Ukraine.

Another problematic form of commemorating Bandera and the OUN-UPA was established by the community of Polish kresowiacy. This group embedded the ethnic cleansing in Volhynia and eastern Galicia in the nationalist narrative of Polish martyrology, denying the Polish nationalist policies in the Second Republic, and atrocities committed by Polish troops against Ukrainian civilians during the Second World

War. In a number of nationalist publications, they instrumentalized the suffering of the victims of ethnic cleansing in Volhynia and eastern Galicia. To understand the nature of the kresowiacy community, one needs to recall two aspects. First, that between 1945 and 1990 communist policy in Poland did not give much or any opportunity to mourn the victims of the OUN and UPA and to come to terms with this difficult aspect of Polish history. Second, that after 1990, the generally uncritical multipatriotic and populist policy of reconciliation between Poland and Ukraine did not pay much respect to the victims of Ukrainian genocidal nationalism and of the Polish military units that murdered Ukrainian civilians. This policy, in which many leading Polish and Ukrainian intellectuals and politicians engaged, preferred to honor anti-Soviet armies, such as the UPA and AK, which fought for the "independence" of their nations.

After the dissolution of the Soviet Union, a number of nationalist factions of the Ukrainian diaspora did not cease to commemorate the *Providnyk*, but a few OUN and UPA veterans—who stayed in Munich after the war and knew Bandera in person—stated in interviews given to me in 2008 that they could not understand the obsessive fascination with Bandera in western Ukraine. They said that this fervent admiration of the *Providnyk* reminded them of the cult they had experienced in the 1930s and 1940s. They also stated that it distorted Bandera as a person and the movement that he represented. Some of them were also concerned about the collective denial of the atrocities committed by the OUN and UPA, which they experienced during the Second World War, although they never wanted to talk about particular war crimes. Similarly, Ukrainians outside the area of the Bandera cult could not comprehend the fascination with the *Providnyk*. The city council of Uzhhorod in Transcarpathia, in reaction to the proposal from eastern Galician Ternopil' to erect a Bandera monument, stated that they "do not share the fascination with" Bandera and "consider agitation for any radical actions as outrageous." Scholars such as Himka and Marples, who had been uncritical of the OUN and UPA for various reasons in the 1980s, rethought their understanding of Ukrainian nationalism in the 1990s and began to investigate this movement. In contrast, several "liberal" post-communist historians from both western and eastern Ukraine expressed the opinion that the history of Bandera and his movement should be distorted, in order to reconcile western and eastern Ukrainians and to help Ukraine to join the European Union.

Half a decade before the Bandera debate, Sofia Grachova criticized the Ukrainian "liberal" historian Iaroslav Hrytsak for marginalizing the pogroms, questioning information about their size, blaming the pogroms on Germans, Soviets, and indirectly on the very victims—Jews, questioning Jewish memoirs because of their "anti-Ukrainian" character, denying the antisemitic element of OUN ideology, adopting the perspective of the OUN-B activist Iaroslav Stets'ko, believing in the stereotype of "Jewish Bolshevism," having more sympathy for traditional than politically active Jews, and several other problematic matters. Grachova's criticism was alarming, because it was essentially correct and because Hrytsak represented the progressive and open-minded factions of Ukrainian historians. Hrytsak's book *Sketch of Ukrainian History*, first published in 1996 and later republished, was extensively used at Ukrainian universities and in schools. Despite its weaknesses related to the Second World War, it has still been one of the best available books on modern Ukrainian history.

The Bandera debate in 2009–2010 has finally demonstrated that not only Ukrainian nationalists but also a number of Ukrainian "liberal" and "progressive" intellectuals are not immune to the Bandera cult and for various reasons refuse to take notice of studies on the subject of Ukrainian nationalism. On the one hand, some of these intellectuals criticize the nationalist historians and far-right activists such as V"iatrovych and Tiahnybok but, on the other hand, they propagate and legitimize the Bandera cult in a more subtle way. Unlike V"iatrovych and Tiahnybok, who try to establish a far-right nationalist Bandera cult, the "liberal" intellectuals vote for the cult of a person who symbolizes resistance. During the Bandera debate, some of them protected Bandera as an "inconvenient hero." Others argued that Bandera is an element of the "regional pluralism of symbols" or an integral element of the Ukrainian collective identity.

The question whether the political conflicts in 2013–2014 and the civil war in 2014 were in some way related to the Bandera cult and the apologetic attitude of some sections of Ukrainian society toward Ukrainian extreme nationalism is not the subject of this study, but it should be briefly discussed because of the disturbing nature and horrific consequences of the violent events of 2013 and 2014 for Ukrainian society and the Ukrainian state. It would be wrong to assume that the Bandera cult or the apologetic attitude to Ukrainian nationalism, led solely or in the first instance, to these violent events. Such an assumption would distort the complex cultural and political relationships between "western" and "eastern" Ukrainians and between Ukraine and Russia. It would also ignore the complicated political situation within Ukraine, and exonerate the policies of Vladimir Putin and other involved parties. Nevertheless, the rise of nationalism in western Ukraine and the inability to rethink Bandera and his epoch has contributed to the polarization and radicalization of postcommunist Ukraine. This process has manifested itself in western Ukraine, in the erection of monuments devoted to Bandera and other nationalists; and in the east, in the preservation of Lenin monuments and other Soviet monuments and the erection of new monuments to Stalin. On the other hand, democracy and the concept of civil society have not played any major role in Ukrainian cultural, intellectual, and political life, and they have sometimes become confused with nationalism and other forms of extremism.

Inability to Mourn, Lack of Empathy, Sacralization, and Trauma

The first open debate about Bandera in 2009–2010 demonstrated that it is possible to discuss Bandera, the OUN, the UPA, the Holocaust, or the Ukrainian contribution to the Holocaust, but it also showed that Ukrainian intellectuals are not prepared to rethink these subjects. One important reason why Ukrainians cannot rethink the "uncomfortable" elements of Ukrainian history is that one needs to feel empathy for the victims of Ukrainian nationalism in order to sympathize with them, and to be able to comprehend all aspects of Ukrainian national history, including the mass violence of the Ukrainian nationalists. Such empathy, however, cannot be established because the Bandera cult and the glorification and sacralization of the perpetrators declare the genocidal policies of the murderers to be correct, and the victims of the OUN and UPA to be guilty of being killed. This kind of thinking simultaneously belittles, denies, and glorifies the crimes committed by the OUN and UPA and invites Ukrainians to identify themselves with the perpetrators, known in the post-Soviet discourse as "national heroes," "eternal heroes," or "heroes of Ukraine." This state of affairs can be also described as a coalition of silence, or collective or organized denial. It comes about to a large extent unconsciously, and it may be compared to the situation in Germany in the first decades after the Second World War. The few individuals who do not admire the perpetrators and who develop empathy for the victims of Ukrainian nationalism are condemned and discredited by other members of the community.

It is interesting to observe that some scholars, mainly "liberals" in postcommunist Ukraine, can better empathize with the Polish than with the Jewish and Ukrainian victims of the OUN-UPA mass violence. These intellectuals confirm that Polish civilians were murdered by the Ukrainian revolutionary nationalists, but they are unable to recognize and state the fact that a substantial number of Jewish and Ukrainian civilians were murdered by the same formations of Ukrainian nationalists for similar reasons. That more research has been done on the ethnic cleansing in Volhynia and eastern Galicia than on the anti-Jewish and anti-Ukrainian terror, can explain this phenomenon only to a certain extent, because the anti-Jewish and anti-Ukrainian mass violence of the OUN-UPA has also been investigated by several scholars and the basic facts about this kind of mass violence have been known for years. The reasons for disavowing the anti-Jewish and anti-Ukrainian mass violence seem, however, to differ from each other. Whereas the reason for the disavowal of anti-Jewish violence seems to be nationalism, which is still deeply rooted in Ukrainian academic and political culture, in the case of the anti-Ukrainian violence it is a deep feeling of shame concerning "national heroes" who had killed members of their own ethnic community.

The thorough and longstanding nationalist sacralization of the *Providnyk* and his movement would be much more difficult without the Soviet occupation of Ukraine, the Soviet terror in western Ukraine, and Soviet propaganda. The Soviet regime not only defeated the OUN and UPA but it also extensively and brutally targeted the civilian population in western Ukraine. Almost every family in eastern Galicia and Volhynia suffered in some manner from the Soviet terror. Many people who supported the UPA were killed, arrested, or deported to the Gulag—as were many who did not support the UPA. In these circumstances, Ukrainians in eastern Galicia, and to a lesser extent in Volhynia, turned Bandera and his followers into a symbol of resistance against the Soviet regime.

The celebration of Bandera not as a "fascist" but only as a symbol of "resistance" is a result of the post-Soviet patriotic sacralization of the *Providnyk* and his movement. It allows the admiration of Bandera, while avoiding the accusation of identifying with and approving of Bandera's genocidal ideas. It suggests that one who has established a positive emotional attitude to Bandera, only honors him because Bandera resisted the Soviet Union and not because he tried to introduce a fascist dictatorship in Ukraine, or voted for wiping out the ethnic and political "enemies of the Ukrainian nation." This also suggests that the OUN and UPA, of which Bandera became a symbol, can be commemorated only as a movement that resisted the Soviet Union and Nazi Germany, and not as a movement that imitated and adopted fascism and killed over 100,000 non-Ukrainian and Ukrainian inhabitants of the western

Ukrainian territories. This kind of memory of Bandera and his movement makes the process of coming to terms with the Ukrainian past impossible. Indirectly, it denies the Holocaust or the Ukrainian contribution to the Holocaust and pays no respect to the victims of Ukrainian nationalism.

The process of mastering its own history is a process of healing a society. It moves the society from a posttraumatic state into a state of awareness of all aspects of its own past. In this sense, the Bandera cult is not only a historical but also a sociological and psychological matter. It suppresses one Ukrainian trauma with the help of another one. The killing of Poles, Jews, and Ukrainians by the Ukrainian nationalists caused a classic perpetrator trauma in western Ukrainian society. This trauma was followed by another one, a victim trauma, caused by the Soviet terror. In the following decades, Ukrainians either had no opportunity to come to terms with their history or deliberately refused to do so. They could mourn neither the perpetrator trauma, nor the victim trauma. Before the dissolution of the Soviet Union, such mourning was impossible because of the Soviet memory politics and the diaspora discourse. After the dissolution of the Soviet Union, the Bandera cult suppressed the memory of the crimes committed by the OUN and UPA with the help of the suffering caused to Ukrainians by the Soviet regime.

An increasing number of Ukrainian historians are aware of the "unpleasant" elements of the Ukrainian history and are concerned about the extensive and ritualized denial of OUN and UPA atrocities. Cultural, social, and political pressure, however, discourages many Ukrainian intellectuals from openly expressing their opinions and constrains them to express only relativized views that appear to be appropriate in the Ukrainian context. Similarly, these scholars do not publish on Ukrainian nationalism in a direct and unapologetic way, because they fear that they will be collectively berated by their colleagues, friends, and relatives. For the same reason, some of them publicly condemn critical research on Ukrainian nationalism and on the Ukrainian contribution to the Holocaust.

In the two decades following the collapse of the Soviet Union, an entire spectrum of methods to protect the nationalist discourse has been developed by various elements of Ukrainian society, and also by a number of non-Ukrainian historians who sympathize with Ukrainian nationalism. These methods were invented and applied in order to discredit scholars who investigate Ukrainian nationalism and thereby uncover new aspects of the ethnic and political violence of Ukrainian extreme nationalism, or the nationalist distortions of Ukrainian history. The spectrum of these methods is wide and has been observed before in similar forms in other debates in which the honor of the nation was at stake. Scholars who investigate the subject may, for example, use "wrong methodology" or may not be "scholarly enough." They may have "bad intentions" toward Ukrainians, or they may investigate the OUN and UPA in the context of Holocaust and fascist studies, and not in the context of Ukrainian studies or the Ukrainian resistance. Similarly, all kinds of real and alleged mistakes are found in the publications of these historians and are presented as sins against science in order to discredit them and thereby to protect the good name of the nation or to maintain good relationships with Ukrainian scholars.

One of the most alarming issues related to the sacralization of Bandera and the OUN and UPA is the question of values represented by Bandera, and of the atrocities conducted by the Ukrainian nationalists. The process of heroization and sacralization does not only whitewash the movement of atrocities and other "unpleasant" aspects such as fascistization or collaboration with Nazi Germany but it also sacralizes the perpetrators. It transforms their genocidal deeds into taboo, a discussion of which is beyond any social norm because it would cause harm to the community. Societies that have established such taboos have usually suffered from a trauma and are very sensitive about their past. They protect distorted and sometimes ridiculous explanations of their past in order to avoid the pain that would result from uncovering their obfuscated history.

The Bandera cult is not the only phenomenon, but certainly one of the most important ones, that does not allow Ukrainians to mourn the past and rethink their history. Although, theoretically, mourning the past appears to be easy, it is not easy at all. It requires a period of latency. The mourning community has to act out and work though the trauma. It needs time to recognize that "its members, instead of being heroes, have been perpetrators who violated the cultural premises of their own identity."[9] Given the state of cultural, social and political affairs and the level of intellectual and political culture in Ukraine, it might take decades until the "heroes" leave Ukraine and enable Ukrainians to mourn and rethink their history. Also, many intermediate stages, which change little or nothing, might occur.

9 Bernhard Giesen, "The Trauma of Perpetrators: The Holocaust and the Traumatic Reference of German National Identity," *Cultural trauma and collective identity*, ed. Jeffrey Alexander (Berkeley, Calif.: University of California Press, 2004), 114.

GLOSSARY

banderivshchyna (Ukr.), *banderovshchina* (Rus.): a term used in Ukrainian and Russian to describe the Bandera movement or the OUN and UPA.

Captive Nations: an organization comprising several anticommunist émigré groups that opposed the Soviet Union and wanted to liberate their countries by means of various nationalist ideologies.

banderophobia: a term used in post-Soviet far-right circles. It defines the critical attitude to Bandera and the OUN as hostility to the Ukrainian culture.

Caudillo (Span.): Leader.

coup d'état (Fr.): "stroke of state," putsch, or an overthrow of government.

Doglavnik (Croat.): deputy leader.

Drahomanivtsi: a pejorative term coined by Dmytro Dontsov, referring to Mykhailo Drahomanov and other moderate earlier Ukrainian thinkers such as Mykhailo Hrushevs'kyi and Ivan Franko.

Ehrenhaft (Ger.): honorable captivity.

Ehrenhäftling or Sonderhäftling (Ger.): "honorary prisoners" or "special political prisoners" were very important political prisoners who received special treatment in Nazi Germany.

Einsatzgruppen (Ger.): "task forces," special troops that killed huge numbers of civilians, primarily by shooting. The Einsatzgruppen (sing. Einsatzgruppe) operated in territories occupied by the German armed forces following the invasion of Poland in September 1939 and Operation Barbarossa in June 1941.

Einsatzkommando (Ger.): "death squad," subgroups of the Einsatzgruppen.

Endecja: National Democracy, a Polish right-wing nationalist political movement active from the late nineteenth century to the end of the Second Polish Republic in 1939. Its main ideological leader was Roman Dmowski.

Führer (Ger.): Leader.

Führerprinzip (Ger.): "leader principle"—prescribed the fundamental basis of political authority in fascist parties, states, and movements.

Gulag (Rus.): a contraction of the name of the government agency that administered the main Soviet forced labor camps, where conditions were extremely poor.

Hilfspolizei (Ger.): native "auxiliary police" who worked for the German occupying authorities. In Ukraine, they were also known also as Ukrainian police. The German administration also called them Schutzmannschaften.

khokhol (Ukr.): the stereotypical Ukrainian Cossack style of haircut that features a lock of hair sprouting from the top or the front of an otherwise closely shaven head; also a pejorative term for ethnic Ukrainians.

kolkhoz (Rus.): collective farm in the Soviet Union.

kresowiacy (Pol.): people resettled from the former eastern Polish territories.

kurkul (Rus.): a prosperous landed peasant in czarist Russia, characterized by the Communists as an exploiter.

oblast (Ukr. and Rus.): area, first level of administrative division of Ukraine.

Ostministerium (Ger.): Reich Ministry for the Occupied Eastern Territories, created in July 1941 by Adolf Hitler and headed by Alfred Rosenberg.

palingenesis: a concept of rebirth or re-creation of a nation coined in fascist studies by Roger Griffin.

panakhyda (Ukr.): memorial service.

perestroika (Rus.): "restructuring," political movement for reformation within the Communist Party of the Soviet Union, associated with Mikhail Gorbachev's politics.

Plast: Ukrainian scout organization founded in Lviv in 1911. It was banned in the Second Republic in 1928 in Volhynia, and in 1930 in eastern Galicia. After the war, Plast was reestablished by Ukrainian political émigrés in various countries of the Western bloc, and in Ukraine after the dissolution of the Soviet Union.

Poglavnik (Croat.): Leader.

Providnyk (Ukr.): Leader.

Prosvita (Ukr.): "Enlightenment," a society created in 1868 in Ukrainian Galicia for preserving and developing Ukrainian culture and education among the population.

raion (Ukr.): district, second level of administrative division of Ukraine.

rynek (Pol.): marketplace.

Sanacja (Pol.): sanation or healing, a political movement that came to power after Józef Piłsudski's coup d'état in May 1926.

Schutzmannschaften (Ger.): collaborationist auxiliary battalions of native policemen in countries occupied by Nazi Germany.

Second Republic: abbreviation of the Second Polish Republic. i.e. the Polish state between 1918 and 1939 (Pol. *II Rzeczpospolita Polska*).

sejm (Pol.): the lower house of the Polish parliament.

Sicherheitsdienst (Ger.): Security Service (SD), the intelligence agency of the Nazi Party. In 1939 it was transferred to the authority of the RSHA.

Sicherheitspolizei (Ger.): Security Police. Between 1936 and 1939 it combined the Gestapo (secret state police) and the Kripo (criminal police). In 1939 it was merged into the RSHA, but the term continued to be used informally until the end of the Third Reich.

Slava Ukraïni! (Ukr.): "Glory to Ukraine!" was a Ukrainian fascist greeting invented by the League of Ukrainian Fascists and taken over by the OUN. The OUN-B extended it while adding *Heroiam Slava!* (Glory to the Heroes!) as a response.

sobornist' (Ukr.): unification of all Ukrainian territories in one state.

svoboda (Ukr.): freedom.

Strasse (Ger.): street.

tryzub (Ukr.): trident, the state arms of Ukraine.

Übermensch (Ger.): superhuman.

Vodca (Slovak): Leader.

vogelfrei (Ger.): outlawed.

völkisch (Ger.): populist or nationalist, and typically racist.

Vozhd' (Ukr. and Rus.): Leader.

Vozhdevi Slava! (Ukr.): "Glory to the Leader!" was a Ukrainian fascist greeting introduced in 1939 by at the Second Great Congress of the OUN in Rome.

Wódz (Pol.): Leader.

BIBLIOGRAPHY

Archival Collections:

Archiwum Akt Nowych w Warszawie, AAN
- Ministerstwo Spraw Zewnętrznych, MSZ
- Ambasada w Rzymie

Archiwum Żydowskiego Instytutu Historycznego, AŻIH
- 229 Teka Lwowska
- 301 Survivor testimonies collected by the Central Jewish Historical Commission
- 302 Memoirs and Survivor testimonies collected by the Central Jewish Historical Commission

Archives of the Stepan Bandera Museum in London, ASBML
- Document collection

Archives of the Shevchenko Scientific Society in New York, ASSS
- Ivan Kedryn-Rudnyts'kyi Archives

Arkhiv Tsentru doslidzhen' vyzvol'noho rukhu, ATsDVR
-Collection of documents and pictures

Archiv, Gedenkstätte und Museum Sachsenhausen, AGMS
- Justiz Sowjetunion, JSU 1 (Soviet Sachsenhausen trial)

Bayerisches Hauptstaatsarchiv, BayHStA
- Landeskriminalamt 271

Biblioteka Narodowa w Waszawie, BN
- Dmitro Dontsov Archives

Bundesarchiv – Militärarchiv in Freiburg, BA-MA
- RW 2 Chef des OKW mit Wehrmachtrechtsabteilung
- RW 4 OKW/Wehrmachtsführungsstab
- RH 24 Generalkommandos der Armeekorps
- RH 26 Divisionen
- RH 2 OKH Operationsabteilung

Bundesarchiv Berlin, BAB
- R 58 Reichssicherheitshauptamt
- R 6 Reichsministerium für die Besetzen Ostgebiete
- NS 26 Hauptarchiv NSDAP
- NS 19 Persönlicher Stab Reichsführer SS

Bundesarchiv Koblenz, BAK
- R 43 II Reichskanzlei
- B 206 Bundesnachrichtendienst
- B 362 Bundesgerichtshof

Bundesbeauftragte für die Unterlagen des Staatssicherheitsdienstes, BStU, Berlin
- MfS Ministerium für Staatssicherheit der DDR
- MfS Hauptabteilung IX
- MfS Zentrale Auswertungs- und Informationsgruppe, ZAIG

Derzhavnyi arkhiv L'vivs'koï oblasti, DALO
- f. 121, L'vivs'ke voievods'ke upravlinnia derzhavnoï politsiï

Federal'naia sluzhba bezopasnosti Rossiiskoi Federatsii, FSB-Archiv
- N 19092, Sachsenhausen Trial

Gosudarstvennyi arkhiv Rossiiskoi Federatsii, GARF
- f. R-9478 Glavnoe upravlenie po bor'be s banditizmom MVD SSR

Haluzevyi Derzhavnyi arkhiv Sluzhby bezpeky Ukraïny, HDA SBU
-f. 13 Interrogation Documents

Karta, Archiwum Wschodnie in Warsaw, KAW
- Collection of Testimonies

Landesarchiv Nordrhein-Westfalen, LN-W
- Staatsanwaltschaft bei dem Landgericht Bonn

National Archives and Records Administration, NARA
- RG 263, E ZZ-18, Stephen (Stepan) Bandera Name File

Politisches Archiv des Auswärtigen Amtes in Berlin, PAAA
- Politische Abteilung XII

Provincial Archives of Alberta, PAA
- Bila knyha OUN. Pro dyversiu-bunt Iary-Bandera

Rossiiskii gosudarstvennyi arkhiv sotsial'no-politicheskoi istorii, RGASPI
- f. 17 Tsentranl'nyi Komitet KPSS

Rossiiskii Gosudarstvennyi voennyi arkhiv, RGVA
- f. 308 Captured Documents of the Polish Intelligence Service.

Staatsarchiv München, StM
- Staatsanwaltschaften
- Pol. Dir. München 9281

Stadtarchiv München
- Pol. Oir. 843.

Taras Shevchenko Library and Archives of the SUB in London, TShLA
- Collection of Photographs

Tsentral'nyi derzhavnyi istorychnyi arkhiv u L'vovi, TsDIAL
- f. 205 Prokuratura Apeliatsiinoho sudu, m. L'viv.
- f. 371 Shukhevych Stepan

Tsentral'nyi derzhavnyi arkhiv hromads'kykh obiednan' Ukrainy, TsDAHO
- f. 1 Tsentral´nyi komitet kompartii Ukrainy
- f. 4620 Kolektsiia dokumentiv z istorii Velykoï Vitchyznianoï viiny 1941–1945 rr.

Tsentral'nyi derzhavnyi arkhiv vyshchykh orhaniv vlady ta upravlinnia Ukrainy, TsDAVOV
- f. 3833 Kraevyi provid Orhanizatsii ukrains'kykh natsionalistiv na zakhidnoukrains'kykh zemliakh

United States Holocaust Memorial Museum, USHMM
- RG 31 Ukraine

Wiener Library for the Study of the Holocaust & Genocide, London
- Collection of Photographs

Zakład Narodowy im. Ossolińskich we Wrocławiu, ZNiO
- Manuscripts

Newspapers:

- *ABN Correspondance,* 1960–1985
- *Avangard. Zhurnal ukraïns'koï molodi,* 1979
- *Banderivets': Informatsiinyi biuleten' Vseukraïns'koï orhanizatsiï "Tryzub" im. Stepana Bandery,* 2000–2006
- *DefendingHistory.com, (http://defendinghistory.com/),* 2009–2011
- *Edmonton Journal, 2010*
- *Express Poranny, Lwów,* 1934–1936
- *Gazeta Lwowska,* 1934–1936
- *Homin Ukraïny,* 1959–2009
- *Ideia i chyn. Orhan Kariovoï Upravy Spilky Ukraïns'koï Molodi v Nimechchyni*
- *Ilustrowany Kuryer Codzienny,* 1934–1936
- *Komar,* 1934
- *Komsomol'skaia pravda,* 1959
- *Labour Focus on Eastern Europe,* 1982
- *Lenins'ka Molod,* 1951
- *L'vivs'ka Hazeta,* 2004
- *L'vovs'kaia Pravda, 1951,* 1988–1990
- *The New York Review of Books,* 2010

- *Neues Deutschland,* 1959
- *Novyi Chas,* 1934–1936
- *Pravda Ukrainy,* 1989–1990
- *Radians'ka Ukraïna. Orhan Tsentralnoho Komitetu KP(b)U, Verkhobnoï Rady i Rady Ministriv Ukraïns'koï RSR,* 1943–1959, 1990
- *Rohatyns'ke Slovo, Rohatyn',* 1941
-*Rozbudova Natsiï,* 1928–1932
- *Rzeczpospolita. Plus Minus,* 2007
- *Samostiina Ukraina,* 1941
- *Der Spiegel,* 1961–1962
- *Surma,* 1928–1932
- *Surma,* 1951
- *Shliakh peremohy,* 1954–1991
- *Süddeutsche Zeitung,* 1950
- *Ukrainian Echo,* 1980–1984
- *The Ukrainian Weekly, New Jersey,* 1985, 1988, 1997
- *Ukraïns'ka dumka,* 1959–1990
- *Ukrains'ke slovo,* 1941
- *Vil'na Ukraïna. Orhan L'vivs'koho Obkomu i Miskomu KP(b)U, Oblasnoï ta Mis'koï Rady Deputativ Trudiashchykh,* 1944–1949
- *Visnyk istoryko-memorial'noho muzeiu Stepana Bandery,* 2006
- *Visti. Hazeta L'vivs'koho Derzhavnoho Ahrarnoho Universytetu,* 2002–2009
- *Vysokyi Zamok,* 1992
- *Vyzvol'nyi shliakh,* 1959–2009
- *Za radiansku Ukraïnu. Hazeta politychnoho upravlinnia viis'k Chervonoï Armiï pivdenno-zakhidnoho napriamku,* 1941
- *Za vil'nu Ukraïnu,* 1990–2004
- *Zaxid.net, (http://zaxid.net/),* 2009–2011

Films:

- Ana Boguslavskaja and Oled Schilowski (film directors), *Die Bandera-Bande: Guerilla-Kämpfer im 2. Weltkrieg.* Discovery Channel 2009.
- Iurii Diukanov (film director), *Try liubovi Stepana Bandery.* Vikna, 1998.
- Deutsche Wochenschau – Nr. 566 / 29 / 10.07.1941.
- Documentary on the unveiling ceremony of the Stepan Bandera monument broadcast by Lviv Television on 13 October 2007.
- A. Fedoriv (film director), *Vidkoly Pamiataie Istoriia,* Ukrainokhroniky 1969.
- Oles' Ianchuk (film director), *Holod-33,* Kinostudia im. Dovzhenka 1991.
- Oles' Ianchuk (film director), *Atentat: Osinnie vbyvstvo v Miunkheni,* Oles'-film 1995.
- Oles' Ianchuk (film director), *Neskorenyi,* Oles'-film 2000.
- Oles' Ianchuk (film director), *Zalizna Sotnia,* Oles'-film 2004.
- Valerii Isakov (film director), *Do poslednei minuty,* Odesskaia Kinostudiia, 1973.
- F. Karpins'kyi (film director), *Z Marshruta Ne Vernulys',* Ukrainokhroniky 1975.
- Vakhtang Kipiani (film director), *Stepan Bandera,* 2009.
- Leonid Lukov (film director), *Ob etom zabyt' nel'zia,* Kinostudia im. Gorkoho, 1954.

- Walter Moßmann, Didi Danquart (film directors), *Menschen und Strassen: Lemberg – geöffnete Stadt,* SWF and arte 1993.
- Serhii Sotnychenko, Taras Tkachenko, and Olena Nozhekina (directors), *Tsina svobody*, Kinotur 2008.
- V. Sychevs'kyi (film director), *Narod Zvynovychuie*, Ukrainokhroniky 1959.
- Ie. Tatarets' (film director), *Voiovnychi Ateïsty*, Ukrainokhroniky 1985.
- L. Udovenko (film director), *Vbyvtsia Vidomyi*, Ukrainokhroniky 1972.
- USHMM Film Archive, tape 402, story RG-60.0441.

Interviews:

Mykhailo Balabans'kyi, 9 May 2008, Volia Zaderevats'ka.
Mykhailo Bilan, 10 July 2008, London.
Mykhailo Klymchuk, 14 May 2008, London.
Irena Kozak, 16 February 2008, Munich.
Andrii Kutsan, 14 February 2008, Munich.
Mykola Horda, 16 May 2008, Lviv.
Oksana Horda, 14 May 2008, Dubliany.
Stepan Lesiv, 18 May 2008, Staryi Uhryniv.
Vasyl' Oles'kiv, 27 November 2008, Berlin/London.
Iurii Nazaryk, 15 May 2008, Lviv.
Andrii Parubyi, 12 May 2006, Lviv.
Andrii Rebet, 22 February 2008, Munich.
Volodymyr Snityns'kyi, 2 June 2008, Dubliany.
Ievhen Stakhiv, 11 November 2008, Berlin/New Jersey.
[name withheld], 17 February 2008, Munich.

Published Works:

Abramson, Henry. *A Prayer for the Government: Ukrainians and Jews in Revolutionary Times, 1917–1920*. Cambridge: Harvard University Press, 1999.

Adamczyk, Mieczysław and Gmitruk, Janusz and Koseski, Adam ed., *Ziemie Wschodnie: Raporty Biura Wschodniego Delegatury Rządu na Kraj 1943–1944*. Warsaw: Muzeum Historii Polskiego Ruchu Ludowego and Wyższa Szkoła Humanistyczna im. Aleksandra Gieysztora, 2005.

Ainsztein, Reuben. *Jewish Resistance in Nazi-Occupied Eastern Europe*. London: Paul Elek, 1974.

Aleksandov, Kirill. *Ofitserskii korpus armii general-leitenanta A. A. Vlasova 1944–1945 gg*. Saint Petersburg: Russko-baltiiskii informatsionnyi tsentr BLITs, 2001.

Aleksandov, Kirill. "Bandera: postskryptum «moskal'skoho» istoryka." In *Strasti za Banderoiu*, edited by Tarik Cyril Amar, Ihor Balyns'kyi, and Iaroslav Hrytsak, 75–89. Kiev: Hrani-T, 2010.

Amar, Tarik Cyril and Balyns'kyi, Ihor, and Iaroslav Hrytsak, ed. *Strasti za Banderoiu*. Kiev: Hrani-T, 2010.

Amar, Tarik Cyril. "A Disturbed Silence: Discourse on the Holocaust in the Soviet West as an Anti-Site of Memory." In *The Holocaust in the East: Local Perpetra-*

tors and Soviet Responses, edited by Michael David-Fox, Peter Holquist, and Alexander M. Martin, 158–84. Pittsburgh: University of Pittsburgh Press, 2014.

Anders, Karl. *Mord auf Befehl: Der Fall Stachynskij*. Tübingen: Fritz Schlichtenmayer, 1963.

Anderson, Benedickt. *Imagined Communities: Reflections on the Origin and Spread of Nationalism*. London: Verso, 1983.

Arendt, Hannah. *Eichmann in Jerusalem: A Report on the Banality of Evil*. New York: Penguin, 1994.

Armstrong, John A. *Ukrainian Nationalism*. New York: Columbia University Press, 1963.

Armstrong, John A. "Heroes and Human: Reminiscences Concerning Ukrainian National Leaders During 1941–1944," *The Ukrainian Quarterly*, LI, no. 2–3 (1995): 213–27.

Arsenych, Petro and Fedoriv, Taras. *Rodyna Banderiv: Do 90-richchnia vid dnia narodzhennia ta 40-richchnia trahichnoï smerti providnyka OUN Stepana Bandery (1909–1959)*. Ivano-Frankivs'k: Nova Zoria, 1998.

Assmann, Aleida. *Der lange Schatten der Vergangenheit: Erinnerungskultur und Geschichtspolitik*. Bonn: C.H.Beck, 2007.

Augsberger, Janis. "Ein anti-analythisches Bedürfnis: Bruno Schulz im Grenzbereich zwischen Poetik und Politik." In *Politische Mythen im 19. und 20. Jahrhundert in Mittel- und Osteuropa*, edited by Heidi Hein-Kircher and Hans Hahn, 25–44. Marburg: Herder Institut, 2006.

Backes, Uwe. "'Rchtsextremismus'—Konzeption und Kontroversen." In *Rechtsextreme Ideologien in Geschichte und Gegenwart*, edited by Uwe Backes, 15–52. Köln: Böhlau, 2003.

Balabans'kyi, Mykhailo. *Muzei-Sadyba Stepana Bandery v seli Volia-Zaderevats'ka*. Volia Zaderevats'ka, 2000.

Balei, Petro. *Fronda Stepana Bandery v OUN 1940 roku*. Kiev: Tekna, 1996.

Bandera, Stepan. *Slovo do Ukraïns'kykh natsionalistiv-revoliutsioneriv za kordonom*. 1948.

Bandera, Stepan. *Perspektyvy ukraïns'koï revoliutsiï*. Munich: Vydavnytsvo Orhanizatsiï Ukraïns'kykh Natsionalistiv, 1978.

Bandera, Stepan. "Interviu nimetskoï radiostatsiï v Kel'ni zi Stepanom Banderoiu." In *Perspektyvy ukraïns'koï revoliutsiï*, edited by Vasyl' Ivanyshyn, 610–17. Drohobych: Vidrodzhennia, 1999.

Bandera, Stepan. "Na pivmeti." In *Perspektyvy ukraïns'koï revoliutsiï*, edited by Vasyl' Ivanyshyn, 604–609. Drohobych: Vidrodzhennia, 1999.

Bandera, Stepan. "Pershe interviu providnyka OUN, Stepana Bandery z chuzhynnymy zhurnalistamy." In *Perspektyvy ukraïns'koï revoliutsiï*, edited by Vasyl' Ivanyshyn, 632–40. Drohobych: Vidrodzhennia, 1999.

Bandera, Stepan. "Proty fal'shuvannia vyzvol'nykh pozytsii." In *Perspektyvy ukraïns'koï revoliutsiï*, edited by Vasyl' Ivanyshyn, 322–38. Drohobych: Vidrodzhennia, 1999.

Bandera, Stepan. "Tretia svitova viina i vyzvolna borot'ba." In *Perspektyvy ukraïns'koï revoliutsiï*, edited by Vasyl' Ivanyshyn, 207–38. Drohobych: Vidrodzhennia, 1999.

Bandera, Stepan. "Znachennia shyrokykh mas ta ïkh okhoplennia." In *Perspektyvy ukraïns'koï revoliutsiï*, edited by Vasyl' Ivanyshyn, 14–17. Drohobych: Vidrodzhennia, 1999.

Bandera, Stepan. *Perspektyvy Ukraïns'koï Revoliutsiï*, edited by Vasyl' Ivanyshyn. Drohobych: Vidrodzhennia, 1999.

Bandera, Stepan. *Perspektyvy Ukraïns'koï Revoliutsiï*. Kiev: Instytut Natsionalnoho Derzhavoznastva, 1999.

Bandera, Stepan. "Do zasad nashoï vyzvol'noï polityky." *In Perspektyvy ukraïns'koï revoliutsiï*, edited by Vasyl' Ivanyshyn, 45–55. Drohobych: Vidrodzhennia, 1999.

Bandera, Stepan. "Khoch iaki velyki zhertvy—borot'ba konechna." In *Perspektyvy ukraïns'koï revoliutsiï*, edited by Vasyl' Ivanyshyn, 355–59. Drohobych: Vidrodzhennia, 1999.

Bandera, Stepan. "Moï zhyttiepysni dani." In *Perspektyvy ukraïns'koï revoliutsiï*, edited by Vasyl' Ivanyshyn, 1–13. Drohobych: Vidrodzhennia, 1999.

Bandera, Stepan. "Nezminna stratehiia Moskvy." In *Perspektyvy ukraïns'koï revoliutsiï*, edited by Vasyl' Ivanyshyn, 391–14. Drohobych: Vidrodzhennia, 1999.

Bandera, Stepan. "Promova na p"iatu zustrich ukraïntsiv ZSA i Kanady 1954 roku." In *Perspektyvy ukraïns'koï revoliutsiï*, edited by Vasyl' Ivanyshyn, 617–22. Drohobych: Vidrodzhennia, 1999.

Bandera, Stepan. "Proty fal'shuvannia." In *Perspektyvy ukraïns'koï revoliutsiï*, edited by Vasyl' Ivanyshyn, 322–28. Drohobych: Vidrodzhennia, 1999.

Bandera, Stepan. "Proty ideinoho rozbroiuvannia vyzvol'noï borot'by." In *Perspektyvy ukraïns'koï revoliutsiï*, edited by Vasyl' Ivanyshyn, 244–53. Drohobych: Vidrodzhennia, 1999.

Bandera, Stepan. "Slovo do Ukraïns'kykh natsionalistiv-revoliutsioneriv za kordonom." In *Perspektyvy ukraïns'koï revoliutsiï*, edited by Vasyl' Ivanyshyn, 77–129. Drohobych: Vidrodzhennia, 1999.

Bandera, Stepan. "Ukraïns'ka Natsional'na Revolutsiia, a ne tilky protyrezhymnyi rezystans." In *Perspektyvy ukraïns'koï revoliutsiï*, edited by Vasyl' Ivanyshyn, 130–70. Drohobych: Vidrodzhennia, 1999.

Bandera, Stepan. "Z nevycherpnoho dzherela." In *Perspektyvy ukraïns'koï revoliutsiï*, edited by Vasyl' Ivanyshyn, 410–14. Drohobych: Vidrodzhennia, 1999.

Bandera, Stepan. "Perspektyvy ukraïns'koï natsional'no-vyzvol'noï revoliutsiï." In *Perspektyvy ukraïns'koï revoliutsiï*, edited by Vasyl' Ivanyshyn, 506–95. Drohobych: Vidrodzhennia, 1999.

Bandera, Stephen. "Family Name Cleared," *Edmonton Journal*, 9 February 2010.

Barkan, Elazar and Cole, Elizabeth A. and Struve, Kai. *Shared History—Divided Memory: Jews and Others in Soviet-Occupied Poland, 1939–1941*. Leipzig: Leipziger Universitätsverlag, 2007.

Bartov, Omer. *Erased: Vanishing Traces of Jewish Galicia in Present-Day Ukraine*. Princeton: Princeton University Press, 2007.

Bartov, Omer. "Eastern Europe as the Site of Genocide." *The Journal of Modern History* Vol. 80, No. 3 (2008): 557–93.

Bartov, Omer. "Wartime Lies and Other Testimonies: Jewish-Christian Relations in Buczacz, 1939–1944." *East European Politics and Societies* Vol. 26, No. 3 (2011): 486–511.

Bastow, Steve. "Integral Nationalism." In *World Fascism: A Historical Encyclopedia*, edited by Cyprian P. Blamires, Vol. 1, 338. Santa Barbara, CA: ABC-CLIO, 2006.

Bauer, Yehuda. *The Death of the Shtetl*. New Haven: Yale University Press, 2009.

Bauerkämper, Arnd. *Die "radikale Rechte" in Großbritanien*. Göttingen: Vandenhoeck & Ruprecht, 1991.

Bauerkämper, Arnd. *Der Faschismus in Europa 1918–1945*. Stuttgart: Reclam, 2006.

Bauerkämper, Arnd. "Transnational Fascism: Cross-Border Relations between Regimes and Movements in Europe, 1922–1939." *East Central Europe* 37 (2010): 214–46.

Beliaiev, Vladimir and Rudnytski, Mikhailo. *Pod chuzhymy znamenamy*. Moscow: Krasnoe znamia, 1954.

Beliaev, Vladimir. *Formula Iada*. Moscow: Sovetskii pisatel', 1972.

Beliaev, Vladimir. *Ia obviniiaiu!* Moscow: Izdatel'stvo politicheskoi literatury, 1978.

Berg, Nicolaus. *Der Holocaust und die westdeutschen Historiker: Erforschung und Erinnerung*. Göttingen: Wallstein, 2003.

Bergesen, Albert. "Die rituelle Ordnung." In *Ritualtheorien: Ein einführendes Handbuch*, edited by Andréa Belliger and David J. Krieger, 49–76. Opladen: Westdeutscher Verlag, 1998.

Berkhoff, Karel and Carynnyk, Marco. "The Organisation of Ukrainian Nationalists and Its Attitude toward Germans and Jews: Iaroslav Stets'ko's 1941 *Zhyttiepys*." *Harvard Ukrainian Studies* Vol. 23, No. 3–4 (1999): 149–84.

Berkhoff, Karel. *Harvest of Despair: Life and Death in Ukraine under Nazi Rule*. Cambridge: Belknap Press of Harvard University, 2004.

Bihl, Wolfdieter. "Aufgegangen in Großreichen: Die Ukraine als österreichische und russische Provinz." In *Geschichte der Ukraine*, edited by Frank Golczewski, 128–57. Göttingen: Vandenhoeck & Ruprecht, 1993.

Bilsky, Leora. *Transformative Justice: Israeli Identity on Trial*. Ann Arbor: University of Michigan Press, 2004.

Bilsky, Leora. "The Eichmann Trial and the Legacy of Jurisdiction." In *Politics in Dark Times: Encounters with Hannah Arendt*, edited by Seyla Benhabib, Roy Thomas Tsao, Peter J. Verovšek, 198–218. Cambridge: Cambridge University Press, 2010.

Binodich, Mark "Controversies surrounding the Catholic Church in Wartime Croatia, 1941–45." *Totalitarian Movement and Political Religions*, Vol. 7, No. 4 (2006): 429–57.

Bizeul, Yves. "Theorien der politischen Mythen und Rituale." In *Politische Mythen und Rituale in Deutschland, Frankreich und Polen*, edited by Yves Bizeul. Berlin: Duncker & Humboldt, 2000.

Boeckh, Katrin. *Stalinismus in der Ukraine: Die Rekonstruktion des sowjetischen Systems nach dem Zweiten Weltkrieg*. Wiesbaden: Harrassowitz, 2007.

Bohunov, Serhii ed., *Poliaky ta Ukraïntsi mizh dvoma totalitarnymy systemamy 1942–1945*, Vol. 4. Warsaw: Instytut Pamięci Narodowej, 2005.

Bohunov, Serhii ed., *Bofony: Hroshovi dokumenty OUN i UPA*. Kiev: Sluzhba Bezpeky Ukraïny, 2008.

Boidunyk, Osyp. "Iak diishlo do stvorennia Orhanizatsiï Ukraïns'kykh Natsionalistiv." In *Ievhen Konovalets' ta ioho doba*, edited by Iurii Boïko, 359–79. Munich: Cicero, 1974.

Boïko, Iurii. "Iak diishlo do stvorennia Orhanizatsiï Ukraïns'kykh Natsionalistiv." In *Ievhen Konovalets' ta ioho doba*, edited by Iurii Boïko. Munich: Cicero, 1974.

Boïko, Iurii, ed. *Ievhen Konovalets' ta ioho doba*, Munich: Cicero, 1974.

Bolianovs'kyi, Andrii. *Dyviziia "Halychyna": Istoriia*. Lviv: A. Bolianovs'kyi, 2000.

Bolianovs'kyi, Andrii. *Ukraïns'ki viis'kovi formuvannia v zbroinykh sylakh Nimechchyny* (1939–1945). Lviv: L'vivskyi natsional'nyi universytet im. Ivana Franka, 2003.

Boll, Bernd. "Zloczow, Juli 1941: Die Wehrmacht und der Beginn des Holocaust in Galizien." *Zeitschrift für Geschichtswissenschaft* Vol. 50 (2002): 899–917.

Boll, Bernd. "Złoczów, July 1941: The Wehrmacht and the Beginning of the Holocaust in Galicia." In *Crimes of War: Guilt and Denial in the Twentieth Century*, edited by Omer Bartov and Atina Grossmann and Mary Nolan, 61–99. New York: The New York Press, 2002.

Borodziej, Włodzimierz. *Geschichte Polens im 20. Jahrhundert*. Munich: C.H.Beck, 2010.

Bociurkiw, Bohdan. *Ukraïns'ka Hreko-Katolyts'ka Tserkva i Radians'ka Derzhava (1939–1950)*. Lviv: Vydavnytsvo Ukraïns'koho Katolyts'koho Universytetu, 2005.

Brandon, Ray. "Hans Koch." In *Handbuch der völkischen Wissenschaften*, edited by Ingo Haar and Michael Fahlbusch, 329–34. Munich: K. G. Saur, 2008.

Brandon, Ray and Lower, Wendy, ed. *The Shoah in Ukraine: History, Testimony, Memorialization*. Bloomington: Indiana University Press, 2008.

Brandon, Ray and Lower, Wendy, "Introduction." In. *The Shoah in Ukraine: History, Testimony, Memorialization*. edited by Ray Brandon and Wendy Lower, 1–22. Bloomington: Indiana University Press, 2008.

Breitman, Richard and Goda, Norman J. W. *Hitler's Shadow, Nazi War Criminals, U.S. Intelligence, and the Cold War*. Washington: National Archives, 2010.

Bronisław Pieracki: Generał brygady, minister spaw wewnętrznych, poseł na Sejm, mąż stanu, człowiek. Warsaw: Instytut Propagandy Państwowo-Twórczej, 1934.

Broszat, Martin. "Die Eiserne Garde und das Dritte Reich. Zum Problem des Faschismus in Ostmitteleuropa." In *Politische Studien* 9 (1958): 628–36.

Browning, Christopher. *Ordinary Men: Reserve Police Battalion 101 and the Final Solution in Poland*. New York: Harper Collins, 1992.

Browning, Christopher. *Remembering Survival: Inside a Nazi Labor Camp*. New York: Norton, 2010.

Bruder, Franziska. "'Der Gerechtigkeit dienen.' Die ukrainischen Nationalisten als Zeugen im Auschwitz-Prozess." In *Im Labyrinth der Schuld: Täter—Opfer—Ankläger*, edited by Irmtrud Wojak and Susanne Meinl, 133–62. Frankfurt: Campus Verlag, 2003.

Bruder, Franziska. "Kollaboration oder Widerstand? Die ukrainischen Nationalisten während des Zweiten Weltkrieges." *Zeitschrift für Geschichtswissenschaft* Vol. 54 (2006): 20–44.

Bruder, Franziska.*"Den ukrainischen Staat erkämpfen oder sterben!" Die Organisation Ukrainischer Nationalisten (OUN) 1929–1948*. Berlin: Metropol Verlag, 2007.

Bul'ba-Borovets', Taras. *Armiia bez derzhavy: Slava i trahediia ukrains'koho povstans'koho rukhu. Spohady*. Kiev: Knyha Rodu, 2008.

Burds, Jeffrey. "AGENTURA: Soviet Informants' Networks and the Ukrainian Underground in Galicia, 1944–1948." *East European Politics and Societies* Vol. 11, No.1 (1996): 89–130.

Burds, Jeffrey. "Ethnicity, Memory and Violence: Reflections on Special Problems in Soviet & East European Archives." *Comma. International Journal of Archives*, No. 3–4 (2002): 69–82.

Burds, Jeffrey. "The Early Cold War in Soviet West Ukraine, 1944–1948." *The Carl Beck Papers in Russian & East European Studies*, Number 1505. Pittsburgh: The Center for Russian and East European Studies, 2001.

Burds, Jeffrey. "Gender and Policing in Soviet West Ukraine, 1944–1948." *Cahiers du Monde russe* Vol. 42, No. 2–4 (2001): 279–320.

Burds, Jeffrey. "Ukraine: The meaning of persecution. An American scholar reflects on the impact of the Ukrainian Jewish experience on international asylum law in the post-Soviet era." *Transitions online*, 2 May 2006, http://www.sovhistory.neu.edu/Burds-Transitions.pdf (accessed, 6 November 2012).

Bussgang, Julian J. "Metropolitan Sheptytsky: A Reassessment," *Polin. Studies in Polish Jewry* Vol. 21 (2009): 401–25.

Bussgang, Julian J. *Mytropolyt Sheptyts'kyi: Shche odyn pohliad na zhyttia i diial'nist'*. Lviv: Drukars'ki kunshty, 2009.

Bußmann, Walter, ed. *Akten zur deutschen Auswärtigen Politik 1918–1945*. Serie D, Band XIII. Göttingen: Vandenhoeck & Ruprecht, 1970.

Carynnyk, Marco. "Blind Eye to Murder: Britain, the United States and the Ukrainian Famine of 1933." In *Famine in Ukraine 1932–1933*, edited by Roman Serbyn and Bohdan Krawchenko, 109–38. Edmonton: CIUS, University of Alberta, 1986.

Carynnyk, Marco. "Foes of Our Rebirth: Ukrainian Nationalist Discussions about Jews, 1929–1947." *Nationalities Papers* Vol. 39, No. 3 (2011): 315–52.

Carynnyk, Marco. "Zolochiv movchyt." *Krytyka* No. 10, Vol. 96 (2005): 14–17.

Chaikivs'kyi, Bohdan. *"Fama": Reklamna firma Romana Shukhevycha*. Lviv: Mc, 2005.

Chaikovs'kyi, Danylo. *Moskovs'ki vbyvtsi Bandery pered sudom*. Munich: Cicero, 1965.

Chartoryis'kyi, Mykola Sydor. *Vid Sianu po Krym: spomyny uchasnyka III pokhidnoï hrupy-pivden'*. New York: Howerla, 1951.

Cherednychenko, Vitalii. *Anatomiia zrady: Ukraïns'kyi burzhuaznyi natsionalizm—znariaddia antyradians'koï polityky imperializmu*. Kiev: Vydavnytstvo Politychnoï Literatury Ukraïny, 1978.

Cherednychenko, Vitalii. *Natsionalizm proty natsiï*. Kiev: Politvydav Ukrainy, 1970.

Chojnowski, Andrzej. *Koncepcje polityki narodowościowej rządów polskich w latach 1921–1939*. Wrocław: Ossolineum, 1979.

Ciesielski, Stanisław and Hryciuk, Grzegorz and Aleksander Srebrakowski, *Masowe deportacje ludności w Związku radzieckim*. Toruń: Adam Marszałek, 2003.

Csáky, Moritz. *Ideologie der Operette und Wiener Moderne: Ein kulturhistorischer Essay*. Vienna: Böhlau, 1998.

Cybulski, Bogdan. "Stepan Bandera w więzieniach II Rzeczypospolitej i próby uwolnienia go przez OUN." *Acta Universitatis Wratislaviensis* 1033 (1989): 67–96.

Cybulski, Henryk. *Czerwone noce*. Warsaw: Wydawnictwo Ministerstwa Obrony Narodowej, 1969.

Cyra, Adam. "Banderowcy w KL Auschwitz." *Studia nad faszyzmem i zbrodniami hitlerowskimi*, Vol. XXX (2008): 383–432.

Dallin, Alexander. *German Rule in Russia 1941–1945: A Study of Occupation Policies*. London: Macmillan, 1957.

Dąbrowska, Maria. *Dzienniki 1933–1945*. Warsaw: Czytelnik, 1988.

David-Fox, Michael and Holquist, Peter and Martin, Alexander M., ed., *The Holocaust in the East: Local Perpetrators and Soviet Responses*. Pittsburgh: University of Pittsburgh Press, 2014.

De Greiff, Pablo. "Theorizing Transnational Justice." In *Transnational Justice*, edited by Melissa S. Williams, Rosenmary Nagy, and Jon Elster, 31–77. New York: New York University Press, 2012.

Dem"ian, Hryhorii. *Stepan Bandera ta ioho rodyna v narodnykh pisniakh, perekazakh ta spohadakh*. Lviv: Afisha, 2006.

Dieckmann, Christoph and Quinkert, Babette and Tönsmeyer, Tatjana, ed. *Kooperation und Verbrechen: Formen der "Kollaboration" im östlichen Europa 1939–1945*. Göttingen: Wallstein, 2003.

Dieckmann, Christoph. "Lithuania in Summer 1941. The German Invasion and the Kaunas Pogrom." In *Shared History—Divided Memory: Jews and Others in Soviet-Occupied Poland, 1939–1941*, edited by Elazar Barkan, Elizabeth A. Cole and Kai Struve, 355–85. Leipzig: Leipziger Universitätsverlag, 2007.

Dietsch, Johan. *Making Sense of Suffering: Holocaust and Holodomor in Ukrainian Historical Culture*. Lund: Lund University, 2006.

Dmitruk, Klim. *Without Homeland*. Kiev: Dnipro Publishers, 1984.

Dontsov, Dmytro. *Natsionalizm*. Lviv: Nove Zhyttia, 1926.

Dorril, Stephen. *MI6: Inside the Covert World of Her Majesty's Secret Intelligence Service*. New York: Simon & Schuster, 2002.

Draus, Jan. *Uniwersytet Jana Kazimierza we Lwowie 1918–1946: Portret kresowej uczelni*. Cracow: Księgarnia Akademicka, 2007.

Dumitru, Diana. "An Analysis of Soviet Postwar Investigation and Trial Documents and Their Relevance for Holocaust Studies." In *The Holocaust in the East: Local Perpetrators and Soviet Responses*, edited by Michael David-Fox, Peter Holquist, and Alexander M. Martin, 142–57. Pittsburgh: University of Pittsburgh Press, 2014.

Duzhyi, Petro. *Stepan Bandera—Symvol natsiï: Eskiznyi narys pro zhyttia i diial'nist' providnyka OUN*, Vol. 1–2. Lviv: Halyts'ka Vydavnycha Spilka, 1996.

Eagleton, Terry. *Ideology: An Introduction*. New York: Verso, 1991.

Eatwell, Roger. *Fascism: A History*. London: Chatto and Windus, 1995.

Eatwell, Roger and Larsen, Stein Ugevlik and Pinto, António Costa, ed. *Charisma and Fascism in Interwar Europe*. London: Routledge 2007.

Eatwell, Roger. "The Nature of 'Generic Fascism': The 'Fascist Minimum' and the 'Fascist Matrix.'" In *Comparative Fascist Studies: New Perspectives*, edited by Constantin Iordachi, 136–61. London: Routledge 2009.

Eikel, Markus and Sivaieva, Valentina. "City Mayors, Raion Chiefs and Village Elders in Ukraine, 1941–4: How Local Administrators Co-operated with the German Occupation Authorities." *Contemporary European History* Vol. 23, No. 3 (2014): 405–28.

"Eiserne Garde," in *Enzyklopädie des Holocaust: Die Verfolgung und Ermordung der europäischen Juden*, edited by Israel Gutman, Vol.1, 403–404. Munich: Piper, 1993.

Elliott, Mark R. "Soviet Military Collaborators during world War II." In *Ukraine during World War II: History and its Aftermath*, edited by Yury Boshyk, 89–104. Edmonton: Canadian Institute of Ukrainian Studies, University of Alberta 1986.

Ennker, Benno and Hein-Kircher, Heidi. *Der Führer im Europa des 20. Jahrhunderts*. Marburg: Verlag Herder-Institut, 2010.

Erlikhman, Vadim. *Poteri narodonaseleniia v XX veke: spravochnik*. Moscow: Russkaia panorama, 2004.

Evan, Thomas. *The Very Best Men: Four who Dared: The Early Years of the CIA*. New York: Simon & Schuster, 1995.

Fäßler, Peter and Held, Thomas and Sawitzki, Dirk. *Lemberg—Lwow—Ľviv: Eine Stadt im Schnittpunkt europäischer Kulturen*. Köln: Böhlau 1995.

Fatran, Gila. "Holocaust and Collaboration in Slovakia in the postwar discourse." In *Collaboration with the Nazis: Public Discourse after the Holocaust*, edited by Roni Stauber, 186–211. New York: Routledge, 2011.

Fenomen Banderofobii v russkom soznanii (Kiev: Ukraïns'ka Vydavnycha Spilka, 2007).

Finder, Gabriel N. and Prusin, Alexander V. "Collaboration in Eastern Galicia: The Ukrainian Police and the Holocaust." *East European Jewish Affairs* Vol. 34, No. 2 (2004): 95–118.

Fischer, Bernd J. ed. *Balkan Strongmen: Dictators and Authoritarian Rulers of South Eastern Europe*. West Lafayette: Purdue UP, 2007.

Flood, Christopher. *Political Myth: A Theoretical Introduction*. New York: Garland Publishing, Inc. 1996.

Frank, Hans. *Das Diensttagebuch des deutschen Generalgouverneurs in Polen 1939–1945*. Stuttgart: Deutsch Vergals-Anstalt, 1975.

Friedländer, Saul. *The Years of Extermination: Nazi Germany and the Jews 1933–1939*. New York: Harper Collins, 1997.

Friedländer, Saul. *Nachdenken über den Holocaust*. Munich: C. H. Beck, 2007.

Friedman, Philip. "Ukrainian-Jewish Relations during the Nazi Occupation." In *Roads to Extinction*, edited by Philip Friedman, Ada June Friedman and Salo Baron, 176–208. New York: Jewish Publication Society, 1980. First published in *YIVO Annual of Jewish Social Science* Vol. 12 (1958–1959): 259–63.

Fröhlich, Elke, ed. *Die Tagebücher von Joseph Goebbels*, Part II, Vol. 7 (Munich: K.G. Saur, 1993).

Furman, Artur. *Krov i vuhillia*. Munich: Ukrainian Publishers, 1961.

Furman, Artur. *Pid praporom Bandery*. London: Ukrainian Publishers, 1964.

Fursenko, Aleksandr and Naftali, Timothy. *'One Hell of a Gamble': Khrushchev, Castro, Kennedy and the Cuban Missile Crisis 1958–1964*. London: John Murray, 1998.

Gasparaitis, Siegfried. "'Verrätern wird nur dann vergeben, wenn sie wirklich beweisen können, daß sie mindestans einen Juden liquidiert haben.' Die 'Front Litauischer Aktivisten' (LAF) und die antisowjetischen Aufstände 1941." *Zeitschrift für Geschichtswissenschaft* Vol. 49 (2001): 886–904.

Geertz, Clifford. *The Interpretation of Cultures*. New York: Basis Books, 1973.

Geissbühler, Simon. *Blutiger Juli: Rumäniens Vernichtungskrieg und der vergessene Massenmord an den Juden 1941*. Padeborn: Schöningh, 2013.

Gellner, Ernest. *Nations and Nationalism*. Oxford: Blackwell, 1983.

Gentile, Emilio. "Fascism as Political Religion." *Journal of Contemporary History*, Vol. 25, Nos. 2–3 (1990): 229–51.

Gentile, Emilio. *The Sacralization of Politics in Fascist Italy*. Cambridge Massachusetts: Harvard University Press, 1996.

Gentile, Emilio. "The Sacralisation of Politics: Definitions, Interpretations and Reflections on the Question of Secular Religion and Totalitarianism," *Totalitarian Movements and Political Religions* Vol. 1, No. 1 (2000): 18–55.

Gentile, Emilio. *The Origins of Fascist Ideology, 1918–1925*. New York: Enigma, 2005.

Gentile, Emilio. "Mussolini as the Prototypical Charismatic Dictator." In *Charisma and Fascism in Interwar Europe*, edited Roger Eatwell, Stein Ugevlik Larsen and António Costa Pinto, 113–27. London: Routledge, 2007.

Gerhard, Jan. *Łuny w Bieszczadach*. Warsaw: Wydawnictwo Ministerstwa Obrony Narodowej, 1959.

Gerlach, Christian. *Extremely Violent Societies: Mass Violence in the Twentieth-Century World*. Cambridge: Cambridge University Press, 2010.

Gerstenfeld-Maltiel, Jacob. *My Private War: One Man's Struggle to Survive the Soviets and the Nazis*. London: Mitchell, 1993.

Giesen, Bernhard. "The Trauma of Perpetrators: The Holocaust and the Traumatic Reference of German National Identity." In *Cultural trauma and collective identity*, edited by Jeffrey Alexander, 112–54. Berkeley, Calif.: University of California Press, 2004.

Gogun, Aleksandr and Vovk, Aleksandr. "Evrei v bor'be za nezavisimuiu Ukrainu." *Korni*, No. 25 (January-March 2005): 133–41

Gogun, Aleksandr. "Evrei v russkom osvoboditel'nom dvizhenii." *Korni*, No. 26 (April-June 2006): 180–88.

Gogun, Alexander. "Stepan Bandera – ein Freiheitskämpfer?" http://gedenkbibliothek.de/downloads/texte/vortragstexte/Dr_Alexander_Gogun_Stepan_Bandera_ein_Freiheitskaempfer_vom_13_10_2009.pdf (accessed 24 October 2011).

Gogun, Aleksandr. *Partyzanci Stalina na Ukrainie: Nieznane działania 1941–1944*. Warsaw: Bellona, 2010.

Goi, Petro, ed. *Zbirka hazetnykh i zhurnal'nykh materialiv pro vbyvstvo Stepana Bandery*. New York, 1999.

Goi, Petro. "Bilia dzherel banderoznavstva," *Zbirka hazetnykh i zhurnal'nykh materialiv pro vbyvstvo Stepana Bandery*, ed. Petro Goi. (New York, 1999), 1–2.

Golczewski, Frank. "Die Ukraine im Zweiten Weltkrieg." In *Geschichte der Ukraine*, edited by Frank Golczewski, 241–60. Vandenhoeck & Ruprecht: Göttingen, 1993.

Golczewski, Frank. "Die Heimatarmee und die Juden," in *Die polnische Heimatarmee: Geschichte und Mythos der Armia Krajowa seit dem Zweiten Weltkrieg*, edited by Bernhard Chiari, 635–76. Munich: Oldenbourg Wissenschaftsverlag, 2003.

Golczewski, Frank. "Die Kollaboration in der Ukraine." In *Kooperation und Verbrechen: Formen der "Kollaboration" im östlichen Europa 1939–1945*, edited by Christoph Dieckmann, Babette Quinkert and Tatjana Tönsmeyer, 151–82. Göttingen: Wallstein, 2003.

Golczewski, Frank. "Shades of Grey: Reflections on Jewish-Ukrainian and German-Ukrainian Relations in Galicia." In *The Shoah in Ukraine: History, Testimony, Memorialization*, edited by Ray Brandon and Wendy Lower, 114–55. Bloomington: Indiana University Press, 2008.

Golczewski, Frank. *Deutsche und Ukrainer 1914–1939*. Paderborn: Ferdinand Schöningh, 2010.

Goldberg, Anatol. *Ilya Ehrenburg: Writing, Politics and the Art of Survival*. London: Weidenfeld and Nicolson, 1984.

Goodfellow, Samuel Huston. "Fascism as a Transnational Movement: The Case of Inter-War Alsace." *Contemporary European History* Vol. 22, No. 1 (2013): 87–106.

Grabner-Haider, Anton. *Ideologie und Religion: Interaktion und Sinnsysteme in der modernen Gesellschaft*. Vienna: Herder, 1981.

Grabowski, Jan. *Hunt for the Jews: Betrayal and Murder in German-Occupied*. Bloomington: Indiana University Press, 2013.

Grelka, Frank. *Die ukrainische Nationalbewegung unter deutscher Besatzungsherrschaft 1918 und 1941/42*. Wiesbaden: Harrassowitz, 2005.

Griffin, Roger. *International Fascism: Theories, Causes and the New Consensus*. London: Arnold, 1998.

Griffin, Roger. *The Nature of Fascism*. London: Printer, 1991.

Griffin, Roger. *Fascism*. Oxford: Oxford University Press, 1995.

Griffin, Roger. "General Introduction." In *International Fascism: Theories, Cases, and the New Consensus*, edited by Roger Griffin, 1–15. Oxford: Oxford University Press, 1998.

Griffin, Roger. "Revolution from the Right: Fascism." In *Revolutions and the Revolutionary Tradition in the West 1560–1991*, edited by David Parker, 185–201. Routledge, London, 2000.

Griffin, Roger and Feldman, Matthew. *Fascism: Critical Concept in Political Science*, edited by Roger Griffin and Matthew Feldman, Vol. 1–5. London and New York: Routledge, 2004.

Griffin, Roger. "General Introduction." In *Fascism: Critical Concept in Political Science*, edited by Roger Griffin and Matthew Feldman, Vol. 1, 1–16. London and New York: Routledge, 2004.

Griffin, Roger and Loh, Werner, and Umland, Andreas ed. *Fascism Past and Present, West and East: An International Debate on Concepts and Cases in the Comparative Study of the Extreme Right*. Stuttgart: Ibidem-Verlag, 2006.

Grose, Peter *Operation Rollback: America's Secret War behind the Iron Curtain*. Boston: Houghton Mifflin, 2000.

Gross, Jan Tomasz. *Polish Society under German Occupation: The Generalgouvernement, 1939–1944*. Princeton: Princeton University Press, 1979.

Gross, Jan Tomasz. *Revolution from Abroad: The Soviet Conquest of Poland's Western Ukraine and Western Belorussia*. Princeton: Princeton University Press, 2002.

Gross, Jan Tomasz. *Neighbors: The Destruction of the Jewish Community in Jedwabne, Poland*. Princeton: Princeton University Press, 2001.

Grünberg, Karol and Sprengel, Bolesław. *Trudne sąsiedztwo: Stosunki polsko-ukraińskie w X–XX wieku*. Warsaw: Książka i Wiedza, 2005.

Hadar, Alizia Rachel. *The Princess Elnasari*. Heinemann: London, 1963.

von Hagen, Mark. "Revisiting the Histories of Ukraine." In *A Laboratory of Transnational History: Ukraine and Recent Ukrainian Historiography*, edited by Georgiy Kasianov and Philipp Ther, 25–50. Budapest: Central European University Press, 2009.

Halan, Iaroslav. *Liudy bez bat'kivshchny*. Kiev: Derzhavne Vydavnytsvo Khudozhnoï Literatury, 1952.

Halan, Iaroslav. *Na sluzhbi u Satany*. Kiev: Derzhavne Vydavnytsvo Khudozhnoï Literatury, 1952.

Halan, Iaroslav. *Liudy bez bat'kivshchny*. Kiev: Derzhavne Vydavnytsvo Khudozhnoï Literatury, 1957.

Halan, Iaroslav. *Liudy bez bat'kivshchyny*. Kiev: Dnipro, 1967.

Halan, Iaroslav. *Lytsary nasylstva i zrady*. Kiev: Radians'kyi Pys'mennyk, 1973.

Handziuk, R. *Stezhkamy Ukraïns'koï Povstans'koï Armiï: Turystychnyi Putivnyk*. Ivano-Frankivs'k: Misto NV, 2007.

Hayes, Carlton Joseph Huntley. *The Historical Evolution of Modern Nationalism*. New York: The Macmillan Company, 1950.

Heer, Hans. "Einübung in den Holocaust: Lemberg Juni/Juli 1941." *Zeitschrift für Geschichtswissenschaft* Vol. 49, No. 5 (2001): 409–27.

Hein, Heidi. *Der Piłsudski-Kult und seine Bedeutung für den polnischen Staat 1926–1939*. Marburg: Verlag Herder Institut, 2002.

Heinen, Armin. *Die Legion "Erzengel Michael" in Rumänien Soziale Bewegung und politische Organisation: Ein Beitrag zum Problem des internationalen Faschismus*. Munich: Oldenbourg, 1986.

Hein-Kircher, Heidi. "Führerkult und Führermythos: Theoretische Reflexionen zur Einführung." In *Der Führer im Europa des 20. Jahrhunderts*, edited by Benno Ennker and Heidi Hein-Kircher, 3–23. Marburg: Verlag Herder-Institut, 2010.

Henke, Lutz and Rossoliński, Grzegorz and Ther, Philipp, ed. *Eine neue Gesellschaft in einer alten Stadt*. Wrocław: ATUT, 2007.

Himka, John-Paul. *Socialism in Galicia: The Emergence of Polish Social Democracy and Ukrainian Radicalism (1860–1890)*. Cambridge Mass.: Harvard Ukrainian Research Institute, 1983.

Himka, John-Paul. "Serfdom in Galicia." *Journal of Ukrainian Studies* Vol. 9, No. 2 (1984): 3–28.

Himka, John-Paul. "Priest and Peasants: The Greek Catholic Church and the Ukrainian National Movement in Austria, 1867–1900." In *The Greek Catholic Church and Ukrainian Society in Austrian Galicia*, edited by John-Paul Himka. Cambridge Mass.: Harvard University Ukrainian Studies Fund, 1986.

Himka, John-Paul. "Introduction." In *Engels and the 'Nonhistoric' Peoples: The National Question in the Revolution of 1848, Roman Rosdolsky*, edited by John-Paul Himka, 3–12. Glasgow: Critique Books, 1986.

Himka, John-Paul. "The Galician Triangle: Poles, Ukrainians, and Jews under Austrian Rule." In *Cross Current: A Yearbook of Central European Culture* Vol. 12 (1993): 125–46.

Himka, John-Paul. "World Wars," *Encyclopedia of Ukraine*, Vol. 5, edited by Volodymyr Kubiiovych, 722–28. Toronto: University of Toronto Press, 1993.

Himka, John-Paul. "Krakivski visti and the Jews, 1943: A Contribution to the History of Ukrainian-Jewish Relations during the Second World War." *Journal of Ukrainian Studies* Vol. 21, No. 1–2 (1996): 81–95.

Himka, John-Paul. *Galician Villagers and the Ukrainian National Movement in the Nineteenth Century*. Basingstoke: Macmillan, 1998.

Himka, John-Paul. "Krakivs'ki visti: An Overview." In *Cultures and Nations of Central and Eastern Europe: Essays in Honor of Roman Szporluk*, edited by Zvi Gitelman, Lubomyr Hajda, John-Paul Himka and Roman Solchanyk, 251–61. Cambridge, Mass.: HURI, 2000.

Himka, John-Paul. "A Central European Diaspora under the Shadow of World War II: The Galician Ukrainians in North America." *Austrian History Yearbook* Vol. 37 (2006): 17–31.

Himka, John-Paul. "How Many Perished in the Famine and Why Does It Matter?" *BRAMA*, 2 February 2008, http://www.brama.com/news/press/2008/02/080202himka_famine.html.

Himka, John-Paul. "Review of Johan Dietsch, 'Making Sense of Suffering' and Stanyslav Vladyslavovych Kul'chyts'kyi, Holod 1932–1933 rr. v Ukraini iak henotsyd/Golod 1932–1933 gg. v Ukraine kak genotsid.'" *Kritika: Explorations in Russian and Eurasian History* Vol. 8, No. 3 (Summer 2007): 683–94.

Himka, John-Paul (Hymka, Ivan). "Dostovirnist' svidchennia: reliatsia Ruzi Vagner pro L'vivskyi pohrom vlitku 1941." *Holokost i suchasnist'* 2, 4 (2008): 43–79.

Himka, John-Paul. "Should Ukrainian Studies Defend the Heritage of OUN-UPA?" 10 February 2010, http://www.ukrainianstudies.uottawa.ca/pdf/UKL441.pdf (accessed 1 November 2011).

Himka, John-Paul. "Refleksje żołnierza Ukraińskiej Powstańczej Armii: Pamiętnik Ołeksandra Powszuka (1943–1944)." In *Prawda historyczna a prawda polityczna w badaniach naukowych*, edited by Bogusław Paź, 179–90. Wrocław: Wydawnictwo Uniwersytetu Wrocławskiego, 2011.

Himka, John-Paul. "The Lviv Pogrom of 1941: The Germans, Ukrainian Nationalists, and the Carnival Crowd." *Canadian Slavonic Papers* Vol. LIII, No. 2–4 (2011): 209–43.

Himka, John-Paul. "Christianity and Radical Nationalism: Metropolitan Andrei Sheptytsky and the Bandera Movement." In *State Secularism and Live Religion in Soviet Russia and Ukraine*, edited by Catherine Wanner, 93–116. New York: Oxford University Press, 2012.

Himka, John-Paul. "The Reception of the Holocaust in Postcommunist Ukraine." In *Bringing the Dark Past to Light: The Reception of the Holocaust in Postcommunist Europe*, ed. John-Paul Himka and Joanna Beata Michlic, 626–53. Lincoln: University of Nebraska Press, 2013.

Hobsbawm, Eric J. *Nations and Nationalism since 1780: Programme, Myth, Reality*. Cambridge: Cambridge University Press, 1992.

Hobsbawm, Eric and Ranger, Terence. *The Inventing of Tradition*. Cambridge: Cambridge University Press, 1992.

Holian, Anna. "Anticommunism in the Streets: Refugee Politics in Cold War Germany." *Journal of Contemporary History*, Vol. 45, No. 1 (2010): 134–61.

Holian, Anna. *Between National Socialism and Soviet Communism: Displaced Persons in Postwar Germany*. Ann Arbor: University of Michigan Press, 2011.

Holovyn, Bohdan. "Sertse, spovnene liubovi, chynyt' liudiam lush dobro." In *Z liuboviu do liudei: Z viroiu v Ukraïnu*, edited by Mykhailo Zubenets', 84–97. Lviv: LNAU, 2008.

Hon, Maksym. *Iz kryvdoiu na samoti: Ukraïns'ko-ievreis'ki vzaiemyny na zakhidnoukraïns'kykh zemiakh u skladi Pol'shchi (1935–1939)*. Rivne: Volyns'ki oberehy, 2005.

Honcharuk, P. S. *Z istoriï kolektivizatsiï sil'skoho hospodarstva zakhidnykh oblastei Ukraïns'koï SSR*. Kiev: Naukova Dumka, 1976.

Honta, Dmytro. "Drukarstvo Zakhidnoï Ukraïny pidchas okupatsiï." Konkurs na spohady, Oseredok Ukrainian Cultural and Educational Centre Winnipeg.

Hordasevych, Halyna. *Stepan Bandera: liudyna i mif*. Kiev: Biblioteka ukraïntsia, 1999.

Hordasevych, Halyna. *Stepan Bandera: liudyna i mif*. Lviv: Spolom, 2000.

Hordasevych, Halyna. *Stepan Bandera: liudyna i mif*. Lviv: Piramida, 2001.

Hots', Petro. *Povernennia u bronzi*. Dubliany, 2001.
Hots', Petro. "Stepan Bandera u Dublianakh." In *U Stepana urodyny*, edited by Petro Hots. Lviv: NVM PT UAD, 2003.
Hots', Petro, ed. *U Stepana urodyny*. Lviv: NVM PT UAD, 2003.
Hots', Petro. *Muzei Stepana Bandery v Dublianakh*. Lviv: Krai, 2005.
Hots', Petro. "Volodymyr Snityns'kyi—dukhovyi bat'ko muzeiu Stepana Bandery u Dublianakh." In *Z liuboviu do liudei: Z viroiu v Ukraïnu*, edited by Mykhailo Zubenets', 194–201. Lviv: LNAU, 2008.
Hots', Petro. "Pam"iatnyk Stepanovi Banderi v Dublianakh." In *Z liubov"iu do liudei: Z viroiu v Ukraïnu*, edited by Mykhailo Zubenets', 221–26. Lviv: LNAU, 2008.
Hrushevs'kyi, Mykhailo. *Istoriia Ukraïny-Rusy*, Vol. 1. Kiev: Persha spilka, 1913.
Hrushevs'kyi, Mykhailo. *History of Ukraine—Rus'. From prehistory to the eleventh century*, edited by Andrzej Poppe and Frank Sysyn, translated by Marta Skorupsky, Vol. 1. Edmonton: Canadian Institute of Ukrainian Studies Press, 1997.
Hrytsak, Iaroslav. "Ukraïns'kyi natsionalizm: Mynule, suchasne, maibutnie." *Vyzvol'nyi shliakh*, Vol. 530, No. 6 (June 1992): 672–73.
Hrycak, Jarosław. *Historia Ukrainy 1772–1999: Narodziny nowoczesnego narodu*. Lublin: Agencja Wschód, 2000.
Hrytsak, Iaroslav. *Narys istoriï Ukraïny: Formuvannia modernoï ukraïns'koï natsiï XIX–XX stolittia*. Kiev: Heneza, 2000.
Hrytsak, Yaroslav and Susak, Victor. "Constructing a National City: Case of L'viv." In *Composing Urban History and the Constitution of Civic Identities*, edited by Czaplicka, John and Ruble, Blair A. and Crabtree, Lauren, 140–64. Washington: Johns Hopkins University Press, 2003.
Hrytsak, Yaroslav. "Ukraïntsi v antyievreis'kykh aktsiiakh u roky Druhoï svitovoï viiny." In *Strasti za natsionalizmom: Istorychni eseï*, edited by Iaroslav Hrytsak, 162–68. Kiev: Krytyka, 2004.
Hrytsak, Iaroslav. "Shche raz pro Iushchenka, shche raz pro Banderu," *Zaxid.net*, 27 January 2010, http://zaxid.net/blogentry/57801/ (accessed 3 November 2011).
Hrytsak, Iaroslav. "Klopoty z pam"iattiu," *Zaxid.net*, 8 March 2010, http://www.zaxid.net/article/60958/ (accessed 3 November 2011).
Hryciuk, Grzegorz. *Polacy we Lwowie 1939–1944: Życie codzienne*. Warsaw: Książka i Wiedza, 2000.
Hunchak, Taras. *Moi spohady—stezhky zhyttia*. Kiev: Dnipro, 2005.
Hundert, Gershon David. *The YIVO Encyclopedia of Jews in Eastern Europe*, Vol. 2. New Haven: Yale Univ. Press, 2008.
Ianiv, Volodymyr. *Shukhevych—Chuprynka: Liudyna i symvol. Dopovid na zhalibni akademiï 19 lystopada 1950 v Miunkheni*. Munich: Molode zhyttia, 1950.
Ianiv, Volodymyr. "Zustrich z polk. Ievhenom Konoval'tsem na tli nastroiv doby." In *Ievhen Konovalets' ta ioho doba*, edited by Iurii Boïko, 426–65. Munich: Cicero, 1974.
Ianiv, Volodymyr. "Stepan Bandera," *Encyclopedia of Ukraine*, Vol. 1, edited by Volodymyr Kubiiovych, 169. Toronto: University of Toronto Press, 1984.
Iashan, Vasyl'. "Polkovnyk Mykhailo Kolodzins'kyi." In *Horodenshchyna: Istorychno-memuarnyi zbirnyk*, edited by Mykhailo H. Marunchak, 632–54. New York: Shevchenko Scientific Society, 1978.
Iliushyn, Ihor. "Kwestia ukarińska w planach polskiego rządu emigracyjnego i polskiego podziemia w latach drugiej wojny światowej." In *Antypolska akcja*

OUN-UPA 1943–1944: Fakty i interpretacje, edited by Grzegorz Motyka and Dariusz Lebionka, 118–20. Warsaw: Instytut Pamięci Narodowej, 2002.

Ilnytzkyi, Roman. *Deutschland und die Ukraine 1934–1945: Tatsachen europäischer Politik*. Vol. 1–2. Munich: UNI, 1958.

Iordachi, Constantin. *Charisma, Politics and Violence: The Legion of the "Archangel Michael" in Inter-war Romania*. Trondheim: Program on East European Cultures and Societies, Norwegian University of Science and Technology, 2004.

Iordachi, Constantin, ed., *Comparative Fascist Studies: New Perspectives*. London: Routledge 2009.

Iordachi, Constantin. "God's Chosen Warriors. Romantic Palingenesis, Militarism and Fascism in Modern Romania." In *Comparative Fascist Studies: New Perspectives*, edited by Constantin Iordachi, 318–54. London: Routledge 2009.

Iordachi, Constantin. "Fascism in Interwar East and Central and Southeastern Europe: Toward a New Transnational Research Agenda." *East Central Europe* 37 (2010), 161–213.

Iukhnovs'kyi, Ihor. "2009 rik—rik Stepana Bandery." In *Stepan Bandera: Zbirnyk materialiv i dokumentiv*, edited by Vladyslav Verstiuk. Kiev: *Ukraïns'kyi Instytut Natsional'noï Pamiaty*, 2009.

Iushchenko, Victor. "Vitannia prezydenta Ukraïny uchasnykam urochystoï akademiï z nakhody 100-richchia vid dnia narodzhennia Stepana Bandery." In *Stepan Bandera: Zbirnyk materialiv i dokumentiv*, edited by Vladyslav Verstiuk. Kiev: *Ukraïns'kyi Instytut Natsional'noï Pamiaty*, 2009.

Ivanyshyn, Vasyl', ed. *Stepan Bandera: Perspektyvy ukraïns'koï revoliutsiï*. Drohobych: Vidrodzhennia, 1999.

Jelinek, Yeshayahu. *The Parish Republic: Hlinka's Slovak People's Party, 1939–1945*. New York: Columbia University Press, 1976.

Jobst, Kerstin. "Die ukrainische Nationalbewegung bis 1917." In *Geschichte der Ukraine*, edited by Frank Golczewski, 158–71. Göttingen: Vandenhoeck & Ruprecht, 1993.

Johnson, Ian. *A Mosque in Munich: Nazis, the CIA, and the Muslim Brotherhood in the West*. Boston: Houghton Mifflin Harcourt, 2010.

Jockusch, Laura. *Collect and Record! Jewish Holocaust Documentation in Early Postwar Europe*. Oxford: Oxford University Press, 2012.

Jones, Eliyahu. *Żydzi Lwowscy w okresie okucpacji 1939–1945*. Łódź: Oficyna Bibliofilów, 1999.

K, V, and T, A. *Chomu svit movchyt'*. Kiev, 1946.

Kal'ba, Myroslav. *U lavakh druzhynnykiv*. Denver: Vydannia Druzhyn Ukrains'kykh Natsionalistiv, 1982.

Kallis, Aristotle A. "Fascism, 'Charisma' and 'Charismatisation': Weber's Model of 'Charismatic Domination' and Interwar European Fascism." *Totalitarian Movements and Political Religions*, Vol. 7, No. 1 (2006): 25–43.

Kallis, Aristotle A. *Genocide and Fascism: The Eliminationist Drive in Fascist Europe*. New York: Routledge, 2009.

Kappeler, Andreas. "Hans Koch (1894–1959)." In *Osteuropäische Geschichte in Wien: 100 Jahre Forschung und Lehre an der Universität*, edited by Arnold Suppan, Marija Wakounig, Georg Kastner, 228–54. Innsbruck: Studien Verlag, 2007.

Kappeler, Andreas. "From an Ethnonational to a Multiethnic to a Transnational Ukrainian History." In *A Laboratory of Transnational History: Ukraine and Re-*

cent Ukrainian Historiography, edited by Georgiy Kasianov and Philipp Ther, 51–80. Budapest: Central European University Press, 2009.

Kasianov, Georgiy and Ther, Philipp ed. *A Laboratory of Transnational History: Ukraine and Recent Ukrainian Historiography*. Budapest: Central European University Press, 2009.

Katchanovski, Ivan. "Terrorists or National Heroes." Paper presented at the Annual Conference of the Canadian Political Science Association, Concordia University, Montreal, Canada, June 1–3, 2010. Forthcoming.

Kazanivs'kyi, Bohdan. *Shliahom Lehendy*. London: Ukraïns'ka Vydavnich Spilka, 1975.

Kentii, V. *Narys istoriï Orhanizatsiï Ukraïns'kykh Natsionalistiv (1929–1941)*. Kiev: Instytut Istoriï Ukraïny, 1998.

Kershaw, Ian. *The 'Hitler Myth': Image and Reality in the Third Reich*. Oxford: Clarendon Press, 1987.

Kershaw, Ian. *Hitler, 1896–1936: Hubris*. New York: W.W. Norton, 1999–2000.

Kershaw, Ian. *Hitler, 1936–1945: Nemesis*. London: Penguin, 2000.

Kessler, Renata, ed. *The Wartime Diary of Edmund Kessler* (Boston: Academic Studies Press, 2010).

Khalili, Laleh. *Heroes and Martyrs of Palestine: The Politics of National Commemoration*. Cambridge: Cambridge University Press, 2007.

Khrushchev, Nikita. *Osvobozhdenie ukrainskikh zemel' ot nemetskikh zakhvatchikov i ocherednye zadachi vosstanovleniia narodnoho khoziaistva sovetskoi Ukrainy*. Moscow: Pravda, 1944.

Klymyshyn, Mykola. *V pokhodi do voli*. Vol. 1–2. Detroit: Ukraïns'ka Knyharnia, 1987.

Knysh, Zynovii. *Dukh, shcho tilo rve do boiu*. Winnipeg: O. D. U., 1951.

Knysh, Zynovii. *Rozbrat: Spohady i materiialy do rozkolu OUN u 1940–1941 rokakh*. Toronto: Sribna Surma, 1960.

Knysh, Zynovii. *Varshavs'kyi protses OUN: Na pidlozhi pol's'ko-ukraïns'kykh vidnosyn tiieï doby*. Toronto: Sribna Surma, 1986.

Kolková, Stanislava. "Das Bild von Jozef Tiso als 'Führer mit christlichem Antlitz' und 'Symbol der slowakischen Unabhängigkeit in Vergangenheit und Gegenwart—Versuch einer Annährung." In *Der Führer im Europa des 20. Jahrhunderts*, edited by Benno Ennker and Heidi Hein-Kircher, 253–75. Marburg: Verlag Herder-Institut, 2010.

Konrad, Mykola. *Natsionalizm i katolytsyzm*. Lviv: Meta, 1934.

Korb, Alexander. "Understanding Ustaša violence." *Journal of Genocide Research* Vol. 12, No. 1–2 (2010): 1–18.

Korman, Aleksander. *Stosunek UPA do Polaków na ziemiach południowo-wschodnich II Rzeczypospolitej*. Wrocław: Nortom, 2002.

Korman, Aleksander. *Ludobójstwo UPA na ludności polskiej: Dokumentacja fotograficzna*. Wrocław: Nortom, 2003.

Korzec, Paweł. "Polen und der Minderheitenschutzvertrag (1918–1934)." *Jahrbücher für Geschichte Osteuropas* 22, 4 (1975): 515–55.

Kosyk, Volodymyr. *Das Dritte Reich und die ukrainische Frage: Dokumente, 1934–1944*. Munich: Ukrainisches Institut, 1985.

Kosyk, Volodymyr. *L'Allemagne national-socialiste et l'Ukraine*. Paris: *Publications de l'Est européen*, 1986.

Kosyk, Volodymyr. *The Third Reich and Ukraine*. New York: Peter Lang, 1993.

Kosyk, Volodymyr. *Ukraïna i nimechchyna u druhii svitovii viini*. Lviv: Naukove tovarystvo im. T. Schevchenka, 1993.

Kosyk, Volodymyr. *Rozkol OUN (1939–1940): Zbirnyk Dokumentiv*. Lviv: L'vivs'kyi Natsional'nyi Universytet, 1999.

Koval, Mykhailo. *Ukraïna v Druhii svitovii i Velykii Vitchyznianii viinakh (1939–1945)*. Kiev, Al'ternatyvy 1999.

Koval, Roman. "Heroi, shcho ne zmih vriatuvaty Bat'kivshchyny." In *Samostiina Ukraïna*, edited by Roman Koval, 5–26. Kiev: Diokor, 2003.

Kozhelianko, Vasyl'. *Defilada v Moskvi*. Lviv: Kal'varia, 2000.

Krajewski, Stanisław. "Auschwitz als Herausforderung." In *Unbequeme Wahrheiten: Polen und sein Verhältnis zu den Juden*, edited by Helga Hirsch, 116–33. Frankfurt am Main: Suhrkamp, 2008.

Krawchenko, Bohdan. "Soviet Ukraine under Nazi Occupation, 1941–44." In *Ukraine during World War II: History and its Aftermath*, edited by Yury Boshyk, 15–37. Edmonton: Canadian Institute of Ukrainian Studies, University of Alberta 1986.

Krentsbakh, Stella. "Zhyvu shche zavdiaky UPA." In *V riadakh UPA: Zbirka spomyniv buv. Voiakiv Ukraïns'koï Povstans'koï Armiï*, edited by Petro Mirchuk and V. Davydenko, 342–49. New York: Nakladom T-va b. Voiakiv UPA v ZDA i Kanadi, 1957.

Kruglov, Alexander. "Jewish Losses in Ukraine, 1941–1944." In *The Shoah in Ukraine: History, Testimony, Memorialization*, edited by Ray Brandon and Wendy Lower, 272–90. Bloomington: Indiana University Press, 2008.

Kruk, Tadeusz. *Karabin i menazka*. Warsaw: Czytelnik, 1964.

Krupnyk, Liubov. "Formovannia svitohliadnykh ustanovok pro Druhu svitovu viinu zasobamy radians'koho kino (materialy TsDAHO Ukraïny 1973 r.)." *Moloda Natsia. Almanakh* Vol. 41, No. 4 (2006): 114–29.

Kubicek, Paul. "What Happened to the Nationalists in Ukraine?" *Nationalism & Ethnic Politics* Vol. 5, No. 1 (1999): 29–45.

Kubiiovych, Volodymyr ed., *Encyclopedia of Ukraine*, Vol. 5. Toronto: University of Toronto Press, 1993.

Kudelia, Serhyi. "Choosing Violence in Irregular Wars: The Case of Anti-Soviet Insurgency in Western Ukraine." *East European Politics and Societies and Cultures*, 26 November 2012: 1–33.

Kul'chyts'kyi, Ivan. "Zamolodu hotuvavsia do naivazhchykh vyprobuvan'..." In *Stepan Bandera: Dokumenty i materialy (1920–1930 rr.)*, edited by Mykola Posivnych, 52–53. Lviv: Afisha, 2006.

Kulińska, Lucyna and Roliński, Adam. *Kwestia ukraińska i eksterminacja ludności polskiej w Małopolsce Wschodniej w świetle dokumentów Polskiego Państwa Podziemnego 1943–1944*. Cracow: Księgarnia Akademicka, 2004.

Kulińska, Lucyna. *Działalność terrorystyczna i sabotażowa nacjonalistycznych organizacji ukraińskich w Polsce w latach 1922–1939*. Cracow: Księgarnia Akademicka, 2009.

Kupchyns'kyi, Oleh, ed., *Dmytro Paliïv: Zhyttia i diial'nist'*. Lviv: Haukove tovarystvo im. Shevchenka, 2007.

Kurylo, Taras and Himka, John-Paul. "Iak OUN stavylasia do ievreiv? Rozdumy nad knyzhkoiu Volodymyra V"iatrovycha." *Ukraïna Moderna* Vol. 13, No. 2 (2008): 252–65.

Kurylo, Taras. "Syla ta slabkist' ukraïns'koho natsionalizmu v Kyievi pid chas nimets'koï okupatsiï (1941–1943)." *Ukraïna Moderna* Vol. 13, No. 2 (2008): 115–30.

Kuzio, Taras. "Radical Nationalist Parties and Movements in Contemporary Ukraine before and after Independence: The Right and Its Politics, 1989–1994." *Nationalities Papers* Vol. 25, No. 2 (1997): 211–42.

Kyrychuk, Iurii. *Ukraïns'ki natsional'nyi rukh 40–50 rokiv XX stolittiia: ideolohia ta praktyka*. Lviv: Dobra sprava, 2003.

Lalande, Julia. *"Building a Home Abroad"—A Comparative Study of Ukrainian Migration, Immigration Policy and Diaspora Formation in Canada and Germany after the World War II* (Dissertation submitted at the University of Hamburg, 2006).

Lambert, Peter and Mallett, Robert. "Introduction: The Heroisation-Demonisation Phenomenon in Mass Dictatorships." *Totalitarian Movements and Political Religions* Vol. 8, No. 3–4 (2007): 453–63.

Le Goff, Jacques. *Geschichte und Gedächtnis*. Frankfurt and New York: Campus Verlag, 1992.

Lebed', Mykola. *Ukraïns'ka Povstans'ka Armiia: Ïï heneza, rist i diï u vyzvol'niï borotbi ukraïns'koho narodu za ukraïns'ku samostiïnu sobornu derzhavu*. Presove biuro UHVR, 1946.

Lebed', Mykola. *Ukraïns'ka Povstans'ka Armiia*. Munich: Suchasnist', 1987.

Lebed', Mykola. *Ukraïns'ka Povstans'ka Armiia: Ïï heneza, rist i diï u vyzvol'niï borotbi ukraïns'koho narodu za ukraïns'ku samostiïnu sobornu derzhavu*. Drohobych: Vidrodzhennia, 1993.

Lenkavs'kyi, Stepan. *Murdered by Moscow: Petlura, Konovalets, Bandera, three leaders of the Ukrainian National Liberation Movement, Assassinated at the Orders of Stalin and Khrushchov*. London: Ukrainian Publishers, 1962.

Lenkavs'kyi, Stepan. *Petlura, Konowalez, Bandera: Von Moskau ermordet*. Munich: Ukrainischer Verlag, 1962.

Levytsky, Marco. "Ukrainian Nationalists Played No Part in Massacre of 4,000 Jews." *Edmonton Journal*, 9 February 2010.

Lewin, Kurt. *Przeżyłem: Saga Świętego Jura w roku 1946*. Warsaw: Zeszyty Literackie, 2006.

Lipstadt, Deborah. *Denying the Holocaust: The Growing Assault on Truth and Memory*. New York: Free Press, 1993.

Lisovyi, R. *Rozlam v OUN: Krytychni narysy z nahody dvatsiatylittia zasnuvannia OUN*. Vydavnytsvo Ukraïna, 1949.

Lizun, R. *Vbyvstvo Stepana Bandery*. Lviv: Chervona Kalyna 1993.

Longerich, Peter, and Pohl, Dieter. *Die Ermordung der europäischen Juden: Eine Umfassende Dokumentation des Holocausts*. Munich: Piper, 1989.

Lower, Wendy. "Pogroms, Mob Violence and Genocide in Western Ukraine, Summer 1941: Varied Histories, Explanations and Comparisons." *Journal of Genocide Research* Vol. 13, No. 3 (2011): 217–46.

Luzzatto, Sergio. *The Body of Il Duce: Mussolini's Corpse and the Fortunes of Italy*. New York: Metropolitan Books, 2005.

Lypovets'kyi, Sviatoslav. *Orhanizatsiia Ukraïns'kykh Natsionalistiv (banderivtsi): Frahmenty diial'nosti ta borot'by*. Kiev: Ukraïns'ka Vydavnycha Spilka, 2010.

MacMillan, Margaret. *Peacemakers: Six Months that Changed the World.* London: John Murray, 2003.

Madajczyk, Czesław. "Vom 'Generalplan Ost' zum 'Generalumsiedlungsplan.'" In *Der "Generalplan Ost." Hauptlinien der nationalsozialistischen Planungs- und Vernichtungspolitik*, edited by Mechtild Rössle and Sabine Schleiermacher, 12–19. Berlin: Akademie-Verlag, 1993.

Madajczyk, Czesław ed. *Vom Generalplan Ost zum Generalsiedlungsplan.* Munich: Saur, 1994.

Makar, Volodymyr. "Postril v obroni mil'ioniv." In *Spomyny ta rozdumy,* Vol. 2, edited by Volodymyr Makar, 286–319. Toronto-Kiev: Afisha, 2001.

Mann, Michael. *Fascists.* Cambridge: Cambridge University Press, 2004.

Margolian, Howard. *Unauthorized Entry: The Truth about Nazi War Criminals in Canada, 1946–1956.* Toronto: University of Toronto Press, 2000.

Mark, Rudolf A. "Die gescheiterten Staatsversuche." In *Geschichte der Ukraine,* edited by Frank Golczewski, 172–201. Göttingen: Vandenhoeck & Ruprecht, 1993.

Mark, Rudolf A., *Galizien unter österreichischer Herrschaft: Verwaltung-Kirche-Bevölkerung.* Marburg: Herder Institut, 1994.

Mark, Rudolf A. "The Ukrainians as Seen by Hitler, Rosenberg and Koch." In *Ukraine: The Challenges of World War II,* edited by Taras Hunczak and Dmytro Shtohryn, 23–36. Lanham: University Press of America 2003.

Marples, David. *Heroes and Villains: Creating National History in Contemporary Ukraine.* Budapest: Central European University Press, 2007.

Marples, David. "Hero of Ukraine Linked to the Murder of 4000 Jews." *Edmonton Journal,* 7 February 2010.

Martin, Terry. *The Affirmative Action Empire: Nations and Nationalism in the Soviet Union, 1923–1939.* London: Cornell University Press, 2001.

Martynets', Volodymyr. *Zhydivska problema v Ukraïni.* London, 1938.

Martynovych, Orest T. "Sympathy for the Devil: The Attitude of Ukrainian War Veterans in Canada to Nazi Germany and the Jews, 1933–1939." In *Re-imaging Ukrainian Canadians: History, Politics, and Identity,* edited by Rhonda L. Hinther and Jim Mochoruk, 173–220. Toronto: University of Toronto Press, 2011.

Marunchak, Mykhailo. *Ukraïns'ki politychni v'iazni v natsysts'kykh kontsentratsyiinykh taborakh.* Winnipeg: Svitova liha ukarïns'kykh politychnykh v'iazniv, 1986.

Maslovs'kyi, Vitalii. *Zbroia Iaroslava Halana.* Lviv: Kameniar, 1982.

Materialy XXV z'ïzdu komunistychnoï partiï Ukrainy. Kiev: Politvydav Ukrainy, 1976.

Matvijeiko, Myron. *A Word to the Younger Generation.* Lviv: Kameniar Publishers, 1981.

Mazur, Grzegorz. *Życie polityczne polskiego Lwowa 1918–1939.* Cracow: Księgarnia Akademicka, 2007.

McBride, Jared. "Ukrainian Neighbors: The Holocaust in Olevs'k" presented at the workshop. *Sixty-Five Years Later: New Research and Conceptualization of the Second World War in Europe,* Stanford University, October 2010.

Mechnyk, Stepan. *Pochatok nevidomoho. Spohady 1945–1954.* Munich: Ukraïns'ke vydavnytstvo, 1984.

Mędykowski, Witold. "Pogromy 1941 roku na terytorium byłej okupacji sowieckiej (Bukowina, wschodnie województwa RP, państwa bałtyckie) w relacjach żydowskich." In *Świat nie pożegnany*, edited by Krzysztof Jasiewicz, 761–809. Warsaw: Instytut Studiów Politycznych, 2004.

Mędykowski, Witold. *W cieniu gigantów: Pogromy 1941 r. w byłej sowieckiej strefie okupacyjnej*. Warsaw: Instytut Studiów Politycznych Polskiej Akademi Nauk, 2012.

Mędrzecki, Włodzimierz. "Polityka narodowościowa II Rzeczypospolitej a antypolska akcja UPA w latach 1943–1944." In *Antypolska akcja OUN–UPA 1943–1944: Fakty i interpretacje*, edited by Grzegorz Motyka and Dariusz Lebionka, 14–18. Warsaw: Instytut Pamięci Narodowej, 2002.

Mel'nychuk, Iurii. *Iaroslav Halan: Literaturno-krytychnyi narys*. Kiev: Radians'kyi pys'mennyk, 1951.

Mel'nychuk, Iurii. "Banderivs'kykh holovoriziv pokarano." *Sluhy zhovtoho diiavola*, edited by Iurii Mel'nychuk, 36–41. Lviv: Knyzhkovo-zhurnal'ne vydavnytsvo, 1957.

Melnychuk, Iurii. "Pid chuzhym porohom." In *Prodai-dushi*, edited by Iurii Mel'nychuk, 164–71. Lviv: Kameniar, 1967.

Mel'nyk, Oleksandr. "Anti-Jewish Violence in Kyiv's Podil District in September 1941 through the Prism of Soviet Investigative Documents." *Jahrbücher für Geschichte Osteuropas* Vol. 61, No. 2 (2013): 233–48.

Mel'nyk, Andryi. "Pamiati vpavshykh za voliu i velych Ukraïny." In *Orhanizatsiia Ukraïns'kyh Natsionalistiv 1929–1954*, 17–48. Paris, 1955.

Mel'nyk, Hryhor. "Stepan Bandera. Prychynky do kharakterystyky osoby." In *Spomyny ta rozdumy*, Vol. 3, edited by Volodymyr Makar, 117–33. Toronto-Kiev: Afisha, 2001.

Melnyk, Michael James. *To Battle: The Formation and History of the 14th Galician Waffen-SS Division*. Solihull: Helion & Co., 2002.

Mick, Christoph. "Kto bronił Lwowa w listopadzie 1918r.? Pamięć o zmarłych, znaczenie wojny i tożsamość narodowa wieloetnicznego miasta." In *Tematy polsko-ukraińskie*, edited by Robert Traba. Olsztyn: Wspólnota Kulturowa Borussia, 2001.

Mick, Christoph. *Kriegserfahrungen in einer multiethnischen Stadt: Lemberg 1914–1947*. Wiesbaden: Harrassowitz, 2010.

Mick, Christoph. "Incompatible Experiences: Poles, Ukrainians and Jews in Lviv under Soviet and German Occupation, 1939–44." *Journal of Contemporary History* Vol. 46, No. 2 (2011): 336–63.

Mikhnovs'kyi, Mykola. "Samostiina Ukraïna." In *Samostiina Ukraïna*, edited by Roman Koval, 28–44. Kiev: Diokor, 2003.

Miljan, Goran. *Fascist Thought in Twentieth Century Europe: Case Study of Ante Pavelić*. MA thesis, Central European University, 2009.

Mirchuk, Petro. *Akt vidnovlennia Ukraïns'koï Derzhavnosty 30 chervnia 1941 roku. Iioho geneza ta politychne i istorychne znachennia*. New York: Vydannia Holovnoï upravy Orhanizatsiï oborony chotyr'okh svobid Ukraïny, 1952.

Mirchuk, Petro. *Koly horiat' lisy*. N.p.: Zahrava, 1947.

Mirchuk, Petro. *Ukraïns'ka Povstans'ka Armiia 1942–1952*. Munich: Cicero, 1953.

Mirchuk, Petro. *Za chystotu pozytsii ukraïns'koho vyzvolnoho rukhu*. Munich: P. Mirchuk, 1955.

Mirchuk, Petro. *Mykola Mikhnovs'kyi: Apostol ukraïns'koï derzhavnosty*. Philadelphia: T-vo ukraïns'koï studiiuiuchoï molodi im. M. Mikhnovs'koho, 1960.

Mirchuk, Petro. *Stepan Bandera: Symvol revoliutsiinoï bezkompromisovosty*. New York: Orhanizatsiia oborony chotyr'okh svobid Ukraïny, 1961.
Mirchuk, Petro. *Ukraïns'ka derzhavnist', 1917–1920*. Philadelphia, 1967.
Mirchuk, Petro. *Narys istoriï OUN*. Munich: Ukraïns'ke vydavnytsvo, 1968.
Mirchuk, Petro. *In the German Mills of Death, 1941–1945*. New York: Vantage Press, 1976.
Mirchuk, Petro. *My Meetings and Discussions in Israel (Are Ukrainians "traditionally anti-Semites"?)*. New York: Ukrainian Survivors of the Holocaust, 1982.
Mirchuk, Petro. *Revoliutsiinyi zmah za USSD: khto taki 'banderivtsi', 'mel'nykivtsi', 'dviikari'*. New York: Soiuz Ukraïns'kykh Politviazniv, 1985.
Mirchuk, Petro. *Narys istoriï OUN: 1920–1939*. Kiev: Ukraïns'ka Vydavnycha Spilka, 2007.
Misiło, Eugeniusz. *Spis tytyłów prasy ukraińskiej w Drugiej Rzeczypospolitej 1918–1939*. Warsaw: Polska Akademia Nauk, 1983.
Mokienko, Valerii. "Das sprachwissenschaftliche Werk Oleksa Horbatschs." *Die Ukraine in Vergangenheit und Gegenwart. Aufsätze zu Geschichte, Sprache und Literatur. Greifswalder Ukrainische Hefte*, edited by Alexander Kratochvil, Vol. 1, No. 1, 10–22. Greifswald: Ernst-Moritz-Arndt-Universität Greifswald, Lehrstuhl für Ukrainistik, 2004.
Morgan, Philip. *Fascism in Europe, 1919–1945*. London: Routledge, 2003.
Mosse, George L. *The Fascist Revolution: Toward a General Theory of Fascism*. New York: H. Fertig, 1999.
Mosse, George L. "Racism and Nationalism." In *The Fascist Revolution: Toward a General Theory of Fascism*, George L. Mosse, 55–68. New York: Howard Fertig, 2000.
Motyka, Grzegorz. "Polski policjant na Wołyniu." *Karta* 24 (1998): 126–40.
Motyka, Grzegorz. *Tak było w Bieszczadach: Walki polsko-ukraińskie 1943–1948*. Warsaw: Oficyna Wydawnicza Volumen, 1999.
Motyka, Grzegorz. "Konflikt polsko-ukraiński w latach 1943–1948: Aktualny stan badań." *Warszawskie Zeszyty Historyczne* 8–9 (1999): 316–29.
Motyka, Grzegorz. "Postawy wobec konfliktu polsko-ukraińskiego w latach 1939–1953 w zależności od przynależności etnicznej, państwoej i religijnej." In *Tygiel Narodów. Stosunki społeczne i etniczne na dawnych ziemiach wschodnich Rzeczypospolitej 1939–1953*, edited by Krzysztof Jasiewicz, 279–408. Warsaw: Rytm, 2002.
Motyka, Grzegorz. "Polska reakcja na działania UPA—skala i przebieg akcji odwetowych." *Antypolska akcja OUN-UPA 1943–1944: Fakty i interpretacje*, edited by Grzegorz Motyka and Dariusz Lebionka, 141–46. Warsaw: Instytut Pamięci Narodowej, 2002.
Motyka, Grzegorz, and Lebionka, Dariusz, ed. *Antypolska akcja OUN-UPA 1943–1944: Fakty i interpretacje*. Warsaw: Instytut Pamięci Narodowej, 2002.
Motyka, Grzegorz. *Ukraińska partyzantka 1942–1960: Działalność Organizacji Ukraińskich Nacjonalistów i Ukraińskiej Powstańczej Armii*. Warsaw: Rytm, 2006.
Motyka, Grzegorz. *Cień Kłyma Sawura: Polsko-ukraiński konflikt pamięci*. Gdańsk: Oskar, 2013.
Motyl, Alexander. *The Turn to the Right: The Ideological Origins and Development of Ukrainian Nationalism, 1919–1929*. Boulder: East European Monographs, 1980.

Motyl, Alexander. "Ukrainian Nationalist Political Violence in Inter-War Poland, 1921–1939." *East European Quarterly* Vol. 19, No. 1, 1985: 45–55.

Motyl, Alexander. "Ukraine, Europe, and Bandera," *Cicero Foundation Great Debate Paper*, No. 10/05, March, 2010, 6–9, http://www.cicerofoundation.org/lectures/Alexander_J_Motyl_UKRAINE_EUROPE_AND_BANDERA.pdf (accessed 4 November 2010).

Mudryk-Mechnyk, Stepan. *Spohad pro Stepana Banderu*. Lviv: Halyc'ka Vydavnycha Spilka, 1999.

Mudryk, Stepan "Spohady pro Stepana Banderu." In *Zhyttia i diial'nist' Stepana Bandery: Dokumenty i materialy*, edited by Mykola Posivnych, 147–77. Ternopil: Aston, 2008.

Müller, Rolf-Dieter. *An der Seite der Wehrmacht. Hitlers ausländische Helfer beim "Kreuzzug gegen den Bolschewismus" 1941–1945*. Berlin: Links, 2007.

Musiał, Bogdan. *"Kontrrevolutionäre Elemente sind zu erschießen." Brutalisierung des deutsch-sowjetischen Krieges im Sommer 1941*. Berlin: Propyläen, 2000.

Neulen, Hans Werner. *An deutscher Seite. Internationale Freiwillige von Wehrmacht und Waffen-SS*. Munich: Universitas, 1992.

Niedzielko, Romuald, ed., *Kresowa księga sprawiedliwych 1939–1945: O Ukraińcach ratujących Polaków poddanych eksterminacji przez OUN i UPA*. Warsaw: Instytut Pamięci Narodowej, 2007.

Nietzsche, Friedrich. "Beyond Good and Evil. Prelude to a Philosophy of Future." In *Cambridge Texts in the History of Philosophy*, edited by Rolf-Peter Horstmann and Judith Norman. Cambridge: University Press, 2002.

Nolte, Ernst. *Der Faschismus in seiner Epoche*. Munich: Piper, 1963.

Olick, Jeffrey. *The Politics of Regret: On Collective Memory and Historical Responsibility*. New York: Routledge, 2007.

Onats'kyi, Ievhen. *U vichnomu misti: Zapysky ukraïns'koho zhurnalista rik 1930*. Buenos Aires: Vydavnytstvo Mykoly Denysiuka, 1954.

Orshan, Iaroslav. *Doba natsionalizmu*. Paris, 1938.

Orzoff, Andrea. "The Husbandman: Tomáš Masaryk's Leader Cult in Interwar Czechoslovakia." *Austrian History Yearbook* 39 (2008): 121–37.

OUN v svitli postanov Velykykh Zboriv. N.p: Zakordonni Chastyny Orhanizatsiï Ukraïns'kykh Natsionalistiv, 1955.

Pan'kivs'kyi, Kost'. *Vid derzhavy do komitetu*. New York and Toronto: Zhyttia i Mysli, 1957.

Pan'kivs'kyi, Kost'. *Roky nimets'koï okupatsiï*. New York: Zhyttia i mysli, 1965.

Panchenko, Oleksandr. *Mykola Lebed': Zhyttia, diial'nist', derzhavno-pravovi pohliady*. Kobeliaky: Kobeliaky, 2001.

Pankowski, Rafał. *The Populist Radical Right in Poland: The Patriots*. New York: Routledge, 2010.

Passmore, Kevin. *Fascism. A Very Short Introduction*. Oxford: Oxford University Press, 2002.

Patryliak, I. K. *Viis'kova diial'nist' OUN (B) u 1940–1942 rokakh*. Kiev: Instytut Istoriï Ukraïny, 2004.

Paulovičová, Nina. "The 'Unmasterable Past'? Slovaks and the Holocaust: The Reception of the Holocaust in Post-communist Slovakia." In *Bringing the Dark Past to Light: The Reception of the Holocaust in Postcommunist Europe*, edited by John-Paul Himka and Joanna Beata Michlic, 549–90. Lincoln: University of Nebraska Press, 2013.

Pavlaković, Vjeran. "Flirting with Fascism: The Ustaša Legacy and Croatian Politics in the 1990s." In *The Shared History and The Second World War and National Question in ex-Yugoslavia*, Conference in Seville, Spain, January-February 2008.

Paxton, Robert O. *The Anatomy of Fascism*. New York: Knopf, 2004.

Payne, Stanley G. *Fascism: Comparison and Definition*. Madison: University of Wisconsin Press, 1980.

Payne, Stanley G. *A History of Fascism, 1914–1945*. Madison: University of Wisconsin Press, 1995.

Payne, Stanley G. "Fascism and Communism." *Totalitarian Movements and Political Religions* Vol. 1, No. 3 (2000): 1–15.

Payne, Stanley G. "Soviet anti-fascism: Theory and practice, 1921–45." *Totalitarian Movements and Political Religions* Vol. 4, No. 2 (2003): 1–62.

Payne, Stanley G. "The NDH State in Comparative Perspective." *Totalitarian Movement and Political Religions* Vol. 7, No. 4 (2006): 409–15.

Penter, Tanja. "Collaboration on Trial: New Source Material on Soviet Postwar Trials against Collaborators." *Slavic Review* Vol. 64, No. 4 (2005): 782–90.

Pereiaslav-Khmel'nyts'kyi i ioho istorychni pamiatky. Kiev: Vydavnytstvo Akademiï Nauk Ukraïns'koï RSR, 1972.

Perepichka, Ievhen. *Fenomen Stepana Bandery*. Lviv: Spolom, 2006.

Petrenko, Olena. "Makellose HeldInnen des Terrors. Die Organisation der Ukrainischen Nationalisten im Spannungsfeld zwischen Heroisierung und Diffamierung." In *Terrorismus und Geschlecht: Politische Gewalt in Europa seit dem 19. Jahrhundert*, edited by Christine Hikel and Sylvia Schraut, 193–210. Frankfurt, Main: Campus-Verlag, 2012.

Petrov, N.V., and Skorkin, K.V. ed. *Kto rukovodil NKVD 1934–1941*. Moscow: Zvenia, 1999.

Philby, Kim. *My Silent War*. St. Albans: Panther, 1973.

Picker, Henry. *Hitler Tischgespräche: Im Führerhauptquartier 1941–1942*. Bonn: Athenäum Verlag, 1951.

Piotrowski, Tadeusz. *Poland's Holocaust: Ethnic Strife, Collaboration with Occupying Forces and Genocide in the Second Republic, 1918–1947*. Jefferson: McFarland, 1998.

Pirie, Paul Stepan. *Unraveling the Banner: A Biographical Study of Stepan Bandera*. MA thesis: University of Alberta, 1993.

Plokhy, Serhii. *Unmaking Imperial Russia: Mykhailo Hrushevskyi and the Writing of Ukrainian History*. Toronto: University of Toronto Press, 2005.

Pohl, Dieter. *Nationalsozialistische Judenverfolgung in Ostgalizien 1941–1944: Organisation und Durchführung eines staatlichen Massenverbrechens*. Munich: Oldenbourg, 1997.

Pohl, Dieter. "Ukrainische Hilfskräfte beim Mord an den Juden." In *Die Täter der Shoah. Fanatische Nationalisten oder normale Deutsche?*, edited by Gerhard Paul, 205–34. Göttingen: Wallstein-Verlag, 2002.

Pohl, Dieter. "Anti-Jewish Pogroms in Western Ukraine." In *Shared History—Divided Memory: Jews and Others in Soviet-Occupied Poland, 1939–1941*, edited by Elazar Barkan, Elizabeth A. Cole and Kai Struve, 305–31. Leipzig: Leipziger Universitätsverlag, 2007.

Pohl, Dieter. "The Murder of Ukraine's Jews under German Military Administration and in the Reich Commissariat Ukraine." In *The Shoah in Ukraine: History,*

Testimony, Memorialization, edited by Ray Brandon and Wendy Lower, 23–76. Bloomington: Indiana University Press, 2008.

Polit, Ireneusz. *Miejsce odosobnienia w Berezie Kartuskiej*. Toruń: Wydawnictwo Adam Marszałek, 2003.

Polonsky, Antony. *The Jews in Poland and Russia, 1350–1880*, Vol. 1. Oxford: The Littman Library of Jewish Civilization, 2010.

Polonsky, Antony. *The Jews in Poland and Russia, 1914–2008*, Vol. 3. Oxford: The Littman Library of Jewish Civilization, 2010.

Poltava, Leonid. *Obraz Stepana Bandery v literaturi i mystetsvi*. New York: Ameryka, 1979.

Poltava, Leonid. *Zhyttia Stepana Bandery*. New York: META, 1987.

Poltava, Petro. *Kto takie banderovtsy i za chto ony boriutsia*. N.p: OUN pod rukovodstvom Stepanan Bandery, 1948.

Poltava, Petro. *Khto taki banderivtsi ta za shcho vony boruts'sia*. Kiev, Lviv: OUN, 1950.

Poltava, Petro. *Khto taki banderivtsi ta za shcho vony boruts'sia*, ed. Iaroslav Radevych-Vynnyts'kyi. Dorohobych: Vidrodzhennia, 1995.

Ponomar'ov, Vitalii. "Deheroïzatsiia Oporu," *Krytyka* 7–8 (2010), 22.

Portnov, Andrij. "Pluralität der Erinnerung: Denkmäler und Geschichtspolitik in der Ukraine." *Osteuropa* Vol. 58, No. 6 (2008): 197–210.

Portnov, Andrii. "Kontekstualizatsiia Stepana Bandery." *Krytyka* 3–4 (2010), 14.

Portnov, Andrei. "Istoria dlia domashnego upotrebleniia." *Ab Imperio* 3 (2012): 309–38.

Posivnych, Mykola. *Varshavs'kyi akt obvynuvachennia Stepana Bandery ta tovaryshiv*. Lviv: Tsentr doslidzhen' vyzvol'noho rukhu, 2005.

Posivnych, Mykola. "Molodist' Stepana Bandery." In *Stepan Bandera: Dokumenty i materialy (1920–1930 rr.)*, edited by Mykola Posivnych, 5–35. Lviv: Afisha, 2006.

Posivnych, Mykola ed. *Stepan Bandera: Dokumenty i materialy (1920–1930 rr.)*. Lviv: Afisha, 2006.

Posivnych, Mykola, "Molodist' Stepana Bandery." In *Zhyttia i diial'nist' Stepana Bandery: Dokumenty i materialy*, edited by Mykola Posivnych, 9–39. Ternopil': Aston, 2008.

Posivnych, Mykola. *Stepan Bandera—zhyttia, prysviachene svobodi*. Toronto: Litopys UPA, 2008.

Posivnych, Mykola, ed. *Zhyttia i diial'nist' Stepana Bandery: Dokumenty i materialy*. Ternopil': Aston, 2008.

Posivnych, Mykola and Hordasevych, Bohdan, ed., *Stepan Bandera: 1909–1959–2009: Zbirnyk statei*. Lviv: Triada Plius, 2010.

Posivnych, Mykola, ed. *Zhyttia i diial'nist' Stepana Bandery: Dokumenty i materialy*. Ternopil: Ason, 2011.

Posivnych, Mykola. "Providnyk OUN." In *Zhyttia i diial'nist' Stepana Bandery: dokumenty i materialy*, edited by Mykola Posivnych, 9–54. Ternopil: Aston, 2011.

Potichnyj, Petro, ed. *Poland and Ukraine: Paste and Present*. Edmonton: Canadian Institute of Ukrainian Studies, 1980.

Potichnyj, Petro and Shtendera, Jevhen, ed. *Political Thought of the Ukrainian Underground, 1943–1951*. Edmonton: Canadian Institute of Ukrainian Studies, 1986.

Potichnyj, Petro and Aster, Howard, ed. *Ukrainian-Jewish Relations in Historical Perspective*. Edmonton: Canadian Institute of Ukrainian Studies, 1990.

Potichnyj, Petro. *Pavlokoma, 1441–1945: Istoriïa sela*. Toronto: Fundatsiia Pavlokoma, 2001.

Potocki, Robert. *Polityka państwa wobec zagadnienia ukraińskiego w latach 1930–1939*. Lublin: Instytut Europy Środkowo Wschodniej, 2003.

Prus, Edward. *Herosi spod znaku tryzuba: Konowalec—Bandera—Szuchewycz*. Warsaw: Instytut Wydawniczy Związków Zawodowych, 1985.

Prus, Edward. *Z dziejów współpracy nacjonalistów ukraińskich z niemcami w okresie II wojny światowej i okupacji*. Katowice: Akademia Ekonomiczna im. Karola Adamieckiego, 1985.

Prus, Edward. *Atamania UPA: Tragedia kresów*. Warsaw: Instytut Wydawniczy Związków Zawodowych, 1988.

Prus, Edward. *Patriarcha galicyjski*. Warsaw: Instytut Wydawniczy Związków Zawodowych, 1989.

Prus, Edward. *Holocaust po banderowsku: Czy Żydzi byli w UPA?* Wrocław: Wydawnictwo Nortom, 1995.

Prus, Edward. *Stepan Bandera (1909–1959): Symbol zbrodni i okrucieństwa*. Wrocław: Wydawnictwo Nortom, 2004.

Prusin, Alexander V. "Revolution and Ethnic Cleansing in Western Ukraine: The OUN-UPA Assault against Polish Settlements in Volhynia and Eastern Galicia, 1943–1944." In *Ethnic Cleansing in Twentieth-Century Europe*, edited by Steven Béla Várdy and T. Hunt Tooley, 517–35. New York: Boulder: Social Science Monographs, 2003.

Prusin, Alexander. "'Fascist Criminals to the Gallows!': The Holocaust and Soviet War Crimes Trials, December 1945–February 1946." *Holocaust and Genocide Studies* Vol. 17, No. 1 (2003): 1–30.

Radonic, Ljiljana. *Krieg um die Erinnerung: Kroatische Vergangenheitspolitik zwischen Revisionismus und europäischen Standards*. Frankfurt am Main: Campus-Verlag, 2010.

Ramet, Sabrina P. "The NDH – An Introduction." *Totalitarian Movement and Political Religions* Vol. 7, No. 4 (2006): 399–408.

Rebet, Lev. *Svitla i tini OUN*. Munich: Ukraïns'kyi Samostiinyk, 1964.

Redlich, Shimon. *Together and Apart in Brzezany. Poles, Jews and Ukrainians 1919–1945*. Bloomington: Indiana University Press, 2002.

Redlich, Shimon. "Metropolitan Andrei Sheptyts'kyi, Ukrainians and Jews during and after the Holocaust." *Holocaust and Genocide Studies* Vol. 5, No. 1 (1990): 39–51.

Redlich, Szymon. "Moralność i rzeczywistość: Metropolita Andriej Szeptycki i Żydzi w czasach Holokaustu i II wojny światowej." *Zagłada Żydów. Studia i materiały* 4 (2008): 241–59.

Reese, Mary Ellen. *Organisation Gehlen: Der Kalte Krieg und der Aufbau des deutschen Geheimdienstes*. Berlin: Rowohlt, 1992.

Reichelt, Katrin. *Lettland unter deutscher Besatzung 1941–1944*. Berlin: Metropol, 2011.

Riabchuk, Mykola. "Bandera's Controversy and Ukraine's Future," *Russkii vopros* 1 (2010) http://www.russkiivopros.com/?pag=one&id=315&kat=9&csl=46#_edn13 (accessed 3 November 2011).

Rish, William Jay. *The Ukrainian West: Culture and the Fate of Empire in Soviet Lviv*. Cambridge Massachusetts: Harvard University Press, 2011.

Rosdolsky, Roman. "The Jewish Orphanage in Cracow." In *The Online Publication Series of the Center for Urban History of East Central Europe*, 4, http://www.lvivcenter.org/en/publications/ (accessed 26 May 2010): 1–4.

Rositzke, Harry. *The CIA's Secret Operations: Espionage, Counterespionage and Covert Action*. Boulder: Westview Press, 1988.

Rossoliński, Grzegorz. "Bandera und Nikifor—zwei Modernen in einer Stadt: Die 'nationalbürgerliche' und die 'weltbürgerliche' Moderne in Lemberg." In *Eine neue Gesellschaft in einer alten Stadt*, edited by Lutz Henke, Grzegorz Rossoliński and Philipp Ther, 109–24. Wrocław: ATUT, 2007.

Rossoliński-Liebe, Grzegorz. "Der polnisch–ukrainische Historikerdiskurs über den polnisch-ukrainischen Konflikt 1943–1947." *Jahrbücher für Geschichte Osteuropas* Vol. 57 (2009): 54–85.

Rossoliński-Liebe, Grzegorz. "Der Raum der Stadt Lemberg in den Schichten seiner politischen Denkmäler." *Kakanien Revisited*, 20 December 2009: 1–21.

Rossoliński-Liebe, Grzegorz. "Obraz Stepana Bandery v pol's'kii natsional'nii svidomosti,' http://zaxid.net/home/showSingleNews.do?obraz_stepana_banderi_v_polskiy_natsionalniy_svidomosti&objectId=1069869 (accessed 1 November 2011).

Rossoliński-Liebe, Grzegorz and Rudling, Per Anders. "Review of Krytyka. Hefte 3–4; 7–8; 9–10. Kiev 2010." *H-Soz-u-Kult*, 15 June 2011, http://hsozkult.geschichte.hu-berlin.de/rezensionen/2011-2-212 (accessed, 1 November 2011).

Rossoliński-Liebe, Grzegorz. "Celebrating Fascism and War Criminality in Edmonton. The Political Myth and Cult of Stepan Bandera in Multicultural Canada." In *Kakanien Revisited*, 12 (2010): 1–16.

Rossoliński-Liebe, Grzegorz. "The 'Ukrainian National Revolution' of Summer 1941." *Kritika: Explorations in Russian and Eurasian History* Vol. 12, No.1 (2011): 83–114.

Rossoliński-Liebe, Grzegorz. "Debating, Obfuscating and Disciplining the Holocaust: Post-Soviet Historical Discourses on the OUN-UPA and other Nationalist Movements." *East European Jewish Affairs* Vol. 42, No. 3, December 2012: 199–241.

Rossoliński-Liebe, Grzegorz. "Der Verlauf und die Täter des Lemberger Pogroms vom Sommer 1941. Zum aktuellen Stand der Forschung." *Jahrbuch für Antisemitismusforschung* 22 (2013): 207–43.

Rossoliński-Liebe, Grzegorz. "Erinnerungslücke Holocaust. Die ukrainische Diaspora und der Genozid an den Juden." *Vierteljahrshefte für Zeitgeschichte* Vol. 62, No. 3 (2014): 397–430.

Rudling, Per Anders. "Organized Anti-Semitism in Contemporary Ukraine: Structure, Influence and Ideology." *Canadian Slavonic Papers* Vol. 48, No. 1–2 (2006): 81–119.

Rudling, Per Anders. "Iushchenkiv fashyst: kult Bandery v Ukraïni ta Kanadi." In *Strasti za Banderoiu*, edited by Tarik Cyryl Amar, Ihor Balyns'kyi and Iaroslav Hrytsak, 237–309. Kiev: Hrani-T, 2010.

Rudling, Per Anders. "Multiculturalism, Memory, and Ritualization: Ukrainian Nationalist Monuments in Edmonton, Alberta." *Nationalities Papers* Vol. 39, No. 5 (2011): 733–68.

Rudling, Per Anders. "The OUN, the UPA and the Holocaust: A Study in the Manufacturing of Historical Myths." *The Carl Beck Papers in Russian & East European*

Studies, Number 2107. Pittsburgh: The Center for Russian and East European Studies, 2011.

Rudling, Per Anders. "Warfare or War Criminality." *Ab Imperio* 1 (2012): 356–81.

Rudling, Per Anders. "Anti-Semitism and the Extreme Right in Contemporary Ukraine." In *Mapping the Extreme Right in Contemporary Europe. From Local to Transnational*, edited by Andrea Mammone, Emmanuel Godin and Brian Jenkins, 189–205. London: Routledge, 2012.

Rudling, Per Anders. "The Return of the Ukrainian Far Right. The Case of VO Svoboda." In *Analysing Fascist Discourse. European Fascism in Talk and Text*, edited by Ruth Wodak and John E. Richardson, 228–55. New York: Routledge, 2013.

Rudnicki, Szymon. "Anti-Jewish Legislation in Interwar Poland." In *Antisemitism and its Opponents in Modern Poland*, edited by Robert Blobaum, 148–88. Ithaca: Cornell University Press, 2005.

Rudnyts'kyi, Stepan. *Ukraine: The Land and Its People: An Introduction to Its Geography*. New York: Ukrainian Alliance of America, 1918.

Rudnyts'kyi, Stepan. "Do osnov ukraïns'koho natsionalizmu." In *Chomu my khochemo samostiinoï Ukraïny*, edited by L. M Harbarchuk, 272–345. Lviv: Vydavnytsvo Svit, 1994.

Rudnyts'kyi, Stepan. *Chomu my khochemo samostiinoï Ukraïny*, edited by L. M. Harbachuk. Lviv: Svit, 1994.

Zynovii Knysh, *Pered pokhodom na skhid: Spokhady i materialy do diialnnia Orhanizatsiï Ukraïns'kykh Natsionalistiv u 1939–1941 rokakh*, Part II (Toronto: Sribna surma, 1959).

Rusnachenko, Anatolii. *Narod zburenyi: Natsional'no-vyzvol'nyi rukh v Ukraïni i natsional'ni rukhy oporu v Bilorusiï, Lytviï, Estniï u 1940–50-xh rokakh*. Kiev: Pul'sary, 2002.

Rusnachenko, Anatolii. "Symvol i ioho krytyky," *Krytyka*, 9–10 (2010), 7.

Russischer Kolonialismus in der Ukraine: Berichte und Dokumente. Munich: Ukrainischer Verlag, 1962.

Sabrin, B. F. *Alliance for Murder: The Nazi-Ukrainian Nationalist Partnership in Genocide*. New York: Sarpedon, 1991.

Sacharow, Vladimir Vladimirovič and Filippovych, Dmitrij Nikolaievič and Michael Kubina, "Tschekisten in Deutschland: Organisation, Aufgaben und Aspekte der Tätigkeit der sowjetischen Sicherheitsapparate in der sowjetischen Besatzungszone Deutschland (1945–1949)." In *Anatomie der Parteizentrale: Die KPD/SPD auf dem Weg zur Macht*, edited by Manfred Wilke, 293–334. Berlin: Akademie Verlag, 1998.

Sandkühler, Thomas. *"Endlösung" in Galizien: Der Judenmord in Ostpolen und die Rettungsinitiativen von Berthold Beitz 1941–1944*. Bonn: Diert, 1996.

Sapiga, D. *Literaturno-memorial'nyi muzei Iaroslava Galana*. Lvov: Kameniar, 1975.

Satzewich, Vic. *Ukrainian Diaspora*. London: Routledge, 2002.

Savaryn, Petro. *Z soboiu vzialy Ukraïnu: Vid Ternopillia do Al'berty*. Kiev: KVITs, 2007.

Shatylov, Mykola. "Vpershe i na zavzhdy. Istorychna konferentsiia ukraïns'kykh natsionalistiv u Kyievi." *Vyzvol'nyi shliakh* Vol. 530, No. 5, (May 1992): 546–48.

Schenke, Cornelia. *Nationalstaat und Nationale Frage: Polen und die Ukrainer 1921–1939*. Hamburg: Dölling und Galitz Verlag, 2004.

Schleichert, Hubert. *Wie man mit Fundamentalisten diskutiert, ohne den Verstand zu verlieren: Anleitung zum subversiven Denken*. Munich: C.H. Beck, 1997.

Schlott, Wolfgang. *Piłsudski-Kult: Die Wiedergeburt einer charismatischen Persönlichkeit in der Solidarność-Ära (1980 bis 1989)*. Bremen: Forschungsstelle Osteuropa, 2003.

Serhiichuk, Volodymyr, ed. *Stepan Bandera. U dokumentakh radians'kykh orhaniv derzhavnoï bezpeky (1939–1959)*, Vol. 1–3 Kiev: Vipol 2009.

Shablii, Oleh. "Peredmova." In Stepan Rudnyts'kyi, *Chomu my khochemo samostiinoï Ukraïny*, edited by L. M. Harbachuk, 5–34. Lviv: Svit, 1994.

Shafeta, P. *People and Cains. Essays, Articles, Pamphlets*. Kiev: Politvidav Ukraini Publishers, 1982.

Shafir, Michael. "Between Denial and 'Comparative Trivialization.' Holocaust Negationism in Post-Communist East Central Europe." *Analysis of Current Trends in Antisemitism* 19 (2002): 1–83.

Shafoval, Mykola, ed., *Universitas Libera Ucrainensis 1921–2006*. Munich: Verlag Steinmeier, 2006.

Shandruk, Pavlo. *Arms of Valor*. New York: Robert Speller & Sons Publishers, 1959.

Shchehliuk, Vasyl'. *"...Iak rosa na sontsi": Politychnyi roman-khronika, napysanyi na osnovi spohadiv kolyshn'oho diicha OUN-UPA L. S. Pavlyshyna*. Lviv: Feniks, 1992.

Shekhovtsov, Anton. "By Cross and Sword: 'Clerical Fascism' in Interwar Western Ukraine." *Totalitarian Movements and Political Religions* Vol. 8, No. 2 (2007): 271–85.

Shekhovtsov, Anton and Umland, Andreas. "Pravoradikal'naia partiinaia politika v postsovetskoi Ukraine i zagadka elektoral'noi marginal'nosti ukraïns'kikh ul'tranatsionalistov v 1994–2009 gg." *Ab Imperio* 2 (2010): 1–29.

Shekhovtsov, Anton. "The Creeping Resurgence of the Ukrainian Radical Right? The Case of the Freedom Party." *Europe-Asia Studies* Vol. 63, no. 2 (2011): 203–28.

Sheptyts'kyi, Andrii. *Pys'ma-poslannia Mytropolyta Andreia Sheptyts'koho ChSVV, z chasiv nimet'koi okupatsii*. Yorkton Sask.: Redeemer's Voice Press, 1969.

Sheremet, Ievhen. *Ukraïntsi za vakhom*. Kiev: Tovarystvo Ukraïna, 1980.

Shermer, Michael and Grobman, Alex. *Denying History: Who Says the Holocaust Never Happened and Why Do They Say It?* Berkeley: University of California Press, 2000.

Shevchenko, Ihor. *Ukraine between East and West: Essays on Cultural History to the Early Eighteen Century*. Edmonton: Canadian Institute of Ukrainian Studies Press, 1996.

Shtohryn, Dmytro. "Volodymyr Ianiv—poet." In Volodymyr Ianiv, *Poeziia*, edited by Dmytro Sapiha, 6–78. Lviv: Kameniar, 2009.

Shukhevych, Stepan. *Moie zhyttia: Spohady*. London: Ukrainian Publishers, 1991.

Shumuk, Danylo. *Za skhidnim obriiem*. Paris: Smoloskyp, 1974.

Siemaszko, Władysław and Siemaszko, Ewa. *Ludobójstwo dokonane przez nacjonalistów ukraińskich na ludności polskiej Wołynia 1939-1945*, Vol. 1–2. Warsaw: Wydawnictwo von borowiecky, 2000.

Siemaszko, Ewa. "Ludobójcze akcje OUN-UPA w lipcu 1943 roku na Wołyniu." In *Antypolska akcja OUN-UPA 1943–1944: Fakty i interpretacje*, edited by

Grzegorz Motyka and Dariusz Libionka, 59–75. Warsaw: Instytut Pamięci Narodowej, 2002.

Simpson, Christopher. *Blowback. America's Recruitment of Nazis and Its Effects on the Cold War*. London: Weidenfeld & Nicolson, 1988.

Siryi, S. (Stepan Bandera). "Do zasad nashoï vyzvol'noï polityky." In *Perspektyvy ukraïns'koï revoliutsiï*, edited by Vasyl' Ivanyshyn, 45–55. Drohobych: Vidrodzhennia, 1999.

Siryi, S. (Stepan Bandera). "Plianovist' revoliutsiinoï borot'by v kraiu," In *Perspektyvy ukraïns'koï revoliutsiï*, edited by Vasyl' Ivanyshyn, 56–76. Drohobych: Vidrodzhennia, 1999.

Siryi, S. (Stepan Bandera). "Znachennia shyrokykh mas ta ïkh okhoplennia." In *Perspektyvy ukraïns'koï revoliutsiï*, edited by Vasyl' Ivanyshyn, 14–17. Drohobych: Vidrodzhennia, 1999.

Šmigel', Michal. *Banderovci na Slovensku 1945–1947: Niektoré aspekty pôsobenia jednotiek Ukrajinskej povstaleckej armády na území krajiny*. Banská Bystrica: Katedra histórie Fakulty humanitných vied Univerzity Mateja Béla, 2008.

Snyder, Timothy. "The Causes of Ukrainian-Polish Ethnic Cleansing 1943." *Past and Present* 179 (2003): 197–234.

Snyder, Timothy. *The Reconstruction of Nations: Poland, Ukraine, Lithuania, Belarus, 1569–1999*. New Haven: Yale University Press, 2003.

Snyder, Timothy. *Sketches from a Secret War: A Polish Artist's Mission to Liberate Soviet Ukraine*. New Haven: Yale University Press, 2005.

Snyder, Timothy. *The Red Prince: The Fall of the Dynasty and the Rise of the Modern Europe*. London: The Bodley Head, 2008.

Snyder, Timothy. "The Life and Death of Western Volhynian Jewry, 1921–1945." In *The Shoah in Ukraine: History, Testimony, Memorialization*, edited by Ray Brandon and Wendy Lower, 77–113. Bloomington: Indiana University Press, 2008.

Snyder, Timothy. *Bloodlands: Europe between Hitler and Stalin*. New York: Basic Books, 2010.

Snyder, Timothy. "A Fascist Hero in Democratic Kiev," 24 February 2010, *The New York Review of Books*, http://www.nybooks.com/blogs/nyrblog/2010/feb/24/a-fascist-hero-in-democratic-kiev/ (accessed 1 November 2011).

Snyder, Timothy. "Declaring People to be Heroes is a Soviet Idea BBC Ukrainian," 15 March 2010, http://www.ukrainianstudies.uottawa.ca/pdf/UKL442.pdf (accessed 1 November 2011).

Sobków, Michał "Rozdroże narodów. W Koropcu." *Karta. Niezależne Pismo Historyczne* 16 (1995): 49–92.

Sodol, Petro. *Ukraïns'ka povstans'ka armiia, 1943–49: Dovidnyk*. New York: Proloh, 1994.

Solonari, Vladimir. "Patterns of Violence: The Local Population and the Mass Murder of Jews in Bessarabia and Northern Bukovina, July–August 1941." *Kritika: Explorations in Russian and Eurasian History* Vol. 8, No. 4 (2007): 749–87.

Solzhenitsyn, Aleksandr I. *The Gulag Archipelago 1918–1956: An Experiment in Literary Investigation*, Vol. 3. New York: Harper & Row, 1974–1978.

Sontheimer, Kurt. *Antidemokratisches Denken in der Weimarer Republik*. Munich: Nymphenburger Verlagshandlung, 1962.

Sorokina, Marina. "People and Procedures. Toward a History of the Investigation of Nazi Crimes in the USSR." In *The Holocaust in the East: Local Perpetrators and*

Soviet Responses, edited by Michael David-Fox, Peter Holquist, and Alexander M. Martin, 118–41. Pittsburgh: University of Pittsburgh Press, 2014.

Sosnovskyi, Mykhailo. *Dmytro Dontsov: Politychnyi portret z istorii rozvytku ideolohii ukrains'koho natsionalizmu*. New York: Trident International, 1974.

Spector, Shmuel. *The Holocaust of Volhynian Jews 1941–1944*. Jerusalem: Achva Press, 1990.

Sporrer, Maria and Steiner, Herbert, eds., *Simon Wiesenthal: Ein unbequemer Zeitgenosse*. Vienna: Orac, 1992.

Stakhiv, Yevhen. *Kriz tiurmy, pidpillia i kordony*. Kiev: Rada, 1995.

Statiev, Alexander. *The Soviet Counterinsurgency in Western Borderlands*. Cambridge: Cambridge University Press, 2010.

Stehle, Hansjakob. "Sheptyts'kyi and the German Regime." *Morality and Reality: The Life and Times of Andrei Sheptyts'kyi*, edited by Paul Robert Magocsi, 125–44. Edmonton: Canadian Institute of Ukrainian Studies, University of Alberta, 1989.

Stepovnyk, Dmytro. *Skulptor Mykhailo Cheresgn'ovs'kyi: Zhyttia i tvorchist'*. Kiev: Vydavnytstvo imeni Olehy Telihy, 2000.

Sternhell, Zeev. *Faschistische Ideologie: Eine Einführung*. Berlin: Verbrecher Verlag, 2002.

Sternhell, Zeev. "fascism." In *Comparative Fascist Studies: New Perspectives*, edited by Constantin Iordachi, 136–61. London: Routledge 2009.

Stets'ko, Iaroslav. *30 chervnia 1941. Prohloshennia vidnovlennia derzhavnosty Ukraïny*. Toronto: Liga Vyzvolennia Ukraïny, 1967.

Stets'ko-Muzyka, Iaroslava. "Z ideiamy Stepana Bandery." In *Zhyttia i diial'nist' Stepana Bandery: Dokumenty i materialy*, edited by Mokyla Posivnych, 189–200. Ternopil: Aston, 2008.

Stobniak-Smogorzewska, Janina. *Kresowe osadnictwo wojskowe 1920–1945*. Warsaw: Oficyna Wydawnicza RYTM, 2003.

Struve, Kai. "Rites of Violence? The Pogroms of Summer 1941." *Polin. Studies in Polish Jewry*, 24 (2012): 257–74.

Stryjek, Tomasz. *Ukraińska idea narodowa okresu międzywojennego: Analizy wybranych koncepcji*. Wrocław: FUNNA, 2000.

Stsibors'kyi, Mykola. *Natsiokratiia*. Paris, 1935.

Stsibors'kyi, Mykola. "Klonim holovy." In *Stepan Bandera: Dokumenty i materialy (1920–1930 rr.)*, edited by Mykola Posivnych, 133–34. Lviv: Afisha, 2006.

Sukhovers'kyi, Mykola. *Moï spohady*. Kiev: Smoloskyp, 1997.

Sushko, Vasyl'. *Zavdannia vykonav*. Lviv: Misioner, 1999.

Szarota, Tomasz. *U progu Zagłady: Zajście antyżydowskie i pogromy w okupowanej Europie: Warszawa, Paryż, Amsterdam, Antwerpia, Kowno*. Warsaw: Wydawnictwo Sic!, 2000.

Szarota, Tomasz. *Stefan Rowecki 'GROT'*. Warsaw: Państwowe Wydawnictwo Naukowe, 1985.

Szende, Stefan (Adolf Folkman). *Der letzte Jude aus Polen*. Zürich: Europa Verlag, 1945.

Szumiło, Mirosław. *Ukraińska Reprezentacja Parlamentarna w Sejmie i Senacie RP (1928–1939)*. Warsaw: Neriton, 2007.

Tal, Haim. *The Fields of Ukraine: A 17-Year-Old's Survival of Nazi Occupation: The Story of Yosef Laufer*. Denver: Dallci Press, 2009.

Taubman, William. *Khrushchev: The Man and His Era*. London: Free Press, 2005.

Teitel, Ruti G. *Transitional Justice*. Oxford: Oxford University Press, 2000.

Tokars'kyi, Iurii. *Dubliany: Istoriia ahrarnykh studii 1856–1946*. Lviv: Instytut Ukraïnoznastva im. I. Krypiakevycha, 1996.

Tomaszewski, Jerzy. *Ojczyzna nie tylko Polaków: Mniejszości narodowe w Polsce w latach 1918–1939*. Warsaw: Młodzieżowa Agencja Wydawnicza, 1985.

Tönsmeyer, Tatjana. "Kollaboration als handlungsleitendes Motiv? Die slowakische Elite und das NS-Regime." In *Kooperation und Verbrechen: Formen der "Kollaboration" im östlichen Europa 1939–1945*, edited by Christoph Dieckmann, Babette Quinkert and Tatjana Tönsmeyer, 25–54. Göttingen: Wallstein, 2003.

Torzecki, Ryszard: *Polacy i Ukraińcy: Sprawa ukraińska w czasie II wojny światowej na terenie II Rzeczypospolitej*. Warsaw: Wydawnictwo Naukowe PWN, 1993.

Totok, William. "Antonescu-Kult und die Rehabilitierung der Kriegsverbrecher." In *Holocaust an der Peripherie: Judenpolitik und Judenmord in Rumänien und Transnistrien 1940–1941*, edited by Wolfgang Benz and Brigitte Mihok, 197–212. Berlin: Metropol, 2009.

Troshchyns'kyi, V. P. *Naimantsi fashyzmu. (Ukraïns'ki burzhuazni natsionalisty na sluzhbi hitlerivtsiv u mizhvoiennyi period 1921–1939 rr.)*. Kiev: Naukova Dumka, 1981.

Trotsky, Leon. *The Permanent Revolution, and Results and Prospects*. New York, Merit Publishers, 1969.

Tsar, Ihor. *Za shcho my liubymo Banderu*. Lviv, 2000.

Tsegel'nyk, Iakiv and Skrypchenko, Iurii. *Literaturno-memorial'nyi muzei Iaroslava Halana*. Lviv: Knyzhkovo-zhurnal'ne vydavnytsvo: 1996.

Umland, Andreas. "Is there a Post-Soviet Fascism? A Brief Deliberation on the Cross-Cultural and Inter-Epochal Study of Right-Wing Extremism in the Post-Cold War Era." *East Central Europe* 37 (2010): 345–52.

Ursprung, Daniel. "Faschismus in Ostmittel- und Südosteuropa: Theorien, Ansätze, Fragestellungen." *Der Einfluss von Faschismus und Nationalsozialismus auf Minderheiten in Ostmittel- und Südosteuropa*, edited by Mariana Hausleitner and Harald Roth, 9–52. Munich: IKGS-Verlag, 2006.

Vasylevych, B. *Post Iaroslava Halana*. Lviv: Kameniar, 1967.

Veryha, Wasyl. *The Correspondence of the Ukrainian Central Committee in Cracow and Lviv with the German Authorities, 1939–1944*, Vol. 1. Edmonton: CIUS, 2000.

Veryha, Vasyl'. *Pid krylamy vyzvol'nykh dum: Spomyny pidkhorunzhoho dyvizi 'Halychna'*. Kiev: Vydavnytsvo imeni Oleny Telihy, 2007.

V"iatrovych, Volodymyr. *Stavlennia OUN do ievreiv: Formuvannia pozytsii na tli katastrofy*. Lviv: Vydavnytstvo Ms, 2006.

V"iatrovych, Volodymyr. "Bandera: stari ta novi mify." *zakhid.net*, 8 January 2009, http://zaxid.net/home/showSingleNews.do?bandera_stari_ta_novi_mifi&objectId=1068824 (accessed 1 November 2011).

Volchuk, Roman. *Spomyny z peredvoiennoho L'vova ta voiennoho Vidnia*. Kiev: Krytyka, 2002.

von Smolka, Stanislau: *Die Reussische Welt: Historisch-Politische Studien: Vergangenheit und Gegenwart*. Vienna: Zentral-Verlagsbüro des obersten polnischen Nationalkomitees, 1916.

Vrets'ona, Ievhen "Moï zustrichi z polkovnykom." In *Ievhen Konovalets' ta ioho doba*, 466–81. Munich: Cicero, 1974.

Vukčević, Slavko. *Zločini na jugoslovenskim prostorima u prvom i drugom svetskom ratu: Zločini Nezavisne Države Hrvatske, 1941–45*, Vol. 1. Belgrade: Vojnoistorijski institut, 1993.

Wachs, Philipp-Christian. *Der Fall Theodor Oberländer (1909–1998): Ein Lehrstück deutscher Geschichte*. Frankfurt: Campus Verlag, 2000.

Ward, James Mace. *Priest, Politician, Collaborator: Jozef Tiso and the Making of Fascist Slovakia*. Ithaca: Cornell University Press, 2013.

Weiner, Amir. *Making Sense of War: The Second World War and the Fate of the Bolshevik Revolution*. New Jersey: Princeton University Press, 2001.

Weiss, Aharon. "The Holocaust and the Ukrainian Victims." In *A Mosaic of Victims: Non-Jews Persecuted and Murdered by the Nazis*, edited by Michael Berenbaum, 109–15. New York: New York University Press, 1990.

Weiss, Aharon. "Jewish-Ukrainian Relations in Western Ukraine During the Holocaust." In *Ukrainian-Jewish Relations in Historical Perspective*, edited by Peter J. Potichnyj and Howard Aster, 409–20. Edmonton: CIUS, 2010.

Weiss-Wendt, Anton. "Hostage of Politics: Raphael Lemkin on "Soviet Genocide." *Journal of Genocide Research* Vol. 7, No. 4 (2005): 551–59.

Welzer, Harald and Moller, Sabine and Karoline Tschuggnall. *"Opa war kein Nazi": Nationalsozialismus und Holocaust im Familiengedächtnis*. Frankfurt am Main: Fischer Taschenbuch Verlag, 2002.

Welzer, Harald and Christ, Michaela. *Täter: Wie aus ganz normalen Menschen Massenmörder werden*. Frankfurt am Main: Fischer Taschenbuch Verlag, 2007.

Wendland, Anna Veronika. *Die Russophilen in Galizien: Ukrainische Konservative zwischen Österreich und Russland, 1848–1915*. Vienna: Verlag der österreichischen Akademie der Wissenschaften, 2001.

Wilczur, Jacek E. *Do nieba nie można od razu*. Warsaw: Oficyna Wydawnicza ECHO, 2002.

Wilson, Andrew. *The Ukrainians. Unexpected Nation*. New Haven: Yale University Press, 2009.

Wippermann, Wolfgang. *Faschismus: Eine Weltgeschichte vom 19. Jahrhundert bis heute*. Darmstadt: Primus Verlag, 2009.

Wołczański, Józef. "Korespondencja arcybiskupa Bolesława Twardowskiego z arcybiskupem Andrzejem Szeptyckim w latach 1943–1944." *Przegląd Wschodni* Vol. 2, No. 2 (6) (1992–93): 465–84.

Wolkowicz, Shlomo. *Das Grab bei Zloczow: Geschichte meines Überlebens: Galizien 1939–1945*. Berlin: Wichern-Verlag, 1996.

Wysocki, Roman. *Organizacja Ukraińskich Nacjonalistów: Geneza, struktura, program, ideologia*. Lublin: Wydawnictwo uniwersytetu Marie Curie-Skłodowskiej, 2003.

Yakovenko, Natalia. "Choice of Name versus Choice of Path: The Names of Ukrainian Territories from the Late Sixteenth to the Late Seventeenth Century." In *A Laboratory of Transnational History: Ukraine and Recent Ukrainian Historiography*, edited by Georgiy Kasianov and Philipp Ther, 117–48. Budapest: Central European University Press, 2009.

Yekelchyk, Serhy. *Stalin's Empire of Memory: Russian–Ukrainian Relations in the Soviet Historical Imagination*. Toronto: University of Toronto Press, 2004.

Yones, Eliyahu. *Die Straße nach Lemberg: Zwangsarbeit und Widerstand in Ostgalizien 1941–1944*, edited by Susanne Heim. Frankfurt am Main: Fischer Taschenbuch Verlag, 1999.

Yones, Eliyahu. *Smoke in the Sand: The Jews of Lvov in the War Years 1939–1944*. Jerusalem: Gefen Publishing House, 2004.

Zabuzhko, Oksana. *Muzei pokynutykh sekretiv*. Kiev: Fakt, 2010.

Zabuzhko, Oksana. *Museum der Vergessenen Geheimnisse*, translated by Alexander Krathochvil. Graz: Droschl, 2010.

Zaitsev, Oleksandr. "Viina iak prodovzhennia polityky. Posivnych Mykola. Voienno-politychna dial'nist' OUN u 1929–1939 rokakh. Lviv, 2010." *Ukraïna Moderna* 18 (2010): 235–45.

Zaitsev, Oleksandr. *Ukraïns'kyi integral'nyi natsionalizm (1920–1930-ti) roky: Narysy intelektual'noï istoriï*. Kiev: Krytyka, 2013.

Zaitsev, Oleksandr, ed., *Natsionalizm i relihiia: Hreko-katolyts'ka tserkva ta ukraïns'kyi natsionalistychnyi rukh v Halychyni (1920–1930-ti roky)*. L'viv: Vydavnytstvo Ukraïns'koho Katolyts'koho Universytetu, 2011.

Żbikowski, Andzej. "Lokalne Pogromy Żydów w czerwcu i lipcu 1941 r. na wschodnich rubieżacj II Rzeczypospolitej." *Biuletyn Żydowskiego Instytutu Historycznego* Vol. 162–163, No. 2–3 (1992): 3–18.

Żbikowski, Andzej. "Anti-Jewish Pogroms in Occupied Territories of Eastern Poland, June-July 1941." In *The Holocaust in the Soviet Union. Studies and Sources on the Destruction of the Jews in the Nazi-Occupied Territories of the USSR, 1941–1945*, edited by Lucjan Dobroszycki and Jeffrey S. Gurock, 173–80. Armonk: M. E. Sharpe, 1993.

Żbikowski, Andrzej ed. *Archiwum Ringelbluma. Relacje z Kresów*, Vol. 3. Warsaw: ANTA, 2000.

Żbikowski, Andrzej. "Pogroms in Northeastern Poland—Spontaneous Reaction and German Instigation." In *Shared History—Divided Memory: Jews and Others in Soviet-Occupied Poland, 1939–1941*, edited by Elazar Barkan, Elizabeth A. Cole and Kai Struve, 315–45. Leipzig: Leipziger Universitätsverlag, 2007.

Żeleński, Władysław. *Akt oskarżenia przeciwko Stefanowi Banderze, Mikołajowi Łebedowi, Darji Hnatkiwskiej, Jarosławowi Karpyncowi, Mikołajowi Klymyszynowi, Bohdanowi Pidhajnemu, Iwanowi Malucy, Jakóbowi Czornijowi, Eugenjuszowi Kaczmarskiemu, Romanowi Myhalowi, Katerzynie Zaryckiej, oraz Jarosławowi Rakowi* (Warsaw: Drukarnia Państwowa, 1935).

Żeleński, Władysław. *Zabójstwo ministra Pierackiego*. Paris: Instytut Literacki, 1973.

Zięba, Andrzej A. "Pacyfikacja Małopolski Wschodniej w 1930 roku i jej echo wśród emigracji ukraińskiej w Kanadzie." In *Przez dwa stulecia XIX i XX w. Studia historyczne ofiarowane prof. Wacławowi Felczakowi*, edited by Wojciech Frazi, 79–99. Cracow: ITKM, 1993.

Zięba, Andrzej A. *Lobbing dla Ukrainy w Europie międzywojennej: Ukraińskie Biuro Prasowe w Londynie oraz jego konkurenci polityczni (do roku 1932)*. Cracow, Księgarnia Akademicka, 2010.

Zubenets', Mykhailo, ed. *Z liuboviu do liudei: Z viroiu v Ukraïnu*. Lviv: LNAU, 2008.

INDEX

***ibidem*-Verlag**

Melchiorstr. 15

D-70439 Stuttgart

info@ibidem-verlag.de

www.ibidem-verlag.de
www.ibidem.eu
www.edition-noema.de
www.autorenbetreuung.de

Printed in Great Britain
by Amazon